The Which?
Guide to
Good Hotels
2005

GW00632753

WHICH? BOOKS

Which? Books is the book publishing arm of Consumers' Association, which was set up in 1957 to improve the standards of goods and services available to the public. Everything Which? publishes aims to help consumers, by giving them the independent information they need to make informed decisions. These publications, known throughout Britain for their quality, integrity and impartiality, have been held in high regard for over four decades.

Independence does not come cheap: the guides carry no advertising, and no restaurant or hotel can buy an entry in our guides, or treat our inspectors to free meals or accommodation. This policy, and our practice of rigorously re-researching our guides for each edition, help us to provide our readers with information of a standard and quality that cannot be surpassed.

The Which?
Guide to
Good Hotels
2005

Edited by Kim Winter

CONSUMERS' ASSOCIATION

The Which? Guide to Good Hotels 2005 (formerly known as
The Which? Hotel Guide) was researched by *Holiday Which?*,
part of Consumers' Association, and published by
Which? Ltd, 2 Marylebone Road, London NW1 4DF
Email address: *whichhotelguide@which.net*

Distributed by The Penguin Group:
Penguin Books Ltd, 80 Strand, London WC2R 0RL

First edition of *The Which? Hotel Guide* September 1990
This edition September 2004
Copyright © 2004 Which? Ltd

Base mapping © European Map Graphics Ltd 2004
Map information © Which? Ltd 2004

British Library Cataloguing in Publication Data
A catalogue record for this book is available from the British Library

ISBN 0 85202 997 7

Warm thanks to Max Fuller, Lindsay Hunt, Andrew Leslie, Paul Pontone,
Kevin Rushby; also to Price Watkins for the cover design and James
Duncan for cover photography.

Editorial and production: Joanna Bregosz, Andrew Grice, Liz Hornby,
Nithya Rae, Ian Robinson, Mary Sunderland, Barbara Toft

For a full list of Which? books, please write to
Which? Books, Castlemead, Gascoyne Way, Hertford X, SG14 1LH
or access our web site at *www.which.net*

Photoset by Tradespools Ltd, Frome, Somerset
Printed and bound in Spain by Bookprint S.L., Barcelona

Holiday Which? regularly inspects holiday destinations in both
Britain and abroad, as well as reporting on airfares, hotel safety and
other issues of interest to holiday-makers. To keep up to date with
the best information, take out a magazine subscription. For details of
a free trial, write to *Holiday Which?*, Consumers' Association, PO
Box 44, Hertford SG14 1SH, tel (0800) 252100.

Contents

How to use the *Guide*

The *Guide's* main entries are divided into four sections: London, England, Scotland and Wales. In the London section, hotels are listed alphabetically by name; in all other sections, they are listed under the nearest town or village. The maps in the central section can be used as a starting point for planning your trip. (The London map locates hotels by name.) Alternatively, if you know the name of a hotel but are unsure about its precise location, use the index at the back of the book. Don't forget that other hotels worth considering are listed in our Round-ups; these also appear on the maps.

All the entries in this year's *Guide* were written between April and June 2004. In the case of the main entries, the narrative about each hotel is based on an inspection by a professional hotel inspector and may be backed up by reports sent in by readers over the past year. The *Guide* relies on proprietors for the factual information about the hotel; they fill in a questionnaire giving details of the number of rooms, facilities offered, restrictions on children, dogs and smoking, prices for rooms and meals, and so on. Telephone and fax numbers, email and web site addresses were all checked just before we went to press but may change.

Key to symbols

This denotes somewhere where you can rely on a good meal – either the hotel features in *The Good Food Guide 2005* or our inspectors were impressed, whether by particularly competent home-cooking or by more lavish cuisine.

This denotes that the hotel is in an exceptionally peaceful location, where you should expect to have a restful stay. We give this symbol to a few city hotels that are relatively peaceful, considering their location.

This denotes that the hotel offers all its twin or double rooms (not including four-posters or suites) for £35 or less *per person per night*, including breakfast, or £50 or less per person if the rate includes dinner. (Many hotels advertise special breaks, and weekend and out-of-season offers, which can mean cheaper room rates than those quoted.)

This denotes that a hotel is child-friendly, with no age restrictions, and offers the basic facilities of cots and highchairs, as well as babysitting and/or baby-listening (some may provide other services as well). The symbol also indicates that where there are restrictions on children in the restaurant or dining room in the evening, early suppers are provided.

NEW ENTRY This denotes that the entry is new to the *Guide* as a main entry in the 2005 edition.

This denotes that the hotel has been singled out for one of our special awards for 2005: see the central colour section.

Other symbols are used to organise our factual information:

◑ Opening and closing periods of both the hotel and any restaurant or dining room.

⬱ Directions to help you find the hotel, and information about whether the hotel has a private car park or is within two miles of a railway station. Some hotels, especially in London, charge for the use of their private car park, so please check when booking.

⛏ Details of the number and type (single, double, four-poster, etc.) of bedrooms and other facilities in the rooms. 'Twin/double' may mean that the beds are of the 'zip-link' type: when booking say whether you want the beds arranged separately or together. All bedrooms have tea/coffee-making equipment unless we specify to the contrary. 'Family rooms available' means that an extra bed can be made available in a twin or double room. All bedrooms are en suite unless we specify otherwise.

⌗ Details of the public rooms at the hotel and other special facilities, including function and conference availability, facilities for children, sports and games at the hotel and nearby leisure facilities. Hotels in England and Wales that are licensed for civil weddings in accordance with the Marriage Act 1949 (as amended) are indicated. In Scotland, religious weddings may be held anywhere; civil weddings, however, can be held only in registrars' offices save in exceptional circumstances.

⛓ Disabled access. We have not inspected hotels specifically from the point of view of disabled readers. The information given here is that supplied by the proprietor, who has assured us that the external and internal doors are at least 75cm wide, and the corridors are at least 90cm wide; also that, if there is a lift, its doors are at least 75cm wide, and the internal measurements are at least 120cm by 90cm, in accordance with British Standards recommendations. Some of the hotels have been inspected for accessibility against a 'National Accessible Standard' by the appropriate national tourist board or by Holiday Care, a national charity that provides holiday and travel information for disabled and older people and their carers. In October 2002 a new National Accessible Scheme was launched, covering three types of impairment – mobility, visual and hearing (see box overleaf for details). For more detailed information about inspected properties please contact Holiday Care on (0845) 124 9971 or look up *www.holidaycare.org*. You can also consult *www.visitbritain.com*. A directory of hotels accessible to people with disabilities is at *www.allgohere.com*.

    Where a hotel is not wheelchair-accessible we have indicated the number of steps at the hotel entrance and into the dining room (or restaurant) if the hotel has ground-floor bedrooms or a lift, to provide people who have limited mobility with information. Always enquire whether the hotel can meet your particular requirements.

● Restrictions on children, dogs, smoking. Some hotels specify minimum ages for children or do not allow them in the restaurant or dining room in the evening – both of which are indicated, if applicable. Restrictions on children in bars are not shown. Guide dogs are often not included in the restriction on dogs; any charge for accommodating dogs is indicated. Rules may change, so it is wise to check on restrictions and charges at the time of booking.

VisitBritain accessibility standards

Accessibility standard for mobility impairment

M1 Typically suitable for a person with sufficient mobility to climb a flight of steps but who would benefit from fixtures and fittings to aid balance.

M2 Typically suitable for a person with restricted walking ability and for those who may need to use a wheelchair some of the time.

M3 Typically suitable for a person who depends on the use of a wheelchair and transfers unaided to and from a seated position.

M4 Typically suitable for a person who depends on the use of a wheelchair and transfers to and from a wheelchair in a seated position. The person also requires personal/mechanical assistance to aid transfer (e.g. carer/hoist).

Accessibility standard for hearing impairment

H1 Minimum entry requirements to meet the VisitBritain accessibility standard for guests with hearing impairment, from mild hearing loss to profoundly deaf.

H2 Recommended (best practice) additional requirements to meet the VisitBritain accessibility standard for guests with hearing impairment, from mild hearing loss to profoundly deaf.

Accessibility standard for visual impairment

V1 Minimum entry requirements to meet the National Accessible Standard for visually impaired guests.

V2 Recommended (best practice) additional requirements to meet the National Accessible Standard for visually impaired guests.

For more information, contact:
Quality Standards Department
VisitBritain
Thames Tower
Blacks Road
London W6 9EL

Details of credit, debit and charge cards accepted at the hotel. Some hotels may levy a surcharge on payment by card.

Prices you can expect to pay up to April 2005 (if the hotel has told us prices are likely to rise before then, we say so). '2004 prices' indicates that prices are valid until December 2004. ('2004 data', on the other hand, indicates that the information is from the previous year's questionnaire.) We give prices *per room for one night*, whether for one person in a single room, for one person alone in a twin or double room (single occupancy), for two people sharing a twin or double room, four-poster or suite, or for a family sharing a room (typically the price indicated for a family room is for 2 adults and 1 child). 'Deposit required' may mean that the hotel will take your credit-card number – and sometimes a deposit – as a surety when you book a room.

Meal prices are given next: breakfast (B), if it is not included in the room price, lunch (L) and dinner (D) if available. Set meal and à la carte (alc) meal prices are given where applicable; these are usually of three or more courses. Where light meals (such as bar food, bistro meals and snacks) are available, this is indicated. Room prices are rounded up to the nearest £1, meal prices to the nearest 50p.

We also indicate whether the hotel offers special-priced, themed or activity breaks; these might include cheaper rates at weekends, or in low season, or for stays longer than a couple of days, and can offer a considerable saving on the standard rate.

(3FOR2) The *Which? Guide to Good Hotels'* voucher scheme. The *Guide* includes four '3 nights for the price of 2' vouchers that readers will be able to redeem against the price of accommodation in participating hotels (the (3FOR2) symbol indicates those taking part in the scheme). Only one voucher may be used per room per booking – e.g., a party of four booking two rooms would need to use two vouchers, but a family of four sharing one room would need only one voucher. The vouchers are redeemable against a pre-booked stay only – the customers must mention their intent to use a voucher at the time of booking and present the voucher on arrival. The vouchers are redeemable against the price of the room and breakfast only (or just the room if breakfast is normally charged separately), not against the price of other meals, services or purchases such as newspapers. Hotels may exclude certain days of the week or times of the year from the scheme, or insist on guests staying half-board, so long as they advise customers of the restrictions at the time of booking. Original vouchers (not photocopies) must be presented. The vouchers are valid from 1 October 2004 to 30 September 2005 and may not be used in conjunction with any other offer.

Introduction

Welcome to *The Which? Guide to Good Hotels 2005*. Regular readers will know by now that the Which? name is a guarantee of ruthless independence and impartiality. We don't take advertising, we don't accept free hospitality, we stay anonymously and we say what we think. Hoteliers don't pay for entry or even see it before it goes to press, let alone write it themselves, as happens with some other guides.

All our inspections are backed up by feedback from you, our readers. If you complain about an establishment, we will send an inspector to check out that complaint. So please let us know about your experiences, good and bad. Although most hoteliers assume that people write to us only when they want to moan, in fact the majority of the letters that we receive are positive – which is heartening, as it means that we are getting our judgements right. And we are constantly struck by the selflessness of those who are willing to let everyone else in on the latest gem they have found. 'It is with extreme reluctance that I write to you about this hotel, as I fear it will be booked up next time I want to go,' is a typical quote. So we are appealing to your altruistic natures to spread a little happiness – use the forms at the back of the guide, or write to us at The Which? Guide to Good Hotels, Freepost, 2 Marylebone Road, London NW1 4DF, or email us at *whichhotelguide@which.net*.

Is it a bar? A gallery? A cinema? A wedding venue?
Does anyone remember the days when hotels were regarded simply as places to stay while we were visiting an area for business or pleasure or to see friends and relatives? Today the emphasis seems to be much more on making hotels destinations to visit in their own right. First came the themed breaks, with hoteliers organising murder mystery weekends or food and wine tastings to fill rooms in the quiet season. But now the trend is to encourage local residents as well as hotel guests to visit the hotel and spend money.

Fashionable bars aim to make their host establishments the places to be seen – and heard of – while well-known chefs take over hotel restaurants. Hotel spas, packed with every treatment imaginable, attract day visitors as well as guests. There are even hotels (Covent Garden and Charlotte Street in London, both part of the Firmdale group) that have in-house cinemas, luring in the after-work crowd with a dinner-and-movie deal. Broomhill Art Hotel in Devon has a ten-acre sculpture park as well as a gallery of changing exhibitions, while the Ceilidh Place in Ullapool has been offering a combination of music, food, poetry and accommodation for years.

Creating a happy buzz in a hotel obviously benefits everyone – nobody likes eating in an empty restaurant that has the atmosphere of a morgue. But we also know that readers get very frustrated when their needs as residents seem to take lower priority than those of outside groups. 'The service was abysmal – they concentrated on the private parties and ignored residents,' complained one correspondent this year. 'The route from the main hotel through the courtyard was blocked by the wedding marquee. The alternative route which we were obliged to take was through the kitchen servicing area and the laundry and not very pleasant. The staff were over-stretched trying to deal with three functions and the hotel guests, and showed signs of stress and tension,' came another report.

One of our inspectors in Scotland this year was turfed out of a restaurant by a private party – and had to make do with a bar meal. Another in south-west England happened to stay in a hotel where a TV crew was filming a pilot for a new dating game show in the restaurant. He was told they'd be finished by 8pm, so he booked a table for 8.30pm. But they still hadn't finished by 10.30pm, so his meal was interrupted by furniture being moved around him and 'London meeja types' braying into mobile phones about what a nightmare the whole exercise was. Was he offered a discount off his dinner for the inconvenience? What do you think?

Hotels must not lose sight of their main priority – their paying guests – or they might as well forget the rooms and stick to the entertainment business.

Looks good – but does it work?

A new phenomenon, in this brand-conscious world, seems to be the number of designers moving on from fashion and homeware into hotels. The partnership between Ian Schrager (hotelier) and Philippe Starck (designer) has been the subject of many column inches in the past. Palazzo Versace in Australia featured in the TV programme *I'm a Celebrity Get Me Out of Here,* and we hear reports that Giorgio Armani and Italian jeweller Bulgari also have plans to set up hotel ventures.

So how much do designers know about running hotels? Designing bedrooms that look good is one thing, but hotels face a lot more wear and tear than the average household. Also, what experience do designers have of maintaining the high standards of service and cleanliness that their guests will expect?

Charlton House in Shepton Mallet, Somerset, shows that such a scheme can work. Roger Saul, founder of the Mulberry home furnishings empire, had his headquarters in Somerset but was frustrated by not having anywhere suitable nearby to entertain visitors. When Charlton House came on the market, he saw a great opportunity – not only to have a suitable venue for hospitality, but also to use the hotel as a shop window for buyers to see how room furnishings would work in real life. 'It's a natural progression for designers who already have a homeware range,' says Lesley Baker, Sales and Marketing Manager of Charlton House. 'People can see it [the look], touch it, use it and decide whether it would work in their own home.' She admits, however, that designers 'ain't got a clue' when it comes to the day-to-day running of a hotel. 'They have to hire professionals to take care of the service, advise on health and safety, run the restaurant, and so on.' If these aspects are satisfactory, the partnership is likely to be a success. But if consumer expectations of service and cleanliness are not met, the brand could even be damaged.

What happened to the Great British Breakfast?

It is a typical consumer expectation to sit down to a good breakfast. Times have moved on since Somerset Maugham opined 'To eat well in England you should have breakfast three times a day'. In fact, all too often, it seems that the pendulum has swung the other way. After an excellent dinner the night before, breakfast is too often a second-rate affair, as if the hotel has run out of steam. 'The scrambled egg was previously cooked and possibly microwaved, arriving in a curious ramekin shape on the plate,' reported one reader. (Funnily enough, the editor had a very similar experience, at a completely different hotel.)

And even for guests who don't opt for a cooked meal, the experience can be disappointing. 'Breakfast was more reminiscent of a seaside boarding house than an establishment calling itself a country-house hotel,' came another complaint. 'We hardly ever choose to eat the full cooked offering, and other options were limited – no fruit other than grapefruit, small glasses of packed long-life orange juice, thin toast, cheap peel-less marmalade (no other jams or honey on the table).'

Some places can't even get the basics right. One disgruntled guest recounts: 'The first morning I ordered coffee, assuming I would be offered perhaps a cafetière (even Little Chef manages this!) or a small jug of milk – even hot maybe – for mixing to my taste. Instead I got a cup full to the brim with black coffee of doubtful freshness and quality and a share in the small jug of cold milk for my wife's tea.'

To add insult to injury, more and more hotels are also charging extra for breakfast, whether cooked or continental – some hotels in London now charge the best part of £25 for a hot breakfast. Ironically, it seems to be the most expensive hotels that are guilty of this practice. In our view, hotels that are charging over £200 a night for a room can afford to include a plate of scrambled eggs in the price.

Technology terrors

DVD players, plasma screen TVs, wireless Internet connections – many hotels are now offering guests the latest in technological wizardry to keep them happy. Even relatively modest places like Castle Cottage in Harlech and the Wheatsheaf in Swinton now have DVD players in some rooms. But sometimes technology can be more of a hindrance than a help.

One of our inspectors checked into a budget chain hotel in Leeds and was given a smart card, which she had to use to operate the lift and get into her room. So far, so good. However, she also had to use it to turn on the TV, and was then faced with five or six pages of 'menus' to try to reach the channel she wanted to watch. In frustration, she called for help. The receptionist was clearly used to coming to the rescue: 'That's OK – nobody can ever fathom out how it works.' Her advice: 'I tell everyone to leave the TV on all the time, or you'll have to go through the whole rigmarole again every time you switch it on.' Anyone for a sing-song round the piano?

Hotel grading

As we went to press yet more discussions were being held between the national tourist boards and the AA and the RAC on the thorny issue of establishing a common hotel-grading scheme across the UK. Currently, VisitBritian and the AA and the RAC use an inspection scheme based on a combination of facilities and quality, while the tourist bodies in Scotland and Wales grade hotels on completely different criteria, based purely on quality. The result is confusion for anyone trying to compare a three-star hotel in London with one in Edinburgh or Cardiff.

Apparently, VisitBritain's own consumer research shows that people value quality above facilities, followed by service, which chimes with the Scottish and Welsh criteria. So it looks as if we may finally be getting a single scheme right across the UK that gives visitors information on what really matters to them. Next – compulsory registration and minimum standards for hotels?

Suits you to a tea

Ah, that great British institution, the tea tray. In all our years of inspecting we have noticed little correlation between the price of a room and what's on the tea tray. We've stayed in three-room B&Bs that offer home-made biscuits and an infinitely wide range of herbal teas, while a very smart restaurant-with-rooms we inspected this year had Villeroy & Boch cups and saucers – but only PG Tips and instant coffee (and awful UHT milk, despite there being a fridge in the room). Another inspector relates how her tea tray, featuring two tea bags, came with a little note explaining that if she wanted any more tea bags they would cost 40p each! What sort of parsimonious impression does that leave?

And finally

I would like to thank all of you for the support and feedback you have provided over the years – please do continue to write in about your experiences, both good and bad. And warm thanks, too, to Patricia Yates for her work over the years, and to Deborah Gittens and Susan Smith for the sterling work they to continue to do to keep the *Guide* running smoothly.

Kim Winter
Editor

Your rights and responsibilities in hotels

A few days away at a hotel is a special treat for many of us, so we don't want anything to spoil it. And when we're travelling on business we don't want any time-wasting hotel hassles. But sometimes things do go wrong and the hotel doesn't live up to expectations.

Below we set out your rights in dealing with hotels and answer some of the questions regularly asked by our readers. This should help you put things straight on the spot, but if it doesn't, we suggest ways to go about enforcing your claim.

When I arrived at the city-centre hotel where I'd booked a weekend break I was told that they had made a mistake and the hotel was full. Owing to a popular conference, the only room I could find was in a more expensive hotel at the other side of town, so I'm out of pocket. What are my rights?

The hotel accepted your booking and was obliged to keep a room available for you. It is in breach of contract and liable to compensate you for additional expenses arising out of that breach – the difference in cost between what you were expecting to pay and what you ended up having to pay, plus any reasonable travelling expenses. Write to the manager explaining what happened, and enclose copies of receipts for your additional expenditure. (See also 'Asserting your rights'.)

After booking I found that I had to cancel. I immediately wrote to advise the owners, but they refuse to return my deposit, and say they expect me to pay additional compensation.

When you book a room and the hoteliers accept your booking you enter into a binding contract with them – they undertake to provide the required accommodation and meals for the specified dates at the agreed price, and you commit yourself to paying their charges. If you later cancel or fail to turn up, the hoteliers may be entitled to keep your deposit to cover administrative expenses, although it should be possible to challenge this if the deposited amount is a very high proportion of the total cost.

If the hoteliers are unable to re-let the room you have booked – and they must try to do so – they can demand from you the loss of profit caused by your cancellation, which can be a substantial proportion of the total price. It's important to give as much notice as possible if you have to cancel: this increases the chances of your room being re-let. If after cancelling you find that the full amount has been charged to your credit card you should raise the matter with your credit-card issuer, which may help you by asking the hotel whether the room was re-let, and requiring it to justify the charge made.

When I phoned to book a room the receptionist asked for my credit-card number. I offered to send a deposit by cheque instead, but the receptionist insisted on taking the number.

Hotels have increasingly adopted this practice to protect themselves against loss when guests fail to turn up. It's reasonable for hotels to request a deposit, and where time permits a cheque should be acceptable. Ultimately it is up to the hotel to decide what type of payment it is willing to accept.

After a long drive I stopped off at a hotel and asked for a room for the night. Although the hotel was clearly not full the owners refused to give me a room. Can they do this?

Hotels and inns are not allowed to refuse requests for food and shelter providing accommodation is available and the guest is sober, decently dressed and able to pay. If you meet these requirements and are turned away by a hotel with a vacancy you are entitled to sue for damages. If proprietors want to be able to turn away casual business, or are fussy about the sort of people they want to stay in their establishment, they are likely to call their establishment 'guesthouse' or 'private hotel'. In any event, it's illegal to exclude anyone on the grounds of race or sex.

When I called to book they told me I would need to pay extra if I wanted to pay by credit card. Is this legal?

Yes. Dual pricing was legalised early in 1991 and some hoteliers have elected to charge guests who pay by credit card extra to recover the commission payable to the card company. You can challenge this if you're not told when you book, or if it's not indicated on the tariff displayed in reception.

I arrived at a hotel in winter and found I was the only guest. Both my bedroom and the public rooms were distinctly chilly. I was uncomfortable throughout my stay and asked the management to turn up the heating, but things didn't improve.

It's an implied term of the contract between you and the hotel that the accommodation will be of reasonable standard, so it should be maintained at a reasonable temperature. You can claim compensation or seek a reduction of the bill. You were right to complain at the time. You are under a duty to 'mitigate your loss' – to keep your claim to a minimum. The most obvious way of doing this is to complain on the spot and give the management a chance to put things right.

I was very unhappy when I was shown to my room. It hadn't been vacuumed, the wastebins were full, the towels hadn't been changed and I found dog hairs in the bed.

You are entitled to a reasonable standard of accommodation having regard to the price paid. But no hotel, however cheap, should be dirty or unsafe. Ask for things to be put right, and if they're not, ask for a reduction of the bill.

While I was in bed a section of the ceiling caved in. I was injured, but I could have been killed.

Hotel owners are responsible for the physical safety of their guests. You have a claim for compensation – seek legal advice to have it properly assessed.

The hotel brochure promised tennis courts. When we arrived the lawns had been neglected and the nets were down. We couldn't play.

A hotel must provide advertised facilities and they must be of a reasonable standard. If it doesn't you can claim compensation, or ask for an appropriate deduction from your bill in respect of the disappointment suffered. You might also want to tell the local trading standards officers, who can prosecute the hotel under the Trade Descriptions Act.

While I was staying at a hotel my video camera was stolen from my room. What are my rights?

Hotel owners owe you a duty of care and must look after your property while it is on their premises. They would be liable for the loss if they were negligent. But you would be unlikely to succeed if you left it clearly visible in a ground-floor room with the door and window unlocked. However, under the Hotel Proprietors Act, providing hotel owners display a notice at reception, they can limit their liability to £50 per item or £100 in total. They can't rely on this limit if the loss was caused by negligence of their staff, although you will have to prove this.

My car was broken into while parked in the hotel car park. I want compensation.

Unless the hotel was negligent, your claim is unlikely to succeed.

My dinner was inedible. Do I have to pay for it?

The Supply of Goods and Services Act obliges hotels to prepare food with reasonable skill and care. The common law in Scotland imposes similar duties. If food is inedible, you should tell the waiter and ask for a replacement dish. If things aren't put right you can ask for a reduction of the billed amount. If you pay in full, possibly to avoid an unpleasant scene, write a note at the time saying that you are doing so under protest and are 'reserving your rights'. This means that you retain your right to claim compensation later.

Asserting your rights

1 Always complain at the time if you're unhappy. It's by the far the best way, and necessary to discharge your obligation to mitigate your loss.

2 If you reach deadlock you can deduct a sum from the bill in recognition of the deficient service received. Remember that the hotel might try to exercise its rights of 'lien' by refusing to release your luggage until the bill is paid. It's probably easier to pay in full, but give written notice that you are paying under protest and are reserving your rights to claim compensation through the courts.

3 Legal advice is available from a number of sources. Citizens Advice Bureaux, Law Centres and Consumer Advice Centres give free advice on consumer disputes. In certain cases your local Trading Standards Department might be able to help. If instructing a solicitor be sure to sort out the cost implications at the outset. Or you can write to Consumers' Association's Which? Legal Service, Castlemead, Gascoyne Way, Hertford SG14 1LH, which, for a fee, may be able to help you. For details on how to join, phone (0800) 252100 or email *wls@which.net*.

4 Once you know where you stand, write to the hotel setting out your claim.

5 If this fails to get things sorted out and you feel that you have a strong case, you can sue for sums of up to £5,000 (£1,000 if it is a personal injury case) under the small claims track of the county court. In the sheriff court in Scotland the small claims limit is usually £750; in Northern Ireland the limit is £2,000. You shouldn't need a solicitor.

LONDON

10 Manchester Street

10 Manchester Street, London W1U 4DG
TEL: 020-7486 6669   FAX: 020-7224 0348
EMAIL: stay@10manchesterstreet.fsnet.co.uk
WEB SITE: www.10manchesterstreet.com

This unfussy townhouse B&B is excellent value for the area and has had a successful face-lift

One of the grandest looking properties on this street near the Wallace Collection, Number 10 has a neoclassical entrance flanked by arched windows and adorned with well-tended shrubs and flowers. The unpretentious interior has no airs and graces, though, and the welcome is warm and friendly. The civilised lounge, with fruit on the mantelpiece, newspapers on one table and coffee cups on another, is a congenial space. Distressed walls, coir carpeting and chocolate sofas feature in the décor and sun streams in through cane blinds. Breakfast is served downstairs in a no-nonsense breakfast room. Comfortable bedrooms, spotless and smelling of polish, have all been given a face-lift this year and shades of grey and beige are found at the windows and on the beds, in line with current fashion. Bathrooms are plain but similarly neat and tidy. A hospitality tray in the rooms is unexpected, considering the free coffee in the lounge, but is a welcome touch. For dinner, there are plenty of eateries nearby; alternatively an outside catering company can provide service to your door.

◗ Open all year   ⤣ Nearest tube station is Baker Street (Metropolitan, Bakerloo, Jubilee, Hammersmith & City and Circle lines)   ⌷ 5 single, 19 twin, 13 double, 9 suites; all with hair-dryer, direct-dial telephone, modem line, TV, CD player; some with trouser press   ⌀ Breakfast room, lounge; cots, highchairs; leisure facilities nearby   ⅙ No wheelchair access; 6 steps into hotel, 7 ground-floor bedrooms, lift   ● No dogs; no smoking in some bedrooms   ⊟ Amex, Delta, MasterCard, Switch, Visa   £ Single £120, twin/double £150, suite £195; deposit required. Cooked B £5. Special breaks available

22 Jermyn Street

22 Jermyn Street, London SW1Y 6HL
TEL: 020-7734 2353   FAX: 020-7734 0750
EMAIL: office@22jermyn.com
WEB SITE: www.22jermyn.com

Intimate hotel on a smart shopping street in Piccadilly

With gentlemen's perfumers, shirt-makers, hat-makers and Fortnum & Mason as neighbours, as well as fine art galleries, private members' clubs and oyster restaurants nearby, you might expect a fair share of foppish male sophisticates to be residing at this prestigious St James address. However, all manner of people pass under the discreet green canopy into the narrow entrance hall, and it is as ideal for business folk as it is for well-heeled families – it has itself been in the same family for the best part of a century (it is currently in Henry Togna's competent hands). Bedrooms and suites are classic in style, all well upholstered in warm tones with welcome extras including video recorders, and CD players in suites. On each floor, you could book interconnecting rooms to create two-bedroom suites, which could suit families or those wanting some space and privacy. There are no public rooms here – 24-hour room service caters for those with out-of-hours hunger pangs, and a continental breakfast, if required, is delivered on a tray to your door.

◗ Open all year   ⤣ Nearest tube station is Piccadilly Circus (Piccadilly and Bakerloo lines)   ⌷ 5 double, 13 suites; family suites available; all with 24-hour room service, hair-dryer, mini-bar, direct-dial telephone, modem line, TV, VCR; suites with CD player; trouser press, tea/coffee-making facilities, fax on request   ⌀ Conferences, social functions; leisure facilities nearby; cots, highchairs, babysitting, baby-listening   ⅙ Wheelchair access to hotel (1 step), 4 rooms specially equipped for disabled people, lift   ● None   ⊟ Amex, Delta, Diners, MasterCard, Switch, Visa   £ Double £247, suite £347 to £394, family suite from £593; deposit required. Continental B £13; alc L £20, D £30; light meals available. Special breaks available

30 Pavilion Road

30 Pavilion Road, London SW1X 0HJ
TEL: 020-7584 4921 FAX: 020-7823 8694
EMAIL: rgr@searcys.co.uk
WEB SITE: www.searcys.co.uk

Cosy rooms without the usual hotel trappings, suitable for people who like to please themselves

Independently minded people will love this B&B on a quiet street in Knightsbridge as it feels more like private lodgings than a hotel in the traditional sense, and guests are given a key to come and go as they please. The immediate environs are nondescript, being next to an NCP car park and a prestigious private catering company, but Harrods, Harvey Nichols, Hyde Park and the museums of Knightsbridge are all within a kilometre's walk – and it's a perfect location for escaping the hustle and bustle of the area.

The ten rooms, on the top floor of this tall, sturdy corner building, are accessed via an initially alarming red cage lift. Those that battle with it will find some of the most affordable, not to mention rather endearing, accommodation in an expensive part of town. Neat bedrooms are spacious and feel like home. Some have queen-sized beds with floral canopies or delicately patterned wallpaper. Shower rooms are rather shoe-horned in. A continental breakfast, included in the rates, is delivered to your door.

◑ Closed Chr & New Year ⊿ Nearest tube station is Knightsbridge (Piccadilly Line) ⌗▸ 2 single, 3 twin, 4 double, 1 family room; all with hair-dryer, trouser press, direct-dial telephone, modem line, TV; some with room service; no tea/coffee-making facilities in rooms ⊘ Roof terrace; conferences; social functions; civil wedding licence; cots, highchairs ⅙ Wheelchair access to rooms, WC, lift ● No dogs; no smoking in bedrooms ⊟ Amex, Diners, MasterCard, Switch, Visa £ Single £95, single occupancy of twin/double £120, twin/double £140, family room £170; deposit required ③FOR②

51 Buckingham Gate

51 Buckingham Gate, London SW1E 6AF
TEL: 020-7769 7766 FAX: 020-7828 5909
EMAIL: info@51-buckinghamgate.co.uk
WEB SITE: www.51-buckinghamgate.com

Perfectly located, top-drawer apartments for fat wallets

Used as lodgings for royal guests in Victoria's time, these luxurious serviced suites still attract visiting dignitaries today. Somewhere between Buckingham Palace and Westminster Cathedral, and near St James and Green Parks, these three intricately adorned Victorian mansions find themselves in a suitably royal location and each, around a fountain courtyard, has its own style. Personal butlers are provided, the concierge can get you into the best London restaurants

at the last minute and if that's not enough pampering, the superb Shiseido Spa, excellent south Indian or modern British cuisine, and cocktails beckon across the courtyard. From modern and minimalist Falconers mansion to Ministers, faithful to its Victorian roots, to Kings, with all the bells and whistles, suites in each of the buildings vary from costly and luxurious to exorbitant and shamelessly magnificent.

◑ Open all year ⊿ Nearest tube stations are St James's Park (Circle and District lines) and Victoria (Circle, District and Victoria lines) ⌗▸ 82 suites; all with room service, hair-dryer, mini-bar, trouser press, direct-dial telephone, fax machine, modem line, TV, CD player, DVD ⊘ 3 restaurants, bar, lounge, games room, garden; conferences; social functions; civil wedding licence; gym, spa; early suppers for children; cots, highchairs, toys, playroom, babysitting ⅙ Wheelchair access to hotel and restaurants (ramps), WC, 1 ground-floor bedroom, 1 room specially equipped for disabled people, lift ● No dogs ⊟ Amex, Delta, Diners, MasterCard, Switch, Visa £ Junior suite £371, 1-bed suite £441 to £529, 2-bed suite £617 to £700, 3-bed suite £917; deposit required (prices valid till Dec 2004). Continental B £17, cooked B £19; set L, D £15; alc L, D £34.50; light meals available. Special breaks available

2

Abbey Court

20 Pembridge Gardens, London W2 4DU
TEL: 020-7221 7518 FAX: 020-7792 0858
EMAIL: info@abbeycourthotel.co.uk
WEB SITE: www.abbeycourthotel.co.uk

Traditional English style in a tree-lined road very near Notting Hill Gate tube

A brass plaque and bright blue door mark the entrance of this tasteful hotel on a street of grand, cream, Victorian terraced houses. Benches in a gravelled space at the front of the house catch the morning sun and the quiet road sees little traffic. The traditional lounge pays homage to the Victorian era, with rich red wallpaper and lacy throws on the chairs, while floral drapes hang at the windows and rugs bedeck the wooden floor of the basement conservatory. Outside is a tiny space with a fishpond and statuette. Bedrooms, which vary in size, come with a smattering of antiques, button-back chairs, china knick-knacks and often chintzy walls or bedspreads. Room 12 has twin brass bedsteads and a mustard and green décor, while room 17 has a prettily draped four-poster. Recently revamped bathrooms, some with Jacuzzi baths, are in cream marble and come with fluffy towelling robes.

◑ Open all year ⁊ Nearest tube station is Notting Hill Gate (Central, District and Circle lines) ⊨ 6 single, 1 twin, 12 twin/double, 3 four-poster; family rooms available; all with room service, hair-dryer, mini-bar, trouser press, direct-dial telephone, modem line, TV ⊘ Breakfast room/conservatory/bar, lounge, garden; conferences and social functions; leisure facilities nearby; cots, highchairs, babysitting ⅃ No wheelchair access; 10 steps into hotel, 20 steps into breakfast room, 3 ground-floor bedrooms ● No dogs; no smoking in some bedrooms ⊡ Amex, Delta, Diners, MasterCard, Switch, Visa £ Single £99 to £105, single occupancy of twin/double £120 to £130, twin/double £140 to £155, four-poster £199 to £250, family room £175 to £195; deposit required. Cooked B £8. Special breaks available

Aster House

3 Sumner Place, London SW7 3EE
TEL: 020-7581 5888 FAX: 020-7584 4925
EMAIL: asterhouse@btinternet.com
WEB SITE: www.asterhouse.com

Appealing South Ken den with a wholesome breakfast

Considering the location – South Kensington, next to Christie's auction rooms, and on a totally unspoilt street of gleaming white period houses – this wonderful B&B remains totally unaffected, and managers Simon and Leonie Tan are infectiously enthusiastic. It's one of the only houses in the street still to have the original black-and-white tiled entrance, and surely the only one to have ducks, from Mandarins to Aylesburys, residing in its small back garden. In spring, two giant chestnut trees coated in pink blossoms create quite a backdrop for breakfast in the bamboo-covered conservatory breakfast room. Inside, more ducks (this time ornamental) adorn the high ledges, pot plants catch the light and newspapers on the table encourage guests to linger over coffee, which can also be taken on the wooden-decked conservatory. The waft of freshly cooked pastries and cakes for breakfast is enough to rouse most guests. Home-made yoghurt and fresh and dried fruits are also on offer, as well as cooked eggs and beans. Bedrooms are decorated in an unfussy, straightforward style. Superior rooms, such as the Garden Suite, tend to have grander bathrooms with tubs rather than showers. Room 5 looks over the ducks below and the four-poster suite is huge.

◑ Open all year ⁊ Nearest tube station is South Kensington (Piccadilly, District and Circle lines) ⊨ 3 single, 7 twin, 3 double, 1 four-poster; all with hair-dryer, direct-dial telephone, modem, TV ⊘ Breakfast room/conservatory/lounge; leisure facilities nearby ⅃ No wheelchair access; 4 steps into hotel, 17 steps into breakfast room, 2 ground-floor bedrooms ● No dogs; no smoking ⊡ Delta, MasterCard, Switch, Visa £ Single £94 to £123, single occupancy £123 to £141, twin/double £141 to £182, four-poster £194 to £229; deposit required

Astons Apartments

31 Rosary Gardens, London SW7 4NH
TEL: 020-7590 6000 FAX: 020-7590 6060
EMAIL: sales@astons-apartments.com
WEB SITE: www.astons-apartments.com

Simple rooms offering great value in a quiet residential part of South Kensington

These bijou, budget billets are in a quiet location a few minutes from the tube and within walking distance of the Science, Natural History and Victoria & Albert museums. Smartly decorated, well-maintained and straightforward are words that could be used to describe the apartments, although large they are not. They do vary in size but some have tiny shower rooms and very compact bedrooms and kitchenettes. However, a lack of clutter and good storage space make them eminently liveable spaces and the prices must be some of the best in London, especially in this part of town. Upgrading to a deluxe designer apartment offers more space, proper good-sized kitchens and attractions such as marble showers and bathrobes. There are no public areas, although guests have access to a small back garden. As there's no lift, those with lots of luggage should consider an apartment on a lower floor.

○ Open all year ⚡ Nearest tube station is Gloucester Road (Circle, District and Piccadilly lines) 🛏 11 single apartments, 9 twin apartments, 24 double apartments, 10 family apartments; all with hair-dryer, direct-dial telephone, modem line, kitchenette, TV; some with trouser press; fax available ⊘ Garden; leisure facilities nearby; cots ♿ No wheelchair access; 5 steps into hotel, 6 ground-floor apartments ● No dogs ☐ Amex, Delta, MasterCard, Switch, Visa £ Single apartment £77, twin/double apartment £106 to £147, family apartment £147 to £194; deposit required

Basil Street Hotel

8 Basil Street, London SW3 1AH
TEL: 020-7581 3311 FAX: 020-7581 3693
EMAIL: info@thebasil.com
WEB SITE: www.thebasil.com

Personal service at this unpretentious hotel with a loyal following

A bastion of old-fashioned hospitality and tradition, this hotel has been in the same family for decades and is known affectionately as 'The Basil' by its devotees. With antiques aplenty, old parquet floors and smartly dressed porters, a timeless country-house feel is created – but in the heart of Knightsbridge. A magnificent staircase leads up to a creaky-floored gallery with chairs and writing desks in window alcoves, along which you approach the dining room (where a pianist plays in the evenings). Roast beef with Yorkshire pudding and Dover sole feature, along with some slightly more contemporary takes on otherwise time-honoured ingredients; in the afternoon, cucumber sandwiches and cream teas are served on delicate china in the lounge bar. Spacious bedrooms in muted colours lead off brightly painted corridors – they vary quite a bit, so regulars develop their own favourites. They are all endearingly old-fashioned, perhaps with chintzy drapes, panelled walls and an antique desk, and come with all the expected modern amenities.

○ Open all year ⚡ Nearest tube station is Knightsbridge (Piccadilly line) 🛏 31 single, 20 twin, 25 double, 4 family rooms; all with room service, hair-dryer, direct-dial telephone, modem line, TV; trouser press on request; no tea/coffee-making facilities in rooms ⊘ Dining room, bar, lounge; conferences and social functions; early suppers for children; cots, highchairs, baby-listening ♿ No wheelchair access; 10 steps into hotel, 3 steps into dining room, WC, lift ● No dogs; no smoking in bedrooms ☐ Amex, Diners, MasterCard, Switch, Visa £ Single £171, twin/double £241, family room £324; deposit required. Continental B £12, cooked B £15.50; set L £15; alc L £25, D £32; light meals available. Special breaks available ③FOR②

Blakes Hotel

33 Roland Gardens, London SW7 3PF
TEL: 020-7370 6701   FAX: 020-7373 0442
EMAIL: blakes@blakeshotels.com
WEB SITE: www.blakeshotels.com

Great for romantic rendezvous, exotic escapism and for lovers of the extraordinary

This is one book that can be judged by its cover! For, although the brass name plaque outside these two terraced mansions in a quiet residential area is rather discreet, the greenish-black paintwork on a road full of creamy-white façades makes a much more dynamic statement. Created by British designer Anouska Hempel, every inch of it provides a feast for the senses, whether it be in reception with light filtering through bamboo blinds illuminating huge baskets of oranges and snuggled-up lovebirds, or in the bedrooms, each a stunning creation with swathes of opulent silks, velvets and voiles on dramatically draped hand-made beds. London has never felt so romantic or exotic or theatrical – it's not surprising that this place attracts its fair share of luvvies and musicians. Venture down the metallic stairs to the low-lit restaurant and bar where east meets west. Orchids top black tablecloths, orange cushions adorn low seating and lacquered walls set the scene in a fantastical extravaganza, the memory of which is sure to endure long past the shock of the credit-card statement.

〇 Open all year   ⚡ Nearest tube station is South Kensington (Piccadilly, Circle and District lines)   🛏 17 single, 2 twin, 14 double, 6 four-poster, 9 suites; family rooms available; all with room service, hair-dryer, mini-bar, modem line, TV, VCR, CD player   ⊘ Restaurant, bar, lounge, garden; conferences; social functions; civil wedding licence; gym, leisure facilities nearby; cots, highchairs, babysitting   ⚬ No wheelchair access; 4 steps into hotel, 20 steps into restaurant, 4 ground-floor bedrooms, lift   ⬤ No dogs; no children in restaurant eves   ▭ Amex, Delta, Diners, MasterCard, Switch, Visa   £ Single £200, twin £200, double £306, four-poster £406, family room from £406, suite from £663; deposit required. Continental B £17.50, cooked B £25; alc D £30; light meals available

The Capital

22–24 Basil Street, London SW3 1AT
TEL: 020-7589 5171   FAX: 020-7225 0011
EMAIL: reservations@capitalhotel.co.uk
WEB SITE: www.capitalhotel.co.uk

Gourmet food, elegant bedrooms and five-star service combine faultlessly

It's a short step to Harrods from the door of this classy red-brick establishment in the heart of Knightsbridge, owned and run by David Levin. A smartly dressed concierge ushers guests in to a fire-warmed lobby with a rug-covered, wooden floor. Modern spotlights and good lamp lighting, a grand marble fireplace and elegant décor set the tone, and staff are warm and welcoming. The snug restaurant, overseen by acclaimed chef Eric Chavot, is a big draw for residents and non-residents alike. Crystal chandeliers sparkle and glow at night and reflect in large mirrors at either end. Expertly hand-crafted dishes – say, pot roast pigeon with potato and bacon galette and mushroom and truffle jus – receive rave reviews from gourmets. Wines on the list include a few produced in the Levins' own Loire vineyard. Bedrooms all differ in style but maintain a Victorian look, with original paintings and antiques adding to their appeal. Guests luxuriate in marble bathrooms and between Egyptian cotton sheets.

〇 Open all year   ⚡ Nearest tube station is Knightsbridge (Piccadilly line). Private car park   🛏 12 single, 23 twin/double, 6 double, 8 suites; all with room service, hair-dryer, mini-bar, direct-dial telephone, modem line, TV; some with trouser press; fax, VCR, CD player available; no tea/coffee-making facilities in rooms   ⊘ Restaurant, bar, lounge; conferences and social functions; leisure facilities nearby; cots, babysitting   ⚬ No wheelchair access   ⬤ No dogs   ▭ Amex, Delta, Diners, MasterCard, Switch, Visa   £ Single from £195, twin/double from £275, suite from £425; deposit required. Continental B £12.50, cooked B £16.50; set L £28.50; alc D £55; light meals available. Special breaks available

Charlotte Street Hotel

15 Charlotte Street, London W1T 1RJ
TEL: 020-7806 2000   FAX: 020-7806 2002
EMAIL: charlotte@firmdale.com
WEB SITE: www.firmdalehotels.com

Tasteful boutique hotel on a happening street

Part of the Firmdale stable (which includes Number Sixteen, Covent Garden and Knightsbridge hotels: see entries), this slick establishment has co-owner Kit Kemp's inimitable stamp all over it. Being near Soho, it's popular with media folk during the week while the brasserie Oscar (muralled with scenes of London life) is a hive of activity. Wild sorrel, star anise, halloumi, pomegranate and papaya feature on an imaginative fusion menu that has touches of Thai, Vietnamese, Japanese, Italian and French, as well as Dover sole, Devon scallops and Irish oysters. Eye-catching sculptures, art, hand-painted furniture and antiques form the focus of comfortable public rooms in gentle colours. Sumptuous bedrooms are beautifully concocted spaces in soothing shades, with pretty printed fabrics and invitingly plump beds. Bathrooms, in granite and oak, are suitably stylish, some with walk-in showers or double sinks.

○ Open all year ⚡ Nearest tube stations are Goodge Street (Northern line) and Tottenham Court Road (Northern and Central lines) 🛏 8 single, 22 twin/double, 8 double, 13 suites; all with room service, hairdryer, mini-bar, direct-dial telephone, modem line, TV, VCR, DVD, CD player; trouser press, fax on request; no tea/coffee-making facilities in rooms 🍽 Restaurant, bar, drawing room, library, private cinema; conferences and social functions; gym; leisure facilities nearby; early suppers for children; cots, highchairs, babysitting ♿ Wheelchair access to hotel (ramp), WC, lift ○ No dogs 🗀 Amex, Delta, MasterCard, Switch, Visa £ Single from £229, twin/double from £271, suite from £388; deposit required. Continental B £15, cooked B £18.50; alc L, D £32; light meals available. Special breaks available

City Inn Westminster [NEW ENTRY]

30 John Islip Street, London SW1P 4DD
TEL: 020-7630 1000   FAX: 020-7233 7575
EMAIL: westminster.res@cityinn.com
WEB SITE: www.cityinn.com

Innovative chain hotel near Tate Britain, with fantastic weekend leisure rates

It's a nice stroll in either direction from the nearest tubes (both roughly the same distance away) to get to this purpose-built, ultra-modern hotel, part of a small but expanding corporate-minded chain. Strip lighting and carpet in red lead the way through an expansive lobby, past mock-suede seating on one side and technicolour modern art on the other, to the City Café. This is a large room well divided up with pillars and screens, which offers light meals at lunch and fine dining at night. Upstairs, the Millbank Lounge is split into zones: in the middle, the red 'chill zone' is a work-free haven, while on either side business folk sit in glass-screened booths, or on beige leather sofas, and tap away on their laptops. Come the weekend, the suits clear out and a DJ moves in and it's a happening place to spend a Friday night – rates at the weekend are slashed to bargain levels (look for leisure packages online). Further up, the large landings are flooded with light, and the city views are great. Bedrooms are streamlined, with chrome and light wood; some have views of Parliament or the Thames. They are all soundproofed and have 'enhanced' air-conditioning, so no dry eyes. Beds come with two soft and two hard pillows (with feather available on request), the neat shower rooms have power showers, and technology includes CD & DVD players and flat-screen TVs.

○ Open all year ⚡ Nearest tube stations are Pimlico (Victoria line) and Westminster (Circle, District and Jubilee lines). Private car park 🛏 75 twin/double, 369 double, 16 suites; all with room service, hair-dryer, mini-bar, ironing facilities, direct-dial telephone, TV, DVD, CD player 🍽 Restaurant, dining room, 2 bars, lounge; conferences and social functions; gym; leisure facilities nearby; early suppers for children; cots, highchairs ♿ Wheelchair access to hotel and restaurant, WC, lift, 26 rooms specially equipped for disabled people. Disabled parking ● No dogs in public rooms ▱ Amex, Delta, Diners, MasterCard, Switch, Visa £ Twin/double £187, suite £517; deposit required. Continental B £13, cooked B £19; set L, D £17.50; alc L, D £25; light meals available. Special breaks available (3FOR2)

The Claverley

13–14 Beaufort Gardens, London SW3 1PS
TEL: 020-7589 8541 FAX: 020-7584 3410
EMAIL: reservations@claverleyhotel.co.uk
WEB SITE: www.claverleyhotel.co.uk

Traditional and well-maintained B&B with modest prices

The Claverley comprises two adjoining stuccoed townhouses on a quiet, tree-lined cul-de-sac only a stroll from Harrods. It offers good rates, considering its prime Knightsbridge placement. In the same safe hands for the last three decades and with a long-serving staff, there is an air of continuity and tradition here. The bedrooms come in different shapes and sizes, and the picture gallery on the Claverley's website showcases most of them. With smart floral drapes and bed canopies, and marbled bathrooms, they are eminently comfortable, if a little old-fashioned in places. Breakfast (included in the room rates) is something to look forward to here. Stewed fruits, grilled kippers and decent Cumberland sausages feature, and salmon kedgeree is served on a couple of mornings a week for a change. The lounge areas downstairs evoke classic English style, with antique desks and wood panelling and good period features. Tea- and coffee-making facilities are available here at all times.

◒ Open all year ⚿ Nearest tube station is Knightsbridge (Piccadilly line) ⛶ 6 single, 5 twin, 2 twin/double, 8 double, 3 four-posters, 4 family rooms; suites available; all with hair-dryer, direct-dial telephone, TV; no tea/coffee-making facilities in rooms ❉ Breakfast room, lounge; leisure facilities nearby; cots ♿ No wheelchair access; 4 steps into hotel, 2 ground-floor bedrooms, lift ● No dogs; no smoking in bedrooms ▱ Amex, Delta, Diners, MasterCard, Switch, Visa £ Single £95 to £120, single occupancy of twin/double £100 to £120, twin/double £125 to £145, four-poster/suite £160 to £180, family room £180 to £195; deposit required. Special breaks available

The Colonnade Town House

2 Warrington Crescent, London W9 1ER
TEL: 020-7286 1052 FAX: 020-7286 1057
EMAIL: res.colonnade@theetoncollection.com
WEB SITE: www.theetoncollection.com

Affordable opulence at excellent prices in Little Venice

The pretty barge- and flower-lined canals nearby give this area its name of Little Venice. Paddington is just two stops away by Tube, so the prices at this hotel are quite a bargain by London standards. The two handsome cream Victorian houses with large bay windows were a hospital in a former life, and Alan Turing, who would later go on to crack the Enigma code, was born here. The walnut-sheathed lift, long enough for a hospital trolley, is the only clue to this institutional past. Minnie the cat passes her time on the comfy sofas in the traditional lounge, which has tasselled drapes and warm red hues, and there's a very civil honesty bar offering port, sherry and spirits. Richly coloured velvet throws adorn the beds in rooms done out in opulent golds, reds and blacks. All have mod cons including CD players, and TVs and tea trays are discreetly hidden away in dark wooden cabinets. JFK is a splendid suite featuring a baronial four-poster built for the president himself.

◒ Open all year; restaurant closed Mon eve ⚿ Nearest tube station is Warwick Avenue (Bakerloo line). Private car park ⛶ 5 twin, 26 double, 3 four-poster, 8 suites; all with room service, hair-dryer, mini-bar, trouser press, direct-dial telephone, modem line, TV, CD player ❉ Restaurant, bar, lounge, patio; leisure facilities nearby; early suppers for children; cots, highchairs ♿ No wheelchair access; 5 steps into hotel, 15 steps into restaurant, 5 ground-floor bedrooms, lift ● No dogs in public rooms ▱ Amex, Delta, Diners,

MasterCard, Switch, Visa £ Single occupancy of twin/double £119 to £148, twin/double £139 to £211, four-poster £216 to £271, suite £231 to £288; deposit required. Continental B £9, cooked B £12.50; set L £15, D £30; alc L £20, D £40; light meals available. Special breaks available (2004 data)

County Hall Travel Inn

Belvedere Road, London SE1 7PB
TEL: (0870) 238 3300   FAX: 020-7902 1619
EMAIL: london.county.hall.mti@whitbread.com
WEB SITE: www.travelinn.co.uk

Location is key at this budget chain hotel

Away from the crowds it certainly isn't: tens of thousands of people pass by this stretch of the South Bank every day, many of them heading for the London Eye or the Aquarium. Access to the handsome building, however, is one block back from the riverside trail. It's a coveted, central location for a budget chain, although unfortunately it's the more upmarket sister hotel next door, the Marriott, that gets the river views – the most you can hope for is a sideways view from some of the family rooms. Costa Coffee and Journey's Friend newsagents are on site and the public areas are getting a major overhaul this year – out with the swirly carpets of the traditional-styled 'Potters Bar' branded eatery and in with 'Slice', which has a more Mediterranean feel and open-plan layout. Bedrooms are what you'd expect of the chain – plain but practical with en-suite bathrooms, and some can sleep a family of four for the same price. Occupancy rates are very high, so book well in advance. Last-minute travellers may find most availability on Sunday nights.

○ Open all year   Nearest tube station is Waterloo (Northern, Jubilee, Bakerloo and Waterloo & City lines) 195 double, 102 family rooms, 16 disabled rooms; all with direct-dial telephone, modem line, TV; hair-dryer on request   Restaurant, bar; conferences; social functions; leisure facilities nearby; cots, highchairs Wheelchair access to hotel (at rear) and restaurant, WC, 16 rooms specially equipped for disabled people, lift. Disabled parking   No dogs; smoking in bar and 50 bedrooms   Amex, Delta, Diners, MasterCard, Switch, Visa   £ All rooms £80 (Fri to Sun); £85 (Mon to Thurs); deposit required. Cooked B £7 (free for accompanied children aged 10 and under); light meals available; service incl

Covent Garden Hotel

10 Monmouth Street, London WC2H 9HB
TEL: 020-7806 1000   FAX: 020-7806 1100
EMAIL: covent@firmdale.com
WEB SITE: www.firmdalehotels.com

Terrific location for a memorable hotel

There is something very civilised about this hotel in the heart of theatreland. It's the kind of place you hanker to return to – and apparently around 80 per cent of guests do just that! A fire-warmed upstairs drawing room in rich red and pink hues is a particularly lovely spot to relax and read, while next door in the small library is where you'll find the honesty bar. The main action, however, is downstairs in buzzing Brasserie Max, with its stripped floors and reasonable prices (it's also the venue for breakfast). Saturday nights are film club nights – Ferrari leather seats furnish the subterranean screening room, and movies include recent releases and old classics. The bedrooms, all individually designed by co-owner Kit Kemp, come in predominantly earthy shades enhancing beautiful fabrics and some great art throughout. All of them (including the one that has what is claimed to be Britain's largest four-poster at eight foot square), have DVD players or videos, CD players and quirky Roberts radios, while bathrooms are stylishly done out in granite and mahogany.

○ Open all year   Nearest tube stations are Covent Garden and Leicester Square (Piccadilly and Northern lines) 6 single, 43 double, 1 four-poster, 8 suites; family rooms available; all with room service, hair-dryer, mini-bar, direct-dial telephone, modem line, TV, VCR, CD player; some with DVD; trouser-press, fax machine on request; no tea/coffee-making facilities in rooms   Restaurant, bar, lounge, library, private cinema; conferences, social functions; gym, beauty treatment room; leisure facilities nearby; early suppers for children; cots, highchairs, toys, baby-sitting ⅃ Wheelchair access to hotel (ramp) and restaurant, 5 ground-floor bedrooms, lift ● No dogs ⌑ Amex, Delta, MasterCard, Switch, Visa £ Single £247, single occupancy £300, twin/double £335 to £412, four-poster £582, family room/suite £412; deposit required. Continental B £16, cooked B £18; set D (Sat only) £30; alc L, D £30; light meals available. Special breaks available

Dorset Square Hotel

39 Dorset Square, London NW1 6QN
TEL: 020-7723 7874   FAX: 020-7724 3328
EMAIL: reservations@dorsetsquare.co.uk
WEB SITE: www.dorsetsquare.co.uk

A classic English country house in the city

There's definitely an old-school air about this civilised hotel on a handsome square that played home to the original Lord's cricket ground back in the eighteenth century. There's an honour cabinet full of drinks in the peaceful lounge, with the newspapers laid out on a low table (along with olives and cheese dips), bookcases of old hardbacks, and a Scrabble board. It's a comfortable spot from which to enjoy the view of the grassed square and its venerable trees. The modern English menu in the basement Potting Shed restaurant – covered in garden implements and terracotta – which includes Atkins options alongside more healthy/vegetarian choices. Wooden stairs lead down to the conservatory, which has murals of Lord's (now a mile to the north) and London Zoo in Regent's Park. Bedrooms, beautifully coordinated, feature luxury bed linen, goose-down pillows and granite bathrooms. Good-value special offers are often available online.

◖ Open all year; restaurant closed Sun eve ⊿ Nearest tube station is Baker Street (Circle, Hammersmith & City, Jubilee, Metropolitan and Bakerloo lines) ⨌ 6 single, 11 twin/double, 17 double, 2 four-poster, 1 suite; all with room service, hair-dryer, mini-bar, direct-dial telephone, modem line, TV; some with VCR; fax available; no tea/coffee-making facilities in rooms ⌀ Restaurant, bar, lounge, garden; conferences and social functions; leisure facilities nearby; early suppers for children; cots, highchairs, babysitting ⅃ Wheelchair access to hotel (ramp) and restaurant, 5 ground-floor bedrooms, lift ● No dogs ⌑ Amex, Delta, MasterCard, Switch, Visa £ Single £165, twin/double £235 to £282, four-poster/suite £353; deposit required. Continental B £12, cooked B £14; set L £20, D £25; alc L, D £30; light meals available. Special breaks available

Durley House

115 Sloane Street, London SW1X 9PJ
TEL: 020-7235 5537   FAX: 020-7259 6977
EMAIL: info@durleyhouse.com
WEB SITE: www.durleyhouse.com

Decidedly upmarket suites in a prestigious location

Gracious apartment blocks surround tree-lined, beautifully tended-to Cadogan Garden in an exclusive part of Knightsbridge, just minutes away from the most modish shopping in London. Durley House is one such, and contains 11 stunning suites with good-sized kitchens. Partridges, one of London's best delis, is just down the road. Alternatively, the Michelin-starred resident chef will cut out the sweat, and butlers will deliver meals to your apartment via the original dumb-waiter system, anytime day or night. The Piano Suite is top-of-the-range, and has its own baby grand and fireplace to boot. Extravagant touches throughout the suites include embroidered bed linen, decadent marble bathrooms and lavish country-house fabrics on well-draped windows. A professional staff caters to your every whim if needs be, but stays discreetly in the background otherwise, adding to the home-from-home feel (well a lavish one anyway!). Ideal for well-heeled families and shoppers with high credit limits.

◖ Open all year ⊿ Nearest tube station is Sloane Square (District and Circle lines) ⨌ 11 suites; all with room service, hair-dryer, mini-bar, trouser press, direct-dial telephone, modem line, TV, VCR, CD player ⌀ Lounge, garden; conferences; social functions; leisure facilities nearby; early suppers for children; cots, highchairs, toys, babysitting, outdoor play area ♿ No wheelchair access; 5 steps into hotel, 1 ground-floor bedroom, lift ● No dogs; no smoking ▭ Amex, Delta, MasterCard, Switch, Visa £ 1-bed suite £494, 2-bed suite £564 to £682; deposit required. Continental B £12.50, cooked B £18.50. Light meals available. Special breaks available

Durrants Hotel

26–32 George Street, London W1H 5BJ
TEL: 020-7935 8131   FAX: 020-7487 3510
EMAIL: enquiries@durrantshotel.co.uk
WEB SITE: www.durrantshotel.co.uk

Tradition and service are watchwords at this charmingly old-fashioned hotel

George Street is a fitting address for this bastion of English hospitality just round the corner from trendy Marylebone High Street. Afternoon tea includes crumpets and scones, home-made biscuits and cake, and is served in the mahogany-panelled restaurant with its leather studded banquet seats and oil portraits. A separate breakfast room has oak panels and small copper tables. Plenty of cosy public rooms along the length of the hotel, which occupies several eighteenth-century terraces, serve as little reading rooms, tea lounges or bars. Not surprisingly, bedrooms are very comfortable, with perhaps padded or mahogany headboards and stripey bedspreads. Nearly all have a bath and shower. This hotel has been in the same family for generations and service is delivered by a professional team, including uniformed doormen. Food continues in a traditional vein, with roasts and grills predominating.

◗ Open all year ⚡ Nearest tube stations are Marble Arch (Central line) and Baker Street (Jubilee, Circle, Bakerloo, Metropolitan and Hammersmith & City lines) ⬅ 16 single, 29 twin, 39 double, 3 family rooms, 5 suites; all with room service, hair-dryer, direct-dial telephone, TV; some with mini-bar, trouser press, modem line; no tea/coffee-making facilities in rooms ⊘ Restaurant, bar, 3 lounges, breakfast room; conferences and social functions; leisure facilities nearby; early suppers for children; cots, highchairs, babysitting ♿ Wheelchair access to hotel (2 steps) and restaurant, 7 ground-floor bedrooms, lift ● No dogs; no smoking in restaurant ▭ Amex, Delta, MasterCard, Switch, Visa £ Single £93 to £110, twin/double £145 to £165, family room £180, suite £285 (2004 prices); deposit required. Continental B £10.50, cooked B £13.50; set L, D £19.50; alc L, D £45; light meals available. Special breaks available

Five Sumner Place

5 Sumner Place, London SW7 3EE
TEL: 020-7584 7586   FAX: 020-7823 9962
EMAIL: reservations@sumnerplace.com
WEB SITE: www.sumnerplace.com

Small, personally run B&B in the heart of South Ken

This immaculately kept and thoroughly comfortable B&B finds itself in the middle of one of Kensington's most striking and best preserved Victorian terraced streets. Gleaming white, with pillared porticos and black glossy railings enclosing paved front terraces, Sumner Place is definitely 'des res', although this B&B doesn't pander to the design-conscious, who'd be better off at 'Number Sixteen' across the road (see entry). The house's good features, such as high ceilings, original sash windows and plaster cornicing, enhance a no-nonsense décor which sees bedrooms decorated mainly in a business-like blue. Most of them have simple shower rooms and dark reproduction furniture – Room 4 has a little extra light and space. Breakfast is served in the cheery conservatory adjoining a tiny paved garden at the back of the house. Guests are given their own front door key to come and go as they please.

◗ Open all year ⚡ Nearest tube is South Kensington (District, Circle and Piccadilly lines) ⬅ 3 single, 5 twin, 5 double; all with room service, hair-dryer, mini-bar, fridge, trouser press, direct-dial telephone, modem, TV; some with tea/coffee-making facilities ⊘ Dining room, conservatory, garden; leisure facilities nearby; cots ♿ No wheelchair access; 6 steps into hotel, 4 steps into dining room, 2 ground-floor bedrooms, lift

● No dogs; no smoking in some public rooms and some bedrooms ⌐ Amex, Delta, Diners, MasterCard, Switch, Visa £ Single £75 to £100, twin/double £115 to £153; deposit required ③FOR②

Franklin Hotel

28 Egerton Gardens, London SW3 2DB
TEL: 020-7584 5533 FAX: 020-7584 5449
EMAIL: bookings@franklinhotel.co.uk
WEB SITE: www.franklinhotel.co.uk

Four red-brick townhouses form this elegant hotel and help to enclose the perfect Egerton Gardens

Whereas many London hotels benefit from a view of a garden in a handsome square, there aren't a great number that have access to these gardens, as keys are often reserved for local residents. But you can sit in the Franklin's immaculate tree-lined garden in a deck chair in summer and actually forget you are in the capital. A nicer backdrop to the plush drawing room, which has deep, comfy sofas, swagged drapes and grand oil paintings, is hard to imagine. A bar, more clubby in feel, operates on an honour basis next door. With so many restaurants in the area, the dining room is used mainly for breakfast – although a full menu is available, as is 24-hour room service. Luxurious bedrooms feature marble bathrooms with brass fittings, beds draped in beautiful fabrics, grand gilded mirrors and squashy sofas. The best choice would be one facing the garden, with floor to ceiling windows and wonderful views.

● Open all year ⚡ Nearest tube station is South Kensington (District, Circle and Piccadilly lines) 🛏 9 single, 5 twin, 22 double, 5 four-poster, 6 suites; all with room service, hair-dryer, mini-bar, direct-dial telephone, modem line, wireless broadband, TV; VCR and CD player in some rooms on request; no tea/coffee-making facilities in rooms ✓ Dining room, bar, 2 lounges, garden; conferences, social functions; leisure facilities nearby; early suppers for children; cots, highchairs, babysitting ᕔ No wheelchair access; 5 steps into hotel, 4 ground-floor bedrooms, lift ● No dogs ⌐ Amex, Diners, MasterCard, Visa £ Single/single occupancy of twin/double £141 to £223, twin/double £165 to £293, four-poster £325 to £385; deposit required. Continental B £11, cooked B £16.50; alc L, D £30; light meals available. Special breaks available

La Gaffe

107–111 Heath Street, London NW3 6SS
TEL: 020-7435 8965 FAX: 020-7794 7592
EMAIL: info@lagaffe.co.uk
WEB SITE: www.lagaffe.co.uk

Family-run restaurant with rooms on one of Hampstead's main streets

This cheerful Italian restaurant with rooms is located in one of London's most desirable residential areas. Despite having plenty of niche designer shops, continental café bars and the lofty Heath on its doorstep the area still manages to retain a villagey feel. In 1962 the Stella family stamped its mark on Hampstead by opening an Italian restaurant, which has been going from strength to strength ever since. A casual wine bar and the slightly smarter restaurant front the road. The latter has walls painted to resemble a Tuscan villa, arched windows and splashes of red. The wide-ranging menu features simple Italian fare such as medallions of veal with wild mushrooms in white wine and grilled halibut with béarnaise sauce, as well as plenty of pastas from gnocchi to pappardelle. Bedrooms range from small cosy twins with co-ordinating bed-drapes to a more luxurious four-poster with a Jacuzzi bath.

● Open all year ⚡ Nearest tube station is Hampstead (Northern line) 🛏 4 single, 4 twin, 6 double, 2 four-poster, 2 family rooms; all with limited room service, hair-dryer, direct-dial telephone, TV; trouser press, fax available ✓ Restaurant, bar, conservatory; social functions; leisure facilities nearby; cots, highchairs ᕔ No wheelchair access; 2 steps into hotel, 2 ground-floor bedrooms ● No dogs; no smoking in bedrooms ⌐ Amex, Delta, MasterCard, Switch, Visa £ Single £70, single occupancy of twin/double £85, twin/double £95, four-poster/family room £125; deposit required. Set L £12.50 (weekends only); alc L, D £20; light meals available ③FOR②

The Gore

190 Queen's Gate, London SW7 5EX
TEL: 020-7584 6601   FAX: 020-7589 8127
EMAIL: reservations@gorehotel.co.uk
WEB SITE: www.gorehotel.com

Eccentric and eye-catching period splendour near the Royal Albert Hall

There are over 5,000 oil paintings, old photos and portraits of anything Victorian covering every inch of the halls, stairwells and bedroom walls at this memorable hotel on a wide residential avenue. This is fitting, since it opened its doors to the public in the 1890s, and the owners (also proprietors of The Rookery and Hazlitt's – see entries) are in the antiques trade. Victoria herself oversees reception, staffed by a young team dressed in black, although would she be amused by the hotel's often irreverent take on her era? This sense of humour is also apparent in the Green Room – a library with grand oils, gilded mirrors and rich red walls. Red leather stools line the length of Bar 190, where distressed leather sofas and pouffes in cosy candlelit alcoves are popular with media types. Through in the bistro there's a buzzy atmosphere on most nights, except Sundays. Bedrooms are painted in rich colours and furnished with startling period fittings, including some impressive beds such as the chunky four-poster in Miss Fanny (a previous owner). Comfort comes first, though, and heavenly pillows and crisp duvets induce a good night's slumber, and showers invigorate, despite the antiquated brass plumbing. Breakfast costs extra; the cold buffet is a satisfying mix of fresh berries, yoghurts and patisserie.

○ Open all year   ⤢ Nearest tube station is Gloucester Road (Piccadilly, Circle and District lines)   🛏 25 single, 2 twin, 16 double, 9 four-poster, 1 suite; family rooms available; all with room service, hair-dryer, mini-bar, direct-dial telephone, modem line, TV; no tea/coffee-making facilities in rooms   ⊘ Restaurant, bar, lounge; conferences and social functions; highchairs   ♿ No wheelchair access   ● Dogs by arrangement only   ⊟ Amex, Delta, Diners, MasterCard, Switch, Visa   £ Single £141 to £212, single occupancy of twin/double £153 to £235, twin/double £165 to £259, four-poster £235 to £394, family room £200 to £247, suite £294 to £405; deposit required. Continental B £10, cooked B £15; set L, D £25; alc L, D £35; light meals available. Special breaks available   ③FOR②

The Goring

Beeston Place, London SW1W 0JW
TEL: 020-7396 9000   FAX: 020-7834 4393
EMAIL: reception@goringhotel.co.uk
WEB SITE: www.goringhotel.co.uk

Sophisticated luxury and fine dining in a decidedly unstuffy combination

Gold-tipped railings, dandy doormen with stripey-cuffed blue coats, and bright red canopies mark the presence of the Goring. In the lobby, beautiful crystal chandeliers catch the light and cast colours on to the marble floor, and a portly Mr Goring, cast in bronze, declares 'I opened this hotel in 1910'. Unlike many other esteemed London establishments, this one is still a family affair and the fourth Mr Goring is about to take the reins. Signs for the 'Ladies Powder Room' signify that there is an enduring sense of tradition here, but not in a staid sense. Not many hotels of this class would have the confidence to incorporate life-size models of shaggy sheep into its décor, but the story behind their presence is quite endearing and the Goring pulls it off. Superlatives abound here – this was the first hotel in the world to have en-suite rooms and it has one of the largest privately owned gardens in London, a stately quadrangle owned by the Duke of Wellington. Public areas are extremely elegant and bedrooms get increasingly plush up through the ranks; some have tiled garden terraces.

○ Open all year   ⤢ Nearest tube station is Victoria (Victoria, Circle and District lines). Private car park   🛏 19 single, 4 twin, 36 twin/double, 9 family rooms, 5 suites; all with room service, hair-dryer, trouser press, direct-dial telephone, modem line, TV; no tea/coffee-making facilities in rooms   ⊘ Restaurant, bar, lounge, conservatory/terrace, IT centre, garden; conferences and social functions; civil wedding licence; leisure facilities nearby; early suppers for children; cots, highchairs, babysitting 🔥 Wheelchair access to hotel (ramp) and restaurant, WC, lift ● No dogs ▭ Amex, Delta, Diners, MasterCard, Switch, Visa £⌐ Single £235, twin/double £300, family room/suite £395; deposit required. Continental B £13.50, cooked B £17.50; set L £29, D £40; light meals available. Special breaks available

Guesthouse West NEW ENTRY

163–165 Westbourne Grove, Notting Hill, London W11 2RS
TEL: 020-7792 9800 FAX: 020-7792 9797
EMAIL: matron@guesthousewest.co.uk
WEB SITE: www.guesthousewest.co.uk

Design on a budget with high-tech gadgetry in an expensive part of town

This immaculately kept three-storey lemon-painted building fronted by a bowling-green-like lawn is set back slightly from the quieter end of Westbourne Grove. A room here costs over £200,000 as part of a new buy-to-let scheme, giving owners a minimum number of nights in their room and a guaranteed rate of return on their money. However, rates for mere overnighters are a boon for those used to over-inflated London prices. Contemporary throughout, this is design on a budget, from the streamlined lounge-bar with low leather chairs on bare floorboards to the chic bedrooms with chrome accents, cream walls and beige or grey and black throws and cushions on crisp white bedlinen. Flat-screen TVs, DVDs and CD players are standard, and all bedrooms have toiletries, proper espresso makers and air-conditioning. Some have French doors to the patio, or light streaming through conservatory roofs. Rates include a simple buffet breakfast at weekends.

❶ Closed last weekend in Aug 🚇 Nearest tube station is Notting Hill Gate (Central, District and Circle lines) 🛏 16 double, 1 four-poster, 3 suites; all with hair-dryer, direct-dial telephone, broadband access, TV, CD players, DVD ✓ Restaurant, bar, lounge, conservatory, garden; leisure facilities nearby; cots 🔥 Wheelchair access to hotel & restaurant, 4 ground-floor bedrooms ● No dogs; no smoking in bedrooms ▭ Amex, MasterCard, Switch, Visa £⌐ Double £147, four-poster/suite £176 (rates incl B Fri to Sun); deposit required. Continental B £10; set L, D £25; light meals available

The Halkin

Halkin Street, London SW1X 7DJ
TEL: 020-7333 1000 FAX: 020-7333 1100
EMAIL: res@halkin.como.bz
WEB SITE: halkin.como.bz

Car park becomes an ultra-sleek zone of tranquillity in the ultimate reincarnation

It is hard, at first, to get a handle on the style at this design hotel on a quiet side street at the back of Buckingham Palace Gardens. The hotel shell is a modern brown brick block, automatic glass doors lead into a bare lobby, weird nets cordon off the minimalist bar area, and a stone Buddha-like statue stands alone. In fact, just over a decade ago a car park stood here and was bequeathed to its oriental owner as a birthday gift! Luckily, she saw the site's potential and so began the transformation into a 'design hotel' in the days before the concept was even taking off. Lift doors open up to large, dark landings, each loosely connected with the four elements – earth, water, fire and air. Bedroom doors are barely even noticeable along the sleek, curved corridors. Inside, an abundance of creamy colours, streamlined furniture and natural fibres combine in a Zen-like design that might be too stark and simplistic for some. Returning from the top-notch and tasteful Thai restaurant to decadent marble bathrooms with spa-quality toiletries and high-tech gadgetry including plasma TVs and electronic consoles could feasibly induce a meditative state.

❶ Open all year 🚇 Nearest tube station is Hyde Park Corner (Piccadilly line) 🛏 6 twin, 18 double, 17 suites; all with room service, hair-dryer, mini-bar, direct-dial telephone, fax machine, modem line, ETV, video, CD player, DVD; no tea/coffee-making facilities in rooms ✓ Restaurant, bar; conferences; social functions;

leisure facilities nearby; cots, highchairs, babysitting ⟨wheelchair⟩ Wheelchair access to hotel and restaurant, WC, lift
● No dogs ▭ Amex, Delta, Diners, MasterCard, Visa £ Twin/double from £364, suite from £581; deposit required. Continental B £20, cooked B £22; set L £26, D £47; alc L £40, D £60; light meals available. Special breaks available

Harlingford Hotel

61–63 Cartwright Gardens, London WC1H 9EL
TEL: 020-7387 1551 FAX: 020-7387 4616
EMAIL: book@harlingfordhotel.com
WEB SITE: www.harlingfordhotel.com

Friendly B&B in an up-and-coming area

This family-run large B&B occupies three townhouses in a handsome Georgian crescent in Bloomsbury and, following a successful makeover, stands head and shoulders above the local competition. Once a frumpy boarding house, the Harlingford now sports fresh colours and contemporary furnishings alongside the original period features. Bedrooms, off warren-like corridors, come in a handful of colour schemes and have been given the same designer treatment, with bold splashes of colour. Some of the bathrooms are on the small side and they are in the process of being refurbished to the same standard as the rest of the hotel. There is no lift here so ask for a ground-floor room if you struggle with stairs. Breakfast – the full English or a decent continental – is a definite plus point and is included in the already low rates. Guests can gain access to the gardens in the private square with a key, and book a spell on the tennis courts.

◑ Open all year 🔼 Nearest tube station is Russell Square (Piccadilly line) 🛏 10 single, 17 twin, 12 double, 3 family rooms; all with hair-dryer, direct-dial telephone, TV ⊘ Breakfast room, lounge, garden; tennis; leisure facilities nearby; cots, highchairs & No wheelchair access; 5 steps into hotel, 4 ground-floor bedrooms ● No dogs ▭ Amex, Delta, MasterCard, Switch, Visa £ Single £75, twin/double £95, family room £105 to £110; deposit required ③FOR②

Hazlitt's

6 Frith Street, Soho Square, London W1D 3JA
TEL: 020-7434 1771 FAX: 020-7439 1524
EMAIL: reservations@hazlitts.co.uk
WEB SITE: www.hazlittshotel.com

Bags of character at this welcoming spot in lively Frith Street

Three characterful red- and sandy-brick houses in Soho form this wonderful hotel that oozes history from every pore. The houses date back to the eighteenth century, as do many of the beautifully carved beeswaxed beds that sit propped up on creaking, wonky floors. Bathrooms are a good feature in all the rooms, and plenty of the plumbing is original (but in very good working order!). Black-and-white tiled floors, brass shower heads as big as plates, or free-standing baths are typical. Old, darkened oils hang on the walls as if untouched for centuries (it comes as no surprise to learn that the owners are in the antiques trade). A blue plaque outside announces that the eponymous writer lived and died here. It's something of a tradition nowadays that visiting authors and novelists leave signed copies of their latest works in the cosy, wood-panelled sitting room. As it's in a lively part of town, there can be noise into the early hours, so if you can't beat 'em, join 'em. A continental breakfast including fresh croissants is delivered to your room on request.

◑ Open all year 🔼 Nearest tube station is Tottenham Court Road (Central and Northern Lines) 🛏 3 single, 1 twin, 12 double, 4 four-poster, 3 suites; all with room service, hair-dryer, mini-bar, direct-line telephone, modem, TV; 3 with VCR; 1 with CD player; no tea/coffee-making facilities in rooms ⊘ Sitting room; leisure facilities nearby; cots, baby-sitting & No wheelchair access; 1 step into hotel, 3 ground-floor bedrooms ● None ▭ Amex, Delta, Diners, MasterCard, Switch, Visa £ Single £182 to £206, twin/double/four-poster £194 to £241, suite £288 to £353; deposit required. Continental B £10. Special breaks available

The Hempel

31–35 Craven Hill Gardens, London W2 3EA
TEL: 020-7298 9000   FAX: 020-7402 4666
EMAIL: reservations@the-hempel.co.uk
WEB SITE: www.the-hempel.co.uk

Harmony prevails amid the minimalism in feng-shui'd Bayswater lodgings

With a design so sublime it sometimes feels more like a work of art than a hotel, The Hempel manages to soothe and drop jaws at the same time. Square ponds framed by stone, gravel and grass make the private garden a fine place to pause awhile and reflect. Its sleek lines are reflected in the white marble lobby with bluish flames appearing through oyster shells in alcoves and flowers floating in giant urns in square sunken seated areas. The I-Thai restaurant downstairs is similarly geometric and fuses Italy with the Orient in its dishes. Textured layers of creams and greys, blacks and whites feature in the uncluttered bedrooms and are set off with orchids, monochromatic art and cushions here and there. The Lioness Den is along Japanese lines with a futon on wooden decking caged in with chrome railings and suspended over the lounge below. Supplements are levied for bedrooms facing the garden.

○ Open all year; restaurant closed Sun eve   Nearest tube stations are Lancaster Gate (Central line) and Paddington (Bakerloo, Circle, District and Hammersmith & City lines). Private car park   4 single, 9 twin/double, 22 double, 10 suites; all with room service, hair-dryer, mini-bar, direct-dial telephone, fax machine, modem line, TV, VCR, CD player   Restaurant, bar, lounge, garden; conferences; social functions; civil wedding licence; leisure facilities nearby; cots, highchairs, babysitting, baby-listening, outdoor play area   Wheelchair access to hotel and restaurant (lift), National Accessible Scheme: mobility impairment, M4, WC, 3 rooms specially equipped for disabled people, lift   No dogs   Amex, Delta, Diners, MasterCard, Switch, Visa   Single £275, twin/double £295, suite £440 to £990; deposit required. Continental B £15, cooked B £17.50; alc L £21.50, D £50; light meals available. Special breaks available

L'Hotel

28 Basil Street, London SW3 1AS
TEL: 020-7589 6286   FAX: 020-7823 7826
EMAIL: reservations@lhotel.co.uk
WEB SITE: www.lhotel.co.uk

Comfortable hotel just doors from Harrods, with a distinctly French feel

A discreet '28' in blue and white tiles on red bricks announces the location of this appealing bolthole a couple of doors from the back of Harrods and just down the road from its swankier sister hotel The Capital (see entry). The basement brasserie (Le Metro), with a chic, modern look, is full to bursting at lunchtime with shoppers laden with the ubiquitous green and gold bags, and is also the venue for breakfast, included in the room rates. The ochre lobby, stencilled with twisting vines and grapes, shows a flourish of creativity and gives the space a warm and welcoming feel. Halls colour-washed in yellows or tangerines lead to just 12 bedrooms. Those facing the street tend to have bigger bathrooms, with plenty of natural light (the hubbub outside dies down at night), whereas those at the back have more living space. All are decorated in warm shades of beige or terracotta, with fabric-covered walls, ceiling fans, or wooden slatted blinds. We had a complaint this year about poor service and lack of storage space and lighting in the bathroom. More reports welcome.

○ Open all year; restaurant closed Sun eve   Nearest tube station is Knightsbridge (Piccadilly line). Private car park (at The Capital)   10 twin/double, 1 double, 1 suite; all with hair-dryer, mini-bar, direct-dial telephone, TV, VCR   Restaurant, bar; social functions; leisure facilities nearby; babysitting   No wheelchair access; 3 steps into hotel, 1 step into restaurant (via rear), 1 ground-floor bedroom specially equipped for disabled people, lift   No dogs in public rooms   Amex, Delta, Diners, MasterCard, Switch, Visa   Single occupancy of twin/double £177, twin/double £177 to £200, suite £212; deposit required. Alc L, D £20; light meals available   (3 FOR 2)

K+K Hotel George

1–15 Templeton Place, London SW5 9NB
TEL: 020-7598 8700   FAX: 020-7370 2285
EMAIL: hotelgeorge@kkhotels.co.uk
WEB SITE: www.kkhotels.com/george

Professional staff at this smart, contemporary hotel in a quiet residential area

This hotel is part of a small Austrian chain which has hit on a formula that works well internationally – it has sister properties in Paris, Munich and Prague among others. This one in Earls Court occupies six cream-and-white stuccoed townhouses and has a large, lawned back garden the length of the block with plenty of tables and chairs. Green-framed glass doors at the entrance open up into a spacious canary yellow reception with spotlights, leafy plants in terracotta pots and mirrored walls. The businesslike lounge sees chrome-rimmed black leather sofas and more sunny yellow, and the garden-side breakfast room successfully combines purple, russet and yellow. A generous continental buffet breakfast, including fruit, cold cuts and cheeses, is included in the rates. Streamlined bedrooms feature wood panelling, fresh white walls, a couple of black-and-white or contemporary framed prints, and beds with crisp white folded duvets. Bathrooms are spick and span, with big mirrors.

○ Open all year   ⊿ Nearest tube station is Earls Court (District and Piccadilly lines). Private car park (£15)   ⌿ 7 single, 67 twin, 42 double, 37 family rooms; all with room service, hair-dryer, mini-bar, direct-dial telephone, modem line, TV   ⊘ Restaurant, bar, lounge, garden; conferences; leisure facilities nearby; early suppers for children; cots, highchairs   ⅃ No wheelchair access; 5 steps into hotel, 8 ground-floor bedrooms, lift   ● No dogs   ▭ Amex, Delta, Diners, MasterCard, Switch, Visa   ⸠£⸡ Single £175, twin/double £210, family room £230; deposit required. Alc L £15, D £17; light meals available; service incl. Special breaks available   ⦅3 FOR 2⦆

Knightsbridge Hotel

10 Beaufort Gardens, London SW3 1PT
TEL: 020-7584 6300   FAX: 020-7584 6355
EMAIL: knightsbridge@firmdale.com
WEB SITE: www.firmdalehotels.com

Intimate B&B with an easygoing manner and bespoke art

The latest house to get the Firmdale treatment, this Georgian edifice is in a peaceful cul de sac graced with trees. Kit Kemp's characteristic flair for interior design is in evidence throughout, with the use of beautiful fabrics, unusual sculptures and eye-catching art without compromising on comfort and amenities. In the African-inspired drawing room, faux furs and exotic fabrics in earthy shades grace the comfy sofas drawn round a sandstone fireplace. The library, in soft pinks and greens, is equally comfortable, with plenty of light pounding through full-length windows, and a walk-in honesty bar – a trademark of this small hotel group that makes it feel all the more like a home from home. Some bedrooms have DVD and all have CD players and grand granite bathrooms. Incredibly feminine fabrics beautify bedrooms in cream or mushroom shades, giving a contemporary, fresh feel throughout.

○ Open all year   ⊿ Nearest tube station is Knightsbridge (Piccadilly line)   ⌿ 7 single, 13 twin/double, 22 double, 2 suites; all with room service, hair-dryer, mini-bar, direct-dial telephone, fax/modem line, TV, VCR or DVD, CD player; trouser press available on request; no tea/coffee-making facilities in rooms   ⊘ Drawing room, library, honesty bar; cots, babysitting   ⅃ No wheelchair access   ● No dogs   ▭ Amex, Delta, MasterCard, Switch, Visa   ⸠£⸡ Single from £177, single occupancy of twin/double from £212, twin £306, double £212, suite from £388; deposit required. Continental B £7, cooked £14; light meals available via room service. Special breaks available

Knightsbridge Green Hotel

159 Knightsbridge, London SW1X 7PD
TEL: 020-7584 6274   FAX: 020-7225 1635
EMAIL: reservations@thekghotel.com
WEB SITE: www.thekghotel.co.uk

Family-owned B&B in a frenetic part of town

The location is not the most auspicious – on the busy Knightsbridge road, with the entrance tucked under a glass canopy between shops selling rugs and phone accessories. However, the rates for this part of town (it's a stone's throw from Hyde Park, Harvey Nichols and Harrods) are definitely something to shout about. A mint-green corridor runs past a plain blue lounge with frosted windows, stripped floors and the morning papers laid out on a table, to the small reception desk. There is no restaurant – breakfast is brought on a tray to your room and ranges from 'express' or 'continental' to 'English'. The last includes sausages and bacon from Harrods. Bedrooms are incredible value, if somewhat plain, and even the singles don't scrimp on space. Many have terracotta and cream colour schemes, although the biggest suite, bigger than many London flats, is in dark blue. All are immaculately kept and spotlessly clean. Service is friendly and personable.

◗ Open all year   ⚡ Nearest tube station is Knightsbridge (Piccadilly line)   🛏 7 single, 4 twin, 4 double, 1 four-poster, 12 suites; family rooms available; all with hair-dryer, trouser press, direct-dial telephone, modem line, TV ✅ lounge; cots ♿ Wheelchair access to hotel (ramp), lift, WC ⬤ No dogs; no smoking ▭ Amex, Diners, MasterCard, Visa £ Single from £90, twin/double/four-poster from £115, suite from £140; family room from £165; deposit required. Continental B £3.50/£7, cooked B £10.50

K-West [see map 3]

Richmond Way, London SW14 0AX
TEL: 020-7674 1000   FAX: 020-7674 1050
EMAIL: bookit@k-west.co.uk
WEB SITE: www.k-west.co.uk

Huge design statement at this super-trendy venue for star-spotting

Shepherd's Bush is a lively, cosmopolitan area most normally associated with the BBC and so it's not surprising that people working in the media frequently find themselves in and around this hi-tech, plate-glass property, formerly the home of the BBC administration centre. It's far from institutional now, and billed itself as 'London's newest design hotel' when it opened. It certainly lives up to its design ideals. Swanky suites and bedrooms come in contemporary neutrals with expensive linens, leathers and suedes. Indulgent bathrooms have state-of-the-art showers, granite surfaces, limestone mosaic tiles and Philippe Starck fittings. Cutting-edge technology includes plasma screens, and CD and DVD players. Young, good-looking staff dressed in black flit around the public areas: a sleek, green and chrome bar and a buzzy restaurant in vivid red and blue. The pièce de résistance is a spa with hot stone treatments and Korean Hand Therapy among those on offer.

◗ Open all year   ⚡ Nearest tube station is Shepherd's Bush (Central line). Private car park 🛏 45 twin/double, 132 double, 33 family rooms, 12 suites; family rooms available; all with room service, hair-dryer, mini-bar, trouser press, ironing facilities, direct-dial telephone, modem line, TV; some with VCR, DVD, CD player ✅ Restaurant, bar, lounge, Internet zone, garden; conferences and social functions; gym, spa; leisure facilities nearby; cots, highchairs ♿ Wheelchair access to hotel and restaurant, WC, 6 ground-floor bedrooms specially equipped for disabled people, lift. Disabled parking ⬤ No dogs; no smoking in some bedrooms ▭ Amex, Delta, Diners, MasterCard, Switch, Visa £ Single occupancy of twin/double £165, twin/double from £193, family room from £277, suite from £294; deposit required. Continental B £9, cooked B £19; set L £14.50; alc L, D £46; light meals available. Special breaks available

Malmaison London NEW ENTRY

18–21 Charterhouse Square, London EC1M 6AH
TEL: 020-7012 3700   FAX: 020-7012 3702
EMAIL: london@malmaison.com
WEB SITE: www.malmaison.com

New outpost for this classy chain in the current epicentre of urban cool

Ten years ago, who outside London had heard of Clerkenwell, or could put it on the map? Things have changed, and it's fitting that this chic, upbeat chain has set up in a handsome red-brick building just a few minutes from the bars and bistros of Smithfield Market. The spotlit lobby makes for a dramatic entrance, all in sleek lines with dark red overtones and single flower stems in tall cylindrical glasses. Downstairs, meals – polenta-crusted sea bass, or the Malmaison mixed-grill meatfest, perhaps – are served in an atmospheric brasserie amid a genial buzz of conversation. Ultra-comfortable bedrooms have crisp white bed linen on oversized beds, aromatic smellies in decent bathrooms with power showers, and mod cons including air-conditioning, CD and mini-disk players, and wall-mounted plasma TVs. Monochromatic urban art, *chaises longues*, and earthy shades are typical of the contemporary look here – and the view over the cobbled square is lovely.

◐ Open all year   🚇 Nearest tube station is Barbican (Circle, Metropolitan and Hammersmith & City lines)
🛏 8 single, 23 twin/double, 64 double, 2 suites; all with room service, hair-dryer, mini-bar, trouser press, direct-dial telephone, modem line, TV, CD player   ✦ Restaurant, bar; conferences; gym; cots, highchairs
♿ Wheelchair access to hotel and restaurant (lift), 5 ground-floor bedrooms, 5 bedrooms specially equipped for disabled people, lift   ● No dogs in public rooms   ▭ Amex, Delta, Diners, MasterCard, Switch, Visa
£ Single £177, twin/double £194 to £212, suite £277; deposit required. Continental B £11, cooked B £14; set L, D £22; alc L, D £35; light meals available. Special breaks available

Mandarin Oriental Hyde Park

66 Knightsbridge, London SW1X 7LA
TEL: 020-7235 2000   FAX: 020-7235 2001
EMAIL: molon-info@mohg.com
WEB SITE: www.mandarinoriental.com

Palatial Knightsbridge hotel with top-notch food and a heavenly spa – for gold card holders only!

Built in 1889 of red brick and Portland stone as gentlemen's apartments, this grand building was projected to be the tallest in London, although luckily it cast no shadow over the Serpentine in Hyde Park opposite, as local residents had feared it might. Stone lions, Corinthian pillars and smartly attired doormen in red coats and top hats mark the entrance on the busy Knightsbridge road. Inside, a lavishly patterned marble floor sits beneath an equally intricate gold ceiling. But it's tastefully done and appears elegant rather than obscenely opulent. The fine dining restaurant, Foliage, reflects the seasons in the colour of the leaves on display, some silk and some picked daily from Hyde Park. The Park restaurant serves mainly Asian cuisine – reserve a table near the window for some great views. A stunningly serene spa gives further opportunity to break the bank. Even the landings all the way up the building have luxurious drapes, plush rugs and crystal chandeliers. Classical music greets guests on entry to suitably refined bedrooms done up in blues and reds and golds with swathes of silk, and marble bathrooms.

◐ Open all year   🚇 Nearest tube station is Knightsbridge (Piccadilly line)   🛏 8 twin, 169 double, 23 suites; all with room service, hair-dryer, mini-bar, direct-dial telephone, modem line, TV, DVD, CD player; tea/coffee-making facilities, fax (suites only) and trouser press on request   ✦ 2 restaurants, bar; conferences and social functions; civil wedding licence; gym, spa; early suppers for children; cots, highchairs, toys   ♿ Wheelchair access to hotel and restaurants, WC, lift   ● No dogs   ▭ Amex, Delta, Diners, MasterCard, Switch, Visa
£ Twin/double from £355, suite from £550; deposit required. Continental B £21, cooked B £25; set L from £31, D from £39; alc L from £35, D from £42; light meals available. Special breaks available

The Milestone

1 Kensington Court, London W8 5DL
TEL: 020-7917 1000   FAX: 020-7917 1010
EMAIL: bookms@rchmail.com
WEB SITE: www.milestonehotel.com

Top-notch service and every conceivable desire catered for at this five-star hotel

The other side of the road from Kensington Palace and Gardens makes a fitting location for such a distinguished hotel, housed in two fine nineteenth-century townhouses. The cosy lounge, with its crackling fire, wood panels and well-draped leaded windows, is a good place to sit and enjoy the view or read the morning papers, and in the evenings a singer or pianist provides the entertainment. Cheneston's (the old name for Kensington) is the restaurant's name. Smartly attired diners sit under an ornate plasterwork ceiling in traditional surroundings. Those after a more casual experience should head for the striking black and white conservatory. Bedrooms are imaginatively and individually decorated, perhaps in regal purples or lovely blue and yellow coordinates. Even the lower grades are supremely comfortable and come with mod cons including DVD and CD players and cosseting extras such as two types of robe and floating votive candles; park-side rooms have a small premium. Further up the scale, bedrooms are more opulent, fabrics are more sumptuous, and designs more decadent. The Safari Suite, for example, is a lavish animal-print concoction with tented walls. A new 'resistance pool' opened in the basement in summer 2004.

◗ Open all year   ⤢ Nearest tube station is High Street Kensington (District and Circle lines)   ⇤ 2 twin, 7 twin/double, 36 double, 12 suites; all with room service, hair-dryer, mini-bar, direct-dial telephone, modem line, TV, VCR, CD player; trouser press on request   ⌑ Restaurant, bar, lounge, conservatory; conferences and social functions; civil wedding licence; gym, heated indoor swimming pool; leisure facilities nearby; cots, highchairs, toys, babysitting, baby-listening   ♿ Wheelchair access to hotel (ramp) and restaurant, WC, 2 ground-floor bedrooms, 1 room specially equipped for disabled people, lift   ⊖ No smoking in restaurant and some bedrooms   ⊏ Amex, Delta, Diners, MasterCard, Switch, Visa   £ Twin/double £341 to £353, family room £382 to £394, suite from £647; deposit required. Continental B £16.50, cooked B £21.50; set L £22; alc L, D £43; light meals available; service incl

Miller's

111A Westbourne Grove, London W2 4UW
TEL: 020-7243 1024   FAX: 020-7243 1064
EMAIL: enquiries@millersuk.com
WEB SITE: www.millersuk.com

Inspired, extraordinary hotel for antiques lovers in Notting Hill

The discreet red door announcing the presence of this gem is actually in Hereford Road, a side street off Westbourne Grove, above a Brazilian restaurant. Once buzzed in, you ascend the red-carpeted stairs past walls richly adorned in eclectic paintings and pictures to reach the hotel. The huge carved fireplace would be the focus of the reception-cum-drawing room, were it not for an Aladdin's cave of curios, antiques, china and portraits that divert the eye away to every nook and cranny of the room. Candelabra on every surface add to the drama, and the flowers and fruit bowls on the polished breakfast table confirm that this is indeed a place of abundance! Arty doors lead to the bedrooms, which are more restrained but are still a feast for the eyes, with oriental rugs strewn on floors and walls bedecked in framed scenes, sketches and old photos. Each of the comfortable rooms is a masterpiece in its own right.

◗ Open all year   ⤢ Nearest tube stations are Bayswater (District and Circle lines) and Notting Hill Gate (District, Circle and Central lines)   ⇤ 4 double, 1 four-poster, 2 suites; all with hair-dryer, direct-dial telephone, modem line, TV, CD player; some with VCR   ⌑ Breakfast room, bar, drawing room; conferences and social functions; leisure facilities nearby; 🔥 No wheelchair access ⬤ None ⌷ Amex, Delta, MasterCard, Switch, Visa £ Single occupancy of double £194 to £217, double £194 to £217, four-poster £217, suite £270; deposit required ③FOR②

Morgan House

120 Ebury Street, London SW1W 9QQ
TEL: 020-7730 2384   FAX: 020-7730 8442
EMAIL: morganhouse@btclick.com
WEB SITE: www.morganhouse.co.uk

Appealing B&B with modest prices near Victoria

A recent traffic-calming scheme has transformed what used to be a busy through-road, so guests of this neat Georgian townhouse, with an incredibly welcoming owner, will find relative tranquillity. It's an interesting area, with antique shops, wine bars, tapas and Italian food, and even a Saturday farmers' market. All the bedrooms are immaculately kept, and many have had new carpets and beds this year. Room 8 at the top of the house has views over the rooftops of Belgravia. Others have wrought-iron bedsteads and crisp cream or pale blue colour schemes. Most bedrooms share neat shower rooms on the landings, although four are en suite. A full cooked breakfast is offered downstairs in a lovely, light room with stripped wooden floors and cream and yellow napery. Guests are also welcome to use a small interior trellised garden, accessed via the office.

◗ Open all year 🔁 Nearest tube station is Victoria (Victoria, Circle and District lines) 🛏 2 single, 2 twin, 1 twin/double, 4 double, 2 family rooms; 7 with shared bathroom; all with hair-dryer, TV ⊗ Breakfast room, conservatory, garden; toys, babysitting; leisure facilities nearby 🔥 No wheelchair access; 5 steps into hotel, 12 steps into breakfast room, 3 ground-floor bedrooms ⬤ No dogs; no smoking ⌷ MasterCard, Visa £ Single £46, single occupancy of twin/double £62 to £76, twin/double £66 to £86, family room £86 to £122; deposit required

Novotel London Euston

100–110 Euston Road, London NW1 2AJ
TEL: 020-7666 9000   FAX: 020-7666 9100
EMAIL: h5309@accor.com
WEB SITE: www.novotel.com

Sparkling new flagship Novotel with bird's-eye views of the capital

Cast aside your preconceptions of this Gallic-owned chain, for this soaring glass tower is firmly in the twenty-first century in its design and attitude. Adjacent to the British Library and just up the road from Bloomsbury, home to the British Museum, it's a busy yet handy base that's easily accessible by tube. First impressions are of a bright, spacious open-plan lobby which fuses with the restaurant and bar. As the glass-sided lift ascends higher, increasingly magnificent views of London unravel, revealing Parliament and the London Eye among other landmarks. Vistas from the small gym on the rooftop should help ease the pain of exercising. Ask for a bedroom as near to the top as you can, for the views. Spacious and streamlined, these are contemporary spaces with stylish colours and bathrooms with round glass sinks and curved-screen showers. Look out for bargain rates online.

◗ Open all year 🔁 Nearest tube station is Euston (Northern and Victoria lines) 🛏 103 twin, 185 double, 21 family rooms, 3 suites; all with room service, hair-dryer, mini-bar, trouser press, direct-dial telephone, modem line, TV, VCR; suites with CD player ⊗ Restaurant, bar, lounge; conferences and social functions; gym, sauna, steam room; cots, highchairs, babysitting 🔥 Wheelchair access to hotel (ramp/lift) and restaurant, National Accessible Scheme: M, WC, 11 rooms specially equipped for disabled people, lift. Disabled parking ⬤ No dogs; no smoking in some bedrooms ⌷ Amex, Delta, Diners, MasterCard, Switch, Visa £ Twin/double/family room £160, suite £500; deposit required. Continental B £9.50, cooked B £14.50; set L, D £15; alc L, D £25; light meals available. Special breaks available

Number Sixteen

16 Sumner Place, London SW7 3EG
TEL: 020-7589 5232 FAX: 020-7584 8615
EMAIL: sixteen@firmdale.com
WEB SITE: www.firmdalehotels.com

Contemporary meets country house in South Kensington

There's something to catch your eye at every turn at this classy townhouse, part of the Firmdale group, recently given a total makeover by co-owner and designer Kit Kemp, and looked after by a genuinely enthusiastic team of staff. At the front is a picture-perfect road of gracious white townhouses, while secreted away at the rear is a delightful leafy garden with a fish pond. Attention is drawn to beautiful antiques, unusual pieces of furniture and brightly coloured art in every room, with clever lighting setting off the stone and pearly shades. Some bedrooms have little garden terraces, while others benefit from garden views, but all have Frette linen on inviting beds, striking fabrics, good pictures and the odd antique. Bathrooms, in floor-to-ceiling granite, have soft white towels and Molton Brown toiletries. A continental breakfast is brought on a tray to your room or served in the garden conservatory.

◖ Open all year ▨ Nearest tube station is South Kensington (Piccadilly, District and Circle lines) ⌕ 5 single, 37 double; all with room service, hair-dryer, mini-bar, direct-dial telephone, fax point, modem, TV; some with DVD, CD player; trouser-press; no tea/coffee-making facilities in rooms ⊘ Honesty bar, lounge, study, conservatory, garden; conferences; social functions; leisure facilities nearby; cots 㫟 No wheelchair access, 3 steps into hotel, 5 ground-floor bedrooms ● No dogs ▭ Amex, Delta, MasterCard, Switch, Visa £ Single from £112, double from £200; deposit required. Continental B £7.50, cooked £9.50; light meals available. Special breaks available

One Aldwych

1 Aldwych, London WC2B 4RH
TEL: 020-7300 1000 FAX: 020-7300 1001
EMAIL: sales@onealdwych.com
WEB SITE: www.onealdwych.com

Art, comfort and modern gadgetry form a winning trilogy at this superb hotel

Walking in to the lofty lobby of this contemporary hotel, you'll find it hard to imagine it in its previous incarnation as a bank. Exquisite flower arrangements stand on tall glass plinths, light floods in through oversized arched windows and a sculpted rower seems to glide across the tiled lobby floor. Indigo restaurant, serving light European food, overlooks the action below, while the underground Axis bistro, with its black leather seating, is more formal and is reached via a separate entrance. A glass and chrome staircase spirals down to a health club with a beautiful pool, which even has an underwater sound system! But the bedrooms really deliver the goods. CD players, fibre-optic reading lights by the bed and TV monitors on bendy stems in front of the bath are among the hi-tech features. Metal mesh cupboards, chrome and glass form part of the décor. Beds are made up with Frette linen and feather-and-down duvets, and most bathrooms have natural light, natural bath products and a separate shower cubicle and tub. Owner Gordon Campbell-Gray's fabulous art collection graces the hotel at every turn, and fresh flowers are in abundance throughout.

◖ Open all year; Axis bistro closed Sun ▨ Nearest tube station is Charing Cross (Bakerloo and Northern lines) ⌕ 3 twin, 17 twin/double, 105 double; suites and family rooms available; all with room service, hair-dryer, mini-bar, trouser press, direct-dial telephone, fax, modem line, TV, CD player; no tea/coffee-making facilities in rooms ⊘ 2 restaurants, bar; conferences and social functions; civil wedding licence; gym, spa, heated indoor swimming pool; cots, highchairs, toys 㫟 Wheelchair access to hotel (lift) and restaurant (ramp), WC, 6 rooms specially equipped for disabled people, lift. Valet parking ● No dogs; no smoking in some bedrooms ▭ Amex, Diners, MasterCard, Switch, Visa £ Single occupancy of twin/double £211 to £441, twin/double £221 to £464, family room £281 to £464, suite £382 to £735; deposit required. Continental B

£14.50, cooked B £19.50; set L £25, D £19.50/£21; alc L £30/£35, D £35/£45; light meals available. Special breaks available

The Pavilion

34–36 Sussex Gardens, London W2 1UL
TEL: 020-7262 0905   FAX: 020-7262 1324
EMAIL: pavilionhotel@aol.com
WEB SITE: www.pavilionhoteluk.com

Totally unique place – great fun for party lovers and pop stars

A place would have to make a name for itself to beat the competition on this busy road near Paddington station, which is chock-full of guesthouses. The Pavilion, an outlandishly flamboyant B&B in a league all of its own, has done just that. The themed bedrooms are often hired by the hour by fashion magazines for photo shoots, and by those who want the right setting for interviewing a band. Luckily, the rooms usually escape the rock-star trashing treatment, which is just as well because such eclectic style would be hard to recreate! King of kitsch is Honky Tonk Afro, in bright canary yellow with leopard prints and a glitter ball. Indian Summer is a cosy four-poster with rich velvets in all shades of pink and purple and gold. Highland Fling is a more masculine wood-panelled room with plenty of tartan and mounted antlers. The tiny shower rooms are often too small to accommodate washbasins, but who cares when you're having this much fun? In fact, the only restraint shown here is in the room rates, which include both VAT (rarely so in London) and continental breakfast – and a cooked version is only £5. Breakfast is brought to your room 'at any time you like'.

❍ Open all year ▨ Nearest tube station is Edgware Road (Bakerloo, District, Circle and Hammersmith & City lines). Private car park ▙ 8 single, 9 twin/double, 9 double, 1 four-poster, 2 family rooms; all with room service, hair-dryer, direct-dial telephone, modem line, TV; some with CD player, DVD ⊘ 2 lounges, garden; conferences and social functions ✦ No wheelchair access; 4 ground-floor bedrooms ➊ No dogs ▭ Amex, Delta, Diners, MasterCard, Switch, Visa £ Single £60, single occupancy of twin/double £85, twin/double/four-poster £100, family room £130; deposit required. Cooked B £5

Pembridge Court

34 Pembridge Gardens, London W2 4DX
TEL: 020-7229 9977   FAX: 020-7727 4982
EMAIL: reservations@pemct.co.uk
WEB SITE: www.pemct.co.uk

Good-sized rooms at this well-maintained B&B near Portobello Market

Two stone pineapples on top of the gateposts – used traditionally to show that the house extends a welcome to guests – mark the entrance of this neo-classical property near Notting Hill tube. The tradition has endured judging by this small hotel's loyal following. Inside, it is home to a collection of framed Victorian memorabilia including babies' dresses, gloves, feathery hats and lacy fans and the joke is that originally it was a 'cheap way to cover the walls' before it got out of hand! A lovely sitting room in blues and yellows has deep, inviting sofas and a further one is found near the comfy basement breakfast room. Housekeeping is impeccable – and things are constantly being improved and freshened up, such as the new red carpets in the halls on our visit. Around three-quarters of the 20 bedrooms are really large. All have a traditional feel with posh drapes and bed canopies and brass bathroom fittings. Cosseting extras include robes and good toiletries, and technology stretches to CD players and videos.

❍ Open all year ▨ Nearest tube station is Notting Hill Gate (Central, District and Circle lines) ▙ 3 single, 3 twin, 13 double, 1 four-poster; family room available; all with room service, hair-dryer, trouser press, direct-dial telephone, modem, TV; some with VCR, CD player; tea/coffee-making facilities on request ⊘ 2 sitting rooms, breakfast room; conferences; leisure facilities nearby; cots, highchairs, babysitting, baby-listening ✦ No wheelchair access, 6 steps into hotel, 3 ground-floor bedrooms ➊ No dogs in public rooms; no unattended dogs in bedrooms ▭ Amex, Delta, Diners, MasterCard, Switch, Visa £ Single £125, single occupancy of twin/double £160 to £165, twin/double £160 to £195, four-poster £195, family room £210; deposit required. Special breaks available

The Portobello

22 Stanley Gardens, London W11 2NG
TEL: 020-7727 2777   FAX: 020-7792 9641
EMAIL: info@portobello-hotel.co.uk
WEB SITE: www.portobello-hotel.co.uk

Plush, occasionally flamboyant bedrooms and a relaxed air at this Notting Hill oasis

This intimate hotel, with potted conifers at the entrance, sits on a short, quiet street in Notting Hill. Light streams in through wooden blinds in the drawing room, illuminating lush plants, grand oil paintings and rich mustard walls. Bedrooms are decorated with panache and imagination, and some, such as Room 16 with its eccentric Victorian bathing machine and round, draped bed, combine eccentric touches with all the comforts you'd expect.

Another top room is Room 13, where a beautiful four-poster has heavenly hosts and windows overlook a charming communal garden. Even standard rooms don't short-change, with thick, silky curtains, enticing beds and perhaps marble bathrooms. Meals are served in the basement dining room; a champagne and smoked salmon breakfast can be served in the drawing room, at polished tables, or delivered upstairs to your room if you prefer.

◑ Closed Chr ⬕ Nearest tube station is Notting Hill Gate (Central, District and Circle lines) ⤙ 6 single, 2 twin/double, 4 double 12 four-poster; family rooms available; all with 24-hour room service, hair-dryer, mini-bar, direct-dial telephone, modem line, TV; CD player on request ⟡ Dining room, bar service, lounge; early suppers for children; cots, babysitting ⅙ No wheelchair access; 6 steps into hotel, 15 steps into dining room, 2 ground-floor bedrooms, lift ⬤ None ▭ Amex, Delta, MasterCard, Switch, Visa £ Single £140, twin/double £160 to £180, four-poster £220 to £260, family room £275; deposit required. Cooked B £11; alc L, D £25; light meals available. Special breaks available

The Queensgate

54 Queen's Gate, London SW7 5JW
TEL: 020-7761 4000   FAX: 020-7761 4040
EMAIL: enquiries@thequeensgate.com
WEB SITE: www.thequeensgate.com

Laid-back and clutter-free B&B in a good location for museum visiting

This contemporary B&B is in a most desirable part of South Kensington and offers views of the Natural History Museum through the trees. Ionic columns stand either side of stone steps that lead into an uncluttered, airy space with cream walls dotted with black and white photos in wooden frames. The café lounge has full-length sash windows and a variety of seating: comfy sofas, tan leather bar stools or diner-like red-leather benches. Here real coffee is served both to passers-by and to residents (who drink for free). Pass the tiny

reception cubby hole (and a friendly face) to ascend the painted white staircase to a barrage of bedrooms in a similarly minimalist style, but with comforts including waffle bathrobes, Molton Brown smellies and Egyptian cotton sheets. Many rooms have a distinguishing feature, whether it be a decked terrace, huge sash windows, or a skylight. Bathrooms, in perhaps black granite or sandstone, have huge chrome rain showerheads.

◑ Open all year ⬕ Nearest tube station is Gloucester Road (Piccadilly, District and Circle lines) ⤙ 5 single, 19 twin/double, 2 suites; all with room service, hair-dryer, trouser press, direct-dial telephone, modem line, TV, DVD, CD player; no tea/coffee-making facilities in rooms ⟡ Bar, lounge, terraces; leisure facilities nearby ⅙ No wheelchair access; 6 steps into hotel, WC, 2 ground-floor bedrooms, lift ⬤ None ▭ Amex, Delta, MasterCard, Switch, Visa £ Single £140, twin/double £160 to £180, suite £220 to £260; deposit required. Light meals available (room service). Special breaks available

The Rookery

12 Peter's Lane, Cowcross Street, London EC1M 6DS
TEL: 020-7336 0931   FAX: 020-7336 0932
EMAIL: reservations@rookery.co.uk
WEB SITE: www.rookeryhotel.com

Idiosyncratic B&B in an area with a fascinating history and exciting future

This hotel is named after the dense slums that filled Clerkenwell in Dickensian days, when the Fagins of the world resided locally, Smithfield was a cattle market and vice girls and pickpockets dodged the Law. Things are rather more salubrious now, and City and media types spend their expense accounts in trendy bars and bistros. The Rookery (whose sister hotels are the Gore and Hazlitt's – see entries) is refreshingly traditional, with flagstone floors, exposed bricks, crackling fires and a liberal smattering of antiques (the owners are in the trade). Characterful bedrooms, named after previous residents of the area (including prostitutes and executioners), contain extravagant period beds with superb mattresses, antique writing desks, Victorian roll-top baths and original brass, copper and nickel plumbing. The top-notch tower suite, Rook's Nest, has views of St Paul's Cathedral and the Old Bailey. Breakfast, taken in bed, consists of freshly baked croissants or 'Rookery Reveille', Greek yoghurt with honey. Light evening meals, too, are available via room service.

○ Closed Chr ⚡ Nearest tube station is Farringdon (Circle, Hammersmith & City and Metropolitan lines) 🛏 6 single, 23 double, 1 four-poster, 3 suites; family rooms available; all with room service, hair-dryer, mini-bar, direct-dial telephone, modem line, TV; two with CD player; no tea/coffee-making facilities in rooms ✧ Lounge, library, conservatory; conferences and social functions; leisure facilities nearby; cots, babysitting ♿ No wheelchair access; 2 steps into hotel, 4 ground-floor bedrooms ● No dogs in bedrooms; no smoking in some bedrooms ▭ Amex, Delta, Diners, MasterCard, Switch, Visa £ Single £224, single occupancy of double £241, double £265, four-poster/family room £324, suite £582; deposit required. Continental B £10; light meals available; service incl. Special breaks available

The Savoy

Strand, London WC2R 0EU
TEL: 020-7836 4343   FAX: 020-7240 6040
EMAIL: info@the-savoy.co.uk
WEB SITE: www.savoygroup.com

Luxurious rooms and faultless service at a London institution

A venerable institution, the Savoy is approached by the only road in the UK where you drive on the right. In the lobby, staff sporting red roses seem to glide between the Corinthian marble pillars. A marble archway leads through to the Savoy Grill. The Banquette is more casual, with cushions on cream leather seating and blood-red walls – although the 'no jeans' policy is still enforced! The grand old dame of the public rooms, the Thames Foyer, on the river side and popular for afternoon teas, was due to be refurbished when we went to press. Start an evening sipping a martini cocktail – it was invented here after all – amid the black and white photography of the American Bar. The best bedrooms look across the river to the London Eye. All are refined and sophisticated with swags, good lamps and squashy sofas. Bathrooms are equally impressive with plenty of marble, heated towel rails and perhaps marble walk-in showers with dinner-plate-size heads.

○ Open all year ⚡ Nearest tube stations are Charing Cross (Bakerloo and Northern lines) and Embankment (Circle and District lines). Private car park 🛏 28 single, 136 twin, 5 family rooms, 68 suites; all with room service, hair-dryer, mini-bar, direct-dial telephone, fax machine, modem line, TV; CD player on request ✧ 4 restaurants, bar, lounge; conferences; social functions; civil wedding licence; gym, spa, heated indoor swimming pool, leisure facilities nearby; highchairs, babysitting ♿ Wheelchair access to hotel and restaurants (lift), WC, 11 rooms partially equipped for disabled people, lift. Disabled parking ● No dogs ▭ Amex, Delta, Diners, MasterCard, Switch, Visa £ Single from £175, single occupancy of twin £340 to £375, twin £405 to £440, family room £580 to £605, suite from £580; deposit required. Continental B £18.50, cooked B £24.50; set L £33.50, D from £43.50. Special breaks available (2004 data)

Sherlock Holmes Hotel

108 Baker Street, London W1U 6LJ
TEL: 020-7486 6161 FAX: 020-7958 5211
EMAIL: info@sherlockholmeshotel.com
WEB SITE: www.sherlockholmeshotel.com

Long-standing hotel given a major makeover by a contemporary international chain

Take away the name and this hip hotel on bustling Baker Street pays only very subtle homage to the fictitious detective. Young staff dressed in designer black serve at the bar, a large buzzy area serving tapas. At the far end is the reception desk and a stylish restaurant with modish hearth features casting a warm glow on the cream seats, from which you can watch the chefs at work in the kitchen. The spacious bedrooms are firmly in the twenty-first century – plenty of chrome, creams and neutrals. The latest wireless technology (coming soon) and lap-top safes should keep those here on business happy. Bathrooms are very modern, with some good features such as mist-free and full-length mirrors. All the rooms are in a similar style, with variations in shape and facilities as you go up through the categories.

◑ Open all year ⊿ Nearest train station: Baker Street (Hammersmith & Circle, Metropolitan, Jubilee and Bakerloo lines) ⟅ 23 twin, 93 double, 4 four-poster, 3 suites; family rooms available; all with room service, hair-dryer, mini-bar, direct-dial telephone, modem, TV; some with CD player ⊘ Restaurant, bar, lounge; gym, leisure facilities nearby; cots, highchairs, babysitting ♿ Wheelchair access to hotel (ramp) and restaurant, WC, 2 rooms specially equipped for disabled people, lift ● No dogs; no smoking in restaurant and some bedrooms ▭ Amex, Delta, Diners, MasterCard, Switch, Visa £ Single occupancy of twin/double £252 to £270, twin/double £252 to £270, four-poster/family room from £288, suite from £476; deposit required. Continental B £12.50, cooked B £16.50; set L £16.50; alc L, D £40; light meals available. Special breaks available

Sloane Hotel

29–31 Draycott Place, London SW3 2SH
TEL: 020-7581 5757 FAX: 020-7584 1348
EMAIL: reservations@sloanehotel.com
WEB SITE: www.sloanehotel.com

Intimate, idiosyncratic boutique hotel behind King's Road

The French owners of this red-brick terraced mansion have combined unusual antiques, beautiful and sensuous fabrics, and dramatic colours together throughout the hotel in a stylish and often theatrical way. Tantalising beds, grand oil paintings and distinctive antiques and *objets d'art* abound, and the overall result will appeal to those seeking somewhere a little bit romantic, or just somewhere unconventional near posh shops. A Louis Vuitton trunk sits at the bottom of one bed draped in silks and velvets in a room with its own decked terrace. In one of the suites, red walls, a thick, cream carpet and leopard-print fabrics blend flamboyantly. In another room, the four-poster is draped in fur covers, and grey silk drapes adorn the windows. There are views past the Battersea Power Station from the great rooftop terrace. Room service is available 24 hours a day, and could include soups, salads and ciabatta.

◑ Open all year ⊿ Nearest tube station is Sloane Square (District and Circle lines) ⟅ 3 single, 6 twin/ double, 5 four-poster, 2 family rooms, 4 suites; all with room service, hair-dryer, direct-dial telephone, modem line, TV, CD player; fax available; no tea/coffee-making facilities in rooms ⊘ Breakfast room, lounge, conservatory, roof terrace; conferences; cots, highchairs, toys, babysitting, baby-listening ♿ No wheelchair access; 5 steps into hotel, 2 ground-floor bedrooms, lift ● No dogs; no smoking in some public rooms and some bedrooms ▭ Amex, Delta, Diners, MasterCard, Switch, Visa £ Single £194, twin/double £253, four-poster/family room £294, suite £329; deposit required. Continental B £10, cooked B £14; alc L £25, D £30; light meals available; service incl

The Stafford

16–18 St James's Place, London SW1A 1NJ
TEL: 020-7493 0111   FAX: 020-7493 7121
EMAIL: info@thestaffordhotel.co.uk
WEB SITE: www.thestaffordhotel.co.uk

Traditional English hospitality and tasteful luxury in the regal heart of the capital

People don't just happen upon The Stafford. This handsome red-brick bolthole is secreted away at the end of a cul-de-sac in Mayfair, just a stone's throw from Green Park and a stroll from Buckingham and St James's palaces. A steady stream of taxis drop off and pick up guests, but apart from that it's amazingly quiet, considering its proximity to Piccadilly. Inside, the hotel is resolutely traditional – crystal chandeliers, plush country-house furnishings, open fires and a sense of calm in the public rooms, which include a refined restaurant. But through in the renowned American Bar, with wood panelling and a ceiling festooned with transatlantic visitors' baseball caps, club ties, and even model aircraft, things move up a gear – martini is the cocktail of choice and diners tuck in to a very British menu including Prince of Wales pork and leek sausages, sirloin steak or good old fish and chips. Bedrooms are either in the main house or in the beautifully converted beamed stables, and none of them disappoints.

◗ Open all year ⚡ Nearest tube station is Green Park (Piccadilly, Jubilee and Victoria lines) 🛏 11 single, 42 twin/double, 4 four-poster, 16 suites; family rooms available; all with room service, hair-dryer, direct-dial telephone, modem line, TV, CD player; some with VCR; no tea/coffee-making facilities in rooms ✅ Restaurant, dining room, bar, drawing room, garden; conferences and social functions; civil wedding licence; leisure facilities nearby; cots, highchairs, babysitting ♿ Wheelchair access to hotel (ramp) and restaurant, WC, 6 ground-floor bedrooms, lift. Valet parking ⬤ No dogs ▭ Amex, Delta, Diners, MasterCard, Switch, Visa £ Single £265, single occupancy of twin/double £288, twin/double £347 to £365, four-poster £365, family room from £459, suite £459. Continental B £19.50, cooked B £22; set L £30; alc L, D £59; light meals available; service incl. Special breaks available

Tophams Belgravia

24–32 Ebury Street, London SW1W 0LU
TEL: 020-7730 8147   FAX: 020-7823 5966
EMAIL: tophams_belgravia@compuserve.com
WEB SITE: www.tophams.co.uk

Good service and cosy bedrooms on a reasonably quiet road near Victoria station

This lovely hotel has been nurtured by the same family for nearly 70 years and has a loyal clientele who return year on year – they know they're on to a good thing! If you like the chrome and light-wood look, go somewhere else, for this is definitely for lovers of tradition. That doesn't mean Tophams is an old relic, and plenty of primary colours, such as the bright blue cloths and red walls of the restaurant, prove that it's not stuck in the past. The service too is attentive and gracious without being overbearing – return a few times and it really could feel as comfortable as home. If you're lucky, the weather may allow you to have breakfast at one of the outside tables in the summer. A cosy lounge looks good in florals and soft greens and pinks – the chintzy element is there, but at just the right level throughout the hotel. Odd plates, pictures and mirrors make the bedrooms, up in the warrens of the corridors, very appealing and homely spaces. Some are split-level, have antique desks in the window and TVs hidden away in cupboards, and have views over the rooftops.

◗ Closed Chr & New Year; restaurant closed Sat & Sun ⚡ Nearest tube station is Victoria (Victoria, District and Circle lines) 🛏 9 single, 2 twin, 19 twin/double, 3 four-poster, 4 family rooms; 2 with shared bathroom; all with room service (restricted), hair-dryer, direct-dial telephone, TV ✅ Restaurant, bar, lounge; conferences and social functions; early suppers for children; cots, highchairs, toys, babysitting ♿ No wheelchair access; 4 steps into hotel, 3 ground-floor bedrooms, lift ⬤ No dogs ▭ Amex, Delta, Diners, MasterCard, Switch,

Visa £ Single £90 to £115, twin/double £100 to £150, four-poster £100 to £150, family room £130 to £260; deposit required. Alc D £22; light meals available; service incl. Special breaks available

Trafalgar Hilton

2 Spring Gardens, Trafalgar Square, London SW1A 2TS
TEL: 020-7870 2900   FAX: 020-7870 2911
WEB SITE: www.hilton.co.uk/trafalgar

Hip bar and contemporary bedrooms in a totally un-Hilton-like experience

Cast aside all your preconceptions of Hiltons. This one, off the south-west corner of Trafalgar Square, breaks the mould in every way – so much so that you won't see a single piece of Hilton branding. The discreet entrance transports you into an expansive lobby-bar, Rockwell, that's hip and modern with stripped floorboards, spotlights and a chrome bar extending the whole length of the room. An impressive number of bourbons – this is London's first bourbon bar – are lined up behind it, and from Thursdays to Saturdays a DJ plays jazz-fusion for a young crowd. Downstairs, Jago is the rather austere restaurant serving European dishes from the open-plan kitchen, with the head chef's Argentinian heritage giving the menu a clear Hispanic leaning. Changing art exhibitions enliven the walls. Bedrooms facing the square are triple-glazed and all come in beige and cream, with a welcome splash of colour confined to a picture frame. They also have CD players, while higher categories have DVD players and a raised seating area.

◐ Open all year   ⟐ Nearest tube station is Charing Cross (Northern and Bakerloo lines)   ⬏ 29 twin, 98 double, 2 suites; all with room service, hair-dryer, mini-bar, direct-dial telephone, modem line, TV, CD player; some with DVD, ironing facilities   ⊘ Restaurant, bar, roof garden; conferences and social functions; leisure facilities nearby   ♿ Wheelchair access to hotel (ramp) and restaurant (lift), WC, 7 rooms specially equipped for disabled people, lift   ⬤ No dogs   ▭ Amex, Delta, Diners, MasterCard, Switch, Visa   £ Twin/double £177 to 282, suite £547; deposit required. Continental B £15.50, cooked B £19.50; alc L, D £32; light meals available

Twenty Nevern Square

20 Nevern Square, London SW5 9PD
TEL: 020-7565 9555   FAX: 020-7565 9444
EMAIL: info@mayflower-group.co.uk
WEB SITE: www.twentynevernsquare.co.uk

Smart boutique hotel with an oriental flavour

This stylish red-brick Georgian townhouse near Earls Court sits on a handsome square with leafy private gardens at its core. It's an eclectic mix of contemporary décor with rich fabrics and Eastern *objets d'art*. So the lounge, with its simple tiled floor and shiny apples on the table, is enriched by vibrant red-trimmed purple drapes. The conservatory has good dark-wicker chairs and round glass-topped tables, oriental lanterns and splashes of red and blue in its stained-glass windows. Here, a luxury continental breakfast featuring cold meats and cheeses and freshly squeezed orange juice is served (and included in the rates), while a full English is available on request for an extra charge. Most of the furniture in the compact, romantic bedrooms is Indonesian, and some of it is elaborately hand-carved. The best room in the house (Room 3) has a carved four-poster on stripped wooden floors and sumptuous beige and burgundy silk drapes. Others see exotic purple and gold silks, linens and cottons. Bathroom smellies are tucked away in carved wooden boxes, sheets are Egyptian cotton, and CD players are in every room.

◐ Open all year   ⟐ Nearest tube station is Earls Court (District and Piccadilly lines). Private car park   ⬏ 4 single, 3 twin, 8 double, 4 four-poster, 1 suite; all with room service, hair-dryer, trouser press, direct-dial telephone, modem line, TV, CD player; no tea/coffee-making facilities in rooms   ⊘ Breakfast room/conservatory, bar, lounge; conferences and social functions; leisure facilities nearby; cots   ♿ No wheelchair access, National Accessible Scheme: mobility impairment M1; 7 steps into hotel, 1 ground-floor bedroom, lift   ⬤ No dogs; no smoking in public rooms and some bedrooms   ▭ Amex, Delta, Diners, MasterCard, Switch,

Visa £ Single £79 to £89, twin/double £99, four-poster £110 to £120, suite £150 to £160; deposit required. Cooked B £5 to £9. Special breaks available

The Victoria [see map 3]

10 West Temple Sheen, London SW14 7RT
TEL: 020-8876 4238   FAX: 020-8878 3464
EMAIL: reservations@thevictoria.net
WEB SITE: www.thevictoria.net

Fairly priced food that pleases gourmets, near the largest royal park in London

The Victoria pub stands in a green and leafy part of London near the north side of Richmond Park, and people flock here mainly for the food. The evening menu changes weekly but could start with spinach, ricotta and walnut tart, be followed by roast brill, and include chocolate pithiviers for dessert. Afternoon teas, organic juices and tapas are also on offer during the day. The bar area, with an open-fire, bare boards and brown leather chairs, is a chic urban space that gives way to the airy conservatory restaurant and some outside seating beyond for summer weather. The stylish bedrooms are reached via the garden or car park and are light and uncluttered in mushroom colours, with more colourful throws. Fall into queensize beds with Egyptian cotton sheets and feather and down duvets, and revive yourself in the morning under a high-pressure shower.

◐ Closed Chr 🔁 Nearest tube station is Richmond (District line). Private car park 🛏 2 twin/double, 5 double; all with room service, hair-dryer, direct-dial telephone, modem line, TV ⊘ Restaurant/conservatory, bar, garden; social functions; leisure facilities nearby; cots, highchairs, outdoor play area ♿ Wheelchair access to hotel (ramp) and restaurant (1 step), 3 ground-floor bedrooms ⊜ No dogs; no smoking in bedrooms ▭ Amex, Delta, MasterCard, Switch, Visa £ Twin/double £100; deposit required. Alc L £25, D £35; light meals available; service incl. Special breaks available (3FOR2)

West Street

13–15 West Street, London WC2H 9NE
TEL: 020-7010 8700   FAX: 020-7010 8601
EMAIL: east.west@egami.co.uk
WEB SITE: www.egami.co.uk

Awesome rooms at this hip theatreland hangout in a quiet street

Three innovative bedrooms are found on the top floors of this fashionable restaurant-with-rooms just down the road from the Ivy in Covent Garden, in a house that was once a 'house of ill repute' for wealthy Japanese businessmen. Guests enter through a glass frontage and heavy curtains into a trendy bar with low leather seating, solid tables, red dabs of colour and a Buddha signalling the oriental leanings of the food. Drinkers snack on sweet chilli chicken or beef satay sticks while the more serious eating action goes on upstairs in the restaurant (known as East@West) with its lacquered ebony and black granite, serving dishes with Vietnamese, Chinese and Japanese influences. The seriously cool bedrooms are each spacious and totally different from the other. The Stone Room has a large private roof terrace with teak loungers and features brown leather and fake fur accessories among the pale cappuccino colours. The White Room is more striking, with Carrara marble flooring and soft red sofa. Lastly, the Loft spreads dark oak over the whole of the top floor and its high ceilings create an immense space.

◐ Closed Chr & New Year; restaurant closed Sun eve 🔁 Nearest tube station is Leicester Square (Northern and Piccadilly lines) 🛏 3 double; all with room service, hair-dryer, mini-bar, direct-dial telephone, modem line, TV, VCR, CD player; no tea/coffee-making facilities in rooms ⊘ Restaurant, dining room, bar; social functions; leisure facilities nearby; cots, highchairs ♿ Wheelchair access to hotel (2 steps) and restaurant, WC, lift ⊜ No dogs ▭ Amex, Delta, MasterCard, Switch, Visa £ Double £294 to £529; deposit required. Set L £20; alc D £47; light meals available

Windermere Hotel

142–144 Warwick Way, London SW1V 4JE
TEL: 020-7834 5163   FAX: 020-7630 8831
EMAIL: reservations@windermere-hotel.co.uk
WEB SITE: www.windermere-hotel.co.uk

Impeccably maintained hotel with the feel-good factor

With neat window boxes, fresh cream paint and tidy railings, the spruce nature of these two townhouses is already apparent before you set foot in the door. For owners Nick and Sylvia Hambi it must be a labour of love, for after nearly 20 years at the helm, their total commitment to the place still shines through – and the awards and favourable reviews just keep coming. No two bedrooms are the same; rooms at the top of the house tend to be a bit smaller, but differences in the rates (which are restrained, for London) reflect this. Common to them all is their homely feel – no cutting-edge designs, just well-coordinated fabrics, shipshape bath or shower rooms, and dark reproduction furniture. Colours vary a lot, so the Cartmel Room's half-tester is dressed in dark greens and russets, other rooms have floral fabrics and cream walls and many have hand-stencilled borders. A hearty breakfast (included in the rates) and good-value meals are served in the cosy basement restaurant.

○ Open all year Nearest tube station is Victoria (District, Circle and Victoria lines) 4 single, 5 twin/double, 10 double, 3 family rooms; 1 single with shared facilities, 1 double with private facilities; all with room service, hair-dryer, direct-dial telephone, modem line, TV; some with trouser press Restaurant, bar, lounge; conferences; leisure facilities nearby; early suppers for children; cots, highchairs, toys No wheelchair access; 3 steps into hotel, steps into restaurant, 4 ground-floor bedrooms No dogs; no smoking in public rooms and some bedrooms Amex, Delta, MasterCard, Switch, Visa Single £69 to £99, twin/double £119 to £145, family room £145; deposit required. Alc D £19; light meals available. Special breaks available

The Zetter NEW ENTRY

86–88 Clerkenwell Road, London EC1M 5RJ
TEL: 020-7324 4444   FAX: 020-7324 4445
EMAIL: info@thezetter.com
WEB SITE: www.thezetter.com

Uber-trendy, well-priced hotel turns up the heat in reinvigorated Clerkenwell

Fabric, one of the trendiest London clubs, is round the corner, *The Guardian's* offices flood the area with media types, and the bars of Smithfield Market beckon nearby – hence the call for Berocca in the mini-bar presumably. This area is seriously cool, and a raft of new ventures, including the Zetter, housed in a converted warehouse, are fanning the flames. The resurgence of retro is clear in the bar with its brown swirly carpet and cylindrical cork stools, in contrast to the contemporary Italian restaurant and spangly-floored lobby. Whereas some trend-setters can be rather shallow, this place has a few environmental principles too – using water drawn from 1,500 feet under. A central, sky-lit well illuminates all the floors on the way and is a great feature. Bedrooms are slightly funky, slightly contemporary and slightly wacky, but not at all over the top. Beds with duck-down pillows and crisp white duvets induce the zzzzz emblazoned down the doors, and hot-water bottles in knitted covers match the fluffy blankets. Monsoon shower heads revitalise in the mornings, if the hangover cures fail, though the views from the rooftop studio balconies might have the same effect.

○ Open all year Nearest tube station is Farringdon (Circle, Hammersmith & City and Metropolitan lines) 4 twin, 44 double, 4 family rooms, 7 suites; all with room service, hair-dryer, direct-dial telephone, modem line, TV, DVD, CD player; some with mini-bar Restaurant, bar, lounge; conferences and social functions; leisure facilities nearby; cots, highchairs Wheelchair access to hotel, 8 steps into restaurant, WC, lift No dogs; no smoking in restaurant and some bedrooms Amex, MasterCard, Switch, Visa Twin/double £155, family room £265, suite £295 to £325; deposit required. Continental B £7.50, cooked B £9; alc L £21, D £28; light meals available. Special breaks available

ENGLAND

ABBERLEY Worcestershire

map 5

Elms Hotel

Stockton Road, Abberley WR6 6AT
TEL: (01299) 896666   FAX: (01299) 896804
EMAIL: reservations@theelmshotel.com
WEB SITE: www.theelmshotel.com

Affordable country house in attractive grounds

Anyone arriving at the Elms Hotel can hardly fail to be impressed by the magnificent flower displays that are a feature of its front entrance. When we inspected, tulips and antirrhinums were in full bloom and their neat rows deftly complemented the classical symmetrical lines of this early Georgian mansion. The hotel has now been added to the Von Essen group's ever-expanding portfolio, but it is unlikely that the sedate, relaxed formula that sums up its style will be changed. The public rooms are nicely proportioned, and the furnishings stick to a traditional country-house look, with tartan and floral fabrics to the fore. Rooms are divided between the main house and the coach house. One of the most attractive is 39B in the coach house – it has a cruck-beam ceiling and a simple, light colour scheme. Other rooms are typified by pale washy tones in beige or green and generally have a good-sized bathroom.

◗ Open all year   ⊿ On A443, 2 miles west of Great Witley (ignore Abberley turning). Private car park   ⊨ 2 single, 8 twin, 9 double, 1 four-poster, 1 family room; all with room service, hair-dryer, direct-dial telephone, modem line, TV; some with trouser press   ⊘ Restaurant, bar, 3 lounges, garden; conferences; social functions; civil wedding licence; tennis, croquet, leisure facilities nearby; early suppers for children; cots, high chairs, babysitting   ⅙ Wheelchair access to hotel and restaurant, 3 ground-floor bedrooms   ● No children under 12 in restaurant eves; dogs in some bedrooms only; smoking in bar and 1 lounge only   ⊟ Amex, Delta, Diners, MasterCard, Switch, Visa   £ Single £110, twin/double £145 to £185, four-poster £185, family room from £165 (rates incl dinner); deposit required. Set L £16.50; light meals available. Special breaks available

ALDEBURGH Suffolk

map 6

Wentworth Hotel

Wentworth Road, Aldeburgh IP15 5BD
TEL: (01728) 452312   FAX: (01728) 454343
EMAIL: stay@wentworth-aldeburgh.com
WEB SITE: www.wentworth-aldeburgh.com

Neat, traditional seaside hotel right on the waterfront

Right on the seafront, but with easy access by road, the Wentworth couldn't be more perfectly located for those wanting to sample the delights of the gentle, old-fashioned resort of Aldeburgh. The same description could be applied to the Wentworth itself – though rooms are continually being spruced up to maintain the high standards the Pritt family have been applying since 1920, there's been no minimalist makeover here, and bedrooms are decked out in bright yellows and blues with patterned wallpapers and comfy chairs. The long dining room is in red with thick red-and-gold curtains and big, imposing portraits. One L-shaped lounge is bright and airy while the other, perhaps more appealing, is full of antiques and bookshelves – a perfect spot for high tea. Take note that there's no lift, so if stairs pose a challenge make sure you ask for one of the ground-floor bedrooms in the main house or in the annexe over the road (which are bigger but lack a sea view).

◗ Closed last week Dec to early Jan   ⊿ Turn off A12 approximately 10 miles north of Woodbridge on to B1094 towards Aldeburgh. In Aldeburgh leave church on left and at bottom of hill turn left into Wentworth Road; hotel is 300 yards on right. Private car park   ⊨ 4 single, 17 twin/double, 10 double, 4 suites; all with room service, hair-dryer, direct-dial telephone, modem line, TV   ⊘ Restaurant, bar, 2 lounges, garden; conferences; social functions; leisure facilities nearby; early suppers for children; cots, highchairs, baby-listening   ⅙ Wheelchair access to hotel (ramp) and restaurant, 5 ground-floor bedrooms   ● No smoking in bedrooms and some public rooms ▭ Amex, Delta, Diners, MasterCard, Switch, Visa £ Single £61 to £81, single occupancy of twin/double £79 to £95, twin/double £105 to £180, suite £152 to £200. Set L £15, D £12 to £18, alc L £17; light meals available

---

ALDERMINSTER Warwickshire   map 5

The Bell

Shipston Road, Alderminster, Nr Stratford-upon-Avon CV37 8NY
TEL: (01789) 450414   FAX: (01789) 450998
EMAIL: thebellald@aol.com
WEB SITE: www.thebellald.co.uk

Rooms for food-lovers in easy-going stylish choice

Originally an eighteenth-century coaching inn, The Bell has now changed its tone – Keith and Vanessa Brewer, the brains behind this popular eatery, are renowned for their excellent home-cooked cuisine rather than fermenting skills. Inside, the traditional rustic charm has been augmented by light modern touches. Inset lighting and sofas contrast pleasantly with the polished flagstone floor and dark, heavy ceiling beams above. The restaurant winds around the old bar areas extending between a cosy annexe and a bright conservatory overlooking the courtyard garden. Food caters for a broad range of tastes – there is home-made steak and kidney pudding for the stolidly English or for the more adventurous, the seriously weird and exotic-sounding bobotie (minced beef with almonds, apricots and a hint of curry powder topped with egg and cream custard). The six bright and colourful bedrooms are set apart from the house in a quiet modern annexe. The Flower room and Green room share a shower room.

◑ Open all year ⚡ On A3400, 3 miles south of Stratford-upon-Avon. Private car park ⛟ 1 twin/double, 3 double, 2 family rooms; 2 with shared facilities; all with hair-dryer, TV; 1 with trouser press ⊘ Restaurant, bar, lounge, conservatory, garden; conferences; social functions; early suppers for children; cots, highchairs, baby-listening ♿ Wheelchair access to hotel and dining room, 2 ground-floor bedrooms, 1 room specially equipped for disabled people ◖ Dogs in bedrooms by arrangement; smoking only in bar ▭ Amex, Delta, Diners, MasterCard, Switch, Visa £ Single occupancy of twin/double £27 to £52, twin/double £45 to £70, family room £60 to £90; deposit required. Alc D £18; light meals available ③FOR②

Ettington Park

Alderminster, Stratford-upon-Avon CV37 8BU
TEL: (01789) 450123   FAX: (01789) 450472
EMAIL: ettington@handpicked.co.uk
WEB SITE: www.handpicked.co.uk/ettingtonpark

Eccentric neo-Gothic country-house with good leisure facilities

Unsurprisingly, this neo-Gothic extravaganza replete with tall chimneys and turrets was the location of a horror film – Robert Wise's *The Haunting*. Inside it is no less flamboyant, brimming with prominent moulded plaster panelling, wrought iron balustrades, carved arches and columns and even a secret doorway disguised as part of a large bookcase. The house also comes with its own ghostly company, although the sociable staff are quick to point out that the spooks are rarely seen and they are all benevolent. Public rooms are palatial and opulent but not in any way stuffy, and the ambience is relaxed and friendly; children would get as much enjoyment from a visit here as adults. Modern country-house cuisine is served attentively by long-aproned staff in the impressive Oak Room Restaurant. Bedrooms are lavishly furnished with views of the garden or the ruined Norman church.

◑ Open all year ⚡ 5 miles south of Stratford-upon-Avon, off A3400 just outside Alderminster. Private car park ⛟ 5 twin, 9 twin/double, 23 double, 2 four-poster, 5 family rooms, 4 suites; all with room service, hair-dryer, trouser press, direct-dial telephone, modem line, TV ⊘ Restaurant, bar, lounge, library, conservatory, garden; conferences; social functions; civil wedding licence; spa, tennis, heated indoor swimming pool; early suppers for children; cots, highchairs ♿ Wheelchair access to hotel (ramp) and restaurant (steps), 6 ground-floor bedrooms, 1 room specially equipped for disabled people, WC, lift ◖ No dogs in public rooms

Amex, Delta, Diners, MasterCard, Switch, Visa £ Single occupancy of twin/double £137, twin/double £158, four-poster/suite £238, family room £218. Set D from £35; alc D £37.50; light meals available; service incl. Special breaks available ③FOR②

ALDFIELD North Yorkshire map 9

Mallard Grange

Aldfield, Ripon HG4 3BE
TEL: (01765) 620242 (AND FAX)
EMAIL: maggie@mallardgrange.co.uk
WEB SITE: www.mallardgrange.co.uk

Friendly farmhouse B&B with a historic past and quality breakfasts

Maggie and Charles Johnson's sixteenth-century farmhouse was once part of the nearby Fountains Abbey estate, and has been worked by the family since the 1930s. Maggie's domain is the B&B side of the business, which she runs with a welcoming and informal charm. You will be greeted with a cuppa, and, whatever you want to do from walking to pottering around the local attractions, she will sit down with maps and talk you through the area's highlights. Four good-sized bedrooms are furnished with antiques and smart fabrics and come with

generous tea trays laden with herb teas and home-made biscuits; bathrooms are classy and modern with huge fluffy towels and upmarket toiletries. The two in the converted blacksmith's shop and carthouse probably have the edge, being bigger, brighter and spacious enough for settees. Maggie is a champion of local produce, so breakfasts feature sausage from the farm next door and prize-winning black pudding from Thirsk, or Whitby kippers. Dinner is not on the menu, but compendious information folders in the rooms suggest the best of local pubs and restaurants.

◗ Closed Chr & New Year ☷ Take B6265 from Ripon towards Pateley Bridge for 2½ miles; Mallard Grange is on right. Private car park ⤶ 2 twin, 2 double; all with hair-dryer, TV ✓ Breakfast room, garden ♿ No wheelchair access; 3 steps into hotel, 2 ground-floor bedrooms ● No children under 12; no dogs; no smoking ▭ MasterCard, Switch, Visa £ Twin/double £65 to £76; deposit required. Special breaks available

---

ALSTON Cumbria map 10

Lovelady Shield

Nenthead Road, Alston CA9 3LF
TEL: (01434) 381203 FAX: (01434) 381515
EMAIL: enquiries@lovelady.co.uk
WEB SITE: www.lovelady.co.uk

An idyllic Pennine bolthole in a dramatic upland setting

The monastic origins of this hotel certainly contribute to its air of tranquil seclusion, but the experience of lodging here these days is anything but austere. This Georgian country house stands on the site of a thirteenth-century convent originally known as Love of Our Lady, hence its name. Convivial hosts Peter and Marie Haynes have been here some six years, and the present style of hospitality is very much their own creation. The surroundings, though, are almost entirely the works of nature: exhilarating roads

scale the Pennine watershed to converge on England's highest market town of Alston. Footpaths from the driveway bridge across the Nent leave keen walkers spoilt for choice. While traditional country house elegance prevails among the antique clocks and silver napkin rings downstairs, the smartly refurbished bedrooms revel in modish neutrals, with sparkling modern bathrooms and many carefully considered accoutrements. Dinners are ambitious affairs, generously served.

◗ Open all year ☷ At junction of A689 and B6294, 2½ miles east of Alston. Private car park ⤶ 2 twin/ double, 7 double, 1 four-poster; all with room service, hair-dryer, direct-dial telephone, modem line, TV; some with DVD; tea/coffee-making facilities on request ✓ Restaurant, bar, lounge, library, garden; conferences, social functions, civil wedding licence; early suppers for children; cots, highchairs ♿ No wheelchair access;

WC ● No children under 8 in restaurant eves; dogs in some bedrooms only; smoking only in bar and library ◻ Amex, Delta, MasterCard, Switch, Visa £ Single occupancy of twin/double £70, twin/double £140, four-poster £220; deposit required. Set Sun L £19.50, set D £34.50; light meals available. Special breaks available ③FOR②

ALSTONEFIELD Staffordshire　　　　　　　　　　　　　　　　　　　　　　　　map 5

Stanshope Hall

Stanshope, Alstonefield DE6 2AD
TEL: (01335) 310278　FAX: (01335) 310470
EMAIL: naomi@stanshope.demon.co.uk
WEB SITE: www.stanshope.net

Beautiful vistas inside and out at this charming Peak District home

With its solid grey-stone exterior built to withstand the Peaks' inclement climate, Stanshope Hall may not look much like a Tuscan villa, but a profusion of murals and *trompe l'oeil* definitely offers a strong hint of the Italianate. One of the best examples is in the cosy Victorian-style drawing room, whose walls (and ceiling) bear a beautiful early-morning moorland scene, but the three bedrooms are not at all left out. There are classical pillars on the walls of the elegantly furnished King Room and a fabulous Renaissance-style fresco in the en suite with its free-standing bath; the pretty Regency Striped Room comes with hand-painted walls and splendid fish in the bathroom; and the cosy Egyptian-themed Twin Room features stunning washed-out rushes over the bath. Breakfasts and three-course dinners (by prior arrangement) are served in the warmly intimate, rich-red-walled dining room.

❍ Closed 24 & 25 Dec　▣ From Ashbourne, take A515 to Buxton; turn left to Thorpe, Ilam and Dovedale; at Ilam memorial turn right (signposted Alstonefield); Stanshope is 3 miles along road. Private car park ⬕ 3 twin/double; family rooms available; all with hair-dryer, direct-dial telephone, TV, VCR　⟨⟩ Dining room, drawing room, garden; early suppers for children; cots, highchairs　& No wheelchair access　● No children in dining room eves; no dogs; no smoking in bedrooms, and in public rooms only if other guests consent ◻ Delta, MasterCard, Switch, Visa £ Single occupancy of twin/double £35 to £45, twin/double £70 to £90, family room £90 to £100; deposit required. Set D £22; light meals available; service incl. Special breaks available ③FOR②

ALTON Staffordshire　　　　　　　　　　　　　　　　　　　　　　　　　　map 5

Alton Towers Hotel

Stoke-on-Trent ST10 4DB
TEL: (01538) 704600/(08705) 001100　FAX: (01538) 704657
EMAIL: alton-towers@alton-towers.com
WEB SITE: www.alton-towers.com

It's non-stop entertainment at this all-frills holiday complex

An extravagant fun-packed waterpark encased in a huge glass bubble is the backdrop to Alton Towers' two colourful interconnected leisure palaces. The vaguely Victorian red-brick Alton Towers is marginally the more sophisticated, but it is still very much geared to children, with a wacky explorer theme instantly apparent in the form of a five-storey fantasy airship (used to host the cabaret) in the atrium-style lobby. The standard rooms in this hotel are comfortably furnished, with twin or double beds plus bunks and lively patchwork quilts, but the stars of the show are the handful of sponsored themed suites, which feature quirky designs (such as submarine-shaped bunks) and interactive features supplied courtesy of big-brand names. On the other side, the colourful-clapboard-clad Splash Landings comes with a Caribbean flavour, so the bedrooms, though similarly outfitted to those next door, are furnished with tropical bedspreads and driftwood headboards. As well as having access to the full range of bars and games rooms, guests can choose to eat at either the Alton Towers' spacious conservatory Secret Garden restaurant, where you can commune with a tree that talks back, or Splash Landings' more-romantic Flambo's restaurant with its duckboards, palm trees and pretty coloured lanterns.

◑ Open all year ⏢ From M1, northbound exit Junction 28, southbound exit Junction 23A, take A50 and follow tourist signs; from M6, northbound exit Junction 16, southbound exit Junction 15, follow tourist signs; hotel is in theme park precincts. Private car park 🛏 169 family rooms, 6 suites; all with room service, hair-dryer, direct-dial telephone, TV; some with mini-bar, trouser press ⍢ Restaurant, 2 bars, lounge, conservatory, games room, garden; conferences; social functions; civil wedding licence; sauna, heated indoor swimming pool; early suppers for children; cots, highchairs, playroom, babysitting, baby-listening, outdoor play area ♿ Wheelchair access to hotel and restaurant, WC, 40 ground-floor bedrooms, 9 rooms specially equipped for disabled people, lift. Disabled parking ● No dogs; smoking in bars only ⊏ Amex, Delta, MasterCard, Switch, Visa £ Single occupancy of twin/double £176 to £261, family room £206 to £298, suite £326 to £472 (rates incl admission to theme park and water-park); deposit required. Set D £17; light meals available. Special breaks available (2004 data)

AMBERLEY West Sussex   map 3

Amberley Castle

Nr Arundel BN18 9ND
TEL: (01798) 831992   FAX: (01798) 831998
EMAIL: info@amberleycastle.co.uk
WEB SITE: www.amberleycastle.co.uk

Five-star luxury within the walls of the imposing castle

As you approach Amberley Castle you cannot fail to be won over by its imposing façade, which surveys the South Downs from behind beautifully landscaped gardens. Built as a hunting lodge for the Bishops of Chichester, the Castle's crenellations and battlements were added during the turbulent fourteenth century, but its fortifications failed to protect it from Cromwell, who reduced the castle to a romantic ruin during the Civil War. The manor house that was built from the rubble is now defended by electric gates and signs discouraging visitors 'who are not expected', warning off the coachloads of sightseers who would otherwise lay siege to the place. But don't be put off, for once across the threshold guests receive a perfectly warm and inviting welcome by staff who manage to be supremely attentive without being obsequious – a fact observed on our inspector's visit, with friendly staff efficiently ushering rain-soaked guests into the elegant library to dry off beside a crackling fire. Public areas are first-rate but also refreshingly unstuffy – opulent and beautifully furnished yet comfortable enough for you to feel you could kick off your shoes and curl up with a good book. Bedrooms – all of which are named after castles – are swanky and luxurious, most with four-posters, elegant fabrics and swish modern gadgets, and good bathrooms. Herstmonceux and Pevensey both have access to the battlements.

◑ Open all year ⏢ Take the B2139 from Storrington or Arundel. Ignore signs to 'Amberley Village' and look for the Union flag which marks the entrance of the driveway. Nearest train station: Amberley. Private car park 🛏 2 twin, 5 double, 6 four-poster, 6 suites; all with room service, hair-dryer, trouser press, direct-dial telephone, modem line, TV, VCR; some with mini-bar, CD player ⍢ 2 restaurants, 3 lounges, library, garden; conferences; social functions; civil wedding licence; tennis, croquet and putting course; leisure facilities nearby ♿ No wheelchair access ● No children under 12; no dogs; no smoking in bedrooms ⊏ Amex, Delta, Diners, MasterCard, Switch, Visa £ Twin/double £190 to £375, four-poster £220 to £335, suite £310 to £335; deposit required. Continental B £10.50, cooked B £16.50; set L £20.50, D £35; alc L, D £45; light meals available. Special breaks available

---

AMBLESIDE Cumbria   map 8

Drunken Duck Inn

Barngates, Ambleside LA22 0NG
TEL: (015394) 36347   FAX: (015394) 36781
EMAIL: info@drunkenduckinn.co.uk
WEB SITE: www.drunkenduckinn.co.uk

A deservedly popular dining pub goes from strength to strength

This award-winning 'Glorious Gastropub' in last year's guide continues to attract accolades from a wide-ranging clientele. Well-heeled metropolitan visitors appreciate the sophistication of its stylishly contemporary bedrooms and country-house sitting room. Foodies flock to sample Nick Foster's imaginative chalkboard creations laced with roast fennel and sun-blushed tomatoes. Venison in cocoa with chestnut polenta, caramelised figs and espresso iced pistachios may seem a little over-elaborate for the average Lakeland lunch, but a hand-pulled pint or two of the Duck's own Barngates microbrewery range of real ales, named after various former pets (Catnap, Cracker etc) may suffice. Tracking down this place, at a remote rural crossroads in the middle of not very much except glorious Langdale scenery, makes patrons feel they deserve a reward, especially if they've arrived on foot. The cosy, hop-garlanded bar with log fires and walls strewn with intriguing photos and cartoons remains the heart of this amiable hostelry.

◐ Closed 24 & 25 Dec 🔁 Take B5286 from Ambleside towards Hawkshead for 2½ miles; turn right and follow signs to Drunken Duck Inn. Private car park 🛏 1 twin, 13 double, 2 suites; all with hair-dryer, direct-dial telephone, TV; no tea/coffee-making facilities in rooms ⊘ Dining room, bar, sitting room, garden; leisure facilities nearby; early suppers for children ♿ No wheelchair access; 1 step into hotel, 1 step into dining room, WC, 2 ground-floor bedrooms ⬤ No dogs in bedrooms; no smoking ▭ Amex, Delta, MasterCard, Switch, Visa £ Single occupancy of twin/double £88, twin/double £115; suite £170; deposit required. Alc L, D £24; light meals available. Special breaks available

Kent House

Lake Road, Ambleside LA22 0AD
TEL: (015394) 33279 (AND FAX)
EMAIL: mail@kent-house.com
WEB SITE: www.kent-house.com

Relaxed and cheerful hosts in the town centre

Keep your eyes peeled for this tall Victorian property of greenish Lakeland slate above a solicitor's office, opposite a bookshop. The one-way system can make access tricky, and parking space beside the house is very limited. The reception entrance is at first-floor level, via a steep drive and a tiny terrace, with tables set outside in fine weather. Our last inspection visit interrupted Gordon and Moira Cox's supper, but they couldn't have been more welcoming. It's surprising to learn that this popular B&B is a new venture for them. Furnishings are simple, homely and traditional. The sitting room is well stocked with games, jigsaws and a collection of DVDs, and the breakfast room is light and bright with china and photos. Bedrooms are fresh and spotless in warm, cheering styles. Kent House's triumph, however, is its breakfast, featuring homemade cinnamon loaf and lemon curd or boiled eggs with soldiers.

◐ Closed 24 & 25 Dec 🔁 Follow signs to town centre and pass Post Office on the right. 100 yards ahead pull into loading bay on the right and look up to the left. Hotel is on a terrace above main road. Private car park 🛏 3 double, 2 family rooms; all with hair-dryer, direct-dial telephone, TV ⊘ Breakfast room, lounge, garden, terrace; leisure facilities nearby; cots, highchairs, toys ♿ No wheelchair access ⬤ No dogs; no smoking ▭ Delta, MasterCard, Switch, Visa £ Single occupancy of double £40 to £50, double £50 to £70, family room £70 to £90; deposit required

The Regent [NEW ENTRY]

Waterhead Bay, Ambleside LA22 0ES
TEL: (015394) 32254 FAX: (015394) 31474
EMAIL: info@regentlakes.co.uk
WEB SITE: www.regentlakes.co.uk

An unexpectedly stylish find on Windermere's lakehead

The winds of change have been blowing through this much-extended, white-painted property opposite the boat steamer terminal in southern Ambleside. Despite the busy Windermere exit road passing directly outside, you'll find the interior a tranquil, well-insulated breath of fresh air. Cool, airy, split-level public areas extend from the reception entrance. The bar-lounge is a symphony of tasteful browns and creams jazzed up with geometric gold-splashed fabrics and frivolously curvaceous, French-style seating. Streamlined blinds billow gracefully at the conservatory extension windows, and nicely framed, arty black-and-white photos deck the walls. Bedrooms are steadily being refurbished, some still harking back to chintzy country-house designs, others dynamically revamped as impressively smart contemporary retreats with CD players and posh soaps. The new garden rooms are the most sought after. Unpretentious modern British menus include plenty of wholesome regional produce, and the heated indoor jet-stream pool is a plus point if Windermere seems on the chilly side.

🌙 Open all year 🚗 On Waterhead Bay in Ambleside. Private car park 🛏 21 twin/double, 7 double, 2 suites; family rooms available; all with room service, hair-dryer, direct-dial telephone, modem line, TV, VCR; some with CD player ✓ Restaurant, bar, 2 lounges, library, garden; conferences; social functions; heated indoor swimming pool; leisure facilities nearby; early suppers for children, cots, highchairs, toys, baby-listening ♿ Wheelchair access to hotel (ramp) and restaurant, 5 ground-floor bedrooms. Disabled parking ● Dogs in bedrooms only (£4.50 a night); smoking in public rooms only 💳 Delta, MasterCard, Switch, Visa £ Single occupancy of twin/double £49 to £100, twin/double £85 to £134, family room from £129, suite £110 to £150; deposit required. Alc L £20, D £25; light meals available. Special breaks available (3 FOR 2)

Rothay Manor

Rothay Bridge, Ambleside LA22 0EH
TEL: (015394) 33605 FAX: (015394) 33607
EMAIL: hotel@rothaymanor.co.uk
WEB SITE: www.rothaymanor.co.uk

A long-established country-house favourite acclaimed for high standards of food, service and accommodation

This pretty Regency-style house, once owned by a well-to-do Liverpool merchant, stands on the Hawkshead side of Ambleside, and thus makes a handy springboard for splendid walks and drives. Admittedly, the one-way system runs audibly close to the hotel's beautifully kept gardens, but sympathetically matched double glazing efficiently screens it from the hotel's elegant confines. The Nixon brothers and their wives have run this well-loved hotel and restaurant with a team of friendly staff for many years and reader reports confirm that standards remain high. Design makeovers have successfully updated some public areas and bedrooms. The bar–lounge has been modernised in fashionable dusky aubergine colours, the non-smoking lounge in dashing creams and golds. The candlelit restaurant is more old-fashioned with polished dark wood and plush upholstery. Bedrooms are all very comfortable and well finished, even the older, smaller ones; the best have garden-view balconies. Cooking is accomplished; afternoon teas are a strong point, and wines generously served.

🌙 Closed 3 to 28 Jan 🚗 On A593, ¼ mile south-west of Ambleside, towards Coniston. Private car park 🛏 1 single, 8 twin/double, 3 double, 4 family rooms, 3 suites; all with room service, hair-dryer, direct-dial telephone, TV; some with VCR; trouser press available ✓ Dining room, bar, 2 lounges, garden; conferences; social functions; leisure facilities nearby; early suppers for children; cots, highchairs, baby-listening ♿ Wheelchair access to hotel (ramp) and restaurant, WC, National Accessible Scheme: mobility impairment M2, 3 ground-floor bedrooms, 2 rooms specially equipped for disabled people. Disabled parking ● No children under 7 in restaurant eves; no dogs; smoking in 1 lounge only 💳 Amex, Delta, Diners, MasterCard, Switch, Visa £ Single from £70 to £80, single occupancy of twin/double £90 to £115, twin/double £120 to £155, family room £145 to £165, suite £160 to £185 (prices valid till Nov 2004); deposit required. Set L £17, D £32; light meals available. Special breaks available

---

The Guide *is totally independent, accepts no free hospitality, and survives on the number of copies sold each year.*

ENGLAND

AMPLEFORTH North Yorkshire   map 9
Shallowdale House

West End, Ampleforth, Nr York YO62 4DY
TEL: (01439) 788325 FAX: (01439) 788885
EMAIL: stay@shallowdalehouse.co.uk
WEB SITE: www.shallowdalehouse.co.uk

Modern country hotel with soothing views and great food

Rest and relaxation are in ample supply at Anton van der Horst and Phillip Gill's elegant 1960s house near the North York Moors. And their visitors know it: around half of them have stayed before and are back for more of the rural tranquillity, easy-going welcome and excellent food that they will find here. When you're not out exploring the ruined abbeys at Byland and Rievaulx, walking in the area or pottering around pretty villages, you could stay put in the house, which is a comfy haven of antiques, Turkish rugs on polished wooden floors and tasteful décor where not a detail jars. Light floods in through vast picture windows where you can bask and enjoy the panoramic views across the undulating dales. One of Phillip's four-course dinners might start with aubergine and red pepper roulade, and be followed by Ryedale lamb, then caramelised apple tart with home-made cinnamon and maple syrup ice cream, and cheese and biscuits to round it all off. Bright and cheery bedrooms have well-matched colour schemes and immaculately kept bathrooms; the one with a wooden decking balcony draped with honeysuckle is the pick of the bunch.

Closed Chr & New Year. In west end of Ampleforth. Private car park. 2 twin, 1 double; all with hair-dryer, TV. Dining room, 2 lounges, gardens; leisure facilities nearby. No wheelchair access. No children under 12; no dogs; no smoking. Delta, MasterCard, Switch, Visa. Single occupancy of twin/double £58 to £68, twin/double £78 to £95; deposit required. Set D £29.50; service incl. Special breaks available

APPLETHWAITE Cumbria   map 10
Underscar Manor

Applethwaite, Keswick CA12 4PH
TEL: (017687) 75000 FAX: (017687) 74904

Elaborate Victorian manor in a breathtaking location at the foot of Skiddaw

'Mind the red squirrels' warn notices in the driveway leading to this imposing Italianate villa. Inside, visitors will find a host of other creatures already in residence: teddy bears seem to occupy every shelf and niche, and a couple more are practising a duet on the hall piano beneath the handsome lanterned stairwell. The jokey teddies, and the romantically florid drapes and swags of fruit and flowers everywhere, may not suit everyone's decorative taste, but only a curmudgeon could resist such a friendly, courteous welcome. This, along with large, luxurious bedrooms, stunning views and impeccable housekeeping, is clearly a winning formula. Hands-on owners Pauline and Derek Harrison, successful Manchester restaurateurs, keep things in the family with Pauline's brother Robert Thornton as head chef. Ambitious French cuisine is served in the flower-festooned conservatory with a flourish of silverware. Residents have use of the opulent on-site health spa, Oxleys.

Closed 2 to 3 days at New Year. Leave M6 at Junction 40 and take A66 towards Keswick for 17 miles; at large roundabout take third exit and turn immediately right to Underscar; entrance is ¾ mile on right. Private car park. 11 double; all with room service, hair-dryer, direct-dial telephone, TV. Restaurant, 2 lounges, conservatory, gardens; gym, spa, heated indoor swimming pool; leisure facilities nearby. No wheelchair access. No children under 12; no dogs; no smoking in restaurant. Amex, MasterCard, Switch, Visa. Single occupancy of double £120, double £180 to £250 (rates incl dinner); deposit required. Set L £28; alc L £41. Special breaks available

ARDINGTON Oxfordshire

map 2

Boar's Head

Church Street, Ardington, Wantage OX12 8QA
TEL: (01235) 833254 (AND FAX)
EMAIL: info@boarsheadardington.co.uk
WEB SITE: www.boarsheadardington.co.uk

You'll be in clover with this fantastic food and equally fine rooms

Imagine soaking your cares away in a splendid, claw-footed bath that is the centrepiece of a swish bathroom big enough to hold a tea party; the sun streams in, lighting up the restful flax-and-biscuit colour scheme, while outside the church bell merrily ding-dongs its way through the hour. Best of all, downstairs a sumptuous repast awaits. If you think this idyll picture is found only in hip, high-flying city hotels, then think again because deep in southern Oxfordshire is this gem of a village pub that dishes up all of the above with lashings of charm without too hefty a price tag. All the bedrooms are stylishly kitted out in contemporary furnishings and colour schemes: Room 1 has the grandstand bathroom, while Room 2 is the biggest, with a sofa bed in the adjoining sitting room making it a family option. Downstairs, the bar-restaurant has brighter shades on the walls and appealingly simple wood furniture acting as a backdrop to Bruce Buchan's top-notch cooking, which marries classic English with French and Spanish. Come the summer, there's also a pleasant, secluded patio for al fresco eating.

○ Open all year　Turn off A417, 2 miles east of Wantage; hotel is in Ardington village, next to church. Private car park　2 double, 1 family room; all with hair-dryer, direct-dial telephone, modem line, TV; 1 with room service　Restaurant/bar, patio; social functions; leisure facilities nearby; early suppers for children; cots, highchairs, toys, baby-listening　No wheelchair access　Dogs and smoking in bar only　Amex, Delta, MasterCard, Switch, Visa　Single occupancy of double from £65, double £75 to £120, family room £145; deposit required. Set Sun L £18.50; alc L, D £25; light meals available　(3 FOR 2)

ARLINGHAM Gloucestershire

map 5

Old Passage Inn

Passage Road, Arlingham, Gloucester GL2 7JR
TEL: (01452) 740547　FAX: (01452) 741871
EMAIL: oldpassage@ukonline.co.uk
WEB SITE: www.fishattheoldpassageinn.co.uk

Isolated, atmospheric location for this inn specialising in seafood

The passage referred to here is the site of the ancient ford on the river Severn crossed by St Augustine in AD 604 to meet Welsh Christians at the Synod of the Oak. Certainly anyone attempting a crossing today would have their attention diverted by the bright green inn with white shutters that now stands on the banks of the river. Run by the Moore family, it is increasingly well known for its excellent seafood, which is served up in a casually smart interior. One guest enjoyed roast skate 'which was so fresh it could have swum to the kitchen itself'. Lobster and *fruits de mer* are among the house specialities. The bedrooms have also been praised, not least for their housekeeping standards, mini-kitchens and digibox video/TV and hi-fi system. 'Friendly staff, cheerful and helpful,' concludes a satisfied report.

○ Closed 22 to 30 Dec; restaurant closed Sun & Mon eves　From M5 Junction 13, take A38 south for ½ mile; take B4071 across ship canal and follow road to Arlingham; continue through Arlingham village and on towards banks of Severn; inn is signed 'The Inn', at river bank. Private car park　3 double; all with room service, hair-dryer, direct-dial telephone, fax, modem line, TV, VCR, CD player, mini-kitchen　Restaurant, garden, terrace, smoking room; conferences; social functions; cots, highchairs, babysitting, baby-listening　No wheelchair access, WC　No dogs; smoking only in smoking room　Amex, Delta, MasterCard, Switch, Visa　Single occupancy of double £65, double £85 to £95; deposit required. Cooked B £5.50; alc L, D £27.50; light meals available

Fox & Goose Inn

Armscote, Stratford-upon-Avon CV37 8DD
TEL: (01608) 682293 (AND FAX)
EMAIL: info@foxandgoose.co.uk
WEB SITE: www.aboveaverage.co.uk

Murder most fowl in England's green and pleasant land

As devotees of Miss Marple are aware, every traditional English village has hidden surprises – and Armscote fits the bill nicely. But the eighteenth-century Fox & Goose with its Cluedo-theme bedrooms could just as easily belong in Alice's wonderland as an Agatha Christie murder mystery. In the dining room a stuffed goose gives chase to a fox and the upright piano at the entrance now tinkles to the tune of cutlery from its converted keyboard. Sue Gray, who runs the Fox & Goose, has a sense of fun and loads of imagination. She has daringly blended the traditional interior with a makeover-modern colour scheme; walls are in vibrant blues, oranges and reds and work surprisingly well against the original rustic features of flagstone floors, wood-panelled areas and exposed ceiling tie beams. The small cosy bar still retains a following of locals, but most guests come here for a pre-dinner aperitif before taking a meal in the adjacent extensive and popular dining room. Bedrooms are named and colour-co-ordinated after Cluedo characters and each queen-size bed has a padded jester's crown as a headboard. The claw-footed baths are the deep free-standing variety set in large attractive bathrooms.

◗ Closed 25 & 26 Dec, 1 Jan ⌷ From Stratford-upon-Avon, take A3400 south for 7 miles; leaving Newbold-on-Stour, follow sign on right to Armscote for 1 mile. Private car park ⌷ 4 double; all with hair-dryer, TV, CD player ⌀ Dining room, bar, garden; conferences, social functions; leisure facilities nearby ⌷ No wheelchair access ◖ Dogs in bar only ⌷ Amex, Delta, MasterCard, Switch, Visa ⌷ Single occupancy of double £45, double £90; deposit required. Alc L £20, D £25; light meals available

Willow Corner

Armscote, Stratford-upon-Avon CV37 8DE
TEL: (01608) 682391
EMAIL: willowcorner@compuserve.com
WEB SITE: www.willowcorner.co.uk

Chocolate-box special in the heart of England

Rupert Brooke's sonnet recalling England, corners and foreign fields must take at least part of the blame for our hotel inspector's feeling of nostalgia evoked by the sight of a three-hundred-year-old low-slung thatched cottage in a pocket-sized cottage garden glowing in the setting sun. Here England as it should be – though isn't and never was – is encapsulated in this perfect summation of a rural idyll. This is a possible clue as to why Trish and Alan Holmes, after a working life of travelling the world fulfilling diplomatic duties, chose to set up shop here and create a homely refuge for the world-weary visitor. Inside the surprisingly roomy cottage, once the village smithy, all is bright and welcoming with tasteful reminders of their previous globetrotting lifestyle, such as the patchwork composed of tiny pieces of wedding saris that takes on a winking life of its own in the sunlight. The cheerfully coloured bedrooms are in reds and creams and come with shower cabinets in large, smart Italian-tiled bathrooms.

◗ Closed Chr & New Year ⌷ Off A3400 in Armscote 2½ miles from Shipston-on-Stour, near Fox & Goose pub. Private car park ⌷ 1 twin, 2 double; all with hair-dryer, TV ⌀ Dining room, lounge, garden; leisure facilities nearby ⌷ No wheelchair access ◖ No children under 15; no dogs; no smoking ⌷ None accepted ⌷ Single occupancy of twin/double £45, twin/double £64; deposit required. Special breaks available

Amerdale House

Arncliffe, Littondale, Skipton BD23 5QE
TEL: (01756) 770250   FAX: (01756) 770266
WEB SITE: www.amerdalehouse.co.uk

Upmarket and traditional country house serving up good food and relaxation

When almost three-quarters of a hotel's guests are repeat visitors, you know that it has come up with a winning formula. Nigel and Paula Crapper have run Amerdale House for 17 years, so the experience they offer is well-honed. Littondale's trails begin straight from the door – perfect for the many guests who are walkers; for less hearty types, Grassington and other Dales villages nearby for pottering about. The imposing Victorian mansion provides perfect seclusion and tranquillity with a mix of comforting chintz and antiques; its airy, uncluttered rooms include a grand drawing room with modern touches such as yellow-washed walls and deep blue plasterwork, an elegant restaurant with polished wooden tables laid with gleaming glass and silverware, and a clubby bar with an impressive array of malts to work your way through before one of Nigel's renowned four-course dinners of food cooked simply, using the freshest ingredients. Bedrooms are done out in soothing colour schemes, with stencilled friezes, smart bathrooms and the occasional period feature such as the marble fireplace in Coverdale. The hotel was up for sale as we went to press.

◗ Closed mid-Nov to mid-Mar ⬚ From Skipton continue on B6160 past Grassington and fork left ½ mile past Kilnsey Crag to Arncliffe; hotel is on edge of village. Private car park ⬚ 2 twin, 7 double, 1 four-poster, 1 family room; all with room service, hair-dryer, direct-dial telephone, TV; some with trouser press ✅ Restaurant, bar, drawing room, library, garden; early suppers for children; cots, highchairs, baby-listening ♿ No wheelchair access; 3 steps into hotel, 1 ground-floor bedroom ◖ No dogs; no smoking in restaurant ☐ MasterCard, Switch, Visa £ Twin/double £162 to £170, four-poster £170, family room rates on application (rates incl dinner)

Callow Hall

Mappleton Road, Ashbourne DE6 2AA
TEL: (01335) 300900   FAX: (01335) 300512
EMAIL: reservations@callowhall.co.uk
WEB SITE: www.callowhall.co.uk

Elegant country-house hotel on the edge of the Peaks

For those who've chosen to leave the helicopter at home and arrive by car, this venerable grey-stone Victorian pile presents a somewhat stern visage from the substantial tree-lined drive. Inside, however, the rich period trappings and general air of hospitality and high living instantly dispel any notions of severity. Plaid carpet and leather chairs given the bar a smarty clubby feel, while warm peach tones set off swagged chintz curtains and a beautiful tiled fireplace in the drawing room. The deep red tones of the restaurant's three rooms provide a stunning, intimate setting in which to savour the applauded five-course set dinner. The bedrooms are individually furnished in period style and tend to come with highly polished wooden beds, chintzy fabrics and plenty of solid antique furniture. The en-suite bathrooms offer good-quality ceramics and old-fashioned brass fittings.

◗ Closed 25 & 26 Dec ⬚ Follow A515 through Ashbourne towards Buxton; turn left at Bowling Green pub, then first right into Mappleton Road; entrance is on right after humpback bridge. Private car park ⬚ 4 twin, 2 twin/double, 7 double, 1 four-poster, 1 family room, 1 suite; all with room service, hair-dryer, trouser press, direct-dial telephone, modem line, TV ✅ Restaurant, bar, drawing room, garden; conferences and social functions; leisure facilities nearby; early suppers for children; cots, highchairs ♿ Wheelchair access to hotel (ramp) and restaurant, WC, 2 ground-floor rooms, 1 room specially equipped for disabled people ◖ No dogs in public rooms; no smoking in restaurant ⊟ Amex, Diners, MasterCard, Switch, Visa £ Single occupancy of twin/double £90 to £110, twin/double £130 to £175, four-poster/family room £175, suite £195 (2004 prices); deposit required. Set L £22.50, D £39.50; alc D £31.50; light meals available. Special breaks available

Omnia Somnia

The Coach House, The Firs, Ashbourne DE6 1HF
TEL: (01335) 300145   FAX: (01335) 300958
EMAIL: alan@omniasomnia.co.uk
WEB SITE: www.omniasomnia.co.uk

A sumptuous, welcoming oasis on the outskirts of town

Paula and Alan Coker Mayes have put a great deal of effort into reviving their red-brick Victorian coach house, which now seems a cut above the rather rundown Victorian house to which it belonged, as well as the adjacent housing estate. Inside, a trio of highly individual bedrooms is testament to their skill. Meridies features a flamboyant medievally inspired black-and-gold four-poster with embroidered love poem;

Occidens is split over two levels, with a seating area downstairs and a cosy little en suite bedroom upstairs; and Oriens comes with its own art gallery as well as a big double en suite bath. Upstairs, the attractive dining room, which overlooks the garden, is gloriously sunny by morning and intimately romantic by evening, when guests can sample dishes from an enticing three-course menu.

◐ Open all year ⟐ From Derby take A52 to Ashbourne; at Plough pub turn left into Old Hill, then left into The Firs; follow sign and fork right, hotel is beyond large Victorian house. Private car park ⌂ 1 double, 1 four-poster, 1 suite; all with room service, hair-dryer, TV, VCR, CD ⟐ Dining room, lounge, garden; leisure facilities nearby ⟐ No wheelchair access; 1 step into hotel, 14 steps into dining room, 2 ground-floor bedrooms (and 1 with steps to bed) ⬤ No children; no dogs; no smoking ⊟ Delta, MasterCard, Switch, Visa £ Double £95, four-poster/suite £90; deposit required. Set D £25; light meals available; service incl. Special breaks available ③FOR②

ASHBURTON Devon map 1

Holne Chase

Two Bridges Road, Nr Ashburton TQ13 7NS
TEL: (01364) 631471   FAX: (01364) 631453
EMAIL: info@holne-chase.co.uk
WEB SITE: www.holne-chase.co.uk

Halcyon retreat for hounds and their humans

Woof! What a place! Seventy acres of fresh air and exciting smells, plenty of woods, and my very own basket to curl up in at the end of the day. The lady of the manor is Batty the basset hound – I'm having a full clip and pedicure tomorrow in the Doggie Spa, to smarten up a bit. Today my mistress has opted for something called a body wrap and Indian head massage, while the master is off fishing on the Dart. Each to their own, I suppose. There's plenty of space in the bedroom, and

they seem very happy with their four-poster. A friendly retriever told me his humans are in the stable block, with a bedroom upstairs and separate sitting area downstairs. We even get our own menu, including smoked salmon and pork chops – though I have to admit the master's main course last night (roast saddle of venison with braised pearl barley and roasted root vegetables) didn't sound bad either! Must go now – saw some rabbits on the lawn earlier ...

◐ Open all year ⟐ Travelling south from Exeter on A38, take second Ashburton turning at Pear Tree Cross and follow signs to Dartmeet; 300 metres after Holne Bridge turn right into hotel drive. Private car park ⌂ 10 twin/double, 6 double, 1 four-poster; suites and family rooms available; all with hair-dryer, direct-dial telephone, TV; some with room service ⟐ Restaurant, bar, drawing room, library, gardens; conferences and social functions; civil wedding licence; leisure facilities nearby; early suppers for children; cots, highchairs, babysitting, baby-listening ⟐ No wheelchair access; 1 step into restaurant, 1 ground-floor bedroom ⬤ No children under 12 in restaurant eves; no dogs in some public rooms; no smoking in restaurant ⊟ MasterCard, Switch, Visa £ Single occupancy of twin/double £95 to £115, twin/double £145 to £165, four-poster £195, family room £235 to £250, suite £195 to £250; deposit required. Set L £20, D £34.50; light meals available; service incl. Special breaks available ③FOR②

ASHEY Isle of Wight   map 2

Little Upton Farm

Gatehouse Road, Ashey, Ryde PO33 4BS

TEL: (01983) 563236 (AND FAX)

EMAIL: alison@littleuptonfarm.co.uk

WEB SITE: www.littleuptonfarm.co.uk

Comfortable B&B on a working farm, moments from the ferry

Peacefully set in rolling countryside just minutes from the Fishbourne ferry, Alison and Howard Johnson's beautiful home has all the ingredients for an agreeable and restful stay. The lovely old farmhouse has a comfortable and homely feel, with a pretty lounge, good-looking breakfast room, and magnificent views over well-tended gardens to the duck pond, paddocks and open countryside beyond. This is a working farm with sheep, cattle, chickens and horses, plus plenty of space to run around in, so there's much to keep children amused, and, as an added treat, Alison and Howard may offer to take them out on their Shetland ponies or for a ride on a tractor. There are also first-rate self-catering units converted from a series of old barns and animal shelters. The two good-sized and beautifully light bedrooms are very attractive; one has light oak beams, raspberry Toile de jouy fabrics and stunning views.

◗ Closed Chr & New Year ⚡ From Fishbourne ferry, turn left on to A3054, then right into Newnham Road, left on to Stroud Wood Road and then right into Gatehouse Road; hotel is on the left. Nearest train station: Ryde. Private car park 🛏 1 twin/double, 1 double; both with hairdryer, TV ⌀ Dining room, lounge, conservatory, garden ⅙ No wheelchair access ● Children under 12 in self-catering units only; no dogs; no smoking ⊟ None accepted £ Twin/double £60 to £70; deposit required

---

ASHWATER Devon   map 1

Blagdon Manor

Ashwater, Nr Beaworthy EX21 5DF

TEL: (01409) 211224 FAX: (01409) 211634

EMAIL: stay@blagdon.com

WEB SITE: www.blagdon.com

Capable and welcoming hosts at this charming country house

Set in 20 acres of idyllic Devonian countryside, this fine seventeenth-century Grade II listed house offers plenty of tranquillity plus some excellent views from its hilltop location. The style here is a creative mix of traditional country house and the more contemporary. So you get flagstone floors, oak beams and antiques, but also warm bright colours and elegant soft furnishings. Steve and Liz Morey bring a friendly and hospitable atmosphere to proceedings: Steve is chef with a penchant for the home-made and also the home-grown while Liz caters for front-of-house, ably assisted by a couple of Labradors, Nutmeg and Cassia. Bedrooms are all different, but show great care and thought with dark-wood furniture and bold colours. Candles, bathrobes and a decanter of sherry complete a very satisfying ensemble.

◗ Closed 2 weeks Jan/Feb and 2 weeks Oct/Nov ⚡ From A388 towards Holsworthy, pass Chapman's Well 8 miles north-east of Launceston; ignore first Ashwater sign and take second turning to Ashwater; turn right, then right again at Blagdon sign; hotel is down second drive on right. Private car park 🛏 1 twin, 1 twin/double, 5 double; all with hair-dryer, direct-dial telephone, TV ⌀ Restaurant, bar, lounge, library, conservatory, garden ⅙ No wheelchair access ● No children under 12; no dogs in restaurant; smoking in bar only ⊟ Delta, MasterCard, Switch, Visa £ Single occupancy of twin/double £72, twin/double £100; deposit required. Set L £17, D £30; set Sun L £19.50

ASKRIGG North Yorkshire map 8

Helm

Askrigg, Leyburn DL8 3JF
TEL: (01969) 650443 (AND FAX)
EMAIL: holiday@helmyorkshire.com
WEB SITE: www.helmyorkshire.com

Top-drawer bedrooms and inspirational views at this rural guesthouse

Barbara and John Drew's guesthouse perches high on the hills of Wensleydale above the hamlet of Askrigg. In the oak-beamed dining room, where oriental rugs lie on the flagstones, there's a breakfast menu that is guaranteed to sort out the most demanding sausage aficionado: try 'hog and hop' (made with herbs and Black Sheep ale), venison or wild boar sausages from a choice of around ten types, or kedgeree, kippers or kidneys to get the day going. (The Drews serve dinner three times a week, but from January 2005 will run Helm as a B&B.) The same concern for quality applies in the immaculate, cottagey bedrooms named after local places. You'll find Victorian mahogany furniture in Askrigg or an art-nouveau washstand in Bainbridge (both these rooms come with wonderful views), and more period charm, oak beams and a claw-foot bath in the Whitfield room.

Closed mid-Nov to 2 Jan; dining room closed Mon to Thur eves From A684 at Bainbridge turn off to Askrigg in front of Rose and Crown Inn, after ½ mile turn right at T-junction, after ¼ mile turn left. Go uphill, keep straight ahead; Helm is last house on right. Private car park 1 twin, 2 double; all with hair-dryer, direct-dial telephone, modem line, TV Dining room, lounge, garden, summerhouse No wheelchair access No children under 10; no dogs; no smoking Delta, MasterCard, Switch, Visa Single occupancy of twin/double £60, twin/double £85; deposit required. Set D £20; service incl. Special breaks available

AUSTWICK North Yorkshire map 8

Austwick Traddock NEW ENTRY

Austwick LA2 8BY
TEL: (01524) 251224 FAX: (01524) 251796
EMAIL: bgdreynolds@aol.com
WEB SITE: www.austwicktraddock.co.uk

Enthusiastic new owners create a classy welcome in a brilliant Dales walking base

Signs in Austwick announce you've just entered the Yorkshire Dales National Park. To prove the point, the three grand Pennine peaks of Whernside soar against the north-eastern horizon, an irresistible challenge to any keen walker. The Austwick Traddock is a substantial, mainly Georgian, property, blending perfectly into the dove-grey stone of this classic village. If you're wondering what a traddock is, think 'trading paddock' – a horse-trading market once took place in the adjoining field. The affable Reynolds family moved in just over a year ago. Few hotels, or hoteliers, make arriving guests feel so instantly welcome. Fires crackle invitingly in the entrance hall, while well-proportioned rooms unfold beyond, dashingly decorated and individually furnished with antiques. Some bedrooms are still being rehabilitated, but the signs look very promising. Cooking sounds good ('Anglo-Saxon' themes, and many New World wines). Reports welcome.

Open all year Just off A65 between Skipton and Kendal, approx 3 miles northwest of Settle. Private car park 2 single, 1 twin, 6 double, 1 family room; all with hair-dryer, TV; some with direct-dial telephone Restaurant, dining room, bar, 2 lounges, garden; social functions; leisure facilities nearby; early suppers for children, cots, highchairs, baby-listening No wheelchair access Dogs in bedrooms only; smoking in bar only Amex, Delta, MasterCard, Switch, Visa Single £50, single occupancy of twin/double £75, twin/double £100 to £110, family room £140; deposit required. Set L (Sun) £17, D £23; light meals available. Special breaks available 3 FOR 2

Map 1

Court Barton Farm NEW ENTRY

Aveton Gifford, Nr Kingsbridge TQ7 4LE
TEL: (01548) 550312   FAX: (01548) 559165
EMAIL: info@courtbarton.freeserve.co.uk

Spruce farmhouse accommodation with friendly, family atmosphere

Although Court Barton is not a working farm, Jackie and Jeremy Harmer are certainly not short of things to keep them occupied. With two ponies, four ducks, several chickens and two guinea pigs – not to mention two children – they have their hands full. When our inspector arrived, Jackie was in the middle of creating a new lawn and was considering getting her son Oliver to help flatten the site on his quad bike! Inside, the stone-built sixteenth-century farmhouse has been lightened and modernised ('I don't like fuss and frills,' says Jackie). So bedrooms have clean, fresh colour schemes, like pale blue or lilac, and furniture in pine or distressed finish. The largest has a bath instead of a shower, and overlooks the Avon valley at the front. The only public area is the pale yellow breakfast room, with a log-burning fire for chilly mornings and an unusual hanging candelabrum. The eggs, of course, come freshly laid from Jackie's own hens. There are also three newly converted self-catering cottages behind.

◗ Closed Chr ⬔ In Aveton Gifford, off A379, 3 miles north-west of Kingsbridge. Private car park 🅿1 twin, 2 double; all with TV, VCR ⟡ Breakfast room, garden; leisure facilities nearby; outdoor play area ♿ No wheelchair access ⬤ No dogs; no smoking ▭ None £ Single occupancy of twin/double £40, twin/double £55 to £60; special breaks available

---

 Map 2

Kerrington House

Musbury Road, Axminster EX13 5JR
TEL: (01297) 35333   FAX: (01297) 35345
EMAIL: enquiries@kerringtonhouse.com
WEB SITE: www.kerringtonhouse.com

Friendly and relaxed guesthouse with beautiful rooms

Some readers of the *Guide* will recall Jim and Hilary Reaney's success at rural Lea Hill in Membury. Having moved on to Axminster – in order to avoid becoming a taxi service for teenage children – and after great trials, they have turned this previously run-down Victorian villa into a winning combination of original features and contemporary brightness. The stripped wood, coir matting and splashes of colour from oriental rugs create a light and cheerful ambience, in tune with the hospitality of Jim and Hilary. The four-course dinners offered Thursday to Saturday give a choice of meat or fish as main course: fillet steak with ragout of wild mushrooms, perhaps, or a Lyme Bay lemon sole with asparagus. On other nights light suppers are available. Bedrooms take the same light-of-touch style as downstairs and add some richer fabrics for extra cosiness. Well-chosen furniture and neat modern shower rooms finish a very attractive ensemble.

◗ Open all year; dining room closed Sun to Wed eves ⬔ From Axminster town centre, take A358 towards Seaton; after ½ mile, turn right into Musbury Road; hotel is on left. Nearest train station: Axminster. Private car park 🅿2 twin, 3 double; family rooms available; all with room service, hair-dryer, direct-dial telephone, TV; trouser press, fax, modem line available ⟡ Dining room, lounge, garden; conferences and social functions; leisure facilities nearby; early suppers for children; cots, highchairs, toys ♿ No wheelchair access ⬤ No dogs; no smoking ▭ MasterCard, Switch, Visa £ Single occupancy of twin/double £68 to £75, twin/double £95 to £105, family room £125 to £130; deposit required. Set D £28; light meals available. Special breaks available

Hartwell House

Oxford Road, Nr Aylesbury HP17 8NL
TEL: (01296) 747444 FAX: (01296) 747450
EMAIL: info@hartwell-house.com
WEB SITE: www.hartwell-house.com

Gracious living in a historic house that exudes elegance from every square inch

Your first hint of the finery that lies ahead is when you turn off the main road and go over a little humpback bridge lined with superbly ornate stonework. On through the gates, the sweeping, circular drive leads to a mellifluous mansion where grand, mullioned windows frame the delicately carved main doorway. Inside, even more grandeur awaits, from the stucco ceiling friezes in the Great Hall to the baroque figures positioned up the banisters of the central staircase. The public rooms drip with art and antiques, and are all opulently decked out, the flouncy femininity of the drawing rooms contrasting well with the dark burgundies and greens of the library. The latter is where Louis XVIII (resident as an exile here between 1809 and 1814) signed his accession to the French throne. Upstairs, Royal Rooms live up to their name (and the king's-ransom price tag) with space and splendour in equal measure. Even the standard rooms are anything but. A swish spa centre, acres of lush grounds, and fine food complete the package, along with little extras such as fresh flowers and local maps in every room.

◗ Open all year 🔁 In Aylesbury take A418 towards Oxford; Hartwell House is 2 miles along this road, on right. Nearest train station: Aylesbury. Private car park 🛏 1 single, 2 twin, 8 twin/double, 29 double, 5 four-poster; family rooms and suites available; all with room service, hair-dryer, trouser press, direct-dial telephone, modem line, TV; some with tea/coffee-making facilities ⊘ 3 dining rooms, bar, 3 drawing rooms, library, garden; conferences and social functions; civil wedding licence; gym, spa, tennis, heated indoor swimming pool; early suppers for children, served in rooms ♿ Wheelchair access to hotel (ramp) and dining rooms, WC, 1 room specially equipped for disabled people, lift. Disabled parking ⬤ No children under 8; no dogs in public rooms or bedrooms in main house; no smoking in some public rooms and some bedrooms ☐ Amex, MasterCard, Switch, Visa 💷 Single £155, single occupancy of twin/double £205, twin/double £260, four-poster/suite/family room £360; deposit required. Cooked B £5; set L £22, D £32; alc L £29, D £46; light meals available; service incl. Special breaks available

Felbrigg Lodge

Aylmerton NR11 8RA
TEL: (01263) 837588 FAX: (01263) 838012
EMAIL: info@felbrigglodge.co.uk
WEB SITE: www.felbrigglodge.co.uk

Get away from it all at this homely, sprawling country establishment

How best to describe Jill and Ian Gillan's secluded retreat? The three remaining guest rooms (the little Yellow Room is likely to be out of action this year) are housed in individual buildings away from the main family house, while the bright dining room and gym/pool occupy outer units within the well-cared-for wooded gardens. But Jill has a horror of them being labelled as annexes, outbuildings or lodges, lest potential guests think she's running some sort of holiday camp. Whatever you call them, the generously sized rooms are all finished in country style and are certainly more upmarket and personal than any *Hi-de-Hi* institution. Jill takes great pride in her professionally run operation, right down to the home-cooked three-course set dinners, which she tells us are firmly of the traditional British variety, handed down to her through generations of her family.

◗ Closed Chr and New Year; dining room closed Tue, Thur and Sun eves 🔁 From A148 Holt to Cromer road, turn off at Roman Camp Inn towards Aylmerton; continue 1 mile to stone cross and turn left; after ½ mile turn right into Felbrigg Lodge after woods. Private car park 🛏 2 twin/double, 1 suite; all with hair-dryer, TV ✅ Dining room, honesty bar, lounge, games room, garden; gym, indoor heated swimming pool, leisure facilities nearby ⓑ No wheelchair access; 1 step into hotel, 1 step into dining room, 3 ground-floor bedrooms ● No children under 10; no dogs; no smoking ⊟ Delta, MasterCard (5% surcharge), Switch, Visa (5% surcharge) £ Single occupancy of twin/double £88 to £100, twin/double £116, suite £148; deposit required (prices valid till Jan 2005). Set D £30. Special breaks available

---

BABWORTH Nottinghamshire　　　　　　　　　　　　　　　　　　　　　　　　map 9

The Barns

Morton Farm, Babworth, Retford DN22 8HA
TEL: (01777) 706336 FAX: (01777) 709773
EMAIL: peter@thebarns.co.uk
WEB SITE: www.thebarns.co.uk

Homely B&B offering a warm rural welcome

There's more than a touch of Lincoln Green about the ivy-swathed frontage of this eighteenth-century red-brick hay barn, which sits conveniently close to the A1, yet far enough away that nothing will disturb you but the occasional tractor. Lynda and Peter Morton haven't been running the place very long, but their efforts are beginning to shine through. Imaginative touches, such as cushions or fabrics hanging behind the beds, make the difference in a handful of prettily countrified, well-appointed bedrooms. En-suite shower rooms are clean and simple and Peter has been busy re-hanging shower doors and installing radiators to make sure that they are comfortable. A cosy breakfast room with antique chairs, low beams and a brick fireplace completes the ensemble.

◖ Open all year 🔢 2 miles east of A1 on B6420, south-west of Babworth. Nearest train station: Retford. Private car park 🛏 1 twin, 4 double, 1 four-poster; family room available; all with hair-dryer, TV; trouser press, fax, CD player available ✅ Breakfast room, small lounge area; leisure facilities nearby ⓑ No wheelchair access; 1 step into hotel, 1 ground-floor bedroom ● No children under 8; no dogs; no smoking ⊟ Amex, Delta, MasterCard, Switch, Visa £ Single occupancy of twin/double £31 to £38, twin/double from £46, four-poster from £60, family room from £62; deposit required. Special breaks available

---

BADBY Northamptonshire　　　　　　　　　　　　　　　　　　　　　　　　　map 5

Windmill at Badby [NEW ENTRY]

Badby Village, Nr Daventry NN11 3AN
TEL: (01327) 702363 FAX: (01327) 311521
EMAIL: info@windmillinn-badby.com
WEB SITE: www.windmillinn-badby.com

Foodies and real-ale enthusiasts unite

Within commuting distance of Northampton the tranquil village of Badby, surrounded by undulating pasture, is a sought-after place to live, and the seventeenth-century Windmill is the sort of thatched cottage people would give their right arms to live in. Luckily, for lovers of food, real ale and a decent glass of wine, John Freestone and Carol Sutton, the enthusiastic proprietors, run the Windmill as a labour of love and it is firmly off bounds to the property prospector. The traditional bar, hung throughout with caricatures of sporting life, has a rustic flavour in keeping with the variety of real ales to be savoured. Provincial and international meals from the award-winning kitchen are served in the attractive restaurant extension, built to blend in. Bedrooms are well equipped, light and pleasant, all with reasonably sized bathrooms with showers. The two single rooms are small and adequate for an overnight stay but perhaps not for lingering.

◖ Open all year 🔢 Village is on A361, 2 miles south of Daventry. Private car park 🛏 2 single, 2 twin, 4 double, 2 family rooms; all with hair-dryer, trouser press, direct-dial telephone, modem line, TV ✅ Restaurant, bar, patio; conferences; social functions; leisure facilities nearby; highchairs ⓑ No wheelchair access ● Smoking in bar only ⊟ Amex, Delta, MasterCard, Switch, Visa £ Single £60, single occupancy of twin/double £60, twin/double £73, family room £85; deposit required. Alc L, D £18; light meals available. Special breaks available

Haigs Hotel

273 Kenilworth Road, Balsall Common, Coventry CV7 7EL
TEL: (01676) 533004   FAX: (01676) 535132
WEB SITE: www.haigshotel.co.uk

Sublime cooking in an innocuous suburban setting

Its rather anonymous Tudorbethan frontage and its location on a busy road might seem inauspicious, but Haigs makes a convenient base for Birmingham airport as well as many of Warwickshire's tourist attractions, and offers some surprising treasures of its own. Under the new owners, the hotel's former poppy-themed restaurant has been lavishly revamped and now looks stylish and modern, with sparkling silverware, beautifully hand-decorated glasses, polished tables and chic leather chairs.

Fortunately, the one thing that hasn't changed is the chef and the superlatives just come flying out over dishes such as wild mushroom and Gruyère soufflé and rabbit casserole in rich mustard sauce. The bedrooms are not in the same league, but they are functionally well-appointed and comfortably furnished in a chintzy way, come with clean, white modern en-suite facilities, and are very good value at the half-board rates.

❶ Open all year; restaurant closed Sun eve   ◪ On A452, 5 miles south of Junction 4 of M6, 4 miles north of Kenilworth; hotel is 200 yards from village centre. Nearest train station: Berkswell. Private car park 🚘 5 single, 8 twin, 10 double; all with room service, hair-dryer, trouser press, direct-dial telephone, modem line, TV; fax available   ⊘ Restaurant, bar, lounge, garden; conferences and social functions; leisure facilities nearby ♿ Wheelchair access to hotel and restaurant, WC, 5 ground-floor bedrooms, 1 room specially equipped for disabled people. Disabled parking   ● No dogs; no smoking in some public rooms and some bedrooms ▭ Amex, Delta, Diners, MasterCard, Switch, Visa   £ Single £75, single occupancy of twin/double £88, twin/double £108; deposit required. Set D £27; alc D £30; light meals available; service incl

Hempstead House

London Road, Bapchild, Sittingbourne ME9 9PP
TEL: (01795) 428020   FAX: (01795) 436362
EMAIL: info@hempsteadhouse.co.uk
WEB SITE: www.hempsteadhouse.co.uk

Family-run Victorian house hotel – with smart new function suite

Since our last visit this well-run hotel on the A2 close to Sittingbourne has been busy rustling up a new wing. The Heritage conference and function suite, plus eight new rooms, have been built in a red-brick extension with its own entrance and bar – along with a new courtyard garden complete with gazebo and a couple of private dining rooms. The original house remains the calm, traditionally decorated hub of the hotel. A small snug lounge has the most Victorian character; the other

lounge is more of an anteroom to the large conservatory-style Lakes Restaurant. Housekeeping is top-notch in the fresh floral bedrooms with their good-sized bathrooms. Those in the new wing have a more luxurious feel in Empire-style gold-and-black colour schemes. The hotel is immaculately kept and a pleasant touch is the family photographs and ornaments on walls and surfaces at every turn in the old house.

❶ Open all year   ◪ On A2, 1½ miles east of Sittingbourne. Nearest train station: Sittingbourne. Private car park 🚘 15 twin/double, 5 double, 7 family rooms; all with room service, hair-dryer, direct-dial telephone, modem line, TV   ⊘ Restaurant, bar, 2 lounges, garden; conferences; social functions; civil wedding licence; outdoor heated swimming pool; leisure facilities nearby; early suppers for children; cots, highchairs, toys, babysitting, baby-listening   ♿ Wheelchair access to hotel and restaurant (ramps), WC, 1 ground-floor bedroom specially equipped for disabled people. Disabled parking   ● No smoking in bedrooms and most public rooms   ▭ Amex, Delta, Diners, MasterCard, Switch, Visa   £ Single occupancy of double

£75 to £95, double £85 to £105, family room £95 to £115; deposit required. Set L £16.50, D £24.50; alc L, D £32.50; light meals available. Special breaks available

---

BARWICK Somerset
map 2

Little Barwick House

Barwick, Nr Yeovil BA22 9TD
TEL: (01935) 423902   FAX: (01935) 420908
EMAIL: reservations@barwick7.fsnet.co.uk
WEB SITE: www.littlebarwickhouse.co.uk

Lovely, relaxing country house with good dining room and food

A curious red-stone gorge leads one into the village of Barwick, a sort of Devonian rose-red Petra, and that sets up Tim and Emma Ford's delightfully secluded country house. The three-storey Georgian house looks out over well-manicured lawns and gardens. Steps lead up into reception hall flanked by restaurant and drawing room. The style is gently elegant, homely and cosy – both Tim and Emma learned their trade under the late Frances Coulson, legendary founder of Sharrow Bay, and the experience shows.

('Emma and Tim are delightful,' wrote one correspondent. 'We highly recommend Little Barwick.') The restaurant is a sophisticated affair with high-backed chairs and polished wooden floor. Cooking favours local ingredients – maybe a goat's cheese starter followed by local lamb with aubergine caviar and globe artichoke. Bedrooms go for natural colours and a light, fresh atmosphere, but readers who otherwise praised Room 3 found the lighting poor and would have liked a storage shelf in the bathroom.

◑ Closed Chr, New Year and 2 weeks in Jan; restaurant closed Sun and Mon eves   ⚡ Take A37 south from Yeovil; after 1 mile, turn left at roundabout; hotel is ¼ mile further on. Nearest train station: Yeovil Junction. Private car park   ⬤⬤ 2 twin/double, 4 double; all with room service, hair-dryer, direct-dial telephone, TV   ⊘ Restaurant, bar, drawing room, conservatory, garden; social functions; leisure facilities nearby; cots, baby-listening   ♿ No wheelchair access   ● No dogs in public rooms, £5 in bedrooms; no smoking in restaurant or bedrooms   ▭ MasterCard, Switch, Visa   £ Single occupancy of twin/double £65 to £110, twin/double £110 to £120; deposit required. Set L £18, D £33; alc L, D £33. Special breaks available

---

BASLOW Derbyshire
map 8

Cavendish Hotel

Church Lane, Baslow, Bakewell DE45 1SP
TEL: (01246) 582311   FAX: (01246) 582312
EMAIL: info@cavendish-hotel.net
WEB SITE: www.cavendish-hotel.net

Long-established, cosy country hotel

If you're planning a visit to Chatsworth, you can reach it via a path that meanders through the grounds to the house itself. And you'll certainly be very comfortable here. Eric Marsh has been running the Cavendish for decades and is still very much front-of-house, greeting guests and checking that they are being looked after. That hands-on approach is undoubtedly one of the main reasons the service is spot on. The atmosphere is traditional and cosy, with a nice warming fire in the lounge where guests chat convivially. To try out the acclaimed

fruitcake, you need to pop into the conservatory-style Garden Room. The slightly more formal restaurant serves good traditional food: double-baked cheese soufflé, roast rump of Castlegate lamb, perhaps bread and butter pudding, if you can fit in a dessert (all portions are a good size). There's a huge choice at breakfast and, in acknowledgement that guests are on holiday, it's served until noon. All bedrooms face the fields of grazing sheep. Older ones have the period character while the newer wing may get you double-aspect views and a DVD player.

◑ Open all year   ⚡ From Chesterfield take A619 to Baslow; hotel is in village centre, off main road. Private car park   ⬤⬤ 8 twin, 12 double, 2 four-poster, 1 family room, 1 suite; all with room service, hair-dryer, mini-bar, trouser press, direct-dial telephone, modem line, TV; 2 with DVD, CD player   ⊘ 2 restaurants, bar, lounge, conservatory, garden; conferences and social functions; cots, highchairs ⟱ Wheelchair access to hotel (ramp) and restaurant, WC, 2 ground-floor bedrooms. Disabled parking ◒ No dogs; no smoking in restaurant ▭ Amex, Delta, Diners, MasterCard, Switch, Visa ⌐£⌐ Single occupancy of twin/double £115, twin/double/four-poster £180, family room £188, suite £215; deposit required. Continental B £9.50, cooked B £15; alc L £25, D £35; light meals available; service incl. Special breaks available

Fischer's Baslow Hall

Calver Road, Baslow, Bakewell DE45 1RR
TEL: (01246) 583259   FAX: (01246) 583818
EMAIL: m.s@fischers-baslowhall.co.uk
WEB SITE: www.fischers-baslowhall.co.uk

Pick your style at this intimate country-house hotel

With its big chimneystacks and small-paned windows in stone-mullioned settings, you'd have to be something of an expert to tell that this striking Tudoresque pile wasn't the real McCoy – in fact, it was built at the start of the last century for a clergyman who had obviously not heard about camels and needles. The interior is equally impressively faux, with grand fireplaces and moulded ceilings finding their match in heraldic papers and opulent fabrics, all adding up to the perfect setting to savour Max Fischer's highly acclaimed cooking. Bedrooms in the main house are tastefully chintzy and come with plenty of character as well as good-quality en-suite facilities. Five new bedrooms in the Garden House are much more contemporary, making use of muted, minimalist décor to set off sumptuous silk bedspreads; their chic bathrooms feature striking stone-effect tiling and slick chrome fittings.

◑ Closed 25 & 26 Dec ⊡ Fischer's Baslow Hall is on right as you leave Baslow village on A623 Stockport road. Private car park ⊏⊐ 2 twin/double, 7 double, 1 four-poster, 1 suite; all with room service, hair-dryer, direct-dial telephone, modem line, TV ⊘ 3 dining rooms, bar/lounge, garden; conferences and social functions; civil wedding licence; leisure facilities nearby; early suppers for children; cots, highchairs, baby-listening ⟱ No wheelchair access; 3 steps into hotel, 4 ground-floor bedrooms ◒ No children under 12 in dining rooms after 7pm; no dogs; no smoking in dining rooms and bedrooms ▭ Amex, Delta, Diners, MasterCard, Switch, Visa ⌐£⌐ Single occupancy of twin/double £100 to £120, twin/double/four-poster £180, suite £150; deposit required. Cooked B £8.50; set L £22.50, D £35; alc D £59; light meals available; service incl. Special breaks available

---

BASSENTHWAITE Cumbria   map 10

Willow Cottage

Bassenthwaite, Keswick CA12 4QP
TEL: (017687) 76440 (AND FAX)
EMAIL: chrisbeaty@amserve.com
WEB SITE: www.willowbarncottage.co.uk

Charming, rustic B&B in a quiet North Lakes village

Not far from the village green and Bassenthwaite's popular Sun Inn (which does decent food if you're after a lunchtime or evening meal), Chris and Roy Beaty's hospitable B&B enterprise occupies a converted Lakeland barn. Exposed stonework and oak timbers are ubiquitous features of the building. Guests enter the cottage past a winsome array of rag dolls and perhaps greeted by the house tabby, emerging in a cosy lounge/dining area generally set up for breakfast with cheerful china displays and Windsor chairs, stone-flagged floors and a wood-burning stove. A stairway leads up to two quaint bedrooms with latched wooden doors and sloping, raftered ceilings. Victorian-style cast-iron baths and brass beds with patchwork quilts add character to these, along with hand-stencilled walls and original floorboards. Who needs TV with views of Skiddaw or Ullock Pike from the windows? Breakfast includes eggs from resident hens, plus emphatically home-made bread and preserves.

◑ Closed Chr ▨ At Keswick on A66, take A591 north at roundabout, signposted Carlisle; after 6½ miles turn right into Bassenthwaite village; cottage is through village on far right-hand corner before little bridge 🛏 1 twin, 1 double; both with hair-dryer ✅ Lounge/dining room, garden ♿ No wheelchair access ● No children under 12; no dogs; no smoking ▭ None accepted £ Twin/double £55; deposit required. Special breaks available

---

BASSENTHWAITE LAKE Cumbria   map 10

The Pheasant

Bassenthwaite Lake, Cockermouth CA13 9YE
TEL: (017687) 76234   FAX: (017687) 76002
EMAIL: info@the-pheasant.co.uk
WEB SITE: www.the-pheasant.co.uk

This well-loved country inn loses none of its personality in a costly bedroom refit

The number of vehicles jockeying for a forecourt parking space indicates this place has no shortage of customers. It's a mere hop and skip from the busy A66 running down Bassenthwaite Lake, though the location seems entirely rural, screened by trees and sheltered by a steep backdrop of forested fellside. It's a rambling, low-slung building in typical Lakeland style, with black-rimmed windows and whitewashed walls. The core of The Pheasant is its snug bar, seemingly fossilised in oxblood varnish and furnished in rustic turned oak. Blizzards of quirky pictures adorn its walls (sporting prints, cartoons, photos of ancient rugby teams and landscape watercolours apparently traded in lieu of the bill). Inventive bar snacks (such as Stilton, walnut & apricot pâté with oatcakes) are served. Beyond lie three attractive lounges in restful country-house styles, and a bevy of refurbished bedrooms with good lighting and efficient power showers.

◑ Closed 25 Dec ▨ 7 miles west of Keswick, just off A66; follow signs for Wythop Mill. Private car park 🛏 1 single, 1 twin, 8 twin/double, 5 double; all with room service, hair-dryer, direct-dial telephone, modem line; TV on request ✅ Dining room, bar, 3 lounges, garden; early suppers for children ♿ No wheelchair access. Disabled parking ● No children under 8; dogs £5 per night; no smoking in bedrooms ▭ Delta, MasterCard, Switch, Visa £ Single £72 to £85, occupancy of twin/double £85 to £95, twin/double £130 to £170; deposit required. Set L £22, D £29; light meals available. Special breaks available

---

BATH Bath & N.E. Somerset   map 2

Apsley House Hotel

141 Newbridge Hill, Bath BA1 3PT
TEL: (01225) 336966   FAX: (01225) 425462
EMAIL: info@apsley-house.co.uk
WEB SITE: www.apsley-house.co.uk

Lovely, spacious house run with civilised good humour

The name of this immaculate family-run hotel will ring bells with students of English history, being normally associated with the Duke of Wellington. The Iron Duke certainly built the place in 1830, possibly for a mistress, which the romantically inclined might connect with the presence of a signalling tower of which only the lower section remains. Otherwise this is a large and dignified stone house with spacious high-ceilinged rooms. Owners Nicholas and Claire Potts manage to strike a good balance in the décor – period charm but not overpowering – and in hospitality – friendly and sociable but tranquil and unfussy. The dining and drawing rooms have elegant flourishes and views to the garden (it was about to be re-landscaped when we visited). The pick of the bedrooms is Wellington, but all are comfortable and on the upmarket side of homely. Ground-floor rooms are handy for garden access. Light suppers are available by prior arrangement.

◗ Closed 5 days Chr 🄕 At junction of A39 and A4, follow signs for Bath; after ½ mile turn left at sign to Newbridge Park, go over bridge and pass car park; turn left up Old Newbridge Hill and right at T-junction; hotel is 300 yards on right. Nearest train station: Bath Spa. Private car park 🚗 3 twin/double, 4 double, 1 four-poster, 2 family rooms; family suites available; all with room service, hair-dryer, trouser press, direct-dial telephone, modem, TV ⊘ Dining room, bar, lounge, garden; leisure facilities nearby 🕭 No wheelchair access ● No dogs; smoking in bar only ▭ Amex, MasterCard, Switch, Visa £ Single occupancy of twin/double £60 to £120, twin/double/four-poster £75 to £160, family room £95 to £160, family suite £95 to £175; deposit required. Light meals available. Special breaks available ③FOR②

Bath Priory

Weston Road, Bath BA1 2XT
TEL: (01225) 331922   FAX: (01225) 448276
EMAIL: mail@thebathpriory.co.uk
WEB SITE: www.thebathpriory.co.uk

Lavish hospitality in an atmosphere of quiet elegance – at a price

There is nothing at all monastic about Bath Priory, but the name itself is misleading: as the building dates back to 1835, it is only the land that has sacerdotal connections. In fact, this deeply comfortable hotel inhabits a world of luxury far removed from that of the hair-shirt. Bedrooms have a gentle elegance and are very well-kept. Those looking over the garden have pleasant views (it is a superb four-acre walled plot and well worth exploring), while recently refurbished rooms get swanky touches such as Bang and Olufsen televisions. Downstairs there are heated indoor and outdoor pools, a steam room and a sauna, while the drawing room is something of an art gallery, revealing the owner's interests in portraiture and sport (Andrew Brownsword also owns Bath Rugby Club). The restaurant offers cooking every bit as sumptuous as the rest of the place.

◗ Open all year 🄕 Off A4, near Victoria Park on north-west side. Nearest train station: Bath Spa. Private car park 🚗 20 twin/double, 5 double, 2 four-poster, 4 suites; family rooms available; all with room service, hair-dryer, trouser press, direct-dial telephone, modem line, TV; no tea/coffee-making facilities in rooms ⊘ Restaurant, 2 dining rooms, drawing room, library, garden; conferences; social functions; civil wedding licence; gym, beauty salon, indoor and outdoor heated swimming pools; early suppers for children; cots, highchairs, toys, babysitting, baby-listening 🕭 Wheelchair access to hotel (1 step) and restaurant, WC, 1 ground-floor bedroom specially equipped for disabled people. Disabled parking ● No dogs; smoking in bedrooms and drawing room only ▭ Amex, Delta, Diners, MasterCard, Switch, Visa £ Single occupancy of twin/double £245 to £360, twin/double £245 to £360, four-poster £360, suite £425, family room from £455; deposit required. Set L £25, alc L, D £49.50; light meals available. Special breaks available

Haydon House

9 Bloomfield Park, Bath BA2 2BY
TEL: (01225) 444919   FAX: (01225) 427351
EMAIL: stay@haydonhouse.co.uk
WEB SITE: www.haydonhouse.co.uk

Eminently elegant and comfortable B&B run with affable charm

In the Edwardian suburbs on the edge of Bath lies Gordon and Magdalene Ashman-Marr's substantial villa. House style here is sociable and civilised – breakfasts around the single table often end up, in Gordon's words, with the atmosphere of 'a forenoon dinner party' (a comment that reveals one of his previous jobs as a submariner). The lounge is similarly set up for conversation, with sofas and armchairs around the coffee table plus plenty of books and family pictures on the shelves. Outside is a bower-like garden with nooks and crannies for a bit more privacy. Bedrooms are all smart and homely, each with its own colour scheme: for example, Elderberry is a creamy fresh concoction of warm pastel shades, Blueberry has a four-poster and Mulberry a spacious attic conversion. All have well-equipped bathrooms and extras such as home-made shortbread. A fridge for fresh milk on the landing and a water dispenser complete a very carefully thought-out and ship-shape operation.

◗ Open all year ⤴ From Bath centre, follow signs for A367 towards Exeter and up Wells Road for ½ mile; at end of short dual carriageway, fork right into Bloomfield Road and second right into Bloomfield Park. Nearest train station: Bath Spa ⤴ 1 twin, 2 double, 1 four-poster, 1 family room; all with limited room service, hair-dryer, direct-dial telephone, TV; some with trouser press; fax machine, modem, VCR and CD player on request ⊘ Breakfast room, lounge, library/study, garden; leisure facilities nearby; cots, highchairs ⅃ No wheelchair access ● Children by arrangement only; no dogs; no smoking ▭ Amex, Delta, MasterCard, Switch, Visa ⌐£⌐ Single occupancy of twin/double £50 to £75, twin/double £80 to £120, four-poster £90 to £125, family room £95 to £160; deposit required. Special breaks available (3FOR2)

Paradise House

86–88 Holloway, Bath BA2 4PX
TEL: (01225) 317723   FAX: (01225) 482005
EMAIL: info@paradise-house.co.uk
WEB SITE: www.paradise-house.co.uk

Top-notch B&B oozing quiet sophistication and friendly charm

Once an undistinguished end-of-terrace house next to the leprosy hospital, Paradise House got the full Georgian upgrade in 1770 to make it what it is now: a spacious and elegant double-fronted house with half an acre of lovely lawned gardens at the rear overlooking the town. Owner David Lanz has done much to keep the atmosphere in keeping with the heritage – fresh, light colour schemes and an understated, elegant style finished off with a smattering of luxurious additions (whirlpool baths in some rooms). Some bedrooms have private access to the garden, others get large bay windows and spacious bathrooms. Evening meals are not served but the town is just a few minutes' stroll away – downhill, so you'll walk it off coming back!

◗ Closed 2 days at Chr ⤴ From Bath ring road take A367 Wells Road for ¾ mile; at shopping centre (Day & Pierce), turn left and continue left into cul-de-sac; hotel is 200 yards on left. Nearest train station: Bath Spa. Private car park ⤴ 4 twin/double, 2 double, 3 four-poster, 2 family rooms; all with hair-dryer, direct-dial telephone, modem line, TV, VCR ⊘ Breakfast room, lounge, garden; leisure facilities nearby; cots, highchairs ⅃ No wheelchair access; 4 ground-floor bedrooms ● No dogs; no smoking ▭ Amex, MasterCard, Switch, Visa ⌐£⌐ Single occupancy of twin/double £65 to £95, twin/double £75 to £155, four-poster £95 to £165, family room £95 to £135; deposit required. Special breaks available

Queensberry Hotel

4–7 Russel Street, Bath BA1 2QF
TEL: (01225) 447928   FAX: (01225) 446065
EMAIL: reservations@thequeensberry.co.uk
WEB SITE: www.thequeensberry.co.uk

This elegant small hotel is making great progress

Laurence and Helen Beere have made an impressive debut as owners at this smart town hotel, well positioned for the sights of Bath. Not that they are debutantes in the hotel business – just the ownership part. And all that experience is being put to good use: a new restaurant (brand new, right down to the cutlery) has given the hotel a plusher, more contemporary feel, with leather seating, modish lighting and abstract art. Reassuringly, however, image is not everything – the basics are done well and the marmalade is still home-made. The à la carte evening menu covers a lot of ground: artfully modern fish dishes feature among the main courses, but desserts such as a toffee-apple bread and butter pudding lend some traditional depth. The bar and reception lounge looked tired when we inspected, but plans are afoot to sweep these into the twenty-first century too. Bedrooms are comfortable, with stylish touches and excellent bathrooms.

◗ Open all year ⤴ In centre of Bath, just north of Assembly Rooms. Nearest train station: Bath Spa. Private car park ⤴ 11 twin/double, 15 double, 1 four-poster, 2 suites; all with room service, hair-dryer, direct-dial telephone, TV; no tea/coffee-making facilities in rooms ⊘ Restaurant, bar, 3 lounges; conferences and social functions; leisure facilities nearby; cots, highchairs, babysitting ⅃ Wheelchair access to hotel (1 step) and restaurant (5 steps, assistance provided), 6 ground-floor bedrooms, lift ● No dogs; no smoking in bedrooms

▭ Delta, MasterCard, Switch, Visa £· Twin/double £100 to £140, four-poster £195 to £285, suite £175 to £255. Continental B £9, cooked B £14; set L £15.50, D £26.50; alc L £22, D £32; light meals available

Royal Crescent Hotel

16 Royal Crescent, Bath BA1 2LS
TEL: (01225) 823333   FAX: (01225) 339401
EMAIL: info@royalcrescent.co.uk
WEB SITE: www.royalcrescent.co.uk

Sumptuous and friendly – a classic country house in the town

They say that if you stay often enough at the Royal Crescent to be considered a regular, then your name appears on the spine of one of the fake books that line the lift, a sort of *trompe l'oeil* library. Certainly every visitor to Bath has probably walked past and admired the façade, as the hotel is at the centre of the most famous sweep of houses in Britain. There is plenty more at the rear too: an acre of pleasant lawned gardens leading to various converted buildings, which include a restaurant, more bedrooms and a rather austere Japanese-themed health spa complete with hot pool and tubs. The atmosphere is upmarket – uniformed porters, etc. – but it's not stuffy. Bedrooms have sufficient Georgian features to maintain the elegant period feel.

◐ Open all year ⚡ In city centre. Nearest train station: Bath Spa. Private car park �ⁿ 31 twin/double, 14 suites; all with room service, hair-dryer, mini-bar, direct-dial telephone, fax/modem line, TV, VCR, CD player; some with DVD; no tea/coffee-making facilities in rooms ⬥ Restaurant, bar, 3 lounges, garden; conferences and social functions; civil wedding licence; gym, spa, indoor heated relaxation pool; leisure facilities nearby; early suppers for children; cots, highchairs, toys, babysitting ⓹ Wheelchair access to hotel (1 step) and restaurant (ramp), 8 ground-floor bedrooms, small lift. Valet parking ⬤ Dogs £25 in bedrooms ▭ Amex, Diners, MasterCard, Switch, Visa £· Twin/double/suite £240 to £715; deposit required. Cooked B £8.50; alc L £25, D £45; light meals available. Special breaks available

Tasburgh House Hotel

Warminster Road, Bath BA2 6SH
TEL: (01225) 425096   FAX: (01225) 463842
EMAIL: hotel@bathtasburgh.co.uk
WEB SITE: www.bathtasburgh.co.uk

Fine B&B offering excellent service and comfortable rooms

Susan Keeling's large red-brick house stands to the south-east of Bath, overlooking the Kennet and Avon Canal. In fact, the grounds lead down to the canal and there is a pleasant stroll to be had along the towpath, either into town or out into the country (where you will find a decent pub for dinner). Susan's friendly and efficient approach lifts the place out of the ordinary into something quite special. Bedrooms are warm and cosy, with bright comfortable modern furnishings and polished bathrooms. Our inspection breakfast confirmed the high standards, with plenty of staff to keep the toast and tea coming plus a good selection of hot dishes. Outside, the gardens are lovely, and there is a terrace with chairs and tables. The only lapse in hospitality was the refusal of the African Grey parrot at the front door to say hello until it was time to say goodbye!

◐ Closed Chr ⚡ From centre of Bath, take A36 (Warminster Road) east; hotel is on left at top of hill. Nearest train station: Bath Spa. Private car park ⟼ 1 single, 1 twin, 2 twin/double, 5 double, 3 family rooms; suites available; all with room service, hair-dryer, direct-dial telephone, fax line, modem line, TV; some with trouser press, VCR ⬥ Restaurant, dining room, bar, lounge, conservatory, garden; conferences; social functions; leisure facilities nearby; cots, highchairs, toys ⓹ No wheelchair access; 2 steps into hotel, 2 ground-floor bedrooms ⬤ No dogs; no smoking ▭ Diners, MasterCard, Switch, Visa £· Single £60, single occupancy of twin/double £75, twin/double £110, family room £140, suite £130; deposit required. Light meals available. Special breaks available

BATHFORD   Bath & N.E. Somerset   map 2

Eagle House

Church Street, Bath BA1 7RS
TEL: (01225) 859946   FAX: (01225) 859430
EMAIL: jonap@eagleho.demon.co.uk
WEB SITE: www.eaglehouse.co.uk

Welcoming hosts and good bedrooms at this family-run B&B

John and Rosamund Napier's spacious Georgian house is well placed for those who want to be close to Bath but out in a country village. It's quite an imposing place, with a pedimented roof, marbled fireplaces and all the neo-classical flourishes expected of the period. But the Napiers bring a light and homely touch to things: you'll find a trampoline and swing out in the one-acre garden and the elegant octagonal sitting room has plenty of board games, books and toys to keep visitors of all ages amused. The spacious bedrooms have stylish touches plus antique furniture dotted throughout. Bathrooms are steadily being upgraded and three of them now have lovely stone floors. If you are given a choice, the best to plump for are those with the valley view at the back of the house. Out in the garden there is also a delightful weatherboarded colonial-style cottage with two bedrooms – perfect for small groups.

◗ Closed 12 Dec to 10 Jan 🔁 From A4, turn on to A363 to Bradford-on-Avon; after 150 yards, fork left up Bathford Hill; turn first right into Church Street; Eagle House is on right. Private car park 🛏 1 single, 2 twin, 1 twin/double, 2 double, 1 family room, 1 suite; all with hair-dryer, direct-dial telephone, modem line, TV; some with VCR ✓ Breakfast room, drawing room, garden; conferences; tennis, leisure facilities nearby; cots, highchairs, toys, babysitting, baby-listening, outdoor play area ♿ Wheelchair access to hotel and breakfast room, 2 ground-floor bedrooms ● Dogs in public rooms by arrangement (£3.50 per night in bedrooms); smoking in drawing room and some bedrooms only 💳 Delta, MasterCard, Switch, Visa £ Single £42 to £62, twin/double £58 to £96, family room £68 to £105, suite £80 to £115; deposit required. Cooked B £4.50. Special breaks available (3FOR2)

BATTLE   East Sussex   map 3

Fox Hole Farm

Kane Hythe Road, Battle TN33 9QU
TEL: (01424) 772053 (AND FAX)
EMAIL: foxholefarm@amserve.com

Top-notch B&B in an idyllic setting

Though it is only minutes away from Battle on the 1066 trail, there's no danger of being disturbed by the tourist hubbub in this tranquil rural retreat, set in lovely gardens complete with duck pond and roaming chickens. The farmland, which is no longer worked, covers 40 acres and is surrounded by 1,000 acres of Forestry Commission land. Friendly hosts Paul and Pauline Collins have restored and extended the former woodman's cottage into a smart, comfortable home and they welcome guests with a winning combination of professionalism, attention to detail and good old-fashioned hospitality. Guests have their own tastefully furnished and good-sized lounge-cum-breakfast area with a huge fireplace, wood-burning stove and wing chairs, and sit at separate tables for breakfast. The three bedrooms are smart and comfortable with neutral carpets, tasteful fabrics and immaculate bathrooms. The Garden Room on the ground floor is perhaps the loveliest, with double-aspect views, while the Ash Room is slightly smaller but equally smart. The Oak Room oozes character with uneven floors, a stepped chimney breast and exposed beams, and has stunning views over the rolling farmland which guests are welcome to explore.

◗ Closed Dec & Jan 🔁 Go west from Battle on A271. Take first right (B2096) towards Heathfield; Fox Hole is ¾ mile on right. Private car park 🛏 3 double; all with TV ✓ Breakfast room/living room, garden; cot, highchair ♿ No wheelchair access; 2 steps into hotel, 1 step into breakfast room, 1 ground-floor bedroom ● No dogs in public rooms; no smoking 💳 Delta, MasterCard, Visa £ Double £53 to £59 (3FOR2)

map 2

Bridge House

Prout Bridge, Beaminster DT8 3AY
TEL: (01308) 862200   FAX: (01308) 863700
EMAIL: enquiries@bridge-house.co.uk
WEB SITE: www.bridge-house.co.uk

Unpretentious and reliably comfortable hotel in this small town

This fine stone-built hotel may be right on the high street, yet it manages to ooze quiet unhurried charm, probably a result of Peter Pinkster's gentle and friendly style. The oldest room in the house started life as a clergyhouse seven centuries ago, but with extensive additions over the years, including recently a couple of conservatories and bedrooms in a converted coach house, this has become a large and comfortable country hotel. There is a strong local art connection and you'll find plenty of paintings dotted around. The spacious bedrooms follow a clean, simple format with fresh pastel colours and well-kept, if occasionally dated, bathrooms. Evening meals follow an uncomplicated country house pattern. 'Dinner was very good,' wrote one regular visitor. 'Simple, well-executed cooking, a great pleasure. Service is a little rustic – not necessarily that quick, but always willing and friendly.'

◖ Closed 30 & 31 Dec ⧅ In centre of Beaminster; down hill from town square; entrance by red telephone box. Private car park ⌂ 1 single, 12 twin, 1 twin/double, 1 family room; all with room service, hair-dryer, direct-dial telephone, modem, TV ⊘ Dining room, bar, sitting room, 2 conservatories, garden; conferences; social functions; cots, highchairs ♿ No wheelchair access; 5 ground-floor bedrooms ⊖ No smoking in bedrooms and some public rooms ▭ Amex, Delta, Diners, MasterCard, Switch, Visa £ Single £57 to £59, single occupancy of twin/double £88 to £93, twin/double £108 to £144, family room £108 to £112; deposit required. Set, alc L £11, D £30; light meals available. Special breaks available

---

map 2

Montagu Arms NEW ENTRY

Palace Lane, Beaulieu SO42 7ZL
TEL: (01590) 612324   FAX: (01590) 612188
EMAIL: reservations@montaguarmshotel.co.uk
WEB SITE: www.montaguarmshotel.co.uk

A stylish village inn in the heart of the New Forest

Though there has been a watering hole here for over 200 years, the building that houses the Montagu Arms has been much remodelled, and the overall effect is a good deal grander than you might expect of a village inn. Step through the doors, and the dimly lit reception – all dark wood with shiny floors, exposed beams and a huge brick fireplace – is in keeping with the smart but austere red-brick frontage. However, at the rear of the hotel, with its sunny conservatory and pretty terraced garden, the feel is rather calmer and lighter. Explore the other public rooms to discover a perfectly manicured lounge with plenty of seating, dark beams and loads of fresh flowers, and a spacious, elegant restaurant where one reader described the food as 'always good, and sometimes very good'. The 'effortless' service receives high praise: 'excellent throughout' pronounces one reader, while another, who returned to his car to find his windscreen had been cleaned, commends the attention to detail, which is 'second to none'. Bedrooms vary considerably in size and character but are stylish and immaculate with well-equipped bathrooms. Front-facing rooms overlooking the road can be noisy despite secondary glazing – better to opt for a rear-facing room overlooking the gardens.

◖ Open all year ⧅ In Beaulieu village. Private car park ⌂ 1 single, 3 twin, 13 double, 3 four-poster, 3 suites; all with room service, hair-dryer, trouser-press, direct-dial telephone, TV; no tea/coffee-making facilities in rooms ⊘ 2 restaurants, 2 bars, 2 lounges, library, conservatory, garden; conferences; civil wedding licence; social functions; leisure facilities nearby; early suppers for children; cots, highchairs, baby-sitting

♿ No wheelchair access ◒ No children under 8 in 1 restaurant; no dogs in bedrooms ▭ Amex, Delta, Diners, MasterCard, Switch, Visa £ Single £100 to £125, single occupancy of twin/double £125 to £145, twin/double £160, four-poster £190, suite £210; deposit required. Set L £21.50, D £35; alc L, D £45; light meals available. Special breaks available

---

BEERCROCOMBE Somerset   map 2

Frog Street Farm

Beercrocombe, Taunton TA3 6AF
TEL: (01823) 480430 (AND FAX)

Excellent farm accommodation with extra interest for horse-lovers

Tucked away in deep and lovely Somerset countryside is Veronica Cole's farmhouse. The working farm is just across the yard and largely given over to horses – racing pictures in the house reflect the equine interests. (Go and say hello to Dubacilla, second in the Gold Cup and fourth in the National, now busy bringing foals into the world.) Originally a fifteenth-century longhouse, the building's rooms necessarily lead on from each other, starting with the dining room. Veronica does dinners by arrangement, using plenty of local produce where she can and lots of home-grown vegetables. Further along the house are two attractive lounges – as you might expect in a house of this vintage the style is beamed ceilings and inglenook fireplaces matched by pretty floral fabrics and ornaments. Bedrooms upstairs have a light and contemporary feel; the twin has its own log-burner and sitting room.

◑ Closed Nov to Mar ⚡ Leave M5 at Junction 25 and take A358 towards Ilminster/Yeovil; leave at Hatch Beauchamp and by Hatch Inn take Station Road for 1 mile; turn left at bottom of hill, over humpback bridge and go down cul-de-sac. Private car park 🛏 1 twin, 2 double; all with hairdryer ✓ Dining room, 2 lounges, garden ♿ No wheelchair access ◒ No children under 11; no smoking ▭ None accepted £ Single occupancy of twin/double £40, twin/double £70. Set D £20; light meals available; service incl

---

BEETHAM Cumbria   map 8

Wheatsheaf at Beetham NEW ENTRY

Beetham, Nr Milnthorpe LA7 7AL
TEL: (015395) 62123   FAX: (015395) 64840
EMAIL: wheatsheaf@beetham.plus.com
WEB SITE: www.wheatsheafbeetham.com

Compliments pour in for this enterprising village dining pub just off the motorway

Canny travellers in this part of the world recognise a useful billet when they see one, and lunchtimes are always popular. Besides being just off the A6 within easy striking distance of the Lakes, the pretty village of Beetham has many charms. One such asset is this strikingly timbered sixteenth-century free house near the church, where Kathryn and Mark Chambers have put their wide-ranging experience of the hospitality trade to excellent use over the past two years. The food is the best sort of gastropub fare, which anyone can enjoy – even humble bangers and mash takes on a sparkling new dimension. The interconnected bar-restaurant areas (some up, some downstairs) are warm and welcoming with plenty of character, while light, uncluttered bedrooms are spruce and neat with decent plumbing and storage. The parrot on the stairs may tell you he loves you, but don't be fooled: he'll say that to anybody.

◑ Closed 25 Dec ⚡ From M6 junction 35, take A6 to Milnthorpe/Kendal; village is 1 mile south of Milnthorpe; hotel is just off main road. Private car park 🛏 1 single, 1 twin, 4 double; family room available; all with room service, hair-dryer, TV ✓ Restaurant, bar, lounge; conferences; social functions; early suppers for children; cots, highchairs ♿ No wheelchair access ◒ No dogs; smoking in bar only ▭ Delta, MasterCard, Switch, Visa £ Single £40 to £55, single occupancy of twin/double £40 to £55; twin/double £40 to £80, family room £50 to £90. Alc L £16, D £24; light meals available. Special breaks available ③FOR②

BERWICK-UPON-TWEED Northumberland   map 10

Number One Sallyport

1 Sallyport, off Bridge Steet, Berwick-upon-Tweed TD15 1EZ
TEL: (01289) 308827 (AND FAX)
EMAIL: info@sallyport.co.uk
WEB SITE: www.sallyport.co.uk

Stylish rooms and good food at a bijou B&B in Berwick's centre

Whatever Elizabeth Middlemiss does, she likes to get it right. Just a short stroll from the River Tweed waterfront, her stone townhouse is a haven of comfy style and fine food, liberally dotted about with eclectic bits and bobs to catch the eye of anyone with a feel for contemporary style. That's not to say that this is a soulless, minimal sort of place: the bedrooms (shoe-free, incidentally) head straight for the comfort zone with touchy-feely fabrics, big beds to sprawl in and classy modern bathrooms with features such as terracotta or mosaic tiles and monsoon shower heads. The vast leather sleigh bed, wooden floors and modular sofa in Smugglers will appeal to style slaves, as will the clean-cut lines of the Manhattan Loft. The Master Bedroom is a more traditional space that blends *toile* wallpaper with a gleaming brass bed and black marble fireplace. By arrangement, Elizabeth cooks Provençal-style dinners in a suitably rustic farmhouse kitchen where guests share a polished table by a huge stone fireplace; breakfasts are a treat too – perhaps vanilla waffles with fresh raspberries, local Craster kippers or a full Scottish breakfast with haggis.

○ Open all year ⚡ Near harbour in Berwick-upon-Tweed. Nearest train station: Berwick-upon-Tweed. Private car park 🛏 3 double; all with hair-dryer, TV, VCR, CD player ⊘ Kitchen/breakfast room, patio; leisure facilities nearby ⅙ No wheelchair access ● No smoking ▭ Amex, Delta, Diners, MasterCard, Switch, Visa £ Single occupancy of double £60 to £75, double £75 to £90; deposit required. Set D £27.50; light meals available. Special breaks available

BEYTON Suffolk   map 6

Manorhouse

The Green, Beyton, Bury St Edmunds IP30 9AF
TEL: (01359) 270960
EMAIL: manorhouse@beyton.com
WEB SITE: www.beyton.com

Suffolk longhouse B&B with eggs direct from the inhabitants

You couldn't argue with the free-range credentials of your breakfast eggs at the Manor House. The chickens wandering around the gardens provide Mark and Kay Dewsbury with around ten eggs a day, destined for frying, poaching, scrambling or just plain boiling (and dipping with soldiers). This is a well-cared-for, unpretentious little B&B with rooms in the main house and out back in the former barn. The renamed Ivory has been recently refurbished and has a nice double aspect and a large bathroom. The dining-room fireplace is flanked by stone allegedly nicked from the abbey at Bury St Edmunds after the dissolution of the monasteries. Dinner is only by special request, though Mark tells us their chickens are definitely not on the menu.

○ Closed Chr ⚡ 4 miles east of Bury St Edmunds. Take Beyton exit off A14; house is in centre of village, by duck pond. Private car park 🛏 2 twin/double, 2 double; all with hair-dryer, TV ⊘ Dining room/lounge, garden ⅙ No wheelchair access; 3 steps into hotel, 2 ground-floor bedrooms ● No children under 12; no dogs; no smoking ▭ None accepted £ Single occupancy of twin/double £45 to £50, twin/double £56 to £60. Set D £17; service incl

BIBURY Gloucestershire

map 2

Bibury Court

Bibury, Cirencester GL7 5NT
TEL: (01285) 740337   FAX: (01285) 740660
EMAIL: info@biburycourt.com
WEB SITE: www.biburycourt.com

Glorious grounds and a relaxed, country-house style that is reassuringly unfussy

Although the exterior of Bibury Court is still that of a Tudor manor house, the owners in the last century opened up the interior and added a feeling of space and light. The location, too, is glorious: set in a bowl of hills, with the babbling river Coln running through the lovely informal English gardens to the rear. Despite the imposing gate and gravel driveway, the house has an unchanging, homely feel. That is not to say that it lacks outstanding features. The bar has a Roaring Twenties atmosphere, with an elaborate art deco etching of nymphs, and the wood-panelled drawing room, with its glass chandeliers, seems to stretch on forever. A notable modern addition is the wood-beamed conservatory, with great views to the garden. Bedrooms are ample and unfussy, and all have good views, either to the front or back, and modern, well-fitted bathrooms.

◑ Open all year   🔲 Behind church in Bibury, next to river. Private car park   🛏 1 twin, 5 twin/double, 6 double, 5 four-poster, 1 suite; family rooms available; all with room service, hair-dryer, direct-dial telephone, TV   ⊘ Restaurant, bar, drawing room, conservatory, gardens; conferences and social functions; civil wedding licence; early suppers for children; cots, highchairs, baby-listening   ♿ No wheelchair access; 3 steps into hotel, 3 steps into restaurant, 1 ground-floor bedroom   ◕ No dogs in restaurant, £5 per night in bedrooms; no smoking in restaurant   ▭ Amex, Delta, Diners, MasterCard, Switch, Visa   £ Single occupancy of twin/double £120, twin/double £135, four-poster/family room £155, suite £220 (prices valid until 1 March 2005); deposit required. Cooked B from £6; set D £35; alc L £25; light meals available. Special breaks available

BIGBURY-ON-SEA Devon

map 1

Burgh Island NEW ENTRY

Bigbury-on-Sea, Kingsbridge TQ7 4BG
TEL: (01548) 810514   FAX: (01548) 810243
EMAIL: reception@burghisland.com
WEB SITE: www.burghisland.com

It's delightful, it's delicious, it's de-lovely – in Devon

If you want to be transported to the Jazz Age, all flappers and boas, it's difficult to think of anywhere better than this. Every detail, from the classic white deco lines of the building to the authentic valve radios and the ziggurat wallpaper panels in the bedrooms, is in place. The Palm Court, with its giant skylight of peacock stained glass above a curving mirrored bar, forms a memorable setting for a pre-dinner cocktail before dinner (black tie is de rigueur). And twice a week there's dancing to a live band in the Ballroom, to tunes of the time, of course. Bedrooms are slowly being refurbished to update facilities while remaining in character; prices depend on size, and include dinner as well as breakfast. One of the nicest is Cunard, with a huge circular balcony overlooking the beach and a lovely big bathroom. Shrimp, the smallest, has a slipper bath in the room and a view over the seawater Mermaid Pool. Not everything is perfect: some of the corridors are rather worn, and the basement leisure facilities (billiard room, table tennis room and children's den) look distinctly tatty. But who cares about that when you're dancing cheek to cheek?

◑ Open all year   🔲 Follow signs to Bigbury-on-Sea. At St Ann's Chapel call hotel from phone box. Do not drive across beach to island. Private car park   🛏 3 twin/double, 3 double, 15 suites; all with room service, hair-dryer, direct-dial telephone, CD player; TV on request   ⊘ 2 restaurants, 2 bars, library, conservatory, 2 games rooms, garden, beach; conferences; civil wedding licence; social functions; tennis, outdoor unheated swimming pool; early suppers for children; playrooms, baby-sitting   ♿ Wheelchair access to hotel, lift   ◕ No children under 3 in hotel and under 12 in restaurant eves; no dogs; smoking in bar only ☐ Delta, MasterCard, Switch, Visa £ Single occupancy of twin/double £200, twin/double/suite from £275 (rates incl dinner); deposit required. Set L £30; light meals available

Henley Hotel

Folly Hill, Bigbury-on-Sea, Kingsbridge TQ7 4AR
TEL: (01548) 810240
EMAIL: enquiries@thehenleyhotel.co.uk
WEB SITE: www.thehenleyotel.co.uk

Model small hotel with enthusiastic proprietor and splendid views

It's not often that our inspectors are greeted with a cry of 'Come and see my roof!', but Martyn Scarterfield is not one to let formality stand in his way. And he's not slow to seize an opportunity either: while the roofers had the scaffolding erected, he used it to paint the exterior of his smart little Edwardian hotel. He's been busy inside too, refurbishing the cosy 'winter lounge' with a leather suite and rugs on stripped boards. But the views from the conservatory dining room remain unchanged and as wonderful as ever, and the homely but uncluttered main lounge, with lots of greenery, is also notably relaxing. Martyn's real strength lies in being able to put himself into his guests' shoes and think about what they want. So he has restructured Room 5, putting the bed by the window ('After all, people come here for the sea views') and moving the bathroom to the back of the room. It's been so successful that he's planning to repeat the exercise in other bedrooms. We say: keep up the good work! 'We were just as happy there this year,' writes a repeat visitor, who praised Martyn's 'excellent' dinners.

◑ Closed Nov to Mar ⚡ From A38, follow signs to Bigbury-on-Sea; hotel is on left as road descends towards seafront. Private car park 🚗 2 twin/double, 4 double; all with room service, hair-dryer, direct-dial telephone, TV ⊘ Dining room/conservatory, bar, 2 lounges, garden ♿ No wheelchair access ● No children under 12; no dogs in public rooms; no smoking ☐ Delta, MasterCard, Switch, Visa £ Single occupancy of twin/double £50 to £58, twin/double £82 to £110; deposit required. Set D £26; light meals available

---

BIGGIN Derbyshire map 5

Biggin Hall

Biggin-by-Hartington, Buxton SK17 0DH
TEL: (01298) 84451 FAX: (01298) 84681
EMAIL: enquiries@bigginhall.co.uk
WEB SITE: www.bigginhall.co.uk

Characterful base in lovely rural setting

Unlike many country seats of similar vintage and distinction, this seventeenth-century mellow-stone house on the edge of the village has something of a workaday, lived-in feel, so you'll find geese strutting about the lawn and it's not too precious to rub shoulders with the next-door caravan site. Inside, the atmosphere is delightfully evocative, from the Historic Lounge with its huge fireplace (often blazing), pieces of old armour and rich Persian rugs on quarry tiles to the low-beamed dining room where more rugs take the chill off stone flags. The bedrooms are split between the main house and a number of converted outbuildings. All of them are comfortably furnished – those in the Bothy are perhaps the nicest – and come with plenty of antiques as well as attractive spreads or pretty floral fabrics, but bathrooms are looking noticeably tired. More reports please.

◑ Open all year ⚡ From A515 between Ashbourne and Buxton take turning to Biggin. Follow road for ½ mile; hotel driveway is next to Waterloo Inn at end of village. Private car park 🚗 1 single, 11 twin/double, 4 double, 1 four-poster, 3 suites; family rooms available; all with hair-dryer, direct-dial telephone, modem, TV, fridge ⊘ Dining room, lounge, library, garden; conferences; social functions ♿ No wheelchair access; 4 ground-floor bedrooms ● No children under 12; no dogs in public rooms and some bedrooms; no smoking in some public rooms and some bedrooms ☐ Amex, Delta, MasterCard, Switch, Visa £ Single £40 to

£70, single occupancy of twin/double £58 to £90, twin/double £66 to £106, four-poster £96 to £146, family room £89 to £156; deposit required. Cooked B £4; set D £15.50; service incl. Special breaks available

BILLINGSHURST West Sussex   map 3

Old Wharf

Newbridge, Wisborough Green, Billingshurst RH14 0JG
TEL: (01403) 784096 (AND FAX)
EMAIL: david.mitchell@farming.co.uk

Immaculate B&B in a lovely canalside setting

Turn off the busy A272 and the Old Wharf appears amid lush water meadows where swans soak up the sun's rays, oblivious to the stresses of negotiating rush-hour traffic. Set well back from the road and shielded by neat gardens complete with croquet lawn, swimming pool and tennis court, the low, square former warehouse is a welcome retreat in a surprisingly peaceful spot right on the canalside. Moira and David Mitchell have converted the building into a smart home and top-notch B&B, incorporating many of the original features from its days as the terminus of the Arun Navigation, including the hoist wheel displayed beneath the eaves above the central staircase. Off the central landing the three bedrooms – Bluebell, Peach and Primrose – are prettily done out, light and fresh with sparkling modern bathrooms. Primrose is the largest, and has a separate sitting area with lovely views. Guests have their own good-sized sitting room, which has French doors leading onto the canalside for leisurely summer strolls, and a lovely brick fireplace where a fire burns on cold winter evenings. Breakfast is a communal affair at a large round table in the cosy breakfast room or, in summer, guests can venture out into the courtyard.

● Closed Chr & New Year 🚗 Head west from Billingshurst on A272 for 2 miles; house is on left-hand side, by banks of canal, just after river bridge. Nearest train station: Billingshurst. Private car park 🛏 2 twin, 1 suite; all with hair-dryer, TV ✔ Breakfast room, sitting room, garden; tennis, heated outdoor swimming pool ♿ No wheelchair access ● No children under 12; no dogs; no smoking 🚭 None accepted £ Single occupancy of twin £50, twin £75, suite £95; deposit required

BIRCH VALE Derbyshire   map 8

Waltzing Weasel

New Mills Road, Birch Vale, High Peak SK22 1BT
TEL: (01663) 743402 (AND FAX)
EMAIL: w-weasel@zen.co.uk
WEB SITE: www.w-weasel.co.uk

An old-world inn with a penchant for foreign cuisine

The atmosphere is solidly traditional at this honey-stone inn nestling in the heart of the Peaks, where an old photo of WG Grace casts a sternly approving gaze over the cosy bar with its invigorating fire. The bedrooms are comfortably kitted out, with a generous smattering of antiques, including a lovely half-tester in Room 6, and old-fashioned fabrics set off against backdrops of neutrally toned walls and moorland vistas. Smartly tiled en-suite facilities tend to come with bath/shower combinations and brass fixtures and fittings. Tapestry chairs and medieval hangings maintain the tone in the intimate, dusky pink restaurant, but just a glance at the eclectically exotic menu is enough to transport you to faraway lands.

● Open all year 🚗 ½ mile west of Hayfield on A6015. Private car park 🛏 1 single, 2 twin, 5 double; all with hair-dryer, trouser press, TV ✔ Restaurant, bar, garden; conferences and social functions; leisure facilities nearby ♿ Wheelchair access to hotel (1 step) and restaurant (1 step), 2 ground-floor bedrooms ● No children under 7 in restaurant eves; no smoking in restaurant or bedrooms 🚭 Delta, MasterCard, Switch, Visa £ Single £48, single occupancy of twin/double £68 to £88, twin/double £78 to £108; deposit required. Alc L £15, D £27.50; light meals available

City Inn Birmingham NEW ENTRY

1 Brunswick Square, Brindley Place, Birmingham B1 2HW
TEL: 0121-643 1003   FAX: 0121-643 1005
EMAIL: birmingham.reservations@cityinn.com
WEB SITE: www.cityinn.com

Up-to-the-minute purpose-built berths for today's discerning travellers

Despite its slightly anonymous location on a bland plaza and beside a multi-storey car park, this slick city-centre establishment (one of the first of a chain that is set to grow) makes an excellent base. There's a luxurious airport-terminal feel to the airy atrium-style lobby/lounge, with its brightly coloured rugs and square, well-upholstered furniture set against a backdrop of brushed chrome and frosted glass. Next door, wooden flooring, smart grey seating and plenty of bits of modern art and artfully arranged twigs set a swish, contemporary tone in the City Café bar-restaurant – even the exotic white flowers look designed. In the identikit bedrooms (featuring all mod-cons), red carpets and chairs make a bold splash against neutral grey and white walls and matching duvets, while full-length windows ensure plenty of light. White-tiled en-suite shower rooms are smartly finished, with grey-green moulded sinks and chrome fittings.

◑ Open all year   ⚡ From M6 Junction 6, take A38 to city centre, and go under the tunnel keeping in the left-hand lane. On emerging from the tunnel follow signs for the International Convention Centre. Stay in the left-hand lane at Paradise Circus and follow signs for the A456. At the third set of traffic lights turn right into Sheepcote Street and hotel is straight ahead. Private car park. Nearest train station: Birmingham New Street
🛏 31 twin/double, 207 double; all with room service, hair-dryer, trouser press, direct-dial telephone, broadband access, TV, CD player   Restaurant, bar, lounge; conferences; gym; leisure facilities nearby; cots, highchairs   ♿ Wheelchair access to hotel and restaurant, WC, lift, 14 rooms specially equipped for disabled people   ● No dogs   ▭ Amex, Delta, Diners, MasterCard, Switch, Visa   £ Twin/double £129; deposit required. Continental B £8.50, cooked B £11.50; set L £12.50, D £16.50; alc L, D £25; light meals available. Special breaks available

Hotel du Vin & Bistro

25 Church Street, Birmingham B3 2NR
TEL: 0121-200 0600   FAX: 0121-236 0889
EMAIL: info@birmingham.hotelduvin.com
WEB SITE: www.hotelduvin.com

Stylish accommodation at this hedonistic urban playground

Birmingham's city centre might seem a million miles from the sultry streets of Havana, yet behind the unobtrusive street front of this early-Victorian hospital building lurks a lingering taste of colonial grandeur. From the lobby with its *trompe l'oeil* stonework and wrought-iron lift cage, to the baroque mirror- and mural-clad bar and the suave restaurant, where bistro dishes are served under brass ceiling fans, everything comes with a playful old-world twist. But it's the bohemian cellar bar with its attendant smoking room – savour a Corona in the company of Che and Fidel – that really sets the mood. Other facilities include a wonderfully decadent-looking shuttered billiard room and an up-to-the-minute, fabulously well-equipped health spa. Bedrooms vary greatly in price, but even the cheapest ones are extremely sophisticated in black and grey schemes and come with lovely en-suite facilities with mosaic floors and sparkling chrome fittings.

◑ Open all year   ⚡ From M6 Junction 6, take A38 to city centre; after flyover keep in left-hand lane and turn off at sign to 'Jewellery Quarter'; at roundabout, take first exit (signed Colmore Row) and turn right opposite cathedral into Church Street. Cross Barwick Street; hotel is on right. Nearest train station: Birmingham New Street   🛏 7 twin/double, 56 double, 3 suites; all with hair-dryer, mini-bar, trouser press, direct-dial telephone, modem line, TV, DVD, CD player   ⊘ Restaurant, 2 bars, games room, courtyard; conferences; social functions; civil wedding licence; gym, spa; early suppers for children; cots, highchairs, baby-sitting   ♿ Wheelchair access to hotel and restaurant (ramp), WC, lift   ● No dogs; no smoking in restaurant

⊟ Amex, Delta, Diners, MasterCard, Switch, Visa ⌊£⌋ Single occupancy of twin/double from £110, twin/double from £110, suite from £195; deposit required (prices valid till autumn 2004). Continental B £9.50, cooked B £13.50; set Sun L £24.50; alc L, D £32

BISHOP'S STORTFORD   Hertfordshire

map 3

The Cottage

71 Birchanger Lane, Birchanger, Bishop's Stortford CM23 5QA
TEL: (01279) 812349   FAX: (01279) 815045
EMAIL: bookings@thecottagebirchanger.co.uk
WEB SITE: www.thecottagebirchanger.co.uk

Neat-as-a-pin B&B with colourful rooms that's handy for Stansted

Here's the thing: you've booked a bargain-basement flight for a cheap weekend away, only to realise that you have to check in even before the sparrows are up, and it's a long drive from home. Enter the Cottage to your rescue. Near enough to be useful but far enough to be quiet, this cheery B&B is just a few miles from Stansted airport and its budget airlines. The original seventeenth-century cottage has been expanded to offer a good number of comfortable bedrooms, while some public rooms lend atmosphere with their wood panelling and big fireplaces. There's a sunny lounge and a long breakfast room with picture windows giving onto the neatly manicured garden. Perhaps the most striking aspect of this winning B&B are the colour schemes, first seen with the exterior's salmon pink walls. Inside, bathrooms come in the likes of aubergine or peacock, while bedrooms are more soothingly lilac, pistachio or even melted butter. Rooms in the old part have creaky floors, but all offer pretty fabrics and a cottagey feel.

◖ Closed Chr & New Year ⚡ From M11 Junction 8, take A120 to Hertford and then B1383 to Newport; after ¼ mile take first right into Birchanger Lane; the Cottage is on left. Nearest train station: Bishop's Stortford. Private car park 🖐 3 single, 5 twin, 7 double; all with TV; some with hair-dryer ✅ Breakfast room/conservatory, 2 lounges, garden; leisure facilities nearby; cots, highchairs ♿ No wheelchair access; 1 step into breakfast room, 4 ground-floor bedrooms ● No dogs; no smoking ⊟ Amex, Delta, Diners, MasterCard, Switch, Visa ⌊£⌋ Single £55 to £60, single occupancy of twin/double £58 to £60, twin/double £78 to £80; deposit required

---

BISHOP'S TACHBROOK   Warwickshire

map 5

Mallory Court

Harbury Lane, Leamington Spa CV33 9QB
TEL: (01926) 330214   FAX: (01926) 451714
EMAIL: reception@mallory.co.uk
WEB SITE: www.mallory.co.uk

A perfect country house with a pleasantly informal air

It would be very hard to find a more pleasing example of a country-house hotel than this venerable Lutyens-style property, where Art Deco features and furnishings provide a comfortable lift to an otherwise classic interior. All public areas show the same impeccable taste, from the comfortable drawing room with its sumptuous fabrics to the oak-panelled dining room and delightful garden room, backed by an ornamental stream. The individually styled bedrooms are just as eye-catching and can be divided broadly between the more traditional, which tend to come with plaids and chintz, and the more modern, such as Berrington with its rich dark plum fabrics, intended to become classics in their own right; all of them have boldly modernist bathrooms, featuring stunning expanses of marble in the pricier rooms. Ten acres of beautifully maintained grounds include water gardens, croquet lawn and a striking outdoor pool.

◖ Open all year ⚡ Two miles south of Leamington Spa, turn off B4087 towards Harbury; hotel is over brow of hill, on right. Nearest train station: Leamington Spa. Private car park 🖐 8 twin/double, 12 double, 9 suites; all with room service, hair-dryer, trouser press, direct-dial telephone, TV; some with mini-bar, modem line, VCR, CD player ✅ Dining room, drawing room, bar, library, conservatory, garden; conferences; social functions; civil wedding licence; unheated outdoor swimming pool; spa and leisure facilities nearby

&. Wheelchair access to hotel (ramp) and dining room, WC, 1 ground-floor bedroom specially equipped for disabled people ● No children under 9; no dogs in public rooms ▭ Amex, Delta, Diners, MasterCard, Switch, Visa £ Single occupancy of twin/double £130 to £250, twin/double £155 to £295, suite £250 to £320; deposit required. Set L £25, D £39.50; alc D £49; light meals available. Special breaks available ③FOR②

BISHOP'S TAWTON Devon　　　　　　　　　　　　　　　　　　　　map 1

Halmpstone Manor

Bishop's Tawton, Barnstaple EX32 0EA
TEL: (01271) 830321   FAX: (01271) 830826
EMAIL: charles@halmpstonemanor.co.uk
WEB SITE: www.halmpstonemanor.co.uk

Romantic atmosphere and good food in a historic home

Delightfully tucked away in the Devon countryside, this stone-built manor house has been pleasing those who take the trouble to find it for a very long time indeed. First positive reports were noted in 1630 and more recent visitors are in agreement. Charles and Jane Stanbury run things as a hospitable family home: the drawing room is an inviting spot with sofas around the fireplace, the dining room likewise with its panelled walls and candlelight gleaming on silver and glass. Bedrooms come with the same sense of elegance and good taste, with antiques dotted around and plenty of luxurious touches. Charles was born in the house, and farms the land. In the evenings, he does front of house, mingling with guests and dispensing drinks, while Jane puts together the well-reported five-course dinners.

◑ Closed Chr & New Year ⬈ Signposted from A377 south of Bishop's Tawton. Private car park 🛏3 twin/double, 2 four-poster; all with room service, hair-dryer, trouser press, direct-dial telephone, TV ⊘ Dining room, bar, drawing room, garden; conferences and social functions; leisure facilities nearby; early suppers for children &. No wheelchair access ● No smoking in bedrooms and some public rooms ▭ Amex, MasterCard, Switch, Visa £ Twin/double £100, four-poster £140; deposit required. Set D £27.50

BLACKPOOL Lancashire　　　　　　　　　　　　　　　　　　　　map 8

Old Coach House

50 Dean Street, Blackpool FY4 1BP
TEL: (01253) 349195
EMAIL: blackpool@theoldcoachhouse.freeserve.co.uk
WEB SITE: www.theoldcoachhouse.freeserve.co.uk

Sold as the Guide went to press

◑ Open all year; restaurant closed Sun to Tue eves ⬈ Off Blackpool South Pier. Nearest train station: Blackpool South. Private car park 🛏2 twin, 1 twin/double, 5 double, 3 four-poster; all with hair-dryer, trouser press, TV ⊘ Restaurant, conservatory lounge, garden; conferences, social functions; leisure facilities nearby; highchairs &. Wheelchair access to hotel (1 step) and restaurant, 2 ground-floor bedrooms ● No young children in restaurant Sat eves; no dogs; no smoking ▭ Diners, MasterCard, Switch, Visa £ Single

---

occupancy of twin/double £50 to £65, twin/double £75 to £95, four-poster £85 to £95; deposit required. Set D £21.50; service incl

Raffles

73–77 Hornby Road, Blackpool FY1 4QJ
TEL: (01253) 294713   FAX: (01253) 294240
EMAIL: enquiries@raffleshotelblackpool.fsworld.co.uk
WEB SITE: www.raffleshotelblackpool.co.uk

A cheerful, welcoming guesthouse near the seafront run with great panache and dedication to detail

Raffles, admirably managed by Graham Poole and his partner and chef Ian Balmforth, has become something of a local legend a minute or two from Blackpool Tower. The property consists of several flower-decked adjoining cottages sporting festive blue awnings over bay windows. It is by no means the cheapest accommodation in town, but you'd be hard pressed to find anywhere offering such excellent value. Knocked-through reception rooms near the main entrance provide a tidy bar-lounge. Bedrooms are cleverly shoehorned into improbable spaces. Some incorporate exotic themes and bold colours, but all are fresh and stylish, and in apple-pie order. Well-lit bathrooms gleam with smart new tiles. Hearty breakfasts and imaginative, well-travelled dinner menus are served, and our last inspection revealed that the kitchens are as spotlessly kept as the rest of the hotel. The ground floor of the end-of-terrace property operates as a Victorian-style tea shop serving home-made cakes and snacks.

❍ Open all year   ⬛ From end of M55, follow signs to Central Car Park; Hornby Road is straight in front of car park exit. Nearest train station: Blackpool North. Private car park   🛏 1 single, 3 twin, 12 double, 1 family room; all with hair-dryer, TV   ⌀ Tea room, breakfast room, bar, lounge; conferences, social functions; leisure facilities nearby; early suppers for children; cots, highchairs, baby-listening   ♿ No wheelchair access; 2 steps into hotel, 2 ground-floor bedrooms   ⬤ No dogs in public rooms; no smoking in some public rooms and some bedrooms   ▭ Delta, MasterCard, Switch, Visa   £ Single £25 to £32, single occupancy of twin/double £40 to £51, twin/double £50 to £64, family room £75 to £96; deposit required. Alc D £11; light meals available; service incl. Special breaks available   ③FOR②

BLACKWELL Warwickshire   map 5

Blackwell Grange

Blackwell, Shipston-on-Stour CV36 4PF
TEL: (01608) 682357   FAX: (01608) 682856
EMAIL: liz@blackwellgrange.co.uk
WEB SITE: www.blackwellgrange.co.uk

Rustic realism and pleasing surroundings

There is something very refreshing about a farm that isn't all apple pie and cream. Blackwell Grange certainly has plenty of the quaint and pastoral to please the eye. The seventeenth-century honey-coloured farm buildings surrounding a charming cottage garden are a delight, and if the peasants don't happen to be gaily skipping around the haystack it's only because they're having a day off. However, this is a working farm with a real yard: the slight dilapidation of the thatched barn only anchors the place in the real world. Liz Vernon-Miller and her husband jointly manage the farm and are proud to talk about their pedigree herd of Vendeen sheep. Inside, the furnishings are substantially rustic, built for comfort and relaxation. Bedrooms (one of which is wheelchair friendly) are spacious and furnished thoughtfully with some engaging family heirlooms.

❍ Closed 25 Dec   ⬛ Take A3400 towards Oxford from Stratford-upon-Avon; after 5 miles turn right by church in Newbold-on-Stour; in Blackwell, fork right. Private car park   🛏 1 single, 2 twin/double; all with hair-dryer; some with TV   ⌀ Dining room, lounge, garden; leisure facilities nearby   ♿ Wheelchair access to hotel (ramp) and dining room, 1 ground-floor bedroom specially equipped for disabled people. Disabled parking   ⬤ No children under 12; no dogs; no smoking   ▭ MasterCard, Visa   £ Single £35, single occupancy of twin/double £45, twin/double £65 to £70; deposit required.   ③FOR②

BLEDINGTON Oxfordshire   map 5

Kings Head Inn [NEW ENTRY]

Bledington, Nr Kingham OX7 6XQ
TEL: (01608) 658365   FAX: (01608) 658902
EMAIL: kingshead@orr-ewing.com
WEB SITE: www.kingsheadinn.net

Country-pub values with a warm atmosphere and comfortable bedrooms

This former sixteenth-century cider house is a low barn-like structure set against a pleasing backdrop of grassy verges and a little brook that ambles through the village. Archie and Nicola Orr-Ewing have maintained this unpretentious approach inside as well, with smooth jazz sounds wafting around. The bar is definitive country pub, with stone floors, low ceilings and a lovely inglenook fireplace, while the menu strays into less traditional areas: a tossed salad of feta, beetroot and toasted pine nuts might be followed by beef fillet with mushrooms, sautéed sweet potatoes and roast shallots – the beef comes from the family's farm nearby. Accommodation is a choice between the quieter, more modern courtyard rooms and those with a bit more character in the main house. Room 1 at the top of the pub is an attractive large double in cream décor with a sloping roof and views to the village, while Room 11 in the courtyard is light and airy and has an iron bedstead and a bright, fresh bathroom.

◖ Closed 25 and 26 Dec ↗ Village is on B4450 between Stow-on-the-Wold and Chipping Norton. Nearest train station: Kingham. Private car park ⬚ 2 twin, 9 double, 1 four-poster; all with hair-dryer, direct-dial telephone, modem line, TV; some with VCR ⊘ Dining room, bar, lounge, garden; conferences; leisure facilities nearby; highchairs   ⅝ No wheelchair access ● No dogs or smoking in bedrooms ☐ Amex, Delta, MasterCard, Switch, Visa £ Single occupancy of twin/double £50, twin £75, double £70, four-poster £100. Set L £16; alc D £22; light meals available (3FOR2)

BLOCKLEY Gloucestershire   map 5

Old Bakery

High Street, Blockley, Moreton-in-Marsh GL56 9EU
TEL: (01386) 700408 (AND FAX)

Upmarket charm and good food in this eye-catching, out-of-the-way Cotswold village

From the roadside there is little clue to the delights that lie in wait in this unremarkable set of thick-walled, Cotswold-stone buildings. A little more of the secret is revealed within the courtyard entrance, where rambling roses creep around the doorway. Inside, however, Linda Helme's natural, unforced hospitality is much in evidence. In essence this is a restaurant-with-rooms, although the food is available only to residents. Crisp white linen covers the dining tables, and antique carved chairs are ready to accommodate diners, who might sit down to ginger, soy and lemongrass broth, then confit of shoulder of lamb with seared lamb cutlet and dauphinoise potatoes, followed by vanilla pannacotta with red berry compote. Each bedroom is named after its colour scheme – Blue, Green, Yellow – although the tones in each are quite subtle, with plain walls, tasteful antiques and sparkling, white-tiled bathrooms.

◖ Closed Dec & Jan, 2 weeks in June ↗ Off A44 between Moreton-in-Marsh and Broadway. Take B4479 to Blockley at Bourton-on-the-Hill. Old Bakery is on corner of High Street and School Lane. Private car park ⬚ 2 double, 1 suite; all with hair-dryer, TV ⊘ Dining room, sitting room/study, bar service, garden ⅝ No wheelchair access ● No children under 14; no dogs; no smoking ☐ Amex, MasterCard, Switch, Visa £ Single occupancy of double £105 to £135, double £160 to £216, suite £196 to £236 (rates incl dinner; 2004 prices); deposit required

 This denotes that the hotel is in an exceptionally peaceful situation where you can be assured of a restful stay.

BOLTON ABBEY   North Yorkshire   map 8
Devonshire Arms

Bolton Abbey, Skipton BD23 6AJ
TEL: (01756) 710441   FAX: (01756) 710564
EMAIL: reservations@thedevonshirearms.co.uk
WEB SITE: www.devonshirehotels.co.uk

Traditional country house, part of the Chatsworth estate

Truth to tell, this doesn't look anything much from the outside – it's not one of the splendid country houses framed by glorious grounds, but a low-lying stone building next to a (pretty quiet) minor road. But inside, the parentage is apparent, with formally dressed, experienced staff, and rooms that showcase the odd bit of art or ornament left over from the family home in Chatsworth. The traditional and modern is cleverly mixed, so there are of course rather grand public rooms with open fires and displays of flowers in which to take afternoon tea or a quick snifter, but also a bright and trendy brasserie to relax in with the papers. This gets busy at lunchtime but the excellent manager forms and reforms seating arrangements to fit everyone in. Bedrooms are either nicely individual in the main house or smaller and less pricey in the Wharfedale wing.

◑ Open all year   ▣ At junction of A59 and B6160, 5 miles east of Skipton; hotel is 250 yards on right, on B6160. Private car park   ⟼ 9 twin, 22 double, 7 four-poster, 1 family room, 2 suites; all with room service, hair-dryer, direct-dial telephone, modem line, TV; some with trouser press, VCR   ⊘ 2 restaurants, 2 bars, 3 lounges, garden; conferences and social functions; civil wedding licence; gym, spa, tennis, heated indoor swimming pool; leisure facilities nearby; cots, highchairs, babysitting, baby-listening   ♿ Wheelchair access to hotel and restaurant, WC, 17 ground-floor bedrooms, 1 room specially equipped for disabled people. Disabled parking   ● No dogs or smoking in some public rooms and some bedrooms   ▭ Amex, Delta, Diners, MasterCard, Switch, Visa   £ Single occupancy of twin/double £160, twin/double £220, four-poster £320, family room £340, suite £380; deposit required. Set L (Sun) £33, D £58; alc L, D (brasserie) £21; light meals available. Special breaks available

BORASTON   Shropshire   map 5
Peacock Inn

Worcester Road, Boraston, Tenbury Wells WR15 8LL
TEL: (01584) 810506   FAX: (01584) 811236
EMAIL: info@thepeacockinn-hotel.co.uk
WEB SITE: www.thepeacockinn.com

Sold as the Guide went to press

◑ Open all year   ▣ On A456 towards Worcester, 1 mile outside Tenbury Wells. Private car park   ⟼ 3 twin/double, 1 double, 2 four-poster; all with room service, hair-dryer, direct-dial telephone, TV   ⊘ Restaurant, bistro/bar, garden; social functions; leisure facilities nearby; early suppers for children; highchairs   ♿ No wheelchair access; 5 steps into hotel, 5 steps into restaurants, 1 ground-floor bedroom   ● Dogs in bar and 1 bedroom only; no smoking in bedrooms   ▭ MasterCard, Switch, Visa   £ Single occupancy £55, twin/double/four-poster £70; deposit required. Set L £10.50; alc L, D £20; light meals available. Special breaks available   ③FOR②

The Millstream

Bosham Lane, Bosham, Chichester PO18 8HL
TEL: (01243) 573234   FAX: (01243) 573459
EMAIL: info@millstream-hotel.co.uk
WEB SITE: www.millstream-hotel.co.uk

Consistently excellent service and pristine bedrooms in a peaceful historic village

There's something very agreeable about stepping through the doors of this much extended eighteenth-century hotel in the heart of Bosham, a pretty quayside village close to Chichester Harbour. You'll no doubt be greeted by a smiling front-of-house assistant – a role recently introduced to ensure guests receive an immediate and warm welcome, and evidence that the Millstream, where flawless service has long been one of the main attractions, isn't content to rest on its laurels. Standards also remain high in the fresh, flower-filled public rooms. A lively team of blue-shirted continental waiters charm the lunchtime crowds with a disarming blend of efficiency and friendliness, contributing to the buzz and chatter as they work the room with considerable panache. The open-plan bar lounge has a small bar with sunny yellow walls, and a cosy lounge with groups of comfy chairs overlooking the millstream which runs through manicured lawns to the front of the hotel. This is a seductive place, understandably popular with locals for tasty lunchtime snacks, and a pleasant spot in which to mull over the menu for more formal dinners in the light, summery restaurant. Bedrooms vary in size but are immaculately kept, well equipped and individually decorated with pretty, well-coordinated colours.

◗ Open all year   ⚡ From Chichester, take A259 to Bosham; turn left at Bosham roundabout and follow signs to hotel. Nearest train station: Bosham. Private car park   ⌣ 4 single, 3 twin, 5 twin/double, 16 double, 2 four-poster, 2 family rooms, 3 suites; all with room service, hair-dryer, trouser press, direct-dial telephone, modem line, TV; some with mini-bar   ⊘ Restaurant, bar, lounge, gardens; conferences and social functions; civil wedding licence; leisure facilities nearby; early suppers for children; cots, highchairs, babysitting, baby-listening   ♿ Wheelchair access to hotel (ramp) and restaurant, WC, 9 ground-floor bedrooms, 1 room specially equipped for disabled people. Disabled parking   ● No dogs; no smoking in bedrooms   ▭ Amex, Delta, Diners, MasterCard, Switch, Visa   £ Single £85 to £95, single occupancy of twin/double £95 to £105, twin/double £135 to £149, four-poster £155 to £169, family room £149 to £164, suite £185 to £199; deposit required. Set L £20, D £26; light meals available. Special breaks available

Botallack Manor

Botallack, St Just, Penzance TR19 7QG
TEL: (01736) 788525

Ross Poldark's manor house and home to an antique-crammed B&B

The *Antiques Roadshow* could fill a whole programme just nosing around the dining room at Joyce Cargeeg's B&B near Land's End. Joyce and housekeeper Delwyn make a great double act, ready to tell the story behind a Chinese throne from the Forbidden City, a mustard yellow porter's chair that's a popular seat for guest photos, or an enchanting series of Arthur Rackham's *Peter Pan* illustrations. It's a veritable treasure trove, and it doesn't stop at the dining room door – each of the bedrooms has its own character and pieces, and regulars ask for their favourite and even complain if a treasured antique switches rooms. Joyce lets only three at a time, but keeps four so that people have a wider choice – just one of many thoughtful touches that make this a really special spot. The building featured in the 1970s TV series *Poldark* and fans from around the world come to stay and pay homage to the cult show.

○ Open all year ⚡ Follow B3306 to 1 mile north of St Just and fork left towards coast; pass Queen's Arms on right; manor is straight ahead at next junction. Private car park 🚗 1 twin, 1 double, 1 four-poster; all with hair-dryer ✓ Breakfast room, garden ♿ No wheelchair access ● No dogs; no smoking ▭ None accepted £ Single occupancy of twin/double from £38, twin/double/four-poster from £52; deposit required

---

BOUGHTON LEES Kent   map 3

Eastwell Manor

Eastwell Park, Boughton Lees, Ashford TN25 4HR
TEL: (01233) 213000   FAX: (01233) 635530
EMAIL: enquiries@eastwellmanor.co.uk
WEB SITE: www.eastwellmanor.co.uk

A country manor house with excellent leisure facilities, indoors and out

The entrance to this rather beautiful manor house of encrusted, mellow stone is impressive, and it comes as some surprise that the house was rebuilt in the 1920s from original materials and salvaged architectural curiosities. The Pavilion leisure centre, on the other hand, is unmistakeably modern, but it is subtly screened by trees and is unobtrusive once you enter the house. Privately owned, the hotel is popular for conferences and weddings, held in a large marquee throughout the summer; although smaller events do take place in the house, it is big enough for them not to intrude. The interior is spacious and comfortable, with wood panelling, leather chesterfields and huge stone fireplaces holding log fires. There's a decent-sized bar full of leather seats, and a separate lounge with stone-framed windows overlooking the acres of topiary in the formal grounds beyond. Bedrooms vary. If you opt for a standard room you may feel it doesn't match up to expectation, with furnishings looking rather weary and the views generally uninspired. Master suites, though, have more character and are more individual and spacious, while the cottage rooms are modern and fresh and have the bonus of small kitchenettes.

○ Open all year ⚡ Leave M20 at Junction 9 and turn into Trinity Road; continue over roundabout to A251; turn left at lights; hotel is ½ mile on left. Nearest train station: Ashford International. Private car park 🚗 3 single, 8 twin, 8 twin/double, 35 double, 3 four-poster, 5 suites; family rooms available; all with room service, hair-dryer, trouser press, direct-dial telephone, TV, DVD, CD player; some with fax, modem line, VCR ✓ 2 restaurants, bar, lounge, garden; conferences and social functions; civil wedding licence; gym, spa, tennis, heated indoor and outdoor swimming pools; early suppers for children; cots, highchairs, babysitting, baby-listening ♿ Wheelchair access to hotel and restaurant (ramps), WC, 4 ground-floor bedrooms, 2 rooms specially equipped for disabled people, lift (not suitable for wheelchairs) ● No children under 7 in restaurants eves; no dogs in some public rooms and some bedrooms (£15 per night) ▭ Amex, Delta, Diners, MasterCard, Switch, Visa £ Single/single occupancy of twin/double £190 to £255, twin/double £220 to £285, four-poster £345 to £395, suite/family room £310 to £395; deposit required. Set L £15, D £37.50; alc L £45, D £50; light meals available. Special breaks available ③FOR②

═══

BOURNEMOUTH Dorset   map 2

Hotel Miramar

East Overcliff Drive, East Cliff, Bournemouth BH1 3AL
TEL: (01202) 556581   FAX: (01202) 291242
EMAIL: sales@miramar-bournemouth.com
WEB SITE: www.miramar-bournemouth.com

Unhurried and supremely professional seaside hotel

A bastion of unaltering seaside tradition, the Miramar was undergoing some changes when we inspected: extensions to both restaurant and lounge that will create fine new terraces for the rooms above. But regulars can rest easy: the tried and tested formula of cheerful courtesy, floral displays and reliable dining is not going to change. The Edwardian building with ocean panoramas was once a favourite of JRR Tolkein, presumably for its quintessential English seaside virtues rather than as inspiration for fantasy. Bedrooms are impeccably neat and welcoming, with comfortable furnishings and undemanding colour schemes. Rooms 104 and 114 will soon have the benefit of large rooftop terraces from which to survey the sea. To enable you to get closer to the water, steps lead down to the beach.

○ Open all year ⟲ Overlooking the sea in East Cliff. Nearest train station: Bournemouth. Private car park ⌂ 3 single, 18 twin/double, 15 double, 1 four-poster, 4 family rooms, 2 suites; all with room service, hair-dryer, trouser press, direct-dial telephone, modem line, TV; some with mini-bar, VCR ✦ Restaurant, 2 bars, 2 lounges, gardens; conferences and social functions; civil wedding licence; leisure facilities nearby; early suppers for children; cots, highchairs ♿ Wheelchair access to hotel and restaurant, WC, 2 rooms specially equipped for disabled people, small lift. Disabled parking ● None 🖃 Amex, Delta, MasterCard, Switch, Visa £ Single £40 to £60, single occupancy of twin/double £65 to £85, twin/double £80 to £120, four-poster £105 to £145, family room £95 to £135, suite £115 to £155; deposit required. Set L £14, D £24; light meals available; service incl. Special breaks available

---

BOURTON-ON-THE-WATER Gloucestershire   map 5

Dial House

High Street, Bourton-on-the-Water GL54 2AN
TEL: (01451) 822244 FAX: (01451) 810126
EMAIL: info@dialhousehotel.com
WEB SITE: www.dialhousehotel.com

Impeccable manners, taste and value for money in archetypal Costwold surroundings

Adrian and Jane Campbell-Howard aim to ensure that 'classy sophistication meets country charm' at their small hotel, and they appear to have achieved this in no small measure. Three small bridges cross the River Windrush in this popular village, but even they don't pre-date this splendid Cotswold mansion, built in 1698, and set back from the tourist bustle across lawns. The eponymous sun dial sits on top of the stone porch. The public areas inside are small and intimate, with leather sofas around a stone fireplace leading through to a wooden bar. Upstairs, the bedrooms are beautifully designed in matching fabrics and bold, rich, colour schemes with antique beds, chandeliers and mirrors. Room 3 has a solid oak four-poster and an ample bathroom with a stand-alone bath and stone-tiled floor. Our inspection meal was excellent: it started with pan-fried wood pigeon on a celeriac remoulade, and moved on to slow-cooked lamb shank with creamed potato and then a flavoursome chocolate and raspberry ganache. All this would be pretty impressive without including the outstanding service and attention to detail of the owners, who are always ready to help out guests with touring tips or the latest football results.

○ Open all year ⟲ In middle of village, set back behind village green, overlooking river's middle bridge. Private car park ⌂ 2 twin, 1 twin/double, 7 double, 2 four-poster, 1 suite; all with room service, hair-dryer, direct-dial telephone, modem line, TV, VCR ✦ Restaurant, bar, lounge, garden; conferences; leisure facilities nearby ♿ Wheelchair access to hotel and restaurant; 7 ground-floor bedrooms ● No dogs; no smoking 🖃 Amex, Delta, Diners, MasterCard, Switch, Visa £ Single occupancy of twin/double £89, twin/double £114, four-poster £150, suite £175; deposit required. Alc L £16, D £30. Special breaks available

---

BOVEY TRACEY Devon   map 1

Edgemoor Hotel

Haytor Road, Bovey Tracey, Newton Abbot TQ13 9LE
TEL: (01626) 832466 FAX: (01626) 834760
EMAIL: edgemoor@btinternet.com
WEB SITE: www.edgemoor.co.uk

New broom sweeping through this traditional hotel on the edge of Dartmoor

You certainly can't accuse Mark Butler of sitting on his hands. He took over the Edgemoor in June 2003, and when our inspector called 11 months later, he had already ticked off everything on his three-year renovation plan. The nineteenth-century creeper-clad building used to be a school, and the original assembly hall/chapel, now the lounge, certainly looks better with the gallery removed. It's an airy space perfect for afternoon tea, with uninterrupted views over the garden and simple cream curtains stylishly draped like Greek togas. The restaurant, in a rather dated 1980s interpretation of country-house style, is due to be refurbished in December 2004, but the pleasant little bar, with a stone fireplace and revamped wine list (including port and Madeira) is a cosy place. Some of the bedrooms also retain their Eighties ambience, while those that have been updated come in more neutral palettes. The ones in the Woodland Wing (formerly classrooms) feel more countrified, with pine furniture, wicker chairs and small patios. Mark's future plans include food and wine weekends – so watch this space.

◑ Open all year   ▣ Turn off A38 on to A3892 towards Bovey Tracey; turn left at second roundabout on to B3387 towards Haytor and Widecombe; after ¼ mile fork left and hotel is ½ mile on right. Private car park ◪ 1 single, 1 twin, 11 twin/double, 3 four-poster; all with room service, hair-dryer, trouser press, direct-dial telephone, TV ⬗ Restaurant, 2 bars, lounge, garden; conferences and social functions; leisure facilities nearby ♿ Wheelchair access to hotel (ramp) and restaurant, 2 ground-floor bedrooms, 1 room specially equipped for disabled people ◗ No children under 14; no dogs in public rooms and some bedrooms; no smoking ▭ MasterCard, Switch, Visa ⌊£⌋ Single £79, single occupancy of twin/double £99, twin/double £120, four-poster £139; deposit required. Alc L £22, D £28.50; light meals available; service incl. Special breaks available

---

Fayrer Garden House Hotel

Lyth Valley Road, Bowness-on-Windermere, Windermere LA23 3JP
TEL: (015394) 88195   FAX: (015394) 45986
EMAIL: lakescene@fayrergarden.com
WEB SITE: www.fayrergarden.com

Lakeshore views from this thoroughly relaxing hotel in award-winning gardens

Iain and Jackie Garside have run this handsome country-house hotel for over 20 years, but show no signs of getting set in their ways. Competition is stiff hereabouts; several similarly impressive Victorian or Edwardian gentlemen's residences with grandstand views of Windermere have been turned into smart hotels. So standards continue to improve and bedrooms are steadily upgraded in a four-tier hierarchy from 'Standard Rooms' (smallish but perfectly formed with restricted views) to 'Lake View Superior Rooms', which luxuriate in four-posters, whirlpool baths and sound systems. Guests soon feel at home, despite the extravagant decorative style. Richly upholstered lounges and a picture-windowed restaurant extension provide generous, tranquil spaces to admire the pastoral views across the gardens to the lakeshore. Prime Lakeland lamb gambol in the intervening fields in spring, and on the menus too, along with Lune salmon, Holker Hall Barbary duck and over a hundred carefully selected wines.

◑ Closed first 2 weeks in Jan ▣ On A5074, just south of Bowness-on-Windermere. Nearest train station: Windermere. Private car park ◪ 2 single, 6 twin, 10 double, 4 four-poster, 2 family rooms; all with room service, hair-dryer, trouser press, direct-dial telephone, TV; some with CD player ⬗ Restaurant, bar, 2 lounges, conservatory, garden; social functions; civil wedding licence; leisure facilities nearby; early suppers for children; cots, highchairs, babysitting, baby-listening ♿ Wheelchair access to hotel (1 step) and restaurant, 6 ground-floor bedrooms, 2 rooms specially equipped for disabled people. Disabled parking ◗ No children under 5 in restaurant eves; no dogs; smoking in bar only ▭ Amex, Delta, MasterCard, Switch, Visa ⌊£⌋ Single from £63, twin/double from £125, four-poster from £180, family room from £130 (prices incl dinner); deposit required. Light meals available. Special breaks available

Lindeth Fell

Lyth Valley Road, Bowness-on-Windermere, Windermere LA23 3JP
TEL: (015394) 43286   FAX: (015394) 47455
EMAIL: kennedy@lindethfell.co.uk
WEB SITE: www.lindethfell.co.uk

Consistent standards of hospitality and service ensure repeat trade at this fine Lakeland hotel

At rhododendron time, Lindeth Fell's 17-acre grounds are a picture, cascading in rainbow drifts down a sloping site to the lake below. Lindeth Fell belongs to the National Gardens Scheme, and is occasionally open to the public. The Edwardian gentleman who first built this house in 1909 certainly picked his spot, and the interior still reflects to some extent the taste and atmosphere of that gracious era. Log fires blaze cheerfully in the generously proportioned, panelled hallway, which opens on to a handsome suite of spacious reception rooms. Antiques, original paintings and delicate plasterwork set the tone. But there's nothing faded or old fogeyish about the friendly, reassuring hospitality here. Pat and Diana Kennedy are practised hosts who are praised by readers as managing to combine professional standards of service and housekeeping with a warm-hearted personal touch. The light, airy bedrooms differ in size and style, but all are beautifully kept and have lovely views.

○ Closed 3 weeks in Jan ⤢ On A5074, 1 mile south of Bowness-on-Windermere. Private car park 🚗 2 single, 1 twin, 6 twin/double, 3 double, 2 family rooms; all with room service, hair-dryer, direct-dial telephone, TV; some with trouser-press ⊘ 3 dining rooms, bar service, 2 lounges, garden; conferences; social functions; leisure facilities nearby; early suppers for children; cots, highchairs, baby-listening ⅚ Wheelchair access to hotel (ramp) and dining room, WC, 1 ground-floor bedroom specially equipped for disabled people ● No children under 7 in dining room, no dogs; no smoking in some public rooms ☐ Delta, MasterCard, Switch, Visa £ Single £80, single occupancy of twin/double from £95, twin/double from £160, family room from £160 (prices incl dinner); deposit required. Set L £15.50; light meals available; service incl. Special breaks available (3FOR2)

Linthwaite House

Crook Road, Bowness-on-Windermere, Windermere LA23 3JA
TEL: (015394) 88600   FAX: (015394) 88601
EMAIL: admin@linthwaite.com
WEB SITE: www.linthwaite.com

Ultra-smart, chintz-free zone with an upbeat colonial air and a spectacular setting

The majestic views from Linthwaite are hard to beat. Set high above Windermere in 14 acres of superbly maintained grounds, this rambling, multi-gabled mansion enjoys the sort of scenery it's impossible to tire of, subtly changing with each season and shift of light. But at closer focal length, the interior offers just as much to catch your eye. The design is effortful ('Ralph Lauren meets Raffles'), from jazzy geometrics and kilims in the reception lobby to a cool cane-and-rattan look in the bar and conservatory. Travelling trunks and fishing rods stacked in the hall, tiny mirrors clustered on dining-room walls, and oodles of decorative Edwardiana perched on plate-rack shelving ensure constant visual stimulus, but the effects are interestingly calming rather than busily cluttered. The same bold streamlining applies to the bedrooms, in classy neutrals or powerful, masculine schemes. All feature high-tech fittings, including CD players, 12-channel TVs and waffle bathrobes.

○ Open all year ⤢ Off B5284, ¾ mile south of Bowness, near Windermere Golf Club. Nearest train station: Windermere. Private car park 🚗 1 single, 4 twin/double, 19 double, 1 family room, 1 suite; all with room service, hair-dryer, trouser press, direct-dial telephone, TV, CD player; some with modem line ⊘ Restaurant, 2 dining rooms, bar, 2 lounges, conservatory, garden; conferences; social functions; civil wedding licence; leisure facilities nearby; early suppers for children; cots, highchairs, baby-listening, outdoor play area ⅚ Wheelchair access to hotel (1 step) and dining rooms, WC, 7 ground-floor bedrooms, 1 room specially equipped for disabled people ● No children under 7 in dining rooms eves; no dogs; smoking in bar only ⌐ Amex, Delta, Diners, MasterCard, Switch, Visa £ Single £115 to £125, single occupancy of twin/ double £115 to £125, twin/double £150 to £180, family room £245 to £295; suite £250 to £295; deposit required. Set L £14.50, Sun £18; D £42; alc L £25; light meals available; service incl. Special breaks available ③FOR②

BRADFORD-ON-AVON Wiltshire   map 2

Bradford Old Windmill

4 Masons Lane, Bradford-on-Avon BA15 1QN
TEL: (01225) 866842   FAX: (01225) 866648
EMAIL: whg@bradfordoldwindmill.co.uk
WEB SITE: www.bradfordoldwindmill.co.uk

Unusual accommodation with home-grown food and well-travelled hosts

There is something quite magical about Peter and Priscilla Roberts' converted windmill. Despite being close to the town centre, it feels delightfully secluded, and they have filled it with quirky objects and features – whether it be a circular bed for a circular bedroom or simply a collection of prehistoric arrowheads lying on the side in the lounge. Somehow they manage to keep all this immaculately clean and shipshape and run two allotments for the table. The commitment this takes in terms of time, however, means that the Roberts are not always around during the day, so guests' access to rooms may be restricted between 10am and 5pm, which may not suit everyone. Priscilla serves up what she terms 'veggie ethnic feasts' for evening meals, and the vegetables she grows for them is eclectic and unusual. You could taste homegrown celeriac or unusual potato varieties such as pink fir apples or Edzell blues. Breakfasts are also taken around the same big old pine table, but carnivores are catered for among the impressive range of choice. All three bedrooms are original and interesting, with Great Spur narrowly coming in as first choice with its hanging cane seat, round bed and view over the town.

● Closed Chr to Feb; dining room closed Sun, Tue & Fri eves ⤢ Entering Bradford-on-Avon from the north on A363, find Castle pub; go down hill towards town centre; after 50 yards turn left into a gravelled drive immediately before first roadside house (no sign on road). Nearest train station: Bradford-on-Avon. Private car park ⌐ 2 double, 1 suite; family room available; all with hair-dryer, TV ✓ Dining room, sitting room, garden; leisure facilities nearby ♿ No wheelchair access ● No children under 6; no dogs; no smoking ⌐ Delta, MasterCard, Switch, Visa £ Single occupancy of double £69 to £99, double £79 to £109, suite £109, family room £119 to £129; deposit required. Set D £21; light meals available; service incl. Special breaks available ③FOR②

Priory Steps

Newtown, Bradford-on-Avon BA15 1NQ
TEL: (01225) 862230   FAX: (01225) 866248
EMAIL: priorysteps@clara.co.uk
WEB SITE: www.priorysteps.co.uk

Delightful family-run small hotel with a sociable atmosphere

Carey and Diana Chapman's late-seventeenth-century house saves its best face for looking out over the back garden – a superb three-storey façade of honey-coloured Bath stone. It's obviously a sun trap because a Black Hamburg vine is doing fine here – well enough for guests to lean out the bedroom window and pluck a bunch of grapes in early autumn. Inside the house the atmosphere is civilised and relaxing: battered leather chairs in the library-cum-lounge plus a catholic selection of reading matter. In the dining room everyone gets together for breakfast – evening meals can be had by prior arrangement. Bedrooms all get a good view across the Avon valley plus plenty of space, period furnishings and homely touches. One of them is named after Mrs Bruce, an indomitable previous resident who flew solo to Japan in 1930 and raced at Brooklands – there is a fascinating collection of artefacts relating to her on the first floor.

◑ Open all year ⚡ From A363, signposted Bath, turn left at sign to Turleigh, 200 yards north of town centre. Nearest train station: Bradford-on-Avon. Private car park 🛏 2 twin, 2 double, 1 suite; family room available; all with hair-dryer, TV ⟐ Dining room, lounge/library, garden; leisure facilities nearby; early suppers for children; highchairs, baby-listening ♿ No wheelchair access ● No dogs; no smoking ⬜ Delta, MasterCard, Switch, Visa £ Single occupancy of twin/double £66 to £68, twin/double/suite £80 to £88, family room £96 to £105; deposit required. Set D £25; service incl. Special breaks available

Woolley Grange

Woolley Green, Bradford-on-Avon BA15 1TX
TEL: (01225) 864705   FAX: (01225) 864059
EMAIL: info@woolleygrange.com
WEB SITE: www.woolleygrange.com

Top-quality facilities for children at this smart hotel

A country house that genuinely caters for all the family is a rare creature indeed, especially when most examples of the genre get by with a 'no under-12s' rule. Not so Woolley Grange, a Jacobean mansion set in 14 acres which manages to please all ages with a dazzling array of facilities topped up with lots of staff and a friendly atmosphere. Public rooms run the full gamut of country-house style – drawing room with log fire and leather sofas, dining room smartened with white linen and modern paintings – while bedrooms get full marks for their smartness

set off with period features and furniture (a further three rooms in a chalet extension have a more contemporary feel). Outside there is a good-sized heated swimming pool, a walled vegetable garden and various playground pieces. Under-8s get the 'Woolley Bears Den', a spacious, well-staffed playroom filled with toys and games. Older children have the Hen House with pool, table football, air hockey and computer games. Both are separate from the main house, which consequently remains elegantly undisturbed.

◑ Open all year ⚡ On B3105, 1 mile north-east of Bradford-on-Avon. Nearest train station: Bradford-on-Avon. Private car park 🛏 1 single, 8 twin/double, 4 double, 6 family rooms, 7 suites; all with room service, hair-dryer, direct-dial telephone, TV, VCR/DVD player ⟐ 2 restaurants, dining room, bar, 2 sitting rooms, library/study, conservatory, games room, garden; conferences; social functions; heated outdoor swimming pool; early suppers for children; cots, highchairs, toys, playrooms, babysitting, baby-listening, outdoor play area ♿ Wheelchair access to hotel (at rear) and restaurant, WC, 3 ground-floor bedrooms ● No children in restaurant eves; dogs in bedrooms £7 ⬜ Amex, Delta, MasterCard, Switch, Visa £ Single £90 to £120, single occupancy of twin/double £86 to £290, twin/double £95 to £225, family room £155 to £340, suite £230 to £330; deposit required. Set L £20, D £35.50. Light meals available. Special breaks available

BRAMPTON Cumbria   map 10

Farlam Hall

Brampton CA8 2NG
TEL: (016977) 46234   FAX: (016977) 46683
EMAIL: farlamhall@dial.pipex.com
WEB SITE: www.farlamhall.co.uk

Impeccable standards of food and accommodation keep this classic country house among the Cumbrian élite

The unshowy but faultlessly landscaped grounds of this acclaimed hotel near Hadrian's Wall are a foretaste of what's inside. Managerial wheels turn so smoothly that motion is barely detectable. Nothing disturbs the tranquillity of these handsomely furnished, softly lit rooms, where antique mirrors reflect fine porcelain, glassware and beautiful flower arrangements. This deceptively large, creeper-clad building

rambles from its Elizabethan manor origins through various afterthoughts of the nineteenth century, when it was lavishly restyled for a wealthy coal-mining family. In the last 30 years, the hard-working Quinion and Stevenson families have steadily achieved a formidable reputation. Barry Quinion's cooking is a high point, amply justifying the minor courtesy of dressing respectably and arriving punctually at dinnertime. But Farlam

Hall feels anything but formal or starchy; service is professional, welcoming and perfectly pitched. Its immaculate bedrooms, though traditional, are subtly updated with sparkling plumbing, Bose radios and wide-screen digital TVs.

◐ Closed 26 to 30 Dec ⟐ On A689 Brampton to Alston road, 2½ miles from Brampton (not in Farlam village). Nearest train station: Brampton. Private car park 🛏 2 twin, 6 twin/double, 3 double, 1 four-poster; family rooms available; all with room service, hair-dryer, trouser press, direct-dial telephone, modem line, TV, CD player; some with VCR, tea/coffee-making facilities ✅ Restaurant, 2 lounges, garden; conferences and social functions; early suppers for children ♿ Wheelchair access to hotel and restaurant (ramps), 2 ground-floor bedrooms ● No children under 5; no smoking in bedrooms or restaurant ▭ MasterCard, Switch, Visa ⌊£⌉ Single occupancy of twin/double £138 to £153, twin/double £255 to £285, four-poster £285, family room £355 (rates incl dinner); deposit required. Special breaks available (3FOR2)

BRANCASTER STAITHE Norfolk   map 6

White Horse [NEW ENTRY]

Brancaster Staithe PE31 8BY
TEL: (01485) 210262   FAX: (01485) 210930
EMAIL: reception@whitehorsebrancaster.co.uk
WEB SITE: www.whitehorsebrancaster.co.uk

Marvellous marsh views on the north Norfolk coast

From the road, there might not be much to grab your attention about this coastal village pub. The building itself is unremarkable – a standard mid-twentieth-century pub. But are the views out back contenders for the best in East Anglia? Tidal marshland stretches under a huge sky from the foot of the gravelled car park to the distant horizon – vast pools of water invaded by tongues of low, lumpy grassland. And, just like the view, the back of the building is much more interesting – a curving extension snakes out towards the sea, topped with an innovative grassed roof. The bedrooms in this extension are all designed so that the patio windows face the water. Décor in here is a little more traditional than in the rooms in the main building, which are bright, modern and simple. It's probably worth paying the extra ten pounds for those on top floor, which have the best of the views. But even if you don't you'll still get a cracking vista from the large conservatory restaurant, with its fish-skewed menu and some interesting desserts, like a gin and tonic sorbet.

◐ Open all year ⟐ On A149 coast road midway between Hunstanton and Wells-next-the-Sea. Private car park 🛏 6 twin/double, 9 double; family rooms available; all with hair-dryer, direct-dial telephone, TV ✅ Dining room, bar, lounge, conservatory restaurant, garden; social functions; leisure facilities nearby; early suppers for children; cots (£4 per night), highchairs, toys ♿ Wheelchair access to hotel and dining area; 8 ground-floor bedrooms, 2 rooms specially equipped for disabled people, WC. Disabled parking ● No dogs in dining area, £4 per dog per night in some bedrooms; no smoking in dining area ▭ Delta, Diners, Switch, MasterCard, Visa ⌊£⌉ Single occupancy of twin/double £62 to £72, twin/double £84 to £104, family room £99 to £119; deposit required (2004 prices). Alc D £25.50; light meals available. Special breaks available

---

BRANSCOMBE Devon   map 2

Masons Arms [NEW ENTRY]

Branscombe, Nr Seaton EX12 3DJ
TEL: (01297) 680300   FAX: (01297) 680500
EMAIL: reception@masonarms.co.uk
WEB SITE: www.masonsarms.co.uk

Popular country pub with swanky rooms and new restaurant

Down the folded Branscombe valley, ten minutes' walk from the sea, is this tremendous pub-with-rooms, recently augmented by a swish new restaurant. The original bar is exactly as you would want: huge stone fireplace (with roast meat cooking several times a week), cosy nooks and an inspiring range of local hand-pulled ales to work through. The no-smoking bar/dining area doesn't have quite the same character, but maybe all energies have gone into creating the Waterfall Restaurant over the courtyard. This is a lovely room, its warm vibrant colours set off by an interesting candelabrum and an extensive menu strong on local produce. Bedrooms in the main building share a cosy upstairs lounge and have attractive oriental bedspreads and some good bathrooms with the occasional whirlpool bath. Other rooms across in the converted cottages are perhaps a little quieter. All show plenty of flair in their furnishings and style.

○ Open all year ⚡ From A3052 take any road signposted to Branscombe; hotel is between village and sea ⬛ 1 twin, 7 twin/double, 6 double, 4 four-poster, 2 family rooms, 2 suites; 2 with shared bathroom; all with room service, hair-dryer, direct-dial telephone, TV ⊘ Restaurant, dining room/bar, lounge, garden; leisure facilities nearby; cots, highchairs ♿ No wheelchair access; 5 steps into hotel, 2 steps into restaurant ● No children under 14 in restaurant eves; no dogs in some bedrooms; no smoking in some public rooms ⬜ MasterCard, Switch, Visa £ Single occupancy of twin/double £30 to £120, twin/double £50 to £150, four-poster £110 to £150, family room £90 to £135, suite £150; deposit required. Set D £30; alc L, D £20; light meals available. Special breaks available

---

BRAY Berkshire
map 3

Waterside Inn [NEW ENTRY]

Ferry Road, Bray SL6 2AT
TEL: (01628) 620691   FAX: (01628) 784710
EMAIL: reservations@waterside-inn.co.uk
WEB SITE: www.waterside-inn.co.uk

Stellar food and equally luminous rooms beside the Thames

There aren't many little Berkshire villages that have not one but two world-class restaurants to draw the culinary crowds, and luckily for diners wanting to sleep off their gastronomic excesses in comfort, one of the two, the aptly named Waterside Inn, also offers sumptuous rooms. Displaying the same French-influenced flair as the finest dishes in the restaurant below, the stylish décor and furnishings have a modern, restful feel – as seen in La Tamise (which, with its terrace, is perhaps our favourite bedroom) where ochre walls offset the sleigh bed with its pale burgundy covers. There's great attention to detail and a host of luxurious extras in every room: flat-screen TVs, fresh fruit, fluffy robes, posh toiletries. And the bathrooms are simply splendid with their wood floors and green marble counters. A small 'honesty kitchen' has a bar with full-size spirit bottles alongside juices, biscuits and a coffee-maker, and while no full breakfasts are offered, continental ones are served in the bedrooms. A nearby cottage houses a swish suite with its own riverside garden. 'Memorable, everything was faultless, and could truly be called perfection, but it was expensive!' was one happy reader's verdict.

○ Closed 26 Dec to 27 Jan; restaurant closed Mon & Tue except Tue eves 1 Jun to 31 Aug ⚡ From M4 Junction 8/9 take A308 towards Windsor then B3028 left to Bray. In village, Ferry Road is second right. Nearest train station: Maidenhead. Private car park ⬛ 2 twin/double, 4 double, 2 four-poster, 1 suite; all with hair-dryer, trouser press, direct-dial telephone, TV; some with CD player; no tea/coffee-making facilities in rooms ⊘ Restaurant, bar, lounge; social functions; civil wedding licence ♿ No wheelchair access ● No children under 12; no dogs; no smoking in bedrooms ⬜ Amex, Delta, Diners, MasterCard, Switch, Visa £ Single occupancy of twin/double £160 to £175, twin/double/four-poster £160 to £175, suite £290 to £320; deposit required. Set L £40/Sun £56, D £85; alc L, D £110

BRIGGSWATH North Yorkshire
map 9

The Lawns

73 Carr Hill Lane, Briggswath, Sleights, Whitby YO21 1RS
TEL: (01947) 810310 (AND FAX)
EMAIL: lorton@onetel.net.uk

Modern, airy guesthouse with a friendly welcome

Jennifer Lorton's guesthouse perches on hills above Whitby with views across rolling green fields; from the door you can embark on circular walks through valleys, across moors and along beaches. It is an unassuming place from the outside, but once indoors you are immediately struck by the spacious rooms and the light that pours in through huge picture windows. A six-foot carved giraffe surveys a smart guest lounge, which has a crisp décor of neutral biscuit tones, stylish cream damask sofas, and ample provision of magazines and CDs. In the bright and modern dining room peace reigns; all tables look out across the fields, a fine backdrop for hearty breakfasts (with home-made bread) and five-course dinners that feature plenty of local produce such as fish from Whitby. The bedrooms are irreproachably smart. The Garden Room is big enough for a plush sofa as well as a huge bed and walk-in wardrobe; two further rooms built under the eaves share the clean-cut modern style and revel in lovely views towards the North York Moors.

◑ Closed Chr & New Year ⤬ From Whitby, take A171 towards Guisborough; after 2 ½ miles turn left on to A169 towards Pickering; turn left after ½ mile into Carr Hill Lane; Lawns is second house on left. Nearest train station: Sleights. Private car park ⤶ 1 twin, 1 double, 1 suite; all with hair-dryer, TV ✅ Dining room, lounge, garden; leisure facilities nearby ♿ Wheelchair access to hotel (1 step) and dining room, 1 ground-floor bedroom ● No dogs; no smoking ▭ None accepted £ Twin/double £54 to £60; suite £60; deposit required. Set D £17.50; service incl. Special breaks available

---

BRIGHTON East Sussex   map 3

Alias Hotel Seattle

The Strand, Brighton Marina, Brighton BN2 5WA
TEL: (01273) 679799   FAX: (01273) 679899
EMAIL: info@aliasseattle.com
WEB SITE: www.aliashotels.com

Laid-back, design-led hotel with stylish bedrooms in Brighton Marina

On first impression Brighton's up-and-coming marina can seem rather bland with its collection of empty buildings, multistorey car parks and out-of-town supermarkets. When we first visited on a cold March evening, it felt positively bleak for the few who had ventured out to wander the boardwalks or sample the eclectic mix of inventive-sounding dishes on the menu at the Café Paradiso, attached to this hotel. With only few diners in the restaurant – of aircraft hangar proportions with a fabulous collection of chandeliers dangling from impossibly high ceilings – the atmosphere can be sadly lacking, particularly when the service is as chilly as the weather outside. But persevere, for a return visit in the sunshine reveals a much livelier spot, with diners savouring both the tasty seafood dishes and stunning views over the bustling waterfront and yacht moorings. In keeping with its prime waterside position, the Seattle is designed in the shape of a ship and a light-hearted nautical theme predominates. In the ultra-modern reception area two camp mannequins in sailor suit and black-tie point the way to the public areas, while in the trendy Saloon lounge, huge model yachts separate islands of comfy seating, and a lovely decked terrace juts like the prow of a ship above the moorings below. Bedrooms are fresh and contemporary with light wood furniture, neutral shades and sparkling modern bathrooms. A sea view is an absolute must.

◑ Open all year ⤬ One mile east of Palace Pier, in Brighton Marina ⤶ 8 twin/double, 63 double; all with room service, hair-dryer, direct-dial telephone, modem line, TV, DVD, CD player ✅ Restaurant, dining room, 2 bars, lounge, sun deck; conferences, social functions, civil wedding licence; leisure facilities nearby; early suppers for children; cots, highchairs, baby-listening ♿ Wheelchair access to hotel and restaurant, National Accessible Scheme: mobility impairment M1, WC, 4 rooms specially equipped for disabled people, lift. Disabled parking ● No dogs ▭ Amex, Delta, MasterCard, Switch, Visa £ Twin/double £95 to £150; deposit required. Continental B £9.50, cooked B £13.50; set L £10; alc L £20, D £24; light meals available. Special breaks available

Blanch House

17 Atlingworth Street, Brighton BN2 1PL
TEL: (01273) 603504   FAX: (01273) 689813
EMAIL: info@blanchhouse.co.uk
WEB SITE: www.blanchhouse.co.uk

Stylish rooms in a trendy hotel moments from the sea

From the outside Blanch House looks fairly typical of Brighton's crop of smart Georgian townhouse hotels. Tucked up a quiet side street in a modest terrace just off the seafront, its traditional creamy stone façade gives few clues that behind the burgundy-trimmed windows lurks a funky style palace with a classy, contemporary feel and innovative design. Perhaps this should come as no surprise, for design-led hotels seem to be mushrooming in trendy Brighton. But Blanch House easily stands out from the crowd – whereas elsewhere the fashion gurus' thirst for smart chic can feel overly manicured and soulless, here designer Amanda Blanch and her husband Chris Edwardes manage to combine design flair with substance, creating a hip, flamboyant bolthole with a pleasingly lived-in and laid-back atmosphere. In the 12 smallish but distinctive bedrooms expect to find strong colours, sumptuous fabrics and lots of quirky, fun touches – Moroccan is all spicy and exotic, Snowstorm has shop display cabinets stuffed with snow globes and a perspex snow curtain dangling over the bed. Of the larger rooms, the masculine blacks, golds and blood-reds of Decadence are suitably decadent, and White is, well, white. Downstairs you will find the stylish '70s lounge-chic cocktail bar and an up-to-date restaurant with a smart but relaxed minimalist feel, both doubling as galleries for local artists.

◑ Closed 25 to 30 Dec; restaurant closed Sun & Mon eves ⚏ From Palace Pier roundabout take Marine Parade exit; turn left at traffic lights into Lower Rock Gardens; take first right then next right into Atlingworth Street. Nearest train station: Brighton ⨎ 9 double, 3 suites; all with hair-dryer, direct-dial telephone, modem line, TV, VCR, CD player ⚑ Restaurant, bar; conferences, social functions, civil wedding licence; leisure facilities nearby; cots, highchairs, baby-listening ⚒ No wheelchair access ⬤ No dogs in restaurant ⊟ Amex, Delta, MasterCard, Switch, Visa £ Single occupancy of double from £100, double from £100, suite £190 to £220; deposit required. Set L £20, D £30; light meals available

Hotel du Vin & Bistro

Ship Street, Brighton BN1 1AD
TEL: (01273) 718588 FAX: (01273) 718599
EMAIL: info@brighton.hotelduvin.com
WEB SITE: www.hotelduvin.com

Contemporary bedrooms with swish bathrooms in a great central location

As positions go this one is practically perfect, for the flamboyant mint-green, mock-Tudor former wine merchant's premises that now houses the Hotel du Vin is right in the thick of things, moments from the Lanes, the sea and Brighton's nightlife. The tried-and-tested formula that devotees of this stylish mini-chain have by now come to expect is reassuringly intact, and there's a familiarly slick, contemporary and resolutely professional feel throughout. Wood-carved seagulls fly above the double-height bar lounge, a stylish and comfortable space where informal business meetings take place at islands of squashy purple suede and brown leather sofas, while weighty timber-slab steps lead up to a gallery which has a funky purple-baize billiard table and more comfy seating. Modern European cuisine is served up by continental waiters in the elegant French-inspired bistro which, with its high-backed leather banquettes, yellow walls and bustling atmosphere, would be perfectly at home on a Parisian boulevard. Bedrooms – either in the main building or in the Pigeon House across the central courtyard area – are good-sized, light and smart, with whitewashed walls, crisp white linen, hi-tech gadgets and luxurious bathrooms.

◑ Open all year ⚏ From A23, follow signs to town centre and seafront; at roundabout opposite pier, turn right; after Ship Street turn right into Middle Street, bear right at end into Ship Street. Nearest train station: Brighton. Private car park ⨎ 3 twin, 31 double, 3 suites; all with hair-dryer, mini-bar, trouser press, direct-dial telephone, TV, DVD, CD player ⚑ Restaurant, 2 dining rooms, bar, lounge, courtyard; conferences; leisure facilities nearby; early suppers for children on request; cots, highchairs ⚒ Wheelchair access to hotel and restaurants, WC, 2 ground-floor bedrooms specially equipped for disabled people ⬤ No dogs; smoking in bar only ⊟ Amex, Delta, Diners, MasterCard, Switch, Visa £ Single occupancy of twin/double from £125, twin/double from £125, suite from £230; deposit required. Continental B £9.50, cooked B £13.50; set L (Sun) £24; alc L, D £35

Hotel Pelirocco

10 Regency Square, Brighton BN1 2FG
TEL: (01273) 327055   FAX: (01273) 733845
EMAIL: info@hotelpelirocco.co.uk
WEB SITE: www.hotelpelirocco.co.uk

Wacky hotel with Pop Art-inspired rooms and a youthful feel

Brighton's coolest hotel is a one-off. Housed in an elegant cream-painted Regency townhouse, it's deceptively traditional from outside, but once through the doorway you'll discover it's anything but. Undeniably original and fun, the Pelirocco's quirky, shabby-chic design was conceived by owners Mick Robinson and Jane Slater and won't be to everyone's taste – inspired by music and youth culture, it has a distinctly edgy and streetwise feel, with a dose of tongue-in-cheek sleaziness thrown in for good measure. A sunny, funkily-furnished breakfast room assumes a totally different character after dark – all dimly lit and vaguely seedy, it doubles as an atmospheric cocktail bar with a chilled vibe and fittingly laid-back service. Although every bedroom has a PlayStation 2, this is unquestionably a place for grown-ups, as is evidenced by the unusual room service menu offering toys of a rather more adult nature. Each of the bedrooms is distinctive and individual, but the place's popularity may be starting to show in wear and tear. We were disappointed when we stayed in Modrophenia, themed around Mods and their links to Brighton – for the price you might expect more than a room reminiscent of a teenager's bedroom, complete with chipped paintwork, scuffed carpets and bathroom fittings that have seen better days. The hotel was up for sale as we went to press.

◑ Closed 25 & 26 Dec   ⤢ Opposite West Pier. Nearest train station: Brighton   ⤙ 5 single, 3 twin, 10 double, 1 suite; family rooms available; all with direct-dial telephone, modem line, TV, CD/DVD player; some with hair-dryer   ⌀ Breakfast room/bar; conferences; leisure facilities nearby   ♿ Wheelchair access to hotel (1 step) and breakfast room, 2 ground-floor bedrooms, 1 room specially equipped for disabled people   ● No dogs; no smoking in bedrooms   ▭ Amex, Delta, MasterCard, Switch, Visa   £ Single £50 to £58, single occupancy of twin/double £80 to £120, twin £90 to £105, double £90 to £130, family room £125 to £135, suite £190 to £250; deposit required

---

Hudson's Hotel [NEW ENTRY]

22 Devonshire Place, Brighton BN2 1QA
TEL: (01273) 683642   FAX: (01871) 224 7591
EMAIL: info@hudonshotel.com
WEB SITE: www.hudsonshotel.com

Friendly, relaxed atmosphere in a gay guesthouse in fashionable Kemp Town

Brighton's growing number of boutique hotels are not everyone's cup of tea. For the city's many gay and lesbian visitors, Hudson's is therefore something of a breath of fresh air, offering a more traditional guesthouse experience. Moments from the sea and handy for Kemp Town's bars and clubs, Stephen Speight and Alex Cooke's immaculate cream-painted townhouse is friendly and unpretentious, and so spick and span that one might imagine Mary Poppins herself to have been drafted in to do the housekeeping. But it is in different character that Julie Andrews makes her appearance, for a small picture of her in a scene from the Sound of Music hangs in the hallway, while a striking photo of fellow gay-icon Audrey Hepburn sits alongside the Klee prints and wall plates in the cheerful café-style breakfast room. Otherwise there are few traces of campery, save for a delicious CD collection, which includes such greats as Shirley Bassey, Eartha Kitt, Ella Fitzgerald and Jason Donovan. The bedrooms are tastefully done out, pristinely kept and comfortably furnished with an eclectic mix of wall hangings and *objets d'art* – as Stephen explains: 'We just choose objects that look nice'. Pick of the rooms is the grandly named 'Hudson's Suite' in the basement, a very spacious king-size room with a well-equipped bathroom and doors leading on to a small patio.

● Open all year 🚪 From A23 follow signs to the seafront; drive past St Peter's Church and take the left filter signposted to the Royal Sussex Hospital into Edward Street. Opposite the Youth Centre turn right into Devonshire Place; hotel is fifth building on the right. Nearest train station: Brighton 🛏 2 twin, 6 double, 1 suite; family rooms available; some with shared facilities; all with hair-dryer, TV, VCR, CD player ✓ Breakfast room, conservatory, garden ♿ No wheelchair access; 2 ground-floor bedrooms ● No dogs; no smoking in public rooms ▭ Delta, MasterCard, Switch, Visa £ Single occupancy of twin/double £35 to £40, twin/double £70 to £80, family room/suite £90 to £100; deposit required (3FOR2)

BRIMFIELD Herefordshire   map 5

Roebuck Inn

Brimfield, Ludlow SY8 4NE
TEL: (01584) 711230   FAX: (01584) 711654
EMAIL: peter@theroebuckinn.com
WEB SITE: www.theroebuckinn.com

Small and welcoming pub with an emphasis on food and conviviality

Peter and Julie Jenkins are now fully settled into gastropub life, after a year at the helm. Peter's former job in the Metropolitan Police is a world away from the demands of this busy roadside establishment in sleepy Brimfield. Inside, small square rooms with wood panelling, carpets or parquet flooring create a distinctive character which is Victorian in feel. On a busy evening it's likely that diners will be eating in every available nook and cranny around the bar area. There's also a restaurant with a very different feel – tangerine walls, blue tablecloths and lots of light. A typical meal might start with smoked chicken ravioli with a white bean cappuccino, and be followed by roast duck breast with rhubarb and honey sauce. Upstairs, the bedrooms are all fairly similar, although only Room 1 has a bath. Room 3, at the back, is quieter with a pale blue and white colour scheme.

● Closed 25 & 26 Dec; restaurant closed Sun in Jan to Mar 🚪 In Brimfield village, just off A49 between Ludlow and Leominster. Private car park 🛏 1 twin, 2 double; all with hair-dryer, trouser press, direct-dial telephone, TV ✓ Restaurant, 2 bars, lounge, courtyard; social functions; leisure facilities nearby; early suppers for children; highchairs ♿ No wheelchair access ● No children in restaurant eves; no dogs; no smoking in restaurant and bedrooms ▭ Delta, MasterCard, Switch, Visa £ Single occupancy of twin/double £50, twin/double £75. Alc L, D £22.50; light meals available

---

BRISTOL Bristol   map 2

The Brigstow [NEW ENTRY]

5-7 Welsh Back, Bristol BS1 4SP
TEL: 0117-929 1030   FAX: 0117-929 2030
EMAIL: brigstow@fullers.co.uk
WEB SITE: www.brigstowhotel.com

A cool and curvaceous take on the boutique style

The Brigstow takes a pattern well established by other modern hotels and moves it up a notch or two. The riverfront building gives a smart first impression, with its stylish curved façade and light airy interiors. A minimalist reception area leads along to a split-level, open-plan bar, lounge and restaurant. The cooking here is brasserie-style and pretty much the dishes you might expect to see: swordfish, sirloin steak, roasted polenta. Bedrooms are impressively chic with their elliptical curves and floor-to-ceiling dark-wood finish. No duvets here – sheets and blankets with pillows and bolsters. Bathrooms offer separate showers and even a plasma screen television over the bath (but don't expect to be reading any subtitles – it's on the small side!)

● Open all year 🚪 In Bristol city centre. Nearest train station: Bristol Temple Meads 🛏 30 twin, 84 double, 1 suite; all with room service, hair-dryer, mini-bar, trouser press, direct-dial telephone, modem line, TV, safe ✓ Restaurant, bar, lounge; conferences; social functions; civil wedding licence; leisure facilities nearby; cots, highchairs ♿ Wheelchair access to hotel and restaurant; 5 rooms specially equipped for disabled people; WC, lift. Disabled parking ● No dogs ▭ Amex, Delta, Diners, MasterCard, Switch, Visa £ Single occupancy of twin/double £89 to £169, twin/double £89 to £169, suite £175 to £250; deposit required (2004 prices). Continental B £9.50, cooked £11.50; set L £14, D £18; alc L £19.50, D £24; light meals available; service incl. Special breaks available

Hotel du Vin & Bistro

The Sugar House, Narrow Lewins Mead, Bristol BS1 2NU
TEL: 0117-925 5577   FAX: 0117-925 1199
EMAIL: info@bristol.hotelduvin.com
WEB SITE: www.hotelduvin.com

Former warehouse given swanky conversion at this city boutique hotel

The recipe for a good Hotel du Vin Bristol appears simple. Take one delightfully *fin de siècle* Parisian bistro, all done up with mirrors and period furnishings, whisk briskly on a floor of well-scrubbed boards. Add friendly, enthusiastic staff, dress with aprons and other appropriate period garb. Ply guests with top-notch cooking and a superior wine list. Stir up to create a pleasant evening buzz then set aside from the other rooms. These should include, in the case of Bristol, a lounging area deeply marinaded in low light and leather seating. On top of this, spread a layer of bedrooms and decorate these with subdued, classic colours and a crisp dressing of white bed linen. Bathrooms should be spacious with bath and separate shower, the latter to have a squashed colander of a shower rose guaranteed to empty a delicious deluge over occupant(s). The recipe works a treat.

○ Open all year   ⚡ From M4 Junction 19 or A4, follow signs to city centre. After passing House of Fraser store on left, turn right at war memorial into opposite carriageway; hotel is down side road after 200 yards. Nearest train station: Bristol Temple Meads. Private car park   🛏 35 twin/double, 5 suites; all with hair-dryer, mini-bar, trouser press, direct-dial telephone, modem line, TV, CD player, DVD   ✓ Restaurant, bar, lounge, games room; conferences; social functions; early suppers for children; cots, highchairs, babysitting   ♿ Wheelchair access to hotel (1 step), restaurant, WC, lift   ● No dogs; no smoking in restaurant   ▭ Amex, Delta, Diners, MasterCard, Switch, Visa   £ Single occupancy of twin/double from £125, twin/double from £125, suite from £190; deposit required (prices valid till autumn 2004). Continental B £9.50, cooked B £13.50; set L (Sun) £24.50; alc L, D £32

BROAD CAMPDEN   Gloucestershire   map 5

Malt House

Broad Campden, Chipping Campden GL55 6UU
TEL: (01386) 840295   FAX: (01386) 841334
EMAIL: info@the-malt-house.freeserve.co.uk
WEB SITE: www.malt-house.co.uk

A memorable, if pricey, treat with fabulous English gardens

In a village of snug honey-stone cottages, the Malt House is a surprising size. The ancient malt house and the cottages that adjoin it have been brought together to create a wonderfully rambling property laced with wisteria. It has plenty of character and charm – spot the elephant motifs that abound in cushions, pictures and curtains, and the collection of tea cups on shelves around one of the two sitting rooms. From the dining room (dinner is available only by arrangement) there are great views of the stunning gardens – an immaculately kept croquet lawn, a thatched summerhouse for afternoon tea, and an orchard up the hillside beyond. Bedrooms are divided between the main house and the annexe; those in the main house have better views of the garden. Hidcote has a kingsize bed and a fireplace and a good-size bathroom with a separate shower as well. Room 7 in the annexe has cool bluey-green tones, distressed furnishings and latticed windows with garden aspects.

○ Closed Chr   ⚡ 1 mile south-west of Chipping Campden, signposted from B4081; on left, 250 yards beyond Bakers Arms pub. Private car park   🛏 4 twin/double, 1 double, 1 four-poster, 1 suite; family room available; all with hair-dryer, TV   ✓ Dining room, 2 sitting rooms, garden; conferences and social functions; leisure facilities nearby; early suppers for children; cots, highchairs, toys, babysitting, baby-listening   ♿ No wheelchair access; 1 ground-floor bedroom   ● No dogs; no smoking   ▭ Amex, Delta, MasterCard, Switch,

Visa £ Single occupancy of twin/double £90, twin/double/four-poster £127, family room £165, suite £140; deposit required. Set D £35; light meals available. Special breaks available ③FOR②

BROADWAY Worcestershire   map 5

Barn House

152 High Street WR12 7AJ
TEL: (01386) 858633
EMAIL: barnhouse@btinternet.com
WEB SITE: www.karenbrown.com/england/barnhouse.html

A combination of grand scale and cosy intimacy at this B&B with notable gardens

There's certainly something a little out of the ordinary about Jane and Mark Ricketts' home. First, the barn in question, to the side of the main house, is an enormous hall full of lofty beams, mullioned windows and a huge stone fireplace. From here it's just a step through French windows into the expansive garden with lawns that stretch away into wilder uncharted parts – ideal for a pre-prandial stroll. If such a scale is unexpected then, you'll be surprised by the 42-foot indoor swimming pool just off the garden path. The property is discreetly tucked away off the eye-catching high street of this Cotswold village, and the rest of the house is simply and traditionally furnished on a more human scale, with guests gathering for breakfast around one big table. Pick of the bedrooms is the garden suite, set away from the main house, which has a lounge with views to the fields and a small kitchen.

○ Open all year 🔁 In upper High Street of Broadway (now a cul-de-sac). Private car park 🛌 2 twin, 2 double, 2 suites; all with hair-dryer, TV; some with trouser press ⊘ Dining room, 2 lounges, library, conservatory, garden; covered heated swimming pool; cots, highchairs ㅤ No wheelchair access ● No dogs in public rooms and some bedrooms; no smoking in bedrooms and some public rooms ☐ None accepted £ Single occupancy of twin/double £65, twin/double £75, suite £65 to £75; deposit required ③FOR②

Mill Hay House

Snowshill Road, Broadway WR12 7JS
TEL: (01386) 852498   FAX: (01386) 858038
EMAIL: millhayhouse@aol.com
WEB SITE: www.millhay.co.uk

A choice Cotswold mansion that opens its doors to discerning B&B guests

Although this house has all the features of a classic Cotswold country house, there is also some Queen Anne brickwork in one wing. Add to this the remains of a twelfth-century watermill and a small lake stocked with trout, and you have a wonderful microcosm of English rural history. This elegant B&B is just outside Broadway, in undulating Cotswold scenery with three acres of gardens. Inside there's a marvellously airy wood-panelled morning room, with large mullioned windows on three sides, which has a clubby sort of atmosphere enhanced by the large leather sofa and armchairs. The breakfast room would not be out of place as a dining room in some smart country-house hotel, while upstairs the bedrooms are of an equally high standard. The pick of the bedrooms is the Regency four-poster room, which has acres of space and great views of the garden, but the twin room and the balcony room are equally luxurious.

○ Open all year 🔁 Turn off Broadway High Street by Main Green and head towards Snowshill; Mill Hay House is 1 mile on right. Private car park 🛌 1 twin, 1 double, 1 four-poster; all with hair-dryer, direct-dial telephone, TV ⊘ Breakfast room, sitting room, garden; leisure facilities nearby ㅤ No wheelchair access ● No children under 12; no dogs; no smoking in bedrooms ☐ Delta, MasterCard, Switch, Visa £ Single occupancy of twin/double £110, twin/double £120, four-poster £160; deposit required. Special breaks available (2004 data)

Grove Thorpe

Grove Road, Brockdish, Diss IP21 4JR
TEL: (01379) 668305
EMAIL: b-b@grovethorpe.co.uk
WEB SITE: www.grovethorpe.co.uk

Fine country B&B with every detail taken care of

Things certainly won't feel crowded for breakfast at Angela and John Morrish's splendid B&B – their new breakfast room is four times larger than the old one. Not much else has changed, and that's no bad thing, as theirs is a superior take on the countryside B&B – immaculate, well equipped and with that all-important cheerful welcome. Bedrooms are feminine and pretty, kitted out with everything you could need, and there's no shortage of space either. Two are in the main house, while a third in the 'Garden Cottage' offers a bit more seclusion. Surrounded by country lanes, rolling meadows and fields of rape, you're likely to bump into at least some domestic or wild creatures, whether you're just strolling around the duck pond or trying your hand at catching one of the fish in the well-stocked lake.

● Closed Chr & New Year 🗲 Take A143 towards Yarmouth; 4 miles after Diss roundabout, pass turning signed Brockdish then turn left into Church Road North; turn right at T-junction; Grove Thorpe is third house on left. Private car park 🛏 2 twin/double, 1 double; all with hair-dryer, TV ⍟ Breakfast room, sitting room, garden; leisure facilities nearby ♿ No wheelchair access; 1 step into house, 1 step into breakfast room, 1 ground-floor room specially equipped for disabled people ● No children under 12; no dogs; no smoking ▭ None accepted £ Single occupancy of twin/double £50 to £60, twin/double £64 to £74; deposit required (3 FOR 2)

Cloud Hotel

Meerut Road, Brockenhurst SO42 7TD
TEL: (01590) 622165   FAX: (01590) 622818
EMAIL: enquiries@cloudhotel.co.uk
WEB SITE: www.cloudhotel.co.uk

Immaculate, well-run hotel in the heart of the New Forest

The Cloud is a pristine small hotel overlooking heathland on the fringes of Brockenhurst, and all reports speak of the warmth and efficiency of the staff. One singles out the 'excellent service', while another praises 'the friendly staff, very comfortable lounges, good food and peaceful location'. But the main ingredient in the Cloud's recipe for success is summarised perfectly by a reader who describes it simply as 'very well run'. Owner and ex-Tiller Girl Avril Owton has been the driving force behind the hotel for 28 years and performs her role with as much gusto as (one imagines) was required for her high-kicking stage performances. The red Tiller bar, complete with safety curtain, houses fascinating memorabilia of her show-business years, and her close eye for detail and a tangible enthusiasm inspire both a faithful clientele and loyal staff, some of whom have been here for 20 years. Public areas are light and have an agreeably laid-back atmosphere, while bedrooms are fresh and comfortable, typically with smart paintwork, new carpets, pine furnishings and modern bathrooms. Again, Avril's touch is firmly in evidence – 'It's very feminine,' she admits, 'but my guests seem to like it.'

● Closed first 2 weeks of Jan 🗲 From M27 Junction 1, take A337 to Lyndhurst/New Forest; on entering Brockenhurst take first right into Meerut Road; hotel is 300 metres on left. Nearest train station: Brockenhurst. Private car park 🛏 3 single, 1 twin, 6 twin/double, 6 double, 1 four-poster, 1 family room; all with hair-dryer, direct-dial telephone, TV; some with trouser press ⍟ Restaurant, bar, 3 lounges, garden; conferences and social functions; leisure facilities nearby; early suppers for children ♿ Wheelchair access to hotel (ramp) and restaurant, 2 ground-floor bedrooms ● No children under 8; no dogs in public rooms, £10 per night in bedrooms; no smoking in restaurant or bedrooms ▭ Delta, MasterCard, Switch, Visa £ Single £68 to

£75, single occupancy of twin/double £102 to £113, twin/double from £120, four-poster £135 to £150, family room £160 to £175; deposit required. Set L (Sun) £17.50, D £28; alc L (midweek) £13.50; light meals available; service incl. Special breaks available ③FOR②

Whitley Ridge

Beaulieu Road, Brockenhurst SO42 7QL
TEL: (01590) 622354   FAX: (01590) 622856
EMAIL: whitleyridge@brockenhurst.co.uk
WEB SITE: www.whitleyridge.co.uk

Unpretentious hotel in a former royal hunting lodge in the middle of the New Forest

Unlike many country-house hotels, Whitley Ridge is not perfectly manicured or flashily restored, and is all the better for it. It is peacefully set down a private road right in the Forest, the cream-painted porch and handsome wisteria-clad façade hiding a refreshingly unassuming and welcoming hotel where the emphasis is less on ostentation and more on comfort and service. The unpretentious bar, lined with prints of French country scenes, is a relaxed spot for pre-dinner drinks, while the elegant and generously proportioned restaurant has smart purple, blue and green high-backed chairs and original Georgian features, including a lovely bay window. One reader describes the menu as 'superb, varied and exciting', reserving special praise for the extensive choice of vegetarian dishes. Bedrooms are immaculate and prettily done out, perhaps with floral or *toile de Jouy* fabrics, and some make a feature of hydrotherapy baths or steam cabins. Those to the front have lovely sash windows with beautiful views.

◑ Open all year ⊿ From A337 at Brockenhurst, take B3055 towards Beaulieu; hotel is 1 mile on left. Nearest train station: Brockenhurst. Private car park ⌁ 2 single, 3 twin, 7 double, 1 four-poster, 1 suite; all with room service, hair-dryer, direct-dial telephone, modem line, TV; some with trouser-press, VCR ⊘ Restaurant, bar, 2 lounges, garden; conferences and social functions; tennis; leisure facilities nearby; early suppers for children; cots, highchairs, babysitting, baby-listening ♿ Wheelchair access to hotel (ramp) and restaurant, 1 ground-floor bedroom ⬤ No dogs in public rooms; no smoking ⊟ Amex, Delta, Diners, MasterCard, Switch, Visa £ Single £68 to £70, twin/double £112 to £120, four-poster £130 to £140, suite £150 to £160; deposit required. Set L £19, D £30; alc L £23, D £36; light meals available; service incl. Special breaks available

---

BROME Suffolk   map 6

Cornwallis Country House NEW ENTRY

Rectory Road, Brome IP23 8AJ
TEL: (01379) 870326   FAX: (01379) 870051
EMAIL: info@thecornwallis.com
WEB SITE: www.thecornwallis.com

New owners and a few new ideas in this classic country-house hotel

Two neat rows of trees line the approach to this country-house hotel, prompting daydreams of driving up to one's own rural retreat in a vintage open-topped car. The hotel is housed in the dower house of Brome Hall, built by Sir Thomas Cornwallis in the sixteenth century. It has recently come under new management, and the administration seems content to leave alone what works but introduce a few ideas here and there. So you're still treated to antique-filled, dark-wood interiors, but in the grounds (which beg to be strolled around) there's some unusual topiary in the form of slightly abstract human shapes standing shoulder to shoulder. Bedrooms vary in style: some are flowery and spotted with antiques; others are plainer and more contemporary. When we inspected, the restaurant seemed strangely spare, with not enough tables to fill the space. There are plans to host performances of Shakespearean plays by a local troupe.

◗ Open all year 🅉 From A140 Norwich to Ipswich road, take B1077 (not B1177) towards Eye; hotel is 20 metres on left. Private car park 🛏 3 twin, 1 twin/double, 5 double, 6 four-poster, 1 family room; all with room service, hair-dryer, trouser-press, direct-dial telephone, modem line, TV ✅ Restaurant, bar, conservatory, garden; conferences; civil wedding licence; social functions; leisure facilities nearby; cots, highchairs ♿ Wheelchair access to hotel and restaurant, 3 ground-floor bedrooms ♠ Dogs in 1 bedroom only (£10); no smoking in some bedrooms ▭ MasterCard, Switch, Visa £ Single occupancy of twin/double £75 to £95, twin/double £95 to £115, four-poster £127 to £170, family room £103 to £123; deposit required. Set L, D £25; alc L, D £26; light meals available ③FOR②

BROMSGROVE Worcestershire   map 5

Grafton Manor

Grafton Lane, Bromsgrove B61 7HA
TEL: (01527) 579007   FAX: (01527) 575221
EMAIL: steplin@graftonmanorhotel.co.uk
WEB SITE: www.graftonmanorhotel.co.uk

Ancient house with grand décor, impressively run by a family team

With 26 acres of ancient parkland, Grafton Manor is cushioned from the humdrum suburban landscape beyond its borders. Steeped in history, the fabric of the house dates back to Elizabethan times; there is also a fifteenth-century private chapel and a sixteenth-century fish stew – a brick building in the local stream. Members of the Morris family have been the custodians of this ancient legacy since 1980 and they have used the style of their namesake William Morris to create a smart Victorian aristocratic look in the public rooms. In the kitchen, Steplin Morris continues to produce good work, in particular his gastronomic passion: Indian cooking. While there are plenty of good European options, a guest might enjoy Gujarati curd curry with red lentil masala pakora, followed by tandoori monkfish with chickpea and coriander sauce. Bedrooms can be quite grand and the best have good views over the grounds, antiques and some bold colours such as the gold theme in the Porch Room.

◗ Open all year 🅉 1½ miles south of Bromsgrove centre, off B4091. Private car park 🛏 1 single, 2 twin, 3 double, 1 four-poster, 2 suites; family rooms available; all with room service, hair-dryer, trouser press, direct-dial telephone, modem line, TV; no tea/coffee-making facilities in rooms ✅ Restaurant, dining room, bar, garden; conferences and social functions; civil wedding licence; leisure facilities nearby; early suppers for children; cots, highchairs ♿ Wheelchair access to hotel (ramp) and restaurant, WC, 1 ground-floor bedroom. Disabled parking ♠ No dogs ▭ Diners, MasterCard, Switch, Visa £ Single £85, single occupancy of twin/double £95, twin/double £105 to £125, four-poster £125, family room £195, suite £145 to £165; deposit required. Set L £20.50, D £28; light meals available; service incl

---

BROXTON Cheshire   map 7

Frogg Manor

Nantwich Road, Broxton, Chester CH3 9JH
TEL: (01829) 782629   FAX: (01829) 782459
EMAIL: info@froggmanorhotel.co.uk
WEB SITE: www.froggmanorhotel.co.uk

A refreshingly light-hearted and idiosyncratic take on the all-too-standardised world of the hospitality trade

'Bats but lovely' is a typical visitor's comment on this place, although perhaps 'Frogs but lovely' would be more accurate. Frogg Manor teems with them, in all shapes, sizes and materials. Not many are actually alive, though the large gardens are full of wildlife. The mostly Georgian house, rather close to the fast-moving A534, is furnished in a medley of Victorian and Georgian styles, somewhat stained and battered in places. Eccentric owner-impresario John Sykes rules this curious domain with an unmatched determination to amuse. He works jolly hard, as host, chef, gardener and bottle-washer, his spry activity belying his 70-odd years. Every night is party night, when guests take to the dance floor after dinner, accompanied by the recorded sounds of yesteryear. Sumptuously individual bedrooms prioritise top-quality bedding, and brim with thoughtful extras, from a micro-pharmacy of tampons, plasters and hangover cures to emergency tights and a drawer full of teas and coffees.

❍ Open all year ⛃ From Chester, head south on A41; turn left on to A534 towards Nantwich. Frogg Manor is approx 1 mile on right. Private car park 🛏 5 double, 2 suite; all with room service, hair-dryer, trouser press, direct-dial telephone, modem line, TV; 1 with VCR ⌑ Restaurant, bar, lounge, conservatory, gardens; conferences and social functions; civil wedding licence; tennis; leisure facilities nearby; early suppers for children; cots, toys ♿ Wheelchair access to hotel (ramp) and restaurant, 1 ground-floor bedroom specially equipped for disabled people. Disabled parking ● No dogs in public rooms; smoking in lounge only ▭ Amex, Delta, Diners, MasterCard, Switch, Visa £ Single occupancy of double £60 to £100, double £80 to £130, suite £150 to £200. Set L, D £22.50; alc L, D £34.50. Special breaks available ③FOR②

BRYHER Isles of Scilly map 1

Hell Bay Hotel NEW ENTRY

Bryher, Isles of Scilly TR23 0PR
TEL: (01720) 422947 FAX: (01720) 423004
EMAIL: contactus@hellbay.co.uk
WEB SITE: www.hellbay.co.uk

Sophisticated island retreat – New England style

The Dorrien-Smiths (owners of Tresco and the hotels there) have extended their reach to the rugged west coast of the small island of Bryher, a short boat ride from Tresco. A five-minute walk from the quay along a track brings you to the hotel, which faces a rock-strewn bay that's buffeted by the Atlantic. The interior of the low-rise buildings, set around a central garden, is stylish and sophisticated, with a New England beach-house feel. Blue and white trims, Lloyd Loom furniture and sun-bleached stripy fabrics decorate comfortable lounges, and the bar terrace has tranquil views over a lake. The restaurant, with huge abstract seascapes and sunsets on off-white walls, serves a contemporary menu that somehow resists a fishy dominance. Bedroom suites can be large and airy, with high rafters and separate seating areas – some have small gardens or terraces with steamer chairs. As well as the pool, there is a well-equipped games room. High teas are served for children, and families are made very welcome.

❍ Closed Jan & Feb ⛃ Fly from Bristol, Southampton, Exeter, Newquay or Land's End, or take helicopter or boat from Penzance, to Tresco or St Mary's, then transfer by boat to Bryher. There are no cars on the Isles of Scilly 🛏 3 family rooms, 22 suites; all with room service, hair-dryer, direct-dial telephone, modem line, TV, VCR, CD player ⌑ Dining room, bar, lounge, games room, garden; conferences; social functions; gym; sauna, heated outdoor swimming pool; early suppers for children, cots, highchairs, toys, playrooms, babysitting, baby-listening, outdoor play area ♿ Wheelchair access to hotel and dining room, 18 ground-floor bedrooms ● No dogs in public rooms; no smoking in bedrooms ▭ Delta, MasterCard, Switch, Visa £ Family room from £250, suite from £220 (rates incl dinner); deposit required. Alc L £20; light meals available. Special breaks available ③FOR②

BUCKDEN Cambridgeshire map 6

Lion Hotel

High Street, Buckden PE19 5XA
TEL: (01480) 810313 FAX: (01480) 811070
EMAIL: reception.lionhotel@virgin.net
WEB SITE: www.lionhotel.co.uk

Atmospheric medieval inn with comfy rooms

Staff at The Lion verge on the omnipresent, with attentive service in the restaurant and regular checks that you're happy by the roving host. If you're sitting in an armchair by the fire, under the magnificent medieval beamed ceiling of the lounge bar, the likelihood is your answer will be a firm yes – country inns don't get much more atmospheric than this. The spokes of the oak beams meet at a central boss carved with a lamb and a Latin motto meaning 'Behold the Lamb of God', attesting to the probable origins of the building as a guesthouse for the Bishop of Lincoln's Palace. The food in the adjoining oak-panelled restaurant is surprisingly adventurous, and even extends to flambéed dishes cooked at your table. Bedrooms are homely, occasionally chintzy, with floral curtains and bedspreads and plastic flowers.

○ Open all year 🚗 Off A1, 4 miles south of Huntingdon. Nearest train station: Huntingdon. Private car park 🛏 2 single, 3 twin, 7 double, 3 four-poster; family rooms available; all with room service, hair-dryer, trouser press, direct-dial telephone, modem, TV ⊘ Restaurant, bar, lounge; conferences; social functions; leisure facilities nearby; cots, highchairs ♿ Wheelchair access to hotel and restaurant (ramp), WC, 5 ground-floor bedrooms, 1 room specially equipped for disabled people ● No dogs ▭ Amex, Delta, MasterCard, Switch, Visa £ Single £45 to £65, single occupancy of twin/double £45 to £74, twin/double £60 to £80, four-poster/family room £70 to £90; deposit required. Set L, D £17.50; alc L, D £22.50; light meals available; service incl. Special breaks available

---

BUCKLAND Worcestershire   map 5

Buckland Manor

Buckland, Nr Broadway WR12 7LY
TEL: (01386) 852626   FAX: (01386) 853557
EMAIL: info@bucklandmanor.com
WEB SITE: www.bucklandmanor.com

A luxury manor-house experience that is reassuringly predictable

Buckland Manor is exactly what one expects from a luxury Cotswold manor-house hotel: pastures and wooded slopes stretching away into the distance, the crunch of gravel underfoot and the sun shining on ancient stone walls. Add to the mix a charming thirteenth-century parish church – the same vintage as the house – tucked up close beside it, and you can see why this hotel holds all the cards. And while conservative English style pervades inside, it is combined with a pleasingly unstuffy atmosphere. Public areas abound, but none is too large or impersonal, each with wood floors, oriental carpets, mullioned windows, antiques and fresh flowers. The understated furnishings are either unpatterned or floral, and long-departed gentry gaze down from walls. The traditional chintz style continues in the bedrooms, most of which have leafy views and impressive bathrooms. The grounds include a tennis court and a lovely formal lawned garden, which diners can enjoy from the cream panelled restaurant – do note there is a dress code. 'Just as good as the last time,' reports a satisfied regular.

○ Open all year 🚗 2 miles from Broadway on B4632. Private car park 🛏 5 twin/double, 5 double, 3 four-poster, 1 family room; all with room service, hair-dryer, direct-dial telephone, TV, CD player; no tea/coffee-making facilities in rooms ⊘ Restaurant, bar, 2 lounges, garden; social functions; tennis; leisure facilities nearby ♿ Wheelchair access to hotel (ramp) and restaurant, 4 ground-floor bedrooms ● No children under 12; no dogs ▭ Amex, Delta, Diners, MasterCard, Switch, Visa £ Single occupancy of twin/double £215, twin/double £270 to £330, four-poster £330 to £360, family room from £360; deposit required. Set L £25.50, alc D £50; light meals available

---

BURFORD Oxfordshire   map 5

The Bay Tree [NEW ENTRY]

Sheep Street, Burford OX18 4LW
TEL: (01993) 822791   FAX: (01993) 823008
EMAIL: info@baytreehotel.info
WEB SITE: www.cotswold-inns-hotels.co.uk

An oasis of refined tranquillity just off Burford's famous main street

Sitting in a pretty side-street, the Bay Tree is slightly removed from the tourist hurly-burly of one of the Cotswolds' most popular honey-pot villages, bestowing a welcome, tranquil feel on this atmospheric Elizabethan house. Every square inch, from the wisteria-clad exterior to the big fireplaces, oozes centuries of history, and the thoughtful décor and furnishings capitalise on this characterful backdrop. With winding staircases, lovely gardens and a plethora of nooks and crannies for cosy seating areas, there's nothing identikit about this hotel. Bedrooms in the main building, which dates from 1585, are named after trees, with Chestnut, a spacious four-poster, being a fine example of the high standards throughout, complete with a smart bathroom and Molton Brown toiletries. Next door is the Cottage, home to more luxury, such as the flagstoned sitting room and half-tester bed found in Tanfield, one of the suites. Yet another building, this one more modern at the back, houses the chintzier garden rooms, which have French balconies overlooking a sunny walled garden.

◐ Open all year ⃞ Sheep Street is first on the left as you descend Burford's High Street from A40. Private car park ⃞ 2 twin, 4 twin/double, 9 double, 7 suites; all with room service, hair-dryer, TV ⃝ Restaurant, bar, library, conservatory, garden; conferences; civil wedding licence, social functions; leisure facilities nearby; cots; high chairs ⃞ No wheelchair access ● No dogs in public rooms ⃞ Diners, MasterCard, Switch, Visa ⃞ Single occupancy of twin/double £119, twin/double from £165 to £195, suite from £215 to £240; deposit required. Set L £19, D £28; alc D 36; light meals available

---

Burford House

99 High Street, Burford OX18 4QA
TEL: (01993) 823151   FAX: (01993) 823240
EMAIL: stay@burfordhouse.co.uk
WEB SITE: www.burfordhouse.co.uk

A right little charmer, offering a perfect mix of comfort and hospitality

The long hill of Burford's renowned High Street is a handsome parade of mellifluous Cotswold stone houses. One of the few to interrupt this dignified sweep is the half-timbered, black-and-white affair at number 99. Its distinctive, zebra-effect upper storey is not, however, the only thing that makes this charming hotel stand out from the crowd, though its best assets are kept well hidden from the milling throng passing the doorstep. Cross the threshold and you'll find not only an inviting townhouse hotel run with friendly flair by Simon and Jan Henty, but a gloriously secret sun-trap garden at the back, which is a popular spot for home-baked high teas on sunny days. Light lunches are also served, but no evening meals are offered. Throughout, the décor and furnishings match the unstuffy elegance of the building itself, with thick carpets, open fires, oil paintings and fresh flowers adding the finishing touches. Whether in the main house or the Courtyard, bedrooms are all splendid, mixing the old – in the form of exposed beams and antiques – with the sparkling new, notably the bathrooms.

◐ Open all year ⃞ Halfway along Burford High Street ⃞ 2 twin, 3 double, 2 four-poster, 1 family room; suite available; all with room service, hair-dryer, direct-dial telephone, TV ⃝ Dining room, 2 lounges, garden; cots, highchairs ⃞ Wheelchair access to hotel (2 steps) and dining room, 1 ground-floor bedroom ● No dogs or smoking in bedrooms ⃞ Amex, MasterCard, Switch, Visa ⃞ Single occupancy of twin/double from £80, twin/double £95 to pound;130, four-poster/family room £130 to £155, suite £205. Light L available. Special breaks available

---

Jonathan's at the Angel

14 Witney Street, Burford OX18 4SN
TEL: (01993) 822714   FAX: (01993) 822069
EMAIL: jo@theangel-uk.com
WEB SITE: www.theangel-uk.com

Sumptuous, imaginative rooms that are as tempting as the top-notch food

A few yards from Burford's buzzy High Street is this winner of a brasserie-with-rooms that manages to provide an awful lot of pleasure in a surprisingly small package. From the outside, it looks resolutely old English, with flower-filled window boxes brightening up the honey-coloured, sixteenth-century stone walls, but step inside and beneath the beams it all feels just a little bit more Mediterranean – the restaurant has a rustic, rural air with its cream walls, wood floors and chunky pine furniture. The food has a modern European edge, so your sirloin might come with onion confit, mash and red wine sauce rather than chips and peas. Breakfasts are just as hearty and mouthwatering. Bedrooms display the same level of individuality, with each of the three strikingly decorated in its own theme – spice-coloured Madras has a canopy bed and exposed stone walls, Simione offers a contemporary blue-green take on classic Italianate style, while chic-rustic Camargue looks straight out of a plush French villa. Throw in a peaceful courtyard and exemplary service led by chef-proprietor Jonathan Lewis, and you're all set for an idyllic stay.

◗ Closed 18 Jan to 6 Feb; restaurant closed Mon & Sun eve From A40, turn into Burford High Street then into Swan Lane; at junction with Barns Lane, turn left into Pytts Lane; Witney Street is at end. Turn left at the Royal Oak pub; the Angel is five houses down on the left 1 twin, 2 double; all with hair-dryer, trouser press, direct-dial telephone, TV, VCR Restaurant, bar, lounge, garden No wheelchair access No children under 9; no dogs; no smoking in bedrooms Delta, MasterCard, Switch, Visa Single occupancy of twin/double £70 to £75, twin/double £85 to £98; deposit required. Set L £18.50; alc L £25, D £27.50; light meals available; service incl 3FOR2

Lamb Inn

Sheep Street, Burford OX18 4LR
TEL: (01993) 823155 FAX: (01993) 822228
EMAIL: info@lambinn-burford.co.uk
WEB SITE: www.lambinn-burford.co.uk

Bags of tradition and character at this old pub, and a bright, new look for some rooms

In a quieter corner of this busy village, the Lamb Inn continues to welcome travellers within its mellow, yellow-stone walls, much as it has done for many a moon. Some come just to revel in the old-world atmosphere of the cosy bar, with its high settle seats and flagstoned floor; others to dine in style in the more elegant restaurant, which overlooks the pretty rear courtyard. For those wanting to linger longer, the bedrooms complete this characterful package. It's definitely worth the little extra for the newly refurbished rooms: when we inspected, six had been completed, and others were in the pipeline. The old-style rooms are still more than comfortable, but feel a little faded compared with the six super-swish affairs, where chic colour schemes and plush fabrics offset perfectly the antique furniture and splendid (though small) bathrooms. One reader was unhappy with the service and attention to detail, though a new manager is now in place and is keen to iron out any such niggles.

◗ Open all year Sheep Street is first on the left as you descend Burford's High Street from A40 3 twin, 11 double, 1 four-poster; suite available; all with room service, hair-dryer, trouser press, direct-dial telephone, TV Restaurant, bar, 2 lounges, library, garden, courtyard; social functions; leisure facilities nearby; early suppers for children; cots, highchairs, baby-listening No wheelchair access; 2 steps into hotel, 3 ground-floor bedrooms No smoking in bedrooms and some public rooms MasterCard, Switch, Visa Single occupancy of twin/double £80 to £100, twin/double £130 to £160, four-poster £175 to £200, suite £300 to £350; deposit required. Alc L £20, D £30; light meals available. Special breaks available

---

BURLTON Shropshire   map 5

Burlton Inn

Burlton, Shrewsbury SY4 5TB
TEL: (01939) 270284 FAX: (01939) 270204
EMAIL: bean@burltoninn.co.uk

Smart, friendly gastropub with up-to-date bedrooms

There's something very cosy and inviting about the Burlton Inn, even for the lonesome hotel inspector. For the last eight years Ann and Gerry Bean have been building up the business at this roadside inn, so that it wins nods of approval for its food and its attractive beer gardens. And now they have gone one step further with a refurbishment of the public areas to add a snug bar, a lounge area with comfy seating, and French windows that invite diners to stroll outside with their pre-prandial drinks. Pot plants and hanging baskets burst with colour in summer. The menu, elegantly written up by Ann, might include a starter of crab and asparagus tartlet, and then chicken, bacon and Brie lasagne. Bedrooms are in a separate block at the back, away from any road noise, and have a fresh, contemporary feel with white walls, colourful prints and equally striking bedspreads. Bathrooms reflect this style.

○ Closed Chr to New Year ⚡ 8 miles north of Shrewsbury on A528. Private car park 🛏️ 2 twin, 3 double, 1 four-poster; family rooms available; all with hair-dryer, TV ⚓ Dining room/bar, lounge, patio; leisure facilities nearby ♿ Wheelchair access to hotel and dining room, WC, 3 ground-floor bedrooms, 1 room specially equipped for disabled people ● None ▭ Delta, MasterCard, Switch, Visa £ Single occupancy of twin/double £50, twin/double £80, four-poster £90, family room £85; deposit required. Alc L, D £23; light meals available

---

BURNHAM MARKET Norfolk   map 6

Hoste Arms

The Green, Burnham Market, Kings Lynn PE31 8HD
TEL: (01328) 738777   FAX: (01328) 730103
EMAIL: reception@hostearms.co.uk
WEB SITE: www.hostearms.co.uk

Stylish hotel constantly renewing and striving for perfection

'A bit like Chelsea-on-Sea' was how one staff member at the Hoste Arms described the pretty, upmarket village of Burnham Market. Paul and Jeanne Whittome's establishment certainly fits the mould with its stylish, innovative interiors that blend the best of tradition and modernity. The seventeenth-century country inn has been added to a number of times, most recently to create the Zulu wing, with a smart but fun African theme, featuring furniture and art brought from South Africa. One room has a rather exciting flat-screen TV that emerges from a plush leather cabinet at the touch of a button. Bedrooms in the main house are more traditional, with countrified bedcovers and large, ostentatious baths. Paul is clearly a hotelier with a mission and is certainly not content to rest on his laurels – recent work has included a complete refit of the kitchens, and opening up his ex-office as a little mezzanine dining area, while gardens continue to be revamped.

○ Open all year ⚡ Hotel overlooks Burnham Market village green, 2 miles from A149. Private car park 🛏️ 5 single, 4 twin, 4 twin/double, 8 double, 4 four-poster, 1 family room, 11 suites; all with room service, hair-dryer, direct-dial telephone, TV; some with trouser press ⚓ 2 restaurants, bar, lounge/conservatory, gardens; conferences; leisure facilities nearby; early suppers for children; cots ♿ Wheelchair access to hotel (ramp) and restaurants (2 steps), WC, 9 ground-floor bedrooms ● Dogs £7.50 ▭ Delta, MasterCard, Switch, Visa £ Single £78 to £138, single occupancy of twin/double £108 to £168, twin/double £108 to £168, four-poster £136 to £206, family room £128 to £188, suite £136 to £206; deposit required. Light meals available

---

BURNSALL North Yorkshire   map 8

Devonshire Fell

Burnsall, Nr Skipton BD23 6BT
TEL: (01756) 729000   FAX: (01756) 729009
EMAIL: reservations@thedevonshirearms.co.uk
WEB SITE: www.devonshirehotels.co.uk

Traditional exterior hides a splash of colour in this modern take on a country-house hotel

If you choose your hotels based on their surroundings, this should go into your collection – a one-time club for gentlemen mill owners who bagged a prime spot looking out over the village of Burnsall and the Wharfe valley. After walking the glorious countryside you can soothe your aching muscles with a swim (or some pampering) at the health club of the sister hotel, the Devonshire Arms, six miles down the road; the facilities are offered free for guests. Both places are owned by the Chatsworth estate, but here the Duchess has used a bright, confident colour palette. Entrance is straight into the brasserie/bar area with stripped wooden floors, lilac walls and contemporary artwork. There is no quiet resident's lounge so you have to mix it with day-trippers popping in for a bite to eat and put up with the boy-band background music, seemingly on a continuous loop. The menu is short and to the point: winter warmers include honey-roast belly of pork on spiced lentils, and sticky toffee pudding and butterscotch sauce. First-floor bedrooms have the bigger windows, so you may prefer a room here. All are sunny, with comfortable beds and good bathrooms. The young staff provide a relaxed and welcoming service.

◑ Open all year ▨ 11 miles east of Skipton on the B6160, approx 6 miles north of its roundabout junction with A59 Shipton to Harrogate road. Private car park �ⱼ 4 twin, 6 double, 2 family suites; all with hair-dryer, direct-dial telephone, TV ⊘ Restaurant, bar, lounge, garden; conferences and social functions; civil wedding licence; leisure facilities nearby; early suppers for children; cots, highchairs, toys, baby-listening ᴧ No wheelchair access ● No dogs or smoking in some public areas and some bedrooms ▭ Amex, Delta, Diners, MasterCard, Switch, Visa £ Single occupancy of twin/double £75, twin/double £115 to £170, family suite £170 to £190; deposit required. Alc L £20, D £25; light meals available. Special breaks available

---

BURPHAM West Sussex   map 3

Old Parsonage

Burpham, Arundel BN18 9RJ
TEL: (01903) 882160 FAX: (01903) 884627
EMAIL: burphamcch@ukonline.co.uk
WEB SITE: www.oldparsonage.co.uk

Recently re-named B&B in a delightful South Downs village

Formerly the Burpham Country House Hotel, this charming B&B has had a recent name-change to represent more accurately its new status following closure of the bar and restaurant. The new name reflects the history of the house, originally the Duke of Norfolk's hunting lodge and later a vicarage. It has an enviable location in the pretty hamlet of Burpham, surrounded by the gently undulating countryside of the peaceful South Downs, yet within easy striking distance of Arundel. Inside, the wide, flower-filled reception hall leads to a small, homely guest lounge, complete with piano and honesty bar, while the former conservatory restaurant is a relaxing setting for breakfast looking out over neatly trimmed lawns and across to the Downs. Upstairs, Rooms 6 and 7 are the flashiest, with huge beds, swish bathrooms, great views and extras such as CDs and sherry. Standard rooms are all fresh, good-sized and well equipped, although Room 1 just has the edge for its lovely views and smart new bathroom with a mosaic-tiled walk-in shower.

◑ Open all year ▨ Take A27 from Arundel towards Worthing; turn left just over railway bridge; after 2 miles hotel is signposted on right. Nearest train station: Arundel. Private car park ⟐postⱼ 1 single, 3 twin, 5 double, 1 four-poster; all with hair-dryer, direct-dial telephone, TV; some with CD player ⊘ Breakfast room, lounge, honesty bar, garden; conferences and social functions; leisure facilities nearby ᴧ Wheelchair access to hotel (1 step) and breakfast room, 1 ground-floor bedroom ● No dogs; no smoking ▭ Amex, Delta, MasterCard, Switch, Visa £ Single £40 to £45, single occupancy of twin/double £60 to £65, twin/double £60 to £120, four-poster £95 to £100; deposit required

---

BURRINGTON Devon   map 1

Northcote Manor

Burrington, Nr Umberleigh, Barnstaple EX37 9LZ
TEL: (01769) 560501 FAX: (01769) 560770
EMAIL: rest@northcotemanor.co.uk
WEB SITE: www.northcote-manor.com

New ownership but no change in the steady, peaceful atmosphere

The long curling drive up through the quiet woods is an appropriate introduction to this secluded country house – one that relies on tranquillity and elegant charm rather than spa centres and all the other modern adornments that are becoming increasingly common. The L-shaped stone-built house was built in the eighteenth century – the sort of place a well-to-do vicar might have once inhabited. The drawing room and reception/bar set the tone: oriental rugs on wooden floors, log fire and views across the lovely lawned grounds. The lounge and restaurant add a more contemporary feel, both being dominated by some colourful murals representing the life at Northcote through the centuries. Cooking is straightforward country house, with a decent list of vegetarian options. Bedrooms without views tend to get an extra such as a four-poster bed or whirlpool bath, but those idyllic rural panoramas are quite special. All rooms are reliably well furnished and comfortable, with smart bathrooms.

○ Open all year ⚡ On A377 about 2 miles north of junction with B3226; entrance is opposite Portsmouth Arms pub. Private car park. Nearest train station: Umberleigh ⌂ 3 twin/double, 3 double, 1 four-poster, 4 suites; all with room service, hair-dryer, direct-dial telephone, TV; some with trouser press; fax, modem line available ✓ Restaurant, bar, 2 lounges, gardens; conferences and social functions; civil wedding licence; tennis; leisure facilities nearby; early suppers for children; cots, highchairs, babysitting, baby-listening ♿ No wheelchair access ● No dogs or smoking in restaurant ⊟ Amex, Delta, MasterCard, Switch, Visa £ Single occupancy of twin/double £99 to £120, twin/double/four-poster £140 to £240, suite £240; deposit required. Set L £25.50, D £35; light meals available. Special breaks available (3FOR2)

BURY ST EDMUNDS Suffolk
map 6

The Angel

3 Angel Hill, Bury St Edmunds IP33 1LT
TEL: (01284) 714000 FAX: (01284) 714001
EMAIL: reservations@theangel.co.uk
WEB SITE: www.theangel.co.uk

Contemporary dining in classic surroundings

Vines creep up the walls of this mainly eighteenth-century hotel facing Bury St Edmunds' central square, which is rather biasedly described by the hoteliers as 'one of the prettiest squares in Britain'. The entrance to the grounds of the former abbey lie directly opposite, and underneath the main building one of the hotel's two restaurants (The Vaults) is housed in a highly evocative twelfth-century vaulted chamber probably once used by monks and travelling pilgrims. Just like the building, the interior doesn't stick to one period. Most of the décor in both the public and private rooms is traditional in tone, with patterned carpets, tapestries and the odd antique. Ten of the bedrooms were refurbished in 2002 – the one we saw had pale lime walls, a large dark-wood bed, modern lamps and a good-sized bathroom. All the higher-grade rooms are kitted out with extras like Playstation 2s. Both The Vaults and the Abbeygate restaurant are firmly contemporary, with bright red walls in the former and deep blue and gold décor in the more formal Abbeygate.

○ Open all year ⚡ Leave A14 and head towards town centre; hotel is in square opposite Abbey Gate. Nearest train station: Bury St Edmunds. Private car park ⌂ 8 single, 6 twin, 2 twin/double, 40 double, 4 four-poster, 4 family rooms, 1 suite; all with room service, hair-dryer, trouser press, direct-dial telephone, modem line, TV ✓ 2 restaurants, bar, lounge; conferences; social functions; civil wedding licence; early suppers for children; cots, highchairs, babysitting, baby-listening ♿ Wheelchair access to hotel (ramp), restaurant, WC, lift, 7 ground-floor bedrooms, 2 rooms specially equipped for disabled people, lift ● No dogs in restaurants, no smoking in restaurants and some bedrooms ⊟ Amex, Delta, Diners, MasterCard, Switch, Visa £ Single £86, single occupancy of twin/double £100, twin/double £120, four-poster £140 to £199, family room £199, suite £210; deposit required. Set L £19, D £26.50; alc L £22, D £26.50; light meals available. Special breaks available

---

Many hotels put up their tariffs in the spring. You are advised to confirm prices when you book.

Ounce House

Northgate Street, Bury St Edmunds IP33 1HP
TEL: (01284) 761779   FAX: (01284) 768315
EMAIL: pott@globalnet.co.uk
WEB SITE: www.ouncehouse.co.uk

A warm welcome at a worn-in, antique-packed family home

Jenny and Simon Pott's personal touch and family history infuse this red-brick Victorian house with an uncommon warmth. The Potts are keen collectors of an eclectic range of antiques. 'Nothing much has changed here, except that there's more! When we see something we like we just have a go at it!' Simon told us, talking enthusiastically about their collecting forays. A highlight of the cluttered but still bright, generous living room is a collection of etchings by Simon's Great Aunt Constance, a renowned artist, while upstairs are some funnies by famous newspaper cartoonists. Bedrooms are in bright but unobtrusive colours with yet more antiques (including a lovely wardrobe picked up for a fiver). The atmosphere is one in which guests are encouraged to feel genuinely at home. 'We just wanted to create the kind of place we'd want to stay in, in a real family home.' This is more than just sales pitch – for example, guests are free to ask at the family kitchen for more ice or lemon for the drinks they've poured themselves in the honesty bar area.

Open all year   Leave A14 at second Bury St Edmunds exit, signposted Bury St Edmunds Central; at roundabout follow signs to Historic Bury St Edmunds; turn left at next roundabout into Northgate Street. House is at the top of the hill, on right. Nearest train station: Bury St Edmunds. Private car park   1 twin, 2 double; all with hair-dryer, trouser press, direct-dial telephone, modem line, TV, CD player   Dining room, bar/library, lounge, snug, garden; leisure facilities nearby; early suppers for children; cots, highchairs, toys, babysitting, baby-listening   No wheelchair access   No dogs; smoking in bar/library only (guests must light candle)   Amex, Delta, Diners, MasterCard, Switch, Visa   Single occupancy of twin/double £60 to £70, twin/double £85 to £95; deposit required. Set D £28 to £30; light meals available; service incl. Special breaks available

Ravenwood Hall

Rougham, Bury St Edmunds IP30 9JA
TEL: (01359) 270345   FAX: (01359) 270788
EMAIL: enquiries@ravenwoodhall.co.uk
WEB SITE: www.ravenwoodhall.co.uk

Tudor-plus country-house grandeur without pretension

Just off the A14 but cushioned from the worst of the traffic noise by its seven acres of grounds and woodland, Ravenwood Hall is a roaming collection of buildings from a variety of periods, starting with the 1530s, but also including a former cricket pavilion transported to the site and now used mainly for functions such as weddings. The interior is old-school luxurious with plenty of antiques, plush curtains and worn-in sofas, in largely Tudor surroundings. Owner Craig Jarvis clearly has an equine passion, with rocking horses popping up both here and in his other hotel, the Black Lion in Long Melford (see entry). Family photos break up the grandeur and give the place a welcome, lived-in feel. Bedrooms in the main house are quite grand, and some have nice features such as a fireplace or a Winnie the Pooh theme. Those in the stable block are a bit more modern and bright. There are plenty of activities on offer including tennis, and pens which, when we inspected, housed an adorable brood of newborn goats which would delight your own kids.

Open all year   Take A14 east out of Bury St Edmunds; turn right to Rougham; left at Blackthorpe Barn; hotel is signposted soon afterwards on right. Private car park   2 twin, 10 double, 2 four-poster; all with room service, hair-dryer, direct-dial telephone, TV   Restaurant, bar, lounge, garden; conferences; social functions; civil wedding licence; heated outdoor swimming pool; leisure facilities nearby; cots, highchairs, toys, babysitting, baby-listening, outdoor play area   Wheelchair access to hotel and restaurant, WC, 3 ground-floor bedrooms   No dogs in restaurant; no smoking in restaurant and bedrooms   Amex, Delta, Diners,

MasterCard, Switch, Visa [£] Single occupancy of twin/double from £81, twin/double from £106, four-poster £149; deposit required. Set L (Sun), D £24; alc D £34; light meals available. Special breaks available

---

BUTTERMERE Cumbria map 10

Wood House

Buttermere, Cockermouth CA13 9XA
TEL: (017687) 70208   FAX: (017687) 70241
EMAIL: woodhouse.guest@virgin.net
WEB SITE: www.wdhse.co.uk

A refined and tranquil country house in a glorious Lakeland setting

It's actually Crummock Water you can see from this isolated location, not Buttermere as JMW Turner entitled his 1798 painting of the scene, in which Wood House makes background interest. The building is a solid stone-built property dating from Georgian times. It is of some historic interest, and is owned by the National Trust, but is also Mike and Judy McKenzie's much-loved home. The gracious interior induces instant calm, being furnished with classy, well-spaced antiques and a judicious selection of vases, pictures and table lamps. Bedrooms are individually decorated in conservative styles, with pastels and florals, all irreproachably spotless (as are the small, pristine bathrooms), but perhaps now looking a little dated. Dinners are served by arrangement, but guests should give Judy some warning as it's a long way to the shops from here, and everything is freshly cooked. Sociophobes should be prepared for pre-dinner sherry and communal dining.

🌓 Closed Nov to Mar   �🡒 Leave M6 at Junction 40; take A66 west and leave at Portinscale, then follow signs for Buttermere; house is ½ mile north of Buttermere on B5289. Private car park 🅿🡒 2 twin, 1 double; all with hair-dryer   ✓ Dining room, drawing room, garden   ৬ No wheelchair access   ⬤ No children under 16; no dogs; no smoking   ⊟ None accepted   [£] Single occupancy of twin/double £48, twin/double £80; deposit required. Set D £26; service incl

---

CALNE Wiltshire map 2

Chilvester Hill House

Calne SN11 0LP
TEL: (01249) 813981/815785   FAX: (01249) 814217
EMAIL: gill.dilley@talk21.com
WEB SITE: www.chilvesterhillhouse.co.uk

Spacious family home with welcoming hosts and a sociable atmosphere

Gill Dilley is one of those individuals who seem to be able to find 25 hours in a day and still remain perpetually cheerful and welcoming. She and husband John have recently restored their country house, which dates from 1885, to its original look, with William Morris patterns and redecorated bathrooms. They run their house in a homely and civilised manner, and guests breakfast together around a single table. Dinners are available too, on request, and much of the fruit and vegetables are either home or locally grown (asparagus is one home-grown speciality from the garden). The smart drawing and sitting rooms feature souvenirs of the Dilleys' lengthy sojourn in Arabia, including five years in Aden when it was Marxist – experiences that make for interesting anecdotes. The spacious and comfortable bedrooms are decorated in keeping with the period of the house.

🌓 Open all year   🚕 1 mile from Calne on A4 towards Chippenham. Take right turn signposted Bremhill and Ratford and immediately turn right again through gateposts. Private car park 🅿🡒 3 twin/double; family rooms available; all with TV; hairdryer available   ✓ Dining room, drawing room, sitting room, garden; small conferences; leisure facilities nearby; cot, highchair, baby-listening   ৬ No wheelchair access   ⬤ No children under 12 exc babes in arms; no dogs; smoking discouraged in bedrooms   ⊟ Amex, Delta, Diners, MasterCard, Switch, Visa   [£] Single occupancy of twin/double £50 to £60, twin/double £80 to £90, family room £110 to £125; deposit required. Set D £20 to £25; service incl

CAMBER   East Sussex   map 3

The Place

New Lydd Road, Camber Sands, Camber, Nr Rye TN31 7RB
TEL: (01797) 225057   FAX: (01797) 227003
EMAIL: enquiries@theplacecambersands.co.uk
WEB SITE: www.theplacecambersands.co.uk

Buzzy restaurant-with-rooms across from stunning dune-backed beach

Huge hopes have been placed on the shoulders of the Place – that it will lead to a much-needed renaissance for this depressed seaside resort. At the very least, let's hope it leads to more of the same. The single-storey motel-like building is run as a relaxed restaurant-with-rooms. Bedrooms are modern and furnished in cool neutrals, with comfortable beds and white cotton bedding. Family rooms have a sofa bed for children, who seem to fit in easily with the mainly young clientele. Bathrooms are clean and white – though the shower was a mere dribble on our inspection visit. The interesting menu, served in the blonde wood and chrome restaurant (no need for jacket and tie, so wear what you feel comfortable in), features plenty of local fish and lamb, and offers half portions for children. Service is spot-on from the young staff. For breakfast there's a help-yourself buffet of yoghurts, croissants, fruit, cereal, cheese and ham – and a toaster so you can ensure your toast is hot – backed up by cafetières of good coffee. It's laid back, as breakfast should be, with guests passing round the papers and children picking up beach towels from reception.

● Closed Chr & New Year ⊿ Heading towards Camber off A259, go past the Rye Golf Club; hotel is ½ mile further on the left, 250 metres past village sign for Camber. Private car park ⊫ 3 twin, 9 double, 3 triple rooms, 3 family rooms; all with TV ⊘ Restaurant, dining room, bar, garden; conferences; social functions; leisure facilities nearby; early suppers for children; cots, highchairs ⑂ Wheelchair access to hotel and restaurant, 18 ground-floor bedrooms, 1 room specially equipped for disabled people. Disabled parking ● No dogs; smoking in some public areas only ▭ Amex, Delta, MasterCard, Switch, Visa £ Twin/double £75 to £80, triple room £90 to £98, family room £120 to £128; deposit required. Alc L £17.50, D £21; light meals available. Special breaks available ③FOR②

CAMBRIDGE   Cambridgeshire   map 6

Hotel Felix

Whitehouse Lane, Huntingdon Road, Cambridge CB3 0LX
TEL: (01223) 277977   FAX: (01223) 277973
EMAIL: help@hotelfelix.co.uk
WEB SITE: www.hotelfelix.co.uk

Don't judge a book by its cover – an interesting meld of old and new

A Victorian building with an unadventurous modern extension opposite some drab office buildings outside Cambridge may be an unlikely place for a stylish boutique hotel, but that's exactly what you find once you've crossed the gravelled car park and ventured inside. The interior is all clean, modern lines and plain colours, with an appealing mixture of furniture styles and specially commissioned modern art. Bedrooms have wide beds with high dark-wood headboards and white linen and similar, unfussy decorative schemes. The Graffiti restaurant serves some adventurous combinations such as baby octopus and dandelion salad and quails 'Felix' with balsamic vinegar and artichoke heart ragù. The hotel takes its name from St Felix of Burgundy who worked in Cambridgeshire in the seventh century, though – perhaps confusingly – its mascot is a dog, not a cat. The sculpture of a dog, believed to be a reproduction of an original of a Molossian breed from Greece, can be seen proudly displayed at the entrance.

● Open all year ⊿ From M11 Junction 13 follow A1303 to Huntingdon Road (A1307), after ¾ mile turn right on to Whitehouse Lane. Nearest train station: Cambridge. Private car park ⊫ 20 twin/double, 27 double, 5 suites; family rooms available; all with room service, hair-dryer, mini-bar, direct-dial telephone, modem line, TV,

CD player; trouser press available ⊘ Restaurant, bar, lounge, garden; conferences; social functions; civil wedding licence; leisure facilities nearby; early suppers for children; cots, highchairs, baby-listening ♿ Wheelchair access to hotel (ramp) and restaurant, WC, 26 ground-floor bedrooms, 3 rooms specially equipped for disabled people, lift ● No dogs in public rooms; no smoking in some public rooms and some bedrooms ▭ Amex, Delta, Diners, MasterCard, Switch, Visa £ Single occupancy of twin/double from £128, twin/double from £158, family room/suite from £245; deposit required. Cooked B £7.50; set L £16.50; alc D £30; light meals available ③FOR②

Meadowcroft Hotel

Trumpington Road, Cambridge CB2 2EX
TEL: (01223) 346120 FAX: (01223) 346138
EMAIL: meadowcroft@meadowcrofthotel.co.uk
WEB SITE: www.meadowcrofthotel.co.uk

Restored Victorian splendour right on the road into town

Blink and you'd miss the signpost for the Meadowcroft as you zip along the main road into Cambridge. If you are in a car you'll be glad of the parking in space-starved Cambridge, and you're only minutes on foot from the historic centre. The hotel itself is a stocky red-brick Victorian retirement home converted into a hotel in 2000. The entrance sports a selection of hats, including a boater and a police helmet, hanging from pegs. Once into the reception area with its impressive wood staircase, you're transported a world away from the road and into an Oxbridge fantasy, with the tick-tock of the grandfather clock accompanied by gentle jazz drifting from the adjoining bar. The lounge has plenty of space even though it is cluttered with antiques and leather-bound books. There is also a restaurant area, but it is used only for breakfast – if you want any other food you have to order it through room service. The rooms are perhaps not quite as impressive, and one reader complained of a bed that was too soft, 'dismal' breakfast, a mark-up on newspapers, as well as a 5am wake-up call not cancelled from a previous guest. More reports, please.

◖ Closed Chr. & New Year ⤢ From M11 Junction 11, head towards Cambridge city centre for 3 miles; Meadowcroft is signposted on right-hand side. Nearest train station: Cambridge. Private car park ⬑ 1 single, 4 twin, 9 double, 2 four-poster, 2 family rooms; all with room service, hair-dryer, direct-dial telephone, modem line, TV ⊘ Dining room, bar, lounge, conservatory, garden; conferences; social functions; leisure facilities nearby; early suppers for children; cot, highchairs, outdoor play area ♿ Wheelchair access to hotel (ramp) and dining room, 2 ground-floor bedrooms ● No smoking ▭ Amex, Delta, MasterCard, Switch, Visa £ Single £85, single occupancy of twin/double £90 to £100, twin/double £100 to £110, four-poster/ family room £120 to £130; deposit required. Light meals available

CANNINGTON Somerset   map 2

Blackmore Farm

Blackmore Lane, Cannington, Bridgwater TA5 2NE
TEL: (01278) 653442 FAX: (01278) 653427
EMAIL: dyerfarm@aol.com
WEB SITE: www.dyerfarm.co.uk

Superb ancient manor offering historic rooms at good prices

The deep lanes that lead up to Ann and Ian Dyer's fifteenth-century manor house provide a spectacular arrival. Suddenly a wonderfully grizzled old giant of a house rises up above you, gnarled wisteria grappling with the porch and arched mullioned windows that promise interesting rooms beyond. The Dyers have kept the house exactly as it should be: stone floors and simplicity. The main hall boasts a single 20-foot-long oak table for breakfasts, while the adjacent rooms, which include a small bar, are lit by wrought-iron candelabras. If you require the full medieval magic, ask for the dramatic Gallery bedroom, which comes with suitably hefty furniture, ancient panelling and a sitting room upstairs in the roof timbers. West bedroom comes in a short second, with a four-poster and views to the Quantocks. Rooms over in the barn conversion don't have the same Gormenghastic glamour but do offer ground-floor access and patio seating areas.

◗ Open all year ⤢ From Bridgwater, take A39 for Minehead; after 3 miles, turn left at Ticknells (just before Cannington village) into Blackmore Lane; follow lane for 1 mile; Blackmore Farm is first on left after Maltshovel pub. Private car park ⤸ 1 twin, 2 double, 1 four-poster, 1 family room, 1 suite; all with hair-dryer, TV ⚭ Breakfast hall, lounge, garden; conferences and social functions; cots, highchairs, toys, babysitting, baby-listening ♿ Wheelchair access to hotel and breakfast room (ramps), 3 ground-floor bedrooms in annexe, specially equipped for disabled people ● No dogs; no smoking ▭ Amex, Delta, Diners, MasterCard, Switch, Visa £ Single occupancy of twin/double £35 to £45, twin/double £55 to £58, four-poster/family room/suite £70 to £75; deposit required

---

CANTERBURY Kent   map 3

Magnolia House

36 St Dunstan's Terrace, Canterbury CT2 8AX
TEL: (01227) 765121 (AND FAX)
EMAIL: magnolia_house_canterbury@yahoo.com
WEB SITE: freespace.virgin.net/magnolia.canterbury

Handsome guesthouse close to the city centre

New owner Isobelle Leggett had just taken the helm when we visited the handsome white house bedecked with pansy-filled window boxes and tubs of shrubs on a residential side street close to the city centre. The welcoming but pepper-pot-sized lounge has books, games and local information and a folder of restaurant recommendations. In sunny weather though you can retire to the lovely gardens with seating tucked away in concealed corners and dense foliage. Guests choose breakfast the night before, and full English breakfast is on offer, with local bacon and sausage plus kippers, smoked haddock or porridge, all taken in the dining room with lacy tablecloths overlooking the garden. Bedrooms are well equipped, and Isobelle has thoughtfully introduced miniature fridges for complimentary wine and fresh milk in each room. The garden room on the ground floor has a four-poster and a good-sized bathroom. Other rooms are less spacious, but comfy and feminine.

◗ Open all year ⤢ Approaching Canterbury from west on A2, turn left at first roundabout, signposted University and Whitstable; St Dunstan's Terrace is third turning on right. Nearest train station: Canterbury West ⤸ 1 single, 2 twin/double, 3 double, 1 four-poster; all with hair-dryer, TV, fridge; 1 with trouser press ⚭ Dining room, lounge, garden; leisure facilities nearby ♿ No wheelchair access; 2 steps into hotel, 1 ground-floor bedroom ● No children under 12; no dogs; no smoking ▭ MasterCard, Switch, Visa £ Single £48 to £55, single occupancy of twin/double £55 to £110, twin/double £85 to £110, four-poster £110 to £125; deposit required. Alc D £25; service incl

Yorke Lodge `NEW ENTRY`

50 London Road, Canterbury CT2 8LF
TEL: (01227) 451243 FAX: (01227) 462006
EMAIL: enquiries@yorkelodge.com
WEB SITE: www.yorkelodge.com

Victorian guesthouse undergoing a full-blossomed facelift

Vicky O'Shea and her husband took over the guesthouse from her aunt back in 2002. Since then they have been busy making their mark on the large Victorian townhouse on a busy road close to the city centre. When our inspector visited the final touches were being made to the large lounge and conservatory bar, with doors leading on to a patio shaded by a magnolia tree which she hopes will be appealing to guests in the evening. Vicky, who grew up in her parents' Canterbury hotel, is keen to lighten and brighten up the house and banish the heavier Victorian-style décor favoured by her aunt. So far she has renovated four of the bedrooms, which are light and fresh in full-blossomed florals and white cotton bedspreads, with modern, white bathrooms and large power showers. Older rooms are spacious and light with heavier décor and clean but decidedly dated bathrooms. The breakfast – a full English – and breakfast room are both traditional in style with various collections of memorabilia on display.

🌙 Open all year ⚡ From M2/A2, at first roundabout turn left into London Road. Nearest train station: Canterbury East. Private car park 🛏 1 single, 2 twin, 3 double, 2 four-poster; family rooms available; all with hair-dryer, TV ⊘ Breakfast room, conservatory bar, lounge, library, patio, garden; leisure facilities nearby; highchairs ♿ No wheelchair access ● No smoking in bedrooms ▭ Amex, Delta, MasterCard, Switch, Visa £ Single £38 to £42, single occupancy of twin/double £42 to £45, twin/double £65 to £75, four-poster £80 to £90. Special breaks available

---

CARLISLE Cumbria   map 10

Number 31 NEW ENTRY

31 Howard Place, Carlisle CA1 1HR
TEL: (01228) 597080 (AND FAX)
EMAIL: pruirving@aol.com
WEB SITE: www.number31.freeservers.com

An elegant Victorian townhouse on a quiet side street near Carlisle's historic centre

Back in the *Guide* after a change of ownership, this well-kept terraced property in a residential area makes a handy base for exploring the city. Pru Irving and her husband recently took over a thriving business and plan to run Number 31 along similar lines, while gradually putting their own ideas into practice. Ground-floor reception rooms include a spacious street-side lounge painted primrose, containing two handsomely upholstered sofas, a tall bay window and original plasterwork. The mantelpiece is decked with striking ornaments and family photographs. The dark-red dining room on the garden side provides an intimate setting for breakfast or three-course dinners (such as spicy baked prawns, chicken stuffed with cheese and asparagus, followed by sticky toffee pudding). The three rag-rolled bedrooms each have a distinctive character, with flamboyant beds or bathrooms. Internet access is available in a box room – a boon for business people who stay during the week. Reports welcome.

🌙 Open all year ⚡ From M6 Junction 43, take road into city centre; after sixth set of lights, take next right. Nearest train station: Carlisle 🛏 1 twin/double, 2 double; all with room service, hair-dryer, trouser press, TV; direct-dial telephone, fax, modem line available ⊘ Dining room, bar service, sitting room, library, garden; conferences; leisure facilities nearby ♿ No wheelchair access ● No children under 16; no dogs; no smoking ▭ Amex, MasterCard, Switch, Visa £ Single occupancy of twin/double £60, twin/double £85. Set D £20; light meals available; service incl

---

CARTMEL Cumbria   map 8

Aynsome Manor

Cartmel, Grange-over-Sands LA11 6HH
TEL: (015395) 36653 FAX: (015395) 36016
EMAIL: info@aynsomemanorhotel.co.uk
WEB SITE: www.aynsomemanorhotel.co.uk

This well-managed, family-owned hotel assures a tranquil and comfortable stay with excellent service

Like the nearby village of Cartmel, Aynsome Manor has a long and distinguished history, dating back well before the present mostly Georgian and Victorian structure. The house is no architectural beauty, but blends into its pastoral south Lakeland surroundings with dignity, overlooking views towards Cartmel Priory that can't have changed much for centuries. The interior is solidly traditional too: a sitting room with a marble Adam fireplace, a fine stairwell surmounted by a lantern cupola, a panelled dining room with a tongue-and-ball ceiling, and an oil portrait of Thomas Machell, self-confident Master of Aynsome. Aynsome's current masters are the Varley family, who have run the hotel with cheerful efficiency for over 20 years. Chris and Andrea ensure a seamless transition from their parents, putting long experience of the hotel trade to good use in attention to every detail, from dressing table lighting to a well-stocked cellar. Bedrooms are steadily being modernised.

○ Closed 2 to 30 Jan ⚏ Leave M6 at Junction 36 and follow A590 towards Barrow-in-Furness; leave dual carriageway at signs for Cartmel; hotel is on right, ½ mile north of Cartmel village. Private car park ⌸ 5 twin, 6 double, 1 four-poster; all with room service, hair-dryer, direct-dial telephone, TV ⊘ Dining room, bar, 2 lounges, garden; leisure facilities nearby; early suppers for children; cots, highchairs ⅙ No wheelchair access ● No children under 5 in dining room eves; no dogs in public rooms; no smoking in bedrooms and most public rooms ▭ Amex, Delta, MasterCard, Switch, Visa £ Single occupancy of twin/double £72 to £88, twin/double/four-poster £114 to £155, family room £139 to £180 (rates incl dinner); deposit required. Set L £15; light meals available. Special breaks available

L'Enclume

Cavendish Street, Cartmel, Grange-over-Sands LA11 6PZ
TEL: (015395) 36362   FAX: (015395) 38907
EMAIL: info@lenclume.co.uk
WEB SITE: www.lenclume.co.uk

Designer style meets top-notch cooking in this high-flying restaurant-with-rooms

If your French vocab has flown the coop, an *enclume* is an anvil. The iron hooping wheel near the entrance confirms the building's original role as village smithy, but prepare to be surprised if you were expecting something quaintly rustic. Despite the ancient beams and original stonework, L'Enclume is uncompromisingly contemporary. It aims at affluent young sophisticates rather than families with children or visitors with conservative notions about food and décor. Chef-patron Simon Rogan's cooking is ultra-ambitious and technically brilliant: multi-course 'taste and texture' menus are his trademark, requiring a brief glossary of arcane ingredients such as barberry bark and mugwort. The restaurant is naturally the focal point, with smooth-flagged flooring and streamlined modern seating, overlooking a secluded garden. The minimalist approach continues through to the bedrooms, elegantly decorated in costly designer fabrics, with sleek gadgetry. The antique furnishings are all for sale. A four-room annexe cottage is available for single lets.

○ Open all year; restaurant closed Mon eve ⚏ From Cartmel village square go through arch into Cavendish Street. Private car park ⌸ 5 double, 2 suites; all with hair-dryer, direct-dial telephone, TV; some with VCR ⊘ Restaurant, conservatory, garden; conferences and social functions; leisure facilities nearby; early suppers for children; cots, highchairs ⅙ Wheelchair access to hotel (1 step) and restaurant (1 step), WC, 3 ground-floor bedrooms specially equipped for disabled people ● No children under 12 in restaurant eves; no dogs in public rooms and most bedrooms; no smoking ▭ Amex, Delta, Diners, MasterCard, Switch, Visa £ Single occupancy of double £80 to £100, double £120 to £170, suite £170 to £200; deposit required. Set L £25, D £50 to £95; alc L, D £45. Special breaks available

Uplands

Haggs Lane, Cartmel, Grange-over-Sands LA11 6HD
TEL: (015395) 36248   FAX: (015395) 36848
EMAIL: uplands@kencomp.net
WEB SITE: www.uplands.uk.com

An elegant restaurant-with-rooms enjoying fine views towards Morecambe Bay

The high volume of repeat trade suggests Tom and Diana Peter have successfully cracked the formula at their attractive country house a mile or so from Cartmel village. Guests approach the house and its formal Italian-style terraced gardens of urns and statuary via an archway artistically draped with wisteria. The elevated site overlooks magnificent views of the Leven estuary; some of the trees in the two-acre grounds have recently been thinned to provide a clearer vista. Few hotels offer more appealing and restful public rooms than the open-plan ground floor of Uplands, exquisitely decorated in lemon and ivory and hung with classy flower prints. But neither décor nor outlook will distract you entirely from Tom's cooking, confidently prepared in a long-practised evolution from John Tovey's celebrated Lakeland style.

Bedrooms share the same fresh, light décor with floral pictures and personal touches, and are steadily being updated in more contemporary themes.

◗ Closed Jan & Feb; restaurant closed Mon eve ⚡ From Cartmel village, take road signposted to Grange opposite Pig and Whistle pub; house is 1 mile on left. Nearest train station: Grange-over-Sands. Private car park 🛏 1 twin, 2 twin/double, 2 double; all with room service, hair-dryer, direct-dial telephone, TV; tea/ coffee-making facilities available ✓ Restaurant, lounge, garden; social functions; leisure facilities nearby ♿ No wheelchair access ● No children under 8; smoking in lounge only ☐ Amex, Delta, MasterCard, Switch, Visa £ Single occupancy of twin/double £84 to £94, twin/double £148 to £168 (rates incl dinner); deposit required. Set L £16.50, D £31. Special breaks available

---

CARTMEL FELL Cumbria
map 8

Lightwood

Cartmel Fell, Grange-over-Sands LA11 6NP
TEL: (015395) 31454 (AND FAX)
EMAIL: enquiries@lightwoodguesthouse.com
WEB SITE: www.lightwoodguesthouse.com

A new generation settles in at this much-loved rural guesthouse

This splendidly peaceful retreat enjoys a remote setting in the southern fells, with views towards the Winster Valley. The main house dates from 1656 and is full of character in typical Lakeland style. It was a working farm until 1970, and a few pet animals are still in residence, but Lightwood's outbuildings are now converted into accommodation units. The main building is cosy and quaint, with creaky floors and cottagey beams. Downstairs lie dining and sitting rooms, including a sun lounge overlooking the gardens. Yvonne and Ian have taken over the management of Lightwood from Yvonne's parents, and it seems very much business as usual, with hearty home-cooked dinners served on request. 'Their welcome is warm and their local knowledge is wide,' according to one reader. Yvonne has the same friendly, outgoing manner with guests. The hyperactive Fideo and Evelyn Cervetti may still be glimpsed wheeling a barrow round the lovely gardens. Maintenance needs tightening up, however, and the elderly pine-cladding and florals are due for a makeover.

◗ Closed Dec & Jan; dining room closed Sun to Wed eves ⚡ Just off A592 at Fell Foot Park. Take steep turn to right signposted Bowland Bridge and Cartmel Fell; continue 2½ miles to Lightwood. Private car park 🛏 1 twin/double, 3 double, 1 family room; all with hair-dryer, TV ✓ Dining room, bar, sitting room, conservatory, garden; aromatherapy treatment room; leisure facilities nearby; cots, highchairs, toys, babysitting, outdoor play area ♿ No wheelchair access; 3 steps into hotel, 2 ground-floor bedrooms ● No dogs; no smoking ☐ MasterCard, Switch, Visa £ Single occupancy of twin/double £28 to £47, twin/ double £64 to £70, family room £75 to £88; deposit required. Set D £19; service incl. Special breaks available (3 FOR 2)

CASTLE ASHBY Northamptonshire
map 5

The Falcon

Castle Ashby, Northampton NN7 1LF
TEL: (01604) 696200 FAX: (01604) 696673
EMAIL: falcon.castleashby@oldenglishinns.co.uk
WEB SITE: www.falconhotel-castleashby.com

Characterful hideaway offering bounteous rural fare

Surrounded by a timeless landscape of low rolling hills of woodland and pasture, Castle Ashby is picturesque and as salubrious as the name suggests, and the delightful sixteenth-century Falcon at the centre of the village provides a popular venue drawing people in from miles around. Michael Eastick and his wife Jennifer are the patient and agreeable architects behind this well-run establishment that seems to provide something for all tastes.

The traditional Cellar Bar, bedecked with trappings of a rural bygone age, offers a selection of beers to please real-ale buffs, along with the designer brands. Michael enjoys his garden and grows many of the vegetables – including over twenty varieties of potatoes – for the restaurant. Conveniently just down the road is a farm selling asparagus and in season there is a speciality asparagus menu for devotees of the vegetable. The warm, rustic dining room extends to a wide, paved garden terrace for al fresco eating and in the extensive garden there is a permanent marquee to accommodate the numerous wedding parties. Bedrooms are comfortable and well equipped.

○ Open all year 🔁 Leave A428 Northampton to Bedford road at signpost to Castle Ashby; hotel is 1 mile along this road. Private car park 🛏 3 single, 3 twin/double, 9 double, 1 family room; all with room service, hair-dryer, trouser press, direct-dial telephone, TV; some with VCR ✔ Restaurant, 2 bars, lounge, garden; conferences; social functions; civil wedding licence; leisure facilities nearby; cots, highchairs ♿ Wheelchair access to hotel and restaurant (ramps), WC, 5 ground-floor bedrooms, 1 room specially equipped for disabled people ◖ No dogs in public rooms; no smoking in restaurant ▭ Amex, Delta, MasterCard, Switch, Visa £ Single £90, single occupancy of twin/double £95, twin/double £113, family room from £128; deposit required. Set L £19, D £27.50; alc D £35; light meals available; service incl (3FOR2)

CASTLE COMBE   Wiltshire   map 2

Manor House

Castle Combe, Chippenham SN14 7HR
TEL: (01249) 782206   FAX: (01249) 783100
EMAIL: enquiries@manor-housecc.co.uk
WEB SITE: www.exclusivehotels.co.uk

Superbly well-groomed country manor in a great location

Castle Combe village is Cotswolds charm at its best – so you certainly won't get the picturesque magic to yourself. Staying in Manor House is one way of securing privileged access: enter via electronically controlled gates and swing up the drive to the wisteria-clad fourteenth-century manor complete with 18-hole golf course, Italianate gardens and swimming pool. The attractive exterior is matched by the interiors: log fires, oak panelling, beams and ornate plasterwork make an enticingly cosy experience. Dinners are taken in the medieval-style gallery restaurant where the cooking is well-reported country house fare. Bedrooms in the main house are full of character with touches of grandeur; those in the nearby cottages are more modest but no less appealing.

○ Open all year 🔁 From M4 Junction 17 follow chequered flag signs to Castle Combe race circuit, then signs to hotel; entrance is over bridge, on right. Private car park 🛏 9 twin, 8 double, 16 four-poster, 15 suites; family rooms available; all with room service, hair-dryer, trouser press, direct-dial telephone, modem line, TV; some with VCR, tea/coffee-making facilities ✔ Restaurant, bar, lounge, library, conservatory, garden; conferences; social functions; civil wedding licence; gym, tennis, heated outdoor swimming pool; leisure facilities nearby; early suppers for children; cots, highchairs, babysitting ♿ Wheelchair access to hotel and restaurant (ramp), WC, 15 ground-floor bedrooms ◖ No children in restaurant after 7pm, dogs in some bedrooms only, £50; no smoking in bedrooms ▭ Delta, MasterCard, Switch, Visa £ Twin from £180, double from £235, four-poster/family room from £295; suite from £340; deposit required. Continental B £13, cooked B £16; set L £19, D £35 to £45; alc D £65; light meals available; service incl. Special breaks available (3FOR2)

CATLOWDY   Cumbria   map 10

Bessiestown Farm

Catlowdy, Nr Longtown, Carlisle CA6 5QP
TEL: (01228) 577219   FAX: (01228) 577019
EMAIL: info@bessiestown.co.uk
WEB SITE: www.bessiestown.co.uk

Sprucely modernised farmhouse accommodation near the Scottish border

In chilly weather it's a windswept and lonely view across moors towards Scotland from this nineteenth-century working sheep-farm, making Bessiestown seem all the more inviting. Here everything is warm and welcoming, especially resident owner Margaret Sisson, who runs this immaculately maintained establishment with natural, practised hospitality, aided by cheerful family helpers. Guests may relax in a spacious and elegant bar-lounge, or a sun lounge of blue-green bamboo overlooking the gardens. The bright dining room has a Victorian fireplace, and wide windowsills decked with homely collections of china cheese dishes or beautifully trimmed gift boxes. Hearty breakfasts feature fresh berries, porridge, black pudding or haggis on request. Simple, generously served two-course dinners appear promptly at 7pm, guaranteeing to keep night starvation at bay, with an extra pudding if you like. The high-quality bedrooms vary, but all are light, fresh and sparkling, every detail carefully considered – mini-fridges stocked with chilled water and fresh milk, for instance.

◐ Closed Chr; dining room closed Sun eve 🔁 From M6 Junction 44 follow A7 to Longtown; at Bush Hotel take road signposted Catlowdy; continue 6 miles to T-junction then turn right; Catlowdy is 1½ miles further on, hotel is first building on left. Private car park 🛏 1 twin, 1 twin/double, 3 double, 1 four-poster, 2 family rooms; all with hair-dryer, TV ⌀ Dining room, bar/lounge, conservatory, games room, garden; social functions; indoor heated swimming pool; leisure facilities nearby; cots, highchairs ♿ Wheelchair access to hotel and dining room, National Accessible Scheme: mobility impairment M3, 3 ground-floor bedrooms ● No dogs; no smoking ▭ Delta, MasterCard, Switch, Visa £ Single occupancy of twin/double £39, twin/double £60 to £65, four-poster £120, family room £75; deposit required. Set D £15; service incl (3FOR2)

CAVENDISH Suffolk   map 6

The George [NEW ENTRY]

The Green, Cavendish CO10 8BA
TEL: (01787) 280298 FAX: (01787) 281703
EMAIL: reservations@georgecavendish.co.uk
WEB SITE: www.georgecavendish.co.uk

Good food in a stylish but sympathetic revamp of a 600-year-old inn

On the green of a picture-pretty Suffolk village lies this timber-framed 600-year-old inn, which has been thoroughly brought up to date by Jonathan and Charlotte Nicholson. The interior shows a light decorative touch, with simple colours and exposed timbers, and artworks depicting jazz and blues masters (as well as rock luminaries like Keith Richards) along with more traditional rural scenes adorning the walls. A small pub bar adjoins the stylishly understated restaurant, which serves excellent, mainly modern, British cooking. Think stripped wood, stocky wooden tables, low ceilings and tables neatly set with delicate silvery lampshades around tea-lights, and a menu ranging from chicken Kiev and chips to wild mushroom risotto with white truffle oil. The rooms continue the unfussy décor in creams and pale colours, with more exposed beams. A little conservatory and beer garden out back complete the picture.

◐ Open all year; restaurant closed Sun eves & Mon 🔁 In Cavendish village 🛏 1 twin/double, 4 double; all with hair-dryer, direct-dial telephone, modem line, TV ⌀ Restaurant, dining room, bar; social functions; highchairs ♿ No wheelchair access ● Dogs in bar and bedrooms only; smoking in bar only ▭ Delta, MasterCard, Switch, Visa £ Single occupancy of twin/double £68 to £78, twin/double £70 to £110. Set L, D (2 courses) £11; alc L, D £25; light meals available (3FOR2)

'There wasn't much point complaining to the hotel. You do not ask a street entertainer if he has a licence for his monkey while the bank behind his pitch is being robbed: the management of this hotel, or group, hasn't the faintest idea of the meaning of "hospitality" to their "guests".'
On a hotel in Kent

'At breakfast I was exposed to English boarding house tastelessness and portion control at its worst.'
On a hotel in Cheshire

map 5

Brockencote Hall

Chaddesley Corbett, Nr Kidderminster DY10 4PY
TEL: (01562) 777876   FAX: (01562) 777872
EMAIL: info@brockencotehall.com
WEB SITE: www.brockencotehall.com

A distinctive French influence sets the tone at this handsome country-house hotel

Joseph and Alison Petitjean pride themselves on bringing a little bit of France into the heart of the English countryside and there's no doubting the success of their enterprise. It probably helps that the house, built in 1880 by a Victorian businessman, has more of the château about it than the normal Gothic pile one usually finds from that period. Add the stillness of the nearby lake, and one could almost be on the Loire. Inside there's a delicate French fanciness to the restaurant, decorated in creams and beiges with matching padded chairs. Chef Jérôme Barbançon completes the perfect Gallic picture with his acclaimed cooking and French serving staff. Perhaps start with frogs' legs with smoked kipper and potato, followed by steamed pike and zander with coriander, and saffron poached pear tart to finish. High standards are there to be seen in the good-size bedrooms, where lush, rich fabrics, used for curtains and bedspreads, set the tone. The superior rooms have whirlpool bathrooms.

○ Open all year   ⊠ Opposite Chaddesley Corbett village, on A448 Bromsgrove to Kidderminster road. Private car park   ⊨ 1 twin, 2 twin/double, 8 double, 4 four-poster, 2 family rooms; all with hair-dryer, direct-dial telephone, modem line, TV, CD player; 2 with trouser press   ⊘ Restaurant, 2 lounges, conservatory, garden; conferences and social functions; tennis; early suppers for children; cots, highchairs, baby-listening   ও Wheelchair access to hotel (ramp) and restaurant, WC, 5 ground-floor bedrooms, 1 room specially equipped for disabled people. Disabled parking   ● No children under 4 in restaurant eves; no dogs; no smoking in public rooms and some bedrooms   ▭ Amex, Delta, Diners, MasterCard, Switch, Visa   £ Single occupancy of twin/double £85 to £120, twin/double £116 to £145, four-poster/family room £144 to £180; deposit required. Set L £17, D £26.50; alc L £28.50, D £43.50; light meals available; service incl. Special breaks available   (3FOR2)

map 3

The Grove   NEW ENTRY

Chandler's Cross, Rickmansworth WD3 4TG
TEL: (01923) 807807   FAX: (01923) 221008
EMAIL: info@thegrove.co.uk
WEB SITE: www.thegrove.co.uk

Untrammelled luxury, with everything you could possibly want – but at a price

Self-billed as 'London's country estate', this sparklingly new, upmarket playground near the M25 certainly has much in common with its metropolitan counterparts, not least high rack rates that don't include VAT or breakfast. But it also has acres of space (including a golf course) and you do get a lot of bang for your buck, letting you revel in the contemporary opulence that abounds in every corner. At the hotel's core is the historic home of the Earls of Clarendon, now rather overwhelmed by the modern but sympathetic extension. The mansion suites are visions of design-led comfort in three themes, one of which – 'hot sexy classic' – features ultra-chic furniture and colours: think black lacquer tables and aubergine curtains – and a baby grand! The more affordable West Wing rooms are smaller but just as swish, with soothingly pastel décor, hi-tech extras such as plasma screens and thoughtful treats such as organic tea and coffee. Public areas, from the hip-cool restaurants to the pamper-palace of a spa, complete this jaw-dropping package, and throughout, striking modern art graces the minimalist walls.

○ Open all year 🔁 From M25, take Junction 19 (if travelling clockwise) or Junction 20 (if travelling anticlockwise); follow brown signs to hotel along A411 towards Watford; private car park. Nearest train station: Watford Metropolitan 🛏 211 twin/double, 16 four-poster/suites; family rooms available; all with room service, hair-dryer, trouser press, direct-dial telephone, modem line, TV, VCR, DVD, CD player ⊘ 3 restaurants, 2 dining rooms, 3 bars, 4 lounges, 1 library, gardens; conferences and social functions; civil wedding licence; gym, spa, tennis, heated indoor and outdoor swimming pools; golf nearby; cots, highchairs, toys, children's club, babysitting, outdoor play area ⅙ Wheelchair access to hotel and restaurant, WC, lift. Disabled parking ● No dogs; no smoking in some public rooms and some bedrooms ⊏ Amex, Delta, Diners, MasterCard, Switch, Visa £ Double £282 to £376, four-poster/suite £376 to £1058; family room rates on application. Cooked B £23; alc L £18/£31/£53, D £23.50/£31/£76.50; light meals available. Special breaks available

---

CHARLBURY   Oxfordshire map 2

Bull Inn

Sheep Street, Charlbury OX7 3RR
TEL: (01608) 810689
EMAIL: dandh.charlbury@virgin.net

A promising start – and a smashing new room – for the new team at this good-value pub

When our inspector called on a sunny April day, Val and Ged Ludden were busy overseeing the finishing touches to their biggest change since taking over a few months before – adding an extra guest room by transforming the previous owner's bedroom. And what a splendid job they have done, giving this characterful village pub a stylish, contemporary addition to the otherwise cosy, cottagey bedrooms. So, if you have a choice, ask for Room 4; it costs a little bit more, but is worth every penny for the super-kingsize bed, peaceful colour schemes, and spacious bathroom with separate shower.

The other rooms are equally spick-and-span but more traditional in appearance and décor, as is the bar-restaurant downstairs, where low-beamed ceilings, exposed stone walls and flagstones predominate. The lighter, airier back room, which leads out to the quiet courtyard, has been spruced up, making it a pleasant spot to enjoy the pub grub on offer. As well as acting as genial hosts, Val and Ged have used their experience in hospitality to iron out past niggles with the Bull, notably starting breakfast at 8.30am, and reducing the room rate if you don't want breakfast at all.

○ Open all year 🔁 In centre of Charlbury. Nearest train station: Charlbury. Private car park 🛏 3 double, 1 suite; all with hair-dryer, TV, DVD ⊘ Restaurant, bar, lounge, garden; conferences and social functions; leisure facilities nearby ⅙ No wheelchair access ● No children under 5; no dogs; no smoking in bedrooms ⊏ Delta, MasterCard, Switch, Visa £ Double £75, suite £85; deposit required. Set Sun L £18.50; alc L, D £20; light meals available ③ FOR ②

CHATTON   Northumberland map 10

Old Manse

New Road, Chatton, Alnwick NE66 5PU
TEL: (01668) 215343
EMAIL: chattonbb@aol.com
WEB SITE: www.oldmansechatton.co.uk

Grand Victorian house run with friendly charm and handy for exploring the countryside and coast

Christine Brown's imposing Victorian manse sits in serene Northumbrian countryside, surrounded by secluded gardens with a fishpond and summerhouse, and still just a short drive from coastal sights such as Bamburgh Castle and Holy Island. Inside, rooms are generously sized, with high

ceilings and plenty of period style. The sitting room has antiques, huge windows and red leather chesterfields, while the breakfast room opens through French windows onto a balustraded patio – great for tea and home-baked scones and cakes in good weather. There are just two bedrooms, furnished with a homely chintzy style: upstairs, the Rosedale room has a four-poster and a double aspect that gives splendid views and, on the ground floor, the flowery Buccleuch suite comes with its own

sitting room and a private patio entrance, which makes for a dog-friendly hideaway. You don't need to roam far and wide to find evening sustenance either: the village inn is just 200 metres away.

◑ Open all year   ◿ At east end of Chatton village, 5 miles west of A1 on B6348. Private car park   🛌 1 four-poster, 1 suite; family rooms available; both with hair-dryer, TV, VCR, CD player   ✓ Breakfast room, sitting room, conservatory, garden   ♿ No wheelchair access; 1 step into hotel, 1 step into breakfast room, 1 ground-floor bedroom   ● No children under 12; dogs in 1 bedroom only; no smoking   ▭ None accepted   £ Single occupancy £32 to £49, four-poster/suite £60 to £64, family room £75 to £79; deposit required

---

CHEDDLETON Staffordshire   map 5

Choir Cottage & Choir House

Ostlers Lane, Cheddleton, Nr Leek ST13 7HS
TEL: (01538) 360561
EMAIL: enquiries@choircottage.co.uk
WEB SITE: www.choircottage.co.uk

Welcoming owners and pleasing bedrooms close to the old town

From the secluded heart of this historic village an old hollow way weaves up to this welcoming B&B, which sits at the edge of a more modern development. Here two worlds come together rather than collide, with the tiny seventeenth-century cottage (whose rent once provided for choir gowns) nestling comfortably beside the sympathetic 1970s house. Two of the three bedrooms are situated in the cottage and therefore have

slightly more character – especially the Pine Room, whose sleeping area is reached up a short flight of wooden steps – but all of them are well decorated and furnished and come with pleasing en-suite facilities and their own entrances. A conservatory, lounge and breakfast room in the house are all tastefully furnished in beige and cream and offer views out over the Churnet valley.

◑ Open all year   ◿ 3 miles south of Leek; in Cheddleton, turn off A520 opposite Red Lion Inn into Hollow Lane; left (200 yards after church) into Ostlers Lane; cottage is on right. Private car park   🛌 1 double, 1 four-poster, 1 family room; all with hair-dryer, TV; some with room service, direct-dial telephone, trouser press   ✓ Breakfast room, lounge, conservatory, garden   ♿ No wheelchair access; 2 steps into hotel, 1 step into breakfast room, 2 ground-floor bedrooms   ● No dogs; no smoking   ▭ None accepted   £ Single occupancy of double £35 to £45, double £60, four-poster £60 to £65, family room £85 to £95; deposit required

---

CHELTENHAM Gloucestershire   map 5

Alias Hotel Kandinsky

Bayshill Road, Cheltenham GL50 3AS
TEL: (01242) 527788   FAX: (01242) 226412
EMAIL: info@hotelkandinsky.com
WEB SITE: www.hotelkandinsky.com

Genteel town villa transformed into an eclectic contemporary hotel

While Cheltenham has never had a reputation as one of England's racier locations, apart from the race festival of course, there's no doubt that some of its older inhabitants have a tale or two to tell about life in some of the more exotic quarters of the world. Certainly the eccentric style of Alias Kandinsky, part of Nigel Chapman's chain, evokes memories of the Raj mixed with contemporary urban flavours. Balinese puppets hang behind the reception desk,

next to a Lord Charles ventriloquist dummy, while guests can slump into a leather sofa that has seen a bit of action in its time. Switching mood, Café Paradiso is all spotlighting and stripped floors, with a pizza oven flaming away in the corner. However, one visitor was not impressed by the food or the standard of service – 'we were looked after by a variety of young staff who didn't have a clue', was the verdict. Each bedroom has a print by the Russian abstract artist Wassily Kandinsky and a tonally matching bedspread. The rooms are not large, but have smart bathrooms and neat modern touches, such as sisal flooring.

○ Open all year ⑦ In centre of Cheltenham. Nearest train station: Cheltenham. Private car park 🅿 8 single, 26 twin, 14 double, 2 suites; all with room service, hair-dryer, direct-dial telephone, modem line, TV, VCR, CD player; trouser press on request ✅ Restaurant, 2 bars, 3 lounges, conservatory, games room, garden; conferences; leisure facilities nearby; cots, highchairs, babysitting, baby-listening ♿ No wheelchair access; 7 steps into hotel, 5 ground-floor bedrooms, lift ● No smoking in restaurant ☐ Amex, Delta, Diners, MasterCard, Switch, Visa £ Single £75, single occupancy of twin/double £90 to 105, twin/double £90 to £105, suite £115; deposit required. Continental B £8, cooked B £11; alc L, D £25 (rates valid till Feb 2005). Special breaks available

Georgian House

77 Montpellier Terrace, Cheltenham GL50 1XA
TEL: (01242) 515577 FAX: (01242) 545929
EMAIL: penny@georgianhouse.net
WEB SITE: www.georgianhouse.net

Intimate Regency terraced B&B with a friendly welcome

When Alex Gamez first came to Britain armed with an economics degree he took a job at the Dorchester in London – and has found himself involved in the hotel business ever since. Nowadays, with wife Penny, he runs this B&B with pride and attention to detail. The delightful terraced house – built in 1807 – speaks for itself, with a tidy front garden and an ironwork porch at the front door. The public rooms are simply decorated with a smattering of antiques and stripped floorboards covered by oriental rugs. Napoleonic prints line the walls of the narrow hallway up to the bedrooms. The best of these is probably the four-poster, larger than the others, with pale lemon walls and a bathroom concealed behind mirrored sliding doors. The other rooms have compact bathrooms, but have enough room for two small armchairs. Each bathroom has an amusing theme such as frogs or pigs pictured on the tiles.

○ Closed Chr & New Year ⑦ Montpellier Terrace is on section of A40 nearest town centre; from west, Georgian House is on right after Montpellier Gardens. Nearest train station: Cheltenham. Private parking in 2 garages 🅿 2 double, 1 four-poster; all with hair-dryer, trouser press, direct-dial telephone, modem line, TV ✅ Breakfast room, drawing room; leisure facilities nearby ♿ No wheelchair access ● No children under 16; no dogs; no smoking ☐ Amex, Delta, Diners, MasterCard, Switch, Visa £ Single occupancy of double £55, double £75, four-poster £85; deposit required

Hotel on the Park

38 Evesham Road, Cheltenham GL52 2AH
TEL: (01242) 518898   FAX: (01242) 511526
EMAIL: stay@hotelonthepark.co.uk
WEB SITE: www.hotelonthepark.com

A Regency villa of grand proportions with equally grand décor

This hotel could be said to be owner Darryl Gregory's labour of love, as for the past 14 years he has constantly tweaked and updated things to produce something gloriously opulent. There's a very bold masculine style to the décor, with swagged curtains in deep, dark colours and striped wallpapers – black and white might not be everyone's choice, but it works well here. The bar is the latest to receive a decadent makeover. There is plenty of humour as well, with a huge teddy bear sitting at one table in the restaurant, and the hotel cat, Emily, portrayed in the mural of the Pittville pump rooms, which are just across the park from the hotel. Bedrooms are individually styled and come with flat-screen TVs as standard, and often stand-alone baths in the bathrooms. William Clifford, a jockey-themed bedroom, now has an added piece of indulgence with a state-of-the-art chromatherapy steam room and foot spa. Perhaps it will come in useful for a jockey wanting to lose a few pounds quickly – the racecourse is very close.

◗ Open all year ⤢ From the town centre one-way system, follow signs for Evesham. Hotel is ½ mile out of town, on left, opposite park. Nearest train station: Cheltenham. Private car park ⛬ 4 twin/double, 6 double, 1 four-poster, 1 suite; all with room service, hair-dryer, direct-dial telephone, modem line, TV, DVD, CD player; some with trouser press ✓ Restaurant, bar/lounge, library, garden; conferences and social functions ⎔ No wheelchair access ◖ No children under 8; no dogs; no smoking in bedrooms ▭ Amex, Delta, Diners, MasterCard, Switch, Visa £ Single occupancy of twin/double from £87, twin/double from £112, four-poster £162, suite £142; deposit required. Continental B £7.50, cooked B £9.50; set L £21, D £30; light meals available. Special breaks available ③FOR②

Milton House Hotel

12 Bayshill Road, Royal Parade, Cheltenham GL50 3AY
TEL: (01242) 582601   FAX: (01242) 222326
EMAIL: info@miltonhousehotel.co.uk
WEB SITE: www.miltonhousehotel.co.uk

Centrally located B&B with hotel-style standards

It's five years since Claude Cittadino swapped the high-rolling pleasures of Monaco for the subtler delights of Cheltenham, and his task of transforming this elegant terraced house is showing signs of matching his ambitious aims. Although this is a B&B, genial Claude brings hotel standards to everything he does, as is reflected in the sharp white tablecloths and the pelmeted curtains in the breakfast room.

A touch of glamour is added by signed photos of Riviera celebrities. Guests relaxing in the tent-like coffee lounge have good views through picture windows over the patio garden, which shelters the bust of a Greek god. Bedrooms have high ceilings and are spick and span, usually with inset bathrooms containing either a small bath or shower. Parking spaces at both the front and back add to the convenience of the central location.

◗ Closed mid-Dec to mid-Jan ⤢ In town centre, close to Montpellier Street roundabout on A40. Nearest train station: Cheltenham. Private car park ⛬ 2 single, 1 twin/double, 4 double, 1 four-poster; all with hair-dryer, direct-dial telephone, TV ✓ Breakfast room, bar, lounge, conservatory, garden; leisure facilities nearby ⎔ No wheelchair access ◖ No children under 8; no dogs; smoking in conservatory only ▭ Amex, Delta, MasterCard, Switch, Visa £ Single £60, single occupancy of twin/double £70, twin/double £95 to £104, four-poster £115; deposit required

Green Bough Hotel

60 Hoole Road, Chester CH2 3NL
TEL: (01244) 326241   FAX: (01244) 326265
EMAIL: luxury@greenbough.co.uk
WEB SITE: www.greenbough.co.uk

Upwardly mobile small hotel, a superior base for exploring historic Chester

Continual improvements are the watchword at Philip and Janice Martin's civilised, much-acclaimed Victorian hotel a mile from the city centre. At first glance, not much distinguishes Green Bough from other guesthouse neighbours, strung out along an unremarkable and rather busy exit route. But the luxuriously furnished, immaculately kept interior of this red-brick, faux-timbered villa indicates what a pride the owners take in it. Original paintings of Italian scenes hang on the walls of the well-cushioned Champagne Bar, where a strikingly carved

eighteenth-century fireplace occupies centre stage. The Olive Tree Restaurant is another important facet of the Green Bough's hospitality – here Savoy-trained chef-patron Philip cooks up a storm of imaginative Mediterranean-influenced fare. The smartly restrained bedrooms and suites feature high-quality fabrics and bathroom fittings, with cast-iron or carved wooden beds, along with a resident teddy and a family of bathtime ducks. A decked roof garden adds an outdoor dimension in summer.

◑ Closed Chr & New Year ⏏ Leave M53 at Junction 12 and follow A56 towards Chester; hotel is ½ mile on right. Nearest train station: Chester. Private car park ⛘ 1 twin/double, 1 four-poster, 6 suites; all with room service, hair-dryer, direct-dial telephone, TV; some with trouser press, VCR, CD player, DVD ✅ Restaurant, bar/lounge, roof garden; conferences and social functions; leisure facilities nearby ♿ Wheelchair access to hotel (ramp) and restaurant, National Accessible Scheme: mobility impairment M2, 3 ground-floor bedrooms. Disabled parking ● No children under 12; no dogs; no smoking 💳 Amex, Delta, Diners, MasterCard, Switch, Visa £ Single occupancy of twin/double £100, twin/double from £145, four-poster £185, suite £250; deposit required. Set D £25; alc D £45; light meals available. Special breaks available

---

CHESTER-LE-STREET Co Durham · map 10

Lumley Castle

Chester-le-Street DH3 4NX
TEL: 0191-389 1111   FAX: 0191-387 1437
EMAIL: reservations@lumleycastle.com
WEB SITE: www.lumleycastle.com

Luxury with a light-hearted touch in a medieval castle

Lumley Castle is an authentic and imposing pile whose tumultuous history stretches back to the fourteenth century when the bold and dashing Sir Ralph Lumley earned his knighthood through bravery in battle, rather than by selling hit singles or making donations to political party funds. Modern-day 'Knights of Lumley Castle' will have achieved their temporary title by paying a small bounty in exchange for a package of exclusive offers and incentives. Far from being a stuffy stately-home hotel, this has staff who are friendly and professional, some kitted out in period costume to add to the flavour of antiquity that the castle already has in spades. There are creaky floors, spiral staircases, secretive passageways and atmospherically lit rooms; and there is, of course, a ghost too. Opulent fabrics, antiques and rich colour schemes make bedrooms memorably comfortable. Dinner varies from a full-on medieval banquet amid armour and pennants in the Elizabethan Hall, or a more intimate experience beneath the arches of the Black Knight restaurant.

◑ Closed 24 to 26 Dec, 1 Jan ⏏ Leave northbound A1(M) at Junction 63 and follow signs for riverside and Lumley Castle. Nearest train station: Chester-le-Street. Private car park ⛘ 8 single, 2 twin, 10 twin/double, 26 double, 10 four-poster, 2 family rooms, 1 suite; all with room service, hair-dryer, trouser press, direct-dial telephone, TV; some with modem line ✅ Restaurant, 2 dining rooms, bar, lounge, library, games room, garden; conferences and social functions; civil wedding licence; leisure facilities nearby; early suppers for children; cots, highchairs, babysitting, baby-listening ♿ No wheelchair access ● No dogs; no smoking in some bedrooms 💳 Amex, Delta, Diners, MasterCard, Switch, Visa £ Single from £115, twin/double from £160, four-poster/family room from £225, suite from £325; deposit required. Continental B £9; set L £18.50, D £30; alc D £40; light meals available; service incl. Special breaks available ③FOR②

CHETTLE Dorset · map 2

Castleman Hotel

Chettle, Blandford Forum DT11 8DB
TEL: (01258) 830096   FAX: (01258) 830051
EMAIL: chettle@globalnet.co.uk
WEB SITE: www.castlemanhotel.co.uk

Delightfully unstuffy atmosphere in grand surroundings

Don't judge a book, or a hotel, by its exterior, you might say when visiting Edward Bourke and Barbara Garnsworthy's restaurant-with-rooms. The façade doesn't promise much but once you're inside, any doubts are overturned by a winning combination of interesting features and relaxing comforts. The Victorian oak library has an impressive Jacobean fireplace – a nice spot for after-dinner coffee – while the lounge is all deep sofas and comfort. Dining takes place underneath a magnificently ornate ceiling with a menu that covers a good range – and includes plenty of local specialities too, particularly in game and fish. Bedrooms might not quite match the downstairs grandeur, but with antique furnishings, smart bathrooms and bags of space they are worthy elements of the whole.

○ Closed 25 & 26 Dec, Feb ⛶ Chettle is signposted from A354 (Blandford to Salisbury road); hotel is signposted in village. Private car park 🚗 1 twin, 6 double, 1 four-poster; all with hair-dryer, direct-dial telephone, TV ⊘ Restaurant, bar, lounge, library, garden; early suppers for children; cots, highchairs, baby-listening ⑁ No wheelchair access ● No dogs; no smoking in restaurant and some public rooms ▭ MasterCard, Switch, Visa £ Single occupancy of twin/double £50; twin/double £75, four-poster £85; deposit required. Set L £18; alc D £23

CHILLATON Devon   map 1

Quither Mill

Quither, Chillaton, Tavistock PL19 0PZ
TEL: (01822) 860160 (AND FAX)
EMAIL: quither.mill@virgin.net
WEB SITE: www.quithermill.co.uk

Well-run and amiable small country house off the beaten track

The long lane down to the hamlet of Quither bodes well for anyone seeking peace and tranquillity. Buzzards stand guard on telegraph poles, and the only sound comes from flocks of sheep in the pastures. Jill and David Wright's mill is at the far end of the few houses, easily spotted because of the huge old wheel – repaired to working order by David, though the overshoot stream is long gone. Internally, the house is beautifully restored and finished: original beams and features mix well with period furniture and cosy décor. The bedrooms are all homely, with extra touches such as crowned beds, bathrobes and magazines. Meals are taken around a single polished table, and dinner is a set four courses offering top-notch home cooking and plenty of local ingredients. The atmosphere is quiet and sociable, and the Wrights make excellent hosts.

○ Closed Chr & New Year ⛶ From Tavistock (Bedford Square) follow Chillaton sign, forking left after 2 miles; after 3 miles, turn right for Quither. Private car park 🚗 1 twin, 1 twin/double, 2 double; all with hair-dryer, TV ⊘ Dining room, lounge, garden; leisure facilities nearby ⑁ No wheelchair access; 1 ground-floor bedroom ● No children under 12; no dogs; no smoking ▭ Delta, MasterCard, Switch, Visa £ Single occupancy of twin/double £53; twin/double £76; deposit required. Set D £21

Tor Cottage

Chillaton, Tavistock PL16 0JE
TEL: (01822) 860248   FAX: (01822) 860126
EMAIL: info@torcottage.co.uk
WEB SITE: www.torcottage.co.uk

Wonderful hospitality and seductively comfortable rooms at this rural B&B

Maureen Rowlatt has won every plaudit and trophy in the book since coming to this charming retreat of a cottage, but there is no laurel-resting here. This year a new cabin, 'Laughing Waters', comes into service and it makes a handsome addition to the distinguished roster of rooms on offer. Like the others it has a self-contained, intimate atmosphere but whereas Art Deco and Craftsmen's Garden are plush, this one has a sturdy, rustic feel with pine cladding, a broad verandah overlooking the stream and a fishing net if you fancy catching tiddlers. Up near the main cottage, Garden offers a different take, with a beautiful vaulted timber roof, sisal carpeting and natural colours. There's one room in the main cottage too – more traditionally country cottage in décor. Breakfasts are comprehensively excellent, but for evening meals you do have to venture out. 'Maureen and her staff are simply the best, with a genuine warmth,' sums up one typically satisfied customer.

○ Closed mid-Dec to mid-Jan ⛶ In Chillaton, with pub and post office on left, drive uphill towards Tavistock; after 300 yards, take right turning signposted 'Bridlepath, No Public Vehicular Access'; cottage is ½ mile along, through second gate. Private car park 🚗 1 twin, 3 double, 1 suite; all with room service, hair-dryer, fridge, TV, VCR, CD player; 1 with direct-dial telephone ⟨✓⟩ Breakfast room/conservatory, 2 lounges, garden; heated outdoor swimming pool; leisure facilities nearby ⟨♿⟩ No wheelchair access; 1 step into hotel, 1 step into breakfast room, 3 ground-floor bedrooms ⬤ No children under 14; no dogs; no smoking ⟨☐⟩ Delta, MasterCard, Switch, Visa ⟨£⟩ Single occupancy of twin/double £89, twin/double/suite £130; deposit required. Light meals available. Special breaks available

---

CHIPPING CAMPDEN Gloucestershire map 5

Cotswold House

The Square, Chipping Campden GL55 6AN
TEL: (01386) 840330 FAX: (01386) 840310
EMAIL: reception@cotswoldhouse.com
WEB SITE: www.cotswoldhouse.com

Opulence and up-to-the-minute style, at a price, in this impressive town mansion

Ian and Christa Taylor have always had big ambitions for Cotswold House and this year sees another leap towards a cool, urban style throughout. Plans were afoot to replace the polite country-house look in the lounge and entrance hall with something more in keeping with Julianna's Restaurant: kaleidoscopic wavy black and white carpet, bold art on the walls and warm-toned wood panelling. Another example is the Hicks brasserie, more in keeping with a scene from *Sex and the City* than *The Vicar of Dibley*, with its marble-topped bar and spotlighting. Bedrooms are similarly striking, with a smattering of antiques; the sharp bathrooms often have separate showers and mosaic tiling. While this is a fine period townhouse, the garden is most unexpected and stretches out with abundant borders and big plant pots. Off here are the converted cottages where rooms in the eaves have exposed beams. Guests can also request specific duvets, pillows and mini-bar items to suit their tastes. And for those who feel things are a still a bit restrained, there's the fabulous Old Grammar School suite, which Johnny Depp apparently found most to his liking on a recent visit.

◖ Open all year ⟨⧉⟩ Off High Street in Chipping Campden. Private car park ⟨🛏⟩ 1 single, 16 twin/double, 1 double, 1 four-poster, 2 suites; family rooms available; all with room service, hair-dryer, mini-bar, direct-dial telephone, fax, modem line, TV, CD player ⟨✓⟩ Restaurant, dining room, bar, lounge, garden; conferences and social functions; civil wedding licence; leisure facilities nearby; early suppers for children; cots, highchairs, babysitting ⟨♿⟩ No wheelchair access; 2 ground-floor bedrooms ⬤ No smoking in bedrooms ⟨☐⟩ Amex, MasterCard, Switch, Visa ⟨£⟩ Single £120 to £125, twin/double £215 to £250, four-poster £250 to £275, family room £250 to £285, suite £375 to £595; deposit required. Set L £20, D £30; alc L £30, D £40; light meals available; service incl

King's Arms [NEW ENTRY]

The Square, Chipping Campden GL55 6AW
TEL: (01386) 840256 FAX: (01386) 841598
EMAIL: info@thekingsarmshotel.com
WEB SITE: www.thekingsarmshotel.com

A modern take on a small village hotel, with smart bedrooms and casual dining

This grand townhouse, dating back to the seventeenth century, has been a hotel since 1927 but just recently it has had a jazzy makeover. Step through the door and you are faced by a curved wooden bar and an improbably outsized blackboard offering plates of charcuterie and delicatessen goodies. The choice then is between the casual brasserie area with stripped floor, bare tables, sofas, armchairs and mood music, or the bistro-style restaurant. Locally sourced, modern British food is served among beamed ceilings and more traditional wooden seating. Bedrooms fulfil the promise of 'no-chintz zone' with muted tones, stylish bedroom lights and chunky wooden furniture. Bathrooms are a highlight, featuring stone-tiled floors and good-quality fittings. Each room comes with a DVD player and there is a free library of films to choose from.

○ Open all year 🛋 In centre of Chipping Campden. Private car park 🛏 3 twin/double, 9 double; all with TV, DVD, CD player ✓ Restaurant, bar, private dining rooms, garden; conferences and social functions; leisure facilities nearby; cots, highchairs, baby-listening ♿ No wheelchair access ● No smoking in restaurant ▭ Amex, MasterCard, Switch, Visa £ Single occupancy of twin/double £60 to £115, twin/double £70 to £120. Alc L £20, D £22.50; light meals available. Special breaks available ③FOR②

CHITTLEHAMHOLT Devon   map 1

Highbullen

Chittlehamholt, Umberleigh EX37 9HD
TEL: (01769) 540561   FAX: (01769) 540492
EMAIL: info@highbullen.co.uk
WEB SITE: www.highbullen.co.uk

Golfing heaven of a country house but plenty more besides

Full marks to Highbullen for its dedication to the cause of the sports hotel. These days that makes for a pretty impressive line-up when it comes to facilities: the Pavilion development boasts indoor golf putting, a 20-metre pool with Jacuzzi facing a magnificent view towards Dartmoor, and even a golf simulator where you can play any of the world's great courses. Elsewhere there are indoor tennis courts, a sauna, and an 18-hole golf course – golf is the reason most guests come here. These are just the new facilities – across the courtyard is the original Victorian Gothic pile of a house, complete with billiard table and cellar bar. Bedrooms in this part are the best bet, being substantially grander than those in the newer annexes.

○ Open all year 🛋 From M5 junction 27 take A361 to South Molton, then B3226. Turn off after about 5 miles to Chittlehamholt; hotel is ½ mile beyond village, on right. Private car park 🛏 2 single, 40 twin/double; all with room service, hair-dryer, direct-dial telephone, TV ✓ 2 restaurants, 2 bars, lounge, library, conservatory, 2 games rooms, garden; conferences; social functions; civil wedding licence; gym, spa, tennis, indoor and outdoor heated swimming pools ♿ No wheelchair access; 2 steps into hotel, 15 steps into restaurant, 1 ground-floor bedroom ● No children under 8; no dogs; no smoking in restaurants ▭ Delta, MasterCard, Switch, Visa £ Single £78, twin/double from £100. Cooked B £8.50; set L from £15, D £25; light meals available; service incl

---

CHOLMONDELEY Cheshire   map 7

Cholmondeley Arms ▐ NEW ENTRY ▌

Cholmondeley, Nr Malpas SY14 8HN
TEL: (01829) 720300   FAX: (01829) 720123
EMAIL: guy@cholmondeleyarms.co.uk
WEB SITE: www.cholmondeleyarms.co.uk

A thoroughly comfortable and civilised pub in an unusual schoolroom setting

This Victorian building may have suffered some sense of rejection when its services as the village school were deemed surplus to requirements in 1982, but its fortunes were completely reversed after its imaginative conversion to the Cholmondeley Arms half a dozen years later. Now aficionados savvy enough to pronounce it 'chumley' beat a path to its barge-boarded gables, confident of receiving a warm welcome from the affable licensees Guy and Carolyn Ross-Lowe, plus some fine ales and decent gastrogrub (game and pickled walnut terrine or devilled kidneys on granary toast, perhaps). The pub's original purpose permeates the lofty, galleried interior, decorated in pinks and greens and a homely mix of simple, authentic-looking wooden furnishings, with open fires, china display plates, alcove bookshelves and old sporting prints.

Bedrooms are provided in the former schoolmaster's house across the yard, unfancy but light and pleasing, in plain colours. Children are still most welcome.

❍ Open all year   🔁 On A49 between Whitchurch and Tarporley; marked 'Bickley Moss' on map. Private car park 🛏️ 1 twin, 4 doubles, 1 family room; all with hair-dryer, direct-dial telephone, TV   ✅ Restaurant, bar, garden; social functions; early suppers for children; cots, highchairs   ♿ No wheelchair access   ⬤ No smoking in bedrooms   ⊟ Delta, MasterCard, Switch, Visa   £ Single occupancy of twin/double £50, twin/double £65, family room from £75. Alc L, D £18; light meals available. Special breaks available (3FOR2)

CHULMLEIGH Devon   map 1

Old Bakehouse

South Molton Street, Chulmleigh EX18 7BW
TEL: (01769) 580074 (AND FAX)
EMAIL: mail@colinandholly.co.uk
WEB SITE: www.colinandholly.co.uk

Well-kept and welcoming small restaurant-with-rooms

Housed in two buildings – the old bakery and shop – Colin and Holly Burls' place is an attractive and carefully run operation. The restaurant has a country-cottage style with low beams, pewter mugs and dried flowers, but look more closely and hints of sophistication appear – the blackboard menu carries dishes such as fillet of plaice in a Beaujolais and port sauce, or duck breast marinated in honey, soy and ginger. There is one bedroom above the restaurant – beams and crooked walls give it a bit more character, though one reader found it 'rather cramped'. The other bedrooms are in a separate building at the back. These are also compact, but there is a small lounge area downstairs and plenty of thoughtful extras: good tea tray, books and bathroom requisites. Not a place to set the pulses racing, one correspondent opined, 'but food was good and hosts friendly.'

❍ Open all year; restaurant closed Sun & Mon eves   🔁 From A377 heading north, turn right 1 mile after Eggesford towards Chulmleigh; hotel is opposite post office in village. Nearest train station: Eggesford 🛏️ 2 twin, 2 double; family rooms available; all with room service, hair-dryer, TV; 1 with trouser press   ✅ Restaurant, bar, lounge, garden; social functions; leisure facilities nearby   ♿ Wheelchair access to hotel (2 steps down) and restaurant (2 steps down), 1 ground-floor bedroom   ⬤ No children under 5; no dogs; no smoking   ⊟ Delta, MasterCard, Switch, Visa   £ Single occupancy of twin/double £33 to £37, twin/double £52 to £62, family room £62 to £72; deposit required. Alc L £14, D £21.50; service incl. Special breaks available

---

CLANFIELD Oxfordshire   map 2

Plough at Clanfield

Bourton Road, Clanfield, Bampton OX18 2RB
TEL: (01367) 810222   FAX: (01367) 810596
EMAIL: theploughatclanfield@hotmail.com
WEB SITE: www.theplough.tablesir.com

A winning mix of old and new in an untouristy corner of the Cotswolds

We are often advised never to judge books by their covers, and the same principle could apply to hotels, especially this one. Pulling up outside this Elizabethan manor house, with wisteria trailing over the aged, golden stone between leaded windows, you might expect a super-plush, super-pricey experience awaiting you inside. But, despite its handy location on the southern edge of the honeypot Cotswolds, the Plough offers period charm at an affordable rate. The interior is a low-key, homely affair, with beams and pillars adding a touch of character to the public rooms, while in the bedroom department there's a hard choice to be made. You could opt for the creaky floors and old-world charm of rooms in the original part of the house, or go for the bigger, smarter ones in the modern (but very tastefully done) extension. We'd plump for the latter, as some of the older rooms need a mini-makeover, particularly the bathrooms, whereas the newer rooms' freshness and comfort more than compensate for the lack of beams. John and Rosemary Hodges continue to infuse the whole proceedings with affable bonhomie.

◗ Closed 24 Dec to 7 Jan; restaurant closed Mon eve 🗲 At junction of A4095 and B4020 between Witney and Faringdon, on edge of Clanfield. Private car park 🛏 2 twin/double, 6 double, 3 four-poster, 1 suite; all with room service, hair-dryer, trouser press, direct-dial telephone, modem line, TV; some with mini-bar, DVD ✔ Restaurant, bar, lounge, garden; conferences; social functions; cots, highchairs ♿ Wheelchair access to hotel and restaurant, 3 ground-floor bedrooms, 1 room specially equipped for disabled people ● No children under 12 exc babes in arms; no dogs or smoking in bedrooms ▭ Amex, Delta, Diners, MasterCard, Switch, Visa £ Single occupancy of twin/double £83 to £90, twin/double £120, four-poster £135, suite £140; deposit required. Set L £19.50, D £28.50; light meals available. Special breaks available

---

CLEARWELL Gloucestershire   map 2

Tudor Farmhouse [NEW ENTRY]

High Street, Clearwell, Nr Coleford GL16 8JS
TEL: (01594) 833046   FAX: (01594) 837093
EMAIL: info@tudorfarmhousehotel.co.uk
WEB SITE: www.tudorfarmhousehotel.co.uk

New owners have made noticeable improvements to this village hotel

After their high-profile appearance in the fly-on-the-wall BBC documentary *Living the Dream*, members of the Evans family are relieved to find themselves back to relative sanity at the Tudor Farmhouse. As well as picking her way past cameras, daughter Hari Evans has been overseeing refurbishment of bedrooms since the family took over the hotel last year. This includes the attractive Cottage suite, which has a fancy new bathroom, and an antique pine bed up the stairs. Other rooms are spread between the medieval farmhouse and the Barn, reached via a pretty ornamental garden. Here too, new furnishings are in place and bathrooms are being replaced, making the room rates rather good value. A small lounge, bar and conservatory area are available for guests, while the restaurant is a larger room with rough stone walls, tapestry chairs and exposed beams. One diner told us the food was excellent, but the speed of service was less so. Guests can also relax in the knowledge that the film makers have no intention of appearing unannounced to see how things are going.

◗ Closed 24 to 26 Dec 🗲 Leave M48 at Junction 2 (Chepstow) and take A466 north through Tintern and Llandogo; turn right after crossing bridge; continue to end, turning left into village; turn right at war memorial; hotel is on left. Private car park 🛏 2 twin, 4 twin/double, 11 double, 3 four-poster, 1 family room, 1 suite; all with room service, hair-dryer, direct-dial telephone, TV; some with modem line, VCR, CD player ✔ Restaurant, dining room, bar, lounge, conservatory, garden; conferences and social functions; leisure facilities nearby; cots, highchairs, baby-listening ♿ Wheelchair access to hotel and restaurant, WC, 7 ground-floor bedrooms ● No dogs in public rooms; no smoking in restaurant and most bedrooms ▭ Amex, Delta, MasterCard, Switch, Visa £ Single occupancy of twin/double £55, twin/double £60 to £80, four-poster £80 to £120, family room £110, suite £150; deposit required. Set L £13; alc L £15, D £25; light meals available; service incl. Special breaks available (3FOR2)

CLEY NEXT THE SEA Norfolk   map 6

Cley Mill

Cley next the Sea, Holt NR25 7RP
TEL: (01263) 740209 (AND FAX)
WEB SITE: www.cleymill.co.uk

Whimsical windmill retreat – but mind the visitors!

The tower of a windmill is certainly an unusual place to bed down for the night, but that's exactly what you'll be doing if you take one of the round rooms in this highly atmospheric little hotel. The tower rooms are probably the pick – if only because of their quirky shape and the glimpses of the sails from the windows, but the others are actually in older parts of the building. Wherever you sleep, you get to enjoy the cosy circular sitting room with sofas clustered around the fireplace, antiques trying to fit themselves up against the walls and a window out on to the marshy grassland of the north Norfolk coast. Breakfast and dinner are taken communally around a row of pine tables, with a set three-course menu in the evenings.

Potential guests should be warned that the mill is open to the public, so you might want to keep your bedroom curtains drawn if you want to protect your privacy during the day.

❍ Open all year ⚡ Follow A149 between Wells-next-the-Sea and Sheringham, enter village; on High Street, turn left at brown sign to Cley Mill. Private car park 🚗 3 twin/double, 5 double; family rooms available; some with TV ✅ Dining room, honesty bar, lounge, garden; social functions; civil wedding licence; early suppers for children ♿ Wheelchair access to hotel (1 step) and dining room (1 step), 5 ground-floor bedrooms ⬤ No smoking in bedrooms ▭ Delta, Diners, MasterCard, Switch, Visa £ Single occupancy of twin/double £76 to £120, twin/double £76 to £120, family room £86 to £130; deposit required. Set D £17.50; service incl. Special breaks available

---

CLIMPING West Sussex   map 3

Bailiffscourt

Climping Street, Climping BN17 5RW
TEL: (01903) 723511   FAX: (01903) 718987
EMAIL: bailiffscourt@hshotels.co.uk
WEB SITE: www.hshotels.co.uk

A fine 'medieval' hotel in a dreamy setting with newly added contemporary bedrooms and a swanky health centre

This medieval-style hamlet of mellow stone, flint-faced, thatched and half-timbered buildings surrounded by idyllic water meadows is an architectural deception with much less of a past than the mullioned windows, Gothic archways and heavy wooden doors would suggest. With the help of leading historians, Bailiffscourt was pieced together from original features taken from ancient houses, and the result is both fascinating and convincing. The smart public areas feel suitably medieval, characterised by uneven floors, heavy beams and bare stone flags and stuffed with fine antiques and tapestries. But Bailiffscourt is no museum piece pickled in aspic; instead there's a thoroughly warm and inviting atmosphere with a lived-in feel, the sort of place where guests can comfortably speak in less than hushed tones and unwind on huge squishy sofas. Bedrooms in the Court House and surrounding buildings are beautifully stylish and luxuriously appointed, several with four-posters and feature bathrooms. Most reflect the hotel's medieval theme, while those in a recently added outbuilding are of a similar high quality but unashamedly contemporary, with leather or mirrored furniture, sliding fabric-covered shutters and sparkling modern bathrooms. Guests also have access to a newly built health centre with top-notch facilities, though with its Canadian oak beams and vaulted ceilings reflecting a contemporary design with a traditional twist, it's worth visiting as much for its architecture as for its swimming pools, hot tub and treatment rooms.

❍ Open all year ⚡ 2 miles south of Arundel, off the A259, following signs for Climping Beach. Nearest train stations: Arundel and Littlehampton. Private car park 🚗 1 twin, 4 twin/double, 21 double, 7 four-poster, 6 suites; all with room service, hair-dryer, direct-dial telephone, TV; some with trouser press, VCR, CD player ✅ Restaurant, bar, 4 lounges, games room, garden; conferences; social functions; civil wedding licence; gym, spa, tennis, indoor and outdoor heated swimming pools; leisure facilities nearby; early suppers for children; cots, highchairs, toys, babysitting, baby-listening ♿ Wheelchair access to hotel and restaurant (1 step), 14 ground-floor bedrooms, 1 room specially equipped for disabled people ⬤ No children under 7 in restaurant eves; no smoking in restaurant ▭ Amex, Delta, Diners, MasterCard, Switch, Visa £ Single occupancy of twin/double from £175, twin/double from £195, four-poster from £250, suite from £355; deposit required. Set L £18.50, D £43.50; light meals available. Special breaks available

map 7

Birches Mill

Clun, Craven Arms SY7 8NL
TEL: (01588) 640409 (AND FAX)
EMAIL: gill@birchesmill.fsnet.co.uk
WEB SITE: www.virtual-shropshire.co.uk/birchesmill

Idyllic setting for simple country pleasures and home cooking

It's little over a decade since Gill Della Casa and Andrew Farmer left city life to come to this riverside retreat by the River Unk. Birches Mill was a working water mill within living memory, but now is the venue for the couple's home cooking, plus the artistic talents of Andrew. Three acres of meadow and vegetable garden lead on to river walks. Inside, a big inglenook fireplace dominates the sitting room where guests can relax in wing armchairs and a high-backed sofa. Dinners are served by arrangement, guests eating together by candlelight, the ingredients often harvested straight from the garden. And at breakfast you can sample home-made jams as well. The bedrooms are cottagey in style, with in one room a Victorian brass bed and a roll-top bath rescued from the cow shed, and in the others touches such as a patchwork quilt and matting flooring.

Closed Nov to early Mar Leave Clun on an A488 to Bishops Castle; after village take first left signposted Bicton; at Bicton take second left (signposted Mainstone). Birches Mill is first right after Llanhedric Farm. Private car park 1 twin, 2 double; all with room service, hair-dryer Dining room, sitting room, garden No wheelchair access No children under 8; no dogs; no smoking None accepted Single occupancy of twin/double £42, twin/double £60 to £72; deposit required. Set D £25; light meals available; service incl

                                    map 1

New Inn

Coleford, Crediton EX17 5BZ
TEL: (01363) 84242 FAX: (01363) 85044
EMAIL: new-inn@reallyreal-group.com
WEB SITE: www.reallyreal-group.com

Good cooking and amiable atmosphere at this village inn

Coleford is a delightful huddle of thatched buildings, at the centre of which is the New Inn, so named because it dates back to only the thirteenth century, presumably. In fact the open-plan bar and dining area don't really harp upon its ancient origins, beyond the expected low beams, coppers collection and horse brasses. You are far more likely to note the unruly and noisy regular, Captain, who greets newcomers gustily and does various impersonations – he's quite good, for a parrot. Food here aims far higher than pub grub – wild boar pâté and blinis feature among the many starters, and lamb meatballs in lemon couscous and coq Dijon on the extensive list of main courses. Bedrooms offer reliable comfort among the roof beams and crooked walls; the woodchip wallpaper looks dated, but things are well-kept and smart. Watch out for Sebastian the friendly ghost: he moves things around occasionally.

Closed 25 and 26 Dec Travelling north from Exeter to Barnstaple on A377, 2 miles beyond Crediton turn left to Coleford. Private car park 1 twin, 4 double, 1 family room; all with hair-dryer, direct-dial telephone, TV Restaurant, bar, garden; cots, highchairs No wheelchair access No dogs in bedrooms; no smoking in restaurant or bedrooms Amex, Delta, Diners, MasterCard, Switch, Visa Single occupancy of twin/double £58 to £68; twin/double £72 to £82, family room £90; deposit required. Alc L, D £19; light meals available; service incl (3 FOR 2)

Report forms are at the back of the Guide; *write a letter or email us if you prefer. Our email address is:* whichhotelguide@which.net

COLERNE Wiltshire   map 2

Lucknam Park

Colerne, Chippenham SN14 8AZ
TEL: (01225) 742777 FAX: (01225) 743536
EMAIL: reservations@lucknampark.co.uk
WEB SITE: www.lucknampark.co.uk

Gently traditional country house with fine sports facilities

The straight mile of beeches and limes is a stirring taster for this seventeenth-century country house, which has managed to survive several changes of ownership and various upheavals over the centuries (in the war Spitfires were parked under the beeches to hide them from the Luftwaffe). Once inside the elegant reception, the atmosphere is quiet and muted, with lovely views from the rooms over the 500 acres of lawns and parkland. Beautiful antique furniture is dotted throughout the hotel, notably in the panelled library and drawing room, which are supremely refined and tasteful. Bedrooms edge things gently towards contemporary with Bose radio/CD players in all, and subtle modern fabrics rather than the chintz you might expect. Five of the rooms have log fires. Plans are afoot to extend the spa facilities, but at the time of inspection there was a fine 20-metre indoor pool with Jacuzzi. Equestrianism is also a speciality, with 25 horses stabled and an Olympic-standard cross-country course.

◐ Open all year 🔲 6 miles north-east of Bath; ¼ mile from crossroads for Colerne. Private car park 🅿 14 twin/double, 13 double, 2 four-poster, 13 suites; all with room service, hair-dryer, direct-dial telephone, modem line, TV, CD player; some with mini-bar, VCR, DVD ✅ 2 restaurants, 1 dining room, bar service, 3 lounges, library, 2 games rooms, gardens; conferences and social functions; civil wedding licence; gym, spa, tennis, heated indoor swimming pool; early suppers for children; cots, highchairs, toys, playroom, babysitting ♿ Wheelchair access to hotel (ramp) and restaurant, WC, 4 ground-floor bedrooms ⬤ No children under 8 in restaurants eves; no dogs; no smoking in restaurants 🔲 Amex, Delta, Diners, MasterCard, Switch, Visa £ Single occupancy of twin/double £225, twin/double from £225, four-poster from £365, family room from £390, suite from £490; deposit required. Continental B £12, cooked B £18; set Sun L £30; alc D £57.50; light meals available; service incl. Special breaks available (3FOR2)

COLN ST ALDWYNS Gloucestershire   map 2

New Inn at Coln

Coln St Aldwyns, Cirencester GL7 5AN
TEL: (01285) 750651 FAX: (01285) 750657
EMAIL: stay@new-inn.co.uk
WEB SITE: www.new-inn.co.uk

A smart country hotel with a pleasing village pub atmosphere

It may have once been an Elizabethan coaching inn, but this creeper-clad building has grown into a far more ambitious operation since those days. Thankfully it has retained the conviviality of a country pub while catering for visitors in search of good food. New owners Roger and Angela Kimmett show every sign of continuing the high standards of their predecessors, and their two daughters were rallying to the cause as well when we inspected. After many years in the USA the Kimmetts have settled in quickly to their new life, and Angela has already made her mark, with examples of her artistic work hanging on the walls. A traditional pub area with a red tiled floor and blackboard menu leads through to a bright, cosy restaurant with pale tartan carpet and lemon walls. Between here and the bar is a small guest lounge with smart new sofas. Bedrooms, in the eaves of the house, are neat and compact with good-quality fabrics. Winson is a superior double with a bathroom on a lower level.

◐ Open all year 🔲 Off main Cirencester to Burford road; follow signs from Bibury. Private car park 🅿 1 single, 2 twin, 8 double, 3 four-poster; all with room service, hair-dryer, trouser press, direct-dial telephone, TV ✅ 2 restaurants, bar, lounge, patio; conferences; leisure facilities nearby ♿ No wheelchair access ⬤ No children under 10; dogs £10 per night; smoking in bar only 🔲 Amex, Diners, MasterCard, Switch, Visa

£ Single £90, single occupancy of twin/double £104, twin/double £120, four-poster £155; deposit required. Bar L £20; set L £24.50, D £35; light meals available. Special breaks available

---

COLWALL STONE Herefordshire map 5

Colwall Park

Walwyn Road, Colwall Stone, Nr Malvern WR13 6QG
TEL: (01684) 540000 FAX: (01684) 540847
EMAIL: hotel@colwall.com
WEB SITE: www.colwall.com

Smart village hotel with a good mix of original features and modern touches

Colwall Park welcomed its first guests in Edwardian days, as a purpose-built hotel in that period's favoured mock-Tudor style. Elgar's inspiration, the Malvern Hills, loom up close by and the hotel nestles in their folds next to the main road through the village – a rather grand building for the modest surroundings. Iain and Sarah Nesbitt are conscientious owners and have made more improvements in the last year. The restaurant now has a more contemporary style, with brown tones to complement the original wood panelling, plus iron chandeliers and steel candlesticks. Modern British menus feature starters such as shellfish minestrone with seared langoustines and fresh crab, followed by beef fillet with wild mushroom charlotte, foie gras and Madeira velouté, and then chocolate and amaretto crème brûlée. Other public rooms are agreeably smart and there's a separate smoker's lounge upstairs. The bigger bedrooms face the road rather than the lawned gardens at the back. Most have new, bright bathrooms and a good range of extras such as satellite TVs.

◑ Open all year ⬛ In centre of Colwall village on B4218 between Malvern and Ledbury. Nearest train station: Colwall. Private car park ⬛ 3 single, 7 twin, 10 double, 1 family room, 1 suite; all with room service, hairdryer, trouser press, direct-dial telephone, modem line, TV; some with VCR ✅ Restaurant, bar, 2 lounges, library, garden; conferences and social functions; leisure facilities nearby; early suppers for children; cots, highchairs, baby-listening ♿ No wheelchair access ⬤ Smoking in bar only ▭ MasterCard, Switch, Visa £ Single £65, single occupancy of twin/double £80, twin/double £110, family room/suite £150; deposit required. Set L £16; alc D £30; light meals available; service incl. Special breaks available (3FOR2)

CONISTON Cumbria map 8

Coniston Lodge

Station Road, Coniston LA21 8HH
TEL: (015394) 41201 (AND FAX)
EMAIL: info@coniston-lodge.com
WEB SITE: www.coniston-lodge.com

Cheerful, family-run guesthouse in a popular Lakeland touring base

This modern, creeper-clad house is built on stilts into a hillside, where it sits quietly just off the main street. It's an easy stroll to pubs or restaurants if Elizabeth Robinson isn't cooking (four-course dinners are available on Wednesday to Saturday only). The lounge and dining room are on the first floor, which opens on to a decked terrace. The busy décor may not suit everyone; every ledge, sill and pelmet is crowded with ornaments, horse brasses, dried flowers, china plates, corn dollies and so forth. Amid this array, a sharp eye may spot one or two interesting bits of memorabilia connected with Donald Campbell, a close family friend, whose fateful attempt on the world water-speed record took place on Coniston Water. Bedrooms, all named after local tarns, are light and well-sized, but rather dated and over-filled with ornaments. On our inspection visit, one badly stained upholstered headboard was due for cleaning or replacement.

◗ Open all year; dining room closed Sun to Tue eves 🔁 Leave A593 between Ambleside and Broughton-in-Furness at crossroads close to petrol station; turn uphill along Station Road; hotel is 50 metres on left. Private car park 🛏️ 3 twin, 2 double, 1 four-poster; all with hair-dryer, trouser press, direct-dial telephone, modem line, TV ✔ Dining room, lounge, garden 🚫 No wheelchair access ● No children under 10; no dogs; no smoking 🗂 Delta, MasterCard, Switch, Visa £ Single occupancy of twin/double £59, twin/double £97, four-poster £107; deposit required. Set D £23.50

CONSTANTINE Cornwall   map 1

Trengilly Wartha

Nancenoy, Constantine, Falmouth TR11 5RP
TEL: (01326) 340332   FAX: (01326) 341121
EMAIL: reception@trengilly.co.uk
WEB SITE: www.trengilly.co.uk

Peace, quiet and a great wine list at this secluded local

As close to the middle of nowhere as you're likely to find in crowded old England lies this multiple-award-winning local pub with rooms. Local because it's buzzing but not full of tourists, award-winning because it combines seclusion (the name means 'settlement above the trees'), a varied menu and a wine list that wouldn't be out of place in an upmarket restaurant, with over 220 wines by the bottle. The Trengilly Classics bar menu includes pub-lunch favourites like scampi and Cornish pasties, while the fixed-price restaurant menu (most dishes also available via the blackboard in the bar) gets more adventurous. Rooms are bright, with pine furniture, and are refreshingly free of frills and chintz. Watch out for the scaldingly hot water in the bathrooms!

◗ Open all year; restaurant closed 25 & 31 Dec 🔁 In Constantine, take Gweek road out of village, by Spar shop; hotel is signposted after 1 mile. Private car park 🛏️ 1 twin, 5 double, 2 family rooms; all with direct-dial telephone, TV; some with hairdryer ✔ Restaurant, bar, lounge, conservatory, garden; social functions; early suppers for children; cots, highchairs, toys, baby-listening 🚫 No wheelchair access; 3 steps into hotel, 3 steps into restaurant, 2 ground-floor bedrooms ● No smoking in some public rooms and some bedrooms 🗂 Amex, Delta, Diners, MasterCard, Switch, Visa £ Single occupancy of twin/double £49, twin/double £78 to £81, family room £110; deposit required. Bar L £8; set D £27; service incl. Special breaks available ③FOR②

COOKHAM DEAN Berkshire   map 3

Inn on the Green [NEW ENTRY]

The Old Cricket Common, Cookham Dean SL6 9NZ
TEL: (01628) 482638   FAX: (01628) 487474
EMAIL: reception@theinnonthegreen.com
WEB SITE: www.theinnonthegreen.com

New owners and a new lease of life for an old favourite

Since arriving in February 2003, Mark Fuller and (chef) Garry Hollihead have transformed this village restaurant-with-rooms into something rather special, waving a particularly stylish magic wand in all the rooms. Rich fabrics and artistic flourishes are offset by natural materials and soothing tones, so that, for example, the bar has stools with black velvet seats while the restaurant has rough-cut wood walls. Each of the nine bedrooms is individual in design: you could go for a Mexican style with a chunky wood bed and terracotta-tiled bathroom (Room 7) or one with a dramatic in-room bath decked out with electric blue tiles (Room 9). Even the smallest bedrooms in a converted coach house are perfectly finished, with smart black slate bathrooms and the same extras, such as DVD players, as the pricier ones. A small courtyard provides the ideal venue for outside dining on warm summer evenings.

◗ Open all year; restaurant closed Sun & Mon eves, Mon to Fri L 🔁 In Cookham Dean turn near war memorial into small lane; inn is signposted to the left. Private car park. Nearest train station: Cookham 🛏️ 8 double, 1 four-poster; all with room service, hair-dryer, direct-dial telephone, TV, CD player, DVD player; some with mini-bar ✔ Restaurant, dining room, bar, 2 lounges, conservatory; conferences; civil wedding licence; social functions; highchairs, baby-sitting, outdoor play area 🚹 Wheelchair access to hotel and restaurant, 4 ground-floor bedrooms ● None ⌐ Amex, Delta, MasterCard, Switch, Visa £ Double £140 to £180, four-poster £190. Set L £20, (Sun) £23.50; alc D £35. Special breaks available

---

CORFE CASTLE Dorset   map 2

Mortons House

45 East Street, Corfe Castle, Wareham BH20 5EE
TEL: (01929) 480988   FAX: (01929) 480820
EMAIL: stay@mortonshouse.co.uk
WEB SITE: www.mortonshouse.co.uk

Welcoming and hospitable atmosphere at this fine old house

An Elizabethan manor house in the heart of Corfe village, Mortons has a perfect location: handy for the ruined castle and the Purbeck coast. The two couples who own it – Andy and Ally Hageman, and Beverley and Ted Clayton – have been busily investing and developing the property. ('Not forgetting that it's what you put in after all the money that really counts.') This year two new rooms in a new-build garden cottage have come on stream. In the main building, oak-panelled rooms create the right period ambience and in the dining rooms the new and well-reported head chef, Neil Patterson, should tackle any previous doubts about the cooking. Bedrooms in the main house have a more historical feel, those in the modern extension are more uniform in character.

● Open all year 🔁 On A351 between Wareham and Swanage, in centre of Corfe Castle village. Private car park 🚗 3 twin, 2 twin/double, 9 double, 1 four-poster, 2 family rooms, 2 suites; all with room service, hair-dryer, direct-dial telephone, modem line, TV; some with trouser press, VCR ⊘ 2 dining rooms, bar, 3 lounges, gardens; conferences and social functions; civil wedding licence; leisure facilities nearby; early suppers for children; cots, highchairs, toys, babysitting, baby-listening ♿ Wheelchair access to hotel (ramp) and dining room, WC, 2 ground-floor rooms ● No children under 5 in dining room eves; no dogs; no smoking in bedrooms ⌐ Delta, MasterCard, Switch, Visa £ Single occupancy of twin/double £75 to £120, twin/double £126 to £145, four-poster/suite £190 to £200, family room £158 to £188; deposit required. Set L £20, D £25; alc D £35. Special breaks available (3FOR2)

COVENTRY West Midlands   map 5

Crest Guesthouse

39 Friars Road, Coventry CV1 2LJ
TEL: 024-7622 7822 (AND FAX)
EMAIL: alanharve@aol.com
WEB SITE: www.smoothhound.co.uk/hotels/crestgue.html

Simple, welcoming establishment set in detached Edwardian villa

This tidily run, homely B&B situated very close to the city centre makes an ideal base for visitors to the historic cathedral town. Downstairs there's a breakfast area at the front of the house with a long-case clock and a polished sideboard on which cereals and juices are set out in the mornings; adjacent to this is a homely lounge where guests can relax on the green velvet settee, perhaps warmed by the gas fire on colder nights or looking out through French windows on to a compact townhouse garden when the sun is shining. Upstairs, there is a choice of four prettily turned out bedrooms with chintzy floral fabrics: two singles that share a bathroom and two en-suite twin rooms; all of them are well appointed, if rather prosaically furnished.

● Closed 25, 26 & 31 Dec 🔁 Turn off inner ring road at Junction 5 and turn left immediately after first set of traffic lights; guesthouse is last house on left. Nearest train station: Coventry. Private car park 🚗 2 single, 2 twin; singles with shared bathroom; some with hairdryer, TV; 1 with trouser press ⊘ Breakfast room/lounge, garden; leisure facilities nearby ♿ No wheelchair access ● No smoking; dogs in bedrooms only ⌐ Delta, MasterCard, Switch, Visa £ Single £33, single occupancy of twin £42, twin £62; deposit required

CRACKINGTON HAVEN   Cornwall   map 1

Manor Farm

Crackington Haven, Bude EX23 0JW
TEL: (01840) 230304

Care and attention combined with a dinner-party atmosphere

You get the impression at this well-tended country house that everything has been carefully put in its place and nothing is left to chance. An intriguing feature is the music room, where guests can tinkle the ivories on Muriel Knight's piano. The room in the East Wing (rooms aren't named or numbered) is the most interesting of the three bedrooms, with stone-framed floor-level windows and ceramics positioned on the low window-ledges. The dining room has a single large table and Muriel says she's trying to foster a dinner-party atmosphere without you having to worry about returning the favour. Guests are oiled with pre-dinner drinks before being treated to one of Muriel's adventurous fixed menus, which could feature risotto cakes with melted cheese, followed by chicken with pistachio stuffing and lemon, and then baked Alaska – cooking is clearly a labour of love in this house!

◐ Closed 25 Dec   ⚡ From Wainhouse Corner on A39 follow sign to Crackington Haven. At beach, turn inland for 1 mile, then left into Church Park Road and first right into lane. Private car park ⟞ 1 twin, 2 double   ⚡ Dining room, bar, 4 lounges, library, TV room, music room, garden ⚡ No wheelchair access ● No children; no dogs; no smoking ⊡ None accepted ⟨£⟩ Single occupancy of twin/double £40 to £45, twin/double £70 to £80; deposit required. Set D £23; service incl

---

CRANBROOK   Kent   map 3

Cloth Hall Oast

Cranbrook TN17 3NR
TEL: (01580) 712220 (AND FAX)
EMAIL: clothhalloast@aol.com

Converted barn and oast house B&B

If you have ever fancied a peek in one of those delightful-looking oast houses seen from the train as you rumble through rural Sussex or Kent then head to Katherine Morgan's fine converted oast – on a secluded lane and away from prying eyes. She has just three rooms and has used her years of experience of offering B&B in the Old Cloth Hall next door in setting up her lovely home for guests. One room has a four-poster, and all are done out in soft colour schemes, with smart and shiny bathrooms. Katherine is happy to offer dinner by arrangement and includes home-made soups and pâtés and a variety of fruit puds for guests who eat dinner and breakfast in the galleried dining room around a polished table looking out on to the garden. There is a small outdoor pool and a deck to bask beside the pond for warm summer days.

◐ Closed Chr   ⚡ 1 mile east of Cranbrook on Tenterden road; turn right just before cemetery. Private car park ⟞ 1 twin/double, 1 double, 1 four-poster; family room available; all with hair-dryer, TV; 2 with trouser press; tea/coffee-making facilities, telephone available   ⚡ Dining room, sitting room, garden; outdoor heated swimming pool; leisure facilities nearby; early suppers for children ⚡ No wheelchair access ● No dogs; no smoking in bedrooms ⊡ None accepted ⟨£⟩ Single occupancy of double £50 to £55, twin/double £85 to £120, four-poster £110 to £120, family room £125; deposit required. Set D £22; light meals available ⟨3FOR2⟩

'I had the misfortune to hit my head four or five times during our stay not only on the sloping ceiling but also in the single dormer window in one corner of the room. Clumsy, you might say, but I would expect to be able to walk around the room with freedom.'
On a hotel in Norfolk

The text of the entries is based on inspections carried out anonymously, backed up by unsolicited reports sent in by readers. The factual details under the text are from questionnaires the Guide sends to all hotels that feature in the book.

CRANFORD Greater London map 3

The Cottage

150 High Street, Cranford, Hounslow TW5 9WB
TEL: 020-8897 1815 FAX: 020-8897 3117
EMAIL: bermuthecottage@tidyworld.co.uk
WEB SITE: www.cottageguesthouse-heathrow.co.uk

Family-run guesthouse with character, handy for Heathrow

This low, two-storey red-brick guesthouse is set back from the High Street moments from the M4 and conveniently placed for Heathrow. Given its location, competition is fierce, but the airport's crop of bland chain hotels are not to everyone's taste, and The Cottage is a good bet for travellers seeking a personal, family-run atmosphere, with the added advantages of off-airport parking, neat, reasonably priced bedrooms and a pretty courtyard garden complete with hanging baskets. Rooms are divided between the main house and the garden annexe and are all good-sized and tastefully done out in cottagey style, though those in the extension – reached via a covered walkway – have the edge for larger-than-average shower cubicles in the modern bathrooms. A similar unflashy but good-quality feel also characterises the public rooms, which are simple, traditional and neat. As with all airport hotels, some noise is to be expected.

◑ Open all year ⊠ From M4 Junction 3 take A312 towards Feltham, turn left at first set of traffic lights, after 200 yards turn left at Jolly Gardener pub, hotel is immediately behind, on left. Nearest train station: Hounslow West. Private car park ⇖ 4 single, 7 twin, 8 double, 2 family rooms; all with hair-dryer, mini-bar, TV ⊘ Dining room, conservatory, garden ♿ Wheelchair access to hotel (ramp) and dining room, 13 ground-floor bedrooms, 1 room specially equipped for disabled people. Disabled parking ● No dogs; no smoking ▭ Delta, MasterCard, Switch, Visa £ Single £50 to £60, single occupancy of twin/double £67, twin/double £67 to £75, family room £75 to £90; deposit required. Special breaks available

CRAYKE North Yorkshire map 9

Durham Ox

Westway, Crayke, Nr Easingwold, York YO61 4TE
TEL: (01347) 821506 FAX: (01347) 823326
EMAIL: enquiries@thedurhamox.com
WEB SITE: www.thedurhamox.com

Lively country pub with smart bedrooms to retire to after indulging in the excellent food

The Ibbotson family's 300-year-old inn is deeply rooted into the local life of Crayke: 'We're the village pub and we don't want to lose that character', says Michael Ibbotson. But although you may bump into the village cricket team celebrating a win with a few pints of hand-pulled ale, it is also a place where food is taken seriously. Since the village shop closed, the pub has even opened an excellent deli selling top-quality local produce. In the characterful bar – a winning mix of flagstones, low dark beams and carved wooden panels – chalkboards display an ambitious spread of modern dishes, based on locally sourced fresh ingredients. Alternatively, there's a quietly elegant table-service restaurant, where photographer Dominic Ibbotson's work is showcased on vibrant blue walls in a romantic candlelit room. Such gastronomic delights beg for a bit of a blowout, and we can assure roving foodies that the bedrooms in converted cottages behind the inn are no half-hearted afterthought. All are suites, the biggest and best of which are mezzanine-style with antique metal beds tucked under A-frame rafters, and feature exposed stone walls. Furnishings are top quality, fabrics exude luxury and bathrooms are no less classy.

◑ Open all year ⊠ Take A19 from York; go through Easingwold market place and straight up towards Crayke; in village, take first left up the hill, pub is on right. Private car park ⇖ 8 suites; family rooms available; all with room service, hair-dryer, TV, VCR, CD player; some with mini-bar ⊘ Restaurant, dining room, bar, lounge, library, garden; conferences; social functions; leisure facilities nearby; early suppers for children; highchairs ♿ Wheelchair access to hotel (ramp) and restaurant, 2 ground-floor bedrooms ● No young children in restaurant, no dogs in public rooms; no smoking ▧ Amex, Delta, MasterCard, Switch, Visa £ Single occupancy of suite £60, suite £80 to £160, family room £125; deposit required. Alc L, D £25; light meals available. Special breaks available

---

CREED Cornwall   map 1

Creed House

Creed, Grampound, Truro TR2 4SL
TEL: (01872) 530372

Wonderful gardens right on your doorstep – and we don't just mean Eden

There's a grand, pleasingly old-fashioned but never pretentious or unwelcoming atmosphere to this B&B in the Cornish countryside perfectly positioned for the Eden Project or the Lost Gardens of Heligan. But you don't need to venture even that far for horticultural splendour, as Lally and William Croggon are rightly proud enough of their own garden to open it occasionally even to visitors not staying the night. Splashes of vibrant purples and pinks, showers of blossom and some exciting exotic specimens make for a gardener's delight. Inside, the bedrooms are decorated with pretty Colefax and Fowler wallpaper and have good beds and linen, and private bathrooms for those which aren't en suite. 'People are paying for B&B so you've got to give them comfy beds and lavish breakfasts,' we were told by the clearly house-proud and chatty Lally. Such breakfasts are served around a large central table (this 'turns into quite a party sometimes') and there's also a lounge with TV, big comfy chairs, bookcases and knick-knacks, which has a relaxed but still grand air.

● Closed Chr and New Year ▩ From Grampound on A390, follow Creed Lane for 1 mile, then turn left opposite Creed church; house is on left. Private car park ⎯ 1 twin, 2 double; hair-dryers available ✓ Breakfast room, lounge, garden ♿ No wheelchair access ● No children under 8; no dogs; no smoking ▧ None accepted £ Twin/double £80

CRICKET MALHERBIE Somerset   map 2

The Old Rectory

Cricket Malherbie, Ilminster TA19 0PW
TEL: (01460) 54364   FAX: (01460) 57374
EMAIL: info@malherbie.co.uk
WEB SITE: www.malherbie.co.uk

Excellent food and charming rooms in rural retreat

This thatched country retreat is the quintessential English rectory – you almost expect a man in a linen jacket and dog collar to be chasing around the delightful garden with a butterfly net. The façade of the house, which was built in the sixteenth century, shows a few additions, notably a brace of arched windows in the Strawberry Hill Gothic style. Owners Michael and Patricia Fry-Foley keep the place impeccably clean and fresh – they have that attention to detail which can make all the difference. Guests eat together around one table and benefit from some very careful sourcing of local produce plus good cooking. You might find locally smoked eel as a starter (most people are immediate converts to that much-maligned dish), then a suprême of guinea fowl wrapped in local ham, followed by apple crumble and custard, and finally a selection of cheeses all made within 25 miles of the house. Bedrooms are all immaculately well presented and cosy with period furniture and prints. The pick are the two at the front which get those unusual Gothic windows. 'Good welcome, room excellent, dinner wonderful, even the garden is lovely,' wrote one very satisfied correspondent. 'Worth making a detour to savour both its charms and the food.'

● Closed Chr ▩ From A358 towards Chard, turn left after Donyatt towards Ilminster, then right to Cricket Malherbie; hotel is 200 metres past church, on left. Private car park ⎯ 1 twin, 4 double; all with hair-dryer, TV; some with VCR ✓ Dining room, bar, lounge, garden; leisure facilities nearby ♿ No wheelchair access

● No children under 16; no dogs; no smoking ⬚ Delta, MasterCard, Switch, Visa £ Single occupancy of twin/double from £55, twin/double from £85; deposit required. Set D £30; service incl. Special breaks available

---

CROFT-ON-TEES Co Durham   map 10

Clow Beck House

Monk End Farm, Croft-on-Tees, Nr Darlington DL2 2SW
TEL: (01325) 721075   FAX: (01325) 720419
EMAIL: david@clowbeckhouse.co.uk
WEB SITE: www.clowbeckhouse.co.uk

Unpretentious family-run hotel with flamboyant rooms and lovely gardens

Heather and David Armstrong's sprawling stone house sits in lovingly tended landscaped gardens amid green fields. The atmosphere here is down to earth and effortlessly friendly: afternoon tea with home-made biscuits will help you unwind in the lounge, which has a bold and bright chinoiserie theme with a blue Chinese carpet and walls panelled with peacock and bamboo motifs. David's dinners are served at antique wooden tables in an impressive split-level barn-style restaurant, where all tables look out into the gardens; food is freshly cooked using ingredients from local suppliers and might feature a tuna steak with dill and cream sauce or duck with caramel, brandy and orange sauce. The bedrooms have real character, top-quality furniture and fabrics and plenty of thoughtful touches worthy of a grander hotel, including disposable slipper socks and upmarket toiletries; all are spacious enough for a sofa or *chaise longue*. A stay in Sunflower ought to make your mouth water for dinner, as it is kitted out in the bright and breezy citrus fruit colours of lime, lemon and tangerine, whereas Daisy has a completely monochrome theme with a black wrought iron four-poster and zebra-skin cushions.

◗ Closed Chr and New Year ⤣ 3 miles south of Darlington on A167, in Croft village ⬚ 1 twin, 12 double; family rooms available; all with room service, hair-dryer, trouser press, direct-dial telephone, modem line, TV, CD player ✓ Restaurant, lounge, garden; conferences; social functions; leisure facilities nearby; early suppers for children; cots, highchairs, toys ♿ Wheelchair access to hotel (ramp) and restaurant (ramp), 8 ground-floor bedrooms, 2 rooms specially equipped for disabled people. Disabled parking ● No dogs ⬚ Amex, Delta, MasterCard, Switch, Visa £ Single occupancy of twin/double £65, twin/double £95, family room £105. Alc D £24; light meals available; service incl

---

CROOKHAM Northumberland   map 10

Coach House

Crookham, Cornhill-on-Tweed TD12 4TD
TEL: (01890) 820293   FAX: (01890) 820284
EMAIL: stay@coachhousecrookham.com
WEB SITE: www.coachhousecrookham.com

New owners at this friendly hotel in splendid Borders country

Leona and Toby Rutter took over the helm of the Coach House in March 2004, and if ever a takeover was destined to go smoothly, this surely was one: Leona worked with previous owner Lynne Anderson for 15 years and knows the business back-to-front. The Rutters have grabbed the hotel with both hands and had already redecorated the dining room when our inspector visited in April. They also plan to convert the library into a new bedroom. Otherwise, the overall style remains the same. In the dining room, you will find lots of stripped pine doors and exposed beams – the house dates from the seventeenth century after all. Bedrooms in the main house have plenty of character thanks to slanted ceilings, wooden rafters and antiques. The other rooms in converted cottages around the courtyard are full of light and furnished in a bright and breezy style; the Orchard room looks into the said orchard through huge picture windows and is especially pleasant. Complimentary afternoon tea with yummy home-made cakes is served in the barn-like lounge, which opens on to a sunny terrace and also offers a particularly well-provisioned honesty bar. Dinner is freshly cooked by Leona, who insists on using local produce, mostly from farms practically within sight of the house.

◑ Open all year ⁊ On A697, 3½ miles south of Cornhill-on-Tweed. Private car park ⌂⌐ 1 single, 5 twin/ double, 5 double; family rooms available; 3 with shared bathroom; all with room service, hair-dryer, direct-dial telephone, TV ⊘ Dining room, breakfast room, bar/lounge, garden, terrace; cots, highchairs ⅙ Wheelchair access to hotel (ramp) and dining room, National Accessible Scheme: mobility impairment M1, WC, 6 ground-floor bedrooms, 3 rooms specially equipped for disabled people. Disabled parking ● No dogs or smoking in public rooms ⊏ Delta, MasterCard, Switch, Visa (2% surcharge on debit and credit cards) £ Single £25, single occupancy of twin/double £34 to £48, twin/double £58 to £86, family room £73 to £107; deposit required. Set D £19.50; service incl ③FOR②

CROSTHWAITE Cumbria   map 8

Crosthwaite House

Crosthwaite, Nr Kendal LA8 8BP
TEL: (015395) 68264
EMAIL: bookings@crosthwaitehouse.co.uk
WEB SITE: www.crosthwaitehouse.co.uk

A timeless English setting for a classic Georgian guesthouse midway between Kendal and Windermere

In springtime, the orchards of the fertile Lyth valley are bright with damson blossom, and lambs frolic over verdant countryside laced with drystone walls. Robin and Marnie Dawson's long-term family home, Crosthwaite House, surveys an enviable slab of this idyllic scene from the tall sash windows of its symmetrical, cream-washed façade. The interior stays faithful to the age and style of the house, original shutters and fireplaces still intact, rugs on polished floorboards, and suitable period furnishings throughout – a leather chesterfield here,

Victorian-style dining chairs there. Lots of house plants, china, books, magazines and games make it feel lived in. Bedrooms are similarly homely, in soothing plain colours. Most have valley views, some overlook the garden, or Crosthwaite's charming church. Good home-cooking from the Aga is served by arrangement (the puddings are legendary), using local produce wherever possible. Self-catering cottages have been converted from various ancient stone outbuildings across the yard.

◑ Closed mid-Nov to mid-Feb ⁊ From A5074 towards Bowness and Windermere, turn right after Lyth Valley Hotel, then left at T-junction; house is on right. Private car park ⌂⌐ 1 single, 2 twin, 2 twin/double, 1 double; all with TV ⊘ Dining room, sitting room; cots, highchairs, baby-listening ⅙ No wheelchair access ● No dogs in public rooms; no smoking ⊏ None accepted £ Single £23 to £25, single occupancy of twin/ double £23 to £25, twin/double £45 to £50. Set D £15; light meals available; service incl

Punch Bowl Inn

Crosthwaite, Nr Kendal LA8 8HR
TEL: (015395) 68237 FAX: (015395) 68875
EMAIL: enquiries@punchbowl.fsnet.co.uk
WEB SITE: www.punchbowl.fsnet.co.uk

A deceptively informal country inn with exceptional food and stylish bedrooms

The fortunes of this rugged seventeenth-century Lakeland pub beside the church took a distinct upswing when top-flight metropolitan chef Steven Doherty moved in. Not that you'd guess he was once head chef at the Roux brothers' Mayfair shrine, Le Gavroche. There's nothing remotely precious about the atmosphere of the Punch Bowl, where the excellent fare apparently aims to please the customer rather than the cook. 'No sauce on it? Half-portions for children? We're

happy to improvise. Please just ask.' How very refreshing. The whole of the pub's rustic beamed and firelit interior is devoted to open-plan bar-dining space ranging around the serving counter, snug booth seating downstairs, airy galleries above. The walls are decked with local artworks and assorted menus from all over the world. Beyond the bars lie the few nicely finished bedrooms, cool and chic in rusts, creams and blues. Book now to avoid disappointment – word's spreading fast.

◑ Open all year; restaurant closed Sun & Mon eves ⚡ On A5074 towards Bowness and Windermere, pass Lyth Valley Hotel on right; at bottom of hill turn right over bridge, signposted Kendal and Crosthwaite; at end of this road, Punch Bowl Inn is on left, next to church. Private car park 🛏 1 twin/double, 2 double; all with hair-dryer, TV ✓ Restaurant, bar, patio; social functions; leisure facilities nearby; early suppers for children; highchairs ♿ No wheelchair access ● No dogs; smoking in bar area only ▭ MasterCard, Switch, Visa £ Single occupancy of twin/double £38, twin/double £65 to £70. Set L £14; alc L, D £25; light meals available; service incl. Special breaks available

---

CROYDE Devon   map 1

Whiteleaf at Croyde

Croyde, Braunton EX33 1PN
TEL: (01271) 890266
WEB SITE: www.thewhiteleaf.co.uk

Handy for the beach and with a reputation for good food

Chef David Rayner worked in grand hotels all around the world before settling with his wife Sue in this rather straggly village five minutes' walk from a glorious beach. The ambitious cuisine rather belies the house's appearance – an undistinguished 1930s detached residence – but this is essentially a family home, with snapshots dotted around on shelves and mantelpieces. The dining room is a smart and comfortable spot, with its warm yellow and terracotta colour scheme. David's cooking is noted for luxuriant sauces and is strong on meats. Bedrooms continue the homely, comfortable feel with stripped pine furniture and floral fabrics. Mini-bars with fresh milk for the tea tray are thoughtfully provided.

◑ Closed 25 & 26 Dec; dining room closed Sun eve ⚡ Off B3231 Braunton to Croyde road, on left before village centre. Private car park 🛏 1 twin, 3 double, 1 four-poster; family room available; all with hair-dryer, mini-bar, direct-dial telephone, TV ✓ Dining room, 2 lounges, garden; social functions; leisure facilities nearby; early suppers for children; cots, highchairs ♿ No wheelchair access ● No dogs in public rooms; no smoking in bedrooms and most public rooms ▭ Delta, MasterCard, Switch, Visa £ Single occupancy of twin/double £40 to £46, twin/double £60 to £72, four-poster £90 to £100, family room £90 to £105; deposit required. Alc D £24; light meals available. Special breaks available

---

CRUDWELL Wiltshire   map 2

Old Rectory

Crudwell, Malmesbury SN16 9EP
TEL: (01666) 577194   FAX: (01666) 577853
EMAIL: office@oldrectorycrudwell.co.uk
WEB SITE: www.oldrectorycrudwell.co.uk

Homely atmosphere and excellent cooking at this country house

Karen and Derek Woods' spacious and attractive Georgian country house has plenty going for it: original features (flagstone floors in reception and oak panelling in the restaurant) plus bedroom views to the garden with its well-trimmed lawns and the village church beyond. There is also a small conservatory that enjoys the same views. Cooking is a major attraction here, the style being modern English with French influences, according to head chef Peter Fairclough. The atmosphere is quiet and relaxing, with homely touches. Bedrooms use swagged drapes, period furnishings, some four-posters and sleigh beds to create sumptuous overtones. Lavender gets a pleasing double aspect and Honeysuckle is a suite with spacious bathroom and a view over the garden's stone-lined carp pond.

◑ Open all year ⚡ In Crudwell village opposite the Plough pub, by church. Nearest train station: Kemble. Private car park 🛏 3 twin/double, 5 double, 4 suites; family rooms available; all with room service, hair-dryer, trouser press, ironing facilities, direct-dial telephone, modem line, TV; some with mini-bar ✓ Restaurant, 2 dining rooms, 2 lounges, conservatory, garden; conferences and social functions; civil wedding licence; leisure facilities nearby; early suppers for children; cots, highchairs, baby-listening ♿ No wheelchair access ● No children under 7 in restaurant eves; no smoking in bedrooms and some public rooms ⊟ Delta, MasterCard, Switch, Visa £ Single occupancy of twin/double £75 to £108, twin/double £98 to £149, family room/suite £170 to £194; deposit required. Set L £18, D £26.50; light meals available

---

CUCKFIELD West Sussex map 3

Ockenden Manor

Ockenden Lane, Cuckfield, Haywards Heath RH17 5LD
TEL: (01444) 416111 FAX: (01444) 415549
EMAIL: ockenden@hshotels.co.uk
WEB SITE: www.hshotels.co.uk

Smart manor-house hotel with views to the South Downs

With echoes of romantic feudalism, the walls of Ockenden Manor gaze down upon the picturesque village of Cuckfield. Set in mature grounds with views across the Sussex countryside, the manor house is predominantly sixteenth century with substantial Victorian additions and a sympathetic modern extension, crowned by a jumble of lichen-covered roofs of varying pitches and heights. Inside, the public areas have been kitted out with flair; the cosy, low-ceilinged bar – built under Henry VIII – is all wood-panelled with a sloping, creaky floor and a stone fireplace (though now housing a real-flame gas fire), while the sitting room, in the Victorian part of the house, has an entirely different character with high ceilings, elegant furnishings and a large bay window with views to the Downs. The restaurant is a striking room with an eight-course tasting menu to match, though less extravagant four-course dinner menus are also on offer. Bedrooms vary considerably in style and size, but all are smart and tasteful with neutral carpets, bold fabrics and well-equipped bathrooms. Feature rooms have the edge for character.

◑ Open all year ⤢ From M23 towards Brighton, take B2115 signposted Cuckfield; on entering village, Ockenden Lane is first right. Private car park ⛽ 1 single, 4 twin/double, 10 double, 3 four-poster, 1 family room, 3 suites; all with room service, hair-dryer, trouser press, direct-dial telephone, TV; some with CD player ⊘ Restaurant, bar, sitting room, conservatory, garden; conferences; social functions; civil wedding licence; leisure facilities nearby; early suppers for children; cots, highchairs, babysitting, baby-listening ♿ Wheelchair access to hotel and restaurant, WC, 2 ground-floor bedrooms ● No dogs in public rooms and some bedrooms ⊟ Amex, Delta, Diners, MasterCard, Switch, Visa £ Single £108, single occupancy of twin/double £155 to £260, twin/double £155 to £285, four-poster £260 to £285, family room £260, suite £260 to £325; deposit required. Set L £19.50, D £38; alc L, D £43. Special breaks available ③FOR②

DARTMOUTH Devon map 1

Little Admiral [NEW ENTRY]

27-29 Victoria Road, Dartmouth TQ6 9RT
TEL: (01803) 832572 FAX: (01803) 835815
EMAIL: info@little-admiral.co.uk
WEB SITE: www.little-admiral.co.uk

Stylish but unstuffy family-friendly place to stay in central Dartmouth

Clare and James Brown had no experience of running a hotel before they took over the Little Admiral two years ago, but they are enjoying it very much, and the business seems to be doing well. Their hotel lies a couple of minutes' walk from the waterfront, and is part of a Regency terrace, with large plate-glass windows looking on to the street. These belong to the restaurant, which is open on Thursday, Friday and Saturday evenings for tapas, fish and steaks, and the lounge, where free tea and coffee are available to residents throughout the day. Both spaces are clean and modern, with white tongue-and-groove panelling, coffee and cream colour schemes, and occasional zings of energy provided by modern seaside paintings or animal-print sofas. The ten rooms upstairs continue in the same vein, with smart wooden beds (including a linenfold panelled four-poster in Room 1), crisp white linen and good-quality bathrooms. The Browns have two children of their own, and are happy to welcome youngsters. Guests staying on Thursday, Friday or Saturday are required to eat in the restaurant on one evening.

◑ Closed Jan; restaurant closed Sun to Wed eves ⚹ Entering Dartmouth from A3122, take third turning on right after mini-roundabout; hotel is on the right in town ↵ 1 twin/double, 8 double, 1 four-poster; family rooms available; all with hair-dryer, direct-dial telephone, TV ✓ Restaurant, bar, lounge; leisure facilities nearby; early suppers for children; cots, highchairs, toys ♿ No wheelchair access ◓ No smoking in bedrooms ☐ Amex, Delta, MasterCard, Switch, Visa £ Single occupancy of twin/double £60 to £75, twin/double £95 to £115, four-poster £130, family room £145; deposit required. Set, alc D £18. Special breaks available (3FOR2)

Royal Castle

11 The Quay, Dartmouth TQ6 9PS
TEL: (01803) 833033   FAX: (01803) 835445
EMAIL: enquiry@royalcastle.co.uk
WEB SITE: www.royalcastle.co.uk

Historic inn that is managing to keep up with the times

Overlooking Dartmouth's 'boat float', the Royal Castle certainly lives up to its name, with a white castellated frontage flying the Union flag. With parts dating from Elizabethan times, the establishment has quite a history: it was originally two separate buildings, now joined together beneath a glass roof, and you can see a complete set of room bells above the reception desk. This heritage is still reflected in some areas – one of the bars retains a huge roasting spit, horse brasses and a stuffed fish – but coexists with other, more modern parts of the hotel. So in the Harbour Bar you can perch on an aluminium bar stool and watch mountain bikers or snowboarders projected onto a flat screen, and the first-floor restaurant combines plasterwork reliefs on the ceiling with a sophisticated monochrome colour scheme. The bedrooms, too, strike a careful balance between traditional and modern. Some retain four-poster or half-tester beds; others come in more contemporary stripes and checks. Rooms with river views cost more; we particularly liked Room 26, aka The Lookout, which has a small raised seating area overlooking the front.

◑ Open all year ⚹ Entering Dartmouth from A3122, head for waterfront and turn right past ferry queue; follow embankment, turn right at Boat Afloat, then right again; hotel is on left. Private car park ↵ 4 twin, 10 double, 5 four-poster, 6 family rooms; all with room service, hair-dryer, direct-dial telephone, modem line, TV ✓ Restaurant, 2 bars, lounge, library; conferences; social functions; civil wedding licence; leisure facilities nearby; early suppers for children; cots, highchairs, babysitting, baby-listening ♿ No wheelchair access ◓ No smoking in bedrooms ☐ Amex, Delta, Diners, MasterCard, Switch, Visa £ Single occupancy of twin/double £71 to £78, twin/double £111 to £180, four-poster £170 to £180, family room £130 to £195; deposit required. Set L £15, D £25; alc L £20, D £30; light meals available; service incl. Special breaks available

DEDHAM Essex   map 6

Dedham Hall

Brook Street, Dedham, Colchester CO7 6AD
TEL: (01206) 323027   FAX: (01206) 323293
EMAIL: sarton@dedhamhall.demon.co.uk
WEB SITE: www.dedhamhall.demon.co.uk

Painters' haven in dreamy surroundings

You don't have to be interested in art to stay at Dedham Hall – but it helps. Everywhere you turn, paintings adorn the walls, and not just Constable-esque landscapes (Dedham markets itself as being the heart of Constable country) but a wide variety of traditional and modern styles from the many artists who come here to teach and learn on the painting weekends. Even if you're not tempted to pick up a brush yourself you're welcome to poke your head into the beautiful light-filled studio-cum-classroom and watch and chat with the painters at work – there's no pretension or separation between the guests coming to paint and those just coming to relax and enjoy the hotel. The house has rambling grounds, including a large pond: the setting is highly evocative of lazy summer days and picnics on the grass. The bedrooms in the house are pretty with floral touches, without ever becoming too florid. The annexe rooms in the grounds are mainly for the week-long painting courses.

○ Closed Chr and New Year; restaurant closed Sun & Mon 🔟 Take Dedham/Stratford St Mary exit off A12; follow signs to Dedham; hotel is at end of High Street on left, down drive. Private car park 🅿 5 double; all with room service, hair-dryer, TV ⊘ Restaurant, dining room, 2 bars, 2 lounges, conservatory, garden; social functions; early suppers for children ♿ Wheelchair access to hotel, restaurant, 12 ground-floor bedrooms, 1 room specially equipped for disabled people ● No dogs; no smoking in bedrooms ▭ Delta, MasterCard, Switch, Visa £ Single occupancy of double £50, double £85; deposit required. Set D £25.50. Special breaks available ③FOR②

Maison Talbooth

Stratford Road, Dedham, Colchester CO7 6HN
TEL: (01206) 322367   FAX: (01206) 322752
EMAIL: maison@milsomhotels.com
WEB SITE: www.milsomhotels.com

Luxurious rooms overlooking a picturesque vale

In true Victorian spirit, Maison Talbooth goes gloriously over the top in its interior design. Each of the luxurious rooms has its own character and decadent features, and many have been recently refurbished. Of the newer ones, Shelley stands out, in greens and browns with a huge cushioned headboard stretching almost to the ceiling, a free-standing spa bath and a wonderful double aspect. Keats, though not one of the redecorated rooms, still shines in oranges with a lovely wooden globe and Jacuzzi. Even the 'standard' room, Kipling, without a bath, has one of the largest shower heads you're ever likely to encounter. The lounge was in the process of being refurbished when we inspected, with the older chintzy furniture gradually being replaced with more contemporary, though still elegant, pieces such as a lovely duck-print sofa. Dinner is served at the nearby Le Talbooth restaurant – it's walking distance but there's a courtesy car if you don't fancy the stroll. Breakfast is brought to your room. A new 'Exclusively Yours' package offers you the chance to pretend the house is yours for the day and hold your own posh house party.

○ Open all year; off-site restaurant closed Sun eve Sept to May 🔟 Leave A12 at Dedham/Stratford St Mary exit; follow signs to Dedham; hotel is over bridge, approx 300 yards along on right. Private car park 🅿 2 twin, 6 twin/double, 1 family room, 1 suite; all with room service, hair-dryer, mini-bar, trouser press, direct-dial telephone, TV ⊘ Restaurant (off site), dining room, lounge, gardens; conferences, social functions, civil wedding licence; leisure facilities nearby; cots, highchairs, babysitting ♿ No wheelchair access; 5 steps into hotel, 7 steps into restaurant, 5 ground-floor bedrooms, WC. Disabled parking ● No dogs ▭ Amex, Delta, Diners, MasterCard, Switch, Visa £ Single occupancy of twin/double £120 to £160, twin/double £165 to £225, family room from £225, suite £225; deposit required. Cooked B £8.50; set L £24.50; alc L, D £45. Special breaks available

Milsoms

Stratford Road, Dedham, Colchester C07 6HW
TEL: (01206) 322795   FAX: (01206) 323689
EMAIL: milsoms@milsomhotels.com
WEB SITE: www.milsomhotels.com

The Milsom family's foray into contemporary chic

Milsoms is a far more stripped-back, contemporary affair than its sister hotel Maison Talbooth (see entry), but the attention to detail and sense of style are just the same. The interiors are done out in solid pale colours with thick woven carpets or big stone tiles. Chunky wooden tables mix with stylish leather, and all the signage is in 'of-the-moment' lower case. Chill-out music wafts over the young couples and families in the bar and patio with its new canopy, creating a mood that's buzzy but relaxed. Rooms are similarly modern and luxurious, and are immaculately turned out. Each is named after a local business, and there are black and white photos of the room's namesakes on the walls. Food is served in the informal bar area and is generally of the modern fusion variety –

write down your own order and take it up to the servery.

○ Open all year ⊡ From A12 towards Ipswich, turn off at first sign to Dedham; turn right over bridge; hotel is on left. Private car park ⟱ 6 twin/double, 9 double; family rooms available; all with room service, hair-dryer, mini-bar, direct-dial telephone, TV ✓ Restaurant, bar, lounge, library, garden; conferences; leisure facilities nearby; early suppers for children; cots, highchairs ♿ Wheelchair access to hotel (ramp) and restaurant, WC, 4 ground-floor bedrooms, 1 room specially equipped for disabled people. Disabled parking ● No dogs in public rooms and most bedrooms, £10 per night; no smoking in bedrooms ⊡ Amex, Delta, Diners, MasterCard, Switch, Visa £ Single occupancy of twin/double £75 to £95, twin/double £95 to £135, family room £155; deposit required. Continental B £7, cooked B £12; alc L, D £25; light meals available

Sun Inn [NEW ENTRY]

High Street, Dedham CO7 6DF
TEL: (01206) 323351 FAX: (01206) 322179
EMAIL: info@thesuninndedham.com
WEB SITE: www.thesuninndedham.com

Traditional English inn with Mediterranean influences

'Sleepy? Hungry? Thirsty?' asks the brochure, and this inn delivers on its promise to help you with all three. Chef Piers Baker bought this coaching inn in the middle of pretty Dedham in 2003 and has successfully transformed it into something of a Mediterranean-influenced oasis without stripping the building of any of its original English character. So the walls of the pub are now in warm yellows, and the menu is decidedly Italian/Spanish, but the oak

beams and eclectic antique furniture remain. The bar is stylish, shabby chic, and the rooms are no less appealing, described as 'boutique hotel meets country inn'. Of the four, Elser is definitely the pick, with extra space, a four-poster bed, and wood panelling. It may shortly be reclassified as a suite with a higher price-tag, but when we inspected, all rooms were priced the same – so grab it while you can.

○ Closed 25 to 28 Dec; dining room closed Sun eves ⊡ From A12 follow signs to Dedham (2 miles); hotel is opposite church ⟱ 3 twin/double, 1 four-poster; all with hair-dryer, TV, VCR, CD player; no tea/coffee-making facilities in rooms ✓ Dining room, bar, lounge, garden, terrace; social functions; leisure facilities nearby; highchairs, toys ♿ No wheelchair access ● No dogs or smoking in bedrooms ⊡ MasterCard, Switch, Visa £ Single occupancy of twin/double £55 to £90, twin/double/four-poster £60 to £150; deposit required. Set L £11.50, D £15; alc L £11.50, D £15; light meals available. Special breaks available (3FOR2)

DITTISHAM Devon   map 1

Fingals

Old Coombe, Dittisham, Dartmouth TQ6 0JA
TEL: (01803) 722398 FAX: (01803) 722401
EMAIL: richard@fingals.co.uk
WEB SITE: www.fingals.co.uk

House-party atmosphere in utterly idyllic surroundings

'We refrained from labelling ourselves as a hotel so that the uninitiated would not come with preconceived ideas,' says Richard Johnston of his lovingly restored farmhouse tucked away in a maze of lanes next to the Dart estuary. Indeed, Fingals is not for those who like to have flunkies at their beck and call, or want everything to work like clockwork. There are no keys, the (proper) bar works on an honesty basis most of the time, and dinner, served around one long

table, may be delayed if everyone is not quite ready (there is a smaller dining room if you prefer to eat separately). So if there's nobody to greet you when you arrive, one of the other guests may pour you a drink, or you can explore the gardens (tennis court, croquet lawn), say hello to the Indian running ducks, or visit the art gallery and studios next door. Alternatively, you can curl up with a glossy magazine in front of the inglenook fireplace, admire the eclectic selection of art – ranging from modern photos to Elizabethan oils – or investigate the selection of DVDs and videos in the TV room. Bedrooms in the main house are certainly the best, with antique beds and modern lighting. Décor is traditional, occasionally dated, but the basics, like water pressure, are good. Standard rooms are less appealing; for a really special occasion, go for the Folly, which overlooks the river. Purists may bemoan the odd cobweb or rotted door frame, but when you're breakfasting on the sunny terrace to the sound of buzzing bees, the weeds between the cracks don't seem to matter.

○ Closed 1 Jan to 31 Mar ⚡ From B3207, take turning to Dittisham 3 miles before Dartmouth; turn left by Sportsman's Arms pub; follow signs to Fingals. Private car park 🛏 2 twin/double, 6 double, 2 four-poster, 1 family room; all with room service, direct-dial telephone; some with TV, CD player ✧ 2 dining rooms, bar, lounge, library, conservatory, games room, garden; conferences, social functions; gym, sauna, tennis, heated indoor swimming pool; early suppers for children; cots, highchairs, baby-listening, outdoor play area ♿ Wheelchair access to hotel (2 steps) and dining room, 2 ground-floor bedrooms; WC ● No dogs or smoking in public rooms ▭ Amex, Delta, MasterCard, Switch, Visa £ Single occupancy of twin/double £65 to £100, twin/double £85 to £120, four-poster £105 to £140, family room £120 to £160; deposit required. Set D £27.50; light meals available; service incl

---

DODDISCOMBSLEIGH Devon
map 1

Nobody Inn

Doddiscombsleigh, Nr Exeter EX6 7PS
TEL: (01647) 252394 FAX: (01647) 252978
EMAIL: info@nobodyinn.co.uk
WEB SITE: www.nobodyinn.co.uk

Splendid food and drink – plus somewhere to sleep off the effects

The original name of this village pub was the New Inn. It was changed in the 1950s, when the owner died and, owing to a mix-up at the mortuary, his coffin was buried without his body inside. The new owner then decided to change the name to NoBody Inn, a move that came under fire at the time for being in bad taste! Today, it's very unlikely that anybody would complain of such a thing, such is the pub's reputation for good food (including local cheeses) and extensive choice of wines and whiskies, as well as beer. Little of the public area seems to have changed, however: the rambling bar's nicotine-coloured walls support copper and brass, tankards hang from beams, and leaded windows look on to a small outside terrace and well-tended flowerbeds. Bedrooms 'over the shop' are compact, with small shower rooms and cottagey décor; there are also more spacious rooms in Town Barton, a separate manor house a couple of hundred yards away, next to the church.

○ Closed 25, 26 Dec & 31 Dec, 1 Jan; restaurant closed Mon and Sun eves ⚡ Leave A38 at Devon & Exeter racecourse (signposted Dunchideock); follow signs to Doddiscombsleigh and Nobody Inn for 3 miles. Private car park 🛏 2 twin, 4 double, 1 four-poster; 2 with shared bathroom; all with hair-dryer, direct-dial telephone ✧ Restaurant, bar, terrace ♿ No wheelchair access; 1 step into hotel, 1 ground-floor bedroom ● No children under 14; no dogs ▭ Amex, Delta, Diners, MasterCard, Switch, Visa £ Single occupancy of twin/double £25 to £50, twin/double/four-poster £40 to £85; deposit required. Alc D £20

DORCHESTER Dorset
map 2

Casterbridge Hotel

49 High East Street, Dorchester DT1 1HU
TEL: (01305) 264043 FAX: (01305) 260884
EMAIL: reception@casterbridgehotel.co.uk
WEB SITE: www.casterbridgehotel.co.uk

Reliable and well-run B&B convenient for Dorchester's centre

On the high street heading out of town, and with Dorchester's architectural prettiness waning slightly, this fine B&B bucks the trend, being a handsome, well-kept building. Stalwart proprietors Rita and Stuart Turner are still involved, but are now taking a back seat and leaving their daughter Vanessa and her husband David in charge more often. The style remains the same: straightforward, comfortable bedrooms, a good breakfast and plenty of local information. Bedrooms are divided between those in the original house and those in the new building at the end of the small patio garden. For quietness these are preferable, and have soft headboards, gentle colour schemes and rattan furniture – Room 25 is a good ground-floor choice with its own patio area. For evening meals there are plenty of options within walking distance.

◖ Closed 24 to 26 Dec   🔁 In centre of Dorchester, 100 yards east of town clock. Nearest train station: Dorchester South or Dorchester West   🛏 4 single, 2 twin, 1 twin/double, 5 double, 1 four-poster, 1 family suite; all with room service, hair-dryer, direct-dial telephone, TV; some with trouser press, VCR   ⊘ Breakfast room/conservatory, bar/library, lounge, courtyard; leisure facilities nearby; highchairs   ♿ Wheelchair access to hotel and breakfast room (ramp), 3 ground-floor bedrooms   ● No dogs; no smoking in most public rooms and most bedrooms   ▭ Amex, Delta, Diners, MasterCard, Switch, Visa   £ Single £50 to £60, single occupancy of twin/double £60 to £75, twin/double £85 to £110, four-poster £98 to £105, family suite £100 to £125; deposit required. Special breaks available   ③FOR②

DORRIDGE West Midlands   map 5

The Forest [NEW ENTRY]

Station Approach, Dorridge, Solihull B93 8JA
TEL: (01564) 772120   FAX: (01564) 772680
EMAIL: info@forest-hotel.com
WEB SITE: www.forest-hotel.com

Chic, sophisticated establishment in olive and burgundy livery

The current owners have done such a good job of transforming what was a 'smoky old railway hotel', which still lies conveniently opposite the station, that it's worth calling at Dorridge just to visit. Neon spotlights sparkle on the marble-topped bar, there's shiny wood panelling on the pillars, and muslin drapes add a note of opulence in the smartly done out bistro-style restaurant with its burgundy leather chairs. The bedrooms are spacious and imaginatively designed, generally coming in one of two 'colour waves'. Floating green or purple backboards – concealing storage space for clothes as well as tea- and coffee-making equipment – make a striking contrast with the cream walls, while crisp white linen is topped off with black cushions and the subtle trademark leafy throws. En-suite facilities are done to the same high standard, with laminate floors, nice white tiling and slick chrome fittings.

◖ Open all year; restaurant closed Sun eve   🔁 From M42 Junction 5, follow A4141 for 2 miles; after Knowle village, follow signs right to Dorridge; after 1½ miles turn left before railway bridge; hotel is 200 yards on left. Nearest train station: Dorridge. Private car park   🛏 1 single, 6 twin, 5 double; family rooms available; all with room service, hair-dryer, direct-dial telephone, TV   ⊘ Restaurant, bar, lounge, patio; conferences; social functions; civil wedding licence; leisure facilities nearby; highchairs   ♿ No wheelchair access   ● No dogs; smoking in bar only   ▭ Amex, Delta, MasterCard, Switch, Visa   £ Single £76, single occupancy of twin/double £88, twin/double £98, family room £123; deposit required. Set L £13, D £17.50 (Mon & Tue); alc L, D £22; light meals available. Special breaks available   ③FOR②

DULVERTON Somerset   map 1

Ashwick House

Dulverton TA22 9QD
TEL: (01398) 323868 (AND FAX)
EMAIL: ashwickhouse@talk21.com
WEB SITE: www.ashwickhouse.co.uk

Wonderful location for this welcoming country house

High up on Exmoor in glorious seclusion sits Richard Sherwood's Edwardian country house, a place set in six acres of lawns that run down to a couple of large ponds and the River Barle. Richard has preserved much of the period flavour of the house – William Morris wallpaper and rugs scattered on parquet flooring – but with significant additions. Hence bold touches in the colour schemes of the library and the sitting room plus small personal idiosyncrasies: the snake charm at the foot of the stairs, the wood-carved legendary beasts of Exmoor lining the driveway, and the mechanical bullfrog that announces the arrival of guests. The atmosphere here is certainly good-humoured, but tranquil too. Dinner menus come on hand-written scrolls, and the cooking is on the lighter side of country-house fare. Bedrooms are spacious and in keeping with the Edwardian flavour of the house; best to choose the south-facing ones for the views.

○ Open all year 🄩 At post office in Dulverton, take B3223 signposted Exford and Lynton; drive over moor, cross 2 cattle-grids and take left turn to Ashwick House. Private car park 🖙 6 twin/double; all with room service, hair-dryer, trouser press, direct-dial telephone, TV; some with mini-bar, CD player; no tea/coffee-making facilities in rooms ⊘ Restaurant, sitting room, library, garden; conferences and social functions; leisure facilities nearby; early suppers for children 🖢 No wheelchair access ● No children under 8; no dogs; no smoking in some public rooms and some bedrooms ⊡ None accepted £ Single occupancy of twin/double £38 to £63, twin/double £104 to £110; deposit required. Set L (Sun) £15, D £22; light meals available. Special breaks available ③FOR②

DUNSLEY North Yorkshire   map 9

Dunsley Hall

Dunsley, Whitby YO21 3TL
TEL: (01947) 893437 FAX: (01947) 893505
EMAIL: reception@dunsleyhall.com
WEB SITE: www.dunsleyhall.com

Elegant country house near to the Whitby coastline

Dunsley Hall is a classic Victorian country house set in lawns and gardens where peacocks roam. It was built from a fortune made in shipping by the Pyman family, who obviously had the sea in their blood, as the house sits just a couple of miles along twisting lanes from the Whitby coast, and several of the bedrooms have sea views. Further nautical nods are to be spotted in the house's stained-glass windows, which combine with oak panels, superbly carved fireplaces, fancy plasterwork and rug-strewn wooden floors to evoke the timeless gentleman's residence. There's a clubby bar to prepare you for a dinner in the impressive venue of the aptly named Oak Room, where elaborate French-influenced fare is served. Despite the grandeur of the surroundings, staff are unstuffily friendly and you'll quickly start to enjoy the informal, yet correctly professional style of service. Opulent bedrooms are furnished with antiques, decorated in rich tones and come with crisply modern bathrooms.

○ Open all year 🄩 In Dunsley village, 3 miles north of Whitby. Private car park 🖙 1 single, 3 twin/double, 9 double, 2 four-poster, 1 family room, 2 suites; all with room service, hair-dryer, trouser press, direct-dial telephone, modem line, TV ⊘ Dining room, bar, lounge, garden; conferences; social functions; civil wedding licence; gym, tennis, heated indoor swimming pool; leisure facilities nearby; early suppers for children; cots, highchairs, baby-listening 🖢 Wheelchair access to hotel and restaurant (ramps), National Accessible Scheme: mobility impairment M2, WC, 2 ground-floor bedrooms. Disabled parking ● No children under 5 in dining room eves; no dogs in public rooms and most bedrooms; smoking in bar and lounge only ⊡ Amex, Delta, MasterCard, Switch, Visa £ Single £80, single occupancy of twin/double £105, twin/double £130, four-poster £151, family room £190, suite £174; deposit required. Set D £28; alc D £37.50; light meals available; service incl. Special breaks available ③FOR②

EARSHAM Norfolk   map 6

Earsham Park Farm

Harleston Road, Earsham, Bungay NR35 2AQ
TEL: (01986) 892180 (AND FAX)
EMAIL: which@earsham-parkfarm.co.uk
WEB SITE: www.earsham-parkfarm.co.uk

Fabulous breakfasts at this working Norfolk farm

It's a bumpy drive along the track to the farmhouse at Earsham Park, but you're rewarded with cracking views over the surrounding rolling farmland (although the main road runs in between). This is very much a working farm, with machinery humming away, a scruffy farm dog and pigs wandering the fields. The pigs are an important component of your stay, for they provide you with one of the best cooked breakfasts you're ever likely to taste – bacon so thick it actually straddles the border between bacon and ham, and sausages so tender they fall apart if you so much as wave your knife in their general direction. Both are available to buy, helpfully packed in polystyrene so they don't defrost too quickly on the drive home. The other attraction in the dining room is the antique map hanging over the fireplace, showing the farm as it was in (many) years gone by. Ask Bobbie Watchorn about it and you'll be treated to a wonderful potted history of the farm featuring kings, earls, beetroots and even a spot of geology. One of the pretty bedrooms, Duck Pond, has stencilled flowers crawling up the walls. A firm sense of humour is also evident in the one named Pig Sty, and the poem in the bathroom about the perils of flushing large objects down the loo.

◖ Open all year   ⤢ Off A143 between Harleston and Bungay; about 3 miles from Bungay turn into private drive. Private car park   ⤶ 1 twin/double, 1 double, 1 four-poster; family rooms available; all with hair-dryer, mini-bar, TV   ⊘ Dining room, lounge, garden; leisure facilities nearby; cots, highchairs   & No wheelchair access   ● Dogs in bedrooms only; no smoking   ⊟ Delta, MasterCard, Switch, Visa   £ Single occupancy of twin/double £40 to £44, twin/double/four-poster £58 to £78, family room £78 to £98; deposit required

---

EAST BARKWITH   Lincolnshire   map 9

Bodkin Lodge

Grange Farm, Torrington Lane, East Barkwith, Market Rasen LN8 5RY
TEL: (01673) 858249 (AND FAX)

Refreshing rural therapy for tired city dwellers

The hospitality shown to their guests by Anne and Richard Stamp ensures a loyal following and a rewarding stay in their spacious, well-planned bungalow. Set on the edge of the family farm in the undulating countryside of Lincolnshire, this is the ideal starting point to begin walking the award-winning farm trail. Anne will happily prepare a picnic lunch for the ramble, although the hearty English breakfast of home-made bread and fresh Lincolnshire farm produce, served in the traditional dining room, is probably enough to set you up for the day. Anne enjoys cooking and by arrangement will provide a candlelit dinner. From the large, garden-facing sitting room, on a clear day the spires of Lincoln cathedral can be seen above the rolling farmland. The sizeable and attractively furnished bedrooms, decked out in restful, light colours, have a self-contained feel – 'a great size and very comfortable' according to one reader, who felt that it was like 'visiting old friends, not a first-time visit to a B&B'.

◖ Closed Chr & New Year and owners' holiday   ⤢ Turn off A157 by war memorial in East Barkwith into Torrington Lane; house is at edge of village, on right. Private car park   ⤶ 1 twin, 1 double; both with room service, hair-dryer, trouser press, TV   ⊘ Dining room, sitting room, garden; swimming and fishing nearby   & Wheelchair access to house and dining room, 2 ground-floor bedrooms. Disabled parking   ● No children under 10; no dogs; no smoking   ⊟ None accepted   £ Single occupancy of twin/double £38, twin/double £56 to £58; deposit required. Set D £16.50; light meals available; service incl

---

The Grange

Torrington Lane, East Barkwith, Market Rasen LN8 5RY
TEL: (01673) 858670
EMAIL: jonathanstamp@farmersweekly.net
WEB SITE: www.thegrange-lincolnshire.co.uk

Comfort, conservation and good food at family-friendly farm

When asking directions to the Grange, it is just as relevant to name the proprietors as the property, since both are equally well known in East Barkwith. Jonathan and Sarah Stamp are the fourth generation to live and farm here, following in the family tradition of providing exemplary hospitality in a traditional farm setting (see Bodkin Lodge). In a previous professional life Sarah was a home economist, and she now uses her expertise to offer traditionally based Lincolnshire dishes. The three-course dinners are available on request and served around one table. Otherwise there is a good pub with grub within walking distance. Jonathan and Sarah are keen conservationists and have introduced wildflower meadows, a tree-planting programme and nest boxes around the farm to encourage wildlife to return to the area, and guests to stroll around the farm. If all this fresh air takes its toll, the guest sitting room is ideal for relaxation – on a cold day there is a roaring wood fire to set a glow to your cheeks. The bedrooms are spacious and light with a fine array of rustic-style furniture.

◗ Closed Chr & New Year ⤬ Turn off A157 at war memorial in East Barkwith into Torrington Lane; continue for ¾ mile; Grange is first farmhouse on right outside village. Private car park ⬅ 2 double; suite available; both with room service, hair-dryer, TV ✅ Dining room, sitting room, garden; tennis; leisure facilities nearby; cots, highchairs ♿ No wheelchair access ⬤ No dogs; no smoking ▭ None accepted £ Double £49; suite £80 (2004 prices). Set D £17; light meals available; service incl (3FOR2)

EASTBOURNE East Sussex   map 3

Brayscroft Hotel [NEW ENTRY]

13 South Cliff Avenue, Eastbourne BN20 7AH
TEL: (01323) 647005
EMAIL: brayscroft@hotmail.com
WEB SITE: www.brayscrofthotel.co.uk

A genuinely warm welcome awaits you in this relaxed non-smoking small hotel

You'd think that life as a cardiac nurse would be much more stressful than running a small hotel in an Edwardian house in a residential area of Eastbourne; Sue Carter will tell you otherwise. She and her husband William took over this business two years ago and have been rushed off their feet ever since, but it's a friendly and homely place to stay. The public lounge is small but well restored, and the bedrooms are also compact. Décor is gradually being upgraded with damask and Toile de Jouy fabrics, *trompe l'oeil* panelling, antique furniture and original artwork throughout. In Room 3, they've gone for a Bloomsbury feel, and you can soak in a roll-top bath from the former home of Elizabeth Browning and Virginia Woolf. In 2005, the single room will be merged with one of the three doubles to make a large double. Dinner is by request and Sue consults guests about what they would like to eat. A typical meal might be mushroom and Parmesan soup, followed by beef fillet poached in red wine on a bed of potatoes and celeriac, served with vegetables from the garden.

◗ Open all year ⤬ From Eastbourne Pier follow Grand Parade towards Beachy Head; past Grand Hotel turn right up South Cliff (hill), then first right into South Cliff Avenue. Nearest train station: Eastbourne ⬅ 1 single, 2 twin, 3 double; all with hair-dryer, TV, mini-cooler ✅ Dining room, bar service, lounge; leisure facilities nearby ♿ No wheelchair access ⬤ No children under 12; dogs by arrangement only; no smoking ▭ Amex, Delta, Diners, MasterCard, Switch, Visa £ Single £30 to £32, single occupancy of twin/double £40 to £42, twin/double £60 to £64; deposit required. Set D £12; service incl (3FOR2)

Grand Hotel

King Edwards Parade, Eastbourne BN21 4EQ
TEL: (01323) 412345 FAX: (01323) 412233
EMAIL: reservations@grandeastbourne.com
WEB SITE: www.grandeastbourne.com

Opulent hotel with plush facilities and a pleasingly warm atmosphere

The Grand is exactly that! Purpose built by the Duke of Devonshire, this hotel's public areas are on an imposing scale, and the ten miles of wide corridors were designed with the hooped skirts of Victorian ladies in mind. While the communal areas are opulently furnished, the bedrooms are understandably more understated, many in the style of a traditional country house, with floral prints and reproduction furniture. Staff are polite and attentive without being deferential, and create a sense of conviviality, all too often absent in a large hotel of this standard. The range of facilities is what you would expect from a top-notch establishment, including a selection of bars and restaurants, both indoor and outdoor pools, a gym, fully equipped spa and putting green. In the renowned Mirabelle restaurant, treat yourself to a cognac at £150 per shot or if your tastes aren't quite as extravagant, the lunchtime bar menu represents much better value for money. The only thing missing is acres of verdant grounds in which to wander, but with views of the English Channel from many bedrooms at the front of the hotel, you have all the sense of space and nature you could need.

❍ Open all year; Mirabelle restaurant closed Sun & Mon eves ⚡ On seafront in Eastbourne, opposite Western Lawns park. Nearest train station: Eastbourne. Private car park ⬅ 60 twin, 46 twin/double, 46 suites; family rooms available; all with room service, hair-dryer, mini-bar, trouser press, direct-dial telephone, modem line, TV; fax, VCR, CD player on request; no tea/coffee-making facilities in rooms ⊘ 2 restaurants, 2 bars, 3 lounges, games room; conferences and social functions; civil wedding licence; gym, spa, heated indoor swimming pool, unheated outdoor swimming pool; leisure facilities nearby; early suppers for children; cots, highchairs, toys, playroom, babysitting, baby-listening 🦽 Wheelchair access to hotel (ramp) and restaurant, National Accessible Scheme: mobility impairment M1, WC, 13 ground-floor bedrooms, 3 rooms specially equipped for disabled people, lift. Disabled parking ● No children under 14 in Mirabelle restaurant eves; no dogs in public rooms; no smoking in restaurants ▭ Amex, Delta, Diners, MasterCard, Switch, Visa £ Single occupancy of twin/double £135, twin/double £165, family room £220, suite £220 to £385; deposit required. Set L £18, D £35; alc L £25, D £38; light meals available; service incl. Special breaks available (3FOR2)

EAST GRINSTEAD West Sussex   map 3

Gravetye Manor

Vowels Lane, East Grinstead RH19 4LJ
TEL: (01342) 810567   FAX: (01342) 810080
EMAIL: info@gravetyemanor.co.uk
WEB SITE: www.gravetyemanor.co.uk

Striking manor house off the beaten track with beautiful gardens and excellent food

As your car sweeps round the lane winding up to Gravetye you know you are in for a treat. Stunning vistas over forest open up at every turn before the imposing mellow stone manor house is revealed. Camouflaged in creepers and with numerous tall chimneys and latticed windows, it's an impressive Elizabethan pile surrounded by equally impressive gardens, the legacy of William Robinson, who developed his ideas for the English natural garden at the Manor. 'Flowers dislike exhaust fumes; please park head-on' is a sign that Gravetye takes its legacy seriously, and one of the indulgences of staying here is exploring the beautiful grounds and tranquil walkways. Another is the deliciously English interior with its wood panelling, country-house furnishings and crackling log fires in huge, intricately carved fireplaces – all conducive to graceful living and relaxation. In the elegant restaurant, Mark Raffan's menu has refreshingly straightforward descriptions and might include Gravetye's home-smoked salmon and breast of young pigeon, followed by warm French apple tart or hot passion fruit soufflé. The stylish bedrooms are named after trees and are typically good-sized, smartly decorated and comfortably furnished with antiques and art relating to nearby Glyndebourne. Those in the older part of the house have the edge for quirkiness.

❍ Open all year ⚡ Leave M23 at Junction 10, take A264 towards East Grinstead; after 2 miles take third exit at roundabout signposted Haywards Heath (B2028). After Turners Hill village, turn left towards West Hoathly, then first left into Vowels Lane. Private car park ⬅ 1 single, 16 twin/double, 1 four-poster; all with room service, hair-dryer, trouser press, direct-dial telephone, TV; no tea/coffee-making facilities in rooms ✓ Restaurant, bar, 3 lounges, garden; conferences; social functions; civil wedding licence; leisure facilities nearby &. No wheelchair access ● No children under 7 exc babes in arms; no dogs; no smoking in restaurant ☐ MasterCard, Switch, Visa £ Single £100 to £160, twin/double £170 to £325, four-poster £230 to £325. Continental B £14, cooked B £16; set L £27, D £37; alc L, D £52; light meals available; service incl

---

EAST HADDON Northamptonshire | map 5

Red Lion Hotel NEW ENTRY

East Haddon, Nr Northampton NN6 8BU
TEL: (01604) 770223   FAX: (01604) 770767
WEB SITE: www.redlionhoteleasthaddon.co.uk

Elegance and traditional country hospitality a hop and a skip from town

East Haddon is a neat, peaceful little haven just seven miles from Northampton, and the thatched seventeenth-century Red Lion Hotel at one end of the village provides a harmonious rural setting for that essential escape from the town. The extensive car park is testimony to its popularity, but once you are within the old-world charm of the hotel it is easy to forget the humdrum and concentrate on the treats ahead. Public rooms are homely and relaxing, and decorated throughout with antique coppers and brasses. The restaurant is elegantly old-fashioned, with heavy tied-back drapes at the high windows, textured floral wallpaper and an abundance of brass jugs and lamps. The cuisine is described as 'traditional English cooking with continental influences' by Ian Kennedy, the proprietor, who runs a tight ship – the service is brisk and polite. Bedrooms are snug and comfortable; all bathrooms come with showers.

◐ Closed 25 Dec ⤤ In East Haddon village, 7 miles northwest of Northampton, off A428. Private car park. Nearest train station: Long Buckby ⤶ 2 twin/double, 2 double, 1 four-poster; family rooms available; all with hair-dryer, direct-dial telephone, TV ✓ 2 restaurants, 2 bars, lounge, garden; conferences; social functions; leisure facilities nearby; cots, highchairs, toys &. No wheelchair access ● No dogs; smoking in bars only ☐ Amex, Delta, Diners, MasterCard, Switch, Visa £ Single occupancy of twin/double £60, twin/ double/four-poster £75, family room £85. Set L £21; alc L, D £27; light meals available ③FOR②

EAST HOATHLY East Sussex | map 3

Old Whyly

East Hoathly, Lewes BN8 6EL
TEL: (01825) 840216   FAX: (01825) 840738
EMAIL: stay@oldwhyly.co.uk
WEB SITE: www.oldwhyly.co.uk

A serene setting and accomplished cooking in this Grade II listed manor house

Sarah Burgoyne is an adept chef and the meals are a real draw at this Wolsey Lodge in the Sussex countryside. In the elegant dining room of this eighteenth-century wisteria-clad mansion, our inspector ate an ornately presented fig and mozzarella salad followed by a perfectly cooked main course of skate wings. The honey in the passion fruit pudding came from Sarah's own bee hives, just as the breakfast eggs came from the free-range hens which greet you as you approach the house on its long gravel drive. Afternoon tea is served in front of a log fire in the drawing room which is as tasteful as the rest of the house. We found that the Tulip bedroom was cold upon arrival but heated up quickly, and our request for a special pillow was met with charm and efficiency. The tranquil views over the extensive gardens, with their lake, pergola, topiary, heated pool and tennis court, and the lack of both televisions and mobile phone reception ensure a thoroughly rejuvenating stay at this country house.

◗ Open all year ⚡ Off A22 East Grinstead to Eastbourne road; heading south, continue ½ mile beyond Halland; take first left off large Shaw roundabout to East Hoathly; hotel is ½ mile on left by postbox; where drive divides into 3, take central gravel drive to Old Whyly. Private car park 🛏 1 twin, 2 twin/double; all with hair-dryer ⚗ Dining room, drawing room, conservatory, garden; social functions; tennis, heated outdoor swimming pool; leisure facilities nearby; early suppers for children, cots, toys ⚹ No wheelchair access ● No children under 8 in dining room eves; no dogs; no smoking in bedrooms ☐ None accepted £ Twin/ double £90 to £110. Set D £25; light meals available; service incl

EAST LAVANT West Sussex

map 3

Royal Oak NEW ENTRY

Pook Lane, East Lavant, Chichester PO18 0AX
TEL: (01243) 527434
EMAIL: nickroyaloak@aol.com
WEB SITE: www.sussexlive.co.uk/royaloakinn

Village inn with good food and contemporary designer bedrooms

Smack in the middle of the pretty Downland village of East Lavant and within spitting distance of Goodwood is this smart village inn. Step inside and you'll see that while the wood and brick floors, low ceilings, open fires and brick chimney breasts remain rooted in a traditional hostelry, the Royal Oak has been done out in less conventional style and rather more flair than you might expect. Take one large room with alcoves and corners providing snug private spaces, then add well-worn leather sofas scattered with cushions, bare pine wood tables, a stack of games and daily newspapers, and the buzz of a youthful lunchtime crowd selecting from chalkboard specials that mix old favourites with Mediterranean cuisine, and the feeling is rather more upmarket brasserie than simple public house. Designer touches also characterise the six resolutely contemporary bedrooms, divided between a converted barn and the space above the bar. Rooms are spacious, supremely comfortable and tastefully decorated with designer paints and neutral shade carpets. Touches of luxury include crisp white linen, top-notch fittings in the bathrooms and state-of-the-art gadgets, including plasma screen TVs and DVD players in all rooms.

◗ Open all year ⚡ From Chichester, take A286 towards Midhurst; after 2 miles turn right at first mini-roundabout, following signs for East Lavant. Cross humpback bridge; hotel car park is on right. Nearest train station: Chichester. Private car park 🛏 1 single, 2 twin, 2 double, 1 suite; family rooms available; all with room service, hair-dryer, mini-bar, direct-dial telephone, modem line, TV, CD player, DVD ⚗ Restaurant, bar, conservatory, garden; leisure facilities nearby; early suppers for children; cots, highchairs ⚹ No wheelchair access ● No dogs; no smoking in bedrooms ☐ Amex, MasterCard, Switch, Visa £ Single £60, single occupancy of twin/double £60 to £70, twin/double £70 to £110, family room £100 to £120, suite £100 to £150; deposit required. Alc L £25, D £30; light meals available. Special breaks available

EAST WITTON North Yorkshire

map 9

Blue Lion

East Witton, Nr Leyburn DL8 4SN
TEL: (01969) 624273 FAX: (01969) 624189
EMAIL: bluelion@breathemail.net
WEB SITE: www.thebluelion.co.uk

Refined country inn with impressive food and fine walking potential

In the eighteenth century travellers and drovers passing through Wensleydale would have stopped to refuel at the Blue Lion. The flagstoned floor and welcoming open fire in the bar would still be recognisable to them, although the emphasis nowadays is firmly on hearty upmarket food chalked up on blackboard menus, rather than quaffing of ale – although they do pull a fine pint of Black Sheep. Make no mistake, this is a popular place, with friendly waiters in long aprons kept hard at it in the evenings and at weekends, so the bare boards and soft lights of the romantic dining room offer a quieter alternative to the busy bar. An impressed correspondent reports an excellent meal of black pudding on bubble and squeak, and chicken breast stuffed with blue Wensleydale on smoked bacon risotto; also a 'huge and immaculate room with tasteful period furniture'. Rooms are indeed very comfortable, with a smart understated décor;

those in the main part of the inn have the edge for character and creaky-floor charm. 'A winning formula', concludes a happy visitor, impressed by the hearty breakfast and charming service.

○ Closed 25 Dec 🅿 On A6108 between Masham and Leyburn. Private car park 🛏 2 twin/double, 9 double, 1 family room; all with direct-dial telephone, TV; hair-dryer on request ⊘ Dining room, 2 bars, gardens; conferences and social functions; leisure facilities nearby; early suppers for children; cots, highchairs, baby-listening 👤 Wheelchair access to hotel (ramp) and dining room, WC, 4 ground-floor bedrooms ● None 💳 Delta, MasterCard, Switch, Visa £ Single occupancy of twin/double £54 to £89, twin/double £69 to £89, family room rates on application; deposit required. Set L, D £28.50; alc L, D £26. Special breaks available

---

EGHAM Surrey map 3

Great Fosters

Stroude Road, Egham TW20 9UR
TEL: (01784) 433822   FAX: (01784) 472455
EMAIL: enquiries@greatfosters.co.uk
WEB SITE: www.greatfosters.co.uk

Elizabethan house with fabulous gardens and characterful rooms

This imposing sixteenth-century manor house sits in a 50-acre estate close to the M25; but the drone of motorway traffic is only dimly audible in the delightful grounds, which come complete with manicured lawns and beautiful topiary gardens with hedged secret areas. Formerly a royal hunting lodge at the heart of Surrey's Royal Windsor Forest, Great Fosters has historic character in spades, with wood-panelled walls, ornate Jacobean ceilings, grand fireplaces and highly polished wood in the public areas, which are smart

and elegant. Bedrooms in the main house range from characterful standard doubles to the top-of-the-range Tapestry room with a fabulous bathroom and huge wall-hangings either side of a stone fireplace. Over in the coach house – close to the hotel's many function suites – accommodation is more standard, while the Cloister Rooms overlooking the courtyard are contemporary and stylish, done out in neutral shades with modern furnishings.

○ Open all year 🅿 Leave M25 at Junction 13 and follow signs to Egham; hotel is on B389 and is signposted from Egham town centre. Nearest train station: Egham. Private car park 🛏 16 single, 2 twin, 2 twin/double, 21 double, 2 four-poster, 2 family rooms, 7 suites; all with room service, hair-dryer, direct-dial telephone, modem line, TV; some with tea/coffee-making facilities, trouser press, CD player ⊘ Restaurant, bar, 2 lounges, gardens; conferences and social functions; civil wedding licence; heated outdoor swimming pool; leisure facilities nearby; cots, highchairs, babysitting 👤 Wheelchair access to hotel (ramp) and restaurant, WC, 1 ground-floor bedroom specially equipped for disabled people. Disabled parking ● No dogs 💳 Amex, Delta, Diners, MasterCard, Switch, Visa £ Single £90, single occupancy of twin/double £90, twin/ double £150 to £160, four-poster £295, family room £150, suite £350 (2004 prices); deposit required. Continental B £9.50, cooked B £15.50; set L £26.50, D £32.50; alc L, D £45; light meals available. Special breaks available

---

Runnymede Hotel

Windsor Road, Egham TW20 0AG
TEL: (01784) 436171   FAX: (01784) 436340
EMAIL: info@runnymedehotel.com
WEB SITE: www.runnymedehotel.com

Bustling business hotel with comfortable bedrooms and good leisure facilities

There is nothing particularly alluring about this modern building of angular red brick and smoked glass close to the M25. But once you've traipsed through the considerable car parks and are inside the hotel, the outlook – over a National Trust towpath and the Thames – is somewhat unexpected. Unsurprising, then, that midweek the public areas are stuffed with mobile-phone-toting business people conducting meetings over lunch either in the attractive waterside restaurant or in Charlie Bell's, a less formal eatery named after a local lock-keeper, where satays and steaks are cooked up on flame-grills and spit-roasts in an open kitchen. At weekends the professionals give way to leisure seekers, drawn by the bustling but relaxed atmosphere and good facilities, including a decent-sized pool, spa and gym. Bedrooms – standard or executive – are tastefully decorated, comfortable and well equipped with smart bathrooms. Fork out the extra tenner or so to upgrade from an executive to a riverside room.

◑ Open all year; restaurant closed Sun eve ⤢ Just off M25 Junction 13, on A308 to Egham and Windsor. Private car park ⬕ 11 single, 37 twin, 132 double; family rooms available; all with room service, hair-dryer, mini-bar, trouser press, direct-dial telephone, modem line, TV ⨂ 2 restaurants, 2 bars, lounge, conservatory, games room, garden; conferences; social functions; civil wedding licence; gym, spa, tennis, heated indoor swimming pool; early suppers for children; cots, highchairs, babysitting ♿ Wheelchair access to hotel and restaurants (ramp), National Accessible Scheme: mobility impairment M3, hearing impairment H2, visual impairment V2, WC, 7 rooms partially equipped for wheelchair users, lift. Disabled parking ● No dogs ▭ Amex, Delta, Diners, MasterCard, Switch, Visa £ Single £78, single occupancy of twin/double £212, twin/double £223, family room from £223. Continental/cooked B £14; set L £22, D £28.50; alc D £35; light meals available. Special breaks available (2004 data)

EMSWORTH Hampshire   map 2

36 On the Quay [NEW ENTRY]

47 South Street, Emsworth PO10 7EG
TEL: (01243) 375592/372257   FAX: (01243) 375593
WEB SITE: www.36onthequay.co.uk

Excellent restaurant with designer bedrooms, smack on the seafront

How reassuring that this immaculate, cream-painted seventeenth-century building should be right where its name suggests: bang on the quayside with lovely views over Emsworth's small harbour. Originally a terrace of cottages, the building variously served as a fishermen's pub and a sailing club before being converted into a restaurant, which chef Ramon Farthing and his wife Karen took on in the mid 1990s. The restaurant remains the heart of the place, a sunny and elegant space decked out in shades of lemon, light blue and green, with well-spaced tables, dark-wood carver chairs and silver cutlery. Menus vary from the whopping 11-course 'Little Big Option' (a reasonably priced tasting menu that promises to be 'varied and balanced with a clean-cut simplicity') to a two- or three-course lunch menu – perhaps pumpkin soup finished with asparagus and fresh white crab meat, followed by breast of farm chicken wrapped in Parma ham and a hot gooseberry soufflé. The bedrooms – appropriately named after spices – are classy and supremely comfortable, with sparkling modern bathrooms. Pick of the bunch is Vanilla, a spacious and stylish room with sloping ceilings, exposed beams and a lovely low bay complete with window seat overlooking the harbour. Cinnamon, a smaller double, is equally tasteful, with a hobbit-sized doorway into a cramped but stylish shower room with a star-shaped shower head resembling an automatic sprinkler system. Cardamom, a tiny fourteenth-century cottage, was about to be finished soon after our inspection.

◑ Closed last week in Oct, first 3 weeks in Jan; restaurant closed Sun eve ⤢ From A259, follow signs to quayside in Emsworth. Nearest train station: Emsworth. Private car park ⬕ 4 double, 1 suite; all with hair-dryer, TV ⨂ Restaurant, bar, garden; baby-listening ♿ No wheelchair access ● Dogs in cottage only ▭ Amex, Delta, Diners, MasterCard, Switch, Visa £ Single occupancy of double £60, double £85, suite £110 to £125; set L £22, D 40; alc L £40

Plantation House

Totnes Road, Ermington, Nr Ivybridge PL21 9NS
TEL: (01548) 831100   FAX: (01548) 831248
EMAIL: enquiries@plantationhousehotel.com
WEB SITE: www.plantationhousehotel.com

Professionally run colonial-style restaurant-with-rooms

Helen and Alan Coby seem to be settling in well in this former rectory looking out over rolling hills. The creamy Georgian façade, complete with wisteria and small sunken garden, looks a picture in late spring, and is only slightly marred by traffic noise from the nearby A3121. The cool, unfussy public rooms on either side of the entrance hall have an airy, colonial feel and long French windows opening onto the front. In the Matisse restaurant, framed prints of collages by the eponymous artist add colour, as does a row of coloured wine goblets along the mantelpiece. Accomplished dinners featuring the best local produce, including seafood, beef and duck, are served up by young, professional staff. On inspection, home-made croissants at breakfast were also good; rather solid scrambled egg less so. Bedrooms, named after cocktails, are very comfortable, even if they lack the stylish simplicity of the downstairs areas. Martini Cocktail, a huge room on the top floor, has Indian bedspreads and a busy orange and green colour scheme. And some details seem out of place in an establishment of this quality: the cups on the tea tray are Villeroy & Boch, but they come with PG Tips teabags, tubes of instant Nescafé, and cartons of UHT milk.

❍ Open all year; restaurant closed Sun eve ⬛ From A38, take Ivybridge exit and follow signs to Ermington; hotel is 200 yards outside village. Private car park ⬛ 2 single, 2 twin/double, 3 double, 1 four-poster, 1 family room; all with room service, hair-dryer, direct-dial telephone, modem line, TV; 1 with VCR ⬥ Restaurant, bar, lounge, garden; conferences; social functions; leisure facilities nearby; early suppers for children; cots, highchairs, baby-listening ♿ No wheelchair access ⬤ No dogs in public rooms; no smoking ▭ Amex, MasterCard, Switch, Visa £ Single £50 to £55, single occupancy of twin/double £59 to £69, twin/double/four-poster £99 to £119, family room £109 to £129; deposit required. Set D £36; alc L £24, D £36; light meals available. Special breaks available (3FOR2)

King John's Lodge

Sheepstreet Lane, Etchingham TN19 7AZ
TEL: (01580) 819232   FAX: (01580) 819562
EMAIL: kingjohnslodge@aol.com
WEB SITE: www.kingjohnslodge.co.uk

Ideal for garden enthusiasts and appreciators of old-world gentility

Tucked discreetly behind a tall hedge just off the hilly Etchingham–Ticehurst road is the atmospheric King John's Lodge. This well-maintained, sprawling Jacobean house is a favourite among gardening enthusiasts. The extensive, tree-lined grounds with impressive water features, formal lawns, shrubberies and a secret garden are the result of Jill and Richard Cunningham's passion for gardening – the family founded the Bed and Breakfast for Garden Lovers Group. The mullion windows, vast stone fireplaces and oak-beamed ceilings reveal an affluent history and a fitting place for a king, even if, so legend has it, King John II of France was staying as unwilling hostage rather than welcome guest in the twelfth century. Comfortable, rustic-style antique furniture and a medley of quaint knick-knacks and family memorabilia enhance the charm of the slightly down-at-heel, old-world gentility of the public areas. A wood-panelled lounge overlooks the gardens and rolling landscape beyond – an ideal place for taking the complimentary afternoon tea in bad weather. A nicely cooked, full English breakfast can be enjoyed in the Edwardian, aristocratic ambience of the high-ceilinged dining room. A winding balustrade staircase leads to the airy, old-fashioned bedrooms. Each pastel-coloured room, with bathroom, is furnished with a brass-framed bed and a miscellany of heavy chests, wall hangings and sofas.

● Closed Chr & New Year 🔁 Turn off A21 at Flimwell and follow A2087 to Ticehurst; turn left past church and first left again; house is 1 mile on left. Nearest train station: Etchingham. Private car park 🛏 1 twin, 2 double, 1 family room ✓ Dining room, 2 lounges, games room, garden; tennis, heated outdoor swimming pool, leisure facilities nearby; cots, highchairs ♿ No wheelchair access ● No children under 7 in dining room eves; no dogs; no smoking in bedrooms and 1 lounge ▭ None accepted £ Single occupancy of twin/double £55, twin/double £80, family room £100; deposit required. Set D £25; service incl

---

EVERSHOT Dorset   map 2

Summer Lodge

Evershot, Dorchester DT2 0JR
TEL: (01935) 482000 FAX: (01935) 482040
EMAIL: reservations@summerlodgehotel.com
WEB SITE: www.summerlodgehotel.com

New owners and a serious makeover at this lovely country house

Summer Lodge is undergoing something of a transformation these days. New owners have taken over, and gone is the quaint and quirky Englishness, in has come the sumptuous and splendid. The changes might not suit everyone: this is a smoothly sophisticated operation that comes at a high price. And yet the bedrooms are magnificent, oozing comfort and relaxation: there is even a flat-screen television tucked inside the four-poster beds. Downstairs, the new bar needs a little bedding in, while the drawing room is a clever mélange of contemporary and traditional: gilt-framed paintings on the walls, deep sofas and a view out into the four-acre garden. Work on this aspect was busily progressing when we visited, with new trees and a herb garden going in. The restaurant stretches alongside the lawns and is decorated with a light touch, with button-back bench seats and high-backed chairs. Menus lean to the richer side of country-house fare.

● Open all year 🔁 1 mile west of A37, midway between Dorchester and Yeovil; entrance to hotel is in Summer Lane. Private car park 🛏 1 single, 1 twin, 15 twin/double, 7 suites; all with room service, hair-dryer, direct-dial telephone, modem line, TV, DVD, CD player; 2 with mini-bar ✓ Restaurant, bar, drawing room, garden; conferences and social functions; civil wedding licence; spa, tennis, heated indoor swimming pool; early suppers for children; cots, highchairs, baby-listening ♿ Wheelchair access to hotel (ramp) and restaurant, 3 ground-floor bedrooms ● No children under 7 in restaurant eves; no dogs in public rooms; smoking in bar and some bedrooms only ▭ Amex, Delta, Diners, MasterCard, Switch, Visa £ Single £83, single occupancy of twin/double £115, twin/double from £280, suite from £490; deposit required. Set L £27, D £32; alc L, D £48; light meals available

---

EVESHAM Worcestershire   map 5

Evesham Hotel

Cooper's Lane, off Waterside, Evesham WR11 1DA
TEL: (01386) 765566 FAX: (01386) 765443
EMAIL: reception@eveshamhotel.com
WEB SITE: www.eveshamhotel.com

Unpretentious fun – and plenty of diversions – at this family-run hotel for all the family

It won't take you very long to guess that there is some eccentricity in the air at John and Sue Jenkinson's hotel. A jolly collection of teddy bears behind the reception desk show that fun is on the agenda. And a glance at the menu, or the hotel directory, both with personal asides by the owners, show that things shouldn't be taken too seriously. The quirky bar area, with a long low bookcase underneath the bar itself, has an enormous collection of drinks on offer, some apparently gifts from friends who understand the Jenkinsons' penchant for obscure drinks. From the restaurant are views to the magnificent cedar tree, planted in 1809, on the ample lawns. This is a hotel which has the child in all of us firmly in mind, and there are plenty of diverting activities available such as the indoor pool, table tennis and table football.

The standard decoration is simple with creams and whites; a programme of refurbishment is ongoing. For a little more adventure guests could try one of the themed rooms, such as the Egyptian Room, with a raised bed like some pharaoh's last resting place, hieroglyphics and murals. Or you could try the Oriental Room, which has wooden cabinets shaped like temples and a mini Japanese garden on the roof outside the window.

◗ Closed 25 & 26 Dec 🗲 Cooper's Lane turns off Waterside (B4035; formerly A44), which runs along the River Avon in Evesham; hotel is on right before junction with Church Street. Nearest train station: Evesham. Private car park 🖐 4 single, 12 twin, 21 double, 1 family room, 1 suite; all with room service, hair-dryer, direct-dial telephone, TV, ironing facilities; some with fridge ⊘ Restaurant, bar, 2 lounges, garden; conferences; heated indoor swimming pool; leisure facilities nearby; early suppers for children; cots, highchairs, toys, babysitting, baby-listening, outdoor play area ♿ No wheelchair access; 10 ground-floor bedrooms ⬤ No dogs in public rooms; no smoking in most public rooms and some bedrooms ▭ Amex, Delta, Diners, MasterCard, Switch, Visa £ Single £77, single occupancy of twin/double £91, twin/double £124, family room £175, suite £201 (rates valid till March 2005). Alc L, D £25; light meals available; service incl. Special breaks available

---

<table>
<tr><td>EXETER Devon</td><td>map 1</td></tr>
</table>

Alias Hotel Barcelona

Magdalen Street, Exeter EX2 4HY
TEL: (01392) 281000 FAX: (01392) 281001
EMAIL: info@aliasbarcelona.com
WEB SITE: www.aliashotels.com

Design-led hotel with young, buzzy vibe

Converting a very institutional Victorian eye infirmary into a microcosm of the Catalan capital might sound like a bit of a challenge, but it's one that the Alias group has met with verve. So the corridors are hung with an eclectic selection of artworks, including framed samples of 1950s wallpaper, and the stairwells feature bright green wavy banister rails, but the original lift, large enough to take a patient trolley, remains intact. Then an eye-catching circular extension has been added at the back to house Café Paradiso, where chefs in the open kitchen turn out wood-fired oven pizzas, pasta, salads and steaks against vibrant blocks of painted colour. The Kino cocktail bar is a more low-lit, end-of-the-evening kind of space, with low leather armchairs and sofas, *film noir* posters and cheery young bartenders flipping bottles as they mix drinks. Bedrooms can be small, but they are stylishly turned out, with cheery throws, custom-made teak furniture, and well-designed bathrooms. We have only a couple of quibbles: a light above the bathroom mirror would make shaving much easier, and why do guests have to ask at reception for their complimentary bottle of mineral water?

◗ Open all year 🗲 Leave M5 at Junction 30, taking A379 to Exeter and Dawlish; at Countess Wear roundabout, take third exit to city centre; follow Topsham Road for 2 miles; follow road right at main junction on to Magdalen Street; hotel is on right. Nearest train station: Exeter St David's. Private car park 🖐 7 single, 39 twin/double; family rooms available; all with room service, hair-dryer, direct-dial telephone, modem line, TV, VCR, CD player ⊘ Restaurant, bar, lounge, library, garden; conferences; social functions; leisure facilities nearby; early suppers for children; cots, highchairs, toys, babysitting ♿ Wheelchair access to hotel (ramp), WC, 2 ground-floor bedrooms, lift. Disabled parking ⬤ Dogs £15 in bedrooms; no smoking in restaurant ▭ Amex, Delta, Diners, MasterCard, Switch, Visa £ Single £85, single occupancy of twin/double £95 to £115, twin/double £95 to £115, family room £115; deposit required. Continental B £8, cooked B £11; set L, D £20/£30; alc L, D £25; light meals available. Special breaks available

---

It is always worth enquiring about the availability of special breaks or weekend prices. The prices we quote are the standard rates for one night – most hotels offer reduced rates for longer stays.

St Olaves Hotel

Mary Arches Street, Exeter EX4 3AZ
TEL: (01392) 217736   FAX: (01392) 413054
EMAIL: info@olaves.co.uk
WEB SITE: www.olaves.co.uk

Charming Georgian hotel, well positioned for the city centre

Tucked away through an archway close to Exeter's town centre is an elegant fountain. Facing it sits this quiet and unassuming hotel. Central to the late-Georgian building is a superb curling staircase with bedrooms leading directly off it – and these are the best rooms to choose, comfortably furnished with some interesting pieces of furniture dotted throughout to create a warm, homely feel.

Downstairs is a small but elegant lounge, a conservatory bar and a classically decorated dining room. The three-course menus offer three or four choices at each stage – a celeriac and pancetta soup to start, perhaps, followed by rump of Dartmoor lamb as main and then a spiced poached pear with nougat parfait. The atmosphere is unstuffy and quiet, but it is best to avoid the rooms across the main road.

◖ Open all year   🚹 In centre of Exeter follow signs for Mary Arches car park; hotel is in same street. Nearest train stations: Exeter Central & Exeter St David's. Private car park   🅿️ 4 twin, 9 double, 4 suites; all with room service, hair-dryer, direct-dial telephone, modem line, TV; some with mini-bar, VCR and trouser press   ⌘ Restaurant, dining room, bar, lounge, library, conservatory, garden; conferences; social functions; civil wedding licence; leisure facilities nearby; early suppers for children; cots, highchairs, baby-listening   ♿ No wheelchair access; 3 steps into hotel, 1 ground-floor bedroom   ⬤ No dogs in public rooms; no smoking in bedrooms   ▭ Delta, Diners, MasterCard, Switch, Visa   £ Single occupancy of twin/double £115, twin/double £125, suite £145; deposit required. Cooked B £4.50; set L £18.50, D £29.50; light meals available; service incl (2004 data)

FALMOUTH Cornwall map 1

Penmere Manor

Mongleath Road, Falmouth TR11 4PN
TEL: (01326) 211411   FAX: (01326) 317588
EMAIL: reservations@penmere.co.uk
WEB SITE: www.penmeremanorhotel.co.uk

A friendly welcome and convenient location just outside Falmouth

You could be forgiven for thinking you're heading in the wrong direction as you drive through Falmouth past an industrial estate. But once at Penmere Manor, you're safely shielded by the trees in the five acres of grounds surrounding this largely modern hotel. The reception has pretty, delicate, flowery wallpaper, but after that the décor becomes slightly corporate in feel. When we inspected, visitors to the lounge had the

opportunity to win a striking bronze statue of a puma by sponsoring a trek to Peru. The bar is a bit of an eccentric mix, with fishtank and children's toys and an interesting table with games built into the tabletop. There's a nice pool and a gym for those who are feeling energetic and a Jacuzzi for those who aren't. Bedrooms are clean and floral, though some of the bathrooms could do with an update.

◖ Closed 24 to 27 Dec   🚹 From Truro take A39 towards Falmouth; turn right at Hillhead roundabout; straight on for 1 mile then turn left into Mongleath Road. Private car park   🅿️ 11 single, 22 twin/double, 4 double; all with room service, hair-dryer, direct-dial telephone, modem line, TV; some with trouser press   ⌘ Restaurant, bar, lounge, library, games room, croquet lawn; conferences and social functions; civil wedding licence; gym, spa, heated indoor and outdoor swimming pools; early suppers for children; cots, highchairs, toys, baby-listening, outdoor play area   ♿ Wheelchair access to hotel (ramp) and restaurant, WC, 14 ground-floor bedrooms. Disabled parking   ⬤ No dogs; no smoking in bedrooms   ▭ Amex, Delta, Diners, MasterCard, Switch, Visa   £ Single £64 to £71, single occupancy of twin/double £75 to £82, twin/double £102 to £146; deposit required. Set D £25; light meals available; service incl. Special breaks available

FAREHAM Hampshire   map 2

Solent Hotel

Rookery Avenue, Whiteley, Fareham PO15 7AJ
TEL: (01489) 880000   FAX: (01489) 880007
EMAIL: solent@shirehotels.co.uk
WEB SITE: www.shirehotels.co.uk

Surprisingly characterful public areas in a business-oriented hotel with first-class leisure facilities

Reclaimed timbers, heavy beams, huge chandeliers, wood floors and crackling fires are not features one might expect in an unremarkable – albeit convenient – setting on the edge of a business park just off the M27. But at this friendly, business-focused hotel, first impressions can be deceptive and the traditional country-house style of the bustling public areas is completely at odds with its modern red-brick chalet-like exterior. Midweek conference and business guests fill cosy alcoves in the open-plan bar and restaurant, which fan out from a welcoming octagonal galleried reception with a roaring fire. At weekends special breaks bring in leisure guests lured by top-notch facilities which have been newly upgraded and extended to include a pool, sauna, steam room and myriad gym and activity studios. Bedrooms lean towards the corporate, with contract furniture and functional but spotless modern bathrooms – all are decorated to a high standard with either pretty flowery or masculine colour schemes.

● Open all year ⊿ Leave M27 at Junction 9, following signs for Whiteley, then signs for hotel; situated on Solent Business Park. Private car park ⊯ 18 twin, 14 twin/double, 61 double, 5 four-poster, 13 suites; family rooms available; all with room service, hair-dryer, trouser press, direct-dial telephone, modem line, TV; some with mini-bar ⊗ Restaurant, bar, lounge, conservatory, games room, garden; conferences and social functions; civil wedding licence; gym, spa, tennis, heated indoor swimming pool; early suppers for children; cots, highchairs, toys, babysitting ⅄ Wheelchair access to hotel and restaurant, WC, 39 ground-floor bedrooms, 3 rooms specially equipped for disabled people, lift. Disabled parking ● No dogs; no smoking in some public rooms and some bedrooms ⊟ Amex, Delta, Diners, MasterCard, Switch, Visa £ Twin/double £126 to £134, four-poster £164, family room £134, suite £194; deposit required. Set L £21; alc L, D £33; light meals available; service incl. Special breaks available ③FOR②

FARNHAM Dorset   map 2

Museum Inn

Farnham, Nr Blandford Forum DT11 8DE
TEL: (01725) 516261   FAX: (01725) 516988
EMAIL: enquiries@museuminn.co.uk
WEB SITE: www.museuminn.co.uk

Excellent food at this stylish and friendly inn

The name comes from local squire Augustus Pitt-Rivers – he of the natural history museum in Oxford and renowned collector of dried human heads, etc. Nothing like that to be found here, of course, although there are some stuffed animals in the stylishly simple bar and dining areas, along with flagged floors, beams and old panelling. Things can get busy at its wooden tables, such is the attraction of the energetic modern cooking. Bedrooms are divided between the main inn and the converted stables. They all get an attractive mix of antiques, prints and thoughtful extras such as home-made biscuits and fresh milk, but those above the bar/restaurant just about get the vote for being that little bit more charming. Breakfast is served either in the cosy, book-lined residents' sitting room or in the more airy dining room. Owners Vicky Elliot and Mark Stephenson keep things humming along with charm and good humour.

● Closed 25, 26 & 31 Dec ⊿ Off A534, 10 miles south of Salisbury. Private car park ⊯ 2 twin/double, 5 double, 1 four-poster; all with hair-dryer, direct-dial telephone, TV; 1 with VCR ⊗ Restaurant/bar, dining room, library, conservatory, garden; conferences; golf, horse-riding nearby ⅄ Wheelchair access to hotel and

restaurant (1 step), WC, 4 ground-floor bedrooms ◖ No children under 8; no smoking in bedrooms
▭ Delta, MasterCard, Switch, Visa £ Single occupancy of twin/double £65 to £110, twin/double £75 to
£95, four-poster £120; deposit required. Alc L, D £25; light meals available

---

FAVERSHAM Kent   map 3

Read's

Macknade Manor, Canterbury Road, Faversham ME13 8XE
TEL: (01795) 535344   FAX: (01795) 591200
EMAIL: enquiries@reads.com
WEB SITE: www.reads.com

Manor house restaurant with sophisticated rooms

Leaving the busy A2 and turning into the drive through mature trees you approach a fine Georgian manor house surrounded by smooth green lawns. To call this a restaurant with rooms doesn't really do the house justice. It is elegantly furnished throughout and has the feel of a rather grand private home lovingly restored. Colour schemes are simple and pale, from the white wood-panelled sitting room with its discreet corner bar and stripped floor with rugs and fresh flowers to the two interlinked rooms that make up the restaurant. The menu is detailed and based on good local produce, supplemented by home-grown fruit and vegetables from the large walled kitchen garden (still in its relative infancy). Whitstable shellfish, local lobster, organically reared pork or duckling 'served three ways' all feature. Each of the six large bedrooms is sophisticated and luxurious. They vary from restrained cool country house with half-testers, floral drapes and gilt frames on walls to more colourful creations with Indian colours or maybe an four-poster bed. Each has a good bathroom (Wisteria has an extra-large shower room). Breakfast is taken in an airy vaulted room, or, in fine weather, on the terrace.

◐ Closed Sun and Mon ⊞ From M2 Junction 6, follow signs to Faversham; at T-junction, turn right on to A2; Read's is ½ mile on right. Nearest train station: Faversham. Private car park ⌂ 5 twin/double, 1 four-poster; all with hair-dryer, direct-dial telephone, modem line, TV, VCR ⊘ Restaurant, breakfast room, honesty bar, sitting room, garden; conferences; social functions; civil wedding licence; leisure facilities nearby; early suppers for children; cots, highchairs ⅙ No wheelchair access ◖ No dogs; smoking in sitting room only ▭ Amex, Delta, Diners, MasterCard, Switch, Visa £ Single occupancy of twin/double £120, twin/double/four-poster £150. Set L £19.50, D £45. Special breaks available

---

FILEY North Yorkshire   map 9

Downcliffe House

6 The Beach, Filey YO14 9LA
TEL: (01723) 513310   FAX: (01723) 512659
EMAIL: info@downcliffehouse.co.uk
WEB SITE: www.downcliffehouse.co.uk

Traditional Victorian seaside hotel with fine views and a warm welcome

Nicholas and Caroline Hunt's imposing mansion has undergone a continuous programme of upgrading and improvements since they took over in 2000. It occupies an enviable spot on Filey's classic promenade, with lovely views over the broad sweep of sand; twin terraces flanking the entrance are just the spot for afternoon tea and home-made cakes or drinks on fine evenings. Inside, the décor doesn't try to compete with the scene outside the grand bay windows; it is spruce and gently traditional with period features such as plaster cornicing and ceiling roses. The dinner menu sticks to tried-and-tested, resolutely traditional favourites; local fish – perhaps haddock with tartare sauce, or sole meunière – is always a feature, or meaty fare such as roast lamb or beef bourguignon. Most bedrooms have sea views – particularly those on the top floor such as Room 8, which also has characterful beams and looks towards Flamborough cliffs, or Room 10 with its corner bath.

◗ Closed Jan; restaurant closed Sun & Mon eves ⏶ On seafront in Filey. From A1039 drive through centre, ignoring signs to beach; at far end of Cargate Hill turn right; hotel is approx 200 yards along. Nearest train station: Filey ⊨ 1 single, 2 twin, 2 twin/double, 2 double, 1 four-poster, 1 family room, 2 suites; all with hair-dryer, direct-dial telephone, TV ⊘ Restaurant, bar, lounge; cots, highchairs � No wheelchair access ● No dogs; smoking in bar only ▭ Delta, Diners, MasterCard, Switch, Visa £ Single £46, twin/double £92 to £106, four-poster/suite £124, family room £115; deposit required. Cooked B £7; set D £22; alc L £18, D £25; light meals available. Special breaks available (3FOR2)

FLAMBOROUGH East Riding of Yorkshire

map 9

Manor House

Flamborough, Bridlington YO15 1PD
TEL: (01262) 850943 (AND FAX)
EMAIL: gm@flamboroughmanor.co.uk
WEB SITE: www.flamboroughmanor.co.uk

Georgian house with interesting history and excellent rooms

After a blustery walk along the windswept cliffs around Flamborough Head, a thick traditional Gansey jumper might seem a good investment. Lesley Berry and Geoffrey Miller can sell you one of these from their shop, as well as putting you up in impeccable style and comfort in their impressive old manor house. Among their multifarious interests, Lesley also trades in antiques, so the house is liberally peppered with curios, and Geoffrey's interest in books (he is the author of several volumes on the First World War) and things nautical is responsible for the sketches of ships on the walls and a huge collection of books. The bedrooms are brimming with character: the main room has as its centrepiece an amazing seventeenth-century Portuguese four-poster, while the second, smaller, room has a more Victorian character, with an antique brass bedstead and a free-standing claw-foot cast-iron bath. In the evening, by prior arrangement, you can dine Wolsey Lodge-style around a communal table.

◗ Closed Chr ⏶ From Bridlington B1255 to Flamborough, pass church on right; house is on next corner (Lighthouse Road/Tower Street). Private car park ⊨ 1 double, 1 four-poster; family room available; both with hair-dryer, TV ⊘ Dining room, lounge, garden; leisure facilities nearby ゟ No wheelchair access ● No children under 8; no dogs; no smoking ▭ Delta, MasterCard, Switch, Visa £ Single occupancy of double £46, double £72, four-poster £82, family room £102; deposit required. Set D £27; service incl

---

FLEET Dorset

map 2

Moonfleet Manor

Fleet Road, Fleet, Weymouth DT3 4ED
TEL: (01305) 786948 FAX: (01305) 774395
EMAIL: info@moonfleetmanor.com
WEB SITE: www.luxuryfamilyhotels.com

Excellent for kids, but pretty spiffing for grown-ups too

In his novel *Moonfleet*, J Meade Falkner weaves an adventurous tale of smuggling and pirates that engulfs his 15-year-old hero. Luckily, at this hotel there's more than enough to keep kids of any age busy without them resorting to midnight rendezvous with shady characters on nearby Chesil Beach. The vast site centres on a Georgian main house, smartly done out in cream-washed walls, surrounded by a hotchpotch of outer buildings housing everything from a skittle alley and squash court to three indoor pools, so that the emphasis is firmly on family fun, both indoor and out. Adults get a look-in too, with a sauna and massage treatments on offer, while a supervised nursery, baby-listening and babysitting are all on hand to give parents a welcome break. The high-ceilinged interior is swishly done, furnished in an Empire-strikes-back style with pot plants, rattan chairs, intriguing prints, and the occasional animal hide adorning the walls. Bedrooms, each named after a character from the novel, are equally comfortable and kitted out in a Raj-comes-home theme, and come complete with snazzy bathrooms.

◗ Open all year 🅉 Off B3157 near Chesil Beach. Private car park 🛏 1 single, 23 twin/double, 11 family rooms, 4 suites; all with room service, hair-dryer, direct-dial telephone, TV; some with VCR, fridge ◈ Restaurant, bar, 2 lounges, library, games room, garden; conferences; social functions; spa, tennis, heated indoor swimming pools; leisure facilities nearby; early suppers for children; cots, highchairs, toys, playroom, babysitting, baby-listening, outdoor play area ♿ Wheelchair access to hotel and restaurant, WC, 3 ground-floor bedrooms, lift ⬤ No dogs in some public rooms ▭ Amex, Delta, Diners, MasterCard, Switch, Visa £ Single £90 to £105, single occupancy of twin/double £124 to £152, twin/double £120 to £190, family room £170 to £210, suite £210 to £285; deposit required (prices valid till Jan 2005). Set L £15, D £25; alc D £30; light meals available. Special breaks available

---

FLETCHING East Sussex   map 3

Griffin Inn

Fletching, Uckfield TN22 3SS
TEL: (01825) 722890 FAX: (01825) 722810
EMAIL: thegriffininn@hotmail.com
WEB SITE: www.thegriffininn.co.uk

Atmospheric family-friendly inn with great food and attractive accommodation

Fletching is a Sussex village that has retained its sixteenth-century veneer, even if its residents are now sons and daughters of office toil rather than the worn-out offspring of the soil. The village's beamed, stucco and brick, cottage-style buildings bristle with high angular chimneys, and the Griffin Inn is no exception. The Inn is directly on the street, but at the rear a spacious and pleasant garden – used for al-fresco drinking and dining (and barbecues in summer) – offers fine views across the undulating countryside. Inside, the extensive, characterful bar is full of locals, who come for the excellent range of dishes chalked up daily on the blackboard. There's also a separate restaurant. The charming bedrooms are well appointed (and telephone-free). The quietest are in the garden-facing coach house, but the most atmospheric are over the pub. Nearly all have stylish, draped four-poster beds and modern 'Victorian-style' bathrooms.

◗ Closed 25 Dec; restaurant closed Sun eve in winter 🅉 Take A22 south from East Grinstead, then A275 from Wych Cross; after 7 miles turn left at sign to Fletching. Private car park 🛏 1 twin, 7 four-poster; all with hair-dryer, TV ◈ Restaurant, 2 bars, garden; social functions (weekdays only); leisure facilities nearby; early suppers for children; highchairs, outdoor play area ♿ Wheelchair access to hotel (2 steps) and restaurant (1 step), 2 ground-floor bedrooms ⬤ No dogs; no smoking in restaurant and bedrooms ▭ Amex, Delta, Diners, MasterCard, Switch, Visa £ Single occupancy of twin £50 to £85, twin £70 to £85, four-poster £70 to £120; deposit required. Set L (Sun) £25; alc L, D £27; light meals available. Special breaks available ③FOR②

FOWEY Cornwall   map 1

Fowey Hall

Hanson Drive, Fowey PL23 1ET
TEL: (01726) 833866 FAX: (01726) 834100
EMAIL: info@foweyhall.com
WEB SITE: www.luxuryfamilyhotels.com

Perfect spot for a posh family getaway

The courtyard rooms of Fowey Hall are named after characters from *The Wind in the Willows* – it is one of several places around the country that claim to have been the inspiration for Toad Hall. Whether this is true or not, just like the book, Fowey Hall has a graceful charm and will appeal to adults and children in equal measure. The secret of keeping the interior so grand and spotless with all those children running around? The hotel has a warehouse full of back-up antiques that can be shipped in at a moment's notice – all part of its ethos (like that of its sister hotels) promising luxury combined with a warm welcome for the little ones. There's a mix of lounging and eating spaces to suit your mood, including a formal dining room with Greek-style columns and wood-panelled walls – a calmer spot away from the kids – and a bright family dining room which still retains a certain summery grandeur. Bedrooms are similarly antique-filled, but never feel cluttered, and all have baby monitors linked to reception so that you can leave your sleeping brood with a clear conscience.

◐ Open all year　🔁 Turn off B3269 following signs to Fowey; at Fowey go straight over mini-roundabout, continue towards town and down a steep hill; turn right into Hanson Drive; Hall is on right. Private car park 🛏️ 1 twin, 5 double, 6 family rooms, 12 suites; all with room service, hair-dryer, direct-dial telephone, modem line, TV, VCR; some with mini-bar; no tea/coffee-making facilities in rooms　✅ 2 dining rooms, 2 lounges, library, games room, garden; conferences; social functions; civil wedding licence; heated indoor swimming pool; leisure facilities nearby; early suppers for children; cots, highchairs, toys, playrooms, babysitting, baby-listening, staffed nursery, outdoor play area　♿ No wheelchair access; 5 steps into hotel, 4 ground-floor bedrooms　● No children in 1 dining room eves; dogs (up to 2) £7 per night; no smoking in bedrooms ▭ Amex, Delta, MasterCard, Switch, Visa　£ Twin/double £175 to £270, family room from £185, suite £185 to £410 (rates incl dinner); deposit required. Set, alc L £17.50; light meals available. Special breaks available

Marina Hotel

The Esplanade, Fowey PL23 1HY
TEL: (01726) 833315　FAX: (01726) 832779
EMAIL: enquiries@themarinahotel.co.uk
WEB SITE: www.themarinahotel.co.uk

Stylish but comfy rooms with some great waterfront views

Plenty of thought has clearly gone into the rooms in this tasteful small hotel ideally situated on the waterfront of one of Cornwall's prettiest villages. In a pleasing mix of antique furniture and contemporary colours, the rooms are fashionable without being intimidatingly stylish. Those with views over the river estuary are the pick, looking out on the boats meandering below the stacked cottages – especially appealing at night. The restaurant is similarly smart but relaxed, with a marine-themed décor, though some may find the jazz music slightly intrusive. As for the menu, make sure you leave room for dessert; if you can't decide, try the selection of six mini-puddings including a profiterole in the shape of a swan. Readers have complained of teething problems with the new annexe rooms in Ashley House – these seemed to have been resolved by the time our inspector stayed, but since none has a waterfront view you're best off staying in the main house anyway. However, we did agree with the criticism of noise from the kitchen and dining room disturbing the peace of the reading room.

◐ Open all year　🔁 Near bottom of main road into town, turn right on to esplanade; hotel is 50 yards along on left. Private car park 🛏️ 2 twin, 15 double, 1 suite; family rooms available; all with room service, hair-dryer, direct-dial telephone, TV; 1 with CD player, VCR　✅ Restaurant, bar, reading room, garden; conferences and social functions; civil wedding licence; leisure facilities nearby; early suppers for children; cots, highchairs, babysitting　♿ No wheelchair access; 15 steps into restaurant, 3 ground-floor bedrooms ● No dogs in public rooms; smoking in bar only ▭ Amex, Delta, Diners, MasterCard, Switch, Visa £ Single occupancy of twin/double £65 to £95, twin/double/family room £124 to £144, suite £144 to £188. Set L £18.50, D £34.50; alc L £22.50, D £55; light meals available; service incl. Special breaks available

Old Quay House 　[NEW ENTRY]

28 Fore Street, Fowey PL23 1AQ
TEL: (01726) 833302　FAX: (01726) 833668
EMAIL: info@theoldquayhouse.com
WEB SITE: www.theoldquayhouse.com

Boutique hotel addition to the growing Fowey fold

Fowey is becoming something of a chic spot down on the south Cornwall coast, with trendy shops and bars joining the traditional pubs and fishing boats. The Old Quay House is a top-notch addition to the fold. It's housed in a nineteenth-century seamen's mission, but the tradition of hospitality is pretty much the only thing that connects it with its past. The interior has been gutted and rebuilt from top to bottom. Stripped wood floors, wicker chairs, chunky dark furniture – it's all very stylish and 'now'. The bedrooms are individually decorated in styles ranging from North African to kitsch decadent, though some share a common motif, such as wickerware throughout or enormous mirrors resting at an angle on the floor. The restaurant has a little terrace overlooking the water and serves an eclectic range of dishes with a Mediterranean and North African influence, such as tagine with feta, spinach and couscous, or chicken breast with chorizo.

○ Open all year; restaurant closed Mon eve ⑦ Follow signs to Fowey town centre; at bottom of steep hill turn left into Lostwithiel Street. Follow road down steep narrow street, go past church on left; hotel is further down on the right. Nearest train station: Par ◄━┓ 4 twin/double, 5 double, 3 four-poster; all with room service, hair-dryer, direct-dial telephone, modem line, TV, VCR; some with CD player ✓ Restaurant, terrace; social functions; leisure facilities nearby ㋡ No wheelchair access ● No children under 12; no dogs; no smoking ▭ Amex, Delta, MasterCard, Switch, Visa £ Single occupancy of twin/double £90 to £120, twin/double/four-poster £100 to £180. Alc L £25, D £32; light meals available. Special breaks available ③FOR②

Sandpipers

Coast Guard Lane, Freshwater Bay, Freshwater PO40 9QX
TEL: (01983) 758500 FAX: (01983) 754364
EMAIL: fatcats@btconnect.com
WEB SITE: www.sandpipershotel.com

Unpretentious, friendly hotel in a gentle seaside village

'If you have to queue, just relax and admire the boats that are passing.' That is Sandpipers' charming way of indicating that it's time to chill out as you leave Yarmouth's ferry port heading for the low-key seaside resort of Freshwater Bay and this calm, homely hotel. Not that its owners, the Chapman family, had much time to relax on our last inspection visit, as they busily prepared for the imminent launch of the hotel's second annual Beer Festival, a celebration of ales from all over the UK. It's perhaps an unlikely place to hold a beer festival, but Sandpipers wears many hats – holiday hotel, restaurant and friendly local. It has an assortment of unfussy outfits to match, from the down-to-earth Fat Cat bar, to cosy, informal lounges and a sunny conservatory-style restaurant where the menu offers a tempting selection of hearty old favourites. Families are well catered for with children's tariffs and early teas, and babysitting is an option for grown-ups seeking a little time off. Bedrooms are spotless, with a comfortably old-fashioned feel. Work on a new wing of bedrooms plus conference and leisure facilities was due to start shortly after our inspection. Reports on this would be welcome.

○ Open all year ⑦ Entrance is at back of main council car park, through 2 brick pillars. Private car park ◄━┓ 1 single, 2 twin, 3 twin/double, 4 double, 2 four-poster; all with room service, direct-dial telephone, modem line, TV; hair-dryer, trouser press available ✓ Restaurant/conservatory, 3 bars, 3 lounges, library, games room, garden; conferences and social functions; leisure facilities nearby; early suppers for children; cots, highchairs, toys, playroom, babysitting, baby-listening, outdoor play area ㋡ No wheelchair access ● No smoking in bedrooms ▭ Delta, MasterCard, Switch, Visa £ Single £30 to £40, single occupancy of twin/double £30 to £50, twin/double £60 to £80, four-poster £80 to £100; deposit required. Alc L £12, D £18; light meals available ③FOR②

Chequers Inn

Froggatt, Calver, Hope Valley S32 3ZJ
TEL: (01433) 630231 FAX: (01433) 631072
EMAIL: info@chequers-froggatt.com
WEB SITE: www.chequers-froggatt.com

Good-value rooms with outstanding new bathrooms

With a pretty valley falling away below and the tree-clad slopes of Froggatt Edge looming behind, the Chequers Inn enjoys a striking setting just outside the little High Peak village of Froggatt. Within the long, low, whitewashed building – which has been welcoming weary travellers since the 1500s – the atmosphere is comfortably traditional. You'll find an eclectic mix of wooden furniture, a stove glowing in a stone fireplace, horse brasses and old tack adorning the walls. The well-regarded menu ranges far and wide, from breast of duck with sweet potatoes and red onion gratin to fillet of pork wrapped in basil and Parma ham with apple jus. Upstairs, the bedrooms are prettily countrified, with floral papers and fabrics and new pine furniture. If you're after a more romantic touch, Room 5 has a richly canopied four-poster, but the en-suite bathroom (waiting to be updated) was not a patch on the newly redone ones in the other bedrooms, which feature power showers and attractive tiling with mosaic inlays.

❶ Open all year ⚡ From Sheffield, take A625 to Froggatt; Chequers Inn is on left as you enter village. Private car park ⬅ 1 twin, 3 double, 1 four-poster; all with hair-dryer, trouser press, direct-dial telephone, modem line, TV ⚑ Restaurant, bar, garden ⚹ No wheelchair access ● No dogs ▭ Amex, Delta, MasterCard, Switch, Visa £ Twin/double £55 to £75, four-poster £65 to £85; deposit required. Alc L £16, D £25; light meals available. Special breaks available

---

GATESHEAD Tyne & Wear   map 10

Eslington Villa

8 Station Road, Low Fell, Gateshead NE9 6DR
TEL: 0191-487 6017 FAX: 0191-420 0667
EMAIL: eslingtonvilla.freeuk.com

Refreshingly relaxed style at this well-presented Victorian villa hotel

Although this imposing mid-nineteenth-century villa occupies high ground above the urban sprawl of the Team Valley Trading Estate, there's nothing impersonal or stuffy about it. It still has the feeling of a home (if a rather grand one), with a very relaxed manner to it. That atmosphere is helped by the generous proportions of the public areas. There's a huge double lounge, with big red sofas and wooden bar at one end, and a large breakfast room with Victorian overtones. The smart conservatory-style dining room is the central focus, offering adventurous dishes such as halibut with roast vine tomatoes and mushroom syrup. Bedrooms are fairly contemporary in style, with only a few hints of period character. Poplar has an attractive blue colour scheme, from its flowered wallpaper to armchairs and blinds in the big bay window. There are views from here down to the pleasant lawned terrace garden.

❶ Closed 3 days Chr, 3 days New Year, bank hols; restaurant closed Sun eve ⚡ Leave A1 at Team Valley and approach Gateshead along Team Valley Trading Estate (Kingsway); at second roundabout turn right into Eastern Avenue, then third left into Station Road; hotel is on left. Nearest train station: Newcastle Central. Private car park ⬅ 2 twin, 15 double; all with room service, hair-dryer, direct-dial telephone, TV; some with trouser press ⚑ Dining room, bar, lounge, conservatory, garden; conferences; social functions; leisure facilities nearby; cots, highchairs ⚹ Wheelchair access to hotel (2 steps) and restaurant, 3 ground-floor bedrooms ● No dogs ▭ Amex, Delta, Diners, MasterCard, Switch, Visa £ Single occupancy of twin/double £60 to £65, twin/double £70 to £75; deposit required. Set L £14.50, D £18.50; alc L, D £25; light meals available. Special breaks available ③FOR②

GILLAN Cornwall   map 1

Tregildry Hotel

Gillan, Manaccan, Helston TR12 6HG
TEL: (01326) 231378 FAX: (01326) 231561
EMAIL: trgildry@globalnet.co.uk
WEB SITE: www.tregildryhotel.co.uk

Domestic comforts and commanding views at this homely Lizard hotel

The Tregildry commands some great views over the Lizard coastline, as well as offering a comfortable home-from-home from which to enjoy them. Peachy colours predominate in the main lounge, with wicker furniture and flowery curtains, while a smaller, second lounge is an ideal spot to sit with a book or a newspaper. Everything is neat and tidy –

testament to the professionalism of owners Huw and Lynne Phillips. The food in the Herra restaurant is as good as the vista, using Cornish produce in modern British cooking with a French/Mediterranean influence. You can retire to the terrace for a post-dinner drink. Bedrooms are a good size, are similarly bright in peaches, yellows and greens and have more wicker furniture. Considerate touches like fridges either in rooms or on landings mean that everyone has fresh milk for their tea.

❍ Closed Nov to Feb ⊿ From B3293 head for Manaccan and then follow signs for Gillan. Private car park ⌂ 1 single, 1 twin, 2 twin/double, 6 double; all with room service, hair-dryer, direct-dial telephone, TV ⊘ Restaurant, bar, 2 lounges, garden ⓧ No wheelchair access ● No children under 8; no dogs in public rooms; smoking in 1 lounge only ⊟ Delta, MasterCard, Switch, Visa £ Single £90 to £99, twin/double £140 to £170 (rates incl dinner); deposit required. Special breaks available

---

GILLINGHAM Dorset   map 2

Stock Hill House

Stock Hill, Gillingham SP8 5NR
TEL: (01747) 823626 FAX: (01747) 825628
EMAIL: reception@stockhillhouse.co.uk
WEB SITE: www.stockhillhouse.co.uk

Welcoming hosts and bags of character at this country house

'A hotel has to have a soul,' says Nita Hauser, explaining the success of the country house she owns with her husband Peter, 'and it needs putting together with love.' Stock Hill, a Victorian house set in delightful Dorsetshire countryside, certainly shows plenty of care and affection throughout. Downstairs there is interest in the various antiques – ships' mastheads, an ancient church door, Italian mirrors – while the atmosphere remains homely and relaxing with loads of fresh flowers around. Food is a major attraction, Peter being the kind of chef who likes to pick the vegetables he's grown shortly before he cooks them. Soft fruit is a speciality too and all the jams are home-made from home-grown fruit. Bedrooms show the same attention to detail as the rest of the house, with excellent bathrooms and touches of luxury: the 200-year-old wrought-iron bed in Room 4, for example.

❍ Open all year ⊿ On B3081, 1½ miles west of Gillingham, 3 miles south of A303. Nearest train station: Gillingham. Private car park ⌂ 1 single, 4 twin, 3 double, 1 four-poster; all with room service, hair-dryer, trouser press, direct-dial telephone, TV; tea/coffee-making facilities on request ⊘ Restaurant, dining room, bar, lounge, garden; conferences; tennis; leisure facilities nearby; early suppers for children ⓧ No wheelchair access; 4 steps into hotel, 3 ground-floor bedrooms ● No children under 7; no dogs; no smoking in bedrooms or restaurant ⊟ MasterCard, Switch, Visa £ Single £105 to £125, single occupancy of twin/double £135 to £165, twin/double/four-poster £190 to £290 (rates incl dinner); deposit required. Set L £25. Special breaks available

---

GITTISHAM Devon   map 2

Combe House

Gittisham, Honiton EX14 3AD
TEL: (01404) 540400 FAX: (01404) 46004
EMAIL: stay@thishotel.com
WEB SITE: www.thishotel.com

Perfect rural retreat in idyllic surroundings – things don't get much better than this

Sitting in the middle of 3,500 acres – yes, that's 3,500 acres – of gardens, wildflower meadows, and woodlands, Combe House could hardly be anything but peaceful. Ken and Ruth Hunt have lost none of their enthusiasm for their beautifully restored Elizabethan manor, and they and their staff bring a down-to-earth friendliness and warmth that banishes any fear of pomposity. The public areas and bedrooms are grand, with requisite antiques, massive fireplaces, fancy plasterwork and panelling, and fresh flowers, but they feel comfortably lived in, not a mere contrived arrangement for an interiors magazine that would be messed up by a human presence. The food, too, forms part of this good life, with vegetables and herbs picked from the walled kitchen garden, and home-cured salmon and sea trout on the menu. For a special occasion, small parties can even dine by candlelight in the restored Georgian kitchen. Bedrooms continue in the palatial vein, with more original features, such as mullioned windows, and amazing bathrooms.

ⓘ Open all year ⚡ From Honiton, take A375 towards Sidmouth; turn off and follow brown sign through beech woods. Private car park ⤺ 7 twin/double, 3 double, 1 four-poster, 2 family rooms, 2 suites; all with room service, hair-dryer, direct-dial telephone, TV; no tea/coffee-making facilities in rooms ⚫ Restaurant, dining room, bar, 2 lounges, garden; conferences; social functions; civil wedding licence; leisure facilities nearby; early suppers for children; cots, highchairs, toys, babysitting, baby-listening, outdoor play area ⓹ No wheelchair access ⬤ No smoking or dogs in restaurant ⊡ Amex, Delta, Diners, MasterCard, Switch, Visa ⓺ Single occupancy of twin/double £125 to £130, twin/double £140 to £158, four-poster £275 to £295, family room from 148, suite £275 to £295; deposit required. Set L £22.50, D £36; light meals available; service incl. Special breaks available

---

GLASTONBURY Somerset
map 2

Number 3

3 Magdalene Street, Glastonbury BA6 9EW
TEL: (01458) 832129 FAX: (01458) 834227
EMAIL: info@numberthree.co.uk
WEB SITE: www.numberthree.co.uk

Personable owner and beautifully decorated rooms at this townhouse B&B

To some, the town of Glastonbury might mean Avalon and ley lines, but Pat Redmond's house appeals to a different kind of long tradition – a smart Georgian townhouse offering civilised Englishness, a sort of B&B version of a country house. The breakfast room is deep red, with plenty of paintings on the walls (given a lift recently by the installation of new inset lighting). Breakfasts come with continental flourishes: lots of fresh fruit, croissants, cheeses and ham. Bedrooms are divided between the main house and the garden house at the rear of the garden; all are stylishly comfortable and strike a good balance between fresh and cosy. The garden provides a well-kept haven in fine weather, there is off-street parking and the Abbey is just across the back wall.

ⓘ Closed Dec & Jan ⚡ Follow signs to Abbey ruins. Private car park ⤺ 1 twin, 3 double, 1 family room; all with hair-dryer, direct-dial telephone, TV ⚫ Breakfast room, garden; cot, highchair ⓹ No wheelchair access; 2 steps into hotel, 6 steps into breakfast room, 1 ground-floor bedroom ⬤ No dogs; no smoking ⊡ Amex, Delta, MasterCard, Switch, Visa ⓺ Single occupancy of twin/double £75 to £100, twin/double £100 to £110, family room £120; deposit required

---

GLEWSTONE Herefordshire
map 5

Glewstone Court

Glewstone, Ross-on-Wye HR9 6AW
TEL: (01989) 770367 FAX: (01989) 770282
EMAIL: glewstone@aol.com
WEB SITE: www.glewstonecourt.com

Hands-on family operation which creates an easy-going, welcoming atmosphere

Externally, Glewstone Court may not win any architectural awards – a central white-painted Georgian part has had two incongruous wings added in pinky grey brickwork – but once inside, the house's dimensions start to speak for themselves. Big windows let light flood in and the family collectables and memorabilia of Bill and Christine Reeve-Tucker add an easy-going feel to the public areas. On our inspection, several guests were enjoying a light lunch in the bar, which is decorated with rugs, comfy sofas and horse-jumping prints. From the alcove window here, there are views across the top of an undulating countryside of pear and cherry orchards. Upstairs, some bedrooms, such as Lucy, Katriona and Rose, bear the names of the Reeve-Tucker daughters. These reflect the

relaxed, thrown-together style with a variety of beds, and often plates on the walls and flower stencilling. Bathrooms are lagging behind in the fashion stakes at present, but our correspondents like the little touches – fresh flowers, hospitality tray with biscuits, and fresh milk and bottled water in a fridge.

◑ Closed 25 to 27 Dec ⬀ Off A40, between Ross-on-Wye and Monmouth. Private car park ⬐ 1 single, 1 twin/double, 5 double, 1 four-poster; family rooms available; all with room service, hair-dryer, direct-dial telephone, TV; some with VCR ✦ 2 restaurants, bar, 2 lounges, garden; conferences and social functions; leisure facilities nearby; early suppers for children; cots, highchairs, toys, babysitting, baby-listening, outdoor play area ⅙ No wheelchair access ● No smoking in some public rooms ▭ Amex, Delta, MasterCard, Switch, Visa £ Single £49, single occupancy of twin/double £65, twin/double £99, four-poster £115, family room £114 (prices valid till Feb 2004); deposit required. Set L (Sun) £17; alc L £21, D £27.50; light meals available; service incl. Special breaks available ③FOR2

GLOSSOP   Derbyshire   map 8

Wind in the Willows

Derbyshire Level, Glossop SK13 7PT
TEL: (01457) 868001   FAX: (01457) 853354
EMAIL: info@windinthewillows.co.uk
WEB SITE: www.windinthewillows.co.uk

Old-fashioned charm aplenty at this country house in the Pennines

There's probably more of the Brontë than the Grahame about this early Victorian country house, with its pervasive air of period romance. From the elegantly furnished lounge with its Regency fireplace to the sumptuous dining room, where such time-honoured offerings as sirloin of Derbyshire beefsteak and rack of lamb are served at carved antique tables, there is a sense that everything is just so. When our inspector arrived, the newly redecorated hall was about

to be redone because the paint had turned out to be the wrong shade. The bedrooms are just as much in keeping, sporting a generous helping of antiques and pretty fabrics, as well as some highly polished half-tester beds. The bathroom in Erika Louise is particularly striking, with its roll-top, claw-foot bath; some of the others are looking a little dated in parts, although they remain pleasantly lavish.

◑ Open all year ⬀ 1 mile east of Glossop on A57, turn down road opposite Royal Oak pub; hotel is 400 yards along on right. Nearest train station: Glossop. Private car park ⬐ 3 twin, 8 double, 1 four-poster; all with hair-dryer, trouser press, direct-dial telephone, TV; some with room service, CD player ✦ Dining room, drawing room, study, conservatory, garden; conferences; social functions; leisure facilities nearby ⅙ No wheelchair access ● No children under 8; no dogs; no smoking in bedrooms ▭ Amex, Delta, Diners, MasterCard, Switch, Visa £ Single occupancy of twin/double £85 to £100, twin/double £115 to £145, four-poster £145; deposit required. Set D £27; light meals available; service incl. Special breaks available ③FOR2

GOLCAR   West Yorkshire   map 9

Weavers Shed

Knowl Road, Huddersfield HD7 4AN
TEL: (01484) 654284   FAX: (01484) 650980
EMAIL: info@weaversshed.co.uk
WEB SITE: www.weaversshed.co.uk

A winning combination of accomplished food and stylish rooms

Although the industrial textile heritage of Yorkshire doesn't make for the most photogenic neighbourhood, you feel transported several hundred miles south

once you're inside Stephen and Tracy Jackson's restaurant-with-rooms. And, much as a French rural *auberge* might pride itself on serving food made from the finest local ingredients, Stephen insists that his menu be based on locally sourced products; this professionalism is pursued to an extent that, in season, much of the vegetables, fruit, herbs and even eggs comes from the restaurant's own kitchen garden. The setting for this fine food is a restaurant that blends features of the original cloth-finishing mill – a low-beamed roof and stone arches – with a rustic flagstoned floor and wall lights made from Sardinian roof tiles. It would be a shame not to take full advantage of the food and excellent cellar which specialises in small interesting producers, so the bedrooms provide stylish havens in which to prepare for and recover from the main event. Decorated in a bright and fresh modern style, these have crisp, good-quality bed linen, shiny modern bathrooms and come with a decanter of sherry.

◑ Closed 25 Dec to 3 Jan; restaurant closed Sun & Mon eves ⚡ From Huddersfield take A62 west; after 1½ miles turn right on to B6111, after ¼ mile turn left at traffic lights, keep on main road for 1 mile; hotel is past church, on right. Nearest train station: Huddersfield. Private car park ⌼ 1 twin, 3 double, 1 four-poster; all with hair-dryer, mini-bar, direct-dial telephone, modem line, TV ⊘ Restaurant, bar, lounge; conferences; social functions; cots, highchairs ♿ No wheelchair access; 2 steps into hotel, 2 ground-floor bedrooms ● No dogs ▭ Amex, Delta, Diners, MasterCard, Switch, Visa £ Single occupancy of twin/double £60, twin/double/four-poster £75; deposit required. Set L £15; alc L, D £31. Special breaks available

---

GRANGE-IN-BORROWDALE Cumbria map 10

Borrowdale Gates Hotel

Grange-in-Borrowdale, Keswick CA12 5UQ
TEL: (017687) 77204   FAX: (017687) 77254
EMAIL: hotel@borrowdale-gates.com
WEB SITE: www.borrowdale-gates.com

An idyllic setting gives this Lakeland hotel a winning hand over many rivals

The picture-postcard scenery of this glorious valley near the shores of Derwent Water is an entrancing blend of rugged fells, lush woodland and stone-walled sheep pasture. Borrowdale Gates is all the more enviable for being just that little way off the beaten tourist trail, quietly set on the edge of Grange village with its charming double-humped bridge. The white-painted, traditionally furnished house, former home of a Methodist minister, has been much extended to accommodate its many visitors. Picture windows from its airy, open-plan restaurant and adjoining lounges overlook sublime views. Although the food has been praised, this year a few dissenting voices have expressed dissatisfaction with service, particularly in relation to the steep tariff. New owners Colin and Carol Slaney have undertaken an ambitious programme of refurbishment, upgrading bedrooms in smart contemporary styles. Not all have equally good views. Reports welcome.

◑ Closed Jan ⚡ From Keswick, follow B5289 with Derwent Water on right; after 4 miles turn right over double humpback bridge into Grange village; hotel is ½ mile through village on right. Private car park ⌼ 3 single, 11 twin, 15 double, family rooms available; all with room service, hair-dryer, trouser press, direct-dial telephone, TV ⊘ Restaurant, bar, 3 lounges, garden; early suppers for children ♿ Wheelchair access to hotel and restaurant (ramp), 10 ground-floor bedrooms, 1 room specially equipped for disabled people ● No children under 12; no dogs; no smoking in restaurant and 1 lounge ▭ Delta, MasterCard, Switch, Visa £ Single £83 to £89, twin/double £156 to £196 (rates incl dinner); deposit required. Set L (Sun) £16, D £34.50; alc L £20; light meals available; service incl. Special breaks available

---

'We have come to the conclusion that as we are now older (in our early 60s) our eyesight is not as good as it was and therefore we need good mirrors and lighting to put on our faces! Is it because the young (we were young once!) do not have the problems and therefore do not think about good mirrors and lighting in their bathroom?'
On a hotel in Somerset

'Question to reception: "Can we use the pool, please?"
Answer: "Well, I don't know. You'll have to go on the waiting list."'
On a hotel in East Yorkshire

GRASMERE Cumbria   map 8

White Moss House

Rydal Water, Grasmere, Ambleside LA22 9SE
TEL: (015394) 35295   FAX: (015394) 35516
EMAIL: sue@whitemoss.com
WEB SITE: www.whitemoss.com

Long-established, elegantly homely hotel-restaurant with Wordsworthian associations

Shielded by tall trees and hedged gardens, the house is successfully distanced from most daytime traffic noise from the passing A591. Behind the solid, creeper-clad house, steep fells loom, and sylvan scenes glide down to the sparkling, reed-pierced fringes of Rydal Water. It's easy to understand why William Wordsworth chose to buy this property for his son in 1729. Inside White Moss House, the atmosphere is tranquil; antique clocks tick gently, and a wood-burning stove glows cheerfully in the handsome, light-filled drawing room. The dining room seems surprisingly modest for a place so focused on its cooking, but Peter Dixon's acclaimed five-course dinners still earn high praise. Bedrooms are pretty and charming, though bathrooms have clearly been a headache to install in this old house, and some are very cramped. Thoughtful personal touches like Radox and reading matter amply compensate for the fact that decorative fashions have moved on a bit.

● Closed Dec & Jan; dining room closed Sun eve ⊠ On A591, at northern end of Rydal Water, halfway between Ambleside and Grasmere. Private car park 🛏 3 twin/double, 2 double, 1 suite; all with hair-dryer, trouser press, direct-dial telephone, TV; some with tea/coffee-making facilities and room service ⊘ Dining room, bar, lounge, garden; leisure facilities nearby; cots, baby-listening 🕭 No wheelchair access ● No toddlers in restaurant at dinner; no smoking in dining room; dogs in suite only ▭ Delta, MasterCard, Switch, Visa £ Single occupancy of twin/double £75 to £97, twin/double £129 to £190, suite £148 to £198 (rates incl dinner); deposit required. Special breaks available

GRASSINGTON North Yorkshire   map 8

Ashfield House

Summers Fold, Grassington BD23 5AE
TEL: (01756) 752584   FAX: (01756) 751891
EMAIL: sales@ashfieldhouse.co.uk
WEB SITE: www.ashfieldhouse.co.uk

Cosy small hotel in a picture-perfect Dales village

New owners Joe Azzopardi and Elizabeth Webb had taken over at Ashfield House just days before our inspector called in April 2004. They have solid foundations on which to stamp their mark, and no plans to wreak major changes. Grassington is a classic Dales honeypot, where amblers and browsers throng the tea shops and galleries around a small cobbled marketplace. All of this touristy commotion is just yards from Ashfield's door – but you're completely unaware of it in the gorgeously secretive garden or with a relaxing drink in one of the two cosy lounges. These are lovely places with the exposed timbers, stone walls and capacious stone fireplaces that are the legacy of the hotel's origins as miners' cottages, but there are shades of modern style in the ochre-washed walls. Bedrooms come with luxury touches such as fluffy bathrobes and freshly ground coffee. 'We want to add in a wow factor to the bedrooms', says Joe, so you can be sure that any moves will be in a positive direction. Joe is also a chef with a lifetime of experience in the world's five-star hotels and a generous attitude to portions, so dinners – based on the best of local produce – are unlikely to disappoint.

● Open all year ⊠ Turn off B6265 into Grassington village square; after 50 yards turn sharp left into Summers Fold. Private car park 🛏 2 twin, 1 twin/double, 4 double; all with hair-dryer, TV ⊘ Dining room, bar, 2 lounges, garden; leisure facilities nearby 🕭 No wheelchair access ● No children under 5; no dogs;

no smoking ⬚ Amex, Delta, MasterCard, Switch, Visa £ Single occupancy of twin/double £71, twin/double £76; deposit required. Set D £20; service incl. Special breaks available (3FOR2)

The Starr

Market Place, Great Dunmow CM6 1AX
TEL: (01371) 874321   FAX: (01371) 876337
EMAIL: starrrestaurant@btinternet.com
WEB SITE: www.the-starr.co.uk

Sophisticated restaurant in a traditional English setting

The Starr remains a classy adaptation of a traditional old English inn. The front bar sticks closer to the pub's origins – it's out back in the restaurant that things get more interesting, with a modern decorative scheme around the timbered beams and a bright new conservatory. A huge cheeseboard overflowing with grapes sets the tone for a menu that looks equally appealing, with dishes such as terrine of wild pigeon and beetroot with fennel and orange salad, or rabbit with wild mushroom mousse and pearl barley and kidney risotto. A sense of humour is evident in the charming 'Hook' private dining room, with a notice warning of 'Danger, low beams' followed by 'Told you so' on the next beam. There are eight rooms in the ex-stable. Each of them is individually furnished – the Oak Room, for example, has a four-poster and roll-top bath.

● Closed 27 to 30 Dec and 2 to 5 Jan; restaurant closed Sun eve 🖬 Off A120 in centre of Great Dunmow. Private car park 🚗 1 twin, 6 double, 1 four-poster; all with hair-dryer, direct-dial telephone, modem line, TV; some with trouser press ⌧ Restaurant, bar, conservatory; conferences; social functions; leisure facilities nearby; early suppers for children; cots, highchairs, babysitting, baby-listening ♿ No wheelchair access; 7 steps into hotel, 2 ground-floor bedrooms ● No dogs in public rooms; smoking in bar only ⬚ Amex, Delta, Diners, MasterCard, Switch, Visa £ Single occupancy of twin/double £75, twin/double £115, four-poster £135; deposit required. Set L £27.50, D £37.50 (3FOR2)

Bredon House [NEW ENTRY]

34 Worcester Road, Great Malvern WR14 4AA
TEL: (01684) 893758   FAX: (01684) 575323
EMAIL: suereeves@bredonhousehotel.co.uk
WEB SITE: www.bredonhousehotel.co.uk

A simple, small B&B where the emphasis is on relaxed hospitality

With its location on the ridge of the Malvern Hills you can be guaranteed a panoramic view of the Severn Valley from whichever room you stay in at Bredon House. This respectable Regency villa, on the main road close to the centre of Great Malvern, has been owned by hands-on proprietor Sue Reeves for the past eight years, and her talent has been to create a calm, restful atmosphere for guests. One couple was struck by Sue's easy-going nature and commented that she made them feel totally relaxed and at home from the moment they arrived. Squashy sofas and low-key antiques and art in the lounge set the tone, while the breakfast room is tastefully furnished with dark varnished tables and a brass chandelier – and of course there's the view again from the picture windows in both. The bedrooms upstairs are better than the ones at garden level: they have strong colour schemes, sofas in the bigger rooms and clean, fresh bathrooms. Room 1 is notable for its antique pine bed and an impressive bathroom with a stand-alone bath and separate shower.

● Open all year 🖬 On A449 in Great Malvern. Private car park. Nearest train station: Great Malvern 🚗 7 double, 2 family rooms; all with room service, hair-dryer, trouser-press, direct-dial telephone, modem line, TV ⌧ Breakfast room, lounge/bar, terrace, garden; social functions; leisure facilities nearby; cots, highchairs, toys, outdoor play area ♿ No wheelchair access ● Dogs £5 ⬚ MasterCard, Switch, Visa £ Single occupancy of double £45; double £72 to £80, family room £90; deposit required (3FOR2)

map 2

Le Manoir aux Quat' Saisons

Church Road, Great Milton, Oxford OX44 7PD
TEL: (01844) 278881   FAX: (01844) 278847
EMAIL: lemanoir@blanc.co.uk
WEB SITE: www.manoir.com

Astonishing in every way: from the food to the décor and the price

Chef-patron Raymond Blanc describes his hotel near Oxford as: 'My dream, my vision, my life', which just about sums up the inspiration and vitality behind this exceptional enterprise, created from a fifteenth-century manor house. Everything is perfect, down to the smallest detail, and is kept that way by a platoon of staff that would put an Edwardian house party to shame. The star attraction is, of course, the renowned restaurant, which dishes up sumptuous feasts with a modern French slant. Much of the produce comes from the extensive, well-manicured gardens, which contain 90 types of vegetables and over 70 types of herbs, some of which are picked each morning for that day's menus. The interior is as tasteful and eye-catching as anything served up in the restaurant, with a swathe of chic public rooms and bedroom styles ranging from contemporary opulence to indulgently traditional. This combination of exquisite food and cosseting luxury is more than enough to soothe anyone's soul – and the bill is accordingly high.

◗ Open all year   ⚡ Off A329, signposted 'Great Milton Manor'. Private car park   🛏 8 double, 5 four-poster, 6 family rooms, 13 suites; all with room service, hair-dryer, trouser press, direct-dial telephone, TV; most with CD player; VCR on request; no tea/coffee-making facilities in rooms   ⚗ Restaurant, bar, 2 lounges, conservatory, garden; conferences; social functions; civil wedding licence; leisure facilities nearby; early suppers for children; cots, highchairs, toys, babysitting, baby-listening   ♿ Wheelchair access to hotel and restaurant, 15 ground-floor bedrooms. Disabled parking   ● No dogs   ▭ Amex, Delta, Diners, MasterCard, Switch, Visa   £ Single occupancy of double £275 to £485, twin/double £275 to £485, four-poster £275 to £875, family room £490 to £875, suite £490 to £1,250; deposit required. Set L £45; alc L, D £90; light meals available; service incl

 map 6

Manor House

Barsham Road, Great Snoring, Fakenham NR21 0HP
TEL: (01328) 820597   FAX: (01328) 820048
EMAIL: gtsnoringmanorho@aol.com
WEB SITE: www.norfolkcountryhouse.co.uk

Idyllic, unaltered English manor house, deep in the Norfolk countryside

'This place is a bit of a time warp, but I make no apology for that – I think it's important to have a place to escape to.' So says considerate host Rosamund Scoles, and escape you certainly will. The only sounds audible when we visited were from the birds in the trees and the animals in the fields, and you feel secluded even from the tiny track that leads you up to this lovely red-brick fifteenth-century manor house. There are towers and a profusion of chimneypots, crumbly flower motifs and flaking faces. Inside, the public rooms are almost as characterful, packed with antiques including a thick Jacobean sideboard which has been in the family forever and stores the silver you'll be eating with around the communal table at dinner. The charm may not quite carry through to the bedrooms, which, though perfectly comfortable, are rather homely, and the bathrooms are beginning to look a little dated.

◗ Closed 24 to 27 Dec   ⚡ Behind church on Barsham Road in Great Snoring. Private car park   🛏 1 twin, 3 twin/double, 2 double; all with room service, hair-dryer, direct-dial telephone, modem line, TV; VCR, CD player on request; tea/coffee-making facilities available   ⚗ Dining room, drawing room, lounge, garden; conferences and social functions; civil wedding licence; leisure facilities nearby; early suppers for children; baby-listening   ♿ No wheelchair access   ● No children in dining room eves; no dogs; no smoking in dining room and some bedrooms ▭ Amex, Delta, Diners, MasterCard, Switch, Visa £ Single occupancy of twin/double £85, twin/double £110 to £130. Set D £28.50; light meals available; service incl

---

GRIMSTON Norfolk map 6

Congham Hall

Lynn Road, Grimston, King's Lynn PE32 1AH
TEL: (01485) 600250   FAX: (01485) 601191
EMAIL: info@conghamhallhotel.co.uk
WEB SITE: www.conghamhallhotel.co.uk

Floral fragrances permeating a classic Georgian home

Congham Hall is a classic Georgian country house in a great location. It's surrounded by its own grounds but stands right on the edge of a pretty village, not too far from the coast, and within reach of King's Lynn if you're in need of the amenities of a larger town. You're not restricted to arriving by car – the hotel comes equipped with a helipad. The interior doesn't stray too far from classic country-house – roomy, light and tasteful, with lots of stripes, florals and pungent pot pourri from the herb gardens. The bedrooms have good views, either over the lawns and parks or on to the walled garden and cricket pitch. The kitchen gardens again come in handy for the Orangery Restaurant which is suitably orange, fresh and airy, with more fine views out through the French windows.

◐ Open all year ⌖ North-east of King's Lynn, turn off A148 at sign for Grimston; hotel is 2½ miles on left. Private car park ⊨ 1 single, 8 twin/double, 3 double, 2 suites; all with room service, hair-dryer, direct-dial telephone, TV; some with trouser press, modem line; tea/coffee-making facilities on request ✓ Restaurant, bar, lounge, garden; conferences and social functions; civil wedding licence; tennis; leisure facilities nearby; early suppers for children; cots, highchairs, babysitting, baby-listening ﹠ Wheelchair access to hotel (ramp) and restaurant, 1 ground-floor bedroom ● No children under 7 in restaurant eves; no dogs; no smoking in bedrooms and some public rooms ▭ Amex, Delta, Diners, MasterCard, Switch, Visa £ Single £99, single occupancy of twin/double £115 to £170, twin/double £165 to £195, suite £250 to £285; deposit required. Set L £16.50, D £36; light meals available. Special breaks available ③FOR②

GRITTLETON Wiltshire map 2

Church House

Grittleton, Nr Chippenham SN14 6AP
TEL: (01249) 782562 (AND FAX)
EMAIL: moore@flydoc.fsbusiness.co.uk

Hospitable hosts and homely comfort at this lovely house

The eighteenth-century vicar who built this fine Georgian residence is reputed to have had 12 daughters, which must have made for some jollity – and that spirit seems to linger. Current owners Michael and Anna Moore certainly bring a good-humoured sociability to proceedings. They came here in 1970 after running flying doctor services in Africa, and have never wanted to move since. Rooms are homely and spacious, particularly the drawing room with its rugs on polished wooden floor, books galore and family heirlooms dotted around. Anna cooks on request, guests gathering around the single huge table – or in summer occasionally choosing to dine on the terrace by the heated indoor pool. Bedrooms are large and homely, with en-suite facilities tucked away behind panelled doors in most, the other having a private bathroom. As we went to press, work was underway to convert the seventeenth-century stable wing to make two more rooms. 'Anna and Michael made us extremely welcome,' reports one visitor, who praised the 'clean and fresh smelling' house and 'lovely' pool.

◐ Open all year ⌖ In Grittleton village, between church and pub. Private car park ⊨ 3 twin, 1 double; all with hair-dryer, TV; fax, modem line available ✓ Dining room, drawing room, garden; conferences; heated indoor swimming pool; leisure facilities nearby; highchair, baby-listening, outdoor play area ﹠ No wheelchair access ● No children aged 2 to 12; no dogs; no smoking in dining room ▭ None accepted £ Single occupancy of twin/double £40, twin/double £68; deposit required. Set D £22.50; service incl. Special breaks available ③FOR②

GUILDFORD Surrey   map 3

Angel Posting House & Livery

91 High Street, Guildford GU1 3DP
TEL: (01483) 564555   FAX: (01483) 533770
EMAIL: angelhotelchotmail.com
WEB SITE: www.slh.com

Atmospheric coaching inn on Guildford's busy cobbled High Street

Inside this black-and-white rabbit warren of a building the modern hustle and bustle of Guildford's shopping streets is quickly left behind. The last of the cobbled High Street's eight coaching inns that provided refuge for passing travellers on the London to Portsmouth road, the Angel has welcomed some notable guests in its time: Jane Austen and Lord Nelson are two of the celebrated visitors after whom some of the bedrooms are named. Rooms are comfortably furnished and well equipped with modern bathrooms, tasteful colour schemes and perhaps elaborate canopies above the beds. Public areas are equally smart and done out in traditional style. The galleried lounge, with its huge brick fireplace, wood-panelled walls and squishy sofas, is an agreeable place in which to mull over the dinner menu, which is served up in the atmospheric thirteenth-century crypt beneath the hotel. Be warned: the High Street is pedestrianised and you may have to park in the nearby Tunsgate car park.

◑ Open all year   ⚡ Halfway up High Street (closed to vehicles 11am to 4pm Mon to Fri & Sun, 9am to 5.30pm Sat). Nearest train station: Guildford   🛏 3 twin, 6 double, 12 suites; all with room service, hair-dryer, direct-dial telephone, TV   ⚒ Restaurant, dining room, bar, lounge; conferences; social functions; leisure facilities nearby; early suppers for children; cots, highchairs, baby-listening   ♿ Wheelchair access to hotel (2 steps) and restaurant (2 steps), lift   ● No dogs; no smoking in bedrooms   ▭ Amex, Delta, Diners, MasterCard, Switch, Visa   £ Single occupancy of twin/double £150, twin/double £150, suite £175 to £195; deposit required. Continental B £9.50, cooked B £13.50; set L £18.50, D £32.50; alc L £18.50, D £32.50; service incl. Special breaks available (2004 data)

HADLEY WOOD Hertfordshire   map 3

West Lodge Park

Cockfosters Road, Hadley Wood, Barnet EN4 0PY
TEL: 020-8216 3900   FAX: 020-8216 3937
EMAIL: westlodgepark@bealeshotels.co.uk
WEB SITE: www.bealeshotels.co.uk

Beautiful grounds and friendly service at this business hotel handily placed near the M25

Once upon a time there was a hunting lodge, situated in the rolling green hills north of London, to which visitors could escape from the seething mass of city life for some rural comforts. Today, though London has grown such that it is at the end of the verdant drive and the old lodge has been much expanded, those wishing for a relaxed break or stylish business base will be amply rewarded. Public rooms exude a confident air, from the elegant, country-house-style hall-lounge to the more modern bar-restaurant, which opens out on to a lovely terrace at the head of the formal gardens. Bedrooms are just as tastefully furnished, perhaps in the traditional, chintzy style in the main building, or maybe something a touch more contemporary in the newer, more spacious affairs in the Chestnut Lodge extension at the back. Some rooms even come with mini-plasma TV screens in the bathrooms! Those looking to unwind can revel in the sauna-spa, while the more energetic might opt for a hearty walk through the extensive arboretum, whose lush leafiness feels a world away from the busy M25 just up the road.

◑ Open all year   ⚡ Leave M25 at Junction 24 and take A111 towards Cockfosters; hotel is 1 mile on left. Nearest train station: Hadley Wood; nearest tube stations: Cockfosters, Oakwood (Piccadilly Line). Private car park   🛏 12 single, 10 twin, 29 double, 3 four-poster, 2 family rooms, 3 suites; all with room service, hair-dryer, trouser press, direct-dial telephone, TV; some with mini-bar, modem line   ⚒ 2 restaurants, bar, lounge, conservatory, garden; conferences, social functions, civil wedding licence; spa; leisure facilities nearby; early suppers for children, served in lounge or bedroom; cots, highchairs, toys, babysitting, baby-listening &. No wheelchair access; 3 steps into hotel, 2 rooms specially equipped for disabled people, lift. Disabled parking ● No dogs; no smoking in some public rooms and some bedrooms ⊟ Amex, Delta, Diners, MasterCard, Switch, Visa £ Single £110 to £115, single occupancy of twin/double £130 to £145, twin/double £150 to £170, four-poster £195 to £250, family room £270, suite £170 to £180; deposit required. Continental B £11, cooked B £13.50; set L £23.50, D £32.50; light meals available. Special breaks available (3 FOR 2)

HALIFAX West Yorkshire   Map 8

Holdsworth House

Holdsworth Road, Holmfield, Halifax HX2 9TG
TEL: (01422) 240024   FAX: (01422) 245174
EMAIL: info@holdsworthhouse.co.uk
WEB SITE: www.holdsworthhouse.co.uk

Seventeenth-century manor house run with professional, modern flair

The industrial world sprang up around this historic Jacobean manor, so the approach to Holdsworth House doesn't set the pulse racing. You enter from the car park at the back, missing its best feature – a stone cross of St John above a centre gable that overlooks a lovely parterre garden. But before you have made your way through to the hotel's more secretive features, there are plenty of creaky floors, panelled and stone walls and low beams to evoke a suitably atmospheric pedigree. The Hall is a tobacco-hued clubby area for browsing the menu before moving

through to the mullioned windows, oak panels and plush drapes of the three restaurant rooms, which hog the finest elements of period character. 'Friendly and efficient' service is the key zone where Holdsworth House really scores well with correspondents: 'family-run, and it shows' – after all, the Pearson family has owned the hotel for forty years. Bedrooms are unlikely to cause complaint: they are competently comfy, with an upmarket corporate edge, designed, perhaps, to appeal to the many business people who keep the hotel busy through the week.

◑ Open all year 🚗 From Halifax, take A629 towards Keighley; after 1½ miles turn right into Shay Lane, signposted Holmfield; hotel is 1 mile on right. Private car park 🚗 10 single, 3 twin, 1 twin/double, 20 double, 1 four-poster, 5 suites; all with room service, hair-dryer, direct-dial telephone, TV; some with trouser press, modem line ✓ Restaurant, bar, lounge, garden; conferences, social functions, civil wedding licence; leisure facilities nearby; early suppers for children; cots, highchairs, babysitting, baby-listening &. Wheelchair access to hotel, 21 ground-floor bedrooms, WC, 2 rooms specially equipped for disabled people. Disabled parking ● No dogs in restaurant; no smoking in restaurant and some bedrooms ⊟ Amex, Delta, Diners, MasterCard, Switch, Visa £ Single £95, single occupancy of twin/double £110, twin/double £120, four-poster £145, suite £180; deposit required. Continental B £8, cooked B £12; set L £16, D £27.50; alc D £32; light meals available. Special breaks available (3 FOR 2)

HALTWHISTLE Northumberland   map 10

Centre of Britain Hotel

Main Street, Haltwhistle NE49 0BH
TEL: (01434) 322422   FAX: (01434) 322655
EMAIL: hotel@centre-of-britain.org.uk
WEB SITE: www.centre-of-britain.org.uk

Ancient building with imaginative Scandinavian interior design

The Centre of Britain Hotel stands out from its dun-coloured neighbours like a canary among pigeons. David Taylor and Grethe Kirkebjerg have taken a historic old building and paired its original features with inventive space-enhancing Scandinavian design; there's also a lot of clever environmentally-aware stuff in the insulation, heating and ventilation

departments that you won't see but whose benefits you will feel if the mercury drops after a rugged day out on the Hadrian's Wall trail. Throughout the building, subtly blended colours merge with the textures of exposed sandstone and beamed ceilings, and its walls showcase art from David and Grethe's own collection as well as temporary exhibitions by a changing cast of artists. The theme continues in the clean lines, pine furniture and wooden beams of the bedrooms: those in the courtyard are smaller, but well designed with a split-level layout, while the rooms in the main house have great character. The new suites with top-notch spa baths and power showers increase the range of rooms. Praise for friendly and professional service, excellent food and eclectic decoration comes from one impressed correspondent.

◑ Open all year   🚆 In Haltwhistle, on A69 between Newcastle and Carlisle. Nearest train station: Haltwhistle. Private car park   🛏 5 twin, 4 double, 3 suites; family rooms available; all with room service, hair-dryer, TV; some with direct-dial telephone   ✓ Restaurant, breakfast room, bar, lounge; conferences and social functions; leisure facilities nearby; early suppers for children; highchairs   ⅙ No wheelchair access   ● No dogs in public rooms   ⊟ Amex, Delta, Diners, MasterCard, Switch, Visa   £ Single occupancy of twin/double £42 to £65, twin/double £54 to £100, family room £95 to £100, suite £80; deposit required. Set D £19; alc L £12, D £20; light meals available; service incl. Special breaks available   (3FOR2)

HAMPTON COURT   Surrey
map 3

Carlton Mitre

Hampton Court Road, Hampton Court KT8 9BN
TEL: 020-8979 9988   FAX: 020-8979 9777
EMAIL: mitre@carltonhotels.co.uk
WEB SITE: www.carltonhotels.co.uk

Handy stopover for Hampton Court Palace right on the Thames

Looking across at the vastness of Hampton Court Palace, it is difficult to imagine how much difference the 36 rooms in this riverside hostelry would have made to Charles II, but evidently juggling guest lists was something of a royal problem in 1665, when the hotel was built to cater for those who could not be accommodated in the Palace. The Carlton Mitre continues to be a convenient stopover for visitors to Hampton Court despite the fact that today few traces of its origins remain.

Behind the red-brick façade, history gives way to function, and a corporate feel now predominates in the public areas, an indication of the hotel's popularity for conferences and events. Predictably, rooms with the best views of the Palace and the river come at a price, but they are generally decent sized, well equipped and pleasantly decorated with flowery fabrics and dark wood furniture.

◑ Open all year   🚆 Opposite Hampton Court Palace, next to bridge. Nearest train station: Hampton Court. Private car park   🛏 6 twin, 28 double, 2 suites; all with room service, hair-dryer, mini-bar, trouser press, direct-dial telephone, TV; some with modem line   ✓ 2 restaurants, bar, lounge, library, terrace, garden; conferences; social functions; civil wedding licence; leisure facilities nearby; early suppers for children; cots, highchairs   ⅙ No wheelchair access, 6 steps into hotel, 4 steps into restaurant, 4 ground-floor bedrooms, lift   ● Dogs in bedrooms only, at management's discretion   ⊟ Amex, Delta, Diners, MasterCard, Switch, Visa   £ Single occupancy of twin/double £180 to £199, twin/double £180 to £199, suite £255 to £300; deposit required. Cooked B £11.50; set D £19; alc D £25; light meals available. Special breaks available

---

HAMSTERLEY FOREST   Co Durham
map 10

Grove House

Hamsterley Forest, Bishop Auckland DL13 3NL
TEL: (01388) 488203   FAX: (01388) 488174
EMAIL: grovehouse@dial.pipex.com
WEB SITE: www.grove-house.biz

Special house lost deep in the woods near Durham

Finding Helene Close's Georgian shooting lodge is something of a Hansel and Gretel experience. At the end of a long dead-end road, the dense groves of Hamsterley Forest part to reveal this elegant house set in fine gardens in a bright clearing. Helene's family

has owned Grove House for generations and it shows: inside, a wonderful collection of German art nouveau furniture combines with big squashy sofas, classic country-house chintz and family photos and paintings to create a memorable décor in its spacious rooms. Look for the detail too: the eye-catching door handles and light fittings in the grand dining room all belong to the art nouveau period too. As the house is not made of gingerbread and spice, and alternative eateries are not exactly thick on the ground in the forest, Helene's dinners are popular and convivial events, cooked from mostly organic top-notch local produce. The bedrooms are all peaceful and comfy: the Middle Room has flowers painted on the door and a window seat looking over the gardens; the smallest is the lovely floral Blue Room, while the Front Room has a wonderfully glam 70s-vintage cherry-pink bathroom that you'll either love or hate.

◑ Closed mid-Dec to mid-Jan ⤢ North of West Auckland, turn off A68 to Hamsterley village (ignore signs to Hamsterley Forest); continue for 2 miles and follow road to right, then left; after ½ mile turn right at Grove House sign; house is over bridge. Private car park ⬚ 1 twin, 1 twin/double, 1 double; family rooms available; all with hair-dryer ⬚ Dining room, 2 lounges, garden ⬚ No wheelchair access ● No children under 10; no dogs; no smoking ⬚ None accepted £ Single occupancy of twin/double £41 to £45, twin/double £61 to £65; family room £85; deposit required. Set D £24; light meals available; service incl

---

HANLEY CASTLE Worcestershire map 5

Old Parsonage Farm

Hanley Castle, Worcester WR8 0BU
TEL: (01684) 310124
EMAIL: opwines@aol.com

House-party style in this countryside home

Ann and Tony Addison always look forward to the arrival of their guests, as it gives them a chance to share in the enjoyment of their attractive home, and also to treat them to a celebration of fine food and wine. 'We do like people who are into food and wine,' Tony told our inspector, and the couple hope that guests will dine at least once during their stay. The aim is to have a house-party atmosphere, so that means no televisions in the bedrooms, and guests eating at the same time, although at separate tables. The public areas in this sturdy, eighteenth-century red-brick farmhouse are bright and friendly in feel, with plenty of family photos and collectibles. The dining room has a big old inglenook fireplace, adding to the cosy atmosphere in which to sample Ann's cooking. The night before our inspection, guests had sat down to duck breast salad, followed by salmon en croûte and then blackberry crème brûlée, plus cheese and biscuits. Tony is a wine importer so there is plenty of choice. Bedrooms are a good size, with simple colour schemes; Pink, the largest, has a corner bath.

◑ Closed mid-Dec to mid-Jan ⤢ Take B4211 out of Upton-upon-Severn for 2 miles towards Worcester; turn left on B4209; farm is 150 yards on right. Private car park ⬚ 1 twin, 2 double; all with room service, hair-dryer; no tea/coffee-making facilities in rooms ⬚ Dining room, bar service, lounge, library, garden; leisure facilities nearby ⬚ No wheelchair access ● No children under 12; no dogs; no smoking ⬚ None accepted £ Single occupancy of twin/double £38, twin/double £56 to £62; deposit required. Set D £19; light meals available; service incl. Special breaks available

---

HAROME North Yorkshire map 9

Star Inn

High Street, Harome, Nr Helmsley YO62 5JE
TEL: (01439) 770397 FAX: (01439) 771833
WEB SITE: www.thestaratharome.co.uk

Top-drawer gastropub with stylish rooms in separate cottage conversions

We've said it before, the Star is a star. It's quite an achievement for Andrew and Jacquie Pern, who have turned the Star around from dereliction to dining heaven in eight years. Nothing has been done by half measures: all rooms are immaculately decorated in a glamorous rustic chic style with a superb level of detail and craftsmanship. The original bedrooms in the fifteenth-century thatched Black Eagle Cottage comprise a pair of suites with open fires and oak timbers, just a short walk away through the quiet village;

thoughtfully, a breakfast hamper is delivered to the door packed with delicious goodies so you don't have to tear yourself out of bed. Eight more – all sybaritic affairs with huge spa baths, or even your own snooker table in Room 5 – are across the road from the inn in Cross House Lodge. The bar of the inn itself is the archetypal rural watering hole, with low beams, log fires and a flagstone floor; you're welcome to eat here if the restaurant is full – a state of affairs that is likely to be the rule rather than the exception, as foodies beat a trail to try Andrew's acclaimed cooking.

❍ Open all year; restaurant closed Sun eve ⧰ From Helmsley, take A170 towards Scarborough; after ½ mile turn right to Harome. Private car park ⧰ 2 twin, 9 double; all with hair-dryer, TV, CD player; some with room service, direct-dial telephone, modem line, VCR, DVD ⧰ Restaurant, bar, lounge, terrace, garden; conferences; social functions; civil wedding licence; heated outdoor swimming pool; early suppers for children; cots, highchairs, toys, babysitting, baby-listening ⧰ Wheelchair access to hotel and restaurant (1 step), WC; 6 ground-floor bedrooms, 2 specially adapted for wheelchair users ● No dogs; no smoking in bedrooms ⧰ Delta, MasterCard, Switch, Visa £ Twin/double £110 to £195; deposit required (prices valid till Jan 2005). Alc L £30, D £35; light meals available

---

HARROGATE North Yorkshire   map 9

Balmoral Hotel

Franklin Mount, Harrogate HG1 5EJ
TEL: (01423) 508208   FAX: (01423) 530652
EMAIL: info@balmoralhotel.co.uk
WEB SITE: www.balmoralhotel.co.uk

Quirky hotel with a cheery welcome and stylish touches near to Harrogate's centre

Mock-Tudor timbered gables and a couple of witch's-hat turrets crown the strangely grandiose façade of the Balmoral Hotel. Inside, too, it is a one-off sort of place, with a rather striking theatricality in its bold colours and contrasting ambiences between bar, restaurant and bedrooms. A straitjacket hangs on the wall of the deep blue bar: not a garment left behind by an absent-minded guest, but part of its escapologist-themed memorabilia dedicated to Harry Houdini. Across the hallway is the Villu Toots restaurant (named after an Estonian calligrapher who did some work for the hotel); this is a modishly minimal chic eatery furnished with cream tables, curvaceous seats, Mark Rothko prints making splashes of colour on beige walls, and high stools where you can perch at a zinc-fronted bar. Bedrooms take the route of traditional romance: most have a grand four-poster or half-tester bed, opulent, richly coloured fabrics, swagged silk curtains and smart modern white bathrooms.

❍ Open all year ⧰ In Harrogate, follow signs for conference centre; hotel is 100 yards further along Kings Road, on right. Nearest train station: Harrogate. Private car park ⧰ 2 single, 3 twin/double, 7 double, 6 four-poster, 2 family rooms, 3 suites; all with room service, hair-dryer, trouser press, direct-dial telephone, TV ⧰ Restaurant, bar, lounge, garden; conferences and social functions; leisure facilities nearby; early suppers for children; cots, highchairs, baby-listening, outdoor play area ⧰ Wheelchair access to hotel and restaurant (ramp), 2 ground-floor bedrooms ● No dogs in public rooms ⧰ Amex, Delta, MasterCard, Switch, Visa £ Single £65 to £85, single occupancy of twin/double £85 to £100, twin/double £90 to £110, four-poster £104 to £124, family room £124 to £144, suite £130 to £150; deposit required. Set D £19; alc D £25; light meals available. Special breaks available ③FOR②

Hotel du Vin & Bistro 【NEW ENTRY】

Prospect Place, Harrogate HG1 1LB
TEL: (01423) 856800   FAX: (01423) 856801
EMAIL: info@harrogate.hotelduvin.com
WEB SITE: www.hotelduvin.com

Style-oriented mini-chain sets up shop in Harrogate

The seemingly unstoppable spread of the Hotel du Vin formula has seen its northernmost outpost open in a townhouse terrace, formerly home to the Harrogate Spa

Hotel. For fans of the HDV product this will be home from home: a modish interior of self-conscious style in subdued masculine hues, wooden floors, butch chocolate leather sofas and informally professional young staff. You walk straight through the door into the Champagne and Claret bar, where trendy lads-about-town cluster round a purple baize pool table, and un-PC notices declare open season on the anti-smoking police – you're welcome to light up anything legal in any public area except the faux-Parisian restaurant. Here, an inspection meal of seared pigeon breast with beetroot and goats' cheese risotto, then sea bass with spinach and sauce vierge proved competent enough, though some may find it irritating to shell out £2.50 a time for the necessary portions of mash, chips and various side dishes required to turn the advertised dishes into a full, and indeed, filling meal. Breakfast too, is charged extra. Bedrooms, like the hotel guests, are sleek, clean-cut and stylish.

❶ Open all year ⚡ At Prince of Wales roundabout in Harrogate, turn into West Park, signposted 'Town Centre'; pass church and take first right into James Street and immediately right into Prospect Place. Nearest train station: Harrogate. Private car park 🚗 3 twin/double, 37 double, 3 suites; all with room service (breakfast only), hair-dryer, mini-bar, trouser press, direct-dial telephone, modem line, TV, DVD, CD player ⚗ Restaurant, bar, lounge, billiards room, courtyard; conferences and social functions; gym; early suppers for children; cots, highchairs, babysitting ♿ Wheelchair access to hotel (ramp) and restaurant, WC, lift ● No dogs; no smoking in restaurant ▭ Amex, Delta, Diners, MasterCard, Switch, Visa £ Twin/double from £85, suite from £185. Continental B £9.50, cooked B £13.50; set Sun L £24.50; alc L, D £34

HARTFIELD East Sussex   map 3

Bolebroke Watermill

Perry Hill, Edenbridge Road, Hartfield TN7 4JP
TEL: (01892) 770425 (AND FAX)
EMAIL: bolebrokemill@btinternet.com
WEB SITE: www.bolebrokemillhotel.co.uk

Ancient water mill in an idyllic rural setting

Tucked away down a bumpy unmade track in the heart of Winnie the Pooh country, Bolebroke Watermill is a beautifully restored eleventh-century corn mill in a wonderfully peaceful rural spot. Set beside a mill pond complete with small island and various roaming ducks, geese and chickens, David Cooper's fine historic home makes for a romantically isolated B&B with rustic character in spades; though the mill closed down in 1948, much of the original internal workings remain, and the interior makes a feature of its exposed timbers and old mill machinery. The simple, comfortable bedrooms are divided between the mill house and the Elizabethan barn, each with a good-sized, comfortable sitting room decorated with all manner of fascinating knick-knacks. Steep stairs in the mill – rather tricky to negotiate – lead up to two pretty bedrooms, Pond and Meadow, which have bathrooms cleverly built into space where corn storage bins used to be. Over in the barn, the three other rooms are equally distinctive – Burrow (on the ground floor with the easiest access) for its low beams, and the two upstairs rooms for their four-poster beds.

❶ Closed 19 Dec to 14 Feb ⚡ Take A264 from East Grinstead towards Tunbridge Wells for 6 miles; at crossroads turn right to Hartfield on B2026; after 1 mile turn left into farm track just past Perryhill Nursery; follow signs down lane. Private car park 🚗 1 twin/double, 2 double, 2 four-poster; all with hair-dryer, TV ⚗ 2 breakfast rooms, 2 lounges, garden; conferences; social functions; leisure facilities nearby ♿ No wheelchair access ● No children under 8; no dogs; no smoking ▭ Amex, MasterCard, Switch, Visa £ Single occupancy of double £55, twin/double £70, four-poster £80; deposit required

---

'In the bathroom there was no ventilation whatsoever. The ceiling fan box was in situ but had not been connected, as there was a loose wire dangling by the wardrobe. There were Happy Shopper toiletries, scratched plastic drinking glasses and small towels.'
On a hotel in Northamptonshire

HARWICH Essex
map 6

The Pier at Harwich

The Quay, Harwich CO12 3HH
TEL: (01255) 241212   FAX: (01255) 551922
EMAIL: pier@milsomhotels.com
WEB SITE: www.milsomhotels.com

Expanding seaside bolthole with good food

Versatility is the name of the game at this Harwich favourite. The front presents a jaunty blue-and-white face to the world, with the Harbourside Restaurant and Ha'Penny Bistro loudly trumpeted at the door. 'Come and enjoy our famous fish and chips' invites the Ha'Penny, a bright, informal space with white and blue plastic chairs, pop music on the radio and mushy peas on the menu. The Harbourside is a more formal affair, with good views over the water, including plenty of cranes (the mechanical rather than the feathered type) and traditional upmarket favourites like lobster thermidor. Seven bedrooms on the second floor are bright and modern, in sandy and seaside colours. The newly acquired building next door has also been completely refurbished, with seven additional bedrooms and a large private lounge decked out with plush modern leather sofas, cream carpets and a subtle nautical theme.

○ Open all year   ⚡ On quay in Harwich, opposite lifeboat station. Nearest train station: Harwich Town. Private car park   ⟱ 4 twin/double, 10 double; family rooms available; all with room service, hair-dryer, mini-bar, direct-dial telephone, TV   ⊗ 2 restaurants, bar, lounge; conferences, social functions, civil wedding licence; leisure facilities nearby; early suppers for children; cots, highchairs   ♿ No wheelchair access   ● No dogs; no smoking in public rooms   ▭ Amex, Delta, Diners, MasterCard, Switch, Visa   £ Single occupancy of twin/double £70 to £83, twin/double £95 to £170, family room from £125; deposit required. Set L £20; alc L, D £26; light meals available

HASSOP Derbyshire
map 9

Hassop Hall

Hassop, Bakewell DE45 1NS
TEL: (01629) 640488   FAX: (01629) 640577
EMAIL: hassophallhotel@btinternet.com
WEB SITE: www.hassophallhotel.com

A noble residence brimming with character

There's no missing the ecclesiastical links at this handsome, Georgian-fronted former stately home set in a picturesque vale. Religious treasures abound, from the neighbouring Catholic classical edifice with its Etruscan temple-style façade, to the snug bar whose lovely old oak box panelling and heraldic painted ceiling were purloined from Sheffield Cathedral, to the rare piece of late-Saxon stonework taken from the old chapel and now incorporated into the reception. However, these are just one aspect of a home that can trace its lineage to Domesday and where formal neoclassical trimmings rub shoulders with a more baronial past. Tradition is just as evident in the dining room, which boasts a cold table to complement the menu's extensive selection of roasts and grills. Bedrooms are very comfortably furnished in period style, although the en-suite facilities are a little dated.

○ Closed Chr; restaurant closed Sun eve   ⚡ 2 miles north of Bakewell on B6001. Private car park   ⟱ 1 twin, 3 twin/double, 5 double, 2 four-poster, 2 family rooms; all with room service, hair-dryer, direct-dial telephone, modem line, TV   ⊗ Restaurant, bar, lounge, garden; conferences and social functions; civil wedding licence; tennis; early suppers for children; cots, highchairs, babysitting   ♿ Wheelchair access to hotel and restaurant (ramp), WC, lift. Disabled parking   ● No dogs in public rooms; no smoking in some public rooms   ▭ Amex, Delta, Diners, MasterCard, Switch, Visa   £ Twin/double/four-poster £79 to £149, family room £149 (2004 prices); deposit required. Continental B £8, cooked B £10; set L £17.50, Sun £27.50, D £28, Sat £40. Special breaks available

Farthings

Hatch Beauchamp, Taunton TA3 6SG
TEL: (01823) 480664   FAX: (01823) 481118
EMAIL: farthing1@aol.com
WEB SITE: www.farthingshotel.com

Friendly and unstuffy atmosphere at this country-house hotel

Hilary and Stephen Murphy's hotel is a handsome-looking place with its white-washed façade trimmed with wrought-iron columns and balcony, plus various flowering baskets in season. At the front is a small bar and lounge done in pretty floral style, and where you may bump into Murphy and Guinness, the two good-natured English pointers who charm guests. The atmosphere here is relaxing and traditional. The restaurant offers a steady list of old favourites with a few more adventurous dishes – breads, desserts and canapés are all home-made. Bedrooms are variable in size and shape, but all are pleasant and comfortable. Those overlooking the garden such as Bay, a spacious double with a sleigh bed, are particularly good – but bathrooms are a little dated in some. Maple Cottage, a suite, is a comfortable alternative for guests with dogs of their own.

◖ Open all year ▨ Off A358, 5 miles south-east of Taunton. Private car park ⛐ 2 twin, 1 twin/double, 4 double, 2 family rooms, 1 suite; all with hair-dryer, direct-dial telephone, TV; limited room service available ⊘ Restaurant, bar, lounge, garden; conferences; social functions; civil wedding licence; leisure facilities nearby; early suppers for children; cot, highchair ♿ Wheelchair access to hotel and restaurant, 1 ground-floor bedroom ● No smoking; dogs in suite only, by arrangement ▭ Amex, Delta, MasterCard, Switch, Visa £ Single occupancy of twin/double £75 to £90, twin/double £105 to £125, family room/suite £135; deposit required. Set (Sun) L £15, D £30; light meals available (prices valid till Mar 2005). Special breaks available (3 FOR 2)

Highlow Hall

Hathersage, Hope Valley S32 1AX
TEL: (01433) 650393 (AND FAX)

Visit the home that inspired Charlotte Brontë

You'd have to look high and low to find another place to match the idyllic romance of this homely-sized sixteenth-century manor house wonderfully tucked away from it all in the depths of the Hope Valley. It's not that time's stood still here, but it's been happily content to drag its heels a little, so you'll still find a host of old-world character in the intimate wood-panelled breakfast room, the pretty, Victorianised sitting room, and especially the original great hall with its stone flags, huge fireplace and wrought-iron chandeliers. Thornfield House in *Jane Eyre* is said to be based on parts of this house. The three good-sized en-suite bedrooms in feminine colours also have plenty of charm – particularly Room 1, which for an extra £5 per night features a stunning carved Tudor four-poster – but it's the ravishing views over the valley that really make them special.

◖ Closed Chr to New Year ▨ From Hathersage, take B6001 (signposted Bakewell); turn off at sign to Abney and continue 1 mile to Hall. Nearest train station: Hathersage. Private car park ⛐ 1 double, 1 four-poster, 1 family room; all with hair-dryer ⊘ Breakfast room, sitting room, garden; leisure facilities nearby ♿ No wheelchair access ● No children under 12; no dogs; no smoking ▭ MasterCard, Visa £ Single occupancy of double £50, double £70, four-poster £75, family room £80; deposit required

---

'The guest–house had its makeover in about 1975. It missed the avocado bathroom suite era by a whisker and landed, and has forever frozen, in a sea of sickly pink.'
On a hotel in Cumbria

Plough Inn

Leadmill Bridge, Hathersage, Hope Valley S32 1BA
TEL: (01433) 650319   FAX: (01433) 651049
WEB SITE: www.theploughinn-hathersage.com

Pleasant rooms and good country fare in the High Peak

A row of carefully arranged pewter tankards hanging from a beam in the main bar strikes a note at once traditional and orderly at this smartly turned-out inn just south of the town. Guests can choose between the cosy bar area with its stylish smokers' chairs and the slightly more formal but nevertheless intimate dining room serving up the likes of rabbit tureen with apple and celeriac rémoulade on a bed of rocket, followed by pot-roast quail with tarragon mash in a red wine jus. However, one reader found the standard of food 'disappointing' this year, though he praised the service, accommodation and breakfast. Bedrooms in the main building are freshly done out and very comfortable, with simple colour schemes, solid built-in beech fittings, and smartly tiled up-to-date en-suite showers; two more rooms in September Cottage at a higher price tag come with more character as well as bathrooms and seating areas.

◗ Closed 25 & 26 Dec   ⊠ From Baslow, take A623 towards Calver; at garage and Discount Centre turn right on to B6001; in Grindleford, turn left 50 yards past garage; continue uphill for about 2 miles; inn is on right just before bridge. Nearest train station: Hathersage. Private car park   ⌂ 3 twin/double, 2 suites; all with room service, hair-dryer, direct-dial telephone, TV, CD player; some with trouser press   ⊘ Dining room, bar, garden; leisure facilities nearby; early suppers for children; cots, highchairs   ♿ Wheelchair access to hotel (1 step) and dining room (1 step), WC, 1 ground-floor bedroom   ⬤ No children under 12 in dining room eves; no dogs; no smoking   ▭ MasterCard, Switch, Visa   £ Single occupancy of twin/double £50 to £70, twin/double £80 to £100, suite £100; deposit required. Alc L, D £22; light meals available. Special breaks available   ③FOR②

Queen's Head

Main Street, Hawkshead, Ambleside LA22 0NS
TEL: (015394) 36271   FAX: (015394) 36722
EMAIL: enquiries@queensheadhotel.co.uk
WEB SITE: www.queensheadhotel.co.uk

Eating, drinking and sleeping are equally enjoyable in this olde-worlde dining pub

Literary associations bring many visitors to Hawkshead, but you don't have to be a fan of Wordsworth or Beatrix Potter to warm to this charming historic village. Its quaint coaching inn is easily identified by a sign depicting a stern likeness of the Virgin Queen, but inside, the atmosphere is warm and welcoming. It's clearly a place for locals as well as tourists. A series of cosily beamed interlocking bars with slate-flagged floors range through the ground floor. Towards the rear lies the dining room, attractively decked in blue-and-white napery, with china plates on oak-panelled walls. Cooking is a strong point at the Queen's Head. Menus range from traditional fish and chips or Herdwick lamb to more adventurous Mediterranean-influenced dishes drizzled with basil oil or topped with tapenade. Bedrooms are smart and colourful, some with romantically draped four-posters. Trout Cottage is a stylish annexe conversion in an adjoining cottage.

◗ Open all year   ⊠ In centre of Hawkshead   ⌂ 2 twin, 7 double, 2 four-poster, 2 family rooms, 1 suite; all with hair-dryer, direct-dial telephone, TV; some with VCR   ⊘ Dining room, bar, lounge, garden; conferences; social functions; leisure facilities nearby; early suppers for children; cots, highchairs, toys, baby-listening   ♿ Wheelchair access to hotel (2 steps) and restaurant, WC, 2 ground-floor bedrooms   ⬤ No dogs; no smoking in bedrooms   ▭ Delta, Diners, MasterCard, Switch, Visa   £ Single occupancy of twin/double £48, twin/double £68 to £84, four-poster £100, family room £124, suite £95; deposit required. Alc L £20, D £25; light meals available. Special breaks available   ③FOR②

Hawnby Hotel

Hawnby, Nr Helmsley YO62 5QS
TEL: (01439) 798202   FAX: (01439) 798344
EMAIL: info@hawnbyhotel.co.uk
WEB SITE: www.hawnbyhotel.co.uk

Peace and quiet and good cooking at a convivial village inn

The Hawnby Hotel is rooted firmly in village life in a tranquil spot among the rolling undulations of the North Yorkshire Moors. On one level, it is the local pub, where the darts team meets up, but – while the hand-pulled Black Sheep ale is a fine pint – the Hawnby amounts to rather more than a simple spit-and-sawdust boozer. With a fat candle on each table and logs stacked by an open fire that scents the place with wood smoke, the bar made a perfect venue for a tasty inspection meal of roast cod with tomato and mozzarella, followed by a massively calorific sticky toffee pudding. For posher surroundings, the Mexborough dining room is smartly furnished and has a separate seating area with squidgy sofas around a stone fireplace; framed prints of game birds are a nod to the shooting parties that frequent the hotel in season. Bedrooms in the main house are traditional and flowery, while the three rooms in the separate Stables annexe are sprucely modern, with wooden floors and good bathrooms with big shower heads; all come with a welcoming glass of sherry, mineral water, biscuits and chocolates.

◗ Open all year   ☒ Hotel is on top of hill in Hawnby. Private car park ⟞⟝ 3 twin, 6 double; all with hair-dryer, direct-dial telephone, TV ⊘ Dining room, bar, lounge, garden; social functions; leisure facilities nearby; cots, highchairs, toys, baby-listening, outdoor play area ⟐ No wheelchair access ● No dogs; smoking in bar only ▭ Delta, MasterCard, Switch, Visa £ Single occupancy of twin/double £49, twin/double £69; deposit required. Alc L, D £17.50; light meals available. Special breaks available ③ᶠᴼᴿ②

Weaver's

13–17 West Lane, Haworth BD22 8DU
TEL: (01535) 643822   FAX: (01535) 644832
EMAIL: weaversinhaworth@aol.com
WEB SITE: www.weaversmallhotel.co.uk

Friendly restaurant-with-rooms in the epicentre of Brontë country

At the summit of Haworth's steep cobbled high street, Weaver's faces the Brontë family parsonage across the town car park. If you have worked up a keen appetite on the wild and windy moors, Jane and Colin Rushworth's quirky enterprise – originally a row of weavers' cottages – offers hearty regional cooking with a serious level of complexity. The bar area, which serves as the breakfast room, glows a warm tangerine hue and is festooned with an entertaining clutter of bobbins from the weaving era, antique mirrors, sepia photos and the odd crystal chandelier. Chirpy young staff keep things ticking over in the restaurant, where an impressive inspection meal kicked off with masala prawns in a sort of Brittany-meets-Bengal pancake, then moved onto a main course of monkfish with red peppers stuffed with smoked sausage risotto, and was rounded off by some excellent northern cheeses. Bedrooms have an eclectic mix of furniture and theatrical splashes of colour against a neutral backdrop; smart white bathrooms are spotless, and foodies will appreciate the freshly ground coffee and home-made biscuits.

◗ Closed Chr and New Year; restaurant closed Sun and Mon eve   ☒ Follow signs to Brontë Parsonage Museum in Haworth ⟞⟝ 1 twin, 2 double; all with hair-dryer, trouser press, direct-dial telephone, TV ⊘ Restaurant, bar, lounge; social functions; leisure facilities nearby; cots, highchairs, baby-listening ⟐ No wheelchair access ● No dogs; no smoking in restaurant and bedrooms ▭ Amex, Delta, Diners, MasterCard, Switch, Visa £ Single occupancy of twin/double £55, twin/double £80 to £85; deposit required. Set L, D £16; alc L £20, D £25; light meals available ③ᶠᴼᴿ②

HEADLAM Co Durham

map 10

Headlam Hall

Headlam, Nr Gainford, Darlington DL2 3HA
TEL: (01325) 730238 FAX: (01325) 730790
EMAIL: admin@headlamhall.co.uk
WEB SITE: www.headlamhall.co.uk

Intimate country-house hotel with impressive facilities

When you arrive at Headlam Hall, passing a cluster of agricultural outbuildings where the odd tractor may be parked, you may be forgiven for thinking you've strayed onto a farm. Indeed, the Robinson family has farmed at Headlam for generations. In summer 2004 the current incumbents opened a new nine-hole golf course on 40 acres of pastureland – an addition that will no doubt go down well with the execs busy in the function suites. Headlam uses its space cleverly, so it manages to feel relaxed for leisure guests whilst functioning as a popular wedding and conference venue: the separate Coach House annexe, which has a pool, gym and sauna, is used to corral corporate and wedding groups, ensuring their privacy while preventing irritation to non-revellers. The main Jacobean and Georgian house is a peaceful, classy place with the requisite creaking oak floors, panelled walls, log fires and décor of classic chintz. Dining rooms are small and intimate; best is the Panelled room, a romantic spot with its antique tables and high-backed chairs. A grand staircase flanked by sandstone pillars leads up to the bedrooms, which use antiques, posh fabrics and good bathrooms to create an upmarket ambience. Those in the Mews annexe have a more modern style, but share the same focus on quality.

○ Closed 25 & 26 Dec 🚫 Turn off A67 at Gainford and follow signs to Hall. Private car park 🛏 6 twin, 15 double, 7 four-poster, 4 family rooms, 2 suites; all with room service, hair-dryer, direct-dial telephone, modem line, TV; some with trouser press ⟨⟩ 3 dining rooms, 2 bars, lounge, conservatory, games room, garden; conferences and social functions; civil wedding licence; gym, tennis, golf, heated indoor swimming pool; early suppers for children; cots, highchairs, toys, baby-listening ♿ Wheelchair access to hotel and dining rooms (ramp), WC, 9 ground-floor bedrooms ● No children under 12 in dining rooms eves; no dogs in public rooms and some bedrooms; no smoking in bedrooms and some public rooms ▭ Amex, Delta, Diners, MasterCard, Switch, Visa £ Single occupancy of twin/double £75, twin/double £90, four-poster £110, family room £100, suite £130; deposit required. Set L £14, D £22; alc L £15, D £25; light meals available; service incl. Special breaks available

HENLEY-ON-THAMES Oxfordshire

map 2

Red Lion Hotel

Hart Street, Henley-on-Thames RG9 2AR
TEL: (01491) 572161 FAX: (01491) 410039
EMAIL: reservations@redlionhenley.co.uk
WEB SITE: www.redlionhenley.co.uk

Perfect position on the Thames for the king of Henley's hotels

Along with Ascot and Wimbledon, and strawberries and cream, an English summer wouldn't be complete without Henley Regatta – or a rainy day or two! Luckily, the Red Lion is well-equipped to deal with both, having a prime, riverside position near the finishing line, and attractive public rooms suitable for whiling away a wet hour or two. Since the fifteenth century, the august red-brick building at the heart of this appealing Oxfordshire town has been acting as one of Henley's focal points, welcoming the great and good through its doors to relax in the convivial, clubby bar or dine in the ancient-meets-modern restaurant. The Tudor origins of the building, in the form of blackened beams or carved four-posters, can be seen in some bedrooms, but all are tastefully furnished and decorated in a traditional style with plenty of floral fabrics. Most face the river, so that you can enjoy those Thames-side views, though with the busy main street outside the door, some will suffer from traffic noise.

○ Open all year ⚡ Beside Henley Bridge. Nearest train station: Henley-on-Thames. Private car park 🅿 3 single, 8 twin, 11 double, 3 four-poster, 1 family room; all with room service, hair-dryer, direct-dial telephone, modem line, TV; some with trouser press; no tea/coffee-making facilities in rooms ⊘ Restaurant, bar; conferences, social functions; leisure facilities nearby; early suppers for children; cots, highchairs, babysitting, baby-listening ⅃ No wheelchair access ● No dogs ▭ Amex, Delta, MasterCard, Switch, Visa £ Single £85 to £99, single occupancy of twin/double £95 to £130, twin/double £95 to £145, four-poster £115 to £165, family room £115 to £170; deposit required. Continental B £8.50, cooked B £12.50; set L £16; alc L £25, D £30; light meals available

---

HEREFORD Herefordshire map 5

Castle House

Castle Street, Hereford HR1 2NW
TEL: (01432) 356321 FAX: (01432) 365909
EMAIL: info@castlehse.co.uk
WEB SITE: www.castlehse.co.uk

A Georgian beauty in a delightful location close to the river

It might be tucked away down a quiet side street next to the banks of the river Wye and an easy stroll from the cathedral, but that is the only thing that is shy and retiring about Castle House. Dutch owners Albert and Monique Heijn have created a big, bold townhouse hotel with lavish décor and an eye to the building's historic features. Antiques and high-quality furnishings are apparent throughout, with oriental rugs over parquet flooring. Bright golds, lemons and reds, with the occasional modern fabric, grace the public rooms. The restaurant has lots of windows and eye-catching prints of ornamental garden plants on the walls, while outside is a terrace down to the river decked with smart garden furniture. Bedrooms are in excellent condition and have names that evoke British history such as Stuart, Cavalier or Albert, reflected in the paintings and colour schemes.

○ Open all year ⚡ In centre of Hereford. Nearest train station: Hereford. Private car park 🅿 4 single, 1 double, 10 suites; family rooms available; all with room service, hair-dryer, mini-bar, direct-dial telephone, modem line, TV, VCR; some with trouser press, CD player; no tea/coffee-making facilities in rooms ⊘ Restaurant, bar, lounge, garden; social functions; leisure facilities nearby; cots, highchairs, baby-listening ⅃ Wheelchair access to hotel and restaurant, National Accessible Scheme: mobility impairment M3, 1 ground-floor bedroom, 2 rooms specially equipped for disabled people, WC, lift ● No smoking in restaurant ▭ Amex, Delta, MasterCard, Switch, Visa £ Single £100, single occupancy of twin/double £140 to £180, double £175 to £225, family room £200 to £250, suite £184 to £225; deposit required. Cooked B £8.50; set L £27; alc D £40; light meals available. Special breaks available ③FOR②

HERMITAGE Dorset map 2

Almshouse Farm NEW ENTRY

Hermitage, Holnest, Nr Sherborne DT9 6HA
TEL: (01963) 210296 (AND FAX)

Welcoming hostess and plenty of bucolic tranquillity at this B&B

Jenny Mayo has been offering B&B at this beautiful ancient farmhouse for 35 years, and the cumulative experience shows: fresh milk on the tea tray, home-made marmalade, home-cured bacon ('as long as it lasts'), and straightforward, homely bedrooms that are immaculately well kept. Bathrooms are on the simple side, but there are other compensations – the dining room, for example, is a lovely fifteenth-century space with a vast stone fireplace and collections of horse tack, various antlers and so on. Outside is a peaceful lawned garden with chairs, and next to it is a farmyard that would keep a bystander amused – horses, cows, dogs and children constantly passing through. For evening meals there is a pub a short drive away.

○ Closed Nov to Feb   ⚡ From Sherborne take A352 towards Dorchester for 5 miles; at Holnest crossroads turn right, signposted Hermitage, for 1 mile; farm on the left. Private car park   🛏 1 twin, 2 double; all with hair-dryer, TV   ⚡ Dining room, lounge, garden   ♿ No wheelchair access   ● No children under 10; no dogs; no smoking   ▭ None   £ Single occupancy of twin/double £30, twin/double £50 to £58

Dene House

Juniper, Hexham NE46 1SJ
TEL: (01434) 673413
EMAIL: info@denehouse-hexham.co.uk
WEB SITE: www.denehouse-hexham.co.uk

Welcoming B&B with cottagey rooms and a tranquil rural location

Margaret and Brian Massey's stone farmhouse is perfectly situated for anyone wanting an out-of-the-way, stress-busting break in glorious Northumberland countryside. The tiny hamlet has the pretty name of Juniper – not that you will see it on any signposts until you're almost upon the house, so make sure you set off with directions. Your arrival will be rewarded with a genuinely warm welcome, tea and home-made cakes. Inside, all is cheerful and cottagey; in the guests' lounge an open fire in a stone hearth warms the soul on grey days,

while a conservatory overlooking the herb garden makes a great place to snooze when the sun shines. The bedrooms are cosily decorated with cheerful patchwork quilts, well supplied with books and fresh milk, immaculately kept and have good bathrooms and showers. Margaret serves up Aga-cooked breakfasts, including home-made bread and preserves, in a sunny farmhouse kitchen – just the job to set you up for another day exploring the wild country around Hadrian's Wall.

○ Open all year   ⚡ Take B6306 from Hexham (south); take first right fork then first left, both signposted Dye House; follow road for 3½ miles; Dene House is 100 yards past Juniper sign. Private car park   🛏 1 single, 1 twin, 1 double; 1 with private facilities; all with hair-dryer   ⚡ Kitchen/breakfast room, lounge, conservatory, garden; leisure facilities nearby; cots, highchairs, toys   ♿ No wheelchair access   ● No dogs; no smoking   ▭ Delta, MasterCard, Switch, Visa   £ Single £25, single occupancy of twin/double £30, twin/double £50; deposit required

---

Langley Castle

Langley on Tyne, Nr Hexham NE47 5LU
TEL: (01434) 688888   FAX: (01434) 684019
EMAIL: manager@langleycastle.com
WEB SITE: www.langleycastle.com

Authentic medieval castle in Hadrian's Wall country

As you approached this crenellated fortress you might not be surprised to see Errol Flynn and sundry men in tights re-enacting historic conflicts, for Langley Castle is exactly Hollywood's image of an English castle. Within its seven-foot-thick walls, the requisite set design – bare-stone walls, stone staircases, suits of armour, arched windows and stained glass – are all present and correct (as is the obligatory ghost) in its grand public spaces, including the vast baronial hall. Naturally, plush furniture and roaring fires soften the edges and take the ambience way

upmarket. Things weren't always like this: after centuries of tumultuous history, the place was derelict until, at the end of the nineteenth century, Cadwallader Bates made it his life's work to restore the pile. The bedrooms all take their names from historical occupants, and are opulently kitted out with antiques and luxurious fabrics. Several have four-posters. Not surprisingly, the castle does a brisk business in weddings and functions, so book ahead and go for one of the rooms in the main fortress.

○ Open all year   ⚡ Leave Hexham towards west on A69; turn left on to A686, signposted Langley Castle, and follow road; hotel is on right. Private car park   🛏 7 double, 8 four-poster, 3 suites; family rooms available; all with room service, hair-dryer, direct-dial telephone, modem line, TV; some with mini-bar   ⚡ 2 restaurants, 2 bars, lounge, garden; conferences and social functions; civil wedding licence; leisure facilities nearby; early suppers for children; cots, highchairs, baby-listening &. Wheelchair access to hotel and restaurant, 8 ground-floor bedrooms, lift ◖ Dogs in some bedrooms only; no smoking in restaurant 💳 Amex, Diners, MasterCard, Switch, Visa £ Single occupancy of double £100 to £160, double £129, four-poster £209, family room £169, suite £149; deposit required. Set L £19, D £30; light meals available. Special breaks available ③FOR②

HIGHER BURWARDSLEY Cheshire   map 7

The Pheasant NEW ENTRY

Higher Burwardsley, Tattenhall CH3 9PF
TEL: (01829) 770434   FAX: (01829) 771097
EMAIL: reception@thepheasant-burwardsley.com
WEB SITE: www.thepheasant-burwardsley.com

A classy inn combining rural charm with metropolitan sophistication

Sheltered by a bowl of wooded hills, this imaginatively converted complex of warm sandstone and half-timbering enjoys breathtaking telescopic views across the Cheshire plains. The location – on the edge of a remote village accessed via a web of tiny lanes – feels like the back of beyond, yet it's not far from main routes to Chester and Crewe. Unobtrusively well kept inside and out, the Pheasant provides stacks of carefully considered sitting and dining space, subtly partitioned in stone or wood, and tastefully furnished in uncluttered, relaxing styles. Bar-lounge areas have open hearths, low tables and an assortment of quality seating on boarded flooring. The airy, stone-flagged conservatory restaurant is more formal, generously decked in white linen and rush-seat ladderback chairs. Bedrooms, some in a converted barn across the courtyard, are varied but quietly refined in restrained modern colours with well-designed bathrooms. Menus are lengthy and inventive, supplemented by daily specials.

◑ Open all year ⁊ In Burwardsley, 2 miles southeast of Tattenhall follow signs for the candle workshop. Private car park ⌐ 2 twin, 4 double, 2 four-poster, 1 family room; suite available; all with hair-dryer, direct-dial telephone, modem line, TV ⊘ Restaurant, dining room, bar, lounge, conservatory, garden; conferences; social functions; leisure facilities nearby; outdoor play area &. Wheelchair access to hotel (ramp) and restaurant, National Accessible Scheme: mobility impairment M2, WC, 3 ground-floor bedrooms ◖ No children under 6 in restaurant; no dogs; no smoking in bedrooms 💳 Amex, Delta, Diners, MasterCard, Switch, Visa £ Single occupancy of twin/double £65, twin/double £70 to £80, four-poster/suite £90, family room £100. Set L £15, D £25; alc L £18, D £27

HINDRINGHAM Norfolk   map 6

Field House NEW ENTRY

Moorgate Road, Hindringham NR21 0PT
TEL: (01328) 878726   FAX: (01328) 878955
EMAIL: stay@fieldhousehindringham.co.uk
WEB SITE: www.fieldhousehindringham.co.uk

Multiple-award-winning B&B – a warm welcome in a modern country style

Field House is a modern home built in time-honoured Norfolk brick and flint, and this combination of traditional but modern runs through the whole place. So décor is sometimes contemporary, sometimes classical, but always welcoming and homely. The sitting room is comfortably furnished with a mixture of antiques and more recent pieces, while the bright dining area features glass-topped square tables and wicker furniture. Bedrooms are in similar country style, with bright pink shiny cushions and little teddy bears welcoming you. Wendy Dolton, now in her third season at Field House, is professional and meticulous but welcoming and unstuffy. 'We try to keep our guests happy,' she told us, and it seems she's succeeding. 'Our room was most luxurious and had every little thing you could possibly want,' wrote one correspondent.

◑ Open all year; dining room closed Mon, Thu, Sun eves ⚡ From Fakenham, take A148 towards Holt; at The Crawfish in Thursford, turn left and follow sign for Hindringham; go through village; at Lower Green turn right into Moorgate Road; hotel is first on left ⤷ 1 twin, 2 double; all with shared bathroom; all with hair-dryer, TV, CD player, DVD, fridge ⚥ Dining room, sitting room, conservatory, garden ♿ No wheelchair access ● No children under 8, and under 12 in dining room; no dogs; no smoking ▭ None accepted £ Twin/double £80 to £90; deposit required. Set D £27; light meals available; service incl

---

HINTON CHARTERHOUSE Bath & N. E. Somerset   map 2

Homewood Park

Hinton Charterhouse, Bath BA2 7TB
TEL: (01225) 723731 FAX: (01225) 723820
EMAIL: res@homewoodpark.com
WEB SITE: www.homewoodpark.com

Well-run country-house hotel with good reputation for its food

With the A36 close by and ready to lead you the six miles into Bath, this lovely Georgian country house is in a handy position. Built in 1780 with later additions, its formal façade is softened by creepers and there are ten acres of lawned gardens to explore. Owned and run by Alan Moxon, the hotel manages to maintain high professional standards but without ever becoming stuffy or losing the friendly, relaxing atmosphere. The lounge and bar are both cosy spots to unwind, combining floral patterns, deep sofas and oil paintings. Next to them the restaurant is made up of three linked rooms – the cooking, under French head chef Jean de la Rouzière, is very well regarded. Bedrooms are prettily decorated and spacious – the pick being those with a view. Bathrooms off the standard rooms can be more of a squeeze.

◑ Open all year ⚡ 6 miles south-east of Bath, on A36 to Warminster. Private car park ⤷ 6 twin/double, 6 double, 1 four-poster, 5 suites; all with room service, hair-dryer, direct-dial telephone, modem line, TV; tea/coffee-making facilities on request ⚥ Restaurant, bar, lounge, library, garden; conferences and social functions; civil wedding licence; heated outdoor swimming pool; early suppers for children; cots, highchairs, baby-listening ♿ Wheelchair access to hotel and restaurant, WC, 2 ground-floor bedrooms ● No smoking ▭ Amex, Delta, Diners, MasterCard, Switch, Visa £ Single occupancy of twin/double £115, twin/double £115 to £190, four-poster £161 to £190, suite £215 to £270; deposit required. Set L £19.50, D £39.50; light meals available; service incl. Special breaks available

---

HOLKHAM Norfolk   map 6

The Victoria

Park Road, Holkham NR23 1RG
TEL: (01328) 711008 FAX: (01328) 711009
EMAIL: victoria@holkham.co.uk
WEB SITE: www.victoriaatholkham.co.uk

Colonial India on the breezy Norfolk coast

The road on which you park your car for the Victoria hotel, just off the main Norfolk coast road, is rather grand. And well it might be, since if you follow it past the hotel you'll find yourself at the entrance to the vast grounds of Holkham Hall, magnificent eighteenth-century home of the Earl of Leicester. The hotel is now being run directly by the estate, and is a little slice of grandeur available to the people. Though there doesn't appear to be any obvious connection, the interior designer has decided to go for a 'colonial India' theme, which certainly makes things interesting, with much of the furniture imported from Rajasthan, pictures of maharajahs and tigers on the walls, and plush fabrics. There are delicate Indian motifs painted on bedroom doors, and the bedroom interiors continue the Indian theme to varying degrees. The inspiration doesn't carry through into absolutely everything – the Holkham Tap bar is more of a traditional English pub, and the restaurant menu features only one Asian dish among otherwise English fare.

◐ Open all year ⊿ 3 miles west of Wells-next-the-Sea, on A149. Private car park ⌂━ 1 twin/double, 6 double, 1 four-poster, 1 family room, 2 suites; all with room service, hair-dryer, mini-bar, direct-dial telephone, TV ⊘ Restaurant, 2 bars, lounge, library, conservatory, garden; conferences and social functions; civil wedding licence; leisure facilities nearby; early suppers for children; cots, highchairs, baby-listening, outdoor play area ⟐ Wheelchair access to hotel and restaurant, 1 ground-floor bedroom, 1 room specially equipped for disabled people ● No children in restaurant after 7pm; no smoking in restaurant and bedrooms ⊟ Delta, MasterCard, Switch, Visa £ Single occupancy of twin/double £90 to £110, twin/double/four-poster £110 to £140, family room £125 to £155, suite £180 to £200; deposit required. Set L £20, D £30; light meals available. Special breaks available ③FOR②

HOLMESFIELD Derbyshire map 9

Horsleygate Hall

Horsleygate Lane, Holmesfield S18 7WD
TEL: 0114-289 0333 (AND FAX)

Unpretentious rural retreat with delightful gardens

More of a farmhouse B&B than you might expect of an establishment with 'Hall' in its title, this attractive Georgian stone guesthouse is tucked away in a valley at the eastern edge of the Peak District. A beautiful garden surrounding the house makes an inviting entrance, but the homely, traditional interior with its rug-strewn flag floors and wood-burning stove is just as appealing when the weather turns. Only one of the three bedrooms is en suite and has a comfortably cottagey feel with its patchwork quilt, pine fittings and stripy wallpaper. The other two rooms share a bathroom but have their own sinks, while all three feature the same lovely Peak views. With a profusion of home-made conserves and free-range eggs to hand, breakfast at the shared table in the sunny dining room is guaranteed to be a treat.

◐ Closed Chr ⊿ Off B6051, north-west of Chesterfield. Private car park ⌂━ 1 twin, 1 double, 1 family room; 2 with shared bathroom ⊘ Breakfast room, sitting room, garden; leisure facilities nearby ⟐ No wheelchair access ● No children under 5; no dogs; no smoking ⊟ None accepted £ Single occupancy of twin/double £35, twin/double £50 to £55, family room £60; deposit required

---

HOPE Derbyshire map 8

Underleigh House

Off Edale Road, Hope S33 6RF
TEL: (01433) 621372   FAX: (01433) 621324
EMAIL: underleigh.house@btinternet.com
WEB SITE: www.underleighhouse.co.uk

A real home from home in a picture-postcard setting

It's clear that Philip and Vivienne Taylor love where they live and enjoy looking after guests. The former is entirely natural given that their home is a beautiful old stone barn brimming with character and set in stunning Peak District valley scenery, while the latter is evident both in their demeanour and in the great attention to detail. Tea and cake is served on arrival, a huge choice at breakfast includes plenty of home-made preserves and locally sourced sausages and eggs, maps of local walks are provided, packed lunches are available, and they're happy for visitors to bring a bottle, although they are licensed. The same commitment can be found in the comfortably cottagey bedrooms, where TVs come with video and DVD (a blank tape is provided and the Taylors are building up their library) and windows feature spectacular views.

◐ Closed Chr & New Year ⊿ Opposite Hope parish church on A6187, take road signposted Edale for just over ½ mile, passing under bridge; just after 'road narrowing' sign, take lane to left at Underleigh sign; continue, bearing right, for about ¼ mile; house is first house on right. Nearest train station: Hope. Private car park ⌂━ 1 twin, 4 double, 1 suite; all with hair-dryer, direct-dial telephone, TV, VCR, DVD, CD player ⊘ Breakfast room, lounge, garden ⟐ Wheelchair access to house (2 steps) and breakfast room (2 steps), 2 ground-floor bedrooms ● No children under 12; no dogs; no smoking ▭ Delta, MasterCard, Switch, Visa £ Single occupancy of twin/double £46 to £50, twin/double £70, suite £85; deposit required. Special breaks available

---

HOPESAY Shropshire   map 7

Old Rectory

Hopesay, Craven Arms SY7 8HD
TEL: (01588) 660245   FAX: (01588) 660502

A fine house in a quiet village, with gardens, food and hospitality to match

As you might expect, it's easy to find the Old Rectory in this delightful hamlet, as it stands right next to the lovely twelfth-century parish church of St Mary. And Roma Villar's house is just as you would hope to find a splendid home in deepest rural England. Dating back to the seventeenth century, its mature gardens have fine copper beeches, redwoods and a dazzling array of azaleas and rhododendrons. Guests can enjoy these as they sit on the York-stone terrace awaiting Roma's home cooking, served on the dot of 8pm, around an oak refectory table. Expect straightforward dishes such as veal, Dover sole or Shropshire lamb, with plenty of seasonal vegetables. Then you can retire to the spacious drawing room with its classy antiques, piano and family photos. The bedrooms are all a good size, with pine furnishings and plenty of light, and come with Roberts radio, television and tea tray with fresh milk.

◗ Closed Chr & New Year ▨ Leave A49 at Craven Arms; take B4368 signposted to Clun; at Aston-on-Clun, turn right over humpback bridge; in Hopesay turn left; house is on left by church. Private car park ⬕ 1 twin, 1 twin/double, 1 double; all with hair-dryer, TV ✅ Dining room, drawing room, garden; leisure facilities nearby ⅙ No wheelchair access ● No children; no dogs; no smoking ▭ None accepted £ Single occupancy of twin/double £50, twin/double £100. Set D £25

HOPWAS Staffordshire   map 5

Oak Tree Farm

Hints Road, Hopwas, Tamworth B78 3AA
TEL: (01827) 56807 (AND FAX)

Luxurious B&B accommodation in a peaceful rural setting

Owner Sue Purkis's maxim is to remember all the things that guests tell her they don't usually get in a hotel – and try to provide them. Thus it's no surprise to find that her immaculately kept guesthouse on a converted farm is thoughtfully provisioned, from goose-down duvets, teddy-bear-shaped hot-water bottles and crisp robes in the bedrooms, to a conservatory sporting a generous plunge pool and attendant steam room. The bedrooms, split between the main house and a converted barn, are all spacious, comfortably furnished and tastefully decorated in soft tones, but vary in appointment; for instance, Room 5 comes with a waterbed, while the en-suite in Room 8 has a large corner bath with an enclosed overhead shower. Breakfasts are taken in an airy room with an attractive brick fireplace and bright lemon and white linen.

◗ Closed 2 weeks at Chr ▨ From A51 Lichfield to Tamworth road, turn into Hints Road at Tame Otter pub; farmhouse is last house on left, where road divides. Private car park ⬕ 1 single, 1 twin/double, 2 twin, 2 double, 1 four-poster; all with room service, hair-dryer, trouser press, direct-dial telephone, modem line, TV, CD player; 2 with VCR ✅ Breakfast room, lounge, conservatory, garden; conferences; heated indoor swimming pool, steam room; leisure facilities nearby ⅙ Wheelchair access to house (2 steps) and breakfast room (1 step), 2 ground-floor bedrooms ● No children; no dogs in public rooms; no smoking ▭ Amex, Delta, MasterCard, Switch, Visa £ Single £57, single occupancy of twin/double £57, twin/double £75, four-poster £100; deposit required

Langshott Manor

Langshott, Horley RH6 9LN
TEL: (01293) 786680   FAX: (01293) 783905
EMAIL: admin@langshottmanor.com
WEB SITE: www.alexanderhotels.com

Comfortable, stylish rooms in a beautiful Elizabethan manor close to Gatwick

Few would expect to find a gorgeous timber-framed manor house on the edge of a modern housing estate, seconds from Horley's busy town centre. Carefully screened by mature beech hedges and surrounded by immaculate formal gardens with a moat to boot, Langshott Manor appears a world away from its surroundings, and, though perfectly placed for Gatwick, it's a cut above your run-of-the-mill airport hotel. Behind the fine red-brick Elizabethan façade and mullioned windows of the main building, huge fireplaces, low-beamed ceilings and wood-panelling feature throughout the flower-filled public areas, which are elegantly furnished and tastefully done out in rich blues and golds. The pristine bedrooms – divided between the original manor, sympathetic extension and annexe Mews – are equally stylish, perhaps with elaborate swags, stripey walls, reproduction furniture and luxurious modern bathrooms. Henry VIII, in the new building, has a stone fireplace, a four-poster you need a ladder to reach and a deck over the moat, while Wisley in the separate Garden Mews has its own small garden and seating area. Superior rooms are no less smart but tend to have only one washbasin and showers over baths instead of the separate walk-in variety found in the feature bedrooms.

◑ Open all year   ▨ From A23 at Chequers roundabout, take Ladbroke Road to Langshott; manor is 1 mile on right. Private car park   ⬛ 4 twin, 13 double, 4 four-poster, 1 suite; all with room service, hair-dryer, mini-bar, trouser press, direct-dial telephone, modem line, TV   ⌖ Restaurant, 3 lounges, garden; conferences; social functions; civil wedding licence; leisure facilities nearby; early suppers for children; cots, highchairs, babysitting   ⅓ Wheelchair access to hotel and restaurant (ramps), 10 ground-floor bedrooms   ● No dogs; no smoking in bedrooms and some public rooms   ▭ Amex, Delta, Diners, MasterCard, Switch, Visa   £ Single occupancy of twin/double £165 to £200, twin/double £185 to £220, four-poster £240 to £260, suite £270 to £290; deposit required. Set L £25, D £37.50; light meals available. Special breaks available (2004 data)

Bell Inn & Hill House

High Road, Horndon on the Hill SS17 8LD
TEL: (01375) 642463   FAX: (01375) 361611
EMAIL: info@bell-inn.co.uk
WEB SITE: www.bell-inn.co.uk

Traditional inn and characterful bedrooms – not to mention great food

The Bell Inn & Hill House, in the pretty village of Horndon on the Hill, is well placed for passing trade just off the A13. The coaching inn has been providing sustenance to passing travellers since the mid-fifteenth century, while some of the roof beams show evidence of being nearly 1,000 years old, having had previous lives as ship's timbers. The bar has a cosy, local feel, but the menu is anything but traditional, offering adventurous fare such as cod gravadlax with red wine, poached egg and pea ravioli, or pan-fried perch with apple and rhubarb risotto and brie ganache. Bedrooms in the inn can be quite grand in a traditional way. Most of the bedrooms are in Hill House, a prestigious local residence until it was converted in 1986. They are quite contemporary in style, with quirky touches like a leopardskin bedcover and black leather sofas.

◑ Closed 25 & 26 Dec   ▨ From A13 at Stanford-le-Hope exit, take B1007 to Horndon on the Hill. Nearest train station: Stanford-le-Hope. Private car park   ⬛ 3 twin, 5 double, 1 four-poster, 1 family room, 5 suites; all with room service, hair-dryer, trouser press, direct-dial telephone, modem line, TV; some with VCR, CD player; fax available ✅ Restaurant, bar, courtyard; conferences; social functions; leisure facilities nearby; cots, highchairs ♿ No wheelchair access; ramps into hotel and restaurant, WC, 4 ground-floor bedrooms ⬤ No dogs in public rooms and some bedrooms; no smoking in restaurant, bar and some bedrooms ⬜ Amex, Delta, MasterCard, Switch, Visa £ Twin/double/four-poster/family room/suite £50 to £85; deposit required. Continental B £4.50, cooked B £9.50; alc L, D £26; light meals available

---

HORRINGER Suffolk　　　　　　　　　　　　　　　　　　map 6

The Ickworth

Horringer, Bury St Edmunds IP29 5QE
TEL: (01284) 735350 FAX: (01284) 736300
EMAIL: info@ickworthhotel.com
WEB SITE: www.luxuryfamilyhotels.com

Fabulous, elegant but uninhibited family retreat

'It's all about not having to compromise just because you've got kids,' says Peter Lord, and that perfectly sums up the ethos of the Ickworth and the other properties in the Luxury Family Hotels stable. The latest addition is nothing short of spectacular, in a huge eighteenth-century manor house surrounded by 1,800 acres of National Trust grounds. The décor strikes a trendy balance between classic and modern, with original features of the house lightened with cool, breezy colour schemes and clean lines. Striking contemporary artworks specially commissioned for the hotel greet you at every turn but never feel out of place. Most of the rooms steer closer to the traditional, but a few are more contemporary, so you can choose according to your taste, though ours would be for the traditional. You could also stay in one of 11 apartments in the grounds. There are options too when it comes to eating – in the basement the informal Café Inferno serves Mediterranean bistro food, and kids can also eat in the sunny conservatory. Then you have a formal dining room where you can take a welcome breather from the little ones – the idea is that this is a holiday for you as well as for the children. Youngsters are more than well catered for with a multitude of activities, both outdoor and in, with a supervised nursery for the littlest ones and Club/Blu with table footie and games consoles for the others.

◖ Open all year ⤢ From A14 take third Bury St Edmunds exit, marked as junction 42; follow brown signs for Ickworth House until you reach a staggered crossroads. Go straight on until T-junction then turn right into Horringer; hotel is on right. Private car park 🚗 7 twin/double, 18 double, 2 four-poster; family rooms and suites available; all with room service, hair-dryer, direct-dial telephone, modem line, TV, DVD ✅ 2 restaurants, lounge, library, study, conservatory, gardens; conferences; social functions; civil wedding licence; spa, tennis, heated indoor swimming pool, leisure facilities nearby; early suppers for children; cots, highchairs, toys, playroom, babysitting, baby-listening, outdoor play area ♿ Wheelchair access to hotel (ramp) and restaurants, WC, lift. Disabled parking ⬤ No dogs in public rooms, £7.50 per night in bedrooms; smoking in library only ⬜ Amex, Delta, Diners, MasterCard, Switch, Visa £ Single occupancy of twin/double from £130, twin/double £250 to £310, four-poster £220 to £290, family room £350 to £445, suite £300 to £390; deposit required. Alc L £20, D £37.50; light meals available; service incl. Special breaks available

---

HUDDERSFIELD West Yorkshire　　　　　　　　　　　map 9

Lodge Hotel

48 Birkby Lodge Road, Birkby, Huddersfield HD2 2BG
TEL: (01484) 431001 FAX: (01484) 421590
EMAIL: contact@birkbylodgehotel.com
WEB SITE: www.birkbylodgehotel.com

Interesting small hotel with good food in a leafy suburb

Ian Barton took over this classy old house a couple of years ago and has ensured that its restaurant is the driving force behind the informally professional small hotel. The building oozes character, thanks to the 1920s owner who had the place kitted out with a host of art-nouveau features by the designer Edgar Wood. Stained glass in the front door sets the tone, then you're into a clubby bar lounge with a casual lived-in feel, full of old Chesterfields, oak panelled walls and worn oriental rugs on oak floors – and don't miss that art-nouveau detail in the ceiling beams and fireplaces. Bedrooms are homely and comfortable with pieces of unusual furniture; some bathrooms are looking a bit dated, but are in line for an ongoing programme of refurbishment. One correspondent reported dust and debris in the dining room while it was being redecorated, and lapses in housekeeping. More reports, please.

❍ Open all year ⚡ Leave M62 at Junction 24 and take A629 towards Huddersfield; at first traffic lights turn left into Birkby Road; after 1 mile, immediately after hospital, turn right into Birkby Lodge Road; hotel is 300 metres on left. Nearest train station: Huddersfield. Private car park 🚗 4 single, 2 twin, 5 double, 1 four-poster, 1 family room; all with room service, hair-dryer, direct-dial telephone, TV; some with modem line ⊘ Restaurant, bar, lounge, library, garden; conferences, social functions, civil wedding licence; leisure facilities nearby; cots, highchairs, baby-listening ♿ No wheelchair access; 4 steps into hotel, 3 ground-floor bedrooms ● No smoking in bedrooms and some public rooms ▭ Amex, Delta, Diners, MasterCard, Switch, Visa £ Single £50 to £60, twin/double £50 to £60, four-poster £120, family room rates on application; deposit required. Continental B £7, cooked B £10; set L £18.50, D £24; light meals available; service incl

---

HURSTBOURNE TARRANT Hampshire   map 2

Esseborne Manor

Hurstbourne Tarrant, Andover SP11 0ER
TEL: (01264) 736444   FAX: (01264) 736725
EMAIL: esseborne@aol.com
WEB SITE: www.essebornemanor.com

Unassuming hotel in a Victorian country house with good food, popular with business guests

This attractive cream-washed Victorian country house sits peacefully amid rolling fields above the lovely Bourne Valley between Andover and Newbury. Comfortably unpretentious, Esseborne Manor is smartly done out in traditional style but remains perfectly homely and relaxing, a winning combination proving particularly popular with business guests, drawn also by its convenient location and good food. Served up in the restful dining room with its open log fires, and prepared from fresh local produce where possible, the three- or four-course menu du vin (served with or without wines specially selected for each course) might include duck liver mousse with candied kumquats and pavé of three fish with sauce vierge, then buttered chicken on crushed potatoes and fine beans followed by lemon tart. Bedrooms are divided among the main house, annexe and cottages and all are well equipped and comfortably furnished with lots of thoughtful extras. Rooms in the house have the edge for character.

❍ Open all year ⚡ On A343, halfway between Newbury and Andover. Private car park 🚗 5 twin/double, 9 double, 1 four-poster; family rooms available; all with room service, hair-dryer, trouser press, direct-dial telephone, modem line, TV, CD player, DVD ⊘ Dining room, bar, lounge, library, garden; conferences; social functions; civil wedding licence; tennis; leisure facilities nearby; early suppers for children; cots, highchairs, baby-listening ♿ Wheelchair access to hotel and restaurant, WC, 6 ground-floor bedrooms. Disabled parking ● No dogs in public rooms ▭ Amex, Delta, Diners, MasterCard, Switch, Visa £ Single occupancy of twin/double £95, twin/double £120, four-poster/family room £150; deposit required. Set L £16, D £22; alc L, D £35; light meals available; service incl. Special breaks available ③FOR2

HUXLEY Cheshire   map 7

Higher Huxley Hall

Red Lane, Huxley, Chester CH3 9BZ
TEL: (01829) 781484   FAX: (01829) 781142
EMAIL: info@huxleyhall.co.uk
WEB SITE: www.huxleyhall.co.uk

Superior manor-farm accommodation in a much-loved family home

The neatly trained trees and hedges along Higher Huxley Hall's private drive signal a place of some distinction. The substantial white-painted house, in immaculately kept gardens, looks mainly Edwardian from outside, but the adjacent complex of farm buildings obviously dates from an earlier era. In fact, parts of the hall go back as far as the thirteenth century, and its domain gets a mention in the Domesday Book. The Marks family has lived here for over 35 years, achieving an air of settled continuity along with impeccable standards of housekeeping. Antiques and classy country-house furnishings fit comfortably into its spacious ground-floor reception rooms, which include a well-proportioned hall lounge, an elegant Georgian drawing room and a bright sun-lounge. A fine feature staircase constructed of Armada oak leads to well-furnished bedrooms with character beams. Pauline's appetising five-course dinners, served in the oldest part of the house, incorporate local market produce.

○ Open all year ☑ From Chester take A41 towards Whitchurch; take fourth left to Waverton and Huxley; go over crossroads, follow canal; just over 1 mile after humpback bridge turn right into drive opposite T-junction with sign for Huxley. Private car park ⬦ 1 single, 1 twin/double, 2 double; all with hair-dryer, direct-dial telephone, modem line, TV ✓ Dining room, lounge, dining room, conservatory, garden; heated indoor swimming pool (summer only) ⬥ No wheelchair access ● No children under 15; no dogs; no smoking ▭ Amex, Delta, MasterCard, Switch, Visa £ Single £50 to £55, single occupancy of twin/double £50 to £65, twin/double £90 to £95; deposit required. Set D £28; light meals available; service incl. Special breaks available (3 FOR 2)

ILMINGTON Warwickshire   map 5

Howard Arms

Lower Green, Ilmington, Shipston on Stour CV36 4LT
TEL: (01608) 682226 (AND FAX)
EMAIL: info@howardarms.com
WEB SITE: www.howardarms.com

Classy gastropub with rooms

On the village green, oozing Cotswold charm, is the characterful seventeenth-century Howard Arms. The aristocratic name comes from a beneficial marriage in the 1800s between the local Canning family and the Howards of Castle Howard fame, but the look is one of rustic abundance: polished flagstones, huge bay windows and massive inglenook fireplaces feature strongly here. Rob and Gill Greenstock chose this setting for their gastropub after a long, time-consuming trawl, and they now have an established reputation for serving good food and fine ales. The mellow gold-coloured dining room, with high arched windows and chunky furniture, is a combination of banqueting hall and bistro, where friendly and efficient staff serve meals such as avocado Caesar salad, baked organic salmon with crab sauce and rhubarb and apple flapjack crumble with custard or cream. The bar, a few steps below, retains its original old-world flavour. Bedrooms are unfussy and tastefully furnished.

○ Closed 25 Dec ☑ In centre of Ilmington village. Private car park ⬦ 1 twin, 2 double; all with hair-dryer, TV ✓ Dining room, bar, garden ⬥ No wheelchair access ● No children under 8; no dogs; smoking in some public rooms only ▭ Delta, MasterCard, Switch, Visa £ Single occupancy of twin/double £70, twin/double £90 to £105; deposit required (prices valid till Jan 2005). Set (Sun) L £18.50; alc L, D £22; light meals available. Special breaks available

---

Folly Farm Cottage

Back Street, Ilmington, Shipston on Stour CV36 4LJ
TEL: (01608) 682425 (AND FAX)
EMAIL: slowe@follyfarm.co.uk
WEB SITE: www.follyfarm.co.uk

The phoenix has risen for this Cotswold gem

It's hard to imagine this compact, seventeenth-century building looking any different from its well-maintained present condition, but when Sheila and Malcolm Lowe took it over 20 years ago it was little more than a basic bungalow showing signs of its past as a ramshackle stable. Now, though, all that has changed, and the Cottage can compare to the best of them in this attractive honey-stoned village conveniently located for Stratford. The house is full of details to make guests feel at home while retaining a sense of independence. So on the first-floor landing by the guest rooms is a small lounge with a fridge for wine or milk or whatever else needs to be kept cool. Beyond the breakfast room is a colourful garden terrace – ideal for sipping chilled white wine on a warm summer evening. The cheerful bedrooms are flower-themed, with four-posters or half-tester. A good range of meals is available a short stroll away at the Howard Arms (see entry).

◐ Closed Chr & New Year ⤴ From B4035 between Chipping Campden and Shipston on Stour, turn north towards Ilmington. Private car park 🛏 1 double, 2 four-poster; all with room service, hair-dryer, TV, VCR ⌀ Breakfast room, lounge, garden; leisure facilities nearby ♿ No wheelchair access ● No children; no dogs; no smoking ⊟ None accepted £ Single occupancy of double £39, double £54 to £66, four-poster £74 to £80; deposit required. Special breaks available

---

Manor House Farm

Ingleby Greenhow, Nr Great Ayton TS9 6RB
TEL: (01642) 722384
EMAIL: mbloom@globalnet.co.uk

Charming hosts and fresh cottagey rooms at a tranquil farmhouse

Manor House Farm lies in a remote and gorgeous area of the North York Moors National Park, so Margaret and Martin Bloom's idyllic house in 164 acres of parkland is a natural magnet for walkers and anyone in search of serious peace and quiet. This is a comfy, homely place and deeply restful; a comforting wood-burning stove warms the convivial lounge, which has a veritable library of books to curl up with on dodgy weather days. Margaret's five-course dinners – largely traditional fare based on local produce – are just the job to refuel after a day striding across moors, and there's a good choice of sensibly priced wines on offer to foster a sociable ambience; menus are discussed when guests book. Three shipshape bedrooms offer plenty of space, have a simple, uncluttered décor and are immaculately kept; a further bonus is the beautiful views to the Cleveland Hills and Captain Cook's monument – it's an interesting thought that he was setting off to the South Pacific around the time the house was built.

◐ Closed Dec ⤴ From Stokesley on A172, take B1257 to Great Broughton. At village hall take road to Ingleby Greenhow; at church in Ingleby, turn into Manor Drive through stone pillars; follow drive for ¼ mile, then fork left to farm. Nearest train station: Battersby Junction. Private car park 🛏 2 twin, 1 double; all with room service; TV, hair-dryer available ⌀ Dining room, bar service, lounge, library, garden; leisure facilities nearby ♿ No wheelchair access ● No children under 12; no dogs; no smoking ⊟ Delta, MasterCard, Switch, Visa £ Twin/double £100 (rates incl dinner); deposit required

---

Crown & Garter NEW ENTRY

Great Common, Inkpen, Hungerford RG16 9QR
TEL: (01488) 668325
EMAIL: gill.hern@btopenworld.com
WEB SITE: www.crownandgarter.com

Bright and breezy rooms attached to an atmospheric village pub

Even when you find little Inkpen – and it is way out in the wilds of southern Berkshire – it's such a straggly (although sweet) village that you'll be hard pushed to locate this down-to-earth pub without some explicit directions. But it's worth the effort, especially on a sunny day when you can enjoy a pint and some slap-up pub grub out in the long, lush garden. Since taking over a couple of years ago, Gill Hern has successfully made the switch from university lecturer to affable pub landlady and has been introducing gentle changes, such as fresher décor and theme nights, from

Latin Summers to Caribbean, to involve the locals. Although the pretty, red-brick pub dates back to the seventeenth century (and has the appropriate character inside), all the bedrooms are in a modern, one-storey extension built around a peaceful central garden, and are decked out in fresh, simple style with exposed floorboards, cheery fabrics and restful colour schemes. Some of the edges are a little rough, but no doubt Gill will soon turn her canny eye to those.

○ Open all year In Kintbury at village store turn left on to Inkpen Road; stay on this road till hotel is on left 3 twin, 5 double; all with room service, hair-dryer, TV, VCR Restaurant, bar, garden; social functions; leisure facilities nearby; highchairs, toys, outdoor play area No wheelchair access; 8 ground-floor bedrooms No dogs in restaurant; smoking in bar only Amex, Delta, MasterCard, Switch, Visa £ Single occupancy of twin/double £50, twin/double £70 (prices valid till Jan 2005); alc L, D £20; light meals available. Special breaks available (3FOR2)

The Swan Inn NEW ENTRY

Inkpen, Nr Hungerford RG17 9DX
TEL: (01488) 668326   FAX: (01488) 668306
EMAIL: enquiries@theswaninn-organics.co.uk
WEB SITE: www.theswaninn-organics.co.uk

Modern comforts at a seventeenth-century pub that is big on organic food

At the lower end of this strung-out village, just near the tiny, triangular green, is this handsome whitewashed pub, which has been sympathetically extended to provide more modern accommodation to complement the olde-worlde feel of the public areas. The spacious bar is pleasant enough, with its beamed ceiling, but it's the restaurant that is the star – a stylish pink-and-white affair beneath an A-frame oak roof that was built using parts of an old ship. And when the sun comes out to play, you can decamp on to the large terrace at the front, which is brimming with tables and benches. The bedrooms were added a few years back, and are kitted out in a simple but attractive way with cream walls, pine furniture, patchwork quilts and smart shower rooms. Just the spick-and-span ticket for a night in the country without breaking the bank. Owners Mary and Bernard Harris are also organic beef farmers, and their meat features on the menus, along with organic veggies and wines, plus local beers. A farm shop out the back sells a tempting spread of organic produce, including the farm's beef.

○ Closed Chr & New Year; restaurant closed Sun to Tues eves 3 miles southeast of Hungerford, in Inkpen village. Private car park 1 single, 3 twin, 6 double; family rooms available; all with hair-dryer, trouser press, direct-dial telephone, modem line, TV Restaurant, dining room, bar, garden; conferences; leisure facilities nearby No wheelchair access No dogs; no smoking in bedrooms Amex, Delta, Diners, MasterCard, Switch, Visa £ Single £40, single occupancy of twin/double £45 to £65, twin/double £75 to £90, family room £100. Set L, D £17; alc L, D £21; light meals available

---

IPSWICH Suffolk   map 6

Salthouse Harbour Hotel NEW ENTRY

1 Neptune Quay, Ipswich IP4 1AS
TEL: (01473) 226789   FAX: (01473) 226927
EMAIL: staying@salthouseharbour.co.uk
WEB SITE: www.salthouseharbour.co.uk

Contemporary style arrives in Ipswich

From the proprietors of the Angel in Bury St Edmunds (see entry) comes this dockside warehouse, neatly refurbished in firmly contemporary style. Everything is very smart and very 'now', for which read neutral colours, natural materials such as wood and slate, and clean lines. A specially commissioned contemporary art programme adds a dash of variety and a splash of colour. Rooms are clean and well equipped without feeling too clinical, with interesting intricately carved dark wood headboards. The bright brasserie, with plenty of exposed brickwork and a black marble bar, serves contemporary European food to the accompaniment of gentle chill-out music, while a big lounge with lots of squashy furniture and bright artworks would benefit from a bit of natural light.

➊ Open all year ⊞ Hotel is halfway along north side of marina in Ipswich. Nearest train station: Ipswich. Private car park 🛏 10 twin/double, 25 double, 6 family rooms, 2 suites; all with room service, hair-dryer, direct-dial telephone, fax, modem line, TV, VCR, CD player ⊘ Restaurant, bar, lounge; social functions; civil wedding licence; early suppers for children; cots, highchairs, baby-listening ♿ Wheelchair access to hotel and restaurant, lift, 2 rooms specially equipped for disabled people ● No dogs in public rooms ▭ Amex, Delta, Diners, MasterCard, Switch, Visa £ Single occupation of twin/double £100 to £120, twin/double £130, family room £145, suite £190; deposit required. Set L, D £25, alc L, D £36; light meals available; service incl. Special breaks available

---

IREBY Cumbria　　　　　　　　　　　　　　　　　　　　　　map 10

Overwater Hall 　NEW ENTRY

Overwater, Ireby CA7 1HH
TEL: (017687) 76566　FAX: (017687) 76921
EMAIL: welcome@overwaterhall.co.uk
WEB SITE: www.overwaterhall.co.uk

Improvements continue at this remarkably friendly place near Bassenthwaite Lake

New arrivals at Overwater may find the castellated, drum-turreted exterior of this unusual Grade II listed Georgian mansion rather daunting, but the welcome couldn't be warmer. The well-mannered house dogs may be first on the doormat (this is a notably pet-friendly establishment); otherwise, owners Stephen Bore or Adrian and Angela Hyde and their staff will soon make you feel at home. The setting, in deep green countryside near Bassenthwaite Lake and the Skiddaw fells, is utterly peaceful, and the hotel is surrounded by some 18 acres of lushly wooded grounds. The interior dimensions are just as grand as the outside, with a finely turned stairwell gliding from the hallway past handsome plasterwork and stately windows. Overwater Hall is currently in a transitional phase, steadily morphing from a period piece of frumpy velour and dizzying carpets into a svelte creation of bold, smart designs. Refurbished bedrooms look very promising, as do the heartily traditional dinner menus. More reports on progress welcome.

➊ Closed 1 to 15 Jan ⊞ Take A591 towards Carlisle from Keswick, turn right after 7 miles at Castle Inn to Ireby; after 2 miles on this minor road turn right at sign for the hotel. Private car park 🛏 3 twin/double, 5 double, 2 four-poster, 1 suite; family rooms available; all with room service, hair-dryer, direct-dial telephone, TV ⊘ Restaurant, bar, 2 lounges, garden; leisure facilities nearby; early suppers for children, cots, highchairs, baby-listening, outdoor play area ♿ No wheelchair access ● No children under 5 in restaurant eves; no smoking in restaurant ▭ MasterCard, Switch, Visa £ Single occupancy of twin/double £95 to £105, twin/double £150 to £170, four-poster/family room £170 to £190, suite £190 to £210 (rates incl dinner); deposit required. Special breaks available

---

IRONBRIDGE Shropshire　　　　　　　　　　　　　　　　　map 5

The Library House

Severn Bank, Ironbridge, Telford TF8 7AN
TEL: (01952) 432299　(AND FAX)
EMAIL: info@libraryhouse.com
WEB SITE: www.libraryhouse.com

Smart, tidy B&B with hosts who show attention to detail

It's easy to miss this quaint Georgian house on arrival in Ironbridge, as it is tucked away up a small alley close to the river. Guests can park for 20 minutes to unload, helped by the owners Chris and George Maddocks, but then they are provided with a car park pass – George can undertake valet parking for you if you wish, while Chris offers you a welcome drink. This is typical of the level of service at the Library House and the reason why guests return year after year. There's an interesting contrast between the country look of the breakfast room, with its wooden tables, dresser and spindle chairs, and the more urban sitting room with its brown leather sofas and cream walls lined with bookcases. Bedrooms have a cosy feel, with a high standard of décor. Wren is the pick – a smallish double with access to a hillside terrace patio and other tiny lawned terraced parts.

◑ Closed Chr 🔁 In Ironbridge town centre, 60 yards from bridge 🛏 1 twin, 3 double; family rooms available; all with hairdryer, TV, VCR ⊘ Breakfast room, sitting room, garden; leisure facilities nearby ♿ No wheelchair access ● No children under 10; no dogs in public rooms; no smoking 🚫 None accepted £ Single occupancy of twin/double £55, twin/double £65, family room £80 to £85; deposit required

---

Severn Lodge

New Road, Ironbridge, Telford TF8 7AU
TEL: (01952) 432147   FAX: (01952) 432148
EMAIL: julia@severnlodge.com
WEB SITE: www.severnlodge.com

A distinctive B&B with an owner of taste and character to match

Seemingly perched precariously on the edge of the Ironbridge gorge, Julia Russell's Georgian home betrays its quirkiness almost immediately. Indian runner ducks scurry about the gravel driveway and the clunk of croquet mallet on ball can be heard from the garden. Julia deals in antiques, but it looks as if she keeps as much as she sells, as every available surface in her home has trinkets and antique clutter. She claims not to have any particular favourite, although Staffordshire items figure prominently. Two Indian statues holding chandeliers stand guard at the entrance to her kitchen, and cabinets of collectibles will keep guests amused for quite some time. Julia serves breakfast in the vestibule, under the gaze of the statues, and likes to offer something a little different each morning, perhaps poached haddock or kedgeree. She is a big fan of pink, but the house has more restrained colour tones. Garden is the pick of the bedrooms, with its large double bed with coronet, cream and beige décor and big stand-alone bath and separate shower. Severn is very feminine, with a matching lavender colour scheme.

◑ Closed first week in Dec to first week in Jan 🔁 Entering Ironbridge on B4373 from north or south, drive past bridge on your left; immediately before Malthouse restaurant, turn right into New Road; house is on right. Private car park 🛏 1 twin, 2 double; all with room service, hair-dryer, TV ⊘ Breakfast room, lounge, garden; leisure facilities nearby ♿ No wheelchair access ● No dogs; no smoking 🚫 None accepted £ Single occupancy of twin/double £55, twin/double £66 to £74; deposit required

---

Higher Cadham Farm NEW ENTRY

Jacobstowe, Exbourne, Okehampton EX20 3RB
TEL: (01837) 851647   FAX: (01837) 851410
EMAIL: kingscadham@btopenworld.com
WEB SITE: www.highercadham.co.uk

Charming farm accommodation in idyllic countryside

Down the lanes of Devon – flower-decked in season – lies Susan Sallis's working farm, but no ordinary farm this. On its 118 acres you can find kingfishers, otters, orchids, owls and plenty more besides. Added to that are sheep, rabbits, chickens and, perhaps most importantly, Susan's welcoming friendliness. The bedrooms are straightforward and simple with pine furniture, floral bedspreads and functional but well-kept shower units. There is a plain restaurant, tea room and small bar with bottles of local cider lined up. Children are well catered for with a playground and trampoline – 'though the dads use that just as much as the kids,' says Susan. Wander a little further and you have the Tarka Trail down to the River Okement. You will be lucky to spot the secretive otters, but other flora and fauna are more easy to find.

◖ Closed Chr; restaurant closed Sun eves ⤵ From Okehampton take A386 towards Hatherleigh; after Folly Gate turn right on to B3072 to Jacobstowe; at junction turn left, then right just after church; hotel is ½ mile down lane. Private car park ⬛⌐ 1 single, 2 twin, 3 double, 1 four-poster, 1 family room; all with hair-dryer; some with TV, VCR ⌀ Restaurant, tea room, bar, lounge, garden; conferences; social functions; cots, highchairs, toys, baby-listening, outdoor play area ⓺ Wheelchair access to hotel and restaurant, National Accessible Scheme: M2, 2 ground-floor bedrooms specially equipped for disabled people. Disabled parking ⬤ No dogs in public rooms; no smoking ⊟ Delta, MasterCard, Switch, Visa £⃝ Single £28, single occupancy of twin/double £30, twin/double/four-poster £55, family room £69; deposit required. Set L £11, D from £12.50; light meals available ⓷ꜰᴏʀ②

KEMERTON Worcestershire map 5

Upper Court

Kemerton, Nr Tewkesbury GL20 7HY
TEL: (01386) 725351   FAX: (01386) 725472
EMAIL: diana@uppercourt.co.uk
WEB SITE: www.uppercourt.co.uk

Fine living at a family manor house set in idyllic gardens

It's hard to imagine a more perfect Georgian manor house – and if the fabulous water gardens, croquet lawn, swimming pool and tennis court are taken into account too, the picture becomes even better. This honey-stone mansion lies just behind the parish churchyard and on the edge of a two-acre lake complete with rowing boat and two islands. Inside, Bill and Diana Herford's home is a country-house delight, with period furnishings, pelmeted curtains, fresh flowers and polished antiques. The dining room looks as if it's set for a grand house party – and indeed, guests sit down to dinner around a single polished table. The bedrooms are decorated in traditional English chintz with neat if unstylish bathrooms. The newly converted Dovecote, a four-poster room, is a romantic hideaway for two overlooking the lake. All the rooms have tea trays and televisions, and you can choose to have breakfast in your room for no extra charge. Alternatively, you may prefer to have your toast on the lawn watching the swans go by.

◖ Open all year ⤵ In Kemerton, turn off the main road at the war memorial; Upper Court is 200 yards down road, behind parish (not RC) church. Private car park ⬛⌐ 1 twin, 1 double, 3 four-poster; all with hair-dryer, TV, VCR, CD player ⌀ Dining room, bar, lounge, library, conservatory, games room, garden; conferences; social functions; tennis, heated outdoor swimming pool (summer only), leisure facilities nearby; cots, highchairs, baby-sitting ⓺ Wheelchair access to hotel (ramp) and dining room, 1 ground-floor bedroom ⬤ No dogs; no smoking in bedrooms ⊟ MasterCard, Switch, Visa £⃝ Single occupancy of twin/double £85, twin/double £85, four-poster £100; deposit required. Set D £35; service incl

---

KENILWORTH Warwickshire map 5

Castle Laurels

22 Castle Road, Kenilworth CV8 1NG
TEL: (01926) 856179   FAX: (01926) 854954
EMAIL: moores22@aol.com
WEB SITE: www.castlelaurelshotel.co.uk

Welcoming guesthouse with abundant period charm

Right in the lee of Kenilworth Castle – hence the appellation – this handsome late-Victorian townhouse enjoys an enviable location just far enough from the centre of the charming old English town to avoid the hustle and bustle. The house has retained much of its original character, so you'll find a beautifully tiled hallway and attractive fireplaces in the comfortable sitting room and elegantly papered breakfast room, as well as swathes of wood panelling and plenty of pretty stained glass throughout. The bedrooms are all similarly decorated, with plain cream walls, red carpets and attractive modern spreads, while en-suite facilities are pleasingly tiled and have decent fittings. Most of the bedrooms feature eye-catching Victorian fireplaces and have pleasant outlooks (the castle itself is obscured by trees), but those in the original house have more character than those in the extension.

○ Closed Chr 🔁 On A452, almost opposite Kenilworth Castle. Private car park 🅿 3 single, 3 twin, 6 double; family rooms available; all with hair-dryer, direct-dial telephone, TV; 1 with trouser press ⊘ Breakfast room, lounge; leisure facilities nearby ⎠ No wheelchair access; 2 steps into hotel, 1 ground-floor bedroom ◖ No dogs; no smoking ▭ Amex, Delta, MasterCard, Switch, Visa £ Single £40, single occupancy of twin/double £52 to £54, twin/double £63, family room £78; deposit required. Light meals available

---

KESWICK Cumbria   map 10

Dale Head Hall

Thirlmere, Keswick CA12 4TN
TEL: (017687) 72478   FAX: (017687) 71070
EMAIL: onthelakeside@daleheadhall.co.uk
WEB SITE: www.daleheadhall.co.uk

Breathtaking vistas of Thirlmere compensate for signal blackspots at this relaxing retreat

Techno-junkies should be aware that there's no television here, and your mobile phone probably won't work either. Helvellyn stands in the path of the transmitting stations, you see, and the otherwise efficient and accommodating owners of Dale Head Hall just haven't got round to shifting the damn thing yet. In daylight hours, at least, a glance out of the window should take your mind off anything remotely digital or analogue. Terraced gardens cascade to the pine-wooded lakeshore in orderly waves, with tables set outside in fine weather. This rather grand house manages to combine historical distinction and a civilised demeanour with complete friendliness. It really is a place to unwind, mostly thanks to its outgoing hosts. The Bonkenburgs run the place with experienced enthusiasm, refurbishing at least three bedrooms every year and keeping everything up to scratch. Decorative styles are conservatively pleasing; smart new bathrooms feature slate surfaces and demisting mirrors. As we went to press the hotel was up for sale.

○ Closed Jan 🔁 Halfway between Keswick and Grasmere on A591, at end of long private drive. Private car park 🅿 2 twin, 6 double, 3 four-poster, 1 family room; all with room service, hair-dryer, direct-dial telephone; some with modem line ⊘ Restaurant, bar, lounge, garden; leisure facilities nearby; early suppers for children; cots, highchairs, baby-listening ⎠ Wheelchair access to hotel (3 steps) and restaurant (1 step), 2 ground-floor bedrooms ◖ No children under 10 at dinner; no dogs; no smoking in bedrooms ▭ Amex, Delta, MasterCard, Switch, Visa £ Single occupancy of twin/double £73 to £83, twin/double £90 to £115, family room £110 to £120; four-poster (rate incl dinner) £200; deposit required. Set D £37.50; service incl. Special breaks available

---

The Grange

Manor Brow, Keswick CA12 4BA
TEL: (017687) 72500
EMAIL: info@grangekeswick.com
WEB SITE: www.grangekeswick.com

A long-established favourite in a secluded but convenient location

Jane and Duncan Miller have run The Grange with great success for many years, and although they're taking things a bit easier these days by limiting service to B&B only, standards of upkeep and housekeeping have clearly not diminished. Furnishings are not the latest thing in designer chic, but the traditional chintzes and fresh, light pastels suit many older guests very well. One great advantage of this well-managed guesthouse is its location. The house is a classic specimen of Victorian Lakeland architecture in local grey-green slate, with lacy bargeboards and festive balustrades. The extensive, well-kept gardens slope away from this elevated site, giving spectacular vistas towards Cat Bells. These fine views are shared by the dining room's large, ornately dressed windows.

Upper bedrooms have the most character, with exposed rafters and sloping attic ceilings; all have a mix of practical modern and older furnishings – a half-tester bed in No 5, for instance.

● Closed 3 Nov to 2 Mar 🚗 Take A591 from Keswick towards Windermere for ½ mile; take first right turn; hotel is 200 yards on right. Private car park 🛏 1 single, 3 twin, 6 double; all with room service, hair-dryer, direct-dial telephone, TV ✓ Breakfast room/conservatory, 2 lounges, garden; leisure facilities nearby ♿ No wheelchair access ● No children under 7; no dogs; no smoking ▭ Delta, MasterCard, Visa £ Single £34 to £48, twin/double £68 to £85; deposit required. Special breaks available

KIMMERIDGE Dorset   map 2

Kimmeridge Farmhouse

Kimmeridge, Wareham BH20 5PE
TEL: (01929) 480990   FAX: (01929) 481503
EMAIL: kimmeridgefarmhouse@hotmail.com

Well-kept rooms and wonderful rural location for this farmhouse B&B

People realised long ago the value of this lovely spot – in the thirteenth century, to be precise. That was when the earliest parts of Annette Hole's house were constructed, but many additions have been made since. There are views of the sea just half a mile away. The land surrounding, all 700 acres of it, is the farm, which produces beef, sheep, pigs and dairy, the meat finding its way on to the table in Annette's cooking. The emphasis is on the home-made and the wholesome. Bedrooms are neat and attractive, with antique pine furniture. A small sitting area is available on the landing where you can leaf through local information on walks and attractions (the coastal path passes nearby and there are the Purbeck Hills to explore). Substantial breakfasts are taken around a single large table and there's the option of a packed lunch too.

● Closed 25 Dec 🚗 From Wareham, take A351 to Swanage and turn right at Corfe Castle; continue through Church Knowle and take second left to Kimmeridge; farmhouse is next to church. Private car park 🛏 1 twin/double, 2 double; all with room service, hair-dryer, TV ✓ Breakfast room, lounge area, garden; leisure facilities nearby ♿ No wheelchair access ● No children under 10; no dogs; no smoking ▭ None accepted £ Twin/double £50 to £58. Packed L £4.50; light meals available

KINGHAM Oxfordshire   map 5

Mill House

Station Road, Kingham, Chipping Norton OX7 6UH
TEL: (01608) 658188   FAX: (01608) 658492
EMAIL: stay@millhousehotel.co.uk
WEB SITE: www.millhousehotel.co.uk

Good food and cheery bedrooms in this quieter corner of the Cotswolds

Entering the reception at Mill House you are literally stepping back in time – the flagstone floor dates back to the original mill that stood here at the time of William the Conqueror's inventory. Evidence of the next 950-odd years is dotted around the building, from the grandfather clock that dates to 1770 when the 'new' mill was built, to the scales used to weigh the Victorians' flour. Best of all is that the more modern extensions and conversions have been so sympathetically done that the whole honey-stone package is a treat, especially when you realise that a trout stream babbles away in the ten acres of gardens. An inglenook fireplace and floral sofas give the lounge an air of homely conviviality, while more low-key elegance is on offer in the smartly turned-out restaurant, where you can dine on good modern British cuisine. Bedrooms are done up in a comfortable, traditional style with sprightly, countrified décor and neat bathrooms.

● Open all year 🚗 South of Kingham village, just off B4450 between Chipping Norton and Stow-on-the-Wold. Nearest train station: Kingham. Private car park 🛏 23 twin/double; all with room service, hair-dryer, direct-dial telephone, TV ✓ Restaurant, dining room, bar, lounge, garden; conferences and social functions; leisure facilities nearby; early suppers for children; cots, highchairs, babysitting, outdoor play area

♿ Wheelchair access to hotel and restaurant (ramp), WC, 6 ground-floor bedrooms ● No dogs in public rooms; no smoking in restaurant ◻ Amex, Delta, Diners, MasterCard, Switch, Visa £ Single occupancy of twin/double £85 to £95, twin/double £120 to £140; deposit required. Set L £16, D £26; alc L £25, D £35; light meals available; service incl. Special breaks available (3FOR2)

KINGSBRIDGE Devon   map 1

Buckland-Tout-Saints Hotel

Goveton, Kingsbridge TQ7 2DS
TEL: (01548) 853055   FAX: (01548) 856261
EMAIL: buckland@tout-saints.co.uk
WEB SITE: www.tout-saints.co.uk

Mellow manor house lost in the maze of lanes of South Hams

You might find this difficult to believe as you navigate the banked lanes and coombs inland from Kingsbridge, but Buckland-Tout-Saints Hotel gets a fair bit of 'walk-in' business. Apparently, people who enjoy 'lane driving' spot the brown hotel sign and decide to follow it to see where they end up! Well, they can thank their lucky stars when their final destination turns out to be this splendid William and Mary manor in the best traditions of country-house lifestyle. The smell of lilies fills the air as soon as you enter the panelled lounge, while a blue-and-white colour scheme highlights the elaborate plasterwork and Adam fireplace in the breakfast room. The clubby bar has more panelling, created from pews from the demolished Carfax Church in Oxford. Bedrooms are named after flowers, and continue the air of quiet luxury, maybe with four-poster beds or coronet drapes. There is the occasional dated bathroom, but all have a member of the 'Teddy Tout-Saints' family in residence.

◐ Closed Jan 🚩 From Totnes take A381 towards Kingsbridge; turn left at brown sign (on right) to Buckland-Tout-Saints. At Goveton bear right up hill; hotel is second on right after church. Private car park 🚘 3 twin/double, 6 double, 1 four-poster, 2 suites; all with room service, hair-dryer, trouser press, direct-dial telephone, TV ★ Restaurant, dining room, bar, lounge, garden; conferences; social functions; civil wedding licence; leisure facilities nearby; early suppers for children; cots, highchairs, babysitting, baby-listening ♿ No wheelchair access ● No dogs in dining areas (£3 charge per night); smoking in bar only ◻ MasterCard, Switch, Visa £ Single occupancy of twin/double from £80, twin/double £150, four-poster £210, suite from £300; deposit required. Set L from £19, D from £37.50; light meals available; service incl. Special breaks available (3FOR2)

KINGSTON BAGPUIZE Oxfordshire   map 2

Fallowfields

Faringdon Road, Southmoor, Kingston Bagpuize OX13 5BH
TEL: (01865) 820416   FAX: (01865) 821275
EMAIL: stay@fallowfields.com
WEB SITE: www.fallowfields.com

Grand beds and a warm welcome in striking distance of Oxford

One thing you can certainly say about Fallowfields is that its beds are big. The majority of its rooms have king-size affairs, including one of the four-posters. Luckily, size isn't everything in the bedroom department, so not only are the fabrics plush and the décor delightful, but all bar one of the rooms have a whirlpool bath, letting you wallow in endless bubbles before retiring. Mainly Victorian Gothic in style, parts of this mellow country house date back over 300 years, but a smart modern extension has been added without reducing any of the charm or character. Public rooms, such as the peaceful lounge, have a relaxed feel, with family photos and an extensive collection of model elephants dotted around. Part of the ten acres of grounds is taken up with a kitchen garden that provides herbs, fruit and vegetables for the light and airy restaurant. And Anthony and Peta Lloyd continue to oversee the whole proceedings with unpretentious amiability.

◑ Closed Chr 🔁 Turn off A420 south-west of Oxford at roundabout signposted to Kingston Bagpuize; turn right at mini-roundabout; turn left at last street lamp in Southmoor, into drive. Private car park 🛏️ 8 twin/ double, 2 four-poster; family rooms available; all with room service, hair-dryer, direct-dial telephone, modem line, TV; some with trouser press, DVD player ✅ Restaurant, dining room, bar, lounge, library, garden; conferences and social functions; civil wedding licence; spa; leisure facilities nearby; early suppers for children; cots, highchairs, toys, babysitting, outdoor play area ♿ Wheelchair access to hotel and restaurant, WC, 1 ground-floor bedroom ● No smoking ▭ Amex, Delta, MasterCard, Switch, Visa £ Single occupancy of twin/double £95 to £115, twin/double/four-poster £140 to £170, family room £150 to £180; deposit required. Set L £25; alc L, D £38; light meals available. Special breaks available ③FOR②

KINGSWEAR Devon

map 1

Nonsuch House

Church Hill, Kingswear, Dartmouth TQ6 0BX
TEL: (01803) 752829 FAX: (01803) 752357
EMAIL: enquiries@nonsuch-house.co.uk
WEB SITE: www.nonsuch-house.co.uk

Fantastic views and hospitality from first-rate upmarket guesthouse

It pays to keep a sharp eye out as you approach the hairpin bend up a steep hill above the Kingswear ferry terminal, for Nonsuch House is fairly inconspicuous from the road. That's because the action in this Edwardian house is all on the other side, from where glorious views over the estuary across to Dartmouth can be savoured. Downstairs, in the conservatory dining room, binoculars are provided for picking out close-up details of Dartmouth Castle, and there's a small sun-trap patio with a trickling lion-head fountain for fine days. Kit Noble's tasty three-course dinners make the most of local seasonal fare – a spring menu, for example, might include wild garlic soup, asparagus wrapped in pancetta, or rhubarb crumble. The three bedrooms also share the vistas, and mix antiques with good-quality fittings, especially in the bathrooms. Kit and his wife Penny have now taken over from Kit's parents, Patricia and Geoffrey, but the gentle, laid-back style of hospitality remains: beds are turned down in the evening, and fresh milk and biscuits are provided.

◑ Open all year; dining room closed Tue, Wed & Sat eves 🔁 2 miles before Brixham on A3022, take A379 towards Dartmouth/Kingswear; after mini-roundabout fork left on to B3205; go downhill through woods, left up Higher Contour Road (signposted Dartmouth Ferry) and down Ridley Hill; Nonsuch is on hairpin bend 🛏️ 3 twin/double; all with room service, hair-dryer, TV ✅ Dining room, lounge, conservatory, garden; leisure facilities nearby; early suppers for children ♿ No wheelchair access; 1 step into house, 17 steps into dining room, 1 ground-floor bedroom ● No children under 10; no dogs; no smoking ▭ MasterCard, Switch, Visa £ Single occupancy of double £70 to £85, double £95 to £110. Set D £25; light meals available; service incl ③FOR②

KINGTON Herefordshire

map 5

Penrhos Court

Penrhos, Kington HR5 3LH
TEL: (01544) 230720 FAX: (01544) 230754
EMAIL: info@penrhos.co.uk
WEB SITE: www.penrhos.co.uk

A farmhouse hotel in authentic surroundings that evoke the Middle Ages

Penrhos Court is not just a successful small hotel and a school for organic cookery – it's really a way of life. Owners Martin Griffiths and Daphne Lambert have built up their business to reflect their own values, and the result is quite impressive. Their professionally run hotel is in a once-derelict farm, dating back to 1280, which they rescued from demolition 30 years ago. This year, two self-catering apartments have been added to the mix, with underfloor heating, smart kitchens with washing machines, and walk-in showers. The main letting bedrooms – converted from the farm outbuildings – are all a good size, with white walls and pine units. Some have showers only. Because of the number of courses run by Daphne, rooms are generally available only at weekends, but it is best to telephone to check on availability during the week. Public rooms are in the ancient half-timbered farmhouse just across the grassy courtyard with its reed-filled pond. Echoes of the medieval origins are found in the stone flag floors, beamed ceilings and huge inglenook fireplace. Guests dine here on simple but inventive dishes, starting perhaps with avocado salad with basil dressing, and moving on to sea bass with ginger and chive cream sauce.

◑ Closed weekdays, excl bank hols, but phone to check ⊿ On A44, 1 mile east of Kington. Private car park ⤶ 4 twin, 7 double, 2 four-poster, 1 family room; all with room service, hair-dryer, direct-dial telephone, modem line, TV ⊗ Restaurant, lounge, snug, gardens; conferences and social functions; civil wedding licence; leisure facilities nearby; cots, highchairs ⅃ Wheelchair access to hotel (ramp) and restaurant, 7 ground-floor bedrooms ● No smoking ▭ Amex, MasterCard, Switch, Visa £ Single occupancy of twin/double £80, twin/double £100 to £140, four-poster £125 to £145, family room £165; deposit required. Set D £33.50; light meals available, service incl. Special breaks available

---

KINNERSLEY Herefordshire map 5

Upper Newton Farmhouse

Kinnersley, Nr Hereford HR3 6QB
TEL: (01544) 327727 (AND FAX)
EMAIL: pearl.taylor@btopenworld.com

Unpretentious rustic farmhouse charm with hearty breakfasts

On arrival at this simple farmhouse, B&B guests are welcomed with tea and biscuits in the drawing room by hosts Pearl and Jon Taylor. It's typical of the couple's conscientious and enthusiastic approach, which is also reflected in the great care they take to produce impressive breakfasts, including freshly baked soda bread and big-yolked duck eggs. The house is a fine example of Herefordshire timber-framing, dating from the seventeenth century with some later additions, and has lovely views towards the Welsh borders and the Black Mountains. The Taylors are happy for guests to take walks around the farm and through the newly planted cider orchards, and can also give advice on the best places to go bird-watching. Accommodation consists of two cottages, each with a sitting room and kitchen. They are decorated in light pastel colours, with exposed beams to the fore. In the main house, in the rafters, is a bold, blue four-poster bedroom.

◑ Open all year ⊿ Off A4112, 13 miles north-west of Hereford. Private car park ⤶ 1 twin, 2 four-poster; all with hair-dryer, TV; direct-dial telephone, fax machine and modem line available ⊗ Dining room, lounge, garden; leisure facilities nearby; cots, highchairs, babysitting, outdoor play area ⅃ No wheelchair access ● No dogs; no smoking ▭ None accepted £ Twin/double/four-poster £50 to £60; deposit required

---

LACOCK Wiltshire map 2

At the Sign of the Angel

6 Church Street, Lacock, Chippenham SN15 2LB
TEL: (01249) 730230 FAX: (01249) 730527
EMAIL: angel@lacock.co.uk
WEB SITE: www.lacock.co.uk

Historic and cosy hotel offering good food

In the heart of a pretty National Trust village stands this half-timbered fifteenth-century wool merchant's house, a place steeped in time and tradition which has, appropriately, been in the care of the Levis family for over half a century. Nowadays Lorna and George Hardy run the place: Lorna is a scion of the Levises and also happens to be a noted chef. The restaurant is certainly the main focus of attention here, an atmospheric spot when log fires and candles are lit. Cooking leans towards the wholesome and traditional, but definitely on the upmarket side. Upstairs is an oak-panelled resident's lounge and bedrooms full of rustic character with sloping walls and creaky floors. However, one reader in the ground-floor room didn't like the fact that his window opened directly on to the street, and that people leant against it.

◑ Closed 22 to 31 Dec ⊞ In Lacock village, 3 miles south of Chippenham. Private car park 🛏 1 twin, 4 double, 1 four-poster; family rooms available; all with room service, hair-dryer, direct-dial telephone, modem line, TV ⊘ Restaurant, lounge, garden; conferences and social functions; civil wedding licence; leisure facilities nearby; highchairs, baby-sitting ♿ No wheelchair access; 1 ground-floor bedroom ● No dogs in public rooms; no smoking in bedrooms ▭ Amex, MasterCard, Switch, Visa £ Single occupancy of twin/double £72 to £85, twin/double £105 to £129, four-poster £132 to £155, family room £125 to £149; deposit required. Alc L, D £30; light meals available. Special breaks available

---

LANGAR Nottinghamshire · map 5

Langar Hall

Langar, Nottingham NG13 9HG
TEL: (01949) 860559   FAX: (01949) 861045
EMAIL: imogen@langarhall.co.uk
WEB SITE: www.langarhall.com

An unforgettable country house of panache, bonhomie and rather good food

Imogen Irving is the personality behind Langar Hall – and what a personality she is. Modelling the Georgian manor house around her own particular taste for the quirky and romantic, Imogen has created a beguiling atmosphere that has become her hallmark. Each bedroom has its own unique character. Flying in the face of feminism, the ultra-feminine Cartland suite (Barbara stayed here) is very pink and white. It's hung with Japanese-style wallpaper and has an icing-finish canopy of little arches overhanging the bath. You can almost touch the neighbouring church from the windows of Bohemia, which is a favourite among romantics because of its warm colours and sentimental verses written on the bathroom walls. Barristers is wood-panelled, while Cricketers has muted green tongue and groove. From the upstairs rooms are splendid views of the extensive gardens tumbling down to medieval carp-ponds and a moat. Staying at Langar without sampling the cuisine would be verging on heresy and, such is its reputation that you won't be dining alone in the colonnaded dining room, with its Romanesque statuary strutting its stuff before a very English inglenook.

◑ Open all year ⊞ Behind the church in Langar. Private car park 🛏 1 single, 3 twin, 3 double, 1 four-poster, 1 family room, 1 suite; all with room service, hair-dryer, trouser press, direct-dial telephone, modem line, TV, CD player ⊘ Restaurant, bar, lounge, library, garden; conferences, social functions, civil wedding licence; leisure facilities nearby; early suppers for children; cots, highchairs, toys, babysitting, baby-listening, outdoor play area ♿ Wheelchair access to hotel (ramp) and restaurant, 1 ground-floor bedroom. Disabled parking ● Dogs £10 in some bedrooms only; no smoking in bedrooms and most public rooms ▭ Amex, MasterCard, Switch, Visa £ Single £60 to £65, single occupancy of twin/double £90 to £98, twin/double £130 to £150, four-poster £185, family room £160 to £180, suite £185. Set L £15, D £30, Sun L £22.50; alc D £35; light meals available. Special breaks available

---

LANGFORD BUDVILLE Somerset · map 2

Bindon Country House

Langford Budville, Wellington TA21 0RU
TEL: (01823) 400070   FAX: (01823) 400071
EMAIL: stay@bindon.com
WEB SITE: www.bindon.com

Characterful country house with good food and rooms

Ten minutes away from the Wellington Monument is Lynn and Mark Jaffa's own tribute to the bellicose Duke, who fought more than a sufficient number of battles for the 12 bedrooms to be named after. The house itself dates back to the 1600s but the impression on arrival is Victorian as the hallway has a teak staircase and gallery topped with a stained-glass lantern. In the two rear bays of the house there is more Wellingtonia: first is the Wellington Bar – all cosy and clubbable with bookcases and panelling – and opposite that, the Bonaparte Lounge. Dotted around are various paintings of battle scenes and military portraits. Under all the military mementoes lies a very well-run and comfortable hotel: the bedrooms are sumptuously furnished with views of the gardens, plus top-notch bathrooms to boot. Dinner is in the Wellesley Restaurant, a handsome space for Scott Dickson's modern country-house cooking. 'Excellent food and service,' wrote one satisfied visitor, who particularly appreciated being invited to choose from the à la carte menu at no additional charge on the last night of a stay.

◐ Open all year ⚡ From B3187 turn off at sign to Langford Budville village; through village, turn right towards Wiveliscombe, then right at next junction; after Bindon Farm take next right at sign for hotel. Private car park 🛏 4 twin/double, 4 double, 2 four-poster, 2 suites; family rooms available; all with room service, hair-dryer, trouser press, direct-dial telephone, TV; some with VCR ⚓ Restaurant, bar, lounge, orangery, gardens; conferences; social functions; civil wedding licence; heated outdoor swimming pool; leisure facilities nearby; early suppers for children; cots, highchairs, toys, babysitting, baby-listening ♿ Wheelchair access to hotel and restaurant, 1 ground-floor bedroom ● No children under 7 in restaurant eves; smoking in bar only ▭ Amex, Delta, Diners, MasterCard, Switch, Visa £ Single occupancy of twin/double £95, twin from £145, double from £115, four-poster from £145, family room/suite £145; deposit required. Set L £17, D £35; alc L, D £42. Special breaks available ③FOR②

LANGHO Lancashire   map 8

Northcote Manor

Northcote Road, Langho, Blackburn BB6 8BE
TEL: (01254) 240555   FAX: (01254) 246568
EMAIL: sales@northcotemanor.com
WEB SITE: www.northcotemanor.com

Fine dining and Ribble Valley views in an elegantly refurbished nineteenth-century mansion

This substantial Victorian property, set just off a busy road, draws much of its clientele from the Blackburn commuter belt. Some traffic is audible outside, but views from the dining room, and many bedrooms, stretch towards the unspoilt expanses of the Forest of Bowland. The food's the thing here. Long-term partners Craig Bancroft (master sommelier) and Nigel Haworth (head chef) are a well-honed team. Culinary fare is ambitious and accomplished, featuring high-quality regional produce (some home-grown in those fine kitchen gardens), backed up by a formidable if rather pricey wine list. Nigel's Lancashire hotpot is much praised (heather-fed, free-range Bowland lambs slowly braised in the Aga – a kitchen cam provides plasma screen viewings of these dastardly murders). Accommodation aspires to equally high standards, with oak-and-leather traditionalism in lounge and bar, and restrained formality in the restaurant. Smart bedrooms are steadily being refurbished and upgraded.

◐ Closed 25 Dec, 1 Jan and bank hol Mon ⚡ Leave M6 at Junction 31 and take A59 Clitheroe road for 9½ miles; hotel is on left just before roundabout at Langho. Private car park 🛏 4 twin, 8 double, 2 four-poster; family rooms and suites available; all with room service, hair-dryer, trouser press, direct-dial telephone, modem line, TV; some with CD player ⚓ Restaurant, bar, lounge, garden; conferences; social functions, civil wedding licence; early suppers for children; cots, highchairs, baby-listening ♿ Wheelchair access to hotel (ramp) and restaurant (2 steps), 4 ground-floor bedrooms ● No dogs; no smoking in some public rooms and some bedrooms ▭ Amex, Delta, MasterCard, Switch, Visa £ Single occupancy of twin/double £110, twin/double £140, four-poster £175, family room £150, suite £175; deposit required. Set L £18.50, D £50; alc L £42, D £42; light meals available. Special breaks available

---

 Denotes somewhere you can rely on a good meal – either the hotel features in the 2005 edition of our sister publication, The Good Food Guide, *or our inspectors thought the cooking impressive, whether particularly competent home cooking or more lavish cuisine.*

LANGTHWAITE North Yorkshire map 9

CB Inn ☐ NEW ENTRY

Langthwaite, Arkengarthdale, Richmond DL11 6EN
TEL: (01748) 884567   FAX: (01748) 884599
EMAIL: info@cbinn.co.uk
WEB SITE: www.cbinn.co.uk

Tastefully revamped inn with smart rooms and accomplished food

Times change. And, in an era of rebranding, familiar old names must follow suit: British Steel became Corus, and the eighteenth-century Charles Bathurst Inn in remote Arkengarthdale became the CB after a total makeover in 1996. The bar has a spruce modern look, with green walls and an expanse of pine floorboards, pine and oak tables and a menu written on a grand mirror above the fireplace. You can still prop up the bar with the locals over a pint of hand-pulled ale, but the focus is more on food these days: serious efforts are being made in the kitchen here, with some pretty ambitious dishes on offer. A particularly fine inspection meal took in a platter of smoked and cured fish, then a tender rare lamb steak, and rounded off with an orange and lemon bread-and-butter pudding. A couple of peaceful guest lounges offer respite from the busy bar: one in the main inn, which has a stone fireplace with a wood-burning stove, and another upstairs in the bedroom wing added in 1999. Warm summery hues, pine beds and furniture, smart modern bathrooms and extra character from exposed ceiling beams make the bedrooms a perfect haven after a day's walking.

◖ Closed 25 Dec   ☑ At Reeth on B6270 take minor road signposted to Langthwaite. Private car park   ⛬ 5 twin, 13 double; all with hair-dryer, direct-dial telephone, TV   ✅ Restaurant, dining room, bar, 2 lounges, games room; conferences; social functions; cots, highchairs, toys, outdoor play area   ♿ No wheelchair access, 1 step into hotel, 4 ground-floor bedrooms   ● Dogs in bedrooms £10 first night, then £7.50 per night; smoking in bar only   ▭ Delta, MasterCard, Switch, Visa   £ Single occupancy of twin/double £60 to £65, twin/double £80 to £95; deposit required. Alc L, D £17.50; light meals available. Special breaks available

LASTINGHAM North Yorkshire map 9

Lastingham Grange

Lastingham, York YO62 6TH
TEL: (01751) 417345   FAX: (01751) 417358
EMAIL: reservations@lastinghamgrange.com
WEB SITE: www.lastinghamgrange.com

Resolutely traditional country-house hotel bordering the North York Moors

You couldn't ask for a more restfully bucolic setting than Dennis and Jane Woods' timeless country-house hotel. Lastingham is a sleepy yellow-stone village on the edge of the North York Moors; walkers have a perfect spot here, with trails beginning practically at the front door. The tone of this gently hospitable hotel is set in the entrance hall with patterned carpets, plates arrayed on a dresser and old-fashioned chintz. But look closer, particularly in the restful lounge, and you will see exotic references to the family's past in the colonial East: inlaid and lacquered oriental cabinets and ornate Asian woodcarvings. An elegant dining room, featuring cabinets of glass and china, and polished antique tables, is the scene for firmly traditional fare made from locally sourced produce – perhaps a main course of plaice with lemon and parsley butter, or venison Madeira. Bedrooms, too, are designed not to rock the boat; bright floral patterns are twinned with antiques, and many have views over the gardens.

◖ Closed Dec to Feb   ☑ 2 miles east of Kirbymoorside on A170, turn north through Appleton-le-Moors to Lastingham. Turn right by church; after 75 yards turn left up hill; hotel is on right. Private car park   ⛬ 2 single, 4 twin, 2 twin/double, 3 double; family rooms available; all with room service, hair-dryer, trouser press, direct-dial telephone, TV   ✅ Dining room, lounge, garden; early suppers for children; cots, highchairs, toys, baby-listening, outdoor play area   ♿ No wheelchair access   ● No dogs in public rooms; no smoking in dining room   ▭ Delta, MasterCard, Switch, Visa   £ Single £60 to £99, single occupancy of twin/double £60 to £99, twin/double/family room £120 to £189; deposit required. Set L £19, D £36.50; alc L £20; light meals available; service incl. Special breaks available ③FOR②

LAVENHAM Suffolk map 6

The Angel

Market Place, Lavenham CO10 9QZ
TEL: (01787) 247388   FAX: (01787) 248344
EMAIL: angellav@aol.com
WEB SITE: www.lavenham.co.uk/angel

Popular inn with straightforward rooms in the heart of historic market town

The Angel looks right at home in the heart of historic medieval Lavenham, so it comes as no surprise to learn that it is the oldest pub in town – first licensed in 1420. The team of Roy and Anne Whitworth and John and Val Barry have been in partnership here for a mere 15 years but preside over a friendly, well-run operation. Upstairs, residents have their own good-sized sitting room – the 'Solar' – which has plenty of light, big sofas and a rare seventeenth-century pargetted plasterwork ceiling. Bedrooms are spotless and straightforward, with all the basics in good nick. Downstairs, the open-plan bar is atmospheric, with curvy wood beams, and is divided into a good, solid local country pub and a slightly smarter restaurant area. The menu changes daily, with a focus on local, seasonal ingredients.

◗ Closed 25 & 26 Dec ⬛ In Lavenham's market place. Private car park ⬚ 1 twin, 6 double, 1 family room; all with room service, hair-dryer, direct-dial telephone, TV ✓ Restaurant, bar, lounge, garden; leisure facilities nearby; early suppers for children; cots, highchairs, toys, baby-listening ♿ Wheelchair access to hotel (ramp) and restaurant, 1 ground-floor bedroom ⬤ Dogs in 1 bedroom only (£10 per stay); no smoking ▭ Amex, Delta, MasterCard, Switch, Visa £ Single occupancy of twin/double £50, twin/double £75, family room £100; deposit required. Alc L, D £18; light meals available. Special breaks available ③FOR②

Great House

Market Place, Lavenham CO10 9QZ
TEL: (01787) 247431   FAX: (01787) 248007
EMAIL: info@greathouse.co.uk
WEB SITE: www.greathouse.co.uk

Characterful French-run restaurant with rooms in a beautiful medieval English setting

Described in the brochure as 'England's finest medieval town', Lavenham is full of charming crooked Tudor houses and winding little streets. The Great House, combining fourteenth- and fifteenth-century beams with a whitewashed Georgian façade, was once home to an important local weaving family but is now more like a small corner of France. Martine and Régis Crépy employ many French staff and the menu is firmly Gallic, well presented and good value. It's served up in a relaxed restaurant with wooden floors and a low beamed ceiling. French doors lead out to a lovely patio for al fresco dining in fine weather, with a stripy awning and plants climbing up the red painted walls. Apart from the dining areas, there isn't much public space, but the spacious bedrooms mean this is no hardship. Tasteful antiques and excellent bathrooms complete the picture.

◗ Closed Jan; restaurant closed Sun & Mon eves ⬛ In Lavenham's market place ⬚ 1 twin, 1 four-poster, 1 family room, 2 suites; all with room service, hair-dryer, direct-dial telephone, TV ✓ Restaurant, lounge/bar, patio, garden; social functions; early suppers for children; cots, highchairs, baby-listening ♿ No wheelchair access ⬤ No dogs in public rooms; smoking in lounge/bar only ▭ Amex, Delta, MasterCard, Switch, Visa £ Single occupancy of twin/double £65 to £99, twin/four-poster/family room/suite £96 to £160; deposit required. Set L £17, D £22; alc L £18, D £35; light meals available. Special breaks available

Lavenham Priory

Water Street, Lavenham CO10 9RW
TEL: (01787) 247404   FAX: (01787) 248472
EMAIL: mail@lavenhampriory.co.uk
WEB SITE: www.lavenhampriory.co.uk

Tasteful Elizabethan furnishings in fabulous thirteenth-century timbered surrounds

Lavenham Priory is a splendid example of a thirteenth-century monks' residence, all crooked beams and wobbly roofs, surrounded by three acres of grounds. As we went to press, Tim and Gilli Pitt were planning a new walled garden – described as 'contemporary but reflecting the medieval origins of the building'. Inside, the feeling is one of refined, tasteful luxury, to which the term B&B barely does justice. The six bedrooms each have their own character and individual features: for example, the grandly named Great Chamber has a polonaise bed and slipper bath, while the Merchant's Chamber has a thick Jacobean four-poster. However, mod cons such as power showers have not been forgotten. The main public area is the dramatic open-plan Great Hall with exposed timbers in the wall and ceiling, and a large inglenook fireplace. Breakfast is a feast.

◐ Closed Chr & New Year ⤷ In centre of Lavenham; at The Swan turn into Water Street, then right after 50 metres into private drive; bear left to Priory's car park. Private car park ⤓ 1 twin, 1 double, 3 four-poster, 1 suite; all with hair-dryer, TV ⨂ Breakfast room, bar, 2 lounges, study, gardens ♿ No wheelchair access ● No children under 10; no dogs; no smoking ☐ Delta, MasterCard, Switch, Visa £ Single occupancy of twin/double £65 to £80, twin/double £85 to £135, four-poster £105 to £135, suite £125 to £145 (prices valid till Jan 2005); deposit required ③FOR②

LAXTON Nottinghamshire	map 9

Dovecote Inn

Laxton, Newark NG22 0NU
TEL: (01777) 871586 (AND FAX)
EMAIL: dovecoteinn@yahoo.com

Cosy, comfy inn with a timewarp setting

England's last open-field village makes a unique and fascinating backdrop to this solidly traditional country inn, which sits right at the heart of the archetypal red-brick settlement. If you want to learn more about the medieval three-field system, the next-door visitor centre has the answers; otherwise you can just soak up the atmosphere in the cosily beamed bar, where plenty of hand-pulled real ales cater for a more phenomenological approach. When you've worked up an appetite, one way or another, there's an intimate dining room, simply furnished and with a nice brick fireplace, where you can sample an appropriately pubby menu, which offers plenty of hearty grills and home-cooked pies. The two en suite bedrooms are located above the visitor centre and have a fresh feel, with bright fabrics, pine furnishings and rugs on stripped boards.

◐ Open all year ⤷ Turn off A1 into Tuxford village; follow signs to Laxton (3 miles). Private car park ⤓ 2 twin; family room available; both with room hair-dryer, TV ⨂ Restaurant, dining room, bar, lounge, games room, garden; leisure facilities nearby; highchairs ♿ No wheelchair access. Disabled parking ● Dogs in games room only; smoking in certain bar areas only ☐ Delta, MasterCard, Switch, Visa £ Single occupancy of twin £35, twin £50, family room £60. Alc L, D £15; light meals available

'The Bloody Mary and Martinis were unavailable as the computer was down! We ordered a bottle of champagne, which arrived, with no glasses, and was placed on the table while glasses for water, champagne and red wine were amassed. We had 12 glasses on one small table at this stage.'
On a hotel in Oxford

LEADENHAM Lincolnshire   map 6

Willoughby Arms [NEW ENTRY]

5 High Street, Leadenham LN5 0PP
TEL: (01400) 272432   FAX: (01400) 273032
EMAIL: geoffpub@tesco.net
WEB SITE: www.willoughbyarms.com

Small pub offering a refuge for adults in atmospheric surroundings

It would be a pity to pass through this typically pastoral Lincolnshire village en route to somewhere else without calling in on the eighteenth-century Willoughby Arms to experience the adult-friendly (children under 14 are off bounds here) hospitality and traditional meals offered by Geoff and Gail Barker. One of our readers described their meal as 'extremely reliable English cuisine; lamb cooked pink, vegetables crisp and just right and excellent apple crumble – nothing fancy but good ingredients in an atmospheric dining room'. The dining room is divided into two parts – with a long hallway between each room – for smokers and non-smokers. The clubby-looking smoking part, in succulent red and cool blue, has propeller ceiling fans, a large wood-carved fireplace and oak wall-panelling. For non-smokers there is a wacky Mediterranean-themed room with a large bronze fountain of frolicking mermaids under an atrium and a large Italianate-style mural. The comfortable bedrooms are a blend of the old-world suffused with light modern touches.

◑ Open all year   ⚡ Off A17 Newark to Sleaford road; hotel is 150 yards from main crossroads in village centre. Private car park   ⬚ 1 twin/double, 3 suites; all with room service, hair-dryer, TV; fax available ⌾ Dining room, bar, lounge; conferences; social functions; leisure facilities nearby   ⎇ No wheelchair access ⬤ No children under 14; no dogs   ▭ Delta, MasterCard, Switch, Visa   ⌷£⌷ Single occupancy of twin/double £45, twin/double £65. Alc L £12.50, D £22.50; light meals available

LEAMINGTON SPA Warwickshire   map 5

York House

9 York Road, Leamington Spa CV31 3PR
TEL: (01926) 424671   FAX: (01926) 832272

Homely guesthouse with a soothing old-world atmosphere

Pleasantly situated a short way off the town's main parade and overlooking the Pump Room Gardens, this tall semi-detached Edwardian town house has been carefully done out to reflect the heyday of the spa. All of the public areas have a chintzy period style, so you'll find a profusion of pretty rose plates, tapestries and pressed flowers in the breakfast room, and lacy tablemats in the elegant drawing room with its beautifully tiled wooden fireplace. Here and in the breakfast room incredibly realistic gas coal fires ensure that you can have a warming glow at a moment's notice. The bedrooms are somewhat more simply furnished and less period in character – they come with colourful modern duvets – but they are still smartly decorated with considerable attention to detail and might have pretty fireplaces or pleasing front views.

◑ Closed Chr   ⚡ From main parade, turn into Dormer Place, left into Dale Street, then left into York Road. Nearest train station: Leamington Spa. Private car park   ⬚ 2 single, 4 twin, 2 double; family room available; 3 with shared bathroom; all with room service, direct-dial telephone, TV; 1 with trouser press; 1 with VCR; hair-dryer available   ⌾ Dining room, drawing room; leisure facilities nearby; cots, highchairs, toys, babysitting ⎇ No wheelchair access   ⬤ Dogs in 1 bedroom only, by arrangement; smoking in lounge and 1 bedroom only   ▭ Diners, MasterCard, Switch, Visa   ⌷£⌷ Single £30 to £35, single occupancy of twin/double £36 to £50, twin/double £50 to £62, family room £70. Light meals available. Special breaks available

42 The Calls

42 The Calls, Leeds LS2 7EW
TEL: 0113-244 0099   FAX: 0113-234 4100
EMAIL: hotel@42thecalls.co.uk
WEB SITE: www.42thecalls.co.uk

Stylishly converted corn mill in Leeds centre

The design at this boutique hotel makes full use of the textures provided by the former corn mill building – painted brick walls, exposed girders, cast-iron pillars and exposed ducting make a modish backdrop for bright flourishes of modern art, and its location overlooking the River Aire is a bonus at breakfast. The sausage menu is impressive, but following the practice of many a boutique hotspot, breakfast is not included; a cooked spread to start the day will set you back £14. Other meal requirements are catered for in suitably cosmopolitan style in Brasserie 44 or Pool Court at 42, which allow you to charge food to your room account. Industrial heritage is again to the fore in stylish bedrooms, which use original features such as iron columns and wooden beams to good effect with bold colour schemes, touchy-feely fabrics and high-tech mod cons. One reader commented on the efficient and friendly service but was 'appalled' by torn curtains, stained chairs and broken furniture. More reports welcome.

◑ Closed 24 to 26 Dec; restaurant closed Sat lunchtime and Sun eve ⊿ In city centre. Nearest train station: Leeds. Valet parking 7am to 11pm ⟼ 2 single, 36 twin/double, 3 suites; all with room service, hair-dryer, mini-bar, trouser press, direct-dial telephone, modem line, TV, CD player; some with DVD ⌀ Restaurant, breakfast room, honesty bar, lounge; conferences; leisure facilities nearby; early suppers for children; cots, highchairs, babysitting ⅊ Wheelchair access to hotel, 1 room specially equipped for disabled people, lift. Disabled parking ● No dogs in public rooms ▭ Amex, Delta, Diners, MasterCard, Switch, Visa £ Single £89 to £140, twin/double £99 to £210, suite £220 to £375; deposit required. Continental B £10, cooked B £14; set L £25, D (Pool Court) £30; alc D £45 (Brasserie 44); light meals available. Special breaks available

Haley's Hotel

Shire Oak Road, Headingley, Leeds LS6 2DE
TEL: 0113-278 4446   FAX: 0113-275 3342
EMAIL: info@haleys.co.uk
WEB SITE: www.haleys.co.uk

Plush business-oriented base in a smart suburb of Leeds

This substantial sandstone house, topped by mock-Tudor timbers and witch's-hat turrets, sits in a leafy street of Headingley, a prosperous, sedate area with its cricket ground and universities. So it seems somehow fitting that the hotel adopts a country-house style of understated elegance and quietly confident class. Antiques, Regency-stripe wallpaper and opulent swagged drapes set an upmarket tone in two lounges that flank the reception desk, and the restaurant is a sophisticated little spot with its high-backed chairs, monogrammed napkins and an exhibition of modern art – all for sale if your wallet is up to it. A classy modern English menu might offer Loch Fyne scallops with mushroom gratin, then venison with haggis, neeps and tatties, and chocolate jus with a passion fruit soufflé for pudding. Bedrooms are split between the main house and Grade II listed Bedford House next door; all are done out in subtly soothing, well-blended colours, have top-quality bathrooms and a cat to put out at night in lieu of a 'do not disturb' sign.

◑ Closed 26 to 30 Dec ⊿ Just off A660 in Headingley; turn off between Yorkshire and HSBC Banks and follow signs to hotel. Nearest train station: Leeds. Private car park ⟼ 8 single, 2 twin, 3 twin/double, 13 double, 1 four-poster, 1 suite; family room available; all with room service, hair-dryer, trouser press, direct-dial telephone, TV ⌀ Restaurant, bar, 2 lounges, library, garden; conferences; social functions; civil wedding licence; leisure facilities nearby; cots, highchairs ⅊ Wheelchair access to hotel (ramp) and restaurant, 2 ground-floor bedrooms ● No dogs; no smoking in some bedrooms ▭ Amex, Delta, MasterCard, Switch, Visa £ Single £85 to £125, single occupancy of twin/double £95 to £115, twin/double/four-poster £110 to

£150, family room £130 to £170, suite £230 to £250; deposit required. Alc D £29.50; light meals available; service incl. Special breaks available ③FOR②

Malmaison Leeds

Sovereign Quay, Leeds LS1 1DQ
TEL: 0113-398 1000   FAX: 0113-398 1002
EMAIL: leeds@malmaison.com
WEB SITE: www.malmaison.com

City bolthole with slinky bedrooms for the style-conscious

The swanky Malmaison chain is not one to let the grass grow beneath its feet. You might walk through its revolving glass portals and think that the plush chic of its lobby is pretty cutting-edge stuff – but no, it will all be refurbished by the end of 2004 to be more in keeping with the latest Malmaison outposts in London and Birmingham. That is to say, masculine, muted neutral tones with every detail thought through to appeal to a young, design-conscious clientele. In the basement of this grand red-brick edifice – the city's former bus garage – the stone-floored brasserie is a darkly intimate place to be seen in as much as to eat. Low jazz wafts beneath its vaulted roof to a bar where black-suited urbanites lounge in plum and chocolate squidgy leather sofas. Once the evening draws to an end, you retire to rooms with bold colour schemes, sexy bathrooms and, in the best, industrial heritage views over the River Aire.

○ Open all year ⓩ In city centre. Nearest train station: Leeds 2 single, 12 twin, 85 double, 1 suite; all with room service, hair-dryer, mini-bar, trouser press, direct-dial telephone, modem line, TV, CD player ⚥ Restaurant, bar; conferences, social functions; gym; leisure facilities nearby; cots, highchairs ⅏ Wheelchair access to hotel (lift) and restaurant, WC, 4 rooms specially equipped for disabled people, lift ● No dogs in public rooms (£10 per night in bedrooms) ⊏ Amex, Delta, Diners, MasterCard, Switch, Visa £ Single £99, single occupancy of twin/double £129, twin/double £129, suite £165; deposit required. Continental B £10, cooked B £12; set L £13, D £14; alc L, D £30; light meals available. Special breaks available

Quebecs

9 Quebec Street, Leeds LS1 2HA
TEL: 0113-244 8989   FAX: 0113-244 9090
EMAIL: res_quebecs@theetongroup.com
WEB SITE: www.theetoncollection.com

Sophisticated boutique hotel in a splendid Victorian building

The former home of the Leeds Liberal Club certainly gave the interior designers of this swish city-slicker hotel plenty of opulent period features to weave into a winning blend. Acreages of oak panels and radiant stained glass windows greet you in reception, then a grand staircase coils upwards to the gentleman's club elegance of the oak bar, where you help yourself (paying later on an honesty system) and settle into a squashy modern sofa to ponder what it would cost to pay modern craftsmen to produce the intricately carved panelling and plasterwork all around. One floor up, and you're back in the twenty-first century for breakfast among pale-wood furniture and vibrant modern art. Bedrooms are a deliciously un-minimal take on modern style: luscious fabrics and muted colours make for plush rooms. Indeed, some, such as the Humbug suite (suites are named after sweets, geddit?), are on an epic, palatial scale. Most memorable is the Bon Bon suite, a quirky octagonal eyrie up in the turret at the top of the building.

○ Closed Chr ⓩ In city centre. Nearest train station: Leeds. Private car park 6 twin/double, 33 double, 6 suites; all with room service, hair-dryer, mini-bar, trouser press, direct-dial telephone, modem line, TV, CD player ⚥ Breakfast room, honesty bar, lounge; conferences; leisure facilities nearby; cots, highchairs ⅏ Wheelchair access to hotel (lift at rear), 4 steps into breakfast room, 8 ground-floor bedrooms, 3 rooms specially equipped for disabled people, lift ● No smoking in some bedrooms ⊏ Amex, Delta, Diners, MasterCard, Switch, Visa £ Single occupancy of twin/double £99 to £125, twin/double £110 to £155, suite £150 to £250; deposit required. Continental B £10.50, cooked B £13.50; light meals available. Special breaks available (2004 data)

ENGLAND

Upper Buckton Farm

Leintwardine, Craven Arms SY7 0JU
TEL: (01547) 540634 (AND FAX)

Fine Georgian farmhouse in stunning surroundings, run as a Wolsey Lodge

You can't get much closer to Herefordshire country life than a stay at Hayden and Yvonne Lloyd's home. Park your car in the farmyard and pass through the garden gate to be welcomed into the unpretentious surroundings of a 400-acre working farm. The Wolsey Lodge system means that guests sit down to dinner at the same time, although not at the same table here. Then they can enjoy hearty good food: a typical menu might be smoked salmon, followed by pork fillet with rhubarb and bramble sauce, and then a choice of pudding – not forgetting a choice of cheeses from the Welsh Borders. Upstairs, the bedrooms are spacious and tidy, with fresh colour schemes and furniture that falls in the category of family heirloom. Each has embroidered cotton sheets, fluffy towels and bathrobes. The highlight, however, is the superb views across the open fields to the River Teme and the Wigmore Rolls hills in the distance.

◗ Closed occasionally ⟲ Take A4113 from Ludlow towards Knighton; at Walford crossroads turn right for Buckton; Upper Buckton is second farm on left. Nearest train station: Bucknell. Private car park 🚗 2 twin/double, 1 double; all with hair-dryer, TV ⟨⟩ Dining room, lounge, garden; early suppers for children ⟨⟩ No wheelchair access ● No children in dining room eves; no dogs; no smoking ☐ None accepted £ Single occupancy of twin/double £52, twin/double £84. Set D £22.50; service incl

Grey Cottage

Bath Road, Leonard Stanley, Stonehouse GL10 3LU
TEL: (01453) 822515 (AND FAX)
WEB SITE: www.greycottage.ik.com

𝒢

A guesthouse with a friendly owner and plenty of nice touches

Although the village is fairly ordinary, behind the nine-foot-high yew hedge that shields Grey Cottage from the outside world life is a little more special. Rosemary Reeves, the lively owner, has created a neat and spotless home with lots of personal touches. The house dates back to the early-nineteenth century and was a Methodist meeting hall at one stage. Its gardens contain a mighty yew, planted in 1840, and a 100-foot sequoia, planted in 1865 – you can sit in the conservatory and enjoy the view. Public rooms are not large, but have a cosy feel, with a chintzy domestic look. Rosemary provides evening meals by prior arrangement, which are served up around a single polished walnut table, and uses local ingredients wherever possible – maybe fresh asparagus, salmon and sticky toffee pudding or perhaps an English cheeseboard, including the local Leonard Stanley cheese. Each bedroom is individually decorated with smart bedspreads and homely extras like radios and mineral water. Bathrooms come equipped with big bath towels and robes.

◗ Closed occasionally ⟲ Leave M5 at junction 13, following A419 towards Stroud for 2 miles; at major traffic lights, take filter road signposted Leonard Stanley; turn right into Downton Road and continue for 1 mile to T-junction with Marsh Garage on right; turn left and cottage is 20 yards on right, on bend. Nearest train station: Stonehouse. Private car park 🚗 1 single, 1 twin, 1 double; all with hair-dryer, trouser press, TV; telephone, fax, modem line, ironing facilities available ⟨⟩ Dining room, sitting room, conservatory, garden; early suppers for children ⟨⟩ No wheelchair access ● No children under 10; no dogs; smoking in conservatory only ☐ None accepted £ Single £47 to £50, single occupancy of twin/double £50, twin/double £57 to £70. Set D £25; light meals available; service incl

Millers

134 High Street, Lewes BN7 1XS
TEL: (01273) 475631   FAX: (01273) 486226
EMAIL: millers134@aol.com
WEB SITE: www.hometown.aol.com/millers134

Wonderfully cluttered, atmospheric B&B, ideally placed on Lewes High Street

Thick beams, wonky angles, creaky staircases, heavy portraits of stern ladies and a dash of cottagey frills are to be found at this fabulously atmospheric, eccentric little B&B. Breakfast is served at a chunky rustic table next to a little seating area, where you can relax in comfy chairs by an iron stove in the fireplace. Teré and Tony Tammar are helpful and interested without being too overbearing – their welcome note in the bedrooms even goes so far as to suggest that night-time requests would not be dismissed out of hand ('We are light sleepers...')! The Rose Room, with its lovely four-poster bed and oriental screen, is full of homely charm, though we found the bath, squashed into the available space, a little on the small size. Parking can be a problem in packed Lewes – if you don't get lucky and bag one of the precious bays over the road you'll have to park in the main car park further through the town.

○ Closed 4 & 5 Nov, 20 Dec to 3 Jan ⚡ In centre of Lewes, just up St Anne's Hill from Shelleys Hotel. Nearest train station: Lewes 🛏 2 four-poster; both with hair-dryer, TV ✅ Breakfast room, sitting area; leisure facilities nearby ♿ No wheelchair access ● No children; no dogs; no smoking ⊟ None accepted £ Single occupancy of four-poster £60, four-poster £66. Special breaks available

Shelleys Hotel

High Street, Lewes BN7 1XS
TEL: (01273) 472361   FAX: (01273) 483152
EMAIL: info@shelleys-hotel-lewes.com
WEB SITE: www.shelleys-hotel.com

Grand high street townhouse in pretty, popular Lewes

'I have stayed in many hotels and this is in my top three,' ends a glowing report from one reader this year. This handsome townhouse, handy for Glyndebourne and Brighton, sits at the top of the busy High Street, but retains a 'peaceful, luxurious ambience'. Make sure you arrive in the evening in time for an aperitif in the bar, so you can luxuriate in one of the plush leather armchairs while you study the menu, before being ushered through to the grand, voluminous dining room. You're better off sticking to the more traditional side of the menu – our inspector's lamb was excellent but he wasn't so sure about some of the more adventurous combinations. Bedrooms are traditionally decorated with lots of plush fabrics and dusky colour schemes; try to get one with a view of the lovely gardens rather than overlooking the main road. Thoughtful extras such as towelling bathrobes have been commented on, along with the comfortable beds. 'Worth a special mention was the muesli: made with cream and nuts, it was absolutely delicious,' purrs one visitor.

○ Open all year ⚡ In centre of Lewes. Nearest train station: Lewes. Private car park 🛏 1 single, 8 twin/ double, 8 double, 1 four-poster, 1 suite; all with room service, hair-dryer, trouser press, direct-dial telephone, TV ✅ Dining room, bar, lounge, garden; conferences and social functions; civil wedding licence; leisure facilities nearby; early suppers for children; cots, highchairs, baby-listening ♿ No wheelchair access ● No dogs in public rooms; no smoking in some public rooms ⊟ Amex, Delta, Diners, MasterCard, Switch, Visa £ Single £80 to £150, twin/double £110 to £185, four-poster £200 to £260, suite £200 to £235; deposit required. Alc L £25, D £35; light meals available; service incl. Special breaks available

Hills Farm

Leysters, Leominster HR6 0HP
TEL: (01568) 750205
EMAIL: conolly@bigwig.net
WEB SITE: www.thehillsfarm.co.uk

Well-established operation at this smart B&B in a modernised farmhouse

These converted farmhouse buildings are the essence of tasteful rural simplicity. A 120-acre working farm surrounds the property, but Jane and Peter Conolly concentrate on seeing to their guests' every need. At the heart of their complex is a fifteenth-century half-timbered farmhouse, with additions in rough stone, well-tended gardens and even a pond. The public areas are bright and airy and have a distinctly rustic feel, with exposed beams, polished floors, an open staircase in the sitting room and simple wooden furniture in the breakfast room. Two bedrooms are in the main house, while three in the upmarket barn conversions have their own front door for added privacy. A bright, fresh feel pervades throughout, with cottagey fabrics to match. The Chapel in the main house is appropriately cavernous, while the barn rooms are also a good size with good-quality pine fittings and soft colour schemes in lavender, lime and lemon.

○ Closed Dec to Feb; dining room closed Sun & Tue eves ⓩ From A49 take A4112 through Kimbolton to Leysters; just after garage turn right to farmhouse. Private car park ⤧ 2 twin, 3 double; all with hair-dryer, TV ⓥ Dining room, sitting room, conservatory, garden ♿ No wheelchair access ● No children under 12; no dogs; no smoking ▭ Delta, MasterCard, Switch, Visa £ Twin/double £66; deposit required. Set D £22; service incl

---

Arundell Arms

Lifton, Nr Launceston PL16 0AA
TEL: (01566) 784666   FAX: (01566) 784494
EMAIL: reservations@arundellarms.com
WEB SITE: www.arundellarms.com

Well-run and immaculately well-kept country hotel

Beside the A30 stands this stalwart of the fishing scene, a place that has long ago shed any of its old associations as a pub and become something much classier and more upmarket. The style is more akin to country house, in fact, with an elegant lounge and a sparkling restaurant that overlooks the rear garden. Cooking follows the country-house line too. The bar offers an alternative dining option or simply a place to unwind and relax – the atmosphere is good-humoured and civilised. Conversation is often of angling experiences, but this is hardly surprising when the hotel boasts 20 miles of private fishing on the nearby Tamar and its tributaries, a private three-acre lake and a fishing school. Bedrooms are divided between those in the main house – more spacious and elegant but closer to the road – and those in the converted Stable Wing – button headboards with pine or cane furniture.

○ Closed 3 days Chr ⓩ 3 miles east of Launceston, just off A30 in Lifton village. Private car park ⤧ 7 single, 10 twin, 1 twin/double, 8 double, 1 suite; all with room service, hair-dryer, direct-dial telephone, modem line, TV; fax available ⓥ Restaurant, 2 bars, lounge, games room, garden; conferences; social functions; civil wedding licence; leisure facilities nearby; early suppers for children; cots, highchairs, babysitting, baby-listening ♿ Wheelchair access to hotel and restaurant (ramp), WC, 4 ground-floor bedrooms ● Dogs £4 per night in bedrooms; no smoking in restaurant ▭ Amex, Delta, Diners, MasterCard, Switch, Visa £ Single £89, single occupancy of twin/double £104, twin/double £136, suite £170; deposit required. Set L £24.50, D £34; alc L, D £40; light meals available. Special breaks available

LINCOLN Lincolnshire map 9

D'Isney Place

Eastgate, Lincoln LN2 4AA
TEL: (01522) 538881   FAX: (01522) 511321
EMAIL: info@disneyplacehotel.co.uk
WEB SITE: www.disneyplacehotel.co.uk

This hotel is due to close in Dec 2004

○ Open all year   ⤢ On Eastgate, 100 yards from cathedral. Nearest train station: Lincoln. Private car park ⌂ 1 single, 3 twin, 11 double, 1 four-poster, 1 suite; family rooms available; all with hair-dryer, direct-dial telephone, TV; some with trouser press   ⊘ Garden; cots   占 No wheelchair access, 9 ground-floor bedrooms   ● No smoking in some bedrooms   ▭ Amex, Delta, Diners, MasterCard, Switch, Visa   £ Single £58 to £68, single occupancy of twin/double £68 to £78, twin/double £92, four-poster £112, family room £102, suite £184 (2004 prices); deposit required. Special breaks available   ③FOR②

LITTLE HAMPDEN Buckinghamshire map 3

Rising Sun [NEW ENTRY]

Little Hampden, Nr Great Missenden HP16 9PS
TEL: (01494) 488393   FAX: (01494) 488788
EMAIL: sunrising@rising-sun.demon.co.uk
WEB SITE: www.rising-sun.demon.co.uk

Cheap and cheerful rooms and food in a leafy corner of Buckinghamshire

With the Prime Minster's country residence just down the road, this could possibly be Mr Blair's local, but staying here is probably a smidge more relaxed than a night at Chequers. Sitting at the end of a single-track road, the Rising Sun's red-and-grey brick exterior belies the fact that this pub dates back 250 years or so. You get more of a feel for its age inside, where the blackened beams, horse brasses, dried hops and wood-burning stoves give the three separate bar areas a really rustic appearance. Blackboards are scrawled with the daily menus: all hearty, comforting pub food such as scampi and chips or curry, as well as some more interesting offerings like roast duck with red wine and black-cherry sauce. Upstairs, the fresh-feeling bedrooms have been decked out in pine furniture and appealing, restful colours: blue and yellow in the spacious double at the back, a more masculine burgundy to match the brick fireplace in the twin.

○ Open all year   ⤢ From Great Missenden take Rignall Road towards Princes Risborough; turn right after 2 miles at signpost to 'Little Hampden only'; hotel is at the end of the lane. Private car park ⌂ 5 twin/double; all with limited room service, TV; hair-dryer, fax, modem line on request; no tea/coffee-making facilities in rooms   ⊘ Restaurant, bar, garden; social functions; leisure facilities nearby   占 No wheelchair access   ● No dogs; no smoking   ▭ Delta, MasterCard, Switch, Visa   £ Single occupancy of twin/double £45, twin/double £70; deposit required. Alc L, D £21; light meals available. Special breaks available

Three Shires Inn

Little Langdale, Ambleside LA22 9NZ
TEL: (015394) 37215   FAX: (015394) 37127
EMAIL: enquiry@threeshiresinn.co.uk
WEB SITE: www.threeshiresinn.co.uk

Inspiring surroundings make this rugged wayside pub memorable

The 'three shires' were the former counties of Cumberland, Westmorland and Lancashire, which met at this point on the steep ascent to the passes of Wrynose and Hardknott. Whichever direction you're heading, by car or Shanks's pony, this welcoming, family-run inn is a fine place to recharge your batteries. Exhilarating Langdale scenes extend in all directions from the simple grey-stone building. The interior may be a little fancier than it was when the pub was first built in 1872, but it is still the sort of no-nonsense place that fell walkers can enter with their boots on, finding plenty of like-minded souls at the slate-flagged bar. Here you can stoke up on Cumberland Ales, wines by the glass, and hearty home-cooked victuals (quick-lunch soups, sausages and baguettes; venison steaks and rabbit ragouts in the adjoining restaurant). Refurbished bedrooms are simple, fresh and pretty, with neat, plain bathrooms. Some have a glorious outlook.

○ Closed midweek Dec and Jan ⌷ Take A593 from Ambleside towards Langdale/Coniston, cross Skelwith Bridge and turn right at sign to the Langdales, Wrynose Pass and Elterwater; follow this road to Little Langdale. Private car park ⌷ 5 twin, 4 double, 1 family room; all with hair-dryer, TV, CD player ✓ Restaurant, 2 bars, 2 lounges, garden; social functions; leisure facilities nearby; early suppers for children; cots, highchairs ⌷ No wheelchair access ● No dogs; no smoking in bedrooms and most public rooms ▢ MasterCard, Switch, Visa £ Single occupancy of twin/double £38 to £65, twin/double £70 to £96, family room £75 to £101; deposit required. Alc L £14, D £18; light meals available. Special breaks available (3FOR2)

Molesworth Manor

Little Petherick, Nr Padstow, Wadebridge PL27 7QT
TEL: (01841) 540292 (AND FAX)
EMAIL: molesworthmanor@aol.com
WEB SITE: www.molesworthmanor.co.uk

Comfortable period house full of original features, offering first-rate B&B

Molesworth Manor isn't really a manor – at its core is a seventeenth-century rectory sold by the church on the understanding that the word 'rectory' would be kept out of the title. But that doesn't mean you can't maintain a lord of the manor fantasy when you stay, especially if you take one of the suites, named Her Ladyship's and His Lordship's. The 'servants' rooms' on the second floor are smaller but still well furnished, with handsome furniture and plenty of original features. Guests have the run of no fewer that three sitting areas, including a cosy lounge, a morning room and a music room with piano. Breakfast is often served in the stone-floored conservatory, and offers a generous selection of cold cuts rather than the traditional fry-up. Jessica Clarke and Geoff French seem to have settled well into their stride since taking over from Jessica's parents a few years ago, redecorating and keeping everything in trim.

○ Closed Nov to Jan ⌷ On A389 from Wadebridge to Padstow; pass through St Issey into Little Petherick; hotel is 300 metres beyond humpback bridge, on right. Private car park ⌷ 1 single, 1 twin, 4 twin/double, 7 double, 1 family room; all with hair-dryer ✓ Breakfast room/conservatory, morning room, TV lounge, music room, library, garden; conferences, social functions; cots, highchairs, toys, babysitting, baby-listening, outdoor play area ⌷ Wheelchair access to hotel (1 step) and breakfast room, WC, 3 ground-floor bedrooms ● No dogs; no smoking ▢ None accepted £ Single £30, single occupancy of twin/double £35 to £56, twin/double £54 to £84, family room £78. Special breaks available (3FOR2)

LITTLE WALSINGHAM Norfolk

map 6

Old Bakehouse

33 High Street, Little Walsingham NR22 6BZ
TEL: (01328) 820454 (AND FAX)
EMAIL: chris.padley@btopenworld.com

Good-value rooms near the site of a popular religious pilgrimage

Little Walsingham attracts visitors out of all proportion to its population of around 1,200 – Old Bakehouse owner Chris Padley told us half a million a year flock into town, many on religious pilgrimages to the local shrine. If the pilgrims are after a solid, good-value place to stay then Chris and Helen's Old Bakehouse could be just the ticket. The oldest parts of the building are over 450 years old, though the façade is Georgian red brick. Décor is homely and rural, with pink the predominant hue, with a slightly more cosmopolitan touch introduced via numerous exhibition posters from around the world. The dining area, all in pink, picks up the town's religious history with brass rubbings framed on the walls, and the food (served every day on request except Mondays) is of a fairly simple traditional English persuasion. Some winding steps take you down to an underground bar, though it's probably fair to say there are better pubs in town if you're planning more than a pre- or post-dinner drink. The three bedrooms are all decorated in a country style, with a couple of twists.

◖ Closed 2 weeks in Jun, Chr and 2 weeks in Jan/Feb; dining room closed Mon eve ⦿ In centre of Little Walsingham on B1105, 5 miles north of Fakenham ⬇ 1 twin, 1 twin/double, 1 double; all with hair-dryer, TV ⬦ Dining room, breakfast room, lounge bar; leisure facilities nearby; highchairs ♿ No wheelchair access ● No dogs; no smoking ▭ Delta, MasterCard, Switch, Visa £ Single occupancy of twin/double £38, twin/double £55; deposit required. Set D £17.50; service incl ③FOR②

LITTLESTONE-ON-SEA Kent

map 3

Romney Bay House

Coast Road, Littlestone-on-Sea, New Romney TN28 8QY
TEL: (01797) 364747 FAX: (01797) 367156

Country house in an isolated spot beside the English Channel

When the coast road peters out and becomes a pot-holed track, just keep going. Go past the decorative Victorian red-brick water tower and soon you will come to this distinctive red-roofed white house standing high amidst green lawns with a slightly scruffy tennis court, beside a stretch of pebble beach overlooking the English Channel. Designed by architect Sir Clough Williams-Ellis for the American actress Hedda Hopper in the late 1920s, the house has an informal air. New owners Clinton and Lisa Lovell, who have both had careers in London hotels, moved to this corner of Kent six years ago and are making their mark on the house. The lounge, with its white sofas and floral fabrics, is traditional in style and leads through to the conservatory restaurant, where Clinton produces a daily set menu – a mix of classical French and modern European dishes based on the best produce from local suppliers. Each of the bedrooms, with views of either the sea or golf course, is immaculately kept, with white walls, attractive, good-quality fabrics – from blue Provençal prints to white cotton bedspreads – and with comfortable chairs from which to enjoy the views.

◖ Closed 1 week Chr; restaurant closed Sun & Mon eves ⦿ At sea front in Littlestone-on-Sea, turn left and follow signs for hotel. Private car park ⬇ 2 twin/double, 6 double, 2 four-poster; all with hair-dryer, TV ⬦ Restaurant, bar, 2 lounges, conservatory, garden; conferences; social functions; tennis; leisure facilities nearby ♿ No wheelchair access ● No children under 14; no dogs; smoking only in bar and 1 lounge ▭ Amex, MasterCard, Switch, Visa £ Single occupancy of twin/double £60 to £95, twin £135, double £85 to £150, four-poster £135; deposit required. Set D £35; light meals available. Special breaks available

The Racquet Club [NEW ENTRY]

Hargreaves Building, 5 Chapel Street, Liverpool L3 9AG
TEL: 0151-236 6676   FAX: 0151-236 6870
WEB SITE: www.racquetclub.org.uk

Clever blending of traditional and modern in august Victorian city-centre building

After an eventful history, stretching back to 1874, the Liverpool Racquet Club settled in these grand premises about 20 years ago. Now brother and sister team Martin and Helen Ainscough have transformed this gentlemen's secret sanctum into a chic operation with spa, gym and two squash courts. Sensibly the Ainscoughs have done little to change the outward appearance; after all, its mock-Renaissance style sets an impressive tone, and the low-key approach continues in the reception area. Wood panelling, tall ceilings and a huge staircase dominate, with small modern design features here and there. A bar and the Ziba brasserie/ restaurant make up the public areas, a sophisticated space with polished wood and marble floors and chrome. Ziba has wacky chandeliers and a huge Florentine-style equestrian painting and serves modern British food with dishes such as stuffed saddle of lamb with pearl barley risotto. Then there's an even bigger bar area with leather pew seating, bright lighting and uniformed staff. Bedrooms are a successful mixture of old and new with themes around key furnishings, such as Japanese or French. Bathrooms are not large, but have inventive touches such as a bright orange shower curtain or red shagpile mat.

◗ Closed 25 & 26 Dec; restaurant closed Sun ⊠ In centre of Liverpool. Nearest train station: Liverpool Lime Street ⏗ 1 twin/double, 7 double; all with room service, hair-dryer, direct-dial telephone, modem line, TV, CD player; some with VCR ⊘ Brasserie/restaurant, 2 bars, lounge, library, games room; conferences; social functions; gym, spa, heated indoor swimming pool; leisure facilities nearby; early suppers for children; cots, highchairs, babysitting ₺ No wheelchair access, lift ● No smoking in some bedrooms ⊟ Amex, MasterCard, Switch, Visa £ Single £105, single occupancy of twin/double £105, twin/double £115; deposit required. Continental B £6, cooked £10; set L £18; alc D £27; light meals available

The Waterdine

Llanfair Waterdine, Nr Knighton LD7 1TU
TEL: (01547) 528214   FAX: (01547) 529992
EMAIL: info@waterdine.com
WEB SITE: www.waterdine.com

Restaurant-with-rooms in a bucolic and timeless setting

It's literally a stone's throw from Wales here – the river Teme, at the bottom of the garden, is the border. The village itself ('the church by the water') was mentioned in the Domesday Book, and this Welsh half-timbered longhouse has some of that ancient quality, even though it was built a good five hundred years later. More recently, Ken and Isabel Adams have turned it into a smart restaurant, retaining the rustic feel and furnishing the small interlocking public rooms in an unpretentious eclectic style. The main restaurant is divided into two areas – the conservatory, with impressive views to the hillsides, and the taproom, the oldest part of the house, with a beamed ceiling and stone floors. A typical menu might start with artichoke risotto with paprika-roasted tomatoes, be followed by rack of Shropshire lamb with provençal vegetables, and end with brioche and butter pudding with minted cream sauce. The bedrooms are quaint and cottagey and have lovely views across the countryside.

◗ Closed 2 weeks in autumn, 1 week in spring; restaurant closed Sun & Mon eves ⊠ 4 miles west of Knighton, in Llanfair Waterdine village. Nearest train station: Knucklas. Private car park ⏗ 3 double; all with hair-dryer, TV ⊘ Restaurant, lounge, bar, garden room, garden; social functions; leisure facilities nearby ₺ No wheelchair access ● No children under 12; no dogs; smoking in part of lounge bar only

MasterCard, Switch, Visa £ Single occupancy of double £60, double £90; deposit required. Set L (Sun) £18, D (Sat) £28; alc L £23, D £26; light meals available. Special breaks available

---

LONG CRENDON Buckinghamshire　　　　　　　　　　　　　　map 2

Angel Restaurant

47 Bicester Road, Long Crendon, Aylesbury HP18 9EE
TEL: (01844) 208268　FAX: (01844) 202497

Appealing roadside restaurant with great food and bijou rooms

Possibly the best way to guests' hearts is through their stomachs, and Trevor Bosch succeeds in capturing both at this intimate restaurant-with-rooms not far from Oxford. The excellent cooking is certainly the big draw, enticing first-timers and regulars inside the cream-washed walls of this former village local; some of those replete punters will be happy to scoot upstairs and sleep off the pleasures of an evening's wining and dining. Trevor's menu encompasses a printed version as well as extensive blackboard selections, and specialises in fish and seafood. You can choose between lighter meals in the stylish yet relaxed beamed bar, with leather chesterfields beside an open fire, or the whole hog in the restaurant proper, the main part of which is an airy conservatory that spills out on to a patio, weather permitting. Upstairs, the sweet bedrooms have plenty of character – wonky walls, low ceilings, mind-your-head doors – to compensate for their lack of size. They're decked out in pretty colours, with good-quality fabrics and pine furniture, snazzy bathrooms completing the picture.

 Open all year; restaurant closed Sun eve 　 Take B4011 from Thame towards Bicester; the Angel is $\frac{1}{2}$ mile beyond Long Crendon village square, on left. Nearest train station: Thame & Haddenham Park. Private car park 3 double; family room available; all with room service, hair-dryer, direct-dial telephone, TV Restaurant/conservatory, bar, lounge, garden; social functions; leisure facilities nearby; cots, highchairs, baby-listening No wheelchair access No dogs; smoking in bar only Amex, MasterCard, Switch, Visa £ Single occupancy of double £65, double £75, family room £85; deposit required. Set L £17; alc L, D £25; light meals available

---

LONG MELFORD Suffolk　　　　　　　　　　　　　　　　map 6

Black Lion

Church Walk, The Green, Long Melford CO10 9DN
TEL: (01787) 312356　FAX: (01787) 374557
EMAIL: enquiries@blacklionhotel.net
WEB SITE: www.blacklionhotel.net

Stylish but sensitive makeover for a traditional village inn

The clutter hasn't completely vanished from this square Georgian inn on the green, but these days it's confined to a photo album at reception chronicling its transformation into a much more stylish affair. The historic building hasn't been forgotten – there are still plush leather armchairs, plenty of antiques and some rather stern looking old portraits – but they're teamed with solid, warm modern colour schemes and, especially in the bedrooms (named after wines), some contemporary twists like leopardskin-patterned cushions, and gold curtains. Refurbishment is complete in six of the ten bedrooms, so you may be wise to ask for one of those. Elsewhere Craig Jarvis, owner of Ravenwood Hall (see entry) continues to indulge in his penchant for rocking horses, proof of the personal touch evident throughout the makeover. The modern restaurant, with high-backed leather chairs and bright yellow walls, serves a heady menu with dishes such as steamed beef and oyster mushroom suet pudding or nut and wild mushroom Wellington with spinach and Madeira jus.

 Open all year 　 On village green, 2 miles north of Sudbury at junction of B1064 and A1092. Private car park 1 twin/double, 4 double, 3 four-poster, 1 family room, 1 suite; all with room service, hair-dryer, direct-dial telephone, TV; 1 with CD player Restaurant, bistro, bar, lounge, garden; conferences, social functions; leisure facilities nearby; early suppers for children; cots, highchairs, toys, babysitting, baby-listening

  No wheelchair access   No dogs in restaurant; smoking in bar only   Amex, Delta, Diners, MasterCard, Switch, Visa   £ Single occupancy of twin/double from £85, twin/double from £110, four-poster £120, family room £140, suite £146; deposit required (prices valid till Oct 2004). Set Sun L £20, D £25; alc L, D £34; light meals available. Special breaks available

---

LOOE Cornwall   Map 1

Talland Bay

Talland, Looe PL13 2JB
TEL: (01503) 272667   FAX: (01503) 272940
EMAIL: info@tallandbayhotel.co.uk
WEB SITE: www.tallandbayhotel.co.uk

Something for everyone at this tidy hotel looking firmly to the future

The subtle regeneration of Talland Bay continues, with more rooms refurbished in a tasteful contemporary style that aims to keep regular guests happy but at the same time attract a new younger clientele. From what we can see so far it's looking as if George and Mary Granville will manage this delicate balancing act in style, as bedrooms and corridors are gradually updated in cleaner lines and colours, but nothing that is too harsh. There are still some bedrooms to keep traditionalists happy, and the public rooms are being left until last, though some modern paintings are creeping in. A new chef is adding a similar zest to the menu – reports would be welcome. There are also plenty of opportunities for activities, whether strolling down to the beach or along the coastal path, swimming in the pool or partaking in a gentle (or not so gentle) game of croquet, badminton or putting.

○ Open all year   From Looe, take Polperro road for 2 miles to sign for hotel at crossroads; turn left down hill; hotel is on left. Private car park   2 single, 8 twin/double, 8 double, 1 four-poster, 2 family rooms, 2 suites; all with room service, hair-dryer, direct-dial telephone, TV   Restaurant, bar, lounge, library, conservatory, garden; social functions; heated outdoor swimming pool; early suppers for children; cots, highchairs, toys, babysitting, baby-listening   No wheelchair access; 3 steps into hotel, 4 ground-floor bedrooms   No children under 5 in restaurant eves; no dogs in public rooms, daily £7.50 in some bedrooms; no smoking in bedrooms and some public rooms   Delta, MasterCard, Switch, Visa   £ Single £105 to £135, single occupancy of twin/double £80 to £120, twin/double £90 to £130, family room £175 to £113, suite £140 to £180; deposit required. Set D £27.50; alc L £15, D £36; light meals available; service incl. Special breaks available

---

LORTON Cumbria   map 10

New House Farm

Lorton, Nr Cockermouth CA13 9UU
TEL: (01900) 85404   FAX: (01900) 85478
EMAIL: hazel@newhouse-farm.co.uk
WEB SITE: www.newhouse-farm.co.uk

Stylish country guesthouse run with flair and enthusiasm

Placid emerald sheep-pasture contrasts with the rugged Buttermere fells around this historic estate farm in Lorton Vale. The north-western lakes are less overrun than the central and eastern sections of the National Park, but plenty of visitors find their way to Hazel Thompson's charming Grade II listed establishment dating from 1650. Classy antiques and a fearless use of colour characterise the rustic beamed and flagstoned interior. Lily scent wafts through the entrance hall, bestrewn with walking sticks and waxed jackets; a jokey fox-pelt snoozes in a jam kettle. Lounge and dining areas feel instantly warm and inviting, as do the cosy bedrooms. Hazel's appetising five-course dinners are a great incentive, while barn lunches and teas are served across the yard. Here a new bedroom conversion has just been completed with a Jacobethan-style four-poster and a vivid scarlet bathroom ('A year ago the horse lived here,' but you'd never guess).

◗ Open all year 🄩 Off B5289 between Lorton and Loweswater, 6 miles south of Cockermouth. Private car park 🛏 1 twin, 3 double, 2 four-poster; all with room service, hair-dryer ✓ Dining room, 3 lounges, garden; hot tub; leisure facilities nearby; early suppers for children 🕭 No wheelchair access ● No children under 6; no dogs in public rooms; no smoking ▭ Delta, MasterCard, Switch, Visa £ Twin/double £98 to £110, four-poster £118 to £130; deposit required. Set D £25; light meals available; service incl. Special breaks available

Winder Hall

Low Lorton, Nr Cockermouth CA13 9UP
TEL: (01900) 85107   FAX: (01900) 85479
EMAIL: nick@winderhall.co.uk
WEB SITE: www.winderhall.co.uk

Period charm in a secluded country manor house

With children, cats and other jobs to think about, it's surprising Ann and Nick Lawler can find time to put so much effort into running Winder Hall. Hotel-keeping is a relatively new venture for them, but confidence and enthusiasm are clearly abundant. It isn't difficult to feel passionate about Winder Hall, a mellow mini-manor of soft grey stone and lattice windows. Part of the ancient Lorton Hall complex dating from the fourteenth century, it adjoins several similarly antique properties in the soft green landscapes of the Cocker valley. Unusual features such as grandly heraldic fireplaces and Victorian mullions stud the interior. The oak-panelled dining room overlooking the fountain garden makes a handsome setting for lavish breakfasts and tasty dinners using carefully sourced regional produce. The firelit lounge is a comfortable place for complimentary afternoon teas with home-baked cakes, or drinks before dinner. Bedrooms are light and spacious, with feature beds and smart bathrooms.

◗ Closed occasionally; dining room closed Tue eve 🄩 On B5289 in Low Lorton, 8 miles west of Keswick via Whinlatter Pass. Private car park 🛏 5 twin/double, 2 four-poster; family rooms available; all with room service, hair-dryer, direct-dial telephone, TV; some with trouser press, VCR ✓ Dining room, lounge, garden; conferences and social functions; civil wedding licence; leisure facilities nearby; early suppers for children; cots, highchairs, toys, babysitting, baby-listening, outdoor play area 🕭 No wheelchair access ● No dogs; no smoking ▭ Delta, MasterCard, Switch, Visa £ Single occupancy of twin/double £65 to £75, twin/double £90 to £110, four-poster £100 to £110, family room £110 to £130; deposit required. Set D £25; alc D £27.50; light meals available; service incl. Special breaks available ③FOR②

LOUGHBOROUGH Leicestershire   map 5

Old Manor Hotel

11-14 Sparrow Hill, Loughborough LE11 1BT
TEL: (01509) 211228   FAX: (01509) 211128
EMAIL: bookings@oldmanor.com
WEB SITE: www.oldmanor.com

Calming churchyard views from hotel at the centre of town

Loughborough is one of those bustling little towns that seem to take pains to direct the motorist through it rather than stay in it, but persevere and make for the old centre, which is an atmospheric world apart from the busier periphery. At its heart, opposite All Saints parish church, is the Manor Hotel. Roger Burdell, its owner, has managed to retain many of the original Tudor features while at the same time suffusing the traditional with lighter, more modern touches. The contemporary-feel restaurant is in shades of ochre with real plants trailing from baskets hanging from the ceiling. The menu offers tasty-sounding Italian-influenced food, with four or five choices at each course. The bedrooms have a more authentic Tudor character with exposed blackened beams and furnished with long hanging drapes at the windows, canopies over the beds and antique-style furniture; one even has a free-standing claw-foot bath in its bedroom. The best views are to be had from rooms at the front of the building overlooking the churchyard.

○ Open all year ⊉ In Loughborough town centre. Nearest train station: Loughborough. Private car park ⟁ 2 single, 5 double, 1 four-poster; all with hair-dryer, direct-dial telephone, modem line, TV ⟨✓⟩ Restaurant, bar, lounge; conferences; social functions; leisure facilities nearby; early suppers for children; cots, highchairs, baby-listening ⟁ Wheelchair access to hotel and restaurant, 1 ground-floor bedroom ⬥ No dogs; no smoking ⊟ Amex, Delta, MasterCard, Switch, Visa ⌁£⌁ Single £70 to £92, single occupancy of double £70 to £92, double £95 to £120, four-poster £110 to £150; deposit required. Continental B £8, cooked B £12.50; set D £32.50; light meals available; service incl. Special breaks available ⟨3FOR2⟩

LOWER BEEDING West Sussex   map 3

South Lodge

Brighton Road, Lower Beeding, Horsham RH13 6PS
TEL: (01403) 892242   FAX: (01403) 892289
EMAIL: enquiries@southlodgehotel.co.uk
WEB SITE: www.exclusivehotels.co.uk

Friendly country-house hotel with splendid conference facilities

Built as a family home for a noted explorer and botanist back in the 1880s, this Victorian country house has been much extended. A sympathetically styled wing, still shiny and new, has smart conference areas and several rooms licensed for weddings. The entrance foyer to the hotel is in similar style, with its marble floor and glitzy chandelier, traditional seat for shoe polishing and an old red telephone box. The main house, however, retains some of its character, with elegant public areas such as the Camellia Restaurant, which has fine views and walls decorated with copies of a collection of china plates –

the originals are now in a London museum. Remarkably, the original wallpaper in the corridor, printed with botanic images, is still complete and is now listed. Bedrooms have been created with flair and are individually styled. High-beamed ceilings, oak floors, four-posters and exposed stone all feature. Bathrooms are top notch, with two or even three basins, huge shower heads, underfloor heating and maybe a Jacuzzi bath. Those facing towards the South Downs, looking over the grounds with the fine rhododendrons and azaleas flowering in spring, have the best views.

○ Open all year ⊉ On A281 Horsham to Brighton road; travelling south, pass Mannings Heath and Monk's Gate; hotel is on right after Leonardslee Gardens on left. Nearest train station: Horsham. Private car park ⟁ 13 twin/double, 16 double, 2 four-poster, 6 family rooms, 3 suites; all with room service, hair-dryer, direct-dial telephone, modem line, TV; some with fax, CD player; no tea/coffee-making facilities in rooms ⟨✓⟩ Restaurant, bar, lounge, library, games room, garden; conferences, social functions, civil wedding licence; gym, tennis; leisure facilities nearby; early suppers for children; cots, highchairs, toys, babysitting ⟁ Wheelchair access to hotel and restaurant, National Accessible Scheme: mobility impairment M1, WC, 1 ground-floor bedroom specially equipped for disabled people. Disabled parking ⬥ No dogs ⊟ Amex, Delta, Diners, MasterCard, Switch, Visa ⌁£⌁ Single occupancy of twin/double £230, twin/double £230, four-poster £306, family room £412, suite £447; deposit required. Continental B £13, cooked B £15; set L £13 to £26, D £45; light meals available; service incl. Special breaks available ⟨3FOR2⟩

LOWER ODDINGTON Gloucestershire   map 5

Fox Inn ⌈NEW ENTRY⌉

Lower Oddington, Moreton-in-Marsh GL56 0UR
TEL: (01451) 870555   FAX: (01451) 870666
EMAIL: info@foxinn.net
WEB SITE: www.foxinn.net

Smart, busy, gastropub with lots of tasteful touches

As with any self-respecting gastropub, word of the Fox Inn has spread far and wide – when we inspected, on a gloomy drizzly day, the atmosphere was brisk and busy as another expectant lunchtime crowd awaited their food. Shiny dark flagstone floors, an inglenook fireplace and hops hanging from the ceiling

characterise the bucolic interior of the bar. However, the style varies noticeably in other parts. The more formal dining area has scarlet walls, brass candlesticks and a changing exhibition of artists' work on view. And for sunny days there's an attractive terrace with an electrically operated awning and overhead heating in case the elements let guests down. Upstairs, owners Ian MacKenzie and Graham Williams have added a continental touch, with French antique beds and rose, peach and blue predominating. Of the three bedrooms, Garden is the largest and Courtyard the smallest. All three have fairly small, though smart, bathrooms.

◑ Closed 25 Dec ⚡ Off A436 in Lower Oddington. Private car park 🛏 3 double; all with hair-dryer, TV, VCR; 1 with trouser press ✅ Bar, garden; conferences; social functions; leisure facilities nearby; highchair ♿ No wheelchair access ◐ No dogs or smoking in bedrooms ☐ Delta, MasterCard, Switch, Visa £ Double £68 to £95; deposit required. Alc L, D £23; light meals available

---

LOWER SLAUGHTER Gloucestershire　　　　　　　　　　　　　　　　map 5

Lower Slaughter Manor

Lower Slaughter, Cheltenham GL54 2HP
TEL: (01451) 820456　FAX: (01451) 822150
EMAIL: info@lowerslaughter.co.uk
WEB SITE: www.lowerslaughter.co.uk

A classic Cotswold manor that treads carefully, but doesn't put a foot wrong

Built in 1658, late into the Cromwell republic, Lower Slaughter Manor reflects some of that puritanical era in its neat, austere structure. Not a window or chimney pot is surplus to requirements, nor a blade of grass out of place on its immaculate lawns. However, any Restoration dandy would feel more than at home in its opulent and colourfully decorated interior. To sum up, this hotel reflects its Englishness in every aspect and manages to create a smart, conservative look without taking itself too seriously. The public rooms are warm and welcoming and keep décor to sensible colours and predictable antiques such as landscape paintings, oriental rugs or the odd grandfather clock. Look out for the fine stucco coffered ceiling in the drawing room and the slight French feel of the salon. All the bedrooms have verdant views in one direction or another, and are individually styled in country-house themes, stripes or floral patterns, with good-size bathrooms.

◑ Open all year ⚡ Situated off A429 towards The Slaughters; approaching village centre on lane, hotel is on right. Private car park 🛏 11 twin/double, 2 four-poster, 3 suites; all with room service, hair-dryer, trouser press, direct-dial telephone, TV, VCR; no tea/coffee-making facilities in rooms ✅ Restaurant, 3 lounges, garden; conferences and social functions; civil wedding licence; tennis; leisure facilities nearby; cots ♿ No wheelchair access ◐ No children under 12 exc babes in arms; no dogs; no smoking in bedrooms ☐ Amex, Delta, Diners, MasterCard, Switch, Visa £ Single occupancy of twin/double £175, twin/double from £220, four-poster/suite £350; deposit required. Set L £22.50, alc D £45; light meals available. Special breaks available

---

LOXLEY Warwickshire　　　　　　　　　　　　　　　　map 5

Loxley Farm

Loxley, Warwick CV35 9JN
TEL: (01789) 840265　FAX: (01789) 840645
EMAIL: loxleyfarm@hotmail.com

Delightful country cottage with a history

Just outside Loxley village, set well back from the main road in its own secluded gardens and positively oozing milk and honey, is Anne and Roderick Horton's superb sixteenth-century cruck cottage. This timber-framed house with its tall brick chimneys sprouting from a low, irregular scalloped thatch is the epitome of the English rural idyll so beloved of card and chocolate box illustrators – and it also comes with historical attachments to please romantics. Charles I took refuge here after being defeated at Edgehill and there are also rumours of a Robin Hood connection with the village. The sloping cottage garden is subdivided by neatly trimmed hedges into lawns bordered by flower beds and studded with fruit trees – perfect for picnics on long drowsy summer days. Breakfasts are served on a single oak table in a characterful room of leaded windows, flagstones and blackened beams. The two guest rooms, set apart from the house in a converted thatched barn, are spacious and virtually self-contained. The

Hayloft Suite has a small kitchen and sitting room while the Garden Suite has an oval conservatory and comes with a fridge and facilities for making hot drinks. Both apartments have en suite bathrooms.

◗ Closed Chr & New Year 🗲 Turn off A422 at sign for Loxley; go through village and turn left at bottom of hill; Loxley Farm is third on right. Private car park 🛌 2 suites; both with hair-dryer, TV ⊘ Breakfast room, garden; leisure facilities nearby; cots, highchairs 🚫 No wheelchair access ● No dogs in public rooms; no smoking ☐ None accepted £ Single occupancy of suite £45, suite £70; deposit required

---

LUDLOW Shropshire   map 7

Dinham Hall

By the Castle, Ludlow SY8 1EJ
TEL: (01584) 876464 FAX: (01584) 876019
EMAIL: info@dinhamhall.co.uk
WEB SITE: www.dinhamhall.co.uk

High standards and a great location at this smart town hotel

The gracious living that takes place at Dinham Hall today is far removed from its previous regime, as a boarding house for Ludlow Grammar School. Thankfully all that remains of that hectic time are some old school photos on the walls and the names of cheeky schoolboys carved into some of the window ledges. Life now is far more in keeping with the quality of this late-eighteenth-century, pale grey stone mansion. A complimentary pot of tea with biscuits welcomes guests, and sherry and fruit are provided in the bedrooms. Public areas are limited to the relaxed drawing room with its huge carved oak fireplace, the small bar just

off it, and the restaurant with its neutral tones and lovely views across the historic rooftops to the woods on the other side of the River Teme. Our inspection meal was meticulous in presentation, and enjoyable, with crab cake, pea purée and crayfish sauce to start, followed by brill with new potatoes, and wonderfully pungent rocket, chorizo and cherry tomatoes, then a crème brûlée with almond tuile for dessert. Bedrooms are well proportioned, with big sash windows. Palmers is impressive, with its huge French bed, flanked by tall bedside lights; it comes with a small lounge and smart, carpeted bathroom.

◗ Open all year 🗲 To left of Ludlow Castle entrance. Nearest train station: Ludlow. Private car park 🛌 1 single, 2 twin, 2 twin/double, 1 double, 3 four-poster, 2 family rooms, 2 suites; all with room service, hair-dryer, direct-dial telephone, TV; some with trouser press, VCR, CD player ⊘ Restaurant, bar, 2 lounges, garden; conferences and social functions; civil wedding licence; leisure facilities nearby; early suppers for children; cots, highchairs, toys 🚫 Wheelchair access to hotel (ramp) and restaurant, 1 ground-floor bedroom ● No children under 8 in restaurant eves; no dogs in public rooms, £9 per night in bedrooms; no smoking in restaurant and bedrooms ☐ Amex, Delta, Diners, MasterCard, Switch, Visa £ Single £95, single occupancy of twin/double £100 to £250, twin/double £130 to £210, four-poster £160 to £210, family room £160 to £280, suite £280; deposit required. Alc L £20.50, D £35; light meals available. Special breaks available (3 FOR 2)

Mr Underhill's

Dinham Weir, Ludlow SY8 1EH
TEL: (01584) 874431
WEB SITE: www.mr-underhills.co.uk

Renowned cooking and a range of stylish bedrooms to match

Work continues at Chris and Judy Bradley's well-established restaurant-with-rooms. Since last year, three impressive new suites have come into commission, using some of the buildings surrounding the original

jumble of creamy orange buildings down by the River Teme: across the road in the Miller's House there are two modern duplex rooms with good attention to detail, and just across the pretty courtyard garden from the main block, the now incongruously named Shed has a spacious room, with a huge picture window that overlooks river and gardens. Bedrooms in the main house are smaller, but baths have been ingeniously fitted in, and there are clear signs that the Bradleys are intent on keeping the improvements going. Apart from a small sofa room, the public areas are given over to the restaurant where guests can sample Chris's cooking. A typical set menu has a starter of butternut squash with Parmesan, brill on pak choi with coriander and ginger, beef with tarragon and cep-scented jus, and finally white chocolate ice cream with sweet chilli syrup.

❍ Closed 25 & 26 Dec, 1 week in July; restaurant closed Tue eve and sometimes Mon eve ⬛ In centre of Ludlow, below castle, on river bank. Nearest train station: Ludlow. Private car park ⬛ 1 twin/double, 5 double, 3 suites; all with room service, hair-dryer, direct-dial telephone, TV; some with mini-bar, VCR, CD player ⬛ Restaurant, small sitting room, garden; leisure facilities nearby; early suppers for children; baby-listening ⬛ No wheelchair access ● No children aged 2 to 8 in restaurant eves; no dogs; no smoking ⬛ Delta, MasterCard, Switch, Visa ⬛ Single occupancy of twin/double £80 to £130, twin/double £95 to £155, suite £175 to £220; deposit required. Set D £36

LYDGATE Greater Manchester   map 8

White Hart Inn

51 Stockport Road, Lydgate, Oldham OL4 4JJ
TEL: (01457) 872566   FAX: (01457) 875190
EMAIL: bookings@thewhitehart.co.uk
WEB SITE: www.thewhitehart.co.uk

Sophisticated hilltop dining pub on the cusp of the Pennines

From the windows of this handsome millstone-grit freehouse in a conservation village just outside Oldham, you sense the call of open countryside in swathes of rising moorland. Originally an eighteenth-century coaching inn, the White Hart has had a chequered history, but has hit the limelight under its present ownership, achieving an enviable reputation for high-quality food and accommodation. Cooking is the mainstay, featuring the on-site Saddleworth Sausage Company's varied offerings and much else besides, plus a formidable wine list and many local ales. The building has been sympathetically extended to the rear, and part of its large grounds are destined for marquee space to keep function trade separate from the rest of the hotel. The spacious interior provides a well-considered series of public rooms, including a smartly contemporary restaurant and a cheerful firelit brasserie with bright red walls. Bedrooms, all named after local personages, have stylish modern furnishings and splendid bathrooms.

❍ Open all year ⬛ 2 miles east of Oldham on A669; turn right at brow of hill on to A6050. Nearest train station: Oldham. Private car park ⬛ 2 twin, 10 double; family room available; all with room service, hair-dryer, trouser press, direct-dial telephone, modem line, TV ⬛ 2 restaurants, 2 bars, 2 lounges, garden; conferences and social functions; civil wedding licence; leisure facilities nearby; cots, highchairs ⬛ No wheelchair access ● No dogs; no smoking in bedrooms ⬛ Amex, Delta, MasterCard, Switch, Visa ⬛ Single occupancy of twin/double £75, twin/double £105, family room £121; deposit required. Set L £17; alc L £24.50; light meals available; service incl. Special breaks available ⬛

LYME REGIS Dorset   map 2

Hotel Alexandra

Pound Street, Lyme Regis DT7 3HZ
TEL: (01297) 442010   FAX: (01297) 443229
EMAIL: enquiries@hotelalexandra.co.uk
WEB SITE: www.lymeregis.co.uk

Well-positioned seaside hotel with gently traditional atmosphere

Something of a Lyme Regis classic, the Alexandra is a cosy seaside hotel run with great charm and courtesy. Set back from the main road, the pebble-dashed building doesn't reveal its advantages until you walk through and see the fine lawned gardens and sea views – a vista that the sitting room, conservatory and restaurant all take in. It's an intimate place rather than grand: lamps and wall-lights add to the atmosphere in the evenings, floors can be creaky and corridors long and winding. The best bedrooms enjoy that sea view. The décor tends to be dated but well kept: floral patterned fabrics, botanic or ornithological prints, and china on the tea tray. Without that view, rooms can be a little anticlimactic: one reader thought that Room 9 was disappointing, especially at 'premium prices', and found the staff 'polite but uninterested'.

○ Closed 19 Dec to 28 Jan ⤷ Head up main street of town (Broad Street) away from sea; take left fork into Pound Street; hotel is on left. Private car park ⤷ 2 single, 5 twin, 8 twin/double, 11 double; family rooms available; all with room service, hair-dryer, direct-dial telephone, TV ⊘ Restaurant, bar, sitting room, conservatory, garden; conferences; social functions; leisure facilities nearby; early suppers for children; cots, highchairs, baby-listening ⅙ No wheelchair access; 3 steps into hotel, 4 steps into restaurant, 3 ground-floor bedrooms ● No children under 10 in restaurant; no dogs in public rooms; £6 in bedrooms; no smoking in restaurant ▭ Delta, MasterCard, Switch, Visa £ Single £35 to £52, single occupancy of twin/double £50 to £75, twin/double £94 to £136, family room £105 to £151; deposit required. Set L £15, D £24.50; light meals available; service incl. Special breaks available

---

LYMINGTON Hampshire
map 2

Stanwell House

14–16 High Street, Lymington SO41 9AA
TEL: (01590) 677123 FAX: (01590) 677756
EMAIL: sales@stanwellhousehotel.co.uk
WEB SITE: www.stanwellhousehotel.co.uk

Traditional Georgian townhouse with a contemporary twist

Right in the thick of things on Lymington's busy High Street, and with its own lively bar and bistro, this enticing townhouse hotel makes for a colourful base from which to discover the town and surrounding area. Affectionately dubbed 'the junk shop' by staff, its vibrant interior – stylishly decorated in shades of mustard, lilac and aubergine, and fringed with sumptuous co-ordinating fabrics – is stuffed with an eclectic mix of antiques, contemporary furnishings and specially commissioned ironwork. The bar, with its stripped wood floors, red velvet-covered stools and blackboards touting tapas, has a laid-back feel, while the cosy bistro buzzes with a spirited lunchtime crowd of locals and guests. Alternatively, you can dine more formally in the restaurant, then repair to the inviting conservatory where comfy wicker chairs and upholstered bench seats are littered with plump cushions covered with brightly coloured silk and velvet. Bedrooms in the main building are the best option and are luxurious and tasteful, with quality furnishings, smart bathrooms and rich colour schemes in keeping with the Georgian origins. Those in the new wing are decidedly more ordinary but are nonetheless comfortable and light.

○ Open all year ⤷ In centre of Lymington. Nearest train station: Lymington ⤷ 8 twin, 12 double, 2 four-poster, 5 suites; all with room service, hair-dryer, trouser press, direct-dial telephone, modem line, TV; some with mini-bar ⊘ 2 restaurants, bar, conservatory, garden; conferences; social functions; civil wedding licence; leisure facilities nearby; cots, highchairs, baby-listening ⅙ No wheelchair access ● No smoking in some public rooms and some bedrooms ▭ Amex, Delta, Diners, MasterCard, Switch, Visa £ Single occupancy of twin/double £85, twin/double £110, four-poster £130, suite £160; deposit required. Set L £13; alc L, D £24.50; light meals available; service incl. Special breaks available ③FOR②

'The bed was six foot across, but the sheets and blanket were those for a five foot bed. Hence with two people in it there was not enough slack in the width of the sheets to cover both bed and occupants properly. Surely it is basic common sense to match the size of the bed linen to the bed for which it is intended?'
On a hotel in Cornwall

LYNMOUTH Devon   map 1

Shelley's

8 Watersmeet Road, Lynmouth EX35 6EP
TEL: (01598) 753219
EMAIL: info@shelleyshotel.co.uk
WEB SITE: www.shelleyshotel.co.uk

Stylish guesthouse B&B close to the sea and run with great charm

Things have come to a pretty pass when you can abscond without paying your hotel bill and the owners simply name the place after you. For that is what Percy Bysshe Shelley did in 1812 after running up a massive £30 tab in Mrs Hooper's Lodging House (he took his ex-girlfriend as well as his new wife on what was a honeymoon). Jane Becker and Richard Briden bought the place in 2000 when it was derelict and spent two years rebuilding before opening under the new name. It sits in a great position right in the heart of Lynmouth. The poet would find it much more comfortable now: re-jigging room layouts means that all bar one bedroom get a sea view – four of them get private conservatory and balcony too. He'd also undoubtedly approve of finding his verses dotted around the place, even on the back of the menu for the excellent breakfasts.

◗ Closed mid-Nov to early Mar ⊠ At main road junction in centre of village, next to Glen Lyn Gorge ⇦ 1 twin, 10 double; all with hair-dryer, direct-dial telephone, TV ⊘ Breakfast room/conservatory, bar, lounge, courtyard; conferences and social functions; leisure facilities nearby ♿ Wheelchair access to hotel (ramp) and breakfast room, 1 ground-floor bedroom specially equipped for disabled people ● No children under 12; no dogs; smoking in bar only ▭ Delta, MasterCard, Switch, Visa £ Single occupancy of twin/double £50 to £75, twin/double £70 to £100; deposit required. Special breaks available (3FOR2)

LYNTON Devon   map 1

Valley House [NEW ENTRY]

Lynbridge Road, Lynton EX35 6BD
TEL: (01598) 752285
EMAIL: info@valley-house.co.uk
WEB SITE: www.valley-house.co.uk

Welcoming hosts and some stylish touches at this interesting house

Until Katherine and Cliff Bench arrived at this mid-1840s vicarage, it was difficult to see quite why it came to be built. Certainly it was secluded, with a great rock wall tight against its back and trees all around – too many trees. Then Cliff and Katherine came and cleared the terraces outside, pruned a few trees and – voilà – fabulous views of the Bristol Channel! They haven't stopped there either: the interior has been extensively remodelled with a swish new lounge bar and a conservatory dining room that is bright and lovely with good views. Katherine's cooking is homely but light of touch and imaginative: a spiced crab and spinach soup might be followed by beef florentine, then baked pears stuffed with Amaretti biscuits and honey in a port syrup. Bedrooms are fresh and light with neat shower rooms. The pick of them has to be Room 2, with its wonderful balcony.

◗ Closed Chr & New Year ⊠ Take A39 following signs to Lynton; turn left on to B3234 at Barbrook and keep straight on the road following signs to Lynmouth; hotel is 150 metres past the Bridge Inn pub on the left. Private car park ⇦ 2 twin/double, 3 double, 1 family room; all with hair-dryer, TV ⊘ Dining room, lounge, conservatory, garden; leisure facilities nearby; early suppers for children ♿ No wheelchair access ● No children under 8; no dogs in public rooms; smoking in some bedrooms only ▭ Amex, Delta, MasterCard, Switch, Visa £ Single occupancy of twin/double £38 to £45, twin/double £50 to £60, family room £65; deposit required. Set D V17; service incl. Special breaks available

If you make a booking using a credit card and find after cancelling that the full amount has been charged to your card, raise the matter with your credit-card company. It will ask the hotelier to confirm whether the room was re-let, and to justify the charge made.

Victoria Lodge

Lee Road, Lynton EX35 6BS
TEL: (01598) 753203
EMAIL: info@victorialodge.co.uk
WEB SITE: www.victorialodge.co.uk

Welcoming hosts and good breakfasts on the hill above the sea

It's a competitive business, running a guesthouse in Lynton, and many go to the wall, but Jane and Ben Bennett's place remains in the vanguard, a paragon of decent rooms, sturdy breakfasts and plenty of good humour. The Lodge was built in 1884 as a family home, and the Bennetts have maintained a period décor, but in the spirit rather than the letter. There is a vast, and ever-growing, collection of period photographs and prints all over the house, plus colour schemes that nod towards the Victorian love of the deep and plush. The lounge stocks lots of local information for walks and restaurants – the Bennetts are impressively up-to-date on new dining options too. Bedrooms are comfortable though most tend to be cosy rather than spacious. In some rooms the brass beds of yesteryear have now given way to the larger six-foot beds of modern taste.

○ Closed Nov to mid-Mar ⚡ In centre of village, opposite post office. Private car park 🚗 1 twin, 6 double, 1 four-poster, 1 family room; all with hair-dryer, TV; some with VCR, CD player ✅ Breakfast room, 2 lounges, garden 🚫 No wheelchair access ● No children under 5; no dogs; no smoking ▢ MasterCard, Switch, Visa £ Single occupancy of twin/double £42 to £68, twin/double £56 to £84, four-poster £80, family room £98; deposit required

---

MAIDENCOMBE Devon   map 1

Orestone Manor

Rockhouse Lane, Maidencombe, Torquay TQ1 4SX
TEL: (01803) 328098 FAX: (01803) 328336
EMAIL: enquiries@orestone.co.uk
WEB SITE: www.orestone.co.uk

Country house in contemporary colonial style by the sea

Elephants, so the saying goes, never forget, and if the number of pachyderm representatives throughout this hotel is anything to go by, staying here should be a memorable experience. Tucked away on a tiny lane off the busy road from Torquay to Teignmouth, this country house is a bit of an unexpected find. The lawns sloping down behind the hotel feature some splendid mature trees, including copper beech, maple and palms, with glimpses of a discreetly screened swimming pool as well as the sea. Inside, colonial style has been given a modern twist, so wicker chairs and cream sofas, rugs on stripped boards, and Chinese lamps happily rub shoulders with more unusual touches, like a dragon suspended in a light well in the restaurant. At the top end of the bedroom price range, the Garden Room, with a tented ceiling, feels like being on a luxury safari, while even the smallest gable rooms have space for a couple of chairs to admire the sea views. The menu may range around the world for inspiration, but is based largely on sourcing good local ingredients, including seafood, beef and lamb. Service is admirably professional.

○ Open all year ⚡ On A379 Torquay to Teignmouth road, turn right down Rockhouse Lane (opposite Brunel Manor); hotel is 50 yards further on. Private car park 🚗 3 twin, 6 double, 1 four-poster, 2 suites; family rooms available; all with room service, hair-dryer, trouser press, direct-dial telephone, TV, VCR, CD player ✅ Restaurant, bar, lounge, library, conservatory, gardens; conferences; social functions; heated outdoor swimming pool, leisure facilities nearby; early suppers for children; cots, highchairs, toys, baby-listening 🚹 Wheelchair access to hotel and restaurant (ramps), WC, 1 ground-floor bedroom. Disabled parking ● No children under 7 in restaurant eves ▢ Amex, Delta, MasterCard, Switch, Visa £ Single occupancy of twin/double £89, twin/double £119, four-poster £149 to £199, family room £169 to £199, suite £199; deposit required. Set L £18; alc L £22, D £35; light meals available (3 FOR 2)

Cottage in the Wood

Holywell Road, Malvern Wells WR14 4LG
TEL: (01684) 575859   FAX: (01684) 560662
EMAIL: reception@cottageinthewood.co.uk
WEB SITE: www.cottageinthewood.co.uk

Comfortable family-run hotel in a picturesque clearing in the woods

This is not really a cottage at all – be prepared instead for a fine Georgian dower house with plenty of space and panoramic views of the Severn Vale. John and Sue Pattin, and their children Dominic and Romy, take a hands-on approach to running this hotel, so you are likely to see them at reception, tending the bar or, in Dominic's case, heading up the kitchen. The style is of a smart and conventional country house, with some bold touches. The restaurant is light and spacious, with 100-year-old Indian prints on the walls and views for up to 30 miles out of the tall windows. On sunny days it's also possible to dine on the terrace outside. The main house has eight comfortable conservative bedrooms, but there are larger ones in more cottagey style in Beech Cottage, even older than the main house. In The Pinnacles, completed in 2003, are more rooms, bright, fresh and well lit – some with balconies.

○ Open all year   ⊿ 3 miles south of Great Malvern off A449; turning is signposted by small postbox and is almost opposite B4209 turning to Upton-upon-Severn. Private car park   ⟵ 8 twin/double, 21 double, 2 four-poster; all with limited room service, hair-dryer, direct-dial telephone, TV, VCR; most with trouser press, modem line   ⊘ Restaurant, bar lounge, terrace, garden; conferences; leisure facilities nearby; early suppers for children; cots, highchairs, baby-listening   & Wheelchair access to hotel and restaurant, 9 ground-floor bedrooms, 1 room specially equipped for disabled people   ● No dogs in public rooms and some bedrooms; smoking only in rear section of bar lounge and some bedrooms   ☐ Amex, Delta, MasterCard, Switch, Visa   £ Single occupancy of twin/double £83 to £105, twin/double £99 to £175, four-poster £155 to £175. Set L £17; alc D £35; light lunches available; service incl. Special breaks available   (3FOR2)

Alias Rossetti

107 Piccadilly, Manchester M1 2DB
TEL: 0161-247 7744   FAX: 0161-247 7747
EMAIL: info@rossetti.com
WEB SITE: www.aliashotels.com

Tongue-in-cheek designer style in a nineteenth-century textile factory

The original industrial role of this handsome sandstone edifice shines through its steel beams and support columns, now waggishly entwined by fragile gilded foliage in the open-plan foyer-restaurant. Other indicators of humour are the mannequin doormen at the entrance, surmounted by a large inflatable globe (allegedly acquired by some means from Scotland Yard). Huge metallic toffee-making cauldrons serve as plant containers. Alias Hotels aficionados will expect the unexpected. So the funky, spacious bedrooms amuse with optical illusion calendars and abstract artworks. The individually styled penthouse suites are wackiest of all: Miles is a lofty, galleried arena with plasma TV and an internet workspace. Each bedroom floor has its own help-yourself 50s-style diner stocked with coffee, cereals, fruit and pastries. Café Paradiso emulates cool metropolitan brasserie; staff are young, laid-back and friendly; service can be a bit hit-and-miss. Downstairs lies a basement bar-disco with a sunken dance-floor and squashy banquette seating.

○ Open all year   ⊿ Between Piccadilly station and Piccadilly Gardens, opposite Hotel Malmaison. Nearest train station: Manchester Piccadilly   ⟵ 11 twin, 45 double, 5 suites; all with room service, hair-dryer, direct-dial telephone, modem line, TV, DVD, CD player; no tea/coffee-making facilities in rooms   ⊘ Restaurant, 2 bars, lounge; conferences and social functions; leisure facilities nearby; cots, highchairs, baby-listening   & Wheelchair access to hotel (ramp) and restaurant, 3 ground-floor bedrooms specially equipped for disabled people; lift   ● None   ☐ Amex, Delta, Diners, MasterCard, Switch, Visa   £ Single occupancy of twin/

double £105, twin/double £130 to £145, suite £330; deposit required. Continental B £8.50, cooked B £13.50; set L, D £17; alc L, D £22; light meals available

Didsbury House

Didsbury Park, Didsbury Village, Manchester M20 5LJ
TEL: 0161-448 2200   FAX: 0161-448 2525
EMAIL: enquiries@didsburyhouse.co.uk
WEB SITE: www.didsburyhouse.co.uk

Fine Victorian house with good standards of service given a modern minimalist makeover

Owner Eamonn O'Loughlin describes this hotel as a 'grown up' version of his original neighbouring enterprise (see entry for Eleven Didsbury Park). Certainly he and his wife, Sally, an interior designer, have taken the best of Eleven and added more features. A cool lounge area with a huge Philippe Starck anglepoise lamp and polished walnut tables leads through to a bar with a zinc counter, black slate floor and displays of exotic fresh flowers. All this is done while retaining the best features of this Victorian villa. So cornicing and ceiling roses remain, as does the grand wooden staircase that acts as a central focus. Upstairs, the bedrooms are spacious and minimalist and the bathrooms are great. There are polished wood floors and good use of primary colours contrasting with the white bed linen. In the bathrooms it's all stone, slate and chrome; some have clawfoot baths.

○ Open all year   From M56 Junction 1 (at M60 ring road), take A34 towards Manchester; filter left on to A5145 towards Didsbury; Didsbury House is on right at second traffic lights. Nearest train station: East Didsbury. Private car park   8 twin/double, 11 double, 8 suites; all with room service, hair-dryer, mini-bar, trouser press, direct-dial telephone, modem line, TV, CD player; some with VCR   Bar, 2 lounges, library, garden; conferences; social functions; gym, spa, leisure facilities nearby; cots, highchairs   Wheelchair access to hotel (ramp), 9 ground-floor bedrooms. Disabled parking   None   Amex, Delta, Diners, MasterCard, Switch, Visa   Single occupancy of twin/double £81 to £135, twin/double £94 to £145, suite £117 to £175; deposit required. Continental B £11.50, cooked B £13. Set D (room service) £20; light meals available. Special breaks available

Eleven Didsbury Park

Didsbury Village, Manchester M20 5LH
TEL: 0161-448 7711   FAX: 0161-448 8282
EMAIL: enquiries@elevendidsburypark.com
WEB SITE: www.elevendidsburypark.com

Manhattan chic meets Manchester style in the leafy suburbs of Didsbury

So successful is Eamonn and Sally O'Loughlin's imaginative reinvention of a classic Victorian townhouse that they have opened a larger and more elaborately serviced version just a few doors along the street (Didsbury House). Guests have access to the facilities of both hotels, but Number Eleven has a loyal band of devotees who prefer its more personal, intimate charms, not to mention its secluded walled garden set with parasoled outdoor furniture. The neat, double-fronted villa expands Tardis-like to the rear, revealing an unexpectedly sophisticated interior of black and neutral furnishings, upmarket coffee-table publications, über-cool flowers and scattered ceiling spotlights. Despite the designer style, it's unpretentious enough to relax in. Interesting soundtracks emanate from the Chinese sideboard used as an honesty bar and music centre. Sleek, well-insulated bedroom boltholes feature Egyptian cotton bed linen, minimalist colour schemes and hedonistic bathrooms. Room service prevents night starvation until 10.30pm; free lifts are offered to local restaurants.

○ Open all year   From M56 Junction 1 (at M60 ring road), take A34 towards Manchester; filter left on to A5145 towards Didsbury; Didsbury Park is on right at second traffic lights; hotel is 150 metres on left. Nearest train station: East Didsbury. Private car park   7 twin/double, 8 double, 5 suites; all with room service, hair-dryer, mini-bar, trouser press, direct-dial telephone, modem line, TV, CD player; some with VCR   Bar,

2 lounges, garden; conferences; social functions; leisure facilities nearby; cots, highchairs   No wheelchair access ● None ⌐ Amex, Delta, Diners, MasterCard, Switch, Visa ⌐£⌐ Twin/double £81 to £145, suite £117 to £175; deposit required. Continental B £11.50, cooked B £13. Set D (room service) £20; light meals available. Special breaks available

Malmaison Manchester

Piccadilly, Manchester M1 3AQ
TEL: 0161-278 1000   FAX: 0161-278 1002
EMAIL: manchester@malmaison.com
WEB SITE: www.malmaison.com

Imaginative transformation of an old city-centre cotton warehouse

The Manchester outpost of the glamorous Malmaison chain occupies a dramatically revitalised industrial building close to the railway station. Most of the hotel's streamlined red-and-black brick façade is unmistakeable new-build, but its historic core is still emblazoned with the Victorian proprietor's name (Joshua Hoyle & Son). The interior is a series of split-level spaces decorated in a boldly minimalist colour palette of black, red, aubergine and taupe. The subtly lit, sunken brasserie dishes up chic modern offerings such as crispy squid and rocket salad, and risotto primavera. Bedrooms are undeniably impressive, featuring dynamic geometric designs, fancy gadgetry, excellent work/storage space and ritzy bathrooms. You can be picky at these prices, though, so we'd suggest that the management redesigns the unhelpful bathroom mirror lighting, ensures that heated towel rails actually work, and adds personal room safes. Our inspection visit chimed with a reader's experience of haughty and inefficient restaurant service, though the food is generally good.

◗ Open all year 📶 In city centre, by Piccadilly station. Nearest train station: Manchester Piccadilly 🛏 20 twin, 134 double, 13 suites; all with room service, hair-dryer, mini-bar, trouser press, direct-dial telephone, modem line, TV, CD player; suites with DVD player ✅ Restaurant, bar, lounge; conferences; social functions; gym, spa; early suppers for children; highchairs   Wheelchair access to hotel, 5 steps into restaurant, 10 rooms specially equipped for disabled people, lift ● No dogs; no smoking in most bedrooms ⌐ Amex, Delta, Diners, MasterCard, Switch, Visa ⌐£⌐ Single occupancy of twin/double £129, twin/double £129, suite £165; deposit required. Continental B £8.50, cooked B £12; set L, D £14; alc L, D £25; light meals available; service incl (prices valid till Jan 2005). Special breaks available

Le Meridien Victoria & Albert

Water Street, Manchester M3 4JQ
TEL: (0870) 400 8585   FAX: 0161-834 2484
EMAIL: rm1452@lemeridien.com
WEB SITE: www.lemeridien.com

A costume-drama setting in an imaginative waterfront conversion

Victorian themes pervade this smartly renovated warehouse hotel dating from 1843 on the banks of the Irwell. Just across the road are the old Granada television studios, which once used these premises for property storage and location filming. The whole Castlefield area is a fascinating conservation zone, notable for its role during the Industrial Revolution and the age of canals and railways. Many features emphasise the building's original role: cast-iron pillars, oak beams and exposed brickwork. Open-plan public areas lead off the handsome, galleried foyer with its grand carpets and huge flower arrangements. Portraits of the original Victorians preside from the balcony above the reception desk. A spacious split-level suite of bar-lounge and dining space overlooks the waterfront, giving masses of room to relax. Appetising menus in Watson's Bar supplement the more formal dining of Sherlock's Restaurant. Bedrooms are spacious, well equipped and tastefully furnished, and are named after popular Granada TV shows.

◑ Open all year 🔲 In city centre beside River Irwell and Granada Studios. Nearest train station: Manchester Piccadilly. Private car park 🛏 1 single, 65 twin, 85 double, 8 suites; family rooms available; all with room service, hair-dryer, mini-bar, trouser press, direct-dial telephone, modem line, TV ✅ 2 restaurants, 2 dining rooms, bar, lounge, conservatory; conferences; social functions; civil wedding licence; leisure facilities nearby; cots, highchairs, babysitting 🦽 Wheelchair access to hotel and restaurant, 4 rooms specially equipped for disabled people, lift. Disabled parking ● No dogs; no smoking in some bedrooms 💳 Amex, Delta, Diners, MasterCard, Switch, Visa £ Single £115, single occupancy of twin/double £170, twin/double £170 to £190, family room £170, suite from £250; deposit required. Continental B £11.50, cooked B £14.50; set L, D £18; alc L £25, D £35. Special breaks available (2004 data)

The Midland

Peter Street, Manchester M60 2DS
TEL: 0161-236 3333 FAX: 0161-932 4100
EMAIL: midlandreservations@paramount-hotels.co.uk
WEB SITE: www.themidland.co.uk

Stately architectural landmark not far from the G-Mex Centre

This grande dame of Manchester's central cityscape has become part of another large hotel group since the previous edition (Paramount, rather than Crowne Plaza). Regular visitors may find it hard to spot the changes, however, as the Midland's sense of history and individuality far transcends any vulgar attempts at corporate branding. Mr Rolls and Mr Royce (who famously met here for the first time in May 1904) are commemorated by the portals of its imposing Edwardian façade. The dizzying glazed atrium of the reception foyer induces a crick in the neck. A pianist plays over afternoon tea and cocktails amid the pillars and parlour palms on the Octagon Terrace, and the French Restaurant is still formidably Gallic in gilt twirls and Regency stripes. Less daunting cooking is available at the Trafford (Sunday roasts and carvery buffets), or at Nico's Brasserie. Bedrooms are predictably opulent, especially the Premium Rooms and Suites.

◑ Open all year 🔲 In city centre, just north of Oxford Road and adjacent to G-Mex Centre. Nearest train station: Manchester Piccadilly 🛏 76 single, 25 twin, 146 double, 42 family rooms, 14 suites; all with room service, hair-dryer, mini-bar, trouser press, direct-dial telephone, TV; VCR, CD player on request ✅ 3 restaurants, 2 bars, lounge; conferences; social functions; civil wedding licence; gym, heated indoor swimming pool; leisure facilities nearby; cots, highchairs 🦽 Wheelchair access to hotel (ramp) and restaurant, WC, 1 room specially equipped for disabled people, lift ● None 💳 Amex, Delta, Diners, MasterCard, Switch, Visa £ Single/twin/double £165, family room £195, suite £250 to £600; deposit required. Continental B £10, cooked B £14; set L £16.50, D £22.50; alc L £20, D £25; light meals available; service incl. Special breaks available

---

MARKINGTON North Yorkshire   map 9

Hob Green

Markington, Harrogate HG3 3PJ
TEL: (01423) 770031 FAX: (01423) 771589
EMAIL: info@hobgreen.com
WEB SITE: www.hobgreen.com

Classic country-house hotel in a huge estate near Harrogate

The Hutchinson family has owned Hob Green, a grand eighteenth-century country home in 800 acres of grounds, for 70 years. This gives the house a timeless quality and a polished style of service that you know is built on tried and tested practice, every detail thought through. A certain amount of refurbishment has taken place in recent years, but there is no *Changing Rooms* makeover gimmickry to scare the horses here. Public rooms have a seamless country-house décor, built on restful pale colours, floral patterns, antiques, sheaves of fresh flowers and oil paintings. The superb gardens are functional as well as decorative: seasonal fruit and vegetables from the kitchen gardens shape the traditional menus throughout the year. Bedrooms are reliably comfortable and many have uplifting views along the valley; classy new bathrooms are gradually replacing their more dated predecessors, and important little details that count are also to be found, such as home-made biscuits and fresh milk.

◑ Open all year ⏾ In Markington village, 8 miles north of Harrogate. Private car park 🔑 1 single, 2 twin, 5 double, 1 four-poster, 2 family rooms, 1 suite; all with room service, hair-dryer, mini-bar, trouser press, direct-dial telephone, modem line, TV; some with trouser press ⌖ Restaurant, lounge, library, conservatory, garden; conferences; social functions; civil wedding licence; leisure facilities nearby; early suppers for children; cots, highchairs, baby-listening, outdoor play area ♿ No wheelchair access ⬤ No dogs in public rooms, no smoking in bedrooms ▭ Amex, Delta, Diners, MasterCard, Switch, Visa £ Single £95, single occupancy of twin/double £105, twin/double £115, four-poster £125, family room £145, suite £140; deposit required. Set L from £15, D £25.50; alc D £29.50; light meals available. Special breaks available

---

MARSDEN West Yorkshire map 8

Olive Branch

Manchester Road, Marsden, Huddersfield HD7 6LU
TEL: (01484) 844487
WEB SITE: www.olivebranch.uk.com

Buzzy restaurant-with-rooms on the edge of Marsden Moor

The Olive Branch is a lively, family-run operation whose engine room is its cheerful restaurant. It started life as a pub, and there's still a pubby feel to the dining areas that are spread around several interconnecting rooms full of rustic wooden tables and chairs. Blackboards list a vast choice of dishes, supplemented by a snowstorm of yellow paper slips advertising the day's specials – perhaps rabbit sausage with leek mash or Loch Fyne scallops with lime garlic butter to start, then mains such as medallions of pork with a stilton and port sauce or sea bass with Chinese noodles and sweet pepper cream.

Three themed bedrooms have a bright and funky décor with stylish flourishes: Serengeti has sensuous velvety fabrics and game-reserve references in its carved giraffe figure and rattan furniture; the low ceilings of the Duck room may be the reason for its name, but there are also numerous images and figurines of our web-footed friends populating the room; finally there's the comfy and bright Topiary room, which you may be relieved to find is not full of sculpted hedges. If noise from the roadside location might be an issue for you, Serengeti faces the hills and is therefore the quietest.

◑ Closed first 2 weeks in Jan; restaurant closed Mon eve ⏾ On A62 between Marsden and Slaithwaite. Private car park 🔑 3 double; all with room service, hair-dryer, direct-dial telephone, TV, VCR ⌖ Restaurant, dining room, bar, garden; conferences; social functions; leisure facilities nearby; cots, highchairs ♿ No wheelchair access ⬤ No dogs; no smoking in some bedrooms ▭ Delta, MasterCard, Switch, Visa £ Single occupancy of twin/double £45, twin/double £60; deposit required. Continental B £5.50, cooked B £10.50; set L £14, D £17; alc L, D £25; light meals available ③FOR②

MARTINHOE Devon map 1

Old Rectory

Martinhoe, Parracombe, Barnstaple EX31 4QT
TEL: (01598) 763368   FAX: (01598) 763567
EMAIL: info@oldrectoryhotel.co.uk
WEB SITE: www.oldrectoryhotel.co.uk

Traditional but unstuffy country house with homely touches

In a great location next to an ancient church, with the North Devon coast nearby, is this substantial Georgian house, much altered over the years but retaining a quiet, tranquil air. Christopher and Enid Richmond keep things fairly low-key and traditional: there's a ticking grandfather clock in the dining room and a pleasant conservatory sitting area

where a 200-year-old Black Hamburg vine shades guests' heads as they sample the welcoming cup of tea and cake. Enid cooks the five-course dinners, using plenty of local ingredients and organic meats. Bread, too, is home-made. Bedrooms have fresh natural colours and pine furniture – a new suite has come into service recently with views towards the church. Bathrooms are smart and modern. Outside are three acres of lovely garden complete with duck pond and the chance to spot local residents such as the buzzards and badgers.

● Closed Nov to Feb 🗲 Off A39, between Parracombe and Lynton, signposted Woody Bay and Martinhoe. Private car park 🛏 1 twin, 2 twin/double, 5 double, 1 suite; all with hair-dryer, TV ⊘ Dining room, 2 lounges, conservatory, gardens ♿ No wheelchair access; 2 steps into hotel, 2 ground-floor bedrooms ● No children under 14; no dogs; no smoking ▭ Delta, MasterCard, Switch, Visa £ Single occupancy of twin/double £62 to £82, twin/double £94 to £124, suite £124 to £154; deposit required. Set D £30; service incl. Special breaks available

---

MARYPORT Cumbria   map 10

The Retreat

Birkby, Maryport CA15 6RG
TEL: (01900) 814056
EMAIL: enquiries@retreathotel.co.uk
WEB SITE: www.retreathotel.co.uk

A friendly, family-run, good-value hotel in a distinguished Victorian residence

This dignified house in a little-traversed part of coastal Cumbria was first built for a retired sea captain in 1850, but the small German flag painted above the main entrance gives a light-hearted clue to the nationality of one of its present owners. Chef-patron Rudi Geissler and his English wife Alison have owned the Retreat since 1985, so are well settled. The listed building retains much of its period character, with generously proportioned reception rooms furnished in classic Victoriana (mahogany cabinets, long-case clocks, balloon-back chairs). The letting bedrooms are similarly traditional in style, dark-wood furnishings offset by light walls and fabrics. Large walled gardens, looking both ornamental and productive, lie to the rear. Rudi's well-prepared four-course dinners require no translation (sirloin steak, roast duckling, grilled lamb chops, etc.). One visitor enthusiastically recommends the Geisslers' helpful, informal brand of hospitality, praising especially Rudi's version of an English Breakfast ('has to be eaten to be believed').

● Closed Chr 🗲 About 2 miles north of Maryport, just off A596 in hamlet of Birkby. Nearest train station: Maryport. Private car park 🛏 3 twin/double; all with room service, hair-dryer, TV ⊘ Restaurant, bar, lounge, garden; leisure facilities nearby ♿ No wheelchair access ● No dogs; no smoking in bedrooms and some public rooms ▭ Delta, MasterCard, Visa £ Single occupancy of twin/double £45, twin/double £55; deposit required. Set D £20; service incl. Special breaks available

---

MASHAM North Yorkshire   map 8

Swinton Park

Masham, Ripon HG4 4JH
TEL: (01765) 680900   FAX: (01765) 680901
EMAIL: enquiries@swintonpark.com
WEB SITE: www.swintonpark.com

Opulent family seat now a stylish castle hotel in the Dales

Swinton Park is an imposing stately pile complete with a crenellated turret above the entrance. It has been around since the seventeenth century, owned by the Cunliffe-Lister family for 120 years, but it was not until the twenty-first century that it became a hotel. Inside, all of the trappings of an elegant stately home are present and correct: rooms are on a grand scale with acres of oak floors, massive ornate fireplaces and ancestral oils of family forbears. The drawing room is a vast ballroom-sized space with a crystal chandelier and plasterwork garlands picked out in gold. Samuel's restaurant fosters a real sense of occasion beneath its gold-leaf ceiling: a modern menu is served at tables decorated with a single lily in a tall vase. No expense has been spared in the top-notch stylish bedrooms. Antiques sit very comfortably with rich colour schemes and luxurious fabrics; sparkling bathrooms are immaculate and, although they might feature the odd claw-foot antique bath, belong firmly in the contemporary world.

○ Open all year ⚡ From A1, take B6267 to Masham; drive through town and follow signs to Swinton. Private car park 🛏️ 2 twin/double, 5 double, 1 four-poster, 4 suites; all with room service, hair-dryer, mini-bar, trouser press, direct-dial telephone, modem line, TV, CD player ✓ Restaurant, bar, drawing room, sitting room, games room, private cinema, gardens; conferences; social functions; civil wedding licence; gym, spa; early suppers for children; cots, highchairs, toys, playroom, babysitting, baby-listening ♿ Wheelchair access to hotel (ramp) and dining room, WC, 3 rooms specially equipped for disabled people, lift. Disabled parking ● No children under 12 in restaurant eves; dogs £10 in bedrooms; no smoking in restaurant ⬚ Amex, Delta, Diners, MasterCard, Switch, Visa £ Single occupancy of twin/double £120, twin/double £120, four-poster/suite £250. Set L £18; alc L £18, D £32, D £32; light meals available. Special breaks available (3FOR2)

MATFEN Northumberland   map 10

Matfen Hall

Matfen, Corbridge NE20 0RH
TEL: (01661) 886500   FAX: (01661) 886055
EMAIL: info@matfenhall.com
WEB SITE: www.matfenhall.com

Big changes at this top-quality country house and golf course

When we visited Matfen Hall in 2004 its new leisure club and treatment spa was nearing completion, so expect mud wraps, 'fire and ice' saunas and other pampering procedures to be on the menu at this grand faux-medieval country house. Since its reincarnation as a hotel in 1999, the Blacket family country seat has undergone radical transformation: millions have been spent, and in the last year alone, the number of rooms has almost doubled. In case the executive cars parked outside and golfing brigade wandering across the greens aren't a giveaway, the enterprise is aimed squarely at a corporate clientele, supplemented by a roaring trade in weddings – 145 were scheduled for 2004. A nineteenth-century ancestor's taste for neo-Gothic grandeur bequeathed the ideal venue for these, in the shape of the Great Hall. The Library restaurant, lined with leather tomes, makes for an equally atmospheric dining experience, with some technically skilled cooking going on behind the scenes. As a leisure guest you won't feel swamped by suits and silly hats, thanks to good separation of the different factions – we're assured that you could come here on a golfing or leisure break and be unaware of wedding parties. Bedrooms are decked out with confident colour schemes, big beds and glitzy white and chrome bathrooms.

○ Open all year ⚡ From A1, take A69 to Hexham; take slip road signposted Horsley and Ovingham; continue along B6318 and turn right at signpost for Matfen Hall. Private car park 🛏️ 1 single, 20 twin, 30 double, 2 four-poster; all with room service, hair-dryer, mini-bar; trouser press, direct-dial telephone, modem line, TV ✓ Restaurant, bar, conservatory, drawing room, garden; conferences; social functions; civil wedding licence; gym, health and beauty spa, golf; early suppers for children; cots, highchairs ♿ No wheelchair access ● No dogs in public rooms; no smoking in restaurant and some bedrooms ⬚ Amex, Diners, MasterCard, Switch, Visa £ Single occupancy of twin/double £102, twin/double £140, four-poster £235; deposit required. Set D £25; alc D £35; light meals available; service incl. Special breaks available

---

The text of the entries is based on inspections carried out anonymously, backed up by unsolicited reports sent in by readers. The factual details under the text are from questionnaires the Guide sends to all hotels that feature in the book.

If you have a small appetite, or just aren't feeling hungry, check if you can be given a reduction if you don't want the full menu. At some hotels you could easily end up paying £30 for one course and a coffee.

Red House Country Hotel

Old Road, Darley Dale, Matlock DE4 2ER
TEL: (01629) 734854   FAX: (01629) 734885
EMAIL: enquiries@theredhousecountryhotel.co.uk
WEB SITE: www.theredhousecountryhotel.co.uk

Relaxing base in the beautiful Derbyshire Dales

Situated just a few miles outside the attractive market town of Matlock, this late-nineteenth-century country house makes a convenient stopover from the M1 as well as an ideal base to explore the Peak District National Park. Inside, the house has an elegant, pleasantly formal feel. A comfortable lounge sporting a splendid local-stone fireplace makes an ideal spot for afternoon tea or for an aperitif before you move into the immaculately laid dining room, which enjoys charming views over the painstakingly pruned gardens. Bedrooms, divided between the main house and the coach house, tend to come with crisp white bed linen and be simply but smartly furnished, although the four-poster rooms and the one with a brass French bed are a little more flamboyant. A next-door Carriage Museum offers hire of a horse-drawn alternative for exploring the local lanes.

○ Closed first 2 weeks of Jan   ⊿ From M1 junction 28 follow signs to Matlock; take A6 to Bakewell, then after 2½ miles take second turning on right. Nearest train station: Matlock. Private car park   1 single, 1 twin, 1 twin/double, 5 double, 2 four-poster; all with room service, hair-dryer, direct-dial telephone, modem line, TV   Dining room, bar, 2 lounges, garden; conferences; social functions; leisure facilities nearby; early suppers for children   Wheelchair access to hotel and dining room, 3 ground-floor bedrooms   No dogs; no smoking   Delta, MasterCard, Switch, Visa   £ Single £60, single occupancy of twin/double £70, twin/double/four-poster £95; deposit required. Set D £23; light meals available; service incl. Special breaks available

Hodgkinson's

150 South Parade, Matlock Bath DE4 3NR
TEL: (01629) 582170   FAX: (01629) 584891
EMAIL: enquiries@hodgkinsons-hotel.co.uk
WEB SITE: www.hodgkinsons-hotel.co.uk

Revitalise yourself at this hotel in Derbyshire's own Little Switzerland

Whilst the town's spa facilities may no longer be on offer, you can still experience the luxury of a bygone era at this elegant Georgian town-house hotel. From the moment you set foot into the beautifully tiled hall, period character radiates at every turn, from the resplendent black marble fireplace in the lounge to the old adverts for soaps and steamers on the stairs. Gold-painted chairs add a touch of opulence in the pleasantly formal, pine-panelled dining room, an appropriate setting for chef and owner Antonio Carrieri's Italian menu. Just as much attention has been lavished on the handful of bedrooms, which tend to come with highly polished antique beds, attractive fireplaces, William Morris papers and appropriately chintzy fabrics. En suite facilities consist of showers rather than baths; the newly refurbished ones (such as Room 1) are worth asking for.

○ Closed 24 to 26 Dec; restaurant closed Sun eve   ⊿ In centre of Matlock Bath, on A6; hotel is on corner of South Parade and Waterloo Road. Nearest train station: Matlock Bath. Private car park   1 single, 1 twin, 6 double; all with direct-dial telephone, TV; hairdryer, iron, internet access available   Restaurant, bar, lounge, garden; conferences; social functions; leisure facilities nearby; early suppers for children; cots, highchairs, toys, baby-listening   No wheelchair access   No dogs in restaurant; no smoking in restaurant and some bedrooms   Amex, Delta, MasterCard, Switch, Visa   £ Single £40, single occupancy of twin/double £50 to £70, twin/double £100, family room £100; deposit required. Set D £16; alc L £12, D £28.50; light meals available; service incl. Special breaks available   (3 FOR 2)

MAWNAN SMITH Cornwall   map 1

Meudon Hotel

Mawnan Smith, Falmouth TR11 5HT
TEL: (01326) 250541   FAX: (01326) 250543
EMAIL: wecare@meudon.co.uk
WEB SITE: www.meudon.co.uk

Traditional English hotel with tropical gardens attached

The gardens of the Meudon Hotel run right down to the sea in a series of terraces, and harbour a surprisingly tropical variety of plant life. The hotel itself comprises a Victorian red-brick mansion with a series of modern extensions tacked on to the side. Inside, the décor is comfy in a worn-in, traditional sort of way, with portraits, squashy chairs, chandeliers and heavily patterned carpets. Bedrooms are similarly homely – ask for one with a refurbished bathroom. The menu at the restaurant doesn't stray too far from home, with the occasional foray on to the Continent complementing firmly British favourites like beef with Yorkshire pudding and honeyed chicken breast, with a good selection of Cornish cheeses available. The staff are friendly and mildly eccentric. Gentlemen are expected to don jacket and tie for dinner.

◗ Closed 1 to 31 Jan   ⊠ Leave A39 at Hillhead roundabout and follow signs to Maenporth (ignore signs to Mawnan Smith). Hotel is ½ mile past Maenporth beach, on left. Private car park   ⨺ 26 twin/double, 1 four-poster, 2 suites; family room available; all with room service, hair-dryer, direct-dial telephone, modem line, TV; some with trouser press, fax, VCR   ⨯ Restaurant/conservatory, bar, 3 lounges, games room, gardens, beach; conferences; social functions; leisure facilities nearby; early suppers for children; cots, highchairs, babysitting, baby-listening, outdoor play area   ⨨ Wheelchair access to hotel and restaurant (lift), WC, 15 ground-floor bedrooms, 3 rooms specially equipped for disabled people, lift. Disabled parking   ⬤ No dogs in public rooms, £7.50 per night in bedrooms; no smoking in restaurant   ⊟ Amex, Delta, Diners, MasterCard, Switch, Visa   £ Single occupancy of twin/double £85 to £125, twin/double £170 to £250, four-poster £205 to £285, family room £213 to £313, suite £250 to £330; deposit required. Set L £19, D £35; alc L £24, D £43; light meals available. Special breaks available

---

MELBOURN Cambridgeshire   map 6

Sheene Mill

30 Station Road, Melbourn SG8 6DX
TEL: (01763) 261393   FAX: (01763) 261376
EMAIL: info@sheenemill.co.uk
WEB SITE: www.sheenemill.co.uk

Celebrity cooking and décor to match

The front of this rambling whitewashed watermill lies right on the road, but out back you're treated to a rural idyll, with gardens looking out over a gentle patch of water with swans and ducks. What probably grabs most people's attention, though, at least at the outset, is the celebrity connection, which owner and TV chef Steven Saunders certainly isn't afraid to trumpet. So the reception features photos of various celeb mates having a good time, and there are plenty of his books on sale. Many of the bedrooms have been decorated by designer friends in very personal style. David Emanuel's suite simply can't be ignored: rugs (white), flouncy bed (white), Arabic-patterned wardrobe (white), original wood beams (er, white). Other rooms are more subtle. The food, of course, is another major draw, with the menu being described as Asian, Pacific, English and French. Steven and Sally Saunders are currently building a new spa (with champagne bar and 'retail outlet') across the road – to be run as a separate business.

◗ Closed 25 & 26 Dec & 1 Jan; restaurant closed Sun eve   ⊠ 8 miles south of Cambridge, off A10. Nearest train station: Meldreth. Private car park   ⨺ 1 single, 1 twin, 6 double, 1 suite; all with room service, hair-dryer, direct-dial telephone, modem line, TV   ⨯ Restaurant, bar, lounge, conservatory, garden; conferences; social functions; civil wedding licence; leisure facilities nearby; early suppers for children; highchairs   ⨨ No wheelchair access   ⬤ Smoking in bar only   ⊟ Amex, Delta, MasterCard, Switch, Visa   £ Single £80, single occupancy of twin/double £85, twin £85, double £95 to £130, suite £120 to £130; deposit required. Set L £18.50, D £30; alc D £35; light meals available

---

MELDRETH Cambridgeshire   map 6

Chiswick House

Meldreth, Royston SG8 6LZ
TEL: (01763) 260242
EMAIL: chiswickhouse@amserve.com

Sweet little farmhouse bursting with history

There's a feeling of comfortable domesticity to this fourteenth-century timbered house, probably in no small part attributable to the warm welcome of John and Bernice Elbourn. The Elbourn family has been here since 1898, not quite as long as some of the drawings on the old wood beams, reputed to be over 500 years old. The flowery rooms (in the main house and stable block) have been recently refitted, but care has been taken not to disturb the character of the building. King James I's royal crest can be found above the fireplace, and it's possible he used the place as a hunting lodge in the seventeenth century. The gardens, which you can enjoy from the terrace, are pretty and overflowing with colour.

◗ Closed Dec & Jan   ⤧ From A10, enter Meldreth village over railway bridge and fork left down Whitecroft Road to house. Nearest train station: Meldreth. Private car park 🅿 2 twin, 4 double; all with hairdryer; TV on request   ⟡ Dining room, drawing room, conservatory, garden ᕗ No wheelchair access, 2 steps into hotel, 4 ground-floor bedrooms ◖ No dogs in public rooms and some bedrooms; no smoking   None accepted   £ Single occupancy of twin/double £44, twin/double £52; deposit required

---

MELLOR Lancashire   map 8

Millstone Hotel

3 Church Lane, Mellor, Blackburn BB2 7JR
TEL: (01254) 813333   FAX: (01254) 812628
EMAIL: millstone@shirehotels.co.uk
WEB SITE: www.shirehotels.co.uk

Chain-owned roadside inn reliably catering for business and leisure travellers

The pleasant village of Mellor lies just off main roads, but this nineteenth-century coaching inn is handy enough to attract plenty of weekday passing trade on the Blackburn-Preston commuter run. It's a tidy-looking building in honey-coloured stone; a latter-day annexe of additional bedrooms lies across the car park. Bar-lounge areas ramble round the serving counter in a series of cosy fireside nooks, walls decked with china and pictures. There are newspapers to read, plus the odd stuffed fish to admire. The more formal oak-panelled restaurant is furnished with dignified tapestry-upholstered dining chairs, tables clad in white linen and good plain glass. Menus look appetisingly straightforward, supplemented by simple bar snacks and a decent range of bin ends. Bedrooms are pleasingly practical in dark-wood repro, with nicely framed prints, light fabrics and efficient little bathrooms. A refurbishment programme is in full swing; some badly stained bar furnishings looked about ready for the skip. More reports would be welcome.

◗ Open all year   ⤧ Leave M6 at Junction 31, following A677 towards Blackburn; take left turn signposted Mellor; hotel is at top of road on right. Private car park 🅿 3 twin, 21 twin/double; family rooms and suites available; all with room service, hair-dryer, trouser press, direct-dial telephone, modem line, TV   ⟡ Restaurant, bar, lounge; conferences and social functions; civil wedding licence; early suppers for children; cots, highchairs, baby-listening ᕗ Wheelchair access to hotel (ramp) and restaurant, 8 ground-floor bedrooms, 1 room specially equipped for disabled people. Disabled parking ◖ No dogs   Amex, Delta, Diners,

MasterCard, Switch, Visa £ Single occupancy of twin/double £48 to £98, twin/double £81 to £125, family room/suite £91 to £125; deposit required. Alc L £19.50, D £25; light meals available; service incl. Special breaks available 3FOR2

MELLOR BROOK Lancashire

map 8

Feilden's Arms NEW ENTRY

Whalley Road, Mellor Brook, Mellor, Blackburn BB2 7PR
TEL: (01254) 769010   FAX: (01254) 814671
EMAIL: kostasnigel@feildens.fsnet.co.uk
WEB SITE: www.feildensarms.co.uk

Lively dining pub serving outstanding cooking in a civilised but informal setting

Easy access to Lancashire's green heart (the Ribble Valley and Forest of Bowland) as well as the densely populated urban corridor of the M65 provide this admirable village hostelry with plenty of custom. It's especially busy at lunchtime, when owner-chef Nigel Smith's culinary team springs into action. Presentation, even of a simple steak-and-onion baguette, indicates precision and confidence in the kitchen, while service is friendly and assured. The pub's spacious interior around a long bar has been gutted, opened up and refurbished in a cottagey, rustic style of cherry-red walls, sporting prints and hop-strewn beams. One section is a quiet library zone of books and bygones; another a buzzy games room with an old-fashioned jukebox. The restaurant rooms are particularly attractive in warm, bright colours; one is a conservatory extension of wicker seating with blue-and-white pottery arrayed on ceiling-height dresser shelves. The smallish bedrooms are unluxurious, but light and agreeable.

◖ Open all year; restaurant closed Sun and Mon eves ⤴ From M6 junction 31 follow A59 (Clitheroe); pass British Aerospace on right; in approx 1 mile turn right at roundabout; bear left; hotel is on left. Private car park ⤓ 1 twin, 3 double; all with hair-dryer, direct-dial telephone, TV ⊘ Restaurant, bar, games room; social functions; highchairs & No wheelchair access ● Dogs in bar only; smoking in public rooms only ▭ Amex, Delta, Diners, MasterCard, Switch, Visa £ Single occupancy of twin/double £48, twin/double £58. Alc L £22, D £25; light meals available; service incl

---

MEMBURY Devon

map 2

Oxenways

Membury, Axminster EX13 7JR
TEL: (01404) 881785   FAX: (01404) 881778
EMAIL: info@oxenways.com
WEB SITE: www.oxenways.com

House-party atmosphere at this equine-oriented establishment

It would be wrong to pigeonhole Ken and Sheila Beecham's place as purely for horsey types – many visitors come for the beautiful surrounding countryside and the sociable nature of the house. Horses, however, are the Beechams' passion: they keep 15 North American specimens and teach the Western method of riding (apparently that doesn't entail firing a Colt 45 at pursuers). The full board package includes the lessons. With 70 acres of gardens and land to use, there is plenty of scope for strolls on foot or on hoof. More entertainment is on hand inside the immaculately well-kept Edwardian house with a hot tub in the conservatory, and a games room. On selected 'dining evenings', things start with drinks in the conservatory, then dinner *en famille* around a single table, before coffee in the lounge. On other nights you need to head for Axminster, which is four miles away. Bedrooms are deliciously luxurious and have superb bathrooms.

◖ Open all year; dining room open some weekends ⤴ From A358 Chard to Axminster road, turn right towards Smallridge; hotel is 2 miles beyond Smallridge, on right. Private car park ⤓ 4 suites; all with hair-dryer; TV, direct-dial telephone, fax, modem line, VCR available; no tea/coffee-making facilities in rooms ⊘ Dining room, bar, lounge, library, conservatory, games room, garden; social functions, civil wedding licence;

gym, spa; leisure facilities nearby   & No wheelchair access   ● No children; no dogs; no smoking   ▭ MasterCard, Switch, Visa   [£] Single occupancy of suite £110 to £155, suite £145 to £170; deposit required. Set L £19, D £29.50; service incl. Special breaks available

---

MEVAGISSEY Cornwall   map 1

Trevalsa Court NEW ENTRY

School Hill, Mevagissey PL26 6TH
TEL: (01726) 842468 FAX: (01726) 844482
EMAIL: stay@cornwall-hotel.net
WEB SITE: www.cornwall-hotel.net

Friendly hotel with bags of style

'The Italians think the Germans have no style. They're wrong,' reads an entry in the Trevalsa Court guest book. Owner Klaus Wagner had always dreamt of owning and running a hotel, and when a deal on his dream property in St Tropez fell through he decided to look to Cornwall. What he found was this rather special little place packed full of interesting features which, though not all belonging to the original building, had been brought together to create a unique ambience. Klaus and friends set about modernising without spoiling, and have created a cosy but luxurious hotel with an eclectic interior décor. Wood-panelled walls in the restaurant and thick stone window frames are teamed with a mixture of antique and contemporary furnishings (ironically, including many imported from Italy). Each bedroom is individually decorated in a similar tasteful style and most have sea views – though you might want to try to get one with a recently refurbished bathroom, as not all have been completed yet.

◐ Closed Dec & Jan; restaurant closed Sun and Mon eves   ⊿ From St Austell, take B3273 towards Mevagissey for 5½ miles; past beach caravan park, turn left at top of hill, go over mini-roundabout; hotel is on left. Private car park 🅿 2 single, 2 twin, 8 double, 2 suites; all with room service, hair-dryer, TV; 2 with CD player ✓ Restaurant, bar, lounge, garden, terrace; conferences; civil wedding licence; leisure facilities nearby & No wheelchair access   ● No children under 12; no dogs; smoking in bar only   ▭ Amex, MasterCard, Switch, Visa   [£] Single £50 to £70, single occupancy of twin/double £70 to £110, twin/double £80 to £140, suite £130 to £165; deposit required. Set D £27; alc D from £21; light meals available; service incl. Special breaks available.

MICKLETON Gloucestershire   map 5

Three Ways House

Chapel Lane, Mickleton, Chipping Campden GL55 6SB
TEL: (01386) 438429 FAX: (01386) 438118
EMAIL: threeways@puddingclub.com
WEB SITE: www.puddingclub.com

A hotel with class and a delicious sense of humour

All is not what it seems within the portals of this distinguished-looking Cotswold hotel – if things are beginning to look sticky it's because 2005 is the twentieth anniversary of the Pudding Club, hosted by the Three Ways House, and celebrations of the most appetising kind are on the menu. Yes, this is a hotel with a delicious sense of humour. Five tasty-looking rooms have been dedicated to the glory of the pudding: Spotted Dick and Custard, for example, has custard-coloured walls, polka-dot fabrics and as its *pièce de résistance* a kitchen cupboard that opens to reveal bunk beds rather than utensils, Summer Pudding is in yellow and orange with delicate *trompe l'oeil* sprays of summer flowers around the walls, and Sticky Toffee and Date is probably best left to the imagination. In contrast to the whimsical décor, Peter Henderson and Simon Coombe, while not lacking in a pleasing sense of the absurd, take their roles as hosts seriously and standards are high.

◗ Open all year 🔟 Mickleton village is on B4632, about 7 miles south of Stratford-upon-Avon. Nearest train station: Honeybourne. Private car park 🛏️ 2 single, 20 twin, 24 double, 2 family rooms; all with room service, hair-dryer, direct-dial telephone, modem line, TV; some with CD player ✍️ Restaurant, bar, lounge, garden; conferences, social functions; civil wedding licence; leisure facilities nearby; early suppers for children; cots, highchairs, baby-listening 🦽 Wheelchair access to hotel (ramp) and restaurant, lift, 14 ground-floor bedrooms, 1 room specially equipped for disabled people ● No smoking in restaurant ═ Amex, Delta, Diners, MasterCard, Switch, Visa ⌐£⌐ Single £72, single occupancy of twin/double £85, twin/double £115 to £140, family room £135; deposit required. Set L £17, D £28.50; light meals available; service incl. Special breaks available ⒊ꜰᴏʀ⒉

MIDDLE WINTERSLOW Wiltshire   map 2

The Beadles

Middleton, Middle Winterslow, Salisbury SP5 1QS
TEL: (01980) 862922   FAX: (01980) 863565
EMAIL: winterbead@aol.com
WEB SITE: www.guestaccom.co.uk/754.htm

Well-kept guesthouse with friendly hosts and good location

Tucked away in a corner of a small village on the southern skirts of Salisbury Plain is Anne and David Yuille-Baddeley's modern Georgian-style house along with their impressive collection of ornaments, pictures and curiosities. This is a house where sociability and conversation are welcomed so it's handy to have so many items that might trigger a chat. There's a comfortable lounge, decked profusely with porcelain, clocks and candlesticks, plus a piano, then a hexagonal conservatory overlooking the lawned garden. Here they keep hens, ducks and geese, all of whom lay for the breakfast table (but the geese are a bit temperamental and the chickens do disappear with the fox occasionally). Anne is a Cordon Bleu cook and does evening meals by arrangement as well as lavish breakfasts – kippers, haddock, porridge and fresh fruit alongside the usual cooked alternatives. Bedrooms are prettily decorated with excellent bathrooms and, of course, plenty of ornaments. 'Exceptional hosts, high-class cooking and pleasant rooms,' wrote one happy correspondent.

◗ Closed New Year; dining room closed Sun, Mon eves 🔟 Turn off A30 at the Pheasant to Middle Winterslow; in village, take first right to West Winterslow, bear right at end of road and then first right up drive after 'Trevano'. Private car park 🛏️ 1 twin, 1 twin/double, 1 double; all with hair-dryer, direct-dial telephone, TV ✍️ Dining room, lounge, conservatory, garden; social functions 🦽 No wheelchair access ● No children under 14; no dogs; no smoking ═ Delta, MasterCard, Visa ⌐£⌐ Single occupancy of twin/double £40 to £45, twin/double £60 to £65; deposit required. Set D £25.50; light meals available; service incl

---

MIDHURST West Sussex   map 3

Angel Hotel

North Street, Midhurst GU29 9DN
TEL: (01730) 812421   FAX: (01730) 815928
EMAIL: info@theangelmidhurst.co.uk
WEB SITE: www.theangelmidhurst.co.uk

Refurbished hotel close to the haunting ruins of Cowdray

Right in the centre of this bustling old market town, the Angel is easy to spot among the shops and townhouses of busy North Street. Disguising a building of Tudor origins, its elegant white Georgian frontage with smart red detailing appears recently made over, a sign that new owners Ian Webb and John Cooper are making their mark on the place. The Tardis-like interior is similarly spruce and though the residents' lounge has been downsized to make way for the Halo bar and brasserie, it remains a cosy and comfortable space in which to relax or mull over the dinner menu. Diners can choose between the contemporary Halo with its range of pastas, steaks, sizzling wok dishes and upmarket burgers, or the more formal Gabriel's restaurant. Inevitably rooms with the most character are those in the oldest part of the hotel – reached off a wood-panelled landing with uneven creaky floorboards – though all are thoughtfully planned, comfortable and tastefully decked out, perhaps with neutral carpets, stripey walls and toile de Jouy fabrics. Given the central, high street position, traffic noise is to be expected.

● Open all year ⚡ In Midhurst's main street. Private car park 🚗 4 single, 1 twin, 9 twin/double, 11 double, 3 four-poster; all with room service, hair-dryer, direct-dial telephone, TV; some with modem line ⚥ Restaurant, brasserie, bar, lounge, garden; conferences and social functions; civil wedding licence; leisure facilities nearby; early suppers for children; cots, highchairs ♿ Wheelchair access to hotel and restaurant, 2 ground-floor bedrooms, 1 room specially equipped for disabled people ● No children in restaurant after 9pm; no dogs in public rooms, £5 per night in bedrooms; smoking in lounge bar only ▭ Amex, Delta, Diners, MasterCard, Switch, Visa £ Single £80, twin/double £110, four-poster £150; deposit required. Set L £20, D £25; light meals available. Special breaks available (3FOR2)

Spread Eagle

South Street, Midhurst GU29 9NH
TEL: (01730) 816911   FAX: (01730) 815668
EMAIL: spreadeagle@hshotels.co.uk
WEB SITE: www.hshotels.co.uk

A creaking, ancient hotel with an up-to-the-minute health spa

Some things just never change, and one of the main reasons for coming to the Spread Eagle is to steep yourself in the historic atmosphere of this fascinating museum piece, a comfortably former coaching inn with values to match. The oldest parts of the hotel are a visual treat, with low beams and uneven floors keeping you on your guard. The core of the original fifteenth-century tavern continues to function as the main bar lounge, which, with its open fireplaces, comfortable leather sofas and creaking floors scattered with rugs, is a popular refuge, while upstairs the magnificent residents' room is similarly ancient with leaded windows, exposed timbers and ivy growing through the ceiling (it's been there for so long that nobody now dares pull it out). Bringing the hotel screeching into the twenty-first century, however, are the leisure facilities, which include a pool, sauna, hot tub and gym. Bedrooms, too, have all the mod cons you might expect but remain fairly traditional. Characterful feature rooms have a distinct edge; of the others, it's worth upgrading from a traditional to a superior for more space and a decent-sized bathroom.

● Open all year ⚡ In Midhurst, by market square in old part of town. Private car park 🚗 13 twin/double, 18 double, 5 four-poster, 3 suites; all with room service, hair-dryer, direct-dial telephone, modem line, TV; some with trouser press ⚥ Restaurant, bar, lounge, conservatory, garden; conferences and social functions; civil wedding licence; gym, spa, heated indoor swimming pool; leisure facilities nearby; early suppers for children; cots, highchairs, baby-listening ♿ No wheelchair access; 8 ground-floor bedrooms ● No smoking in restaurant and some bedrooms ▭ Amex, Delta, Diners, MasterCard, Switch, Visa £ Single occupancy of twin/double £85 to £140, twin/double £99 to £165, four-poster/suite £225 (2004 prices); deposit required. Set L £18.50, D £35; alc L, D £40; light meals available. Special breaks available (3FOR2)

MILBORNE PORT Somerset	map 2

Old Vicarage

Sherborne Road, Milborne Port, Nr Sherborne DT9 5AT
TEL: (01963) 251117   FAX: (01963) 251515
EMAIL: theoldvicarage@milborneport.freeserve.co.uk
WEB SITE: www.milborneport.freeserve.co.uk

Good food and imaginative décor

Dominating the sleepy village of Milborne Port are the towering chimneys and façade of this imposing Victorian building. Not that there is anything stern or Victorian about the way Jörgen Kunath and Anthony Ma have decorated the place. Antiques and curios from around the world, particularly South-East Asia, are to be found throughout, and these work well against the background of bare stonework, modern colour schemes and period furniture. The lounge has deep armchairs, sofas and an open fire, plus views to the lawns and ornamental pond. The cooking is a highlight here: the Old Vicarage has an excellent reputation for bright, modern cuisine suffused with a little Asian influence. Note that dinner is served only on Fridays and Saturdays. Bedrooms in the main house take Indian or Chinese themes and are lovely. Over in the coach house are more rooms, one of which has recently been doubled in size with a split-level loft conversion.

Closed 1 week in Sept, all Jan; dining room closed Sun to Thur ⚡ 2 miles east of Sherborne, off A30 at western end of Milborne Port. Nearest train station: Sherborne. Private car park 🚗 2 twin, 3 double, 1 family room; all with hair-dryer, direct-dial telephone, TV ⚒ Dining room/conservatory, bar/lounge, garden ♿ No wheelchair access; 5 steps into hotel, 3 ground-floor bedrooms, 1 room partially equipped for disabled people ⬤ No children under 5; no dogs in public rooms and some bedrooms ▭ Amex, Delta, MasterCard, Switch, Visa £ Single occupancy of twin/double £57 to £78, twin/double £70 to £102, family room £86 to £128; deposit required. Set D £27. Special breaks available

---

MINCHINHAMPTON Gloucestershire   map 2

Burleigh Court Hotel [NEW ENTRY]

Burleigh, Minchinhampton GL5 2PF
TEL: (01453) 883804   FAX: (01453) 886870
EMAIL: info@burleighcourthotel.co.uk
WEB SITE: www.burleighcourthotel.co.uk

A fine house and gardens complemented by smart décor

Perched on the steep slopes of the Cotswold ridge, with views across the Golden Valley, this is one of the finest Georgian mansions in the area and dates back to 1800. The Noble family has owned it for only a short time but those running it have been quick to improve things and yet keep a sense of history about the place. Creamy sofas contrast with pale blue curtains in the corner lounge, while there is a clubby feel in the wood-panelled bar, with its deep, rich-red sofas. The dining room has a striking purple colour scheme and a light, airy feel enhanced by the French windows that lead out to the terraced gardens. In the 1930s the house was purchased by Sir Guy Granet and it's still possible to see the servant-paging system in the hallway, with a buzzer for 'Sir Guy's bathroom'. It was he who employed Clough Williams-Ellis to redesign the garden and install a heated outdoor pool that is still in use today. Bedrooms are prettily decorated and of a good size with smart bathrooms. The Coach House rooms, close to the pool, have a more secluded feel.

Closed Chr ⚡ Leave Stroud on A419, heading towards Cirencester; 2½ miles outside Stroud take a right turn, which is signposted Burleigh and Minchinhampton. Go up the side of the hill, after 500 yards take sharp left turn, signposted Burleigh Court. Take left turn and hotel is on the right after 300 yards. Private car park. Nearest train station: Stroud 🚗 14 twin/double, 2 family rooms, 2 suites; all with room service, hair-dryer, direct-dial telephone, TV, VCR ⚒ Restaurant, dining room, bar, lounge, garden; conferences; civil wedding licence; social functions; heated outdoor swimming pool; leisure facilities nearby; early suppers for children, cots, highchairs, toys, baby-listening ♿ Wheelchair access to hotel (ramp) and restaurant, WC, 2 ground-floor bedrooms ⬤ No dogs in some bedrooms; no smoking in dining room ▭ Diners, MasterCard, Switch, Visa £ Single occupancy of twin/double £80 to £90, twin/double £105 to £125, family room/suite £145. Set L £18, D £26.50; light meals available; service incl. Special breaks available

---

Hunters Lodge

Dr Brown's Road, Minchinhampton, Stroud GL6 9BT
TEL: (01453) 883588   FAX: (01453) 731449
EMAIL: hunterslodge@hotmail.com

A classic Cotswold home and B&B with scintillating gardens

You will find Hunters Lodge 650 feet up, on a ridge of the south Cotswolds, just off the wide open spaces of Minchinhampton Common. A busy road runs nearby, but once you're through the door, this impressive Cotswold stone house exudes its own wonderful oasis of calm. Peter and Margaret Helm's gracious and much-loved family home has acquired family mementoes and pleasing antiques through the years, many of which can be seen in the lounge, against a backdrop of the showpiece gardens outside. These have mature trees, pretty borders and sleek lawns as well as a small reed-filled water feature. You are welcome to wander in them, or on chilly days, just relax in a bamboo chair in the modern conservatory and take in the view.

Bedrooms are spacious and comfy with simple colour schemes and chintzy furnishings. During breakfast, served around a solid polished dining table, you can consult Peter on the forthcoming day's itinerary, as he is an official Gloucestershire tourist guide.

❍ Closed Chr 🚗 Turn off A419 at Brimscombe, signposted to Minchinhampton and Burleigh; follow this road to open common at top of hill; turn left at T-junction and take second right into Dr Brown's Road. Private car park 🅿️ 2 twin/double, 1 family room; all with hair-dryer, TV ⌀ Dining room, lounge, conservatory, garden; leisure facilities nearby ♿ No wheelchair access ● No children under 10; no smoking ▭ None accepted £ Single occupancy of twin/double £35 to £40, twin/double £50 to £55, family room £70; deposit required

---

MOBBERLEY Cheshire map 8

Laburnum Cottage

Knutsford Road, Mobberley, Knutsford WA16 7PU
TEL: (01565) 872464 (AND FAX)

Neat, family-run guesthouse offering excellent value in a much-travelled part of Cheshire

Laburnum Cottage looks a modest property from the busy road between Knutsford and Mobberley (a well-used commuter route), but appearances are deceptive. The house extends into a sizeable conservatory to the rear, overlooking ample, well-kept gardens and an elaborate water feature. Rod and Carmen Messenger have run this useful little business for many years, steadily building up a solid reputation and a regular client base, including some weekday women business travellers. The interior is cosily homely, featuring lots of plants, photos and ornaments. Rod cooks tasty evening meals on request, which are excellent value (you might be offered toasted goat's cheese and a simple roast, with apple pie to follow). A glass of wine is proffered (though there's no licence). The tidy little bedrooms are fresh and clean in floral pastels. Largest, with a private bath, is Room 5, but ask for a rear room if you're a light sleeper.

❍ Open all year 🚗 On B5085, 1 mile from Knutsford. Nearest train station: Knutsford. Private car park 🅿️ 2 single, 2 twin, 1 double; all with hair-dryer, TV ⌀ Dining room, sitting room, conservatory, garden; social functions; early suppers for children; cots ♿ No wheelchair access; 1 step into hotel, 1 ground-floor bedroom ● Dogs by arrangement only; smoking only in annexe ▭ Amex, Delta, MasterCard, Switch, Visa £ Single £44, single occupancy of twin/double £44, twin/double £57; deposit required. Set D £14; light meals available; service incl

---

MORETON Oxfordshire map 2

The Dairy

Moreton, Nr Thame, Oxford OX9 2HX
TEL: (01844) 214075 (AND FAX)
EMAIL: thedairy@freeuk.com
WEB SITE: www.thedairy.freeuk.com

Tranquil surroundings and comfortable lodging in a welcoming B&B

The long, sweeping gravel drive leads you to a dark-timber, low-slung building that wouldn't look out of place on a prairie ranch but equally seems in complete harmony with the green fields of this bucolic corner of Oxfordshire. In its former life this was a milking parlour, but Peter Cole has successfully transformed it into a welcoming, relaxing B&B that offers a quiet night's rest to tourists and business travellers alike – the M40 is just a few miles away. High, A-frame beams and light streaming in give the barn-like central room an added feeling of space, so that the long, polished pine table that hosts communal breakfasts actually seems rather small. With the open-plan kitchen, a forest of foliage, wood floors and some comfy sofas, Peter's design for the interior has a stylish but informal air that is replicated in the three ground-floor bedrooms. Each offers a modern take on country living with exposed brick walls, brass bedsteads, old-wood furniture and big, mirrored wardrobes. Room 3 opens out onto a sweet patio, though with camping and caravans permitted in the small back garden, you might lack privacy.

◗ Open all year ⚡ Turn off A329 to Moreton; turn left at war memorial; hotel is 150 metres on left. Private car park 🛏 3 double; all with hair-dryer, TV; trouser press available ✅ Breakfast room, lounge, gardens ♿ No wheelchair access; 2 steps into hotel, 3 ground-floor bedrooms ● No children under 12; no dogs; no smoking ▭ Amex, MasterCard, Visa £ Single occupancy of double £65, double £89; deposit required

---

MORSTON Norfolk   map 6

Morston Hall

Morston, Holt NR25 7AA
TEL: (01263) 741041 FAX: (01263) 740419
EMAIL: reception@morstonhall.com
WEB SITE: www.morstonhall.com

Leading light on the Norfolk food scene

It's food first at Morston Hall – even the brochure features a sample recipe (for a rather nice-looking summer pudding) from Galton Blackiston's house cookbook. Delia has used his recipes in her books too – high praise indeed! The building is a classic example of a Norfolk brick-and-flint country house dating back to Jacobean times. Public rooms are well kept and quite grand, though not necessarily design-matched. All the rooms are named after Norfolk country houses and are for the most part spacious and comfortable. The more recently refurbished rooms are best, with cleaner, paler colours – some of the others are starting to look a little dated in places.

◗ Closed Jan ⚡ On A149, 2 miles west of Blakeney. Private car park 🛏 1 twin, 5 double, 1 suite; all with room service, hair-dryer, direct-dial telephone, TV, VCR, DVD, CD player ✅ Restaurant, 2 lounges, conservatory, garden; conferences and social functions; leisure facilities nearby; early suppers for children; cots, highchairs, toys, babysitting, baby-listening ♿ Wheelchair access to hotel (ramp) and restaurant, WC, 1 ground-floor bedroom ● No dogs in public rooms; no smoking in restaurant ▭ Amex, Delta, Diners, MasterCard, Switch, Visa £ Single occupancy of twin/double £145, twin/double/suite £240 to £250 (rates incl dinner); deposit required. Set L £26; light meals available. Special breaks available

---

MORTEHOE Devon   map 1

Cleeve House Hotel

North Morte Road, Mortehoe, Woolacombe EX34 7ED
TEL: (01271) 870719
EMAIL: info@cleevehouse.co.uk
WEB SITE: www.cleevehouse.co.uk

Friendly and homely coastal hotel with high standards

Mortehoe is a pretty village at the top of the hill above Woolacombe, and Anne and David Strobel's rather unprepossessing house is tucked off the main road. If the house looks a bit bland, remember that it is the Strobels' dedicated hospitality that makes the place tick. They bring bags of good humour and thoughtful care to proceedings. What is more, they are always searching for improvements, the latest being a plan to enlarge the dining room. There is a brace of comfortable lounges with pine furniture, and the dining room is neat and simple. David is the chef, putting together a country-house type of menu; breakfasts are memorable with home-laid eggs, home-made bread and muesli, plus lots of choices such as eggy bread and West Country kippers. Bedrooms are bright and cheerful with pine furniture and immaculate bathrooms.

● Closed Oct to Mar; dining room closed Wed eve, and 21 Jul to 31 Aug ⤵ Leave Barnstaple on westbound A361; at Mullacott Cross turn left on to B3343; Mortehoe is 2 miles further on; turn right at Power garage; hotel is 50 yards on left. Private car park 🛏 1 twin, 1 twin/double, 3 double, 1 family room; all with room service, hair-dryer, TV ◈ Dining room, bar, 2 lounges, garden; golf nearby ♿ Wheelchair access to hotel (ramp) and dining room, WC, 1 ground-floor bedroom, specially equipped for disabled people. Disabled parking ● No children under 12; no dogs; smoking in bar only ▭ Delta, MasterCard, Switch, Visa £ Single occupancy of twin/double £46 to £48, twin/double £68 to £72, family room £85 to £90; deposit required. Set D £20; service incl. Special breaks available

---

MOULSFORD Oxfordshire

map 2

Beetle & Wedge

Ferry Lane, Moulsford, Wallingford OX10 9JF
TEL: (01491) 651381   FAX: (01491) 651376
EMAIL: kate@beetleandwedge.co.uk
WEB SITE: www.beetleandwedge.co.uk

A riverside setting adds something extra to an already special hotel

With the Thames gliding blissfully past, there are few more delightful places along the river's banks than the Water Garden of this special little hotel. You can just imagine Jerome K. Jerome, a former resident, lingering here, mulling over the fate that should befall his three men and their boat. To sit out beside the water, enjoying an early evening drink, is the perfect prelude to a memorable meal in the elegant conservatory dining room. This extends out from the comfy, cosy lounge with its wood-panelled walls and squishy sofas. A less formal venue, the Boathouse, which lies across the drive, was being extensively remodelled and expanded when we inspected (and is expected to be open by the time you read this). Upstairs in the wisteria-clad main building are the well-appointed bedrooms, some of which benefit from river views. Good-quality furniture and tasteful colour schemes that mix greens, creams, blues and yellows make them a delight, while free-standing baths are the highlight of every bathroom.

● Open all year; dining room closed some eves (Boathouse open) ⤵ In Moulsford turn towards river via Ferry Lane. Nearest train stations: Goring, Streatley. Private car park 🛏 5 twin/double, 5 double; family room available; all with limited room service, hair-dryer, direct-dial telephone, modem line, TV ◈ 2 restaurants, bar, lounge, garden; conferences and social functions; leisure facilities nearby; early suppers for children; cots, highchairs, babysitting, baby-listening, outdoor play area ♿ Wheelchair access to hotel and restaurants, WC, 2 ground-floor bedrooms ● No dogs in public rooms and some bedrooms; no smoking in bedrooms and some public rooms ▭ Amex, Delta, Diners, MasterCard, Switch, Visa £ Single occupancy of twin/double £135, twin/double £175; family room £200. Set L, D £37.50; alc L, D £35; light meals available. Special breaks available

---

MUDDIFORD Devon

map 1

Broomhill Art Hotel

Muddiford, Barnstaple EX31 4EX
TEL: (01271) 850262   FAX: (01271) 850575
EMAIL: info@broomhillart.co.uk
WEB SITE: www.broomhillart.co.uk

Idiosyncratic country hotel run with flair and friendliness

It must be one of the most unusual hotel driveways: a quarter mile of track winding down, then up, through the woods past fantastical constructions, a giant red stiletto and any number of other weird but wonderful sculptures. Rinus and Aniet van de Sande's hotel sets out to offer decent rooms, good food and highly interesting surroundings. They succeed with ease on the latter two, but the rooms could do with more attention. Furniture is serviceable pine, there is plenty of hot water and everything is scrupulously clean. However, bare lightbulbs in bathrooms, no shampoo and a clapped-out television, as our inspector found, might not suit everyone. So much for the drawbacks, but the plus points are significant. Food is excellent and the dining room lovely. Across the hall – well-stocked with newspapers – is a fascinating art gallery which, in a very real sense, continues outside in the woods. No matter if you dislike modern sculpture, this place will give much to think about and challenge preconceptions.

○ Open all year; dining room closed Sun to Wed eves ⊿ From M5 Junction 27, take A361 to Barnstaple then B3230 to Ilfracombe; Broomhill is signposted on left. Nearest train station: Barnstaple. Private car park ⊨ 1 twin, 4 double, 1 family room; all with direct-dial telephone, TV ⊘ Dining room, bar, 2 lounges, study, garden; conferences; social functions; tennis, heated outdoor swimming pool; leisure facilities nearby; early suppers for children; cots, highchairs, baby-listening ♿ No wheelchair access ● No children under 12 in dining room eves; no dogs; no smoking in bedrooms ▭ MasterCard, Visa £ Single occupancy of twin/double £33 to £38, twin/double £55 to £65, family room £65 to £75; deposit required. Set L £12.50, D £18; light meals available; service incl

MULLION Cornwall   map 1

Polurrian Hotel

Mullion, Helston TR12 7EN
TEL: (01326) 240421 FAX: (01326) 240083
EMAIL: polurotel@aol.com
WEB SITE: www.polurrianhotel.com

Traditional family holidays on offer in a spectacular location

The Polurrian's location encapsulates all that's appealing about Cornwall. Perched at the top of 300-foot cliffs, it's dramatic, windswept and romantic. The building is a large Edwardian pile rebuilt on the site of the original 1904 hotel, which burned down shortly after a visit from Winston Churchill. The dining room is smart, in creams and yellows, with gorgeous views, and the lounge has also recently been refurbished. Leisure facilities, including pool and squash courts, continue to expand, with some new additions in the gym, and there's plenty on offer for the kids such as high teas, videos, and mountain bike and wet-suit hire. Rooms are simple and straightforward with few frills – the nicest are on the top floor, and the even-numbered ones have sea views.

○ Open all year ⊿ Mullion is signposted from A3083 at Penhale, between Helston and the Lizard. Private car park ⊨ 1 single, 6 twin, 18 double, 3 four-poster, 10 family rooms, 1 suite; all with room service, hair-dryer, direct-dial telephone, TV; some with trouser press ⊘ Restaurant, 2 bars, 3 lounges, study, 2 games rooms, garden; conferences; social functions; civil wedding licence; gym, spa, heated indoor and outdoor swimming pools, tennis, leisure facilities nearby; early suppers for children; cots, highchairs, toys, playrooms, babysitting, baby-listening, outdoor play area ♿ Wheelchair access to hotel and restaurant, WC, 8 ground-floor bedrooms. Disabled parking ● Dogs £6 per night; no smoking in some public rooms and some bedrooms ▭ Amex, Delta, Diners, MasterCard, Switch, Visa £ Single £64 to £130, twin/double/four-poster £128 to £260, family room from £128, suite £153 to £285 (rates incl dinner); deposit required. Set L £10 (prices valid till Dec 2004). Special breaks available

MUNGRISDALE Cumbria   map 10

Mill Hotel

Mungrisdale, Penrith CA11 0XR
TEL: (017687) 79659 FAX: (017687) 79155
EMAIL: quinlan@evemail.net
WEB SITE: www.themillhotel.com

Small hotel-restaurant unobtrusively set in the northern fells

Richard and Eleanor Quinlan have been offering their well-honed style of dinner, bed and breakfast at this white-painted seventeenth-century mill cottage for many years now. Satisfied visitors return for repeat helpings of their thoughtful hospitality, not to mention Eleanor's splendid five-course dinners (choice is limited; imagination runs free). It isn't a grand place; the clematis-clad exterior is simple and tucked almost invisibly behind its confusingly named neighbour, the Mill Inn. But the surroundings are glorious – a backdrop of high fells shouldering into the skyline, and a mare's-tail stream leaping through a fern-filled gully. The interior is small-scale and homely: chintzy lounges piled high with enticing books, and a simple, intimate restaurant of wheelback chairs, each polished table attentively set with flowers and candles. Richard is an avid collector of paintings and antiques, and an amateur artist too. Bedrooms are restfully understated in muted colours with lots of personal touches.

① Closed 1 Nov to 1 March 🔁 2 miles north of A66, midway between Penrith and Keswick. Private car park 🛏 3 twin, 1 twin/double, 5 double, 2 with shared bathroom; all with room service, hair-dryer, TV ✅ Restaurant, 2 lounges, conservatory, garden; early suppers for children; cots, highchairs, baby-listening ♿ No wheelchair access; 9 steps into hotel, 1 step into restaurant, 2 ground-floor bedrooms ● No dogs in public rooms; no smoking in restaurant ▭ None accepted £ Single occupancy of twin/double £35 to £55, twin/double £70 to £110. Set D £32; light meals available (3 FOR 2)

NANTWICH Cheshire   map 7

Curshaws at the Cat [NEW ENTRY]

26 Welsh Row, Nantwich CW5 5ED
TEL: (01270) 623020   FAX: (01270) 613350
EMAIL: kathy@curshaws.com
WEB SITE: www.curshaws.com

Black-and-white property transformed into a design-led restaurant-with-rooms

This quaint row of seventeenth-century cottages, in Cheshire 'magpie' timbering, has had a chequered history: it once housed a nightclub of dubious repute, and was latterly left derelict. Now imaginatively refurbished by entrepreneurial restaurateurs, the establishment has taken on a new lease of life. The original street-side complex contains a chic split-level bar-brasserie serving modern European grazing food of the tapas and chips variety. Downstairs is a wine bar, all tub chairs and angular banquette seating in dark leather; upstairs lies a streamlined restaurant in black, chrome and beechwood furnishings beneath pitched rafters. Service is amiably erratic. The ambience is predictably youthful; sound levels rise as crowds pour in. Beyond the glazed rear walls extends a heated, furnished courtyard and a purpose-built accommodation wing housing sleek, fashionably minimalist bedrooms (lightwood surfaces, recessed spotlights, neutral fabrics splashed with colour). Best is the Octagon Room (bed-foot Jacuzzi, 40-inch plasma TV and DVD player).

① Closed 24 & 25 Dec 🔁 Leave M6 at junction 15 and follow signs to Nantwich; pass Safeway on right, straight across roundabout, left at next lights and left again into car park. Nearest train station: Nantwich. Private car park 🛏 3 twin/double, 7 double, 1 suite; family rooms available; all with room service, hair-dryer, mini-bar, trouser press, direct-dial telephone, modem line, TV; 1 with VCR, CD player, DVD ✅ Restaurant, bar-brasserie, wine bar, conservatory, patio/terrace; conferences; social functions; leisure facilities nearby; early suppers for children; cots, highchairs ♿ No wheelchair access ● No children in restaurant eves; no dogs in public rooms; no smoking in restaurant and some bedrooms ▭ Amex, Delta, Diners, MasterCard, Switch, Visa £ Single occupancy of twin/double £50 to £85, twin/double £70 to £105, family room £105, suite £170; deposit required. Alc L, D £30; light meals available; service incl

---

NAYLAND Suffolk   map 6

White Hart

11 High Street, Nayland, Colchester CO6 4JF
TEL: (01206) 263382   FAX: (01206) 263638
EMAIL: nayhart@aol.com
WEB SITE: www.whitehart-nayland.co.uk

French style in English packaging

Bang in the middle of the implausibly sweet Suffolk village of Nayland, with rickety beamed houses and pastel-coloured cottages all around, the White Hart looks like a whitewashed traditional English country inn. But step inside and you'll find yourself transported right across the Channel, as the décor and menu have been given a thoroughly French polish by Frank Deletang and Karine Bordas. The original wonky timber beams remain, but the colour schemes are modern and bold, with yellow walls and terracotta-coloured tiles on the floors in the downstairs bar/restaurant area.

A glass cutaway in the floor reveals the cellar below the dining room. Traditional dishes are given a contemporary presentation: melt-in-the-mouth suckling pig with Calvados sauce might be served on lightly spiced greens. Service is professional and courteous without being obsequious. The bedrooms follow a similar decorative scheme with bold colours and many original features such as frescoes on the walls.

● Closed 26 Dec to 9 Jan ▣ In village of Nayland; turn off A134 on to B1087 between Colchester and Sudbury. Private car park ⬅ 1 twin, 5 double; family rooms available; all with hair-dryer, trouser press, direct-dial telephone, modem line, TV ✅ Restaurant, terrace, garden; conferences; social functions; civil wedding licence; leisure facilities nearby; early suppers for children; cots, highchairs ♿ No wheelchair access ● No dogs; no smoking in bedrooms ▭ Amex, Delta, Diners, MasterCard, Switch, Visa £ Single occupancy of twin/double £69 to £75, twin/double £82 to £95, family room £112 to £125; deposit required. Set L £13, D £21.50; alc L £19, D £26; light meals available. Special breaks available (3FOR2)

Buckle Yeat

Near Sawrey, Hawkshead, Ambleside LA22 0LF
TEL: (015394) 36446
EMAIL: info@buckle-yeat.co.uk
WEB SITE: www.buckle-yeat.co.uk

Tiggywinkle charm at a simple seventeenth-century cottage B&B

Literary pilgrims pour into the pretty village of Near Sawrey to visit Hill Top, former home of Beatrix Potter, and to soak up the quintessentially English scene of quaint cottages brimming with flowers. Buckle Yeat is a typical example of the sort of place that might have featured in the Potter tales, as indeed it did in more than one of them. But the connections are not laboured, and no sentimentalised animals or superfluous knick-knacks litter the interior. Once

through the entrance door, guests find themselves in an inviting, firelit sitting room of softly gleaming antiques and restful wing armchairs. The adjacent tea rooms also serve as a breakfast area, furnished in rustic pine with plain white walls and a cast-iron Victorian range. Bedrooms, up steep, narrow stairs, ring the changes in crisp florals, with character added by exposed beams and window seats in the thick walls. Several new shower rooms are planned.

● Open all year ▣ In centre of Near Sawrey. Private car park ⬅ 1 single, 2 twin, 4 double; family rooms available; all with hair-dryer, TV ✅ Breakfast room, sitting room, garden; leisure facilities nearby; cots, highchairs ♿ No wheelchair access; 1 ground-floor bedroom ● No dogs in public rooms; no smoking in bedrooms ▭ Amex, Delta, MasterCard, Switch, Visa £ Single £30 to £32, single occupancy of twin/double £45, twin/double £60 to £64, family room £75 to £80; deposit required

---

Ees Wyke

Near Sawrey, Hawkshead, Ambleside LA22 0JZ
TEL: (015394) 36393 (AND FAX)
EMAIL: mail@eeswyke.co.uk
WEB SITE: www.eeswyke.co.uk

A restful setting in a delightful Lakeland village

Readers' letters confirm continued satisfaction with Richard and Margaret Lee's late-Regency country-house hotel, beautifully located near Esthwaite Water. The Lees seem to have settled down very well in their first season, preferring to get essentials such as

food and service right rather than refurbishing everything all at once. Inherited decorative schemes and structural alterations seem a bit of a mixed bag, some bedrooms stylishly modern, others conservatively chintzy with cramped bathrooms, but all are light with fine outlooks. Good-value dinners are much praised, and breakfasts too. It seems impossible to mention any building in Near Sawrey without finding some connection with its famous former resident Beatrix Potter, who lived at nearby Hill Top. Ees Wyke was the holiday home she stayed in as a young woman, acquiring a lasting affection for this tranquil village. Looking at the stunning views from the restaurant's double-aspect picture windows, it's easy to understand why. 'We were very impressed with the easy relaxed manner of Richard Lee,' writes a satisfied visitor.

○ Open all year ⚡ On B5285 1½ miles from Hawkshead, in direction of Windermere ferry. Private car park 🛏 1 twin, 7 double; all with hair-dryer, TV ⚶ Dining room, 2 lounges, garden; conferences and social functions ⅙ No wheelchair access; 1 ground-floor bedroom ● No children under 12; no dogs in public rooms; no smoking ▭ Delta, MasterCard, Switch, Visa £ Twin/double £130 to £144 (rates incl dinner); deposit required. Special breaks available ③FOR②

Sawrey House

Near Sawrey, Hawkshead, Ambleside LA22 0LF
TEL: (015394) 36387   FAX: (015394) 36010
EMAIL: mail@sawreyhouse.com
WEB SITE: www.sawreyhouse.com

Gracious country house with gorgeous views and appetising dinners

Fields, fells and woods, plus a few sheep, fill the tall windows of this former Victorian vicarage overlooking the pine-clad shores of Esthwaite Water. It's a solid, gabled building of dark slate, its bay window framed in Virginia creeper, while terraced gardens cascade towards National Trust surroundings. Colin and Shirley Whiteside have put their considerable home-making skills to good use here, creating a tasteful but completely relaxing ambience of classic English style. Soft lighting and firelight glow on antiques and good pictures, bronze statuary, china and fresh flowers in the lounge. Dinners are a positive asset: chef Bryan Parsons rustles up ambitiously inventive concoctions like white crab risotto with globe artichoke, or rhubarb and elderflower sorbet. These are served in the candlelit restaurant, accompanied by piano music. Bedrooms vary, furnished with antiques or good-quality modern pieces, and draped in floral chintz. The hotel was up for sale as we went to press.

○ Closed Dec & Jan ⚡ On B5285 from Hawkshead, in Near Sawrey village, on right. Private car park 🛏 1 single, 4 twin/double, 5 double, 1 four-poster, 1 family room; all with hair-dryer, direct-dial telephone, TV ⚶ Restaurant, bar, lounge, garden; conferences, social functions; leisure facilities nearby ⅙ Wheelchair access to hotel (ramp) and restaurant, WC, 2 ground-floor bedrooms ● No children under 10; no smoking ▭ Delta, MasterCard, Switch, Visa £ Single £45 to £55, single occupancy of twin/double £70 to £75, twin/double £90 to £120, four-poster £120 to £150, family room £100 to £130; deposit required. Set D £35. Special breaks available

---

NETTLEBED Oxfordshire   map 2

White Hart Hotel [NEW ENTRY]

28-30 High Street, Nettlebed RG9 5DD
TEL: (01491) 641245   FAX: (01491) 649018
EMAIL: info@whitehartnettlebed.com
WEB SITE: www.whitehartnettlebed.com

A splash of contemporary comfort within easy reach of historic Henley

Grey is definitely the new magnolia, at this super-stylish hotel anyway – there isn't a hint of creamy, off-white to be seen. External woodwork comes in battleship hue, while the bedrooms marry it very effectively with pale blue, chocolate brown, black and white. But fear not, this hotel is not grey to the core: lively, young staff and a very raspberry wall in the restaurant inject plenty of vitality to the whole operation, overseen by Chris Barber, formerly Prince Charles's personal chef. A sweep of public rooms occupies the main inn, and all are equally attractive in a modern way, such as the grey, green and black

The Which? Guide to
Good Hotels 2005
voucher scheme

3for2

*Valid at participating hotels, as
listed in The Which? Guide
to Good Hotels 2005,
until 30 September 2005*

See terms and conditions overleaf

The Which? Guide to
Good Hotels 2005
voucher scheme

3for2

*Valid at participating hotels, as
listed in The Which? Guide
to Good Hotels 2005,
until 30 September 2005*

See terms and conditions overleaf

The Which? Guide to
Good Hotels 2005
voucher scheme

3for2

*Valid at participating hotels, as
listed in The Which? Guide
to Good Hotels 2005,
until 30 September 2005*

See terms and conditions overleaf

The Which? Guide to
Good Hotels 2005
voucher scheme

3for2

*Valid at participating hotels, as
listed in The Which? Guide
to Good Hotels 2005,
until 30 September 2005*

See terms and conditions overleaf

Terms and Conditions

- The vouchers in *The Which? Guide to Good Hotels 2005* are valid from 1 October 2004 until 30 September 2005. Only one '3 nights for the price of 2' voucher may be used per room per booking – i.e., a party of four booking two rooms would need to use two vouchers, but a family of four sharing one room would need only one voucher. No photocopies or other reproductions of vouchers will be accepted. The vouchers may not be used in conjunction with any other offer.

- The vouchers are redeemable against a pre-booked stay only – the customer must mention his or her intent to use a voucher at the time of booking and present the voucher on arrival. The vouchers are redeemable against the price of the room and breakfast only (or just the room if breakfast is normally charged separately), not against the price of other meals, services or purchases such as newspapers.

- Participating establishments, which are highlighted in the pages of *The Which? Guide to Good Hotels 2005* by a symbol (3for2) at the end of entries, may exclude certain days of the week or times of the year from the scheme so long as they advise customers of the restrictions at the time of booking.

Terms and Conditions

- The vouchers in *The Which? Guide to Good Hotels 2005* are valid from 1 October 2004 until 30 September 2005. Only one '3 nights for the price of 2' voucher may be used per room per booking – i.e., a party of four booking two rooms would need to use two vouchers, but a family of four sharing one room would need only one voucher. No photocopies or other reproductions of vouchers will be accepted. The vouchers may not be used in conjunction with any other offer.

- The vouchers are redeemable against a pre-booked stay only – the customer must mention his or her intent to use a voucher at the time of booking and present the voucher on arrival. The vouchers are redeemable against the price of the room and breakfast only (or just the room if breakfast is normally charged separately), not against the price of other meals, services or purchases such as newspapers.

- Participating establishments, which are highlighted in the pages of *The Which? Guide to Good Hotels 2005* by a symbol (3for2) at the end of entries, may exclude certain days of the week or times of the year from the scheme so long as they advise customers of the restrictions at time of booking.

Terms and Conditions

- The vouchers in *The Which? Guide to Good Hotels 2005* are valid from 1 October 2004 until 30 September 2005. Only one '3 nights for the price of 2' voucher may be used per room per booking – i.e., a party of four booking two rooms would need to use two vouchers, but a family of four sharing one room would need only one voucher. No photocopies or other reproductions of vouchers will be accepted. The vouchers may not be used in conjunction with any other offer.

- The vouchers are redeemable against a pre-booked stay only – the customer must mention his or her intent to use a voucher at the time of booking and present the voucher on arrival. The vouchers are redeemable against the price of the room and breakfast only (or just the room if breakfast is normally charged separately), not against the price of other meals, services or purchases such as newspapers.

- Participating establishments, which are highlighted in the pages of *The Which? Guide to Good Hotels 2005* by a symbol (3for2) at the end of entries, may exclude certain days of the week or times of the year from the scheme so long as they advise customers of the restrictions at the time of booking.

brasserie-bistro or the candy-striped reception. Bedrooms in this building might suffer from traffic noise on the main road outside the front door, so light sleepers should request one of the six rooms located in a purpose-built extension at the back.

Wherever you lay your weary head, it will be surrounded by chic furnishings and modern art – and little rubber ducks will be waiting for you in the sparklingly smart bathroom.

○ Open all year; main restaurant closed Thurs to Sat ⏩ Between Wallingford and Henley-on-Thames on A4130 in Nettlebed. Private car park ⏩ 1 twin, 11 suites; all with room service, hair-dryer, direct-dial telephone, modem line, TV, CD player ⏩ Restaurant, bistro, bar, lounge; conferences; social functions; leisure facilities nearby; highchairs, outdoor play area ⏩ Wheelchair access to hotel and restaurants (1 step), WC, National Accessible Scheme M2, 1 ground-floor bedroom specially equipped for disabled people. Disabled parking ● No children under 16 in main restaurant eves; no dogs; no smoking in bedrooms ⏩ Delta, Diners, MasterCard, Switch, Visa ⏩ Twin £105 to £125, suite £135 to £145. Cooked B £8; set L £10, D £15; alc L £35, D £55; light meals available

---

NEW MILTON Hampshire
map 2

Chewton Glen

Christchurch Road, New Milton BH25 6QS
TEL: (01425) 275341 FAX: (01425) 272310
EMAIL: reservations@chewtonglen.com
WEB SITE: www.chewtonglen.com

Superb facilities and attentive staff in a lavish country house

Luxury hospitality is at its very best at Chewton Glen and carries an appropriate price-tag, but if you dig deep into your pockets this premier-league country house makes for the perfect retreat for a blow-out, pampering break. Inside, the striking eighteenth-century red-brick mansion is unstuffy. Sumptuous but not overly ostentatious, the spacious public areas are beautifully done out, light and supremely comfortable. The staff – at once ubiquitous and unobtrusive – blend that elusive concoction of efficiency, friendliness and discretion that characterises impeccable service. In the restaurant, an eclectic menu makes maximum use of fresh local produce such as wild mushrooms, vegetables and game from the New Forest, and seafood from local Christchurch and Lymington, and the excellent food is one of the many treats in staying here. Another is the superb spa, which, with every imaginable activity and a beautiful indoor pool, is just the thing for working off the excesses of the five-course *menu gourmand*. Decent-sized bedrooms with pretty colour schemes, flashy modern gadgetry and suitably indulgent bathrooms complete the superlative, relaxing whole.

○ Open all year ⏩ From A35, turn towards Walkford; drive through village and follow sign for Chewton Glen on left before roundabout. Nearest train station: New Milton. Private car park ⏩ 35 twin/double, 23 suites; all with room service, hair-dryer, mini-bar, trouser press, direct-dial telephone, modem line, TV, VCR, CD player; tea/coffee-making facilities on request ⏩ Restaurant, bar, 3 lounges, games room, gardens; conferences and social functions; civil wedding licence; gym, spa, tennis, indoor and outdoor heated swimming pools, golf; early suppers for children; baby-listening ⏩ Wheelchair access to hotel and restaurant (ramp), WC, 10 ground-floor bedrooms. Valet parking ● No children under 5; no dogs; no smoking in some public rooms ⏩ Amex, Delta, Diners, MasterCard, Switch, Visa ⏩ Twin/double £199 to £445, suite £315 to £780. Continental B £20, cooked B £25; set L from £20, D £57.50; alc L £45, D £70; light meals available; service incl. Special breaks available

---

NEWBROUGH Northumberland
map 10

Allerwash Farmhouse

Newbrough, Hexham NE47 5AB
TEL: (01434) 674574 (AND FAX)

Welcoming countryside guesthouse B&B with charming hosts who know how to entertain

Ian and Angela Clyde's Georgian stone-built farmhouse is lost among the quiet back roads around Hexham, making a wonderfully tranquil base for exploring Hadrian's Wall country. The area provides nature's bounty at its finest from local farms, and fresh fish and seafood from the nearby Northumberland coast – all very convenient for a cook with Angela's two decades of experience at the local General Havelock Inn. With just two bedrooms to cater for, evening meals are a chatty, dinner-party sort of affair – starting, perhaps, with crab tart, then moving on to a main course of roast duck with honey and oyster sauce. The smart dining room and lounge are decorated with warm colours, while the bedrooms have a Victorian character with antiques or stripped wood furniture, rich colours and William Morris-patterned wallpapers. Extras such as bathrobes and home-made cakes and biscuits increase the feelgood factor still further.

○ Open all year ⚡ On B6319, 5 miles west of Hexham. Private car park 🛏 1 twin, 1 double; both with hair-dryer, modem line ⟡ Dining room, lounge, garden ♿ No wheelchair access ● No children under 8; no dogs; no smoking ▭ None accepted £ Single occupancy of twin/double £58, twin/double £85; deposit required. Set D £26.50

NEWCASTLE UPON TYNE Tyne & Wear
map 10

Malmaison Newcastle

Quayside, Newcastle upon Tyne NE1 3DX
TEL: 0191-245 5000   FAX: 0191-245 4545
EMAIL: newcastle@malmaison.com
WEB SITE: www.malmaison.com

Contemporary character smack in the middle of the Toon

With the striking Millennium Bridge and showpiece Baltic Exchange the banks of the Tyne are looking decidedly stylish nowadays. So it's good to see that this link in the Malmaison chain, a converted riverside warehouse, is keeping up appearances itself. There's a fabulous view of the sights from the Gallic restaurant, with its aubergine-and-cream colour scheme, wood and leather chairs, and chunky metal light fittings. Our inspection meal matched the mood well with a starter of red onion and goat's cheese tart, followed by rib-eye steak with thick chips and finally a chocolate mousse. Public areas are otherwise confined to the Art Deco-style lobby, with sleek curvy lines on the reception desk and desk lights. Bedrooms continue the theme with dark-wood furniture and elegant, if slightly small, black-and-white bathrooms with power showers. The hotel also comes with a 'hi-tech fitness facility' and pampering boutique.

○ Open all year ⚡ Hotel is on quayside, next to Millennium Bridge. Nearest train station: Newcastle Central 🛏 11 twin, 83 double, 10 family rooms, 16 suites; all with room service, hair-dryer, mini-bar, trouser press, direct-dial telephone, modem line, TV, CD player ⟡ Restaurant, bar; conferences; social functions; gym, spa, leisure facilities nearby; cots, highchairs ♿ Wheelchair access to hotel and restaurant, WC, 5 rooms specially equipped for disabled people, lift ● No dogs in public rooms ▭ Amex, Delta, Diners, MasterCard, Switch, Visa £ Single occupancy of twin/double £129, twin/double £129, family room £145, suite £165 to £195. Continental B £10, cooked B £12; set L £13, D £14; alc L, D £30; light meals available. Special breaks available

---

NEWQUAY Cornwall
map 1

Sands Family Resort

Watergate Road, Porth, Newquay TR7 3LX
TEL: (01637) 872864   FAX: (01637) 876365
EMAIL: reception@sandsresort.co.uk
WEB SITE: www.sandsresort.co.uk

Good-value family resort with plenty of personality

Sands may be a big modern building standing on the main road out of overcrowded Newquay, but don't let that put you off. Some quirky shapes, welcoming Mediterranean colours, all the facilities a child could ask for and more, plus some great views over nearby golden beaches and rolling countryside – all come at a reasonable price. It's by no means top-end luxury (you'd have to pay top-end prices for that), but here you will find more personality than you might expect from a family complex. It's bright and modern, and there are plenty of imaginative touches, for example cheerful multicoloured windows of sea scenes (made by the multi-talented gardener!) that cast a pleasing glow over the beachcombers' bar, or the jungle theme to the pool. The bedrooms are a little sparse but with plenty of space to accommodate your brood, and with everything else on offer there's not much chance you'll want to linger in your room in any case.

◑ Open all year **⊡** From A392 to Newquay, turn right at Quintell Downs roundabout; in Newquay, turn right to Porth at two mini-roundabouts; hotel is past beach, up hill. Nearest train station: Newquay. Private car park **🛏** 2 single, 2 twin, 3 twin/double, 2 double, 60 family rooms/suites; all with room service, direct-dial telephone, modem line, TV; most with VCR, DVD, CD player; some with hair-dryer **✅** Restaurant, bar, 3 lounges, games room, garden; conferences and social functions; civil wedding licence; gym, spa, tennis, heated indoor swimming pool, unheated outdoor swimming pool; early suppers for children; cots, highchairs, toys, playrooms, babysitting, baby-listening, outdoor play area, children's clubs **♿** Wheelchair access to hotel and restaurant, WC, 10 ground-floor bedrooms. Disabled parking **●** No dogs; smoking in 1 lounge only **▭** Delta, MasterCard, Switch, Visa **£** Single £42 to £80, twin/double £84 to £160, family room/suite £84 to £200; deposit required. Set D £18; light meals available; service incl. Special breaks available

---

NEWTON-LE-WILLOWS North Yorkshire   map 8

The Hall

Newton-le-Willows, Bedale DL8 1SW
TEL: (01677) 450210

Characterful Wolsey Lodge with plenty of art and a relaxed atmosphere

This peaceful Georgian manor house lies in a quintessentially English hamlet just a handily short drive off the A1, but far enough away that you are never aware of its thundering presence. Inside the buttoned-down walls of Oriella Featherstone's elegant house you'll find a surprisingly arty collection of rooms with an agreeably Bohemian edge. Tapestries, kilims and eclectic *objets* combine with classic antiques, gilt-framed mirrors and chandeliers to ensure that there's always a talking point within sight. The snug lounge is a place to shut yourself in on a cold day, while the grand dining room has as its centrepiece an imposing old table large enough to seat a sizeable dinner party gathering, in the Wolsey Lodge style. The three bedrooms are floral and feminine compared with the treasure trove downstairs, but antiques and oil paintings play their part in their décor too. Apollo is a huge room that swallows its seven-foot-square bed with ease, and still has space for a capacious bathroom big enough for a sofa; Aphrodite is light and airy and comes with its own private bathroom; while Pollux is a comfy twin that looks into the paddocks and courtyard.

◑ Open all year **⊡** Leave A1 at Leeming Bar and turn off A684 to Bedale; turn right at main street; ¼ mile out of Bedale, turn left to Newton-le-Willows; turn right at T-junction, left at crossroads, then immediately right through the Hall's gates. Private car park **🛏** 1 twin, 1 double, 1 suite; all with hair-dryer, TV **✅** Dining room, honesty bar, lounge, study, garden **♿** No wheelchair access **●** No children under 13; dogs by arrangement; no smoking in bedrooms **▭** None accepted **£** Single occupancy of twin/double £55, twin/double £90, suite £100; deposit required. Set D £25; service incl

---

NEWTON-ON-THE-MOOR Northumberland   map 10

Cook & Barker Inn

Newton-on-the-Moor, Felton, Morpeth NE65 9JY
TEL: (01665) 575234 (AND FAX)
WEB SITE: www.cookandbarkerinn.co.uk

Handily located inn with new rooms and a popular restaurant

Perched on high ground above Alnmouth Bay, this village inn has grown a bit in recent years. The substantial annexe housing bedrooms behind the original pub was almost complete on our inspection visit, with a gym soon to be added. A correspondent had earlier reported some disruption to housekeeping routine and teething problems with the new rooms, but our inspector found the recent additions to be comfy and smart. Décor is summery in hue and bathrooms are good modern jobs with tiled walls, strong showers and posh smellies; big TVs and DVD players in most rooms complete the complement of twenty-first-century extras. The place certainly has ambition in matters culinary too: you can eat in either a classic convivial bar, which is geared more to diners than drinkers, or in the rustic main restaurant, a vast split-level area, busy with throngs of diners; high barn-style rafters hung with pots, pans and farming implements give a nod to the building's history as a blacksmith's shop. Our inspection meal was competent stuff, starting with tempura prawns, then a tasty if unauthentic bouillabaisse, served by keen, well-trained young staff. More reports welcome.

○ Closed 25 Dec 🚗 Just off A1, about 5 miles south of Alnwick. Private car park 🛏 1 single, 5 twin, 10 double, 1 four-poster, 2 family rooms; all with room service, hair-dryer, TV; some with DVD ✓ Restaurant, bar, lounge, garden; conferences; social functions; leisure facilities nearby; early suppers for children; cots, highchairs ♿ Wheelchair access to hotel and restaurant (ramps), 7 ground-floor bedrooms, 1 room specially equipped for disabled people ● No dogs; no smoking in restaurant or bedrooms ▭ Amex, Delta, MasterCard, Switch, Visa £ Single £45, single occupancy of twin/double £65, twin/double £65, four-poster £75, family room £110; deposit required. Set D £17.50; alc L £15, D £24; light meals available. Special breaks available (3FOR2)

NORTH WALSHAM Norfolk   map 6

Beechwood Hotel

Cromer Road, North Walsham NR28 0HD
TEL: (01692) 403231   FAX: (01692) 407284
EMAIL: info@beechwood-hotel.co.uk
WEB SITE: www.beechwood-hotel.co.uk

Well-run hotel with that elusive certain something in spades

When we inspected, Lindsay Spalding was brimming with enthusiasm about the new bedrooms currently under construction on the side of her ivy-covered Georgian hotel. At the time of writing there was little to see except the underfloor heating, but it's clear that they're certainly going to be spacious ('The six-foot four-poster is going to get lost in here!'), and the sneak preview of the luxurious fabrics Lindsay and Don Birch have taken great delight in choosing indicate that the décor will be in the same tasteful period style as the rest of the rooms. Current bedrooms have occasional innovative touches like a wardrobe in one which lights up when you open the doors, luxuries like roll-top or slipper baths, and colour schemes which are dense without feeling overly oppressive. The restaurant is in three sections and can be arranged to create a sense of intimacy on slower nights but opened up to encourage a buzzy atmosphere when busy, adapting chameleon-like to its situation. But it is Lindsay and Ron's joie de vivre that steals the show. One correspondent summed things up by saying he couldn't put his finger on why they came away feeling as pleased as they did – but was left with 'an overwhelming sense that nothing you might ask for would be too much trouble – except that on most occasions you didn't have to ask because it had already been offered. The truly impressive thing was the way that attitude of mind had embedded itself in the young staff as well'.

○ Open all year 🚗 Leave Norwich on B1150. On entering North Walsham, turn left at first set of traffic lights and right at the next; hotel is 150 yards on left. Nearest train station: North Walsham. Private car park 🛏 2 twin/double, 9 double, 6 four-poster; all with room service, hair-dryer, direct-dial telephone, modem line, TV, CD player; some with modem line, VCR ✓ Restaurant, bar, drawing room, garden; conferences; social functions; leisure facilities nearby; early suppers for children ♿ Wheelchair access to hotel (ramp) and restaurant, WC, 2 ground-floor bedrooms ● No children under 10; dogs £6 per night; no smoking ▭ Delta, MasterCard, Switch, Visa £ Single occupancy of twin/double £66, twin/double £90 to £110, four-poster £160; deposit required. Set L £18, D £32; light meals available. Special breaks available (3FOR2)

Hundred House

Bridgnorth Road, Norton, Nr Shifnal TF11 9EE
TEL: (01952) 730353   FAX: (01952) 730355
EMAIL: reservations@hundredhouse.co.uk
WEB SITE: www.hundredhouse.co.uk

A Victorian fantasy – there might even be fairies at the bottom of the garden

'We ate, we drank, we went swinging – then we slept. Brilliant!' That was the verdict of one couple quoted in the Hundred House brochure. We should perhaps explain at this point that each bedroom here contains a swing! It's by no means the only sign of eccentricity to be found. The Phillips family has designed something approaching a Victorian fairy tale. Bedrooms have big brass bedsteads, glass chandeliers and decoration festooned with flower motifs. There's also a little heart-shaped pin cushion in every room. Then, reached along a path behind the main buildings, is a fascinating secret garden. It's almost grotto-like, with strange mossy stones and sculptures ancient and modern. This is certainly a place where your imagination can run riot. The main part of the operation is a busy pub and restaurant and the mood here is altogether more sombre in feel – it's so dark that the lights are turned on much of the time. There is wood panelling, stained glass, seating divided by wooden pews and a forest of dried flowers hanging from the ceiling.

◑ Open all year ▨ In village of Norton, midway between Bridgnorth and Telford on A442. Private car park 🛏 1 single, 1 twin/double, 5 double, 3 four-poster; family rooms available; all with room service, hair-dryer, direct-dial telephone, TV ✔ Restaurant, bar, garden; conferences; social functions; leisure facilities nearby; early suppers for children; cots, highchairs, baby-listening ♿ No wheelchair access ● No dogs in public rooms, £10 per night in bedrooms ▭ Delta, MasterCard, Switch, Visa £ Single £69, single occupancy of twin/double £85, twin/double £99 to £125, four-poster £125, family room £125; deposit required. Alc L, D £28; light meals available. Special breaks available

By Appointment

25–29 St George's Street, Norwich NR3 1AB
TEL: (01603) 630730 (AND FAX)

Theatrical flamboyance tucked away in central Norwich

Arriving at By Appointment as a first-timer, you may find yourself a little confused to read the handwritten note on the front door directing you down a side-alley past a scruffy yard and in through the kitchen door, so that even the kitchen staff can join in the welcome ritual. First-timers, however, may be lucky to get in, as people tend to become smitten by this fabulously charming restaurant-with-rooms and come back again and again. The interior is an antique-lover's paradise, with barely room to move in some parts of the tiny maze of rooms in this ex-merchant's house. At times it can feel like a stage-set waiting to leap into life, with old-fashioned grooming kits inviting you to sit at your dresser gazing wistfully into the mirror combing your hair, and battered suitcases looking as if they're ready to be whisked off on some exotic adventure. Owners Timothy Brown and Robert Culyer throw themselves into their role as hosts, revelling in attention to detail, reading out the day's menu (homely British and French cooking) to the guests at dinner and organising events such as special themed evenings.

◑ Open all year; restaurant closed Sun and Mon eves ▨ On junction of St George's Street and Colegate. Nearest train station: Norwich Thorpe. Private car park 🛏 1 single, 1 twin, 2 double; all with hair-dryer, trouser press, direct-dial telephone, TV ✔ Restaurant, 2 lounges; social functions; leisure facilities nearby ♿ No wheelchair access ● No children under 12; no dogs; no smoking in bedrooms ▭ Delta, MasterCard, Switch, Visa £ Single £70, single occupancy of twin/double £85, twin/double £95; deposit required. Alc D £30

Catton Old Hall

Lodge Lane, Catton, Norwich NR6 7HG
TEL: (01603) 419379   FAX: (01603) 400339
EMAIL: enquiries@catton-hall.co.uk
WEB SITE: www.catton-hall.co.uk

Surprisingly rural retreat in Norwich suburbia

The sundial above the front door of this seventeenth-century gentleman's home reads 'Redeem the time'. Slightly cryptic perhaps, but Catton Old Hall is certainly a good time-saving option if you're coming in from Norwich airport but don't want to settle for a chain hotel. The Old Hall stands a little on its own, the surrounding village now having been swallowed up by suburbia, but Roger and Anthea Cawdron go to great lengths to offset any disadvantages they can't change about their location. Housekeeping is top notch, and décor and furnishings are of the highest quality in the bedrooms, dining area and characterful sitting room with its large inglenook fireplace and timbered ceiling. Bedrooms are generally of the pink variety – Anna Sewell (named after the author of *Black Beauty*) is particularly romantic, with strawberry-cream walls. A fixed-menu dinner is available by prior arrangement, cooked by Andrea to old family recipes.

◗ Open all year; dining room closed Sun eve   ⤵ From ring road take B1150 towards North Walsham; at Woodman pub go straight on for ½ mile then turn left into White Woman Lane; at traffic lights keep in left lane and cross over into Lodge Lane; hotel is on right. Private car park   🛏 2 twin/double, 4 double, 1 four-poster; all with hair-dryer, trouser press, direct-dial telephone, modem line, TV   ✓ Dining room, bar, sitting room, garden; leisure facilities nearby; cots, highchairs   ♿ No wheelchair access   ● No children under 14 exc babes in arms; no dogs in public rooms; smoking in sitting room only   ▭ Amex, Delta, Diners, MasterCard, Switch, Visa   £ Single occupancy of twin/double £60 to £70, twin/double £65 to £90, four-poster £100 to £120; deposit required. Set D £24.50; light meals available. Special breaks available   ③ FOR ②

The Old Rectory

103 Yarmouth Road, Thorpe St Andrew, Norwich NR7 0HF
TEL: (01603) 700772   FAX: (01603) 300772
EMAIL: enquiries@oldrectorynorwich.com
WEB SITE: www.oldrectorynorwich.com

Georgian home within river-reach of Norwich

Chris, Sally and James Entwistle's red-brick Georgian home overlooks the beautiful Yare Valley, close enough to Norwich to make a river-bus trip into town an appealing prospect. In the summer you can enjoy the view from the well-tended gardens or take a dip in the heated outdoor pool. Or if things get a little chillier, move into the conservatory and settle into the bamboo furniture to sip your tea. The parquet-floored dining room has plates displayed on the elegant cream and blue panelled walls; here you can sample the hearty English cooking on offer on the set menu. Bedrooms are immaculately kept, well furnished and comfortable, in an occasionally frilly style, with fine bed linen and bathrobes on offer, and cuddly toys on each bed for those who are missing their own.

◗ Closed 22 Dec to 5 Jan; dining room closed Sun eve   ⤵ From city centre, follow signs for A47 (Great Yarmouth) down Prince of Wales Road; at right of traffic lights go straight ahead, over river, passing train station on right; continue straight on; just after Oakland's Hotel turn left at sign for Old Rectory. Private car park   🛏 1 twin, 7 double; family rooms available; all with room service, hair-dryer, direct-dial telephone, modem line, TV; some with CD player, DVD   ✓ Dining room, drawing room, conservatory, garden; conferences and social functions; heated outdoor swimming pool; leisure facilities nearby; early suppers for children; cots, highchairs, baby-listening, outdoor play area   ♿ No wheelchair access   ● No dogs in public rooms and most bedrooms; no smoking in dining room and bedrooms   ▭ Amex, Delta, MasterCard, Switch, Visa   £ Single occupancy of twin/double £68, twin/double £88, family room £108; deposit required. Set D £21; light meals available; service incl. Special breaks available

Greenwood Lodge [NEW ENTRY]

5 Third Avenue, Sherwood Rise, Nottingham NG7 6JH
TEL: 0115-962 1206 (AND FAX)
EMAIL: pdouglas71@aol.com
WEB SITE: www.greenwoodlodgecityguesthouse.co.uk

Tranquil, hospitable hideaway within walking distance of busy city centre

It helps to have a city street map and a sense of adventure when locating this pleasing haven of peace, but it's worth the effort needed to find it. Greenwood Lodge is tucked away in a quiet cul-de-sac, and it's difficult to imagine that the bustling city centre is a mere fifteen-minute walk away. The very patient Doug and Sue Pearse (our inspector turned up late after losing himself in the city's one-way system and was still welcomed with a smile) have decorated their Victorian townhouse predominantly in rich papers and fabrics. The sitting room bursts with antique bric-à-brac, lots of comfortable armchairs, and crammed bookshelves. Nicely prepared breakfasts are cooked to order and served in the spacious conservatory, which is interestingly decked out with art nouveau pieces and adorned with *trompe l'oeil* trailing vines, flowers and fruit. The appealing cottage-look bedrooms have substantial beds and come with en-suite facilities.

◗ Closed 23 to 28 Dec   ▨ From city centre take A60 Mansfield Road, turn on to B682 (Sherwood Rise); Third Avenue is third turning on left. Nearest train station: Nottingham. Private car park ⬚ 1 single, 1 twin, 1 double, 3 four-poster; all with hair-dryer, trouser press, TV ✓ Sitting room, conservatory, garden; leisure facilities nearby ♿ No wheelchair access ● No children under 12; no dogs; no smoking ⬚ Delta, MasterCard, Switch, Visa £ Single £41, single occupancy of twin/double £48 to £52, twin/double/four-poster £65 to £73; deposit required

Hart's [NEW ENTRY]

Standard Hill, Park Row, Nottingham NG1 6FN
TEL: 0115-988 1900   FAX: 0115-947 7600
EMAIL: info@hartsnottingham.co.uk
WEB SITE: www.hartsnottingham.co.uk

Chic modernity in the heart of Nottingham's historic centre

Contrasting with its historic neighbours in the old merchant area of the city is the modern streamlined Hart's hotel. Set at the top of a steep hill, it has a small secluded garden of tree-edged clipped lawns with a good view across the city and, very important around here, a car park. This is a place for those who dislike the floral fuss of more traditional hotels. There is a distinctly minimalist feeling inside: a two-sided fireplace has flames licking around smooth beach pebbles and chic co-ordinated furniture is positioned in neat configurations around the periphery of the uncluttered floor. To offset the stylised décor, colours are bold and warm and nowhere more so than in the quirky restaurant with its vibrant abstract paintings and colourful furnishings. The menu is simple and well executed with meals such as smoked Gressingham duck, orange and hazelnut salad as a first course and roasted partridge, fondant potato and cep sauce to follow. Bedrooms are neat and smart, and if they are a touch anonymous in style, they are at least comfortable and nicely put together.

◗ Open all year   ▨ In centre of Nottingham off Maid Marian Way. Nearest train station: Nottingham. Private car park ⬚ 13 twin/double, 17 double, 2 suites; all with room service, hair-dryer, mini-bar, direct-dial telephone, modem line, TV, CD player; DVD in suites ✓ Restaurant, 2 bars, garden, terrace; conferences; social functions; civil wedding licence; gym; leisure facilities nearby; early suppers for children; cots, highchairs, babysitting ♿ Wheelchair access to hotel and restaurant, WC, lift. Disabled parking ● No dogs in public rooms, no smoking in bedrooms ⬚ Amex, Delta, MasterCard, Switch, Visa £ Single occupancy of twin/double £115, twin/double £115 to £155, suite £235; deposit required. Continental B £8.50, cooked £13.50; set L £15, alc L £27.50, D £29.50; light meals available. Special breaks available ③FOR2

Lace Market Hotel

29-31 High Pavement, The Lace Market, Nottingham NG1 1HE
TEL: 0115-852 3232   FAX: 0115-852 3236
EMAIL: reservations@lacemarkethotel.co.uk
WEB SITE: www.lacemarkethotel.co.uk

A breath of fresh air in the heart of the city's historic district

In the tranquil centre of Nottingham's historic Lace Market, close to several trendy bars, this super-cool hotel offers style without pretensions and service that is unobtrusive and professional. Mark Cox is the innovator behind the funky establishment that has knocked chintz out of the repertoire and replaced it with modern sophistication. Although the building has a Regency and Victorian heritage, inside there is little evidence of the past – apart from a gastropub called the Cock and Hoop, Mark's latest addition, which he proudly describes as a faithful reproduction of a Victorian alehouse. By contrast, the chic restaurant has pewter-effect moulded panels on the vaulted ceiling and opaque mirrors around the walls, giving an atmospheric, cinematic effect. Bedrooms are painted in warm ochre colours with comfortable modern furniture and hypoallergenic bedding. Some have high-powered, skin-stripping drench showers.

◑ Open all year   ⌷ In city centre. Follow brown tourist information signs for Galleries of Justice (immediately opposite hotel). Nearest train station: Nottingham   ⌷ 6 single, 15 twin/double, 13 double, 8 suites; all with room service, hair-dryer, mini-bar, direct-dial telephone, modem line, TV, CD player; some with trouser press, VCR   ⌧ Restaurant, 2 bars, lounge; conferences; social functions; leisure facilities nearby; cots, highchairs   ⌷ No wheelchair access; lift   ● No children in restaurant eves; no dogs in public rooms, £25 in bedrooms; smoking in bar only   ⌷ Amex, MasterCard, Switch, Visa   ⌷ Single £65 to £90, single occupancy of twin/double £95 to £110, twin/double £95 to £110, suite £165 to £199; deposit required. Continental B £8, cooked B £13; set L £15; alc L, D £24; light meals available. Special breaks available   ③FOR②

OAKAMOOR Staffordshire   map 5

Bank House

Farley Road, Oakamoor, Stoke-on-Trent ST10 3BD
TEL: (01538) 702810 (AND FAX)
EMAIL: john.orme@dial.pipex.com
WEB SITE: www.smoothhound.co.uk/hotels/bank.html

Civilised haven in the beautiful Churnet Valley, close to Alton Towers too

With a series of terraced ponds sloping gently down past a well laid out Italianate garden, then a peachery, and finally what is to become a bog garden, all set against the idyllic backdrop of Stoney Dale, you might think you were in the grounds of a small country-house hotel. In fact, this immaculately kept home, set in a sympathetically extended old red-brick farmhouse, is run as a simple B&B by the very pleasant and enthusiastic retired couple John and Muriel Egerton-Orme. Inside, guest facilities run to a comfortable drawing room, with an ornate Balinese coffee table and incredible built-in cast-iron fireplace, and an airy breakfast room, which has a single solid table. Two twin rooms are pleasantly furnished in traditional English style, with pretty floral fabrics and solid furnishings, while a third bedroom boasts an attractive antique four-poster. Bathrooms are spacious and come with bidets.

◑ Closed Chr   ⌷ Follow signs for Alton Towers via Alton village, passing theme park main entrance (on right); after road turns sharply left, continue 400 yards, then turn left down narrow lane, signposted Farley; house is second on left. Private car park   ⌷ 2 twin, 1 four-poster; family rooms and suite available; all with hair-dryer, trouser press, direct-dial telephone, TV   ⌧ Breakfast room, bar service, drawing room, library, garden; cots, highchairs, toys, baby-listening   ⌷ No wheelchair access   ● Dogs by arrangement only; no smoking   ⌷ Delta, Diners, MasterCard, Switch, Visa   ⌷ Single occupancy of twin £48 to £55, twin £65 to £80, four-poster £75, family room £75 to £96, suite £130; deposit required. Special breaks available

OAKHAM Rutland | map 5

Barnsdale Lodge

The Avenue, Rutland Water, North Shore, Nr Oakham LE15 8AH
TEL: (01572) 724678   FAX: (01572) 724961
EMAIL: enquiries@barnsdalelodge.co.uk
WEB SITE: www.barnsdalelodge.co.uk

Good food to be enjoyed in distinctive surroundings

Rutland is awash with lovely honey-coloured stone farmhouses but few will offer such highly individualistic interiors as the extensive Barnsdale Lodge. On entering you get the distinct impression that this is a place much cherished by its owner Thomas Noel and his welcoming staff; there is a refreshing symmetry here between sumptuous formality and more down-to-earth informality and almost everywhere are hung the humorous, detailed cartoons of Sue McCartney Snape depicting the eccentricities of well-heeled country life. Excellently prepared meals can be enjoyed in the super-plush surroundings of the interconnecting gourmet dining room or the spacious, airy conservatory, which is festooned with watering cans and other garden paraphernalia. The large garden courtyard has ample garden furniture among an abundance of flowering shrubs and strongly coloured flowers. Bedrooms have a quirky peculiarity lending each a unique flavour so that in one you might enjoy a nostalgic return to childhood with *Wind in the Willows* upholstery and in another the luxury of a *chaise* and super-king-size bed in a room done out in bold blues and reds.

○ Open all year   ⊡ On A606 between Stamford and Oakham, 3 miles outside Oakham. Nearest train station: Oakham. Private car park ⊨ 8 single, 8 twin, 2 twin/double, 22 double, 2 four-poster, 2 family rooms, 2 suites; all with room service, hair-dryer, trouser press, direct-dial telephone, TV ⊘ 3 dining rooms, bar, lounge, conservatory, garden; conferences; social functions; civil wedding licence; leisure facilities nearby; cots, highchairs, outdoor play area ♿ Wheelchair access to hotel and dining rooms (ramps), National Accessible Scheme: M2, WC, 28 ground-floor bedrooms, 2 rooms specially equipped for disabled people. Disabled parking ● Dogs £10 in bedrooms; no smoking in some bedrooms ▭ Amex, Delta, Diners, MasterCard, Switch, Visa £ Single £75, single occupancy of twin/double £85, twin/double £100, four-poster/family room/suite £120; deposit required. Set D £15, D £18.50; alc L, D £36; light meals available. Special breaks available (3FOR2)

ORFORD Suffolk | map 6

Crown and Castle

Orford, Nr Woodbridge IP12 2LJ
TEL: (01394) 450205
EMAIL: info@crownandcastle.co.uk
WEB SITE: www.crownandcastle.co.uk

Trendy but unpretentious inn on the east coast

The castle in the name is presumably the old Norman keep yards from the front door of this mainly Victorian hotel on Orford's market square. There's nothing old about the interior though – Ruth and David Watson have strictly avoided country-house clichés, so the feel is modern, but also relaxed and unpretentious. The Trinity restaurant is a place to tuck yourself into and relax on velvet banquettes. Ruth is very much front-of-house, ensuring friendly and approachable service. There's rather less of her than there used to be, and her book of diet-friendly recipes, *Fat Girl Slim*, is given to guests on special two-night breaks. Bedrooms are decorated in neutrals with splashes of colour (and striking pebble lino in the sparkling white bathrooms). Rooms in the main house may have views over to the sea, while those in the garden chalets have French windows opening on to a terrace for fine days.

○ Closed 24 to 27 Dec & 3 to 6 Jan; restaurant closed Sun eve Nov to Feb (excl bank hols) ⊡ From A12 near Saxmundham, take B1078 to Orford; hotel is on corner of market square. Private car park ⊨ 3 twin, 14 double, 1 family room; all with room service (breakfast only), hair-dryer, direct-dial telephone, TV, VCR ⊘ Restaurant, dining room, bar, family parlour, garden; conferences; early suppers for children; cots, highchairs, toys, babysitting, baby-listening   Wheelchair access to hotel and restaurant; 11 ground-floor bedrooms ● No children under 9 in restaurant eves; no dogs in some public rooms, £10 in bedrooms; smoking in bar only   Delta, MasterCard, Switch, Visa £ Single occupancy of twin/double £72 to £150, twin/double £90 to £150, family room £130 to £155. Alc L £21.50, D £27.50; light meals available. Special breaks available

---

OSMOTHERLEY North Yorkshire   map 9

The Three Tuns

9 South End, Osmotherley, Northallerton DL6 3BN
TEL: (01609) 883301   FAX: (01609) 883988
EMAIL: info@thethreetuns.net
WEB SITE: www.thethreetuns.net

Stylish brasserie-with-rooms in a bucolic spot near the North York Moors

The oh-so-English setting, opposite the village hall in a picturesque village within sight of the Cleveland Hills, and the honey-stone exterior of the Three Tuns scream 'traditional village pub' – except for one detail: a scribbled modern hieroglyph on its sign, which gives the only clue to what lies beyond the front door. Inside, surprise, surprise! This place is very hip, with lovely burr oak tables and high-backed chairs on a bleached stone floor and light oak half-panelled walls with wrought-iron candleholders. The menu offers suitably contemporary European-influenced cuisine. Next door in Moon House, guests can choose from a good range of videos and CDs and flop out in a swish modern lounge with blue leather sofas and a glowing wood-burning stove. Smart and stylish bedrooms feature solid pine beds, lots of exposed wood and stone textures, trendy spotlights and good-quality modern bathrooms; style fans will also appreciate details such as the chrome kettles and designer bottled water.

---

❶ Open all year ▨ From A19, take A684 and follow road into Osmotherley; where this road forks to right, hotel is straight ahead. Nearest train station: Northallerton. Private car park ⬚ 1 twin, 5 double, 1 family room; all with hair-dryer, direct-dial telephone, TV ⟡ Restaurant, bar, lounge, garden; conferences; social functions; highchairs & No wheelchair access; 1 ground-floor bedroom ● No dogs; smoking in bar only ⬚ Amex, MasterCard, Switch, Visa £ Twin/double £65, family room £75. Set L, D £10; alc L £20, D £28; light meals available; service incl (2004 data)

OXFORD Oxfordshire   map 2

Burlington House

374 Banbury Road, Oxford OX2 7PP
TEL: (01865) 513513   FAX: (01865) 311785
EMAIL: stay@burlington-house.co.uk
WEB SITE: www.burlington-house.co.uk

Superlative B&B with exceedingly good hosts and even better breakfasts

Slightly removed from the tourist bustle of the city centre – it's a short bus ride or leisurely stroll up the Banbury Road – is this very smart, yellow-brick Victorian house that now functions as a winningly good B&B, run with panache and imagination. The interior has a stylish, modern feel to it, most noticeably in the bedrooms, where the attention to detail is meticulous, so that you get home-made biscuits on your tea tray as well as a swish room to sleep in. Particularly memorable is the chic, oval bathroom in Room 10, on the ground floor, which looks as if it has been transported in from an architectural magazine. Public rooms are small-scale, with a dinky lounge and pleasant pink and blue dining room, setting for the sumptuous breakfasts that involve free-range eggs and home-made bread. One contented reader could 'not find anything to criticise', heaping praise on the coffee ('very good indeed') and the proprietors ('flair and good humour'), while another simply said, 'I recommend this establishment without hesitation'. 'Their standards get better and better,' concurred another.

◐ Open all year ⌁ Leave A40 at Cottesloe roundabout and take Banbury Road towards town centre, signposted Summertown; hotel is fourth turning on left, on corner of Hernes Road. Nearest train station: Oxford. Private car park 🛏 6 single, 3 twin/double, 2 double; 2 with shared bathroom; all with hair-dryer, direct-dial telephone, modem line, TV ✓ Breakfast room, lounge, garden; leisure facilities nearby ♿ Wheelchair access to hotel (ramp) and breakfast room, 2 ground-floor bedrooms, 1 room specially equipped for disabled people ⬤ No children under 12; no dogs; no smoking ▭ Amex, Delta, MasterCard, Switch, Visa £ Single £58, single occupancy of twin/double £65 to £70, twin/double £85; deposit required

Old Bank

92–94 High Street, Oxford OX1 4BN
TEL: (01865) 799599 FAX: (01865) 799598
EMAIL: info@oldbank-hotel.co.uk
WEB SITE: www.oldbank-hotel.co.uk

Swish and stylish modern hotel bang in the middle of the historic city

Sitting right at the heart of the busy city centre, this former Barclays Bank has an exterior just as grandiose, though noticeably more sombre, than many of the colleges nearby. The restful hues of the sandstone walls are continued inside, where a pastel palette of flax, mushroom, honey, and cream predominates, exuding a sense of stylish yet inviting minimalism. The Quod restaurant winningly weaves an old-meets-new picture, with a metal-topped bar and leather seating contrasting nicely with the chunky stone pillars, opening out on to a sunny, peaceful back courtyard. Bedrooms are just as chic, and bathrooms opulently kitted out, though those guests in search of chintzy flowery fabrics may be disappointed. The modern approach stretches to the technology as well, with broadband connection and CD player in each room, plus DVD players for hire. Some rooms have the sought-after inspiring views of Oxford's skyline. Its days as a financial institution are long gone, but be warned: this old bank is still cashing in by charging guests extra for breakfast.

◐ Closed Chr ⌁ In centre of Oxford. Nearest train station: Oxford. Private car park 🛏 4 single, 36 twin/double, 2 suites; all with room service, hair-dryer, direct-dial telephone, modem line, TV, CD player; some with mini-bar, trouser press, DVD ✓ Restaurant, dining room, 2 bars, lounge, garden; conferences and social functions; leisure facilities nearby; early suppers for children; cots, highchairs, babysitting ♿ Wheelchair access to hotel and restaurant, WC, 1 ground-floor bedroom, specially equipped for disabled people, lift ⬤ No dogs; no smoking in bedrooms ▭ Amex, Delta, Diners, MasterCard, Switch, Visa £ Single £140, twin/double £160 to £235, suite £265 to £320 (2004 rates); deposit required. Continental B £9, cooked B £12; set L £14, D £18; alc L, D £25; light meals available; service incl. Special breaks available
⓷FOR②

Old Parsonage

1 Banbury Road, Oxford OX2 6NN
TEL: (01865) 310210 FAX: (01865) 311262
EMAIL: info@oldparsonage-hotel.co.uk
WEB SITE: www.oldparsonage-hotel.co.uk

A city-centre hotel that's disguised as a country-house charmer

In a city that itself is not short on history, this upmarket hotel has plenty of its own: begun in 1640-60, it survived the Civil War despite being on the front line, so that its characterful wooden doors and stout mullioned windows are original. There's even an underground passage linking it to the church next door, though guests don't see that. Instead, they're treated to a beautifully appointed interior, with the focus of the public rooms being the smart restaurant, whose deep-red walls are festooned with art. A front courtyard allows al fresco dining, but traffic noise is a constant companion, so more secluded, tranquil spots are the secret little garden at the back or the sun-trap roof terrace. Bowls of fruit (apples in summer, satsumas in winter) are placed in the corridors for guests' pleasure, and there are bicycles and even a punt available for free use. Bedrooms successfully mix flowery fabrics, antique furniture and restful colours, while bathrooms are smartly done out. One reader commented on the slow, disorganised restaurant service; we hope that recent management changes in that area will rectify this. As at its sister hotel, Old Bank, breakfast incurs an extra charge.

● Closed 23 to 26 Dec   ⏢ At north end of St Giles, fork right into Banbury Road; hotel is on left after first junction. Nearest train station: Oxford. Private car park   ⬛ 6 twin/double, 18 double, 4 suites; all with room service, hair-dryer, direct-dial telephone, modem line, TV; some with trouser press   ⊘ Restaurant/bar, lounge, garden; leisure facilities nearby; cots, highchairs, toys, baby-listening   ♿ No wheelchair access; 10 ground-floor bedrooms   ● No dogs in public rooms; no smoking in bedrooms and some public rooms   ▭ Amex, Delta, Diners, MasterCard, Switch, Visa   £ Single occupancy of twin/double £130, twin/double £160, suite £200. Continental B £10, cooked B £12.50; alc L, D £28, light meals available. Special breaks available

---

PADSTOW   Cornwall   map 1

Number 6

6 Middle Street, Padstow PL28 8AP
TEL: (01841) 532093
WEB SITE: www.number6inpadstow.co.uk

Calming, modern B&B with a funky twist

Number 6 is a bright recent addition to the Padstow scene, and is run with the enthusiasm of the newcomer by Paul and Brenda Harvey. Most of the décor is dizzyingly white, colour being applied via exuberant accessorising – funky cushions, fabrics and furniture. The white bedrooms (even the little TV in one room is white) have splashes of lilac, lime and pale blues – and, unexpectedly, cuddly toys and oversized children's books (for big kids only, as no children are allowed). The lounge spaces have plenty of low, soft furnishings such as beanbags and frizzy cushions resembling curled-up poodles, and carefully chosen pots, plates and pictures, plus some pretty fairy-lights. The adjoining (mainly white) bar and dining area, similarly chilled-out, is now principally for house guests, which Paul says is working better and creates more of a house dinner-party atmosphere. 'Our aim is for people to come as strangers, leave as friends, then return with their friends.' They're certainly doing something right – apparently one couple has visited no fewer than seven times in the last 18 months!

● Open all year   ⏢ Middle Street is off Duke Street, near quayside in Padstow   ⬛ 3 double; all with hair-dryer, TV, CD player   ⊘ Dining room, bar, 3 lounges, garden; conferences and social functions; leisure facilities nearby   ♿ No wheelchair access   ● No children; no dogs; no smoking   ▭ MasterCard, Switch, Visa   £ Double from £125; deposit required. Set D £29.50; light meals available

---

Seafood Restaurant, St Petroc's Hotel, Rick Stein's Café

Riverside, Padstow PL28 8BY
TEL: (01841) 532700   FAX: (01841) 532942
EMAIL: reservations@rickstein.com
WEB SITE: www.rickstein.com

Wide choice of high-quality accommodation, and the food's not bad either

Padstow has been cheekily renamed Padstein as Rick's influence grows with each new addition to the fold (the latest venture a posh new fish and chip shop). But there's no sign of a dropping off in standards. Bedrooms are spread over three properties scattered around town: at the flagship Seafood Restaurant itself, at the more informal Café and at St Petroc's hotel. Rooms are stylish without being overly fussy, and are a mix of traditional and modern styles. With so many different rooms to choose from, it might be a good idea to visit the website before you book – there are pictures of every room and 360-degree views of many. Those at the Café are the simplest – a cut above your average B&B. Rooms at the Seafood Restaurant are split between the main building and St Edmund's, just behind. The main building's rooms are bright and airy with some lovely furniture, but St Edmunds probably has the poshest, featuring cherrywood four-posters from South Africa and sunlight filtering in through shuttered windows. At St Petroc's the focus seems to switch to the hotel rather than the food (though there is a bistro attached), with a variety of comfy sofas to relax in in the guests' lounge, a reading room and a patio overlooking the rooftops of Padstow.

❍ Closed 25 & 26 Dec 🔁 Seafood Restaurant is on quayside in Padstow; St Petroc's Hotel is just above Strand; for Rick Stein's Café, go to Seafood Restaurant for key and directions. Private car park (St Petroc's) 🛏 3 twin, 18 double, 9 four-poster, 3 family rooms; all with hair-dryer, direct-dial telephone, TV; some with mini-bar, trouser press, modem line, VCR, DVD, CD player ✦ 3 restaurants, 2 bars, lounge, library, conservatory, 3 gardens; conferences and social functions; cots, highchairs, babysitting 🚹 No wheelchair access; between 2 and 6 steps into buildings, 3 ground-floor bedrooms ● No children under 4 in Seafood Restaurant; no dogs in public rooms and some bedrooms; no smoking in St Petroc's Hotel bistro or Rick Stein's Café ▭ Amex, Delta, MasterCard, Switch, Visa £ Twin/double/four-poster/family room £85 to £235; deposit required. Seafood Restaurant alc L, D £40/£50, St Petroc's bistro alc L, D £25, Café alc L, D £20; light meals available. Special breaks available

---

PAINSWICK Gloucestershire   map 5

Painswick Hotel

Kemps Lane, Painswick GL6 6YB
TEL: (01452) 812160   FAX: (01452) 814059
EMAIL: reservations@painswickhotel.com
WEB SITE: www.painswickhotel.com

Pure pleasure in Painswick's smartest hotel

Despite being one of the largest houses in town, Painswick Hotel is not that easy to spot. Like many other buildings here, it was built in pale Cotswold stone, and is tucked away down a lane behind the glorious fourteenth-century St Mary's church. In fact everything about the hotel feels tranquil and still, encouraging guests to linger in the public areas, perhaps playing one of the board games on offer as a fire crackles in the grate. Furnishings are in traditional styles, but fresh, bright and up-to-date. Ownership has changed since last year, but standards remain the same. There is a choice of a library and two lounges, one offering help-yourself tea and coffee. The restaurant has pale-wood panelling below terracotta walls and attracts non-resident clients. Our inspection meal began with a couple of *amuse-bouches*, and moved on to lobster ravioli with wilted chard, and halibut with curried scallop and sag aloo. Bedrooms are smart, if slightly formulaic, with plenty of floral patterns, a wide mix of colour schemes and decent bathrooms.

❍ Open all year 🔁 Painswick is on A46, between Stroud and Cheltenham. On turning right past St Mary's church, hotel is situated behind. Private car park 🛏 2 single, 5 twin/double, 10 double, 2 four-poster; all with room service, hair-dryer, direct-dial telephone, TV ✦ Restaurant, 2 dining rooms, bar, 2 lounges, library, garden; conferences and social functions; civil wedding licence; leisure facilities nearby; early suppers for children; cots, highchairs, toys, babysitting, baby-listening 🚹 No wheelchair access ● No children under 6 in restaurant eves; no dogs in public rooms and some bedrooms; no smoking in some public rooms and some bedrooms ▭ Amex, Delta, MasterCard, Switch, Visa £ Single £85, single occupancy of twin/double £100, twin/double £140, four-poster £210; deposit required. Set L £19, D £31; light meals available; service incl. Special breaks available (3 FOR 2)

PAULERSPURY Northamptonshire   map 5

Vine House

100 High Street, Paulerspury, Towcester NN12 7NA
TEL: (01327) 811267   FAX: (01327) 811309
EMAIL: info@vinehousehotel.com
WEB SITE: www.vinehousehotel.com

Top-notch food in quaint country-cottage hotel

Paulerspury is tiny, and quiet enough to look as if it only just made the upgrade from hamlet to village. The eighteenth-century, vine-clad Vine House is one of those cosy looking cottages in perfect tune with its peaceful surroundings. The entrance to the hotel is rather confusingly reached through the pretty walled garden at the rear of the cottage, the front door no longer being in use. The interior has the appearance of being put together with a lot of care and by someone with an eye for detail. Julie Springett describes her small hotel as a 'Tinkerbell-style cottage' and such is the effect of the high-chintz bedrooms with antique beds and flowery wallpaper that it would be no surprise to see Wendy and the gang hovering outside the bedroom windows. The provincial-look restaurant, run by Julie's husband Marcus, has a small yet varied menu specialising in delicious meals that juxtapose the traditional with contemporary styles and are prepared from fresh and local produce.

◖ Closed 2 weeks at Chr; restaurant closed Sun eve ⤴ Just off A5 in village of Paulerspury, 2 miles south of Towcester. Private car park 🛏 1 single, 1 twin, 4 double; all with hair-dryer, direct-dial telephone, TV ⌁ Restaurant, bar, lounge, library, garden; conferences and social functions; leisure facilities nearby; early suppers for children; baby-listening ♿ No wheelchair access ● No dogs; no smoking in public rooms ▭ Delta, MasterCard, Switch, Visa £ Single £59, twin/double £85; deposit required. Set L, D £30 ③FOR②

Penellick

Pelynt, Looe PL13 2LX
TEL: (01503) 272372 (AND FAX)
EMAIL: penellick@hotmail.com
WEB SITE: www.cornwall-online.co.uk/penellick

Superb service in a homely setting with excellent hosts and cooking

Tucked well into deep countryside is Ann and Micky Macartney's wonderful house, parts of which date back to the fourteenth century. The house is full of books, curios and period furniture and the couple manage to bring an easy, unforced hospitality to things – ever-helpful but never overpoweringly so. Pick of the bedrooms must be the double, with its red canopied bed and striking gold flourishes in the fabrics and colour scheme. On the landing is a sitting area that guests share, complete with more books, a log burner and a rocking sheep. Dinner is taken down the stairs in a cosy and homely small dining room. Ann's cooking and the care taken over the table and service are superior to that in far grander establishments. The proportion of home-made, local and organic ingredients is high. One reader praised the service and the food, but found the accommodation too 'darkly Bohemian' for his taste.

◖ Open all year ⤴ From Looe, take A387 towards Polperro; turn right on to B3359 signposted Pelynt; after almost 1 mile, take second of two lanes on left; after ½ mile turn left at T-junction; house is at end of lane. Nearest train station: Looe. Private car park 🛏 1 single, 1 double; family room available; both with shared bathrooms; both with hair-dryer; telephone, fax machine, modem line available ⌁ Dining room, sitting room, garden; leisure facilities nearby; early suppers for children; cots, highchairs, toys, babysitting, baby-listening ♿ No wheelchair access ● No dogs; no smoking ▭ None accepted £ Single £30 to £38, twin/double £60 to £76, family room from £60; deposit required. Alc D £21.50; light meals available; service incl ③FOR②

Abbey Hotel

Abbey Street, Penzance TR18 4AR
TEL: (01736) 366906   FAX: (01736) 351163
EMAIL: hotel@theabbeyonline.com
WEB SITE: www.theabbeyonline.com

Magical hotel hitched to a modern Michelin-starred restaurant

Natural light pours into the comfortably shabby, antique-filled drawing room of the Abbey from the fairytale walled garden, and you could easily imagine you're sitting in a long-lost children's book, the kind where magical adventures happen in big old houses belonging to kindly aunts. There are games, toys, books, clocks, portraits. As you wander the corridors outside, the colours are constantly changing, deep reds suddenly giving way to more subdued colours. Rooms are individually decorated and individually priced. Number 6 is a triple in the attic, cute and rickety, with the door through to the single room made to look like a secret entrance through a bookcase. Number 1 is probably the pick: it is light and airy with original wood-panelled bath jutting out of the bathroom wall, a delicately painted lampstand, a working coal fire and a great harbour view. Rooms do have TVs, but there are no phones and no locks on the doors. Next door, Ben Tunnicliffe runs his Michelin starred restaurant. Dark, red plaster arches with almost no decoration make up the downstairs bar, then when your food is ready you emerge into the light to seagrass flooring, glass-topped tables and black and white Eve Arnold prints.

◐ Closed Jan; Abbey restaurant closed Sun & Mon eves ⤵ Entering Penzance, take seafront road; after 300 yards, just before bridge, turn right; after 10 yards, turn left and drive up slipway; hotel is at top. Nearest train station: Penzance. Private car park ⬅ 1 twin, 2 twin/double, 4 double, 1 four-poster, 1 suite; family room available; all with room service, hair-dryer, TV; some with CD player ✓ Restaurant, dining room, bar, lounge, garden; conferences; social functions; leisure facilities nearby; early suppers for children, cots, babysitting, baby-listening ⅙ No wheelchair access ● No smoking in bedrooms ⊟ MasterCard, Switch, Visa £ Single occupancy of twin/double £75 to £95, twin/double from £100, four-poster £155 to £165, family room £200 to £215, suite £175 to £185; deposit required. Set L £20, alc D £37; light meals available. Special breaks available

---

Summer House

Cornwall Terrace, Penzance TR18 4HL
TEL: (01736) 363744   FAX: (01736) 360959
EMAIL: reception@summerhouse-cornwall.com
WEB SITE: www.summerhouse-cornwall.com

Aptly named hotel and restaurant offering style and comfort without leaving a luxury-sized dent in your wallet

Linda and Ciro Zaino clearly thought long and hard about the image they wanted to project after they decided to change the name of their hotel five years ago. The Summer House certainly does what it says on the tin – summery by name and summery by nature. Not only does it close for the winter, but you get breezy, bright yellow and blue colour schemes, a menu that shows a lightness of touch and, above all, a warm welcome from your hosts. There are plenty of interesting contemporary artworks around, most notably some striking abstract photography. Linda talks most enthusiastically about her bright, boldly decorated rooms, and describes herself as 'ruthless', but she's referring to her knowing what she wants and how to get it rather than her manner with guests, which – judging by her chatty demeanour – is anything but. Ciro serves up a three-course dinner every day except Monday and Tuesday, with plenty of seafood cooked in a light, interesting style, for example pan-fried sea bass with a touch of Pernod.

◐ Closed Dec to Feb; restaurant closed Mon & Tue eves ⤵ In Penzance, continue along seafront road on to promenade; at Queens Hotel, take next right into small news; hotel is 200 yards on left. Nearest train station: Penzance. Private car park ⬅ 1 twin/double, 4 double; all with hair-dryer, TV ✓ Restaurant, lounge, garden; social functions; leisure facilities nearby; early suppers for children ⅙ No wheelchair access ● No children under 13; no dogs; no smoking in bedrooms ⊟ Delta, MasterCard, Switch, Visa £ Single occupancy of twin/double £70 to £75, twin/double £75 to £95; deposit required. Set D £24.50

'The owner met us in the hall. The hotel literature said that he was an ex-schoolteacher, but I could well have believed that he used to work in a funeral parlour but was dismissed for being too lugubrious.'
On a hotel in the Scottish Borders

'One would have needed to be a contortionist to be able to pull off toilet paper while sitting on the lavatory.'
On a hotel in Hampshire

Ednovean Farm

Perranuthnoe, Penzance TR20 9LZ
TEL: (01736) 711883   FAX: (01736) 710480
EMAIL: info@ednoveanfarm.co.uk
WEB SITE: www.ednoveanfarm.co.uk

Top-class B&B – a truly winning combination of seclusion, sumptuous rooms and great views

Bump up and down on the potholed road, stop, open the gate, drive past a hay-filled barn, stop, close the gate – it's a bit of a struggle but it's absolutely worth it for this really special coastal B&B. Christine and Charles Taylor have managed to strike a perfect balance between the carefully chosen and the charmingly offhand in their decorative selections. So the lounge adjoining the homely open-plan kitchen-dining area is chock-full of mismatched antiques collected since childhood, while the bedrooms are luxurious and stylish. Each guest room has a colour scheme –

choose from Pink, Blue or Apricot – but none of these is in any way overwhelming. It's more that the splashes of colour in each are carefully coordinated. Pink is probably the pick of the bunch – warm and welcoming, never sickly and girlie. There's a lovely red hand-embroidered wall hanging (imported from the East via Penzance) and a large but cosy bathroom which (like the others) has hand-made soaps and shampoos. Blue is a larger room, if you prefer, with a new roll-top bath. As if all that were not enough, there's a nascent Italian garden and a fabulous view out to sea over St Michael's Mount.

○ Closed Chr & New Year ⬚ From A394 east of Marazion, turn off at Dynasty Restaurant towards Perranuthnoe; farm drive is on left on bend by postbox; pass four houses, fork right into car park/farmyard. Private car park ⬚ 2 double, 1 four-poster; all with hair-dryer, TV, CD player; 2 with private terrace ⬚ Breakfast room, lounge, garden ⬚ No wheelchair access; 3 ground-floor bedrooms ● No children; no dogs; no smoking ⬚ Amex, Delta, MasterCard, Switch, Visa £⬚ Double/four-poster £75 to £85; deposit required

The Barn

Pensham Hill House, Pensham, Pershore WR10 3HA
TEL: (01386) 555270   FAX: (01386) 552894

A B&B in a modern barn-conversion away from the main house

You could say that this is a plum location, as the town of Pershore is the self-proclaimed 'capital of the plum', thanks to the number of fruit orchards found around here. The Barn in question is a converted nineteenth-century farm outbuilding adjoining Pensham Hill House, the home of Gina Horton. The chalet-style building has three ground-floor bedrooms and a shared sitting room, so it is ideal for larger parties or extended family. It's been sympathetically restored in a cosy,

rustic, look, retaining some of the original rafters. The sitting room is spacious, with plenty of sofas and armchairs and a wood-burning stove as a feature, and there are French windows to a small terrace outside, which has views over the Avon valley and towards Bredon Hill. Pretty bedrooms have chintzy fabrics; one has a double whirlpool bath, and another an en-suite sauna. Guests can also use the pool and tennis court by prior arrangement.

○ Open all year ⬚ Just outside Pershore on B4084 to Evesham. Nearest train station: Pershore. Private car park ⬚ 1 twin, 2 double; all with hair-dryer, TV; 1 with trouser press ⬚ Dining room, sitting room, garden; tennis, unheated outdoor swimming pool (by arrangement); leisure facilities nearby ⬚ No wheelchair access; 3 ground-floor bedrooms ● No children under 12; no dogs; no smoking ⬚ None accepted £⬚ Single occupancy of twin/double £43 to £45, twin/double £65 to £75; deposit required

Old Railway Station

Petworth GU28 0JF
TEL: (01798) 342346   FAX: (01798) 343066
EMAIL: mlr@old-station.co.uk
WEB SITE: www.old-station.co.uk

First-class B&B in an elegant colonial-style station and luxurious Pullmans

Though no trains have passed this way for many a year, railway enthusiasts – and others – will feel they've died and gone to heaven at this beautifully restored colonial-style station just outside Petworth. Built in 1894, the good-looking, cream-painted station building is kept resolutely in period by owner Lou Ripley but is no stuffy museum piece; instead it's a fascinating, elegant and superbly comfortable B&B stuffed with character and period features. The impressive former waiting room, with its lofty vaulted ceiling, ticket-office windows, louvre shutters and bare wood floors makes for a comfortable and stylish lounge, where salmon-painted wood walls are lined with old photos and lanterns original to Brighton station. Breakfast is served here, or, in summer, on the station platform, where tables and chairs are put out overlooking the steeply banked track gardens. Most of the bedrooms are found in the sidings along the platform in three lovingly restored railway carriages – Flora, Mimosa and Alicante – the stuff of every schoolboy's dreams. The most prestigious (according to experts) is Flora, the newest addition, for she served on the Golden Arrow and boasts lovely marquetry throughout to prove it. All, though, are beautifully done out, typically compact but comfortable, perhaps with brass beds, some of them king-size, and well-equipped bathrooms which manage to include a bath and full-height shower. The two bedrooms in the main station building – one downstairs and one under the eaves, reached by an industrial fire-escape staircase – are no less appealing.

○ Open all year   On A285 about 2 miles south of Petworth; at Badgers Pub, pull in to front of pub and take slip road to station. Private car park   1 twin/double, 7 double; all with hair-dryer, TV   Breakfast/ sitting room, library, terrace, garden; leisure facilities nearby; cots   Wheelchair access to hotel and restaurant, National Accessible Scheme M1, 1 ground-floor bedroom, specially equipped for disabled people   No children under 10; no dogs; no smoking in bedrooms   Delta, Diners, MasterCard, Switch, Visa   Single occupancy of twin/double £50 to £80, twin/double £66 to £138; deposit required. Cooked B £8. Special breaks available

White Swan

Market Place, Pickering YO18 7AA
TEL: (01751) 472288   FAX: (01751) 475554
EMAIL: welcome@white-swan.co.uk
WEB SITE: www.white-swan.co.uk

Old coaching inn with a modern twist in the bedroom and dining departments

History, atmosphere and cosiness make for solid foundations in any inn. Add to these sterling qualities a switched-on attitude to contemporary style and you have, in the White Swan, a winner. The immediate impression is that of a classy, upmarket place. Food and wine are taken seriously here: spot the cases from grand Bordeaux appellations that are inlaid into the bar itself, paintings of superstar wine bottles on the walls, and a good spread of hand-pulled ales and wine by the glass. Two convivial rooms front the house, both with pubby tables, log fires and exposed beams that make it hard to choose which one to take a seat in, although in practice your choice will be dictated by available space – make no mistake, this is a busy inn, kept ticking over by cheery, professional staff who are on the ball. Exemplary Whitby fish with mushy peas and fat, crisp chips made for a satisfying inspection lunch in the bar, or you could go more upmarket for dinner in the main restaurant, where rough flagstone floors, cerise walls and polished, candlelit tables create a romantic ambience. Rooms keep up the overall tone of understated style, with a mix of antiques, muted colours, plush fabrics and smart white-tiled modern bathrooms.

○ Open all year In centre of Pickering's market place. Private car park 10 twin/double, 2 suites; family rooms available; all with room service, hair-dryer, direct-dial telephone, modem line, TV, DVD; some with trouser press, CD player; fax machine available Restaurant, bar, sitting room; conferences; social functions; leisure facilities nearby; early suppers for children; cots, highchairs, baby-listening No wheelchair access No children in restaurant after 8pm; no dogs in restaurant, £7.50 per stay in bedrooms; no smoking in restaurant or bedrooms Amex, Delta, MasterCard, Switch, Visa Single occupancy of twin/double £75 to £85, twin/double £120 to £130, family room £120 to £195, suite £140 to £170; deposit required. Alc L £20, D £25; light meals available. Special breaks available (3FOR2)

PICKHILL North Yorkshire
map 9

Nag's Head

Pickhill, Nr Thirsk YO7 4JG
TEL: (01845) 567391 FAX: (01845) 567212
EMAIL: enquiries@nagsheadpickhill.freeserve.co.uk
WEB SITE: www.nagsheadpickhill.co.uk

Unpretentious hospitality at this handily located country inn

Just a mile or so from the A1, but far enough to be comfortably out of earshot, the Nag's Head is well worth seeking out, whether you need to break a long journey with an overnight stop, or as a base for the Dales attractions or a flutter on the gee-gees at local racecourses. Raymond and Edward Boynton have run the place for over 30 years, so it has the feel of a long-established inn. There's a proper pubby locals' bar with a glowing coal fire and a draughts board set into the flagstone floor – games are played with pints instead of pieces to liven things up. The lounge lacks the bar's authentic ambience, but is a plusher place and more geared towards diners than drinkers – food is, after all, taken quite seriously here, with heaps of modern British dishes chalked up on boards. Posher still is the stylish main restaurant, which has a light, woody décor of oak flooring, pale-wood chairs and polished antique tables. The best rooms are in the Friar Villa annexe: these have a plain and simple modern style with pine furniture and smart bathrooms; those in the main building have an older, more floral look with the bathrooms showing signs of wear and tear.

○ Open all year From A1, 8 miles from Thirsk, take Masham turn-off; Pickhill is signposted from B6267 in Ainderby Quernhow; hotel is in centre of village. Private car park 2 single, 5 twin, 7 double, 1 suite; family rooms available; all with room service, hair-dryer, direct-dial telephone, modem line, TV; some with trouser press, VCR, CD player Restaurant, 2 bars, lounge, garden; conferences; social functions; leisure facilities nearby; early suppers for children; cots, highchairs Wheelchair access to hotel and restaurant (ramps), WC, 2 ground-floor bedrooms No dogs in public rooms and some bedrooms; no smoking in some public rooms and some bedrooms Delta, MasterCard, Switch, Visa Single £45, single occupancy of twin/double £50, twin/double £70, family room/suite £80; deposit required. Set L £16, D £23; alc L, D £25; light meals available; service incl. Special breaks available (3FOR2)

POLPERRO Cornwall
Map 1

Cottage Restaurant

The Coombes, Polperro, Looe PL13 2RQ
TEL: (01503) 272217

Well-tended country rooms in a lovely Cornish coastal village

Polperro is the very vision of a picture-pretty Cornish village, and as you approach the Cottage Restaurant down the holidaymaker-choked hill you'll pass numerous B&Bs, postcard sellers and fudge shops. The oldest parts of the building date back to the sixteenth century, though there have been plenty of additions right up to the 1990s. The restaurant areas have low beams and whitewashed walls and adjoin a little bar with horse brasses, Toby jugs, curly plastic flowers and a heavy antique sideboard filled with blue and white china. The well-regarded food is firmly traditional British – Guinness and mushroom pie or grilled sea bass being prime menu samples. Bedrooms are appositely cottagey. Room 5 is possibly the pick – up a couple of steps, it feels a little more secluded.

◑ Closed Dec and Jan; restaurant closed Nov to Mar ⬕ 300 metres towards village from main car park, on the right ⬔ 5 double; all with hair-dryer, trouser press, TV ⬗ Restaurant, bar, garden ⬕ No wheelchair access; 2 ground-floor bedrooms ⬤ No children under 5; no dogs; no smoking ⬚ Delta, MasterCard, Switch, Visa ⬚ Double £60 to £64; deposit required. Alc D £25; service incl

---

POOLE Dorset

map 2

Mansion House

Thames Street, Poole BH15 1JN
TEL: (01202) 685666   FAX: (01202) 665709
EMAIL: enquiries@themansionhouse.co.uk
WEB SITE: www.themansionhouse.co.uk

Attractive hotel with personable staff, good restaurant and comfortable rooms

Among the quaint streets of old Poole, and close to the waterfront, lies this handsome Georgian house with ivy-clad façade. The reception is particularly grand, rising through three floors, with balustrades curling upwards. Downstairs there is a bistro, recently brought up to date with a more contemporary look – modern art on the walls and polished wood tables – and the smart restaurant, cosy and intimate with wood panelling and soft lighting. The well-reported cooking covers a good range of options including plenty of seafood. Upstairs, bedrooms that have been refurbished recently go for richer colours – lots of old gold matched with tasselled curtains and soft headboards – while the older décor is generally lighter in tone. Owners Jackie and Gerry Godden run the place with a sure touch, creating a gently sophisticated but welcoming atmosphere.

◑ Open all year; restaurant closed Sun eve (except bank hols) ⬕ Approaching Poole from Southampton on A31, follow signs for Channel ferry; at lifting bridge, turn left on to Poole Quay; take first road on left (Thames Street); hotel is opposite church. Nearest train station: Poole. Private car park ⬔ 9 single, 5 twin, 14 double, 2 four-poster, 2 family rooms; all with room service, hair-dryer, trouser press, direct-dial telephone, TV ⬗ 2 restaurants, 2 bars, lounge; conferences and social functions; civil wedding licence; leisure facilities nearby; early suppers for children; cots, highchairs, babysitting, baby-listening ⬕ No wheelchair access ⬤ No children under 5 in restaurant eves; no dogs; no smoking in most public rooms and some bedrooms ⬚ Amex, Delta, Diners, MasterCard, Switch, Visa ⬚ Single £75 to £95, single occupancy of twin/double £90 to £99, twin/double £120 to £130, four-poster £135 to £145, family room £140 to £150. Set L £18.50, D £26.50; light meals available. Special breaks available ⬚

PORLOCK WEIR Somerset

map 1

Andrew's on the Weir

Porlock Weir, Minehead TA24 8PB
TEL: (01643) 863300   FAX: (01643) 863311
EMAIL: info@andrewsontheweir.co.uk
WEB SITE: www.andrewsontheweir.co.uk

Attentive hosts and excellent food at this coastal restaurant-with-rooms

This interesting little seaside settlement is worth a detour in itself, but many visitors simply motor down the lovely coastal lane to eat at Andrew Dixon's place. In fact the success of this restaurant-with-rooms has meant big changes in the offing, with the bar at the front moving to the rear of house and the restaurant expanding to take in more sea-view tables. This won't change the essential nature of the operation, which is relaxing and friendly, a style matched by zealous determination to produce good food. Seafood gets particular praise, as do the British cheeses, and breakfasts are comprehensive to say the least. Bedrooms adopt a pretty, cottagey look with floral patterns and good bathrooms. Three of them have sea views across the front garden and car park to the Bristol Channel.

● Closed Jan; restaurant closed Sun eve to Tues lunch ☑ From M5 Junction 25, go through Taunton and take A358 to Minehead, then A39 to Porlock; turn right on to B3225 to Porlock Weir. Private car park ⌂ 1 twin, 3 double, 1 four-poster; all with hair-dryer, TV ✅ Restaurant, bar, lounge, garden; social functions ⅙ No wheelchair access ● No children under 12; no dogs in public rooms; smoking in lounge only ▭ Amex, Delta, MasterCard, Switch, Visa £ Single occupancy of twin/double £65 to £95, twin/double £75 to £95, £120; deposit required. Set L £15; alc L, D £35. Special breaks available ③FOR②

PORTLOE Cornwall
Map 1

The Lugger

Portloe, Truro TR2 5RD
TEL: (01872) 501322   FAX: (01872) 501691
EMAIL: office@luggerhotel.com
WEB SITE: www.luggerhotel.com

Contemporary chic hidden in an old smuggler's den

Portloe is a picturesque little cove squeezed snugly into the spectacular headlands of the Roseland Peninsula. It's just the sort of place you'd expect to find the seventeenth-century smuggler's inn that houses The Lugger, but perhaps not the swish modern interiors you'll find when you step inside. We're not quite sure what the billing as 'designed for international travellers' means, but don't let it put you off; what you get here is tasteful contemporary luxury which doesn't come cheap. The restaurant, overlooking the water, has high-backed chairs and smart table settings, and lunch can be served on the terrace, weather permitting. Bedrooms are of the pale colour schemes teamed with straight-lined furniture variety common to today's boutique hotels, though it's a shame that not many are able to take advantage of the sea view.

● Open all year ☑ From St Austell take A390 to Truro, then B3287 to Tregony, turn left on to A3078 towards St Mawes; after 2 miles fork left for Veryan and Portloe; turn left at T-junction for Portloe. Private car park ⌂ 11 twin/double, 10 double; all with room service, hair-dryer, direct-dial telephone, TV, VCR ✅ Restaurant, bar, lounge, study, terrace; spa; leisure facilities nearby; highchairs ⅙ No wheelchair access; 1 ground-floor bedroom ● No children under 12; no dogs; no smoking in bedrooms ▭ Amex, Delta, MasterCard, Switch, Visa £ Single occupancy of twin/double £132 to £235, twin/double £155 to £275; deposit required. Set L £20, D £37.50; light meals available. Special breaks available

---

PORTSCATHO Cornwall
Map 1

Driftwood Hotel

Rosevine, Nr Portscatho, Truro TR2 5EW
TEL: (01872) 580644   FAX: (01872) 580801
EMAIL: info@driftwoodhotel.co.uk
WEB SITE: www.driftwoodhotel.co.uk

Chilled-out contemporary style complete with private beach

The terraced lawns of the Driftwood Hotel offer great views out to sea, and if you fancy a dip in the water, you've the enviable luxury of a private beach available just three minutes' walk away. The mood that Paul and Fiona Robinson are aiming for is one of unalloyed relaxation – everything is pale, stylish and tasteful and there's little to grab the eye or distract you from your contemplative repose. The hotel name is reflected in the occasional use of driftwood in the décor, and the scheme has a generally nautical bent. The restaurant takes advantage of the sea view with a picture window facing the water, and there's a new chef in the kitchen, the ex-head of One Aldwych in London. Virtually all the bedrooms have sea views, and there's a cabin right on the beach if you feel the need to get away even from the tranquillity of the hotel.

◗ Closed mid-Dec to early Feb (exc New Year) 🔁 Take A3078 towards St Mawes; hotel is signposted 2 miles south of Ruan High Lanes, off A3078. Private car park 🛏 1 twin, 3 twin/double, 5 double, 2 family rooms; all with room service, hair-dryer, direct-dial telephone, TV, VCR ⊘ Restaurant, bar, sitting room, drawing room, gardens; social functions; early suppers for children; cots, highchairs, playroom 🔥 No wheelchair access; 1 ground-floor bedroom ⬤ No dogs; no smoking ⊟ Amex, MasterCard, Switch, Visa £ Single occupancy of twin/double £130, twin/double £170, family room £200; deposit required. Set D £34. Special breaks available

Rosevine Hotel

Rosevine, Portscatho, Truro TR2 5EW
TEL: (01872) 580206   FAX: (01872) 580230
EMAIL: info@rosevine.co.uk
WEB SITE: www.rosevine.co.uk

Traditional comforts in a splendid bay-side location

The Rosevine is an unashamedly old-fashioned sort of place – if you're tired of trendy boutique hotels, incomprehensible modern art and fashionable fusion food, this could be just your sort of retreat. Everything from the spacious dining room to the drawing room (ideal for high teas) and bedrooms in the main house and rose garden annexe are smartly decorated and furnished in a traditional country-house style – comfy chairs, patterned rugs, flowery borders and drapes and swags. The beach is mere minutes away from the bottom of the gently sloping subtropical gardens, and at low tide you can walk all the way to the pretty village of Portscatho, returning via the coastal path if you miss the tide on the way back. If things are a bit too nippy for a swim in the sea, the indoor pool (complete with paddling pool for little ones and decorated with a cheerful jungle fresco) is an option. Or there's the sun lounge for simply gazing at the views.

◗ Closed Nov, Dec & Jan 🔁 Take A3078 towards St Mawes; 3 miles before St Mawes follow signs to Rosevine and to Rosevine Hotel. Private car park 🛏 8 twin/double, 6 family rooms, 3 suites; all with room service, hair-dryer, trouser press, direct-dial telephone, TV, DVD ⊘ Dining room, bar, drawing room, conservatory, games room, garden; social functions; indoor heated swimming pool; leisure facilities nearby; early suppers for children; cots, highchairs, toys, playroom, babysitting, baby-listening, outdoor play area 🔥 Wheelchair access to hotel and restaurant (ramps), WC, 3 ground-floor bedrooms. Disabled parking ⬤ No dogs in public rooms; smoking in bar only ⊟ Amex, Delta, MasterCard, Switch, Visa £ Single occupancy of twin/double £108 to £189, twin/double £168 to £252, family room £189 to £283, suite £252 to £378; deposit required. Set D £36; alc L £26, D £36; light meals available. Special breaks available

POSTBRIDGE Devon   map 1

Lydgate House

Postbridge, Yelverton PL20 6TJ
TEL: (01822) 880209   FAX: (01822) 880202
EMAIL: lydgatehouse@email.com
WEB SITE: www.lydgatehouse.co.uk

Fine small hotel offering good food and comfortable rooms

Tucked well back from the main road over Dartmoor and close to the East Dart River stands Cindy and Peter Farrington's substantial country house, mostly late Victorian but parts of which are over 200 years old. The setting is a key reason for coming to stay: it gives guests access to wild nature walks along the river, including meadows where five species of orchid flower grow. The house itself is 'friendly and relaxing' with excellent river views from the recently extended conservatory dining room. Cindy is the chef and her menus cover a good range of imaginative dishes with three or four alternatives at each course. One guest described dinner as 'good, plain cooking', but objected to being charged extra for coffee. Next door is a pleasant and homely lounge with deep cream-coloured sofas arranged around a log burner – stacks of local guides, information and maps are available. Bedrooms follow the same cosy and homely line with the Farringtons' thoughtful approach evident – there is a large basket of useful extras in each bathroom. The ground-floor room lacks any views but does have a sitting area and living flame gas fire.

◐ Closed Jan ⌨ Off B3212, midway between Moretonhampstead and Princetown; turn south between humpback bridge and East Dart pub. Private car park ⬤⇝ 2 single, 1 twin/double, 4 double; all with hair-dryer, TV ✅ Dining room/conservatory, bar, lounge, garden; conferences ♿ No wheelchair access; 1 ground-floor bedroom ⬤ No children under 12; no smoking ☐ MasterCard, Switch, Visa £ Single £50 to £55, single occupancy of twin/double £80 to £100, twin/double £100 to £130; deposit required. Alc D £28; service incl. Special breaks available

---

PRESTBURY Cheshire   map 8

The White House Manor

New Road, Prestbury, Macclesfield SK10 4HP
TEL: (01625) 829376 FAX: (01625) 828627
EMAIL: info@thewhitehouse.uk.com
WEB SITE: www.thewhitehouse.uk.com

Superior hotel-restaurant in an affluent commuter village

Within striking distance of Greater Manchester, Prestbury is definitely on the des-res list of North Cheshire's dormitory settlements. Secluded from passing traffic by tall conifers, this nineteenth-century townhouse on the edge of the village has a distinctly upscale air, an impression perpetuated by its classily sophisticated interior. The Orangery is a strikingly elegant though restful sitting room, but it is the bedrooms that really pack a punch, each individually decorated with great panache and no expense spared. Glyndebourne (sumptuously French with a high-tech sound system), Trafalgar (military and naval themes) or Earl Grey (beautifully displayed bone china and a bewildering array of teas) are just three typically extravagant boltholes. Elaborate bathrooms are a recurring theme; Turkish steam showers and whirlpool baths feature in several rooms. The acclaimed restaurant occupies a separate building in the village centre, similarly stylish and ambitious in etched glass and limed woodwork, with refined contemporary cooking.

◐ Closed 25 & 26 Dec; restaurant closed Sun eve ⌨ 2 miles north of Macclesfield on A538. Nearest train station: Prestbury. Private car park ⬤⇝ 3 single, 1 twin, 5 double, 2 four-poster; all with room service, hair-dryer, mini-bar, trouser press, direct-dial telephone, modem line, TV, CD player ✅ Restaurant, bar, sitting room, conservatory, garden; conferences; leisure facilities nearby ♿ Wheelchair access to hotel (ramp) and restaurant, 2 ground-floor bedrooms ⬤ No children under 10; no dogs; no smoking in bedrooms and some public rooms ☐ Amex, Delta, MasterCard, Switch, Visa £ Single £75, single occupancy of twin/double £90, twin/double £110, four-poster £130; deposit required. Continental B £6.50, cooked B £9.50; set L £16, D £19; alc L, D £24; light meals available. Special breaks available

---

PURTON Wiltshire   map 2

Pear Tree at Purton

Church End, Purton, Swindon SN5 4ED
TEL: (01793) 772100 FAX: (01793) 772369
EMAIL: relax@peartreepurton.co.uk
WEB SITE: www.peartreepurton.co.uk

Handy location for this well-run country-house hotel

A host who has looked after royalty should know a thing or two about pampering guests – Francis and Anne Young got the experience with the late King Hussein of Jordan and it shows in the immaculate professional operation they run at this sixteenth-century vicarage (the church is further away than you'd expect – the house was moved almost a century ago). Business travellers appreciate the smoothly executed service and the convenient location for the M4, but there is much else to praise. The building itself is country house par excellence with homely library, clubby bar and conservatory restaurant all decorated with fresh flowers. Outside are lawned gardens with croquet hoops. Bedrooms are impeccably well kept and smart. Décor is rather traditional; there are more fresh flowers, and luxuries such as sherry and digital television to complete a very attractive package.

◑ Closed 26 to 30 Dec ⚡ Leave M4 at Junction 16 and follow signs to Wootton Bassett, then Purton; at end of High Street, turn right at Spar shop; hotel is ¼ mile on left. Private car park ⌁ 8 twin/double, 5 double, 2 four-poster, 2 suites; family room available; all with room service, hair-dryer, trouser press, direct-dial telephone, modem line, TV; some with VCR, CD player; no tea/coffee-making facilities in rooms ⌀ Restaurant, bar, lounge, library, conservatory, garden; conferences; social functions; civil wedding licence; leisure facilities nearby; early suppers for children; cots, highchairs, baby-listening, outdoor play area ⌁ Wheelchair access to hotel (ramp) and restaurant, WC, 6 ground-floor bedrooms. Disabled parking ● No dogs in public rooms ☐ Amex, Delta, Diners, MasterCard, Switch, Visa £ Single occupancy of twin/double £110, twin/double £110, four-poster £135, family room £145, suite £160; deposit required. Set L £18.50, D £32.50; light meals available; service incl. Special breaks available

---

RAMSGILL North Yorkshire

map 8

Yorke Arms

Ramsgill-in-Nidderdale, Harrogate HG3 5RL
TEL: (01423) 755243   FAX: (01423) 755330
EMAIL: enquiries@yorke-arms.co.uk
WEB SITE: www.yorke-arms.co.uk

Upmarket rural inn with seriously good food and classy bedrooms

The Yorke Arms may sound like a pub, but visitors at Frances and Bill Atkins' creeper-swathed stone inn are unlikely to be here just for the beer. Tapestry hangings, pewter jugs and plates, flagstones and carved settles create a country feel in the bar, while stripped wooden floors with oriental rugs and huge mirrors make for a lighter touch in the main restaurant. Frances' cuisine is inventive stuff, firmly rooted in French tradition. You'll find local beef and Nidderdale lamb, hare and partridge, Whitby crab and turbot, and luxury ingredients such as lobster and foie gras – most of which will put in an appearance at some point during the blowout seven-course tasting menu. Of course you don't have to eat to the point of incapacitating yourself – there is a variety of menus and formulas to cater for most appetites, starting with simpler fare in the bar – but if you have come to eat yourself to a standstill, the bedrooms are elegantly furnished to aid digestion.

◑ Open all year ⚡ From Harrogate take A61 to Ripley, then follow B6165 to Pateley Bridge; turn right up Low Wath road to Ramsgill. Private car park ⌁ 2 single, 4 twin/double, 7 double, 1 four-poster; all with hair-dryer, direct-dial telephone, TV; some with mini-bar, trouser press, VCR ⌀ Restaurant, bar, lounge, garden; conferences; social functions; leisure facilities nearby ⌁ No wheelchair access; 3 steps into hotel, 2 steps into restaurant, 4 ground-floor bedrooms ● No children under 12; dogs in bar only; smoking in bar only ☐ Amex, Delta, Diners, MasterCard, Switch, Visa £ Single £100 to £125, single occupancy of twin/double £120 to £150, twin/double £200 to £250, four-poster £260 to £340 (rates incl dinner); deposit required. Set L £17.50, Sun L £29; alc L £40; light meals available

---

REDWORTH Co Durham

map 10

Redworth Hall

Redworth, Durham DL5 6N6
TEL: (01388) 770600   FAX: (01388) 770654
WEB SITE: www.paramount-hotels.co.uk

Professionally run country-house hotel good for business and leisure

Redworth Hall ticks most of the boxes for character you might expect in a country house that started life as an Elizabethan manor. A grand coiling staircase, mullioned windows with stained glass heraldic panels and the baronial Great Hall provide plenty of period feel, but time doesn't stand still, so nowadays the atmosphere is fairly corporate during the week. When we visited, eight conference groups were milling around, with men in shirts and ties, mobiles in hand pacing the car park. And, naturally, weddings – over 100 annually take place here – are big business too. Although character has inevitably been sacrificed to cater for the various types of clientele, staff are on the ball and friendly, and there are enough nooks, crannies and quiet corners to find a bit of personal space. The modern brasserie-style Conservatory – a buzzing place that caters for up to 200 diners on a weekend evening – is the more casual of two dining venues; the 1744 restaurant is more formal. Bedrooms in the main house are the ones with grandest style and period features, while those in the newer section come in a variety of sizes and price bands. All are modern with confident colour schemes and upmarket fabrics.

○ Open all year ⊿ Between Darlington and Bishop Auckland, follow brown signs to hotel. Private car park ⌁ 2 single, 27 twin, 51 double, 3 four-poster, 14 family rooms, 3 suites; all with room service, hair-dryer, trouser press, fax/modem line, TV ⌀ 2 restaurants, bar, lounges, gardens; conferences; social functions; civil wedding licence; gym, spa, tennis, heated indoor swimming pool; early suppers for children (served in rooms); cots, highchairs, playroom, babysitting, outdoor play area ⌖ Wheelchair access to hotel (ramp) and restaurant, National Accessible Scheme M1, WC, 10 ground-floor bedrooms, 2 rooms specially equipped for disabled people, lift. Disabled parking ● No dogs in public rooms ⊟ Amex, Delta, Diners, MasterCard, Switch, Visa £ Single £120, single occupancy of twin/double £120, twin/double/family room £135, four-poster suite £190. Set D £18; alc L, D £20; light meals available; service incl. Special breaks available

---

REETH North Yorkshire   map 8

Arkleside Hotel

Reeth, Richmond DL11 6SG
TEL: (01748) 884200 (AND FAX)
EMAIL: info@arklesidehotel.co.uk
WEB SITE: www.arklesidehotel.co.uk

Small Swaledale hotel with the right location and attitude for walkers

Richard Beal and Dorothy Kendall's cosy little hotel lies just off the postcard-perfect village green of Reeth surrounded by open Dales countryside that is heaven for hikers. Don't let first impressions fool you: once you're beyond the courtyard entrance, the stone-built house opens up Tardis-like into a series of convivial rooms that focus on a pleasant terraced garden perched like a balcony over Swaledale. When bad weather puts the block on outdoor activities, you can stare wistfully at the superb views from a squashy bentwood seat in the conservatory lounge, or deaden the pain by a wood-burning stove in the bar. Of course it helps that Richard and Dorothy are keen walkers themselves and organise special walking weekends through the year, so you're never far from advice, maps and guides. Above all, this is a 'put your feet up' sort of place for relaxing. Bedrooms are homely, with a floral cottagey décor; the best get cracking views or are cosily tucked under the eaves.

○ Closed Jan ⊿ 100 yards from post office in Reeth. Private car park ⌁ 2 twin, 7 double, 2 suites; all with hair-dryer, TV ⌀ Restaurant, bar/lounge, conservatory, garden; conferences ⌖ No wheelchair access; 4 steps into hotel, 4 steps into restaurant, 2 ground-floor bedrooms ● No children under 10, no children under 16 in restaurant; dogs in bedrooms only; smoking in bar only ⊟ Delta, MasterCard, Switch, Visa £ Single occupancy of twin/double £58, twin/double £86, suite £100; deposit required. Alc D £24. Special breaks available

Burgoyne Hotel

On The Green, Reeth, Richmond DL11 6SN
TEL: (01748) 884292 (AND FAX)
EMAIL: enquiries@theburgoyne.co.uk
WEB SITE: www.theburgoyne.co.uk

Classy rooms and charming owners at an upmarket Georgian hotel on a quintessentially English village green

When you have spent the day hiking over the Swaledale hills or pottering around picturesque villages it is good to retire to a bit of a luxury bolthole. Derek Hickson and Peter Carwardine's classic double-fronted Georgian house fits the bill admirably. Its period style combines rich colour schemes, fancy plasterwork, antiques and opulent fabrics. Of the two drawing rooms that flank the front door, the smokers' room probably pips the smoke-free zone for character: it is a deeply peaceful spot with logs crackling in a triple-arched fireplace – great for an aperitif before moving into the deep-green dining room for Peter's four-course dinners; expect traditional English fare with a continental slant, based on fresh local produce. Even the tea trays in the impeccable bedrooms come with classy china; all but one of the rooms face across the green to the hills beyond and share a décor of understated elegance, where not a detail jars.

◐ Closed 2 Jan to 13 Feb 🔁 Hotel overlooks village green in Reeth. Private car park ⬛ 3 twin, 4 double, 1 four-poster; all with room service, hair-dryer, trouser press, direct-dial telephone, TV ⌀ Dining room, 2 drawing rooms, garden; conferences, social functions; early suppers for children; baby-listening ♿ No wheelchair access; 6 steps into hotel, 1 ground-floor bedroom specially equipped for disabled people ● No children under 10; no dogs in dining room; smoking in 1 drawing room only ▭ MasterCard, Switch, Visa £ Single occupancy of twin/double from £100, twin/double from £110, four-poster from £160; deposit required. Set D £26.50. Special breaks available

---

RHYDYCROESAU Shropshire   map 7

Pen-y-Dyffryn

Rhydycroesau, Oswestry SY10 7JD
TEL: (01691) 653700   FAX: (01691) 650066
EMAIL: stay@peny.co.uk
WEB SITE: www.peny.co.uk

Superb location and attentive service at this charming country house

Head west out of Oswestry, and on the last hill in Shropshire you will find this country-house gem, a perfect setting for sunset over the Welsh mountains. Audrey and Miles Hunter have been owners of this striking, pale grey Victorian rectory for more than 15 years and have created a tasteful upbeat hotel that pleases both old and young alike. Although things are run slickly and efficiently, the Hunters have kept a homely feel to the décor. The lounge has low bookcases, pelmeted curtains, a gently ticking clock, unfussy lamps and plenty of fresh flowers. Bedrooms are split between the main house and the Coach House. There is little to choose between them, as all have excellent bathrooms and good lighting with light fresh colour schemes. The Coach House bedrooms have their own private patios and are popular with dog owners. Guests can relax here or head off into the south-facing rhododendron gardens – it's hard to believe that this is almost 1,000 feet above sea level.

◐ Closed 20 Dec to 20 Jan 🔁 From Oswestry town centre follow sign for Llansilin (B4580); hotel is 3 miles west of Oswestry, on left. Private car park ⬛ 1 single, 4 twin, 6 double, 1 family room; all with room service, hair-dryer, trouser press, direct-dial telephone, modem line, TV; 3 with spa bath; 1 with CD player; 1 with Jacuzzi ⌀ Dining room, bar, 2 lounges, garden; leisure facilities nearby; early suppers for children; baby-listening ♿ Wheelchair access to hotel (ramp but further steps) and dining room, 1 ground-floor bedroom specially equipped for disabled people ● No children under 3; no dogs in public rooms eves; smoking in bar only ▭ Amex, Delta, MasterCard, Switch, Visa £ Single £78, single occupancy of twin/ double £78, twin/double £104 to £140, family room £143; deposit required. Set D £29; light meals available. Special breaks available ③FOR②

RINGLESTONE Kent   map 3

Ringlestone Inn

Ringlestone, Nr Harrietsham, Maidstone ME17 1NX
TEL: (01622) 859900   FAX: (01622) 859966
EMAIL: bookings@ringlestone.com
WEB SITE: www.ringlestone.com

Country inn with attractive bedrooms and good ale

Follow the signs for Ringlestone out of Maidstone and you'll end up in the wrong place altogether! Instead, aim for Harrietsham and you'll have better luck. This traditional old inn of weatherboard and brick, deep in the countryside, is a popular place for a spot of lunch or an evening meal – especially with families, as children can come too – so book your table in advance. The dark interior is cosy with candlelight, even during the day, and a warm, welcoming open fire. Food based on plenty of produce from the heart of Kent is served in all of the three interlinked bars and in a small dining room. Each of the three bedrooms is in the farmhouse building across the road, which rules out the usual and expected 'above the bar' murmur that

affects many pub rooms. Two have space for armchairs and heavy wooden furniture and are stylish with cream colour schemes. They are also well equipped – they come with CD players – and have good bathrooms.

● Closed 25 Dec ⊉ From M20 junction 8, take A20 towards Leeds Castle; turn left to Hollingbourne at roundabout opposite Great Danes Hotel, continue through village to top of hill; turn right at crossroads and follow signs to Ringlestone. Nearest train station: Hollingbourne. Private car park 🛏 2 twin/double, 1 four-poster; family rooms available; all with hair-dryer, trouser press, direct-dial telephone, TV, CD player, fridge ⊘ Dining room, 3 bars, lounge, gardens; conferences; social functions; leisure facilities nearby; cots, highchairs ⅟ No wheelchair access ● No dogs or smoking in bedrooms ▭ Amex, Delta, Diners, MasterCard, Switch, Visa £ Single occupancy of twin/double £89 to £120, twin/double/four-poster £99 to £120, family room £109 to £130; deposit required. Continental B £12, cooked B £15; alc L £18, D £22.50; light meals available. Special breaks available ③FOR②

RIPLEY North Yorkshire   map 8

Boar's Head

Ripley, Nr Harrogate HG3 3AY
TEL: (01423) 771888   FAX: (01423) 771509
EMAIL: reservations@boarsheadripley.co.uk
WEB SITE: www.boarsheadripley.co.uk

Comfort, tradition and rather good food in a historic postcard village

The village of Ripley is something of a time-warp. The medieval castle, town hall, and the sprinkling of houses around the cobbled square on which the Boar's Head sits, are mostly owned by the Ingilby family, which has presided over this honeypot village for nearly seven centuries. And it still likes to be involved with the running of the hotel: Lady Ingilby designs the bedrooms, contributing family antiques from the castle's attics, while Sir Thomas takes a personal interest in sourcing, and of course tasting, all of the wines. Bedrooms are rather grand affairs and

good-sized, whether they are of the standard variety in the courtyard or the top-notch ones in the main house, such as Cathedral with its cherubic ceiling frescoes; all come with home-made biscuits, bathrobes and posh smellies. The insistence on quality carries through to dining: choose between a candlelit bistro for robust fodder such as venison sausages with mustard mash, or the elegant and romantic restaurant for creative and ambitious fare – perhaps red mullet on vanilla lemon mash.

● Open all year ⊉ 3 miles north of Harrogate on A61. Private car park 🛏 25 twin/double; all with room service, hair-dryer, trouser press, direct-dial telephone, TV ⊘ Restaurant, bar, 2 lounges, garden; conferences; social functions; civil wedding licence; tennis; leisure facilities nearby; early suppers for children; cots, highchairs, babysitting, baby-listening, outdoor play area ⅟ Wheelchair access to hotel (2 steps or ramp at rear) and restaurant, WC, 5 ground-floor bedrooms. Disabled parking ● No dogs in some public rooms; no smoking in some public rooms and some bedrooms ▭ Amex, Delta, Diners, MasterCard, Switch, Visa £ Single occupancy of twin/double £105, twin/double £125 to £150; deposit required. Set L £15, D £30; light meals available. Special breaks available

---

ROCK Cornwall   map 1

St Enodoc Hotel

Rock, Wadebridge PL27 6LA
TEL: (01208) 863394   FAX: (01208) 863970
EMAIL: enodochotel@aol.com
WEB SITE: www.enodoc-hotel.co.uk

Stylish design-led hotel in suburban seaside surrounds

Built for the Siamese royal family, St Enodoc is now a stylish hotel, and despite the

surrounding suburbia, there are some great views and the beach is within easy reach. The spirit of the overall design scheme by well-known London interior designer Emily Todd-Hunter has been retained through a recent refurbishment – lots of bright seaside colours and stripy carpets. You've a choice of two lounges, a cosy one to the left, and a recently redesigned funky modern one to the right, in cream and red to match the strawberries and cream you'll be eating there. This is the only room where you won't find contemporary local art in – as Kim Oxenham has decided to

reflect his Aussie origins instead. The restaurant is a split-level affair: up top there's a bar and café-type seating, while the lower level has white-linened restaurant tables overlooking the patio and the sea. Kids are well catered for with some good family rooms, including kitchenettes for a spot of self-catering and one suite with an Xbox. There's also a playroom with plenty to amuse.

○ Closed 2 Jan to mid-Feb ⊿ From A39 Bodmin to Wadebridge road, take B3314 at Wadebridge and head towards Rock; hotel is in middle of village. Private car park ⟞ 8 twin/double, 7 double, 5 family suites; all with hair-dryer, direct-dial telephone, modem line, TV; some with VCR, DVD ⊘ Restaurant, bar, 2 lounges, library, 2 games rooms, garden; conferences; social functions; gym, heated outdoor swimming pool; leisure facilities nearby; early suppers for children; cots, highchairs, toys, playroom, babysitting, baby-listening ⅃ No wheelchair access ● No dogs; smoking in bar only ▭ Amex, Delta, MasterCard, Switch, Visa £ Single occupancy of twin/double £75 to £150, twin/double £100 to £210, family suite £290; deposit required. Alc L £20.50, D £33.50; light meals available. Special breaks available ③FOR②

Mizzards Farm

Rogate, Petersfield GU31 5HS
TEL: (01730) 821656   FAX: (01730) 821655
EMAIL: julian.francis@hemscott.net

High standards in a beautifully furnished B&B in a secluded country setting

The grassy mounds in the long narrow track that leads to Mizzards Farm bear testimony to the fact that the lane is little used. Yet as the secluded sixteenth-century farmhouse appears into view – surrounded by acres of lawns, immaculate sculpture-filled gardens and peaceful open country – it's not difficult to see why Mizzards Farm's faithful followers return here year after year to savour its idyllic setting. Guests are drawn here as much for the Francis family's hospitality and the comfortable interior as the relaxing situation. Inside, visitors have use of a

spacious, airy drawing room, which, with its open fire, restrained décor and quality furniture, is a lovely space in which to unwind, while breakfast is served in a baronial-style room complete with a high ceiling, gallery and stone fireplace. The largest of the three bedrooms has a luxurious marbled bathroom plus a bed raised on a plinth and electrically operated curtains so you don't have to stir of a morning to enjoy lovely views down to the lake. The two other rooms are smaller but stylish with smart modern bathrooms.

○ Closed Chr and New Year ⊿ Travel south from crossroads in Rogate; cross bridge and after 300 yards turn right down lane. Private car park ⟞ 1 twin/double, 1 double, 1 four-poster; all with hair-dryer, TV ⊘ Breakfast room, drawing room, conservatory, garden; heated outdoor swimming pool ⅃ No wheelchair access ● No children under 9; no dogs; no smoking ▭ None accepted £ Single occupancy of twin/double £50, twin/double £65 to £70, four-poster £75

Brookhouse Hotel

Brookside, Rolleston on Dove, Nr Burton on Trent DE13 9AA
TEL: (01283) 814188   FAX: (01283) 813644
EMAIL: info@brookhousehotel.fs.world.co.uk

A traditionally themed, romantic period house

A quintessentially red-brick English village is the setting for this imposing seventeenth-

century creeper-clad edifice, bounded on one side by the eponymous brook and approachable by bridge or ford as well as road. Inside, a labyrinthine jumble of corridors and anonymous portals will miraculously deposit you without fail at the galley-like bar. Here you can peruse a classically styled menu before moving into the restaurant, whose almost spartan simplicity – white walls, black beams, bare polished tables – is offset by the silverware and crystal goblets sparkling in the candlelight. After coffee in the conservatory, the bedrooms all make suitably romantic retreats, with an array of delightful antique beds (including some four-posters and half-testers), perhaps decked out with Nottingham lace, nestling amid cosy, well-furnished surrounds. Carpeted en suites come with good fittings. When we inspected, service was slightly brusque.

◗ Open all year; restaurant closed Sun eve 🚉 In centre of Rolleston on Dove. Nearest train station: Tutbury. Private car park 🛏 8 single, 1 twin, 8 double, 2 four-poster, 1 suite; all with room service, hair-dryer, direct-dial telephone, modem line, TV; some with trouser press, CD player ✓ Restaurant, bar, lounge/conservatory, garden; conferences and social functions; leisure facilities nearby ♿ No wheelchair access; 1 step into hotel, 4 ground-floor bedrooms ● No children under 12; no dogs in public rooms; no smoking in restaurant ▭ Amex, Delta, Diners, MasterCard, Switch, Visa £ Single £79, single occupancy of twin/double £89, twin/double £109, four-poster £115, suite £145; deposit required. Set L £14.50, alc L, D £32; light meals available. Special breaks available (3FOR2)

ROMALDKIRK Co Durham   map 10

Rose & Crown

Romaldkirk, Barnard Castle DL12 9EB
TEL: (01833) 650213   FAX: (01833) 650828
EMAIL: hotel@rose-and-crown.co.uk
WEB SITE: www.rose-and-crown.co.uk

Excellent food and stylish bedrooms at an upmarket coaching inn

Having made it as far as Romaldkirk, a remote hamlet in Teesdale, it would be a shame not to stop for the night, particularly when there's a village inn as inviting as the Rose & Crown to hand. But you're in for a surprise if you think – as its simple exterior suggests – that this is a basic pub. Inside, there are fresh flowers and gleaming brasses in the welcoming bar, part of which has been converted into a relaxed brasserie, or residents can retreat with an after-dinner brandy to a lounge with a ticking grandfather clock. Christopher and Alison Davy make sure that food takes centre stage here, so the main restaurant's polished oak panels, sparkling glass and silverware provide a suitably classy and intimate setting for some pretty complex modern English cooking – expect the likes of woodpigeon breasts with parsnip tartlet, juniper berry sauce and grilled pancetta. Bedrooms, shared between the main house and a converted stables annexe, are irreproachably plush with a blend of bold colour schemes, top-quality fabrics and glitzy bathrooms.

◗ Closed Chr 🚉 6 miles north-west of Barnard Castle on B6277. Private car park 🛏 3 twin, 5 twin/double, 1 double, 1 family room, 2 suites; all with room service, hair-dryer, trouser press, direct-dial telephone, TV; some with CD player ✓ Restaurant, brasserie, bar, lounge; leisure facilities nearby; early suppers for children; cots, highchairs, toys, baby-listening ♿ No wheelchair access; 5 ground-floor bedrooms ● No children under 6 in restaurant eves; no dogs in public rooms; smoking in front bar only ▭ MasterCard, Switch, Visa £ Single occupancy of twin/double £75 to £90, twin/double £110 to £124, family room £122 to £136, suite £130 to £144 (prices valid till Jan 2005); deposit required. Set L £16, D £26; light meals available; service incl. Special breaks available (3FOR2)

Denotes somewhere you can rely on a good meal – either the hotel features in the 2005 edition of our sister publication, The Good Food Guide, *or our inspectors thought the cooking impressive, whether particularly competent home cooking or more lavish cuisine.*

ROMSEY Hampshire
map 2

Berties NEW ENTRY

80 The Hundred, Romsey SO51 8BX
TEL: (01794) 830708   FAX: (01794) 507507
EMAIL: sales@berties.co.uk
WEB SITE: www.berties.co.uk

Informal restaurant with good-value food and simple, comfortable rooms

This popular restaurant-with-rooms sits right in the centre of town in a one-time workhouse (and later an inn) of sixteenth-century origins. Deceptively small from the outside, the restaurant spills over into the smart Georgian building next door, providing for two distinct dining spaces: non-smokers can admire the original Adams fireplace in the generously proportioned Georgian section, while smokers are housed in the older part, where the shape of the former inn's snug can still be made out, and low ceilings, dark-wood tables and candles lend a more intimate, romantic feel. The walls throughout the restaurant and the small courtyard garden are decorated with colourful paintings by local artist Jenny Muncaster, while chalkboards list the daily specials, which might include Berties' famous fishcakes or pan-seared scallops. The reasonably priced menu combines culinary nostalgia with innovative modern cuisine. Bedrooms are straightforward and fresh with sparkling bathrooms and plain colour schemes lifted by omnipresent wall art.

○ Open all year; restaurant closed Sun eve ⏩ In the centre of Romsey. Private car park. Nearest train station: Romsey ⇙ 2 single, 2 twin, 1 twin/double, 3 double, 1 family room; all with TV; some with hair-dryer ✦ Restaurant, dining room, bar, conservatory; conferences; social functions; leisure facilities nearby; highchairs ♿ No wheelchair access ● No dogs in public rooms; no smoking in bedrooms ▭ Amex, Delta, Diners, MasterCard, Switch, Visa £ Single £40 to £53, twin/double £55 to £75, family room £60 to £75. Set L, D £15; alc L, D £25; light meals available ③FOR2

ROSS-ON-WYE Herefordshire
map 5

Wilton Court Hotel

Wilton Lane, Wilton, Ross-on-Wye HR9 6AQ
TEL: (01989) 562569   FAX: (01989) 768460
EMAIL: info@wiltoncourthotel.com
WEB SITE: www.wiltoncourthotel.com

A red sandstone manor house with lovely river views and affable hosts

They came from Shangri-La, but they have found their own corner of heaven in the Herefordshire countryside on the banks of the River Wye. Roger and Helen Wynn spent many years in the hotel trade, including at the Dorchester and Shangri-La in Hong Kong, and have now taken on this project with gusto. They have sympathetically refurbished this sturdy Elizabethan manor, with much of the work done to the bedrooms. Room 9 is now much larger, with double windows to the garden and river beyond, while other rooms have been given a cottagey makeover using Sanderson fabrics to maintain the traditional character. Six bedrooms have full river views and the rest have partial ones. The public rooms include an atmospheric bar with dark-wood panelling and an open fire, a small lounge that includes objects collected on the Wynns' Far East travels, and a bright sunny restaurant with a conservatory and Lloyd Loom chairs, which successfully lighten the mood.

○ Open all year; restaurant closed Sun eve ⏩ From M50 Junction 4, take A40 towards Monmouth; at third roundabout, turn left past Esso garage (signposted Ross-on-Wye), and take first right before the bridge. Hotel is on right, facing river. Private car park ⇙ 1 single, 3 twin/double, 4 double, 1 four-poster, 1 family room; all with hair-dryer, direct-dial telephone, TV, VCR; some with trouser-press; limited room service available ✦ Restaurant, bar, lounge, conservatory, garden; conferences; social functions; leisure facilities nearby; early suppers for children; cots, highchairs ♿ No wheelchair access ● No smoking in bedrooms ▭ Amex, Delta, MasterCard, Switch, Visa £ Single £60, single occupancy of twin/double £65 to £85, twin/double £80 to £105, four-poster £105 to £115, family room £120 to £145; deposit required. Alc L £15, D £26; light meals available; service incl. Special breaks available (3 FOR 2)

ROWSLEY Derbyshire   map 9

East Lodge

Rowsley, Matlock DE4 2EF
TEL: (01629) 734474   FAX: (01629) 733949
EMAIL: info@eastlodge.com
WEB SITE: www.eastlodge.com

Every inch a classic country-house hotel

It's not hard to see why this dignified Victorian country house, set back from the road amid well-landscaped grounds, has acquired a reputation locally as the place for special occasions. With its smart plaid fabrics and stripy wallpapers, it has an elegant feel, but is much too vibrant to come across as stuffy. In the last year a new bar has been built in the comfortably informal conservatory, making it as much a place for a pre-dinner drink as an afternoon tea. Meanwhile, the dining room in its green and yellow livery remains a suitably formal setting for a menu exuding the assurance of time-honoured dishes making use of top-quality produce. The bedrooms are conservative in tone, with smart furnishings, floral designs and pleasant views; en-suite facilities are smartly tiled and come with sparkling chrome fittings.

● Open all year 🔋 At junction of A6 and B6012, 3 miles south of Bakewell. Private car park 🛏 5 twin/double, 6 double, 2 four-poster, 1 suite; all with room service, hair-dryer, trouser press, direct-dial telephone, modem line, TV, CD player, DVD ✅ 2 restaurants, dining room, bar, lounge, conservatory, garden; conferences; social functions; civil wedding licence; leisure facilities nearby; early suppers for children ♿ Wheelchair access to hotel and restaurant, WC, 1 ground-floor room specially equipped for disabled people. Disabled parking ● No children under 12; no dogs; no smoking   Amex, MasterCard, Switch, Visa £ Single occupation of twin/double £80; twin/double £100; four-poster £140; suite £160; deposit required. Set L £13, D £26; light meals available. Special breaks available. (3 FOR 2)

The Peacock at Rowsley [NEW ENTRY]

Bakewell Road, Rowsley DE4 2EB
TEL: (01629) 733518   FAX: (01629) 732671
EMAIL: reception@thepeacockatrowsley.com
WEB SITE: www.thepeacockatrowsley.com

An up-to-date twist in a tried and trusted setting

A fresh contemporary makeover has transformed this grand seventeenth-century stone pad in a charming High Peak village, bringing a host of striking original features into line with the dictates of today's style gurus. The bar retains the most period character, although the semi-spartan combination of wood panelling and bare-stone walls seems much in keeping with the sisal carpets and clean-lined design throughout. A trio of dining areas is more avant garde, making bold use of colour (for instance, green curtains against purple walls) as well as blending modernist and antique furnishings to create an apt setting for a modern, mostly Mediterranean-inspired, menu. Upstairs, the stylish bedrooms come in a mix of cool tones and strong purple back-walls, with dark antique wood and the odd cast-iron fireplace contrasting well with crisp white embroidered linen; en-suite facilities are a pleasing blend of cream tiles and swish chrome fittings.

● Open all year 🔋 On A6, 3 miles from Bakewell and 5 from Matlock. Private car park 🛏 2 single, 8 twin/double, 5 double, 1 four-poster; all with room service, hair-dryer, direct-dial telephone, TV, CD player; some with mini-bar, DVD player; trouser-press on request ✅ Restaurant, 2 dining rooms, bar, lounge, garden; conferences; civil wedding licence; social functions; fishing, free golf nearby; early suppers for children; cots, highchairs ♿ No wheelchair access ● No dogs in public rooms; smoking in bar and bedrooms only ▭ Amex, MasterCard, Switch, Visa £ Single £55 to £65, twin/double £100 to £135, four-poster £145; deposit required. Cooked B £5.50, set L £20.50, D (Sun) £20.50, alc D £34; light meals available. Special breaks available

---

ROYDHOUSE West Yorkshire map 9

Three Acres Inn

Roydhouse, Shelley, Huddersfield HD8 8LR
TEL: (01484) 602606   FAX: (01484) 608411
EMAIL: 3acres@globalnet.co.uk
WEB SITE: www.3acres.com

Moorland vistas at a busy food-oriented inn

Fine food is very much the driving force behind this friendly inn, whose hilltop location is unmissably flagged by the towering Emley Moor television mast. One way in to the bar and restaurant is through an excellent deli selling a cornucopia of goodies to bring the foodie agenda firmly to the fore. Further credentials are added by fresh shellfish on ice, delivered daily from Cornwall, which make for a mouthwatering display at one end of the restaurant. This room has a relaxed atmosphere and attractive décor, featuring a blizzard of knick-knacks, prints of old menus, plants and a piano. The extensive menus range from exotica such as Chinese roast belly pork with plum and black bean sauce through to local classics such as Yorkshire pudding with onion gravy or steak, kidney and mushroom pie with home-made brown sauce. Characterful features such as exposed beams, stone fireplaces and moorland views add extra value to simple, comfy rooms that are divided between the main house and a more peaceful cottage annexe.

◖ Closed 24 Dec to 4 Jan ⚡ 5 miles south of Huddersfield, between Emley, Shelley and Kirkburton, ¼ mile from Emley Moor mast. Private car park 🅿 7 single, 2 twin, 10 double, 1 suite; all with hair-dryer, trouser press, direct-dial telephone, modem line, TV ⊘ 2 restaurants, 2 bars, garden, terrace; early suppers for children; cots, highchairs, baby-listening ♿ Wheelchair access to hotel (ramp) and restaurant (ramp), 6 ground-floor bedrooms. Disabled parking ● No dogs, no smoking in bedrooms ▭ Amex, Delta, MasterCard, Switch, Visa £ Single £55 to £60, twin/double £75 to £80, suite £100 to £120. Set Sun L £19, D £30; alc L £30, D £32.50; light meals available

---

RUAN HIGH LANES Cornwall map 1

Polsue Manor

Ruan High Lanes, Truro TR2 5LU
TEL: (01872) 501270   FAX: (01872) 501177
WEB SITE: www.polsuemanor.co.uk

Fine country-house B&B run with plenty of zest

A sweeping mahogany staircase greets you in the entrance hall to this lovely Georgian country house, setting the scene for a good old-fashioned dose of rural splendour, run with youthful exuberance by Graham and Annabelle Sylvester and their young family (sheepdogs included). The dining room is perhaps most striking, with a polished wood floor and a fireplace in black marble. Breakfast is served here around a single large table. The lounge is bright, with light flooding in through French windows on to comfortable chintzy furnishings. Bedrooms are straightforwardly well kept in a traditional country style – one has a four-poster with cheery yellow canopy. There are four acres of well-kept grounds to investigate, and south Cornwall's Roseland Peninsula has plenty of sandy beaches and striking coastal walks for when you're ready to head out.

◖ Open all year ⚡ Take A3078 towards St Mawes; in Ruan High Lanes take second right at telephone box to Philleigh for 1 mile; house is on left. Private car park 🅿 2 twin/double, 1 double, 1 four-poster; all with direct-dial telephone, TV ⊘ Breakfast room, sitting room, garden; social functions; leisure facilities nearby; cots, highchairs, toys, babysitting, baby-listening ♿ No wheelchair access ● Dogs £3.50 per night in bedrooms; no smoking ▭ Delta, MasterCard, Switch, Visa £ Single occupancy of twin/double £50, twin/double/four-poster £80; deposit required

Stone House

Rushlake Green, Heathfield TN21 9QJ
TEL: (01435) 830553 FAX: (01435) 830726
WEB SITE: www.stonehousesussex.co.uk

Gracious country living and superb food in an elegant ancestral home

Jane and Peter Dunn's impressive country house sits within beautiful gardens on the corner of a thousand-acre plot just a hop, skip and jump from the village green. Stone House – really part stone, part timber-framed since the elegant frontage was added by Wyatt in 1778 – has been in the Dunn family since the fifteenth century, and this fine ancestral home provides a perfect base for a relaxing break away from the hustle and bustle. In the Georgian part of the house, the book-lined library is smart but unstuffy, while on the other side of the grand hallway with its double staircase and black-and-white marble floor, the generously proportioned drawing room is also a lovely place for lounging in front of a fire or enjoying views of the gardens through tall sash windows. Pick of the bedrooms are the two four-poster rooms in the Georgian Front – luxurious and spacious with enormous, well-equipped bathrooms in which you could easily live. The bed in the Pink Four-Poster Room is particularly fine and has unusual ribbon carving so exquisite it has allegedly been copied both by royalty and a famous pop star. Though less grand, rooms in the Tudor part are equally tasteful and comfortable. If you can tear yourself away, you're welcome to explore the extensive grounds and the delightful walled garden, where master chef Jane grows many of the vegetables, herbs and salads for her mouthwatering menus, served in the ancient panelled dining room. A bistro-style lunch is now also an option, while luxury picnic dinners – with a waiter thrown in – can be arranged for those attending nearby Glyndebourne.

● Open all year ⤢ In village, with green on right, turn left and continue to crossroads; entrance is on left. Private car park ⤸ 3 twin/double, 2 four-poster, 1 suite; all with room service, hair-dryer, direct-dial telephone, TV; some with trouser press; fax available on request ⊘ Dining room, drawing room, bar service, library, games room, gardens; conferences; social functions ⅄ No wheelchair access ● No children under 9; no dogs in public rooms ⊟ Delta, MasterCard, Switch, Visa £ Single occupancy of twin/double £80 to £115, twin/double £120 to £145, four-poster/suite £180 to £235; deposit required. Set L, D £25; light meals available; service incl ③FOR②

Jeake's House

Mermaid Street, Rye TN31 7ET
TEL: (01797) 222828 FAX: (01797) 222623
EMAIL: stay@jeakeshouse.com
WEB SITE: www.jeakeshouse.com

High standards and attention to detail in a historic B&B with immaculate rooms

There's something reassuringly traditional about Jeake's House, a beautiful creeper-clad B&B that stands alongside tall red-brick town houses and ancient half-timbered properties on one of Rye's loveliest cobbled streets. Hands-on hosts Jenny Hadfield and Richard Martin are evidently proud of its rich history – originally built by a wool-merchant in 1689, it later became a Baptist school, then home to the American poet Conrad Aiken – and the house has been smartly restored in keeping with its past. Detail is obviously of importance: 'One coat was too pink; I had to put on three coats before I was happy with it but then I had to change the pictures,' says Jenny of the Russian-red walls in the breakfast room, between serving up hearty plates of Full English, devilled kidneys or oak-smoked haddock. Breakfast is a civilised affair and soft chamber music is piped through the galleried, double-height room – should it remind you of a church it might be because this eighteenth-century addition was originally a Quaker meeting house, then a chapel. Careful planning and close attention to detail also characterise the bedrooms, some

Hotels
of the Year

Here is our pick of hotels for this edition of
The Which? Guide to Good Hotels.

They are not necessarily the most sumptuous or
the most expensive in the book – in some cases,
far from it – but we felt they deserved special
mention this year, not just in their particular category
but for all-round excellence.

**Ravishing restaurants-
with-rooms**

Country-house comforts

Coastal corkers

Urban chic

Glorious gastropubs

Brilliant B&Bs

Notable new entries

Dial House

Ravishing restaurants-with-rooms

Dial House
Bourton-on-the-Water

Masons Arms
Branscombe

By Appointment
Norwich

The Peacock at Rowsley
Rowsley

Masons Arms

Kinnaird

Country-house comforts

Aynsome Manor
Cartmel

Bailiffscourt
Climping

Kinnaird
Dunkeld

Edenwater House
Ednam

Fairyhill
Reynoldston

Holbeck Ghyll
Windermere

Holbeck Ghyll

Harbourmaster Hotel

Coastal corkers

Harbourmaster Hotel
Aberaeron

Summer Isles Hotel
Achiltibuie

Bae Abermaw
Barmouth

Abbey Hotel
Penzance

Abbey Hotel

Champany Inn

Glorious gastropubs

Applecross Inn
Applecross

Boar's Head
Ardington

Durham Ox
Crayke

Champany Inn
Linlithgow

Stagg Inn
Titley

Urban chic

Langs Hotel
Glasgow

Old Bank
Oxford

Lowry Hotel
Salford

Old Bank

The Lynch

Brilliant B&Bs

Tasburgh House
Bath

Ounce House
Bury St Edmunds

Earsham Park Farm
Earsham

Nonsuch House
Kingswear

The Old Vicarage
Rye

The Lynch
Somerton

Thomas Luny House
Teignmouth

The White Hart

Notable new entries

Gordon's
Inverkeilor

The White Hart
Winchcombe

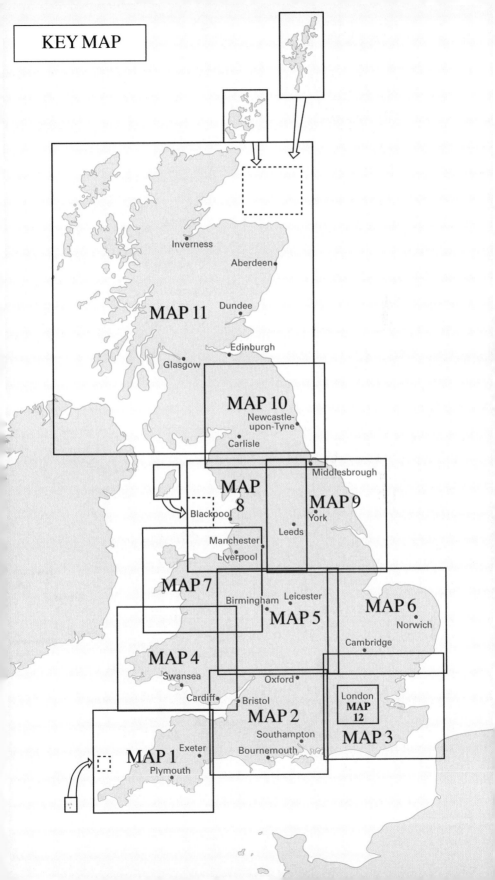

KEY MAP

MAP 1

- ▲ Hotel in main section
- △ *Round-up entry*
- ◨ Hotels in main and Round-up sections

0		5		10 miles
0			15 kms	

© Copyright

Lundy Isl

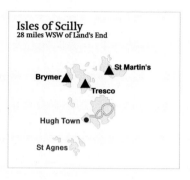

Isles of Scilly
28 miles WSW of Land's End

▲ St Martin's

▲ Brymer

▲ Tresco

Hugh Town ●

St Agnes

B
E

Crackington H

Tintagel ●

Port Isaac Bay

Port Isaac △

B

▲ Rock

Padstow ◨

Little ▲ Petherick ● Wadebridge

Watergate Bay

Bodmin ●

Newquay ◨

C O R N W A

Ligger Bay

▲ St Blazey

St Austell △

Fow

St Au

▲ Creed

St Ives Bay

● Redruth

△ *Truro*

Ruan High ▲ Lanes ▲ Portloe

▲ Mevagissey

St Ives ▲

Veryan ▲

Veryan Bay

Botallack ▲

St Hilary ▲

St Mawes ▲ ▲ Portscatho

Penzance ▲

Constantine ▲

Falmouth ▲

Perranuthnoe ▲

△ *Porthleven*

Mawnan ◨ Smith

Falmouth Bay

Land's End ●

Land's End

Mount's Bay

▲ Gillan

Mullion ▲

Lizard Point

The Channel Islands are not
covered in this edition

MAP 2

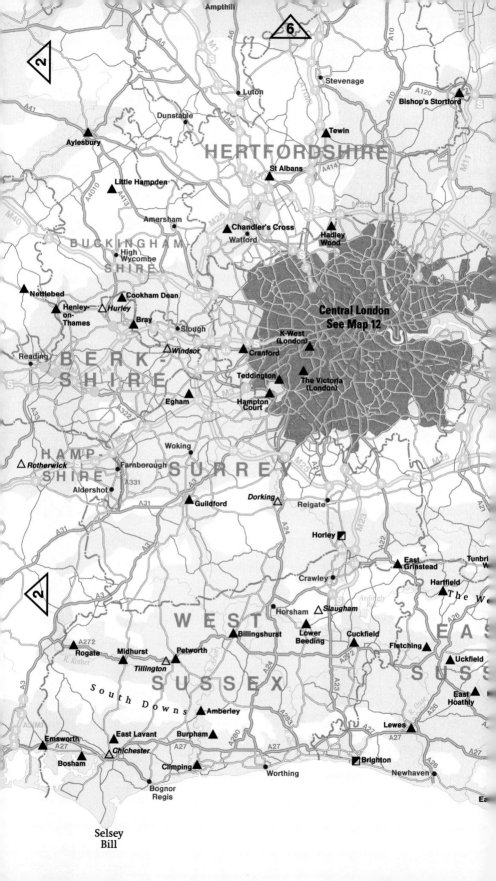

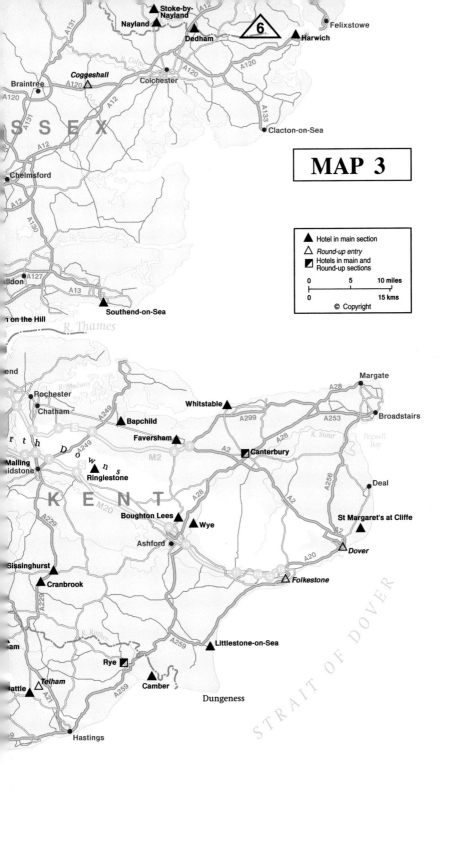

MAP 3

Legend:
- ▲ Hotel in main section
- △ *Round-up entry*
- ◪ Hotels in main and Round-up sections

0 — 5 — 10 miles
0 — — 15 kms
© Copyright

Stoke-by-Nayland
Nayland
Dedham
Felixstowe
Harwich
6
Coggeshall
Colchester
Braintree
A131
A120
A12
A120
A120
A120
A133
Clacton-on-Sea
S S E X
Chelmsford
A12
A130
A127
ildon
A13
on the Hill
Southend-on-Sea
R. Thames
R. Thames

end
Rochester
Chatham
Whitstable
Margate
A28
A299
A253
Broadstairs
Pegwell Bay
R. Stour
A249
Bapchild
Faversham
Canterbury
A2
r t h
D o w n s
A249
M2
A256
Malling
idstone
Ringlestone
Deal
K E N T
A229
M20
A28
A2
Boughton Lees
Wye
St Margaret's at Cliffe
Ashford
Dover
A20
Sissinghurst
Cranbrook
Folkestone
A229
R. Rother
am
A259
Littlestone-on-Sea
Rye
S T R A I T   O F   D O V E R
attle
Telham
Camber
A21
A259
Dungeness
Hastings

MAP 4

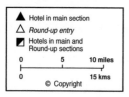

▲ Hotel in main section
△ *Round-up entry*
◩ Hotels in main and
Round-up sections

0   5   10 miles
0   15 kms

© Copyright

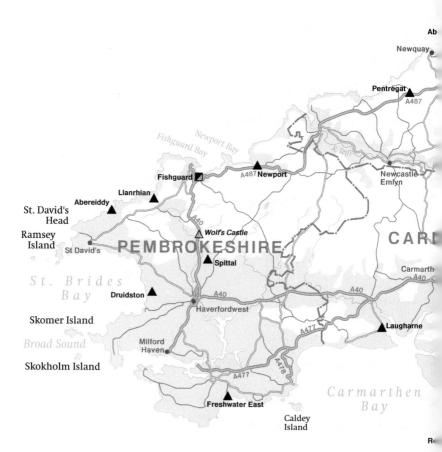

C A R D I G A

B A Y

Ab

Newquay

Pentregat ▲
A487

Newport Bay
Fishguard Bay

Fishguard ◩

A487 Newport

R. Teifi

Newcastle
Emlyn

Llanrhian ▲

Abereiddy ▲

St. David's
Head

△ *Wolf's Castle*

PEMBROKESHIRE

CAR

Ramsey
Island

St David's

Spittal ▲

Carmarth

A40

A40

St. Brides
Bay

Druidston ▲

Haverfordwest

Skomer Island

A477

Laugharne ▲

Broad Sound

Milford
Haven

Skokholm Island

A478

A477

Carmarthen
Bay

Freshwater East ▲

Caldey
Island

R

B R I S T O

MAP 5

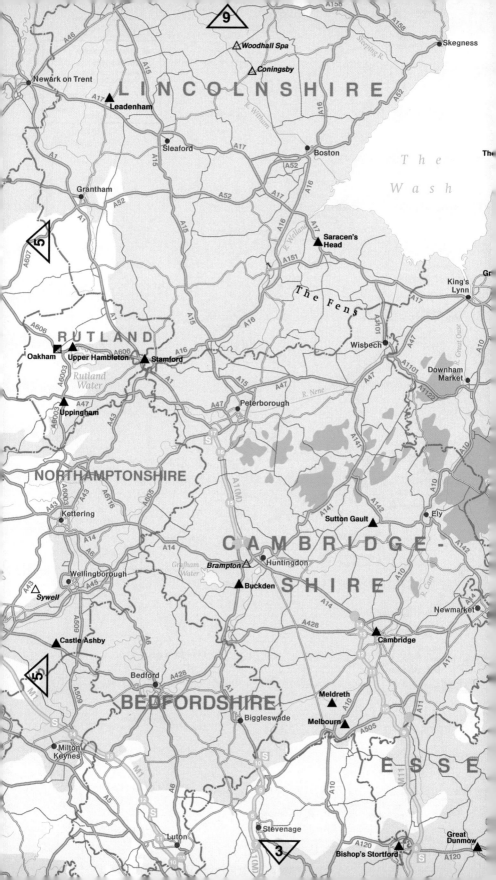

MAP 6

△ Hotel in main section
△ Round-up entry
◣ Hotels in main and Round-up sections

0   5   10 miles
0   15 kms
© Copyright

NORTH SEA

9

Brancaster Staithe
Holkham
Morston
Cley next the Sea
Cromer
Burnham Market
Wells-next-the-Sea
Blakeney
Aylmerton
Little Walsingham
Hindringham
Great Snoring
Wolterton
North Walsham
Fakenham
Wellingham
East Dereham
Norwich
Great Yarmouth
R. Bure
R. Yare
A47
A146
A143
R. Waveney
Lowestoft
A146
A12
Earsham
A140
Diss
A1066
Brockdish
Southwold
Thetford
Brome
Walberswick
R. Blyth
A134
A11
A134
A143
A140
A12
R. Alde
Bury St Edmunds
A14
Beyton
Snape
Aldeburgh
A134
Needham Market
Lavenham
Orford
A14
Woodbridge
A134
Long Melford
Ipswich
Sudbury
A12
Stoke-by-Nayland
A45
A14
A12
Nayland
Harwich
Felixstowe
Dedham
A131
R. Colne
A12
A120
Coggeshall
A120
Colchester
A120

NORFOLK

SUFFOLK

A148
A1065
A148
A47
A11
A140
A11
A134
A14

3

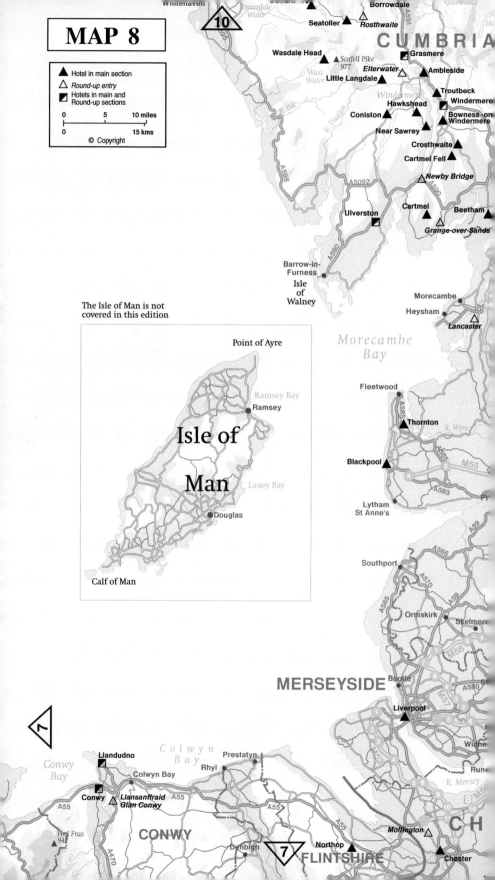

MAP 8

- ▲ Hotel in main section
- △ Round-up entry
- ◪ Hotels in main and Round-up sections

0 5 10 miles
0   15 kms
© Copyright

CUMBRIA

Whitehaven
Ennerdale Water
Borrowdale
Seatoller △ Rosthwaite
Wasdale Head
Scafell Pike 977
West Water
Elterwater
Grasmere
Ambleside
Little Langdale
Windermere
Troutbeck
Hawkshead
Windermere
Coniston
Bowness-on-Windermere
Near Sawrey
Crosthwaite
Cartmel Fell
Newby Bridge
Ulverston
Cartmel
Beetham
Grange-over-Sands
Barrow-in-Furness
Isle of Walney
Morecambe
Heysham
Lancaster

The Isle of Man is not covered in this edition

Point of Ayre

Ramsey Bay
Ramsey

Isle of

Man

Laxey Bay

Douglas

Calf of Man

Morecambe Bay

Fleetwood
Thornton
R. Wyre
Blackpool
M55
Lytham St Anne's

Southport

Ormskirk
Skelmersdale

MERSEYSIDE

Bootle
Liverpool
Widnes
Runcorn
R. Mersey

C H

Llandudno
Colwyn Bay
Prestatyn
Rhyl
Conwy
Colwyn Bay
Llansantffraid Glan Conwy
Conwy Bay
Foel Fras 942

Mollington

CONWY

Denbigh
Northop

FLINTSHIRE

Chester

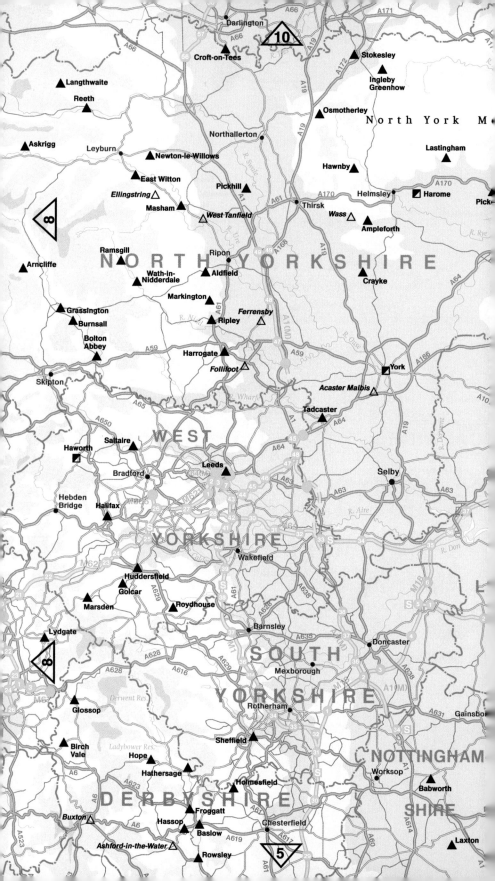

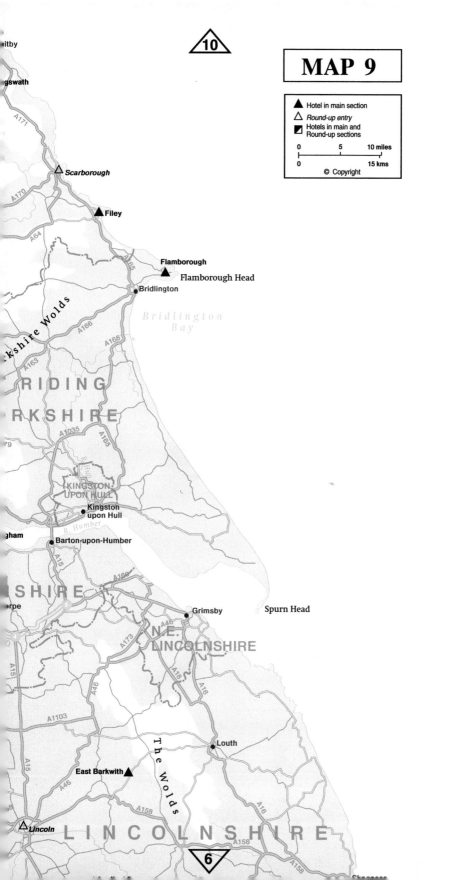

MAP 9

▲ Hotel in main section
△ *Round-up entry*
◤ Hotels in main and
Round-up sections

0   5   10 miles
0   15 kms
© Copyright

itby

gswath

A171

A170

△ *Scarborough*

A64

▲ Filey

A65

Flamborough
▲
Flamborough Head

● Bridlington

*Bridlington
Bay*

kshire Wolds

A166

A165

A163

RIDING

RKSHIRE

A1035

A165

79

KINGSTON-
UPON HULL

● Kingston
upon Hull

R. Humber

gham

● Barton-upon-Humber

A15

SHIRE

rpe

A160

Grimsby
●

Spurn Head

A46

A173

N.E.
LINCOLNSHIRE

A18

A16

A15

A1103

A46

The Wolds

Louth
●

A15

East Barkwith ▲

A46

A158

A16

△ *Lincoln*

LINCOLNSHIRE

A158

A158

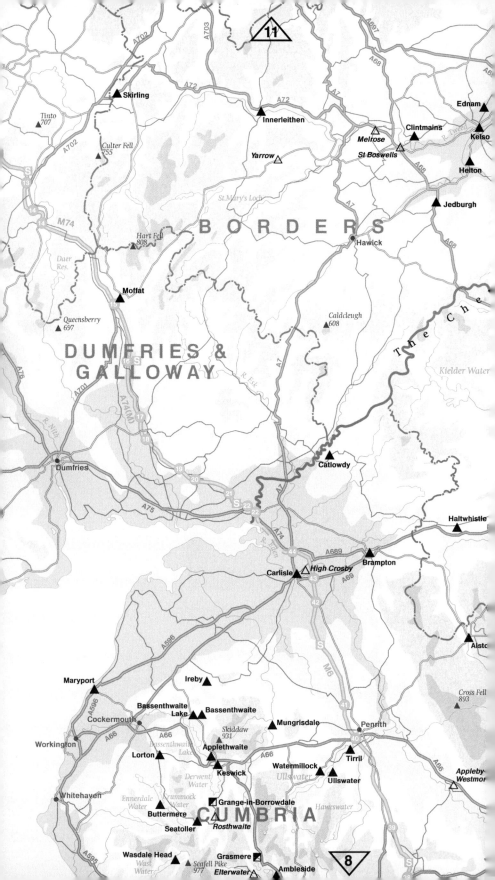

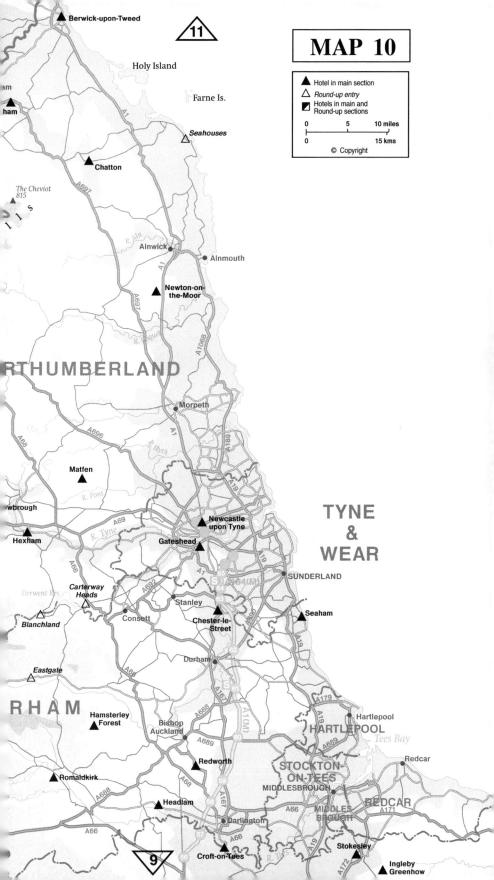

MAP 11

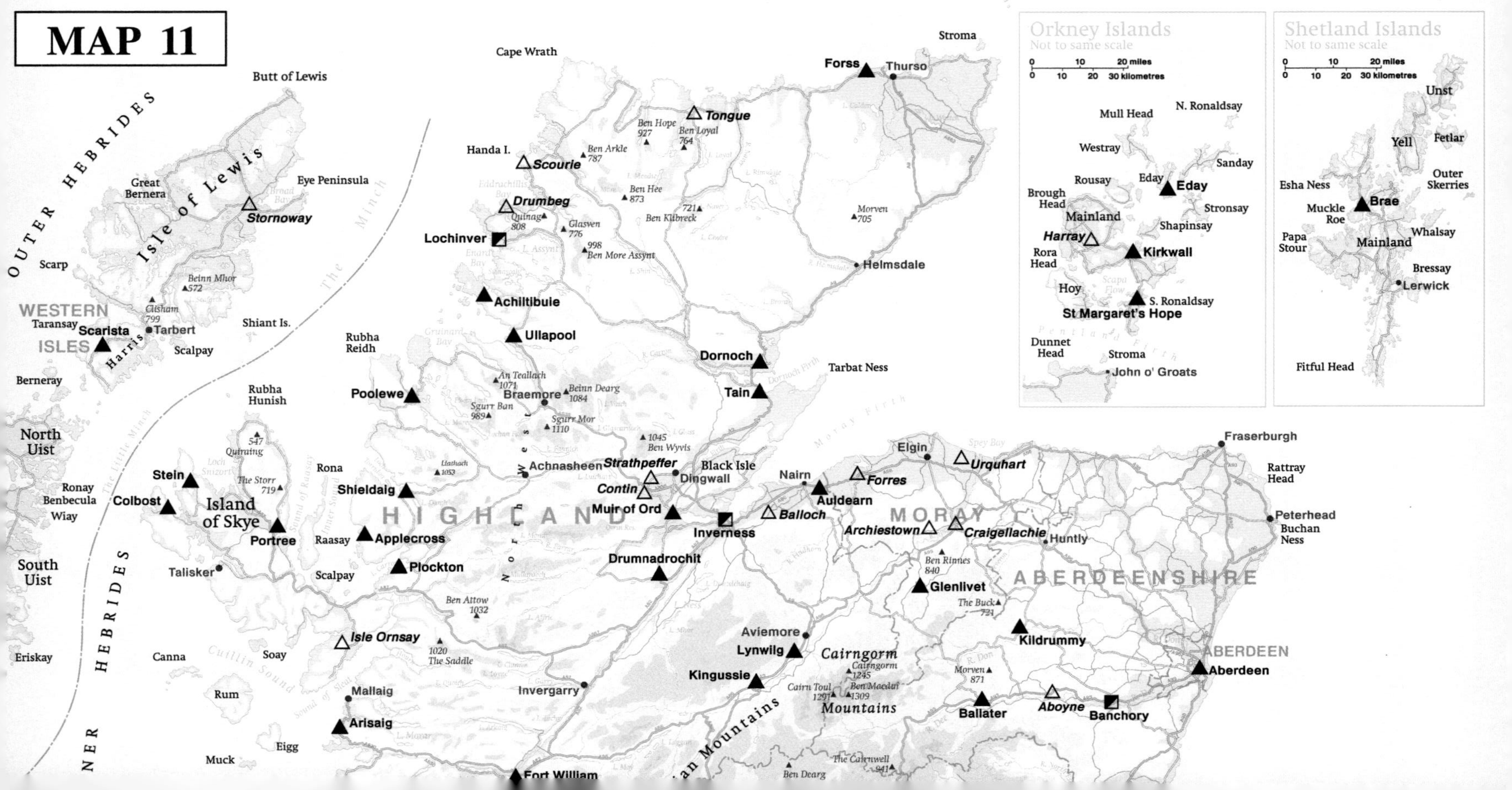

Shetland Islands
Not to same scale

0   10   20   30 kilometres
0   10   20 miles

Unst
Fetlar
Yell
Outer Skerries
Whalsay
Brae
Muckle Roe
Mainland
Bressay
Lerwick
Esha Ness
Papa Stour
Fitful Head

Orkney Islands
Not to same scale

0   10   20   30 kilometres
0   10   20 miles

Mull Head
N. Ronaldsay
Sanday
Stronsay
Westray
Rousay
Eday
Shapinsay
Kirkwall
Brough Head
Mainland
Harray
S. Ronaldsay
St Margaret's Hope
Hoy
Rora Head
Stroma
Dunnet Head
John o' Groats

Stroma
Forss
Thurso
Helmsdale
Tarbat Ness
Morven
705

Cape Wrath
Handa I.
Tongue
Ben Loyal
764
Ben Hope
927
Ben Arkle
787
Ben Hee
873
Ben Klibreck
721
Scourie
Drumbeg
Quinag
808
Glasven
776
Ben More Assynt
998
Lochinver
Achiltibule
Ullapool
Dornoch
Tain
Braemore
An Teallach
1075
Beinn Dearg
1084
Sgurr Mor
1110
Sgurr Ban
983
Achnasheen
Strathpeffer
Contin
Ben Wyvis
1045
Black Isle
Dingwall
Muir of Ord
Inverness
Drumnadrochit
Rubha Reidh
Poolewe
Shieldaig
Plockton
Applecross
Rona
Raasay
Scalpay
Ben Attow
1032
The Saddle
1020
Isle Ornsay
Mallaig
Arisaig
Invergarry
Fort William

Butt of Lewis
Eye Peninsula
Stornoway
ISLE OF LEWIS
WESTERN ISLES
Beinn Mhor
572
Shiant Is.
Tarbert
Scalpay
Harris
Great Bemera
Taransay
Scarista
Gillam
799
Scarp
Ronay
Benbecula
Wiay
North Uist
Berneray
South Uist
Eriskay

OUTER HEBRIDES

Rubha Hunish
Quiraing
The Storr
719
Island of Skye
Portree
Stein
Colbost
Talisker
Sligachan
Cuillin Hills
INNER HEBRIDES
Canna
Rum
Soay
Eigg
Muck

Fraserburgh
Rattray Head
Peterhead
Buchan Ness
ABERDEEN
Aberdeen
Banchory
Aboyne
Kildrummy
Ballater
Morven
871
The Buck
721
ABERDEENSHIRE
Huntly
Ben Rinnes
840
Glenlivet
Craigellachie
Archiestown
MORAY
Elgin
Urquhart
Forres
Auldearn
Balloch
Nairn
Lynwilg
Aviemore
Cairngorm
Cairngorm
1245
Ben Macdhui
1309
Cairn Toul
1291
Cairngorm Mountains
Kingussie
Ben Dearg
The Cairnwell
Grampian Mountains

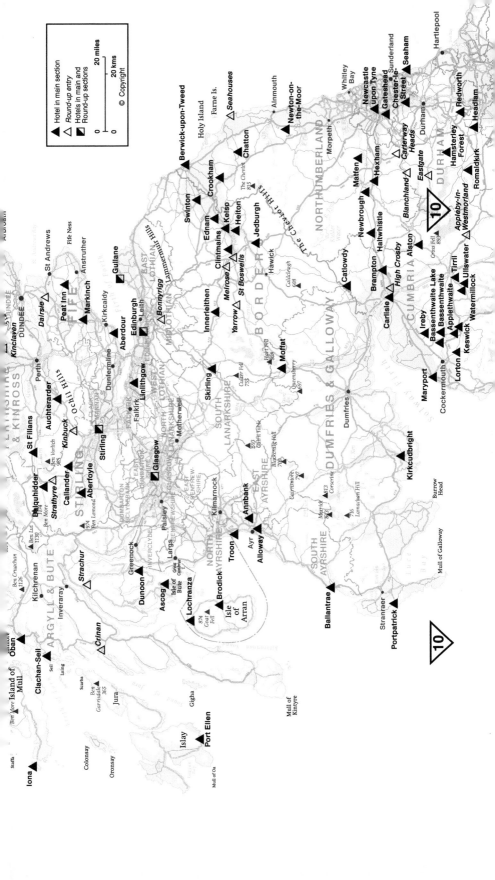

Central London

MAP 12

	Hotel in main section
▲	Round-up entry
△	

0   440   880 yds
0   800m

© Copyright

Hotel howlers

'The reading room is situated between the dining room and the kitchen. There may have been only us in it, but it was impossible to read anything of substance: there is no window in the room but a window-shaped opening into the dining room. So instead of quiet, you get the dining room Muzak. When the kitchen door is opened you get a 'double whammy' stereo effect of kitchen noise and what sounded like loud pop one side plus Muzak from the dining room on the other. Relaxing? Solitude? No way.'
On a hotel in Cornwall

'My wife started running a bath and then turned down the beds. They both looked as if they had been slept in, and we called the receptionist, who promptly told us that the bed linen had definitely been laundered but that they never ironed the sheets. We then said that we would accept that the linen was clean but pointed out that both blankets had body stains and pubic hairs on them and that we required clean blankets. After about 10 minutes the receptionist returned with the message that there were no spare blankets in the hotel and that she was unable to help any further.'
On a hotel in Sussex

'There was an overriding impression of staff who were ill at ease. In the restaurant they were all taking themselves very seriously and resolutely without humour, and everywhere else one felt they couldn't have cared less what you thought about anything! When we left, the man who took our credit card (when he eventually finished his phone call) never once asked if we had enjoyed our stay, hope to see us again or wished us a nice onward trip – perhaps he already knew what the answer might have been.'
On a hotel in Cornwall

'We arrived at 2.30pm, having driven 350 miles, to meet a girl at reception who told us three times that the room would be available only after 2pm. When I questioned what this meant, her colleague pointed out that it was well after 2pm and she laughed and said that she lost track of time. No apology followed.'
On a hotel in Edinburgh

with creaking floors and low beams, which are comfortable, prettily done out and immaculately maintained with lots of thoughtful extras.

◑ Open all year ⚡ Centrally located in old Rye. Nearest train station: Rye. Private car park 🚗 1 single, 1 twin, 3 double, 1 four-poster, 2 family rooms, 3 suites; 1 with shared bathroom; all with hair-dryer, direct-dial telephone, TV; some with trouser press ✓ Breakfast room, bar, lounge, library, parlour; leisure facilities nearby ⅙ No wheelchair access ● No children under 11; no dogs in breakfast room, £5 per day in bedrooms; no smoking in breakfast room ▭ MasterCard, Switch, Visa £ Single £39, single occupancy of twin/double £70 to £79, twin/double £94, four-poster £104, family room £129, suite £106 to £118; deposit required

Little Orchard House

West Street, Rye TN31 7ES
TEL: (01797) 223831 (AND FAX)
EMAIL: info@littleorchardhouse.com
WEB SITE: www.littleorchardhouse.com

Delightful B&B on a central cobbled street lined with ancient houses

Just off a cobbled lane in the heart of Rye, Sarah Brinkhurst's appealing eighteenth-century town house is well placed for exploring the ancient town but you'd do well to book ahead for Little Orchard House has just two smart rooms. Hayloft – a characterful split-level room – has a pretty, pine four-poster on the lower level and a well-equipped bathroom on the upper, while the romantic Garden Room houses an enormous four-poster built from an oak tree that came down in a hurricane. Both have TVs with video recorders, hair-dryers, hot-water bottles and handy fridges for storing milk and cold drinks. Guests are welcome to use the beautiful walled garden, which has an eighteenth-century smuggler's watchtower, while inside, the inviting sitting room is stuffed with fascinating curios and artwork and is a lovely place in which to relax in front of an open fire. Breakfast, around a long pine table in the kitchen, is a real treat and might include organic apple juice and yoghurt, local award-winning pork and sage sausages, locally farmed free-range bacon and Romney Marsh mushrooms. Special diets and vegetarians are happily catered for.

◑ Open all year ⚡ West Street is off High Street in Rye. Nearest train station: Rye. Private car park 🚗 2 four-poster; both with hair-dryer, TV, VCR, fridge; trouser press available ✓ Breakfast room, sitting room, library, garden; leisure facilities nearby ⅙ No wheelchair access ● No children under 12; no dogs; no smoking ▭ Delta, MasterCard, Switch, Visa £ Single occupancy of four-poster £50 to £70, four-poster £76 to £100; deposit required

The Old Vicarage

66 Church Square, Rye TN31 7HF
TEL: (01797) 222119 FAX: (01797) 227466
EMAIL: info@oldvicaragerye.co.uk
WEB SITE: www.oldvicaragerye.co.uk

Friendly B&B with attentive hosts and comfortable rooms in a fabulous central location

'Last time we saw you, you stayed in here,' said hostess Julia Masters as she ushered our inspector into one of the smart bedrooms overlooking the church – impressive stuff given this particular inspector last visited the Old Vicarage some ten years ago. During its long history, the Old Vicarage (it was last used as such in 1896) has seen many changes so it's good to know that the welcome – typically with a pot of tea and a slice of home-made fruitcake – remains warm at Julia and husband Paul's well-established B&B, which continues to go from strength to strength. The immaculate, Suffolk-pink-painted building that stands at the top of the old town, bang opposite the churchyard, would have been timber-framed in the fifteenth century but is now predominantly Georgian in design. Inside, a cosy lounge has light-wood floors, comfy leather sofas and a lovely window seat which Paul has built into the gorgeous curved bay, added during the eighteenth-century modernisations. This is a restful space in which to enjoy a complimentary sherry before heading off for dinner, while a tray of port awaits your return in the small library. Paul's carpentry skills extend upstairs to the bedrooms, where he has fashioned some of the doors and wardrobes from reclaimed oak floorboards. Each of the rooms is light, tastefully decorated and pristinely kept with pretty colour schemes and spotless bathrooms. A lavish breakfast of home-made jams, muesli and yoghurt followed by free-range eggs, mushrooms and tomatoes from local farms and sausages made by the local butcher will round off your stay rather nicely.

◐ Closed Chr ⚡ Enter old town by Landgate Arch into High Street; take third left into West Street; hotel is by St Mary's Church. Nearest train station: Rye. Private car park 🛏 1 twin/double, 2 four-poster, 1 suite; family rooms available; all with hair-dryer, TV; some with trouser press ⎰ Breakfast room, lounge, library, garden; leisure facilities nearby 🚶 No wheelchair access ● No children under 8; no dogs; no smoking ⌷ None accepted £ Single occupancy of double £55 to £80, twin/double £68 to £94, four-poster £68 to £90, family room £95 to £120, suite £85 to £110; deposit required. Special breaks available

ST ALBANS Hertfordshire — map 3

St Michael's Manor

St Michael's Village, Fishpool Street, St Albans AL3 4RY
TEL: (01727) 864444 FAX: (01727) 848909
EMAIL: reservations@stmichaelsmanor.com
WEB SITE: www.stmichaelsmanor.com

An all-round good egg in the heart of town

Visitors heading to this ancient town to explore the famous abbey or the remains of Roman Verulamium might like to consider stopping a while longer, and exceedingly well-placed for that, in a quiet heritage street, is this rather fine hotel. Under the expert direction of Richard Newling Ward, the latest member of the family to be in charge, St Michael's Manor manages to be elegant without being starchy, with a welcome that hits just the right note. The graceful lounge, with its chandeliers, plush swagged curtains and a restful yellow décor, is the grandest of the public rooms, while the restaurant is a touch more intimate. Bedrooms, all named after trees in the pleasant gardens, mirror the understated elegance found throughout the hotel – rich fabrics, tasteful furnishings, smart (but sometimes small) bathrooms and a pleasing attention to detail with hot-water bottles, bathrobes, home-made biscuits, fresh milk and bowls of fruit on hand for everyone.

◐ Open all year ⚡ Hotel is 10 minutes' walk from town centre; Fishpool Street is to the south-west of the centre. Nearest train station: St Albans. Private car park 🛏 2 single, 3 twin, 15 double, 1 four-poster, 1 suite; all with room service, hair-dryer, direct-dial telephone, TV ⎰ Restaurant, bar, 2 lounges, conservatory, gardens; conferences; social functions; civil wedding licence; leisure facilities nearby; cots, highchairs, babysitting 🚶 No wheelchair access, WC ● No dogs in bedrooms; smoking in some bedrooms ⌷ Amex, Delta, Diners, MasterCard, Switch, Visa £ Single £140, single occupancy of twin/double £150 to £175, twin/double £175 to £185, four-poster £300, family room/suite £240; deposit required. Continental B £9, cooked B £16; alc L £26.50, D £37.50; light meals available. Special breaks available (3FOR2)

ST BLAZEY Cornwall — map 1

Nanscawen Manor House

Prideaux Road, Luxulyan Valley, St Blazey, Par PL24 2SR
TEL: (01726) 814488
EMAIL: keith@nanscawen.com
WEB SITE: www.nanscawen.com

Spacious B&B near the Eden Project with delightful gardens of its own

Keith Martin is certainly proud of his involvement in setting up Cornwall's now legendary Eden Project – signed copies of Tim Smit's books sit on the coffee table, and Keith runs a website packed with pictures of its development. If you're looking for a comfortable base from which to set out for Eden, you won't find a much better location than this, just two miles down the road. And if it's horticultural splendour you're after you've the added bonus of the superb gardens of the house right on your doorstep, which can be enjoyed from the pool or whirlpool spa. Inside, this is a relaxing, no-nonsense country home – a mix of pine and antique furniture, cuddly toys and flowery fabrics, with plenty of space in a remarkably roomy complex behind the sixteenth-century façade. The huge drawing room is in pale colours with piles of games for older children and an antique sideboard offering drinks for grownups. Breakfast is served in a bright conservatory which has coffeewood chairs from Rick Stein's. Upstairs, bedrooms are traditionally styled, and Rashleigh in particular is so spacious you could hold a small tea dance there!

○ Open all year ⚡ From A390, heading towards St Austell, turn right in St Blazey opposite garage, signposted Luxulyan; hotel is ¾ mile on right. Nearest train station: Par. Private car park 🚗 1 twin/double, 1 double, 1 four-poster; all with hair-dryer, direct-dial telephone, TV, spa bath ✓ Breakfast room/conservatory, drawing room/bar, garden; heated outdoor swimming pool ⅙ No wheelchair access ● No children under 12; no dogs; no smoking ▭ MasterCard, Switch, Visa £ Single occupancy of double £79 to £89, twin/double £89 to £99, four-poster £89; deposit required (prices valid till March 2005)

ST BRIAVELS Gloucestershire
map 2

Cinderhill House

St Briavels, Lydney GL15 6RH
TEL: (01594) 530393 FAX: (01594) 530098
EMAIL: cinderhill.house@virgin.net
WEB SITE: www.cinderhillhouse.co.uk

Ancient house, panoramic location and plenty of character at this intimate home

Since our last inspection, owner Gillie Peacock has been finding out more about her extraordinary house. An expert visiting the neighbouring Norman castle popped in and told her that originally Cinderhill was a medieval hall house, dating back to 1286, with just one room that accommodated both man and beast. Things have moved on a bit since then – King John is said to have stayed – and hospitality seems to have always figured highly in events here. Yet the medieval character is still very strong, particularly in the sitting room, with its stone fireplace, thick walls and window seats. From the dining room there are great views of the Wye valley, and French windows lead to a small terraced garden. Dinners are provided on request and might feature leek and potato soup, supreme of chicken with garlic, rosemary and pancetta, and Gillie's speciality tarte Tatin. Bedrooms are straightforward with the odd grand touch; bathrooms are very good. There are also three self-catering cottages in the grounds.

○ Closed Chr & New Year ⚡ From B4228 turn off into village; at castle take Cinderhill (steep road); house is 100 yards on right. Private car park 🚗 1 twin, 2 twin/double, 1 four-poster; all with hair-dryer; 1 with TV ✓ Dining room, lounge, games room, garden; leisure facilities nearby; early suppers for children ⅙ No wheelchair access ● No children under 8; no dogs; no smoking ▭ None accepted £ Single occupancy of twin/double £45, twin/double £88 to £92, four-poster £96; deposit required. Set D £23; light meals available. Special breaks available

---

ST HILARY Cornwall
map 1

Ennys

Trewhella Lane, St Hilary, Penzance TR20 9BZ
TEL: (01736) 740262 FAX: (01736) 740055
EMAIL: ennys@ennys.co.uk
WEB SITE: www.ennys.co.uk

Well-travelled and well-heeled atmosphere at this country B&B

There's a well-travelled, cosmopolitan feel to this traditional Cornish country manor. Behind the Georgian façade you'll find things are modern and stylish without overwhelming the character of the building, and there's plenty of interesting detail to catch the eye – a gorgeous golden embroidered throw from India, a traditional Buddhist 'thangka' painting from Nepal, carved tables imported from Burma. The sitting room had just been refurbished in contemporary style when we inspected, and owner Gill Charlton was waiting for a new granite fireplace carved by a friend to cap it off. Bedrooms are individually decorated. Some are bright and modern, others a little more traditional, though no less thoughtfully decorated, with, for example, a dark-wood four-poster and some tasteful wallpaper featuring rural scenes. Rounding things off nicely is a pleasingly shaped outdoor pool and a grass tennis court if you fancy imagining yourself starring at Wimbledon.

◗ Closed 1 Nov to 15 Mar 🔁 2 miles east of Marazion on B3280; just before Relubbus, turn left into Trewhella Lane. Ennys is 1 mile along. Private car park 🛏 1 twin/double, 2 four-poster, 2 family suites; all with hair-dryer, TV, VCR ✅ Breakfast room, sitting room, garden; tennis, heated outdoor swimming pool; leisure facilities nearby; babysitting ♿ No wheelchair access ⬤ No children under 3; no dogs; no smoking ▭ Delta, MasterCard, Switch, Visa £ Single occupancy of twin/double £50 to £80, twin/double £80, four-poster £85 to £95, family suite £105 to £130; deposit required

---

ST IVES Cornwall   map 1

Blue Hayes NEW ENTRY

Trelyon Avenue, St Ives TR26 2 AD
TEL: (01736) 797129 FAX: (01736) 799098
EMAIL: bluehayes@btconnect.com
WEB SITE: www.bluehayes.co.uk

Sparkling modern luxury with great views over St Ives

'Without doubt the find of the holiday,' writes one reluctant correspondent reporting on Blue Hayes this year. Reluctant, for he fears his glowing write-up may mean 'endless trouble getting a reservation again'. It's a bit of a walk uphill after a night out in the main town centre, but your reward is a cracking view out over St Ives' golden sands from the balcony, which also looks out over the gardens with a huge pine tree lying prostrate but still alive (lit in blue at night), having survived being blown over in the 1970s. The white exterior of this 1920s building is a taste of things to come – you can have the décor in any colour you like as long as it's cream. The occasional splash of colour is provided by the cushions or curtains – there's very little in the way of any other decorative embellishment. The lounge area, with its high, vaulted ceiling is probably the pick of the public rooms, and there's also a dining area where light suppers are served if you don't fancy the walk into town. Bedrooms are luxurious and still predominantly cream and minimalist. Service comes in for praise, too, from the 'jovial' proprietor to the 'efficient, friendly and knowledgeable' waiting staff at breakfast.

◗ Closed Dec and Jan 🔁 From A3074 into St Ives, go past Tesco roundabout, down hill and past garage on right, then turn right into car park. Nearest train station: St Ives. Private car park 🛏 4 twin/double, 1 four-poster; all with hair-dryer, fax, modem line, TV ✅ Dining room, bar, lounge, library, garden, terrace; conferences; social functions; civil wedding licence; leisure facilities nearby ♿ No wheelchair access ⬤ No children under 10; no dogs; no smoking ▭ Amex, Delta, MasterCard, Switch, Visa £ Single occupancy of twin/double £85 to £115, twin/double £130 to £140, four-poster £150 to £170; deposit required. Light meals available

---

One Sea View Terrace

1 Sea View Terrace, St Ives TR26 2DH
TEL: (01736) 798001 FAX: (01736) 791802
EMAIL: oneseaviewterrace@hotmail.com
WEB SITE: www.seaview-stives.co.uk

Minimalist chic minus the pretensions at this stylish hilltop B&B

Public space is limited at One Sea View Terrace – the small lounge is really more of a reception area, but the two perfectly formed bedrooms are so comfortable and enticing that you're barely likely to notice. As the name suggests, there are cracking sea views from both rooms (the upper one, being higher, just has the edge) and they are decorated in a cool white minimalist style, but without ever being as cold or clinical as that description might suggest. Far from it, in fact – you're plied with luxuries like big fluffy towels and hand-made toiletries, and the breakfasts (taken in your room) are made with plenty of fresh ingredients. 'The best B&B we've ever stayed in!' reports one enthusiastic reader, who praised the 'attention to detail' and 'very high standard of service and cleanliness'. The only thing we can think of that isn't utterly relaxing about the whole place is the walk back up the hill from town after dinner!

❍ Open all year 🔁 Entering St Ives on A3074, at Porthminster Hotel continue left as far as Dunmar Hotel; turn sharp left, then first right into Sea View Terrace. Nearest train station: St Ives. Private car park 🛏️ 2 twin/double; both with hair-dryer, TV, CD player, fridge ✓ Lounge/reception, patio; leisure facilities nearby ♿ No wheelchair access; 5 steps into hotel, 1 ground-floor bedroom ● No children under 12; no dogs in public rooms; no smoking ▭ MasterCard, Switch, Visa £ Single occupancy of twin/double £85, twin/double £95; deposit required

Primrose Valley Hotel [NEW ENTRY]

Porthminster Beach, St Ives TR26 2ED
TEL: (01736) 794939 (AND FAX)
EMAIL: info@primroseonline.co.uk
WEB SITE: www.primroseonline.co.uk

Smart family-run and family-friendly hotel less than a minute from the sand

If you've a good arm, Primrose Valley is possibly a literal stone's throw from the golden Porthminster Beach at St Ives. But seashore proximity is not all it has going for it. Since newcomers to the hotel scene Susan and Andrew Biss took the place over in 2001 they've been steadily ploughing through a top-to-bottom refurbishment which is now almost complete. They've gone for a bright, modern look which is smart but comfortable. Downstairs there's a little exposed brick bar with slate-tiled floor and photographs of classic stars (Elvis, the Rat Pack) and a large open-plan lounge/dining area with stripped and varnished wood floor, sofas around a square fireplace alcove and high-backed leather dining chairs. Décor in the bedrooms varies – some rooms are brighter and airier, others more cosy. Superior rooms may have a brick fireplace or balcony. On our inspection we were accompanied around the hotel by Susan and Andrew's little daughter Poppy, so it's clear that there's no policy that children should be seen and not heard – games, kids' DVDs and baby monitors mean that the whole family is catered for.

❍ Closed Nov to Jan exc New Year; dining room closed Wed eves and Oct to May 🔁 On entering St Ives on A3074 turn left just after local hospital sign into Primrose Valley. Bear left under bridge and take next left after 50 metres; hotel signposted from there. Private car park. Nearest train station: St Ives 🛏️ 1 single, 1 twin/double, 5 double, 3 family rooms; all with hair-dryer, TV; 2 with CD player, DVD ✓ Dining room, bar, lounge; early suppers for children, cots, highchairs, toys, baby-listening ♿ No wheelchair access ● No dogs; smoking in bar only ▭ Delta, MasterCard, Switch, Visa £ Single £38 to £54, single occupancy of twin/double £66 to £86, twin/double £66 to £99, family room £95 to £125; deposit required. Alc D £20; light meals available. Special breaks available

---

ST KEYNE Cornwall   map 1

The Well House

St Keyne, Liskeard PL14 4RN
TEL: (01579) 342001 FAX: (01579) 343891
EMAIL: enquiries@wellhouse.co.uk
WEB SITE: www.wellhouse.co.uk

Attention to detail and a personal touch

The Well House was built in 1894 by a tea planter with estates in Assam, and Nick Wainford and Ione Nurdin have maintained a sense of grandeur while modernising and adding their own personal touches throughout. 'We like to have little bits like that – we try to make it special,' says Nick, pointing out a framed preserved bug on one wall. Other favourites singled by Nick included an evocative little watercolour purchased with a fiver he found on the street, and a print of an exquisitely detailed watercolour of a brood of ducklings. The most recently made-over room is the dining room, in contemporary style with extremely comfortable high-backed black leather Italian chairs. There's plenty of space given to each diner – no cramming them in here, and it is attention to details like that that are sure to make your stay a pleasant one. Bedrooms are similarly smart and modern, with pale colours predominating, enlivened by splashes of bolder colour here and there.

◗ Closed 1 week in Jan 🚉 Go through St Keyne, past church, and take road to St Keyne Well; hotel is ½ mile from church. Nearest train station: St Keyne. Private car park 🚗 3 twin, 5 twin/double, 1 family room; all with room service, hair-dryer, trouser press, direct-dial telephone, TV; no tea/coffee-making facilities in rooms ✷ Dining room, bar, lounge, garden; social functions; tennis, heated outdoor swimming pool; leisure facilities nearby; early suppers for children; cots, babysitting, baby-listening ♿ No wheelchair access ● No children under 8 in restaurant eves; no dogs in public rooms ▭ Delta, MasterCard, Switch, Visa £ Single occupancy of twin/double £80 to £95, twin/double £115 to £170, family room £180; deposit required. Set L £23.50, D £32.50; light meals available. Special breaks available

---

ST MARGARET'S AT CLIFFE Kent   map 3

Wallett's Court

Westcliffe, St Margaret's at Cliffe, Dover CT15 6EW
TEL: (01304) 852424   FAX: (01304) 853430
EMAIL: stay@wallettscourt.com
WEB SITE: www.wallettscourt.com

Family-run country house with a modern twist and small but well-formed spa

Away from the village, which is remarkable for its steep descent to the beach at the foot of the famed white cliffs, Wallett's Court is surrounded by rolling arable land and has distant sea views. It's privately owned and now managed by Gavin Oakley. The appealing white farmhouse at its hub is traditional in style. A long sitting room with a wood-burning stove at one end, oak beams, exposed brickwork and a variety of comfortable upholstered chairs and sofas and well-polished furniture is an inviting spot in which to await dinner. In the light restaurant, which extends into a large conservatory with views on to the garden with a fantastic tree house, petanque pitch and smooth lawns, you can see a carefully handwritten history of the house, which dates back to the Norman Conquest. The bedrooms in the main house have the most history, with four-posters to match, but newer rooms in the surrounding converted barn and farm outbuildings are equally attractive. They have contemporary colour schemes, creamy carpets and maybe a vaulted ceiling, sofa and armchairs or a big brass bed. All have good modern bathrooms. The spa is an added delight, from the neat pool, Jacuzzi and sauna to a treatment room hidden away in the trees.

◗ Closed 24 to 26 Dec 🚉 From M20 or A2 take A258 Dover to Deal road; take first right for Westcliffe; hotel is 1 mile on right. Private car park 🚗 2 twin, 9 double, 2 four-poster, 1 family room, 2 suites; all with room service, hair-dryer, trouser press, direct-dial telephone, modem line, TV ✷ Conservatory/restaurant, bar, sitting room, library, garden; conferences; social functions; gym, spa, tennis, heated indoor swimming pool; early suppers for children; cots, highchairs, babysitting, baby-listening, outdoor play area ♿ No wheelchair access; National Accessible Scheme: mobility impairment M1, 2 steps into hotel, 1 step into restaurant, 7 ground-floor bedrooms, WC ● No children under 8 in restaurant eves; no dogs; no smoking in some public rooms ▭ Amex, Delta, Diners, MasterCard, Switch, Visa £ Single occupancy of twin/double £79, twin/double £99, four-poster £159, family room £129, suite £159; deposit required. Set L £19.50, D £35; light meals available. Special breaks available

map 1

St Martin's on the Isle

Lower Town, St Martin's TR25 0QW
TEL: (01720) 422090   FAX: (01720) 422298
EMAIL: stay@stmartinshotel.co.uk
WEB SITE: www.stmartinshotel.co.uk

You know you're in very special territory as your boat glides towards the jetty and a manager stands ready to escort you to reception and to see your luggage is whisked away, ever so discreetly, to your room. The porter, like all the other staff you'll encounter throughout your stay, will address you by name; everyone conspires to make you feel like a Very Important Person; there's even chilled champagne in the room to get your visit off with a bang! The determinedly unflashy, low-slung building is attractively fringed by a patch of sandy beach, and many of the rooms have terraces opening out to the swathe of lawn that flanks it. Once indoors you are in modern country-house territory, with public areas glorying in their modish split-levels and classy fabrics. Bedrooms are tastefully furnished and decorated in an opulent yet restrained style, with lots of pampering treats like Molton Brown toiletries, snug dressing gowns and a turn-down service. Dinner is accomplished and inventive: perhaps fillet of sea bass with herb-scented crab, followed by Barbary duck with celeriac purée and redcurrant and lime sauce, and a diet-busting coconut rice pudding with roasted pineapple and piña colada sorbet. Service manages to be simultaneously correct yet friendly. With all these superlatives it seems churlish to table one minor quibble: given the general excellence, it's a little disappointing to encounter a hot breakfast buffet, rather than the perfectly executed, cooked-to-order full English you might expect.

◖ Closed Dec to Feb ◿ Take a helicopter, boat or plane from Penzance, or plane from Bournemouth, Southampton, Bristol, Exeter, Newquay or Land's End to St Mary's. Then take boat to St Martin's. There are no cars on the Isles of Scilly; no air or sea service on Sunday ⌔ 18 twin/double, 10 family rooms, 2 suites; all with room service, hair-dryer, direct-dial telephone, TV ⌀ Restaurant, bar, lounge, library, games room, garden, private quay; conferences; social functions; civil wedding licence; heated indoor swimming pool; early suppers for children; cots, highchairs, toys, babysitting, baby-listening ও No wheelchair access ● No children under 9 in restaurant eves; no dogs in public rooms ⊟ Amex, Delta, Diners, MasterCard, Switch, Visa £ Single occupancy of twin/double £127 to £380, twin/double £115 to £380, family room £290 to £380, suite £340 to £430 (rates incl dinner; prices valid till Mar 2005); deposit required. Special breaks available

map 1

Hotel Tresanton

Lower Castle Road, St Mawes, Truro TR2 5DR
TEL: (01326) 270055   FAX: (01326) 270053
EMAIL: info@tresanton.com
WEB SITE: www.tresanton.com

Design-led luxury with plenty for the kids too

Just down the hill from the splendid St Mawes castle lies this white-painted little (or so it seems) hotel. Looks nice enough you might think, but with nowhere to park your car you may well just drive on. If you've got the budget, that could well be a mistake, as behind the unprepossessing exterior lies one of Cornwall's most exciting and luxurious hotels. Designer-owner Olga Polizzi has clearly invested huge amounts of her time in making sure that every last detail is just so but at the same time the hotel is infused with an eclectic personal touch. The various buildings of this originally 1940s seaman's club form a series of terraces up the hillside, separated by pretty gardens, paths and walkways, and didgeridoos, huge ammonites, tribal masks, ceramic hats and a bronze sheep are just a few of the carefully chosen pieces on display inside. Lovely contemporary mosaics by Paul Marks turn up in the restaurant and cinema room, among other places. The hotel isn't specifically marketed at families, but there's plenty for youngsters to do. All bedrooms have sea views.

○ Open all year ⟦▨⟧ On seafront in St Mawes, 200 yards east of castle. Private car park ⟦⟧ 14 twin, 13 double, 2 suites; all with room service, hair-dryer, direct-dial telephone, modem line, TV, VCR; tea/coffee-making facilities on request ⟨✓⟩ Restaurant, bar, 2 lounges, private cinema, terrace, garden; conferences; social functions; civil wedding licence; early suppers for children; cots, highchairs, toys, babysitting, baby-listening ⟦⟧ No wheelchair access ● No children under 8 in restaurant eves; no dogs ⟦⟧ Amex, MasterCard, Switch, Visa ⟦£⟧ Single occupancy of twin/double £141 to £226, twin/double £165 to £265, suite £265 to £365; deposit required. Set L £26, D £35; light meals available; service incl

Rising Sun

The Square, St Mawes, Truro TR2 5DJ
TEL: (01326) 270233   FAX: (01326) 270198
EMAIL: therisingsun@btclick.com
WEB SITE: www.innsofcornwall.com

Harbourside pub decked out with care and attention

'A winner!' applauds one reader, who praises this small hotel 'delightfully situated on the quayside' with 'immaculately clean' rooms. From the outside, it looks like a fairly ordinary pub, but it's certainly a cut above the average. Inside there are contemporary colours, tiled floors, lots of comfy furnishings and chunky low tables made of distressed wood that's clearly enjoyed a former life. Bedrooms are light, pretty and cheerful, with a gentle seaside theme apparent in shells scattered around bathrooms, and with the occasional chintzy fabric here and there. The bar is unpretentious, serving tasty, uncomplicated bar food while chef Ann Long's restaurant menu gets praised for being 'varied and innovative'. 'Eating in the conservatory-style restaurant was a pleasure,' reports another happy visitor, and 'the young staff were uniformly helpful and friendly – the hotel absolutely came up to our expectations.'

○ Open all year ⟦▨⟧ On harbour in St Mawes. Private car park ⟦⟧ 1 single, 2 twin, 4 double, 1 family room; all with room service, hair-dryer, direct-dial telephone, TV ⟨✓⟩ Restaurant, bar, lounge, terrace; social functions; cots, highchairs, baby-listening ⟦⟧ No wheelchair access, WC ● Smoking in bar only ⟦⟧ MasterCard, Switch, Visa ⟦£⟧ Single £50 to £65, single occupancy of twin/double £50 (low season only), twin/double £100 to £130, family room £125 to £162; deposit required. Set D £30; light meals available

SALCOMBE Devon   map 1

Soar Mill Cove Hotel

Soar Mill Cove, Salcombe TQ7 3DS
TEL: (01548) 561566   FAX: (01548) 561223
EMAIL: info@soarmillcove.co.uk
WEB SITE: www.soarmillcove.co.uk

Luxurious comfort in sensational location

Despite the signposts encouraging you on, the approach to Soar Mill Cove, along single-track lanes past wind-stunted trees, feels rather like the road to nowhere. Even when you've arrived, you don't see the hotel until the track sweeps around in front, so unobtrusive is this low, whitewashed building of stone and slate. Sensibly, given the isolated splendour of its location – above a beautiful sandy bay along a stretch of coastline owned by the National Trust – this luxurious bolthole concentrates on providing soothingly traditional comforts rather than competing in the style stakes. Top-quality furnishings are much in evidence, from the damask-patterned sofas in the lounge to the well-spaced tables in the restaurant – both rooms have full-length windows along the front to give the views centre stage. We had a complaint this year about a limited choice of food and 'bland and uninteresting' desserts. A smaller bar with leather sofas is tucked away behind. Bedrooms are individually furnished, many with coronet drapes and good bathrooms – each has its own private terrace. The pricier ones get those sea views at the front. For days when the weather refuses to co-operate, there's an indoor pool and a spa. And for once, children of all ages are welcome.

◗ Closed Nov to Feb ⎘ From A381, turn right at Marlborough and follow signs towards sea and hotel. Private car park ⬜⟶ 8 twin/double, 1 double, 1 four-poster, 8 family rooms, 4 suites; all with room service, hair-dryer, trouser press, direct-dial telephone, modem line, TV, CD player, VCR/DVD ⊘ 2 restaurants, bar, lounge, games room; beauty treatment suite, sauna, tennis, heated indoor and outdoor swimming pools; early suppers for children; cots, highchairs, toys, playroom, baby-listening, outdoor play area ♿ Wheelchair access to hotel (no steps at 1 entrance) and restaurant, all bedrooms on ground floor. Disabled parking ◗ No children under 8 in restaurant after 8.30pm; no dogs in public rooms; smoking in bar only ⊏ Delta, MasterCard, Switch, Visa £ Single occupancy of twin/double £100 to £170, twin/double £200 to £230, four-poster £220 to £250, family room £250 to £300, suite £250 to £350; deposit required. Set L £29, D £39; light meals available; service incl. Special breaks available

Tides Reach

South Sands, Salcombe TQ8 8LJ
TEL: (01548) 843466   FAX: (01548) 843954
EMAIL: enquire@tidesreach.com
WEB SITE: www.tidesreach.com

Oh, we do like to be beside the seaside, especially with lots of facilities

The Edwards family has owned and run Tides Reach for over 30 years, and under John Edwards, whose hand is currently on the tiller, the message seems to be steady as she goes. The location is superb – in a tiny cove overlooking the safe beach of South Sands at the mouth of the estuary – and if the architecture won't win many prizes, at least it ensures that every room has a sea view. Large picture windows in the main lounge frame those vistas nicely; the adjoining conservatory-style sun lounge and restaurant look over the large ornamental pond and gardens, which are lit up at night. One thing that won't be on the menu, however, will be the inhabitants of the aquarium in the bar – Leroy and Snip Snip, the resident lobsters, are far too fondly regarded for that! Of the various categories of bedroom, the premier rooms have more space and the best outlook (often with a balcony), while views from the estuary wing are more oblique. Furnishings are carefully co-ordinated and well kept. For rainy days, when the beach is less inviting, there's a fully equipped leisure centre, including an indoor pool.

◗ Closed Dec & Jan ⎘ Follow A381 from A38 to Salcombe, then follow signs to South Sands. Private car park ⬜⟶ 2 single, 6 twin, 16 twin/double, 6 double, 3 family rooms, 2 suites; all with room service, hair-dryer, direct-dial telephone, modem line, TV; some with trouser press ⊘ Restaurant/conservatory, bar, 3 lounges, games room, garden; gym, spa, heated indoor swimming pool ♿ Wheelchair access to hotel (ramp) and restaurant, 2 rooms specially equipped for disabled people, lift. Disabled parking ◗ No children under 8; no dogs in some public rooms, £5 in bedrooms; no smoking in some public rooms and some bedrooms ⊏ Amex, Delta, Diners, MasterCard, Switch, Visa £ Single £66 to £120, single occupancy of twin/double £66 to £120, twin/double £130 to £226, family room from £224, suite £172 to £240 (rates incl dinner); deposit required. Light meals available; service incl. Special breaks available ③FOR②

SALFORD   Greater Manchester   map 8

Lowry Hotel

50 Dearmans Place, Chapel Wharf, Salford M3 5LH
TEL: 0161-827 4000   FAX: 0161-827 4001
EMAIL: enquiries@thelowryhotel.com
WEB SITE: www.roccofortehotels.com

Urban chic that is a class act in this city-centre hotel

If you approach this hotel from the front you might wonder what all the fuss is about – it's surely just another office block with a large car park. But, seen from the other side, where the wall of gently curving glass overlooks the River Irwell, and Calatrava's pencil-thin pedestrian bridge that straddles it, is a rather different prospect. What impresses about the interior is the effortless use of space. There's the yawning reception area, sleek and polished with a wide staircase, then the river bar divided by slatted wooden screens to create an intimate Oriental effect, and the River Room restaurant in pale brown and pinkish tones, with the feel of a 1920s cocktail bar. All are suffused with light from the large picture windows. Marco Pierre White, while not in the kitchen himself, advises on the dishes served and his reputation attracts the crowds. Our inspection meal was a competent red mullet saltimbocca with olive couscous and osso buco sauce followed by champagne and strawberry baked Alaska. Bedrooms are immense in grey, black and beige tones, with huge windows and electric curtains that give you the feeling you are about to host a board meeting for a funky advertising agency. If a hotel is judged on the generosity of its toiletries then the Lowry is a clear winner. And, for a big hotel, service was excellent with pleasant cheery staff, eager to please.

◑ Open all year 🅿 In the city centre over looking River Irwell. Nearest train station: Manchester Piccadilly. Private car park 🅿 158 double, 7 suites; family rooms available; all with room service, hair-dryer, mini-bar, trouser press, direct-dial telephone, fax, modem line, TV, CD player; some with DVD ⊘ Restaurant, bar, lounge, library; conferences; social functions; civil wedding licence; gym, spa, leisure facilities nearby; early suppers for children; cots, babysitting ⅃ Wheelchair access to hotel (ramp) and restaurant, WC, 17 ground-floor bedrooms, 10 rooms specially equipped for disabled people, lift. Disabled parking ◔ None ▭ Amex, Diners, MasterCard, Switch, Visa ⒑ Single occupancy of twin/double from £189, twin/double from £214, suite from £500; deposit required. Continental B £12.50, cooked B £16.50; set L, D £17; alc L, D £45; light meals available. Special breaks available

---

SALTAIRE West Yorkshire   map 8

Beeties

7 Victoria Road, Saltaire, Shipley BD18 3LA
TEL: (01274) 595988   FAX: (01274) 582118
EMAIL: jayne@beeties.co.uk
WEB SITE: www.beeties.co.uk

Stylish restaurant-with-rooms in a World Heritage model village

When wool baron and philanthropist Sir Titus Salt built the model village of Saltaire for the workers in his textile mill (we can only assume that this decent chap's workplace was less satanic than his rivals') it is unlikely that they would have popped out for roast sea bass with tapenade or scallops with herb and truffle risotto after a hard shift. Nowadays the delights of good food and art have come to Saltaire – along with its industrial World Heritage status – and you can sample both at the same time in Jayne Dixon-Hall and chef Wayne Brimicombe's welcoming set-up. The Gallery restaurant not only serves the aforementioned dishes, but also showcases work by resident artist Marek Skoczylas against a summery blue and cream backdrop; alternatively, the tapas bar serves up platters of toothsome Mediterranean-influenced nibbles. Five dinky bedrooms are on the top floor, attractively turned out with chunky pine furniture and pretty patchwork bedspreads.

◑ Closed New Year 🅿 From Bradford, take A650 to Shipley and follow signs to Saltaire for ½ mile; hotel is in centre of village. Nearest train station: Saltaire 🅿 2 single, 3 double; all with room service, hair-dryer, trouser press, direct-dial telephone, TV; some with modem line ⊘ Restaurant, bar; conferences; social functions; leisure facilities nearby ⅃ No wheelchair access ◔ No dogs; no smoking in bedrooms ▭ Amex, Delta, MasterCard, Switch, Visa ⒑ Single £35 to £45, single occupancy of double £42 to £52, double £50 to £60; deposit required. Set D £16; alc D £30; light meals available ③ꜰᴏʀ②

SANDIWAY Cheshire   map 7

Nunsmere Hall

Tarporley Road, Oakmere, Sandiway, Northwich CW8 2ES
TEL: (01606) 889100   FAX: (01606) 889055
EMAIL: reservations@nunsmere.co.uk
WEB SITE: www.nunsmere.co.uk

Immaculate standards inside and out ensure a luxurious and peaceful stay

Aerial views of Nunsmere Hall confirm ground-level impressions that the building is virtually moated by a huge, curving lake. The approach drive sweeps through wooded parkland, bright with bulbs and rhododendrons in spring, to an unusually elegant late-Victorian mansion of brick and red sandstone. Built for a wealthy shipping magnate around 1900, the house clearly spells gracious living, a style emulated under its present ownership. The tariff is predictably high, but for this, guests have the run not only of the lavishly furnished house, but also of its impeccably kept gardens. Seemly terraces and sunken lawns provide soothing vistas from the tall windows of a series of gracious public rooms. Oriental curios add a touch of colonial spice (the owners, the McHardys, previously worked in the Far East). Bedrooms are truly sumptuous, each individually designed in lavish country-house style. Cooking is unmistakeably *gastronomique*, menus incorporating sautéed frogs' legs, lobster ravioli and Lancashire quail.

❍ Open all year　☒ Off A49, 4 miles south-west of Northwich. Private car park 🅿 2 twin, 8 twin/double, 19 double, 3 four-poster, 4 suites; all with room service, hair-dryer, trouser press, direct-dial telephone, modem line, TV　⚓ Restaurant, bar, lounge, library, games room, garden; conferences; social functions; civil wedding licence; leisure facilities nearby; early suppers for children; cots, highchairs, baby-listening ♿ No wheelchair access; 3 steps into hotel, 2 ground-floor bedrooms, WC, lift ● No children under 12 in restaurant eves; no dogs; no smoking in some bedrooms ☐ Amex, Delta, Diners, MasterCard, Switch, Visa ⓔ Single occupancy of twin/double £140, twin/double £195 to £230, four-poster £270, suite £350; deposit required. Continental B £14.50, cooked B £19.50; set L £26.50; alc D £40; light meals available; service incl. Special breaks available (prices valid till Dec 2004) ③FOR②

SANDYPARK Devon　　　　　　　　　　　　　　　　　　　　　map 1

Mill End

Sandypark, Chagford TQ13 8JN
TEL: (01647) 432282　FAX: (01647) 433106
EMAIL: info@millendhotel.com
WEB SITE: www.millendhotel.com

Unpretentious and welcoming country hotel in lovely countryside

Owner Keith Green was just standing back to admire his newly refurbished restaurant when our inspector called. It certainly does look smart, with an elegantly retro touch in the colours and styling picked out by inset lighting and candles. From one window you get a glimpse of the old waterwheel turning gently and the sound of the millstream dashing beneath. Mill End was a mill for about a century until it became a hotel in the 1920s. Rooms are spacious with hints of old character but generally the atmosphere is one of a country house. The living room is delightful, warmed by a log fire and with plenty of cosy corners to find among the chesterfields and armchairs. Refurbished rooms tend to be the best choices, but all are well furnished with a good mix of antique and contemporary furniture. 'Our immediate feeling on arrival that we would like to stay longer at this hotel was confirmed at all times,' writes one reader, who was planning to return.

❍ Open all year　☒ From A30 east of Okehampton, take A382 south towards Bovey Tracey; stay on A382 for Chagford; hotel is on right, before Chagford. Private car park 🅿 2 single, 3 twin/double, 8 double, 2 suites; all with room service, hair-dryer, trouser press, direct-dial telephone, TV; some with VCR　⚓ Restaurant, bar, 3 lounges, gardens; conferences; social functions; leisure facilities nearby; early suppers for children; cots, highchairs ♿ Wheelchair access to hotel and restaurant, WC, 3 ground-floor bedrooms ● No children under 12 in restaurant eves; no dogs or smoking in public rooms ☐ MasterCard, Switch, Visa ⓔ Single £70 to £100, single occupancy of twin/double £70 to £100, twin/double £100 to £140, suite £160 to £200; deposit required. Set L £20, D £35; alc D £35; light meals available. Special breaks available ③FOR②

SARACEN'S HEAD Lincolnshire　　　　　　　　　　　　　　　　map 6

Pipwell Manor

Washway Road, Saracen's Head, Holbeach, Spalding PE12 8AL
TEL: (01406) 423119　(AND FAX)
EMAIL: honnor@pipwellmanor.freeserve.co.uk
WEB SITE: www.smoothhound.co.uk/hotels/pipwell.html

A rural idyll with vast skies, big vistas and loads of quiet

Close to the Wash in low-lying arable farmland, this is an area of big skies and wide-open spaces, and a cycle ride away from the sea and enough bird life to please twitchers. This Georgian manor house B&B presided over by John and Lesley Honnor is something of a rural retreat, offering tranquillity in acres of pleasant gardens with paddocks and spacious lawns scattered with mature trees and shrubs. For boys who love toys the garden's eye-opener feature should appeal: winding its way around the grounds is John's wonderful extensive model railway. Lesley has a horror of fussy soft furnishings, and the attractively spacious and uncluttered bedrooms are done out in pastel colours with rustic furniture. A lack of televisions and telephones adds to the atmosphere of peace and quiet. Breakfast – with home-made jams and marmalade on the menu – is taken around one table, and there's a homely sitting room with comfy sofas perfect for reclining after an exhausting day out in all that fresh air and countryside. Lunch and dinner can be taken at the village pub.

○ Closed Chr & New Year ⚡ Off A17, 1 mile north-west of Holbeach, in centre of Saracen's Head village. Private car park ⤶ 1 twin, 2 double; all with hair-dryer; fax available ⟨✓⟩ Breakfast room, sitting room, conservatory, garden ⟨&⟩ No wheelchair access ● No children under 10; no dogs; no smoking ⌐ None accepted ⌐£⌐ Single occupancy of twin/double £36 to £40, twin/double £50

SEAHAM Co Durham   map 10

Seaham Hall Hotel

Lord Byron's Walk, Seaham SR7 7AG
TEL: (0191) 516 1400   FAX: (0191) 516 1410
EMAIL: reservations@seaham-hall.com
WEB SITE: www.seaham-hall.com

Ultra-stylish stately home with state-of-the-art spa and a price tag to match

Cool rules at Seaham Hall. The exterior of this elegant house perched on a headland over the moody North Sea may say dignified Georgian pile, but the interior makes a style statement as loud as any metropolitan boutique hotel. Everything is designed to iron out the stress-induced wrinkles in body and mind. Muted hues of mushroom, charcoal, biscuit and cream serve to focus the attention on oriental antiques and the artwork of contemporary painters and sculptors. Inventive food is presented, equally, with a designer's eye. The clean lines of minimal geometric furniture don't feel nearly as severe as they look: comfort is the prime objective here. When hotel staff show you around a room it is usually a superfluous exercise; here, the guided introduction to your seriously stylish and luxurious abode is vital if you're to find your way around the cutting-edge flight deck control panels that adjust light, sound from downloadable CDs, and temperature. Needless to say, décor in all rooms is a style slave's fantasy. When you're ready to be pampered into submission, the oriental-flavoured Serenity Spa awaits through an underground walkway.

○ Open all year ⚡ From A1 Junction 62, take A690 towards Sunderland then turn on to southbound A19; after 2 miles take B1404 towards Seaham, turn left and go straight on at traffic lights; hotel is ½ mile on right. Nearest train station: Seaham. Private car park ⤶ 19 suites; all with room service, hair-dryer, mini-bar, direct-dial telephone, TV, CD player ⟨✓⟩ 2 restaurants, bar, drawing room, ballroom, garden; conferences; social functions; civil wedding licence; gym, spa, indoor heated swimming pool; early suppers for children; cots, highchairs, toys, babysitting ⟨&⟩ Wheelchair access to hotel and restaurant, WC, National Accessible Scheme M2, H1, 4 ground-floor bedrooms, 1 room specially equipped for disabled people, lift. Disabled parking ● No dogs; smoking only in drawing room ⌐ Amex, Delta, Diners, MasterCard, Switch, Visa ⌐£⌐ Suite £195 to £565; deposit required. Cooked B £9; set L £21, D £40; alc L, D £48; light meals available

---

'The walls were paper-thin and our next-door neighbour managed to keep us awake with his snoring. General crashing and banging in the morning did not help.'
On a hotel in Cornwall

Seatoller House

Borrowdale, Keswick CA12 5XN
TEL: (017687) 77218   FAX: (017687) 77189
EMAIL: seatollerhouse@btconnect.com
WEB SITE: www.seatollerhouse.co.uk

An unforced house-party atmosphere prevails at this convivial walking base

Seatoller is a classic Lakeland village on Keswick's famous 'Borrowdale Loop', at the foot of Honister Pass. High fells rise sharply from the valley floor, an obvious temptation for ramblers. The frighteningly energetic members of the Lake Hunts Ltd, who own the hotel, chase each other over the hills at intervals in a spirit of schoolboyish camaraderie. Visitors to this low-slung, stone-built seventeenth-century building need dread no compulsory activity. Easy-going new managers Daniel Potts and Lynne Moorhouse continue a tradition of relaxed sociability. Guests breakfast and dine together, possibly mingling in the boot room or the Tea Bar, where you can fill a flask or help yourself to home-made cake. Alternatively, curl up on the window seats of the oak-panelled library and recharge your batteries by a roaring fire. Bedrooms are simple and cottagey in honey-coloured pine and florals. All have their own bathrooms, though not necessarily en suite.

◗ Closed 28 Nov to 7 Mar; dining room closed Tue eve ⚡ 8 miles south of Keswick on B5289. Private car park ⌫ 3 twin, 1 double, 6 family rooms; no tea/coffee-making facilities in rooms ⌀ Dining room, tea bar, honesty bar, sitting room, library, boot room, garden ⅙ No wheelchair access; 1 step into hotel, 1 step into dining room, 2 ground-floor bedrooms ⬤ No children under 5 in dining room eves; no dogs in public rooms; smoking in sitting room only ⬜ Delta, MasterCard, Switch, Visa £ Single occupancy of twin/double £28 to £34, twin/double £51 to £64, family room £64 to £77 (2004 prices); deposit required. Set D £15; service incl

Seaview Hotel

High Street, Seaview PO34 5EX
TEL: (01983) 612711   FAX: (01983) 613729
EMAIL: reception@seaviewhotel.co.uk
WEB SITE: www.seaviewhotel.co.uk

Good food and excellent service in a friendly seaside hotel

Given its position, just a stone's throw from the seafront in the heart of this genteel Victorian resort, it's not surprising that the hotel should adopt a seafaring theme. A tall yacht mast juts above the front terrace, which is not unlike a ship's deck with its blend of highly polished steel and bare wood – a hint of the nautical flavour that lies behind the smart Edwardian bay-windowed façade. The Pump bar, popular with locals for lunch, makes the most of the seaside connection and is stuffed with all manner of knick-knacks, including mounted port-holes, lobster pots, ship's wheels and dozens of photos of military vessels. The smallish Front Restaurant, with its terracotta walls, blue fabric-covered chairs and crisp white table linen, is reserved for non-smokers, while smoking is permitted in the Sunshine Room – light and airy with a contemporary feel – which has a fancy smoke-extraction system. Where possible, produce is sourced locally from farmers and fishermen and the menu might include Isle of Wight roasted tomato and balsamic soup, and fricassee of Godshill chicken with pancetta and wild mushrooms. Upstairs, a cosy sitting room has squishy armchairs and a lovely bay window from which to watch the ferries go by, while bedrooms – all individual – vary in size and décor but are tasteful and comfortable with simple bathrooms.

◑ Open all year 🚗 Take B3330 from Ryde and follow signs to Seaview. Private car park 🛏️ 2 single, 9 twin/double, 2 double, 3 family rooms, 1 suite; all with room service, hair-dryer, direct-dial telephone, TV 🐾 2 restaurants, 2 bars, lounge, patio; conferences and social functions; leisure facilities nearby; early suppers for children; cots, highchairs, toys, babysitting, baby-listening ♿ Wheelchair access to hotel and restaurants (ramp), WC, 2 ground-floor bedrooms. Disabled parking ● No children under 5 in restaurants eves; no dogs in restaurants; no smoking in 1 restaurant and some bedrooms ⊟ Amex, Delta, Diners, MasterCard, Switch, Visa £ Single £70 to £100, twin/double £70 to £170, family room £190 to £240 (2004 prices); deposit required. Set L (Sun) £17; alc L, D £30; light meals available. Special breaks available (3FOR2)

SEDBUSK North Yorkshire   Map 8

Stone House

Hawes DL8 3PT
TEL: (01969) 667571   FAX: (01969) 667720
EMAIL: daleshotel@aol.com
WEB SITE: www.stonehousehotel.com

Relaxed Edwardian country-house hotel in a lovely Wensleydale location

Stone House looks down from a perch high on a valley side across Wensleydale to the Pennines beyond. Walkers can start their day straight from the door of this lovely mellow stone house with its creeper-covered gables, and after the day's exertions are over you couldn't ask to return to a more welcoming and unstuffily relaxed base, run with friendly charm by family team Chris Taplin and brother-in-law Peter Westwood. There's a certain masculine clubbiness to the public rooms, which becomes more evocative when you know that PG Wodehouse met a gardener named Percy Jeeves while visiting friends here. Bertie Wooster would certainly feel at home with a pre-dinner tipple by the log fire in the cosy oak-panelled lounge or in the book-lined billiards room before proceeding to table for straightforward hearty Yorkshire fare made from fresh local ingredients. Try to bag one of the bedrooms with the great view, such as Room 5, which has a four-poster and other furniture carved by a family forebear. Dog-owners – who are made very welcome – may prefer one of the cheerful conservatory rooms that open straight into the gardens.

◑ Closed Jan 🚗 From Hawes take road signposted Muker for ½ mile; turn right towards Askrigg; hotel is 500 yards on left. Private car park 🛏️ 1 single, 7 twin, 12 double, 3 four-poster; family rooms available; all with hair-dryer, direct-dial telephone, TV; some with VCR 🐾 Dining room, bar, lounge, library, games room, garden; early suppers for children; cots, highchairs ♿ Wheelchair access to hotel (ramp) and dining room, WC, 6 ground-floor bedrooms ● Smoking only in bar ⊟ Delta, MasterCard, Switch, Visa £ Single £45, single occupancy of twin/double £45 to £90, twin/double £77 to £99, four-poster/family room £103, suite £96; deposit required. Set D £24 (prices valid till Jan 2005). Special breaks available

---

SELSIDE Cumbria   Map 8

Low Jock Scar

Selside, Kendal LA8 9LE
TEL: (01539) 823259 (AND FAX)
EMAIL: ljs@avmail.co.uk
WEB SITE: www.smoothhound.co.uk/hotels/lowjocks

Beautiful streamside gardens surround this isolated stone-built guesthouse

Philip Midwinter interrupted his mini-tractor lawn-mowing duties to bid us a cheerful, courteous greeting on our last inspection stay. The six-acre grounds certainly require some attention to maintain them in such colourful glory. Low Jock Scar nestles invisibly in a craggy, wooded setting just off the A6, easy to reach, but completely secluded. The house, sympathetically remodelled in classic Lakeland stone and slate from an older dwelling, is as well kept as its gardens. Visitors feel immediately at home in its spacious, restful lounge, pleasingly sprinkled with antiques and ornaments, and well stocked with maps, books and board games. Alison Midwinter's appetising cooking, served in the plant-festooned conservatory, is a strong point. Book ahead for dinner, as it's quite a trek to find alternative fodder in the evenings. Most of

the neat, simply furnished bedrooms have their own bathrooms. One enthusiastic correspondent especially praised the food and the hosts' friendly, flexible manner.

◑ Closed 1 Nov to mid-Mar ⚡ 5 miles north of Kendal on A6 (1 mile past Plough Inn). Private car park 🛏 2 twin, 3 double; 2 with shared bathroom; hairdryer available ✓ Dining room/conservatory, bar service, lounge, gardens 👌 Wheelchair access to house (1 step) and dining room, 2 ground-floor bedrooms ● No children under 12; no dogs in public rooms; no smoking ▭ Delta, MasterCard, Switch, Visa £ Single occupancy of twin/double £42, twin/double £52 to £64. Set D £20; light meals available; service incl

---

SHANKLIN Isle of Wight

map 2

Foxhills

30 Victoria Avenue, Shanklin PO37 6LS
TEL: (01983) 862329 FAX: (01983) 866666
EMAIL: info@foxhillshotel.co.uk
WEB SITE: www.foxhillshotel.co.uk

Relaxing small hotel with spa facilities and pampering beauty treatments

Foxhills does an excellent job of looking after its guests – many of whom are drawn by the soothing whirlpool spa or tempting array of health and beauty therapies on offer at this small-scale hotel moments from the sea. On an attractive residential avenue close to the old village centre, Foxhills is a good-looking, smartly maintained Victorian villa. Its pretty terraced gardens lead down to a stream and make for a restful base for a pampering break. Inside is smart and tasteful but thoroughly comfortable and relaxed; there's a spruce lounge in period style with a wood-burning

stove, high-backed chairs and piano, while in the cheerful Garden Room restaurant – prettily decked out in check fabrics and flowery stencilling – the menu may include a risotto of baby spinach and wild mushrooms and roast leg of Isle of Wight lamb, finishing with bread and butter pudding or strawberry brûlée. Bedrooms are neatly furnished, pristine and unfussy, perhaps with floral fabrics, lavender or fudge colour schemes or toile de Jouy wallpaper and modern bathrooms.

◑ Closed Jan; restaurant closed Mon eve ⚡ From centre of Shanklin take A3020 towards Newport; Foxhills is less than ½ mile on left. Nearest train station: Shanklin. Private car park 🛏 1 twin, 3 twin/double, 2 double, 1 four-poster; all with room service, hair-dryer, mini-bar, direct-dial telephone, modem line, TV ✓ 2 restaurants, lounge, garden; conferences; social functions; spa; leisure facilities nearby 👌 Wheelchair access to hotel (ramp); 1 ground-floor bedroom ● No children under 15; no dogs; no smoking ▭ MasterCard, Switch, Visa £ Single occupancy of twin/double £55 to £90, twin/double £90, four-poster £100; deposit required (prices valid till Jan 2005). Set L £13.50, D £25; light meals available

---

SHEFFIELD South Yorkshire

map 8

Hotel Bristol

Blonk Street, Sheffield S1 2AU
TEL: 0114-220 4000 FAX: 0114-220 3900
EMAIL: sheffield@hotel-bristol.co.uk
WEB SITE: www.hotel-bristol.co.uk

Modern city-centre hotel with urban chic style

On the principle that you shouldn't judge a book by its cover, reserve judgement on the Hotel Bristol until you're inside the rather brutalist structure and out of sight of the urban wasteland surroundings – a car park and the inner ring road make unlovely neighbours. Inside, a funky modern makeover has transformed this former office

block into an upbeat, briskly efficient base in Sheffield's quayside quarter just a short stroll from the centre. On the first floor the P!casso restaurant is a vast open-plan affair, all terracotta tiles, mirrored pillars and muralled walls inspired by the eponymous artist's work, where modern, colourful food is served and TV screens are tuned to music

---

channels – grab a newspaper from one of the racks and it makes an airy venue for breakfast too. The style carries over into the bedrooms which have clean lines, neutral colour schemes, big beds and crisp linen; smart bathrooms with mosaic tiles have strong showers to blast you into life in the morning.

○ Closed 24 to 26 Dec 🚇 From M1 Junction 33, follow signs to city centre; turn right at Sheaf Quays and go under bridge; at traffic lights signposted M1, turn left; go over bridge and after 100 metres turn left immediately before Esso garage; hotel is next to NCP. Nearest train station: Sheffield City Station 🛏 71 twin, 40 double; all with room service, hair-dryer, trouser press, direct-dial telephone, modem line, TV, VCR ⊘ Restaurant, bar, lounge; conferences; social functions; leisure facilities nearby ♿ Wheelchair access to hotel (1 step) and restaurant, WC, 5 rooms specially equipped for disabled people, lift ● No children under 12; no smoking in bedrooms and some public rooms ▭ Amex, Delta, Diners, MasterCard, Switch, Visa £ Single occupancy of twin/double £53 to £79, twin/double £53 to £79; deposit required. Set L £10, D £15; alc L £18, D £22; light meals available; service incl. Special breaks available (3 FOR 2)

Whitley Hall

Elliott Lane, Grenoside, Sheffield S35 8NR
TEL: 0114-245 4444 FAX: 0114-245 5414
WEB SITE: www.whitleyhall.com

Old-fashioned comfort at a country-house hotel where Sheffield seems a long way off

You can understand why the Fearn family was drawn to this spot in the triangle between Rotherham, Barnsley and Sheffield: the suburban sprawl suddenly melts away as you turn down the quiet lane leading to Whitley Hall, which is further buffered from its surroundings by 30 acres of gardens, wood and ponds, complete with resident peacock. This lovely old house dates back to the sixteenth century, a pedigree that ensures plenty of creaky-floored character to go with mullioned windows, oak panelling and carved fireplaces, and a priest hole above the stone fireplace in the clubby bar. Some details jar slightly – pieces of rather corporate furniture, busy carpets, for example – but the overall style is homely and unpretentious, as is the resolutely English cuisine served in the smart yellow dining room. Bedrooms come in all shapes and sizes: at the top of the scale is a former billiards room kitted out with a wonderful carved four-poster, while standard rooms are comfy but unlikely to set the style pulse racing.

○ Open all year 🚇 Off A61 Sheffield to Barnsley road at Grenoside. Nearest train station: Chapeltown. Private car park 🛏 2 single, 4 twin, 12 double, 2 four-poster; family rooms and suites available; all with room service, hair-dryer, trouser press, direct-dial telephone, TV ⊘ Restaurant, 2 bars, lounge, garden; conferences; social functions; civil wedding licence; early suppers for children; cots, highchairs, baby-listening ♿ No wheelchair access ● No dogs; no smoking in some public rooms ▭ Amex, Delta, Diners, MasterCard, Switch, Visa £ Single £70 to £79, single occupancy of twin/double £70 to £79, twin/double £92 to £99, four-poster £120, family room £132, suite £170; deposit required. Set L, D £15; alc L, D £26.50; light meals available

---

SHEPTON MALLET Somerset   map 2

Charlton House

Charlton Road, Shepton Mallet BA4 4PR
TEL: (01749) 342008 FAX: (01749) 346362
EMAIL: enquiry@charltonhouse.com
WEB SITE: www.charltonhouse.com

Affable but upmarket country house decorated with undoubted flair

Anyone familiar with the Mulberry style of soft furnishings will immediately recognise them in Charlton House, a grand country house on the edge of Shepton Mallet. Everywhere you will find deep rich fabrics, heavy tassels, warm russet colours and a love of natural stone and wood. Public rooms are open-plan: a cosy lounge area with oriental rugs on bare floorboards leads into a bar and conservatory restaurant. Staff are attentive and personable, the atmosphere quiet but not hushed. If anything grates at all it's a slight sense that this is all a shop window, but then so what – it's a persuasively comfortable concoction. Bedrooms continue the sumptuous mix: cushions galore, deep drapes, stylish furniture; three of them have log fires too. Popular for weddings and functions, the hotel keeps those aspects discreetly separate from the rest. When we inspected, work on an ambitious health spa was in progress.

◗ Open all year ⚡ On A361, ½ mile from Shepton Mallet towards Frome. Private car park 🅿 6 twin, 8 double, 3 suites; four-posters and family rooms available; all with room service, hair-dryer, direct-dial telephone, TV; no tea/coffee-making facilities in rooms ⓥ Restaurant, bar, 2 lounges, conservatory, beauty treatment rooms, gardens; conferences, social functions, civil wedding licence; leisure facilities nearby; early suppers for children; cots, highchairs, toys, outdoor play area ♿ Wheelchair access to hotel (ramp) and restaurant (ramp), WC, 1 ground-floor bedroom. Disabled parking ● No dogs in public rooms and most bedrooms; no smoking in restaurant ▭ Amex, Delta, Diners, MasterCard, Switch, Visa £ Single occupancy of twin/double £130, twin/double £165, four-poster/suite/family room £295; deposit required. Set L £18.50; alc L, D £45; light meals available. Special breaks available

---

Daneswood House

Cuck Hill, Shipham, Winscombe BS25 1RD
TEL: (01934) 843145   FAX: (01934) 843824
EMAIL: info@daneswoodhotel.co.uk
WEB SITE: www.daneswoodhotel.co.uk

Relaxed, traditional comfort with good food and a lovely location

It was lead mining that first brought people to this spectacular part of the Mendip hills. Then, much later, Edwardian visitors arrived at Daneswood House to try its homeopathic health hydro. Today David and Elise Hodges dispense their own brand of therapy with a hotel that offers a relaxing atmosphere and high-quality food. It all starts, really, with the view. From the house there are uninterrupted vistas across the Bristol Channel to Wales and down to some interesting terraced gardens at the front. The interior retains its period charm with a dark Victorian feel to the décor and plenty of antiques scattered about. The small sitting room conservatory has unusual Art Nouveau tiled tables. There's a faded but comfortable feel to the bedrooms, although some guests felt some rooms were shabby and poorly maintained. Room 2 has a great view, with a padded window seat to enjoy it from, large chunky furniture and a bathroom in good condition. Reports on the food have been good – judgements backed up by a memorable inspection meal. The bad service also complained of was not experienced by either of our inspectors this year.

◗ Closed 24 Dec to 4 Jan ⚡ 1 mile off A38 towards Cheddar. Private car park 🅿 3 twin/double, 9 double, 1 four-poster, 4 suites; family rooms available; all with room service, hair-dryer, trouser press, direct-dial telephone, TV ⓥ Restaurant, bar, sitting room, conservatory, garden; conferences; social functions; leisure facilities nearby; early suppers for children; cots, highchairs, baby-listening ♿ No wheelchair access ● Dogs in 1 bedroom only; smoking only in bar and some bedrooms ▭ Amex, Delta, Diners, MasterCard, Switch, Visa £ Single occupancy of twin/double £90, twin/double £105, four-poster £125, suite £150; deposit required. Set L £20; alc L, D £32; light meals available; service incl. Special breaks available ③FOR②

Innsacre Farmhouse

Shipton Gorge, Bridport DT6 4LJ
TEL: (01308) 456137 (AND FAX)
EMAIL: innsacre.farmhouse@btinternet.com
WEB SITE: www.innsacrefarmhouse.com

Sociable and welcoming house in lovely rural location

'Please don't tell anyone about this place,' pleads one correspondent. Sorry, but the secret's out. Jayne and Sydney Davies have doubled in size recently – that is, they have gone from owning 11 acres to 22, something which is cause for great delight as it puts their lovely secluded farmhouse at the centre of a broad swathe of hillside pasture, woodland, orchards and garden. The plan is to create woodland walks through an area planted with 21 indigenous tree species. Their converted seventeenth-century house fits perfectly into such an environment: downstairs is a single large room divided into lounge and dining areas with a huge stone fireplace and plenty of cosy corners to curl up in. The dining area has been given a facelift recently to give it a more sophisticated feel but Jayne's cooking stays the same: familiar dishes done with imagination and flair. Organic and local are the principles by which she works when sourcing ingredients. Bedrooms are full of character with antique furniture, striking colour schemes and good bathrooms.

○ Closed Oct, Chr for 2 wks; dining room closed Sat eve Easter to Oct ⚡ Travelling west from Dorchester, turn off A35 after 13 miles at second turning signposted Shipton Gorge and Burton Bradstock; farmhouse is first entrance on left. Private car park ⚡ 1 twin, 3 double; all with TV; hair-dryer available ⚡ Dining room/lounge, bar, garden; leisure facilities nearby ⚡ No wheelchair access ● No children under 9; no smoking ▭ Delta, MasterCard, Switch, Visa £ Single occupancy of twin/double £55, twin/double £75 to £85; deposit required. Set D £19.50; service incl

---

SHIPTON-UNDER-WYCHWOOD Oxfordshire map 5

Lamb Inn

Simons Lane, Shipton-under-Wychwood OX7 6DQ
TEL: (01993) 830465 FAX: (01993) 832025
EMAIL: lamb@suwychwood.fsbusiness.co.uk
WEB SITE: www.traditionalvillageinns.co.uk

Plenty of character and exceptional comfort in the heart of the Cotswolds

There's not much more to Shipton than a clutch of golden stone houses around the village green, but tucked away in a quiet corner is a super pub that deftly combines old-world charm and modern comfort. Within its aged walls the bedrooms have been designed with outstanding imagination to raise them more than a cut above the usual pub accommodation. The names reflect the love of travel that has inspired the owner, Simon Clifton – so Spice Route has a dramatically carved four-poster bed as its centrepiece, while Roman Road shows pleasing attention to detail with urn-print curtains and a stone bust. All are very comfortably kitted out, while the bijou bathrooms have mosaic tiles, posh smellies and fluffy towels. Downstairs, the rustic-chic bar and restaurant mix a sense of style with local informality, so that you can enjoy a pint in the noisy, flagstoned bar and move on to the quieter dining areas at the back. Our inspector's stay was marred by an under-par breakfast that failed to match the good meal the night before, and by being in one of the front bedrooms, which are not peaceful until the bar has closed. More reports, please.

○ Open all year ⚡ From Oxford follow A40 to Burford; at roundabout take A361 right to Shipton; hotel is just off this road at southern end of village. Private car park ⚡ 3 double, 2 four-poster; all with hair-dryer, TV ⚡ Restaurant, bar, garden; social functions; cots, highchairs ⚡ No wheelchair access ● No dogs or smoking in bedrooms ▭ Amex, Delta, MasterCard, Switch, Visa £ Single occupancy of double £60 to £110, double £80 to £130, four-poster £80 to £140; deposit required. Set L, D £12.50; alc L, D £27.50; light meals available (3 FOR 2)

SIDMOUTH Devon map 2

Hotel Riviera

The Esplanade, Sidmouth EX10 8AY
TEL: (01395) 515201 FAX: (01395) 577775
EMAIL: enquiries@hotelriviera.co.uk
WEB SITE: www.hotelriviera.co.uk

A paragon of civilised seaside hospitality

On Sidmouth's unspoiled seafront the Riviera stands out, a large wedding cake of a building, all dazzling white with generous bay windows rising through three floors. The hotel has been run by the same family for over 30 years now and the consummate professionalism shines through: 'Rooms were scrupulously clean,' wrote one happy correspondent, 'beds excellent and linen immaculate. Staff were outstandingly efficient and friendly.' Downstairs are the spacious lounge, bars and dining room, all prettily decorated in pinks and whites with lots of fresh flowers on display. Bedrooms are comfortable and cosy, with soft headboards and well-kept bathrooms. The main choice is between sea view – those with bay windows are particularly attractive – or the quieter rear view.

◑ Open all year ⚡ At centre of Esplanade. Private car park 🛏 7 single, 5 twin, 8 twin/double, 5 double, 2 suites; family rooms available; all with room service, hair-dryer, direct-dial telephone, TV, VCR; some with trouser press, CD player ✓ Dining room, 2 bars, lounge, conservatory, ballroom, patio; conferences, social functions; leisure facilities nearby; early suppers for children; cots, highchairs, babysitting, baby-listening ♿ Wheelchair access to hotel (ramp) and restaurant, WC, 2 rooms specially equipped for disabled people, lift. Disabled parking ● Dogs £9.50 per day; no dogs in public rooms; no smoking in restaurant ▭ Amex, Diners, MasterCard, Switch, Visa £ Single from £97, twin/double from £172, suite from £258, family room rates on application; deposit required. Set L £22, D £33; alc L, D £40; light meals available. Special breaks available

---

SISSINGHURST Kent   map 3

Sissinghurst Castle Farm

Sissinghurst, Cranbrook TN17 2AB
TEL: (01580) 712885   FAX: (01580) 712601
EMAIL: sissinghurstcastlefarm@farmersweekly.net
WEB SITE: www.kent-esites.co.uk/sissinghurstcastlefarm

A winner with visitors to Sissinghurst gardens – and good value too

Patricia and James Stearns' home is the sort of farmhouse B&B you find only occasionally these days: it's well priced and welcoming, does a good breakfast and has bundles of character. In addition, it is in the happy position of being right next to Sissinghurst gardens. James Stearn grew up in this large Victorian house built in 1855 for Lord Cornwallis's estate, and the family has been doing B&B for many years. The wide hall, complete with a mounted deer's head and pots of jam for sale, leads through to a large, paisley-wallpapered breakfast room overlooking attractive gardens. Guests eat around a long T-shaped table. Hot food is cooked to order, and there are the usual cereal and fruit choices to start. Bedrooms vary from floral, in the blue and white Laura Ashley Room 4 (redecorated for a photo shoot), to simple and uncoordinated on the second floor. One room has its own bathroom and one has a shower unit in the room. The others share a large bathroom in the hall; this has a free-standing bath with an overhead shower, and there is room for a sofa too.

◑ Closed Chr ⚡ 1 mile out of Sissinghurst towards Biddenden; turn left down lane marked Sissinghurst Castle Gardens; farmhouse is on right. Private car park 🛏 1 single, 2 twin, 2 double, 1 family room; 4 with shared bathroom; all with hair-dryer, TV ✓ Breakfast room, garden; leisure facilities nearby; highchair ♿ No wheelchair access ● No children under 6; no dogs; no smoking ▭ None accepted £ Single occupancy of twin/double from £30, twin/double from £60, family room from £65

SOMERTON Somerset   map 2

The Lynch

4 Behind Berry, Somerton TA11 7PD
TEL: (01458) 272316   FAX: (01458) 272590
EMAIL: the_lynch@talk21.com
WEB SITE: www.thelynchcountryhouse.co.uk

Charming host and good rooms at this B&B

The great selling point of this fine Georgian house is soon apparent to visitors: Roy Copeland, downright affable, entertaining. ever-helpful It's and hardly surprising, as he's been entertaining all his life, mostly in big bands – hence the grand piano and other instruments in the sunny breakfast room (our inspection breakfast in here was excellent). Aside from Roy, however, the house is good value too: spacious, well-proportioned rooms on three floors rising up to an observatory at the top equipped with a telescope. Bedrooms are spotlessly clean and tidy with a homely atmosphere and occasional fine touches such as a brass four-poster or a roll-top bath. Outside there are some lovely woods and lawned gardens complete with duck-filled pond. For dinner, the town centre is less than five minutes' walk away.

○ Closed Chr and 31 Dec ⤧ Leave M3 at Junction 8 and take A303; at Podimore roundabout, join A372 and follow signs to Somerton; hotel is at junction of North Street and Behind Berry. Private car park ⛌ 2 twin, 3 twin/double, 2 four-poster, 1 family room; all with hair-dryer, direct-dial telephone, TV ⌀ Breakfast room, lounge, garden; social functions � Wheelchair access to hotel (2 steps) and breakfast room, 3 ground-floor bedrooms in annexe ● No dogs in public rooms; no smoking ▭ Amex, Delta, Diners, MasterCard, Switch, Visa £ Single occupancy of twin/double £45 to £60, twin/double £49 to £85, four-poster £95, family room £64 to £110; deposit required

---

SOUTHEND-ON-SEA Essex   map 3

Pebbles

190 Eastern Esplanade, Thorpe Bay, Southend-on-Sea SS1 3AA
TEL: (01702) 582329 (AND FAX)
EMAIL: pebbles_guesthouse@yahoo.co.uk
WEB SITE: www.smoothhound.co.uk

No-nonsense B&B that's a cut above the competition

If you're after a place to while away the hours in luxurious surrounds, look elsewhere. But if what you need is somewhere to rest your head when exploring the area or a stop-off on a business trip that won't break the bank, then this simple, unfussy B&B could be just the ticket. There's nothing even as fancy as a lounge on offer here, but what you do get is spotless and exceptionally well maintained and run by Colin and Edna Christian. If the weather is good you won't need a lounge anyway as the little roof terrace at the back is a nice place to relax, with a spot of greenery adding some charm (the place has been several times winner of the 'Southend in Bloom' competition). Décor throughout is clear and white with pine furniture and occasional contemporary touches such as art prints adding a splash of glamour to the proceedings.

○ Open all year ⤧ On seafront, 1¼ miles east of pier. Nearest train station: Southend East ⛌ 1 single, 2 twin, 3 double; all with hair-dryer, TV ⌀ Breakfast room, roof terrace; leisure facilities nearby � No wheelchair access ● No children under 6; no dogs; no smoking ▭ MasterCard, Switch, Visa £ Single £35, twin/double £55; deposit required

---

SOUTHWOLD Suffolk   map 6

The Crown

90 High Street, Southwold IP18 6DP
TEL: (01502) 722275 FAX: (01502) 727263
EMAIL: crownhotelreception@adnams.co.uk
WEB SITE: www.adnams.co.uk

Some elegant touches complement a traditional old inn

The Crown sits just a few doors away from its sister hotel The Swan (see entry below), both owned by the famed local Adnams brewery. Of the two The Crown is the cosier, more modest affair, but that doesn't mean it lacks grace. The main front bar has the feel of a smartened-up village pub, with bright yellow walls and chunky wood furniture, and a good selection of wine as well as beer available. The tiny back bar has a theme reflecting Southwold's maritime heritage, while the restaurant is more formal and elegant in an interesting curved shape, with a menu weighted towards local fresh fish. Bedrooms are fairly simple in light colours and with smart white bathrooms – nothing flash, but they are comfortable and good quality.

◑ Open all year ▣ In centre of Southwold. Private car park ▙ 1 single, 1 twin, 8 double, 2 family rooms, 1 suite; all with limited room service, hair-dryer, direct-dial telephone, TV; some with VCR, CD player ✅ Restaurant, 2 bars, lounge, patio; leisure facilities nearby; early suppers for children; cots, highchairs, toys ⟨ No wheelchair access ⬤ No children under 5 in restaurant eves; no dogs; no smoking in bedrooms ☐ Delta, Diners, MasterCard, Switch, Visa £ Single from £77, twin/double from £110, family room from £155, suite from £150; deposit required. Set L £21.50, D £29.50; light meals available. Special breaks available

The Swan

Market Place, Southwold IP18 6EG
TEL: (01502) 722186 FAX: (01502) 724800
EMAIL: swan-hotel@adnams.co.uk
WEB SITE: www.adnams.co.uk

Southwold's centrepiece offering upmarket but relaxed accommodation

The Swan might be the classier of Adnams' Southwold establishments, but that doesn't mean it's overly pretentious or showy (though you should be warned that there's a 'no jeans and trainers' policy in the evenings). The building dominates Southwold's marketplace, and you get the feeling you're staying somewhere of local import from the moment you walk through the door and are greeted by a portrait of local heiress Philippa Bedingfield of Darsham. There is a profusion of public rooms to choose from, from a pubby bar to a country-house-style drawing room and a reading room with views of the marketplace. Bedrooms are divided between buildings and style. One reader, who stayed in one of the new rooms in the extension, was full of praise, especially for the bed: 'the most comfortable in any hotel we've ever stayed in'. Garden rooms have been popular in the past with dog owners; others find them 'tacky'. But there is general agreement about the 'unforced, relaxed, friendly charm of the staff' and 'really good value for money'.

◑ Open all year ▣ On Southwold's market square. Private car park ▙ 3 single, 38 twin/double, 1 four-poster; family rooms and suites available; all with room service, hair-dryer, direct-dial telephone, modem line, TV; some with trouser press, CD player, DVD; tea/coffee-making facilities in some rooms only ✅ Dining room, bar, drawing room, reading room, garden; conferences; social functions, civil wedding licence; leisure facilities nearby; early suppers for children; cots, highchairs ⟨ Wheelchair access to hotel (ramp) and restaurant, WC, 17 ground-floor bedrooms, lift. Disabled parking ⬤ No children under 5 in restaurant eves; dogs in Garden rooms only, £5 per night; no smoking in some public rooms and some bedrooms ☐ MasterCard, Switch, Visa £ Single £75 to £85, single occupancy of twin/double £105 to £110, twin/double £140 to £160, four-poster £180 to £190, family room £165 to £175, suite £200 to £210; deposit required. Set L £23, D £32; light meals available. Special breaks available

---

STADHAMPTON Oxfordshire map 2

The Crazy Bear

Bear Lane, Stadhampton, Oxford OX44 7UR
TEL: (01865) 890714 FAX: (01865) 400481
EMAIL: sales@crazybearhotel.co.uk
WEB SITE: www.crazybearhotel.co.uk

Colour and quality in equal measure, and designed with extravagant flair

From the outside, this is the quintessential English village inn with creepers trailing over the old stone walls and pub benches outside. The back garden-cum-patio, with its classical statuary and big London bus, hints a little of the unorthodoxy inside, but even so the kaleidoscope of colour and quirkiness can be startling. The dark, intimate bar has black-and-gold chequered walls and a copper-topped counter alongside an aged fireplace and rough stone floors; the main restaurant is a pink-and-purple treat with wine bottles adorning the ceiling, while the Thai brasserie has deep-red walls and a mirrored ceiling. Bedrooms continue the high quality yet eccentric theme with zebra-patterned carpets, turquoise walls and stylish art deco-esque fittings. Suites are more restrained in colour, perhaps caramels and creams, but have deep baths at the foot of the bed and giant coiled-spring radiators to liven things up. One reader noted some irritating niggles in the suites, such as no shaver point, bottled liquid soap instead of a bar, and no wastebin in the bedroom area, but praised the 'very good food and friendly, efficient staff'.

○ Open all year　⚡ Entering Stadhampton on A329 southbound, bear left immediately after petrol station and take next left into Bear Lane. Private car park　⚑ 8 double, 4 suites; all with room service, hair-dryer, direct-dial telephone, modem line, TV, DVD, CD player; no tea/coffee-making facilities in rooms　⊘ 2 restaurants, bar, garden; conferences, social functions, civil wedding licence; leisure facilities nearby; early suppers for children; highchairs　♿ No wheelchair access; 2 steps into hotel, 6 steps into restaurant, 2 ground-floor bedrooms　● No dogs　▭ Amex, Delta, MasterCard, Switch, Visa　£ Single occupancy of double £90 to £120, double £130 to £300, suite £270 to £300; deposit required. Set L, D £15; alc L, D £30; light meals available. Special breaks available (2004 data)

STAITHES　North Yorkshire	map 9

Endeavour

1 High Street, Staithes TS13 5BH
TEL: (01947) 840825
EMAIL: theendeavour@ntlworld.com
WEB SITE: www.endeavour-restaurant.co.uk

Cheerful fish-oriented restaurant-with-rooms in a historic fishing village

The cobbled streets of the old fishing and smuggling village of Staithes were built when the main form of transport was the ship rather than cars, so it is lucky that the Endeavour has its own little car park among the jumble of cottages clustered at the foot of its steep hill. Brian Kay and Charlotte Willoughby's restaurant is named of course after Captain Cook's famous ship, a nod to the days when he was apprenticed to a haberdasher and grocer in Staithes before making a rather momentous career move. Inside, the tiny fisherman's cottage is a haven of good humour and fine fishy flavours. A bright yellow and blue restaurant is the main focus of the piscine pleasures on offer; fresh locally caught fish might end up on your plate in the form of sea bass with plum and star anise compote or monkfish with watercress sauce – and the menu does not shun carnivores and vegetarians. Three bedrooms are done out in a fresh and uncluttered modern style, with illuminated stained-glass features. All come with video players and an impressive film library, bathrobes and complimentary sherry.

○ Open all year; restaurant closed Sun & Mon eves　⚡ Off A174 Whitby to Saltburn road; enter village: Endeavour is at bottom of hill, in High Street, on right. Private car park　⚑ 3 double; all with hair-dryer, TV, VCR　⊘ Restaurant, bar; social functions; highchairs　♿ No wheelchair access　● No dogs; smoking in bar area only　▭ Amex, Delta, MasterCard, Switch, Visa　£ Double £65 to £75; deposit required. Alc D £30. Special breaks available

---

STAMFORD　Lincolnshire	map 6

George of Stamford

71 St Martins, Stamford PE9 2LB
TEL: (01780) 750750　FAX: (01780) 750701
EMAIL: reservations@georgehotelofstamford.com
WEB SITE: www.georgehotelofstamford.com

Layers of history are visibly woven into this venerable medieval inn

Just off the centre of town this striking coaching inn hasn't just survived intact from a thousand years of often turbulent history, it has also expanded extensively over the centuries to incorporate its sizeable medieval neighbours into the fabric. Many of the additions are intact, but they are often located in the unlikeliest of places: the thick exterior walls of a twelfth-century hospital can now be seen deep inside the present building, ancient stone fireplaces incongruously line a hallway where once they were part of a grand public room and a thirteenth-century church was transmuted into a wing of the hotel. The cloistered garden and quadrangle also bear testimony to a varied past and inside, the place has such an abundance of quaint little lounges, bars and eateries that it is difficult to know what to sample first. The main restaurant is of the atmospheric genre of dark oak panelling, heavily draped mullioned windows and a large stone fireplace, while the garden restaurant is an altogether lighter affair with exposed stone walls, large atrium and a mass of plant life around a central colonnade. Bedrooms are comfortable and full of character – the quietest overlook the courtyard.

◑ Open all year ⧅ From A1 north of Peterborough, at roundabout take road signposted Stamford B1081. Hotel is at bottom of hill by first set of traffic lights. Nearest train station: Stamford. Private car park ⧅ 10 single, 9 twin, 24 double, 3 four-poster, 1 suite; family rooms available; all with 24-hour room service, hair-dryer, trouser press, direct-dial telephone, modem line, TV; no tea/coffee-making facilities in rooms ⧅ 2 restaurants, 2 bars, 2 lounges, gardens; conferences, social functions, civil wedding licence; leisure facilities nearby; early suppers for children; cots, highchairs, babysitting ⧅ No wheelchair access ● No children under 10 in main restaurant eves; no dogs in restaurant; no smoking in main restaurant before 10pm ⧅ Amex, Delta, Diners, MasterCard, Switch, Visa £ Single £78 to £90, single occupancy of twin/double £95 to £120, twin/double £110 to £225, four-poster £180 to £225, family room from £130, suite £150; deposit required. Set L £17.50 (Mon to Sat, 2 courses); alc L, D £34; light meals available. Special breaks available

---

STANTON WICK   Bath & N. E. Somerset   map 2

Carpenters Arms

Stanton Wick, Nr Pensford BS39 4BX
TEL: (01761) 490202   FAX: (01761) 490763
EMAIL: carpenters@buccaneer.co.uk
WEB SITE: www.the-carpenters-arms.co.uk

Lovely bar and restaurant plus decent rooms at this roadside inn

Look carefully at the façade of this pretty inn and you will see it was once three miners' cottages – the old coal workings are up the lane. Once inside the door, the origins disappear in a carefully designed open-plan bar and restaurant area. Bare stone walls, plaid carpets, log fires and polished wood create a cosy and sociable ambience. There is a second restaurant too, newly refurbished but similar in style. Cooking covers the whole range from upmarket sandwiches to steaks and seared salmon. Bedrooms have seen new bathrooms put in with power showers; the rooms themselves have had new mattresses and bedding (sheets and blankets are preferred here). Décor is in keeping with the period and atmosphere of the place: spriggy wallpapers, pine furniture and botanical prints for a fresh, cottage-like feel.

◑ Closed 25, 26 Dec ⧅ From A37 south of Bristol, take A368 towards Chew Valley Lake; Stanton Wick signposted off to right. Private car park ⧅ 3 twin/double, 9 double; all with hair-dryer, trouser press, direct-dial telephone, TV ⧅ 2 restaurants, bar, lounge, patio; conferences; social functions; leisure facilities nearby; cots, highchairs, limited babysitting ⧅ No wheelchair access; 3 steps into hotel, 1 step into restaurant ● No dogs in bedrooms and most public rooms; smoking only in bar and 1 restaurant ⧅ Amex, Delta, MasterCard, Switch, Visa £ Single occupancy of twin/double £65, twin/double £90; deposit required. Alc L, D £25; light meals available. Special breaks available

---

STOCKCROSS   Berkshire   map 2

Vineyard at Stockcross

Stockcross, Newbury RG20 8JU
TEL: (01635) 528770   FAX: (01635) 528398
EMAIL: general@the-vineyard.co.uk
WEB SITE: www.the-vineyard.co.uk

Every conceivable luxury on offer, as well as thousands of wines

If you hadn't already guessed from the name, the fact that every bedroom contains a copy of the comprehensive wine list is a very clear indication that this upmarket pad is oenophile heaven – even the rooms are named after French or Californian wines.

The trouble is, if we are being pedantic, there is no vineyard here at all (it's actually in Napa Valley, California) and the closest you'll get is admiring the wall murals in the Music Room or the arty photos of all things viticultural. Or, of course, sampling one of the 23,000 bottles stored in the hotel's wine cellar, which, in keeping with the obtuse terminology, is upstairs! Public rooms, such as the split-level restaurant, are elegance itself, which even extends to the outer courtyard with its central feature of floating flames. Bedrooms range from pamper-me-silly normal rooms to height-of-luxury suites, mainly in the new Atrium wing, and come in tasteful colour schemes that might be ultra-modern or reassuringly chintzy. Bathrooms are equally swish, with lots of marble in evidence. For even more opulence, head to the spa and lounge beneath the dramatic glass dome.

◑ Open all year ⚡ From M4 Junction 13, take A34 towards Newbury; turn off at third exit signposted Hungerford; turn right at roundabout; at next roundabout turn right following sign for hotel; hotel is ¼ mile on right. Private car park ⬅ 3 twin, 11 double, 2 four-poster, 31 suites; all with room service, hair-dryer, mini-bar, trouser press, direct-dial telephone, modem line, TV, CD player; no tea/coffee-making facilities in rooms ⌀ Restaurant, 2 bars, lounge, conservatory, garden; conferences; social functions; civil wedding licence; gym, spa, heated indoor swimming pool; leisure facilities nearby; early suppers for children; cots, highchairs ♿ Wheelchair access to hotel and restaurant, 10 ground-floor bedrooms, WC, lift ● No dogs; no smoking in bedrooms ⊟ Amex, Delta, Diners, MasterCard, Switch, Visa £ Single occupancy of twin/double £194, twin/double £288, four-poster/suite £353 to £746; deposit required (prices valid till Jan 2005). Set L £25, D £33; alc L, D £55; light meals available (3FOR2)

---

map 6

Angel Inn

Stoke-by-Nayland, Colchester CO6 4SA
TEL: (01206) 263245   FAX: (01206) 263373
WEB SITE: www.horizoninns.co.uk

Contemporary dining and traditional rooms in an-old fashioned village setting

You'll find The Angel on a sleepy road through a traditional Suffolk village, cute pink and white houses surrounding and the countryside laid out for you across the road. Bedrooms are of the country chintz variety, and the bathrooms especially will benefit from the refurb the rooms are due this year. Downstairs in the bar and restaurant areas (which you'll have to use if you want to relax away from your room as there's no guests' lounge) there's already been something of a makeover in the last couple of years, shifting the décor towards a simpler, more contemporary style with commissioned artworks, mainly with foodie subject matter like huge lobsters, on plain-coloured walls. For the most part the modernisation works well and doesn't try to overpower the building – original features are allowed to shine, such as a vertiginous well in the middle of the main restaurant, spookily lit from beneath. The menu, on numerous little chalkboards above the bar, is modern European dishes like char-grilled lamb on cheddar mash with mint hollandaise, or seared tuna niçoise.

◑ Closed 25 & 26 Dec, 1 Jan ⚡ In centre of village at junction of B1087 and B1068. Private car park ⬅ 1 twin/double, 5 double; all with hair-dryer, direct-dial telephone, TV ⌀ Restaurant, bar, garden ♿ No wheelchair access; 1 ground-floor bedroom ● No children under 8; no dogs; no smoking in bedrooms ⊟ Delta, MasterCard, Switch, Visa £ Single occupancy of twin/double £60 to £70, twin/double £75 to £85. Alc L £16.50, D £23

The Guide *office can quickly spot when a hotelier is encouraging customers to write a letter recommending inclusion. Such reports do not further a hotel's cause.*

Prices are what you can expect to pay in 2005, except where specified to the contrary. Many hoteliers tell us that these prices can be regarded only as approximations.

Chapters

27 High Street, Stokesley TS9 5AD
TEL: (01642) 711888   FAX: (01642) 713387
EMAIL: info@chaptershotel.co.uk
WEB SITE: www.chaptershotel.co.uk

Characterful small hotel with busy dining scene in a lively market town

This eighteenth-century coaching inn at the centre of Stokesley has certainly seen some changes and is about to see more. Switched-on owners Alan and Catherine Thompson are certainly receptive to the demands of their customers: they have noticed that families have started to make inroads into their solid base of business customers, so they plan to knock through walls to make larger family rooms. The bistro restaurant, too, is due for a makeover: when our inspector called in spring, plans were afoot to turn it into a tapas bar. In the other foodie options it's business as usual: at the rear, the Garden Room stays darkly romantic in boldly stylish shades of burgundy and blue, and for an espresso and snack, the deli and café is still a short stroll along the high street. Overall, Chapters' style relies on bold, eye-catching colour schemes and pulls off quite a flamboyant effect. Bedrooms have either clean-cut modern lines with pale wooden beds, wooden slatted blinds and oriental rugs against a neutral background, or a more Victorian feel with a colonial edge thanks to rattan furniture and warm ochre hues. All have crisp modern bathrooms. Some signs of wear and tear were noticeable, which ongoing refurbishment ought to put right. Reports on progress welcome.

◗ Closed 1 Jan; restaurant closed Sun eve ⚡ In centre of Stokesley 🚗 4 single, 1 twin, 7 twin/double, 1 four-poster; family rooms available; all with room service, direct-dial telephone, modem line, TV; some with hair-dryer ⚄ 2 restaurants, 2 bars, lounge, garden; conferences; social functions; civil wedding licence; leisure facilities nearby; early suppers for children; cots, highchairs, baby-listening ♿ No wheelchair access ⬥ No dogs; no smoking ▭ Amex, Delta, Diners, MasterCard, Switch, Visa £ Single £66 to £68, single occupancy of twin/double £68 to £70, twin/double/four-poster £80 to £85, family room £85. Set L £14.50; alc D £28; light meals available; service incl. Special breaks available (3FOR2)

Ston Easton Park

Ston Easton, Nr Bath BA3 4DF
TEL: (01761) 241631   FAX: (01761) 241377
EMAIL: info@stoneaston.co.uk
WEB SITE: www.stoneaston.co.uk

Lovely house and grounds plus understated, genteel atmosphere

The long drive curling through parkland gives you plenty of time to admire this handsome eighteenth-century house landscaped by the man who coined the term 'landscape gardening', Humphrey Repton. Interior design is very much in keeping with the period – high ceilings and ornate plasterwork matched by classical furnishings and lit with Chinese vase lamps. The Palladian saloon is particularly grand and has fine views of the ornamental river behind the house. Next to it, the dining room is light and airy rather than cosy, dinner menus being staunchly country house. Bedrooms maintain the high standards with old-fashioned chintzy elegance. Period furniture, smart bathrooms and extras such as sherry and fresh flowers complete the picture. Standard rooms tend to be smaller and with less expansive views but are good value.

◗ Open all year ⚡ On A37, just north of Shepton Mallet, in village of Ston Easton. Private car park 🚗 2 single, 10 twin/double, 3 double, 6 four-poster, 3 suites; 2 with shared bathroom; all with room service, hair-dryer, trouser press, direct-dial telephone, TV; some with VCR, CD player ⚄ Restaurant, 3 lounges, 3 libraries, games room, gardens; conferences and social functions; civil wedding licence; tennis; leisure facilities nearby; early suppers for children; cots, highchairs, babysitting, baby-listening ♿ No wheelchair access ⬥ No smoking in bedrooms ▭ Amex, Delta, Diners, MasterCard, Switch, Visa £ Single £120 to £180, twin/double £150 to £195, four-poster £210 to £395, suite rates on application; deposit required. Set L £17.50, D £34.50; alc D £39.50; light meals available; service incl. Special breaks available ③FOR②

STOW-ON-THE-WOLD Gloucestershire　　　　　　　　　　　　　　　　　　　　map 5

Grapevine Hotel

Sheep Street, Stow-on-the-Wold GL54 1AU
TEL: (01451) 830344 FAX: (01451) 832278
EMAIL: enquiries@vines.co.uk
WEB SITE: www.vines.co.uk

A well-situated Cotswold hotel with all the trimmings

'Everything a hotel should be, or used to be in the past, and we really could not find anything to complain about.' There seems to be a touch of disappointment in the words of this reporter on a stay at the Grapevine, but it's clear what he means. Janine and Mark Vance are now well into their stride at this neat, stone-built inn in an enviable location in the centre of Stow. Much of the activity centres around the Grapevine restaurant, named after the remarkable Hamburg vine which stretches across the ceiling, and the Gigot bar, the low-lit alternative dining option. As is usual in old Cotswold houses, bedroom sizes are not large, but the standard of decoration is high, and sloping ceilings and rough stone walls in some of the bedrooms add to the interest. Our happy guest also noted that his 'faultless' bedroom was well stocked with extras, including packets of soup on the tea tray in addition to tea, coffee and biscuits, and large dispensers of toiletries in the bathroom. There is praise, too, for the 'highest level of service'.

◑ Open all year ⚡ From A429 (Fosseway) in Stow-on-the-Wold, take A436 towards Chipping Norton; hotel is 500 yards on right, opposite green. Private car park. Nearest train station: Kingham ⊨ 1 twin, 12 twin/double, 8 double, 1 four-poster; family rooms available; all with room service, hair-dryer, direct-dial telephone, modem line, TV; some with trouser press, mini-bar ⊘ Restaurant, bar, 2 lounges, library, patio; conferences; civil wedding licence; social functions; cots, highchairs, baby-sitting ⅙ No wheelchair access; 2 steps into restaurant, 3 ground-floor bedrooms ● Dogs in bar and bedrooms only; smoking in bar only ▭ Amex, Delta, MasterCard, Switch, Visa £ Single occupancy of twin/double from £110, twin/double from £130, four-poster/family room from £150; deposit required. Set, alc L £15, D £28; light meals available. Special breaks available ③FOR②

STRATFORD-UPON-AVON Warwickshire　　　　　　　　　　　　　　　　　map 5

Victoria Spa Lodge

Bishopton Lane, Stratford-upon-Avon CV37 9QY
TEL: (01789) 267985 FAX: (01789) 204728
EMAIL: ptozer@victoriaspalodge.demon.co.uk
WEB SITE: www.stratford-upon-avon.co.uk/victoriaspa.htm

Welcoming B&B with noteworthy history, just outside Stratford

In 1837 the young Princess Victoria opened this purpose-built hotel, strategically positioned to accommodate visitors for a Georgian spa enterprise that folded soon after it had been set up. Marooned without its spa, the hotel became a private house boasting such notable residents as the cartoonist Captain Bruce Bairns and the founder of the Birmingham Repertory Company, Sir Barry Jackson. Paul and Dreen Tozer now preside over this lovely piece of Victoriana with evident affection. The handsome breakfast room is well lit and retains much of its character. Bedrooms are all pleasantly furnished, with Number 3 being the pick – a spacious room in rose-tints and rich red where Victoria stayed during her inaugural visit. The hotel is off a quiet lane in an attractive leafy garden and, although there is still no spa, Stratford is a picturesque walk away along the adjacent canal towpath.

◗ Closed 24, 25 & 31 Dec ▢ At intersection of A46 and A3400, take road signposted Bishopton; hotel is along on right. Nearest train station: Stratford-upon-Avon. Private car park ⬛ 1 twin, 3 double, 3 family rooms; all with hair-dryer, TV ⊘ Breakfast room, lounge, garden; leisure facilities nearby; cots, highchairs, outdoor play area ⅙ No wheelchair access ● No dogs; no smoking ▢ MasterCard, Switch, Visa £ Single occupancy of twin/double £50, twin/double £65, family room £80; deposit required

---

STUCKTON Hampshire   map 2

Three Lions

Stuckton, Nr Fordingbridge SP6 2HF
TEL: (01425) 652489   FAX: (01425) 656144
WEB SITE: www.thethreelionsrestaurant.co.uk

Country restaurant with excellent, welcoming hosts and comfortable bedrooms

What a find the Three Lions proves to be, tucked down a quiet country lane close to Fordingbridge. The bedrooms – each guarded by a cuddly ginger lion – are supremely comfortable, done out in calming country style with pastel walls, flowery fabrics and pine furniture, plus there's a decent-sized garden where children have their own play area, and a sauna and outdoor Jacuzzi thrown in for good measure. But the icing on the cake has to be the breezy restaurant, undoubtedly the heart of the place, where seriously good food is served up with little unnecessary fuss or fanfare in perfectly unpretentious surroundings. Jane Womersley is a charming hostess and performs her front-of-house duties with significant aplomb, chatting warmly but never lingering too long, and expertly anticipating the particular needs of her guests, be they ex-Prime Ministers or local couples celebrating an anniversary. Husband Mike's skills as chef are no less considerable and his balanced and carefully prepared daily menu – listed with no-nonsense descriptions on a chalkboard by the bar – might include delicately cooked rösti of kidneys, followed by Quantock duck with mango or venison scented with myrtle and delicious caramelised bananas with brûlée custard. Happily, breakfast doesn't disappoint either – strong black coffee, beautifully presented fresh fruit drizzled with passion fruit juice, then fresh croissants and home-baked bread are just the thing to set you up for the day.

◗ Closed last 2 weeks in Jan and 1 week in Feb ▢ From Fordingbridge on B3078 to Godshill, pass A338 flyover and turn right after garage on left; take next left towards Stuckton; hotel is on left. Private car park ⬛ 2 twin/double, 2 double; family room available; all with hair-dryer, TV, VCR ⊘ Restaurant, dining room, bar, lounge, conservatory, garden; conferences; social functions; leisure facilities nearby; early suppers for children; cots, highchairs, toys, baby-listening, outdoor play area ⅙ Wheelchair access to hotel and restaurant, 2 ground-floor bedrooms specially equipped for disabled people ● No dogs; smoking in bar only ▢ Delta, MasterCard, Switch, Visa £ Single occupancy of twin/double £59 to £75, twin/double £65 to £95, family room £115 to £125; deposit required. Cooked B £6.50; set L £16; alc L £30, D £33; light meals available. Special breaks available

---

STURMINSTER NEWTON Dorset   map 2

Plumber Manor

Sturminster Newton DT10 2AF
TEL: (01258) 472507   FAX: (01258) 473370
EMAIL: book@plumbermanor.com
WEB SITE: www.plumbermanor.com

Dependable bastion of traditional values in a welcoming package

With rolling farmland all around, this mullioned seventeenth-century house is a tranquil spot three miles out of Sturminster Newton. The house has been in the same family, the Prideaux-Brunes, since being built and oil portraits of ancestors hang on the walls. Not that this is a stuffy sort of place: traditional certainly, but friendly too and one that aims to create the atmosphere of staying in a private house. There is a relaxing sitting room with bar and a series of restaurant rooms that feature grand fireplaces, barrel-vaulted ceilings and plenty of oil paintings. Brian Prideaux-Brune is the chef, producing a reliable and well-reported menu of French-influenced cooking. Bedrooms are spacious, immaculately well kept and traditional in style – those over in the converted stable courtyard are slightly more modern in appearance. In recent years the two-acre gardens around the house have been extensively remodelled and there are pleasant walks down to the River Divelish (a stream really) with places to sit en route.

○ Closed Feb ◪ In Sturminster Newton take A357 towards Sherborne; then first left, following brown tourist signs to hotel. Private car park ▙▙ 14 twin/double, 2 double; all with room service, hair-dryer, trouser press, direct-dial telephone, TV ⊘ Restaurant, bar, lounge, garden; conferences; social functions; tennis; early suppers for children; cots, highchairs ☒ Wheelchair access to hotel and restaurant, WC, 6 ground-floor bedrooms, 2 rooms specially equipped for disabled people ● Dogs in bedrooms only; no smoking ☐ Amex, Diners, MasterCard, Switch, Visa £ Single occupancy of twin/double from £90, twin/double £110 to £170. Set L (Sun) £21.50, D £26; service incl. Special breaks available

---

SUTTON COLDFIELD West Midlands   map 5

New Hall

Walmley Road, Sutton Coldfield B76 1QX
TEL: 0121-378 2442   FAX: 0121-378 4637
EMAIL: jayne.shorter@thistlehotels.com
WEB SITE: www.thistlehotels.com/newhall

An appropriately baronial setting for a royal pampering

Although this hotel is now part of the Thistle group, the only obvious 'chain' at what is thought to be the oldest inhabited moated manor house in England is the drawbridge (off limits except at weddings). Inside, the atmosphere is very much English country house, with a host of fabulous period details offering reminders of the house's lineage, especially in the Tudor dining room with its impressive fireplace, moulded ceiling and oak-panelled walls. For relaxing, you can choose from the elegant lounge, with its beautiful mullioned windows, or the cosy, clubby cocktail bar. In fine weather, there's also the option of sitting amid the topiary on the secluded patio. Most of the traditionally decorated bedrooms are situated in a big, sympathetic extension and come with chintz fabrics, appealing views and slick, neutrally toned en-suite bathrooms. Plentiful facilities include a croquet lawn, nine-hole golf course, tennis courts and a complete health spa.

○ Open all year ◪ Just off B4148 near Walmley. Nearest train station: Sutton Coldfield. Private car park ▙▙ 4 single, 15 twin, 29 double, 4 four-poster, 8 suites; all with room service, hair-dryer, trouser press, direct-dial telephone, modem line, TV; some with VCR, CD player, mini-bar ⊘ Dining room, bar, lounge, conservatory, garden; conferences; social functions; civil wedding licence; gym, spa, tennis, heated indoor swimming pool, leisure facilities nearby; early suppers for children; cots, highchairs, babysitting, baby-listening ☒ Wheelchair access to hotel and dining room (ramp), WC, 20 ground-floor bedrooms, 1 room specially equipped for disabled people. Disabled parking ● No dogs; no smoking in some public rooms and some bedrooms ☐ Amex, Delta, Diners, MasterCard, Switch, Visa £ Single £190, twin/double £220 to £260, four-poster £280, suite £300; deposit required. Continental/cooked B £15.50; set L £18, D £33; alc L, D £45; light meals available; service incl. Special breaks available

---

SUTTON GAULT Cambridgeshire   map 6

Anchor Inn

Sutton Gault, Ely CB6 2BD
TEL: (01353) 778537   FAX: (01353) 776180
EMAIL: anchorinnsg@aol.com
WEB SITE: www.anchor-inn-restaurant.co.uk

Peaceful Fenland pub with a pair of charming rooms

If the flood defences protecting the Anchor go, so does most of Cambridgeshire, says Robin Moore, proprietor of this splendid little Fenland gastropub. The ditches were originally dug by Scottish prisoners of war, whom the original seventeenth-century parts of the inn were built to house. The interior is rustic but in a simple, understated way rather than a flowery, fussy one. The excellent food is served in any of three or four areas, each of which has its own charms such as timber beams, dark-wood panelling or a low brick fireplace. At the time of going to press there were only two rooms, though plans were afoot to add another two. The twin has pine furniture, cream carpets and a tiny but perfectly well-formed bathroom with shower, while the suite has a comfy little living room separated from the bedroom by the bathroom.

◑ Closed 24 to 26 Dec ⚡ Signposted off B1381, 6 miles west of Ely, in Sutton Gault. Private car park 🛏️ 1 twin, 1 suite; both with hair-dryer, direct-dial telephone, TV ⊘ Dining room, terrace; social functions; leisure facilities nearby; highchairs ♿ No wheelchair access ● No dogs; smoking only in part of dining area ▭ Amex, Delta, MasterCard, Switch, Visa £ Single occupancy of twin £50 to £70, twin £75 to £85, suite £95 to £105; deposit required. Set Sun L £20; alc L, D £27; light meals available. Special breaks available

---

SWAFFHAM Norfolk map 6

Strattons

4 Ash Close, Swaffham PE37 7NH
TEL: (01760) 723845   FAX: (01760) 720458
EMAIL: enquiries@strattonshotel.com
WEB SITE: www.strattonshotel.com

Eco-friendliness without skimping on luxury

Les and Vanessa Scott continue to prove that you don't have to sacrifice luxury in the pursuit of environmental friendliness. Running through the whole operation, often behind the scenes, is a genuine desire to tread lightly – not just pay lip service by skimping on towel washing – though the tone is never preachy. Rooms are eclectically decorated in a lavish ornamental style, mixing modern and traditional to create an effortlessly appealing blend. The majority of the bedrooms are in the main house, a mix of eighteenth-century Palladian and Victorian. Each is individually decorated – examples include the Venetian Room with a *Birth of Venus* painted on the bathroom wall, the Victorian Room with a splendidly flouncy white bed and ruddy leaves varnished onto the wood floor, or the Opium Room in the ex-groom's cottage, which has a wonderful carved headboard from an opium bed (opium not included) and a bath at the foot of the bed beyond carved Corinthian columns. Public rooms are similarly elaborate, with artworks by local artists for sale.

◑ Closed 24 to 26 Dec; restaurant closed Sun eve ⚡ At north end of marketplace, behind shop fronts. Private car park 🛏️ 1 twin, 3 double, 4 suites; family rooms available; all with room service, hair-dryer, direct-dial telephone, TV; mini-bar, VCR, CD player in suites ⊘ Restaurant, drawing room, garden; conferences; leisure facilities nearby; early suppers for children; cots, highchairs, toys, babysitting, baby-listening ♿ No wheelchair access; 8 steps into hotel, 8 steps into restaurant, 1 ground-floor bedroom ● No smoking ▭ MasterCard, Switch, Visa £ Single occupancy of twin/double from £80 to £100, twin/double £100 to £140, family room £195 to £215, suite £180 to £200; deposit required. Set D £35; light meals available; service incl. Special breaks available

---

SWAY Hampshire map 2

The Nurse's Cottage

Station Road, Sway, Lymington SO41 6BA
TEL: (01590) 683402 (AND FAX)
EMAIL: nurses.cottage@lineone.net
WEB SITE: www.nursescottage.co.uk

Country restaurant with excellent, welcoming hosts and comfortable bedrooms

Tony Barnfield's astonishing attention to detail and attentiveness are, one imagines, not far removed from that of the district nurses who formerly occupied this small turn-of-the-twentieth-century cottage, and after whom each of the guest bedrooms is now named. His apparent quest to provide the ultimate B&B experience means that you'd be hard pressed to think of anything that hasn't already been thought of in the immaculately kept and superbly well-equipped bedrooms. They are stuffed with all manner of home-from-home extras, including fresh flowers and fruit, a hairdryer, CD player and a fridge with water, juice and fresh milk. Of course there's a TV and video, too, plus a blank cassette to record your favourite programme should it clash with dinner. This is served up in the conservatory restaurant: perhaps a delicate mushroom millefeuille, followed by breast of guinea fowl in a tarragon, white wine and cream sauce and a selection of tasty West Country cheeses. The extensive wine list has more than 60 wines from 16 countries; don't worry if you have trouble choosing as, of course, Tony has helpfully selected a baker's dozen of the most highly recommended wines, available by the glass in the restaurant, and, should you wish, as a collection to take home.

◖ Closed 3 weeks in Nov, 3 weeks in Mar ☒ In centre of Sway village, close to shops. Nearest train station: Sway. Private car park 🚗 1 single, 1 twin, 1 double; all with room service, hair-dryer, mini-bar, trouser press, direct-dial telephone, modem line, TV, VCR, CD player ⊗ Restaurant, garden; social functions ♿ Wheelchair access to hotel and restaurant (ramps), National Accessible Scheme: mobility impairment M1, hearing impairment H1, WC, 3 ground-floor bedrooms, 1 room specially equipped for disabled people ● No children under 10; no dogs in public rooms; no smoking ▭ Amex, Delta, MasterCard, Switch, Visa £ Single £75, single occupancy of twin/double £85, twin/double £140 to £150 (rates incl dinner); deposit required. Set Sun L £16.50. Special breaks available ③FOR②

Hazlewood Castle

Paradise Lane, Hazlewood, Tadcaster LS24 9NJ
TEL: (01937) 535353   FAX: (01937) 530630
EMAIL: info@hazlewood-castle.co.uk
WEB SITE: www.hazlewood-castle.co.uk

Function-oriented hotel with an interesting past and strong focus on food

Hazlewood Castle's impressive history is first documented in the Domesday Book, and until celeb chef John Benson-Smith turned it into a hotel in 1997, the low crenellated castle was a rather run-down monastery. Inside there's still plenty of period detail, although what period precisely depends where exactly you are – expect acreages of oak panelling, baronial stone fireplaces and rooms on a massive scale such as the Great Hall, a suitably memorable backdrop for the massive turnover in weddings and conference groups. Thanks to a sensitive separation policy, however, leisure guests need not fear invasion by hordes clad in tailcoats and powder-puff dresses. Eating is taken care of in the twenty-first century surroundings of the 1086 restaurant, all sinuous sofas and stylish black tables and chairs on dark stone floors, or more lightly, in the trendy Prickly Pear café where funky citrus fruit seats stand out against a pale wooden floor. Irreproachably plush bedrooms are unlikely to disappoint: some, such as Hibiscus, are theatrical with leopard-print throws and brazen cherry, green and gold hues, while others – Elderflower, for example – are more pastelly and traditional. Bathrooms, too, tick all of the style boxes.

◖ Open all year ☒ Near Junction 45 of A1(M); hotel drive is south of A64; follow brown signs. From A1(M) northbound, take A64 towards York, turn first left on to A659 towards Tadcaster and follow brown signs. Private car park 🚗 10 twin/double, 2 four-poster, 9 suites; family rooms available; all with room service, hair-dryer, mini-bar, trouser press, direct-dial telephone, fax, modem line, TV ⊗ 2 restaurants, bar, lounge, library, garden; conferences, social functions, civil wedding licence; leisure facilities nearby; early suppers for children; highchairs ♿ No wheelchair access ● No children under 12 in main restaurant eves; no dogs; smoking in library only ▭ Amex, Delta, Diners, MasterCard, Switch, Visa £ Single occupancy of twin/double £120, twin from £140, double £190, four-poster £320, suite from £255, family room from £310; deposit required. Set Sun L £29.50, set D £19.50; alc D £33; light meals available. Special breaks available

The Swan

50 High Street, Tarporley CW6 0AG
TEL: (01829) 733838   FAX: (01829) 732932

A comfortable coaching inn experience in one of Cheshire's 'Best-Kept Villages'

Locals maintain that Tarporley is really a town, albeit a miniature one, complete with bank, post office and an irresistible chocolate shop a few yards from this handsome inn. The Swan's oldest sections date back to the sixteenth century, though its dignified, double-bayed façade, like the rest of Tarporley's historic High Street, is mellow red-brick Georgian. An ample range of well-furnished public rooms stretches throughout the ground floor. Décor manages to impart a stylishly contemporary but traditional feel to the antique, oak-timbered, stone-flagged interior. Smart plaid carpets and checked upholstery blend with well-framed flower prints and hunting scenes against Farrow & Ball 'heritage' colour schemes. Bedrooms vary from smallish but comfortably conservative rooms in the main building to dashing recent conversions in the coach-house annexe across the rear car park. Service is friendly and unstuffy; menus combine traditional steaks and sirloins with elegant modern ingredients like red onion marmalade, chilli salsa and sunblushed tomatoes.

◑ Open all year ▨ On High Street in Tarporley. Private car park ▙ 3 single, 4 twin, 6 double, 2 four-poster, 1 suite; all with room service, hair-dryer, trouser press, direct-dial telephone, TV ✅ Restaurant, bar, lounge; conferences; social functions; civil wedding licence; leisure facilities nearby; early suppers for children; cots, highchairs, toys ♿ Wheelchair access to hotel (no steps at rear) and restaurant, WC, 3 ground-floor bedrooms specially equipped for disabled people. Disabled parking ● No dogs; no smoking in bedrooms ▭ Amex, MasterCard, Switch, Visa £ Single £52, single occupancy of twin/double £70, twin/double £77, four-poster £90, suite £120. Set L, D £10; alc L, D £29.50; light meals available. Special breaks available

Horn of Plenty

Gulworthy, Tavistock PL19 8JD
TEL: (01822) 832528 (AND FAX)
EMAIL: enquiries@thehornofplenty.co.uk
WEB SITE: www.thehornofplenty.co.uk

Top-notch country house in a superb location

After a brief hiatus when the hotel was up for sale, it is good to report that this fine Victorian house is back on track doing what it is best at – namely, providing excellent food and superior accommodation. There are new developments too – the garden has been tackled, and runaway rhododendrons cut back to reveal original Victorian beds and terraces. The views across the Tamar Valley are just as good as they ever were, but there are new vantage points from which to enjoy them. Within the house the atmosphere is amiably sophisticated. The spacious conservatory dining room also looks out across the valley, a fine place to enjoy Peter Gorton's well-reported cooking. Bedrooms are divided between the main house and a converted garden wing at the rear. Those in the house are more opulent and have real character with period furniture, cushions galore and sumptuous bathrooms. Rooms in the garden wing are fresher and more contemporary in style, each with a small outside seating area.

◑ Closed 24 to 26 Dec ▨ 3 miles west of Tavistock on A390, turn right at Gulworthy Cross and follow signs to hotel. Private car park ▙ 10 twin/double; all with room service, hair-dryer, mini-bar, direct-dial telephone, TV, VCR ✅ Restaurant, lounge, library, drawing room, garden; conferences, social functions, civil wedding licence; early suppers for children; cots, highchairs ♿ Wheelchair access to hotel (ramp) and restaurant, WC, 4 ground-floor bedrooms in annexe ● No children under 10 in restaurant eves; no dogs in public rooms and most bedrooms; 2 or more dogs £10; smoking in drawing room only ▭ Amex, Delta, MasterCard, Switch, Visa £ Single occupancy of twin/double £105 to £190, twin/double £115 to £200;

deposit required. Set L £18.50, D £30; alc L £23.50, D £39.50; light meals available. Special breaks available
③FOR②

TEDDINGTON Surrey   map 3

The Park

Park Road, Teddington TW11 0AB
TEL: 020-8614 9700   FAX: 020-8614 9701
EMAIL: theparklodge@dial.pipex.com
WEB SITE: www.galleongroup.co.uk

Lively brasserie with smart modern bedrooms a short hop from central London

How handy this smart café bar and brasserie is! Set on a residential street around the corner from Teddington's shops and within spitting distance of the station, The Park is understandably popular with business travellers during the week, while at weekends special rates lure visitors to nearby Bushy Park, Hampton Court and Kew Gardens. The large, informal brasserie is a lively spot for a light lunch – perhaps a chicken and brie burger, a blue cheese and walnut salad or a rib platter to share from the eclectic contemporary menu – while main courses for dinner might include pan-fried red snapper, scallops wrapped in smoked bacon or Moroccan lamb tagine. Bedrooms – most of which are in a separate modern block across the car park – are unfussy but well-equipped and comfortable, with tasteful modern colour schemes, good-quality furniture and spotless bathrooms. Weekend prices do not include breakfast.

◐ Closed 25 Dec   ⚡ Park Road runs between Bushy Park and west end of Teddington High Street (A313); hotel is just off this junction. Nearest train station: Teddington. Private car park 🛏 36 double, 6 family rooms; all with room service, hair-dryer, direct-dial telephone, TV ⚉ Restaurant, bar, lounge, terrace; leisure facilities nearby ♿ Wheelchair access to hotel (ramp) and restaurant, WC, 10 ground-floor bedrooms, 4 rooms specially equipped for disabled people, lift. Disabled parking ● No dogs; no smoking in some bedrooms and some public rooms ☐ Amex, Delta, Diners, MasterCard, Switch, Visa £ Single occupancy of twin/double £70 to £105, twin/double £70 to £115, family room £80 to £125. Continental B £5, cooked B £7 (included in room price midweek); set L £12; alc L, D £19; light meals available. Special breaks available
③FOR②

TEFFONT EVIAS Wiltshire   map 2

Howard's House

Teffont Evias, Salisbury SP3 5RJ
TEL: (01722) 716392   FAX: (01722) 716820
EMAIL: enq@howardshousehotel.com
WEB SITE: www.howardshousehotel.com

Small hotel with a gentle, relaxing atmosphere and personable staff

The village of Teffont Evias is a delightfully pretty one: thatched cottages around a stream are presided over by a castellated manor house and church. Noele Thompson's lovely pearly-grey house sits close to both these landmarks, a 1623 building with unlikely-looking Alpine-style eaves and an otherwise Georgian appearance. It's the kind of place where guests are made to feel they are staying with friends, the sort who employ a very good chef, put fruit in bedrooms and generally pamper their visitors generously. The restful sitting room and restaurant both look out on a garden terrace beyond which is a croquet lawn and vegetable garden (its produce goes into the pot). Bedrooms are a good size and feature comfortable beds, sparkling bathrooms and plush fabrics. Ask for those with views to the village.

◐ Closed 5 days Chr   ⚡ 9 miles west of Salisbury, turn off B3089 at Teffont Magna towards Teffont Evias. Private car park 🛏 1 twin, 6 double, 1 four-poster, 1 family room; all with room service, hair-dryer, direct-dial telephone, modem, TV; tea/coffee-making facilities on request ⚉ Restaurant, sitting room, garden; social functions; leisure facilities nearby; early suppers for children; cots, highchairs ♿ No wheelchair access

● Dogs £7 per night; no smoking in restaurant ☐ Amex, Delta, MasterCard, Switch, Visa £ Single occupancy of twin/double £95, twin/double £145, four-poster £165, family room £175; deposit required. Set L £22.50, D £24; alc D £36. Special breaks available

---

TEIGNMOUTH Devon   map 1

Thomas Luny House

Teign Street, Teignmouth TQ14 8EG
TEL: (01626) 772976
EMAIL: alisonandjohn@thomas-luny-house.co.uk
WEB SITE: www.thomas-luny-house.co.uk

First-rate hospitality, comfort and breakfasts in excellent B&B

In its heyday, Teignmouth was a favourite of the fashionable seafaring crowd, including some of Nelson's admirals and captains, so it is not surprising that marine artist Thomas Luny was also attracted to the town. The smart Georgian townhouse that he built, complete with secluded front courtyard, now belongs to John and Alison Allan, who pay tribute to Luny's memory at the same time as providing thoroughly modern facilities for today's guests. So new arrivals are offered tea and home-made cake, either in the elegant blue drawing room – where they can admire family photos and antiques or browse through copies of *National Geographic* or glossy magazines – or, in fine weather, in

the neat little walled garden at the back. They are also given the option of having early-morning tea brought to their room, or being provided with tea-making facilities. The room named after the eponymous artist has a suitably nautical theme, with a ship's lantern, rope-patterned wallpaper border, and watercolours of sailing vessels on the walls. The Chinese room has an oriental-style half-tester, while the four-poster bed in the Bitton room bears an inscription from the *Ancient Mariner*. Excellent breakfasts include fruit salad and compote, yoghurts, cereals, and home-made bread and local cheeses as well as a cooked option.

○ Open all year ☑ In Teignmouth, follow signs to quay; after turning off inner relief road, take first left into Teign Street. Nearest train station: Teignmouth. Private car park ⟵ 2 twin/double, 1 double, 1 four-poster; all with hair-dryer, direct-dial telephone, modem line, TV ⊘ Breakfast room, drawing room, garden; leisure facilities nearby ⟵ No wheelchair access ● No children under 12; no dogs; no smoking ☐ MasterCard, Visa £ Single occupancy of twin/double £50 to £60, twin/double/four-poster £65 to £85; deposit required. Special breaks available

---

TEMPLE CLOUD Bath & N.E. Somerset   map 2

Old Court

Main Road, Temple Cloud, Bath BS39 5DA
TEL: (01761) 451101   FAX: (01761) 451224
EMAIL: oldcourt@gifford.co.uk
WEB SITE: www.theoldcourt.com

Idiosyncratic origins but a comfortable and welcoming B&B all the same

Next to the A37 Bristol road stands this rather imposing Victorian Gothic Revival building, a place that has been dedicated to receiving guests right from the start. That is, if you count the prisoners who filled the cells – it was once town gaol, police station and courtroom all rolled into one. The old courtroom, all 45 feet long, is now the lounge, while the three cells have become comfortable, if rather small, bedrooms (there are still bars at the windows). Bathrooms are

squeezed in somehow. Upstairs are more spacious rooms, beautifully decorated with plush furnishings and power showers in the bathrooms – a couple also have whirlpool baths. Explore the various landings and staircases and eventually you will find a way up the spiral staircase to a room at the top which those former felons could only have dreamed about – with a Jacuzzi and sauna. Dinner is served only to groups and by arrangement.

○ Open all year 🔁 Entering Temple Cloud on northbound A37, at top of hill turn right into Temple Inn Lane, just before Temple Inn pub, opposite Texaco petrol station; fork right immediately into access road, across cattle grid, and turn into gates. Private car park 🛏️ 2 twin, 1 twin/double, 3 double, 1 four-poster, 1 suite; family rooms available; all with hair-dryer, TV; some with modem line, VCR ⊘ Dining room, lounge, games room, garden; conferences; social functions; civil wedding licence; spa; early suppers for children; cots, toys, babysitting ♿ No wheelchair access; 3 ground-floor bedrooms ● No dogs in public rooms, £5 per night in bedrooms; no smoking ▭ Delta, Diners, MasterCard, Switch, Visa £ Single occupancy of twin/double £50, twin/double £55 to £90, four-poster £75, family room from £60, suite £120; deposit required. Set L £12.50, D £18.50. Special breaks available ③FOR②

TETBURY Gloucestershire   map 2

Calcot Manor

Tetbury GL8 8YJ
TEL: (01666) 890391   FAX: (01666) 890394
EMAIL: reception@calcotmanor.co.uk
WEB SITE: www.calcotmanor.co.uk

A contemporary attitude and facilities that blend in with solid country-house values

This is the very model of a modern Cotswold country house. Pristine honey-stone Cotswold buildings that date back to the Middle Ages, spa and leisure facilities that would do an Olympic bid proud, plus an enlightened attitude to children, all add up to an impressive operation. The style of the public rooms is mainstream country house without a hair out of place – smart armchairs in tartan, red and green stripes and the odd well-placed antique. This year the Conservatory restaurant has had a refit in a more contemporary, spacious feel, with extra light provided by an expanded conservatory frontage. In addition there's a trendy champagne bar, a display kitchen and a mosaic-tiled wood-burning oven. A third of the bedrooms are in the main house and the rest are in cottage suites suitable for families (baby-listening is offered), or around the courtyard. Again, everything is in perfect condition in a traditional English country style and with big bathrooms. Also available are a resident nanny and a Playzone for those who should be neither seen nor heard.

○ Open all year 🔁 3 miles west of Tetbury on A4135, just before intersection with A46. Private car park 🛏️ 13 twin/double, 5 double, 2 four-poster, 10 family rooms; all with room service, hair-dryer, direct-dial telephone, modem line, TV; some with tea/coffee-making facilities, trouser press, VCR, CD player ⊘ Restaurant/conservatory, dining pub, 2 bars, lounge, garden; conferences and social functions; civil wedding licence; gym, spa, tennis, heated indoor and outdoor swimming pools; early suppers for children; cots, highchairs, toys, playroom, babysitting, baby-listening, outdoor play area ♿ Wheelchair access to hotel (ramp) and restaurant, WC, 17 ground-floor bedrooms, 1 room specially equipped for disabled people. Disabled parking ● No children in conservatory restaurant eves; no dogs ▭ Amex, Delta, Diners, MasterCard, Switch, Visa £ Single occupancy of twin/double £150, twin/double/four-poster from £190, family room from £235, suite from £250; deposit required. Alc L, D £35; light meals available; service incl

---

TEWIN Hertfordshire   map 3

Tewin Bury Farm   [NEW ENTRY]

B1000 Hertford Road, Nr Welwyn AL6 0JB
TEL: (01438) 717793   FAX: (01438) 840440
EMAIL: hotel@tewinbury.co.uk
WEB SITE: www.tewinbury.co.uk

Characterful converted farm that serves its business – and other – clients well

Business hotels can sometimes be so disappointing, with bland, identikit rooms and a lack of imagination. Nothing could be further from the truth for this smashing spot in the heart of Hertfordshire, which manages to cater effortlessly for the corporate and leisure crowds – and remain a working, 400-acre farm. The old farmhouse has been tastefully converted so that the former kitchen, with its vast brick fireplace, now makes an attractive reception, and the rest of the ground floor is given over to comfy lounges with stripped floors and squishy sofas. Bedrooms maintain the deft old-meets-new combination, with beams much in evidence, and all are thoughtfully decorated and furnished with a sense of tradition, so while some have patchwork quilts, others are more modern in grey-and-cream to complement the old wood furniture. Many of the farm's outbuildings, including the seventeenth-century tithe barn, have been converted, some containing bedrooms, others attractive meeting rooms, and of course a restaurant, where brick walls, exposed beams and hearty food give it a cheery country air.

◖ Closed 24 to 26 Dec ⦀ From A1(M) Junction 6, follow signs for A1000 (Welwyn Garden City) through Digswell; ignore Tewin sign left, pass layby, hotel is 100 yards on left. Nearest train station: Welwyn Garden City. Private car park ⤙ 6 twin/double, 14 double, 3 four-poster, 6 family rooms; all with room service, hair-dryer, direct-dial telephone, modem line, TV, iron; some with trouser press ⊘ Restaurant, bar, lounges, garden; conferences; social functions; civil wedding licence; leisure facilities nearby; cots, highchairs ♿ Wheelchair access to hotel and restaurant, WC, lift; 21 ground-floor bedrooms, 2 specially equipped for disabled people ● No children aged 2 to 12; no dogs; no smoking in restaurant ⊟ Amex, Delta, Diners, MasterCard, Switch, Visa £ Single occupancy of twin/double from £99, twin £106, double £116, four-poster £126, family room £141; deposit required. Set D £22.50; alc L £18, D £22.50; light meals available. Special breaks available ③FOR②

Lifeboat Inn

Ship Lane, Thornham, Hunstanton PE36 6LT
TEL: (01485) 512236   FAX: (01485) 512323
EMAIL: reception@lifeboatinn.co.uk
WEB SITE: www.lifeboatinn.co.uk

Atmospheric smugglers' inn right on the edge of the marsh

The delightfully atmospheric interior and the grand views over the sometimes foreboding marshland remain as enticing as ever at this former alehouse. The lounge is mildly grand, with stuffed birds around the walls and a grandfather clock in the corner, but probably the nicest place to sit is the nookish old bar, scattered with farming implements. Generous bar meals are served here, or you can opt for an eclectic restaurant menu in the Mediterranean-style conservatory, where vines hanging above your head give the light a pleasing dappled effect. Bedrooms are in a cheerful modern country style with lots of chunky pine and check patterns. There are more bedrooms down the road in the village at the sister establishment Old Coach House Inn, where you can dine on pizzas and pasta in the bright, modern bistro. The Old Coach House rooms are fine, but since you don't get either the views or breakfast on site, you're probably better off sticking to the Lifeboat and perhaps making a foray for dinner one evening.

◖ Open all year ⦀ Signposted off A149, 4 miles from Hunstanton. Private car park ⤙ 11 twin/double, 1 double; family rooms available; all with limited room service, hair-dryer, direct-dial telephone, TV ⊘ Restaurant, bar, lounge, conservatory, garden; conferences; social functions; leisure facilities nearby; early suppers for children; cots, highchairs, outdoor play area ♿ Wheelchair access to hotel and restaurant (1 step), WC, 1 ground-floor bedroom ● No smoking in bedrooms ⊟ Delta, MasterCard, Switch, Visa £ Single occupancy of twin/double £59 to £65, twin/double £78 to £110, family room £93 to £125; deposit required. Set D £26. Special breaks available

---

River House

Skippool Creek, Thornton-le-Fylde, Nr Thornton FY5 5LF
TEL: (01253) 883497   FAX: (01253) 892083
EMAIL: enquiries@theriverhouse.org.uk
WEB SITE: www.theriverhouse.org.uk

Riverside restaurant-with-rooms with idyllic views and positive personality

Stranded boats loll sleepily in the mud at low water, bobbing briskly as the tide returns to this quiet but ever-changing backwater down a bumpy cul-de-sac on the River Wyre. Bill and Linda Scott's dignified, brick-built house dates from the last year of the Georgian era (1830), surveying the waterfront from a site sufficiently elevated to avoid wetting its foundations. River House is clearly a long-established family home, full of character and more than a little battered in places. The focal point is the restaurant, in a cushioned conservatory extension with views over secluded rear gardens. Bill is a confidently inventive cook and genial host, his relaxed style disguising the fact that he is a serious food technologist with a thriving business in high-quality microwaveable dishes. Linda helps with puddings and starters and ensures the accommodation side of things runs smoothly. Bedrooms are comfortably old-fashioned, some featuring eyepopping original Victorian plumbing.

◑ Closed 25 & 26 Dec, 1 Jan; restaurant closed Sun eve From M55 Junction 3, take A585 for Fleetwood; follow road through three sets of traffic lights; at roundabout take third exit towards Little Thornton; immediately on right is Wyre Road, leading to Skippool Creek; house is at end of road, on left. Nearest train station: Poulton-le-Fylde. Private car park 🚗 3 twin/double, 1 double; all with room service, hair-dryer, direct-dial telephone, TV ✅ Restaurant, bar, lounge, conservatory, garden; conferences and social functions; leisure facilities nearby ♿ No wheelchair access ● No children under 7 in restaurant eves ☐ MasterCard, Switch, Visa £ Single occupancy of twin/double £70, twin/double £90. Set D £25; alc D £35. Special breaks available (3FOR2)

Tilston Lodge

Tilston, Malpas SY14 7DR
TEL: (01829) 250223 (AND FAX)

Welcoming Victorian country guesthouse in extensive, well-kept grounds

Rolling Cheshire farmland stretches in all directions from the tranquil village of Tilston. On its fringes stands Kathie and Neil Ritchie's substantial nineteenth-century house, originally built as a hunting lodge. A mini-menagerie of pets and livestock (speciality sheep and poultry, cats and retrievers) gives a smallholding feel to the property, whose domain runs to 16 acres of landscaped gardens, orchards and grazing land. Internal reorganisation means that guests now have an extra sitting room, and the run of the front of the house. The large, comfortable letting bedrooms contain lots of treats, such as sweets, sherry and home-baked biscuits, as well as varied reading matter and a generous array of toiletries. Breakfasts incorporate home-made and regional produce, including fruit from the gardens, plus unusual blue-shelled eggs from the resident free-range hens. Additional facilities run to a garden hot tub and safe-keeping for bikes (the house is on the Cheshire Cycle Way).

◑ Open all year In Tilston village, turn left at T-junction (signposted Malpas); lodge is 200 yards on right. Private car park 🚗 1 twin, 2 four-poster; family rooms available; all with hair-dryer, TV, CD player; 1 with trouser press ✅ Dining room, 2 sitting rooms, garden; hot tub; leisure facilities nearby; cots ♿ No wheelchair access ● No dogs; no smoking ☐ None accepted £ Single occupancy of twin £45 to £50, twin £70, four-poster £76. Special breaks available

---

Queen's Head Inn [NEW ENTRY]

Tirril, Penrith CA10 2JF
TEL: (01768) 863219 FAX: (01768) 863243
EMAIL: tirrilpub@yahoo.co.uk
WEB SITE: www.queensheadinn.co.uk

Enjoyable drinking and dining pub with Wordsworthian connections on the edge of Ullswater

In the gentle green countryside of the Eamont valley, this traditional village free house was once owned by the Wordsworth family. It has long been a popular local, but its growing reputation now attracts visitors from further afield. The oldest section of this low-slung, white-painted building dates from 1719. Extensive bar-dining areas ramble round the main serving counter, warmed by four open fireplaces, including a fine inglenook complete with its original meat-smoking hooks. Dark panelling, flagstoned floors, low beams and settle seating characterise the older parts, while its recently expanded dining areas are more routinely furnished. The Tirril Brewery's real ales, brewed just up the road, are a great attraction; so too is an extensive selection of food incorporating local Lakeland produce, plus inventive foreign cuisine and vegetarian dishes. Simple, practical, well-kept bedrooms, with nice outlooks and fresh clean décor, represent excellent value a stone's throw from the National Park boundary.

◑ Open all year; restaurant closed 25 Dec ☑ From Penrith take A6 south towards Shap through Eamont Bridge; turn right at mini-roundabout by Crown Inn; continue for 1½ miles to Tirril; hotel is in middle of village on right. Private car park ⊨ 1 twin, 6 twin/double; all with hair-dryer, TV ⊘ Dining area, bar; social functions; leisure facilities nearby; highchairs ⴲ No wheelchair access ● Children under 3 or over 13 only ⬚ Delta, MasterCard, Switch, Visa £ Single occupancy of twin/double £40, twin/double £70; deposit required. Alc L £12, D £16; light meals available. Special breaks available

---

TITCHWELL Norfolk map 6

Titchwell Manor

Titchwell, Nr Brancaster, King's Lynn PE31 8BB
TEL: (01485) 210221 FAX: (01485) 210104
EMAIL: margaret@titchwellmanor.com
WEB SITE: www.titchwellmanor.com

A smart modern makeover with some fine Victorian features

If you can ignore the coast road that runs past the front door, Titchwell Manor has a cracking vista out to the huge Norfolk coastal horizon. An alternative viewpoint was under construction when we inspected, as the gardens were being given a makeover to bring them in line with the refurbished interior. The new style, then, is one of gentle modernity, leaving original features like the splendid Victorian tiled floor in the reception but complementing them with pale, clean colours and relaxed contemporary furnishings. It's all rather soothing, and even in muggy weather you won't miss the views, with a series of photos of the big skies on the walls of the comfy lounge, where voluminous sofas and plates of cake tempt you to linger. Owner Margaret Snaith's son is head chef, so this really is a family affair, and he serves up a seafood-slanted menu, always with one eye on the presentation (as praised by a regular visitor). The best of the bedrooms are those upstairs, but those downstairs are popular with pet-owners.

◑ Open all year ☑ On A149 between Thornham and Brancaster. Private car park ⊨ 1 single, 1 twin, 4 twin/double, 3 double, 3 family rooms; all with room service, hair-dryer, direct-dial telephone, modem line, TV; some with trouser press, CD player ⊘ Restaurant, bar, 2 lounges, conservatory, garden; social functions; leisure facilities nearby; early suppers for children; cots, highchairs, toys, playroom, baby-listening, outdoor play area ⴲ Wheelchair access to hotel and restaurant, National Accessible Scheme: mobility impairment M1, WC, 7 ground-floor bedrooms, 1 room specially equipped for disabled people ● No children under 12 in restaurant eves; dogs in some bedrooms only, £5 per night; no smoking in bar, lounge and some bedrooms ⬚ Amex, Delta, MasterCard, Switch, Visa £ Single £55 to £65, twin/double £100 to £116, family room £115 to £150; deposit required. Set L £10; alc L £20, D £25; light meals available; service incl. Special breaks available (3FOR2)

If you make a booking using a credit card and find after cancelling that the full amount has been charged to your card, raise the matter with your credit-card company. It will ask the hotelier to confirm whether the room was re-let, and to justify the charge made.

Where we know that an establishment levies a surcharge if you pay by credit card we say so. It is always best to check when booking whether the card you want to use is acceptable.

TITLEY Herefordshire   map 5

Stagg Inn [NEW ENTRY]

Titley, Kington HR5 3RL
TEL: 01544) 230221   FAX: (01544) 231390
EMAIL: reservations@thestagg.co.uk
WEB SITE: www.thestagg.co.uk

Unassuming gastropub that does the simple things well

There's been an inn on this site since medieval times, but the building today is an unremarkable mix of Georgian and Victorian. What makes this pub superior, however, is the friendliness of the welcome from Nicola and Steve Reynolds, the quality of its food and the simple comfort of its bedrooms. Beyond the dark confines of the bar, there is a feel of a domestic house about the place. As guests climb the stairs they might pass a coat on the banisters, while books and CDs are jammed into the cabinets on the way to the bedrooms. There are just two bedrooms upstairs. The double has an iron bedstead, with matching curtains and a clean, fresh feel, plus a small but impressive shower room with gleaming blue tiles. Down the road at the vicarage, close to the church, there are some more smart bedrooms. But the highlight of any stay is Steve's cooking. An excellent inspection meal started with scallops that melted in the mouth, matched nicely with celeriac purée, followed by a choice fillet of Herefordshire beef with rösti, shallots and morels and finally pannacotta spiced with rhubarb and ginger. Not surprisingly, the restaurant was full.

◐ Closed 1 week in spring and first 2 weeks Nov; restaurant closed Sun and Mon eves ⚡ On B4399 between Kington and Presteigne. Private car park 🚗 1 twin, 4 double; family rooms available; all with hair-dryer, TV; some with mini-bar, CD player ✅ Restaurant, bar, lounge, garden; social functions; highchairs, toys ♿ No wheelchair access ● Dogs in bar and one bedroom only; smoking in bar only ▭ Delta, MasterCard, Switch, Visa £ Single occupancy of twin/double £50 to £70, twin £90, double £70 to £90, family room £110; deposit required. Alc L, D £25; light meals available (3FOR2)

TOPSHAM Devon   map 1

The Galley [NEW ENTRY]

41 Fore Street, Topsham, Exeter EX3 0HU
TEL: (01392) 876078
EMAIL: fish@galleyrestaurant.co.uk
WEB SITE: www.galleyrestaurant.co.uk

Seventeenth-century fishy restaurant-with-rooms in delightful riverside town

It's difficult to categorise the establishment of Mark Wright and Paul Da-Costa-Greaves (which, we suspect, is exactly as they like it). First, there's the restaurant – a Grade II listed building, all beams and brickwork, in the quaintly charming town of Topsham. Although it specialises in seafood (with a menu divided under the intriguing headings of 'Teasing the palate', 'Feeding the desire', and 'Keeping the passion alive'), there's also a separate, largely fishy, tapas menu. Then there are the 'nautical cabins', which are anything but. The Captain's Suite, reached from the top floor of the restaurant via a short but narrow staircase, is delightful, with a separate sitting/dining room, a bedroom with a king-size pine bed and matching furniture, and a view over the Exe. A bathroom equipped with every extra you can imagine, as well as a separate bath and shower, lies at the foot of the stairs. Other rooms, like Cabin Boy and Second Mate, are in a separate seventeenth-century cottage just up the road – but again, every detail has been thought of. Continental breakfast, left in a fridge in the room, consists of a bento box containing cold salmon, cream cheese, Danish pastries and fruit (cereals, juice, tea and coffee are also provided).

◐ Closed Chr & New Year ⚡ Head towards quay in Topsham; hotel is behind Lighter Inn, overlooking river. Nearest train station: Topsham. Private car park 🚗 1 twin, 1 double, 1 suite; all with room service, hair-dryer, mini-bar, direct-dial telephone, fax, modem line, TV, VCR, CD player ✅ Restaurant, bar, lounge, garden; leisure facilities nearby ♿ No wheelchair access ● No children under 12; no dogs; no smoking ≡ Amex, Delta, Diners, MasterCard, Switch, Visa £ Single occupancy of twin/double £63 to £75, twin/double/suite £125 to £150; deposit required. Cooked B £10; alc L, D £30; light meals available (3 FOR 2)

TORQUAY Devon   map 1

Mulberry House

1 Scarborough Road, Torquay TQ2 5UJ
TEL: (01803) 213639

Pristine restaurant-with-rooms run with an excellent eye for detail

Lesley Cooper celebrates 20 years at Mulberry House in 2004, but when asked how she will be marking the occasion, she replied, with a typical modest shrug, 'Oh, I expect we may have a small party.' Her neat white Grade II-listed Victorian villa occupies a corner position on a street of other B&Bs, with a pretty rose and a couple of palms adorning the exterior. Inside, the ground floor is taken up with the restaurant, which exudes an air of calm, with a ticking clock and prints depicting the five senses hanging above the marble mantelpiece. Lesley's cooking features plenty of seafood, simply treated – maybe marinated anchovies with parmesan, fresh herbs and green salad, or pan-fried sole with olive oil and herbs and home-made tartare sauce – but there are meaty and vegetarian options too. All this – along with the home-made chutneys and jams for sale – is produced in a tiny galley kitchen, which guests can visit if they want. Upstairs, guests are equally cosseted, in pretty bedrooms decked out with antique pine. One room has its bathroom across the corridor (robes are provided); the other two have powerful 'body-jet' showers en suite. The hospitality tray on the landing even includes wine as well as tea and coffee.

◎ Open all year; restaurant closed Sun eve ◹ From middle of Torquay seafront, turn up Belgrave Road; Scarborough Road is first right; house is on left at end. Nearest train station: Torquay 🚊 1 twin, 2 double; all with room service, hair-dryer, TV ✓ Restaurant, lounge area, patio; social functions; leisure facilities nearby; early suppers for children; babysitting, baby-listening ♿ No wheelchair access ● No dogs; no smoking ≡ None accepted £ Single occupancy of twin/double £45, twin/double £70; deposit required. Alc L, D £25; light meals available; service incl

---

TOTNES Devon   map 1

Kingston House

Staverton, Totnes TQ9 6AR
TEL: (01803) 762235   FAX: (01803) 762444
EMAIL: info@kingston-estate.co.uk
WEB SITE: www.kingston-estate.co.uk

Fascinating B&B in unique historical house

'This is surely Devon's most obscure but gracious bed and breakfast.' A quote, not from a reader, but from Simon Jenkins' *England's Thousand Best Houses*, serves only to emphasise that Elizabeth and Michael Corfield's home is not your average B&B. Their elegant, neoclassical house, completed by 1735, sits amid 13 acres of grounds, including a pleached lime walk and walled rose and vegetable gardens (a new formal garden was being planned when we inspected). The interior retains many fascinating features – notably a splendid marquetry staircase containing six different types of wood. On the first floor, the central saloon was originally designed as a Catholic chapel (the Rowe family, who built the house, were supporters of James II, a devout Catholic), and still features a plaster relief of the Flight into Egypt and roundels of St Peter and St Paul (there's also a priest's hole). And there can't be many bedrooms like the Blue Suite, where you can sleep in a copy of a 1735 angel tester, wash in a bathroom with fifteenth-century linenfold panelling, or admire a hand-painted china closet. The Green and Red Suites are nearly as impressive; if you prefer more privacy, there are also converted self-catering cottages.

◑ Closed Chr & New Year ⚡ From A38, take A384 Totnes road at Buckfastleigh; after 2½ miles turn left to Staverton; take left fork at Sea Trout Inn and follow signs to Kingston. Private car park ⬅ 3 suites; all with room service, hair-dryer, direct-dial telephone; fax, modem line available ⬥ Dining room, saloon, library, gardens; conferences; social functions; civil wedding licence ⬥ No wheelchair access ⬤ No children, dogs or smoking in main house ▭ Amex, Delta, Diners, MasterCard, Switch, Visa £ Single occupancy of suite £90 to £100, suite £140 to £160; deposit required. Set D £32.50; light meals available; service incl. Special breaks available

Old Forge

Seymour Place, Totnes TQ9 5AY
TEL: (01803) 862174 FAX: (01803) 865385
EMAIL: enq@oldforgetotnes.com
WEB SITE: www.oldforgetotnes.com

Small is beautiful in this very friendly B&B near the centre of Totnes

Christine Hillier and David Miller are continuing on their quest to update and streamline accommodation at the Old Forge, and very successful they are too. Six-hundred-year-old buildings may have historical appeal (and this one certainly does, being the former workshops of the Duke of Somerset, housing a blacksmith, wheelwright, carpenter and coach-builder), but they can often be dark, cramped and gloomy. Christine's solution has been to bring modern, light beech furniture and natural matting into the dining room, and put down a slate floor in the conservatory to contrast with cream-coloured chairs, giving a more contemporary air. The Jacuzzi is still there, screened off by a trellis supporting abundant passion flowers and bougainvillea. Upstairs, bedrooms remain small, but have been shorn of frills and flowers, with Indian blue-and-white cutwork or elephant print bedspreads providing a more streamlined feel. Some of the en-suite shower rooms have also been given a makeover. The Old Court Room is bigger than most, and can be used as a family room. It has a small roof terrace with decking that overlooks the ancient blacksmith's lock-up, whose chains are still intact – an excellent warning for children who won't do as they're told!

◑ Open all year ⚡ From town centre (at monument), cross the Old Totnes Bridge and take second turning on right. Nearest train station: Totnes. Private car park ⬅ 2 twin, 6 double, 1 family room, 1 suite; all with room service, hair-dryer, direct-dial telephone, TV; modem line, trouser press available ⬥ Dining room, lounge, bar service, conservatory, garden; hot tub; leisure facilities nearby; cots, highchairs ⬥ Wheelchair access to hotel (1 step, ramp available) and dining room, WC, 3 ground-floor bedrooms. Disabled parking ⬤ No dogs; no smoking ▭ MasterCard, Switch, Visa £ Single occupancy of twin/double £50 to £66, twin/double £56 to £76, family room £89, suite £89; deposit required. Special breaks available ③FOR②

TRESCO Isles of Scilly   map 1

Island Hotel

Tresco TR24 0PU
TEL: (01720) 422883   FAX: (01720) 423008
EMAIL: islandhotel@tresco.co.uk
WEB SITE: www.tresco.co.uk

Luxurious island getaway with a family welcome

In a stunning position overlooking white-sand beaches, this low-rise modern hotel is at the helm of the Tresco Estate, under the ownership of the Dorrien-Smith family. It's on the other side of the island from the main ferry, shop and pub, but luggage and guests are transported effortlessly across the island by golf buggy. Public areas are generous and light and open out on to terraces and gardens surrounded by agave and palms, which extend down to the sea. The décor is cheerful and informal with white basket chairs and stripy fabrics at tables in the lounge bar, where guests and families wander in from the terrace for a tasty lunch. The remarkable feature of the large dining room is the beautiful view over to the sand-fringed island of St Martin's. Otherwise, furnishings are fairly standard with chrome and wickerwork seating and crisp white tablecloths. The menu is inventive, making use of organic produce where possible. There is an enclosed pool and water sports on site, and families with children are made very welcome. Bedrooms come in various sizes with bright co-ordinated colour schemes. Some are huge, with large luxurious bathrooms, and have terraces or spacious balconies.

❍ Closed Nov to Feb ⤴ Take helicopter from Penzance to Tresco. Or fly from Bristol, Exeter, Newquay, Plymouth or Land's End to St Mary's, then take connecting launch to Tresco. Or take ship from Penzance to St Mary's, then launch. On Tresco you are collected by hotel's transport. There are no cars on the Isles of Scilly; no air or sea service on Sunday ⌁ 5 single, 40 twin/double, 3 suites; family rooms available; all with room service, hair-dryer, direct-dial telephone, TV, VCR; some with mini-bar, CD player ⊘ Restaurant, dining room, bar, lounge, study, games room, terrace, gardens; conferences, social functions; tennis, heated outdoor swimming pool; early suppers for children; cots, highchairs, toys, playroom, babysitting, baby-listening, outdoor play area ♿ Wheelchair access to hotel and restaurant, WC, 20 ground-floor bedrooms, 2 rooms specially equipped for disabled people ● No dogs; no smoking in bedrooms and several public rooms ▭ Delta, MasterCard, Switch, Visa £ Single £117 to £257, single occupancy of twin/double £175 to £236, twin/double £240 to £384, family room £256 to £416, suite £328 to £566 (rates incl dinner). Alc L £37.50; service incl. Special breaks available

New Inn [NEW ENTRY]

Tresco, Isles of Scilly TR24 0QQ
TEL: (01720) 422844 FAX: (01720) 423200
EMAIL: newinn@tresco.co.uk
WEB SITE: www.tresco.co.uk

Snug pub that is the hub of the island and pub

This pub-restaurant and hotel has become the hub of the island, attracting day trippers for lunch on the large patio, or those self-catering on the island for dinner. It's an easy stroll to the inn from the quay and island shop, and there are great sea views. Although the bar is extensive, the actual hotel is snug. The sitting room, which acts as an entrance hall for residents, is not wholly successful, but the restaurant, away from the hustle and bustle of the bar, is more appealing. Service is friendly and copes well with large family groups, sorting out highchairs and warming bottles for young children. Evening meals are well presented and cooked and may include dishes such as courgette and rocket salad, monkfish on fennel with new potatoes, and good home-made bread. The bar is large and airy, and the terrace is an appealing place to while away a warm evening. The bedrooms are full of blue-stained wooden furniture and are cheerfully decked out with floral curtains and bedspreads. They all have good bathrooms.

❍ Open all year ⤴ Helicopter, light aircraft and ferry services from mainland ⌁ 14 twin/double, 2 double; family rooms available; all with hair-dryer, direct-dial telephone, TV ⊘ Restaurant, 2 bars, sitting room; tennis, heated outdoor swimming pool; leisure facilities nearby; early suppers for children; cots, highchairs, baby-listening ♿ No wheelchair access ● No dogs; no smoking in restaurant ▭ Delta, MasterCard, Switch, Visa £ Single occupancy of twin/double £113 to £164, twin/double £150 to £218, family room £176 to £218 (rates incl dinner). Special breaks available

---

TROUTBECK Cumbria   map 8

Queen's Head

Townhead, Troutbeck, Windermere LA23 1PW
TEL: (015394) 32174 FAX: (015394) 31938
EMAIL: enquiries@queensheadhotel.com
WEB SITE: www.queensheadhotel.com

A magnet for visitors at the foot of the Kirkstone Pass

Guests have a choice of presiding queens here – signs outside depict both the first Elizabeth, from whose reign this historic coaching inn is said to date, and the second, in whose time many subtle improvements have taken place. Oak beams, inglenook fireplaces and slate-flagged floors provide an authentic olde-worlde setting (the main bar is surmounted by part of an ornate Jacobethan four-poster bed). Cumbrian real ales can be enjoyed by a roaring log fire, or at tables outside, contemplating an impressive eyeful of Troutbeck fells. Interlocking dining areas of cushioned settles ramble rearwards and downstairs, where you can sample a choice of gastrofare ranging from shanks of lamb and haunches of venison to bean and lentil strudel. Bedrooms are smart and bold, many with four-posters and lovely views. Bathrooms combine gleaming modern plumbing with occasional feature beams or exposed stonework. It's very popular; a two-night minimum stay is required on summer weekends.

○ Closed 25 Dec ⚡ On A592, halfway between Windermere and Kirkstone Pass, ½ mile north of caravan site. Private car park 🅿️ 1 twin/double, 5 double, 8 four-poster; all with TV ⊘ Dining area, bar; cots, highchairs ♿ No wheelchair access ● No dogs or smoking in bedrooms ▭ Delta, MasterCard, Switch, Visa £ Single occupancy of twin/double £60 to £70, twin/double £95, four-poster £105; deposit required. Set L, D £15.50; alc L, D £20; light meals available. Special breaks available (3FOR2)

TUNBRIDGE WELLS Kent
map 3

Hotel du Vin & Bistro

Crescent Road, Tunbridge Wells TN1 2LY
TEL: (01892) 526455   FAX: (01892) 512044
EMAIL: info@tunbridgewells.hotelduvin.com
WEB SITE: www.hotelduvin.com

Handsome town house hotel with informal stylish interiors

Even if you are not fortunate enough to be able to hang around till cork-popping time, the bottles of Dom Perignon sitting on ice by mid-morning create an expansive, optimistic feel. The bar and lounge areas, in rich, deep colours like olive green, dark red and black, extend from one end of the building to the other, and there are lots of corners and comfortable chairs to cosy up in and admire copies of well-known modern paintings decorating the walls. The informal brasserie, with festoons of dried hops (well, we are in Kent) serves up a modern French menu along with simple classics such as wiener schnitzel or Spanish charcuterie. It overlooks the sunny terrace, where relaxing on the smart teak furniture and green cushions is an inviting prospect. The most deluxe – and therefore expensive – of the bedrooms is Yering Station. Its sunny dual aspect overlooks the park, while creamy coffee colours and dark, sleek teak furnishing sets off plasma TVs and DVD and CD players and a sumptuous bathroom. Standard rooms are less notable but still stylishly simple, with off-white walls and slate or brown fabrics and good-quality furnishings. Some of the smart bathrooms have free-standing baths.

○ Open all year ⚡ At intersection of Mount Pleasant Road and Crescent Road/Church Road, take Crescent Road; hotel is 150 yards on right, just past Phillips House. Nearest train station: Tunbridge Wells. Private car park 🅿️ 35 double; all with room service (breakfast only), hair-dryer, mini-bar, trouser press, direct-dial telephone, TV, CD player ⊘ Restaurant, bar, lounge, garden; conferences; social functions; early suppers for children; cots, highchairs ♿ Wheelchair access to hotel (2 steps) and restaurant, WC, lift ● No dogs ▭ Amex, Delta, Diners, MasterCard, Switch, Visa £ Double £95 to £175; deposit required. Continental B £9.50, cooked B £13.50; set Sun L £23.50; alc L, D £32

TWO BRIDGES Devon
map 1

Prince Hall

Near Two Bridges, Tavistock PL20 6SA
TEL: (01822) 890403   FAX: (01822) 890676
EMAIL: info@princehall.co.uk
WEB SITE: www.princehall.co.uk

Superb Dartmoor location for this unpretentious hotel

Down a half-mile of lane and feeling for all the world like somewhere removed from the rest of civilisation, this substantial country house was, appropriately perhaps, built in 1787 for the man who first transported convicts to Australia. Except his remote billet was a good deal more comfortable than theirs. Rooms are spacious and often with good views across the pastures to the River Dart, and the atmosphere is country house without being stuffy. The corner sitting room has excellent views and there is a cosy bar with fire. Cooking is country house with some international flourishes – Dorset

mussels Thai-style, for example, as a starter – but with more traditional staples too, such as roast local lamb in rosemary and garlic for a main course. Bedrooms are all spacious and have a fresh and well-kept feel. Those with views down to the river – Haytor and Yestor, for example – are the ones to ask for.

○ Closed mid-Dec to early Feb ⚡ On B3357, 1 mile east of Two Bridges junction. Private car park 🚪 3 twin/double, 3 double, 2 four-poster; all with room service, hair-dryer, direct-dial telephone, TV ⊘ Restaurant, bar/lounge, sitting room, garden; social functions; leisure facilities nearby ♿ No wheelchair access ● No children under 10 ▭ Amex, MasterCard, Switch, Visa £ Single occupancy of twin/double £60 to £155, twin/double/four-poster £140 to £170; deposit required. Set D £35; light meals available; service incl. Special breaks available (3FOR2)

<hr>

UCKFIELD East Sussex　　　　　　　　　　　map 3

Hooke Hall

250 High Street, Uckfield TN22 1EN
TEL: (01825) 761578　FAX: (01825) 768025
EMAIL: a.percy@virgin.net
WEB SITE: www.hookehall.co.uk

Good-quality, characterful rooms in fine Queen Anne home

A few steps away from the shops of Uckfield High Street, this large, creeper-clad Queen Anne townhouse is the characterful home of Juliet and Alister Percy. The number of its guest bedrooms sets it somewhere between a large guest house and a small hotel, and each room is individually styled with good pieces of furniture and interesting objects and antiques. All but one are saucily named after mistresses of one kind or another, and on the first floor the grandest of the rooms lead off a wide hallway filled with sofas and antiques and botanical prints. Mme de

Pompadour in pink is one of the largest, with a fine four-poster bed and oriental paintings, while Nell Gwynne has a half-tester bed and a bath in an alcove. Casanova is the exception, a neat smaller room on the second floor. Downstairs there is a small green sitting room hung with portraits and a tapestry. An honesty bar is concealed behind a panelled door. The breakfast room, in bold reds and greens, feels more like a hotel restaurant – probably because of the number of individual tables. Breakfast is charged separately, and is cooked to order.

○ Closed Chr ⚡ At northern end of High Street in Uckfield. Nearest train station: Uckfield. Private car park 🚪 7 twin/double, 2 double, 1 four-poster; family rooms available; all with hair-dryer, trouser press, direct-dial telephone, modem line, TV; some with mini-bar ⊘ Breakfast room, study/sitting room, honesty bar, garden; leisure facilities nearby; babysitting, baby-listening ♿ No wheelchair access ● No children under 10 exc babes in arms; no dogs; no smoking in bedrooms ▭ MasterCard, Visa £ Single occupancy of twin/double £50 to £55, twin/double £70 to £75, four-poster £100 to £120, family room £90; deposit required. Continental B £6.50, cooked B £8.50 (3FOR2)

<hr>

UFFINGTON Oxfordshire　　　　　　　　　　map 2

The Craven

Fernham Road, Uffington SN7 7RD
TEL: (01367) 820449　FAX: (01367) 820351
EMAIL: carol@thecraven.co.uk
WEB SITE: www.thecraven.co.uk

Oodles of character and conviviality a couple of miles from the famous White Horse

You might be forgiven for thinking that Carol Wadsworth wants to keep her house a secret –

the lack of signage means that you can easily drive past without spotting it. Our inspector did. Twice! In reality all you have to do is look out for the most picture-perfect building in the village, and you'll be in the right place. With its pretty, quintessential English cottage garden and lovely thatched roof, this former farmhouse could feature on any chocolate box. Dating back to 1650, it exudes old-world charm from every quirky corner – beamed ceilings, cosy rooms, bowed walls and large fireplaces. Meals are taken *en famille* around a robust, pine table in the farmhouse kitchen, where a dresser holds Carol's extensive collection of milk jugs. A three-course dinner can be provided on request. Bedrooms have a cheery, cottagey feel to them, and though not all are en suite they are all comfortably kitted out with handsome beds and pretty linens. Primrose, with its Victorian mahogany half-tester, is in the converted barn next door, whereas Magnolia, which looks out over the garden, features its own huge, stone fireplace.

◑ Open all year 🔁 Uffington village lies 5 miles west of Wantage, between the B4508 and B4507. Cottage is on northern edge of village. Private car park 🛏1 twin, 2 double, 1 four-poster, 1 family room; 2 with shared bathroom; all with room service, hair-dryer ⊘ Dining room/kitchen, sitting room, garden; social functions; leisure facilities nearby; early suppers for children 🔥 No wheelchair access; 1 step into dining room, 3 ground-floor bedrooms, 1 room specially equipped for disabled people. Disabled parking ● No dogs; no smoking 💳 MasterCard, Switch, Visa £ Single occupancy of twin/double £40 to £50, twin/double £75 to £85, four-poster £90, family room £80; deposit required. Set D £23; light meals available ③FOR②

ULLSWATER Cumbria
map 10

Sharrow Bay

Ullswater, Penrith CA10 2LZ
TEL: (017684) 86301 FAX: (017684) 86349
EMAIL: info@sharrowbay.co.uk
WEB SITE: www.sharrowbay.co.uk

A change of ownership at this long-established and much-loved country-house hotel

Devotees of Sharrow Bay need fear no ripples on the mirror-smooth managerial surface of this classic lakeshore hotel overlooking dazzling views of Ullswater. Its stalwart band of loyal retainers remains the same, and the timeless quality of its ultra-discreet, unflashy luxury seems unchanged. It was the first and is for many people still the definitive country-house hotel. The décor is gradually becoming more streamlined – fewer dust-catching, Frenchified *objets* everywhere, while the new Garden Room lounge seems almost stark. A fresh, contemporary style blows through the spacious annexe bedrooms. Elsewhere, antiques, original artworks, porcelain and crystal still abound amid ornately draped chintz and classy flowers. Food remains one of the greatest pleasures at Sharrow Bay, whether you opt for a six-course dinner extravaganza or a lavish English tea. Bedrooms are romantic, impeccably maintained retreats equipped with every imaginable comfort. So far, an expense rarely regretted. Reports welcome on the new regime.

◑ Open all year 🔁 Leave M6 at Junction 40 and follow signs for Ullswater; at Pooley Bridge, turn right for Howtown; follow road for 2 miles to lakeside. Private car park 🛏2 single, 19 twin/double, 3 suites; all with room service, hair-dryer, direct-dial telephone, fax, TV; some with mini-bar, trouser press, CD player; no tea/coffee-making facilities in rooms ⊘ 2 dining rooms, 3 lounges, garden; conferences; social functions; civil wedding licence; leisure facilities nearby 🔥 Wheelchair access to hotel and dining room, WC, 6 ground-floor bedrooms, 1 room specially equipped for disabled people ● No children under 13; no dogs or smoking in bedrooms 💳 Amex, Delta, MasterCard, Switch, Visa £ Single £150, single occupancy of twin/double £210 to £250, double £160 to £235, suite £225 to £235 (rates incl dinner); deposit required. Set L £38.50, light meals available

---

Use the index at the back of the book if you know the name of a hotel but are unsure about its precise location.

map 8

Bay Horse Hotel

Canal Foot, Ulverston LA12 9EL
TEL: (01229) 583972   FAX: (01229) 580502
EMAIL: reservations@thebayhorsehotel.co.uk
WEB SITE: www.thebayhorsehotel.co.uk

Waterfront views and ambitious cooking distinguish this pub-restaurant-with-rooms

The approach to the Bay Horse, via a futuristic-looking pharmaceutical plant, is bewildering, but perseverance is rewarded by a stunning *pieds-dans-l'eau* setting on Morecambe Bay. The building is a low-key affair, a conversion of an eighteenth-century inn that once served as a coaching post on the perilous route across the sands to Lancaster. The modest entrance leads into a homely pub, cosy with brass and copper. But the real ale casque mark on the hand-pumps indicates this place is a cut above your average local. At mealtimes attention focuses on the conservatory restaurant, all candles and matching napery, where owner-chef Robert Lyons masterminds impressive gastronomic performances as tides swirl past the windows. The smallish bedrooms share the same seductive views from private terraces. The chintzy décor is looking weary, however, and a recent visitor was disappointed by lapses in service and housekeeping. Time for a makeover, perhaps? More reports welcome.

○ Open all year ⚡ From A590 on outskirts of Ulverston, follow signs for Canal Foot. Nearest train station: Ulverston. Private car park 🛏 3 twin, 6 double; all with room service, hair-dryer, trouser press, direct-dial telephone, modem line, TV; no tea/coffee-making facilities in rooms ✅ Restaurant, bar/lounge; social functions ♿ No wheelchair access ● No children under 12; smoking in bar only ▭ Amex, MasterCard, Switch, Visa £ Single occupancy of twin/double £80, twin/double from £150; deposit required. Set L £19, D £28.50; alc L, D £35; light meals available; service incl. Special breaks available

                                           map 6

Hambleton Hall

Upper Hambleton, Oakham LE15 8TH
TEL: (01572) 756991   FAX: (01572) 724721
EMAIL: hotel@hambletonhall.com
WEB SITE: www.hambletonhall.com

Rural pursuits at country house offering rooms with a view

This striking Victorian mansion, enjoying a secluded position on a peninsula with superb views across Rutland Water, is surrounded by extensive stepped gardens that beg to be strolled around. The neat lawns are studded with a varied collection of trees and shrubs and are crowned with huge cypress trees. This is very much an outdoors sort of place and the friendly and efficient staff are happy to give advice on the range of activities on offer in and around the hotel. The interior is no less impressive than its many-gabled façade. Wood-panelled walls, gilt-framed mirrors and grand oil paintings create an atmosphere of comfortable opulence. Dinner menus, themselves sumptuous affairs, offer meals such as pan-fried foie gras, roasted loin of fallow venison and hot passion fruit soufflé. The spacious and sophisticated bedrooms are done out in muted colours, all rooms overlook the grounds and the superior and master bedrooms have views of the lake.

○ Open all year ⚡ Off A606, 3 miles south-east of Oakham. Private car park 🛏 15 twin/double, 1 four-poster, 1 suite; all with room service, hair-dryer, direct-dial telephone, modem line, TV; some with fax, CD player; no tea/coffee-making facilities in rooms ✅ Restaurant, bar, lounge, garden; conferences; social functions; civil wedding licence; tennis, heated outdoor swimming pool; leisure facilities nearby; early suppers for children; cots, highchairs, babysitting, baby-listening ♿ Wheelchair access to hotel (ramp) and restaurant, WC, lift ● No dogs in public rooms, £10 per night in bedrooms ▭ Amex, MasterCard, Switch, Visa

£ Single occupancy of twin/double £165 to £190, twin/double £190 to £355, four-poster £205 to £260, suite £500 to £600; deposit required. Cooked B £12; set L £27, D £35; alc L, D £60; light meals available. Special breaks available

---

UPPINGHAM Rutland   map 5

Lake Isle

16 High Street East, Uppingham, Oakham LE15 9PZ
TEL: (01572) 822951   FAX: (01572) 824400
EMAIL: info@lakeislehotel.com
WEB SITE: www.lakeislehotel.com

Lovers of the grape will feel at home in this appealing market town hotel

Uppingham is a quiet market town with something of a scholastic feel to it – possibly because of its ties with Uppingham School (founded in 1584). But bookshops apart, the recent addition of some attractive boutique-style shops and coffee bars has injected a little zest into this very English town. Lake Isle Hotel, once a baker's shop, then a deli, is within easy striking distance of the hub. From the street the understated eighteenth-century building is pleasant enough, but it isn't until the entrance is reached at the side that the full extent of the place is revealed. Three cottages have been knocked into one, forming an attractive courtyard with patio furniture surrounded by tubs of flowers and colourful hanging baskets. Inside, a few steps down from the sombre old-fashioned reception, is the light-coloured restaurant with wall-to-ceiling tongue and groove and innocuous-looking contemporary paintings gracing the walls. The proprietors, Richard and Jeanine Burton, have a bit of a passion for the grape, and reflecting their interest they have named each of the delightful bedrooms after a French wine-growing area. The spacious deluxe Dom Perignon is a favourite, done out in rich burgundies and with its own whirlpool bath.

○ Open all year; restaurant closed Sun eve & Mon lunch   ⤺ On Uppingham's High Street. By car, turn into Queen Street, then first right and first right again. On foot, reached via Reeves Yard. Private car park ⇱ 1 twin, 1 twin/double, 6 double, 1 family room, 3 suites; all with room service, hair-dryer, trouser press, direct-dial telephone, modem line, TV ⊘ Restaurant, dining room, bar, lounge, garden; conferences; social functions; early suppers for children; cots, highchairs, babysitting, baby-listening ⅙ No wheelchair access ● No dogs in public rooms; smoking in bar only ⊟ Amex, Delta, Diners, MasterCard, Switch, Visa £ Single occupancy of twin/double £55, twin £70, twin/double £70 to £85, family room from £75, suite £60 to £85; deposit required. Alc L £12.50, D £22.50; light meals available. Special breaks available

---

VERYAN Cornwall   map 1

Nare Hotel

Carne Beach, Veryan, Truro TR2 5PF
TEL: (01872) 501111   FAX: (01872) 501856
EMAIL: office@narehotel.co.uk
WEB SITE: www.narehotel.co.uk

Top-quality facilities, plenty of space and a cracking view

The perfect spot from which to enjoy the perfect views the Nare commands over the sweeping bay is at the foot of the gardens, by the chunky stone tables made from mill wheels, with bright flowerbeds behind. It may be a tad hyperbolical, but not without at least some justification does it make the rather bold claim to be 'surely the most beautifully situated hotel in the British Isles'. The hotel itself is a rambling modern building in a mix of cream rendering and grey stonework. Inside, the atmosphere is carefully balanced between welcomingly relaxed and satisfyingly formal (jackets and ties are the norm at dinner), with fresh, plain-coloured walls complemented by more heavily patterned soft furnishings and rugs and a wide range of spaces to relax in, including a smart cocktail bar, colourful drawing room, conservatory and sun lounge. Bedrooms are similarly traditional but smart; those at the deluxe end of the scale have private patios to take advantage of those cracking sea vistas. Recreational facilities are top-notch too – there's a full complement of gym, sauna, steam room, beauty clinic, snooker room, croquet lawn, tennis courts, both indoor and outdoor pools and even a hotel sailing boat!

◑ Open all year ⚡ 1 mile south-west of Veryan, on Carne Beach. Private car park 🛏 6 single, 21 twin/double, 5 double, 3 family rooms, 4 suites; all with room service, hair-dryer, direct-dial telephone, TV; some with trouser press, VCR ✓ Restaurant, dining room, bar, lounge, drawing room, library, conservatory, games room, garden; social functions; gym, spa, tennis, heated indoor and outdoor swimming pools; leisure facilities nearby; early suppers for children; cots, highchairs, babysitting, baby-listening, outdoor play area ৬ Wheelchair access to hotel and dining rooms, 5 ground-floor bedrooms, 1 room specially equipped for disabled people, lift. Disabled parking ● No children under 10 in restaurant eves; no dogs or smoking in some public rooms ▭ MasterCard, Visa £ Single £110 to £180, single occupancy of twin/double £193 to £245, twin/double £220 to £280, family room £395 to £413, suite £430 to £520; deposit required. Set D £38; alc L £20, D £35; light meals available. Special breaks available

---

VIRGINSTOW Devon
map 1

Percy's Country Hotel

Coombeshead Estate, Virginstow EX21 5EA
TEL: (01409) 211236   FAX: (01409) 211460
EMAIL: info@percys.co.uk
WEB SITE: www.percys.co.uk

Superb food and rooms at this flagship for honest, straightforward hospitality

Many moons ago Tina and Tony Bricknell-Webb did what many other urban dwellers dream of and sank their hopes (and money) into a run-down farm in deepest Devon. It wasn't always an easy transition – their previously docile Doberman displayed murderous tendencies and killed several sheep, while money disappeared faster than swallows in September. But now they have things pretty well set up. The smart restaurant is a showcase for Tina's stylish yet uncomplicated cooking. Lamb is home-grown, as are the eggs (from hens and geese), breads are home-made and fish bought from Looe. Our inspection meal of warm scallops followed by steamed turbot with asparagus was faultless, Tony providing just the right amount of welcome and conversation. Across the courtyard in a barn conversion the rooms match that approach, with their simple colours and top-quality furnishings. Sheets and pillows are excellent; there is a good tea tray and DVD player, and a power shower in the bathroom.

◑ Open all year ⚡ Virginstow is off A388 Launceston to Holsworthy road; follow signs from St Giles on the Heath on A388, from Metherell Cross on A3079, or from A30. Private car park 🛏 8 twin/double; all with hair-dryer, mini-fridge, direct-dial telephone, modem line, TV, DVD ✓ Restaurant, bar, 3 lounges, garden; conferences and social functions; leisure facilities nearby ৬ Wheelchair access to hotel and restaurant, WC, 4 ground-floor bedrooms. Disabled parking ● No children under 12; no dogs in public rooms; no smoking ▭ Delta, MasterCard, Switch, Visa £ Single occupancy of twin/double from £90, twin/double from £150; deposit required. Set L from £20, D £37.50. Special breaks available ⑶ꜰᴏʀ②

WALBERSWICK Suffolk
map 6

Bell Inn

Ferry Road, Walberswick, Southwold IP18 6TN
TEL: (01502) 723109   FAX: (01502) 722728
EMAIL: bellinn@btinternet.com
WEB SITE: www.blythweb.co.uk/bellinn

Unpretentious village pub on a lovely stretch of the Suffolk coast

Perfectly situated near the green of this remote coastal Suffolk village, the Bell Inn is just the kind of friendly, no-nonsense pub that's fast disappearing under a tide of trendification. From the outside the angles look quite neat, but inside things take a turn for the wobbly, with wonky floor tiles and crooked beams, along with intimate alcoves and open fires. The menu sticks mainly to the traditional – just the kind of hearty food you'd

ENGLAND

want to return to after a long day's walking along the dramatic coastline – and you've a choice of the atmospheric main bar or the bright, attractive restaurant in which to take

your meals. Bedrooms are generally quite small, but are cosy and carefully decorated, for example, with patchwork quilts.

◑ Closed 25 Dec; restaurant open Fri & Sat eves only ⬚ In centre of Walberswick. Private car park ⬚ 1 twin, 4 double, 1 family room; all with hair-dryer, TV ⬚ Restaurant, 2 bars, games room, garden; social functions; cots, highchairs, toys ⬚ Wheelchair access to hotel and dining room, WC, 2 ground-floor bedrooms ● No smoking in bedrooms ⬚ Delta, MasterCard, Switch, Visa ⬚ Single occupancy of twin/double £60 to £70, twin/double £70 to £75, family room £100; deposit required. Alc L, D £17.50; light meals available. Special breaks available ⬚

WAREHAM Dorset   map 2

Priory Hotel

Church Green, Wareham BH20 4ND
TEL: (01929) 551666   FAX: (01929) 554519
EMAIL: reservations@theprioryhotel.co.uk
WEB SITE: www.theprioryhotel.co.uk

Welcoming small hotel with good food and rooms

Under a higgledy-piggledy collection of mossy roofs between the church and the river is this lovely small hotel, something of a classic of its kind, offering the kind of discreet and homely charm that others aspire to. All the public rooms reinforce this character: there is a cosy bar, a drawing room with rugs on floorboards and a piano, and an intimate cellar restaurant that utilises the original features of ceiling beams, stone floor and walls. Best of all is the garden breakfast room with its views over the lawns

that run up to the riverbank. The gardens are a big attraction here, running all along the water in a series of walled enclosures. Bedrooms are traditionally elegant with extra touches of luxury in bathrobes, mini-bar, satellite television and the occasional fancy bath – two are lotus-shaped. Rooms with river views are preferable, either in the main house or over in the Boathouse. 'An impressive example of informal perfection', wrote one correspondent.

◑ Open all year ⬚ Leave A351 for Wareham along North Causeway and enter North Street; turn left past town hall and right into Church Street, leading to green. Nearest train station: Wareham. Private car park ⬚ 2 single, 5 twin/double, 6 double, 2 four-poster, 3 suites; all with hair-dryer, mini-bar, direct-dial telephone, modem line, TV; tea/coffee-making facilities, room service available on request ⬚ Restaurant, breakfast room, bar, drawing room, garden; conferences; social functions; leisure facilities nearby ⬚ No wheelchair access; 4 ground-floor bedrooms ● No children under 8; no dogs ⬚ Delta, Diners, MasterCard, Switch, Visa ⬚ Single £110, single occupancy of twin/double £120 to £160, twin £210, double £140 to £170, four-poster £245, suite £295; deposit required. Set D £35; alc L £26.50; light lunches available. Special breaks available ⬚

WARWICK Warwickshire   map 5

Rose and Crown [NEW ENTRY]

30 Market Place, Warwick CV34 4SH
TEL: (01926) 411117   FAX: (01926) 492117
EMAIL: roseandcrown@peachpubs.com
WEB SITE: www.peachpubs.com

Trendy set-up offering good food and appealing rooms

'It doesn't cost more to do it beautifully', our inspector was told on visiting this recently revamped eatery, drinkery and sleepery (not to mention meetery!) on one of Warwick's main plazas. Whether that's a general rule, prices here are very reasonable, especially for the bedrooms, and they've certainly achieved

the aesthetic. A spruce Georgian façade fronts an extremely swish contemporary bar/bistro, where bold use of colour – fuchsia and white in the dining area and sage and apricot in the bar – creates an intimate, informal setting to enjoy dishes turned out by a well-trained kitchen. Upstairs, the handful of bedrooms are equally modern and appealing, with strong blocks of colour creating a stylish backdrop for smart spreads and pieces of modern art. En-suite facilities are less dapper, but well tiled and perfectly adequate.

◗ Open all year ⚡ From M40 follow signs for Warwick town centre. Nearest train stations: Warwick Town and Warwick Parkway ⬅ 2 twin/double, 3 double; family rooms available; all with hair-dryer, direct-dial telephone, modem line, TV ✓ Restaurant, bar, terrace; conferences; leisure facilities nearby; highchairs ♿ No wheelchair access ● No dogs or smoking in bedrooms ▭ Amex, Delta, Diners, MasterCard, Switch, Visa £ Single occupancy of twin/double £65 to £75, twin/double £75 to £85, family room £85; deposit required. Alc L, D £20; light meals available ③ FOR ②

WASDALE HEAD Cumbria

map 8

Wasdale Head Inn

Wasdale Head, Nr Gosforth CA20 1EX
TEL: (019467) 26229   FAX: (019467) 26334
EMAIL: wasdaleheadinn@msn.com
WEB SITE: www.wasdale.com

Spectacularly located mountain inn with oodles of character

The trio of peaks framing Wasdale Head are the highest in England, forming the famous silhouette logo of the Lake District National Park. Here, at the remote dead-end of scree-sided Wastwater (England's deepest lake), stands this rugged gabled inn, open to visitors all year. On any fine weekend, the firelit Ritson's Bar is packed with hikers and climbers refuelling on Cumberland sausages and home-brewed ales, and spilling into the beckside beer gardens. Menus feature hearty stuff like fillet of beef and rack of lamb.

Packed lunches can be provided on request. The public areas of the hotel are surprisingly comfortable, though highly traditional in style. Historic climbing photographs deck oak-panelled walls. Bedrooms vary from smallish, chalet-style cabins in the main house to spacious, smartly contemporary suites in the barn annexe. Self-catering apartments are also available. A drying room and steam room help you unwind after conquering the three gables.

◗ Open all year; restaurant closed occasionally midweek in winter ⚡ Turn off A595 for Gosforth or Holmrook, then follow signs for Wasdale Head. Private car park ⬅ 3 single, 2 twin, 5 double, 1 four-poster, 1 family room, 3 suites; all with hair-dryer, direct-dial telephone, modem line; some with room service, mini-bar, VCR ✓ Dining room, 2 bars, lounge, garden; conferences; social functions; leisure facilities nearby; early suppers for children ♿ No wheelchair access, 2 ground-floor bedrooms. Disabled parking ● No dogs in some public rooms and some bedrooms; no smoking in some public rooms and some bedrooms ▭ Amex, Delta, MasterCard, Switch, Visa £ Single £49, single occupancy of twin/double £69, twin/double £98, four-poster £110, family room/suite £98; deposit required. Continental B £4.50, cooked £9.50 (breakfast included in all room rates except suite); set D £25; light meals available; service incl. Special breaks available

---

WATERLIP Somerset

map 2

Burnt House Farm

Waterlip, West Cranmore, Shepton Mallet BA4 4RN
TEL: (01749) 880280   FAX: (01749) 880004
EMAIL: pam@burnthousefarmbandb.co.uk
WEB SITE: www.burnthousefarmbandb.co.uk

Attentive and welcoming hosts at this working farm

The Hoddinott family have farmed here for several generations, nowadays concentrating their 190 acres on organic beef production. Pam Hoddinott operates the B&B side and is a dedicated and thoughtful hostess, the sort who thinks of what you need before you do so yourself. Hence there is home-made cake on arrival with every kind of tea and hot

drink imaginable on offer, and bedrooms get all kinds of extras to suit every situation – even a puncture repair kit for cyclists. The farmhouse is impeccably well kept: there is an attractive lounge with wood-burning stove, low-beamed ceiling and plenty of local information, then a main dining room with single polished wood table, the spot for sampling Pam's breakfasts. Eggs are free-range and organic from their own hens, bread is home-made (organic flour) and every day sees some type of fruit – stewed rhubarb perhaps or plums. The three bedrooms go for rich colours and plenty of luxurious touches. Only one of them is en suite.

○ Open all year ⚡ On A361 Shepton Mallet to Frome road, turn off where signposted to Waterlip at a crossroads just east of Doulting; farmhouse is on left after ½ mile. Private car park ⬜1 twin, 1 double, 1 family room; all with room service, hair-dryer, trouser press, TV ⊘ Breakfast room, lounge, games room, garden; hot tub; leisure facilities nearby; outdoor play area ⅙ No wheelchair access ● No children under 4; no dogs; no smoking ⬜ None accepted £ Single occupancy of twin/double £30 to £40, twin/double £52, family room £63. Light meals available. Special breaks available

---

WATERMILLOCK Cumbria map 10

Old Church Hotel

Old Church Bay, Watermillock, Penrith CA11 0JN
TEL: (017684) 86204
EMAIL: info@oldchurch.co.uk
WEB SITE: www.oldchurch.co.uk

A superb lakeshore setting makes this tranquil country house unforgettable

Comfortably distanced from the oversubscribed touring route along Ullswater by a private drive, Kevin and Maureen Whitemore's white-painted Georgian house enjoys truly exceptional views. Velvet lawns stretch from its front door to the mirror-like water's edge. In spring, the gardens are a Wordsworthian delight of daffodils and other bulbs. It's a deceptively large building, gracious but domesticated inside, and immaculately kept with softly gleaming antiques and intact period features (original cornices, handsome fireplaces, a fine wide stairwell). Decorative schemes downstairs are bold and striking; there's no timidity about the choice of colour schemes and wallpapers, but all work well in these elegantly proportioned rooms. Kevin's home-cooked dinners (served at 8p.m.) are worth staying in for (e.g. tomato and tarragon soup, breast of Gressingham duckling, sticky toffee pudding). Bedrooms differ in size and style, and all are pleasingly decorated in restful colours. Best, of course, face the lake, so it's worth paying a premium for these.

○ Closed Nov to Feb; dining room closed Sun eve ⚡ From M6 Junction 40, take A66 to Keswick; at roundabout take A592 to Ullswater and Glenridding; hotel is 3 miles from Pooley Bridge. Private car park ⬜1 twin, 9 double; all with room service, hair-dryer, direct-dial telephone, TV ⊘ Dining room, bar, lounge, garden; civil wedding licence; social functions ⅙ No wheelchair access ● No dogs; no smoking ⬜ Amex, Delta, MasterCard, Switch, Visa £ Single occupancy of twin/double from £65, twin from £130, double from £145; deposit required. Set D £30; light meals available; service incl

---

Rampsbeck Country House

Watermillock, Penrith CA11 0LP
TEL: (017684) 86442 FAX: (017684) 86688
EMAIL: enquiries@rampsbeck.fsnet.co.uk
WEB SITE: www.rampsbeck.fsnet.co.uk

A hostess with the mostest at this beautiful lakeside property

Marion Gibb has been welcoming guests to the glorious eighteenth-century house she owns with husband Tom and her mother for quite a few years now, but her smile is as radiant as ever. A stay in this grandstand location overlooking Ullswater would make most people happy; having the permanent run of these eighteen-acre grounds must be sublime. Views extend across the lake towards Martindale and Howtown, best enjoyed from the dining room's picture windows. The gracious drawing room shares similar views, but guests may also relax in the log-fired hall or the refurbished bar, which opens on to immaculate gardens through French windows. Bedrooms are all exceptionally handsome, some deluxe standard with private balconies and lake views, but none a short straw. Service strikes just the right note of courteous, unstarchy friendliness. Cooking is accomplished Anglo-French stuff (pan-fried loin of hare; wild mushroom velouté, roasted squab etc.), with an enterprising wine-list.

● Closed 4 Jan to mid-Feb 🚗 From M6 junction 40, follow A592 for Ullswater; at T-junction at lake, turn right, still on A592; hotel is 1¼ miles along lakeshore. Private car park 🛏 1 single, 6 twin/double, 10 double, 1 four-poster, 1 suite; all with room service, hair-dryer, direct-dial telephone, TV; tea/coffee-making facilities, trouser pres available ⟡ Dining room, bar, drawing room, hall, gardens; conferences; social functions; leisure facilities nearby; early suppers for children ⟐ No wheelchair access; 3 steps into hotel, 1 ground-floor bedroom ● No dogs in public rooms and most bedrooms; no smoking in most public rooms and some bedrooms ⟦ Delta, MasterCard, Switch, Visa £ Single £65 to £70, single occupancy of twin/double £75 to £95, twin/double £110 to £180, four-poster/suite £220 to £230; deposit required. Set L £28, D £39; light meals available (lunch only). Special breaks available

---

WATH-IN-NIDDERDALE North Yorkshire　　　　　　　　　　　map 9

Sportsman's Arms

Wath-in-Nidderdale, Pateley Bridge, Harrogate HG3 5PP
TEL: (01423) 711306　FAX: (01423) 712524

Stylish and characterful inn in remote Nidderdale

If you're in search of rural peace, the sleepy village of Wath is an ideal time-warp setting reached by a hump-backed packhorse bridge. This is shooting and fishing territory, with parties descending to bag grouse on the moors and pull trout from the local waterways. Naturally, local bounty figures highly on the menu of this pub. The posh bar was in line for a makeover when we visited in spring 2004. Among the references to sporting pursuits – fishing rods and framed prints of dogs with mouthfuls of feathered game – plenty of chalkboard choices are displayed. The smoked Nidderdale trout with lemon and horseradish certainly hit the spot at lunch for our inspector. More formal evening dining takes place in a classy setting of lemon and blue with tasselled curtains and a collection of huge clocks rescued from railways, market and town halls; a correspondent proclaimed dinner 'really good... full even on a Monday', with commendable use of local ingredients and professional service. Bedrooms have a country-style décor, with antique pine panelling, smart gingham fabrics and top-quality bathrooms; those in the barn conversion have characterful exposed beams.

● Closed 25 Dec 🚗 From Pateley Bridge, follow signs for Ramsgill but turn off at Wath after 2 miles. Private car park 🛏 2 twin, 9 double; all with room service, hair-dryer, direct-dial telephone, TV ⟡ Dining room, bar, 2 lounges, garden; conferences; social functions; leisure facilities nearby; early suppers for children; highchairs ⟐ No wheelchair access; 4 ground-floor bedrooms, 1 room specially equipped for disabled people ● No dogs; no smoking in bedrooms and dining room ⟦ Delta, MasterCard, Switch, Visa £ Single occupancy of twin/double £50 to £90, twin/double £60 to £100, four-poster £60 to £100; deposit required. Set L £25, D £20; alc D £26; light meals available. Special breaks available (2004 data)

WELLINGHAM Norfolk　　　　　　　　　　　　　　　　　map 6

Manor House Farm

Wellingham, Fakenham PE32 2TH
TEL: (01328) 838227　FAX: (01328) 838348

Working farmhouse B&B offering comfort and great walks under big skies

Wellingham isn't even big enough to warrant a village pub – it's really just a church, a few houses and a phone box. And of course the Ellis' delightful working farm and B&B. There's plenty to explore around the rambling farm, including formal gardens, a field of deer and pens for the chickens, before you head off out into the vast fields of crops for a wander under Norfolk's famous big skies. Back indoors you'll be able to relax in one of the comfortable, tasteful country-style bedrooms, refreshingly plain in bright colours with pictures of rural scenes. One twin has a nice high sloping ceiling (though remember to close the blinds on the skylights if you don't want to wake with the dawn) and an interesting abstract chicken wall hanging. Bathrooms come with luxurious fluffy towels and bathrobes, though our inspector found the shower was uncomfortably powerful.

○ Open all year ⤢ In Wellingham, ½ mile from A1065 between Fakenham and Swaffham; farm is next to church. Private car park ⬛ 2 twin/double, 2 double; all with hair-dryer, TV; some with VCR, CD player; fax available ⬗ Breakfast room, lounge, conservatory, gardens; leisure facilities nearby; outdoor play area ♿ Wheelchair access to hotel and breakfast room, WC, 2 ground-floor bedrooms, 1 room specially equipped for disabled people ● No children under 10; no dogs in hotel (kennel available); no smoking in bedrooms ▭ None accepted £ Single occupancy of twin/double £45, twin/double £65 to £80; deposit required

---

WELLS Somerset
map 2

Canon Grange

Cathedral Green, Wells BA5 2UB
TEL: (01749) 671800
EMAIL: canongrange@email.com
WEB SITE: www.canongrange.co.uk

A fine B&B with a wonderful location and hospitable owners

As if a medieval façade to their house were not sufficient, Ken and Annette Sowden's place also boasts a fabulous view from the pale-green dining room down Cathedral Close. Rising up before you at breakfast is Wells Cathedral's magnificent west front – a view enjoyed by two of the bedrooms: Room 3 on the first floor and the single room (which does not have an en suite bathroom). Other bedrooms facing the street are equally attractive, however, with rugs on stripped floorboards, various curios dotted about and occasionally a marble fireplace. Breakfasts offer a varied choice of dishes and are highly praised. Ken and Annette run things with calm assurance and much friendliness – Ken is particularly knowledgeable on the area and local history.

○ Open all year ⤢ From A371 follow hospital A&E signs, turn into St Andrew Street; hotel is beyond cathedral ⬛ 1 single, 3 twin/double, 1 family room; all with room service, hair-dryer, TV ⬗ Dining room; leisure facilities nearby; early suppers for children; cots, toys ♿ No wheelchair access; 1 ground-floor bedroom ● No dogs; no smoking ▭ Delta, MasterCard, Visa £ Single occupancy of twin/double £35, twin/double £54 to £57, family room £64; deposit required. Set D £18; light meals available; service incl; special breaks available ③FOR②

WELLS-NEXT-THE-SEA Norfolk
map 6

Crown Hotel [NEW ENTRY]

The Buttlands, Wells-next-the-Sea NR23 1EX
TEL: (01328) 710209   FAX: (01328) 711432
EMAIL: reception@thecrownhotelwells.co.uk
WEB SITE: www.thecrownhotelwells.co.uk

A warm welcome at Pacific-influenced English country inn

This sixteenth-century coaching inn has recently been passed around like a hot potato – current owners Chris and Jo Coubrough are the third in quick succession. We're pleased to report that the place appears to be in capable hands. The latest refurbishment sticks to the contemporary style of the last, but stamps Chris's exuberant Kiwi style throughout, with bright zesty colours in the public rooms, pale, soothing whites in the bedrooms and local photography on the walls. The atmosphere is welcoming and youthful – Chris describes the place as 'a young family hotel owned by young people without kids'. All the staff are employed on a profit-sharing basis, so the place is 'full of people who want to be here'. Chris's claims are borne out by one reader, who told us: 'The new owners were terrific hosts, and their attitude permeated to all their staff. We have never felt so welcome and so at home in any hotel we've stayed at in recent years.' The praise extended to the kitchen: 'We loved the influence of Asia and New Zealand', and they also felt that prices were reasonable, though we thought they may be a little on the high side for the simple rooms, some of which were showing signs of damp on the walls.

◗ Open all year ⚡ On The Buttlands, the green in centre of Wells-next-the-Sea. Private car park 🛏 2 twin, 7 double, 2 family rooms; all with hair-dryer, direct-dial telephone, modem line, TV ✅ Restaurant, bar, conservatory, sun deck; conferences; social functions; leisure facilities nearby; early suppers for children; cots, highchairs, baby-listening ♿ No wheelchair access ● No dogs or smoking in bedrooms ▭ Amex, Delta, MasterCard, Switch, Visa £ Single occupancy of twin/double £60 to £95, twin/double £95 to £150, family room £125 to £150; deposit required. Set D (5 courses) £30, alc L, D £20; light meals available. Special breaks available 3FOR2

WEST MALLING Kent   map 3

Scott House

37 High Street, West Malling ME19 6QH
TEL: (01732) 841380   FAX: (01732) 522367
EMAIL: mail@scott-house.co.uk
WEB SITE: www.scott-house.co.uk

Georgian B&B hidden behind interior design shop

On the busy High Street above and beside a small interior design and reproduction furniture shop in a large Georgian town house is the Smiths' home and well-run business. You enter through the shop – a fairly cluttered space – but beyond it, the house opens up to reveal a finely proportioned hall and staircase, which leads to the comfortable bedrooms. Each is, as expected, cleverly designed and tastefully done out. Four-poster and half-tester beds dominate. Rooms have painted wall-panelling, artfully placed mirrors to give a feeling of space and cleverly concealed storage. Fabrics are good quality, the beds are firm, and each bedroom has a smart modern shower room. Guests are generally visiting local businesses in the area and few linger in the airy sitting room with its comfortable sofas, preferring to retire to bed in the evenings to watch TV after dinner at a nearby restaurant. Breakfast is taken downstairs at individual polished tables, where Mr Smith can provide anything from full English to a kipper or two.

◗ Closed Chr and New Year ⚡ West Malling is on A228, 1 mile from M20 junction 4. Nearest train station: West Malling 🛏 1 single, 1 twin, 2 double, 1 four-poster; all with hair-dryer, trouser press, modem line, TV ✅ Breakfast room, sitting room; leisure facilities nearby ♿ No wheelchair access ● No children under 10; no dogs; no smoking ▭ Amex, Delta, Diners, MasterCard, Switch, Visa £ Single £59, single occupancy of twin/double £59, twin/double/four-poster £79; deposit required 3FOR2

WESTON-UNDER-REDCASTLE Shropshire   map 5

The Citadel

Weston-under-Redcastle, Shrewsbury SY4 5JY
TEL: (01630) 685204 (AND FAX)
EMAIL: griffiths@thecitadelweston.co.uk
WEB SITE: www.thecitadelweston.co.uk

Castle living in a Wolsey Lodge in splendid grounds

The Citadel is a red castle, but evidently not the red castle of village repute. Rather, it was built at the beginning of the nineteenth century as a dower house for the Hill family who lived in nearby Hawkstone Hall. If it looks a little like an overblown folly then it certainly fits in with the fascinating woodlands nearby, which contain magical paths, caves, monuments, grottoes and an obelisk. Sylvia and Beverley Griffiths welcome guests to their intriguing home, which is eminently suited to house-party entertainment. There's a sweeping staircase, a circular sitting room with plasterwork ceiling and a billiards room for after-dinner amusement. Step through the French windows from here and you are into well-tended gardens filled with rhododendrons and azaleas. Guests sit down to dinner around one table at about 7.30p.m. and a typical menu might start with asparagus with anchovies and Parmesan, followed by lamb with Shrewsbury sauce, then gooseberry crumble and local cheeses. Bedrooms have a lavish feel, with two of the rooms occupying turrets. Work has been done on upgrading the bathrooms and by later this year all should have a bath and separate shower.

◐ Closed Chr & Easter; dining room closed Sun eve ⬚ 12 miles north of Shrewsbury, turn off A49 towards Weston/Hawkstone Park; hotel is ¼ mile beyond Weston towards Hodnet, on right. Private car park ⬚ 2 twin/double, 1 double; all with room service, hair-dryer, trouser press, TV ⊘ Dining room, sitting room, billiards room, gardens; leisure facilities nearby ⬚ No wheelchair access ● No children under 10; no dogs; no smoking ⬚ MasterCard, Switch, Visa £⬚ Single occupancy of twin/double £65, twin/double £84 to £104; deposit required. Set D £25 to £28; light meals available; service incl ⬚

WEYMOUTH Dorset map 2

Seaham Guesthouse

3 Waterloo Place, Weymouth DT4 7NU
TEL: (01305) 782010
EMAIL: stay@theseaham.co.uk
WEB SITE: www.theseaham.co.uk

Superlative seaside B&B in a fine location

At the quieter end of the seafront stands Tania Petford's imposing four-storey terrace house of 1845 vintage, all painted sparkling white. The house is everything you could ask of a seaside B&B: immaculately well kept, tastefully decorated in fresh and bright style, ten minutes' walk from a whole host of restaurants and pubs, and most importantly it is a hundred yards from the beach. There is a pleasant breakfast room decorated with paintings and sketches of local scenes, then a small sitting room with local information. Bedrooms with a sea view will be most visitors' favourites: Room 2 occupies a large first-floor bow window while Room 5 is right at the top of the house and has a double aspect. All rooms are equipped with straightforward, well-maintained shower rooms.

◐ Closed Chr ⬚ In Weymouth, follow signs for seafront and head towards church; hotel is just before church. Nearest train station: Weymouth ⬚ 5 double; all with hair-dryer, TV; ironing facilities available ⊘ Breakfast room, sitting room; leisure facilities nearby ⬚ No wheelchair access ● No children; no dogs; no smoking ⬚ Amex, Delta, MasterCard, Switch, Visa £⬚ Twin/double £54 to £70; deposit required. Special breaks available

---

WHIMPLE Devon map 1

Woodhayes Country House & Cottage

Whimple, Exeter EX5 2TD
TEL: (01404) 822237 FAX: (01404) 822337
EMAIL: info@woodhayes-hotel.co.uk
WEB SITE: www.woodhayes-hotel.co.uk

Peaceful country house offering top-notch B&B

This handsome, mid-eighteenth century property stands next to the apple orchards that provided its wealth for many years – mainly through cider. There are two acres of lovely lawned grounds, too, and so, despite the convenient proximity of the A30, it seems lost in deep countryside. Lynda and Eddie Katz have been here for eight years, their style being one of unforced and unfussy hospitality. There is an elegant but homely sitting room, an attractive honesty bar and a bright breakfast room. Breakfasts always include fresh fruits and local sausages, bacon and eggs, and there are various specials which might include a Devonian hog's pudding. Bedrooms are spacious and pretty, with bathrooms occasionally old-fashioned but very well kept.

◐ Closed Nov to Feb ⬚ Turn off A30 Exeter to Honiton road at Daisymount junction; follow brown signs to Woodhayes. Nearest train station: Whimple. Private car park ⬚ 2 twin/double, 4 double; family rooms available; all with hair-dryer, direct-dial telephone, modem line, TV; 2 with CD player ⊘ Breakfast room, bar, sitting room, garden; leisure facilities nearby; toys, babysitting ⬚ No wheelchair access ● No dogs; smoking in bar only ⬚ Amex, Delta, Diners, MasterCard, Switch, Visa £⬚ Single occupancy of twin/double £65, twin/double £90, family room £110; deposit required. Special breaks available ⬚

map 8

Inn at Whitewell

Whitewell, Forest of Bowland, Clitheroe BB7 3AT
TEL: (01200) 448222   FAX: (01200) 448298
WEB SITE: www.greatinns.co.uk

A quirky inn at an idyllic riverside spot in the Forest of Bowland

This historic inn on the banks of the Hodder attracts hordes of visitors and walkers on fine weekends. It's a rambling, stone-built place, bits dating back to the fourteenth century. Its long-term owners, the Bowman family, are as determinedly eccentric as the building itself. There's nothing off the peg here; pictures and talking-point artefacts bestrew the interior of stone-flagged floors, mullioned windows and wood panelling. An on-site wine-shop replaces anything as dreary as a reception desk. Both wines and victuals deserve sampling (e.g. Whitewell fish pie, home-made ice cream, an adventurous cheeseboard). Bedrooms are dashingly attractive affairs full of character and antique furnishings, plus high-tech sound systems and eye-popping period bathrooms. However, one reader this year complained about poor housekeeping and service. More reports please.

◑ Open all year   🔁 Whitewell is 6 miles north-east of Clitheroe. Private car park   🅿 1 twin, 4 twin/double, 11 double, 1 suite; family rooms available; all with room service, hair-dryer, direct-dial telephone, TV, VCR, CD player; no tea/coffee-making facilities in rooms   ⬦ Dining room, bar, lounge/hall, garden; conferences; social functions, civil wedding licence; early suppers for children; cots, highchairs, baby-listening   ♿ No wheelchair access; 1 step into hotel, 1 step into restaurant, 2 ground-floor bedrooms in annexe   ● None   ▭ Delta, MasterCard, Switch, Visa   £ Single occupancy of twin/double £69, twin/double £94 to £120, family room from £114, suite £140; deposit required. Alc L £17, D £26; light meals available; service incl

                                                              map 3

Hotel Continental

29 Beach Walk, Whitstable CT5 2BP
TEL: (01227) 280280   FAX: (01227) 280257
EMAIL: reservations@hotelcontinental.co.uk
WEB SITE: www.hotelcontinental.co.uk

Informal seafront hotel with cheery brasserie

Just one of the various outlets of the Whitstable Oyster Fishery Company, the Hotel Continental is a short walk east of the harbour, overlooking the Thames estuary and close to the town's leisure pool. On the ground floor, the light and airy bar and brasserie have huge windows and red and mustard paintwork with wicker tables and chairs (no cushions!) and a decorative Victorian tiled floor. There are sofas and easy chairs too, and daily papers piled up by the door. Deep-fried cod in beer batter, mussels and fishcakes are lunchtime staples in the bar, while in the restaurant flashes of red and white gingham tablecloths may be glimpsed beneath whole lobsters or platters of Aberdeen beef. The bedrooms in the hotel are small but fresh and pretty with yellow walls, light furniture and turquoise bathrooms. Hanging rails rather than wardrobes are common. Four rooms come with a balcony, though the most popular rooms are in the eight fisherman's huts on the other side of the harbour. Each has a concrete terrace and a couple of deckchairs to sit out on. One reader this year was disappointed by breakfast ('rather lukewarm') and coffee 'of doubtful freshness'.

◑ Closed Chr   🔁 On the seafront in Whitstable. Nearest train station: Whitstable. Private car park   🅿 10 twin, 10 double, 3 family rooms; additional rooms in huts on beach; all with hair-dryer, direct-dial telephone, modem line, TV   ⬦ Restaurant, bar, lounge; conferences; leisure facilities nearby; early suppers for children; cots, highchairs   ♿ No wheelchair access   ● No dogs; no smoking in bedrooms and some public rooms   ▭ Amex, Delta, Diners, MasterCard, Switch, Visa   £ Single occupancy of twin/double £52 to £70, twin/double £65 to £135, family room £100 to £150, suite £110 to £150; deposit required. Alc L, D £20; light meals available. Special breaks available

Old House NEW ENTRY

The Square, Wickham PO17 5JG
TEL: (01329) 833049   FAX: (01329) 833672
EMAIL: oldhousehotel@aol.com
WEB SITE: www.oldhousehotel.co.uk

Contemporary twists in a relaxed period hotel with good food and designer bedrooms

Wickham's wide market square, with its timbered medieval shop-fronts and smart period townhouses, has been at the centre of village activity since the Middle Ages. In the thick of things right on the Square, the Old House shows its age in the best possible way: a typical early-Georgian townhouse with three elegant storeys of immaculate white windows and creeper-clad red brick. Inside, things are rather more twenty-first century, for owners Paul and Lesley Scott have embellished their historic canvas with contemporary chic in a stylish makeover which cleverly combines trendiness with tradition, creating a delightful small hotel with an agreeably laid-back atmosphere. The centre of activity is the smart brasserie-style restaurant which, with its wood floors, wood-burning stove and modern artwork by local artists (including Lesley's own sculpture), is an informal but elegant place for dinner. There's a flavour of France about the menu: perhaps twice-baked Roquefort cheese soufflé, followed by chicken coq au vin or smoked pavé of salmon, finishing with apple Tatin and Calvados sorbet. Of the eight well-equipped rooms, Room 1, with its two gold-silk window seats overlooking the square, a cast-iron fireplace and a four-poster with a silk-edged canopy, was our favourite, though suffering from a little noise. Seven more rooms are to be added by August 2004.

◑ Closed 26 to 31 Dec; restaurant closed Sun eve   ⊡ From M27 Junction 7, follow A334 through Botley to Wickham; hotel is on the Square on left after lights at pedestrian crossing. Private car park   ⌂⌐ 2 twin, 5 double, 1 four-poster; family rooms available; all with room service, hair-dryer, trouser press, direct-dial telephone, modem line, TV, CD player, DVD   ⊘ Restaurant, bar, lounge, garden; conferences; social functions; leisure facilities nearby; early suppers for children; cots, highchairs, baby-listening   ও No wheelchair access   ● No dogs; no smoking in bedrooms   ⊟ Amex, Delta, MasterCard, Switch, Visa   £ Single occupancy of twin/double £80, twin/double from £85, four-poster from £120, family room from £105; deposit required. Cooked B £7.50; set L £20; alc L, D £27.50; light meals available

Coombe Farm

Widegates, Looe PL13 1QN
TEL: (01503) 240223
EMAIL: coombe_farm@hotmail.com
WEB SITE: www.coombefarmhotel.co.uk

The warmest of welcomes and an on-site menagerie at this charming country B&B

The roll call of resident animals at Coombe Farm could take some time – with a sweet-natured retriever, one rabbit, one guinea pig, three ponies, a horse and any number of peacocks and peahens (we lost count), there's no danger of forgetting you're in the country here. With woods, streams and ponds to explore in the grounds, and a swimming pool out by the farmhouse, there's no shortage of things to do either, even before you head out into the countryside around the nearby town of Looe. Unfortunately, if you do want to linger and the weather's not playing ball you're a bit stuck, as there are no public rooms, meaning you're confined to your bedroom in the farmhouse outbuildings. Not that there's anything wrong with them – far from it; there are some lovely features such as a large walk-in shower with striking chunky blue tiles in Room 9, and a big granite-framed fireplace in the spacious 10. Breakfast is brought to your room by the friendly

Martin Eades, happy to cater to your every whim and to call ahead and make reservations for dinner at one of the local pubs or restaurants.

◑ Open all year ⏏ On B3253 just south of Widegates village. Private car park ⟵ 3 twin/double; family rooms available; all with hair-dryer, direct-dial telephone, modem line, TV ✦ Gardens; heated outdoor swimming pool; leisure facilities nearby; babysitting ♿ No wheelchair access; 3 ground-floor bedrooms (2 steps) ● No smoking ⬚ Amex, Delta, MasterCard, Switch, Visa £ Single occupancy of twin/double £45 to £60, twin/double £64 to £78, family room £80 to £97; deposit required

---

WILMCOTE Warwickshire   map 5

Pear Tree Cottage

7 Church Road, Wilmcote, Stratford-upon-Avon CV37 9UX
TEL: (01789) 205889   FAX: (01789) 262862
EMAIL: mander@peartreecot.co.uk
WEB SITE: www.peartreecot.co.uk

Enchanting Elizabethan cottage in Shakespeare's home patch

Set in a picture-perfect English village, Ted and Margaret Mander's Elizabethan cottage bulges and tilts in the best tradition of charming historical architecture. Parish records have it that the Bard's parents once owned the Cottage, and for added piquancy, Anne Hathaway's own listing house can be seen from the garden. This large garden of lawns, fruit trees and flowerbeds is divided into delightful secluded sections making it a popular picnicking spot for the romantically inclined guest. Inside, the breakfast room and sitting room are atmospheric; the walls are stone-exposed or white, the low ceilings are beamed and Ted and Margaret's impressive collection of Staffordshire china, arranged on a huge wooden dresser, complements the tasteful simplicity of the décor. Bedrooms are attractively furnished with brass- or wood-framed beds and done out in cheerful pastoral shades – guests have the use of a small kitchen. There is one self-catering apartment with a fully equipped kitchen.

◑ Closed 24 Dec to 1 Jan ⏏ Turn off A3400 2½ miles north-west of Stratford-upon-Avon; turn left at village green and first left again. Nearest train station: Wilmcote. Private car park ⟵ 1 twin, 3 double, 1 family room; all with hair-dryer, TV ✦ Breakfast room, 2 sitting rooms, gardens; leisure facilities nearby; outdoor play area ♿ No wheelchair access; 2 ground-floor bedrooms ● No children under 3; no dogs; no smoking ⬚ None accepted £ Single occupancy of twin/double £38 to £40, twin/double £56 to £60, family room £70

WIMBORNE MINSTER Dorset   map 2

Beechleas

17 Poole Road, Wimborne Minster BH21 1QA
TEL: (01202) 841684   FAX: (01202) 849344
EMAIL: information@beechleas.co.uk
WEB SITE: www.beechleas.co.uk

Sold as the Guide went to press

◑ Closed 24 Dec to mid-Jan 🚲 Take A31 to Wimborne Minster; at roundabout take B3073; at next roundabout take A349 towards Poole; hotel is on right. Private car park 🛏 3 twin/double, 3 double, 1 family room, I suite; all with room service, hair-dryer, direct-dial telephone, modem line, TV; CD player, VCR available ⚒ Restaurant/conservatory, drawing room, garden; conferences, social functions; leisure facilities nearby; early suppers for children; cots, highchairs, babysitting, baby-listening ♿ Wheelchair access to hotel and restaurant, WC, 2 ground-floor bedrooms. Disabled parking ⬤ No dogs in public rooms; no smoking in bedrooms ▭ Amex, Delta, Diners, MasterCard, Switch, Visa £ Single occupancy of twin/double £69 to £99, twin/double £99 to £119, family room £130, suite £149; deposit required. Set L £22.50 to £24.50, D £27 to £29; light meals available. Special breaks available

---

WINCANTON Somerset   map 2

Holbrook House Hotel

Wincanton BA9 8BS
TEL: (01963) 824466   FAX: (01963) 32681
EMAIL: enquiries@holbrookhouse.co.uk
WEB SITE: www.holbrookhouse.co.uk

Good range of leisure facilities and a relaxing, modern atmosphere at this country house

Though attractively symmetrical and certainly substantial, there is something quite plain about this Georgian country house – perhaps that's what made it popular with the various military men who have lived here. Once you are through the 17-acre grounds and past the front door, however, the sumptuary factor rises fast: a plush reception lounge leads on to an elegant dining room, bar and library, all combining luxury with modern flourishes.

The cooking matches this style, with one dessert choice revealing the hedonistic tendencies: baked white chocolate soufflé tart set on frozen cucumber with pink champagne. Upstairs, the bedrooms are spacious and done in fairly traditional country-house style – the Garden rooms adopt a simpler tone with pine furniture and smaller dimensions.

◑ Open all year 🚲 Holbrook House is between Wincanton and Castle Cary, 5 minutes off A303. Private car park 🛏 10 twin/double, 5 double, 2 four-poster, 1 family room, 3 suites; all with room service, hair-dryer, trouser press, direct-dial telephone, TV; CD player, iron; no tea/coffee-making facilities in rooms ⚒ Dining room, bar, lounge, library, garden; conferences; social functions; civil wedding licence; gym, spa, tennis, indoor heated swimming pool, leisure facilities nearby; early suppers for children; cots, highchairs, toys, playroom, babysitting, baby-listening, outdoor play area ♿ Wheelchair access to hotel and restaurant, WC, 5 ground-floor bedrooms, 2 rooms specially equipped for disabled people. Disabled parking ⬤ No children under 8 in restaurant; no dogs; no smoking in some bedrooms ▭ Amex, Delta, Diners, MasterCard, Switch, Visa £ Single occupancy of twin/double £90 to £135, twin/double £150 to £175, four-poster/suite £195 to £245. Set L £20, D £37; alc L £20, D £37; light meals available. Special breaks available ③FOR②

WINCHCOMBE Gloucestershire   map 5

Isbourne Manor House

Castle Street, Winchcombe GL54 5JA
TEL: (01242) 602281 (AND FAX)
EMAIL: felicity@isbourne-manor.co.uk
WEB SITE: www.isbourne-manor.co.uk

Elegant, leafy B&B on the edge of this pretty town

The fine pale-stone features of this house come into sight as you drive down the hill out of Winchcombe's high street. Although it is ostensibly Georgian, Elizabethan features lurk beneath, and the house's name derives from the babbling river Isbourne that passes by the lovely gardens of Felicity and David King's home. As one might expect in this very

English setting, the interior exudes affluent charm, and antiques abound. Guests can sit down to breakfast in the dining room to Felicity's home-made marmalades and jams. All three bedrooms are spacious and light. The biggest is Sudeley, with a four-poster bed, en-suite bath and separate shower. Probably the prettiest is Langley, a double with a brass Victorian half-tester and light, fresh décor. Finally, Beesmore, in the eaves, is a twin with its own sun terrace. Extras in the bedrooms include bathrobes, tea trays, iced water and plenty of books and magazines.

◑ Closed Chr ⏁ In Winchcombe, turn into Castle Street by White Hart Hotel; hotel is at bottom of steep hill. Private car park 🛏 1 twin, 1 double, 1 four-poster; all with hair-dryer, TV ⟨✓⟩ Breakfast room, drawing room, gardens; leisure facilities nearby ♿ No wheelchair access ● No dogs; no smoking ▭ None accepted £ Single occupancy of twin/double £55 to £60, twin/double £65 to £80, four-poster £80 to £90; deposit required

---

The White Hart **NEW ENTRY**

High Street, Winchcombe GL54 5LJ
TEL: (01242) 602359   FAX: (01242) 602703
EMAIL: enquiries@the-white-hart-inn.com
WEB SITE: www.the-white-hart-inn.com

Full marks to this Cotswold pub with Swedish overtones

'A taste of Sweden in the Cotswolds' is the unlikely promise of the White Hart, but it certainly lives up to expectations. Everything – from the food and colour schemes to the Scandinavian serving staff – is authentic. Members of the Burr family who run the inn have strong Swedish connections, and they are definitely playing to their strengths by emphasising it. Wisely, they haven't touched the exterior, which is still reassuringly half-timbered. Inside there's a long bar area with bare wood tables, chairs and floor enclosed by creamy lemon walls. This leads through to a distinctive small restaurant in Gustavian style. Here, a grey colour scheme is matched with blue and white striped cushions on the grey painted chairs. An inspection meal included a pleasant smorgasbord of a selection of fish and meat dishes, herring, shrimp in sauces and slices of ham and beef. The classy bedrooms take various themes – some are in Swedish style, but others branch out to take in the Scottish Highlands or Morocco. New England is a small double with a red, white and blue theme, a smattering of antiques and a small well-equipped shower room.

◑ Closed 25 Dec ⏁ On High Street in Winchcombe. Private car park 🛏 1 twin, 3 twin/double, 2 double, 1 four-poster, 1 family room; suites available; all with hair-dryer, direct-dial telephone, modem line, TV, VCR; fax available on request ⟨✓⟩ Restaurant, pizzeria, 2 bars, patio; conferences; social functions; leisure facilities nearby; early suppers for children, cots, highchairs, babysitting ♿ No wheelchair access ● No children in restaurant after 9pm; no dogs in restaurant (£10 per stay); no smoking in restaurant and some bedrooms ▭ Amex, Delta, MasterCard, Switch, Visa £ Single occupancy of twin/double £55 to £85, twin/double £75 to £125, four-poster £85 to £115, family room £75 to £95; deposit required. Set L £15, D £20; alc L £19, D £25; light meals available. Special breaks available (3 FOR 2)

Hotel du Vin & Bistro

14 Southgate Street, Winchester SO23 9EF
TEL: (01962) 841414   FAX: (01962) 842458
EMAIL: info@winchester.hotelduvin.com
WEB SITE: www.hotelduvin.com

Consistently high standards in a stylish city-centre hotel

This venture in Winchester was the first of this successful mini-chain's growing number of stylish boutique hotels housed in historic buildings – here a handsome red-brick Georgian townhouse with an immaculate frontage. It recently celebrated its tenth birthday, but happily, there are no signs of its advancing years and the Hotel du Vin's stylish, contemporary design and high-quality feel continue to seduce. After a dinner chosen from the daily-changing menu of dishes in the Paris-inspired bistro, you can retire to the squishy purple velvet and aubergine leather sofas amid the *trompe l'oeil* wall-paintings of the lounge. Bedrooms – off smartly painted French grey corridors with seagrass carpeting – are sponsored by champagne and wine houses or breweries.

Cream of the crop is Tattinger, a swanky suite (with a price-tag to match) in which the lounge walls are daubed with paintings inspired by the works of Grand Masters. Less grand rooms, all of which are comfortable and stylishly done out with luxurious linen, high-tech gadgets and serious showers, are unlikely to disappoint either.

○ Open all year ▨ In Winchester city centre. Nearest train station: Winchester. Private car park ⛟ 3 twin, 19 double, 1 four-poster; all with room service (breakfast only), hair-dryer, mini-bar, trouser press, direct-dial telephone, TV, CD player, DVD ✔ Restaurant, bar, lounge, garden; conferences, social functions, civil wedding licence; leisure facilities nearby; early suppers for children; cots, highchairs, babysitting ♿ Wheelchair access to hotel and restaurant, WC, 4 ground-floor bedrooms ● No dogs; no smoking in restaurant ▭ Amex, Delta, Diners, MasterCard, Switch, Visa £ Twin from £115, double from £125, four-poster £185. Continental B £9.50, cooked B £13.50; alc L, D £35

Wykeham Arms

75 Kingsgate Street, Winchester SO23 9PE
TEL: (01962) 853834   FAX: (01962) 854411
EMAIL: wykehamarms@accommodating-inns.co.uk

A thriving old inn with excellent food

Tucked behind the cathedral close and around the corner from the college, the Wykeham Arms can be tricky to find – but your efforts won't go unrewarded. The Wyk – as it is known locally – is a pub with a difference, a beguiling warren of a place where cheerful staff cope admirably with the bustle of locals and visitors drawn by its friendly atmosphere and enormous character. The bar is difficult to take in all at once for it is stuffed with an amazing array of interesting knick-knacks, curious and engaging clutter, from old school desks and bits of military memorabilia to more than a thousand tankards (some of the locals have their own) and unclaimed lost property which is simply hung on the walls. Meals are a cut above standard pub fare, and the menu might include sautéed breast of free-range organic chicken served on a creamy risotto of bacon, pumpkin and Savoy cabbage or seared loin of tuna on a prawn couscous. Bedrooms are divided between the space above the bar and the annexe in St George Street, where rooms have only marginally less character, and have access to a snug lounge with an open fire plus a lovely patio garden within earshot of the cathedral bells.

○ Closed 25 & 31 Dec; dining room closed Sun eve ▨ Immediately south of cathedral by Kingsgate, at junction of Canon Street and Kingsgate Street. Nearest train station: Winchester. Private car park ⛟ 2 single, 2 twin, 1 twin/double, 7 double, 1 four-poster, 1 suite; all with hair-dryer, mini-bar, direct-dial telephone, TV; some with modem line ✔ Restaurant, bar, lounge, garden; conferences; leisure facilities nearby ♿ No wheelchair access ● No children under 14; dogs in bar and 1 bedroom only (£5 charge); smoking in bar only ▭ Amex, Delta, Diners, MasterCard, Switch, Visa £ Single £55, single occupancy of twin/double £85 to £88, twin/double £90 to £98, four-poster £120, suite £135; deposit required. Alc L £20, D £25; light lunches available

WINDERMERE Cumbria   map 8

Coach House [NEW ENTRY]

Lake Road, Windermere LA23 2EQ
TEL: (015394) 44494
EMAIL: enquiries@lakedistrictbandb.com
WEB SITE: www.lakedistrictbandb.com

Dynamically decorated guesthouse with charming owners

Mark and Jenny Johnson's late-Victorian coach-house is set back from the road, enjoying a peaceful rear outlook over streamside gardens and woodland. The vibrantly colourful interior is a breath of fresh air, the sort of voguishly contemporary place that features in style magazines. From the sisal-floored reception hall (a mini-perch with magazines), a bright breakfast room/conservatory leads off, furnished with beechwood chairs and gingham-clothed tables. Modern blinds screen the windows, and old-fashioned radiators add a retro touch. Though not large or luxurious, the five bedrooms are instantly cheering in lime green, clear pink, sunshine yellow or mulberry. Practical modern lighting, comfortable wrought-iron beds and controllable heating and ventilation indicate the effects are more than merely cosmetic.

Spotlessly tiled shower rooms (described as 'wickedly invigorating') feature smart black-and-white chequerboard flooring, shower radios and hair-dryers in neat little bags. Breakfast includes French pastries, fruit, freshly ground cafétière coffee and a range of teas.

○ Closed 23 to 26 Dec 🔁 From M6 Junction 36, take A590 then A591. In Windermere, turn left following signs for Bowness and lake; hotel is ½ mile on right. Nearest train station: Windermere. Private car park 🛏️ 4 double, 1 family room; all with hair-dryer, TV ✅ Breakfast room/conservatory, garden; leisure facilities nearby 🔓 No wheelchair access ● No children under 7; no dogs; no smoking 🗔 Delta, MasterCard, Switch, Visa £ Single occupancy of double £37 to £51, double £50 to £68, family room £60 to £78; deposit required. Special breaks available

Gilpin Lodge

Crook Road LA23 3NE
TEL: (015394) 88818   FAX: (015394) 88058
EMAIL: hotel@gilpinlodge.com
WEB SITE: www.gilpinlodge.com

Understated luxury in all departments at this splendid Lakeland retreat

'Late Victorian', say some; 'Edwardian', assert others. Spanning both reigns, this deceptively modest gabled house in 22 acres of lovely grounds dates from 1901, but it has been discreetly extended in recent years, and plans are afoot to add a few more bedrooms soon. This indicates the success John and Christine Cunliffe have made of Gilpin Lodge, a chart-topper even near Windermere, where there are more smart country-house hotels than you can shake a stick at. It excels without architectural grandeur or a spectacular

setting, simply by being a superbly good hotel – and a fine restaurant too. Immaculately furnished with gorgeous flowers, antiques and vibrant colour schemes, it's impossible to find a wrong note anywhere. The main lounge is a *tour de force*, and there isn't a bedroom you wouldn't want to stay in. Smart sofas, window-seats and easy chairs give them a suite-like feel, and every detail is elegant and sophisticated, including bathrooms.

○ Open all year 🔁 From M6 Junction 36, take A590 and A591 to roundabout north of Kendal, then B5284 for 5 miles. Nearest train station: Windermere. Private car park 🛏️ 7 twin/double, 3 double, 4 four-poster; all with room service, hair-dryer, mini-bar, trouser press, direct-dial telephone, TV; some with CD player ✅ Restaurant, 2 lounges, gardens; leisure facilities nearby 🔓 No wheelchair access ● No children under 7; no dogs; smoking in one lounge only 🗔 Amex, Delta, Diners, MasterCard, Switch, Visa £ Single occupancy of twin/double £160, twin/double £220 to £290, four-poster £250 to £290 (rates incl dinner); deposit required. Set L £19.50, D £42.50; alc L £20; light lunches available (exc Sun). Special breaks available

Holbeck Ghyll

Holbeck Lane, Windermere LA23 1LU
TEL: (015394) 32375   FAX: (015394) 34743
EMAIL: stay@holbeckghyll.com
WEB SITE: www.holbeckghyll.com

A spectacular location for this fine Victorian mansion

A majestic panorama of Windermere and the rugged Langdale fells surrounds this handsome country house, originally built as a hunting lodge for the ebulliently wealthy Lord Lonsdale of Automobile Association and boxing fame. Terraced gardens with mature specimen trees enhance the scenes from large

bay windows. Arts and Crafts details and one or two life-size model sheep enliven a well-preserved period interior of fine woodwork, etched glass and plaster mouldings. The firelit entrance hall makes a welcoming lounge space, society magazines arrayed on a huge oak table. Food is a high point at Holbeck

Lodge (traditional British with French influences), stretching from *amuse-bouches* to a diplomatic Anglo-Gallic cheeseboard. Service is attentively friendly, and leisure facilities impressive, including jogging trails and a palatial health spa. Bedrooms are spacious and very comfortable. Newest ones are in the lodge; a gradual programme of refurbishment is bringing them all into the 21st century.

○ Open all year ▨ 3 miles north of Windermere on A591; turn right into Holbeck Lane after Brockhole Visitors' Centre; hotel is 1½ miles on left. Private car park ⛬ 15 twin/double, 2 four-poster, 3 suites; family rooms available; all with room service, hair-dryer, trouser press, direct-dial telephone, TV, CD player; some with tea/coffee-making facilities, mini-bar, DVD ✅ Restaurant, bar, hall, lounge, garden; conferences; social functions; civil wedding licence; gym, spa, tennis; early suppers for children; cots, highchairs, babysitting, baby-listening ♿ Wheelchair access to hotel (ramp) and restaurant, National Accessible Scheme: mobility impairment M1, WC, 3 ground-floor bedrooms ● No children under 8 in restaurant eves; no dogs in public rooms, £4.50 per night in bedrooms; no smoking in some public rooms and some bedrooms ▭ Amex, Delta, Diners, MasterCard, Switch, Visa £ Single occupancy of twin/double £125 to £200, twin/double £190 to £340, four-poster £250 to £340, family room £250 to £370, suite £250 to £340 (rates incl dinner); deposit required. Set L £27.50, D £47.50; light meals available. Special breaks available

Low House NEW ENTRY

Cleabarrow, Windermere LA23 3NA
TEL: (015394) 43156
EMAIL: info@lowhouse.co.uk
WEB SITE: www.lowhouse.co.uk

Classy, affordable B&B in a charming seventeenth-century country house

This unassuming but eminently desirable stone-built property dates from 1692, sheltered by a natural windbreak of trees on a blissfully quiet lane. Beyond pretty cottage gardens, a couple of latched gates are all that separate you from the sort of scene Constable might have painted, a truly picturesque composition of classic English countryside. Inside, elegantly domesticated sitting and dining rooms with antiques, books and log fires promise a thoroughly restful stay. The three letting bedrooms overlooking garden views are similarly soothing with tasteful country furnishings, skirted tables and chintzy curtains. 'Mediterranean' breakfasts can be served upstairs on request. It's hard to believe the bustling resorts of Bowness and Windermere are within easy walking distance. Energetic guests won't baulk at the mile or so stroll to the town or lakeshore, but if you prefer to travel in style, you can book the family Bentley for sightseeing outings or restaurant visits.

○ Closed 24 to 26 Dec ▨ From Kendal take B5284 signed Crook and Hawkshead ferry; after 5 miles pass Windermere golf course on left; after another 100 yards turn right towards Heathwaite; hotel is 100 yards on right. Nearest train station: Windermere. Private car park ⛬ 1 twin/double, 2 double; family rooms available; all with room service, hair-dryer, TV, VCR ✅ Breakfast room, sitting room, library, garden; leisure facilities nearby ♿ No wheelchair access ● No children under 8; no dogs; no smoking ▭ Delta, Diners, MasterCard, Switch, Visa £ Single occupancy of twin/double £60 to £85, twin/double £70 to £90, family room £105 to £135; deposit required ③FOR②

Miller Howe

Rayrigg Road, Windermere LA23 1EY
TEL: (015394) 42536 FAX: (015394) 45664
EMAIL: lakeview@millerhowe.com
WEB SITE: www.millerhowe.com

Flamboyantly individual hotel serving outstanding food

The humdrum roadside entrance to Miller Howe gives little warning of the retinal shocks to follow. Beyond the house, gardens cascade past an ornate water feature to a stunning vista of tree-lined Windermere and a skyline pierced by the Langdale Pikes. Interior décor is just as attention-seeking, with gilt cherubs and tasselled curtains setting a distinctly thespian tone in public rooms. Hardly home-from-home for most of us, but hey, you're not at home. The view is perhaps best appreciated through the arcaded windows of the airy, split-level dining room, the focal point of Miller Howe. The cooking is classic French with North-country overtones (Flookburgh shrimps and Kentmere lamb). Bedrooms are steadily being redone in varying degrees of refined extravagance, and contain every imaginable comfort from binoculars to brollies. For all its show-stopping qualities, Miller Howe remains a restful bolthole, underpinned by polished, well-paced service. Relax, indulge, enjoy – at least until the bill arrives.

○ Open all year ⊿ On A592 between Windermere and Bowness. Nearest train station: Windermere. Private car park ⊨ 8 twin/double, 3 double, 4 suites; all with room service, hair-dryer, trouser press, direct-dial telephone, TV, CD player; no tea/coffee-making facilities in rooms ⊘ Restaurant, 3 lounges, conservatory, garden; conferences, social functions, civil wedding licence; leisure facilities nearby; cots, highchairs, babysitting ⅙ Wheelchair access to hotel (ramp) and restaurant, National Accessible Scheme: mobility impairment M2, 1 ground-floor bedroom specially equipped for disabled people ● No children under 8 exc babes in arms; dogs £5 per night; smoking in 1 lounge and on some bedroom balconies only ⊟ Amex, Delta, MasterCard, Switch, Visa £· Twin/double £240 to £280, suite £260 to £350 (rates incl dinner); deposit required. Set L £19.50; light meals available. Special meals available

The Samling

Ambleside Road, Windermere LA23 1LR
TEL: (015394) 31922   FAX: (015394) 30400
EMAIL: info@thesamling.com
WEB SITE: www.thesamling.com

Luxury bolthole with a house-party atmosphere

This exclusive retreat was once the domain of beautiful people wealthy enough to commandeer the whole place. Built in the late 1700s, the deceptively cottage-like property with its neatly embroidered gables enjoys the most glorious vistas over Windermere from an elevated site just outside Ambleside. The mind can only boggle at what The Samling's 67 acres of prime lakeshore real estate would currently fetch on the open market. You don't have to be famous or beautiful to enjoy it for a while these days, however – merely affluent. A couple's average spend for a weekend is around £1,000, but for this you can expect untrammelled pampering, exquisite cooking and ultra-sophisticated contemporary style. Public rooms feel anything but hotelish – there's no bar or reception area, just original artwork, perfect flowers, neutral colours. Dinner has the intimacy of a private club. Bedrooms are dashingly colourful and interesting, with romantic bathtubs built for two.

○ Open all year ⊿ On A591 north of Windermere, turn right after Low Wood Hotel. Private car park ⊨ 5 double, 6 suites; all with room service, hair-dryer, direct-dial telephone, TV, VCR, CD player; no tea/coffee-making facilities in rooms ⊘ Restaurant, drawing room, library, games room, garden; conferences; social functions; civil wedding licence; hot tub; leisure facilities nearby; early suppers for children; cots, highchairs ⅙ Wheelchair access to hotel (ramp) and restaurant, 1 ground-floor bedroom ● No dogs ⊟ Amex, MasterCard, Switch, Visa £· Single occupancy of double from £175, double from £175, suite from £325; deposit required. Set L, D £45; alc L, D £45; light meals available; service incl (3FOR2)

WINSTER Derbyshire   map 5

Brae Cottage

East Bank, Winster, Matlock DE4 2DT
TEL: (01629) 650375

Cottagey bedrooms in a secluded village setting

It's well worth wending your way through the warren of old streets that make up the utterly unspoilt little lead-mining town of Winster to reach this secret bolt-hole. The prettily countrified guest rooms are situated in a separate building behind the 300-year-old cottage, beyond a paved area that provides parking for skilled navigators. Both rooms are tastefully decorated in pale colours, with gingham fabrics on black wrought-iron beds and new tongue-and-groove wood flooring – Room 2 is cosier, while airier Room 1 comfortably fits a sofa bed as well as its own seating area; each comes with a tidy en-suite electric shower. A charming dining room full of polished antique furniture and Delft china makes an atmospheric setting for candlelit breakfasts served upon lacy table settings.

○ Open all year ⧉ 2 miles north of Matlock, turn off A6 on to B5057 to Winster; in village turn left off Main Street just after Market House; cottage drive is on right before fork. Private car park ⧉ 1 twin/double, 1 double; family room available; both with hair-dryer, TV ⧉ Breakfast room, garden; leisure facilities nearby ⧉ No wheelchair access; 2 ground-floor bedrooms ● No dogs in public rooms; no smoking ⧉ None accepted £ Single occupancy of twin/double £35 to £40, twin/double £44 to £60, family room £55; deposit required

---

WINTERINGHAM   North Lincolnshire   map 9

Winteringham Fields

Winteringham, Scunthorpe DN15 9PF
TEL: (01724) 733096   FAX: (01724) 733898
EMAIL: wintfields@aol.com
WEB SITE: www.winteringhamfields.com

A gourmet experience with exceptional service in ambient surroundings

It is with good reason that Annie and Germain Schwab have built up a considerable reputation for offering superb food, warm hospitality and ambient surroundings in the 16 years that they have been running Winteringham Fields. On entering the honey-coloured, sixteenth-century manor house the sensation is of having arrived somewhere special. The staff are welcoming and service is outstanding in this opulently furnished retreat. The bar/lounge is in rich purples and gold with comfortable deep armchairs and sofas in front of a wood fire – lit on chillier evenings – and the conservatory, packed with lovely old-fashioned armchairs, extends to a garden terrace. Meals are served in a well-appointed U-shaped restaurant, embellished with lilac drapes and statues of exotic turbaned figures that double up as light fittings. Bedrooms are atmospheric and named after local historic notables. The one called Robert Marmion, after the man who owned the village in the tenth century, is one of the most memorable: the red and green wood-beamed room has antique furniture, an elegant king-size bed and walk-in steam room and shower. There is a more modern-attired suite in the courtyard annexe.

○ Closed 2 weeks Chr, last week Mar, first 10 days Aug; restaurant closed Sun & Mon eves ⧉ 4 miles west of Humber Bridge, off A1077 in centre of village, at crossroads. Private car park ⧉ 1 twin, 1 twin/double, 5 double, 1 four-poster, 2 suites; all with room service, hair-dryer, direct-dial telephone, TV; some with tea/coffee-making facilities ⧉ Restaurant, bar/lounge, conservatory/lounge, gardens ⧉ Wheelchair access to hotel and restaurant, 3 ground-floor bedrooms ● No dogs in public rooms; no smoking in bedrooms ⧉ Amex, Delta, MasterCard, Switch, Visa £ Single occupancy of twin/double £90 to £130, twin/double £145 to £200, four-poster/suite £200; deposit required. Cooked B £12; set L £31 to £33, D £38; alc L, D £68; service incl

---

WIRKSWORTH   Derbyshire   map 5

Old Lock-up   [NEW ENTRY]

North End, Wirksworth DE4 4FG
TEL: (01629) 826272   (AND FAX)
EMAIL: wheeler@theoldlockup.co.uk
WEB SITE: www.theoldlockup.co.uk

The one place to enjoy a night in the cells

The first to stay at this early Victorian police station might have been 'prisoners, murderers and malcontents', but the only dissatisfied visitors today are likely to be those about to be released. With an emphasis on breaks for couples (at least at weekends), Vivien and Tony Wheeler have turned this former penitentiary into a romantic haven, although plenty of tongue-in-cheek mementoes, from antique truncheons to sets of handcuffs, set a light-hearted tone. Two bedrooms in the main house have a chintzy period character, while two more in the former coach house, including the lovely lemon and white Hayloft, are simpler and lighter in style, but come with the same antique beds and pretty embroidered spreads. A fifth bedroom in a petite converted chapel next door is sumptuous with its deep-red and white colour scheme and arched Gothic lancet windows. Facilities include a spa bath for two.

○ Open all year ⚡ From A6 at Cromford, turn off to Wirksworth; North End is first right as you enter the town. Nearest train station: Cromford ⬜ 1 twin, 1 twin/double, 3 double; all with room service, hair-dryer, TV; some with trouser press; VCR available ⊘ Dining room, bar, lounge, garden; leisure facilities nearby 👤 Wheelchair access to hotel and dining room (ramps), WC; 1 ground-floor bedroom ● No children; no dogs; no smoking ▭ None accepted £ Single occupancy of twin/double from £45, twin from £80, double from £90; deposit required (prices valid till Feb 2005). Set L £20, D £25; alc L £20, D £25; light meals available; service incl. Special breaks available ③FOR②

WITHYPOOL Somerset   map 1

Royal Oak Inn

Withypool TA24 7QP
TEL: (01643) 831506   FAX: (01643) 831659
EMAIL: enquiries@royaloakwithypool.co.uk
WEB SITE: www.royaloakwithypool.co.uk

A fine country inn with excellent bedrooms and convivial upmarket bar

Gail Sloggett, owner of the Royal Oak, was just seeing the local hunt off when our inspector arrived – her inn is very much part of local life. Gail's cheerful and friendly presence is a big plus, too, as is the fine bar with its log fire, candles and hand-pulled pints. Next door, the dining room moves things up a notch or two in sturdy elegance – a lovely blue room with polished wooden tables and a decorative trim of blue-and-white porcelain. Cooking covers a good range – anything from home-made steak and kidney pudding to moules marinière, or sticky toffee pudding to passion fruit tart with mango coulis. Bedrooms are delightful: interesting beds and oriental rugs matched with excellent bathrooms – all rooms have a bath.

○ Open all year ⚡ In Withypool village, off B3223 approx 7 miles north of Dulverton. Private car park ⬜ 2 twin/double, 6 double; all with room service, hair-dryer, direct-dial telephone, TV ⊘ Dining room, 2 bars, patio; early suppers for children; cots, babysitting 👤 No wheelchair access; 4 steps into hotel ● No smoking in bedrooms ▭ Delta, Diners, MasterCard, Switch, Visa £ Single occupancy of twin/double £65, twin/double £100 to £110; deposit required. Set L £20, D £25; alc L, D £25; light meals available

---

WITNEY Oxfordshire   map 5

The Fleece [NEW ENTRY]

11 Church Green, Witney OX28 4AZ
TEL: (01993) 892270 (AND FAX)
EMAIL: thefleece@peachpubs.com
WEB SITE: www.peachpubs.com

Trendy brasserie with great position and young, friendly staff

Witney's church green is rather a large affair adding a peaceful corner to this otherwise bustling market town, and standing on one side, amid a row of honey-stone houses, is this dapper brasserie with rooms. Chairs and tables spill out on to the sunny, part-grassy pavement, while inside, the bar-cum-restaurant is very spruce indeed. The modern décor encompasses exposed floorboards, deep leather chairs, and flax-coloured walls that give way to a deeper burgundy at the back. It's a buzzy place, especially on market days, when shoppers pop in for a quick bite – the oversized menu offers salads and pizzas as well as sausage and mash or whole seabass. Upstairs, the ten bedrooms are equally stylish, though plans are afoot for a mini makeover to bring in some fresher colour schemes to update the caramel-aubergine combination that is pleasant enough but perhaps a little dark. Tastefully furnished, the bedrooms have smart bathrooms to complete the package. 'A very pleasurable experience; the stay enjoyable, the food superb,' was one reader's comment.

◐ Closed Dec 25 ⬒ Leave A40 following signs to Witney town centre. At top of the town turn into the Green; the inn is on the left. Private car park ⬑ 1 single, 1 twin/double, 8 double; all with hair-dryer, direct-dial telephone, modem line, TV ⬗ Restaurant, bar, terrace; conferences; highchairs ⅙ Wheelchair access to hotel (ramp) and restaurant, WC, 1 ground-floor bedroom specially equipped for disabled people. Disabled parking ◐ No dogs or smoking in bedrooms ⬜ Amex, Delta, Diners, MasterCard, Switch, Visa £ Single £75, single occupancy of twin/double £75, twin/double £85. Alc L, D £20; light meals available (3FOR2)

WOLTERTON Norfolk   map 6

Saracen's Head

Wolterton, Erpingham NR11 7LX
TEL: (01263) 768909   FAX: (01263) 768993
EMAIL: saracenshead@wolterton.freeserve.co.uk
WEB SITE: www.saracenshead-norfolk.co.uk

Escape the rat race in favour of fine dining and bucolic pursuits

If the middle of nowhere really did exist, Robert Dawson-Smith's relaxed village inn would be at its heart. Built in 1806 as a coaching inn for Wolterton Hall, the house's leaning roof and pebbled courtyard are hallmarks of the Tuscan style in which it was built. Internally, a full renovation has been overseen by daughter Rachel, recently returned to Norfolk after giving up a career in advertising. In the public areas she has created a Bloomsbury theme, with colourful décor and an eclectic mix of ornamentation, while pine and patchwork lend a pastoral feel to the bedrooms. The only thing likely to disturb your sleep here is the cacophonous dawn chorus. Alongside contributing to the running of the hotel, Rachel runs a rustic furniture workshop from the former stables, operating under the same strict opening times as the restaurant and bar. But the real treasure at the end of your hunt for the Saracen's Head is the food: Robert mixes local and Mediterranean influences to produce a sumptuous range of dishes, all served up in three cosy parlour rooms.

◐ Closed 25 & 26 Dec ⬒ Turn off A140 at brown tourist sign to Wolterton Hall, go through Erpingham, pass pub and continue ¼ mile, ignoring right turn to Aldborough, continue straight on past church on left; hotel is ½ mile on right. Private car park ⬑ 1 twin, 3 double; family room available; all with hair-dryer, TV ⬗ Dining rooms, 2 bars, garden; conferences; social functions ⅙ No wheelchair access ◐ No dogs in public rooms; no smoking in bedrooms ⬜ Amex, Delta, MasterCard, Switch, Visa £ Single occupancy of twin/double £45, twin/double £75, family room £85; deposit required. Alc L, D £23; light meals available. Special breaks available

---

WOODBRIDGE Suffolk   map 6

Seckford Hall

Woodbridge IP13 6NU
TEL: (01394) 385678   FAX: (01394) 380610
EMAIL: reception@seckford.co.uk
WEB SITE: www.seckford.co.uk

Stunningly preserved Elizabethan grandeur suffused with a gentle formality

Seckford Hall is a delightful red-brick Elizabethan pile, a real English country treat with leaded windows, creeping vines and tall, slender chimneys. The interior is beautifully preserved – wood floors, carved beams, atmospheric nooks and crannies are everywhere. There are a plethora of public spaces in various states of grandeur, perhaps the most striking of which is the Great Hall with fabulous carved wood panelling and screens – and a carpet that can certainly be described as cheerful. Décor in the bedrooms is quite flouncy, and there are some magnificent features such as a massive four-poster that may have been used by Elizabeth I herself, brought from Windsor Castle to the

Tudor room. Newer buildings inhabit the grounds surrounding the main building, housing more bedrooms and a leisure club as well as another, less formal restaurant you can frequent if you don't fancy donning the mandatory jacket and tie in the main restaurant.

◗ Closed 25 Dec ⚡ Hotel is signposted on A12 near Woodbridge. Private car park 🛏 3 single, 9 twin, 2 twin/double, 12 double, 4 four-poster, 2 suites; family rooms available; all with room service, hair-dryer, trouser press, TV; some with mini-bar ⌷ 2 restaurants, bar, 3 lounges, gardens; conferences; social functions; civil wedding licence; gym, indoor heated swimming pool, leisure facilities nearby; early suppers for children; cots, highchairs, babysitting, baby-listening, outdoor play area ♿ No wheelchair access; 1 step into dining room, 9 ground-floor bedrooms, 1 room specially equipped for disabled people ● Dogs £7.50 per night; no smoking in bedrooms ☐ Amex, Delta, Diners, MasterCard, Switch, Visa £ Single from £85, single occupancy of twin/double from £105, twin/double from £130, four-poster from £140, family room from £195, suite from £170; deposit required (prices valid till Sep 2004). Set L £18; alc L, D £29; light meals available; service incl. Special breaks available

---

WOODSTOCK Oxfordshire   map 5

Kings Arms [NEW ENTRY]

19 Market Street, Woodstock OX20 1SU
TEL: (01993) 813636   FAX: (01993) 813737
EMAIL: enquiries@kings-woodstock-fsnet.co.uk
WEB SITE: www.kings-hotel-woodstock.co.uk

Lovely Georgian building with swish, modern bedrooms and a lively air

Sitting as it does at the gates of Blenheim Palace, the honeypot village of Woodstock fairly bristles with hotels, restaurants, tea rooms and boutiquey shops. Right in the thick of things is a handsome, cream Georgian building which at first glance seems little more than a central watering hole for the passing throngs. But step inside, and it opens out into a stylish bar with exposed floorboards and high-backed settles that leads on to an equally smart yet relaxed restaurant at the back. A simple menu offers old favourites like beer-battered cod, as well as more innovative dishes such as duck breast on sweet potato rösti. Visitors and locals alike saunter in for a drink or more, giving the place a buzzy atmosphere. Upstairs, the bedrooms (all named after British kings) have been recently refurbished and are serenely decorated in natural tones that mix brown, cream, beige and white to complement the predominantly wood and leather furniture. Chic bathrooms have a similar contemporary feel.

◗ Open all year ⚡ In centre of Woodstock 🛏 1 twin, 14 double; all with room service, hair-dryer, direct-dial telephone, modem line, TV ⌷ Restaurant, bar, lounge; social functions; leisure facilities nearby; early suppers for children ♿ No wheelchair access ● No children under 12; no dogs; smoking in bar only ☐ Amex, Delta, MasterCard, Switch, Visa £ Single occupancy of twin/double £70, twin/double £130; deposit required. Set/alc L £20, D £25; light meals available. Special breaks available (3FOR2)

Shipton Glebe

Woodstock OX20 1QQ
TEL: (01993) 812688   FAX: (01993) 813142
EMAIL: stay@shipton-glebe.com
WEB SITE: www.shipton-glebe.com

Relaxing, elegant B&B with smashing breakfasts and welcoming atmosphere

If Woodstock's daily merry-go-round of coach parties and day-trippers seems too overwhelming, the answer is to stay just beyond the village, but still within walkable distance of the area's big attraction, Blenheim Palace. Fitting this bill is Shipton Glebe, a splendid B&B run with charm and vitality by the affable Teddy Bevan. The smart, cream-painted house sits in ten acres of grounds, much of which can be seen from the tranquil, airy conservatory where breakfast is served – and Teddy rustles up a glorious morning feast to match the view. Our inspection meal was of fresh fruit salad brimming with berries, and perfectly done poached eggs. Of the bedrooms, Room 2 stands out just by virtue of its size; you could house a family of four in there easily. Instead, two of you can luxuriate in a vast bed as well as a sink-into-me sofa. The only drawback is that the French doors open on to the gravel drive, so it's not entirely private. Tasteful furnishings and thoughtful decoration are much in evidence, with sunny yellows cheering up the bathrooms. Plenty of reading material, from old novels to local tourist info, is on hand for whiling away the worst of British weather.

○ Open all year ⚡ From A44, turn on to A4095 towards Kirtlington, then take second road on left; hotel is first house visible. Private car park 🚗 2 twin, 1 double, 1 family room; all with room service, hair-dryer, direct-dial telephone, TV ⊘ Breakfast room/conservatory, dining room ♿ No wheelchair access; 1 ground-floor bedroom specially equipped for disabled people ● No children under 12; no smoking ▭ Delta, MasterCard, Switch, Visa £ Single occupancy of twin/double £60 to £75, twin/double £85 to £90; deposit required (2004 data)

WOOKEY HOLE Somerset   map 2

Glencot House

Glencot Lane, Wookey Hole, Wells BA5 1BH
TEL: (01749) 677160   FAX: (01749) 670210
EMAIL: relax@glencothouse.co.uk
WEB SITE: www.glencothouse.co.uk

Lots of character and lovely grounds at this unusual country house

Set in 18 acres of gardens and parkland, including a cricket pitch, this grand Victorian house modelled itself on the early seventeenth century when it was built. That's not the only curious thing about it, current owner Jenny Attia is a passionate collector and has filled the rooms with a glorious panoply of curiosities and memorabilia: clocks, chandeliers and ornaments galore to add to the house's own stock of walnut panelling, carved ceilings and huge inglenook fireplaces. The drawing room is especially attractive, having views down to the River Axe which passes through the gardens. There is an interesting library too, complete with piano. All in all it is a fascinating but idiosyncratic kind of country house imbued with homely values. Bedrooms are not as grand as the downstairs rooms and they vary considerably, from four-poster with *chaise longue* to single with shower only.

○ Closed New Year ⚡ From Wells, follow signs to Wookey Hole; on entering village, look for pink cottage on left; take sharp left 100 yards further on. Private car park 🚗 3 single, 1 twin, 2 twin/double, 2 double, 5 four-poster; all with room service, hair-dryer, direct-dial telephone, TV ⊘ Dining room, bar, drawing room, library, games room, gardens; conferences; social functions; heated indoor swimming pool, leisure facilities nearby; early suppers for children; cots, highchairs, toys, baby-listening ♿ No wheelchair access ● No children under 5 in dining room eves; dogs in 1 bedroom only; smoking in public rooms only ▭ Amex, Delta, MasterCard, Switch, Visa £ Single £68, single occupancy of twin/double £72 to £85, twin/double £94 to £96, four-poster £122 to £124; deposit required. Set D £26.50; light meals available. Special breaks available

WOOLACOMBE Devon   map 1

Little Beach Hotel [NEW ENTRY]

The Esplanade, Woolacombe EX34 7DJ
TEL: (01271) 870398   FAX: (01271) 871398
EMAIL: info@surfersworld.co.uk
WEB SITE: www.surfersworld.co.uk

Beach boys and girls will love this affable sandside hotel

You don't have to be a surfer dude to enjoy this bright and breezy small hotel on Woolacombe's seafront, but a love of the great outdoors is probably advisable. The downstairs has been stripped down to basics and has white walls, bare wood and a bar serving straightforward bistro fare. The sole concession to entertainment is a flat-screen television on one wall running surfer footage – most guests prefer to stare longingly out of the big front windows to the seascape outside. The atmosphere is energetic and convivial but not overpoweringly so. Upstairs, the best bedrooms face the sea but all offer fresh, simple comforts with natural colours and plenty of white. You wouldn't sit in here watching the world go by anyway – not when surf's up.

❍ Open all year 🅩 On the seafront in Woolacombe. Private car park 🛏 1 single, 3 twin, 6 double, 1 family room; all with TV; some with hair-dryer, VCR ⊘ Restaurant, bar, lounge, garden; conferences, social functions; leisure facilities nearby; babysitting, baby-listening ᵹ No wheelchair access; 2 ground-floor bedrooms ● No smoking in bedrooms ▭ Amex, Delta, MasterCard, Switch, Visa £ Single £20 to £25, single occupancy of twin/double from £30, twin/double £60 to £90, family room from £60; deposit required. Alc D £22; service incl. Special breaks available

---

WORFIELD Shropshire
map 5

Old Vicarage

Worfield, Bridgnorth WV15 5JZ
TEL: (01746) 716497   FAX: (01746) 716552
EMAIL: admin@the-old-vicarage.demon.co.uk
WEB SITE: www.oldvicarageworfield.com

Smart, small Edwardian country hotel with hands-on owners

Next year is the centenary of the Old Vicarage's construction, and it can rarely have looked in better shape in all that time. David and Sarah Blakstad have worked hard to get the hotel up to their own high standards – David spent five years at Claridges – but it's now paying off. From its polished parquet floors to its stained-glass front windows and the gleaming conservatory, the couple have managed to retain the character of the house while running an efficient operation. The public rooms all have views out to lawns and open countryside, so you can feast on these as well as dishes like roasted poussin with rösti and rosemary cream sauce, in the restaurant. The neat bedrooms are divided between the main house and the coach house and typically have antique wooden beds, big televisions – a video library is available – and high-standard bathrooms.

❍ Open all year 🅩 At top of hill in Worfield. Private car park 🛏 4 twin, 8 double, 1 four-poster, 1 suite; family rooms available; all with room service, hair-dryer, mini-bar, trouser press, direct-dial telephone, modem line, TV, VCR ⊘ Restaurant, bar, conservatory, garden; conferences; social functions; early suppers for children; cots, highchairs, toys, babysitting, baby-listening ᵹ Wheelchair access to hotel (ramp) and restaurant, WC, 2 ground-floor bedrooms, 1 room specially equipped for disabled people ● No children under 12 in restaurant; no dogs in public rooms, £10 in bedrooms; smoking in conservatory only ▭ Amex, Delta, Diners, MasterCard, Switch, Visa £ Single occupancy of twin/double £90, twin/double £100, four-poster £175, family room £135, suite £175; deposit required. Set L £23.50; alc D £35; light meals available. Special breaks available (3FOR2)

WYE Kent
map 3

Wife of Bath [NEW ENTRY]

4 Upper Bridge Street, Wye, Ashford TN25 5AF
TEL: (01233) 812540   FAX: (01233) 813033
EMAIL: reservations@wifeofbath.com
WEB SITE: www.wifeofbath.com

Restaurant-with-rooms in the heart of the village

In the centre of the High Street, this handsome, solid white house built in the eighteenth century (one-time home of the village doctor) is a well-established restaurant-with-rooms. To one side of the front door is the small bar with its old tiled floor and yellow walls and bench seating, while on the other are two interconnecting rooms with a bay window to the front which make up the restaurant. Kentish scenes decorate the walls, and in this fairly traditional setting a menu featuring locally grown produce such as asparagus and Kent duckling is served with a slight Asian influence – maybe lime salsa, soy and ginger dressing – along with more traditional combinations such as beef in a port wine sauce. Each of the five rooms is individually styled with white walls and fresh floral fabrics – Yeomans has high cruck beams and a pine four-poster. Two rooms are in the small cottages to the rear beside the car park – they share a small kitchen, where guests can prepare their own continental breakfasts if they so wish. Alternatively, full English breakfast is served in the house.

○ Closed 2 weeks Chr, 2 weeks in Aug; restaurant closed Sun & Mon eves ⊠ Wye village is off A28, a few miles north-east of Ashford. Drive into village; hotel is on right. Nearest train station: Wye. Private car park ⊨ 3 twin, 2 double, 1 four-poster; all with hair-dryer, direct-dial telephone, TV; some with trouser press ⊘ Restaurant, bar, garden; social functions ⟂ Wheelchair access to hotel and restaurant, 2 ground-floor bedrooms ● No dogs; no smoking ▭ Amex, Delta, MasterCard, Switch, Visa £ Single occupancy of twin/double £55, twin/double £75, four-poster £95; deposit required. Cooked B £7.50; set L £19.50, D £24.50; alc L, D £32.50. Special breaks available

---

YARMOUTH Isle of Wight   map 2

George Hotel

Quay Street, Yarmouth PO41 0PE
TEL: (01983) 760331   FAX: (01983) 760425
EMAIL: res@thegeorge.co.uk
WEB SITE: www.thegeorge.co.uk

Elegant townhouse hotel in a fabulous quayside setting

Though in a prime position overlooking the Solent, yards from the water's edge, this fine seventeenth-century Georgian townhouse is a world apart from the hubbub of the historic harbour and Lymington-bound ferry. Behind the pristine cream-washed façade with its flower-filled window boxes lies a peaceful retreat from the bustling village. From the calm of the wood-panelled lounge with its elegant furnishings, open fire and lived-in feel, to the sunny waterside garden, the hotel is conducive to relaxation. The cheerful brasserie, with its wood floors, pine furniture and flowery fabrics, is pleasingly unstuffy, while the smart restaurant – all deep red with stripy high-backed chairs and crisp white linen – is a more formal space designed for fine dining. You might perhaps choose poached oysters with parsley and caviar, then wild sea bass with seared scallop, cauliflower and olive oil purée, finishing with hot chocolate fondant with raspberries and coconut sorbet. Bedrooms are luxurious, decent-sized, light and airy, maybe with wood panelling and an antique four-poster or two. For a splurge, it may be worth splashing out on one of the sea-facing rooms with large balconies overlooking the Solent.

○ Open all year; main restaurant closed Sun & Mon eves ⊠ In centre of Yarmouth's square ⊨ 2 single, 13 double, 1 four-poster, 1 suite; all with room service, hair-dryer, direct-dial telephone, TV ⊘ 2 restaurants, bar, lounge, garden, private beach; conferences; social functions; civil wedding licence; early suppers for children; cots, highchairs ⟂ No wheelchair access ● No children under 12; no dogs in public rooms ▭ Delta, Diners, MasterCard, Switch, Visa £ Single £130, single occupancy of twin/double £130, twin £175, double £195, four-poster/suite £235; deposit required. Restaurant: set D £45; brasserie: alc L from £32.50, D from £35. Special breaks available

---

YATTENDON Berkshire   map 2

Royal Oak

The Square, Yattendon, Thatcham RG18 0UG
TEL: (01635) 201325   FAX: (01635) 201926
EMAIL: oakyattendon@aol.com

Friendly welcome at this village restaurant-cum-pub with tidy rooms

Tiny Yattendon is only a couple of miles from the M4, though you have to meander down country lanes to reach it as the nearest motorway exits are at either Reading or Newbury, both pretty much equidistant. That slight removal from the rush of traffic gives the village, and its central pub, a sleepily welcome air that invites you to linger longer. Most of the ground floor is given over to the pleasures of food and drink, either in the understated bar which has a cosy, local feel, or one in of the two eating areas. More relaxed is the brasserie, with its lovely fireplace, beamed ceiling and half-panelled walls, whereas the restaurant is a formal affair with smart tableware. Separating the two, a pleasant lounge marries big chintzy sofas and a fresh, restful décor. Things are just as spruce upstairs, where the cheery bedrooms are done out in pretty colours – maybe blue and gold, or pink and peach – and furnished with low-key elegance. After 30 years in the brewing trade, new proprietor William Boyle is turning his hand to hospitality and no doubt will soon turn his attention to those corners of the hotel that are looking a bit tired.

◑ Closed 1 Jan ⦿ In centre of Yattendon village. Private car park ⏛ 1 twin, 4 double; suite available; all with room service, hair-dryer, direct-dial telephone, TV ⟡ Restaurant, dining room, bar, lounge, garden; conferences, social functions; leisure facilities nearby; cots, highchairs ♿ No wheelchair access ● No children under 6 in restaurant eves; no smoking in bedrooms or restaurant ▭ Amex, Delta, MasterCard, Switch, Visa £ Single occupancy of twin/double £75 to £105, twin/double £105 to £130, suite £140; deposit required. Continental B £8, cooked B £11; set £15, alc L, D £28, service incl. Special breaks available ⒊FOR⒉

YELVERTON Devon
map 1

Old Orchard NEW ENTRY

Harrowbeer Lane, Yelverton PL20 6DZ
TEL: (01822) 854310 (AND FAX)
EMAIL: babs@baross.demon.co.uk
WEB SITE: www.baross.demon.co.uk/theoldorchard

Warm-hearted and homely B&B on the edge of Yelverton

With Dartmoor, Plymouth and the Eden Project all within striking distance, Ross and Barbara Greig's homely B&B is certainly well placed. The 1970 house is spacious, airy and beautifully kept with plenty of décor features considered the epitome of cool in those days: open-tread stairs, decorative slate and parquet floors. Barbara and Ross bring a welcoming friendliness to proceedings, greeting new arrivals with tea and scones and putting fresh milk in bedrooms along with fruit and biscuits. There is a pleasant and homely lounge with television, videos, games and lots of local information. Next door is the breakfast room where guests gather around a single large table (Barbara uses all organic foods). Bedrooms are very homely and comfortable with soft colours and floral patterns – it's not the cutting edge of style but it is dependably cosy and warm. The twin ventures out further than the others with an Egyptian theme.

◑ Open all year ⦿ From A38 at Plymouth take A386 for Tavistock; past Yelverton roundabout, take second right; at T-junction turn left up hill; hotel is second house on left. Private car park ⏛ 1 twin, 1 double; both with hair-dryer, TV; fax, laundry available ⟡ Breakfast room, lounge, garden; leisure facilities nearby; cots, highchairs, toys, babysitting ♿ No wheelchair access; 5 steps into hotel ● No smoking ▭ None accepted £ Single occupancy of twin/double £32, twin/double £51 to £56; deposit required. Light meals available ⒊FOR⒉

YORK North Yorkshire
map 9

Easton's

90 Bishopthorpe Road, York YO23 1JS
TEL: (01904) 626646 (AND FAX)
EMAIL: infoateastons@tiscali.co.uk

Comfy Victorian B&B just a short stroll from York's city walls

Anyone who has ever been to York will tell you what a boon it is to be able to park the car, so Lynne Keir's handily located B&B already scores bonus points. The double-fronted Victorian terrace has a façade of cream-glazed bricks, a period theme that continues inside its sizeable rooms. A tiled entrance hall opens on to a lounge and breakfast room scented with great sheaves of lilies and grandly adorned with fancy plaster friezes, grand marble fireplaces, antiques and William Morris-patterned wallpaper.

Bedrooms come in a variety of shapes and sizes, but all have a discernibly Victorian edge with more decorative wallpaper, patchwork bedspreads, and stripped pine doors. Room 8 is one of the nicest – light and airy with a double aspect, although its roadside position might be a problem for light sleepers; the top floor, too, has some characterful, quieter options, such as Room 5 with its sloping ceiling and antique wooden bed. One correspondent reported numerous problems with one room that was musty and dusty, but these faults appear to have been sorted out and were not visible on our inspection. There were, however, some signs of overdue maintenance in bathrooms. More reports welcome.

◑ Closed Chr & New Year ⏚ In York city centre. Nearest train station: York. Private car park ⏚ 1 twin, 8 double, 1 family room; all with hair-dryer, TV ⊘ Breakfast room, lounge, garden ⅓ No wheelchair access, 1 ground-floor bedroom ● No children under 5; no dogs; no smoking ⊟ None accepted £ Single occupancy of twin/double £36 to £40, twin/double £46 to £75, family room £66 to £77; deposit required. Special breaks available

---

Middlethorpe Hall

Bishopthorpe Road, York YO23 2GB
TEL: (01904) 641241   FAX: (01904) 620176
EMAIL: info@middlethorpe.com
WEB SITE: www.middlethorpe.com

Luxurious country-house style on the edge of town

Middlethorpe Hall has certainly seen good times and bad times since it was built in 1699: the solid red-brick house has been home to high society, then reached a rather low ebb as a nightclub before full restoration as a hotel brought back the top hat and champagne crew from York's nearby racecourse. A formal air hangs over its opulent public rooms – all classic stately-home pomp with their oak panels, oil paintings, antiques and twinkling chandeliers amid plush swagged curtains and chintzy sofas. The modern world puts in an appearance on your plate in the panelled grandeur of the Oak dining room, or the lighter surroundings of the Pineapple room; the dress code and formally correct service, however, still have roots in a bygone age. Contemporary pampering is at hand in a health and fitness spa unobtrusively disguised in a pair of converted cottages. Very plush bedrooms are in either the main house – generally grand affairs with high ceilings and period features – or in converted courtyard buildings; these have a lighter, more contemporary style with bold colours and bright fabrics, and, on the upper floors, exposed rafters.

◑ Open all year ⏚ 1½ miles south of York, beside York racecourse. Nearest train station: York. Private car park ⏚ 4 single, 10 twin/double, 5 double, 2 four-poster, 8 suites; all with room service, hair-dryer, trouser press, direct-dial telephone, modem line, TV; 3 with tea/coffee-making facilities ⊘ 2 dining rooms, drawing room, bar service, 2 libraries, gardens; conferences; social functions; civil wedding licence; gym, spa, heated indoor swimming pool; leisure facilities nearby ⅓ Wheelchair access to hotel (ramp) and dining room, WC, 9 ground-floor bedrooms in courtyard annexe, 1 suite specially equipped for disabled people ● No children under 8; no dogs; no smoking in dining room, some public rooms and some bedrooms ⊟ MasterCard, Switch, Visa £ Single £109 to £115, single occupancy of twin/double £140 to £155, twin/double £165 to £215, four-poster £285, suite £230 to £370; deposit required (prices valid till April 2005). Continental B £11.50, cooked B £15; set D £38, alc L £18.50; light meals available; service incl (prices valid till April 2005). Special breaks available

SCOTLAND

The Marcliffe at Pitfodels

North Deeside Road, Aberdeen AB15 9YA
TEL: (01224) 861000   FAX: (01224) 868860
EMAIL: stewart@marcliffe.com
WEB SITE: www.marcliffe.com

Expansion plans at this happy hybrid of city business hotel and country house

South of the border the old cliché is that the Scots are mean; in Scotland itself the baton passes to residents of the granite city. A stay at the Spence family's smart but welcoming hotel should kill such prejudices stone dead, run as it is with quiet good humour and generosity of spirit. Set in seven acres of grounds in the city's outskirts, the Marcliffe is a curiosity; the original white-harled building, sweeping staircase, flagstoned hallway, and swathes of plaid echo the country-house tradition. A modern extension, and a plethora of executive-friendly facilities like modem lines in many of the straightforward bedrooms, and conference rooms anchor it equally in the business market. Diners can choose between an airy conservatory bistro and the more formal Invery Restaurant; as you'd expect, local fish and seafood and Aberdeen Angus steak feature prominently. As we inspected, work was starting on smart new suites and a gym.

◖ Open all year ⤢ From A90 heading north, turn left on to A93 towards Braemar; hotel is 1 mile on right. Private car park ⤶ 12 twin, 23 twin/double, 5 family rooms, 2 suites; all with room service, hair-dryer, mini-bar, direct-dial telephone, TV, iron; some with trouser press, modem line, VCR, CD player ⨂ Restaurant, conservatory/dining room, bar, lounge, games room, garden; conferences; social functions; gym; leisure facilities nearby; early suppers for children; cots, highchairs, babysitting ♿ Wheelchair access to hotel and restaurant, National Accessible Scheme: mobility impairment M2, WC, 12 ground-floor bedrooms, 1 room specially equipped for disabled people, lift. Disabled parking ● No dogs in public rooms; no smoking in some public rooms and some bedrooms ▭ Amex, Diners, MasterCard, Switch, Visa £ Single occupancy of twin/double £115 to £155, twin/double £130 to £175, family room £150 to £195, suite £295; deposit required. Set Sun L £24.50; alc L, D £38 (2004 prices); light meals available; service incl. Special breaks available

Hawkcraig House

Hawkcraig Point, Aberdour KY3 0TZ
TEL: (01383) 860335
EMAIL: hawkcraig@btopenworld.com
WEB SITE: hawkcraighouse.co.uk

Delightful hosts and good food at a homely guesthouse with views over one of Scotland's national icons

Rail buffs from across the globe come to Elma Barrie's waterfront guesthouse just to enjoy the rail journey back and forth to Edinburgh across the famous bridge, visible from her upstairs lounge; it's a striking sight, especially when juxtaposed with the new Fife to Zeebrugge ferry which sails past nightly. What makes guests return, however, is the warm welcome, and Elma's accomplished repertoire of classic dishes, from local crab soup to Pittenweem halibut and clootie dumpling. Such pre-arranged dinners are served in a dainty blue dining room enlivened with Delft figures and artwork by Russell Flint. Guests have the run of a couple of sitting rooms. The upper has the better views. The other is a cosy affair presided over by a marvellously evocative photograph of Elma's grandfather. Bedrooms are simply decorated and comfortably furnished. Expect to be lulled to sleep by the Forth lapping at the shore.

◖ Closed Nov to Mar ⤢ Turn off A921 in Aberdour and follow Hawkcraig road to a large car park; drive through and down a very steep access road. Nearest train station: Aberdour. Private car park ⤶ 1 twin, 1 double; both with hair-dryer, TV; tea/coffee-making facilities on request ⨂ Dining room, 2 sitting rooms, conservatory; leisure facilities nearby ⅃ No wheelchair access; 4 steps into hotel, 18 steps into dining room, 2 ground-floor bedrooms ● No children under 10; no dogs; no smoking ⊟ None accepted £ Single occupancy of twin/double £36, twin/double £52. Set D £24; service incl

---

Creag-Ard House

Aberfoyle, Stirling FK8 3TQ
TEL: (01877) 382297 (AND FAX)
EMAIL: cara@creag-ardhouse.co.uk
WEB SITE: www.creag-ardhouse.co.uk

Great views and fine malts at a friendly guesthouse by the shores of Loch Ard

If you're minded to explore Loch Lomond & the Trossachs National Park, Cara and David Wilson's congenial Victorian guesthouse on the outskirts of the resort of Aberfoyle makes the ideal base. That said, the views of Loch Ard from the lounge/breakfast room and the two premier bedrooms are so inspiring that you might feel inclined to leave the bonnie, bonnie banks of Loch Lomond to the bumper-to-bumper day-trippers, and toast your good fortune with a selection from David's collection of malts. The public rooms understandably focus on the views, but if you can tear your gaze from the loch you'll find a pleasant interior, with stripped floorboards, cheerful, sunny décor and rustic-style wheelback chairs that seem entirely apposite when you tuck into a breakfast accompanied by warm home-baked scones. The bedrooms are tastefully decorated in smart blues and yellows or muted autumnal shades, and feature a sprinkling of antiques.

◑ Closed Nov to Feb   ⤢ From Aberfoyle take B829 towards Kinlochard. Creag-Ard House is 1¼ miles along the road, overlooking Loch Ard on the right-hand side. Private car park ⤴ 2 twin, 4 double; all with hair-dryer ⌀ Breakfast room, lounge, garden; tennis, private fishing; leisure facilities nearby ⅃ No wheelchair access ● No children under 12; no dogs in public rooms; no smoking ⊟ Delta, MasterCard, Switch, Visa £ Single occupancy of twin/double £45 to £60; twin/double £60 to £80; deposit required

---

Summer Isles Hotel

Achiltibuie, Nr Ullapool IV26 2YG
TEL: (01854) 622282   FAX: (01854) 622251
EMAIL: info@summerisleshotel.co.uk
WEB SITE: www.summerisleshotel.co.uk

A romantic and sophisticated seaside retreat

Sixteen miles down a single-track road on a peninsula overlooking the Summer Isles and the Hebrides is this oasis of civilisation, once an inn for fishermen and deer-stalkers. Gerry and Mark Irvine are charming hosts who are very aware of the needs of their guests and run a warm-hearted yet unobtrusive service for all. Gerry's own artwork adorns the walls of the public areas and these bursts of bold colour are a vibrant contrast to the tranquil, neutral décor of the bedrooms. The rooms in the main part of the hotel are stylish and comfortable, containing a mix of antiques and modern decorative twists such as ornamental driftwood, but it was the spacious 'Boat House' which our inspector fell in love with, featuring exposed stone walls, a wood-burning stove and split-level living space. The menus of both the hotel restaurant and the more informal and extremely popular Summer Isles Bar focus on local seafood and with over 500 bins of wine to choose from, you're bound to find something to suit your taste.

◑ Closed mid-Oct to Easter   ⤢ 10 miles north of Ullapool on A385, turn left onto a single-track road to Achiltibuie; village is 15 miles along; hotel is 1 mile further, on left. Private car park ⤴ 2 twin, 3 twin/double, 5 double, 3 suites; family rooms available; all with hair-dryer, direct-dial telephone; some with TV; no tea/coffee-making facilities in rooms ⌀ Restaurant, 2 bars, 2 lounges; early suppers for children ⅃ No

---

wheelchair access ◗ No children under 8; no dogs in public rooms; no smoking in bedrooms and most public rooms ⬚ MasterCard, Switch, Visa £ Single occupancy of twin/double £75, twin/double from £117, family room £210, suite from £190; deposit required. Set D £46; alc L £15; light meals available; service incl

---

ALLOWAY South Ayrshire map 11

Ivy House Hotel

2 Alloway, Ayr KA7 4NL
TEL: (01292) 442336 FAX: (01292) 445572
EMAIL: enquiries@theivyhouse.uk.com
WEB SITE: www.theivyhouse.uk.com

Smart hotel with popular restaurant, ideally situated for pilgrimages to the Bard's birthplace

Friday lunchtime and the restaurant at George and Eleanor Willock's rather stylish hostelry is buzzing with the Ayrshire contingent of the ladies who lunch. Even if the skies outside are so leaden that they would have failed to move the loquacious Burns to poetry, the Mediterranean colours, modish fabrics and modern art of the hotel's Courtyard Café and adjacent bar are instantly cheering. Whether you opt for brasserie fare like the smoked haddock gratin or classical à la carte offerings like grilled escalope of salmon and seared scallops, efficient service comes courtesy of sleek staff in long aprons, and there's a choice of cosy lounges to retire to over coffee. But it's in the bedrooms – striking spaces boasting contemporary colour schemes and light fittings – that the place comes into its own. 'Vintage' is a well-equipped symphony in green, and 'Blue Haven' a sure-fire enigma: there's nothing blue about it!

◑ Open all year; restaurant closed Sun eve ⬚ In centre of Alloway, 2 miles south of Ayr town centre. Nearest train station: Ayr. Private car park 🚗 1 twin, 2 double, 1 four-poster, 1 suite; all with room service, hair-dryer, direct-dial telephone, modem line, TV, VCR, CD player ✓ Restaurant, bar, lounges, conservatory, garden; conferences, social functions; leisure facilities nearby; highchairs ⓖ No wheelchair access ◗ No dogs; no smoking in bedrooms or restaurant ⬚ Amex, Delta, MasterCard, Switch, Visa £ Single £120, single occupancy of twin/double £120, twin/double/four-poster/suite £150; deposit required. Set L £14, D £20. Alc L, D £28; light meals available

---

ANNBANK South Ayrshire map 11

Enterkine House

Annbank, Ayr KA6 5AL
TEL: (01292) 520580 FAX: (01292) 521582
EMAIL: mail@enterkine.com
WEB SITE: www.enterkine.com

A world away from nearby Prestwick

There's something of that slightly wistful between-the-wars air about Oswald Browne's substantial whitewashed country house, set in large grounds some distance from the rather nondescript village of Annbank. It certainly feels a time-traveller's jaunt away from nearby Prestwick Airport, and its Ryanair-inspired bustle. The absence of a formal reception desk at the house helps to foster the illusion that you might be arriving for the social whirl of a country house-party, though this is no dark Scots baronial pile. Instead you are instantly enveloped in a sense of space and light, with white panelling and parquet flooring setting a bright, airy note in the hallway. Cool colours predominate in the capacious drawing room, while the restaurant blazes in sunshine yellow and fiery orange. Chef Douglas Smith's menu gallops around the globe, perhaps offering intriguing possibilities such as oriental confit spring rolls before a Scottish Buccleuch beef fillet. Bedrooms are in classic country-house mode.

◑ Open all year ⌧ On B742 on the outskirts of Annbank. Private car park ⨧ 5 twin/double, 1 double; suites available; all with room service, hair-dryer, trouser press, direct-dial telephone, TV ✓ Restaurant, drawing room, library, conservatory, garden; conferences and social functions; leisure facilities nearby; early suppers for children; highchairs, baby-sitting, outdoor play area ⧓ Wheelchair access to hotel (lift) and restaurant, WC, lift ● No dogs in public rooms ▭ Amex, Delta, Diners, MasterCard, Switch, Visa £ Single occupancy of twin/double £55 to £110, twin/double £110 to £220, suite £150 to £220; deposit required. Alc L £16.50, D £23.50/£37.50; light meals available; service incl. Special breaks available ③FOR②

APPLECROSS Highland   map 11

Applecross Inn

Applecross, Wester Ross IV54 8LR
TEL: (01520) 744262   FAX: (01520) 744400
EMAIL: applecrossinn@globalnet.co.uk
WEB SITE: www.applecross.uk.com

A remote inn which more than lives up to its Gaelic name of 'The Sanctuary'

Judith Fish will emphatically tell you that her business is not a gastropub, though the trendiest bars in Kensington could learn a few things about hospitality from her. She'd describe it as an old-style village inn, and certainly when we were inspecting, the lost mountaineers who arrived well after normal ordering hours appreciated the understanding welcome and sustenance they received. The bedrooms are bright and cheery and there is a formal restaurant should you want it, but the cosy bar is the real heart of Applecross, serving up real ales and man-sized portions to locals and holidaymakers alike. Claire Mansfield has maintained the high standards of the former chef, yet stamped the kitchen with her own ideas, bringing more vegetarian options to the menu and increased composting and recycling behind the scenes. Local specialities naturally feature, including a large selection of seafood but also spilling into the dessert menu – the raspberry cranachan was a divine concoction of Drambuie-soaked oatmeal, raspberries, honey, meringue and cream. The views of Raasay, Skye and the Cuillins are pretty stunning too and if you're lucky, you may well spy deer, seals, otters or eagles as you watch the sun go down.

◑ Closed 20 Dec to 1 Jan ⌧ In Applecross village. Private car park ⨧ 1 single, 2 twin/double, 2 double, 2 family rooms; 4 with shared facilities; all with hair-dryer ✓ Dining room, bar/restaurant, lounge, garden; social functions; early suppers for children; cots, highchairs, toys ⧓ No wheelchair access ● No children in restaurant eves, no dogs in public rooms, £5 in bedrooms; smoking in bar only ▭ Delta, MasterCard, Switch, Visa £ Single £28, single occupancy of double £35 to £45, twin/double £55 to £70, family room £70 to £90; deposit required. Set D £25; alc L £15, D £25; light meals available

---

ARISAIG Highland   map 11

Old Library

Arisaig PH39 4NH
TEL: (01687) 450651   FAX: (01687) 450219
EMAIL: reception@oldlibrary.co.uk
WEB SITE: www.oldlibrary.co.uk

A picture-postcard setting for this restaurant-with-rooms

The oldest part of this whitewashed house was built in 1750 as stables for the original Arisaig House, which later burnt to the ground. It is right on the waterfront and commands panoramic views of Loch nan Ceall and the Inner Hebrides, including Eigg and Rum. Proprietor Jilly's attitude is 'If it ain't broke, don't fix it,' and so has changed little in the couple of years she's been here with husband Michael. The dining room upholstery and curtains are in 'Lindsay ancient' tartan, muted shades of red and purple complementing the white walls. Bedrooms in the back extension aren't as character-filled as those at the front, which have stunning views, king-sized beds and power showers. In the restaurant, the couple know that with local ingredients this fresh, you don't need to add too much, so the predominantly seafood menu is simply cooked: monkfish, scallops and salmon

steaks marinated in herbs and oil, then grilled or baked.

❶ Open all year ⑦ On waterfront, in centre of Arisaig. Nearest train station: Arisaig ⬛ 1 twin, 5 double; all with hair-dryer, direct-dial telephone, TV ⑦ Restaurant, garden; leisure facilities nearby ⑤ No wheelchair access ● No dogs; no smoking ▭ Amex, Delta, MasterCard, Switch, Visa ⑤ Single occupancy of twin/double from £40, twin/double from £60; deposit required. Alc L £15, D £22; light meals available

---

Balmory Hall

Isle of Bute PA20 9LL
TEL: (01700) 500669 (AND FAX)
EMAIL: tony@balmoryhall.com
WEB SITE: www.balmoryhall.com

Unabashed luxury with a total lack of pretension in a country house with a definite wow factor

A one-time Salvation Army home for elderly gentlemen of the road may seem an unlikely entrant to the luxury B&B market, but thanks to the vision of Tony and Beryl Harrison that's exactly the role that the lovingly restored Balmory Hall can claim. Set amid lush parkland, the Hall's façade confides a certain diffident affluence, but it's once the door opens to reveal a hallway of stupendous grandeur that visitors realise that they've arrived somewhere very special indeed; one

might be forgiven for thinking that the classical music that drifts from the gracious drawing room-cum-breakfast area is intended simply to mask the sound of jaws hitting the floor, as their owners take in the flamboyant fusion of classical columns, playful cherubs and gilded balustrade. The bedrooms are barely less opulent, with sumptuous soft furnishings, and pampering extras from CD players to living flame fires. Gourmet breakfasts provide the perfect finishing touch.

❶ Open all year ⑦ About 3 miles south of Rothesay ferry terminal. From terminal, follow coast road A644 for 3 miles; at 30mph derestriction sign turn right into Balmory Road; hotel is 120 yards, at end of road. Private car park ⬛ 1 twin, 1 double, 1 four-poster; all with hair-dryer, TV, CD player; 1 with trouser press ⑦ Breakfast room, drawing room, garden ⑤ No wheelchair access; 10 steps into hotel, 1 ground-floor bedroom ● No children under 12; no dogs; no smoking ▭ Delta, MasterCard, Switch, Visa ⑤ Single occupancy of twin/double £60 to £75, twin/double £124, four-poster £144; deposit required

---

Gleneagles

Auchterarder PH3 1NF
TEL: (01764) 662231 FAX: (01764) 662134
EMAIL: resort.sales@gleneagles.com
WEB SITE: www.gleneagles.com

Peerless leisure facilities at a slick resort operation that proves big needn't be bad

In an unworthy moment it flashed across our inspector's mind that the Ferrari nonchalantly positioned beside the main entrance resembled a photo-shoot prop; a variant on the old estate agent's trick of flaunting glamour to make a property seem aspirational. A quick recce of the car park, however, revealed that the Italian dream machine wasn't without a stable-mate or two; at Gleneagles such stunts just aren't necessary. The hotel's sheer scale, coupled

with interior art deco flourishes, invites respect, but it's the evident professionalism of the staff and the variety of activities on offer – from shooting to falconry, riding to fishing and golf to spa treatments – that makes this resort unique. Food comes in many guises, but the tone is set by the capacious Strathearn Restaurant, where the likes of pan-roasted Crinan scallops, Highland venison and ginger and rhubarb crème brûlée wave a flag for tradition. Bedrooms are all you'd expect.

○ Open all year ⚡ On A823, just off A9, midway between Stirling and Perth. Nearest train station: Gleneagles. Private car park 🚗 8 single, 47 twin, 205 double, 13 suites; family rooms available; all with room service, hair-dryer, mini-bar, trouser press, direct-dial telephone, modem line, TV; some with VCR, CD player ✅ 4 restaurants, 3 bars, library, conservatory, games room, garden; conferences and social functions; gym, spa, tennis, heated indoor swimming pool, outdoor hot pool, other leisure facilities; early suppers for children; cots, highchairs, playroom, babysitting ♿ Wheelchair access to hotel and restaurants (ramps), WC, 11 ground-floor bedrooms, 3 rooms specially equipped for disabled people, lift. Disabled parking ● No dogs in public rooms, £15 per night in bedrooms; no smoking in some bedrooms 💳 Amex, Delta, Diners, MasterCard, Switch, Visa £ Single and family room rates on application, twin/double from £265, suite from £605; deposit required. Set D £45 (Strathearn); alc D and light meals available. Special breaks available

---

AULDEARN Highland   map 11

Boath House

Auldearn, Nairn IV12 5TE
TEL: (01667) 454896   FAX: (01667) 455469
EMAIL: wendy@boath-house.com
WEB SITE: www.boath-house.com

Georgian country-house hideaway with accomplished cuisine in tranquil surroundings

Don and Wendy Matheson's Grade-A listed Georgian mansion on the Moray Firth has been superbly restored, and their warm welcome makes this a hotel you will want to return to again and again. Bedrooms are immaculately finished, one even having double slipper baths in which you can recline to enjoy views of the lochan and the surrounding 20 acres of grounds, fruit and vegetable gardens and beehives. Décor in the public areas is fresh and bold and includes plenty of contemporary art. The five-course table d'hôte menus have received much praise and might feature a celeriac and lemon velouté with truffle dumplings, roasted saddle of black-faced lamb on artichoke hearts with chive flower fritters, and a double chocolate brownie with vanilla and jasmine ice cream. Service is discreet, professional and friendly. Complete the relaxing element to your stay with a visit to the in-house spa, which specialises in ayurvedic treatments, a branch of beauty therapy which aims to calm and harmonise.

○ Closed Chr ⚡ Leave Nairn on eastbound A96; hotel is 2 miles on left. Private car park 🚗 4 twin/double, 2 four-poster; all with room service, hair-dryer, direct-dial telephone, TV, CD player ✅ Restaurant, 2 lounges, library, conservatory, garden; conferences; social functions; spa; early suppers for children; cots, highchairs, babysitting, baby-listening ♿ Wheelchair access to hotel (ramp) and restaurant, WC, 1 ground-floor bedroom, specially equipped for disabled guests. Disabled parking ● No dogs in public rooms; no smoking 💳 Amex, MasterCard, Switch, Visa £ Single occupancy of twin/double £110, twin/double £170, four-poster £200; deposit required. Set L £29.50, D £45. Special breaks available

---

BALLANTRAE South Ayrshire   map 11

Glenapp Castle

Ballantrae KA26 0NZ
TEL: (01465) 831212   FAX: (01465) 831000
EMAIL: info@glenappcastle.com
WEB SITE: www.glenappcastle.com

One of Scotland's élite corps of hotels – just the ticket for a major splurge

In one of Robert Louis Stevenson's swashbucklers his protagonist is known as the Master of Ballantrae. This fictional creation may be the master, but there's no doubt that in modern Ballantrae the king of the castle is most definitely Graham Cowan who, with wife Fay, runs Glenapp as a dauntingly exclusive, but refreshingly unstuffy, country house in the grand tradition. And they really don't come much grander. There's nothing at the entrance to indicate that this impressive faux-medieval-cum-baronial pile is a hotel, so admission is secured via a controlled-entry system that opens the gates to those passing muster, allowing them to negotiate the winding woodland road, and discover the delights of manicured lawns and arboretum. Inside, the tone is set by a magnificent oak-panelled hallway, which opens out to reveal a succession of light, airy rooms of impeccable taste and traditional style. Bedrooms and food reflect similar lofty standards.

● Closed Nov to Mar (open for exclusive use at New Year) ⚡ Head south out of Ballantrae village; cross bridge over River Stinchar and turn first right; 1 mile ahead are gates to Glenapp Castle. Private car park ⬛↵ 7 twin, 8 double, 2 four-poster, 2 suites, family suites available; all with room service, hair-dryer, trouser press, direct-dial telephone, modem line, TV, VCR, CD player; tea/coffee-making facilities on request ⬧ 2 dining rooms, lounge, library, gardens; conferences; social functions; tennis; early suppers for children; cots, highchairs, toys, babysitting, baby-listening, outdoor play area ♿ Wheelchair access to hotel (ramp) and dining rooms (lift), restaurant (ramp), WC, lift, 7 ground-floor bedrooms, 1 room specially equipped for disabled guests ● No children under 6 at dinner; no dogs in public rooms and some bedrooms; smoking in library only ▭ Amex, Delta, MasterCard, Switch, Visa £ Single occupancy of twin/double £255 to £395, twin/double/four-poster £365 to £515, family suite £505 to £525, suite £425 to £445 (rates include dinner); deposit required. Special breaks available (3FOR2)

BALLATER Aberdeenshire   map 11

Balgonie Country House

Braemar Place, Ballater AB35 5NQ
TEL: (013397) 55482   FAX: (013397) 55497
EMAIL: balgoniech@aol.com
WEB SITE: www.balgonie-hotel.co.uk

Accomplished food at a confident country house in the heart of Royal Deeside

In this neck of the woods the words 'country house' usually conjure up a flamboyant, but essentially rather dark and sombre, baronial pile. John and Priscilla Finnie's *belle époque* house, built with a nod to Arts & Crafts style amid three acres of garden appears therefore as something of a mould-breaker, with its deep soffits, pavilion-style balustrade and clean lines blurred only by a veil of creeper cladding. Indoors the décor favours pastels or neutral colours which accentuate the sense of space and light, and this together with the modern art in the bar adds a contemporary vigour to essentially traditional rooms. Stained glass, Paisley-pattern upholstered chairs and Margaret Loxton vineyard prints add a dash of colour to the dining room, where the likes of spinach soup, spiced crab cake with avocado, and seared bass with saffron tagliatelle consistently impress. A sprinkling of antiques adds character to the comfortable bedrooms.

● Closed Jan and Feb ⚡ At western edge of Ballater, off A93. Private car park ⬛↵ 1 single, 3 twin, 5 double; all with room service, hair-dryer, direct-dial telephone, modem line, TV; tea/coffee-making facilities on request ⬧ Dining room, bar, lounge, gardens; social functions; early suppers for children; cots, highchairs ♿ No wheelchair access ● No dogs in public rooms ▭ Amex, Delta, Diners, MasterCard, Switch, Visa £ Single £60 to £80, single occupancy of twin/double £60 to £80, twin/double £100 to £135; deposit required. Set L £19.50, D £35; light meals available. Special breaks available (3FOR2)

Darroch Learg

Braemar Road, Ballater AB35 5UX
TEL: (013397) 55443   FAX: (013397) 55252
EMAIL: info@darrochlearg.co.uk

Elegant but comfortable country house with great views, good food and thoughtful owners

When our inspector called, Fiona Franks was setting things up for one of the monthly classical concerts that help anchor this imposing, detached Victorian house firmly within the local community. And this quietly elegant but essentially unflashy hotel is the sort of place where locals and visitors alike can feel at home from the get-go, thanks to a winning array of public rooms. These range from a comfy lounge that teams plaid sofas and floral drapes, through a cosy smokers' retreat with honesty bar, to a bright restaurant with lashings of modern art and contemporary halogen lighting. David Mutter's cooking skilfully harnesses the traditional and the modish, so you might follow breast of squab with roast saddle of Deeside hare and a classic lemon tart. Bedrooms in the original house feature lofty ceilings and fine antiques – but those in the extension may compensate with picture windows that frame terrific views of Lochnagar.

❍ Closed Chr & 3 weeks in Jan ⛫ At western edge of Ballater, off A93. Private car park 🛏️ 7 twin/ double, 3 double, 2 four-poster; family rooms available; all with room service, hair-dryer, trouser press, direct-dial telephone, TV ⊘ Restaurant, 3 lounges, conservatory, gardens; conferences; social functions; early suppers for children; cots, highchairs, toys ♿ Wheelchair access to hotel (ramp) and restaurant, National Accessible Scheme: mobility impairment M3, 1 ground-floor bedroom ● No dogs in public rooms; smoking only in smoking room ▭ Amex, Diners, MasterCard, Switch, Visa £ Single occupancy of twin/double £65 to £87, twin/double £90 to £164, four-poster £120 to £204, family room £140 to £224; deposit required. Set L £22, D £38.50; light meals available; service incl. Special breaks available

---

BALQUHIDDER Stirling map 11

Monachyle Mhor

Balquhidder, Lochearnhead FK19 8PQ
TEL: (01877) 384622   FAX: (01877) 384305
EMAIL: info@monachylemhor.com
WEB SITE: www.monachylemhor.com

Expansion under way at this innovative hotel that's setting the pace for bedroom design among Scotland's rural hotels

Tom Lewis just isn't one to rest on his laurels. Not content with installing a clutch of bedrooms that bring cutting-edge metropolitan style to the remote shores of Loch Voil, he's adding a brace of master suites that will only serve to confirm this couthy-looking, pink-harled, vernacular-style hotel with sensitively converted outbuildings as one of Scotland's most inviting. And reasons to visit aren't in short supply. For a start there's the glorious lochside position. Then you have a bijou bar with its settle and blazing fire, a cosy retreat with melt-in-the-mouth scones or shortbread on a damp or dreich day. Best of all is Tom's largely home-grown or locally sourced food; an inspection lunch of celeriac and apple soup followed by wild River Forth salmon with a ginger and spring onion crust was perfectly judged and brilliantly executed. Bedrooms eschew conventional rustic whimsy for bold, modern style, and state-of-the-art gadgets.

❍ Closed Jan ⛫ 11 miles north of Callander, turn off A84 at King's House Hotel; continue on glen road for 6 miles; hotel is on right. Private car park 🛏️ 1 twin/double, 3 double, 1 family room, 6 suites; all with hair-dryer, direct-dial telephone, TV, CD player; some with modem line, DVD ⊘ Dining room, bar, lounge, conservatory, garden; conferences; early suppers for children ♿ Wheelchair access to hotel and restaurant, WC, 3 ground-floor bedrooms. Disabled parking ● No children under 12; dogs in 2 bedrooms only; no smoking in bedrooms ▭ MasterCard, Switch, Visa £ Single occupancy of twin/double £65 to £95, twin/ double £95, family room £140, suite £145 to £220; deposit required. Set L £21.50, D £37; alc L £21.50; light meals available

---

BANCHORY Aberdeenshire map 11

Banchory Lodge

Dee Street, Banchory AB31 5HS
TEL: (01330) 822625   FAX: (01330) 825019
EMAIL: enquiries@banchorylodge.co.uk
WEB SITE: www.banchorylodge.co.uk

Traditional Deeside hotel, run with a sense of old-fashioned courtesy

Hospitality has been offered at Margaret Jaffray's genteel Deeside hotel since its days as a sixteenth-century coaching inn, and a Georgian makeover and more recent extension merely serve to underline its timeless quality. The position, right on the Dee where it meets the River Feugh, is just about the area's finest, and the vernacular architecture chimes perfectly with its setting. The interior is a pleasing assembly of wood panelling, ornate cornicing and abundant paintings, and the furnishings and décor, from gilt mirrors to well-dressed windows and sunny colour-schemes, complement the classical proportions of the main public rooms. The somewhat hearty food has a slant as traditional as the dining room in which it is served; perhaps asparagus and prawn roulade, followed by duo of duck and venison on a woodland mushroom sauce, and sticky toffee pudding. Bedrooms are modelled in pretty country-house style. Staff are warm and friendly.

◖ Open all year ⚡ In Banchory, turn south down Dee Street; hotel is 400 yards on left. Private car park 🛏 4 twin, 10 double, 2 four-poster, 6 family rooms; all with room service, hair-dryer, direct-dial telephone, TV ⚕ Dining room, breakfast room, bar, 2 lounges, games room, garden; conferences and social functions; leisure facilities nearby; early suppers for children; cots, highchairs, baby-listening, outdoor play area ⅙ No wheelchair access ● None ▭ Amex, Delta, Diners, MasterCard, Switch, Visa £ Single occupancy of twin/double £75, twin/double/four-poster £130, family room £140; deposit required. Set L (Sun) £18.50, D £24.50; light meals available; service incl. Special breaks available

---

BRAE Shetland   map 11

Busta House

Brae, Shetland ZE2 9QN
TEL: (01806) 522506   FAX: (01806) 522588
EMAIL: reservations@bustahouse.com
WEB SITE: www.bustahouse.com

Unpretentious and comfortable island hotel in the Guide's *most northerly location*

This hotel has a mixed clientele: it provides a good stopping-off point for business people en route to the oil terminal at Sullom Voe, and is also frequented by travellers touring the Shetland Islands. The hotel reflects this in its style, which is a blend of country-house hotel and corporate features such as modem connection in some rooms. The oldest part of the house is a well-maintained stone building dating from 1588 with crow-step gables and its very own ghost: a seventeenth-century woman deemed unsuitable to marry, searching in vain for her dead lover and long-lost son. The more modern extensions are well harmonised and the views of Busta Voe and the harbour are excellent. Bedrooms are adequately though not extravagantly furnished and all have been re-decorated in the past year. With a four-course restaurant menu for £30 including dishes like paupiettes of haddock fillet with smoked salmon, baked with pink prawns and citrus butter, this hotel plays to its strengths in terms of local seafood. The bar menu is equally good value.

◖ Closed 2 weeks at Chr ⚡ Hotel is signposted on main road, 2 miles north of Brae. Private car park 🛏 2 single, 11 twin, 7 double, 1 four-poster, 1 suite; all with room service, hair-dryer, trouser press, direct-dial telephone, some with modem line, TV ⚕ Restaurant, bar, sitting room, library, garden; social functions; early suppers for children; cots, highchairs, toys ⅙ No wheelchair access ● No dogs in public rooms; no smoking in some public rooms and some bedrooms ▭ Amex, Delta, Diners, MasterCard, Switch, Visa £ Single £75, single occupancy of twin/double £80, twin/double £100 to £110, four-poster £110, suite £140. Set D £30; alc L £15, D £30; light meals available; service incl

---

BRODICK North Ayrshire   map 11

Kilmichael Country House

Glen Coy, Brodick, Isle of Arran KA27 8BY
TEL: (01770) 302219   FAX: (01770) 302068
EMAIL: enquiries@kilmichael.com
WEB SITE: www.kilmichael.com

Elegant, secluded country house on lovely Costa Clyde island

The island of Arran is famous for mustard and its aromatic unguents – things to add a bit of spice or froth to life. You might also add a little pizzazz to a jaded lifestyle by spending a few days at Geoffrey Botterill and Anthony Butterworth's handsome, immaculately whitewashed seventeenth-century house, situated a couple of miles from Arran's main ferry terminal at Brodick. Once across the threshold guests encounter a series of graceful and effortlessly tasteful rooms, featuring restful colour schemes, rich soft furnishings and a liberal sprinkling of intriguing artefacts from India and the East. Dinner, served in the airy dining room, might involve the likes of Arran hot smoked salmon, chicken with smoked mussels and mango parfait with its own wee pavlova. There are antiques aplenty in the impressive bedrooms, some of which are in the main house and the rest (including the delightful Smithy, Byre and Dovecote rooms) in the Courtyard. All are unimpeachably restful.

❍ Closed Nov to mid-March; restaurant closed Tue eve ⟲ From ferry drive in direction of Lochranza, carry along seafront; at sports ground turn inland between floodlight and church; hotel is at end of private drive. Private car park 🛏 1 twin, 2 double, 2 four-poster, 2 suites; all with room service, hair-dryer, trouser press/iron, direct-dial telephone, TV, CD player; some with VCR ⊘ Dining room, 2 bar/lounges, study, garden; leisure facilities nearby ♿ Wheelchair access to hotel (1 step) and dining room, WC, 6 ground-floor bedrooms. Disabled parking ● No children under 12; no dogs in public rooms; smoking in 1 lounge only ⊟ Delta, MasterCard, Switch, Visa £ Single occupancy of twin/double room £85 to £95, twin/double £120 to £150, four-poster £140 to £170, suite £160 to £190; deposit required. Set D £35; service incl. Special breaks available

---

CALLANDER Stirling
map 11

Leny House

Leny Estate, Callander FK17 8HA
TEL: (01877) 331078 FAX: (01877) 331335
EMAIL: res@lenyestate.com
WEB SITE: www.lenyestate.com

Delightful Trossachs views at a superb and warmly run country-house B&B

If Dr Finlay, whose television adventures were filmed in these parts, had ever needed to prescribe an antidote to urban stress, a short stay at Leny House would have fitted the bill admirably. It's not just that this is a fine, baronial house with all the turrets and crow-stepped gables your heart could desire, or that the interiors are sumptuous, or even its noble pedigree in hospitality (its first B&B guests were Jacobites marching to their doom in 1745). The clincher is the winning personality of chatelaine Frances Roebuck, who seems as comfortable feeding her angora goats as she is discussing the finer points of interior design, and is completely lacking in pretension. She and her furniture restorer have collaborated in creating stylish, memorable bedrooms and impeccably elegant, appositely grand public rooms. Imaginative breakfasts are served house-party style in a gracious dining room. The Lade Inn on the estate serves evening meals in convivial, traditional surroundings.

❍ Closed Oct to Easter ⟲ On A84, 1 mile north-west of Callander. Private car park 🛏 1 twin, 2 four-poster; all with hair-dryer, trouser press, TV ⊘ Breakfast room, drawing room, garden; leisure facilities nearby ♿ No wheelchair access ● No children under 12; no dogs; no smoking ⊟ Delta, MasterCard, Switch, Visa £ Twin/four-poster £120; deposit required

---

  Denotes somewhere you can rely on a good meal – either the hotel features in the 2005 edition of our sister publication, The Good Food Guide, *or our inspectors thought the cooking impressive, whether particularly competent home cooking or more lavish cuisine.*

'It appeared to be a relief when on the last night we were not in for dinner and nobody was staying for the next three days. "You know, we like to be full at weekends, but with our other business it's a break if we are not busy during the week."'
On a hotel in Derbyshire

map 11

Willowburn Hotel

Clachan-Seil, Isle of Seil, Oban PA34 4TJ
TEL: (01852) 300276   FAX: (01852) 300597
EMAIL: willowburn.hotel@virgin.net
WEB SITE: www.willowburn.co.uk

Smashing views and friendly folk, a world away from bustling Oban

The Bridge over the Atlantic sounds like an engineering project to overshadow the Channel Tunnel; in fact it's a photogenic humpback construction dating back to 1793, which links Clachan-Seil ('the Isle of Willows') to mainland Argyll a few miles south of Oban. Even after a couple of centuries the island feels like a place apart, and this – and the self-evident care with which the couple run operations – may explain why, even on a Monday night in April, Chris and Jan Wolfe's venture offered no vacancies. The building is a low-slung, whitewashed affair, with hanging baskets (and a patrol of ducks) to add colour. It's a civilised place, with neat, comfortable bedrooms, and books to browse while relaxing in the cosy lounge; but the telescope at the picture window tells its own story – this is a place to look out across the Sound, rather than in. Dinner is a five-course set menu, included in room rates, and majors on local ingredients, including lobster.

❶ Closed Dec to Feb   ↗ Take A816 south from Oban for 7 miles; turn right on to B844 at Kilninver; follow road for 7 miles, cross humpback bridge and hotel is ½ mile on left. Private car park   ⬅ 1 single, 1 twin, 2 twin/double, 3 double; all with hair-dryer, TV, CD player   ✓ Dining room, bar, lounge, garden   ᚻ No wheelchair access   ● No children under 8; no dogs in some public rooms; no smoking   ☐ Delta, MasterCard, Switch, Visa   £ Single £72, single occupancy of twin/double £102, twin/double £144 (rates incl dinner); deposit required. Special breaks available

 map 11

Clint Lodge

Clintmains, St Boswells, Melrose TD6 0DZ
TEL: (01835) 822027   FAX: (01835) 822656
EMAIL: clintlodge@aol.com
WEB SITE: www.clintlodge.co.uk

The country-house experience delivered with warmth and good humour

As well as holding large tracts of the Highlands, the Dukes of Sutherland own a hunting lodge near Melrose, at the other end of Scotland. For this we should give thanks, as the lodge operates as a smart guesthouse, enabling those unlikely ever to trouble a ducal guest-list to enjoy a taste of aristocratic living. Passage into this other world is eased with grace and warmth by Bill and Heather Walker, who have the knack of making guests relax, whether they've come to shoot or fish or prefer enjoying the area's literary and historical beats. There are fine, late-Victorian features including elaborate cornicing and gilded mirrors in the gracious drawing room, and candelabra add to the sophisticated atmosphere in the dining room, where Heather's menus might feature smoked haddock fish cakes and Border lamb. Dinners are enjoyed house-party style, with Bill presiding as host. Bedrooms are distinctly top-drawer, and views are simply stunning.

❶ Open all year   ↗ From A68 at St Boswells, take B6404 for 2 miles, then turn left on to B6356 (signposted Clint Lodge, Scott's View and Earlston); drive through Clintmains village veering left and follow road to Clint Lodge, on right after 1 mile. Private car park   ⬅ 1 single, 4 twin/double; all with hair-dryer, trouser press, TV   ✓ Dining room, drawing room, sitting room, conservatory, garden; conferences and social functions; leisure facilities nearby; early suppers for children; cots, highchairs, toys, outdoor play area   ᚻ No wheelchair access   ● No smoking in bedrooms   ☐ MasterCard, Switch, Visa   £ Single £42, single occupancy of twin/double £50 to £60, twin/double £70 to £84. Set D £25   ③FOR②

COLBOST Highland

map 11

Three Chimneys

Colbost, Dunvegan, Isle of Skye IV55 8ZT
TEL: (01470) 511258 FAX: (01470) 511358
EMAIL: eatandstay@threechimneys.co.uk
WEB SITE: www.threechimneys.co.uk

Forget the pressures of modern life in these converted crofters' cottages

Shirley and Eddie Spear are design-conscious in all that they've set out to achieve in this remote corner of the Isle of Skye. Their attention to detail cannot be faulted – look for the Caithness slate on the floors of the restaurant, or on the doors of the bedrooms. The interior design of both the Three Chimneys restaurant and the guest rooms in the House Over-by was largely done by local designers and artists. Bedrooms are modern but not minimalist, with flat-screen televisions, laminate floors, French doors leading onto the meadows beyond and rich tangerine and mustard soft furnishings. Shirley's innovative evening menus undoubtedly attract many visitors, but the Scottish breakfast, featuring smoked venison and kedgeree, is a tempting option in its own right. The fact that the past year has been 'heinously busy' is a testament to the success of their vision, despite the doubts which many had years ago about the wisdom of opening a top-of-the-range restaurant-with-rooms in such an isolated location.

◖ Closed 3 weeks in Jan ⤴ From Dunvegan take B884 single-track road signposted Glendale; Colbost is 5 miles along. Private car park ⟵ 1 twin, 5 double; family rooms available; all with hair-dryer, mini-bar, direct-dial telephone, TV, DVD, VCR, CD player; some with room service ⊘ Restaurant, bar, lounge area, breakfast room, garden; social functions; leisure facilities nearby; early suppers for children; cots, highchairs, toys, baby-listening ♿ Wheelchair access to hotel (ramp) and restaurant, 6 ground-floor bedrooms, 1 room specially equipped for disabled people. Disabled parking ● No children under 8 in restaurant eves; no dogs; no smoking ▭ Amex, Delta, MasterCard, Switch, Visa £ Twin/double £155 to £215, family room from £215. Set L £25, D £45; light lunches available. Special breaks available

DORNOCH Highland

map 11

2 Quail

Castle Street, Dornoch IV25 3SN
TEL: (01862) 811811
EMAIL: goodhotel@2quail.com
WEB SITE: www.2quail.com

Hospitable owners ensure a comfortable stay in this pretty seaside village

It took Michael and Kerensa Carr two years to strip all the wood in their Victorian home but it was a worthwhile project as the cottage now exudes an air of homeliness and intimacy, reflected by the scale of the operation, which has capacity for a mere twelve diners and six overnight guests. Michael formerly worked at both Le Caprice and the Ritz, so his credentials as a top-quality chef aren't disputed, although our inspector found the breakfast menu of a Scottish grill or kippers somewhat predictable. Samples of the evening menus looked more inviting and the couple certainly know their wines. Having had negative experiences of unreliable paid staff, Michael and Kerensa prefer to do everything themselves, right down to the washing up, ensuring high standards of service throughout. The three bedrooms are spacious and comfortably furnished in a range of period styles, and Molton Brown smellies always add a touch of luxury to the bathroom, even if the mechanical toilet is a necessary evil of staying in such a charming conservation area.

◖ Closed Chr, 2 weeks in Feb/Mar, restaurant closed Sun & Mon eves ⤴ Entering Dornoch on A949, restaurant is on left 200 yards before cathedral ⟵ 1 twin, 1 twin/double, 1 double; family rooms available; all with hair-dryer, direct-dial telephone, modem line, TV; 1 with VCR ⊘ Restaurant, lounge, library; cots, baby-listening ♿ No wheelchair access ● No children under 8 exc babes in arms; no dogs; no smoking

Amex, Delta, MasterCard, Switch, Visa £ Single occupancy of twin/double £60 to £85, twin/double £70 to £85, family room £90 to £120; deposit required. Set D £35.50

DRUMNADROCHIT Highland   map 11

Polmaily House

Loch Ness, Drumnadrochit, Inverness IV63 6XT
TEL: (01456) 450343   FAX: (01456) 450813
EMAIL: polmaily@btinternet.com
WEB SITE: www.polmaily.co.uk

An action-packed break beckons at this family-friendly hotel

'Never work with children or animals' goes the old saying, but Sonia Whittington-Davis has chosen to do both at her Victorian hotel, set in the countryside near Loch Ness. As you advance up the long tree-lined driveway, the large grounds give a good indication of what to expect: forget manicured topiaries and think equipment-strewn lawns instead. Activities available include swimming, trampolining, horse riding, tennis, fishing, snooker, and use of a range of videos and computer consoles and games for teenagers. For adults there are sun beds and holistic massage. Pets' feeding hour will bring animal-loving children into contact with many species, from goats to golden-mantle posellas (parrots to you and me), while the evening Monster Club will bring parents into contact with the after-dinner liqueur of their choice and a bit of well-earned peace and quiet. The hotel's Mauritian chef produces a variety of uninteresting dishes, and now there's a Dutch head waiter so a cosmopolitan angle to your break is possible even in the Scottish Highlands. Bedrooms are spacious and functional.

◑ Open all year 🗲 From Inverness take A82 to Drumnadrochit, then take A831 towards Cannich for 2 miles; hotel is on right. Private car park 🛏 2 single, 1 twin, 2 double, 2 four-poster, 6 suites; family rooms available; all with room service, hair-dryer, direct-dial telephone, TV, VCR, ironing facilities ⧆ Restaurant, bar/conservatory, lounge, library, games rooms, garden; conferences and social functions; tennis, heated indoor swimming pool, horse riding, fishing; early suppers for children; cots, highchairs, toys, playroom, babysitting, baby-listening, outdoor play area, evening club ♿ Wheelchair access to hotel and restaurant, WC, 1 ground-floor bedroom specially equipped for disabled people ● No dogs in public rooms; no smoking in restaurant and bedrooms ▢ MasterCard, Switch, Visa £ Single £40 to £72, single occupancy of twin/double £65 to £122, twin/double/four-poster £80 to £144, family room £105 to £187; suite from £80 (prices valid till Feb 2005); deposit required. Set D £22; alc L £14; light meals available. Special breaks available ③FOR②

DUNKELD Perthshire & Kinross   map 11

Hilton Dunkeld House

Dunkeld PH8 0HX
TEL: (01350) 727771   FAX: (01350) 728924
EMAIL: reservations.dunkeld@hilton.com
WEB SITE: www.hilton.co.uk/dunkeld

A chain hotel with character – plus a splendid location and a full menu of activities

If only all chain hotels were like this! From the moment you drive through the turreted archway and past the twin gatehouses there's a hint that this one is a little different: you glimpse the Tay meandering through the 280-acre estate, and the towered house, built a century ago by the Duke of Atholl, hoves into view. A later extension may resemble an Alpine resort sanatorium, but full-blooded Scottish baronial style reasserts itself as soon as you enter the reception, which has stained glass and burnished wood. Venture into the bar or airy Garden Restaurant, and manager Philip Rolfe's admirably friendly and professional staff look after you with warmth and aplomb, whether you want a delicious lunchtime hot green foccacia salad, a hearty dinner of venison or beef, or simply a peaty malt. Public areas are sprinkled with plaids, and restful bedrooms feature warm and autumnal tones.

◑ Open all year 🔁 From Perth take A9 towards Inverness; after 12 miles turn right and follow signs for Blairgowrie. In Dunkeld, pass car park on left and follow hotel signposts to right. Nearest train station: Dunkeld & Birman. Private car park 🛏 21 twin, 8 twin/double, 55 double, 1 four-poster, 3 family rooms, 8 suites; all with room service, hair-dryer, trouser press, direct-dial telephone, modem line, TV; some with ironing facilities ⌁ Restaurant, bar, 2 lounges, garden; conferences and social functions; gym, spa, tennis, heated indoor swimming pool; leisure facilities nearby; early suppers for children; cots, highchairs, babysitting, baby-listening 🦽 Wheelchair access to hotel (ramp) and restaurant, WC, 23 ground-floor bedrooms, 2 rooms specially equipped for disabled people, lift. Disabled parking ⬤ No dogs; no smoking in some bedrooms 🔲 Amex, Delta, Diners, MasterCard, Switch, Visa £ Single occupancy of twin/double £158, twin/double £178 to £199, four-poster £238 to £258, family room £153 to £203, suite £228 to £248. Set L £19.50, D £29; alc L £23; light meals available

Kinnaird

Kinnaird Estate, Dunkeld PH8 0LB
TEL: (01796) 482440   FAX: (01796) 482289
EMAIL: enquiry@kinnairdestate.com
WEB SITE: www.kinnairdestate.com

Calm and gracious country house within a vast Highland sporting estate

If you have a penchant for nostalgia and the good things in life, Kinnaird is the place for you. There's something about this hybrid Georgian-Edwardian mansion that conjures up a world in which the First World War never happened, the Union flag still flutters over half the globe, and news comes via uniformed telegram boys on bicycles rather than by shrill mobile phones. More remarkably, it pulls off the trick of achieving this, plus an air of grandeur, without being stuffy. A judicious eye for design has teamed all the characteristics of the classic country house – the rich fabrics, blazing fires, acres of wood-panelling – with striking works of art, including bronzes by Nick Deans (who designed the ladies *en déshabillé* flanking the entrance) and magnificent frescoes. Modern-accented food – perhaps poussin, followed by brill with fried langoustine and ginger risotto – makes the dining experience memorable. Sumptuous bedrooms feature living-flame fires and decanters of Kinnaird's own spiced whisky liqueur.

◑ Open all year 🔁 From Perth, take A9 until 1½ miles beyond Dunkeld; stay on A9 (do not enter village), then take B898 towards Dalguise; hotel is signposted 4½ miles on right. Private car park 🛏 8 double, 1 suite; all with room service, hair-dryer, trouser press, direct-dial telephone, modem line, TV, VCR, CD player; no tea/coffee-making facilities in rooms ⌁ 2 dining rooms, 2 lounges, study, games room, beauty treatment room, gardens; conference and social functions; tennis; leisure facilities nearby; early suppers for children 🦽 Wheelchair access to hotel (ramp) and dining rooms, WC, 1 ground-floor bedroom, lift ⬤ No children under 12; no dogs; no smoking in dining rooms 🔲 Amex, MasterCard, Switch, Visa £ Single occupancy of double £225 to £375, double/suite £275 to £425 (rates incl dinner); deposit required. Set L £30; light meals available

The Pend

5 Brae Street, Dunkeld PH8 0BA
TEL: (01350) 727586   FAX: (01350) 727173
EMAIL: molly@thepend.sol.co.uk
WEB SITE: www.thepend.com

Fine furniture, imaginative food and an extensive wine list

Peter and Marina Braney are careful, professional and considerate hosts, so it may exasperate them that the fan mail to this central, Georgian guesthouse is addressed to housemates Molly and Bridie. But since the girls are photogenic West Highland terriers, who patrol the Pend to ensure that new arrivals get the friendliest of welcomes, the couple are phlegmatic about playing second fiddle. And they do so with aplomb. Guests eat in the welcoming dining room with its honesty bar and posh swag-and-tail drapes. There is a wine list with over 100 bins, designed to accompany imaginative dinners: perhaps roast garlic and goats' cheese with French bread croûtons, followed by roast mallard with rose-petal confit, and ricotta winter pudding. Better still are the spacious, handsome guest bedrooms (which share two bathrooms), simply decorated in contemporary colours, but furnished with delightful antiques, and buttressed with surprising extras such as mini-fridges. And all for a bargain price, bang in the centre of this popular tourist village.

◖ Open all year 🔁 In centre of Dunkeld. Brae Street is off High Street, opposite road to market cross and cathedral; house is 30 yards up hill, on right. Nearest train station: Dunkeld & Birnam. Private car park 🛏 1 double, 2 family rooms; all with shared bathrooms; all with hair-dryer, TV; 1 with trouser press, VCR ⌀ Dining room/bar; leisure facilities nearby; early suppers for children; cots, highchairs, toys, babysitting, baby-listening ♿ No wheelchair access; 2 steps into hotel, 20 steps into dining room, 2 ground-floor bedrooms ● No smoking in dining room ⊟ Amex, Delta, Diners, MasterCard, Switch, Visa £ Single occupancy of double £33, double £65, family room rates on application; deposit required. Set D £22.50; light meals available; service incl ③FOR②

DUNOON Argyll & Bute
map 11

Enmore Hotel

111 Marine Parade, Dunoon PA23 8HH
TEL: (01369) 702230   FAX: (01369) 702148
EMAIL: enmorehotel@btinternet.com
WEB SITE: www.enmorehotel.co.uk

A tale of two design styles at this family-run hotel on the Holy Loch

The long, whitewashed Georgian building, sitting with a certain prim elegance overlooking the Firth of Clyde, and with a backdrop of the Cowal peninsula, looks like the epitome of tradition – and, as you enter the public areas, that is exactly what you get. The blue and cream reception hallway, the autumnally toned sitting room and hunting prints in the dining room all provide nothing to frighten the horses. Despite 25 years at the helm, however, Angela and David Wilson still have a few tricks up their sleeves, and they reveal these with a flourish as guests are ushered to the bedrooms, which flaunt a distinctly contemporary, and sometimes racy, sensibility, whether in the blue and lilac frenzy of Room 5, with its split-level layout and heart-shaped double spa bath, or the grandeur of the four-poster and flamboyant gilded swan bathroom fittings in Room 8. David's menus often feature locally smoked salmon and other native delights.

◖ Closed mid-Dec to mid-Feb 🔁 On seafront at Kirn, 1 mile north of centre of Dunoon on A815. Private car park 🛏 2 twin/double, 3 double, 3 four-poster, 1 family room; all with room service, hair-dryer, mini-bar, direct-dial telephone, TV; 2 with VCR, 1 with trouser press, CD player ⌀ Restaurant, bar, lounge, garden; conferences and social functions; leisure facilities nearby; early suppers for children; cots, highchairs, toys, babysitting, baby-listening ♿ No wheelchair access ● No smoking in bedrooms ⊟ Amex, Delta, MasterCard, Switch, Visa £ Single occupancy of twin/double £59 to £75, twin/double £75 to £90, four-poster £110 to £150, family room £100 to £140; deposit required. Set L £23, D £26; alc L £25, D £29; light meals available; service incl. Special breaks available

---

EDAY Orkney
map 11

Sui Generis Guest Rooms **NEW ENTRY**

Redbanks, Eday KW17 2AA
TEL: (01857) 622219 (AND FAX)
EMAIL: guestrooms@suigenerisfurniture.co.uk
WEB SITE: www.suigenerisfurniture.co.uk/guest.htm

Stylish accommodation at this far-flung furniture emporium

The name means 'one of a kind' and, for once, that's no exaggeration. You won't have stayed anywhere quite like Colin and Sherry Kerr's endearingly eccentric creation, which is located a few minutes' walk from the ferry terminal on the island of Eday. The couple are refugees from southern England, and Colin saw the then-derelict croft as the ideal base for his business as a bespoke furniture maker. We're talking master craftsman here – his work has been commissioned for St Magnus Cathedral. The croft includes a gallery, but several of Colin's very individual pieces are on display in the guesthouse. The Sequoia sitting room is a remarkable, bohemian space with a warming peat fire, where guests take breakfast and evening meals. Sherry's hearty dinners include vichyssoise, shepherd's pie and chocolate marquise. The well-equipped bedrooms feature beautiful craft furniture and striking décor – the double has green-waxed oak panelling amid a nautical design, while the twin has a slightly more contemporary feel. Both have remarkably arty, en-suite shower cabinets with designs by Colin.

● Closed Oct to Mar ☑ Leaving ferry terminal, take first road left; Sui Generis is first crofthouse on right, at 300 yards. Private car park 🛏 1 twin, 1 double; both with shared WC; both with hairdryer, TV; fridge available ✅ Dining/sitting room, library, gardens ᵹ No wheelchair access; 2 steps into dining/sitting room, 2 ground-floor bedrooms ● No children under 10; no dogs, no smoking in bedrooms ☐ None accepted £ Single occupancy of twin/double £45, twin/double £70; deposit required. Set L, D £10; light meals available; service incl

---

EDINBURGH Edinburgh   map 11

The Bonham

35 Drumsheugh Gardens, Edinburgh EH11 2TB
TEL: 0131-226 6050   FAX: 0131-226 6080
EMAIL: reserve@thebonham.com
WEB SITE: www.thebonham.com

Modern mix of styles in a Victorian townhouse

Drumsheugh Gardens is an ordinary looking terrace of large Victorian townhouses, but the Bonham has made a valiant attempt to stand out from the crowd. From its trademark crimson spiral *chaise longue* in the lounge to its eclectic range of antique or reproduction bath tubs, via the fabric sculptures haunting the main stairs, it offers the largely business clientele who frequent it something different from the run-of-the-mill. Its virtues are its range of good-sized bedrooms, some colourful, some soothing; its efficient service; and its large, bright restaurant, which runs the length of the house and is decorated with appropriate culinary photographs. Here, the lunchtime offering is especially popular and good value, the two-course option being perhaps sugar snap and lettuce soup followed by wild mushroom, grape and Shropshire blue risotto.

● Open all year ☑ From the West End (Hope Street), follow Queensferry Street through two sets of traffic lights; turn left into Drumsheugh Gardens, then first right; hotel is at end on right. Nearest train stations: Edinburgh Haymarket and Edinburgh Waverley. Private car park 🛏 10 single, 36 twin/double, 2 suites; family rooms available; all with room service, hair-dryer, mini-bar, trouser press, direct-dial telephone, modem line, TV, CD player ✅ Restaurant, lounge; conferences and social functions; leisure facilities nearby; cots, highchairs ᵹ Wheelchair access to hotel (ramp at rear) and restaurant, WC, 1 room specially equipped for disabled people, lift ● No dogs; no smoking in most public rooms and most bedrooms ☐ Amex, Delta, Diners, MasterCard, Switch, Visa £ Single £145, single occupancy of twin/double £165; twin/double £170 to £195, family room £225 to £245, suite £295 to £330; deposit required. Cooked B £7.50; set L £15; alc D £30; light meals available. Special breaks available

---

The Howard

34 Great King Street, Edinburgh EH3 6QH
TEL: 0131-557 3500   FAX: 0131-557 6515
EMAIL: reserve@thehoward.com
WEB SITE: www.thehoward.com

Classy town hotel with quiet charm

Perfect for celebrities, who would attract little more than a raised eyebrow here, the Howard hides behind its simple brass plaque in one of Edinburgh's smartest Georgian streets. Soothing colour schemes, a peaceful drawing room, and a liberal sprinkling of polished antiques create a relaxing townhouse atmosphere, while the smoothly efficient staff act much like personal butlers. Rooms are exceedingly tasteful, not always huge, but universally comfortable. The Tower suites in the basement are perhaps not as nice as the smaller rooms upstairs, which get more light and better views. The Atholl restaurant offers classy food, such as white bean and blue cheese soup, grilled tuna with scallops and summer berry mille-feuille, in a sunny front room.

◐ Closed 25 to 28 Dec **⚡** On Great King Street, east of Dundas Street. Nearest train station: Edinburgh Waverley. Private car park **🛏** 2 single, 1 twin, 10 double, 1 four-poster, 4 suites; all with room service, hair-dryer, trouser press, direct-dial telephone, modem line, TV, CD player **✓** Restaurant, breakfast room, lounge; conferences; social functions; cots, highchairs, babysitting **&** No wheelchair access; 1 ground-floor bedroom **◐** No dogs; no smoking in restaurant **▭** Amex, Delta, Diners, MasterCard, Switch, Visa £ Single £108 to £145, single occupancy of twin/double £175 to £210, twin/double £180 to £295, four-poster £296 to £355, suite £356 to £475; deposit required. Set L, D £32.50; light meals available; service incl. Special breaks available

---

Malmaison Edinburgh

1 Tower Place, Leith, Edinburgh EH6 7DB
TEL: 0131-468 5000   FAX: 0131-468 5002
EMAIL: edinburgh@malmaison.com
WEB SITE: www.malmaison.com

A smart, genial business hotel in a prime position on Leith's waterfront

A few years ago, the Edinburgh Malmaison stood virtually on its own in the soon-to-be-reclaimed surroundings of Leith docks. The vision that led the chain to purchase the isolated old Seamen's Mission has been rewarded. Now, expensive apartments, tranquil water vistas, young trees and smart street furniture speak of an area on the move, and of money to be spent. Only the fading carved 'Sailors' Home' above the doorway reminds you of the less prosperous past. Blessed with a good building (and a whole unobtrusive block of new rooms), the Edinburgh Malmaison seems to be keeping standards high. There's a subtle change of emphasis, with less in-your-face branding than of old, a slight smartening of menu and surroundings in the refurbished bistro restaurant, and less banging on about the wonders of the mini-bars. A hotel (and perhaps a chain) now confident of itself, in other words. With good reason. It's pleasing to find that the new rooms are as sizeable and as comfortable as the old ones, and that housekeeping standards are well up to scratch. The staff are friendly and efficient, too. On a sunny day, there's a patch of grass on which to enjoy a drink or snack from the bar, and reckon that life as a guest here is not at all bad.

◐ Open all year **⚡** Take A900 from city centre to Leith; hotel is situated on waterfront. Nearest train station: Edinburgh Waverley. Private car park **🛏** 18 twin, 74 double, 3 four-poster, 6 suites; family rooms available; all with room service, hair-dryer, mini-bar, trouser press, direct-dial telephone, modem line, TV, CD player **✓** Restaurant, bar; conferences; social functions; gym; leisure facilities nearby; cots, highchairs, babysitting, baby-listening **&** Wheelchair access to hotel and restaurant, WC, 4 rooms specially equipped for disabled people, lift. Disabled parking **◐** No dogs **▭** Amex, Delta, Diners, MasterCard, Switch, Visa £ Twin/double/family room from £135, four-poster/suite £170; deposit required. Continental B £9, cooked B £12; set L, D £13; alc L, D £25. Special breaks available

---

The Scotsman Hotel

20 North Bridge, Edinburgh EH1 1YT
TEL: 0131-556 5565   FAX: 0131-652 3652
EMAIL: reservations@thescotsmanhotelgroup.co.uk
WEB SITE: www.thescotsmanhotel.co.uk

Newspaper's HQ converted into a smart hotel

From one of the best locations in Edinburgh, perched high above Princes Street Gardens, you can see nearly everything going on in the east end of Edinburgh. The proprietors of Scotland's best-known newspaper endowed their Victorian baronial building with a marble-swathed reception area and a massive lobby. The lobby, now additionally garnished with curving steel staircases, has become the brasserie and breakfast bar of the hotel, while green-uniformed staff cluster to welcome you in the reception area. Bedrooms are smartly outfitted in smoky tweeds and blues. Each has the *de rigueur* Edinburgh Monopoly set and bath or shower rooms in charcoal, white or grey. As you rise higher in the building, the views generally get more magnificent and the prices more astounding. Alas, not every room has a view, and it has

taken some crafty interior design in the sitting room (calfskin sofas, raffia and glass coffee tables) to distract the eye from the blank walls outside the window. Down in the Vermilion restaurant, backlit wine bottles and crisp cream table linen do the same job, as perhaps would the foie gras, saddle of lamb with onion purée, or pear tarte Tatin.

◗ Open all year 🗲 On North Bridge, next to Waverley station, between the Royal Mile and Princes Street. Nearest train station: Edinburgh Waverley. Valet parking 🛏 13 twin/double, 43 double, 13 suites; family rooms available; all with room service, hair-dryer, mini-bar, trouser press, direct-dial telephone, modem line, TV, DVD, CD player ⊘ Restaurant, brasserie/breakfast bar, drawing room; conferences and social functions; gym, spa, heated indoor swimming pool, private cinema; leisure facilities nearby; cots, highchairs, babysitting ♿ Wheelchair access to hotel (ramp) and restaurant (lift), WC, 2 rooms specially equipped for disabled people, lift ⬤ No children in Vermilion restaurant eves; no dogs or smoking in some public areas; dogs £25 in bedrooms ▭ Amex, Delta, Diners, MasterCard, Switch, Visa £ Single occupancy of twin/double from £185, twin/double from £195, suite from £365, family room rates on application; deposit required. Continental B £14.50, cooked B £17.50; set D £39; alc L £27.50, D £30.50; light meals available. Special breaks available

Seven Danube Street

7 Danube Street, Edinburgh EH4 1NN
TEL: 0131-332 2755 FAX: 0131-343 3648
EMAIL: seven.danubestreet@virgin.net
WEB SITE: www.sevendanubestreet.com

An admirable B&B in a tranquil area of Edinburgh's New Town

Fiona Mitchell-Rose's house is in one of the rather grand stone terraces down beside the Water of Leith, only a few minutes by bus from the city centre but well removed from its noise and bustle. Guests can enjoy the late-Georgian proportions of the splendid breakfast room, where bookcases on one side and a big black marble fireplace on the other frame the tall windows. It's a homely room, with a collection of decanters on view, and other curiosities, such as an egg-decapitator (which might well double as a thumbscrew) making an unexpected

appearance. Bedrooms, on the basement level, are sweetly stylish. The big double has a half-tester with a chintzy canopy; the single is snug and neat, and there's a view of the garden from the room to the rear. There are an additional two rooms in the same mode in a separate flat just round the corner, which is usually let as self-catering. In Fiona's words, breakfasts consist of home-made everything you can think of, while she makes a praiseworthy attempt to seek out the best blends of coffee that she can.

◗ Closed Chr 🗲 In city centre, ½ mile north of Princes Street, between Queensferry Road and Raeburn Place. Nearest train stations: Edinburgh Waverley and Edinburgh Haymarket 🛏 1 single, 1 twin/double, 1 double; all with hair-dryer, direct-dial telephone, modem line, TV ⊘ Breakfast room, garden; leisure facilities nearby; cots, highchairs, toys ♿ No wheelchair access ⬤ No dogs in public rooms; no smoking ▭ MasterCard, Switch, Visa £ Single £55 to £70, single occupancy of twin/double £60 to £90, twin/double £95 to £130; deposit required

Six Mary's Place

6 Mary's Place, Raeburn Place, Edinburgh EH4 1JH
TEL: 0131-332 8965 FAX: 0131-624 7060
EMAIL: info@sixmarysplace.co.uk
WEB SITE: www.sixmarysplace.co.uk

Friendly, comfortable and well-designed guesthouse

The Stockbridge area of Edinburgh is close to the centre, but has managed to keep a

genuine village atmosphere, and here Mary's Place is set slightly back from the main street. In a row of neat, late-Georgian houses, Number Six is run in admirable style by Forth Sector, a mental health charity. There are a lot of plus points, the chief one being the relaxed and cheerful atmosphere. It's a place where everyone is obviously welcome, and this is mirrored in the clean, bright design. Big, colourful squashy sofas in the living room go surprisingly well with the Georgian features. Coffee and tea are always on, as is the free internet access. The bedrooms, equipped with IKEA-style furniture and with pastel-coloured televisions, are peaceful; the shower rooms are spotless. A big basement space makes a wonderful family room, with laminated floor, pale lemon walls and wiggly mirrors. Breakfast – all vegetarian, with hash browns or veggie haggis – is eaten in a warm conservatory extension. Beyond it, a surprisingly spacious garden beckons, with benches and a trickling fountain.

◗ Closed Chr ⤢ From Princes Street, go north up Frederick Street and Howe St; turn left to N.W. Circus Place and continue into Raeburn Place; hotel is directly opposite Shelter shop. Nearest train stations: Edinburgh Waverley and Edinburgh Haymarket ⬅ 2 single, 2 twin, 3 double, 1 family room; all with hairdryer, direct-dial telephone, modem line, TV ✅ Breakfast room/conservatory, living room, garden; conferences and social functions; leisure facilities nearby; cots, highchairs, toys ♿ No wheelchair access ● No dogs; no smoking ▭ Delta, MasterCard, Switch, Visa £ Single £40 to £50, single occupancy of twin/double £60 to £70, twin/double £70 to £90, family room £120 to £150; deposit required ③FOR②

The Witchery by the Castle │NEW ENTRY│

Castlehill, The Royal Mile, Edinburgh EH1 2NF
TEL: 0131-225 5613   FAX: 0131-220 4392
EMAIL: mail@thewitchery.com
WEB SITE: www.thewitchery.com

Beguiling, extravagant rooms in a historic location

James Thomson's passion for culling panelling, church furniture and Gothic antiques from ancient buildings has enabled him to add five more lavishly decorated rooms to the Witchery, meaning that romantic weekends may not have to be booked quite so far in advance. The location, at the very gates of Edinburgh Castle, could hardly be better, while the narrow alleyways leading between sixteenth-century stone houses create a frisson of expectations before you even set foot in the rooms. Once inside, you find an antiquarian's imagination run riot, with swathes of velvet, carved wood, and quirky antiques. In the bedrooms, organ pipes form the bedhead in The Vestry while church vestments hang on the back of the door; The Library is crowded with statuettes and candlesticks – its bathroom is lined with leather bookends, while at the press of a button, a vast television rises from a chest like a vampire from a coffin. Bathrooms are even more extravagant than the bedrooms, with huge roll-top baths, and there are small, tucked-away kitchens too. The restaurant is almost sober by comparison. But here too, the same joyous mixture of genuine history and wonderful pastiche sit side by side. A turret stair leads from one corner of the carefully contrived courtyard, and you sit under a Scottish painted ceiling based on ones from Holyrood Palace while working your way through shellfish bisque, pumpkin risotto, and brioche bread and butter pudding with blueberries.

◗ Closed 24 to 26 Dec ⤢ At top of Royal Mile, at entrance to castle. Nearest train station: Edinburgh Waverley ⬅ 7 suites; all with room service, hair-dryer, direct-dial telephone, TV, DVD, CD player ✅ 2 restaurants, courtyard; social functions; leisure facilities nearby ♿ No wheelchair access ● No dogs ▭ Amex, Delta, Diners, MasterCard, Switch, Visa £ Suite £250; deposit required. Alc L, D £35; light meals available

'Breakfasts were dismal, with badly prepared grapefruit, tiny portions of very dry smoked haddock and ineptly poached eggs. The coffee was some of the thinnest we've ever had.'
On a hotel in Cambridgeshire

'Rare, medium and well done all appeared to mean the same thing, and the vegetables turned up very late.'
On a hotel in Gloucestershire

map 11

Edenwater House

Ednam, Kelso TD5 7QL
TEL: (01573) 224070   FAX: (01573) 226615
EMAIL: relax@edenwaterhouse.co.uk
WEB SITE: www.edenwaterhouse.co.uk

Sophisticated food and bags of bonhomie at this small and civilised Borders country house

When our inspector called, Jeff Kelly was busy in the garden, tweaking the colonnade (reclaimed from a local stables) that he had recently added to the garden façade of this pleasing former manse. The pillars, and a new pergola, enhance an already idyllic garden, lapped by the races of Eden Water. Things are equally special indoors, with public areas flooded by light, the better to enjoy the sculptures, paintings and *objets d'art* that bestow a distinctive flavour, not least in the artfully arranged but decidedly restful drawing room. Jacqui Kelly is a collector of antique linen, and crisply handsome table settings are a suitable canvas for her set menus. These promise all manner of mouthwatering treats; perhaps fillet of sea bass on lemon spinach, followed by suprême of guinea fowl basted with foie gras, and cheese with sautéed pears, with a wine list of similar calibre. Bedrooms, like the hosts, are warm and inviting.

◑ Closed first 2 weeks in Jan & Aug; dining room closed Sun to Tue   ▣ Take B6461 from Kelso to Ednam; house overlooks river, next to church. Private car park   ⤶ 1 twin/double, 2 double; all with hair-dryer, TV   ⟋ Dining room, drawing room, study, garden; social functions; leisure facilities nearby   ㅤ No wheelchair access   ● No children under 10; no dogs; no smoking   ▭ Delta, MasterCard, Switch, Visa   £ Single occupancy of twin/double £55 to £65, twin/double £90 to £95. Set D £35; service incl. Special breaks available

map 11

The House of Mark

Invermark, Glenesk by Edzell, Brechin DD9 7YZ
TEL: (01356) 670315
EMAIL: bea.houseofmark@btinternet.com
WEB SITE: www.thehouseofmark.com

Homely, welcoming guesthouse with a sense of fun

Even among the unjustly neglected Angus glens, Glenesk is little visited, partly because of its no-through-road status. For those lucky enough to be in the know, that is its major charm. Bea Rawlinson's externally plain but comfortable and welcoming enterprise, sprinkled with family photos and treasures, provides another. Her guests may conclude they've stepped into a Tardis, as the house seems emphatically bigger within, where a nostalgic, traditional style, choreographed around some very fine pieces of furniture, prevails. Restrained colours and tied-back drapes add a hint of formality to the lounge, while meals are enjoyed in a large, yet cosy, dining-kitchen, with plaid wall-covering, striking sideboard and wood-burning stove. Bea's food is imaginative and often rich; perhaps pheasant and pasta soup, followed by mountain hare with walnuts, and fig and port ice-cream. Bedrooms are tasteful and comfortable. The standing stones in the garden provide a talking point; they're a recent addition by mischievous Bea.

◑ Open all year   ▣ From A90 north of Brechin, take B966 through Edzell; after 1 mile, cross North Esk river and take road on left signposted Glenesk, Tarfside, Invermark; continue for 15 miles to house. Private car park   ⤶ 2 twin, 1 double; 2 with shared bathroom; all with hair-dryer; no tea/coffee-making facilities in rooms   ⟋ Dining room/kitchen, lounge, garden; cots   ㅤ No wheelchair access   ● No children under 12, no dogs; no smoking   ▭ None accepted   £ Twin/double £52 to £60. Set D £18; packed lunches available; service incl   (3 FOR 2)

Isle of Eriska

Eriska, Ledaig, Oban PA37 1SD
TEL: (01631) 720371   FAX: (01631) 720531
EMAIL: office@eriska-hotel.co.uk
WEB SITE: www.eriska-hotel.co.uk

Yet more opportunities for pampering about to be unveiled at this grand but convivial country house

You might think that the combination of a flamboyant and opulent Victorian pile, the location (a private island reached by a bridge), plus a millennium of history (the island's name commemorates Norseman Eric the Red) would tempt hoteliers to rest on their laurels. No danger of that when the hoteliers are the Buchanan-Smiths who, with three decades of stewardship under their belts, continue exploring ways of making the guest experience even more special. This means sensibly celebrating the turreted building's stately features, including its panelled grand hall and classically elegant drawing room, cherishing rituals like morning coffee and afternoon tea, yet finding ways to innovate. The most recent involve sumptuous conversions of outbuildings, and expansion of the spa and treatment facilities, allowing guests to detoxify in luxury. Food is accomplished, with favourites like roast pork, Highland venison and apple crumble sensitively tweaked for modern sensibilities. Bedrooms offer top-drawer style and comfort.

◖ Closed Jan ⚡ From A85 north of Oban, turn over bridge on to A828 at Connel; continue for 4 miles to north of Benderloch; follow signs from here to Eriska. Private car park 🛏 2 single, 15 twin/double, 4 suites; all with room service, hair-dryer, trouser press, direct-dial telephone, modem line, TV; some with VCR, CD player; 1 with fax ✓ Dining room, bar, drawing room, lounge, library, conservatory, garden; conferences; social functions; gym, spa, tennis, heated indoor swimming pool; early suppers for children; cots, highchairs, babysitting, baby-listening ♿ Wheelchair access to hotel (ramp) and dining room, National Accessible Scheme: mobility impairment M2, WC, 2 ground-floor bedrooms specially equipped for disabled people. Disabled parking ● No dogs in public rooms; no smoking in dining room ▭ Amex, Delta, MasterCard, Switch, Visa £ Single £140 to £200, twin/double £260, suite £350; deposit required. Alc D £38.50; light meals available; service incl. Special breaks available

Forss House

Forss, Thurso KW14 7XY
TEL: (01847) 861201   FAX: (01847) 861301
EMAIL: john@forsshousehotel.co.uk
WEB SITE: www.forsshousehotel.co.uk

A peaceful hotel as far north on the mainland as you can get

Approaching from the south on a dreary day, Forss House appears grey and dour, but the perception of new arrivals quickly changes when they see the 271 malt whiskies on offer in the bar and log fires blazing in reception. Bedrooms are named after Scottish places and are furnished in a straightforward style, with pine and palatable amounts of tartan materials. New owners Ian and Sabine Richards have begun a major upgrade of the hotel and are hoping to attract more corporate clients, so it will be interesting to see if the hotel is still as popular with recreational fishing parties when we next visit. The conservatory is a bright and airy location for breakfast with views over the Caithness countryside (you can fish in Forss Falls only ten metres from the door), while the dining room is more formal but no less elegant. The new chef continues to use locally sourced ingredients, such as beef, for example, served with shallot marmalade and braised celery Madeira jus.

◖ Open all year ⚡ On A836, 5 miles west of Thurso, beside Bridge of Forss. Private car park 🛏 7 twin, 6 double; all with room service, hair-dryer, trouser press, direct-dial telephone, modem line, TV ✓ Restaurant, bar, lounge, conservatory, garden; conferences and social functions; leisure facilities nearby; early suppers for children; cots, highchairs   ♿ Wheelchair access to hotel and restaurant, 6 ground-floor bedrooms, 1 room specially equipped for disabled people   ● Dogs in some bedrooms only; no smoking in bedrooms   ▭ Amex, Delta, MasterCard, Switch, Visa   £ Single occupancy of twin/double £60, twin/double £95. Set D £27.50; light meals available; service incl. Special breaks available   (3FOR2)

FORT WILLIAM Highland   map 11

The Grange

Grange Road, Fort William PH33 6JF
TEL: (01397) 705516   FAX: (01397) 701595
EMAIL: info@thegrange-scotland.co.uk
WEB SITE: www.thegrange-scotland.co.uk

Turrets and bay windows, sculpted trees and garden statues herald your arrival at this top-of-the-range B&B

Joan and John Campbell took years to renovate this Victorian house, stripping it to the brick and ignoring the architect's advice when their vision was stronger than his doubts. Each bedroom is of a high standard, with extras such as binoculars and sherry, but each has a character of its own. The Rob Roy room was Jessica Lange's choice when she was here shooting the film of the same name. Its colonial-style bed and marble bathroom lend it an air of grandeur, making it a favourite with regular guests. The Terrace room, perhaps predictably, has a private terrace, a Victorian slipper bath and Louis

XV king-sized bed while the Turret and Garden rooms are furnished in French oak and have views of Loch Linnhe. In the spacious lounge Joan has hit the right balance between the contemporary and the traditional, and her design ideas, such as display bowls of conkers, work well. Breakfasts are a real treat, with light alternatives to the usual options such as oatcakes, fruit and yoghurt platters or poached salmon on potato pancakes with chive crème fraîche. Joan is a bubbly hostess who easily manages all with good grace.

◑ Closed late Oct to Mar   ⊉ Off A82, at top of Ashburn Lane. Nearest train station: Fort William. Private car park ⟵ 4 double; all with hair-dryer, TV   ⊘ Lounge, breakfast room, garden; leisure facilities nearby   ♿ No wheelchair access; 1 ground-floor bedroom   ● No children under 13; no dogs; no smoking   ▭ MasterCard, Visa   £ Twin/double £88 to £98; deposit required

Inverlochy Castle

Torlundy, Fort William PH33 6SN
TEL: (01397) 702177   FAX: (01397) 702953
EMAIL: info@inverlochy.co.uk
WEB SITE: www.inverlochycastlehotel.com

Billing itself as 'Scotland's finest country house hotel' Inverlochy Castle certainly charges top-notch prices and has an illustrious list of former guests ranging from Queen Victoria to Robert De Niro. Compared to Utopia by one guest, according to the visitors' book, it may well be another man's idea of claustrophobia if a sedate pace of life and collars and ties are not to your taste. Gentlemanly pursuits are de rigueur here, from catching one's own fish for dinner to clay-pigeon and pheasant shooting on the

3,000 acres of castle land. Indoors, the elegance of the Great Hall cannot be denied, with its Venetian crystal chandeliers and French Empire-style frescoed ceilings. In the restaurant, the prodigious furniture was a gift from the King of Norway. Here you can expect to feast on dishes such as loin of rabbit with risotto and an asparagus velouté. Upstairs, bedrooms are of course sumptuous and your every need is catered for by the faultless management and their team of complaisant staff.

◑ Closed 6 to 12 Jan   ⊉ On A82, 3 miles north of Fort William town centre. Nearest train station: Fort William. Private car park ⟵ 1 single, 11 twin/double, 2 double, 3 suites; all with room service, hair-dryer, trouser press, direct-dial telephone, TV, VCR; some with modem line, CD player; no tea/coffee-making facilities in rooms   ⊘ 3 dining rooms, 2 lounges, library, games room, garden; conferences, social functions; tennis;

leisure facilities nearby; early suppers for children; cots, highchairs, toys, babysitting, baby-listening ♿ No wheelchair access ● No children in dining rooms eves; no dogs in public rooms; no smoking in bedrooms 🗀 Amex, Delta, MasterCard, Switch, Visa £ Single £205 to £290, single occupancy of twin/double £205 to £290, twin/double £330 to £475, suite £400 to £550; deposit required. Set L £28, D £52.50; light meals available. Special breaks available

---

GLASGOW Glasgow   map 11

Express by Holiday Inn NEW ENTRY

165 West Nile Street, Glasgow G1 2RL
TEL: 0141-331 6800   FAX: 0141-331 6828
EMAIL: info@hiexpressglasgow.co.uk
WEB SITE: www.hiexpressglasgow.co.uk

The best value of Glasgow's chain hotels, with high standards of housekeeping

About five minutes away from the main shopping streets, and a stone's throw from the Royal Concert Hall, the Holiday Inn Express is ideally located for a quick in-and-out trip to Glasgow. If you can do without the extra frills, such as room service, an all-night bar and a cooked breakfast, which drive prices up in the big corporate places, this hotel should do you well. Standards are obviously high, with fabrics and furniture extremely well maintained. The rooms, although again without unnecessary extras, are far from small, and most contain convertible sofa beds, should there be more than two of you. The colour scheme is bright and cheerful in reds and turquoises. A bright, first-floor breakfast room is the setting for buffet-style continental breakfast, and there is a small, comfortable area to relax in by the reception desk. A number of places to eat are nearby, and the 'big sister' Holiday Inn is just next door.

◑ Open all year   🔁 In Glasgow city centre, near Royal Concert Hall. Nearest train station: Glasgow Central, Glasgow Queen Street   🛏 4 single, 42 twin, 42 family rooms; all with hair-dryer, direct-dial telephone, modem line, TV   ⊘ Breakfast room, bar, lounge; conferences; leisure facilities nearby; cots   ♿ Wheelchair access to hotel and breakfast room, WC, lift, 9 bedrooms specially equipped for disabled people   ● Smoking in some bedrooms only   🗀 Amex, Delta, Diners, MasterCard, Switch, Visa   £ All rooms £56 to £89; deposit required. Special breaks available

---

Langs Hotel

2 Port Dundas Place, Glasgow G2 3LD
TEL: 0141-333 1500   FAX: 0141-333 5700
EMAIL: reservations@langshotels.co.uk
WEB SITE: www.langshotels.co.uk

Cool, retro and sharp – a hotel in the here and now

At the heart of Glasgow, Langs clearly wants to beat in time with the urban bustle. Its exterior is big, stark and arresting, in clay-coloured stone and exposed metalwork. The reception area almost seamlessly segues into a trendy lounge with blue leather seating, which in turn evolves into a long bar with retro canteen tables and chairs and huge picture windows, like an upmarket Edward Hopper scene. Diners then have a choice of two directions, geographically speaking, for their meal. Upstairs is Las Brisas, with its wood-lined walls, serving Mediterranean cooking, while on the ground floor, Oshi serves a fusion of Eastern and European food, such as sushi or five-spiced duck with sweet potato dauphinoise, asparagus tempura and plum sauce. Bedrooms continue the retro theme and have a functional feel, with stripped floors in dark-stained beechwood and a huge TV/wardrobe unit on one wall. The best features are the bathrooms, with sandstone floors and a walk-in shower with mosaic tiles. Needless to say, facilities include 'the latest in entertainment technology' in the rooms, and a spa to get the urban jungle out of your system.

○ Open all year ⊿ In city centre opposite Royal Concert Hall. Nearest train stations: Glasgow Queen Street & Glasgow Central 🛏 14 twin, 57 double, 29 suites; family rooms available; all with room service, hair-dryer, direct-dial telephone, modem line, TV, CD player ✧ 2 restaurants, 2 bars, reception/lounge; conferences and social functions; gym, spa; leisure facilities nearby; early suppers for children; cots, highchairs ♿ Wheelchair access to hotel (ramp) and restaurant (lift), WC, 5 rooms specially equipped for disabled people, lift ● No children under 12; no dogs; no smoking in some public rooms and some bedrooms ▭ Amex, Delta, Diners, MasterCard, Switch, Visa £· Single occupancy of twin/double £100, twin/double/family room £110, suite £140; deposit required. Set L £13.50, D £14.50; alc L £20, D £25; light meals available; service incl ③FOR②

GULLIVET Moray

Minmore House

Glenlivet AB37 9DB
TEL: (01807) 590378   FAX: (01807) 590472
EMAIL: minmorehouse@ukonline.co.uk
WEB SITE: www.minmorehousehotel.com

Upgrades on the agenda at this self-assured family-run hotel in the heart of whisky country

The original owner of this house has made lots of people very happy; the founder of The Glenlivet distillery built Minmore House in 1820. These days the responsibility for ensuring high spirits has passed to Victor and Lynne Janssen, who come to Moray by way of South Africa, but who seem happy with the stag's head, portrait of the Queen Mother and swatches of plaid that label the place as unmistakably Scottish. The clubby bar is a cosy spot in which to sample a dram or two from Victor's extensive collection of malts, while lighter tones prevail in the kick-your-shoes-off lounge with its ceramics and wide-ranging library of books. Fine views are on the menu in the smart restaurant, together with the likes of pumpkin soup, venison with seasonal vegetables and orange pannacotta. The spacious, well-furnished bedrooms are named after local malts, with the remaining dated bathrooms scheduled for a revamp.

○ Closed Feb & 1 week Nov ⊿ From A95 northbound from Grantown-on-Spey, turn south on to B9008 towards Glenlivet; hotel is 400 yards before distillery, at top of hill. Private car park 🛏 2 single, 4 twin, 3 double, 1 suite; family rooms available; all with room service, hair-dryer, direct-dial telephone; some with TV ✧ Restaurant, bar, lounge, gardens; conferences, social functions; tennis, unheated outdoor swimming pool; early suppers for children; cots, highchairs, babysitting ♿ No wheelchair access ● No children under 5 in restaurant eves; no dogs in public rooms, £5 in bedrooms; smoking in bar only ▭ Amex, Delta, MasterCard, Switch, Visa £· Single £50 to £55, single occupancy of twin/double £65 to £70, twin/double £100 to £110, suite £140 to £160, family room £125; deposit required. Alc L £25, D £35; light meals available. Special breaks available ③FOR②

Greywalls

Muirfield, Gullane EH31 2EG
TEL: (01620) 842144   FAX: (01620) 842241
EMAIL: hotel@greywalls.co.uk
WEB SITE: www.greywalls.co.uk

First-rate choice for golfers, gardeners and lovers of twentieth-century architecture

When it comes to designing the perfect twentieth-century country dwelling, partnerships don't come much more distinguished than that of Sir Edwin Lutyens and Gertrude Jekyll, and they are the team responsible for the gracious sometime holiday home that abuts the famous championship golf course of Muirfield. There's a seductive quality to the curvilinear, honey-stoned house that is sustained as you enter within through a series of archways, to explore a well-endowed library and a clubby bar bedecked with *Vanity Fair* caricatures and jaunty golfing memorabilia. Food in the neat, traditional dining room has a distinctly modern twist: perhaps sea bass with a saffron risotto cake, followed by Scottish spring lamb with chorizo & sunblushed tomato, and layered rhubarb & ginger sherbet. Service is adroit.

For maximum character choose one of the bedrooms in the original house; golfers might, however, be seduced by the links views from the smart rooms of the newer wing.

● Closed Nov to Mar ⚡ Off A198 in Gullane village. Nearest train station: Drem. Private car park 🛏3 single, 4 twin, 14 twin/double, 2 double; all with room service, hair-dryer, direct-dial telephone, TV; no tea/coffee-making facilities in rooms ⚥ Dining room, bar, 3 lounges, library, conservatory, gardens; conferences; social functions; tennis, leisure facilities nearby; early suppers for children; cots, highchairs, babysitting ♿ Wheelchair access to hotel and main dining room, 5 ground-floor bedrooms ● No dogs in public rooms; no smoking in dining rooms ▭ Amex, Delta, Diners, MasterCard, Switch, Visa £ Single £135, single occupancy of twin/double from £170, twin/double £265; deposit required. Set D £45; light meals available. Special breaks available ③FOR②

HEITON Borders — map 11
The Roxburghe
Heiton, Kelso TD5 8JZ
TEL: (01573) 450331   FAX: (01573) 450611
EMAIL: hotel@roxburghe.net
WEB SITE: www.roxburghe.net

Country-house grandeur with the emphasis on sports and rural pursuits

Were you to indulge in all the activities on offer at the Duke of Roxburghe's splendid retreat – from golf to clay-pigeon shooting, trout fishing to mountain-biking – you'd be ready to sink into the inviting, deep-red sofas clustered around the magnificent Jacobean-style fireplace just behind the grand reception area. If that sounds a little tame, you might recharge your batteries with a snifter in the smart, decidedly masculine, library bar, before repairing to the elegant restaurant where bold red walls are lined with equestrian prints. The food has a modern twist; perhaps sautéed squid, lemon and avocado, followed by seared scallops, sun-blushed tomato risotto and salsa, and warm spiced apple cake with Stichill clotted cream. Liqueurs are best taken in the restful drawing room, where coffee-and-cream décor provides a lighter touch. Bedrooms are spacious, occasionally vast, and while most are decorated in traditional country-house style, some standard rooms feature a more contemporary look.

● Open all year ⚡ Hotel is signposted off A698 Jedburgh to Kelso road, just south of Heiton village. Private car park 🛏2 single, 7 twin, 7 double, 4 four-poster, 2 suites; all with room service, hair-dryer, TV; some with VCR, CD player; trouser press on request ⚥ Dining room, library/bar, drawing room, conservatory, garden; conferences, social functions; golf, croquet, fishing; early suppers for children; cots, highchairs, outdoor play area ♿ Wheelchair access to hotel (ramp) and dining room, WC, 2 ground-floor bedrooms specially equipped for disabled people. Disabled parking ● None ▭ Amex, Diners, MasterCard, Switch, Visa £ Single £125, single occupancy of twin/double £145, twin/double £140 to £185, four-poster £230, suite £280; deposit required. Set D £29; alc L £16; light meals available; service incl. Special breaks available

INNERLEITHEN Borders — map 11
Caddon View
14 Pirn Road, Innerleithen EH44 6HH
TEL: (01896) 830208   FAX: (01896) 831807
EMAIL: caddonview@aol.com
WEB SITE: www.caddonview.co.uk

Delightful bedrooms and cheerful hosts in a wonderful Victorian house

Classic French cuisine from a Scots-Asian couple in a sleepy Borders town may seem an unlikely combination, but – as served up by Elena and Amar Djellil – it's certainly a winning one. Elena's bubbly personality is the perfect complement to the Victorian brio of the house, with its pointy gables, tall chimneys and rooms of extravagant proportions. Guests relax in a spacious but homely lounge, with a wood-burning stove and striking floral arrangements, before adjourning to the restaurant. This is distinctly smart, with swag-and-tail drapes, a raspberry-and-cream colour scheme, and just a hint of Gallic chic. Amar's menus feature dishes like pheasant terrine with an onion jam, followed by fillet of bream and seared scallops with a bouillabaisse sauce, and crème brûlée. The bedrooms are stylish and agreeable, with décor in restful creams and golds, and luxurious bathrooms.

◖ Closed mid-Feb to mid-Mar ⚡ On A72, 6½ miles south of Peebles; just before leaving Innerleithen, turn right into Horsbrugh Street, then sharp right into hotel drive. Private car park ⬚ 1 single, 2 twin, 2 double, 3 family rooms; all with hair-dryer, TV, 1 with VCR ⚇ Restaurant, lounge, conservatory, garden; social functions; leisure facilities nearby; early suppers for children; cots, highchairs, toys ♿ No wheelchair access; 2 ground-floor bedrooms ● No dogs; smoking in lounge only ▭ Delta, MasterCard, Switch, Visa £ Single £43 to £47, single occupancy of twin/double £58 to £61, twin/double £76 to £84, family room £86 to £94; deposit required. Set D £27; service incl. Special breaks available

---

INVERKEILOR Angus　　　　　　　　　　　　　　　　　　　　map 11

Gordon's NEW ENTRY

Main Street, Inverkeilor, by Arbroath DD11 5RN
TEL: (01241) 830364　(AND FAX)
EMAIL: gordonsrest@aol.com
WEB SITE: www.gordonsrestaurant.co.uk

Plaudits galore for an exciting restaurant-with-rooms

The hinterland between Arbroath and Montrose might seem an unlikely location to launch an ambitious restaurant-with-rooms, but that is what Gordon and Maria Watson have done just off the A92 trunk road in the sleepy village of Inverkeilor. Behind an unremarkable façade, the restaurant adopts a terracotta-and-gold colour scheme, and a profusion of signature fleurs-de-lys. Gordon's food is the main event. An inspection meal of tian of Arbroath smokie cheesecake with gazpacho dressing, followed by suprême of pheasant with hazelnut mousse, cep risotto and thyme jus, and chocolate mousse with melting chocolate centre and honeycomb ice cream, was consistently good. 'My wife and I found every aspect of this small, family-run restaurant-with-rooms to be excellent,' wrote one satisfied correspondent, while one local deemed it 'an oasis in very rural countryside', and another, 'worth a detour'. Bedrooms assume a modern retro style. Service, including turn-down of beds, is personal yet efficient.

◖ Closed Jan; restaurant closed Mon eve ⚡ Off A92 between Arbroath and Montrose; follow signs for Inverkeilor. Private car park ⬚ 1 twin, 2 double; all with room service, hair-dryer, TV; no tea/coffee-making facilities in rooms ⚇ Restaurant, garden; social functions; leisure facilities nearby ♿ No wheelchair access ● No children under 12; no dogs; no smoking ▭ Delta, MasterCard, Switch, Visa £ Single occupancy of twin/double £47, twin/double £80; deposit required. Set L £22, D £33

INVERNESS Highland　　　　　　　　　　　　　　　　　　map 11

Dunain Park

Inverness IV3 8JN
TEL: (01463) 230512　FAX: (01463) 224532
EMAIL: dunainparkhotel@btinternet.com
WEB SITE: www.dunainparkhotel.co.uk

A fine country hotel providing traditional comforts

Overlooking the Caledonian Canal, this eighteenth-century Italianate mansion is well situated for those preferring a rural location from which to visit Inverness. Edward Nicoll is a charming host, while wife Ann ably manages the cuisine from behind the scenes. Beyond the croquet lawn, a sauna and swimming pool are housed in a Scandinavian-style outbuilding and the range of activities beyond the hotel is wide:

hampers, golf tee-off times at 16 courses, dolphin watching, horse riding, salmon and trout fishing and hiking routes can all be arranged. The atmosphere is not overly formal, although men may be uncomfortable without a collared shirt in the three intimate dining areas. Residents have to chose their main course in advance. The wine list has many options under the £20 mark and our inspector found the house wine very palatable. After dinner, retire to the lounge for coffee and petits fours where gilt and chintz dominate and where you will find family photographs, as well as pictures of the Nicolls with Sean Connery, Prince Edward and other illustrious former guests. Some bedrooms have four-poster or half-tester beds and marble-lined bathrooms while all are spacious and continue the floral theme.

○ Closed 5 to 21 Jan 🚗 Just off A82, 2 miles from Inverness town centre. Nearest train station: Inverness. Private car park 🔌 3 twin/double, 1 double, 1 four-poster, 2 family rooms, 6 suites; all with room service, hair-dryer, trouser press, direct-dial telephone, TV; some with fridges, VCR ⊘ 3 dining rooms, 2 lounges, bar, garden; indoor heated swimming pool, leisure facilities nearby; early suppers for children; cots, highchairs, baby-listening ♿ Wheelchair access to hotel, restaurant, 3 ground-floor bedrooms, 1 suite partially adapted for disabled guests ● No dogs in public rooms; smoking in 1 lounge only ☐ Amex, Delta, Diners, MasterCard, Switch, Visa £ Twin £158, double £178, four-poster £218, family room £203, suite £243; deposit required. Alc D £30; light meals available. Special breaks available

Millwood House

36 Old Mill Road, Inverness IV2 3HR
TEL: (01463) 237254   FAX: (0870) 429 6806
EMAIL: gill@millwoodhouse.co.uk
WEB SITE: www.millwoodhouse.co.uk

A luxury B&B with amiable hosts

This top-notch B&B may not be the easiest to find, but Gillian and Bill Lee will provide detailed directions and it does have the advantages of plenty of parking space and proximity to the city centre. Gillian's housekeeping is of the highest possible standard, both internally and externally, and guests are free to use the well-tended garden with its pond and pergola. The Tartan room is the largest of the bedrooms and features a sitting area and antique hand-crocheted bedspread, while the Garden room has a king-size bed and Georgian-style bow window overlooking the garden. The Rose room is not the sugary shades of pink you might find in a different hotel – instead the theme is restricted to floral wallpaper. This room has an adjacent private bathroom. Extras such as bathrobes contribute to the impression of this being an above-average establishment. Breakfast options include haggis, French toast with cinnamon and maple syrup and river trout with bacon, as well as all the usuals. Guests eat communally around a central polished table and Gillian and Bill's personal touch helps to make it a relaxed affair.

○ Closed Chr & New Year 🚗 Near golf course, at junction of Old Mill Road and Damfield Road. Nearest train station: Inverness. Private car park 🔌 3 double; all with hair-dryer, TV ⊘ Breakfast room, sitting room, garden ♿ No wheelchair access; 3 steps into hotel, 2 ground-floor bedrooms ● No children under 12; no dogs; no smoking ☐ Delta, Diners, MasterCard, Visa £ Double £71 to £89; deposit required

Moyness House [NEW ENTRY]

6 Bruce Gardens, Inverness IV3 5EN
TEL: (01463) 233836 (AND FAX)
EMAIL: info@moyness.co.uk
WEB SITE: www.moyness.co.uk

A good-value guesthouse close to Inverness town centre

Richard and Jenny Jones have a pragmatic approach to their guesthouse: they want to retain the period theme but are not 'Victorian obsessives', so the house, built by a carpenter in 1881, contains a mixture of modern and original features. Other former residents include the Provost of Inverness Cathedral and author Neil Gunn. The Joneses are relaxed and welcoming hosts and are happy to provide information on local events and nightlife. There is a spacious family room and the other bedrooms are just as comfortable, some with elegant touches such as a stained glass skylight. All of them benefit from quality fabrics and lots of natural light.

There is a walled garden for guest use and the house, although in a residential area, is well located for the town centre, with plenty of parking available. Request a rear or side room if you are a light sleeper.

○ Open all year ⟶ From A9 or town centre, follow signs for A82 Fort William holiday route; from Glenurquhart Road (A82) turn right opposite council offices into Bruce Gardens. Nearest train station: Inverness. Private car park ⟶ 1 single, 2 twin, 3 double, 1 family room; all with hair-dryer, TV ⊘ Breakfast room, lounge, garden; leisure facilities nearby; cots, highchairs, toys, outdoor play area ⟶ No wheelchair access, 2 ground-floor bedrooms partially equipped for disabled people ○ Dogs in bedrooms only, by prior arrangement; no smoking ⟶ Amex, MasterCard, Switch, Visa ⟨£⟩ Single £35 to £38, twin/double £70 to £76, family room from £80; deposit required. Special breaks available

---

IONA Argyll & Bute
map 11

Argyll Hotel

Isle of Iona PA76 6SJ
TEL: (01681) 700334   FAX: (01681) 700510
EMAIL: reception@argyllhoteliona.co.uk
WEB SITE: www.argyllhoteliona.co.uk

Appealing accommodation on a favourite Scottish island

Scottish Christianity has its origins on this lovely isle which, ten years ago, become the focus of renewed attention when it became the last resting place of the late Labour Party leader John Smith. Day-trippers flock to Iona on the short ferry crossing from Mull, but to get any sense of the serenity that makes the island so special you need to stay overnight, and Claire Bachellerie and Daniel Morgan's pleasant and homely waterfront hotel is the best place to do that. There are three lounges and a conservatory with spectacular views, all

comfortably kitted out, and designed to encourage sociability between the assorted band of pilgrims, seekers of spirituality and bird-watchers who make the Argyll their base. Food is straightforward; perhaps scallop chowder, followed by venison and Iona rabbit daube and a home-baked fruit pie. Smart table-settings and friendly service by personable young staff help make it memorable. Bedrooms team cosy pine and period pieces.

○ Closed Dec & Jan ⟶ 200 yards from ferry jetty on Iona ⟶ 6 single, 2 twin, 6 double, 1 family room, 1 suite; 1 with shared bathroom; 1 with mini-bar, 1 with TV; hair-dryer on request; fax, modem line, TV available ⊘ Restaurant, dining room, bar, 3 lounges, conservatory, garden; conferences, social functions; leisure facilities nearby; early suppers for children; cots, highchairs, baby-listening ⟶ No wheelchair access ○ No smoking in some public rooms ⟶ Delta, MasterCard, Switch, Visa ⟨£⟩ Single £61 to £65, twin/double £82 to £142, family room £149 to £157, suite £170 to £178; deposit required. Alc L, D £17; light meals available

---

JEDBURGH Borders
map 11

Hundalee House

ℒ

Jedburgh TD8 6PA
TEL: (01835) 863011 (AND FAX)
EMAIL: sheila.whittaker@btinternet.com
WEB SITE: www.accommodation-scotland.org

Georgian style and elegance at modest cost

When our inspector called, Peter Whittaker was busy on his tractor, attending to the family farm. There could hardly be a greater contrast between the honest toil (and soil) of the farmer and the gracious, elegant and dignified interior of this delightful Georgian

manor house. With mullioned windows and 10 acres of woodland grounds and garden to explore, and a gryphon standing guard, the house evokes a sense of grandeur that is sustained as you cross the threshold to encounter the fox heads, bristle of antlers, and wall-mounted guns of the sweeping hallway. Egyptian dogs flank the grand fireplace in the stately sitting room, where a collection of novelty teapots steams aside any hint of formality. Best of all perhaps is the striking and delightful green room where

Sheila Whittaker serves breakfasts guaranteed to create a sense of occasion. The bedrooms, including a couple of four-posters, are lovingly furnished with splendid antiques.

◑ Closed Nov to Mar 🔀 1 mile south of Jedburgh, off A68. Private car park 🛏 1 twin, 1 double, 2 four-poster, 1 family room; all with hair-dryer, TV ✓ Breakfast room, sitting room; leisure facilities nearby; highchairs ♿ No wheelchair access ● No dogs; no smoking ⊟ None accepted £ Single occupancy of twin/double £25 to £35, twin/double £40 to £48, four-poster £45 to £50, family room £50 to £60

Ednam House

Bridge Street, Kelso TD5 7HT
TEL: (01573) 224168   FAX: (01573) 226319
EMAIL: contact@ednamhouse.com
WEB SITE: www.ednamhouse.com

Timeless Georgian house where anglers are the core constituency

With many hotels beset by chasing the next big thing and embracing the latest passing fad (however ridiculous), it's refreshing to come across an old trouper like Ednam House that carries on nonchalantly offering comfortable accommodation with a total disregard for the vagaries of fashion. With 75 years of service to those who come to fish the Tweed under their belts, the Brooks family continues to offer a wilful lack of modishness that suits their regulars very well. The prime, riverside position and

gracious lines of the Georgian house play no small part in Ednam's appeal, but there's a pleasing solidity to the plethora of rods and stuffed fish in the dark reception hallway, and the shabby-chic grandeur of the lounge with its cherub plasterwork and pedimented doors. Menus in the bright restaurant offer uncomplicated fare like pea and mint soup and Tweed Valley lamb, and bedrooms adopt a similar straightforward, traditional approach.

◑ Closed Chr and New Year 🔀 100 yards from town square in Kelso. Private car park 🛏 8 single, 19 twin/double, 4 double, 1 suite; all with room service, hair-dryer, trouser press, direct-dial telephone, TV; some with VCR ✓ Restaurant, 2 bars, 3 lounges, library, garden; conferences; social functions; leisure facilities nearby; early suppers for children; cots, highchairs, toys, baby-listening ♿ No wheelchair access ● None ⊟ MasterCard, Switch, Visa £ Single £70, single occupancy of twin/double from £75, twin/double from £93, suite from £190. Set D £25; light meals available; service incl. Special breaks available

---

Ardsheal House [NEW ENTRY]

Kentallen of Appin PA38 4BX
TEL: (01631) 740227   FAX: (01631) 740342
EMAIL: info@ardsheal.co.uk
WEB SITE: www.ardsheal.co.uk

A punctilious welcome awaits you at this lovely country home

After approaching this hotel through its 780 acres of land, you will invariably be greeted by Neil Sutherland sporting both the family tartan and impeccable manners. The original building dates back to the 1400s, although much of what you see now was built in 1880, and the Sutherlands have owned it since 1906, except for a brief period when it had to be sold to pay unexpected death duties. In the

sitting room and dining room many of the chunky antiques have an Asian influence, as Neil's father was born in India and Neil himself worked in Hong Kong for over two decades. If you look closely you may also see evidence of his days as an officer in the Highland Regiment. Bedrooms are fussier than the central areas, with plenty of floral patterns, but have views of Loch Linnhe, the surrounding grounds and farmland. Dinner is served in either the formal dining room, beneath imposing portraits of family ancestors, or the plant-filled conservatory. Neil's wife Philippa cooks up delights such as artichoke and Parma ham galette followed by chocolate French toast, but only in the winter; in the summer her other passion of gardening takes up all her time, and local restaurants provide alternative options.

○ Closed Chr   ⚡ Signed from A828 5 miles south of Ballachulish Bridge in village of Kentallen. Private car park ⇱ 1 single, 2 double, 1 four-poster; all with hair-dryer   ⊘ Dining room, bar, sitting room, games room, conservatory, garden; leisure facilities nearby; cots, highchairs, toys, outdoor play area   占 No wheelchair access   ● Smoking in sitting room only   ▭ Amex, Delta, MasterCard, Switch, Visa   £ Single £45 to £55, twin/double/four-poster £90 to £110; set D £29.50

KILDRUMMY Aberdeenshire   map 11

Kildrummy Castle Hotel

Kildrummy, Alford AB33 8RA
TEL: (019755) 71288   FAX: (019755) 71345
EMAIL: bookings@kildrummycastlehotel.co.uk
WEB SITE: www.kildrummycastlehotel.co.uk

Flamboyant baronial pile in an interesting spot

Arrivals need to be clear that their stay will be at Kildrummy Castle Hotel, rather than at the adjacent, and extensively ruined, Z-plan fortress that is the original, thirteenth-century Kildrummy Castle. Not that the nineteenth-century interloper lacks its own sense of romance; here you will find all the steep gables, castellations and balustrades your heart could desire. The sense of grandeur continues once you open the door to find an extravagant oak-panelled hallway, with a stunning lion-flanked staircase beneath a giant stained-glass window. This sets the tone for a series of majestic public rooms, whether elegant and dainty, like the Wedgwood-blue drawing room, or clubby and masculine like the library and bar. Food served in the traditionally elegant restaurant plays to local strengths and has a hearty flavour; perhaps Scotch broth, followed by lemon sole, escalope of salmon and cheese. Bedrooms are well proportioned, richly decorated in country-house style, and feature some fine antiques.

○ Closed 3 Jan to 6 Feb   ⚡ Off A97 Huntly to Ballater road, 2½ miles south of junction with A944. Private car park ⇱ 1 single, 6 twin, 5 double, 2 four-poster, 2 family rooms, all with room service, hair-dryer, trouser press, direct-dial telephone, TV   ⊘ Restaurant, bar/lounge, drawing room, library, games room, garden; conferences; early suppers for children; cots, highchairs, outdoor play area, babysitting, baby-listening 占 No wheelchair access   ● No dogs in public rooms; no smoking in restaurant or drawing room ▭ MasterCard, Switch, Visa   £ Single £80 to £90, twin/double £142 to £152, four-poster £168 to £178, family room £157 to £167. Set L £19, D £34; alc D £31; service incl. Special breaks available   ③FOR②

KINGUSSIE Highland   map 11

The Cross

Tweed Mill Brae, Ardbroilach Road, Kingussie PH21 1LB
TEL: (01540) 661166   FAX: (01540) 661080
EMAIL: relax@thecross.co.uk
WEB SITE: www.thecross.co.uk

Restaurant-with-rooms well placed for the A9 and access to the hills

Reminders that 'The Cross' was once a tweed mill are gentle – a display loom and books about Scottish tweed are visible, for example – and proprietors David and Katie Young are keen 'not to force tartan down people's throats'. Nevertheless, they are having a tweed designed especially for them, but as a former AA hotel inspector, David is well placed to gauge how far this should be a theme. Having focused on the interior of the hotel for the past couple of years they are now improving the grounds, creating a petanque court and developing a natural pond. The side patio overlooks the River Gynack and inside the small restaurant is a contemporary mixture of pine, exposed beams, stone work and fresh flowers. Menus change monthly and contain components regularly found in the most avant-garde of city bistros: sweet potato mash, fried polenta and celeriac dauphinoise are amongst the side dishes which may tempt you. Bedrooms are bright and spotless and touches such as lavender and lemongrass shampoo handmade in Arran make a lasting impression.

◗ Closed Chr and Jan; restaurant closed Sun and Mon eves   ⚡ From traffic lights in centre of village, travel 300 yards uphill along Ardbroilach Road, then left down private drive. Nearest train station: Kingussie. Private car park   ⤙ 1 twin, 1 twin/double, 6 double; family room available; all with hair-dryer, direct-dial telephone, CD player; some with TV, VCR; tea/coffee-making facilities available on request   ⚒ Restaurant, 2 lounges, garden, patio; conferences; social functions; leisure facilities nearby; highchairs   ♿ No wheelchair access   ● No dogs; smoking in 1 lounge only   ▭ Amex, Diners, MasterCard, Switch, Visa   £ Single occupancy of twin/double from £80, twin/double/family room £120 to £180; deposit required. Set D £33.50; service incl. Special breaks available

---

KINLOCH Perthshire & Kinross   map 11

Kinloch House

Kinloch, Blairgowrie PH10 6SG
TEL: (01250) 884237   FAX: (01250) 884333
EMAIL: reception@kinlochhouse.com
WEB SITE: www.kinlochhouse.com

Reinvigorated for the twenty-first century, an accomplished country house with a new lease of life

Nearby Blairgowrie is the centre of Scotland's berry and soft fruit farming industry, and there's no doubt that in the hands of the Allen family (for so long the force behind Airds at Port Appin) this doughty baronial house is a plum. From the moment you stand engulfed in the grand, imposing hallway, with its magisterial oak panelling, its blazing fire, bristle of antlers and sonorous clock, all seems well with the world. Guests come to shoot, fish or simply indulge themselves in the health and fitness centre. Décor has been nudged upmarket under the Allens' stewardship, and each public room has its adherents: the revamped conservatory, the inviting library and the elegant, coral-walled drawing room with its magnificent fireplace. A series of archways add intimacy to the smart restaurant where Highland salmon and fillet of hare are among the local fare. Bedrooms are tasteful and comfortable, and come with complimentary whisky.

◗ Closed 17 to 30 Dec   ⚡ On A923, 3 miles west of Blairgowrie. Private car park   ⤙ 3 single, 12 twin/double, 1 four-poster, 2 suites; all with room service, hair-dryer, trouser press, direct-dial telephone, modem line, TV; no tea/coffee-making facilities in rooms   ⚒ Restaurant, bar, lounge, drawing room, library, conservatory, garden; conferences and social functions; gym, heated indoor swimming pool; early suppers for children; cots, highchairs, babysitting, baby-listening   ♿ Wheelchair access to hotel and restaurant, 4 ground-floor bedrooms   ● No children under 8 in restaurant eves; no dogs in bedrooms or public rooms, kennels available; no smoking in bedrooms and some public rooms   ▭ Amex, Delta, MasterCard, Switch, Visa   £ Single £125, single occupancy of twin/double £125 to £152, twin/double/four-poster £250 to £290, suite £330. Cooked B £15; set L £18.50, D £39; light lunch available; service incl. Special breaks available

---

KIRKCUDBRIGHT Dumfries & Galloway   map 11

Gladstone House

48 High Street, Kirkcudbright DG6 4JX
TEL: (01557) 331734 (AND FAX)
EMAIL: hilarygladstone@aol.com
WEB SITE: www.kirkcudbrightgladstone.co.uk

Comfortable rooms and agreeable hosts at a welcoming townhouse B&B

Kirkcudbright is a long-established artists' colony, and its quaint and colourful streets and easy access to the Heritage Coastline make it a powerful magnet for those eager to gen up on the Scottish Colourists and the famous illustrator Jessie M. King. Hilary and

Gordon Cowan have been at the helm of this dignified townhouse for a couple of years now, and bring a cheery helpfulness to the task of steering visitors to the best walks, gardens and museums the area has to offer. With these duly explored, visitors can return to enjoy a bright, attractive upstairs sitting room, filled with light and a goodly selection of books and magazines. Bedrooms are cosy and agreeably furnished, with interesting views across the roofscape towards the harbour. Breakfast is something to look forward to, with smart table-settings and dishes like smoked salmon with poached eggs.

◖ Open all year　🗂 On High Street (L-shaped), opposite Osbourne's antique shop　🛏 1 twin, 2 double; all with hair-dryer, TV　✇ Dining room, sitting room, garden; leisure facilities nearby　♿ No wheelchair access　● No children under 14; no dogs; no smoking　▭ MasterCard, Visa　£ Single occupancy of twin/double £35 to £39, twin/double £55 to £60; deposit required. Set D £17.50; service incl. Special breaks available

---

KIRKWALL Orkney   map 11
Foveran Hotel

St Ola, Kirkwall KW15 1SF
TEL: (01856) 872389   FAX: (01856) 876430
EMAIL: foveranhotel@aol.com
WEB SITE: www.foveranhotel.co.uk

A rural location, sea views and tasty food within easy reach of Kirkwall

Set amid lush pastureland dotted with sheep, cattle plus the odd Shetland pony, and with fine views over the anchorage of Scapa Flow, the Foveran feels rather further from the bustle of Kirkwall than the three-mile measure suggests. There's nothing remarkable about the modern, low-slung, pebbledash buildings that make up the Doull family's venture – in fact it's rather anonymous – but the tranquillity of the location, and the gentle courtesy and friendliness of the staff, will ensure it lingers in the memory. The preponderance of pine – from wood-clad ceilings to high-backed chairs – adds a Scandinavian flavour that's more Sven-Goran Eriksson than Svein Breast-Rope (leading light in the Norse era Orkneyinga Saga). Autumnal colours predominate in the cosy lounge, where guests peruse a menu that features well-executed local dishes: 'the highlight for us was the monkfish in oatmeal with seared scallops,' reports a satisfied diner. Bedrooms are light, bright and comfortable. 'Thoroughly recommended,' concludes a positive report.

◖ Restricted opening Nov to Mar, closed 2–3 weeks Apr and Oct　🗂 From centre of Kirkwall, take A964 towards Orphir for 3 miles; turn left at signpost to hotel (on right-hand side of road). Private car park　🛏 3 single, 2 twin, 3 double; all with room service, hair-dryer, direct-dial telephone, modem line, TV　✇ Restaurant, bar, lounge, garden; social functions; leisure facilities nearby; early suppers for children; cots, highchairs, toys, baby-listening, outdoor play area　♿ Wheelchair access to hotel (ramp), 2 ground-floor bedrooms　● No dogs; no smoking　▭ Delta, MasterCard, Switch, Visa　£ Single £53 to £55, single occupancy of twin/double £75 to £80; twin/double £85 to £90; deposit required. Alc D £25; light meals available

---

LINLITHGOW West Lothian   map 11
Champany Inn

Champany Corner, Linlithgow EH49 7LU
TEL: (01506) 834532   FAX: (01506) 834302
EMAIL: reception@champany.com
WEB SITE: www.champany.com

A meaty restaurant-with-rooms with accommodation to match, close to Edinburgh airport

It is said that Mary, Queen of Scots, who was born in Linlithgow Palace, considered this her favourite picnic spot *à la campagne* – hence the name Champany. Nowadays, even Mary herself might be impressed by the fare on offer at these low, whitewashed, rustic buildings that date from her era. Clive and Anne Davidson specialise in serving

Aberdeen Angus beef and Shetland salmon in the restaurant and the adjoining less formal Chop and Ale House. Certainly no one should pass up the chance to taste one of these dishes, and our inspector duly obliged with a resounding thumbs up for his chargrilled rib-eye steak. As if to match the food, the bedrooms have a very masculine and clubby feel, with dark walls and carpets and tartan bedspreads and curtains. All are an excellent size, and come with huge, well-designed bathrooms.

Closed 25 & 26 Dec and 1 & 2 Jan; Champany restaurant closed Sun eve (Ale House open) From Edinburgh, leave M9 at Junction 3, turn right towards Bo'ness for approx 200 yards then turn right at next junction; hotel is on corner. Nearest train station: Linlithgow. Private car park 16 twin/double; all with hair-dryer, trouser press, direct-dial telephone, modem line, TV 2 restaurants, bar, breakfast room, lounge, garden; conferences and social functions; leisure facilities nearby; early suppers for children; highchairs, baby-listening Wheelchair access to hotel and restaurant (1 step), WC, 16 ground-floor bedrooms, 1 room specially equipped for disabled people. Disabled parking No children under 8 in Champany restaurant eves; no dogs; no smoking in bedrooms Amex, Delta, Diners, MasterCard, Switch, Visa Single occupancy of twin/double £105, twin/double £125; deposit required. Set L £17; alc L, D £45; light meals available. Special breaks available

LOCHINVER Highland
map 11

The Albannach

Baddidarrach, Lochinver IV27 4LP
TEL: (01571) 844407 FAX: (01571) 844285
EMAIL: the.albannach@virgin.net
WEB SITE: www.thealbannach.co.uk

Go with a lover and you'll not want to leave this sumptuous bolthole

Lesley Crosfield fell in love with Colin Craig because of his handsome knees. If that is the secret of an illustrious hotelier partnership, so be it. Lesley is an alumna of four art colleges and her impeccable taste is obvious: no expense has been spared on Farrow and Ball paints, etoile and Jacquard fabrics and William Morris-style furniture, not to mention flat-screen televisions should you tire of the view of Loch Suilven and the Canisp Mountains from your bed. Bedrooms are light and spacious, while public areas feature rich colours and dark wood. Colin's geniality knows no bounds – he is an expansive host whose gentle humour will put you at ease. The couple have exploited their artisan connections and many features of the house have their own story: Colin's brother is a Liberty named craftsman whose copper and pewter designs recur throughout. No short cuts have been taken in the kitchen either: five-course menus use only organic, free-range, seasonal and local produce, and the range of wines and European beers reflects the couple's modern tastes. All in all, this is an idyllic place to snuggle up and recharge your batteries in front of the fire.

Closed mid-Nov to mid-Mar, all year Mon; restaurant closed Mon eve Entering Lochinver on A837, turn right over old stone bridge at foot of hill, signposted Baddidarrach; after ½ mile cross cattle-grid and turn left. Private car park 1 twin/double, 3 double, 1 four-poster; all with hair-dryer, direct-dial telephone, modem line, TV, CD player, DVD; limited room service Dining room, sitting room, conservatory, garden; social functions; leisure facilities nearby No wheelchair access; 1 ground-floor bedroom No children under 12; no dogs; no smoking MasterCard, Switch, Visa Single occupancy of twin/double £102 to £140, twin/double £194 to £234, four-poster £222 to £234, deposit required (rates incl dinner)

LOCHRANZA North Ayrshire
map 11

Apple Lodge

Lochranza, Isle of Arran KA27 8HJ
TEL: (01770) 830229 (AND FAX)

Super guesthouse with good food and smashing hill views

The great green bulk of Creag a' Mhadaidh rears above the lovely gardens that form one of the highlights of a stay at John and Jeannie Boyd's pristine former manse on the outskirts of the ferry port of Lochranza. The neatness of the lawns and flowerbeds is reflected indoors, where bright heathery colours set a cheerful tone in a sitting room rich in walking and bird books, as well as board games, which are just the ticket to keep you occupied if inclement weather makes a trek up Goatfell – Arran's landmark mountain – unappealing. Crystal and candlelight lend a cosy ambience to the dining room where Jeannie's set dinners win plaudits: perhaps smoked haddock and mushroom vol-au-vents, followed by roast chicken with celery, apple and almond stuffing, and rum and banana brown bread ice cream. 'As good as ever,' writes a happy visitor. The bedrooms, which are named after varieties of apple, team fine antiques with tasteful soft-furnishings. Service is friendly and charming.

◑ Closed Chr & New Year; restaurant closed Tue eve ⚡ Take A481 north from Brodick to Lochranza (about 14 miles); in village, pass distillery and Apple Lodge is 300 yards on left, opposite golf course. Private car park 🛏 1 twin/double, 1 double, 1 four-poster, 1 suite; all with hair-dryer, TV ⚙ Dining room, breakfast room, sitting room, garden ♿ No wheelchair access; 1 ground-floor bedroom ⬤ No children under 12; no dogs; no smoking ▭ None accepted £ Single occupancy of twin/double £47, twin/double £66, four-poster £70, suite £76; deposit required. Set D £20

LYNWILG Highland map 11

Lynwilg House

Lynwilg, Aviemore PH22 1PZ
TEL: (01479) 811685 (AND FAX)
EMAIL: marge@lynwilg.co.uk
WEB SITE: www.lynwilg.co.uk

Swish hillside guesthouse well placed for Aviemore

A farmhouse on the Kinara estate in the 1920s, this guesthouse is on a peaceful rural lane close to the Cairngorms but within a few minutes' drive of Aviemore. Horses graze, flowers grow and you can feel yourself beginning to relax in the capable hands of Alan and Marjory Cleary. Marjory has known this house since childhood when it belonged to her grandfather's friend, and after a long spell in Ireland, she returned to claim it for her own. Energetic guests can borrow the couple's maps, bend their ear for route advice and then head off into the nearby hills, perhaps using a walking stick from the collection if necessary. Marjory is an enthusiastic housekeeper and the drawing room in particular is elegantly furnished in shades of blue and gold, with plump sofas and antique furniture framing the large fireplace. She also has a passion for cooking: 'dinner was excellent' writes a reporter, and breakfast presents many delicious options such as home-made yoghurt, muesli and bread, and herb omelettes as well as the traditional fry-up. Bedrooms are named after sunset hues visible outside – the Red, Peach and Pink rooms – and vary in size. 'We would thoroughly recommend Lynwilg House,' concludes a contented guest.

◑ Closed Nov & Dec ⚡ Travelling north on A9, turn off left about 1 mile before Aviemore, at Lynwilg; continuing north, hotel is first house on left. Nearest train station: Aviemore. Private car park 🛏 1 twin, 2 double; family rooms available; all with hair-dryer, TV ⚙ Dining room, drawing room, lounge, garden; leisure facilities nearby; cots, highchairs ♿ No wheelchair access ⬤ No children under 5; dogs in 1 bedroom only; no smoking ▭ MasterCard, Visa £ Single occupancy of twin/double £35 to £40, twin/double £60 to £70, family room £75 to £85. Set D £18; alc D £22; service incl

---

MARKINCH Fife map 11

Balbirnie House

Balbirnie Park, Markinch, Glenrothes KY7 6NE
TEL: (01592) 610066   FAX: (01592) 610529
EMAIL: info@balbirnie.co.uk
WEB SITE: www.balbirnie.co.uk

Swish yet unstuffy country house with notably obliging and attentive staff

High living has long been on the agenda at this handsome, neo-classical Georgian country house, with gardens landscaped in the style of Capability Brown. Balbirnie was, in its previous heyday, home to the aristocratic Balfour family, which begat the statesman responsible for the famous 1917 Declaration. These days, after a thoroughly successful refurbishment, there's no need to wait for a Prime Ministerial invitation (or indeed summons) to enjoy its signature room, the spectacular Long Gallery – a delightful vaulted space awash with *trompe l'oeil* cherubs – the clubby library bar, or bright and modern Orangery Restaurant. Dinner here, served by noticeably solicitous staff, adopts a modern slant, and might involve avocado and crab gateau, followed by roast loin of venison, and banana brûlée. The elegant bedrooms incorporate excellent bathrooms, classy soft furnishings, and a number of fine, original features that are showcased to good effect by smart, reproduction marquetry furniture.

○ Open all year North of Glenrothes on A92, turn on to B9130 and follow signs to Markinch and Balbirnie Park. Nearest train station: Markinch. Private car park 2 single, 13 twin, 11 double, 2 four-poster, 2 suites; family rooms available; all with room service, hair-dryer, trouser press, direct-dial telephone, modem line, TV Restaurant, library/bar, 3 lounges, garden; conferences; social functions; leisure facilities nearby; early suppers for children; cots, highchairs, babysitting Wheelchair access to hotel (ramp) and restaurant, WC, 7 ground-floor bedrooms, 1 room specially equipped for disabled people. Disabled parking No dogs in public rooms; no smoking in restaurant Amex, Delta, Diners, MasterCard, Switch, Visa Single £130, single occupancy of twin/double £160, twin/double £190, four-poster £250, family room from £210, suite £250; deposit required. Set L £14.50, D £32.50; alc L £18; light meals available. Special breaks available

---

MOFFAT Dumfries & Galloway   map 11

Beechwood Country House

Harthope Place, Moffat DG10 9HX
TEL: (01683) 220210 FAX: (01683) 220889
EMAIL: enquiries@beechwoodcountryhousehotel.co.uk
WEB SITE: www.beechwoodcountryhousehotel.co.uk

Nice folk and smashing food at a modest and friendly country house on the outskirts of the popular spa town

The revamping efforts of Cheryl and Stavros Michaelides brought Beechwood back to the pages of the *Guide* last year after a period of absence, and the past twelve months have seen them consolidating their civilised approach to hotel-keeping. The handsome house enjoys a fairly secluded location, and the couple exploit this by creating public rooms full of art, roaring fires and family photos to provide an authentic country-house atmosphere, although Moffat's woollen mills and coffee shops are just a few minutes away. There's an urbanity to the dining room, with crisp linen and smart table settings creating an appropriate backdrop for interesting, well-executed food with a modern twist, perhaps risotto of king prawns with chillies, sweet peppers and ginger, followed by loin of venison, topped with foie gras mousse, pudding, and an impressive trolley groaning with gourmet Scottish cheeses. Bedrooms are comfortable, and thoughtfully kitted out with pampering extras, from generous bales of towels to sherry and flowers.

○ Closed 1 Jan to 13 Feb North of Moffat town centre turn off main road between St Mary's church and school; turn left at T-junction; hotel drive is a few yards along. Private car park 3 twin, 3 double, 1 family room; all with hair-dryer, direct-dial telephone, TV; one with VCR Dining room, bar, lounge; conferences; social functions; leisure facilities nearby; early suppers for children; cots, highchairs, toys, baby-listening, outdoor play area No wheelchair access No children under 12 in dining room eves; smoking only in bar Delta, MasterCard, Switch, Visa Single occupancy of twin/double £62, twin/double £96, family room £124; deposit required. Alc D £25; service incl (prices valid till Feb 2005). Special breaks available

---

Report forms are at the back of the Guide; *write a letter or email us if you prefer. Our email address is:* whichhotelguide@which.net

All rooms have tea/coffee-making facilities unless we specify to the contrary.

Well View

Ballplay Road, Moffat DG10 9JL
TEL: (01683) 220184
EMAIL: info@wellview.co.uk
WEB SITE: www.wellview.co.uk

Comfortable, genteel retreat with classic – and classy – cuisine

For a certain generation of *Guide* user, Janet and John were the decorous duo who steered novice readers into the wonderful world of books. With careers in teaching behind them, Well View's own Janet and John – the Schuckardts – can probably make similar claims, but these days they're content to offer agreeable accommodation and top-notch food to visitors to their imposing Moffat house. Public rooms have a quiet, understated formality that's best illustrated in the gracious dining room, with its ornate coving and splendid floral displays. Janet's set menus are thoughtful, carefully balanced affairs, perhaps cream of tomato and harissa soup with warm hand-made rolls, followed by Thai smoked salmon with melon and tarragon dressing, and Aberdeen Angus beef on a bed of roasted root vegetables. Choice comes into play only at the dessert stage, but vegetarians can order in advance. Bedrooms team homely fabrics and gentle colours to restful effect. One correspondent found the welcome perfunctory. More reports, please.

○ Closed part Feb, Sep, Oct; dining room closed Mon to Thu from Nov to March Follow A708 out of Moffat towards Selkirk; turn first left after fire station; hotel is 300 yards on right. Private car park 1 twin, 1 twin/double, 1 double; all with hair-dryer, TV; some with trouser press Dining room, lounge, garden No wheelchair access No children under 6; no dogs; no smoking Amex, Delta, MasterCard, Switch, Visa Single occupancy of twin/double £60 to £70, twin/double £90 to £110. Set L £16, D £30; service incl. Special breaks available

---

MUIR OF ORD Highland   map 11

Dower House

Highfield, Muir of Ord IV6 7XN
TEL: (01463) 870090 (AND FAX)
EMAIL: stay@thedowerhouse.co.uk
WEB SITE: www.thedowerhouse.co.uk

The emphasis is on the food in this Ross-shire cottage orné

A dagger dripping blood is the ominous signpost insignia indicating the entrance to this former dower house. It is the crest belonging to the original owners, the Gallanders family, and signifies their role in the brutal Highland clearances. Fortunately, the gabled, wisteria-framed entrance to what is now Robyn and Mena Aitchison's small hotel, the children's tree house and their down-to-earth approach rapidly banish any sense of foreboding you may have had. Robyn is the chef and describes his cooking style as 'modern British with a hint of the Middle Eastern', a result of spending his childhood in Iraq. Above all he aims to avoid 'Scottish stodge' and does so with panache, producing dishes which rely on local game and fish as well as the vegetables and herbs from their own garden. All of the bedrooms are tasteful and understated, but Room 3 is the best choice, with its half-tester bed, claw-foot bath and views of the garden. Room 5 comes a close second, especially if you fancy tinkling the ivories of the organ installed therein.

○ Closed Chr 1 mile north of Muir of Ord on A862 Dingwall road, turn left after double-bend sign into hotel's maroon gates. Nearest train station: Muir of Ord. Private car park 2 twin, 2 double, 1 suite; all with room service, hair-dryer, direct-dial telephone, TV Dining room, lounge, garden; social functions; leisure facilities nearby; early suppers for children; cots, highchairs, toys, baby-listening Wheelchair access to hotel (ramp) and dining room, WC, 5 ground-floor bedrooms No children under 5 in dining room, no dogs in public rooms; no smoking in bedrooms Delta, MasterCard, Switch, Visa Single occupancy of twin/double £65 to £85, twin/double £110 to £130, suite £120 to £150; deposit required. Set L £22, D £35; light meals available; service incl

Kilchrenan House

Corran Esplanade, Oban PA34 5AQ
TEL: (01631) 562663   FAX: (01631) 570021
EMAIL: info@kilchrenanhouse.co.uk
WEB SITE: www.kilchrenanhouse.co.uk

Superior seafront B&B in the bustling Argyll resort

You may need to bathe in the roll-top claw-foot of Room 5 in order to fully appreciate just how different Alison Bell and Kenny McLeod's enterprise is from the other B&Bs lining the Corran Esplanade. You get a clue from the architecture; the house has a decidedly Gothic bent, a style that's pretty thin on the ground in these parts, and the distinctive tower is sure to catch the eye. Textile magnate Sydney Courtauld, who commissioned the house in 1883, clearly had an eye for unusual features, because the interior still sports an amazing cantilevered staircase with twisted spindle balustrade, in addition to more usual period features. These include the intricate cornicing in the light and bright lounge and breakfast room. The latter is the venue for generous Scottish breakfasts that boast smoked fish and Kenny's traditional porridge as well as the usual grill. Bedrooms are smart, comfortable and tasteful.

◑ Closed Dec & Jan ⤢ On seafront, beyond St Columba's Cathedral. Nearest train station: Oban. Private car park ⤒⎯ 1 single, 2 twin, 5 double, 1 four-poster, 1 family room; all with room service, hair-dryer, direct-dial telephone, TV; some with modem line ⟡ Breakfast room, lounge, garden; conferences; social functions; leisure facilities nearby ⚑ No wheelchair access ● No dogs; no smoking ▭ MasterCard, Switch, Visa £ Single £35 to £40, single occupancy of twin/double £48 to £60, twin/double/four-poster £68 to £80, four-poster £70 to £80, family room £85 to £95; deposit required. Special breaks available

Manor House

Gallanach Road, Oban PA34 4LS
TEL: (01631) 562087   FAX: (01631) 563053
EMAIL: manorhouseoban@aol.com
WEB SITE: www.manorhouseoban.com

Style and comfort in a smart hotel overlooking Oban Bay

If you need to make an early-morning crossing to Mull or Barra you could hardly be closer to the ferry terminal. But the Manor House is more than a convenient billet allowing you to maximise your shut-eye. From the moment you spot the grand staircase in reception it is apparent that this is a hotel that's several notches above the resort norm. Public areas adopt a style that's emphatically nostalgic, and oscillates somewhere between townhouse (a vestibule of Minton tiles) and country house (the obligatory Scottish stag's head). Pre-dinner drinks are taken overlooking the harbour in the nautically themed bar, before heading into the rather stylish restaurant, where candle flames flicker to illuminate warm wood panelling, deep-green walls and flourishes of Black Watch tartan. Menus make judicious use of local fare from salmon to venison, with Western Isles seafood (and lobster on summer Thursday nights) to boot. Bedrooms, most with sea views, are smart and well-equipped.

◑ Open all year ⤢ From A816, follow signs to Oban ferry terminal; continue up Gallanach Road; hotel is 200 yards past terminal on right. Nearest train station: Oban. Private car park ⤒⎯ 3 twin, 8 double; all with hair-dryer, direct-dial telephone, TV; room service available ⟡ Restaurant, bar, 2 lounges, garden; leisure facilities nearby ⚑ No wheelchair access; 1 ground-floor bedroom ● No children under 12; no dogs in public rooms; no smoking in bedrooms ▭ Amex, Delta, MasterCard, Switch, Visa £ Single occupancy of twin/double £65 to £105, twin/double £98 to £134. Set D £29.50; alc L £11.50, D £29.50; light meals available. Special breaks available

Peat Inn

Peat Inn, Cupar KY15 5LH
TEL: (01334) 840206   FAX: (01334) 840530
EMAIL: reception@thepeatinn.co.uk
WEB SITE: www.thepeatinn.co.uk

Top-notch restaurant-with-rooms, with a refreshingly unaffected attitude

Turning up for dinner at one of the nation's top restaurants can be daunting, what with the temper tantrums of celebrity chefs, agonising over suitable attire and getting apprehensive about the superior ways of sniffy maître d's. None of these need cause you a moment's worry at David and Patricia Wilson's admirably unpretentious restaurant-with-rooms in its unlikely Fife backwater. The restaurant retains the human scale of its coaching inn origins, with lots of nooks and crannies, plus comfy sofas to sink into with

aperitifs, the menu or liqueurs. David's menus encourage self-indulgence; perhaps lobster salad with avocado, followed by venison fillet on wild mushroom cake, and iced lemon parfait with orange sorbet. For the full gastronome's experience, tables of diners can work through a seven-course tasting menu – ideal for those who just can't choose. All but one of the bedrooms in the adjacent residence is split-level. Period French furniture and classy fabrics exude style.

○ Closed 25 & 26 Dec, 1 Jan; restaurant closed Sun and Mon eves ⊿ At junction of B940 and B941, 6 miles south-west of St Andrews. Private car park ⌐ 1 twin, 4 twin/double, 2 double, 1 four-poster; all with room service, hair-dryer, direct-dial telephone, TV ⊘ Restaurant, lounge, garden; social functions; leisure facilities nearby ﾚ Wheelchair access to hotel (ramp) and restaurant, WC, 8 ground-floor bedrooms, 1 room specially equipped for disabled people ● No dogs or smoking in public rooms ▭ Amex, Delta, MasterCard, Switch, Visa ⌐£⌐ Single occupancy of twin/double £95, twin/double/four-poster £165, family room £190; deposit required. Set L £22, D £32; alc D £36; service incl. Special breaks available ③FOR②

Plockton Hotel

Harbour Street, Plockton IV52 8TN
TEL: (01599) 544274   FAX: (01599) 544475
EMAIL: info@plocktonhotel.co.uk
WEB SITE: www.plocktonhotel.co.uk

A pretty lochside cottage in a National Trust village, good for stopping off before journeying to Skye

A ship's chandlery in the 1800s, this waterfront hotel is in two distinct parts. Black and cream masonry are juxtaposed strikingly against one another, the quaint image completed by heather-filled window boxes. Plockton is obviously not crime capital of the world, and the owners (members of the Pearson family) are a trusting lot: our inspector arrived late at night to find a friendly note on the open entrance detailing directions to the bedroom. Bedrooms all have unpronounceable Gaelic places names such as 'U' Inneac Chruinn' and are decked out in modern furniture and neutral colours.

Bedrooms can be a bit of a lottery: Rooms 6 and 7 are spacious with embroidered bedspreads while Room 4 is cramped and on a noisy corridor thoroughfare. Poems and paintings from regular customers (among them Scottish painter Hamish MacDonald) adorn the walls and the entire interior has a newly renovated feel. The dining room has beechwood flooring, stained-glass windows and removable partitions which transform it into a ceilidh area. Son Alan does much of the cooking and has developed the menus specifically with healthy eating options in mind.

○ Closed 1 Jan ⊿ Hotel is 7 miles round the coast from Kyle of Lochalsh on the mainland opposite the Isle of Skye ⌐ 1 single, 2 twin, 4 twin/double, 7 double, 1 family room; all with room service, hair-dryer, direct-dial telephone, TV; trouser press, fax, modem line and VCR available ⊘ Dining room, bar, lounge, garden; conferences; social functions; leisure facilities nearby; early suppers for children; cots, highchairs, baby-listening   ♿ Wheelchair access to hotel, dining room, WC, 3 ground-floor bedrooms, 1 room specially equipped for disabled people   ● Dogs in public bar only; smoking in public areas only   ▭ Amex, Delta, MasterCard, Switch, Visa   £ Single £45, single occupancy of twin/double £55, twin/double £90, family room £100; deposit required. Alc L £11; D £27.50; light meals available. Special breaks available

---

POOLEWE Highland   map 11

Pool House

Poolewe IV22 2LD
TEL: (01445) 781272   FAX: (01445) 781403
EMAIL: enquiries@poolhousehotel.com
WEB SITE: www.poolhousehotel.com

An intense design experience of opulent splendour is masked by the mundane exterior of this family-run hotel

Once owned by Osgood MacKenzie, the originator of nearby Inverewe Gardens, this house has a legacy of innovation and design, which current owners Peter and Margaret Harrison have respected, with their taste for the lavish in everything from toiletries to doorknobs. Named after battleships which set sail from Loch Ewe during World War II, each of the five suites in this sumptuous hotel has its own style. With features such as canopied Jacobean bedsteads, French marquetry furniture and a Victorian canopy bath (one of only four of its type in the country) it's easy to see how. The couple are unswervingly passionate about the details of the design of their hotel without being too precious or over the top, whilst their approachable demeanour and myriad of stories make this a hotel with pure class in every sense of the word. Their son-in-law is a gourmet chef who serves up a six-course table d'hôte menu, completing the luxurious experience. All of this, combined with an equally impressive exterior landscape, makes for an inspiring visit.

◑ Closed Jan   ◲ On A832, 6 miles north of Gairloch, in centre of Poolewe village. Private car park   ⬛ 1 single, 5 suites; all with room service, hair-dryer, trouser press, direct-dial telephone, TV, VCR   ⊘ 2 dining rooms, bar, lounge, library, games room, garden; social functions; leisure facilities nearby   & No wheelchair access   ● No children under 14; no dogs; smoking in bar only   ▭ Amex, Delta, MasterCard, Switch, Visa   £ Single £160 to £175, suite £230 to £395; deposit required. Set L £30, D £45. Special breaks available (3 FOR 2)

PORT APPIN Argyll & Bute   map 11

Airds Hotel

Port Appin, Appin PA38 4DF
TEL: (01631) 730236   FAX: (01631) 730535
EMAIL: airds@airds-hotel.com
WEB SITE: www.airds-hotel.com

Newish owners making their mark with revamped bedrooms at this famous foodie temple

A few hotels in this *Guide* are veritable institutions, and there is no doubt that Airds is one of those. It's both interesting, and a relief, therefore, to see the old stalwart flourishing under the regime of Shaun and Jennifer McKivragan, who've now had a couple of seasons at the helm. The eighteenth-century former ferry inn retains most of the features that made it so seductive to regulars: the simple, white-harled walls, air of civilised conviviality, smart yet relaxing lounges and crisply elegant restaurant are all gently refreshed, yet essentially familiar. Menus still espouse culinary excellence; perhaps lightly grilled tuna with soft herb salad, parsnip and apple soup, Gressingham duck and prune and Armagnac soufflé. Airds has always mounted impressive artwork, and curios like the African sculpture in the conservatory are joined by striking paintings by Shaun's father. The bedrooms adopt a bright, restrained country-house style; some boast sleek flat-screen televisions and DVD players.

Closed after New Year till end Jan ☑ Turn off A828 at Appin at sign for Port Appin and Lismore ferry. Private car park 🛏 2 twin, 4 twin/double, 5 double, 1 suite; all with room service, hair-dryer, direct-dial telephone, TV; some with CD player, DVD; tea/coffee-making facilities available on request ✅ Restaurant, bar service, 2 lounges, conservatory, garden; conferences; social functions; leisure facilities nearby; early suppers for children; cots, highchairs, toys, babysitting ♿ No wheelchair access; 2 ground-floor bedrooms ● No children under 8 in restaurant eves; dogs in conservatory and bedrooms only; smoking in 1 lounge and conservatory only ☐ Delta, MasterCard, Switch, Visa £ Twin/double £230 to £320, suite £280 to £360 (rates incl dinner); deposit required. Set L £22; light meals available; service incl. Special breaks available

---

PORT ELLEN **Argyll & Bute** map 11

Glenmachrie Country Guesthouse

Port Ellen, Isle of Islay PA42 7AQ
TEL: (01496) 302560 (AND FAX)
EMAIL: glenmachrie@lineone.net
WEB SITE: www.glenmachrie.com

The warmest of welcomes at smashing guesthouse with lovely owner

The much-loved traditional song 'Westering Home' is a paean of praise to the folks of Islay, who are described as 'canty and couthy and kindly, our best' – a pretty fair portrait of Glenmachrie's Rachel Whyte, who offers the epitome of farmhouse hospitality. Rachel welcomes new arrivals with tea and home-baked scones, maps and guidebooks, willing and eager to point guests to the best spots to see seals or deer, cycle, or just enjoy a leisurely walk. You'll need to indulge in some physical activity to work up the appetite to do justice to Rachel's impressive dinners, perhaps fillet of home-smoked Glenmachrie river salmon, then Rayburn-roasted roe venison haunch, poached figs with a quenelle of crème fraîche, and a cheeseboard with home-baked oatcakes. In any event you'll retire replete to one of the neat, pastel bedrooms. Breakfast is another gargantuan affair, with porridge joining a superb Highland grill.

Open all year ☑ On coastal side of A846, 4 miles north of Port Ellen, south of airstrip. Private car park 🛏 2 twin, 1 twin/double, 2 double; all with room service, hair-dryer, trouser press, TV ✅ Dining room, lounge, library, garden; conferences; social functions; leisure facilities nearby; cots, highchairs, toys, outdoor play area ♿ Wheelchair access to house (ramp) and dining room, WC, 1 ground-floor bedroom partially equipped for disabled people ● No children under 5; no dogs in public rooms; no smoking ☐ None accepted £ Single occupancy of twin/double £60, twin/double £80; deposit required. Alc D £28; light meals available; service incl

---

PORTPATRICK **Dumfries & Galloway** map 11

Knockinaam Lodge

Portpatrick, Stranraer DG9 9AD
TEL: (01776) 810471 FAX: (01776) 810435
EMAIL: reservations@knockinaamlodge.com
WEB SITE: www.knockinaamlodge.com

Classic country house offering a touch of luxury in unspoilt setting

The postal address may be Portpatrick, but the reality of David and Sian Ibbotson's Victorian country house is a good deal more bucolic. It takes a long and winding rustic road to deliver visitors to Knockinaam's memorable position, on a narrow bay by a rocky shore. There's a discernible sense of tranquillity, even isolation, in this location, yet creature comforts have peacefully co-existed with this sense of seclusion at least since the days when Churchill chose it for a hush-hush wartime pow-wow, when the house's Scots baronial elements lent an apposite sense of grandeur. These days relaxation is top of the agenda, and the Ibbotsons use the Lodge's panelled lounge, snug bar and gracious drawing room with fine cornicing to create a retreat that's stylish, yet just informal enough to encourage you to put your feet up. 'The service is attentive from well-trained staff and the house is as comfortable as ever,' writes one reader, though he also found the portions at dinner small, if beautifully presented.

◐ Open all year ⊿ On A75 or A77, follow signs to Portpatrick; 2 miles west of Lochans, turn left at Knockinaam Lodge sign; follow signs for hotel for 3 miles. Private car park ⟟ 1 twin, 4 twin/double, 3 double, 1 suite; all with room service, hair-dryer, direct-dial telephone, TV, VCR; no tea/coffee-making facilities in rooms ⊘ Dining room, bar, lounge, drawing room, garden; conferences; social functions; leisure facilities nearby; early suppers for children; cots, highchairs, babysitting, baby-listening ⅄ No wheelchair access ● No children under 12 in restaurant eves; no dogs in public rooms, £10 in bedrooms; no smoking in some public rooms and most bedrooms ▭ Amex, MasterCard, Switch, Visa ⌷£⌷ Single occupancy of twin/double £125 to £165, twin/double £200 to £350; deposit required. Set L £30, Sun L £22.50, D £45; light meals available. Special breaks available

---

PORTREE Highland   map 11

Viewfield House

Portree, Isle of Skye IV51 9EU
TEL: (01478) 612217   FAX: (01478) 613517
EMAIL: info@viewfieldhouse.com
WEB SITE: www.viewfieldhouse.com

A fascinating family history and verdant grounds at this Isle of Skye hotel

If taxidermy is your passion then the imposing central hall of Hugh and Linda Macdonald's country hotel will be of great interest: there are mounted tigers, foxes and birds of prey, all shot by Hugh's ancestors. Viewfield House has been in the family for generations and various grandiose additions have been made to the original Victorian structure. In the publicity material Hugh remonstrates with a past architect, saying he would 'gladly hang him from the tower ... since his additions leak and cost a fortune to maintain'. But well maintained they are and in keeping with the original style of the house. In 2003 the couple finally hearkened to the winds of change and replaced the dining room wallpaper for the first time since 1887! By candlelight, family portraits will stare solemnly as you use their silver to eat your Aberdeen Angus or monkfish in house-party style. Each bedroom has its own history, Room 4 being the former schoolroom of Hugh's great-grandfather for example, and all are on an impressive scale, containing a wealth of period features. The young couple's personal approach is considerate: 'unobtrusive, but always there when needed', praised one happy reader.

◐ Closed mid-Oct to mid-Apr ⊿ On southern edge of Portree, just off A87; hotel driveway is opposite BP petrol station. Private car park ⟟ 2 single, 2 twin, 3 twin/double, 5 double; 2 with shared facilities; all with hair-dryer, direct-dial telephone, modem line ⊘ Dining room, drawing room, library/TV room, gardens; leisure facilities nearby; early suppers for children; cots, highchairs, toys, baby-listening ⅄ Wheelchair access to hotel (ramp) and dining room, 1 ground-floor bedroom specially equipped for disabled people ● No dogs in public rooms; no smoking in bedrooms and some public rooms ▭ MasterCard, Switch, Visa ⌷£⌷ Single £40 to £50, twin/double £80 to £100; deposit required. Set D £25. Special breaks available

---

ST FILLANS Perthshire & Kinross   map 11

Four Seasons Hotel

St Fillans, Crieff PH6 2NF
TEL: (01764) 685333   FAX: (01764) 685444
EMAIL: info@thefourseasonshotel.co.uk
WEB SITE: www.thefourseasonshotel.co.uk

Welcoming host, good food and comfortable bedrooms at one of the finest locations in Scotland

Songs extol Loch Lomond, and Loch Ness has its monster attraction, but you'll search hard to find an inland loch to trump the beauty of Loch Earn. And Andrew Low's modest but ambitious hotel has the finest position on it. There's nothing particularly aesthetic about the whitewashed building, but the juxtaposition of loch and forested hills bedazzle, and the windows of the lounge and bright Meall Reamhar Restaurant (which majors on fish and game) frame them beautifully. One of Andrew's projects has been bestowing a funkier feel on the Tarken Bar, with talking-point photographs from his southern hemisphere travels, contemporary lighting, and food like salt and pepper squid, smoked haddock risotto and pecan sticky toffee pudding. The individually furnished bedrooms make the most of the spectacular views, and feature fine furniture, from marquetry headboards to the brass and iron bed in the strikingly oval Room 23. More basic accommodation is offered in the adjacent chalets.

○ Closed Jan, Feb ⚡ On A85, at western end of St Fillans, overlooking Loch Earn. Private car park 🛏5 twin, 7 double, 6 family rooms; all with room service, hair-dryer, direct-dial telephone, TV, CD player; VCR available ⚐ Restaurant, bar, lounge, library, garden; conferences; social functions; leisure facilities nearby; early suppers for children; cots, highchairs, toys, babysitting, baby-listening ♿ Wheelchair access to hotel (ramp) and restaurant, 3 ground-floor bedrooms ● No dogs in some public rooms; no smoking in some public rooms and some bedrooms ▭ Delta, MasterCard, Switch, Visa £ Single occupancy of twin/double £78, twin/double £80 to £106, family room £100 to £133; deposit required. Set D (4 courses) £32; alc L, D £19.50; light meals available. Special breaks available

---

ST MARGARET'S HOPE Orkney   map 11

The Creel

Front Road, St Margaret's Hope KW17 2SL
TEL: (01856) 831311
EMAIL: alan@thecreel.freeserve.co.uk
WEB SITE: www.thecreel.co.uk

Comfy rooms, thoughtful staff and the best food in Orkney

Dining alone can be dispiriting, so it's uplifting when a restaurateur or hotelier makes a special effort to ensure that a solo diner feels just a little bit pampered. Thus our inspector found herself occupying a prized window table in Alan Craigie's agreeable restaurant-with-rooms, mesmerised by the mainland ferry cruising out to sea, lights ablaze against the night sky. Attention to detail is important here, from the carefully chosen artwork that makes galleries of the restaurant and breakfast room, to the lovely big bath-sheets that await you in the spacious, comfortable but homely bedrooms. Most artful of all is the food, which uses local ingredients – and a flair for canny simplicity – to impress with dishes such as crab salad with avocado and grapefruit, and diver-collected scallops and plaice with braised fennel. Breakfast can be a fishy affair, too – Inverawe kippers or smoked haddock should kick-start your day rather nicely.

○ Closed Nov to Mar ⚡ 13 miles south of Kirkwall on A961. Private car park 🛏2 twin, 1 double; all with hair-dryer, TV ⚐ Restaurant, breakfast room, lounge; social functions; early suppers for children ♿ No wheelchair access ● No dogs; smoking in 1 public room only ▭ Switch, Visa £ Single occupancy of twin/double £60, twin/double £90 to £100. Set, alc D £30

SCARISTA Western Isles   map 11

Scarista House

Scarista, Isle of Harris HS3 3HX
TEL: (01859) 550238   FAX: (01859) 550277
EMAIL: timandpatricia@scaristahouse.com
WEB SITE: www.scaristahouse.com

Soak up the Hebridean flavour of this tranquil and windswept island retreat

On their website, Tim and Patricia Martin list one of the activities on offer at their Georgian former manse on the Isle of Harris as 'nothing'. By this of course they mean nothing but walking on the nearby sandy beaches and heather-covered mountains, admiring stunning sunsets and eating and drinking the best of local fare. The hotel kitchen specialises in organic and local ingredients, and as many dishes as possible are home-made. The manse house, along with the two cottage annexes, has scenic views from all bedrooms, rendering the need for televisions redundant. Max, the resident cat, guards an open fire in the library, in which guests can take afternoon tea and browse the large collection of CDs and, of course, books. Antiques and unobtrusive service contribute to the civilised atmosphere in which it's easy to unwind. And if you really must do something other than 'nothing', Tim and Patricia will gladly point you in the direction of tennis, golf, archaeology, pottery and rock-climbing.

◗ Closed Chr and occasionally in winter ⚡ From Tarbert, take A859 south-west for 15 miles; hotel drive is first on left after 'Scarasta Bheag' sign. Private car park 🛏 2 twin, 3 double; all with hair-dryer, direct-dial telephone; fax, modem line available ⚙ Dining room, drawing room, library, garden; conferences; social functions; early suppers for children; cots, highchairs, baby-listening 🦽 Wheelchair access to hotel (2 steps) and dining room, WC, 2 ground-floor bedrooms ● No children under 8 in dining room eves; no smoking ▭ MasterCard, Switch, Visa £ Single occupancy of twin/double £88, twin/double £130 to £140; deposit required. Set D £35. Special breaks available

---

Tigh an Eilean

Shieldaig, on Loch Torridon, Wester Ross IV54 8XN
TEL: (01520) 755251   FAX: (01520) 755321
EMAIL: tighaneileanhotel@shieldaig.fsnet.co.uk

Classy accommodation in an unspoilt fishing village

Located in one of the most dramatic landscapes in Scotland, Shieldaig is a picture-postcard village built during the Highland clearances, with 3,000-foot mountains giving way to a rugged coastline, Loch Torridon and the Isle of Pines. Tigh an Eilean, or 'House of the Islands', is nestled on the waterfront street in a whitewashed cottage and is run with panache by Christopher and Cathryn Field. There are many cosy nooks and crannies in this eighteenth-century building, one neat room leading into another: the reception into the lounge and then into the restaurant or the residents' honesty bar, which in turn leads to the kitchen. Throughout there's a homely atmosphere with low ceilings, narrow corridors and sculpted art in unexpected wall recesses. Upstairs, rooms are decorated in shades of the seaside and have co-ordinating bathrooms.

◗ Closed end Oct to mid-Mar ⚡ On lochside in Shieldaig village, off A896 🛏 3 single, 4 twin, 3 double, 1 family room; all with hair-dryer; room service available on request ⚙ Restaurant, library/bar/TV lounge, sitting room; social functions; leisure facilities nearby; early suppers for children; cots, highchairs, toys, babysitting, outdoor play area 🦽 No wheelchair access ● No dogs in public rooms; no smoking in some public rooms ▭ MasterCard, Switch, Visa £ Single £55, single occupancy of twin/double £55, twin/ double £120, family room £120. Set D £32.50; light meals available. Special breaks available ③FOR②

Skirling House

Skirling, Biggar ML12 6HD
TEL: (01899) 860274   FAX: (01899) 860255
EMAIL: enquiry@skirlinghouse.com
WEB SITE: www.skirlinghouse.com

Accomplished guesthouse offering friendly accommodation in an architectural hybrid

'London's big, but Biggar's Biggar' boast the T-shirts from the small but self-confident community just down the road from the village where Bob and Isobel Hunter have opened their fine, yet somewhat eclectic, home to guests. The house stands, somewhat discreetly, at the heart of the village, but its provenance is something to shout about, for Skirling House is that most unusual of cross-breeds, a seventeenth-century farmhouse remodelled à la mode by an Edwardian Arts and Crafts architect. Thus a rustic clapboard façade presages the unexpected sumptuousness of a Florentine carved ceiling. Bob's food is of the mouth-watering, slightly decadent variety: perhaps quail's eggs in a Parma ham nest, followed by tenderloin of pork with a fig and thyme stuffing, and gooseberry and elderflower fool with shortbread biscuit. The same sort of imagination comes into play at breakfast time, when dishes like French toast with caramelised apples and black pudding offer respite from, or just an alternative to, the usual grill. Bedrooms are as handsome as you'd expect.

● Closed Jan & Feb 🔋 Just north of Biggar turn off A702 on to A72 and continue into Skirling; house is by village green. Private car park ⛟ 1 twin, 1 twin/double, 3 double; all with hair-dryer, direct-dial telephone, TV, VCR, CD player ⊘ Dining room/conservatory, drawing room, library, garden; tennis; early suppers for children; cots, highchairs, toys, baby-listening ♿ Wheelchair access to hotel and dining room (1 step), WC, 1 ground-floor bedroom ● No dogs in public rooms; no smoking ▭ Delta, MasterCard, Switch, Visa £ Single occupancy of twin/double £48 to £50, twin/double £75 to £80; deposit required. Set D £25 (2004 price); service incl ③FOR②

STEIN Highland map 11

Stein Inn

Macleod's Terrace, Stein, Waternish, Isle of Skye IV55 8GA
TEL: (01470) 592362 (AND FAX)
EMAIL: angus.teresa@steininn.co.uk
WEB SITE: www.steininn.co.uk

Down-to-earth hospitality on this windswept peninsula

Angus and Teresa McGhie's traditional-style inn is certainly off the beaten track and so they believe they attract 'independently minded people' with the aim of providing 'all things to all people'. The neat white cottage is the oldest inn on Skye, dating back to 1790, and there are always locally produced real ales on tap in the cosy bar, where farm equipment mounted ornamentally on the walls is a reminder of the rural location. It would be difficult not to feel content when nestled in the low-beamed bar, fire blazing and a dramatic sunset and choppy sea loch between you and the Outer Hebrides. Both the lunchtime and evening menus are affordable and of good quality, if slightly unadventurous, limited to basics such as steak and ale pie and chicken suprme. The same could be said of the bedrooms, with their fresh colours and pine furniture, all named after places in the village. Book-lined walls and tartan sofas characterise the tiny residents' lounge, which is a snug place to curl up in with a liqueur, while the indoor children's play area will keep younger members of the family occupied.

● Open all year; dining room closed some Mon eves 🔋 From A850 about 3 miles north of Dunvegan, turn on to B886 towards Waternish; after 3 miles, at T-junction, turn left towards water and inn. Private car park ⛟ 1 single, 2 twin/double, 2 double; family rooms available; all with hair-dryer; 1 with trouser press ⊘ Dining room, bar, lounge, games room, garden; cots, highchairs, toys, playroom ♿ No wheelchair access ● No smoking in bedrooms ▭ MasterCard, Switch, Visa £ Single room £25, single occupancy of twin/double £32, twin/double £49 to £64; family room £74; deposit required. Alc L £10, D £14; service incl. Special breaks available

---

STIRLING Stirling map 11

Ashgrove House

2 Park Avenue, Stirling FK8 2LX
TEL: (01786) 472640 (AND FAX)
EMAIL: ashgrovehouse@strayduck.com
WEB SITE: www.ashgrove-house.com

Grand but welcoming B&B bang in the centre of Scotland's newest city

There are some distinctly grand residences in the Allan Park area of Stirling, and Hamish and Dorothy Mailer's distinguished Victorian dwelling is up there with the best of them. The honey-stoned mansion has such a sense of opulence and grandeur that it's something of a relief to find the Mailers such friendly and straightforward people. The interior features acres of wood panelling, which instantly bestow a baronial glow, and (unusually for a B&B) guests can choose between two formal lounges. The lower has a more feminine look with a fireplace guarded by twin Oriental dogs (booty from the couple's annual jaunts to Malaysia), Jazz Age figurines and a collection of wall-mounted plates. The upper (and more popular) lounge is a lovely room, with parquet flooring, swagged drapes and a focal point portrait of

a lady. Elegant plasterwork runs the writ of the house. Breakfasts offer some unusual savouries, while sumptuous bedrooms follow architectural and historical themes.

◐ Closed mid-Oct to 1 Apr ⊉ In centre of Stirling, opposite St Columba's church. Nearest train station: Stirling. Private car park 🛏 1 twin, 1 double, 1 four-poster; suite available; all with hair-dryer, TV, CD player; 1 with VCR ⊘ Breakfast room, 2 lounges, garden; leisure facilities nearby ♿ No wheelchair access ⬤ No children under 15; no dogs; no smoking ▭ Delta, Diners, MasterCard, Switch, Visa £ Single £50, single occupancy of twin/double £50, twin/double/four-poster £70, suite £80; deposit required. Special breaks available

---

STRONTIAN Highland	map 11

Kilcamb Lodge

Strontian PH36 4HY
TEL: (01967) 402257 FAX: (01967) 402041
EMAIL: enquiries@kilcamblodge.co.uk
WEB SITE: www.kilcamblodge.co.uk

Take a short ferry ride to this secluded haven

New owners Sally and David Fox favour a hands-on approach and have invigorated this country-house hotel with their energetic innovations. The refurbishment of the Victorian bath house and the construction of luxury accommodation in both the penthouse and a tree house are projects which should add uniqueness to this already top-quality rural retreat. In the hallway, the large stained-glass window is an exact replica of the one in the village church, a legacy from the former dowager owner, and the recurring thistle motif is a reminder of your Scottish location.

Bedroom colours reflect those outside the window: you can nature-watch over the verdant grounds and Loch Sunart. The reception and drawing room are similarly tasteful and mercifully un-twee, with chunky furniture, deep-pile carpets and modern prints. Note that younger children are no longer accepted, and dinner is now served from 7.30 to 8.30pm. Food is locally sourced: venison from the Isle of Mull, and the day's fishing catch left on the pier for hotel staff to collect – ensuring as fresh a gastronomic experience as you are likely to find anywhere.

◐ Closed Jan ⊉ From A82 just north of Onich, take Corran ferry across to Ardgour; turn left from ferry and follow A861 west for 13 miles to Strontian; in village cross over river; hotel is 200 metres on left. Private car park 🛏 12 twin/double; suites available; all with hair-dryer, direct-dial telephone, TV, CD player; 2 with mini-bar ⊘ Restaurant, lounge bar, drawing room, library, garden; social functions; leisure facilities nearby ♿ No wheelchair access ⬤ No children under 12; no dogs in public rooms, £3.50 in bedrooms; no smoking ▭ Amex, Delta, MasterCard, Switch, Visa £ Single occupancy of twin/double £75, twin/double £130 to £145, suite £190; deposit required. Set D £35; alc L £15; light meals available. Special breaks available (3FOR2)

SWINTON Borders	map 11

The Wheatsheaf [NEW ENTRY]

Main Street, Swinton TD11 3JJ
TEL: (01890) 860257 FAX: (01890) 860688
EMAIL: reception@wheatsheaf-swinton.co.uk
WEB SITE: www.wheatsheaf-swinton.co.uk

New owners committed to upholding standards at this agreeable Border Country restaurant-with-rooms

Straddling the formal and the informal can be a hard act to pull off, but Chris and Jan Winson, the newish owners of this long-time favourite, seem to have pulled it off with aplomb. There's a dash of local colour in the

couthy Fish Lounge with its piscatorially themed wall-covering and prints. It's the natural complement to the light, pine-rich conservatory dining room with its humorous Margaret Loxton prints of French vineyard scenes. Tradition reasserts itself in the lounge area, where settles, tartan chairs and a blazing fire make a cosy, and engaging, combination. The restaurant teams décor in rich colours, spindle-back chairs and smart swag-and-tail drapes. Food is interesting, perhaps goujons of halibut in a Parmesan batter with pesto mayonnaise, followed by loin of venison on celeriac rémoulade, and sticky ginger and pear pudding. Bedrooms feature cheerful pine or French-style antiques, plush soft furnishings and glitzy bathrooms. Some offer video and DVD players.

◑ Closed 24 to 26 and 31 Dec, 1 Jan ⬆ Swinton village. Private car park ⌣ 1 twin/double, 6 double; all with hair-dryer, direct-dial telephone, TV; some with VCR, CD player ⊘ Restaurant, dining room/ conservatory, bar, lounge; conferences; social functions; leisure facilities nearby; early suppers for children; cots, highchairs ♿ No wheelchair access ● No children in restaurant eves; no dogs in public rooms; no smoking ▭ Delta, MasterCard, Switch, Visa £ Single occupancy of twin/double £62 to £90, twin/double £62 to £120; deposit required. Alc L £18, D £25; light meals available. Special breaks available ③FOR②

TAIN Highland

map 11

Mansfield House

Scotsburn Road, Tain IV19 1PR
TEL: (01862) 892052   FAX: (01862) 892260
EMAIL: info@mansfieldhouse.en.com
WEB SITE: www.mansfieldhouse.en.com

A friendly ghost and castellations galore make this baronial mansion an atmospheric choice

This fort-like hotel, situated in the heart of whisky distillery country, has changed hands recently: former owners the Lauritsons have gone and the Edinburgh Inns group has taken over. Still, the quality remains high. At the top of the landscaped grounds you'll be greeted by a Scottish saltire, tartan uniforms and a blazing fire. The bar area is enlivened by interesting photographs of the RAF Falcons and Red Arrows performing their annual display nearby. The hotel also has its own ghost, former owner Mrs Fowler, who regularly haunts 'The Tower', a regal junior suite with a private terrace, situated in the turrets of the house's central tower. Some of the other bedrooms are also spacious and may have views over the Dornoch Firth. Antique furnishings are teamed with modern bathrooms. The kitchen serves up hearty portions at reasonable prices and also offers a fine dining menu during the summer months.

◑ Open all year ⬆ Approaching Tain from south, ignore first entrance and continue on A9 for ½ mile; turn right to hotel. Nearest train station: Tain. Private car park ⌣ 1 single, 6 twin, 6 double, 1 four-poster, 2 family rooms, 4 suites; all with room service, hair-dryer, trouser press, direct-dial telephone, TV; some with mini-bar, VCR, CD player ⊘ 2 restaurants, bar, lounge, library, garden; conferences; social functions; leisure facilities nearby; early suppers for children; cots, highchairs, toys, babysitting, baby-listening ♿ No wheelchair access; 6 ground-floor bedrooms ● No children in restaurant after 8pm; no dogs in some public rooms and some bedrooms; smoking in bar only ▭ Amex, MasterCard, Switch, Visa £ Single £65 to £85, twin/double £80 to £150, four-poster £140 to £170, family room £250, suite £140 to £250; deposit required. Alc L £15, D £18. Special breaks available

---

TROON South Ayrshire

map 11

Lochgreen House

Monktonhill Road, Southwood, Troon KA10 7EN
TEL: (01292) 313343   FAX: (01292) 318661
EMAIL: lochgreen@costleyhotels.co.uk
WEB SITE: www.costleyhotels.co.uk

Slick hybrid of a business and leisure hotel with bags of tradition – and a discreet (and discrete) new suite worthy of James Bond

A location near one of Scotland's championship golf courses is always going to be a banker in attracting a certain type of well-heeled guest. Catherine and Bill Costley have pulled off the difficult trick of catering to the needs and demands of the Pringle-clad brigade, while serving those who've come on business, or just for a traditional seaside holiday, equally well. Public rooms adopt a fresh, light look that counterpoints the traditional panelling and plasterwork of this early-twentieth-century building in full-blooded baronial style. Despite some fine furniture, Lochgreen House, with its informal brasserie and mirror glass wall, exudes a modern sensibility that ensures it never quite feels like a traditional country-house hotel, though the Malt Room with its behind-lock-and-key collection pays homage to that tradition. Diners can expect the likes of marinated sea bream and medallions of Caledonian beef before retiring to tasteful, generously equipped bedrooms. The free-standing, four-bedroomed suite is a hi-tech affair, with all the gadgets and funky modern fittings your heart could desire.

○ Open all year 🗗 Take B749 to Troon; hotel is on left after 1 mile. Nearest train station: Troon. Private car park ⬛ 1 twin/double, 41 double, 2 suites; all with room service, hair-dryer, trouser press, direct-dial telephone, TV; some with VCR, CD player ✅ 2 restaurants, 2 bars, 3 lounges, study, garden; conferences; social functions; tennis; leisure facilities nearby; cots, highchairs, early suppers for children; babysitting ♿ Wheelchair access to hotel (ramp) and restaurant, WC, 8 ground-floor bedrooms, lift ● No dogs; no smoking ▭ Amex, Delta, MasterCard, Switch, Visa £ Single occupancy of twin/double £99, twin/double £130 to £160, suite £200; deposit required. Set L £22.50, D £35; light meals available

---

ULLAPOOL Highland map 11

Ceilidh Place

14 West Argyle Street, Ullapool IV26 2TY
TEL: (01854) 612103 FAX: (01854) 612886
EMAIL: info@theceilidhplace.com
WEB SITE: www.theceilidhplace.com

There's something for everyone in this informal hostelry on the coast

Owned by the Urquhart family, the Ceilidh Place is a whitewashed cottage hotel, restaurant and bookshop, which functions as something of a political and cultural arts venue for the town. Events include live bands and exhibitions of paintings: when we inspected, a visiting speaker reflected upon her experiences as an aid worker in Iraq. The restaurant menu has aspirations to the cosmopolitan, including ingredients such as tabbouleh, but the inclusion of Cullen Skink, haggis and several local ales also reflects their pride in Scottish cuisine. The entrance is decorated with a Gaelic inscription, the bookshop full of local literature and so, given the proud emphasis on Scottish heritage, it is no surprise to learn that Jean Urquhart is an SNP councillor. Bedrooms themselves have no dominant style, but each has some interesting features and a hot-water bottle. Across the road, bunkhouse-style accommodation is available for those with a smaller budget who don't mind sharing a bathroom. As well as the relaxed dining area and conservatory there is a rustic-style Parlour Bar and cosy residents' lounge in which to continue topical debates.

○ Open all year 🗗 In centre of Ullapool; turn first right past pier. Private car park ⬛ 3 single, 4 twin, 6 double; 3 with shared bathrooms; some with modem line; tea/coffee-making facilities, hair-dryer, direct-dial telephone, fax, TV available ✅ Restaurant, 3 bars, lounge, conservatory, garden; conferences; social functions; leisure facilities nearby; early suppers for children; cots, highchairs, toys, baby-listening ♿ No wheelchair access ● No dogs in public rooms, £5 per stay in bedrooms; no smoking in restaurant ▭ Amex, Delta, Diners, MasterCard, Switch, Visa £ Single £40 to £55, single occupancy of twin/double £50 to £75, twin/double £80 to £100; deposit required. Alc L £20, D £24; light meals available. Special breaks available ③FOR②

The Guide *office can quickly spot when a hotelier is encouraging customers to write a letter recommending inclusion. Such reports do not further a hotel's cause.*

Don't forget that other hotels worth considering are listed in our Round-ups near the back of the Guide.

Tanglewood House

Ullapool IV26 2TB
TEL: (01854) 612059 (AND FAX)
EMAIL: tanglewoodhouse@ecosse.net
WEB SITE: www.tanglewoodhouse.co.uk

Successful modern architecture at this house-party-style accommodation

At her house perched on heather-clad cliffs overlooking Loch Broom and the Scoraig Peninsula, Anne Holloway claims to have the 'most scenic washing line in Scotland'. Construction of the building began in the early 1970s but is an ongoing project, with a new terrace just completed. The former owner/architect had the sense to design the curved house only one room deep, hence all have the natural advantage of a sweeping perspective. The open-plan lounge and dining room have the most panoramic views, as well as wooden rafters, a wood burner, original artwork and a Broadwood grand piano with a fascinating history. Bedrooms are equally comfortable, the Green Room having a balcony and antique furniture throughout, although with feather pillows and duvets, Siamese cats and friendly dogs, this is not a place to head for if you are prone to allergies. Outside, the walled garden is an earlier construction than the house and although now charmingly ramshackle, still produces all the vegetables and fruit Anne needs. Her years spent in Japan and Hong Kong are sometimes reflected in her style of cooking, and her accommodating sociability cannot fail to put you at ease.

○ Closed Chr & New Year; restaurant closed Sun eve ⚡ Approaching Ullapool from the south on A835 from Inverness, look out for four 40mph signs. Turn left immediately after the 4th and over cattle grid and take left fork to the house. Private car park 🛏 2 twin, 1 double; all with hair-dryer, TV, VCR ⊘ Dining room, lounge, conservatory, garden, private beach; social functions; leisure facilities nearby; early suppers for children; cots, highchairs, toys, babysitting, outdoor play area ⅙ No wheelchair access ● No children under 8 exc babes in arms; no dogs in public rooms; no smoking ▭ MasterCard, Visa (note: 4% surcharge) ⌐£⌐ Single occupancy of twin/double £58, twin/double £76 to £84; deposit required. Set L £7.50, D £28

WALES

Harbourmaster Hotel

Pen Cei, Aberaeron SA46 0BA
TEL: (01545) 570755 FAX: (01545) 570762
EMAIL: info@harbour-master.com
WEB SITE: www.harbour-master.com

Fine Welsh cooking and lovely harbour views at a friendly, stylish hotel

With streets of multicoloured Georgian homes, dolphin-spotting trips out in Cardigan Bay, and its focal harbour, coastal Aberaeron makes an attractive base. This Regency hotel is a great little place to anchor yourself, with picturesque views over the tidal harbour from every room and just the sound of seagulls and distant jangling of boat masts at night. The Harbourmaster, once the home of the harbour traffic controller, has been transformed into an upmarket, stylish hotel that will easily satisfy a young metropolitan crowd. Yet there's no mistaking that you're in Wales – locally born hosts Glyn and Menna Heulyn ensure menus are bilingual, cooked breakfast includes delicious laverbread (a national speciality of seaweed fried in oatmeal) and the open-plan restaurant and bar often buzz with Welsh conversation. The small bar's blackboard menu offers tapas, while in the wood-panelled restaurant, efficient waitresses serve well-presented dishes such as locally caught lobsters or chargrilled Welsh Black beef fillet with rosemary mash. Up the spiral staircase, the luxurious bedrooms (named after old local ships) are decorated in marine colours, with chic furnishings and stripped wood furniture. Expect plenty of special details, from aromatherapy soap and cafetière coffee to hand-painted room key fobs and even a book of the tide times.

● Closed 24 Dec to 10 Jan; restaurant closed Sun eve ⚡ In Aberaeron follow signs for Tourist Information Centre and Sea Aquarium; hotel is on quayside. Private car park ⬌ 2 single, 2 twin/double, 2 double, 1 suite; all with room service, hair-dryer, direct-dial telephone, modem line, TV; some with CD player ✓ Restaurant, bar ⚹ No wheelchair access ● No children under 5; no dogs; smoking in bar only ▭ Delta, MasterCard, Switch, Visa £ Single £55 to £65, single occupancy of twin/double £75 to £85, twin/double £95 to £115, suite £115; deposit required. Alc L £21.50, D £25; light meals available. Special breaks available

Penhelig Arms Hotel

Terrace Road, Aberdovey LL35 0LT
TEL: (01654) 767215 FAX: (01654) 767690
EMAIL: info@penheligarms.com
WEB SITE: www.penheligarms.com

Rooms with a view and food with a flourish in an enjoyable waterfront inn

Sandwiched between Aberdovey's old harbour and a request stop on a quaint branch railway line, this characterful, cream-painted hostelry can be reached without a car. No doubt former seafaring patrons (shipwrights and fishing folk) arrived by boat before downing a noggin in the panelled, firelit bar. Today the cosily nautical Fisherman's Bar forms the core of a well-patronised local, but the adjacent hotel attracts a wider clientele in search of outstanding food and thoroughly comfortable accommodation. Affable owner Robert Hughes masterminds the kitchen (inventive fishy fare and a splendid array of wines by the glass). The restaurant, decorated in cool, contemporary blue-greys, echoes the briny scenes from the windows. Nearly all the bedrooms, too, overlook fine views of the Dovey Estuary towards Snowdonia. The newer ones in the Bodhelig annexe just behind the main building are the best, spacious and sophisticated with top-range plumbing and underfloor heating.

● Closed 25 & 26 Dec ⚡ From Machynlleth take A493 coastal road to Aberdovey; go underneath railway bridge and turn right at roundabout; hotel drive is to right of car park. Nearest train station: Penhelig Halt (request stop). Private car park ⬌ 4 single, 8 twin/double, 2 double, 1 suite; all with room service, hair-dryer, direct-dial telephone, TV; some with mini-bar; 1 with CD player ⊘ Restaurant, 2 bars, lounge, library; early suppers for children; cots, highchairs, baby-listening ⅙ No wheelchair access ⬤ Smoking in upper bar and lounge only ⊟ Delta, MasterCard, Switch, Visa £ Single £45, twin/double £78 to £98, suite £110 to £145; deposit required. Set L (Sun) £15, D £26; light meals available; service incl. Special breaks available

Trefeddian Hotel

Aberdovey LL35 0SB
TEL: (01654) 767213 FAX: (01654) 767777
EMAIL: info@trefwales.com
WEB SITE: www.trefwales.com

A relaxing family hotel with excellent facilities for all age groups

Generations of the Cave-Browne-Cave family have run this substantial, white-painted, seaside property for the best part of a century now, and Peter Cave manages to combine the reassurance of long-term ownership with a firm commitment to appropriate modernisation. Having many loyal regulars, and such a blizzard of past accolades, would tempt many similarly popular hotels to rest on their laurels. But the Trefeddian shows no signs of slackening standards. The spacious public rooms are immaculately kept, offering a warm welcome to holidaymakers of all ages, from babes in arms to pensioners. It has especially good facilities for families. Huge picture windows give uninterrupted views over a dune-fringed golf course to the sea; for less hardy souls, the covered, heated swimming pool in the grounds is an enticing option. Refurbished bedrooms on upper floors are opulently stylish, with glorious big bathrooms and elegant splashes of colour against pale walls. A steady upgrade continues.

❶ Open all year ⤢ From Machynlleth, take A493 coastal road to Aberdovey and go through village; hotel overlooks golf course. Nearest train station: Aberdovey. Private car park ⬅ 10 single, 26 twin, 9 double, 1 four-poster, 13 family rooms; all with room service, hair-dryer, direct-dial telephone, TV ⊘ Dining room, bar, 2 lounges, library, games room, garden; conferences, social functions (Christmas only); tennis, heated indoor swimming pool; leisure facilities nearby; early suppers for children; cots, highchairs, toys, playroom, babysitting, baby-listening ⅙ Wheelchair access to hotel and dining room, WC, lift. Disabled parking ⬤ No highchairs in dining room eves; dogs in one public room and some bedrooms only; no smoking in bedrooms and most public rooms ⊟ Delta, MasterCard, Switch, Visa £ Single £73 to £93, single occupancy of twin/double £93, twin/double £146 to £166, four-poster £176 to £216, family room £160 to £200 (rates incl dinner); deposit required. Set L £16; light meals available. Special breaks available

ABEREIDDY Pembrokeshire

map 4

Crug-Glas

Abereiddy, Solva, Haverfordwest SA62 6XX
TEL: (01348) 831302 (AND FAX)
EMAIL: crug-glascountryhouse@yahoo.co.uk
WEB SITE: www.crug-glas.co.uk

Rural refinement near St David's

This austere-fronted, Georgian house attached to a beef and arable farm and surrounded by miles of pastoral scenery is also in a fabulous spot if you're keen on history or hiking. The cathedral and Bishop's Palace at St David's are just four miles away, and the Coastal Path even closer. The farm was once one of the Bishop's residences, but in recent times it has belonged to five generations of the Evans family. Janet has avoided the cottagey décor found in many farmhouse B&Bs, instead going for a refined, upmarket look that could suit a grand country house. So the smart sitting room teams antiques and ceramics with period plasterwork, and the bedrooms not only have elegant furnishings but may also feature fireplaces, ornate carved-wood four-posters and claw-foot baths. Our favourite is the huge Room 5, a recently upgraded gem of a suite up in the eaves, where you'll be treated to lovely rustic views and original beams. All rooms have thoughtful extras like bathrobes and video recorders. Janet will gladly prepare packed lunches, while her set dinner might feature wild pheasant in fruit sauce or salmon steaks in white wine.

🌑 Closed Chr 🔁 On A487 between St David's and Haverfordwest. Private car park 🅿️ 1 twin, 1 double, 2 four-poster, 1 suite; all with room service, hair-dryer, TV, VCR; some with CD player ✓ Breakfast room, sitting room, garden; leisure facilities nearby ♿ No wheelchair access ⬤ No children under 12; no dogs; no smoking 🔲 MasterCard, Switch, Visa £ Single occupancy of twin/double £30 to £50, twin/double £60 to £80, four-poster £90, suite £110. Alc D £20; service incl

---

ABERSOCH Gwynedd   map 7

Porth Tocyn Hotel

Bwlch Tocyn, Abersoch, Pwllheli LL53 7BU
TEL: (01758) 713303   FAX: (01758) 713538
EMAIL: bookings@porthtocyn.fsnet.co.uk
WEB SITE: www.porth-tocyn-hotel.co.uk

Food as grand as the views, plus comfy rooms

A couple of miles from the busy beaches of honeypot Abersoch is a handsome, whitewashed hotel that occupies a splendid spot overlooking the bay. Its core of leadminers' cottages has been oft expanded with modern but harmonious additions, so that the ground floor is now a succession of comfortable public rooms stretching along behind the manicured lawns. Sea views abound, especially from the popular, buzzy dining room (be sure to book ahead even if you are staying). This is the scene of delicious dinners featuring lots of local seafood and a wondrous cheeseboard. Bedrooms – which have no keys – are cosy rather than luxurious, but it's worth splashing out for the sea views. Children will be catered for with their own games room and a summertime pool, while adults can revel in their reading beside a log fire. The friendly and efficient staff are overseen with aplomb by the Fletcher-Brewer family, now in its third generation of ownership.

🌑 Closed mid-Nov to mid-Mar 🔁 2 miles south of Abersoch, through hamlets of Sarn Bach and Bwlch Tocyn; follow brown signs to hotel. Private car park 🅿️ 3 single, 1 twin, 12 double, 1 family room; all with hair-dryer, direct-dial telephone, TV; no tea/coffee-making facilities in rooms ✓ Dining room, bar, 6 lounges, conservatory, garden; tennis, heated outdoor swimming pool (May to Sept); early suppers for children; cots, highchairs, children's room, baby-listening ♿ Wheelchair access to hotel and dining room, WC, 3 ground-floor bedrooms ⬤ No small children in dining room eves; no dogs in public rooms; no smoking in dining room and bedrooms 🔲 MasterCard, Switch, Visa £ Single £60 to £79, twin/double £81 to £149, family room £95 to £174; deposit required. Cooked B £5.50; set L (Sun) £20.50, D £29.50/£36; light meals available. Special breaks available

---

BARMOUTH Gwynedd   map 7

Bae Abermaw

Panorama Hill, Barmouth LL42 1DQ
TEL: (01341) 280550   FAX: (01341) 280346
EMAIL: enquiries@baeabermaw.com
WEB SITE: www.baeabermaw.com

Chic contemporary interiors wonderfully offset by stunning views

Sitting in a perfect location – high above a busy but somewhat down-at-heel seaside resort – this hotel benefits from wonderful bay views without suffering from passing traffic and milling throngs. As you pull up alongside the imposing grey-stone edifice, offset by crisp white paintwork, it looks rather subdued, even forbidding, but inside it's all very calm and relaxing. Pale colours – white, cream, flax and beige – abound in the stylishly contemporary interior, with its stripped floorboards and modern furnishings, while deep blue curtains and chairs add a splash of colour to the smart restaurant. Upstairs, the bedrooms continue the chic minimalist feel, with a vast amount of white and cream serving to highlight the occasional low beam, black fireplace or pale wood furniture. Swish bathrooms have splendidly powerful showers to wash away the salt and sand from a day at the beach. The friendly service is as impressive as the mouthwatering food.

○ Open all year ⚡ In Barmouth, follow A496 to Dolgellau along High Street; take turning signposted 'Panorama Hill', hotel is 100 yards. Nearest train station: Barmouth. Private car park 🅿 12 twin/double, 2 family rooms; suites available; all with room service, hair-dryer, direct-dial telephone, modem line, TV ⚐ Restaurant, 2 bars, lounge, garden; conferences and social functions; civil wedding licence; leisure facilities nearby; early suppers for children; cots, highchairs, baby-listening 🚫 No wheelchair access ● No dogs; smoking in bars only ☐ Delta, MasterCard, Switch, Visa £ Single occupancy of double £79 to £94, twin/double/suite £116 to £138, family room £126 to £148; deposit required. Set L £16.50; alc D £28; service incl. Special breaks available ③FOR②

BEAUMARIS Isle of Anglesey   map 7

Ye Olde Bull's Head

Castle Street, Beaumaris LL58 8AP
TEL: (01248) 810329   FAX: (01248) 811294
EMAIL: info@bullsheadinn.co.uk
WEB SITE: www.bullsheadinn.co.uk

A triumphantly successful contemporary reinvention of a classic ancient hostelry

Admittedly, this fifteenth-century inn doesn't date back quite as far as its near neighbour the castle, which was the last and most perfectly designed one built for Edward I by Master James of St George. But the Bull's Head had a walk-on part in the Civil War, and hosted Dickens and Dr Johnson. The street façade is elegantly Georgian, though hints of the inn's antiquity are evident in the mighty portal enclosing the coaching yard. In the bar, blazing fires glimmer traditionally on ornamental harness and weaponry, but the rest of the hotel has had a startlingly sophisticated makeover in strong and subtle colours, using a judicious selection of dashing fabrics and furnishings. The hotel's reputation resides substantially in its kitchens, from which a dazzling choice of brasserie fare and ambitious modern European cooking emerges at very reasonable prices. Service is faultlessly courteous. Bedrooms, though named after historic or Dickensian characters, are flamboyantly contemporary in style.

○ Closed 25 & 26 Dec and 1 Jan; main restaurant closed Sun eve ⚡ In centre of Beaumaris. Private car park 🅿 4 twin, 6 double, 1 four-poster, 2 suites; family rooms available; all with room service, hair-dryer, direct-dial telephone, modem line, TV ⚐ 2 restaurants, bar, lounge; social functions; leisure facilities nearby; cots, highchairs 🚫 Wheelchair access to hotel (1 step) and brasserie, WC, 2 ground-floor bedrooms ● No children under 7 in main restaurant eves; no dogs; smoking in bar only ☐ Amex, Delta, MasterCard, Switch, Visa £ Single occupancy of twin/double £67 to £70, twin/double £95 to £97, four-poster £110 to £115, family room £125 to £130, suite £120 to £145; deposit required. Set L, D £16 (brasserie); alc D £32; light meals available. Special breaks available

---

BEDDGELERT Gwynedd   map 7

Sygun Fawr

Beddgelert, Caernarfon LL55 4NE
TEL: (01766) 890258 (AND FAX)
EMAIL: sygunfawr@aol.com
WEB SITE: www.sygunfawr.co.uk

Down-to-earth accommodation in a stone-built country house amid gorgeous scenery

Solid stone walls and tightly fitted slates protect this low-slung, rambling manor house from the elements, and there must be some heavy weather from time to time in this mountainous retreat just outside one of Snowdonia's most popular walking bases. Snugly nestled in 20 acres of grounds at the foot of a bracken-covered hillside, this peaceful haven, reached up a narrow track, couldn't seem further away from it all. The interior is homely and cosy, with beams, inglenooks and open stonework offsetting cottagey dark-wood furnishings. You could well find owner Ian Davies in the kitchen, busily chopping things up for the appetising no-nonsense dinners (choiceless until

pudding stage, but changed daily and very good value). Bedrooms are variable – some smartly chintzy, others pretty but dated, with Laura Ashley much in evidence. All are trim and comfy, complete with a resident teddy bear. A conservatory extension has been added to the lounge and dining areas.

◖ Closed Jan; restaurant closed Tue eve ◪ From centre of Beddgelert, take A498 north towards Capel Curig for ½ mile; turn off right, over bridge; follow hotel signs along single-track road. Private car park ⌂ 1 twin, 2 twin/double, 9 double; all with hair-dryer ◈ Restaurant, bar, 2 lounges, conservatory, garden; early suppers for children; cots, highchairs ♿ No wheelchair access; 3 steps into hotel, 2 steps into restaurant, 1 ground-floor bedroom ◗ Dogs in bar and some bedrooms only, £3 per night; smoking in bar only ▭ Delta, Switch £ Single occupancy of twin/double £49, twin/double £68 to £79; deposit required. Set D £17.50; service incl. Special breaks available ③FOR②

BETWS-Y-COED Conwy   map 7

Pengwern Country House [NEW ENTRY]

Allt Dinas, Betws-y-Coed LL24 0HF
TEL: (01690) 710480
EMAIL: gwawr.pengwern@btopenworld.com
WEB SITE: www.snowdoniaaccommodation.com

A sense of artistry inspires this distinctive Victorian B&B

Betws-y-Coed is one of Snowdonia's most popular holiday centres, and at busy times it can be difficult to find any sort of bed for the night. It's rewarding, therefore, to report such an appealing discovery. Pengwern is a new venture for Welsh-speaking owners Ian and Gwawr Mowatt, who display an infectious enthusiasm for this house. It's a solid, traditional-looking, stone-and-slate building about a mile outside the village. Standing on a steep wooded hillside above the A5, it enjoys glimpses of the Lledr Valley. In the

1880s Pengwern was something of an artists' colony, and its three letting rooms are named after leading residents. Each is furnished with handsome Victorian-style beds and baths, and plenty of interesting pictures. Slate floors and stone fireplaces are carefully preserved in the rest of the house, but surefooted modern touches complement the elegantly unstuffy period style. The adjoining galleried Studio makes an attractive self-catering cottage.

◖ Open all year ◪ From Betws-y-Coed take A5 towards Llangollen. Hotel is on the left, roughly 1 mile from Waterloo bridge. Private car park. Nearest train station: Betws-y-Coed ⌂ 1 twin, 1 double, 1 four-poster; all with hair-dryer ◈ Breakfast room, lounge, garden; leisure facilities nearby ♿ No wheelchair access ◗ No dogs; no smoking ▭ Delta, MasterCard, Switch, Visa £ Twin/double/four-poster £64 to £70; deposit required

---

BRECON Powys   map 4

Cantre Selyf

5 Lion Street, Brecon LD3 7AU
TEL: (01874) 622904 FAX: (01874) 622315
EMAIL: enquiries@cantreselyf.co.uk
WEB SITE: www.cantreselyf.co.uk

Delightful townhouse B&B with period charm in the centre of town

Right on the edge of the Brecon Beacons National Park and close to the Black Mountains, Brecon is a popular base for walkers, but also has its own highlights including the cathedral and canal boat trips.

But Cantre Selyf, set back from the main street and dating back to the seventeenth century, is also one of the town's historic sights and reason enough to stay in Brecon. Helen and Nigel Roberts (not forgetting

Dodger the dog) have been welcoming guests to the townhouse and its lovely walled garden for nearly ten years now and have managed to retain many period features. Dark wood boards and beams are complemented by intricate mouldings, tastefully decorated furnishings and a smattering of antiques. The bedrooms continue the traditional theme with perhaps French-style beds or a pretty fireplace. Helen no longer serves evening meals but there are several restaurants right on the doorstep. She has, instead, concentrated on upgrading the breakfast options with daily specials, so you might be offered waffles, French toast or poached haddock to set you up for a day in the hills.

◑ Closed Dec & Jan ⤴ From High Street in Brecon, turn left at HSBC bank, then first right; Cantre Selyf is large yellow house on left. Private car park ⤵ 1 twin, 1 twin/double, 1 double; family rooms available; all with room service, hair-dryer ⊘ Dining room, lounge, garden; leisure facilities nearby ♿ No wheelchair access ⬤ No dogs; no smoking 🗀 None accepted £ Single occupancy of twin/double £48, twin/double £70, family room £90 (3 FOR 2)

CAPEL GARMON Conwy map 7

Llannerch Goch NEW ENTRY

Capel Garmon, Betws-y-Coed LL26 0RL
TEL: (01690) 710261
EMAIL: which@betwsycoed.co.uk
WEB SITE: www.betwsycoed.co.uk

High-quality B&B in Snowdonian sheep-farming country

This attractive seventeenth-century house is almost hidden in rolling, rural countryside. A car is essential, but it's hard to imagine you're only a short drive from one of Snowdonia's most popular holiday bases. Large gardens contain a mini-waterfall and space to sit outside, and, although this isn't a working farm, about four acres of attached land are the domain of assorted poultry and ponies. Eirian Ifan runs a civilised and immaculate B&B in her home of slate, stone and Welsh oak. Furnishings seem at first glance artlessly rustic, but reveal a deft eye for stylish designer fabrics and bold use of colour. Bedrooms are extremely pretty, and the practicalities haven't been forgotten. Well-insulated replacement windows (some still with original shutters) make ventilation controllable, and bathrooms are modern and spotless. A sun lounge and games room provide more guest space than many B&Bs offer. A holiday cottage is available for self-catering.

◑ Closed Dec & Jan ⤴ Off A5, 2 miles south-east of Betws-y-Coed. Private car park. Nearest train station: Betws-y-Coed ⤵ 1 twin, 1 twin/double, 1 double; family room available; all with hair-dryer, TV ⊘ Breakfast room, 2 lounges, games room, garden; leisure facilities nearby ♿ No wheelchair access ⬤ No children under 8; no dogs; no smoking 🗀 None accepted £ Single occupancy of twin/double £32 to £35, twin/double £50 to £60, family room £62 to £72

Tan-y-Foel

Capel Garmon, Betws-y-Coed LL26 0RE
TEL: (01690) 710507 FAX: (01690) 710681
EMAIL: enquiries@tyfhotel.co.uk
WEB SITE: www.tyfhotel.co.uk

Dashing contemporary design and brilliant cooking make this idyllic hideaway a memorable treat

So enthusiastic was the vacuuming on our last visit (mid-morning, off-season) that it took ten minutes to attract anyone's attention. But a glance inside reveals how much care is lavished on this stone-built, part-sixteenth-century property. Beyond its six acres of beautifully manicured grounds, a bowl of lushly wooded, mountain-ringed Conwy valley scenery enfolds it in peace. Tan-y-Foel's lily-scented interior, however, presents stiff competition to these natural Snowdonian wonders. The décor is arresting yet relaxing, a confident application of clean-lined modern furnishings, dynamic colours, lavish fabrics and carefully selected *objets* in every room. It could hold its own in the trendiest urban enclave, yet suits this country house perfectly. The effects are more than merely cosmetic: bedrooms are highly practical as well as being sumptuously designed. The welcoming Pitman family soon puts new arrivals at their ease. Janet, a master chef, prepares acclaimed, inventive, daily changing menus using much local produce.

◗ Closed Dec, part Jan 🚇 From northbound A470, 2 miles north of Betws-y-Coed, turn right (signposted Capel Garmon); go 1 mile uphill towards village; hotel is on left. Private car park 🚗 4 twin/double, 2 four-poster; all with room service, hair-dryer, direct-dial telephone, TV, ironing facilities ✅ Dining room, lounge, garden; leisure facilities nearby 🚶 No wheelchair access; 3 steps into hotel, 1 step into restaurant, 2 ground-floor bedrooms ⬤ No children under 7; no dogs; no smoking ☐ MasterCard, Switch, Visa £ Single occupancy of twin/double £99 to £120, twin/double/four-poster £143 to £157; deposit required. Alc D £36. Special breaks available

---

CARDIFF Cardiff   map 4

The Big Sleep Hotel

Bute Terrace, Cardiff CF10 2FE
TEL: 029-2063 6363   FAX: 029-2063 6364
EMAIL: bookings.cardiff@thebigsleephotel.com
WEB SITE: www.thebigsleephotel.com

Minimalist décor matched with minimal prices at this city-centre hotel

First impressions of the Big Sleep are perhaps inauspicious – a boxy tower block formerly owned by the Gas Board, sitting on top of a communal car park. But once inside, you should soon be disarmed by the combination of striking aesthetics and rooms that are excellent value for a city-centre hotel. The retro chic décor swings from pastel mirror frames and icy cool tones in some bedrooms to bright orange lift doors and a love-it-or-hate-it fiery-red bar. Owner Cosmo Fry is responsible for both the hotel's design and the furniture, much of which comes from his formica factory. Investor (and actor) John Malkovich has also made his mark by appearing (in photos) in many rooms – mainly those on the ninth floor, which have great picture windows, fleecy beanbags and crisp white linen. The décor in the standard rooms is less individually creative, but several (such as Room 1002) have excellent views. Go for a higher floor to get the best of these, perhaps of the Millennium Stadium, Cardiff Bay or as far as the Severn Bridge. Breakfast is a continental buffet.

◗ Closed 25 Dec 🚇 In city centre, opposite Cardiff International Arena. Nearest train station: Cardiff Central. Private car park 🚗 30 twin, 42 double, 6 family rooms, 2 suites; all with direct-dial telephone, modem line, TV; hair-dryers available ✅ Breakfast room, bar; conferences; leisure facilities nearby; cots, highchairs 🚶 Wheelchair access to hotel and breakfast room, WC, 2 rooms partially equipped for disabled people, lift. Disabled parking ⬤ No dogs in public rooms ☐ Amex, Delta, Diners, MasterCard, Switch, Visa £ Twin/double/family room £45 to £99, suite £99 to £135; deposit required

---

The Town House   [NEW ENTRY]

70 Cathedral Road, Cardiff CF11 9LL
TEL: 029-2023 9399   FAX: 029-2022 3214
EMAIL: thetownhouse@msn.com
WEB SITE: www.thetownhousecardiff.co.uk

Impressively smart but cosy B&B not far from the castle

Cathedral Road has been designated a conservation area, and no wonder, with its lengthy strip of semi-detached, Gothic Victorian townhouses. One such building is this appealing B&B, which has plenty of period detail – original floral-designed plasterwork, stained-glass windows and the hallway's mosaic floor. Hospitable hosts Paula and Charles Mullins have been here since 1998, offering a smart yet homely place to stay. Family photos and shelves of books share wall space with elegant paintings in the cosy but sizeable lounge, and chinaware adds decorative charm to the open-plan breakfast room. Guests tend to sit together around the one table at breakfast, where they can choose hash browns or pancakes with maple syrup in addition to the usual British fare. Bedrooms are in a traditional style with smartly designed curtains and bedspreads, and televisions are neatly hidden in cabinets; the shower rooms are quite small but spotless. Cathedral Road can get busy, so light sleepers may prefer to avoid front-facing rooms, which don't have double glazing. A major bonus is that Cardiff Castle and the city's shops are within walking distance.

○ Open all year 🗷 Heading west along Castle Street (A4161), pass castle and turn right at traffic lights into Cathedral Road; hotel is 800 metres on right. Private car park. Nearest train station: Cardiff Central 🚄 3 single, 1 twin, 3 twin/double, 1 family room; all with direct-dial telephone, TV; hair-dryer on request ✓ Breakfast room, lounge, conservatory, garden; leisure facilities nearby; cots, toys ⅛ No wheelchair access ● No dogs; no smoking ▭ Amex, Delta, MasterCard, Switch, Visa £ Single £45 to £55, single occupancy of twin/double £48 to £58, twin/double £55 to £65, family room £65 to £75

CLYTHA Monmouthshire
map 2

Clytha Arms

Clytha, Abergavenny NP7 9BW
TEL: (01873) 840206
EMAIL: clythaarms@tiscali.co.uk
WEB SITE: www.clytha-arms.com

Creative meals at this family-run, down-to-earth inn

Planning an invasion of the Welsh Marches' many castles (such as nearby Raglan)? Then consider as a base the welcoming Clytha Arms, which is within striking distance of several. The focal point is the convivial bar, which offers several real ales as well as games such as table skittles. Andrew and Beverley Canning run the inn with down-to-earth joviality and there's a cheeky humour, seen in the collection of fun teapots and the schoolboy mural in the gents. Daughter Sarah is just as much a key ingredient to the hostelry's success, and her imaginative cooking extends to the Welsh breakfasts, which might include wild boar sausage, laverbread with cockles, or Marmite fritters. The low-ceilinged restaurant is informal but smartly decorated with French pictures. Our only niggle was that, on our visit, some chairs were looking rather worn in the next-door lounge bar. Each bedroom has its own charm. Room 1 goes for the cottagey look, with teddies on twin pine beds. It is worth paying more for delightfully traditional Room 3, which has a larger bathroom, a four-poster and a spacious sitting area.

○ Closed 25 Dec; restaurant closed Sun & Mon eves 🗷 On B4598 old Raglan to Abergavenny road, south of A40, 6 miles from Abergavenny (no exit at Clytha from A40). Private car park 🚄 1 twin, 2 double, 1 four-poster; all with hair-dryer, TV ✓ Restaurant, bar/lounge, garden; conferences and social functions; early suppers for children; cots, highchairs, toys, outdoor play area ⅛ No wheelchair access ● No dogs; smoking in bar only ▭ Amex, Delta, Diners, MasterCard, Switch, Visa £ Single occupancy of twin/double £50, twin/double £70, four-poster £90; deposit required. Set L, D £19; alc L, D £30; light meals available; service incl

CONWY Conwy
map 7

Castle Hotel NEW ENTRY

High Street, Conwy LL32 8DB
TEL: (01492) 582800 FAX: (01492) 582300
EMAIL: mail@castlewales.co.uk
WEB SITE: www.castlewales.co.uk

Smart central hotel with a long history

Not many of medieval Conwy's buildings could be described as modern, and this fine old coaching inn is no exception. It stands on the site of a Cistercian monastery, its earliest sections dating back to the fifteenth century. The striking brick-and-granite façade is the result of a Victorian makeover, which created a handsome addition to the historic High

Street. The enterprising members of the Lavin family are in the process of an ambitious refurbishment, which has already turned the top floor into unexpectedly luxurious bedrooms. The Caer Rhun suite is a hedonistic eye-popper with leopardskin fabrics, lamps trimmed with ostrich feathers and a double whirlpool bath beyond wildest fantasies (the floor beneath has been appropriately strengthened!). Some rooms suit slimmer budgets, but all have character, as does the spacious trio of public areas downstairs. The colourful restaurant is decked with large canvases of Shakespearean scenes by a Victorian artist once in residence.

◑ Open all year　🛋 In Conwy one-way system, hotel is halfway along High Street on left. Private car parks. Nearest train station: Llandudno Junction　🛏 4 single, 2 twin, 5 twin/double, 12 double, 1 four-poster, 2 family rooms, 2 suites; all with room service, hair-dryer, trouser press, direct-dial telephone, modem line, TV; 3 with CD player　🍽 Restaurant, bar, lounge; conferences and social functions; leisure facilities nearby; early suppers for children; cots, highchairs, babysitting, baby-listening　♿ No wheelchair access　● No dogs in public rooms; no smoking in most public rooms and most bedrooms　🗀 Amex, Delta, MasterCard, Switch, Visa　£ Single £65 to £79, single occupancy of twin/double £84 to £124, twin/double £90 to £130, four-poster £130 to £155, family room £110 to £130, suite £130 to £250; deposit required. Set Sun L £16; alc L £20, D £30; light meals available. Special breaks available　③ᶠᵒʳ②

Sychnant Pass House [NEW ENTRY]

Sychnant Pass Road, Conwy LL32 8BJ
TEL: (01492) 596868
EMAIL: bre@sychnant-pass-house.co.uk
WEB SITE: www.sychnant-pass-house.co.uk

A spacious, cheerful, family-friendly house in a lovely position

'Now we're not a hotel, you know,' says owner Bre Carrington-Sykes, anxious not to overinflate expectations. But this charming place is way above average in any hospitality league, and is popular for excellent home cooking as well as fine accommodation. It's a substantial Edwardian house in a peaceful setting on the fringes of the National Park near Conwy, with two acres of garden. New arrivals step straight into a large, inviting lounge in blues and yellows, generously decked with stylish, comfy-looking seating. Beautifully dressed windows take full advantage of the views. Games, books, music and chess sets provide indoor entertainment, along with many teddies and soft toys. Families are most welcome here, but the atmosphere is civilised, and grown-up standards of behaviour are tactfully insisted on. The two interlocking restaurant rooms are pretty in pine with lots of blue and white china, pictures, candles and ornaments. Several smartly decorated bedrooms have private terraces.

◑ Closed Chr　🛋 From one-way system in Conwy, turn into Upper Gate Street; go straight up hill for 1½ miles. Private car park. Nearest train station: Conwy　🛏 3 twin/double, 1 double, 2 four-poster, 4 suites; family rooms available; all with hair-dryer, mini-bar, trouser press, TV, VCR, CD player　🍽 Restaurant, 2 lounges, library, gardens; social functions; civil wedding licence; leisure facilities nearby; cots, highchairs, toys, playroom, babysitting, baby-listening, outdoor play area　♿ No wheelchair access, 2 ground-floor bedrooms　● No smoking in bedrooms and most public rooms　🗀 MasterCard, Switch, Visa　£ Single occupancy of twin/double from £55, twin/double from £80, four-poster from £90, family room from £105, suite from £120; deposit required. Set D £20; alc D £25; light meals available

---

CRICKHOWELL Powys　　　　　　　　　　　　　　　　　　map 4

Bear Hotel

High Street, Crickhowell NP8 1BW
TEL: (01873) 810408　FAX: (01873) 811696
EMAIL: bearhotel@aol.com
WEB SITE: www.bearhotel.com

Historic watering hole serving good, modern fare in the town centre

It's no wonder that the charming town of Crickhowell has become a tourist hub. Head out a short way in any direction and you'll find something worth visiting, perhaps the spectacular Brecon Beacons, the Black Mountains, the Big Pit Mining Museum or Llanthony Priory. The black-and-white Bear Hotel makes a good base for all this sightseeing, thanks to a fine blend of ancient charm and a flair for turning out high-quality meals. Its medieval origins are recalled in the timber beams, old settles, stone walls and floors that characterise the various bar areas (no fewer than four to choose from!), and really played upon with Tudor images and chandeliers in the function hall. Overall, the décor is often steadfastly traditional, with floral-patterned carpets and walls, and lacy tablecloths in one dimly lit restaurant. The main, low-beamed restaurant is a better venue for tasting the hotel's inventive country cooking. Rooms are shared between the main building and the converted stable block. Some are rather dated, although superiors such as Room 10 may have warm tones and lovely antique furniture. Light sleepers may be wise to avoid the rooms facing the main street.

◑ Open all year; restaurant closed Sun eve ▨ On A40 between Abergavenny and Brecon, in centre of Crickhowell. Private car park ⊨ 8 twin, 18 double, 2 four-poster, 4 family rooms, 2 suites; all with room service, hair-dryer, direct-dial telephone, modem line, TV ⊘ Restaurant, 2 dining rooms, bar, 2 lounges; garden; conferences; social functions; leisure facilities nearby; cots, highchairs, baby-listening � Wheelchair access to hotel and dining rooms, WC, 6 ground-floor bedrooms ◔ No children under 8 in dining rooms eves ▭ Amex, MasterCard, Switch, Visa ⌸ Single occupancy of twin/double £67 to £108, twin/double £75 to £140, four-poster £85 to £95, family room £100, suite £140; deposit required. Alc D £35; light meals available; service incl

---

Gliffaes Country House

Crickhowell NP8 1RH
TEL: (01874) 730371 FAX: (01874) 730463
EMAIL: calls@gliffaeshotel.com
WEB SITE: www.gliffaes.com

Fine cuisine at a traditional country house with Italian influences

Perched high above the River Usk, this multi-gabled stone house with distinctive campaniles boasts some superb terrace views. And although the Brecon Beacons and Black Mountains may be on the doorstep, you could find it hard to stray beyond the hotel grounds, given the temptation of 33 acres of landscaped gardens and woodland to explore and numerous activities. Whether it's an afternoon spent down at the river where the hotel has fishing rights (salmon is popular here), or playing tennis or croquet, the elegant sitting rooms should make an inviting homecoming, with wood-panelled walls and perhaps a log fire. In fact, the décor has the expected 'country-house' features throughout, such as ornate mirrors and parquet floors, but the atmosphere doesn't feel pretentious. Sumptuous Italianate colours enrich the bedrooms, particularly Rooms 2 and 6 (the latter has a balcony and a splendid bathroom with roll-top bath). A good alternative could be Room 3, known as the 'old library' and boasting wood panelling. Gliffaes also takes pride in its cuisine; the chefs make a point of using mostly regional produce, focusing on traditional country cooking with international twists.

◑ Closed 3 to 19 Jan ▨ 1 mile off A40, 2½ miles west of Crickhowell. Private car park ⊨ 4 single, 9 twin, 7 double, 1 four-poster, 1 suite; family rooms available; all with room service, hair-dryer, direct-dial telephone, modem line, TV; some with DVD ⊘ Dining room, bar, 2 sitting rooms, conservatory, games room, gardens; conferences; social functions; civil wedding licence; fishing, tennis; leisure facilities nearby; early suppers for children; cots, highchairs, baby-listening ⅃ No wheelchair access ◔ No children under 8 in restaurant eves; no dogs in hotel (kennels available); no smoking in bedrooms ▭ Amex, Delta, Diners, MasterCard, Switch, Visa ⌸ Single £65, single occupancy of twin/double £85 to £126, twin/double £126 to £180, four-poster £155, family room £165; deposit required. Set D £29.50, Sun L £23.50; light meals available; service incl. Special breaks available

---

If you make a booking using a credit card and find after cancelling that the full amount has been charged to your card, raise the matter with your credit-card company. It will ask the hotelier to confirm whether the room was re-let, and to justify the charge made.

DRUIDSTON Pembrokeshire   map 4

The Druidstone

Druidston Haven, Nr Broad Haven, Haverfordwest SA62 3NE
TEL: (01437) 781221   FAX: (01437) 781133
EMAIL: jane@druidstone.co.uk
WEB SITE: www.druidstone.co.uk

Splendid isolation to suit families, high above the beach

They may have lived here for decades, but Rod and Jane Bell are still ringing the changes at the Druidstone. The latest additions to this Victorian stone house are two new, luxurious bedrooms up in the eaves. These are pricier than the other, more simply furnished, rooms but are well worth the extra – the décor stirs thoughts of being below deck on ship, the pine bathrooms are immaculate and you even get a balcony to enjoy the superb view over the Pembrokeshire coast. Some of the other rooms can be rather small, with shared bathrooms. Downstairs, the toy-filled front lounge is an obvious sign of the hotel's down-to-earth, child-friendly style. Parents won't find breakable ornaments to fret about and the sandy beach, just down the steep path from the cliff top, should appeal to children. In fact, the hotel welcomes groups of children on trips funded by the Prince's Trust, several times a year. Early suppers are served to youngsters, while there is a good choice of Welsh and international dishes for adults, who can enjoy sea views from the dining room. The bar area was looking rather tired on our visit. More reports would be welcome.

◑ Open all year; dining room closed Sun eve ⤢ From Haverfordwest, take B4341 to Broad Haven; turn right at sea; after 1½ miles turn left to Druidston Haven; hotel is ¾ mile on left. Private car park ⤙ 2 single, 4 twin/double, 3 double, 2 family rooms; 6 with shared bathrooms; hair-dryer on request ✦ Dining room, bar, lounge, gardens; conferences and social functions; civil wedding licence; early suppers for children; cots, highchairs, toys ♿ No wheelchair access ● No dogs in dining room; no smoking in bedrooms and most public rooms ▭ Amex, Delta, MasterCard, Switch, Visa £ Single £40, single occupancy of twin/double £50, twin/double £80 to £130, family room £140 (prices valid till 1 Feb 2005). Alc L £21, D £25; light meals available; service incl

---

EGLWYSFACH Powys   map 4

Ynyshir Hall

Eglwysfach, Machynlleth SY20 8TA
TEL: (01654) 781209   FAX: (01654) 781366
EMAIL: info@ynyshir-hall.co.uk
WEB SITE: www.ynyshir-hall.co.uk

Spectacularly gracious country-house hotel in gorgeous grounds

Owners Joan and Rob Reen were in personal charge at reception on our last inspection visit. This hands-on approach to hotel-keeping is evident throughout Ynyshir Hall, where no detail escapes attention. Extravagant flower arrangements are on display, lights are on, and fires lit, even when most guests are out – though one guest found the heating off in their room when they arrived on a chilly day. This white-painted Georgian longhouse is stunningly beautiful, each room a design masterpiece containing many of Rob's own striking landscape paintings. Bedrooms are gloriously individual creations: Goya dashingly handsome in blue and gold silk, Renoir classically restrained in pale lemon and inlaid walnut, and Matisse outrageously romantic in cerise and candy pink with painted clouds and a marble bathroom. 'Comfortable and very well equipped', was one correspondent's verdict. Cooking is accomplished, and uses carefully sourced ingredients. One couple praised the ingredients and 'meticulous care', as well as the excellent breakfasts, but found the meal rather 'long drawn out' for their taste. In the splendid gardens – a sheltered 14-acre site – considered plantings ensure a continuous succession of colour: azalea time provides more fireworks than usual and a mature parrotia is beautiful through all the seasons.

◗ Closed Jan ⬚ 6 miles south-west of Machynlleth on A487. Private car park ⬚ 5 twin/double, 1 four-poster, 3 suites; all with room service, hair-dryer, direct-dial telephone, TV; some with CD player; no tea/coffee-making facilities in rooms ⬚ 2 dining rooms, bar, lounge, garden; conferences and social functions; leisure facilities nearby ⬚ No wheelchair access; 3 steps into hotel, 3 ground-floor bedrooms ● No children under 9; dogs in some bedrooms only; no smoking ⬚ Amex, Delta, Diners, MasterCard, Switch, Visa £ Single occupancy of twin/double £100 to £190, twin/double £160 to £250, four-poster £195 to £250, suite £195 to £330; deposit required. Set L £32, D £48 to £58; light meals available; service incl. Special breaks available

map 4

Felin Fach Griffin

Felinfach, Brecon LD3 0UB
TEL: (01874) 620111 FAX: (01874) 620120
EMAIL: enquiries@eatdrinksleep.ltd.uk
WEB SITE: www.eatdrinksleep.ltd.uk

Cosy, unpretentious gastropub near the Brecon Beacons

Charles Inkin and his team have concocted a winning recipe. Take one old farmhouse (set back a little from the road to Brecon). Add the staple country ingredients – flagstone floors, original beams, stone walls – with a hint of Tuscan flavouring. Blend with rich colouring, soft toffee sofas and a dash of cool creams, and warm with a lovely fireplace and an Aga. The result? One tasty-looking Griffin! The management's emphasis now, though, has turned to providing high-quality, cosmopolitan cooking using locally sourced ingredients – such as venison with braised red cabbage and dauphinoise potatoes – backed up with a large wine list. The overall ambience is cosy and convivial, particularly in the lounge bar, and lacks the pretensions of other gastropubs. The bar counter of shiny slate, originally a milking parlour partition, doubles as the reception desk. The bedrooms are modern and stylish, in crisp, pale tones, offering several novels in place of televisions. Room 3 stands out: it has a sofa at the end of an ornate four-poster bed.

◗ Closed 25 & 26 Dec and first week in Jan ⬚ Take A470 from Brecon towards Hay-on-Wye; inn is 4 miles from centre of Brecon, on left. Private car park ⬚ 2 twin/double, 2 double, 3 four-poster; all with hair-dryer, direct-dial telephone ⬚ Restaurant, lounge bar, garden; social functions; leisure facilities nearby; highchairs ⬚ No wheelchair access ● Dogs £10 in bedrooms; no smoking in bedrooms ⬚ Delta, MasterCard, Switch, Visa £ Single occupancy of twin/double £68, twin/double £93, four-poster £115; deposit required. Alc L £20, D £23; light meals available

map 4

Manor Town House

Main Street, Fishguard SA65 9HG
TEL: (01348) 873260 (AND FAX)
EMAIL: davies.themanor@amserve.net

Thoughtful home cooking and super views at a traditional townhouse

It doesn't take long to realise that Ralph and Beatrix Davies are devout collectors. Manor Town House brims with global decorative interest, from Indian camelhair rugs and Guatemalan cushions to Victorian furniture and old paintings. So it's no great surprise that the warm-toned smoker's lounge was actually Ralph's antiques shop until 2003. The house itself dates back to the 1790s, and it has been run by these hospitable hosts for around 15 years now. Much of the success is down to the set dinners, home-cooked by Beatrix, which might include local lamb with aubergine caviar. You can expect fresh flowers and candles on your table in the intimate basement restaurant, but on fine mornings, ask to have breakfast down in the gazebo. The view down to Lower Town harbour is tremendous from the end-of-garden terrace, and an incentive to get out and explore the Pembrokeshire coastal path. Bedrooms vary in style but are quite traditional, with generally tiny shower rooms and sinks in bedrooms. Go for rear-facing rooms such as 1 or 5, which avoid street noise and offer sea views.

◑ Closed occasionally ⚡ From central roundabout in Fishguard, head north on A487 towards Cardigan; hotel is 200 yards on left. Nearest train station: Fishguard Harbour Ferry Terminal 🚶 1 single, 2 twin, 3 double; family rooms available; all with hair-dryer, TV ✓ Restaurant, bar, 2 lounges, gazebo, garden; cots, highchairs ♿ No wheelchair access ● No dogs in public rooms; no smoking in most public rooms and all bedrooms ▭ MasterCard, Visa £ Single £38, single occupancy of twin/double £45, twin/double £60 to £70, family room £85; deposit required. Alc D £22; light meals available; service incl. Special breaks available

FRESHWATER EAST Pembrokeshire
map 4

Portclew House [NEW ENTRY]

Freshwater East, Pembroke SA71 5LA
TEL: (01646) 672800   FAX: (01646) 672810
EMAIL: enquiries@portclewhouse.co.uk
WEB SITE: www.portclewhouse.co.uk

Good-value B&B in an elegant Georgian country house

The sweeping, sandy bay at Freshwater East has just one of the many stunning beaches along this scenic stretch of the Pembrokeshire Coastal Path. Head back up to the top of the hill (less than a mile) and you'll find this pastel yellow, listed mansion with its typically Georgian porch. Steven and Sarah Jackson have been welcoming guests since 2001, offering packed lunches, luggage storage and clothes-drying facilities that will gladden the heart of many a walker. Substantial, Aga-cooked breakfasts are served in an exquisite breakfast room that springs straight out of a Jane Austen novel, with its ornate leaf-design coving, marble fireplace and Regency-stripe paper. Decorative china on an impressive Welsh dresser adds to the charm, but on a sunny day you might just be tempted out to eat on the balcony terrace looking on to the garden and pond. The spacious bedrooms are elegant and well appointed, with Edwardian furniture and fresh-looking bathrooms. Our inspector's favourite was Room 4, with its view to the Preseli mountains. The nearest dinner options are within walking distance.

◑ Closed Chr ⚡ From A477, turn off at Milton for Lamphey; in Lamphey take B5484 for Freshwater East. Nearest train station: Lamphey. Private car park 🚶 1 single, 3 twin, 2 double, 1 family room; all with room service, direct-dial telephone, modem line, TV; some with trouser press; hair-dryer on request ✓ Breakfast room, lounge, garden; leisure facilities nearby; cots, highchairs, outdoor play area ♿ No wheelchair access ● No smoking ▭ MasterCard, Switch, Visa £ Single £25 to £32, single occupancy of twin/double £25 to £42, twin/double £50 to £64, family room £55 to £76; deposit required (3 FOR 2)

HARLECH Gwynedd
map 7

Castle Cottage

Pen Llech, Harlech LL46 2YL
TEL: (01766) 780479   FAX: (01766) 781251
EMAIL: glyn@castlecottageharlech.co.uk
WEB SITE: www.castlecottageharlech.co.uk

A new look for an ancient building a stone's throw from Harlech Castle

Castle Cottage is one of the oldest properties in town, burrowed into the same rocky dais as Edward I's mighty thirteenth-century fortress, and aptly quaint inside. But what chef-patron Glyn Roberts describes as 'a massive declutter' has recently taken place at this much-loved restaurant-with-rooms. Fans of the leitmotif pigs that once adorned every nook of Castle Cottage need not be dismayed: a shelf of mini-porkers still rootles round the stairwell. But the winds of change are certainly blowing through this charming place, the aim being to provide some much-needed breathing space. This year, four new and bigger bedrooms are available in an adjoining building, in a sleeker, contemporary style of which Glyn is very proud. He has plans, too, to enlarge some of the original rooms above the restaurant and give them en-suite bathrooms. The driving force behind this highly successful family-run business is the cooking, which has achieved a solid reputation among locals and visitors alike for excellent value and accomplished handling of top-quality regional produce.

◑ Closed 3 weeks in Jan ⊅ Just off High Street, behind castle. Nearest train station: Harlech ⤶ 7 twin/ double, 1 double; family rooms available; all with hair-dryer, modem line, TV, VCR, CD/DVD player; trouser press on request ⊗ Restaurant, bar, lounge; social functions; leisure facilities nearby; early suppers for children; cots, highchairs ⇖ No wheelchair access; 2 ground-floor bedrooms ⬤ No dogs; smoking in bar only ⊟ Delta, MasterCard, Switch, Visa £ Single occupancy of twin/double from £53, twin/double from £80, family room from £100; deposit required. Set D £27 ③FOR②

HAY-ON-WYE Powys

map 5

Old Black Lion

26 Lion Street, Hay-on-Wye, Hereford HR3 5AD
TEL: (01497) 820841 FAX: (01497) 822960
EMAIL: info@oldblacklion.co.uk
WEB SITE: www.oldblacklion.co.uk

Charming, old-world inn – a good central base for bibliophiles

Don't judge a book by its cover. The Old Black Lion's rather plain exterior belies a wealth of seventeenth-century charm inside, with creaking, sloping floors, narrow corridors and bowed, stoop-inducing ceilings that look as though they have barely changed since (allegedly) Oliver Cromwell stayed here. After a day spent scouring the town for good books or antiques, or walking along nearby Offa's Dyke, guests should find the rustic main bar (with lots of bulky timber posts, pine tables and a wood burner) a particularly appealing spot in which to wind down and taste the eponymous ale. Expect a mix of smart furnishings, teddies and the odd antique in the bedrooms; shower rooms are quite small. Go for one of the rear-facing rooms, which avoid potential street noise and give countryside views. Best of these is the atmospheric Cromwell Suite, where the ornate bed is tucked beneath a beamed, mezzanine lounge area. Rooms in the annexe have a more modern, cottagey look, with immaculate, slate-tiled shower rooms.

◑ Closed 25 & 26 Dec and 2 weeks in Jan ⊅ In centre of Hay-on-Wye. Private car park ⤶ 2 single, 2 twin, 5 double, 1 suite; all with hair-dryer, direct-dial telephone, TV ⊗ Restaurant, bar, garden; social functions; leisure facilities nearby ⇖ No wheelchair access; 2 ground-floor bedrooms ⬤ No children under 5; no dogs; smoking in bar only ⊟ MasterCard, Switch, Visa £ Single £40 to £50, single occupancy of twin/double £55 to £65, twin/double £60 to £85, suite £90 to £110; deposit required. Alc L £20, D £25; light meals available; service incl. Special breaks available

---

LAUGHARNE Carmarthenshire

map 4

The Cors

Newbridge Road, Laugharne, Carmarthen SA33 4SH
TEL: (01994) 427219

Fine Welsh cooking at an intimate restaurant-with-rooms

The cult of Dylan Thomas lives on in his home town, where tourists flock to the poet's Boathouse residence as well as the town's medieval castle. Both of these are walkable from this well-hidden, beige-stone house, which is set back from the street behind a large, exotically landscaped garden, featuring bamboo, reeds and little ponds. The greenery extends to the conservatory, which is dedicated purely to plants. In fact, owner Nick Priestland admits, 'I prefer to garden rather than cook'. Nevertheless, Nick is noted for his skilful modern Welsh cuisine. So over in the intimate, candlelit dining room, the daily-changing menu might include roasted figs with gorgonzola and Parma ham, or beef fillet with green peppercorns in a red wine jus. The general décor leans towards shabby chic, with modernist artworks, antiques and stripped-wood floors. The two bedrooms have a simple appeal, with solid furniture, and look over the garden. On our visit, we thought the entrance sign looked rather tired, and the outside of the house could benefit from a lick of paint. More reports, please.

◖ Closed Mon to Wed; restaurant closed Mon to Wed eves ⚡ Turn right at first crossroads in centre of Laugharne; Cors is at bottom of hill, on right. Private car park 🅿 2 double; both with room service, hair-dryer ✧ Dining room, bar, lounge, conservatory, gardens; leisure facilities nearby ⟨ No wheelchair access ⬤ No children under 12; no dogs; no smoking in bedrooms ▭ None accepted £ Single occupancy of double £30 to £35, double £60 to £70. Set L £15, D £19; alc D £26; light meals available; service incl

Hurst House NEW ENTRY

East Marsh, Laugharne, Carmarthen SA33 4RS
TEL: (01994) 427417   FAX: (01994) 427730
EMAIL: info@hurst-house.co.uk
WEB SITE: www.hurst-house.co.uk

Stylish luxury at a remote, newly converted farmhouse

City-slickers searching for a Welsh antidote to the urban jungle should find this suitably remote. Hurst House sits one mile back from the sea in a pancake-flat landscape punctuated by wind-shaped trees, grazing livestock and a huddle of caravans. It is hard to imagine how this cream, Georgian building looked inside when it was a farmhouse, now that it has been transformed into a boutique hotel. Occasional rustic touches remain, such as the high beams and wood-burner in the bar, but overall the décor follows a classy, metropolitan style. Trendy artworks adorn the walls while exotic ornaments and large mirrors add interest to one of the three dining areas. Here, you might choose locally caught sea bass from the wide-ranging menu. The bedrooms team rich, bold colours with wood beams and offer views to the sea or fields. We liked Room 102, with its intriguingly ornate fireplace and claw-foot bath. The hotel is still a work in progress – on our visit, a bar had yet to be built on the rear patio terrace, the car park faced dilapidated farm outbuildings (due to become bedrooms eventually) and plans were afoot to install a spa centre and indoor pool.

◖ Open all year ⚡ From St Clears, take A4066 to Laugharne; continue through to Broadway; after Broadway take immediate left down into marshes, signposted. Private car park 🅿 7 twin/double; suite available; all with room service, hair-dryer, direct-dial telephone, TV, VCR, DVD, CD player ✧ Restaurant, bar, lounge, library, garden; conferences and social functions; leisure facilities nearby; early suppers for children; cots, highchairs, toys, babysitting, baby-listening ⟨ Wheelchair access to hotel and restaurant; 1 ground-floor bedroom ⬤ None ▭ Amex, Delta, MasterCard, Switch, Visa £ Twin/double £150, suite £200. Continental/cooked B £10; alc L £15, D £30; light meals available

---

LLANARMON DYFFRYN CEIRIOG Wrexham   map 7

West Arms

Llanarmon Dyffryn Ceiriog, Llangollen LL20 7LD
TEL: (01691) 600665   FAX: (01691) 600622
EMAIL: gowestarms@aol.com
WEB SITE: www.thewestarms.co.uk

Appealing seventeenth-century inn hidden in quintessential Welsh countryside

It takes some effort to reach this snug outpost deep in the Ceiriog Valley, and guests are advised that their mobile phone won't work after Chirk or Oswestry. But you will be justly rewarded with a village whose pace of life is refreshingly unhurried and by scenic surroundings that make idyllic walking territory. A brook flows past the gabled West Arms, a seventeenth-century cattle-drovers' inn whose age shows in the profusion of blackened beams, low ceilings, flagged floors and flaming inglenooks. The comfortable lounge bar is ideal for a pre-prandial tipple; look out for the unusual seat – probably a confessional – which came from the local monastery. The small but smart restaurant plays host to a mixture of traditional country dishes and more continental offerings such as risotto. Books and new video players, recently added to the bedrooms, should stave off boredom on rainy days, and complimentary sherry is another thoughtful touch. The older 'character' rooms are aptly named, with charming beams and a four-poster or French-style bed, but it is also worth considering the cheaper, garden-view rooms, particularly since their bathrooms have recently been upgraded with separate baths and showers.

○ Open all year ⊡ From Oswestry take B4579, or from Chirk take B4500. Follow signs to Glyn Ceiriog/ Ceiriog Valley, then to Llanarmon DC. Hotel is on right just over bridge. Private car park ⊨ 1 single, 1 twin, 6 twin/double, 4 double, 1 four-poster, 1 family room, 2 suites; all with room service, hair-dryer, TV, VCR; most with direct-dial telephone, modem line ✓ Restaurant, bar, 2 lounges, library, conservatory, garden; conferences, social functions, civil wedding licence; leisure facilities nearby; early suppers for children; cots, highchairs, baby-listening 𝄞 Wheelchair access to hotel (1 step) and restaurant, WC, 5 ground-floor bedrooms, 3 rooms specially equipped for disabled people. Disabled parking ● No smoking in restaurant ▭ MasterCard, Switch, Visa £ Single £28, single occupancy of twin/double from £53, twin/double from £85, four-poster £174, family room £203, suite from £174; deposit required. Set L (Sun) £18, D £32; light meals available. Special breaks available ③FOR②

LLANDDEINIOLEN Gwynedd
map 7

Ty'n Rhos

Seion, Llanddeiniolen LL55 3AE
TEL: (01248) 670489   FAX: (01248) 670079
EMAIL: enquiries@tynrhos.co.uk
WEB SITE: www.tynrhos.co.uk

Immaculately kept country hotel with views towards the Menai Strait

A thoroughly relaxing stay seems guaranteed in this converted farmhouse, whose picture windows frame tranquil slabs of coastal plain between Snowdon and the sea. The building itself isn't particularly distinguished, but standards of upkeep are extremely high inside and out, the gardens being as trim and tidy as the light, spacious interior. Décor is tastefully elegant – antiques and country pieces are thoughtfully interspersed with high-quality modern furnishings. Housekeeping is impeccable, but guests' comfort is the main priority.

Interlocking public rooms include a cosy bar and airy lounge, both with open fires and plenty to read. Beyond lies a plant-festooned conservatory with wicker seating, where drinks are served. The sunny dining room is the centre of attention in the mornings and evenings, when guests are treated to interesting breakfasts (Menai oysters and laver bread if you're lucky) and accomplished set dinners using local produce. Each bedroom is individually designed with great decorative flair.

○ Closed 17 Dec to 10 Jan ⊡ Off B4366 in hamlet of Seion, between the B4547 and the A4244, 1½ miles north-east of Bethel. Private car park ⊨ 2 single, 2 twin, 4 twin/double, 3 double; all with room service, hair-dryer, direct-dial telephone, modem line, TV; some with VCR ✓ Dining room, bar, lounge, conservatory, garden; conferences; social functions; leisure facilities nearby; early suppers for children 𝄞 Wheelchair access to hotel (2 steps) and restaurant (2 steps), 3 ground-floor bedrooms, 1 room specially equipped for disabled people ● No children under 6; no dogs; smoking in lounge only ▭ Amex, Delta, MasterCard, Switch, Visa £ Single £55, single occupancy of twin/double £65 to £85, twin £86, double £86 to £120; deposit required. Set D £23.50; light meals available. Special breaks available

---

LLANDRILLO Denbighshire
map 7

Tyddyn Llan

Llandrillo, Corwen LL21 0ST
TEL: (01490) 440264   FAX: (01490) 440414
EMAIL: tyddynllan@compuserve.com
WEB SITE: www.tyddynllan.co.uk

Top-notch cuisine is the focus at this refined Georgian country house

Tyddyn Llan describes itself as a restaurant-with-rooms, but that seems rather modest, considering that this stone building, just outside the quiet village of Llandrillo, is

actually a large country house with several tastefully furnished lounge areas. But Bryan and Susan Webb are keen to attract guests here with the promise of fine but unpretentious cuisine, and they don't disappoint. No-nonsense, flavoursome dishes, such as roast pigeon with Savoy cabbage parcels, are served with efficiency in the appealing, wood-panelled restaurant. The menus offer a good choice, backed up by a gargantuan wine list. With Snowdonia National Park only a short drive away, there is ample opportunity to build up an appetite with outdoor activities, although some may be content with a spot of croquet on the hotel's trim lawn. The bedrooms are as scrumptious as the cooking, decorated in stylish colours, and often fitted with antique beds. For that extra touch of luxury and privacy, a ground-floor suite has been added recently, with its own private garden.

❍ Closed 17 to 27 Jan ⚡ From A5 at Corwen, take B4401 through Cynwyd to Llandrillo; house is on right as you leave village. Private car park 🚗 4 twin, 1 twin/double, 7 double, 1 suite; family rooms available; all with hair-dryer, direct-dial telephone, TV, CD player ✓ Restaurant, bar, 2 lounges, garden; conferences and social functions; civil wedding licence; leisure facilities nearby; early suppers for children; cots, highchairs ♿ Wheelchair access to hotel and restaurant, WC, 1 ground-floor suite. Disabled parking ● No dogs in public rooms; smoking in bar only ▭ MasterCard, Switch, Visa £ Single occupancy of twin/double £55 to £65, twin/double £120 to £150; family room £140 to £170, suite £160 to £200; deposit required. Set Sun L £19.50; alc L £23.50, D £35; light meals available. Special breaks available (3 FOR 2)

LLANDUDNO Conwy map 7

Abbey Lodge NEW ENTRY

14 Abbey Road, Llandudno LL30 2EA
TEL: (01492) 878042 (AND FAX)
EMAIL: enquiries@abbeylodgeuk.com
WEB SITE: www.abbeylodgeuk.com

Fresh and friendly B&B offering great rates near the seafront

Just a few minutes' walk from Llandudno's popular seafront is a road brimming with B&Bs and hotels, among which the fragrantly floral Abbey Lodge stands out at first glance. Inside and out, it's smartly decorated with a stylish yet comfortable colour scheme and furnishings, one example being the cosy sitting room with its inviting burgundy squishy sofas, an open fire and plenty of magazines to browse. The generous breakfasts (and weekend evening meals on request) are taken *en famille* at the big dining table, giving you a chance to meet your fellow guests. Upstairs, bedrooms are not huge, but they are well appointed, often with smashing bathrooms – for example, Beaumaris's bathroom comes complete with a Gothic arched window. There's a pleasant garden at the back for summertime relaxing, while Trish and Geoffrey Howard's jolly, personable style puts guests at ease.

❍ Closed 15 Dec to 15 Jan ⚡ From the promenade, with sea on right, turn left at T-junction into Gloddaeth Street; go straight ahead at two roundabouts, then first right; at top, turn right at T-junction; hotel is on left. Private car park. Nearest train station: Llandudno 🚗 1 twin, 3 double; all with room service, hair-dryer, trouser press, TV; fax, modem line available ✓ Breakfast room, sitting room, library, garden ♿ No wheelchair access ● No children under 12; no dogs; no smoking ▭ None accepted £ Single occupancy of twin/double £45 to £50, twin/double £65

Bodysgallen Hall

Llandudno LL30 1RS
TEL: (01492) 584466 FAX: (01492) 582519
EMAIL: info@bodysgallen.com
WEB SITE: www.bodysgallen.com

A fascinating, historic country-house hotel offering a taste of the high life

Bodysgallen dates back to medieval times, when its thirteenth-century watchtower formed part of Conwy's Anglo-Welsh border defences, commanding strategic views towards Snowdonia's mountains. Through subsequent centuries additions have been made in mellow sandstone, the latest being a state-of-the-art spa complex and a number of self-catering units in the grounds. The property is protected under covenant by the

National Trust and its owners, Historic House Hotels, spared no expense when painstakingly restoring the property to its former glory. Its period features (superb oak panelling, original fireplaces) provide a splendidly authentic foil for sumptuous, traditional country-house furnishings. Fresh flowers, blazing fires and gleaming antiques create a scene fit for an interior design magazine. Bedrooms, all different, are classically pretty and have lots of luxury extras. Food is predictably ambitious. Magnificent gardens, with a maze of topiaried terraces, add exterior 'rooms' to the house.

○ Open all year ⊡ Leave A55 on A470 towards Llandudno; hotel is 2 miles on right. Private car park ⛽ 3 single, 19 twin/double, 8 double, 2 four-poster, 3 family rooms; suites available; all with room service, hair-dryer, trouser press, direct-dial telephone, TV; some with tea/coffee-making facilities, modem line, VCR, CD player ✓ Dining room, bar, 3 lounges, library, garden; conferences and social functions; civil wedding licence; gym, spa, tennis, heated indoor swimming pool 🦽 Wheelchair access to hotel (ramp) and restaurant, WC, 2 ground-floor bedrooms, 1 room specially equipped for disabled people. Disabled parking ● No children under 8; no dogs; no smoking in bedrooms ▭ Delta, MasterCard, Switch, Visa £ Single room £120, single occupancy of twin/double from £130, twin/double from £165, four-poster £290, family room £300, suite from £195; deposit required. Cooked B £15; set L £22, D £38; light meals available; service incl. Special breaks available

Osborne House

17 North Parade, Llandudno LL30 2LP
TEL: (01492) 860330   FAX: (01492) 860791
EMAIL: sales@osbornehouse.com
WEB SITE: www.osbornehouse.com

Dazzlingly imaginative restoration of a distinguished Victorian townhouse

This Grade II listed building at the smart end of Llandudno's seafront began life as the holiday home of a wealthy Liverpool brewer, then slipped into decline. After a decade in the hands of the Maddocks family, its fortunes have revived dramatically. Dedicated craftsmanship and painstaking hard work have paid off, and the hotel has become a must-try experience for affluent young professionals escaping urban stress. A stage-set lounge/dining area occupies the entire reception floor, each section more theatrically designed than the last in black, white and gold, with period features and genuine antiques at every turn: crystal chandeliers, Persian rugs, rococo mirrors. The food, sophisticated but refreshingly simple, is surprisingly good value (dressed fresh crab, local belly of pork). Sumptuous bedrooms extend the romantic fantasy on three upper floors. Four-posters or canopied beds swathed in airy white drapes, gas-flame fireplaces and roll-top baths greet new arrivals, along with complimentary champagne. Classic, but sparklingly contemporary too. Bring a friend, and enjoy!

○ Closed 10 days at Chr ⊡ On promenade in Llandudno, opposite pier. Nearest train station: Llandudno Junction. Private car park ⛽ 6 suites; all with room service, hair-dryer, trouser press, direct-dial telephone, fax line, modem line, TV, DVD, CD player ✓ Restaurant, bar, lounge, library, conservatory; conferences; leisure facilities nearby 🦽 No wheelchair access ● No children under 16; no dogs; no smoking in public rooms ▭ Amex, Delta, Diners, MasterCard, Switch, Visa £ Single occupancy of suite £155 to £200; suite £145 to £200; deposit required. Alc L £15, D £20; light meals available ③FOR②

LLANFACHRETH Gwynedd   map 7

Ty Isaf Farmhouse

Llanfachreth, Dolgellau LL40 2EA
TEL: (01341) 423261 (AND FAX)
EMAIL: raygear@tyisaf78.freeserve.co.uk
WEB SITE: www.tyisaf78.freeserve.co.uk

Charming, simple guesthouse in a friendly seventeenth-century longhouse

Llanfachreth lies in a tangle of rural lanes north of Dolgellau, with mountain and forest scenery all around. Ty Isaf stands near the stumpy-spired church, and all you see beyond its cottage gardens are streams, meadows and bracken-clad hills. Until fairly recently it was a working farm, and a few creatures still scratch round the gardens. Hens provide the breakfast eggs, and you may spot the odd pet llama or stray deer. Raymond and Lorna Gear's stone-built home isn't luxurious, but it has an immediately welcoming atmosphere. There's a spacious lounge with a wood-burning stove

and plenty of games and magazines. Simple three-course evening meals (by arrangement) and breakfast are served at a single polished table. The three letting bedrooms are quaint and countrified, with spriggy wallpapers, pine furnishings, sloping ceilings and latched doors. They have suitably rustic names like Hay Loft and Straw Store. One has a half-bath, the others showers only.

◖ Closed mid-Dec to Jan and for owners' holidays ⊿ From A470 Dolgellau bypass, take turning to Bala then first left to Dolgellau; turn right to Llanfachreth. Private car park 🛏 1 twin, 2 double; all with hair-dryer ⬙ Dining room, lounge, study, garden ⅋ No wheelchair access ⬤ No children under 13; dogs by arrangement; no smoking ▭ None accepted £ Single occupancy of twin/double £25 to £35, twin/double £50; deposit required. Set D £16.50; service incl. Special breaks available (3 FOR 2)

LLANFIHANGEL-YNG-NGWYNFA Powys
map 7

Cyfie Farm [NEW ENTRY]

Llanfihangel-yng-Ngwynfa, Nr Llanfyllin, Welshpool SY22 5JE
TEL: (01691) 648451   FAX: (01691) 648363
EMAIL: info@cyfiefarm.co.uk
WEB SITE: www.cyfiefarm.co.uk

Friendly hosts and far-reaching views at an old longhouse

When Claire and Neil Bale stayed at Cyfie Farm for their silver anniversary, they fell so in love with it that they decided to buy it! And it's easy to see why. This 20-acre working farm is perched above a valley deep in the Powys countryside, surrounded by miles of bucolic beauty that can't have changed since the farm's longhouse was built in the seventeenth century. Attractions nearby include Powis Castle and Lake Vyrnwy, although you may prefer to simply stay put and get acquainted with farm life, maybe watching sheep-dipping or holding a newborn lamb. Lamb may turn up in a rosemary and wine sauce at the Bales' five-

course set dinner, served around one table on Wednesday to Saturday evenings. There is no communal lounge because every bedroom suite has its own sitting area, complete with hearth and DVDs. There are plenty of other thoughtful touches, such as individually wrapped chocolates, the hotel's own filtered spring water, and umbrellas. Choosing a favourite is hard – perhaps the rustic Stable Suite, dotted with antiques and Shetland paintings, or the beamed Wheat Suite which has great hill views from upstairs. For our inspector, the Barley Suite had the edge, with its own kitchen, a bread-oven feature and a spacious bathroom.

◖ Closed mid-Nov to mid-Feb; dining room closed Sun to Tue ⊿ From Welshpool take A490 to Llanfyllin; then B4393 towards Lake Vyrnwy; after 4 miles turn left on to B4382, signposted Llanfihangel/Dolanog. At bottom of Llanfihangel bear right; straight on past cemetery, over crossroads towards Dolanog, then take first left; Cyfie is third farm on left. Private car park 🛏 3 suites; all with hair-dryer, TV, VCR, CD player; fax, modem line available ⬙ Dining room, library, conservatory, garden ⅋ No wheelchair access ⬤ No children under 10; no dogs; no smoking ▭ Amex, Delta, Diners, MasterCard, Switch, Visa £ Single occupancy of suite £60, suite £75 (2004 prices); deposit required. Set D £17.50; light meals available; service incl. Special breaks available

---

LLANGAMMARCH WELLS Powys
map 4

Lake Country House

Llangammarch Wells LD4 4BS
TEL: (01591) 620202   FAX: (01591) 620457
EMAIL: info@lakecountryhouse.co.uk
WEB SITE: www.lakecountryhouse.co.uk

Unwind at an elegant former spa resort in beguiling grounds

During the early twentieth century, tourists and leaders flocked to this mock-Tudor hotel, to sample the waters at the only barium spa resort in Britain. Its heyday may be long gone – no spa is available these days – but now the hotel offers plenty of other enticements. For starters, there are 50 acres of splendid grounds. Walking the woodland paths or going to the eponymous lake to fish for trout or see the resident swans is a delight. Golf, tennis and billiards are among other boredom-busting options. The inviting lounges have the usual country-house refinements such as antiques, family portraits and chandeliers, and on our visit,

the former bar was due to reopen as another lounge, which will be oak-panelled with oil paintings. The set menu in the smart restaurant might include tenderloin of pork with fresh linguini and calvados sauce. The bedrooms are tastefully decorated, and offer novels and sherry. The Master bedroom (a standard room), where Kaiser Wilhelm stayed in 1912, has an ornately carved bed, but its bathroom is small. One reader mentioned poor service and extreme variations in shower temperature. Parking space in the grounds is also limited. More reports, please.

❍ Open all year ⚡ From Brecon, take B519 across Mount Eppynt (6 miles); at foot of hill, turn left at crossroads; hotel is 1 mile along. Private car park. Nearest train station: Llangammarch Wells 🛏 2 twin/double, 6 double, 11 suites; all with room service, hair-dryer, direct-dial telephone, TV; no tea/coffee-making facilities in rooms ✅ Restaurant, 3 lounges, bar service, games room, gardens; conferences and social functions; civil wedding licence; tennis, golf, fishing; early suppers for children; cots, highchairs, babysitting, baby-listening ♿ Wheelchair access to hotel (ramp) and restaurant, 2 ground-floor bedrooms, 1 room specially equipped for disabled people ● No children under 8 in restaurant eves; no dogs in public rooms and some bedrooms (£6 per night); no smoking in some public rooms and some bedrooms ▭ Amex, Delta, Diners, MasterCard, Switch, Visa £ Single occupancy of twin/double/suite £105 to £170, twin/double £140 to £200, suite £240 (2004 prices); deposit required. Set L £24.50, D £37.50; light meals available; service incl. Special breaks available ③FOR②

LLANGOLLEN Denbighshire   map 7

Gales

18 Bridge Street, Llangollen LL20 8PF
TEL: (01978) 860089   FAX: (01978) 861313
EMAIL: richard@galesofllangollen.co.uk
WEB SITE: www.galesofllangollen.co.uk

Historic wine bar with stylish rooms right in the town centre

Oenophiles with a thirst for wine-related paraphernalia should head for this corking wine bar in the centre of Llangollen. Long-established, Gales sells various items in its reception shop, although it is the bar and bedrooms that are the major draw. Unsurprisingly, the dual-level bar is the focal point, a distinctive area with bare wood floors and Art Deco posters on wood-panelled walls. It is a convivial place to sit back with one of the many wine options and chat about the day's activities – whether a narrowboat trip along Llangollen canal or a

rather speedier white-water rafting experience on the River Dee, which is right on the doorstep. Bistro-style daily specials are chalked up on the blackboard, based on locally sourced produce where possible. A covered walkway now links the main building and the annexe, which dates back to the seventeenth century. The well-designed, uncluttered bedrooms are divided between both buildings and variously feature ornate French-style beds, smart white furnishings and exposed timbers. Some have been refreshed recently with new carpets.

❍ Closed 24 Dec to 2 Jan; restaurant closed Sun eve ⚡ In Llangollen town centre. Private car park 🛏 6 twin, 6 double, 1 family room, 2 suites; all with hairdryer, direct-dial telephone, TV ✅ Restaurant/bar; conferences; leisure facilities nearby; cots, highchairs ♿ Wheelchair access to hotel (1 step) and restaurant (1 step), 1 ground-floor bedroom ● No dogs in bedrooms; no smoking in some bedrooms ▭ Amex, Delta, Diners, MasterCard, Switch, Visa £ Single occupancy of twin/double £40 to £50, twin/double £50 to £60, family room £57.50 to £67.50, suite £60 to £70; deposit required. Cooked B £5; alc L £11, D £17; light meals available

map 4
Old Post Office

Llanigon, Hay-on-Wye HR3 5QA
TEL: (01497) 820008
WEB SITE: www.oldpost-office.co.uk

Intimate cottage with inviting rooms, near Hay-on-Wye

In 1980, this whitewashed stone cottage ended its time as Llanigon's post office and store. Now the nearest shops are two miles away in that booklovers' centre, Hay-on-Wye, although the cottage must still be the most visited place in this hamlet. Linda Webb has lived here for about 15 years and continues to enjoy catering for B&B guests. On your arrival, she will probably invite you into the sunny lounge for a pot of tea and will gladly give recommendations for eateries in Hay and around. Breakfast is a strictly vegetarian affair, including perhaps potato cakes and mushrooms, and is served on stylish crockery in the smart breakfast room. It's a shame that the wood burner never gets used, though. Plenty of seventeenth-century charm remains up in the bedrooms, usually in the form of chunky beams. The rooms are modestly furnished and tend to be rather small, perhaps with sinks nearer the bed than the shower room. The attic room has double-aspect Black Mountain views; another, spacious room has its own external entrance, whitewashed stone walls and (curiously) a ledge of antique phials.

◗ Open all year ⌷ From Hay-on-Wye, take B4350 Brecon road for ½ mile; turn left at sign to Llanigon; after a mile, turn left just before school; B&B is white house on right. Private car park ⌷ 1 twin/double, 2 double; all with hair-dryer ⌀ Breakfast room, lounge; leisure facilities nearby ⌷ No wheelchair access ● No children under 7; no smoking ⌷ None accepted £ Single occupancy of twin/double £20 to £50, twin/double £40 to £60; deposit required

map 4
Trevaccoon NEW ENTRY

Llanrhian, St David's, Haverfordwest SA62 6DP
TEL: (01348) 831438 (AND FAX)
EMAIL: flynn@trevaccoon.co.uk
WEB SITE: www.trevaccoon.co.uk

Well-run, upmarket Georgian country house offering B&B and sea views

With the picturesque Pembrokeshire National Park literally across the road, and superb views stretching to the coast, Trevaccoon is already on to a winner. Add to that Caroline Flynn's sensitive restoration of this pale pink Georgian gem – seen in the decorative coving, original arches and vaulted ceilings – and you've got a perfect combination. Whether you're tucking into kippers or exotic fruits in the breakfast room or relaxing by the fire in the elegant sitting room, the vista is impressive. Caroline has a passion for pottery, and if the sight of her colourful floral jugs around the house inspires you to try throwing clay, lessons may be available. She also wants guests to feel at home, so a communal kitchenette with fresh milk is provided, as well as many books and games to keep all ages happy. Yet more thoughtful touches, such as port decanters, fresh flowers and bathrobes, appear in the bedrooms. Each room, named after a local beach or bay, is decorated differently in stylish, muted tones, and most feature charming local paintings, original sash window shutters and a slick-looking bathroom. The sweet harbour village of Porthgain, about two miles away, is the nearest place for dinner.

◗ Closed occasionally ⌷ Take A487 linking Fishguard and St David's; about 9 miles from Fishguard (6 miles from St David's), turn towards sea at Croes Goch crossroads; after 1 mile turn left at Llanrhian crossroads; house is on left after ½ mile. Private car park ⌷ 2 twin, 1 double, 2 family rooms; all with hair-dryer, TV; fax, telephone, ironing facilities available ⌀ Breakfast room, sitting room, kitchenette, garden; meetings and social functions; leisure facilities nearby; cots, highchairs, toys, baby-listening, outdoor play area ⌷ Wheelchair access to hotel and breakfast room; 1 ground-floor bedroom partially equipped for disabled people ● No dogs; no smoking ⊟ None accepted £ Single occupancy of twin/double £55 to £70, twin/double £70 to £85, family room £125; deposit required. Special breaks available

---

LLANWRTYD WELLS Powys map 4

Carlton House

Dol-y-coed Road, Llanwrtyd Wells LD5 4RA
TEL: (01591) 610248 FAX: (01591) 610242
EMAIL: info@carltonrestaurant.co.uk
WEB SITE: www.carltonrestaurant.co.uk

Impressive home cooking matched with cosy, good-value rooms

Mary Ann Gilchrist has been delighting visitors to this townhouse restaurant-with-rooms for more than a dozen years. The dinners still work their magic, partly through Mary Ann's skilful combination of ingredients (such as fillet steak with porcini, smoked pancetta and polenta), but also through the personal touches. A lemon sorbet laced with gin and tonic was given as an *amuse-bouche* to our incognito inspector, who had previously ordered a 'G & T'. The deliciously moist bread and butter pudding was also notable on this visit. The small lounge has an abundance of cosy seats in which to chat over an aperitif (and plenty of board games too), while eclectic modern paintings and oriental ornaments add interest to the informal, wood-panelled restaurant. Bold, black-cherry walls on the landings give a hint of the character to come in the bedrooms, which, despite not being luxurious, are homely and good-value. Each has a distinct style, such as oriental Room 1, with its marquetry furniture and Chinese-style lampstand, or the cheery tartan Room 5, with its Scottish pictures, new emerald carpet and plaid fabrics.

◐ Closed Dec; restaurant closed Sun eve exc bank hols ⤢ In centre of Llanwrtyd Wells. Nearest train station: Llanwrtyd Wells ⤢ 2 twin/double, 4 double; all with hair-dryer, TV ⊘ Restaurant, lounge; early suppers for children; cots, highchairs, baby-listening ⅙ No wheelchair access ● No dogs in public rooms; no smoking in some public rooms ⊟ Delta, MasterCard, Switch, Visa £ Single occupancy of twin/double £30 to £45, twin/double £50 to £80; deposit required. Set L £24.50, D (not Fri/Sat) £24.50; alc L, D £40. Special breaks available ③FOR②

LLWYNHENDY Carmarthenshire map 4

Llwyn Hall [NEW ENTRY]

Llwynhendy, Llanelli SA14 9LJ
TEL: (01554) 777754 FAX: (01554) 744146
EMAIL: llwynhall@hotmail.com
WEB SITE: www.llwynhall.com

Stylish intimacy at a family-run country house near Llanelli

Richard Burrows is a creative man. In the 1990s, he took on the challenge of restoring a derelict Victorian, gabled house and has transformed it with panache into an appealing yellow and snow-white confection with a homely, traditional style inside. More recently, he has put his training with Laura Ashley to good use, designing and making many of the house's curtains and other stylish furnishings, as well as decorating with hand-printed wallpaper. Richard's attention to detail also appears in stained-glass windows, ornate mouldings in the snug lounge, and the attractive bedrooms, which all offer biscuits and DVD players. They are generally light, with pine furniture and perhaps old fireplaces. The premier four-poster room has a great rural view as well as a gilt angel above the claw-foot bath! Half the bedroom accommodation (including a luxury twin) is in a cottage, Han y Bont, 300 yards from the house. Breakfast is an event, with such possibilities as cockles and laverbread, kippers and home-baked bread. Llwyn Hall is a couple of miles from the centre of Llanelli, although bird watchers will be pleased to know that the Millennium Wetlands Centre is even closer.

○ Open all year From A484 east of Llanelli, follow brown tourist signs for Llwyn Hall. Private car park 1 single, 1 twin, 5 double, 1 four-poster; all with hair-dryer, TV, VCR, DVD, CD player; some with room service Restaurant, bar service, lounge, conservatory, garden; conferences and social functions; civil wedding licence; leisure facilities nearby; highchairs No wheelchair access ● Children by arrangement only; no dogs in public rooms and most bedrooms; no smoking Amex, Delta, MasterCard, Switch, Visa £ Single £45, single occupancy of twin/double £45 to £55, twin/double £65 to £75, four-poster £75; alc L £16/£18, D £27.50; light meals available. Special breaks available

---

LLYSWEN Powys

map 4

Llangoed Hall

Llyswen, Brecon LD3 0YP
TEL: (01874) 754525 FAX: (01874) 754545
EMAIL: enquiries@llangoedhall.com
WEB SITE: www.llangoedhall.com

First-rate luxury, and prices to match, at a venerable country house

Even from the first glimpses of Llangoed Hall as you approach down the long driveway to the grand entrance, you may feel that you have suddenly been time-warped back to the Edwardian era. The austere stone building itself, typically mullioned and covered in creepers, dates back in part to that period (the origins are Jacobean), while a generous spread of antiques and ancient wall hangings are matched with an air of polite formality in the public rooms. There are several elegant, interlinking lounges, dotted with model trains belonging to owner Sir Bernard Ashley, plus the Jacobean snooker room with a library's worth of books. The hotel's surroundings are suitably bucolic, with a forest, acres of meadows leading to the River Wye and mountain views in the distance. Fruits and herbs from the walled garden may turn up in the light, Regency-style dining room, where creative dishes on the set menus blend Mediterranean influences with traditional British fare. Breakfast options include laverbread and brioche. The bedrooms are suitably furnished in typically country-house style (often with fruity and floral patterns), and have smart, capacious bathrooms.

○ Open all year 11 miles north-east of Brecon on A470 towards Builth Wells. Private car park 2 single, 10 double/twin, 8 four-poster, 3 suites; all with room service, hair-dryer, direct-dial telephone, TV; no tea/coffee-making facilities in rooms Dining room, 3 lounges, library/games room, conservatory, garden; conferences, social functions, civil wedding licence; tennis, croquet; leisure facilities nearby; early suppers for children No wheelchair access ● No children under 8, no dogs in hotel (heated kennels available); no smoking in bedrooms Amex, Delta, Diners, MasterCard, Switch, Visa £ Single from £140, single occupancy of twin/double from £140 to £160, twin/double £180 to £200, suite £340 to £360; deposit required. Alc L £28.50, D £43; light meals available, service incl. Special breaks available

---

MENAI BRIDGE Isle of Anglesey

map 7

Wern Farm NEW ENTRY

Pentraeth Road, Menai Bridge LL59 5RR
TEL: (01248) 712421 (AND FAX)
EMAIL: wernfarmanglesey@onetel.com
WEB SITE: www.angleseyfarms.com/wern

Book ahead to avoid disappointment at this sought-after farm guesthouse

Peter and Linda Brayshaw have happily exchanged doing the milking on their 260-acre mixed farm for another kind of early morning start. They have been known to serve breakfast at 5am for guests with planes to catch, but try not to make a habit of this. It's obvious, though, that they love what they're doing. The original seventeenth-century house, now painted a cheery yellow, has been sympathetically extended and modernised. Guests arrive (via the Internet) from all over the world, many for a second helping of the Brayshaws' exemplary hospitality, so the three letting bedrooms are often full. The interior is homely, comfortable and spotlessly kept in light colours. Furnishings are generally simple, but bedrooms have many thoughtful touches and the house is full of books and games, plus local information and restaurant suggestions. Welsh teas are served to new arrivals, and breakfasts in the Victorian conservatory sound a feast.

⭕ Closed Dec and Jan 🗺 From A5/A55 take second exit (Junction 8) after crossing Britannia Bridge, signed A5025 Amlwch/Benllech. After roundabout, pass large garage; hotel is ½ mile on right. Private car park 🛏 1 twin/double, 1 double, 1 family room; all with hair-dryer, trouser press, TV ✓ Lounge, conservatory/breakfast room, games room; tennis; highchairs, toys, babysitting ♿ No wheelchair access ⬤ No dogs; no smoking ▭ MasterCard, Switch, Visa £ Twin/double £60 to £70, family room £70 to £80

MILEBROOK Powys   map 4

Milebrook House

Milebrook, Knighton LD7 1LT
TEL: (01547) 528632   FAX: (01547) 520509
EMAIL: hotel@milebrook.kc3ltd.co.uk
WEB SITE: www.milebrookhouse.co.uk

Tasteful rooms at an informal country house bordering England

Positioned on the border with England, Offa's Dyke is a long-standing reminder of ancient Anglo-Welsh hostility. These days, the Dyke brings people together as visitors walk the classic Offa's Dyke path, often basing themselves near its centre in Knighton. Neighbouring Milebrook House, which provides lovely views to these well-trodden hills, is a smart, creeper-clad, Georgian building where explorer Wilfred Thesiger once resided. Beryl Marsden is the genial, down-to-earth hostess, while her husband Rodney works his magic on the attractively landscaped gardens, tending vegetables that will appear on the varied menus. Lunch out on the terrace overlooking the gardens might precede a game of croquet or fishing on the River Teme. The boldly decorated restaurant rooms are refreshingly informal while interesting ornaments pepper other public rooms, such as the genteel bar. One reader enjoyed her evening meal 'with a quite extensive choice, prompt service and reasonably priced wine'. However, she was less impressed with the lack of choice at breakfast and was kept awake by traffic noise. Go for one of the tastefully furnished rooms at the side or rear, such as the newer, fresh-looking rooms in the extension, with their marble-tiled bathrooms.

⭕ Open all year 🗺 2 miles east of Knighton, on A4113 Ludlow road. Nearest train station: Knighton. Private car park 🛏 4 twin, 6 double; family rooms available; all with room service, hair-dryer, direct-dial telephone, TV ✓ Restaurant, bar, lounge, library, garden; conferences; social functions; leisure facilities nearby; early suppers for children ♿ Wheelchair access to hotel (1 step) and restaurant, National Accessible Scheme: mobility impairment M3, 2 ground-floor bedrooms, 1 room specially equipped for disabled people. Disabled parking ⬤ No children under 8; no dogs; smoking in bar only ▭ Delta, Diners, MasterCard, Switch, Visa £ Single occupancy of twin/double £58 to £62, twin/double £89 to £95, family room £114 to £120; deposit required (prices valid till Jan 2005). Set L £13, D £25.50; alc L £25.50, D £30.50; light meals available. Special breaks available

---

NANTGWYNANT Gwynedd   map 7

Pen-y-Gwryd Hotel

Nantgwynant, Caernarfon LL55 4NT
TEL: (01286) 870211
WEB SITE: www.pyg.co.uk

Rugged walkers' inn, a character-forming but friendly Snowdonian base-camp

Lightning strikes routinely interrupt electricity supplies in this area, but on a clear day, the vistas of ice-gouged Snowdonian massifs mirrored in the hotel's spring-fed natural swimming pool are unforgettable. This stone-built inn has a couple of centuries of history behind it, and more than its fair share of tales to tell, as witnessed by the signatures of Himalayan heroes scrawled on taproom ceilings, and the wartime evacuees' graffiti etched on dining-room windows. The hotel's training-camp role for the 1953 Everest expedition has endowed it with an enduring cachet among walkers and climbers, and its yesteryear institutional ambience survives unchallenged. Bedrooms are small and spartan, cheered only by colourful Welsh bedspreads. This is not a place for cissies expecting door keys, televisions or en-suite showers. But if you're down the mountain fast enough you can be first in line for that amazing original Victorian bathroom before the dinner gong bangs at 7.30p.m.

◗ Closed Nov & Dec and midweek in Jan & Feb ⚡ From Betws-y-Coed, take A5 west to Capel Curig; turn left on to A4086; hotel is 4 miles on. Private car park ⬅ 1 single, 6 twin, 8 twin/double, 1 four-poster; 11 with shared bathroom; hair-dryer available; no tea/coffee-making facilities in rooms ✓ Dining room, bar, lounge, games room, garden; conferences; unheated outdoor natural pool; leisure facilities nearby; early suppers for children; cots, highchairs, outdoor play area ♿ Wheelchair access to hotel and dining room, WC, 1 ground-floor bedroom. Disabled parking ● No dogs in dining room, £2 in bedrooms, no smoking in bedrooms ▭ None accepted £ Single room £28, single occupancy of twin/double £38, twin/double £56 to £68, four-poster £74. Set D £20; service incl

---

NEWPORT Pembrokeshire map 4

Cnapan

East Street, Newport SA42 0SY
TEL: (01239) 820575
EMAIL: cnapan@online-holidays.net
WEB SITE: www.online-holidays.net/cnapan

Relaxed, family-run restaurant-with-rooms, a short walk from the beach

This Newport is not the large industrial town near Cardiff but its infinitely smaller and more charming namesake by the Pembrokeshire coast. Only a few minutes' walk from East Street (the town's main street), you'll hit the beach and coastal path. Beyond the pedimented porch of this pale pink Georgian house lies an unassuming family home, decorated with porcelain sets and ancestral photos on the upstairs walls. Two of the most recent generations (the Coopers and Lloyds) have been entertaining and feeding guests at Cnapan for two decades, attracting guests back with dishes such as pan-fried strips of Welsh black beef in creamy brandy sauce. The rear garden makes a pleasant alternative to the bar for a pre-prandial tipple, while the dining room itself looks traditionally rustic, with exposed stone walls, chintzy cloths and pine settles. The lounge is suitably inviting, with several cosy sofas around the wood burner. The bedrooms have light, country furnishings; our favourite was Room 4, with its sofa in the bay window. Some rooms face the town's church and castle but may be prone to traffic noise; the shower rooms are a little pokey.

◗ Closed Chr, Jan & Feb; dining room closed Tue eve ⚡ In centre of Newport, about 7 miles from Fishguard, on A487. Private car park ⬅ 3 twin/double, 1 double, 1 family room; all with room service, hair-dryer, TV ✓ Dining room, bar, lounge, garden; leisure facilities nearby; early suppers for children; cots, highchairs, toys, baby-listening ♿ No wheelchair access ● No dogs; smoking in bar only ▭ Delta, MasterCard, Switch, Visa £ Single occupancy of twin/double £35 to £42, twin/double £70, family room £79 (2004 prices); deposit required. Alc L £13.50, D £24; light meals available

---

NORTHOP Flintshire map 7

Soughton Hall

Northop, Mold CH7 6AB
TEL: (01352) 840811   FAX: (01352) 840382
EMAIL: info@soughtonhall.co.uk
WEB SITE: www.soughtonhall.co.uk

Impressive Italianate mansion, much used for functions and weddings

A setting in 150 acres of fine parkland with an approach via a stately avenue of lime trees sets the tone for this grand country house, built originally as a bishop's palace in 1715.

Victorian owner William John Bankes stamped his love of all things oriental on the house, adding Islamic turrets and sumptuous mouldings. The imposing interiors with their marble fireplaces and period antiques lend themselves to grand occasions, so Soughton Hall is very popular for the posher sort of civil wedding. Bedrooms – all but the Butler's Suite on upper floors and reached by a warren of steep stairways – are traditionally chintzy, with a sprinkling of antique brass beds and character bathrooms. One cottage-style suite is in a separate annexe. The Stables brasserie in raftered outhouses offers an alternative to the frescoed formality of the main restaurant with its breezy Racecourse Menu (dishes include Thai-style fishcakes with chilli and coriander salad, and farmhouse sausages). One reader, who found the dinner excellent and praised the 'efficient and friendly service', was less impressed by the 'very poor' breakfast, and the fact that she was overcharged.

○ Open all year 🔁 Turn off A55 on to A5119 (signposted Mold); pass through Northop village; hotel is ¾ mile on left. Nearest train station: Flint. Private car park 🚗 2 twin, 5 double, 2 four-poster, 1 family room, 4 suites; all with room service, hair-dryer, direct-dial telephone, modem line, TV; some with trouser press, VCR, CD 🅥 2 restaurants, bar, drawing room, library, gardens; conferences; social functions; civil wedding licence; tennis; leisure facilities nearby; cots, highchairs 🦽 Wheelchair access to hotel and restaurant, WC, 1 ground-floor bedroom ● No dogs in public rooms; no smoking in bedrooms ▭ Amex, MasterCard, Switch, Visa £ Single occupancy of twin/double £100, twin from £150, double from £120, four-poster £170, family room £180, suite from £150; deposit required. Alc L £17.50, D £25; light meals available; service incl. Special breaks available

---

PENMACHNO Conwy   map 7

Penmachno Hall NEW ENTRY

Penmachno, Betws-y-Coed LL24 0PU
TEL: (01690) 760410   FAX: (01690) 760410
EMAIL: enquiries@penmachnohall.co.uk
WEB SITE: www.penmachnohall.co.uk

Dashingly renovated stone-built rectory in idyllic rural setting

Errant sheep making night raids on the garden seem the most serious threats to the good life here. Penmachno is a quiet village on the edge of the Snowdonia Forest Park near Betws-y-Coed. Smitten by this attractive Victorian former rectory, Lauraine and Simon Awdry moved in recently with their young family. They have great plans for further development, but it already looks in fine fettle, full of individual touches and interesting furnishings. Smart, strong colours and paint effects suit the house well (rich burgundy in the dining room, blues and yellows in the lounge). Even the recently refurbished bedrooms are colour-coded (Orange, Yellow and Blue). One has a king-size sleigh bed; a couple have cast-iron roll-top baths. All have super views over the gardens and the Machno Valley. The Awdrys plan to offer tailor-made breaks, both energetic (climbing, horse-riding) and leisurely (Welsh learning weekends, artists' breaks). A five-course dinner is by arrangement, with menus discussed at breakfast time, and evening meals are served house-party style.

○ Closed Chr and New Year 🔁 From A5 just south of Betws-y-Coed, at Conwy Falls, take B4406 to Penmachno; in village take turning straight ahead alongside right of Eagles pub; house is just after stone bridge. Private car park 🚗 1 twin/double, 2 double; all with hair-dryer, ironing facilities, TV, CD player 🅥 Dining room, lounge, garden; social functions; leisure facilities nearby; early suppers for children; toys, baby-listening 🦽 No wheelchair access ● No dogs; no smoking ▭ MasterCard, Switch, Visa £ Twin/double £60 to £75; deposit required. Set D £23; service incl. Special breaks available ③FOR②

Denotes somewhere you can rely on a good meal – either the hotel features in the 2004 edition of our sister publication, The Good Food Guide, *or our inspectors thought the cooking impressive, whether particularly competent home cooking or more lavish cuisine.*

All entries in the Guide *are rewritten every year, not least because standards fluctuate. Don't trust an out-of-date edition.*

PENMAENPOOL Gwynedd | map 7

George III Hotel

Penmaenpool, Dolgellau LL40 1YD
TEL: (01341) 422525   FAX: (01341) 423565
EMAIL: reception@george-3rd.co.uk
WEB SITE: www.mortal-man-inns.co.uk

Panoramic pub in unusual premises overlooking the Mawddach Estuary

Notwithstanding the fairly busy road behind, this handsome old inn couldn't enjoy a more appealing setting, with a grandstand view of an ancient tollbridge spanning reflective, estuarial expanses between gentle, wooded hills. The pub is even older than its name suggests, its earliest sections dating back to the mid-seventeenth century. Remodelled in the late Victorian era, the original coaching inn and ship's chandlery were merged into a rambling hotel. An annexe was added later – part of a Victorian railway station rendered obsolete by the unlamented Dr Beeching. The interior is reassuringly unsurprising: interlocking bar and lounge areas decked in horse-brasses, copper and china, and plenty of timber and exposed stonework. Hearty bar meals (steak and kidney pie or faggots in onion gravy) ring the changes on more refined Mediterranean specialities (pan-fried or slow-roasted things drizzled in oil and garlic). Bedrooms are comfortably traditional, the views in most compensating for rather elderly bathrooms.

◑ Open all year 🅿 At Dolgellau, turn off A470 on A493 towards Tywyn; after approx 2 miles turn right for toll bridge and first left for hotel. Private car park 🛏 4 twin, 7 double; all with hair-dryer, direct-dial telephone, TV ✓ Dining room, bar/lounge, garden; conferences and social functions; leisure facilities nearby; highchairs ♿ No wheelchair access; 6 steps into hotel, WC, 5 ground-floor bedrooms ⬤ No smoking in some public areas and some bedrooms ▭ Amex, MasterCard, Switch, Visa £ Single occupancy of twin/double £56, twin/double £98; deposit required. Alc L £16, D £23; light meals available. Special breaks available

---

PENTREGAT Ceredigion | map 4

The Grange NEW ENTRY

Pentregat, Nr Llangranog SA44 6HW
TEL: (01239) 654121 (AND FAX)
EMAIL: theresekimber@freenetname.co.uk

Welcoming countryside bolthole with Georgian elegance

Therese Kimber hails from across the water in Limerick, a town known for its Georgian architecture. So no wonder she feels right at home in this pastel pink, foursquare building from the eighteenth century. Accessed by a long lane from the main road, and surrounded by fields of black cattle and scampering rabbits, the Grange is a good-value hideaway for the world-weary. A sense of elegance pervades this gracious guesthouse, from the pillared porch and arched dormer window to the decorative plasterwork, original doors and fanlight in the hallway. Therese runs the Grange alone but with bags of enthusiasm, serving guests tea and biscuits on arrival, chatting with them in the lounge in the evening, where she lights a log fire. Family photos, board games and an honesty bar add to the homely feel. On request, Therese will also prepare straightforward set dinners, served in the smartly traditional dining room, once used for meat-salting. Chintzy fabrics are the norm in the symmetrical bedrooms, and although these are rather small, their bathrooms are the highlight. Each has a charming archway, appealing tiles and a claw-foot bath without any shower: 'to enforce relaxation', says Therese.

◑ Open all year 🅿 Halfway between Cardigan and Aberaeron, off A487 on Cardigan side of Pentregat. Private car park 🛏 1 twin, 1 twin/double, 2 double; family room available; all with hair-dryer, TV ✓ Dining room, 2 lounges, garden; cots, highchairs ♿ No wheelchair access ⬤ No dogs in public rooms; no smoking ▭ None accepted £ Single occupancy of twin/double £40 to £45, twin/double £60 to £65, family room £65 to £75; deposit required. Set D £17.50; light meals available ③FOR②

Egerton Grey

Porthkerry, Rhoose, Barry CF62 3BZ
TEL: (01446) 711666   FAX: (01446) 711690
EMAIL: info@egertongrey.co.uk
WEB SITE: www.egertongrey.co.uk

Gentle country-house elegance close to Cardiff airport

As Cardiff airport becomes an increasingly popular base for cheap flights abroad, nearby Egerton Grey will no doubt attract more pre-flight holidaymakers. But this stone country house's setting by the sea, in appealingly landscaped gardens, makes it equally pleasant as a base if your holiday is in South Wales. In keeping with its heritage – it was a rectory in the nineteenth century – the rooms exude a suitably restrained refinement, with decorative mouldings, ticking clocks and oil paintings on wood-panelled walls. Many an hour could be spent curled up with a book by the open fire in the cosseting sitting room, while the conservatory and drawing room windows provide splendid views towards a striking viaduct and on to the sea. The wood-panelled restaurant makes a smart venue for dinner, which focuses on modern country cooking such as roast rump of lamb with hazelnut mash and port wine sauce. A traditional country-house style underlies the elegant bedrooms; some have sweet fireplace features and antiques, and most bathrooms have roll-top baths. Rear-facing rooms, such as Uncle Fred's, enjoy the best seaward views.

◗ Open all year   🔁 From M4 Junction 33, follow signs to airport by-passing Barry; at small roundabout by airport turn left towards Porthkerry; turn left again after 500 yards, down narrow lane between thatched cottages. Nearest train station: Barry Town. Private car park   🛏 1 single, 2 twin, 4 double, 1 four-poster, 2 suites; family rooms available; all with room service, hair-dryer, trouser press, direct-dial telephone, modem line, TV   ✔ Restaurant, bar, sitting room, drawing room, library, conservatory, garden; conferences and social functions; civil wedding licence; leisure facilities nearby; early suppers for children; cots, highchairs, toys, babysitting, baby-listening   ♿ No wheelchair access   ● No dogs in public rooms; no smoking   ▭ Amex, Delta, MasterCard, Switch, Visa   £ Single £80, single occupancy of twin/double £95, twin/double £100 to £115, four-poster £130, family room £125, suite £130; deposit required. Set L, D £19; alc L, D £36; light meals available. Special breaks available   (3FOR2)

Hotel Portmeirion and Castell Deudraeth

Portmeirion, Penrhyndeudraeth LL48 6ET
TEL: (01766) 770000   FAX: (01766) 771331
EMAIL: hotel@portmeirion-village.com
WEB SITE: www.portmeirion-village.com

Unique Italianate fantasy village incorporating many different elements

Portmeirion evokes many things, from the familiar flower-and-fruit pottery to the classic '60s TV series, *The Prisoner*. But primarily, Clough Williams-Ellis's extraordinary 1920s creation is a hotel. Or, these days, two very different hotels – one a chintzy jumble of vaguely Mediterranean and oriental themes in Italian ice-cream colours, the other a folly castle kitted out in contemporary minimalism. The estate is a charitable trust, earning its keep partly by charging day visitors an entrance fee, so it's scarcely a secluded hideaway. But the setting, on a private wooded peninsula by a superb sandy beach, with panoramic estuary views, is splendid. Accommodation is dispersed between the main hotel by the waterfront, various separate buildings teetering on steep cliffs, and Castell Deudraeth just outside the village entrance. Some units are self-catering, but all are furnished and equipped to high standards. The newer suites in Castell Deudraeth are exceptionally large and luxurious.

◑ Open all year 🔲 In Portmeirion village. Private car park. Nearest train station: Minffordd 🔔 8 twin, 3 twin/double, 19 double, 2 four-poster, 4 family rooms, 15 suites; all with hair-dryer, direct-dial telephone, TV; some with room service, modem line, CD player ✅ Restaurant, dining room, 2 bars, 3 lounges, gardens; conferences and social functions; civil wedding licence; heated outdoor swimming pool, beauty salon; leisure facilities nearby; early suppers for children; cots, highchairs, babysitting, outdoor play area ♿ Wheelchair access to some bedrooms and restaurant (chair lift), WC, 5 ground-floor bedrooms, lift (Castell Deudraeth). Disabled parking ● No dogs; no smoking in some public rooms 🔲 Amex, Delta, Diners, MasterCard, Switch, Visa £ Single occupancy of twin/double £110, twin/double £135 to £175, four-poster £175, family room £155, suite £155 to £240; deposit required. Continental/cooked B £12; set L £12.50, D £22.50; alc L £16, D £37.50; light meals available; service incl. Special breaks available

---

PWLLHELI Gwynedd   map 7

Plas Bodegroes

Nefyn Road, Pwllheli LL53 5TH
TEL: (01758) 612363   FAX: (01758) 701247
EMAIL: gunna@bodegroes.co.uk
WEB SITE: www.bodegroes.co.uk

A supremely enjoyable and surprisingly affordable country-house restaurant-with-rooms

Chris Chown's splendidly inventive cooking is the main reason to choose this charming Georgian manor on the Lleyn peninsula; it's hard to imagine where you could eat better for the price in this part of Wales. But the accommodation is brilliant value too, each bedroom beautifully designed in good-looking Scandinavian style with pale, streamlined surfaces and dynamic use of colour. The house is exceptionally pretty, with a Regency verandah floating like a ballerina's skirt around its ground floor. An avenue of magnificent beech trees and parkland (with hooting owls) screens it from passing traffic. The interior is voguishly sophisticated and thoroughly interesting, full of original art and eye-catching objects – Venetian carnival masks in the elegantly simple dining rooms, a bowl of sea shells on the landing. Yet there's no stuffy pretension about this place; service is attentive but completely relaxing, and it's as enjoyable for lone diners as for couples or groups.

◑ Closed Sun & Mon exc bank hols; closed Dec to Feb 🔲 1 mile west of Pwllheli on A497 Nefyn road. Nearest train station: Pwllheli. Private car park 🔔 1 single, 2 twin, 1 twin/double, 6 double, 1 four-poster; all with room service, hair-dryer, direct-dial telephone, TV; some with CD player; no tea/coffee-making facilities in rooms ✅ 2 dining rooms, bar, lounge, gardens; leisure facilities nearby; early suppers for children; cots, highchairs, baby-listening ♿ No wheelchair access ● No dogs in public rooms; no smoking 🔲 Delta, MasterCard, Switch, Visa £ Single £45, single occupancy of twin/double £70 to £120, twin/double £90 to £160, four-poster £140; deposit required. Set Sun L £17.50; alc D £38. Special breaks available

---

REYNOLDSTON Swansea   map 4

Fairyhill

Reynoldston, Swansea SA3 1BS
TEL: (01792) 390139   FAX: (01792) 391358
EMAIL: postbox@fairyhill.net
WEB SITE: www.fairyhill.net

Low-key luxury and sensational Welsh cooking in the heart of the Gower

The Gower peninsula can lay claim to some of Wales' best sandy beaches. But though these are just a short distance from Fairyhill, guests searching for natural beauty without the crowds can find it by ambling around the hotel's woodlands and down to its tranquil lake and trout stream. Ignore the disappointingly plain façade of this Georgian house, because there's plenty of elegance inside. Cosy sofas and log fires are warming enticements to both the Regency-striped bar and the lounge. The latter leads through the French doors on to the terrace, where you could borrow binoculars and spot wildlife on and around the croquet lawn. Fresh flowers appear on well-spaced tables in the restaurant, which looks surprisingly understated, given the high quality of the modern cooking here. A flair for interesting adaptations of Welsh ingredients even extends to the breakfast menu, which offers pikelets with Welsh honey, or dry cured bacon with laverbread and cockle cake. The walled garden provides many of the vegetables. The individually styled bedrooms look smart without being pretentious, with some rooms simply furnished in light chintz, and all have little luxuries such as CD and DVD players.

⚫ Closed 3 to 21 Jan ⃞ Take B4295 west from Swansea for 9 miles, through Gowerton and Crofty; hotel is signposted on left. Private car park ⃞ 8 twin/double; all with room service, hair-dryer, direct-dial telephone, modem line, TV, DVD, CD player; some with trouser press, VCR; tea/coffee-making facilities on request ✓ Restaurant, bar, lounge, health therapy rooms, multi-media room, gardens; conferences and social functions ⃞ No wheelchair access ⚫ No children under 8; no dogs; no smoking in restaurant ⃞ Delta, MasterCard, Switch, Visa ⃞ Single occupancy of twin/double £120, twin/double £140 to £190; deposit required. Set L £19, D £37.50; alc L £25; service incl. Special breaks available

---

ST BRIDES WENTLOOGE Newport

map 4

Inn at the Elm Tree

St Brides Wentlooge, Newport NP10 8SQ
TEL: (01633) 680225   FAX: (01633) 681035
EMAIL: inn@the-elm-tree.co.uk
WEB SITE: www.the-elm-tree.co.uk

Wayside inn with individually styled, cottagey bedrooms

On the misty meadows of the Severn estuary, this nineteenth-century former barn is one of the biggest buildings in the area. And its prominence has increased since being remodelled four years ago and hailed as Wales' 'first inn of the new century'. Certainly the welcome is warm and the look is modern. Guests park at the back and walk through a small landscaped area straight into the body of the inn, which is shared between the lounge and the restaurant. In the lounge there is grey seating, in soft leather, where diners can peruse the menu before being seated at one of the fancy metal chairs in the restaurant. Food is described as British with a bit of European influence, using Welsh Black beef and coastal seafood such as lobster, oysters and cockles. The bedrooms are all individually styled in a cottagey way. Country quilts, pine furnishings and Laura Ashley drapes are typical. Bathrooms gleam and there are corner baths and spa baths. Although there was some irritating muzak playing in the corridors, our inspector thought a complaint about 'motel' type accommodation to be wide of the mark.

⚫ Open all year ⃞ In centre of St Brides Wentlooge village, on B4239 south of Newport. Private car park ⃞ 1 twin, 6 double, 2 four-poster, 1 family room; water bed available; all with room service, hair-dryer, trouser press, direct-dial telephone, modem line, TV ✓ Restaurant, bar, lounge, patio; conferences and social functions ⃞ Wheelchair access to hotel and restaurant, 2 ground-floor bedrooms, 1 room specially equipped for disabled people. Disabled parking ⚫ No children under 12; no dogs or smoking in public rooms ⃞ Amex, Delta, MasterCard, Switch, Visa ⃞ Single occupancy of twin/double from £80, twin/double £90, four-poster £110, family room £115; deposit required. Set L £12.50, D £13.50; alc L £22, D £26; light meals available

---

West Usk Lighthouse

Lighthouse Road, St Brides Wentlooge, Newport NP10 8SF
TEL: (01633) 810126
EMAIL: lighthouse1@tesco.net
WEB SITE: www.westusklighthouse.co.uk

Eccentric charm at a wildly remote lighthouse offering B&B

There's a distinctly 'end of the world' feel at West Usk. At the end of a mile-long, bumpy track, this unusual, drum-shaped lighthouse is surrounded by flat, windswept fields, the sandflats of the Severn estuary and, in another direction, the less romantic sight of a decommissioned power station. Head up to the lantern room or roof terrace for the best panoramic views over to the Bristol Channel. Hospitable Frank Sheahan and his family are the current lighthouse keepers, serving cooked breakfasts around one table in the homely breakfast room. A Dalek in the hallway, signed by Jon Pertwee, is just one of the quirky features in this Tardis-like house. The memorable, wedge-shaped bedrooms fan out from the spiral staircase and have plenty of maritime character. The yellow four-poster room is decorated with model ships and mural of a 1920s cruise liner, while seascape models cling to the ceiling in another. The price you pay for such splendid isolation is that the nearest evening meals are a three-mile drive away, but if you need more than a simple escape from civilisation to wind down, Danielle Sheahan's soothing therapies should do the trick.

◑ Open all year ⌷ Leave M4 at Junction 28 and take A48 for Newport; take B4239 for St Brides Wentlooge; after 2 miles (before St Brides), turn left at B&B sign next to cattle bridge, into long private road. Private car park ⌂ 2 double, 1 four-poster; family room available; all with TV ⌀ Breakfast room, lounge, roof garden; flotation tank; leisure facilities nearby ♿ No wheelchair access ● No dogs or smoking in bedrooms ⫐ Amex, Delta, Diners, MasterCard, Switch, Visa £ Single occupancy of double £55 to £75, double £85, four-poster £98 to £110, family room £95; deposit required ③FOR②

SKENFRITH Monmouthshire map 2

The Bell at Skenfrith

Skenfrith, Monmouth NP7 8UH
TEL: (01600) 750235 FAX: (01600) 750525
EMAIL: enquiries@skenfrith.com
WEB SITE: www.skenfrith.com

Top-notch bedrooms, great food and rustic chic at a border coaching inn

The tiny village of Skenfrith is dominated by its medieval, red-stone castle, one of a trio worth a visit in this Marches region. Beside the castle flows the River Monnow, which doubles as the border with England, while across the road stands this former coaching inn. Janet and William Hutchings renovated it from scratch in 2000, creating a smart but rustic-styled inn that wouldn't look out of place in the French countryside. Settles, farming utensils and a lovely inglenook offer charm aplenty in the flagstoned bar – a great setting for one of the real ales or hundred-odd wines. Old photos of village locals adorn the walls in the light, informal restaurant, where service is friendly and efficient. Menus offer plenty of choice, perhaps braised lamb shoulder with provençale aubergine and Madeira jus. No expense has been spared in the uncluttered, stylish bedrooms, which are named after fly-fishing bait. Along with specially built beds and antiques, there are treats such as DVD players, CD speakers in the bathrooms, robes and home-made biscuits. Whickham's Fancy enjoys window-seat views over the river, while the beamed attic suite comes with hill views from your bath.

◑ Closed 2 weeks Jan/Feb ⌷ By the bridge in Skenfrith. Private car park ⌂ 1 twin, 1 twin/double, 4 double, 2 four-poster; all with hair-dryer, direct-dial telephone, modem line, TV, DVD, CD player ⌀ Restaurant, 2 bars, garden; conferences and social functions; early suppers for children; cots, highchairs, toys ♿ No wheelchair access ● No children under 8 in restaurant eves; no smoking in bedrooms ⫐ Amex, Delta, MasterCard, Switch, Visa £ Single occupancy of twin/double £90 to £130, twin/double £130, four-poster £150. Alc L £18, D £32.50; light meals available

---

SPITTAL Pembrokeshire map 4

Lower Haythog Farm

Spittal, Haverfordwest SA62 5QL
TEL: (01437) 731279 (AND FAX)
EMAIL: nesta@lowerhaythogfarm.co.uk
WEB SITE: www.lowerhaythogfarm.co.uk

Home comforts, inventive meals and a warm welcome down on the farm

If you're searching for perfect peace in pastoral Pembrokeshire, look no further than this remote working farm. The house itself, medieval in origin, has been run by the delightful Nesta Thomas, aided by husband Bill and now daughter-in-law Joss, for more than three decades. Yet this local lady has lost none of her enthusiasm for providing creative, Aga-cooked meals and chatting to guests with advice on nearby sights and walks. You could simply explore the farm's enormous 250 acres, including its wooded valley and ponds, or get a taster of agricultural life by feeding calves or watching sheep-shearing. Nesta is eager for guests to feel at home, whether it's in the oak-beamed lounge or in the small, stone-walled dining room. Here you could dine on Gressingham duck with ginger and lime inside the inglenook; guests can bring their own wine. Breakfast inspiration includes Glamorgan (vegetarian) sausages and laverbread, waffles with pancetta and even apricots soaked in Earl Grey! The bedrooms are quite small, furnished in a typically cottagey style, with cherrywood furniture, and views over the farmyard or the pretty, well-tended garden. A gorgeously rustic, two-storey cottage is also available for self-catering.

◑ Open all year; dining room closed Sun and Wed eves 🔁 From Haverfordwest, take B4329 towards Cardigan; farm entrance is 5 miles along on right, just before railway bridge. Private car park 🛏 2 twin, 2 twin/double, 1 double, 1 family room; all with hair-dryer, TV, mini-fridge ⊘ Dining room, lounge, garden; leisure facilities nearby; cots, highchairs, toys, outdoor play area ⅃ No wheelchair access; 2 ground-floor bedrooms ● Dogs by arrangement only; no smoking ▭ None accepted £ Single occupancy of twin/double £30 to £40, twin/double £50 to £70, family room £75 to £105; deposit required. Set D £20; light meals available

SWANSEA Swansea   map 4

Morgans

Somerset Place, Swansea SA1 1RR
TEL: (01792) 484848   FAX: (01792) 484849
EMAIL: info@morganshotel.co.uk
WEB SITE: www.morganshotel.co.uk

All's ship-shape at this swanky, central hotel

Here in the heart of Swansea's trendy maritime quarter (near the Dylan Thomas Theatre and Maritime Museum) stands this impressive, late-Victorian building, formerly the offices of the port authority and distinguished by its cupola and clock tower. Features such as detailed stained-glass designs and ornate mouldings add plenty of historic charm inside as well, but Martin and Louisa Morgan have made sure that the hotel is squarely anchored in the 21st century. Angular leather chairs and dark-wood panelling and floors are a common theme, with ship-funnel-style metal pillars in the main restaurant. Here, dishes might include cider-braised rabbit with Dijon mustard and field mushrooms, while the Plimsoll Café serves bistro meals. The bedrooms, named after ships, are suitably contemporary in style and fittings, often with coffee-and-cream tones and large bedheads. Not only will you find luxuries like Egyptian cotton sheets, DVD players and plasma screens, but rooms such as John Bright might well seduce romantic couples with their double showers.

◑ Open all year 🔁 From M4 Junction 42 take A483, follow signs for city centre then turn left into Somerset Place after Sainsburys. Nearest train station: Swansea 🛏 20 twin/double; all with room service, hair-dryer, mini-bar, trouser press, direct-dial telephone, modem line, CD player, DVD ⊘ 2 restaurants, 2 bars, lounge, library; conferences; social functions; civil wedding licence; leisure facilities nearby; early suppers for children; cots, highchairs, babysitting, baby-listening ⅃ Wheelchair access to hotel (ramp) and restaurants (lift), WC, 6 ground-floor bedrooms, 1 room specially equipped for disabled people, lift ● No dogs; no smoking ▭ Amex, Delta, Diners, MasterCard, Switch, Visa £ Single occupancy of twin/double £100 to £250, twin/double £100 to £250, family room £100 to £250; deposit required. Set L £10 to £15; alc L, D £27; light meals available; service incl. Special breaks available

If you have a small appetite, or just aren't feeling hungry, check if you can be given a reduction if you don't want the full menu. At some hotels you could easily end up paying £30 for one course and a coffee.

Parva Farmhouse

Tintern, Chepstow NP16 6SQ
TEL: (01291) 689411/511   FAX: (01291) 689557
EMAIL: parva_hoteltintern@hotmail.com
WEB SITE: www.hoteltintern.co.uk

Cosy riverside cottage in the Wye Valley

From the picturesque ruins of Gothic Tintern Abbey, head through this popular Wye Valley village which follows the river's curve. One mile on, you will find the seventeenth-century Parva farmhouse, a rough stone cottage that has great views to the steep, forested hills. Dereck and Vickie Stubbs will gladly advise on various local walks, such as the Wye Valley path, which passes the house. On rainy days, the low-slung lounge with its chesterfields and wood burner makes a cosy, if old-fashioned, place to squirrel away with one of the games or books. Equestrian fans, perhaps having been to the nearby Chepstow races, may also appreciate the horsey knick-knacks here. Those wanting to fish on the Wye should find more interest in the flies, rods and piscatorial paintings gracing the intimate, inglenook restaurant. Here, the reasonably priced four-course dinner might include poached halibut, washed down perhaps with wine from the vineyard just up the road. The bedrooms have a smart, cottagey style with chintzy fabrics, pine doors, low ceilings and creaky floors; most have lovely views over the river. The hotel was up for sale as we went to press.

● Open all year On A466 at northern edge of Tintern village. Private car park 3 twin, 2 double, 1 four-poster, 3 family rooms; all with room service, hair-dryer, direct-dial telephone, TV Restaurant, bar, lounge, garden; leisure facilities nearby; early suppers for children; cots, highchairs, toys, baby-listening No wheelchair access; 3 steps into hotel, 1 ground-floor bedroom ● No children under 4 in restaurant eves; dogs £3.50 in bedrooms; no smoking in bedrooms Amex, MasterCard, Switch, Visa Single occupancy of twin/double £55, twin/double £76, four-poster £86, family room £95; deposit required. Set D £21; service incl. Special breaks available

The Newbridge [NEW ENTRY]

Tredunnock, Nr Usk NP15 1LY
TEL: (01633) 451000   FAX: (01633) 451001
EMAIL: thenewbridge@tinyonline.co.uk
WEB SITE: www.thenewbridge.co.uk

Upmarket riverside inn with new, tip-top bedrooms

The bucolic beauty of the Usk Valley and its sinuous river is just one of the reasons to come to the Newbridge. The views are best from the restaurant terrace, although you may prefer to sit at tables down on the grassy riverbank, beside the eponymous arched bridge – which actually dates back to 1850. The restaurant's simple, cream exterior belies the upmarket, 'rustic chic' style inside, redolent of a smart Tuscan inn, and an annexe added in 2002 enables diners to sleep here too. The restaurant is a stylish blend of rugs on stripped-wood floors, brick and terracotta walls, exposed beams and chunky candles. Up the spiral stairs, the mezzanine level has colourful artworks from Irish painter Graham Knuttel, and is a disarming venue for a feast of fine country cooking, such as wild mushroom charlotte with tomato and tarragon beurre blanc. Breakfast, in contrast, is a simple, continental buffet. The splendid bedrooms mix a modern, rustic-style décor with spacious marble-tiled bathrooms. The best, and priciest, is Room 6, with its lovely sunken bath, and the only room to benefit from a decent view, thanks to its balcony.

● Open all year Leave M4 at Junction 24 and take A449 towards Monmouth; turn off to Usk on A472; just after bridge in Usk turn left for Caerleon; continue through Llangybi and on for 1 ½ miles; turn left opposite Cwrt Bleddyn Hotel; inn is other side of Tredunnock on riverbank. Private car park 2 twin/double, 3 double, 1 four-poster; all with hair-dryer, direct-dial telephone, modem line, TV ⊗ Restaurant, bar, lounge, garden; conferences and social functions; civil wedding licence; leisure facilities nearby; cots, highchairs ⎣ No wheelchair access; 2 ground-floor bedrooms ● No dogs; no smoking in bedrooms ⊟ Amex, Delta, Diners, MasterCard, Switch, Visa ⸤£⸥ Single occupancy of twin/double from £80, twin/double £90 to £115, four-poster £120 to £125; deposit required. Alc L £16, D 28; light meals available. Special breaks available ③FOR②

TYN-Y-GROES Conwy   map 7

Groes Inn NEW ENTRY

Nr Conwy LL32 8TN
TEL: (01492) 650545   FAX: (01492) 650855
EMAIL: thegroesinn@btinternet.com
WEB SITE: www.groesinn.com

Historic inn overlooking Conwy Valley, serving good food and ales

The oldest sections of this famous, white-painted roadside pub are fifteenth-century, and a sign outside claims it as the first licensed house in Wales (1573). Inside, it's warm, inviting and surprisingly spacious, a maze of attractive bar, lounge and dining areas unfolding around the central serving hatch. A conservatory extension adds dining space, and outdoor tables are available. Walls, beams, fireplaces and shelves are festooned with collections of bric à brac: hats, postcards, jugs, plaques. Chalkboard specials supplement an already wide-ranging menu, offering everything from a ham sandwich to effortful concoctions like mixed-berry champagne jelly with rose-petal ice cream. There's a fair range of wines, including some halves. Next to the pub stands a modern accommodation wing, a matching pastiche of the original low-slung, slate-roofed building. Bedrooms are smart, spacious and comfortable, some with balconies or terraces overlooking the quiet fields and mountains behind.

❍ Open all year ⤢ From Conwy castle, take B5106 towards Trefriw, passing under double arches of town walls; hotel is just over 2 miles on right. Private car park ⨼ 10 twin/double, 3 double, 1 four-poster; family rooms available; all with room service, hair-dryer, direct-dial telephone, TV; some with trouser press ⊗ Restaurant, bar, lounge, library, conservatory, garden; conferences; social functions; leisure facilities nearby; cots, highchairs, baby-listening ⎣ Wheelchair access to hotel and restaurant; 1 ground-floor room specially equipped for disabled people ● No children under 12 in restaurant eves; no dogs in public rooms ⊟ Amex, Delta, Diners, MasterCard, Switch, Visa ⸤£⸥ Single occupancy of twin/double from £79, twin/double from £95, four-poster £145, family room from £100; deposit required. Set L £15.50, D £28; bar L, D £15; light meals available; service incl. Special breaks available

Round-ups

Again this year we are including a collection of hotels that are worth considering but do not quite merit a full entry. Those marked with an asterisk are new to the *Guide* this year. We would be particularly pleased to get feedback on hotels in this section. The price given for each hotel is the standard cost of a twin–bedded or double room with breakfast unless otherwise indicated, and is the latest available as we go to press. Prices may go up at some point in 2005.

LONDON

SW3 THE BEAUFORT   020-7584 5252
Welcoming and immaculately kept hotel on a wide cul-de-sac in Knightsbridge. Bedrooms are plush and stylish and civilities extended to guests include afternoon tea and a complimentary bar.   £229

SW6 CHELSEA VILLAGE HOTEL   020-7565 1400
Two hotels, shops, conference rooms, a handful of eateries and bars, and a football-themed attraction make up this large complex behind the football ground. Well-kept bedrooms offer families excellent value.   £110-£204

SW3 EGERTON HOUSE HOTEL   020-7589 2412
Sister hotel to the Franklin (see entry), Egerton House is a more intimate operation, but with equally high standards of décor. Bedrooms, about ten of which have garden views, are beautifully done out with good fabrics and feature marble bathrooms.   £222

SW7 THE GAINSBOROUGH HOTEL   020-7957 0000
Reasonable prices at this well-maintained, white neoclassical townhouse (sister hotel to the Gallery, see below), just minutes from South Kensington tube. Bedrooms are traditional in style and vary in size.   £141

SW7 GALLERY HOTEL   020-7915 0000
Decent rates for the area and a convenient location near the tube and Museums make the Gallery worth considering for a night or two. Public areas are loosely Victorian in feel, with plenty of deep colours, oil paintings and panelling.   £141

EC2 GREAT EASTERN HOTEL   020-7618 5010
Victorian splendour and modern luxuries create a sound platform for this former railway hotel. Bedrooms pamper, and public areas include the Japanese 'Miyabi' and the elegant 'Aurora' restaurants.   £200 to £346

SW1 LIME TREE HOTEL   020-7730 8191
Friendly staff and great rates make this family-run B&B, on a quiet and pleasant street near Victoria Station, a decent base. Larger doubles and triple rooms are available if you need more space.   £147

WC1 MYHOTEL BLOOMSBURY   020-7667 6000
Contemporary, 'feng-shuied' design hotel with a Yo! Sushi restaurant and holistic gym. Buzzy, central location; compact standard rooms.   £282

W1 No 5 MADDOX STREET   020-7647 0200
These swanky contemporary suites, featuring bamboo floors, faux fur and leather, alongside cutting edge technology, are near Bond Street and Mayfair. Some have tiny pebbled terraces.   £229

EC2 THREADNEEDLES   020-7657 8080
In the heart of the City, this fashionable hotel is in the handsome premises of a former bank whose period features, such as the stained glass dome and marble columns, are intact. The décor is contemporary and neutral, with fabrics, flowers and modern art providing splashes of colour.   £203 to £314

ENGLAND

Acaster Malbis (North Yorkshire)
MANOR COUNTRY
HOUSE (01904) 706723
Friendly country house in lovely
grounds, just a short drive from York.
There's a private lake and the nearby
River Ouse to keep anglers happy.
Rooms are light, comfy and spacious
with a homely decor. £68 to £76

Aldeburgh (Suffolk)
BRUDENELL (01728) 452071
A neat, contemporary alternative to some
of the more traditional establishments in
the upmarket seaside resort of
Aldeburgh. Everything is bright and airy
and the beachfront location is hard to
beat. £124

Appleby-in-Westmorland (Cumbria)
APPLEBY MANOR (017683) 51571
Enjoying superb Eden valley scenery on
the edge of a historic, castle-crowned
village, this impressive sandstone
country manor has award-winning
gardens and excellent leisure facilities.
Family owners and exceptionally
friendly staff maintain it
immaculately. £128

Ashford-in-the-Water (Derbyshire)
RIVERSIDE HOTEL (01629) 814 275
Pretty, comfortably furnished bedrooms
and elegant eating and seating areas are
the hallmark at this laid-back, ivy-clad
Georgian residence. Upstairs rooms
feature river views, but the nearby A6
may cause some traffic noise. £135
(B&B, midweek only) £215 to £220 (D,
B&B, weekends)

Ashprington (Devon)
WATERMAN'S ARMS (01803) 732214
Delightfully located inn in riverside
location, with picnic benches allowing
you to watch ducklings while you eat.
Traditional pub interior of beams,
brasses, and hanging tankards.
Bedrooms in the new block are larger,
but all are furnished in a pretty cottagey
style. From £59

Bantham (Devon)
SLOOP INN (01548) 560489
Nautically themed pub with popular
bar, near splendid beaches. Rooms are
simple and on the small side. Guests
should be aware that the pub is closed in
the afternoon, so if you arrive before
6pm there may be nobody to greet
you. From £70

Barnsley (Gloucestershire)
VILLAGE PUB * (01285) 740421
This humble village house exterior hides
a sharp, sophisticated pub and a
pleasant patio garden at the back.
Choose between four-poster bedrooms
or those with iron bedsteads. None of
the rooms is that large, but all of them
show a natty sense of style.
£80 to £125

Bath (Bath & N.E. Somerset)
ROYAL YORK
TRAVELODGE (0870) 191 1718
Continental breakfast on a tray at the
room door, simple décor and facilities in
well-kept rooms – welcome to Bath's
chain hotel hidden behind a Georgian
facade. Despite the lean nature of the
enterprise this hotel is excellent value
for its location in central Bath. £84

Berkswell (Warwickshire)
NAILCOTE HALL 024-7646 6174
A huge range of leisure facilities,
including a stunning Roman-bath-style
pool, nine-hole golf course, tennis courts
and a gymnasium, make this
seventeenth-century manor house a
complete holiday destination. Bedrooms
tend to be romantic in a chintzy old-
fashioned style, but with Rick's, 'the
place for entertainment', on hand, this is
not a place to get away from it all.
£100 to £140

Blakeney   (Norfolk)
THE WHITE HORSE   (01263) 740574
Comfortable local pub right on the
expansive Norfolk marshland. The
bright, yellow-walled restaurant serves
up some excellent local seafood, and this
year previous negative comments about
service have been contradicted by a
reader who said 'excellent in all
respects. . .professional but warm and
welcoming.'   £60 to £100

Blanchland   (Northumberland)
LORD CREWE ARMS   (01434) 675251
Atmospheric inn that was once attached
to Blanchland Abbey – so it comes with
an interesting history, and is chock-full
of bare stone walls, exposed beams and
creaking floors. Some bedrooms have
more of the ancient character than others,
but all are very comfy.   £120

Bodinnick   (Cornwall)
OLD FERRY INN   (01726) 870237
Just up the hill from the short car ferry to
Fowey, with good views over the water
from the simple, unpretentious rooms,
the Old Ferry Inn is a solid pubby
option. Don't expect anything too
sophisticated – the pub areas could be
described as eccentric, and the restaurant
menu majors on traditional favourites
like scampi, steak and kidney pie and
curry.   £65

Brampton   (Cambridgeshire)
THE GRANGE   (01480) 459516
Relaxed, friendly Georgian hotel with
past lives including a stint as a wartime
base for the American airforce. The
location may be less than perfect for the
tourist trade but there's plenty of effort
going into retaining a lot more character
than many hotels aimed at the business
customer. Rooms are undergoing a
gradual refurb, so ask for one of the
newer ones.   £90

Brighton   (East Sussex)
NEO HOTEL *   (01273) 711104
This funky boutique hotel sits on the
western edge of Brighton, just moments
from the sea. Inside, the lovely Regency
townhouse has been smartly done out
with contemporary designer touches,
rich fabrics and tasteful furnishings.
Bedrooms are stylish, some with original
cornices and sash windows, and a
luxurious feel. Some lean towards the
small side and can suffer from street
noise. Reports welcome.   £85 to £125

Broadway   (Worcestershire)
LEASOW HOUSE   (01386) 584526
A large B&B operation in a renovated
Cotswold farmhouse, plus two more
bedrooms in the converted barn.
Sapphire, a bedroom in the main house,
has exposed beams and lovely views to
distant hills. Bull Pen in the barn is
bright and airy and is adapted for
disabled guests.   £57 to £67

Broxton   (Cheshire)
BROXTON HALL   (01829) 782321
This rambling manor in classic Cheshire
'magpie' timbering dates from the late-
seventeenth century, and has a
distinguished history. The interior is full
of character, and the four-acre gardens
are a delight (notice the venerable
weeping cherry and mulberry). Antique-
sprinkled furnishings are comfortably
traditional.   £80 (Sat £145, D, B&B)

Buckingham   (Buckinghamshire)
VILLIERS HOTEL   (01280) 822444
Set around a cobbled courtyard that once
stabled 150 horses, this central former
hostelry has as its focus an atmospheric
beamed bar that dates back 400 years.
The 46 spacious bedrooms are stylishly
furnished and many face out on to the
courtyard.   £110 to £120

Buxton   (Derbyshire)
**BUXTON'S VICTORIAN
GUEST HOUSE**   (01298) 78759
If you want to try a slice of comfortable
nineteenth-century living, it would be
hard to do better than this completely
period establishment overlooking the
Pavilion Gardens in the heart of this
classic spa town.   £64

Canterbury (Kent)
FALSTAFF HOTEL (0870) 6096102
Central fifteenth-century inn with
corporate-style bedrooms. The breakfast
room has too few tables to take all the
guests, so at busy times you may have to
join a queue for your coffee and toast.
We've had complaints about
housekeeping, service and food this year
– more reports, please. £112

Carterway Heads (Northumberland)
MANOR HOUSE INN (01207) 255268
Go for one of the rear-facing rooms at
this roadside inn: you not only hear less
traffic noise from the A68, but also get
lovely views as a bonus. Bedrooms are
good quality and come with a pleasant
pine and floral décor. Upmarket food is
on offer in the lively pub and pricier
main restaurant. £160

Cheltenham (Gloucestershire)
LYPIATT HOUSE (01242) 224994
This is a grand, creamy-yellow-coloured
Cheltenham villa with plenty of original
features. There is a lofty drawing room,
with lots of racing scenes on the walls,
and an attractive conservatory with
wicker chairs. The bedrooms get better
towards the top of the house – Birdlip
has recently been renovated, with good
pine furnishings, stripped floors and a
bright fresh bathroom. £80 to £90

Chichester (West Sussex)
FRIARY CLOSE (01243) 527294
Though well placed for visiting the city
centre, this three-storey Georgian
townhouse is in a quiet position and has
a lovely walled garden, while inside, the
bedrooms are neat, fresh and
comfortably furnished. Breakfast is a
buffet affair, served in the simple
breakfast room. £56

Chippenham (Wiltshire)
THE ANGEL (01249) 652615
In Chippenham's market place lies this
fine Georgian house, the elegant period
façade hiding a contemporary interior
with striking colour schemes and swish
design features. £86 to £124

Clawton (Devon)
COURT BARN (01409) 271219
This lovely sixteenth-century house in
extensive tranquil grounds is run with
unpretentious charm and good humour.
Bedrooms are staunchly traditional and
bathrooms dated in parts, but the place
is comfortable and relaxing.
£80 to £110

Coggeshall (Essex)
THE WHITE HART HOTEL (01376) 561654
There are some lovely features in this
wood-beamed inn – most notably the
small guests' lounge with a fantastic
fireplace, its thick beams curving gently
up to a point. Dining rooms are graceful
and atmospheric, but the overall tone
can be a little corporate. £85 to £95

Colyford (Devon)
SWALLOW EAVES (01297) 553184
Substantial 1920s residence, set in
lawned gardens beside the main road to
nearby Lyme Regis. Bedrooms are well
kept, bright and comfortable. Owners
are particularly hospitable and good-
humoured, and also totally unapologetic
about the layout of their lounge, with all
the chairs facing each other. 'It makes
people talk,' they say, 'and that's what
our guests like.' £78

Coningsby (Lincolnshire)
LEAGATE INN (01526) 342370
An appealing sixteenth-century, family-
friendly pub located a short distance
from the village and aviation highlights.
The traditional bar has snug ante-
chambers, and the attractive brick-
exposed restaurant – with low-key
ambient music – offers good pub grub.
Bedrooms are pleasingly furnished and
spacious; some have spa baths. £65

Cross Houses (Shropshire)
**UPPER BROMPTON
FARM** (01743) 761629
This Georgian farmhouse, on a working
farm, is close to the River Severn and has
lovely countryside walks straight out of
the door. All the bedrooms are en suite
and have four-poster, brass or mahogany
beds. This is a B&B, but evening meals
are served on request in the period
dining room. £75

Dodington   (Somerset)
CASTLE OF COMFORT   (01278) 741264
Formerly a coaching inn and a cider house, this cosy but unfussy hotel is on the A39 between Minehead and Bridgewater. Pleasant gardens and smart, well-kept rooms. 'Beautifully restored and well above average,' wrote one satisfied correspondent, who also praised the attention to detail.   £95

Dorking   (Surrey)
BURFORD BRIDGE HOTEL   (0870) 400 8283
Though there's little worth going out of your way for, this long low white-washed hotel makes for a handy enough pitstop, just off the busy A24 a few miles from Dorking centre and convenient for Polesden Lacey and Box Hill. The hotel leans to the corporate, but bedrooms are comfortable and well equipped, and for the summer months there's a swimming pool in the gardens.   £128 to £140

Dover   (Kent)
NUMBER 1 GUEST HOUSE (01304) 202007
Central townhouse with two basement bedrooms decked out in lace, sleeping two to four people. Early riser continental and full English breakfasts are served in the bedrooms. Secure parking is available.   £54

Eastgate   (Durham)
ROSE HILL FARM   (01388) 517209
A working sheep farm high above Weardale with charming hosts, superb views and lots of peace and quiet. Guests are welcome to see how the farm works, so it's splendid for children, and it's also great for walkers, who can set off straight from the door.   £43

Easton   (Devon)
EASTON COURT   (01647) 433469
Historic Tudor thatched longhouse with various changes and additions over the years, making for a pleasant small hotel. It stands by the road but has four acres of gardens behind. Rooms are comfortable with excellent facilities.   £65

Ellingstring   (North Yorkshire)
HAREGILL LODGE   (01677) 460272
Perfect tranquillity at this excellent B&B on a friendly working farm near to Masham. The elegant farmhouse dates from the eighteenth century and has a lovely lived-in ambience. Three comfy bedrooms are decorated with pretty, feminine flourishes and have fine rural views.   £50

Elterwater   (Cumbria)
BRITANNIA INN   (015394) 37210
Idyllic Langdale surroundings make this sturdy Cumbrian inn by the village green eternally popular with walkers and real-ale enthusiasts. Food is hearty and varied, and simple bedrooms have been recently refurbished. Book ahead to avoid disappointment.   £84 to £92

Exeter   (Devon)
SOUTHGATE HOTEL   (01392) 412812
An exemplary business-oriented hotel a few minutes' walk from central Exeter. Its new-build, neo-Georgian architecture is bland, but the rooms are certainly comfortable and well organised. With spacious restaurant and open-plan lounges it manages to retain a friendly, welcoming atmosphere. Plans for ambitious extensions were in hand as we went to press.   £130 to £136

Ferrensby   (North Yorkshire)
GENERAL TARLETON   (01423) 340284
A wayside inn that is now more of a restaurant-with-rooms, it still retains a convivial pubby atmosphere in the beamed bar/brasserie. Inventive modern British cooking makes it quite a foodie magnet, and newly redecorated rooms offer a smart haven to allow maximum indulgence. We had a complaint from a guest in Room 9 about noise from the kitchen and cold store.   £85

Folkestone   (Kent)
CLIFTON HOTEL   (01303) 851231
A Best Western Victorian-style hotel in the centre of the Leas with good views of the English Channel. It is close to the town centre and handy for Le Shuttle and ferry terminal to France.   £85

Follifoot (North Yorkshire)
RUDDING PARK HOTEL (01423) 871350
Golf, leisure and business venue handy
for Harrogate. Upmarket country-club
style of service with a modern slant to
the décor. Dining is in either the stylish
Clocktower or the more formal
Mackaness room. Bedrooms have a
smart contemporary feel, but are not
especially memorable. £165

Fowey (Cornwall)
THE GALLEON INN (01726) 833014
Popular pine-clad pub in the classy
riverside town of Fowey. Bedrooms are
in a modern block and are bright and
well kept. There are shiny new
bathrooms and two have a water view. A
good-value option for families, with
plenty of three- and four-berth
rooms. £60 to £70

Golant (Cornwall)
**CORMORANT ON THE
RIVER** (01726) 833426
A splendid location overlooking a river
estuary busy with bird life and some
thoughtfully decorated rooms. We've
had a few negative reports this year
about the standards of décor and value
for money. More reports welcome.
£90

Grange-In-Borrowdale (Cumbria)
LEATHES HEAD * (017687) 77247
Spacious, stone-built Edwardian house
in glorious valley scenery, comfortably
distant from one of Lakeland's most
popular touring routes. Period features
enhance the well-kept, practically
furnished interior, which includes an
attractive sun lounge of wicker seating.
Home-cooked dinners offer plenty of
choice. £138 (D, B&B)

Grange-over-Sands (Cumbria)
CLARE HOUSE * (015395) 33026
This well-kept, highly traditional
guesthouse has lots of nineteenth-
century period character. The best
bedrooms, some in a newer extension
wing, enjoy lovely views over lovely big
gardens towards Morecambe Bay. Room
rates include home-cooked dinner.
£116 (D, B&B)

Grange-over-Sands (Cumbria)
GRAYTHWAITE MANOR (015395) 32001
A rambling Victorian mansion in
splendid landscaped gardens sloping
towards Morecambe Bay. The firelit,
oak-panelled lounges provide plenty of
comfortable place to sit and enjoy the
views, as do the large, calm bedrooms,
which are steadily being modernised
without alarming the regular
clientele. £55

Grasmere (Cumbria)
ROTHAY GARDEN (015394) 35334
On the edge of one of Lakeland's most
popular villages, this efficiently
managed, much-extended Victorian
hotel in grey-green slate enjoys tranquil
views over immaculate gardens,
especially from its conservatory
restaurant. Décor blends traditional
country-house chintz with upbeat
contemporary styles. A satisfied reader
warmly commends both food and
service. £110 to £144

Great Malvern (Worcestershire)
THE RED GATE (01684) 565013
Situated in a tree-lined avenue close to
the railway station, this large Victorian
red-brick house contains a genteel and
comfortable B&B, run with great
attention to detail by David Watkins.
Bedroom decoration is jolly, with pine
beds and wall stencilling as common
features. There's a pretty south-facing
lawned garden at the back. £72

Harome (North Yorkshire)
PHEASANT HOTEL (01439) 771241
Friendly family-owned hotel
overlooking the duck pond in a tiny
tranquil village. The original
blacksmith's forge is now a beamed bar
with a cosy inglenook. Bedrooms are
comfy with a homely, old-fashioned
décor. £144 (D, B&B)

Haworth (West Yorkshire)
HOLE FARM (01535) 644755
Wake up to ducks, chickens and cows
and wonderful views across the moors at
this friendly farmhouse above Haworth,
in Brontë country. There's just one
bedroom, but it's a cracker – cosy and
bright, with a big metal-framed bed and
smart, spotless bathroom. £60

High Crosby   (Cumbria)
CROSBY LODGE   (01228) 573618
This mellow castellated pile lies in green countryside near Hadrian's Wall. Inside, it has a friendly, relaxing atmosphere and handsome public rooms furnished with antiques and fresh flowers. Bedrooms are bright and spacious, with lots of character and serene views.   £130

Hindon   (Wiltshire)
ANGEL INN   (01747) 820696
This one-time village inn is now more of a trendy gastropub with sturdily stylish design in the bar and restaurant: flagstone floors in the former, natural fibre matting in the latter. Bedrooms and bathrooms vary in style but are all comfortable.   £76

Holne   (Devon)
CHURCH HOUSE INN   (01364) 631208
Once the home of author Charles Kingsley, this fourteenth-century inn on the edge of Dartmoor is a friendly, old-fashioned pub – no fruit machines or juke boxes here. Visitors come for walking, fishing, or riding, and there's a good range of food, including home-made desserts. Bedrooms are small and simple, decorated in cottagey style.   £66

Horley   (Surrey)
THE LAWN   (01293) 775751
Straightforward, friendly B&B with terrific attention to detail in a smart red-brick former school house complete with turret, just a few miles from Gatwick. Guesthouse competition is fierce in this neck of the woods but the Lawn stands out from the crowd with its spruce rooms, thoughtful extras and free daytime transfers to the airport (at night a fixed-price taxi service is available). The reception area is festooned with handy information for travellers; there's even a PC with a broadband connection so guests can book a last-minute, no-frills flight!   £55

Hurley   (Windsor & Maidenhead)
YE OLDE BELL   (01628) 825881
Rooms in the old inn (dating back to 1135) have a smidgen more character than those in the converted outbuildings, but all are well kitted out and comfortable, if a little corporate. An atmospheric bar, elegant restaurant and good conference facilities complete the picture at this Ramada franchise.   £99

Huxham   (Devon)
BARTON CROSS   (01392) 841245
This thatched seventeenth-century inn has a wonderful bar and restaurant, full of period charm – and good, imaginative food too. Bedrooms, however, lack the same flair, being comfortable but unexciting.   £98

Ironbridge   (Shropshire)
THE MALTHOUSE   (01952) 433712
There is a trendy, upbeat feel to this converted malthouse on the banks of the River Severn in view of the bridge. The bar area is decorated with modern art and there is often live music. The restaurant has a more urban, modernist feel with an interesting international menu. The bedrooms have simple fresh colour schemes and good fittings.   £69

Isley Walton   (Leicestershire)
DONINGTON PARK FARMHOUSE HOTEL   (01332) 384518
This appealing seventeenth-century farmhouse, convenient for East Midlands Airport, has a robust weekend function trade and is an ideal location for motor racing enthusiasts. The attractive wood-panelled restaurant has an appetising-looking menu and the pick of the bedrooms is in the converted barn annexe.   £50 to £65

Kirkby Lonsdale   (Cumbria)
SNOOTY FOX   (01524) 271308
Atmospheric seventeenth-century pub in an attractive market town on Lancashire/Cumbrian borders. Log fires, original timbers, stone-flagged floors and quirky wall-clutter add personality. A go-ahead new manager has plenty of ideas for improvement, especially extending the range of food served. Bedrooms are simply furnished but perfectly adequate.   £64

Knutsford (Cheshire)
LONGVIEW (01565) 632119

A Victorian villa, conveniently located on outskirts of town but within walking distance of centre. New owners are steadily reshaping this long-established small hotel in their own image, while retaining some former features, including the famous basement Bunker Bar, where white-suited wonder Martin Bell masterminded his election campaign. Progress reports welcome. £80 to £92

Lancaster (Lancashire)
EDENBRECK HOUSE (01524) 32464

Large, individually designed house in a tranquil spot on the edge of town, overlooking beautiful gardens and unspoilt valley scenery. Clearly a much-loved family home, this spacious, comfortable B&B feels very relaxing. Bedrooms are all light and pleasingly decorated in traditional styles. £50

Leicester (Leicester City)
SPINDLE LODGE 0116-233 8801

Set in a leafy conservation district of the town, this family-run Victorian house is a popular choice for those wanting to be in a tranquil area yet within walking distance of the city centre. £50 to £55

Lincoln (Lincolnshire)
ST CLEMENTS LODGE* (01522) 521532

Within easy walking distance of the cathedral and castle, the lodge is a convenient and homely base for visiting Lincoln's historic centre. The pleasing dining room is simply furnished and the nicely decorated bedrooms are large and bright, with some lovely detailed touches. £56

Llanfair Waterdine (Shropshire)
MONAUGHTY POETH (01547) 528348

Traditional farm B&B on the Welsh border run by the Williams family. It's a simple homely farmhouse with chintzy fabrics and personal mementoes, and there are views of sheep grazing from the light and airy breakfast room. The two bedrooms are a good size and have a comfortable, peaceful feel. £47

Macclesfield (Cheshire)
CHADWICK HOUSE (01625) 615558

This conveniently located, family-run B&B near the town centre comprises a handsome pair of adjoining neoclassical townhouses, conspicuously well kept inside and out. Public areas consist of a ground-floor bar-breakfast room of rush-seat chairs and honey-pine furnishings. Neat, practical bedrooms are pleasantly decorated in clean blues and creams with small tidy shower-rooms. Front windows are well insulated against traffic noise. £55

Madeley (Shropshire)
CLARION HOTEL
MADELEY COURT (01952) 680068

A remarkable sixteenth-century manor house, including a gatehouse with pepperpot towers, and an impressive lake very close to the house at the back. It includes two restaurants, one in the great hall with an inglenook fireplace and a more intimate cellar bistro. The bedrooms in the main house have a lot of character, the newer ones less so. £125

Manchester (Greater Manchester)
ETROP GRANGE 0161-499 0500

Sympathetically extended Georgian house very close to Manchester Airport's Terminal 2 (complimentary transfer by chauffeured limousine). It's a handsome building of some distinction, now part of a hotel chain. Though spacious and comfortable inside, much of its trade consists of conferences and functions, so it can seem a little impersonal. £119 to £176

Mawnan Smith (Cornwall)
BUDOCK VEAN (01326) 252100

Rambling extended 1930s country house wonderfully located in grounds leading down to the river. Leisure facilities are top notch, including a full golf course – décor and management are firmly corporate in style. £132 to £192 (D, B&B)

Mollington   (Cheshire)
CRABWALL MANOR   (01244) 851666
Not far from Chester, this extensive complex of hotel and leisure facilities is shielded from busy arterial routes by landscaped parkland. The centrepiece is a Grade II listed castellated building dating from the mid-seventeenth century. Now part of a hotel chain, the atmosphere is comfortable but corporate, lending itself particularly to business conferences and weekend breaks.
£181

Needham Market   (Suffolk)
PIPPS FORD   (01449) 760208
Some of the rooms could probably do with a spruce up, and the personal touch may have been lost now that there's a manager in charge, but this B&B still offers some atmospheric charm. Despite being literally just off a busy roundabout, the setting is surprisingly secluded and rural. We've had complaints about food and maintenance this year – more reports welcome.
£69 to £79

Newby Bridge   (Cumbria)
LAKESIDE *   (015395) 30001
Much-extended Victorian hotel by the steamer terminal at the southern end of Windermere. The enviable waterfront location and smart facilities keep rack rates high, but good-value breaks are available. It is popular with groups and can seem quite crowded. John Ruskin's bar-brasserie makes a pleasantly informal venue for light meals and snacks.   £190 to £220

Newquay   (Cornwall)
HEADLAND HOTEL *   (01637) 872211
Huge red-brick slice of Victoriana with some wonderful architectural details, away from Newquay's tacky town centre. Waves crash on the rocks almost right outside the dining room windows. A refurbishment in a more contemporary style is only partly complete – reports on progress would be welcome.
£77 to £173

Norbury   (Shropshire)
SUN INN   (01588) 650680
This beautiful backwater deep in the valley of Long Mynd is being put on the map by this atmospheric pub full of dark timbering and huge fireplaces and a pretty and secluded garden outside. The no-frills accommodation has eclectic, old-fashioned furniture, comfy beds and tiny shower rooms.   £70 to £80

Oakfordbridge   (Devon)
BARK HOUSE HOTEL   (01398) 351236
Situated to capitalise on the lovely views of the Exe Valley, this wisteria-clad cottage gets sparkling reports for friendly service and food. Public areas are charmingly romantic, bedrooms are cheerful and sunny. 'We felt thoroughly spoiled,' wrote one correspondent.
£79

Oakham   (Rutland)
LORD NELSON'S HOUSE   (01572) 723199
Tucked away in a corner is this characterful – if rather tired-looking in parts – fourteenth-century townhouse. The atmospheric 'Nick's restaurant' has an excellent-looking menu and the stylish bedrooms are vibrant and highly individual (available from Tuesday through to Saturday).   £80

Oxford   (Oxford)
GABLES GUESTHOUSE   (01865) 862153
Sally Tompkins is as cheery and welcoming as the profusion of flowers outside her neat, pebbledash home. Spick and span rooms, a sunny, peaceful garden and interesting breakfasts (such as cinnamon toast or eggs Benedict) and keen prices compensate for being a short bus ride from the centre.   £60 to £64

Padstow   (Cornwall)
THE OLD CUSTOM HOUSE   (01841) 532359
Smart, well-maintained little place housed in four buildings on the harbour-front in popular Padstow. There's a chic wood-beamed bar and even a beauty parlour, but things can feel somewhat corporate at times. Parking is across the road in the town car park at £4 for 24 hours.   £100 to £115

Plymouth (Devon)
ATHENAEUM LODGE (01752) 665005
Smart and well-run B&B in a convenient location for the city and the Hoe. What the rooms lack in character and bathroom space, they work hard to overcome with thoughtful extras and tidy neat décor. 'Delightful,' wrote one satisfied correspondent. Others have praised the 'excellent' breakfast and the fact that the Kewells 'have thought of everything'. £36 to £50

Port Isaac (Cornwall)
SLIPWAY HOTEL (01208) 880264
Unpretentious village pub, right on the beachfront in pretty Port Isaac. The atmosphere is youthful and friendly and the recently refurbished restaurant is looking good. Your only problem could be parking – beach spaces are available only until the tide comes in, so overnight parking is at the top of the long, steep hill. £90 to £100

Porthleven (Cornwall)
THE HARBOUR INN (01326) 573876
Pine-panelled, fairly standard pub in the pretty harbourside village of Porthleven. The bedrooms are a good cut above usual pub rooms though, tastefully decorated with some nice modern touches. £69

Rosthwaite (Cumbria)
HAZEL BANK (017687) 77248
Stone-built Victorian country-house hotel on the edge of a delightful Borrowdale village. Regular visitors appreciate the warm, family welcome, attentive service and good home-cooking. Furnishings and décor are highly traditional, in keeping with its age and style, but housekeeping is irreproachable, and inclusive rates are good value, especially if booked well ahead. £168 (D, B&B)

Rotherwick (Hampshire)
TYLNEY HALL (01256) 764881
In a beautiful setting on top of a hill and surrounded by acres of mature grounds complete with lake, arboretum and bluebell woods, this handsome red-brick country house has a corporate feel, though excellent health facilities bring in the leisure crowd at weekends. £165

Ryde (Isle of Wight)
NEWNHAM FARM (01983) 882423
This comfortable, homely B&B is housed in a lovely stone seventeenth-century farmhouse surrounded by tranquil gardens and pretty countryside, just a few miles from the Fishbourne ferry. Breakfast – a hearty affair which might include locally smoked haddock or salmon, organic sausages, home-made muesli and honey from the farm – is served outside overlooking the pond in summer, or in the cosy dining-room with its wood-burning stove and wood-block flooring, made from oak cut from the woods and laid green. Bedrooms are good-sized, fresh and modern with lovely views over the surrounding countryside which guests are welcome to explore (wellies and dogs are happily provided on request!) £70

Rye (East Sussex)
MERMAID INN (01797) 223065
This ancient half-timbered inn with a lovely central courtyard is on one of Rye's most picturesque cobbled streets, well placed for exploring the historic citadel. Inside, bedrooms are luxurious and public areas well turned out, though the signed photos of Richard and Judy and other famous visitors sit rather strangely alongside the low beams, crackling open fires and leaded windows. Dinner in the smart restaurant is well presented but unexceptional. The service veered from the uninterested to the downright rushed when we inspected. £160 to £200

Rye (East Sussex)
WHITE VINE HOUSE (01797) 224748
If you fancy a coffee or a light lunch, the wood-panelled parlour or cheerful sunflower room in this lovely Georgian townhouse make it as good a place as any to rest your feet and your credit cards after a morning's retail therapy in Rye's upmarket tourist shops. Bedrooms are simple with an old-fashioned feel and some period features. £80 to £125

St Austell   (Cornwall)
CARLYON BAY HOTEL   (01726) 812304
Traditional English hotel taking up a
large clifftop chunk of Carlyon Bay near
St Austell. Public rooms are palatial in
scale, furnished in grand corporate style.
It's the sort of place where gentlemen are
requested to wear ties after 7pm, and the
attached championship golf course tends
to dominate proceedings.   £170 to £260

St Austell   (Cornwall)
THE LODGE   (01726) 815543
Friendly B&B in a suburban house near
Carlyon Bay and St Austell, an ideal
place for older guests as all the rooms are
on the ground floor. You're well placed
for trips to nearby gardens like Heligan
and the Eden Project.   £90

Scarborough   (North Yorks)
INTERLUDES   (01723) 360513
Charming small hotel with a strongly
theatrical slant in a conservation area
between the castle and the beach. Many
guests are here for a visit to the Stephen
Joseph Theatre, so thespian
memorabilia abounds in the boldly
decorated bedrooms. If you want a view
over the bay go for one on the top
floor.   £60

Seahouses   (Northumberland)
OLDE SHIP HOTEL   (01665) 720200
A wonderful nautical bar is the engine
room of this small hotel in a traditional
bucket-and-spade seaside port. The best
rooms in the Fishers Yard annexe have
views over the harbour to Bamburgh
Castle and the Farne Islands. One reader
this year complained about the food and
'amateur' service.   £90 to £96

Seaview   (Isle of Wight)
PRIORY BAY   (01983) 613146
In a stunning setting – perched on a
hillside overlooking the sea – this good-
looking country house has luxurious
public rooms with high ceilings, modern
colour schemes and superb views
through huge picture windows. For all
that, the feeling is rather corporate and
disappointingly bland. Bedrooms are a
mixed bag, so you need to choose
carefully; rooms in the house have the
edge over those in the self-catering
annexe – note that children are not
allowed in the hotel's principal
rooms.   £170 to £210

Shalstone   (Buckinghamshire)
HUNTSMILL FARM   (01280) 704852
Carefully run B&B offering three smart,
spick-and-span bedrooms in a converted
ex-stable block and cattle yard, which
retains vestiges of its former life with
exposed beams and slate roofs. Set amid
Fiona and Chris Hildon's arable farm, its
surrounding acres of pasture provide
plenty of bucolic views and rural
tranquillity.   £50

Shurdington   (Gloucestershire)
THE GREENWAY   (01242) 862352
A compact Cotswold country manor
house, with a pleasant unhurried feel.
There are lovely views to the countryside
and the Cotswold hills, plus a croquet
lawn at the back of the house. Bedrooms
are spacious, and bathrooms have a real
touch of luxury.   £150

Slaugham   (West Sussex)
CHEQUERS INN   (01444) 400239
Within a historic village with
connections to Admiral Nelson's family,
this cheerful traditional village pub has
an appealing restaurant and a friendly
local ambience. Bedrooms are simply
furnished and comfortable.   £85

Snape   (Suffolk)
THE CROWN INN   (01728) 688324
This bright, family-run country inn was
positively frenzied when we inspected
at lunchtime, the enticing menu
obviously working its magic on visitors.
The four-poster room is lovely, and the
bar has a curving wood enclosure billed
as 'probably the finest Suffolk settle in
existence'.   £70

Stow-on-the-Wold   (Gloucestershire)
UNICORN HOTEL   (01451) 830257
A traditional Cotswold inn, close to a
busy junction, with the public rooms
made up of a woody and convivial bar
area and a smart restaurant. The
bedrooms are a good size and neatly
decorated. Check ahead, as there are
plans to add a spa and expand the
hotel.   £78 to £105

Stratford-upon-Avon (Warwickshire)
THE SHAKESPEARE (0870) 400 8182
Creaking floorboards, low ceilings and beams a-plenty characterise this sprawling seventeenth-century, centrally located, chain hotel. Public rooms are sombre and cosy, and the well-equipped bedrooms have bucketloads of character, especially in the older section. £110 to £130

Stratford-upon-Avon (Warwickshire)
STRATFORD VICTORIA (01789) 271001
Close to the station and convenient for the town's amenities, this large, corporate-style hotel has plenty to interest the eye. Red phone boxes in the lobby and a penny farthing bicycle in the porch contrast with the Elizabethan-feel lounge and bar with dark wood-panelled walls and highly ornate high-backed chairs. Bedrooms are nicely furnished, spacious and well equipped. £83

Sturminster Newton (Dorset)
FIDDLEFORD MILL HOUSE (01258) 472786
Superb location for this magnificent Grade I listed former mill on the River Stour. Period details such as sixteenth-century plasterwork add to the flavour, while the bedrooms are comfortably furnished and spacious. £60

Sywell (Northampton)
AVIATOR HOTEL (01604) 642111
This pleasing Art Deco hotel is an obvious choice for aviation enthusiasts as well as appealing to visitors who require something a bit different, or those needing a base near Northampton or Kettering. The wood-panelled rooms full of aviation memorabilia have a distinctly clubby atmosphere. The three Art Deco bedrooms, kept to their original style, are in the main building. £63

Telham (East Sussex)
LITTLE HEMINGFOLD HOTEL (01424) 774338
Idyllically set in 40 acres of beautiful grounds perfect for walkers and dog-lovers, this straightforward homely farmhouse has a friendly, relaxed atmosphere and unfussy, comfortable bedrooms either in the main house or in a converted cottage and stables around the courtyard. Dinner in the rustic restaurant is prepared from fresh local produce where possible; perhaps leek and potato soup or aubergine and mushroom gratin, followed by fillet of pork with apples and calvados. £92

Thornbury (Gloucestershire)
THORNBURY CASTLE (01454) 281182
This Tudor castle/palace retains a regal splendour, with morning-suited staff, wine from its own vineyard and baronial trappings such as wood panelling, oriel windows and bedrooms with a medieval style. The historic parkland is close to the River Severn. £140 to £350

Thurlestone (Devon)
THURLESTONE HOTEL * (01548) 560382
'Old fashioned but with a real heart,' comes a reader's report on this hotel. 'Alive with confident, helpful staff who are well trained and keen to make your stay a good one.' The rooms are certainly comfortable, and the range of leisure facilities is excellent. Changes were afoot when we inspected, with plans to renovate the restaurant and build a new outdoor pool with al fresco eating area. Reports welcome. £150 to £236

Tillington (West Sussex)
HORSE GUARDS INN (01798) 342332
In a pretty village a couple of miles from Petworth, this pale-stone village pub has reasonably priced rooms (a hearty full English breakfast is thrown in), plus above-average and well-presented pub food, served up in the characterful dining areas or bustling low-beamed bar, popular with locals. Bedrooms are spacious and simple with exposed heavy beams and exceptionally low doorways, but are showing signs of wear and tear. Service can be patchy, with staff ranging from utterly charming to downright frosty during our inspector's stay. £70

Trumpet   (Herefordshire)
VERZONS COUNTRY INN * (01531) 670381
This fine Georgian red-brick house has fabulous views towards the Malvern Hills. The new owners are in the process of modernising the public areas, with a vibrant stripped-floor brasserie and cool, spacious dining room, both serving excellent food. Bedrooms are of ample size and well equipped with smart furnishings.   £78

Truro   (Cornwall)
ALVERTON MANOR   (01872) 276633
A rather grand affair housed in a Victorian Gothic ex-nunnery in the middle of bustling Truro. Staff are friendly without being uncomfortably slick, though things can feel a little corporate at times, with slightly incongruous modern colours in many rooms.   £115

Tunbridge Wells   (Kent)
THE SPA HOTEL   (01892) 520331
Eighteenth-century mansion house with leisure facilities including an indoor pool, and acres of grounds with well-kept but unexciting bedrooms.   £127

Two Bridges   (Devon)
TWO BRIDGES   (01822) 890581
Right in the centre of Dartmoor, this substantial and extensive inn can be a welcome sight in bad weather. When the sun shines, the location is magnificent. Full of character and with sumptuous touches, this is an unstuffy and relaxing hotel with very good bedrooms.   £120

Ulverston   (Cumbria)
VIRGINIA HOUSE   (01229) 584844
Georgian townhouse B&B in the older quarter of a small south Lakeland market town. Public rooms run to a bar with banquette seating, and a chintzy dining room with a little lounge area at one end. Bedrooms are smallish, in conventional pastels and florals. Buffet-style breakfasts include fresh fruit, yoghurt and vegetarian options.   £55 to £58

Upper Slaughter   (Gloucestershire)
LORDS OF THE MANOR   (01451) 820243
A classic Cotswold manor house plus sympathetically converted buildings and well-tended grounds with a small lake. It has an updated English country-house look, but with familiar features like ancestral portraits, leather chairs and mullioned windows. The bedrooms in the newer parts lack a little character. One reader complained this year of 'abysmal' service and 'poor value for money', though the food was good. More reports, please.   £160

Warwick   (Warwickshire)
OLD FOURPENNY SHOP HOTEL   (01926) 491360
You may not get a tot of rum and a cup of coffee for four pennies anymore, but this eighteenth-century coaching-inn-turned-hotel on a quiet residential street still offers well-appointed chintzy bedrooms and snug traditional public areas.   £85

Wass   (North Yorkshire)
WOMBWELL ARMS   (01347) 868280
Upmarket country inn at the foot of the Hambleton Hills. Good hearty food is served in the authentically rustic bar and a smarter main restaurant. Bedrooms are cheerful and smartly furnished.   £70

Welland   (Worcestershire)
HOLDFAST COTTAGE   (01684) 310288
A small family-run hotel in a leafy location, close to the Malvern Hills, that has been receiving good reports. Originally a seventeenth-century cottage, it was enlarged in Victorian times and includes a dining room that overlooks the garden and airy bedrooms in traditional fabrics.   £84 to £94

West Tanfield   (North Yorkshire)
BRUCE ARMS   (01677) 470325
Top-drawer modern English food is the focus at this convivial bistro with bedrooms in a pretty village. Three comfy bedrooms are at hand to allow diners to take full advantage of the culinary pleasures. They are furnished with pine and patchwork bedspreads, and come with smart, white shower rooms.   £60

Wilmington (Devon)
HOME FARM HOTEL   (01404) 831278
This thatched farmhouse is right on the
A35, which can be busy, but it has much
going for it: friendly owners, well-kept
and comfortable bedrooms, plus a
converted barn that makes for a cosy and
intimate restaurant and bar area.   £70

Winchcombe (Gloucestershire)
SUDELEY HILL FARM   (01242) 602344
A glimpse of real farm life is guaranteed
at Barbara Scudamore's B&B. Pick your
way past the farm equipment, including
dogs and a combined harvester, to get to
this characterful farmhouse. The large
double bedroom in cream and rose is the
pick of the crop, with views down to
Winchcombe plus a corner bath.   £52

Windermere (Cumbria)
STORRS HALL *   (015394) 47111
Palatial lakeshore mansion with
wonderful views and a considerable
history. Inside, elegant reception rooms
unfold from an imposing entrance hall
with a lantern stairwell. Handsome
antiques, paintings and *objets d'art* match
splendid period features. For all its
daunting grandeur, staff are remarkably
courteous, helpful and welcoming.
Bedrooms are predictably magnificent,
some with truly enormous
bathrooms.   £150

Windsor (Windsor & Maidenhead)
**SIR CHRISTOPHER
WREN'S HOUSE**   (01753) 861354
Excellent, city-centre location right on
the Thames for this fine red-brick house
that was home to the architect
extraordinaire. Helpful, efficient staff,
characterful public areas, and spacious,
tastefully decorated bedrooms, some of
which have river views.   £156 to £232

Wolverhampton (West Midlands)
ELY HOUSE HOTEL   (01902) 311311
Despite being only five minutes' walk
from the city centre and convenient for
all of Birmingham's facilities, this
detached Georgian townhouse displays
a refined and venerable air and comes
with well-appointed, tastefully
decorated bedrooms.   £79

Woodhall Spa (Lincolnshire)
PETWOOD HOTEL   (01526) 353105
Set in its own extensive woodland, this
large, impressive mock-Tudor
Edwardian house was the officers' mess
for the famous 'Dambusters' 617
Squadron during the Second World War.
The hotel is ideally suited to hosting
functions in its spacious and attractive
wood-panelled public rooms.   £130

Woodstock (Oxford)
THE LAURELS   (01993) 812583
Attractive Victorian house, which used
to be home to Tim Henman's
grandparents, in a quiet side-street not
far from Blenheim Palace. Three prettily
floral bedrooms, all non-smoking, plus
affable, knowledgeable hosts in Nikki
and Malcolm Lloyd.   £55 to £60

Yarcombe (Devon)
**BELFRY COUNTRY
HOUSE HOTEL**   (01404) 861234
A former Victorian schoolhouse
converted to a hotel with six bedrooms,
all with neat and fresh shower rooms.
Owners are friendly and enthusiastic,
the atmosphere relaxing and cosy.
£80

York (York)
THE HAZELWOOD   (01904) 626548
Smart townhouse B&B on a quiet street
close to York Minster. The guest lounge
and some bedrooms have been
refurbished in the last year; all have an
upmarket style of décor and most have
some period Victorian character from
high ceilings or tiled fireplaces. We've
had a complaint this year about traffic
noise and poor maintenance.
£75 to £80

SCOTLAND

Aboyne (Aberdeenshire)
STRUAN HALL   (01339) 887241
This interesting Gothic-influenced
house began life five miles to the east,
but was brought stone-by-stone to its
present location in this well-heeled
village a century ago. The public rooms
are graciously proportioned, but
essentially homely, and bedrooms boast
fresh, simple décor, decent furniture and
thoughtful extras like fresh milk.
Imaginative breakfasts offer treats like a
hot banana sandwich or French toast
with cinnamon and maple syrup.   £64

Archiestown (Moray)
ARCHIESTOWN HOTEL   (01340) 810218
Friendly, thoughtfully run village-centre
hotel, popular with parties of anglers.
The restaurant design pays homage to
their passion with a fascinating
collection of ephemera, which means
that solo diners need never be bored
while sampling the well-executed, often
fishy, menu. Bedrooms are
straightforward and comfortable.   £94

Balloch (Highland)
CULLODEN HOUSE   (01463) 790461
Come to this Palladian mansion in April
to see the spectacle of Jacobite role-
players commemorate the death of
Bonnie Prince Charlie at the Battle of
Culloden. The colours of the hotel's
signature tartan reflect the famous battle:
purple for the heather, yellow
representing the moorland and red for
spilt blood. The extensive grounds are
well kept and the interior retains a
multitude of original features – this all
comes at a price.   £199 to £279

Banchory (Aberdeenshire)
RAEMOIR HOUSE   (01330) 824884
Spacious, often pretty, individually
decorated bedrooms and a bar
constructed from a venerable four-poster
bed are the high-spots at this substantial
country house set in 3,500 acres on the
outskirts of this affluent Deeside village.
Nine-hole pitch-and-putt and croquet on
offer to ball-game enthusiasts.   £95

Bonnyrigg (Midlothian)
DALHOUSIE CASTLE   (01875) 820153
All the medieval atmosphere and
architectural flamboyance you could
possibly want, buttressed by a
refreshingly unstuffy atmosphere at this
venerable pile in a country location, but
within striking distance of
Edinburgh.   £190

Contin (Highland)
COUL HOUSE HOTEL *   (01997) 421487
Two large and impressive octagonal
rooms have earned this Victorian
country house in the Strathconnan
Valley its grade A listed status. The new
owners were working in the USA when
it came up for sale and bought it, unseen,
over the Internet. It is hoped that such
daring will translate into inspired
restoration during their current plans for
extensive upgrading. One reader has
praised the staff ('attentive but
unobtrusive') and the 'excellent'
food.   £78 to £118

Craigellachie (Moray)
CRAIGELLACHIE HOTEL   (01340) 881204
This haven for lovers of fishing and malt
whisky hit the headlines when it hosted
a summit in December 2003 to broker
peace between feuding factions in the
South Caucasus region. Besides taking
its place on the international diplomatic
circuit it's an agreeable combination of
atmospheric bars – the Quaich offers
over 300 malts – and restaurants, with
chain hotel-style bedrooms.   £125

Crinan (Argyll & Bute)
CRINAN HOTEL   (01546) 830261
A great, white leviathan of a building,
with blazing fires, vibrant artwork and
friendly staff – and all at the picturesque
spot where Loch Fyne meets the
Atlantic. Our inspector's room was smart
and comfortable with cheerful modern
fabrics, though the bathroom had seen
better days. Service on this visit was
unimpeachable. More reports,
please.   £190

Dairsie (Fife)
TODHALL HOUSE   (01334) 656344
Formal, elegant country-house B&B
with lovely open views of the
surrounding countryside and across to St
Andrews Bay, manicured gardens and
gracious bedrooms with immaculate
bathrooms. John and Gill Donald are
unfailingly courteous hosts, and the
house is open from March to October
only.   £58

Drumbeg (Highland)
DRUMBEG HOUSE *   (01571) 833236
The exterior grey pebble dash and
corrugated iron roof of Michel and
Carolyn Hédoin's hotel is uninviting but
one look at the restaurant menu will
tempt you in. Although it advertises
itself as a seafood restaurant, a variety of
charcuterie is also on offer, sourced from
Michel's native France. Bedrooms are
straightforward, although a process of
renovation is ongoing throughout.
£54 to £82

Edinburgh (Edinburgh)
RICK'S RESTAURANT
*BAR*ROOMS *   0131-622 7800
The bar/restaurant side of this
'contemporary' city-centre outfit is
beginning to look a little tired.
Bedrooms, however, are calm, cool and
convenient.   £130

Edinburgh (Edinburgh)
22 MURRAYFIELD
GARDENS   0131-337 3569
New bedrooms this year in this
comfortable B&B close to the rugby
stadium. A peaceful garden and an
elegant sitting room are big
advantages.   £80

Edinburgh (Edinburgh)
41 HERIOT ROW *   0131-225 3113
A two-room B&B in a flat in Edinburgh's
poshest street. Great views, some nice
design, a bright and sunny living room
and good fellowship from journalist
owner Erlend Clouston. No signage, just
ring the bell.   £95

Edinburgh (Edinburgh)
MELVIN HOUSE HOTEL   0131-225 5084
Opulent woodcarving in the public
rooms and a lovely but little-used library
are the chief features of this simple hotel,
run with quiet professionalism. The
bedrooms are ordinary in contrast to the
rest. Those at the top of the house have
great views.   £120

Forres (Moray)
KNOCKOMIE HOTEL   (01309) 673146
Interesting late-Edwardian house built
in Arts & Crafts style, but with a fun
bistro, striking restaurant with a
smattering of Anglo-Indian style, and
cosy bar. Bedrooms are comfortable,
often smart, yet with an air of old-
fashioned unpretentiousness.   £131

Glasgow (Glasgow)
ART HOUSE *   0141-240 1002
A strange but interesting hotel created
from the old education department.
There is an ancient lift in the central
stairwell, art exhibitions on the top floor,
original stained glass and bedrooms
swathed in velvet. The restaurant is
done up like a very stylish diner. Some
room prices are a fraction stiff. The hotel
was on the market as we went to
press.   £111

Glasgow (Glasgow)
BRUNSWICK MERCHANT
CITY HOTEL *   0141-552 0001
A modern block shoehorned into a
narrow space in Glasgow's Merchant
city. Most rooms are tiny, and some
refurbishment is needed, but the
relaxed, mildly crazy atmosphere in the
downstairs café bar may appeal.
£65 to £95

Glasgow (Glasgow)
RAB HA'S *   0141-572 0400
Four stylishly refurbished bedrooms in
an old Glasgow pub come complete with
dark wood, chrome and flat-screen telly.
Prices are keen for this central location.
The bar is atmospheric; the restaurant
considerably less so.   £65 to £75

Glasgow (Glasgow)
TOWN HOUSE   0141-357 0862
A relaxing place to stay out by Glasgow
University. There's a large living room
with plenty of books, and light meals on
offer in the evening. 'Oscar-winning
black pudding from Orkney' for
breakfast. Bedrooms are gradually being
refurbished.   £70

Gullane (East Lothian)
GOLF INN HOTEL   (01620) 843259
Vibrant colour-schemes characterise the
bedrooms at this cheerful, creeper-clad
inn a short distance from the golfer's
delights of Muirfield. This, plus bright
airy public rooms and a good reputation
for seafood, make it a favourite retreat for
refugees from Edinburgh's bustle.
£90

Harray (Orkney)
RICKLA *   (01856) 761575
Two very comfortable and stylish suites
in this small B&B in a secluded position
with fantastic views. Breakfast features a
feast of Orkney produce including
brown trout, cheeses, home-made
yoghurt and all the elements of a full
Scottish breakfast. A minimum of two
night stays preferred.   £75

Inverness (Highland)
SEALLADH SONA   (01463) 239209
Breakfast is the highlight at this bargain
B&B, and includes options such as
venison sausages, hot fruit compote, rice
banrock and a continental buffet.
Situated on the banks of the Caledonian
Canal just out of the town centre, this
stone cottage has functional bedrooms
and a relaxed atmosphere.   £56 to £64

Isle Ornsay (Isle of Skye)
EILEAN IARMIN   (01471) 833332
Named after an Ossianic hero and with
an emphasis on Gaelic language, this
hotel conveys the pride of its owners in
their Highland connections. The
atmosphere is one of old-world charm,
and the setting on the tranquil shoreline
conducive to repose and luxuriating.
£125 to £235

Kentallen (Highland)
THE HOLLY TREE   (01631) 740292
There are few reminders that this hotel is
housed in a former railway station;
instead, a Charles Rennie Mackintosh
theme dominates. The style throughout
is contemporary, and the menu heavily
weighted in favour of locally caught
seafood.   £110

Killiecrankie (Perthshire & Kinross)
KILLIECRANKIE HOTEL   (01796) 473220
No-nonsense country inn, well placed
for exploring the nearby National Trust
site and taking in the theatrical offerings
down the road at Pitlochry. Bedrooms
are cheerful, and correspondents this
year have praised the food and the
friendliness and efficiency of the staff.
More reports, please.   £178 (D, B&B)

Kinbuck (Stirling)
CROMLIX HOUSE   (01786) 822125
Blazing wood fires, wood panelling,
friendly staff and a wealth of baronial
features give a natural graciousness to
this formal country house in extensive
grounds, close to Dunblane. Bedrooms
are comfortable, but appeared old
fashioned and rather tired on this year's
inspection. More reports, please.
£275

Kinclaven (Perthshire & Kinross)
BALLATHIE HOUSE   (01250) 883268
An exuberant Victorian hunting lodge
with fine views over the River Tay, a
roster of sedate leisure pursuits for those
left cold by fishing and shooting, and an
air of effortless self-assurance. Rooms in
the modern Riverside annexe are
comfortable and well equipped, but try
to bag one in the main house if you want
more character.   £178

Lochinver (Highland)
INVER LODGE HOTEL   (01571) 844496
A 1980s-build hotel offering quality
service and comfort but lacking in
character, despite the hunting
paraphernalia on the walls and the
impressive views over Lochinver Bay.
Facilities include a sauna, billiard
rooms, a sun bed and fishing.
£150 to £250

Melrose (Borders)
BRAIDWOOD   (01896) 822488
Cheerful, unpretentious new owners at this neat Georgian house with comfortable bedrooms, a few steps away from Melrose Abbey. Reports, please. £50

Melrose (Borders)
BURT'S HOTEL   (01896) 822285
Bags of bustle, interesting, well-executed bar food, plus thoughtful, attentive staff, all expertly choreographed by a hands-on family management team. Bedrooms are comfortable and well equipped, with neat, fresh décor.   £98

Pitlochry (Perthshire & Kinross)
LOCH TUMMEL INN   (01882) 634272
Glorious vistas from this simple roadside inn at Strathtummel, a short drive from the famously lovely Queen's View. Bedrooms are comfortable but old fashioned; bathrooms might benefit from a makeover.   £75 to £100

Salen (Argyll & Bute)
GLENFORSA HOTEL   (01680) 300377
New owners are implementing a slate of radical refurbishments at this log-cabin style family hotel with wonderful views of the Sound of Mull and cheerful, if basic, accommodation.   £85

Scourie (Highland)
SCOURIE HOTEL   (01971) 502396
If you are a fishing enthusiast this hotel will cater for your every need, from 25,000 acres of hill-loch fishing to boats, ghillies, permits and equipment. If not, the puffin colony on Handa Island and Britain's highest waterfall are nearby and the food and accommodation adequate.   £60 to £80

St Boswells (Borders)
DRYBURGH ABBEY HOTEL   (01835) 822261
An energetic manager is knocking this imposing hotel, right by the medieval Abbey, into shape for the twenty-first century. A rolling programme of refurbishment and renewal focuses on the bedrooms, and signs so far are promising. Reports on progress welcome.   £124

Stirling (Stirling)
PARK LODGE   (01786) 474862
Creeper-clad Regency house within walking distance of the city centre, featuring a grand interior packed with *trompe l'oeil* effects and magnificent plasterwork, plus Georges Marquetty's classic French cuisine. Bedrooms are comfortable, though simpler.   £90

Stornoway (Western Isles)
PARK GUEST HOUSE   (01851) 702485
Well located for ferry transfers to the mainland, this guest house on the Isle of Lewis offers hearty food and informal service, but lacks private parking facilities or a good view. The interior décor reflects the house's Victorian roots, with William Morris-style wallpaper adding some character.   £42 to £58

Strachur (Argyll & Bute)
CREGGAN'S INN   (01369) 860279
Cheerful, long-established hostelry, family-run, and occupying a prime position on the shores of Loch Fyne. Terrific views from spacious, airy but rather bland public rooms. The refurbished bedrooms are smart and comfortable. Reports welcome, particularly regarding the food.   £110

Strathpeffer (Highland)
CRAIGVAR   (01997) 421622
Handily located right next to the newly restored Victorian spa pavilion, this B&B is a real budget find. Margaret Scott is a jolly hostess, who keeps an immaculate house with lots of extras on offer such as sherry, bathrobes and tennis equipment. The breakfast menu is extensive too. £52 to £64

Strathyre (Stirling)
CREAGAN HOUSE   (01877) 384638
A programme of refurbishment is about to roll through the public areas of this medieval-style restaurant, with cosy rooms and recently re-vamped showers. Gordon Gunn's French-influenced cuisine is hearty fare.   £95

Tongue (Highland)
BEN LOYAL HOTEL (01847) 611216
The bedrooms and bar are uninspiring while the food, although of good quality, is expensive. What sets this hotel apart is the view from its dining room: floor to ceiling windows provide vistas of the Viking castle Varrick, and Ben Hope (the most northerly Munro), as well as Ben Loyal and the Kyle of Tongue.
£50 to £64

Urquhart (Moray)
OLD CHURCH (01343) 843063
Curiously pleasing cocktail of Scottish vernacular architecture, Scandinavian style and Native American-influenced décor in this fun, energetically run converted church in Speyside. £48

Yarrow (Borders)
THE GORDON INN * (01750) 82222
Try to bag the ground-floor four-poster room at this modest roadside inn with Walter Scott connections, interesting, well-judged food and a surprisingly contemporary bar with a fine array of malts and cigars. £55

WALES

Abersoch (Gwynedd)
NEIGWL * (01758) 712363
Immaculate, personally run seaside hotel with superb bay views from the bar-lounge and adjacent dining room (some bedrooms too). Room rates include set dinners, flexibly priced for smaller appetites. Bedrooms are decorated in clean, light schemes, with modern fittings and autumnal duvets. Resort and harbour lie within easy walking distance. £110

Aberystwyth (Ceredigion)
CONRAH COUNTRY HOUSE HOTEL (01970) 617941
This family-run hotel, about four miles south of the town, lacks the grandeur of some country houses, although public areas do sport oil paintings and stained-glass windows. Picture windows in the smart restaurant give views to the vegetable garden and the hills beyond. The spacious, rustic-styled courtyard bedrooms are preferable to those in the main house. £120

Cardiff (Cardiff)
EXPRESS BY HOLIDAY INN 029-2044 9000
This business-oriented, waterside hotel stands between the city centre and the attractions of Cardiff Bay. Expect an informal, spick-and-span place, with bright, cheery colours and light pine furniture. The bedrooms – smart, if rather impersonal – now include air conditioning. Only breakfast is served, but there's a restaurant opposite.
£69 to £100

Conwy (Conwy)
BERTHLWYD HALL (01492) 592409
A quiet, rambling Victorian guesthouse with plenty of period character. Rooms are very spacious and are furnished with antiques and traditional pieces chosen to suit the style of the house. Welcoming owners offer simple dinners at very reasonable prices. £65

Fishguard (Pembrokeshire)
3 MAIN STREET
This Georgian townhouse is no longer classed as a restaurant-with-rooms, because Inez Ford now offers simpler dinners, on request, only to overnight guests. The three en-suite bedrooms feature Art Deco touches; choose the back room for its view over the cliffs. Breakfast may include home-baked croissants and scones. £70

Gellilydan (Gwynedd)
TYDDYN DU FARM * (01766) 590281
This guesthouse on a working sheep farm in southern Snowdonia offers charming, well-equipped accommodation, including several self-contained suites in converted outbuildings. Though comfortably modernised throughout, the seventeenth-century buildings retain cosy period features such as a large inglenook fireplace. Home-cooked dinners by prior arrangement (guests are welcome to bring their own wine).
£60 to £76

Harlech (Gwynedd)
HAFOD WEN * (01766) 780356
Unusual Dutch-colonial style property with a large sundeck balcony running along the seaward façade and eight acres of terraced gardens. Inside, the house is full of antiques, books, curios and original art, some by members of the artistic Chapman family. The Victorian-style dining room provides an intimate setting for simple, inexpensive home-cooked dinners, and the bedrooms are generously proportioned and interestingly furnished.   £74 to 76

Holyhead (Isle of Anglesey)
YR HENDRE * (01407) 762929
A boon for prospective ferry travellers, this long-established B&B in a comfortable 1920s house on the edge of town offers a great welcome, an excellent breakfast and home-like rooms. Furnishings are a mix of antiques and more functional modern pieces. Friendly owners go to endless trouble for visitors, including transporting them to and from the port or station on request.   £55

Llanaber (Gwynedd)
LLWYNDU FARMHOUSE (01341) 280144
Idiosyncratic sixteenth-century farm guesthouse (originally Elizabethan) halfway up a hillside above Cardigan Bay. The interior is cosy and cottagey, full of beams, exposed stonework and quirky features (such as a priest's hole now used as a walk-in wardrobe). Some furnishings are perhaps ready for a makeover.   £74

Llandudno (Conwy)
BELMONT (01492) 877770
This well-kept Victorian block occupies a prime location on Llandudno's seafront. Affiliated to the Royal Blind Society, it has many specially adapted features (automatic doors, wide corridors, menus in Braille, etc). It takes many groups and is somewhat institutional, but seems well kept, bright, clean and friendly.   £60 (£30 per person most rooms are single)

Llandudno (Conwy)
ST TUDNO (01492) 874411
An exceptionally well-kept hotel on Llandudno's elegant Victorian seafront. Under the same family ownership for many years, it has achieved a solid reputation for good service and high standards of accommodation. The heated swimming pool is an added bonus. 'Service is exemplary – they remember your name and your room number (even when you forget),' reports a happy regular.   £132

Llanerchymedd (Isle of Anglesey)
LLWYDIARTH FAWR * (01248) 470321
Good-value B&B in an elegant Georgian farmhouse deep in rural Anglesey. This is a working farm, and obviously a much-loved family home. The welcome is exceptionally warm.   £60

Llanrwst (Gwynedd)
GWYDIR CASTLE (01492) 641687
An authentic early-Tudor courtyard house (open to visitors) provides an atmospheric setting for a couple of B&B rooms. Don't expect luxury or even any great degree of comfort, but fabrics and furnishings are suitably imposing and the ornamental grounds are splendid.   £65 to £75

Llansanffraid Glan Conwy (Conwy)
OLD RECTORY (01492) 580611
A handsome, well-kept Georgian house set high over the Conwy Estuary. The interior is elegant and tasteful, with many antiques and paintings. Service is attentive, especially in the evenings, when elaborate gourmet dinners are served.   £129 to £159

Penmaenpool (Gwynedd)
PENMAENUCHAF HALL (01341) 422129
Large Victorian mansion in secluded location near the Mawddach Estuary. Inside, it is handsomely furnished and spacious, with plenty of antiques and period character. Staff seemed in short supply on our last inspection visit.   £120

Pentraeth (Isle Of Anglesey)
PARC YR ODYN *   (01248) 450566
This substantial modern family farmhouse overlooks 150 acres of working farmland, mostly grazing for sheep and horses, and it is very well maintained, and surrounded by tidy gardens. There are just two letting bedrooms, both well equipped and nicely decorated with super big bathrooms (one has a Jacuzzi).   £60

Pontyclun (Rhondda Cynon Taff)
MISKIN MANOR   (01443) 224204
This traditional country house, conveniently (and audibly) close to the M4, is set in substantial, wooded grounds. The hotel is geared up for weddings and conferences, with a leisure complex and banqueting hall (complete with minstrels' gallery). Plans for 2005 include adding an orangery. Bedrooms are decked out cheerfully with tasteful furnishings.   £100 to £136

St Fagans (Cardiff)
THE OLD POST OFFICE *   029-2056 5400
This unassuming restaurant-with-rooms near Cardiff was the village's post office in the 1980s. Now the décor is clinically minimalist, with pine fittings and abstract photos from the much-visited, neighbouring Folk Museum. The inventive dishes are flavoursome and well presented; the service attentive and professional. Good-sized, cool-looking bedrooms have marshmallow-white linen and powerful showers.   £75

Swansea (Swansea)
WINDSOR LODGE   (01792) 642158
The city centre may only be a stroll away, yet this small, sky-blue hotel is on a quiet street. The lounge is inviting and smartly furnished, while several artworks are the backdrop for thoughtful, Welsh and continental dishes in the restaurant. The 19 bedrooms vary in size but are comfortable and clean.   £65 to £75

Talsarnau (Gwynedd)
MAES-Y-NEUADD   (01766) 780200
An imposing country house with a long history. The interior gives mixed impressions: the cheerful lounge and cosy inglenook bar are undeniably pleasing, but its highly regarded restaurant seems rather bland, as are some of the bedrooms. Fine grounds. £165

Tal-y-Llyn (Gwynedd)
TYNYCORNEL   (01654) 782282
A substantial white-painted complex in a glorious lakeshore setting, sheltered by steep hills behind. Although not strong on personality, it is well kept, light and spacious, and the bar-lounge is decorated with bird paintings by a local artist. Bedrooms vary; some has been smartly refurbished, others are a little faded.   £100

Trearddur Bay (Isle of Anglesey)
TREARDDUR BAY HOTEL *   (01407) 860301
Extensive resort hotel on one of Anglesey's best beaches, which explains much of its appeal to families with children. Guests of all ages, however, appreciate the civilised atmosphere here. All bedrooms have side sea views; best and largest are the seabird suites, which have their own balconies. A bit more attention could be paid to practical details, like surface space in bathrooms.   £120 to £124

Wolf's Castle (Pembrokeshire)
WOLFE INN   (01437) 741662
Food is the focus of this Italian-run inn on the A40. While the bar itself is tiny, there are four dining areas, including one beamed, hunting-themed room. A good variety of evening meals and breakfast buffet options will keep the wolf from the door. The three bedrooms are simply furnished in cottagey style.   £60 to £80

Hotels noted for serving good food

Hotels where you can rely on a good meal – either the hotel features in *The Good Food Guide 2005* or our inspectors were impressed, whether by particularly competent home-cooking or by more lavish cuisine – are listed below.

London
The Capital
Charlotte Street Hotel
The Gore
The Halkin
Mandarin Oriental Hyde Park
One Aldwych
The Savoy
The Victoria
West Street
The Zetter

England
Alderminster, The Bell
Ambleside, Drunken Duck Inn
Ambleside, Rothay Manor
Ampleforth, Shallowdale House
Applethwaite, Underscar Manor
Ardington, Boar's Head
Arlingham, Old Passage Inn
Arncliffe, Amerdale House
Ashbourne, Callow Hall
Ashbourne, Omnia Somnia
Ashwater, Blagdon Manor
Aylesbury, Hartwell House
Balsall Common, Haigs Hotel
Barwick, Little Barwick House
Baslow, Cavendish Hotel
Baslow, Fischer's Baslow Hall
Bassenthwaite Lake, The Pheasant
Bath, Bath Priory
Bath, Queensberry Hotel
Bath, Royal Crescent Hotel
Beercrocombe, Frog Street Farm
Beetham, Wheatsheaf at Beetham
Berwick-upon-Tweed, Number One Sallyport
Bigbury-on-Sea, Henley Hotel
Birch Vale, Waltzing Weasel
Birmingham, Hotel du Vin & Bistro
Bishop's Tachbrook, Mallory Court
Bishop's Tawton, Halmpstone Manor
Blockley, Old Bakery
Bolton Abbey, Devonshire Arms
Boughton Lees, Eastwell Manor
Bourton-on-the-Water, Dial House
Bowness-on-Windermere, Lindeth Fell
Bowness-on-Windermere, Linthwaite House
Brampton, Farlam Hall
Branscombe, Masons Arms
Bray, Waterside Inn
Brighton, Hotel du Vin & Bistro
Brimfield, Roebuck Inn

Bristol, Hotel du Vin & Bistro
Bromsgrove, Grafton Manor
Burford, Jonathan's at the Angel
Burlton, Burlton Inn
Burnham Market, Hoste Arms
Burnsall, Devonshire Fell
Burrington, Northcote Manor
Cambridge, Hotel Felix
Cartmel, Aynsome Manor
Cartmel, L'Enclume
Cartmel, Uplands
Castle Combe, Manor House
Cavendish, The George
Chaddesley Corbett, Brockencote Hall
Chandler's Cross, The Grove
Charlbury, Bull Inn
Chettle, Castleman Hotel
Chipping Campden, Cotswold House
Cholmondeley, Cholmondeley Arms
Chulmleigh, Old Bakehouse
Coleford, New Inn
Colerne, Lucknam Park
Coln St Aldwyns, New Inn at Coln
Constantine, Trengilly Wartha
Cookham Dean, Inn on the Green
Crackington Haven, Manor Farm
Crayke, Durham Ox
Cricket Malherbie, The Old Rectory
Crosthwaite, Punch Bowl Inn
Croyde, Whiteleaf at Croyde
Crudwell, Old Rectory
Cuckfield, Ockenden Manor
Dedham, Milsoms
Dedham, Sun Inn
Doddiscombsleigh, Nobody Inn
Dorridge, The Forest
East Barkwith, Bodkin Lodge
East Barkwith, The Grange
Eastbourne, Grand Hotel
East Grinstead, Gravetye Manor
East Hoathly, Old Whyly
East Witton, Blue Lion
Emsworth, 36 on the Quay
Ermington, Plantation House
Evershot, Summer Lodge
Exeter, Alias Hotel Barcelona
Farnham, Museum Inn
Faversham, Read's
Fleet, Moonfleet Manor
Fletching, Griffin Inn
Fowey, Marina Hotel
Froggatt, Chequers Inn
Gateshead, Eslington Villa

Gillan, Tregildry Hotel
Gillingham, Stock Hill House
Gittisham, Combe House
Golcar, Weavers Shed
Grange-in-Borrowdale, Borrowdale Gates Hotel
Grasmere, White Moss House
Great Dunmow, The Starr
Great Milton, Le Manoir aux Quat' Saisons
Grimston, Congham Hall
Grittleton, Church House
Halifax, Holdsworth House
Harome, Star Inn
Harrogate, Balmoral Hotel
Harrogate, Hotel du Vin & Bistro
Harwich, The Pier at Harwich
Hathersage, Plough Inn
Haworth, Weaver's
Hereford, Castle House
Higher Burwardsley, The Pheasant
Hinton Charterhouse, Homewood Park
Holkham, The Victoria
Horndon on the Hill, Bell Inn & Hill House
Horringer, The Ickworth
Huddersfield, Lodge Hotel
Hurstbourne Tarrant, Esseborne Manor
Ilmington, Howard Arms
Kingham, Mill House
Kingswear, Nonsuch House
Kington, Penrhos Court
Lacock, At the Sign of the Angel
Langar, Langar Hall
Langford Budville, Bindon Country House
Langho, Northcote Manor
Langthwaite, CB Inn
Lavenham, The Angel
Lavenham, Great House
Leeds, 42 The Calls
Leeds, Haley's Hotel
Leeds, Malmaison Leeds
Leintwardine, Upper Buckton Farm
Lifton, Arundell Arms
Liverpool, The Racquet Club
Llanfair Waterdine, The Waterdine
Long Crendon, Angel Restaurant
Looe, Talland Bay
Ludlow, Dinham Hall
Ludlow, Mr Underhill's
Lydgate, White Hart Inn
Maidencombe, Orestone Manor
Manchester, Malmaison Manchester
Manchester, The Midland
Marsden, Olive Branch
Masham, Swinton Park
Matfen, Matfen Hall
Mawnan Smith, Meudon Hotel
Melbourn, Sheene Mill
Mellor Brook, Feilden's Arms
Mickleton, Three Ways House
Milborne Port, Old Vicarage
Morston, Morston Hall

Moulsford, Beetle & Wedge
Muddiford, Broomhill Art Hotel
Mungrisdale, Mill Hotel
Nantwich, Curshaws at the Cat
Nayland, White Hart
Near Sawrey, Ees Wyke
Near Sawrey, Sawrey House
Nettlebed, White Hart Hotel
New Milton, Chewton Glen
Newcastle, Malmaison Newcastle
Norwich, By Appointment
Nottingham, Hart's
Nottingham, Lace Market Hotel
Orford, Crown and Castle
Oxford, Old Parsonage
Padstow, Seafood Restaurant, St Petroc's Hotel, Rick Stein's Café
Painswick, Painswick Hotel
Paulerspury, Vine House
Pelynt, Penellick
Penzance, Abbey Hotel
Penzance, Summer House
Pickering, White Swan
Polperro, Cottage Restaurant
Poole, Mansion House
Porlock Weir, Andrew's on the Weir
Portscatho, Driftwood Hotel
Postbridge, Lydgate House
Prestbury, The White House Manor
Ramsgill, Yorke Arms
Rhydycroesau, Pen-y-Dyffryn
Ripley, Boar's Head
Rock, St Enodoc Hotel
Romaldkirk, Rose & Crown
Romsey, Berties
Rowsley, The Peacock at Rowsley
Roydhouse, Three Acres Inn
Rushlake Green, Stone House
St Briavels, Cinderhill House
St Keyne, The Well House
St Margaret's at Cliffe, Wallett's Court
St Martin's, St Martin's on the Isle
St Mawes, Hotel Tresanton
St Mawes, Rising Sun
Seaham, Seaham Hall Hotel
Seaview, Seaview Hotel
Shepton Mallet, Charlton House
Shipham, Daneswood House
Shipton Gorge, Innsacre Farmhouse
Southwold, The Crown
Southwold, The Swan
Stadhampton, The Crazy Bear
Staithes, Endeavour
Stanton Wick, Carpenters Arms
Stockcross, Vineyard at Stockcross
Stoke-by-Nayland, Angel Inn
Stokesley, Chapters
Stuckton, Three Lions
Sturminster Newton, Plumber Manor
Sutton Gault, Anchor Inn
Swaffham, Strattons

Sway, The Nurse's Cottage
Tadcaster, Hazlewood Castle
Tavistock, Horn of Plenty
Teffont Evias, Howard's House
Thornham, Lifeboat Inn
Thornton, River House
Tirril, Queen's Head Inn
Titchwell, Titchwell Manor
Titley, Stagg Inn
Torquay, Mulberry House
Tunbridge Wells, Hotel du Vin & Bistro
Ullswater, Sharrow Bay
Ulverston, Bay Horse Hotel
Upper Hambleton, Hambleton Hall
Virginstow, Percy's Country Hotel
Wareham, Priory Hotel
Warwick, Rose and Crown
Watermillock, Rampsbeck Country House
Wath-in-Nidderdale, Sportsman's Arms
Whitewell, Inn at Whitewell
Wickham, Old House
Winchester, Hotel du Vin & Bistro
Winchester, Wykeham Arms
Windermere, Gilpin Lodge
Windermere, Holbeck Ghyll
Windermere, Miller Howe
Windermere, The Samling
Winteringham, Winteringham Fields
Withypool, Royal Oak Inn
Wolterton, Saracen's Head
Wookey Hole, Glencot House
Worfield, Old Vicarage
Wye, Wife of Bath
Yarmouth, George Hotel
Yattendon, Royal Oak
York, Middlethorpe Hall

Scotland

Aberdour, Hawkcraig House
Achiltibuie, Summer Isles Hotel
Annbank, Enterkine House
Applecross, Applecross Inn
Auchterarder, Gleneagles
Auldearn, Boath House
Ballantrae, Glenapp Castle
Ballater, Balgonie Country House
Ballater, Darroch Learg
Balquhidder, Monachyle Mhor
Clachan-Seil, Willowburn Hotel
Colbost, Three Chimneys
Dornoch, 2 Quail
Dunkeld, Kinnaird
Edinburgh, The Bonham
Edinburgh, The Witchery by the Castle
Ednam, Edenwater House
Eriska, Isle of Eriska
Fort William, Inverlochy Castle
Glasgow, Langs Hotel

Gullane, Greywalls
Inverkeilor, Gordon's
Kingussie, The Cross
Kirkwall, Foveran Hotel
Linlithgow, Champany Inn
Lochinver, The Albannach
Lochranza, Apple Lodge
Moffat, Beechwood Country House
Moffat, Well View
Muir of Ord, Dower House
Peat Inn, Peat Inn
Plockton, Plockton Hotel
Port Appin, Airds Hotel
Port Ellen, Glenmachrie Country Guesthouse
St Fillans, Four Seasons Hotel
St Margaret's Hope, The Creel
Scarista, Scarista House
Shieldaig, Tigh an Eilean
Strontian, Kilcamb Lodge
Swinton, The Wheatsheaf
Troon, Lochgreen House
Ullapool, Tanglewood House

Wales

Aberaeron, Harbourmaster Hotel
Aberdovey, Penhelig Arms Hotel
Abersoch, Porth Tocyn Hotel
Barmouth, Bae Abermaw
Beaumaris, Ye Olde Bull's Head
Capel Garmon, Tan-y-Foel
Clytha, Clytha Arms
Crickhowell, Bear Hotel
Crickhowell, Gliffaes Country House Hotel
Druidston, The Druidstone
Eglwysfach, Ynyshir Hall
Felin Fach, Felin Fach Griffin
Fishguard, Manor Town House
Harlech, Castle Cottage
Laugharne, The Cors
Llanddeiniolen, Ty'n Rhos
Llandrillo, Tyddyn Llan
Llandudno, Bodysgallen Hall
Llandudno, Osborne House
Llangammarch Wells, Lake Country House
Llangollen, Gales
Llanwrtyd Wells, Carlton House
Llyswen, Llangoed Hall
Newport, Cnapan
Northop, Soughton Hall
Porthkerry, Egerton Grey
Portmeirion, Hotel Portmeirion and Castell Deudraeth
Pwllheli, Plas Bodegroes
Reynoldston, Fairyhill
Skenfrith, The Bell at Skenfrith
Tredunnock, The Newbridge
Tyn-y-Groes, Groes Inn

Hotels in a peaceful location

Hotels in an exceptionally peaceful location, where you should expect to have a restful stay, are listed below. A few city hotels that are relatively peaceful considering their location are also included.

London
The Stafford

England
Abberley, Elms Hotel
Aldfield, Mallard Grange
Alston, Lovelady Shield
Alstonefield, Stanshope Hall
Ampleforth, Shallowdale House
Applethwaite, Underscar Manor
Arlingham, Old Passage Inn
Armscote, Willow Corner
Arncliffe, Amerdale House
Ashbourne, Callow Hall
Ashburton, Holne Chase
Ashwater, Blagdon Manor
Askrigg, Helm
Austwick, Austwick Traddock
Aylesbury, Hartwell House
Aylmerton, Felbrigg Lodge
Bassenthwaite Lake, The Pheasant
Battle, Fox Hole Farm
Beercrocombe, Frog Street Farm
Bibury, Bibury Court
Bigbury-on-Sea, Burgh Island
Biggin, Biggin Hall
Bishop's Tachbrook, Mallory Court
Bishop's Tawton, Halmpstone Manor
Blackwell, Blackwell Grange
Botallack, Botallack Manor
Bowness-on-Windermere, Lindeth Fell
Bowness-on-Windermere, Linthwaite House
Brampton, Farlam Hall
Brockenhurst, Whitley Ridge
Bryher, Hell Bay Hotel
Buckland, Buckland Manor
Burpham, Old Parsonage
Burrington, Northcote Manor
Buttermere, Wood House
Cannington, Blackmore Farm
Cartmel, Aynsome Manor
Cartmel, Uplands
Cartmel Fell, Lightwood
Castle Ashby, The Falcon
Castle Combe, Manor House
Chettle, Castleman Hotel
Chillaton, Quither Mill
Chillaton, Tor Cottage
Chittlehamholt, Highbullen
Climping, Bailiffscourt
Clun, Birches Mill
Colerne, Lucknam Park
Constantine, Trengilly Wartha

Crackington Haven, Manor Farm
Creed, Creed House
Cricket Malherbie, The Old Rectory
Croft-on-Tees, Clow Beck House
Crosthwaite, Punch Bowl Inn
Dittisham, Fingals
Dulverton, Ashwick House
Dunsley, Dunsley Hall
East Barkwith, Bodkin Lodge
East Barkwith, The Grange
East Grinstead, Gravetye Manor
East Hoathly, Old Whyly
Etchingham, King John's Lodge
Evershot, Summer Lodge
Gillan, Tregildry Hotel
Gillingham, Stock Hill House
Gittisham, Combe House Hotel
Glossop, The Wind in the Willows
Grange-in-Borrowdale, Borrowdale Gates Hotel
Great Snoring, Manor House
Grimston, Congham Hall
Hamsterley Forest, Grove House
Harome, Star Inn
Hartfield, Bolebroke Mill
Hassop, Hassop Hall
Hathersage, Highlow Hall
Hathersage, Plough Inn
Hawnby, Hawnby Hotel
Headlam, Headlam Hall
Hexham, Dene House
Higher Burwardsley, The Pheasant
Holmesfield, Horsleygate Hall
Hope, Underleigh House
Hopesay, The Old Rectory
Hopwas, Oak Tree Farm
Horringer, The Ickworth
Hurstbourne Tarrant, Esseborne Manor
Ingleby Greenhow, Manor House Farm
Ireby, Overwater Hall
Keswick, Dale Head Hall
Kimmeridge, Kimmeridge Farmhouse
Kingham, Mill House
Kingsbridge, Buckland-Tout-Saints Hotel
Langford Budville, Bindon Country House
Langthwaite, CB Inn
Lastingham, Lastingham Grange
Leintwardine, Upper Buckton Farm
Leysters, Hills Farm
Little Langdale, Three Shires Inn
Looe, Talland Bay
Lorton, New House Farm
Lorton, Winder Hall

Lower Beeding, South Lodge
Loxley, Loxley Farm
Maidencombe, Orestone Manor
Malvern Wells, Cottage in the Wood
Markington, Hob Green
Martinhoe, Old Rectory
Masham, Swinton Park
Matfen, Matfen Hall
Matlock, Red House Country Hotel
Mawnan Smith, Meudon Hotel
Membury, Oxenways
Moreton, The Dairy
Morston, Morston Hall
Mullion, Polurrian Hotel
Mungrisdale, Mill Hotel
Near Sawrey, Ees Wyke
Near Sawrey, Sawrey House
Newbrough, Allerwash Farmhouse
Newton-Le-Willows, The Hall
Oakamoor, Bank House
Pelynt, Penellick
Perranuthnoe, Ednovean Farm
Portscatho, Driftwood Hotel
Portscatho, Rosevine Hotel
Postbridge, Lydgate House
Ramsgill, Yorke Arms
Rhydycroesau, Pen-y-Dyffryn
Ringlestone, Ringlestone Inn
Rogate, Mizzards Farm
Romaldkirk, Rose & Crown
Ruan High Lanes, Polsue Manor
Rushlake Green, Stone House
St Blazey, Nanscawen Manor House
St Briavels, Cinderhill House
St Hilary, Ennys
St Keyne, The Well House
St Margaret's at Cliffe, Wallett's Court
St Martin's, St Martin's on the Isle
Salcombe, Soar Mill Cove Hotel
Sandiway, Nunsmere Hall
Sandypark, Mill End
Saracen's Head, Pipwell Manor
Seatoller, Seatoller House
Sedbusk, Stone House
Selside, Low Jock Scar
Shipton Gorge, Innsacre Farmhouse
Sissinghurst, Sissinghurst Castle Farm
Sturminster Newton, Plumber Manor
Sutton Gault, Anchor Inn
Tavistock, Horn of Plenty
Teffont Evias, Howard's House
Thornton, River House
Tilston, Tilston Lodge
Totnes, Kingston House
Two Bridges, Prince Hall Hotel
Ullswater, Sharrow Bay
Upper Hambleton, Hambleton Hall
Veryan, Nare Hotel
Virginstow, Percy's Country Hotel
Wasdale Head, Wasdale Head Inn
Watermillock, Old Church Hotel

Watermillock, Rampsbeck Country House
Wath-in-Nidderdale, Sportsman's Arms
Wellingham, Manor House Farm
Whimple, Woodhayes Country House and Cottage
Wilmcote, Pear Tree Cottage
Wincanton, Holbrook House Hotel
Windermere, Gilpin Lodge
Windermere, Holbeck Ghyll
Windermere, Low House
Windermere, The Samling
Winteringham, Winteringham Fields
Wolterton, Saracen's Head
Woodstock, Shipton Glebe
Wookey Hole, Glencot House
Worfield, Old Vicarage

Scotland
Aberfoyle, Creag-Ard House
Achiltibuie, Summer Isles Hotel
Annbank, Enterkine House
Applecross, Applecross Inn
Ascog, Balmory Hall
Auldearn, Boath House
Ballantrae, Glenapp Castle
Balquhidder, Monachyle Mhor
Brodick, Kilmichael Country House
Callander, Leny House
Clachan-Seil, Willowburn Hotel
Clintmains, Clint Lodge
Colbost, Three Chimneys
Drumnadrochit, Polmaily House
Dunkeld, Hilton Dunkeld House
Dunkeld, Kinnaird
Eday, Sui Generis Guest Rooms
Ednam, Edenwater House
Edzell, The House of Mark
Eriska, Isle of Eriska
Fort William, Inverlochy Castle
Glenlivet, Minmore House
Kentallen, Ardsheal House
Kingussie, The Cross
Kinloch, Kinloch House Hotel
Kirkwall, Foveran Hotel
Lochinver, The Albannach
Lynwilg, Lynwilg House
Markinch, Balbirnie House
Muir of Ord, Dower House
Peat Inn, Peat Inn
Portpatrick, Knockinaam Lodge
Scarista, Scarista House
Shieldaig, Tigh an Eilean
Stein, Stein Inn
Strontian, Kilcamb Lodge
Ullapool, Tanglewood House

Wales
Abereiddy, Crug-Glas
Beddgelert, Sygun Fawr
Capel Garmon, Llannerch Goch
Capel Garmon, Tan-y-Foel

Conwy, Sychnant Pass House
Crickhowell, Gliffaes Country House Hotel
Eglwysfach, Ynyshir Hall
Laugharne, Hurst House
Llanarmon Dyffryn Ceiriog, West Arms Hotel
Llanddeiniolen, Ty'n Rhos
Llandrillo, Tyddyn Llan
Llandudno, Bodysgallen Hall
Llanfachreth, Ty Isaf Farmhouse
Llanfihangel-yng-Ngwynfa, Cyfie Farm
Llangammarch Wells, Lake Country House

Llanigon, Old Post Office
Llanrhian, Trevaccoon
Llyswen, Llangoed Hall
Menai Bridge, Wern Farm
Northop, Soughton Hall
Penmachno, Penmachno Hall
Pentregat, The Grange
Pwllheli, Plas Bodegroes
Reynoldston, Fairyhill
St Bride's Wentlooge, West Usk Lighthouse
Spittal, Lower Haythog Farm
Tredunnock, The Newbridge

Good-value hotels

Hotels offering all their twin or double rooms (not including four-posters or suites) for £35 or less per person per night, including breakfast – or £50 or less per person if the rate includes dinner – are listed below. (Many hotels advertise special breaks, and weekend and out-of-season offers, which can mean cheaper room rates than those quoted.)

England

Alderminster, The Bell
Ambleside, Kent House
Armscote, Willow Corner
Ashey, Little Upton Farm
Aveton Gifford, Court Barton Farm
Babworth, The Barns
Bassenthwaite, Willow Cottage
Battle, Fox Hole Farm
Beercrocombe, Frog Street Farm
Beyton, Manorhouse
Blackpool, Raffles
Blackwell, Blackwell Grange
Botallack, Botallack Manor
Briggswath, The Lawns
Cannington, Blackmore Farm
Cartmel Fell, Lightwood
Catlowdy, Bessiestown Farm
Chatton, Old Manse
Cheddleton, Choir Cottage & Choir House
Cholmondeley, Cholmondeley Arms
Chulmleigh, Old Bakehouse
Coventry, Crest Guesthouse
Crosthwaite, Crosthwaite House
Crosthwaite, Punch Bowl Inn
East Barkwith, Bodkin Lodge
East Barkwith, The Grange
Eastbourne, Brayscroft Hotel
Grittleton, Church House
Hamsterley Forest, Grove House
Hanley Castle, Old Parsonage Farm
Hartfield, Bolebroke Watermill
Hathersage, Highlow Hall
Hawnby, Hawnby Hotel
Hermitage, Almshouse Farm
Hexham, Dene House
Holmesfield, Horsleygate Hall
Hope, Underleigh House
Huddersfield, Lodge Hotel
Ilmington, Folly Farm Cottage
Ingleby Greenhow, Manor House Farm
Inkpen, Crown & Garter
Ironbridge, The Library House
Jacobstowe, Higher Cadham Farm
Kenilworth, Castle Laurels
Kimmeridge, Kimmeridge Farmhouse
Kinnersley, Upper Newton Farmhouse
Laxton, Dovecote Inn
Leadenham, Willoughby Arms
Leamington Spa, York House
Leonard Stanley, Grey Cottage
Lewes, Millers
Leysters, Hills Farm
Little Hampden, Rising Sun
Little Walsingham, Old Bakehouse
Loxley, Loxley Farm
Lynton, Valley House
Marsden, Olive Branch
Maryport, The Retreat
Meldreth, Chiswick House
Mellor Brook, Feildens Arms
Middle Winterslow, The Beadles
Minchinhampton, Hunters Lodge
Mobberley, Laburnum Cottage
Muddiford, Broomhill Art Hotel
Near Sawrey, Buckle Yeat
Newton-on-the-Moor, Cook and Barker Inn
Osmotherley, The Three Tuns
Pickhill, Nag's Head
Polperro, Cottage Restaurant
Rogate, Mizzards Farm
Saltaire, Beeties
Saracen's Head, Pipwell Manor
Seatoller, Seatoller House
Selside, Low Jock Scar
Sissinghurst, Sissinghurst Castle Farm
Southend-on-Sea, Pebbles
Stratford-upon-Avon, Victoria Spa Lodge
Tilston, Tilston Lodge
Tirril, Queen's Head Inn
Torquay, Mulberry House
Waterlip, Burnt House Farm
Wells, Canon Grange
Weymouth, Seaham Guesthouse
Wilmcote, Pear Tree Cottage
Windermere, Coach House
Winster, Brae Cottage
Yelverton, Old Orchard

Scotland

Aberdour, Hawkcraig House
Applecross, Applecross Inn
Dunkeld, The Pend
Eday, Sui Generis Guest Rooms
Edzell, The House of Mark
Jedburgh, Hundalee House
Kirdcudbright, Gladstone House
Lochranza, Apple Lodge
Lynwilg, Lynwilg House
Port Ellen, Glenmachrie Country Guesthouse

Stein, Stein Inn
Stirling, Ashgrove House

Wales

Betws-y-Coed, Pengwern Country House
Brecon, Cantre Selyf
Capel Garmon, Llannerch Goch
Cardiff, The Town House
Clytha, Clytha Arms
Fishguard, Manor Town House
Freshwater East, Portclew House

Laugharne, The Cors
Llandudno, Abbey Lodge
Llanfachreth, Ty Isaf Farmhouse
Llangollen, Gales
Llanigon, Old Post Office
Menai Bridge, Wern Farm
Nantgwynant, Pen-y-Gwryd Hotel
Newport, Cnapan
Pentregat, The Grange
Spittal, Lower Haythog Farm

Child-friendly hotels

Hotels that do not have age restrictions and offer the basic facilities of cots and highchairs, as well as babysitting and/or baby-listening, are listed below. Where there are restrictions on children in the restaurant or dining-room in the evening, early suppers are provided.

London
22 Jermyn Street
51 Buckingham Gate
Abbey Court
Basil Street Hotel
Charlotte Street Hotel
Covent Garden Hotel
Dorset Square Hotel
Durley House
Durrants Hotel
Franklin Hotel
The Goring
The Halkin
The Hempel
The Milestone
Novotel London Euston
Pembridge Court
Sherlock Holmes Hotel
Sloane Hotel
The Stafford
Tophams Belgravia

England
Abberley, Elms Hotel
Aldeburgh, Wentworth Hotel
Alderminster, The Bell
Alton, Alton Towers Hotel
Ambleside, The Regent
Ambleside, Rothay Manor
Ardington, Boar's Head
Arlingham, Old Passage Inn
Arncliffe, Amerdale House
Ashburton, Holne Chase
Austwick, Austwick Traddock
Bapchild, Hempstead House
Baslow, Fischer's Baslow Hall
Bath, Bath Priory
Bath, Queensberry Hotel
Bath, Royal Crescent Hotel
Bathford, Eagle House
Beaulieu, Montagu Arms
Bibury, Bibury Court
Birmingham, Hotel du Vin & Bistro
Blackpool, Raffles
Bolton Abbey, Devonshire Arms
Bosham, The Millstream
Boughton Lees, Eastwell Manor
Bowness-on-Windermere, Fayrer Garden House Hotel
Bowness-on-Windermere, Lindeth Fell
Bowness-on-Windermere, Linthwaite House
Bradford-on-Avon, Woolley Grange

Brighton, Alias Hotel Seattle
Brighton, Blanch House
Brighton, Hudson's Hotel
Bristol, Hotel du Vin & Bistro
Broad Campden, Malt House
Brockenhurst, Whitley Ridge
Bryher, Hell Bay Hotel
Burford, Lamb Inn
Burnsall, Devonshire Fell
Burrington, Northcote Manor
Bury St Edmunds, The Angel
Bury St Edmunds, Ounce House
Bury St Edmunds, Ravenwood Hall
Cambridge, Hotel Felix
Cannington, Blackmore Farm
Cartmel Fell, Lightwood
Castle Combe, Manor House
Chaddesley Corbett, Brockencote Hall
Chandler's Cross, The Grove
Cheltenham, Alias Hotel Kandinsky
Chester-le-Street, Lumley Castle
Chettle, Castleman Hotel
Chipping Campden, Cotswold House
Chipping Campden, King's Arms
Clearwell, Tudor Farmhouse
Climping, Bailiffscourt
Colerne, Lucknam Park
Colwall Stone, Colwall Park
Constantine, Trengilly Wartha
Corfe Castle, Mortons House
Crosthwaite, Crosthwaite House
Crudwell, Old Rectory
Cuckfield, Ockenden Manor
Dartmouth, Royal Castle
Dedham, Maison Talbooth
Dittisham, Fingals
Dunsley, Dunsley Hall
Eastbourne, Grand Hotel
East Witton, Blue Lion
Egham, Great Fosters
Egham, Runnymede Hotel
Ermington, Plantation House
Evershot, Summer Lodge
Evesham, Evesham Hotel
Exeter, Alias Hotel Barcelona
Exeter, St Olaves Hotel
Falmouth, Penmere Manor
Fareham, Solent Hotel
Fleet, Moonfleet Manor
Fowey, Fowey Hall
Fowey, Marina Hotel
Freshwater Bay, Sandpipers

Gittisham, Combe House
Glewstone, Glewstone Court
Great Dunmow, The Starr
Great Milton, Le Manoir aux Quat' Saisons
Grimston, Congham Hall
Guildford, Angel Posting House & Livery
Hadley Wood, West Lodge Park
Halifax, Holdsworth House
Harome, Star Inn
Harrogate, Balmoral Hotel
Harrogate, Hotel du Vin & Bistro
Hassop, Hassop Hall
Hawnby, Hawnby Hotel
Haworth, Weaver's
Headlam, Headlam Hall
Henley-on-Thames, Red Lion Hotel
Hereford, Castle House
Hexham, Langley Castle
Hinton Charterhouse, Homewood Park
Holkham, The Victoria
Horley, Langshott Manor
Horringer, The Ickworth
Huddersfield, Lodge Hotel
Hurstbourne Tarrant, Esseborne Manor
Ipswich, Salthouse Harbour Hotel
Ireby, Overwater Hall
Jacobstowe, Higher Cadham Farm
Kemerton, Upper Court
Keswick, Dale Head Hall
Kingham, Mill House
Kingsbridge, Buckland-Tout-Saints Hotel
Kingston Bagpuize, Fallowfields
Kinnersley, Upper Newton Farmhouse
Langar, Langar Hall
Langford Budville, Bindon Country House
Langho, Northcote Manor
Lastingham, Lastingham Grange
Lavenham, The Angel
Lavenham, Great House
Leamington Spa, York House
Leeds, 42 The Calls
Lewes, Shelleys Hotel
Lifton, Arundell Arms
Little Petherick, Molesworth Manor
Liverpool, The Racquet Club
Long Crendon, Angel Restaurant
Long Melford, Black Lion
Looe, Talland Bay
Lorton, Winder Hall
Loughborough, Old Manor Hotel
Lower Beeding, South Lodge
Lyme Regis, Hotel Alexandra
Lymington, Stanwell House
Maidencombe, Orestone Manor
Malvern Wells, Cottage in the Wood
Manchester, Alias Rossetti
Manchester, Le Meridien Victoria & Albert
Markington, Hob Green
Masham, Swinton Park
Matlock Bath, Hodgkinson's
Mawnan Smith, Meudon Hotel

Mellor, Millstone Hotel
Mickleton, Three Ways House
Midhurst, Spread Eagle
Minchinhampton, Burleigh Court Hotel
Morston, Morston Hall
Moulsford, Beetle & Wedge
Muddiford, Broomhill Art Hotel
Mullion, Polurrian Hotel
Mungrisdale, Mill Hotel
Newquay, Sands Family Resort
Norton, Hundred House
Norwich, The Old Rectory
Nottingham, Hart's
Oakamoor, Bank House
Orford, Crown and Castle
Oxford, Old Bank
Oxford, Old Parsonage
Padstow, Seafood Restaurant, St Petroc's Hotel, Rick Stein's Café
Painswick, Painswick Hotel
Pelynt, Penellick
Penzance, Abbey Hotel
Pickering, White Swan
Poole, Mansion House
Portscatho, Rosevine Hotel
Purton, Pear Tree at Purton
Redworth, Redworth Hall
Ripley, Boar's Head
Rock, St Enodoc Hotel
Romaldkirk, Rose & Crown
Roydhouse, Three Acres Inn
Ruan High Lanes, Polsue Manor
St Albans, St Michael's Manor
St Ives, Primrose Valley Hotel
St Margaret's at Cliffe, Wallett's Court
St Martin's, St Martin's on the Isle
St Mawes, Hotel Tresanton
St Mawes, Rising Sun
Salcombe, Soar Mill Cove Hotel
Sandiway, Nunsmere Hall
Seaham, Seaham Hall Hotel
Seaview, Seaview Hotel
Sheffield, Whitley Hall
Shipham, Daneswood House
Sidmouth, Hotel Riviera
Stamford, George of Stamford
Stanton Wick, Carpenters Arms
Stokesley, Chapters
Ston Easton, Ston Easton Park
Stow-on-the-Wold, Grapevine Hotel
Stuckton, Three Lions
Sutton Coldfield, New Hall
Swaffham, Strattons
Tetbury, Calcot Manor
Titchwell, Titchwell Manor
Tresco, Island Hotel
Tresco, New Inn
Upper Hambleton, Hambleton Hall
Uppingham, Lake Isle
Veryan, Nare Hotel
Wells-next-the-Sea, Crown Hotel

Whitewell, Inn at Whitewell
Wickham, Old House
Wincanton, Holbrook House Hotel
Winchcombe, The White Hart
Winchester, Hotel du Vin & Bistro
Windermere, Holbeck Ghyll
Woodbridge, Seckford Hall
Wookey Hole, Glencot House
Worfield, Old Vicarage
Yelverton, Old Orchard

Scotland

Aberdeen, The Marcliffe at Pitfodels
Auchterarder, Gleneagles
Auldearn, Boath House
Ballantrae, Glenapp Castle
Banchory, Banchory Lodge
Colbost, Three Chimneys
Drumnadrochit, Polmaily House
Dunkeld, Hilton Dunkeld House
Dunkeld, The Pend
Dunoon, Enmore Hotel
Edinburgh, The Howard
Edinburgh, Malmaison Edinburgh
Edinburgh, The Scotsman Hotel
Eriska, Isle of Eriska
Fort William, Inverlochy Castle
Glenlivet, Minmore House
Gullane, Greywalls
Inverness, Dunain Park
Iona, Argyll Hotel
Kelso, Ednam House
Kildrummy, Kildrummy Castle Hotel
Kinloch, Kinloch House Hotel
Kirkwall, Foveran Hotel
Markinch, Balbirnie House
Moffat, Beechwood Country House

Muir of Ord, Dower House
Plockton, Plockton Hotel
Port Appin, Airds Hotel
Portpatrick, Knockinaam Lodge
Portree, Viewfield House
St Fillans, Four Seasons Hotel
Scarista, Scarista House
Shieldaig, Tigh an Eilean
Skirling, Skirling House
Tain, Mansfield House
Troon, Lochgreen House
Ullapool, Ceilidh Place

Wales

Aberdovey, Penhelig Arms Hotel
Aberdovey, Trefeddian Hotel
Abersoch, Porth Tocyn Hotel
Barmouth, Bae Abermaw
Conwy, Castle Hotel
Conwy, Sychnant Pass House
Crickhowell, Bear Hotel
Crickhowell, Gliffaes Country House
Druidston, The Druidstone
Laugharne, Hurst House
Llanarmon Dyffryn Ceiriog, West Arms Hotel
Llangammarch Wells, Lake Country House
Llanrhian, Trevaccoon
Llanwrtyd Wells, Carlton House
Newport, Cnapan
Porthkerry, Egerton Grey
Portmeirion, Hotel Portmeirion and Castell Deudraeth
Pwllheli, Plas Bodegroes
Swansea, Morgans
Tintern, Parva Farmhouse
Tyn-y-Groes, Groes Inn

Non-smoking establishments

Hotels that state they are completely non-smoking are listed below.

London
Aster House
Durley House
Knightsbridge Green Hotel
Morgan House

England
Aldfield, Mallard Grange
Ambleside, Drunken Duck Inn
Ambleside, Kent House
Ampleforth, Shallowdale House
Armscote, Willow Corner
Ashbourne, Omnia Somnia
Ashey, Little Upton Farm
Askrigg, Helm
Aveton Gifford, Court Barton Farm
Axminster, Kerrington House
Aylmerton, Felbrigg Lodge
Babworth, The Barns
Bassenthwaite, Willow Cottage
Bath, Haydon House
Bath, Paradise House
Bath, Tasburgh House Hotel
Battle, Fox Hole Farm
Beercrocombe, Frog Street Farm
Berwick-upon-Tweed, Number One
Sallyport
Beyton, Manorhouse
Bigbury-on-Sea, Henley Hotel
Billingshurst, Old Wharf
Bishop's Stortford, The Cottage
Blackwell, Blackwell Grange
Blockley, Old Bakery
Botallack, Botallack Manor
Bourton-on-the-Water, Dial House
Bovey Tracey, Edgemoor Hotel
Bradford-on-Avon, Bradford Old Windmill
Bradford-on-Avon, Priory Steps
Briggswath, The Lawns
Broad Campden, Malt House
Brockdish, Grove Thorpe
Brockenhurst, Whitley Ridge
Burpham, Old Parsonage
Buttermere, Wood House
Cambridge, Meadowcroft Hotel
Cannington, Blackmore Farm
Canterbury, Magnolia House
Carlisle, Number 31
Cartmel, L'Enclume
Cartmel Fell, Lightwood
Catlowdy, Bessietown Farm
Chatton, Old Manse
Cheddleton, Choir Cottage & Choir House
Cheltenham, Georgian House
Chester, Green Bough Hotel
Chillaton, Quither Mill
Chillaton, Tor Cottage
Chulmleigh, Old Bakehouse
Clun, Birches Mill
Coniston, Coniston Lodge
Coventry, Crest Guesthouse
Crackington Haven, Manor Farm
Cranford, The Cottage
Crayke, Durham Ox
Creed, Creed House
Cricket Malherbie, The Old Rectory
Crosthwaite, Crosthwaite House
Earsham, Earsham Park Farm
East Barkwith, Bodkin Lodge
East Barkwith, The Grange
Eastbourne, Brayscroft Hotel
Ermington, Plantation House
Flamborough, Manor House
Fowey, Old Quay House
Glastonbury, Number 3
Grassington, Ashfield House
Hamsterley Forest, Grove House
Hanley Castle, Old Parsonage Farm
Hartfield, Bolebroke Mill
Hatch Beauchamp, Farthings
Hathersage, Highlow Hall
Hathersage, Plough Inn
Hermitage, Almshouse Farm
Hexham, Dene House
Hindringham, Field House
Hinton Charterhouse, Homewood Park
Holmesfield, Horsleygate Hall
Hope, Underleigh House
Hopesay, Old Rectory
Hopwas, Oak Tree Farm
Huxley, Higher Huxley Hall
Ilmington, Folly Farm Cottage
Ingleby Greenhow, Manor House Farm
Ironbridge, The Library House
Ironbridge, Severn Lodge
Jacobstowe, Higher Cadham Farm
Kenilworth, Castle Laurels
Keswick, The Grange
Kimmeridge, Kimmeridge Farmhouse
Kingston Bagpuize, Fallowfields
Kingswear, Nonsuch House
Kington, Penrhos Court
Kinnersley, Upper Newton Farmhouse
Lavenham, The Angel
Lavenham, Lavenham Priory
Leintwardine, Upper Buckton Farm
Lewes, Millers
Leysters, Hills Farm
Little Hampden, Rising Sun
Little Petherick, Molesworth Manor
Little Walsingham, Old Bakehouse

Lorton, New House Farm
Lorton, Winder Hall
Loughborough, Old Manor Hotel
Loxley, Loxley Farm
Ludlow, Mr Underhill's
Lynton, Victoria Lodge
Martinhoe, Old Rectory
Matlock, Red House Country Hotel
Meldreth, Chiswick House
Membury, Oxenways
Middle Winterslow, The Beadles
Minchinhampton, Hunters Lodge
Moreton, The Dairy
Near Sawrey, Ees Wyke
Near Sawrey, Sawrey House
Newbrough, Allerwash Farmhouse
North Walsham, Beechwood Hotel
Nottingham, Greenwood Lodge
Oakamoor, Bank House
Oxford, Burlington House
Padstow, Number 6
Pelynt, Penellick
Perranuthnoe, Ednovean Farm
Pershore, The Barn
Polperro, Cottage Restaurant
Portscatho, Driftwood Hotel
Postbridge, Lydgate House
Rogate, Mizzards Farm
Rowsley, East Lodge
Ruan High Lanes, Polsue Manor
Rye, Little Orchard House
Rye, The Old Vicarage
St Blazey, Nanscawen Manor House
St Briavels, Cinderhill House
St Hilary, Ennys
St Ives, Blue Hayes
St Ives, One Sea View Terrace
Saracen's Head, Pipwell Manor
Selside, Low Jock Scar
Shanklin, Foxhills
Shipton Gorge, Innsacre Farmhouse
Sissinghurst, Sissinghurst Castle Farm
Somerton, The Lynch
Southend-on-Sea, Pebbles
Stokesley, Chapters
Stratford-upon-Avon, Victoria Spa Lodge
Sturminster Newton, Plumber Manor
Swaffham, Strattons
Sway, The Nurse's Cottage
Teignmouth, Thomas Luny House
Temple Cloud, Old Court
Tilston, Tilston Lodge
Topsham, The Galley
Torquay, Mulberry House
Totnes, Old Forge
Uffington, The Craven
Virginstow, Percy's Country Hotel
Waterlip, Burnt House Farm
Watermillock, Old Church Hotel
Wells, Canon Grange
West Malling, Scott House

Weston-under-Redcastle, The Citadel
Weymouth, Seaham Guesthouse
Widegates, Coombe Farm
Wilmcote, Pear Tree Cottage
Winchcombe, Isbourne Manor House
Windermere, Coach House
Windermere, Low House
Winster, Brae Cottage
Wirksworth, Old Lock-up
Woodstock, Shipton Glebe
Wye, Wife of Bath
York, Easton's

Scotland

Aberdour, Hawkcraig House
Aberfoyle, Creag-Ard House
Arisaig, Old Library
Ascog, Balmory Hall
Auldearn, Boath House
Callander, Leny House
Clachan-Seil, Willowburn Hotel
Colbost, Three Chimneys
Dornoch, 2 Quail
Edinburgh, Seven Danube Street
Edinburgh, Six Mary's Place
Ednam, Edenwater House
Edzell, The House of Mark
Fort William, The Grange
Inverkeilor, Gordon's
Inverness, Millwood House
Inverness, Moyness House
Jedburgh, Hundalee House
Kirdcudbright, Gladstone House
Kirkwall, Foveran Hotel
Lochinver, The Albannach
Lochranza, Apple Lodge
Lynwilg, Lynwilg House
Moffat, Well View
Oban, Kilchrenan House
Port Ellen, Glenmachrie Country
Guesthouse
Scarista, Scarista House
Skirling, Skirling House
Stirling, Ashgrove House
Strontian, Kilcamb Lodge
Tain, Mansfield House
Troon, Lochgreen House
Ullapool, Tanglewood House

Wales

Abereiddy, Crug-Glas
Betws-y-Coed, Pengwern Country House
Brecon, Cantre Selyf
Capel Garmon, Llannerch Goch
Capel Garmon, Tan-y-Foel
Cardiff, The Town House
Eglwysfach, Ynyshir Hall
Freshwater East, Portclew House
Llandudno, Abbey Lodge
Llanfachreth, Ty Isaf Farmhouse
Llanfihangel-yng-Ngwynfa, Cyfie Farm

Llanigon, Old Post Office
Llanrhian, Trevaccoon
Llwynhendy, Llwyn Hall
Menai Bridge, Wern Farm
Penmachno, Penmachno Hall

Pentregat, The Grange
Porthkerry, Egerton Grey
Pwlleli, Plas Bodegroes
Spittal, Lower Haythog Farm
Swansea, Morgans

Dog-friendly hotels

Hotels that allow dogs to stay with you in at least one bedroom are listed below. Please check each hotel's entry for its terms of acceptance.

London
22 Jermyn Street
City Inn Westminster
Colonnade Town House
The Gore
Hazlitt's
L'Hotel
Malmaison
The Milestone
Miller's
Pembridge Court
The Portobello
The Queensgate

England
Abberley, Elms Hotel
Aldeburgh, Wentworth Hotel
Alderminster, The Bell
Alderminster, Ettington Park
Alston, Lovelady Shield
Ambleside, The Regent
Ashbourne, Callow Hall
Ashburton, Holne Chase
Ashwater, Blagdon Manor
Austwick, Austwick Traddock
Aylesbury, Hartwell House
Badby, Windmill at Badby
Bapchild, Hempstead House
Barwick, Little Barwick House
Bassenthwaite Lake, The Pheasant
Bath, Royal Crescent Hotel
Bathford, Eagle House
Battle, Fox Hole Farm
Beaminster, Bridge House
Beercrocombe, Frog Street Farm
Berwick-upon-Tweed, Number One Sallyport
Bibury, Bibury Court
Bigbury-on-Sea, Henley Hotel
Biggin, Biggin Hall
Birch Vale, Waltzing Weasel
Bishop's Tachbrook, Mallory Court
Bishop's Tawton, Halmpstone Manor
Blackpool, Raffles
Bolton Abbey, Devonshire Arms
Boughton Lees, Eastwell Manor
Bournemouth, Hotel Miramar
Bovey Tracey, Edgemoor Hotel
Bradford-on-Avon, Woolley Grange
Brampton, Farlam Hall
Brancaster Staithe, White Horse
Branscombe, Masons Arms
Brighton, Blanch House
Broadway, Barn House

Brockenhurst, Cloud Hotel
Brome, Cornwallis Country Hotel
Broxton, Frogg Manor
Bryher, Hell Bay Hotel
Burford, The Bay Tree
Burford, Lamb Inn
Burlton, Burlton Inn
Burnham Market, Hoste Arms
Burnsall, Devonshire Fell
Burrington, Northcote Manor
Bury St Edmunds, Angel
Bury St Edmunds, Ravenwood Hall
Cambridge, Hotel Felix
Cambridge, Meadowcroft Hotel
Canterbury, Yorke Lodge Hotel
Cartmel, Aynsome Manor
Cartmel, L'Enclume
Cartmel, Uplands
Castle Ashby, The Falcon
Castle Combe, Manor House
Cavendish, The George
Chatton, Old Manse
Cheltenham, Alias Hotel Kandinsky
Chipping Campden, Cotswold House
Chipping Campden, King's Arms
Cholmondeley, Cholmondeley Arms
Clearwell, Tudor Farmhouse
Cley next the Sea, Cley Mill
Climping, Bailiffscourt
Coln St Aldwyns, New Inn at Coln
Colwall Stone, Colwall Park
Constantine, Trengilly Wartha
Cookham Dean, Inn on the Green
Coventry, Crest Guesthouse
Crayke, Durham Ox
Crookham, Coach House
Crosthwaite, Crosthwaite House
Croyde, Whiteleaf at Croyde
Crudwell, Old Rectory
Cuckfield, Ockenden Manor
Dartmouth, Little Admiral
Dartmouth, Royal Castle Hotel
Dedham, Milsoms
Dittisham, Fingals
Dunsley, Dunsley Hall
Earsham, Earsham Park Farm
Eastbourne, Brayscroft Hotel
Eastbourne, Grand Hotel
East Witton, Blue Lion
Emsworth, 36 on the Quay
Ermington, Plantation House
Evershot, Summer Lodge
Evesham, Evesham Hotel
Exeter, Alias Hotel Barcelona

Exeter, St Olaves Hotel
Farnham, Museum Inn
Fleet, Moonfleet Manor
Fowey, Fowey Hall
Fowey, Marina Hotel
Freshwater Bay, Sandpipers
Gillan, Tregildry Hotel
Gittisham, Combe House Hotel
Glewstone, Glewstone Court
Grasmere, White Moss House
Great Dunmow, The Starr
Great Malvern, Bredon House
Halifax, Holdsworth House
Haltwhistle, Centre of Britain Hotel
Hampton Court, Carlton Mitre
Harrogate, Balmoral Hotel
Hassop, Hassop Hall
Hatch Beauchamp, Farthings
Headlam, Headlam Hall
Hereford, Castle House
Hexham, Langley Castle
Hinton Charterhouse, Homewood Park
Holkham, The Victoria
Hopwas, Oak Tree Farm
Horndon on the Hill, Bell Inn & Hill House
Horringer, The Ickworth
Huddersfield, Lodge Hotel
Hurstbourne Tarrant, Esseborne Manor
Inkpen, Crrown and Garter
Ipswich, Salthouse Harbour Hotel
Ireby, Overwater Hall
Ironbridge, The Library House
Jacobstowe, Higher Cadham Farm
Kingham, Mill House
Kingsbridge, Buckland-Tout-Saints Hotel
Kingston Bagpuize, Fallowfields
Kington, Penrhos Court
Lacock, At the Sign of the Angel
Langar, Langar Hall
Langford Budville, Bindon Country House
Langthwaite, CB Inn
Lastingham, Lastingham Grange
Lavenham, The Angel
Lavenham, Great House
Leamington Spa, York House
Leeds, 42 The Calls
Leeds, Malmaison Leeds
Leeds, Quebecs
Lewes, Shelleys Hotel
Lifton, Arundell Arms
Liverpool, The Racquet Club
Long Melford, Black Lion
Looe, Talland Bay
Lorton, New House Farm
Loxley, Loxley Farm
Ludlow, Dinham Hall
Lyme Regis, Hotel Alexandra
Lymington, Stanwell House
Lynton, Valley House
Maidencombe, Orestone Manor
Malvern Wells, Cottage in the Wood

Manchester, Alias Rossetti
Manchester, Didsbury House
Manchester, Eleven Didsbury Park
Manchester, The Midland
Markington, Hob Green
Masham, Swinton Park
Matfen, Matfen Hall
Matlock Bath, Hodgkinson's
Mawnan Smith, Meudon Hotel
Melbourn, Sheene Mill
Meldreth, Chiswick House
Mellor Brook, Feilden's Arms
Mickleton, Three Ways House
Midhurst, Angel Hotel
Midhurst, Spread Eagle
Milborne Port, Old Vicarage
Minchinhampton, Burleigh Court
Minchinhampton, Hunters Lodge
Mobberley, Laburnum Cottage
Morston, Morston Hall
Moulsford, Beetle & Wedge
Mullion, Polurrian Hotel
Mungrisdale, Mill Hotel
Nantwich, Curshaws at the Cat
Near Sawrey, Buckle Yeat
Near Sawrey, Ees Wyke
Near Sawrey, Sawrey House
Newcastle, Malmaison Newcastle
Newton-Le-Willows, The Hall
North Walsham, Beechwood Hotel
Norton, Hundred House
Norwich, Catton Old Hall
Norwich, The Old Rectory
Nottingham, Hart's
Nottingham, Lace Market Hotel
Oakamoor, Bank House
Oakham, Barnsdale Lodge
Orford, Crown and Castle
Oxford, Old Parsonage Restaurant and Bar
Padstow, Seafood Restaurant, St Petroc's
Hotel, Rick Stein's Café
Painswick, Painswick Hotel
Pickering, White Swan
Pickhill, Nags Head
Porlock Weir, Andrew's on the Weir
Portscatho, Rosevine Hotel
Postbridge, Lydgate House
Purton, Pear Tree at Purton
Redworth, Redworth Hall
Reeth, Arkleside Hotel
Reeth, Burgoyne Hotel
Rhydycroesau, Pen-y-Dyffryn
Ripley, Boar's Head
Rolleston on Dove, Brookhouse Hotel
Romaldkirk, Rose & Crown
Romsey, Berties
Ross-on-Wye, Wilton Court Hotel
Rowsley, The Peacock at Rowsley
Ruan High Lanes, Polsue Manor
Rushlake Green, Stone House
Rye, Jeake's House

St Ives, One Sea View Terrace
St Keyne, The Well House
St Martin's, St Martin's on the Isle
St Mawes, Rising Sun
Salcombe, Soar Mill Cove Hotel
Salcombe, Tides Reach
Salford, Lowry Hotel
Sandypark, Mill End
Seatoller, Seatoller House
Seaview, Seaview Hotel
Sedbusk, Stone House
Selside, Low Jock Scar
Sheffield, Hotel Bristol
Shepton Mallet, Charlton House
Shipham, Daneswood House
Shipton Gorge, Innsacre Farmhouse
Sidmouth, Hotel Riviera
Somerton, The Lynch
Southwold, The Swan
Stamford, George of Stamford
Ston Easton, Ston Easton Park
Stow-on-the-Wold, Grapevine Hotel
Sturminster Newton, Plumber Manor
Swaffham, Strattons
Sway, The Nurse's Cottage
Tavistock, Horn of Plenty
Teffont Evias, Howard's House
Temple Cloud, Old Court
Thornham, Lifeboat Inn
Thornton, River House
Tirril, Queen's Head Inn
Titchwell, Titchwell Manor
Titley, Stagg Inn
Two Bridges, Prince Hall Hotel
Ulverston, Bay Horse Hotel
Upper Hambleton, Hambleton Hall
Uppingham, Lake Isle
Veryan, Nare Hotel
Virginstow, Percy's Country Hotel
Walberswick, Bell Inn
Wasdale Head, Wasdale Head Inn
Watermillock, Rampsbeck Country House
Whitewell, Inn at Whitewell
Widegates, Coombe Farm
Winchcombe, The White Hart
Winchester, Wykeham Arms
Windermere, Holbeck Ghyll
Windermere, Miller Howe
Winster, Brae Cottage
Winteringham, Winteringham Fields
Withypool, Royal Oak Inn
Wolterton, Saracen's Head
Woodbridge, Seckford Hall
Woodstock, Shipton Glebe
Wookey Hole, Glencot House
Woolacombe, Little Beach Hotel
Worfield, Old Vicarage
Yarmouth, George Hotel
Yattendon, Royal Oak
Yelverton, Old Orchard

Scotland

Aberdeen, The Marcliffe at Pitfodels
Aberfoyle, Creag-Ard House
Achiltibuie, Summer Isles Hotel
Annbank, Enterkine House
Applecross, Applecross Inn
Auchterarder, Gleneagles
Auldearn, Boath House
Ballantrae, Glenapp Castle
Ballater, Balgonie Country House
Ballater, Darroch Learg
Balquhidder, Monachyle Mhor
Banchory, Banchory Lodge
Brae, Busta House
Brodick, Kilmichael Country House
Clachan-Seil, Willowburn Hotel
Clintmains, Clint Lodge
Drumnadrochit, Polmaily House
Dunkeld, The Pend
Dunoon, Enmore Hotel
Edinburgh, The Scotsman Hotel
Edinburgh, Seven Danube Street
Eriska, Isle of Eriska
Forss, Forss House
Fort William, Inverlochy Castle
Glasgow, Express by Holiday Inn
Glenlivet, Minmore House
Gullane, Greywalls
Heiton, The Roxburghe
Inverness, Dunain Park
Inverness, Moyness House Hotel
Iona, Argyll Hotel
Kelso, Ednam House
Kentallen, Ardsheal House
Kildrummy, Kildrummy Castle Hotel
Lynwilg, Lynwilg House
Markinch, Balbirnie House
Moffat, Beechwood Country House
Muir of Ord, Dower House
Oban, Manor House
Peat Inn, Peat Inn
Port Appin, Airds Hotel
Port Ellen, Glenmachrie Country
Guesthouse
Portpatrick, Knockinaam Lodge
Portree, Viewfield House
St Fillans, Four Seasons Hotel
Scarista, Scarista House
Shieldaig, Tigh an Eilean
Skirling, Skirling House
Stein, Stein Inn
Strontian, Kilcamb Lodge
Swinton, The Wheatsheaf
Tain, Mansfield House
Ullapool, Ceilidh Place
Ullapool, Tanglewood House

Wales

Aberdovey, Penhelig Arms
Aberdovey, Trefeddian Hotel
Abersoch, Porth Tocyn Hotel

Beddgelert, Sygun Fawr
Druidston, The Druidstone
Cardiff, The Big Sleep Hotel
Conwy, Castle Hotel
Conwy, Sychnant Pass House
Crickhowell, Bear Hotel
Eglwysfach, Ynyshir Hall
Felin Fach, Felin Fach Griffin
Fishguard, Manor Town House
Freshwater East, Portclew House
Laugharne, Hurst House
Llanarmon Dyffryn Ceiriog, West Arms
Llandrillo, Tyddyn Llan
Llanfachreth, Ty Isaf Farmhouse
Llangammarch Wells, Lake Country House

Llanigon, Old Post Office
Llanwrtyd Wells, Carlton House
Llwynhendy, Llwyn Hall
Nantgwynant, Pen-y-Gwryd Hotel
Northop, Soughton Hall
Penmaenpool, George III Hotel
Pentregat, The Grange
Porthkerry, Egerton Grey
Pwllheli, Plas Bodegroes
St Brides Wentlooge, Inn at the Elm Tree
St Brides Wentlooge, West Usk Lighthouse
Skenfrith, The Bell at Skenfrith
Spittal, Lower Haythog Farm
Tintern, Parva Farmhouse
Tyn-y-Groes, Groes Inn

Hotels licensed to hold civil weddings

Hotels in England and Wales that are licensed for civil weddings, in accordance with the Marriage Act 1949 (as amended), are listed below. The situation is different in Scotland, where religious weddings may be held at any hotel or indeed anywhere else; civil weddings, however, can be held only in registrars' offices save in exceptional circumstances.

London
30 Pavilion Road
51 Buckingham Gate
Blakes Hotel
The Goring
The Hempel
Mandarin Oriental Hyde Park
The Milestone
One Aldwych
The Savoy
The Stafford

England
Abberley, Elms Hotel
Alderminster, Ettington Park
Alston, Lovelady Shield
Alton, Alton Towers Hotel
Amberley, Amberley Castle
Ashburton, Holne Chase
Aylesbury, Hartwell House
Bapchild, Hempstead House
Baslow, Fischer's Baslow Hall
Bath, Bath Priory
Bath, Royal Crescent Hotel
Beaulieu, Montagu Arms
Bibury, Bibury Court
Bigbury-on-Sea, Burgh Island
Birmingham, Hotel du Vin & Bistro
Bishop's Tachbrook, Mallory Court
Bolton Abbey, Devonshire Arms
Bosham, The Millstream
Boughton Lees, Eastwell Manor
Bournemouth, Hotel Miramar
Bowness-on-Windermere, Fayrer Garden House
Bowness-on-Windermere, Linthwaite House
Bray, Waterside Inn
Brighton, Alias Hotel Seattle
Brighton, Blanch House
Bristol, The Brigstow
Brome, Cornwallis Country Hotel
Bromsgrove, Grafton Manor
Broxton, Frogg Manor
Burford, The Bay Tree
Burnsall, Devonshire Fell
Burrington, Northcote Manor
Bury St Edmunds, The Angel
Bury St Edmunds, Ravenwood Hall
Cambridge, Hotel Felix
Castle Ashby, The Falcon
Castle Combe, Manor House

Chandler's Cross, The Grove
Chester-le-Street, Lumley Castle
Chipping Campden, Cotswold House
Chittlehamholt, Highbullen
Cley next the Sea, Cley Mill
Climping, Bailiffscourt
Colerne, Lucknam Park
Cookham Dean, Inn on the Green
Corfe Castle, Mortons House
Crudwell, Old Rectory
Cuckfield, Ockenden Manor
Dartmouth, Royal Castle
Dedham, Maison Talbooth
Dorridge, The Forest
Dunsley, Dunsley Hall
Eastbourne, Grand Hotel
East Grinstead, Gravetye Manor
Egham, Great Fosters
Egham, Runnymede Hotel
Evershot, Summer Lodge
Exeter, St Olaves Hotel
Falmouth, Penmere Manor
Fareham, Solent Hotel
Faversham, Read's
Fowey, Fowey Hall
Fowey, Marina Hotel
Great Milton, Le Manoir aux Quat' Saisons
Great Snoring, Manor House
Grimston, Congham Hall
Hadley Wood, West Lodge Park
Halifax, Holdsworth House
Hampton Court, Carlton Mitre
Harome, Star Inn
Harwich, The Pier at Harwich
Hassop, Hassop Hall
Hatch Beauchamp, Farthings
Headlam, Headlam Hall
Hexham, Langley Castle
Hinton Charterhouse, Homewood Park
Holkham, The Victoria
Horley, Langshott Manor
Horringer, The Ickworth
Huddersfield, Lodge Hotel
Hurstbourne Tarrant, Esseborne Manor
Ipswich, Salthouse Harbour Hotel
Kingsbridge, Buckland-Tout-Saints Hotel
Kingston Bagpuize, Fallowfields
Kington, Penrhos Court
Lacock, At the Sign of the Angel
Langar, Langar Hall
Langford Budville, Bindon Country House

Langho, Northcote Manor
Leeds, Haley's Hotel
Lewes, Shelleys Hotel
Lifton, Arundell Arms
Lorton, Winder Hall
Lower Beeding, South Lodge
Lower Slaughter, Lower Slaughter Manor
Ludlow, Dinham Hall
Lydgate, White Hart Inn
Lymington, Stanwell House
Manchester, Le Meridien Victoria & Albert
Manchester, The Midland
Markington, Hob Green
Masham, Swinton Park
Matfen, Matfen Hall
Melbourn, Sheene Mill
Mellor, Millstone Hotel
Membury, Oxenways
Mevagissey, Trevalsa Court
Mickleton, Three Ways House
Midhurst, Angel Hotel
Midhurst, Spread Eagle
Minchinhampton, Burleigh Court Hotel
Mullion, Polurrian Hotel
Nayland, White Hart
New Milton, Chewton Glen
Newquay, Sands Family Resort
Nottingham, Hart's
Oakham, Barnsdale Lodge
Painswick, Painswick Hotel
Poole, Mansion House
Purton, Pear Tree at Purton
Redworth, Redworth Hall
Ripley, Boar's Head
Rowsley, East Lodge
Rowsley, The Peacock at Rowsley
St Albans, St Michael's Manor
St Ives, Blue Hayes
St Martin's, St Martin's on the Isle
St Mawes, Hotel Tresanton
Salford, Lowry Hotel
Sandiway, Nunsmere Hall
Seaham, Seaham Hall Hotel
Sheffield, Whitley Hall
Shepton Mallet, Charlton House
Southwold, The Swan

Stadhampton, The Crazy Bear
Stamford, George of Stamford
Stockcross, Vineyard at Stockcross
Stokesley, Chapters
Ston Easton, Ston Easton Park
Stow-on-the-Wold, Grapevine Hotel
Sutton Coldfield, New Hall
Tadcaster, Hazlewood Castle
Tarporley, The Swan
Tavistock, Horn of Plenty
Temple Cloud, The Old Court
Tetbury, Calcot Manor
Tewin, Tewin Bury Farm
Totnes, Kingston House
Ullswater, Sharrow Bay
Upper Hambleton, Hambleton Hall
Watermillock, Old Church Hotel
Whitewell, Inn at Whitewell
Wincanton, Holbrook House Hotel
Winchester, Hotel du Vin & Bistro
Windermere, Holbeck Ghyll
Windermere, Miller Howe
Windermere, The Samling
Woodbridge, Seckford Hall
Yarmouth, George Hotel
York, Middlethorpe Hall

Wales

Barmouth, Bae Abermaw
Conwy, Sychnant Pass House
Crickhowell, Gliffaes Country House Hotel
Druidston, The Druidstone
Llanarmon Dyffryn Ceiriog, West Arms Hotel
Llandrillo, Tyddyn Llan
Llandudno, Bodysgallen Hall
Llangammarch Wells, Lake Country House
Llwynhendy, Llwyn Hall
Llyswen, Llangoed Hall
Northop, Soughton Hall
Porthkerry, Egerton Grey
Portmeirion, Hotel Portmeirion and Castell Deudraeth
Swansea, Morgans
Tredunnock, The Newbridge

Hotels with swimming pools

Hotels that have swimming pools – outdoor or indoor, heated or unheated – are listed below.

London
The Milestone
One Aldwych
The Savoy

England
Alderminster, Ettington Park
Alton, Alton Towers Hotel
Ambleside, The Regent
Applethwaite, Underscar Manor
Aylesbury, Hartwell House
Aylmerton, Felbrigg Lodge
Bapchild, Hempstead House
Bath, Bath Priory
Bath, Royal Crescent Hotel
Bigbury-on-Sea, Burgh Island
Billingshurst, Old Wharf
Bishop's Tachbrook, Mallory Court
Bolton Abbey, Devonshire Arms
Boughton Lees, Eastwell Manor
Bradford-on-Avon, Woolley Grange
Broadway, Barn House
Bryher, Hell Bay Hotel
Bury St Edmunds, Ravenwood Hall
Castle Combe, Manor House
Catlowdy, Bessietown Farm
Chandler's Cross, The Grove
Chillaton, Tor Cottage
Chittlehamholt, Highbullen
Climping, Bailiffscourt
Colerne, Lucknam Park
Cranbrook, Cloth Hall Oast
Dittisham, Fingals
Dunsley, Dunsley Hall
Eastbourne, Grand Hotel
East Hoathly, Old Whyly
Egham, Great Fosters
Egham, Runnymede Hotel
Etchingham, King John's Lodge
Evershot, Summer Lodge
Evesham, Evesham Hotel
Falmouth, Penmere Manor
Fareham, Solent Hotel
Fleet, Moonfleet Manor
Fowey, Fowey Hall
Grittleton, Church House
Harome, Star Inn
Headlam, Headlam Hall
Hinton Charterhouse, Homewood Park
Hopwas, Oak Tree Farm
Horringer, The Ickworth
Huxley, Higher Huxley Hall
Kemerton, Upper Court
Langford Budville, Bindon Country House

Liverpool, The Racquet Club
Looe, Talland Bay
Maidencombe, Orestone Manor
Manchester, The Midland
Midhurst, Spread Eagle
Minchinhampton, Burleigh Court Hotel
Muddiford, Broomhill Art Hotel
Mullion, Polurrian Hotel
New Milton, Chewton Glen
Newquay, Sands Family Resort
Norwich, The Old Rectory
Pershore, The Barn
Portscatho, Rosevine Hotel
Redworth, Redworth Hall
Rock, St Enodoc Hotel
Rogate, Mizzards Farm
St Blazey, Nanscawen Manor House
St Hilary, Ennys
St Keyne, The Well House
St Margaret's at Cliffe, Wallett's Court
St Martin's, St Martin's on the Isle
Salcombe, Soar Mill Cove Hotel
Salcombe, Tides Reach
Seaham, Seaham Hall Hotel
Stockcross, Vineyard at Stockcross
Sutton Coldfield, New Hall
Tetbury, Calcot Manor
Tresco, Island Hotel
Tresco, New Inn
Upper Hambleton, Hambleton Hall
Veryan, Nare Hotel
Widegates, Coombe Farm
Wincanton, Holbrook House Hotel
Woodbridge, Seckford Hall
Wookey Hole, Glencot House
York, Middlethorpe Hall

Scotland
Auchterarder, Gleneagles
Dornoch, 2 Quail
Drumnadrochit, Polmaily House
Dunkeld, Hilton Dunkeld House
Edinburgh, The Scotsman Hotel
Eriska, Isle of Eriska
Glenlivet, Minmore House
Inverness, Dunain Park
Kinloch, Kinloch House Hotel

Wales
Aberdovey, Trefeddian Hotel
Abersoch, Porth Tocyn Hotel
Llandudno, Bodysgallen Hall
Nantgwynant, Pen-y-Gwryd Hotel
Portmeirion, Hotel Portmeirion and Castell Deudraeth

Hotels with spa facilities

Hotels that offer spa facilities on the premises are listed below.

London
51 Buckingham Gate
K-West
Mandarin Oriental Hyde Park
One Aldwych
The Savoy

England
Alderminster, Ettington Park
Applethwaite, Underscar Manor
Aylesbury, Hartwell House
Bath, Royal Crescent Hotel
Birmingham, Hotel du Vin & Bistro
Bolton Abbey, Devonshire Arms
Boughton Lees, Eastwell Manor
Chandler's Cross, The Grove
Chittlehamholt, Highbullen
Climping, Bailiffscourt
Colerne, Lucknam Park
Eastbourne, Grand Hotel
Egham, Runnymede Hotel
Evershot, Summer Lodge
Falmouth, Penmere Manor
Fareham, Solent Hotel
Fleet, Moonfleet Manor
Hadley Wood, West Lodge Park
Horringer, The Ickworth
Kingston Bagpuize, Fallowfields
Liverpool, The Racquet Club
Manchester, Didsbury House
Manchester, Malmaison Manchester
Masham, Swinton Park
Matfen, Matfen Hall

Membury, Oxenways
Midhurst, Spread Eagle
Mullion, Polurrian Hotel
New Milton, Chewton Glen
Newcastle, Malmaison Newcastle
Newquay, Sands Family Resort
Portloe, The Lugger
Redworth, Redworth Hall
Salcombe, Tides Reach
Salford, Lowry Hotel
Seaham, Seaham Hall Hotel
Shanklin, Foxhills
St Margaret's at Cliffe, Wallett's Court
Stockcross, Vineyard at Stockcross
Sutton Coldfield, New Hall
Temple Cloud, Old Court
Tetbury, Calcot Manor
Veryan, Nare Hotel
Wincanton, Holbrook House Hotel
Windermere, Holbeck Ghyll
York, Middlethorpe Hall

Scotland
Auchterarder, Gleneagles
Auldearn, Boath House
Dunkeld, Hilton Dunkeld House
Edinburgh, The Scotsman Hotel
Eriska, Isle of Eriska
Glasgow, Langs Hotel

Wales
Llandudno, Bodysgallen Hall

Index of entries

Index of entries

All entries are indexed below, including those in the Round-ups. An asterisk indicates a new entry.

Report form

To: *The Which? Guide to Good Hotels*,
FREEPOST, 2 Marylebone Road, London NW1 1YN

Name of hotel

Address

I visited this hotel on:

My report is:

I am not connected in any way with the management
or proprietor of this hotel.

My name is:

Address:

Report form

To: *The Which? Guide to Good Hotels*,
FREEPOST, 2 Marylebone Road, London NW1 1YN

Name of hotel

Address

I visited this hotel on:

My report is:

I am not connected in any way with the management or proprietor of this hotel.

_____

My name is:
_____

Address:
_____

Report form

To: *The Which? Guide to Good Hotels,*
FREEPOST, 2 Marylebone Road, London NW1 1YN

Name of hotel

Address

I visited this hotel on:

My report is:

I am not connected in any way with the management or proprietor of this hotel.

My name is:

Address:

Report form

To: *The Which? Guide to Good Hotels*,
FREEPOST, 2 Marylebone Road, London NW1 1YN

Name of hotel

Address

I visited this hotel on:

My report is:

I am not connected in any way with the management or proprietor of this hotel.

My name is:

Address:

Report form

To: *The Which? Guide to Good Hotels*,
FREEPOST, 2 Marylebone Road, London NW1 1YN

Name of hotel

Address

I visited this hotel on:

My report is:

I am not connected in any way with the management or proprietor of this hotel.

My name is:

Address:

As a result of your sending us this report form, we may send you information on **The Which? Guide to Good Hotels** and **The Good Food Guide** in the future. If you would prefer not to receive such information, please tick this box [   ].